AF597642

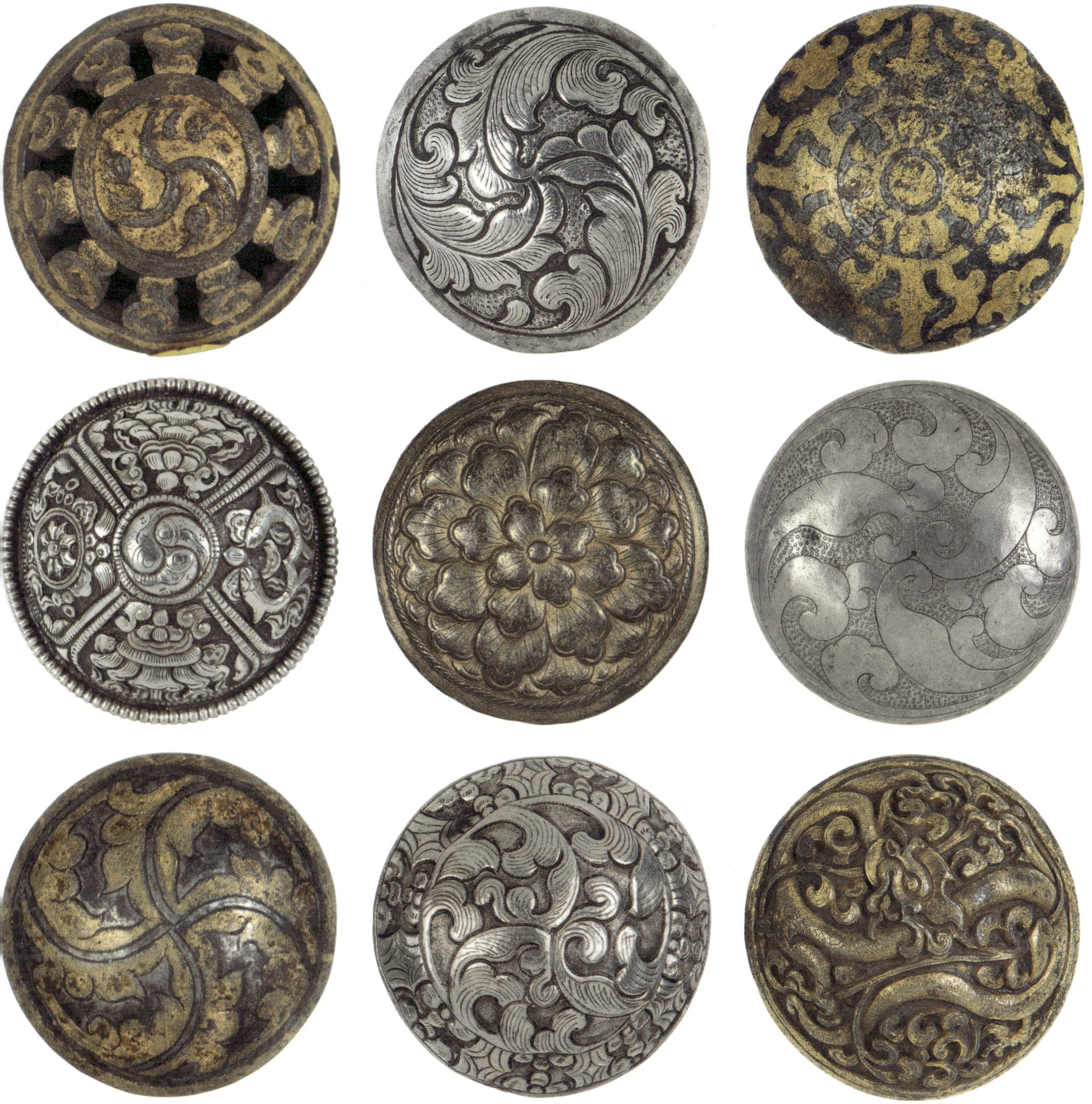

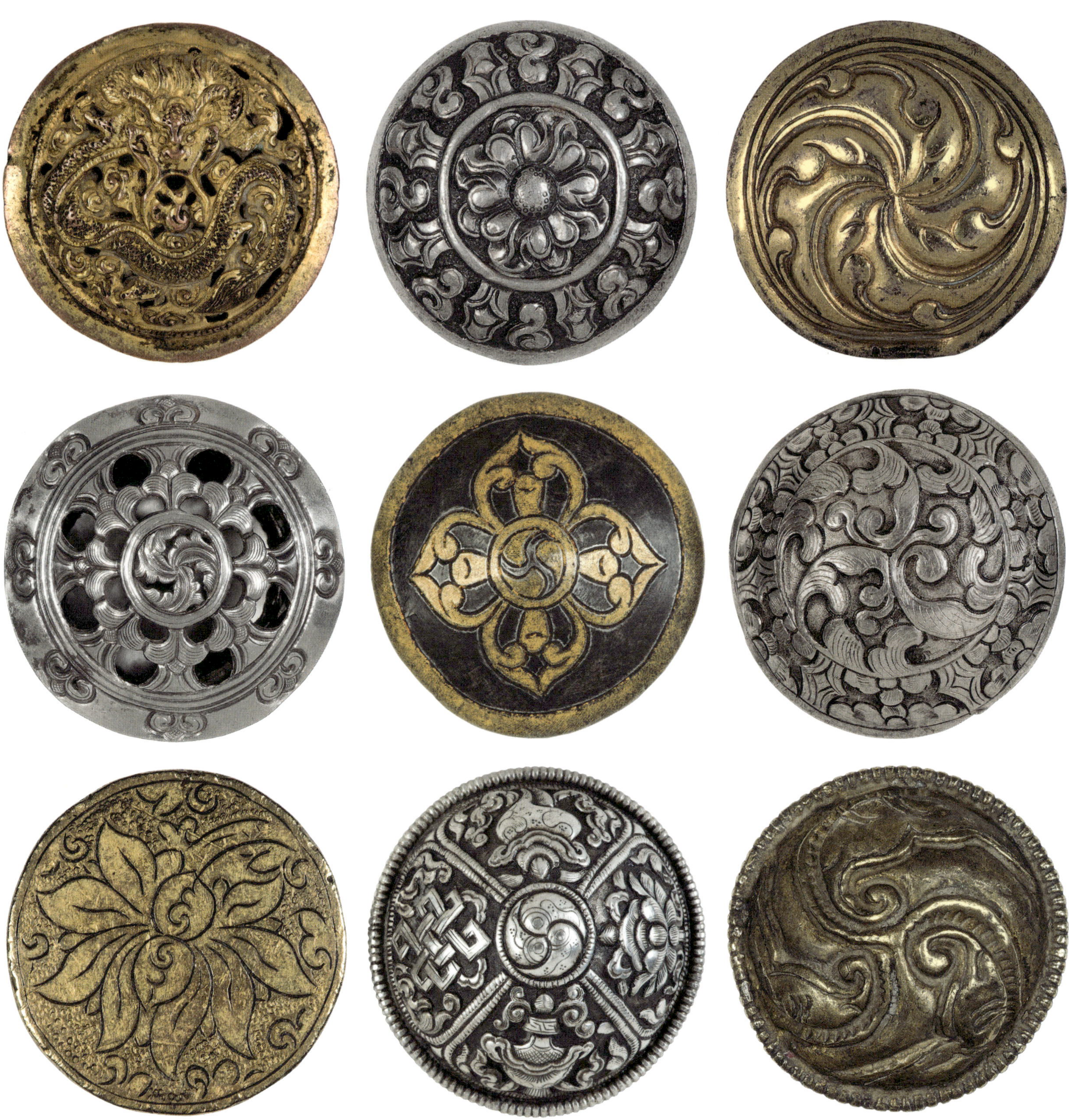

FROM THE LAND OF THE SNOW LION

The Ernst von Siemens
Art Foundation supported
this publication

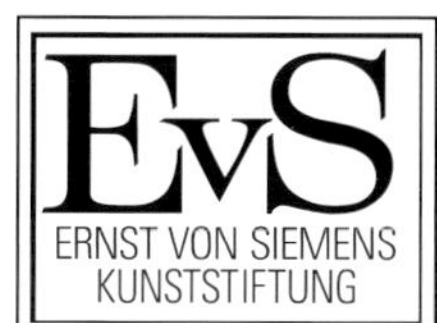

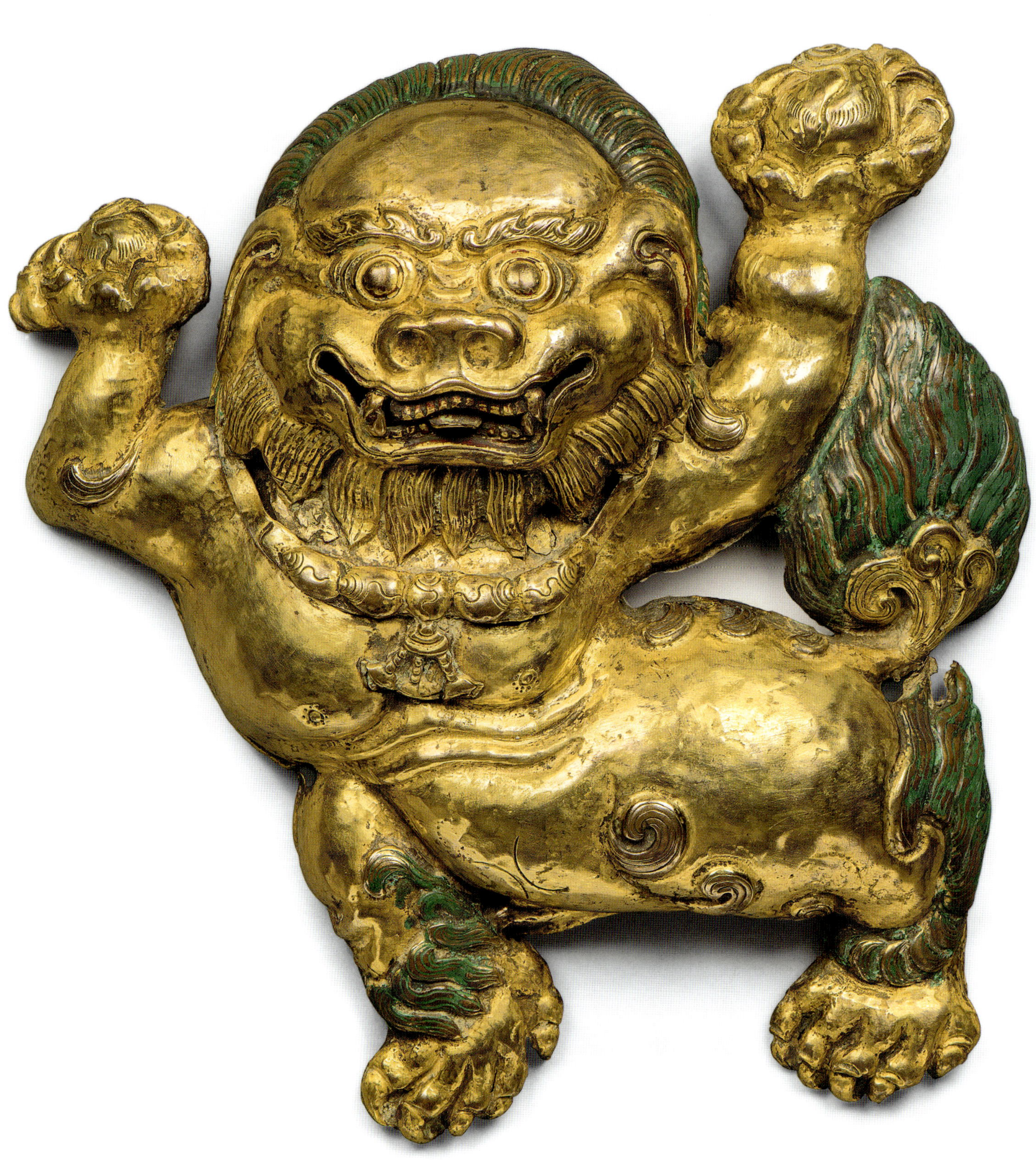

Michael Buddeberg
Bruno J. Richtsfeld (eds.)

FROM THE LAND OF THE SNOW LION

Tibetan Treasures from the 15th to 20th Century: The Justyna and Michael Buddeberg Collection

HIRMER

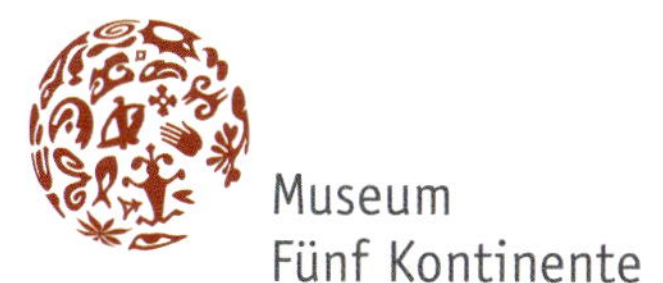

TABLE OF CONTENTS

METALWORK AND JEWELLERY

TIBETAN FURNITURE

APPENDICES

Karl Steiner with guide Sonam and monks in Bardan Gompa monastery, Zanskar, August 2012

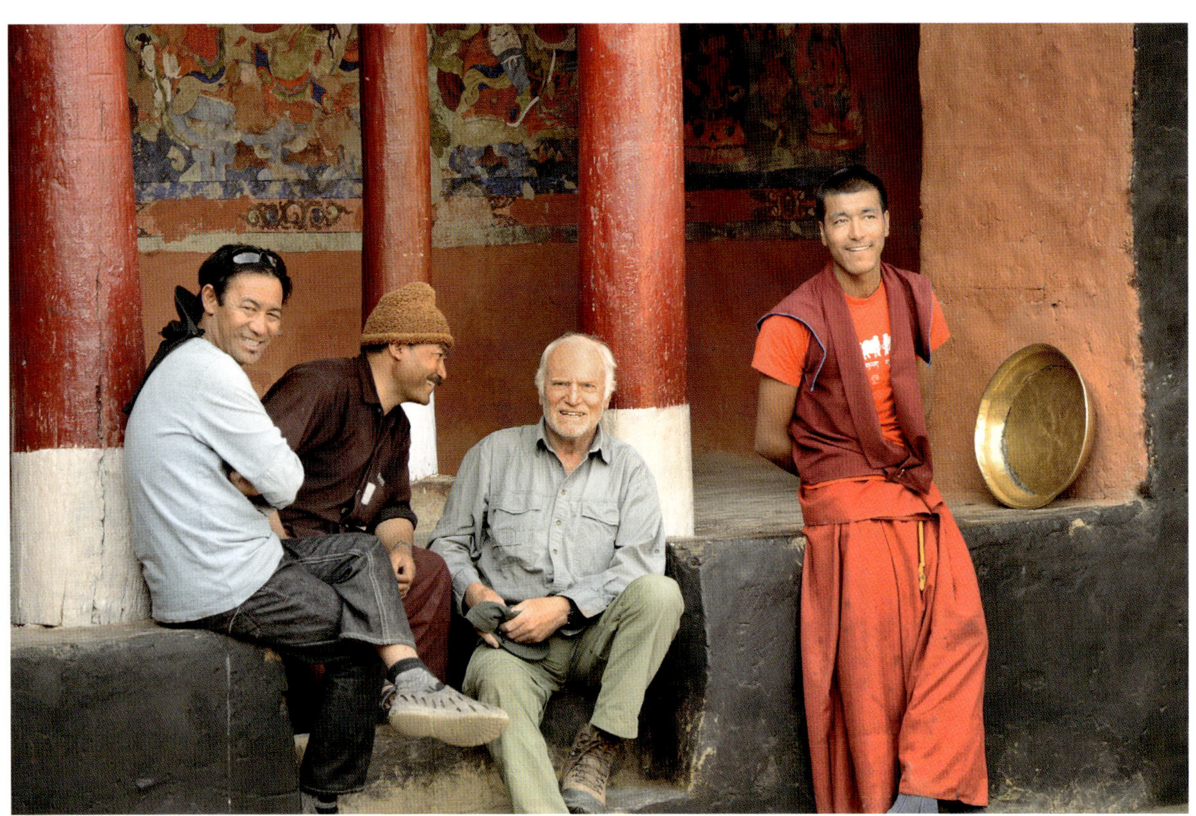

This book is dedicated to our friend, fellow collector and travel companion Karl Steiner (1937–2014).

Justyna and Michael Buddeberg

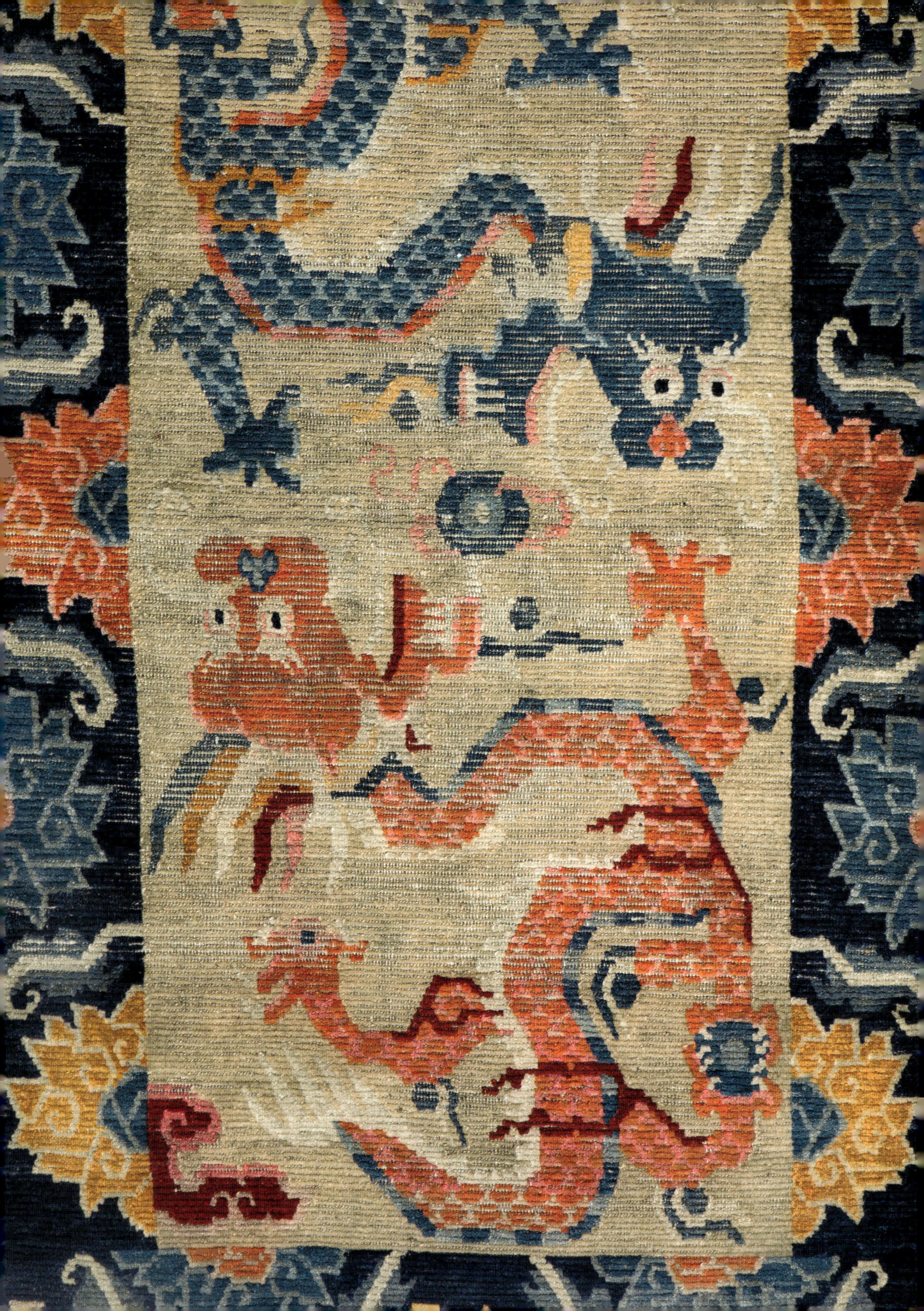

FOREWORD

Detail of Fig. 32 in the contribution by Elena Tsareva

How could museums exist without the generous contributions of ardent collectors who have often spent decades with great patience, a schooled eye and unerring intuition for the quality and distinctiveness of the objects that create their unique collections, which they then are willing to donate to a museum? The museums would unquestionably be much poorer, not only in the number of objects that could enhance an existing collection but also entirely new objects that would complement a museum's collections. The museum would also forgo the objective discussion with the collector and his expertise about the objects that are so dear to him. For several decades, the collectors Justyna and Dr. Michael Buddeberg have been travelling in Tibet and its neighbouring Himalayan countries. Their love for the country, the people and their material culture is deeply evident in their collection. The Museum Fünf Kontinente already has an extensive and valuable Tibet collection. The Buddebergs' collection will be a welcome enrichment, both for its academic and for its historical interest.

Justyna and Dr. Michael Buddeberg earn my heartfelt thanks for the generous gift of their Tibet collection, especially the rugs, which significantly enhance the international importance of the Asian and carpet collections of the Museum Fünf Kontinente. My thanks is even greater, as Dr. Buddeberg and my colleague Dr. Bruno J. Richtsfeld have assumed responsibility for the publication of the book to accompany the exhibition of the collection. Dr. Richtsfeld has also curated the exhibition, for which he deserves a second thanks. Although rugs until now have not been a subject of his research, they have aroused his anthropological curiosity and opened a new view of our collections. Dr. Uta Weigelt, Ines von Ketelhodt, Ulrich Berkmann and Paul Harris M.A. are responsible for the editorial and graphic conception of the book, filled with invaluable academic professionalism; my hearty thanks to all, also for text editing. For the accurate translation of the contributions from English and into English, I thank Dr. Ute Weber, Dr. Sabine Lang, Paul Harris M.A. and Lawrence E. Fogelberg. Jürgen Kleidt from Hirmer Publishers deserves special thanks for his patient coordination of the whole project. They are all owed additional thanks for their help with the English version of the book. All the authors of the contributions are also to be thanked that their immense knowledge has made the catalogue a standard work on various aspects of Tibetan material culture. Once again, the Munich exhibition design company "Die Werft" has assisted the museum with the best presentation of the objects. I therefore also thank Matthias Nolz, Swen Sieber and Christian Raißle.

My special thanks go to the Ernst von Siemens Kunststiftung for its generous support, which has also made possible the publication of the extensive catalogue in both languages. From this and the great efforts of all, it is hoped that a work has been created which will be a pleasure to the friends of Tibet throughout the world.

Dr. Christine Kron
Director

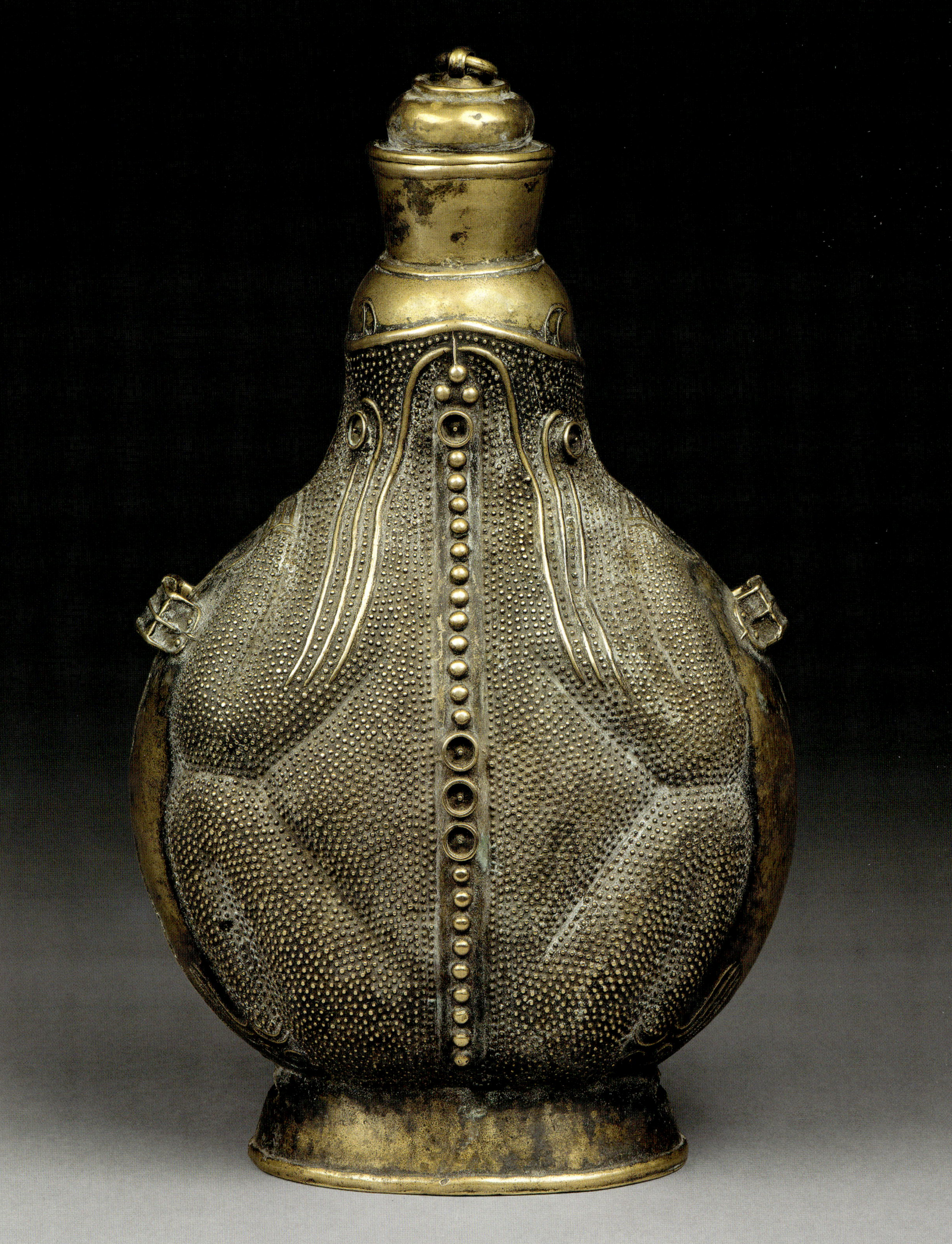

Bruno J. Richtsfeld, Stephanie Kleidt[1]

TIBETICA

The Collection of the Museum Fünf Kontinente

THE COLLECTIONS OF THE 19TH CENTURY

Fig. 1: Toad-shaped flask from the Heinrich Harrer collection, acquired for the museum with the support of the Preetorius Foundation. 19th c., bronze, wood, 33×20×12 cm, Museum Fünf Kontinente, Inv. no. 2016-20-1

The foundation for the Tibet collection of the Museum Fünf Kontinente was laid by the three Schlagintweit brothers from Munich: Hermann (1826–1882), Adolph (1829–1857) and Robert (1833–1885), who had made a name for themselves as alpinists and explorers from the mid-19th century onwards. Among the ethnographic objects they brought back from their expedition to India and the Himalayas from 1854 to 1857, those from the Tibetan cultural sphere played an important role despite being few in number.[2]

One of Alexander von Humboldt's (1769–1859) lifetime dreams seemed to come true when the brothers, after studying geography and geology, joined his circle in Berlin in 1849: an expedition to further explore the Himalayas. Humboldt was the Schlagintweit brothers' "spiritus rector" and diplomatic mediator. When the Prussian Minister of Culture refused to finance the enterprise despite its support by King Friedrich Wilhelm IV (1795–1861, ruled 1840–1861), von Humboldt proposed to approach the British East India Company (EIC) for funding. As employees of the EIC, the brothers were to complete the mapping of terrestrial magnetism in India up to 37° latitude north, up to the Hindu Kush and the Karakorum. Humboldt's idea fell on fertile ground in England, and in autumn 1854 the Schlagintweit brothers set out for India.

Their scientific interest focused on the mountainous regions not yet systematically explored. Committed to Humboldt's holistic approach and in addition to their primary task, they not only observed the interrelations between geography, geology, climate, and the botanical and biological world, but also compiled extensive natural history collections. Their panoramic study also included anthropological measurements and observations of the various ethnic groups whose material culture was likewise documented with significant objects, with a particular focus on Tibetan Buddhism. Since the Tibetan government was not allowing Westerners into the country at that time, it was impossible for the brothers to visit inner Tibet. Hence, their knowledge was limited primarily to Ladakh with its culture dominated by Lamaism. For the acquisition of Buddhist objects they employed an influential Sikkimese of Tibetan descent as an agent, Chibu Lama from Darjeeling. He arranged the purchase of objects from the monasteries of Saimonbong, Mangnang, Narigun, Lama Yuru, Tassiding, Pemiongtsi and Tamlung. Chibu Lama was especially helpful when it came to purchasing religious and historical texts of Tibetan origin. A catalogue of this collection lists 207 works.[3] During a visit to Hemis monastery (1856) near Leh in Ladakh, following a dance performance Hermann Schlagintweit was able to acquire six Cham dance masks along with accessories to the dancers' costumes. The brothers counted them among the gems of their collection. (However, the masks lacked the characteristic, religiously important bone decoration, which was apparently removed before the masks were sold.)[4]

The importance of the Buddhist objects is further illustrated by the fact that a fourth, younger brother, the lawyer Emil Schlagintweit (1835–1904), educated himself in Tibetology and wrote a book about Buddhism in Tibet, primarily based on the material collected by his brothers.

To some extent, the Schlagintweit collection owes its existence to the hopes of Friedrich Wilhelm IV and von Humboldt that museums in Berlin would profit from duplicates in the collection (which officially belonged to the EIC). After their return from India in 1857, the brothers Hermann and Robert[5] themselves worked towards the establishment of a natural science and ethnographic museum in Berlin and had copies made of important unique items. The most

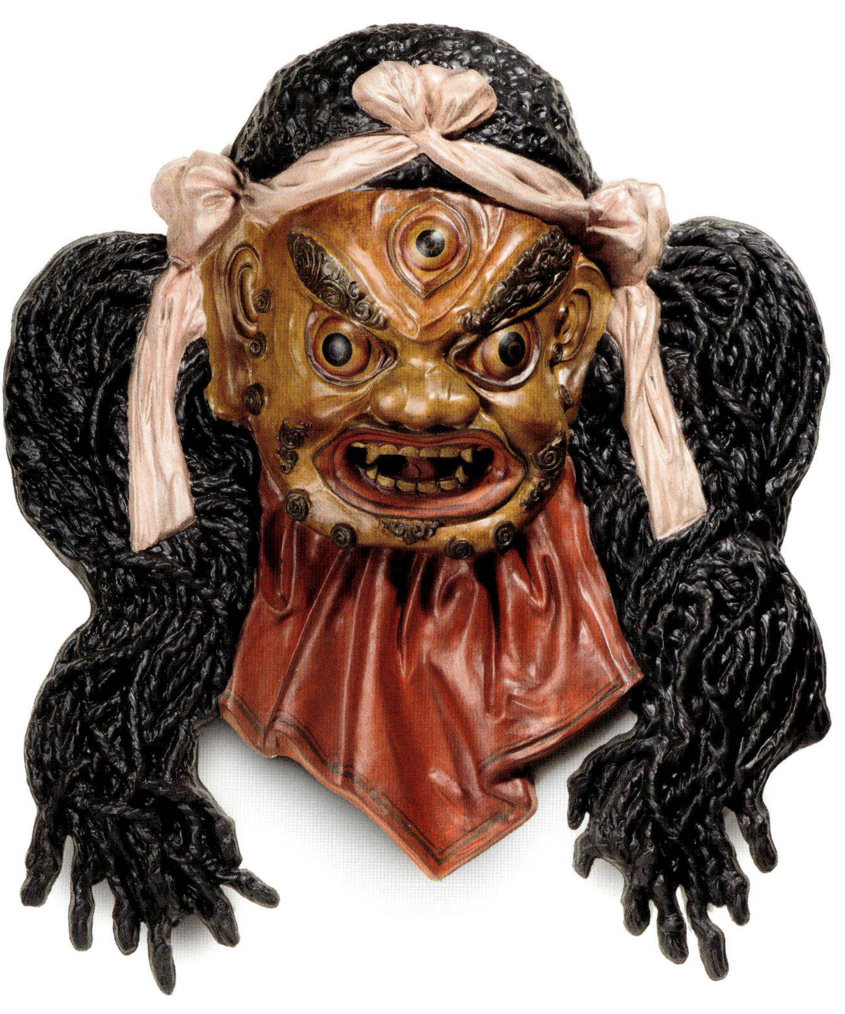

Fig. 2: Schlagintweit-commissioned replica of the mask of the god Pehar from Hemis monastery in Ladakh. Such masks were worn at religious dances (Tib. *cham*) performed during important monastery and New Year's celebrations. Berlin 1857, "Steinpappe", paint, 97.5×75×25 cm, Museum Fünf Kontinente, Inv. no. Schl. 871

prominent pieces were the dance masks which the Berlin-based Carl Gropius factory reproduced in the often then used "Steinpappe" technique, a mixture of papier mâché, clay, whiting, and linseed oil.[6] They were then painted. Casts of *mani* stones and statuettes were reproduced in zinc, probably in the Moritz Geiss zinc foundry in Berlin which had already produced mountain reliefs for the brothers. The original wood blocks were used to reprint the Tibetan texts on prayer flags and related items.

Such replicas, including the masks and *mani* stones, form the bulk of the 58 objects that came to the "Vereinigte Sammlungen" (Combined Collections) in Munich in 1859. This was due to the wish expressed by the Bavarian King Maximilian II (1811–1864, ruled 1848–1864), who was a supporter of the Schlagintweit brothers, that part of the collections should come to Bavaria. Other supporters received such gifts as well, such as the Grand Duke Carl Alexander of Sachsen-Weimar-Eisenach (1818–1901, ruled 1853–1900), who received 12 original *mani* stones in 1858, for which he expressed his cordial thanks.[7]

When Friedrich Wilhelm IV was declared incapable of ruling in late 1858, the Schlagintweit brothers saw no future for themselves in Berlin any more. In autumn 1860 they took their collection to the former hunting lodge of Jägersburg near Forchheim which they had acquired with the intention of using it as a museum to present their collection to interested visitors. In 1861, they again tried to establish their own museum, offering their collection to the Bavarian State. In their letter to the king, they wrote: "We would consider it especially fortunate if our collections, which are now in Jägersburg Castle near Forchheim, could be appropriately displayed and seen to, similar to the rich and varied treasures of art and science already represented here [in Bavaria]. Perhaps Your Majesty would kindly allow us to additionally suggest establishing a separate geographical-ethnological museum, for which our collection would provide the first – but we daresay fairly copious – material. As far as we know, on the continent no such collection is displayed which has ethnography as its subject …"[8] This museum project was as unsuccessful as the one in Berlin, and the brothers were forced to offer their collection (except for the ethnographic items) for sale in printed catalogues.

However, Hermann was apparently able to impress King Ludwig II of Bavaria (1845–1886, ruled 1864–1886). When the monarch wanted the impression of an Indian fairytale landscape in his famous winter garden on the roof of the Munich Residence in 1870/71, the "renowned Orient traveller" was consulted.[9] Hermann's sketches of huts in the Khasia Hills served as inspiration for the "Indian fisher's hut" at the artificial lake. For its authentic furnishing, the king bought from the Schlagintweits textiles and rugs, furniture and baskets, an incense burner, as well as a red paddle with painted flowers, a gift from the Raja of Kashmir. Furthermore, the large Himalayan landscape panorama painting (1870/71) for the winter garden drafted by Christian Jank (1833–1888) was based on a watercolour Hermann made in 1855 of Mount Everest, which he believed he could identify as the Gaurisankar.[10] Jank is also listed as one of the artists who retouched the Schlagintweit brothers' watercolours.

In 1881 and after long negotiations, Hermann had to sell the most important part of the ethnographic collection to the financially strong Museum für Völkerkunde in Berlin (now Ethnologisches Museum); other items also went there in 1883. However, up to 1884 further pieces from the collection went to the Ethnological Collection in Munich (independent since 1862, now Museum Fünf Kontinente), ap-

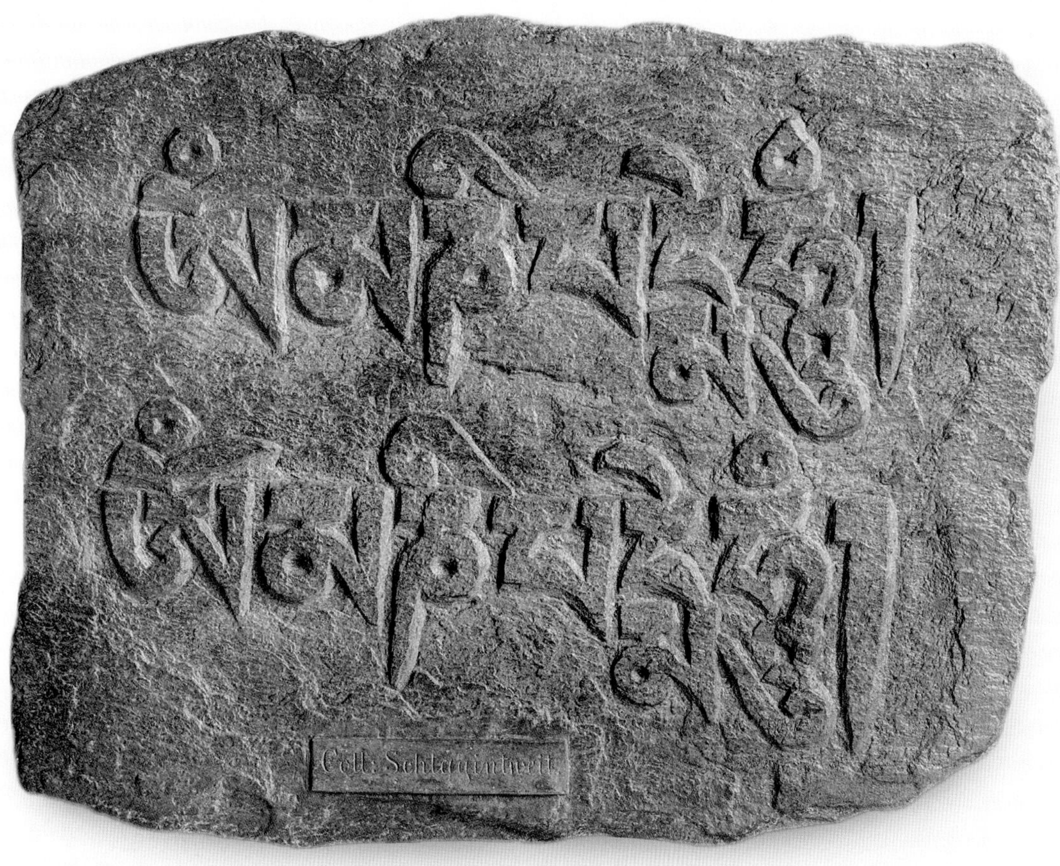

Fig. 3: Schlagintweit-commissioned Zinc cast of a *mani* stone mounted on a wooden display frame. Berlin 1857, zinc, 30.2 × 38 × 0.4 cm, Museum Fünf Kontinente, Inv. no. Schl. 874

parently on the basis of earlier agreements with its director, Moritz Wagner (1813–1887). These included original Tibetan items: *mani* stones, musical instruments, prayer wheels, a Buddhist rosary and a few household items. In comparison to the Schlagintweit collection from India, the Tibetan items in Munich were, admittedly, quite a few less in number. Moritz Wagner thanked Emil Schlagintweit, the common heir of his two deceased brothers, for his cooperation: "[...] let me repeat my warmest thanks for the great sacrifice you have made in a truly patriotic spirit in selling the beautiful collection of your meritorious brothers to the ethnographic collection of the Bavarian State at such a reasonable price."[11] The major part of the Tibet collection consists of replicas of *thangka* paintings, prayer flags and written documents. Hence, the collection is mostly of scientific interest today. Nonetheless, the originals and replicas may be considered to be the first objects ever seen in Bavaria illustrating Tibetan culture.

As the original Cham dance masks were destroyed in Berlin during World War II, the replicas commissioned by the brothers are of particular interest today. They provide a good impression of originals from Hemis, which were arguably the first Tibetan dance masks to come to Europe from the forbidden country. The Museum Fünf Kontinente possesses replicas of the masks; other sets of the dance-mask replicas are housed in the Lower Saxony State Museum in Hanover, the National Museum of Ethnology (Rijksmuseum voor Volkenkunde) in Leiden, and the National Museum of Denmark (Nationalmuseet) in Copenhagen.

In 1895, the Royal Ethnographic Museum in Munich received an additional collection of 83 objects collected by Munich-born Friedrich (known as "Friedl") Martin (1860–?): this time originals of everyday and sacred objects from Tibet.

After studying law in Munich, Friedl Martin moved to what was then the Dutch East Indies (now Indonesia), probably at the suggestion of his brother, Dr. Ludwig Martin, who was a doctor in Deli in Sumatra. Friedl became an assistant on a plantation in Sumatra. From 1889 onwards he donated collections he had compiled in Ceylon, Sumatra, and elsewhere in the East Indian archipelago to the Munich museum.

In recognition of his generosity he was awarded with medals and titles. In 1892/93, he travelled in the Congo region in Africa and returned with another collection of ethnographic objects for the museum. A collection given in 1895 included objects from Sumatra, but the greater portion were objects from Tibet and Nepal. Nothing is known about how they were acquired; the museum's archives yield no information. We can only surmise that Martin bought them during a stay in India, perhaps in the then capital Calcutta and/or in Darjeeling.[12]

ACCESSIONS IN THE 20TH CENTURY

In Darjeeling and the nearby Ghoom (Ghum) monastery on the border to the kingdom of Sikkim, Lucian and Christine Scherman were able to expand the museum's collection by acquiring 171 selected objects from Bhutan, Sikkim and Tibet (September 1911). Since 1907 Scherman had been director of the Ethnographic Collection in Munich; from October 1910 until December 1911 he and his wife were able to take a research and acquisition tour of British India (now India, Pakistan and Burma). In Darjeeling, Scherman had an audience with the thirteenth Dalai Lama who lived there in exile, having fled to British India when an army of the Qing Dynasty, then ruling the Chinese Empire (1644–1911) invaded Lhasa. After the collapse of the Qing Dynasty and the end of the empire in February 1912, the religious and secular leader of the Tibetans returned to Lhasa and declared the independence of Tibet, which, however, none of the subsequent Chinese governments has ever recognised.[13]

Among the persons close to the Dalai Lama, Scherman met the Sikkimese-Tibetan police chief, Laden-La (1876–1936), who was in charge of organising the Dalai Lama's stay in India. Laden-La helped Scherman acquire objects for the Tibet collection, and even shortly before his death in 1936 sent six objects to the museum and offered them for purchase.[14]

In 1903, Count Maximilian Maria Karl Desiderius von Montgelas (1860–1938), then military attaché to the German Embassy in Peking, gave the museum three statues of Lamaist deities as well as a comprehensive pantheon of 458 paintings of Lamaist deities and teachers, presumably painted in Peking for use in the city's Tibetan-Mongolian temples. In 1902, he had already passed on six miniature *thangkas* to the museum, which were a donation from Baron Victor von Grot who was director and manager of a gold mine in Urga (now Ulaanbaatar, Ulan Bator). This collection was extended in 1904 when Prince Rupprecht von Bayern gave the museum another 19 miniature *thangkas* which he had acquired during his trip to Asia in 1902/03, either in Peking or at the pilgrimage site of Wutaishan.[15]

Peking was one of the centres of Tibetan-Mongolian Buddhism with about 7,000 monks (1912) and several high-ranking incarnates residing in and near the city. The support for this type of Buddhism by the emperors of the Manchu Qing dynasty (1644–1911) resulted from the claim of each emperor that he was a *Chakravartin*, a universal ruler in the Buddhist sense, whose patronage united many peoples. The Manchu emperors were declared by the Lamaist clergy to be incarnations of Manjushri, the *Bodhisattva* of wisdom, and Tibetan and Mongolian as well as Manchu and Chinese were the most important official languages in the empire. In the political context, this support by the Qing rulers was one of the measures employed to tie the Tibetan and Mongolian populace to the dynasty and make them loyal vassals.

As a result, it was easy to purchase Tibetan Buddhist cult and devotional items at the time. For example, Max Buchner (1846–1921), the second director of the Ethnographic Collection in Munich, was able to buy six copper figures of Lamaist deities on his trip through Australia, New Guinea and East Asia (1888–1890) in the so-called Mongolian market situated in the Diplomatic Quarter of Peking.

Before World War I and thanks to Scherman's contacts, the Austrian explorer and zoologist Erich Zugmayer (1879–1938) gave objects from Tibet and Ladakh to the museum. In 1906 he had made an extensive trip through Kashmir, East Turkestan and north-western Tibet during which he collected ethnographic items.

World War I and the ensuing disastrous economic situation in Germany rendered it next to impossible for German researchers to make extended trips in Central Asia. However, in the course of the 1920s and 1930s research was resumed on the remote fringes of that culture area, e.g., in Peking with its Lamaist temples and monasteries. It was possible to collect not only curiosities but also items complying with scholarly standards. A few researchers, such as Wilhelm Filchner (1877–1957), were able to do research in Inner Asia and Tibet. Sven Hedin's (1865–1952) interdisciplinary and international Sino-Swedish Expedition (1927–1935) was partially supported by German funding.

On the other hand, collectors in Peking and northern China profited from the downfall and corruption of the still existent imperial household and the clergy. Although the last Manchu emperor, Xuantong (1906–1967), known as Puyi, had abdicated in February 1912, he continued to

Fig. 4: Statue of the teacher Padmasambhava (Tib. *Guru Rinpoche*), who according to legend helped Buddhism achieve victory in Tibet in the 8th century. Statue from the collection of the Sikkimese-Tibetan police chief Sonam Wangphal Laden-La which he sent to Munich in 1936. Late 19th or early 20th c., gilded thin copper, paint, wood, 31.5×24×15 cm, Museum Fünf Kontinente, Inv. no. 36-18-1

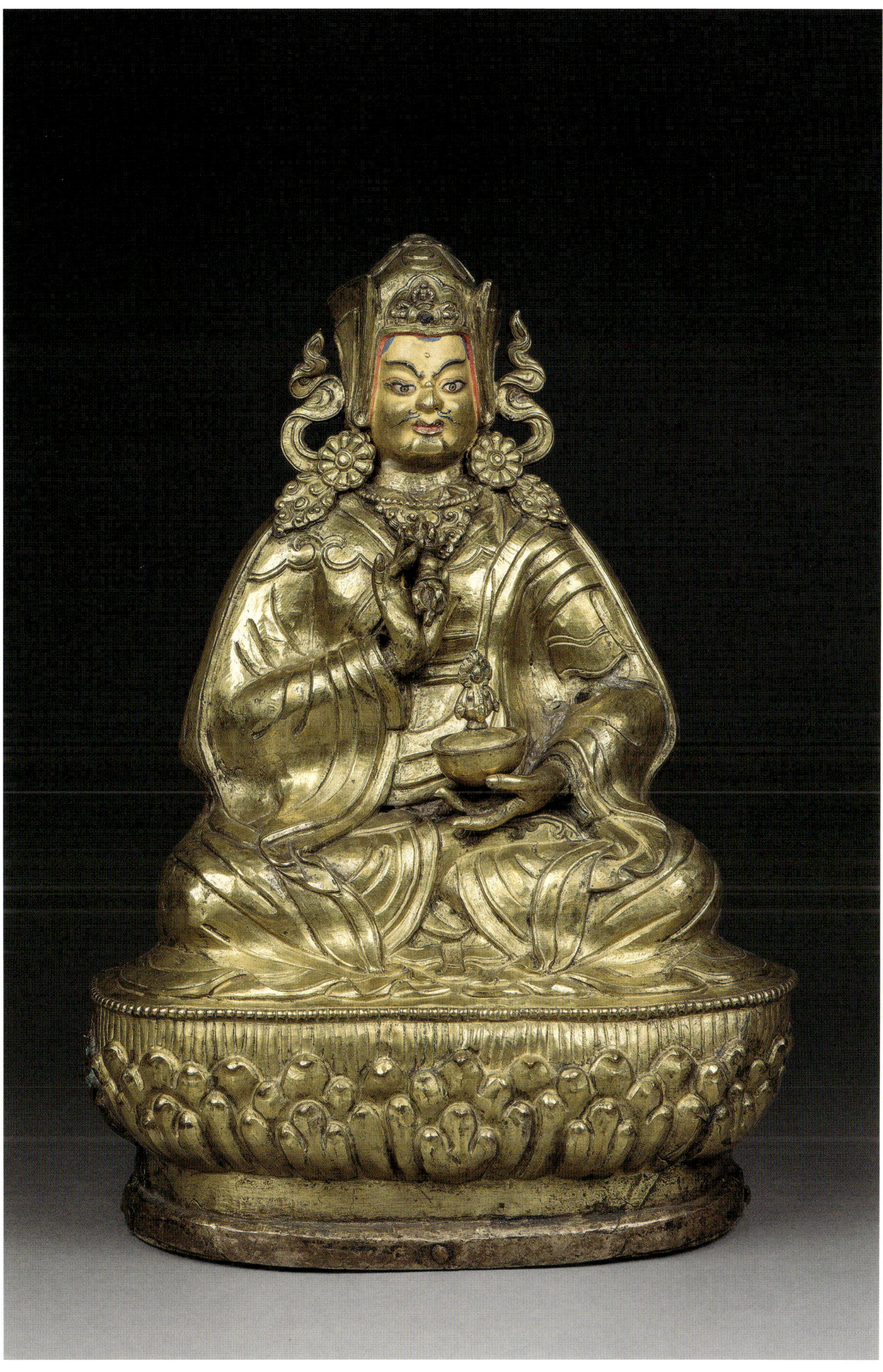

reside as a shadow emperor in a part of the imperial palace until 1924. Thievery and corruption were encouraged by the lack of central power and the fact that parts of the palace collections had not yet been forfeited to the Chinese government but were still the personal property of the former ruling family. Eunuchs enriched themselves by smuggling works of art, valuable texts, etc. out of the palace collections and into Peking's antique markets. This continued until 1923 when part of the palace was set on fire out of fear of discovery and to hide the thievery.[16] After 1912 many monasteries no longer received financial support from the state and fell into decline. Antique dealers and collectors also acquired objects and collections from former nobles, high-ranking monks and previously influential persons, who were now impoverished and had to dispose of their belongings.

It can be assumed that the Bavarian Lt. General Wilhelm Täubler acquired the Tibetan and Chinese objects in his collection from antique dealers in Peking and northern China. It was inherited by the museum in 1939. According to the sparse notes in the museum's archives, he collected these and other Chinese objects during his "journeys around the world". Since the documents in the archives only concern the terms of the purchase and give no information about the collection and collector, nothing is presently known about the collector.

It was only ten years after World War I that a portion of the Central Asian collection of August Hermann Francke (1870–1930) and Hans Körber (1886–1979) came to the museum. In the context of his preparing a Tibetan translation of the Bible, the British and Foreign Bible Society had obliged the "Herrnhuter" (Moravian Brethren) missionary Francke to visit the Tibetan-speaking region every three years to brush up on his language skills. When Scherman learned that a new trip was planned for 1914 he convinced Francke to travel overland and collect for the museum. Francke had already been a Moravian Brethren missionary in Ladakh from 1896 until 1910 and was one of the most distinguished specialists on Tibetan history, language, and folklore. As a travel companion he suggested the young Hans Körber, who spoke Chinese, to Scherman. Scherman agreed, and the two men travelled from Germany via Russia and West Turkestan, which was controlled by Russia at the time, into the western part of Chinese-controlled East Turkestan/Xinjiang in China, and then over the Karakorum Pass to Ladakh. Along the way they compiled large collections from the Mongolian Kalmyks as well as in East Turkestan and in Ladakh. On the Karakorum Pass, they learned from the Italian researcher Filippo de Filippi (1869–1938) that World War I had broken out. Shortly after their arrival in Ladakh, Francke and Körber were interned in the prisoner-of-war camp of Ahmednagar where Körber was detained until 1919, whereas Francke, well-known to the British as a Tibetologist and missionary, was released in 1916. Until the end of the war he served as a translator and paramedic in Transylvania, where he was again imprisoned. Francke and Körber had become so completely estranged – maybe already during the trip but definitely during their imprisonment – that they were never reconciled for the rest of their lives. However, their individual correspondence with Scherman continued.[17]

The Kalmyk objects and those collected in Russian Turkestan had been lost by war's end,[18] but not so the boxes with archaeological finds from East Turkestan. Francke and Körber had entrusted them to Swedish missionaries in Kashgar who were not able to ship the boxes before the outbreak of the war and therefore kept them for the war's duration. To everyone's great surprise, the crates with these archaeological and the ethnological objects from Ladakh (in all ca. 2,000 items) arrived at last in Berlin and Munich in 1928, thanks to financial support by the Emergency Association of German Science. Francke began to study and catalogue the 9th-century Tibetan literary monuments from East Turkestan, but died before he could complete the task.

Thanks to this collection, the Museum Fünf Kontinente is one of three museums in Germany that has comprehensive archaeological collections from East Turkestan/Xinjiang; the other two are the Ethnological Museum Berlin (Grünwedel/Le Coq collection) and the Überseemuseum Bremen (Trinkler collection). Among other written Central Asian documents, these holdings of the Munich archaeological collection also include Tibetan scripts.[19] These archaeological holdings were complemented in 1983 by Hans Weihreter, who gave the museum a collection of 17 *thokcha*. These are usually metal objects of pre- or early historical origin found in the soil; the Tibetans believed they fell from heaven and considered them powerful amulets.

During the period from 1930 to 1960, a number of individual Tibetan items were added to the holdings. Then another large collection – remarkable for having been compiled on site – came to the museum: the Ernst Schäfer collection. The zoologist Ernst Schäfer (1910–1992) led his own expedition to Tibet in 1938/39 after already having been a member of two expeditions to West China and East Tibet (1931/32 and 1934/36) led by the American explorer Brooke Dolan (1908–1945). Due to the war between China

Fig. 5: Statue of Yamantaka, conqueror over death and patron deity of the Gelugpa school of Tibetan Buddhism, from the collection of the publisher and Indian Honorary Consul General Robert Gedon (1909–1989). 18th c., gilded bronze, 17 × 16 × 7 cm, Museum Fünf Kontinente, Inv. no. 77-7-34

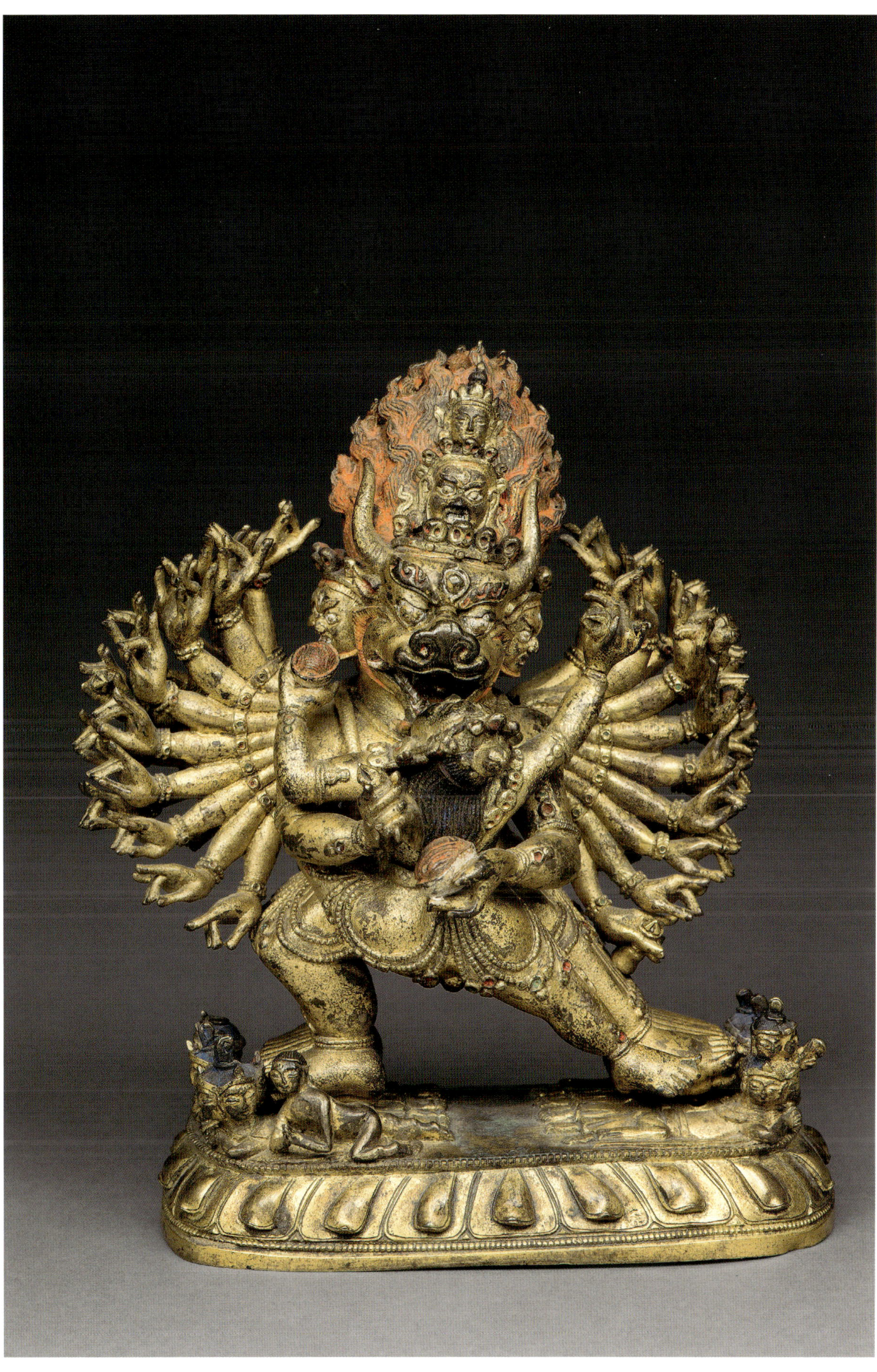

Fig. 6: Photograph of a horse with under-saddle rug on the Nathu Lu Pass between Sikkim and Tibet, taken by Ernst Krause during the Deutsche Tibet-Expedition Ernst Schäfer 1938/39

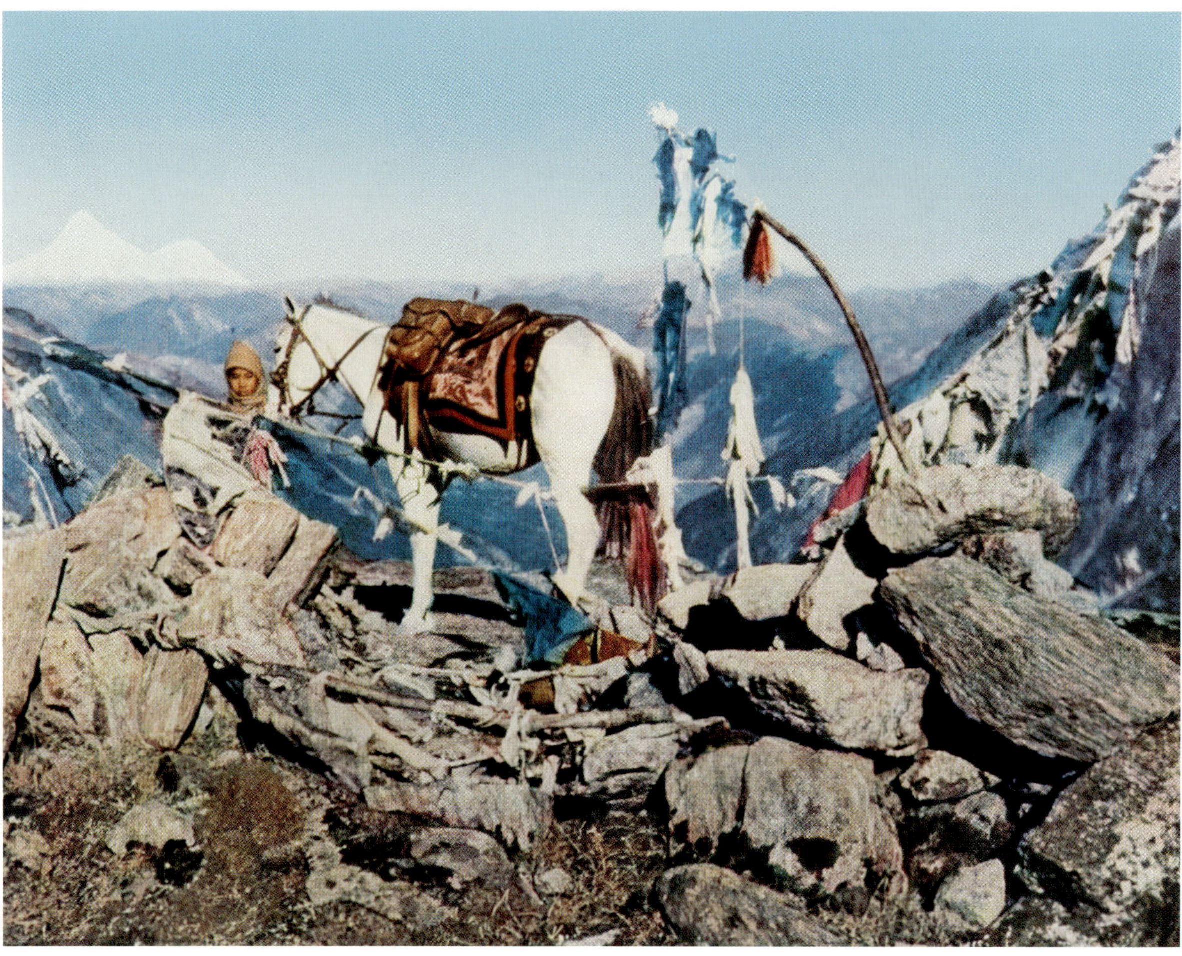

and Japan, which had broken out in 1937, the route from the Chinese coast to his desired destination – East Tibet – was closed. From the British he received permission to do research on the Sikkimese-Tibetan border, but he was not allowed to cross that border. Through clever negotiations with Tibetan dignitaries, however, he succeeded in getting an invitation from the Tibetan government. Thus Schäfer's party was the first German expedition officially invited to enter Lhasa, the Tibetan capital, which was otherwise closed to western travellers. During their visit, Schäfer and his four companions were able to observe and film the New Year's celebrations, which in the holy city were particularly elaborate. Schäfer also received permission to travel to other important regions in Central Tibet, which strained the already bad relations with Hugh Richardson (1905–2000), Great Britain's Resident in Lhasa. The imminent outbreak of war between Germany and Great Britain thwarted any further travel plans and forced Schäfer and his party to leave for Germany without delay. During the expedition, the team's anthropologist and ethnographer, Bruno Beger (1911–2009), collected more than 2,000 ethnographic objects in Sikkim and Tibet, which he either bought in the markets or was given out of gratitude for the medical aid he delivered. The original list of the items with their prices has survived. The collection mainly has everyday utensils; religious objects make up only a small portion. Among those, however, one is quite outstanding, a complete edition of the *Kangyur*, the Tibetan-Buddhist collection of all the important Buddhist teachings. These 108 volumes were a gift of the noble Phala family and are today kept in the Bavarian State Library.

Schäfer's expedition to Tibet is often described as being in the spirit of National Socialism, and as research undertaken in collaboration with Heinrich Himmler's institution "Ahnenerbe" (Research and Teaching Community of the Ancestral Heritage). Schäfer was definitely not adverse to a patriotic German attitude and was willing to avail himself – as far as was possible in a dictatorial system – of the existing structures for his own ambitious plans. However, an assessment of the expedition as a National Socialist undertaking in the spirit of Himmler's pseudo-scientific theory is countered by the fact that Schäfer rejected funding by the "Ahnenerbe"; instead, he organised support from private donors, corporations, and the German Research

Foundation. By his choice of team members Schäfer circumvented Himmler's recommendations as well, and in contrast to many pseudo-scientists of the "Ahnenerbe", his reputation as a serious scientist was never at stake. Originally he named his expedition the "Schäfer Expedition 1938/39", but under pressure from the "Ahnenerbe" he had to rename it the "Deutsche Tibet-Expedition Ernst Schäfer". He did not, however, name it the "Deutsche SS Tibetexpedition Ernst Schäfer", a designation that was used in the media at the time and is often quoted today.[20] After his return, the ambitious Schäfer, one of Himmler's few "model scientists", became increasingly caught in the maelstrom of the "Ahnenerbe." In 1942, he renamed his newly founded "Research Institute for Inner Asia and Expeditions" in Munich to "Sven Hedin Institute for Inner Asian Studies", and soon assumed a key role in the "Ahnenerbe".[21]

The renaming celebration was attended by the famous Central Asia explorer and eponym of the institute, Sven Hedin. In his honour and due to the increasing bombing of Munich, Bruno Beger built the Tibet diorama in the Haus der Natur in Salzburg from early autumn 1942 onward using objects from the collection. In January 1943, Hedin arrived by special train in Salzburg. At the opening of the exhibit he officially dedicated the new institute that was now named after him. Schäfer donated all the ethnographic items on display to his friend Paul Eduard Tratz (1888–1977), the founder (1924) and first director of the Haus der Natur.[22]

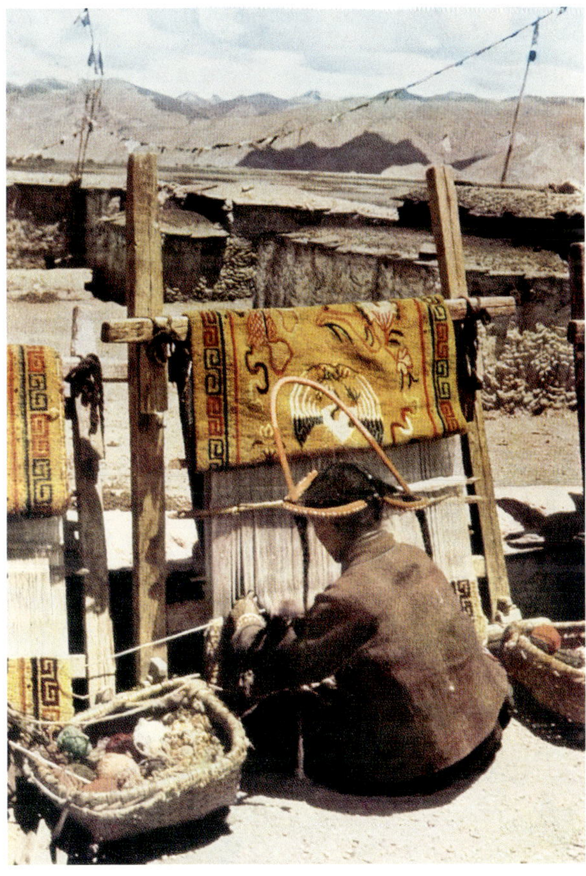

Fig. 7: Photograph of rug making on the flat roof of a house in the town of Gyantse, taken by Ernst Krause during the Deutsche Tibet-Expedition Ernst Schäfer 1938/39

At the end of 1943, due to the increased bombing, the institute and collection were moved from Munich to Mittersill (Pinzgau, Austria) on Schäfer's initiative. There, the Tibet collection was seized by the American forces and brought to the Central Collecting Point in Munich. The objects in Salzburg remained there and are still on exhibition in the Haus der Natur.[23]

How the collection was transferred from the Central Collection Point to the Ethnological Museum around 1970 could only be reconstructed from the statements of now deceased employees, since there are no written documents in the museum's archives.[24] According to them, following a notice by the relevant authorities as to the transfer of the collection to the museum, the then technical director, Günter Sandner, arranged the transportation, as Director Andreas Lommel was unappreciative of the collection because it had no works of art, which for him were the only true document of any people's skill and, therefore, the only objects worthy of display. Sandner eventually arranged transportation using the technical staff of the museum. The objects were stored in the underground buildings between the former "Führerbau" (now College of Music and Theatre Munich) and the former administration building of the NSDAP (now Munich House of the Cultural Institutes); these buildings had been the original site of the Central Collecting Point. The museum personnel picked them up in the passages and brought them to the museum, where they were catalogued in 1974 and exhibited in 1982/83 in the major Tibet exhibition: "Der Weg zum Dach der Welt" (The Way to the Roof of the World).[25] Thanks to Schäfer's collection (1,109 inventory numbers), the museum's holdings of everyday Tibetan objects are outstanding in the world. Together with the photographic material, they are unique documents of the life of the Tibetan population prior to 1951.

An additional collection of 94 objects, predominantly cult items compiled by the Düsseldorf collector Ludwig L. Hassenpflug, was purchased by the museum in 1969/70. This collection consists mostly of religious works of art including 53 *thangkas*. However, the records in the archives are so meagre that no precise information about the collector exists yet.

The latest major collection to reach the museum was the 239 objects from the Austrian journalist, writer and expert on Tibetan culture and religion, Blanche Christine Olschak (1913–1989), who lived in Zurich from 1946 until her death.

From the late 1960s into the 1980s, it was above all Olschak's popular scientific works that were instrumental in publicising Tibetan culture in the West. During many trips to the Himalayan countries with Tibetan culture, she compiled a collection of Tibetan items, the most precious of which are religious objects. After her passing, the museum bought the collection and brought it to Munich in 1991.

Following the major Tibet exhibition in 1982/83, the Tibetan dealer Namgyal Gongpo Ronge stayed in contact with the museum, to which he sold and donated a collection of 45 everyday objects, including a nomad tent and yak-hide boat, in 1983, 1984, 1988, 2003 and 2005. Another small nomad tent was acquired in 2010 thanks to Michael Buddeberg's contacts to Tibet and support by the Preetorius Foundation. This tent and the boat were first shown in 2010 in the exhibition "Tibet, Religion, Art, Myth" in the Knauf-Museum in Iphofen, organised jointly by the Museum Fünf Kontinente and the Knauf-Museum.

Not only these extensive collections have contributed to the enlargement of the Tibetan holdings of the Museum Fünf Kontinente but also many benefactors and friends of the museum have donated individual objects or small numbers of objects. For example, between 1903 and 1953 Crown Prince Rupprecht von Bayern undertook a trip to Asia in 1902/03 and gave the museum not only a considerable number of objects from China and Japan but also 25 Tibetan-Mongolian items, including two large temple paintings on cloth, which he had collected in Peking and in the mountain pilgrimage region of Wutaishan. Not all benefactors can be named here, but let us mention three more as "pars pro toto". Friedrich A. Peter (1904–1988), a descendent of Friedrich E. Peter[26] who was a missionary in Leh, Ladakh before World War I and a bishop, gave the museum 17 objects from Ladakh and left another 25 objects to the museum in his will, including a silver container for tea which possibly came from the royal family of Ladakh. The Tibetologist Eva Dargyay gave the museum 17 objects, household items, clothing and women's jewellery from Ladakh. Korinna Harrer, the widow of Heinrich Harrer (1912–2006), gave the museum a set of sheets with musical notes from her husband's collection, as well as a pamphlet with medical images from the holdings of the Chagpori medical school in Lhasa which was destroyed in 1959 by Chinese grenades during the Tibetan unrest.

Formerly, the museum only had 23 Tibetan rugs of varying quality. With the addition of the collection of Justyna and Michael Buddeberg and, through their mediation, 37 rugs from the collection of Karl Steiner (1937–2014), the museum now has an internationally important collection in that field as well, which closes a gap in the museum's comprehensive holdings of carpets and rugs.

NOTES

1 The section about the Schlagintweit brothers was written by Stephanie Kleidt, curator of the exhibition "Über den Himalaya. Die Expeditionen der Brüder Schagintweit nach Indien und Zentralasien 1854 bis 1858" (Over the Himalayas. The Expeditions of the Schlagintweit Brothers to India and Central Asia, 1854 to 1858) in the Alpine Museum in Munich (19 March 2015 to 26 June 2016) and co-editor of the catalogue of the same name (Brecius & Kaiser & Kleidt 2015). During her research, Ms. Kleidt acquainted herself in depth with the Schlagintweit collection in Munich and Berlin. The rest of the article is by Bruno J. Richtsfeld.

2 See also Appel & Stelzig 2012: 23b–26b, Schlagintweit 1982, Kick 1982, Körner 1982, Lindgren 1982, Polter 1982 and Seeberger 1982. In the museum are 112 objects from the Schlagintweit collection. For the history of the collection see Kleidt 2015.

3 The bulk of this collection was sold by the heir Emil Schlagintweit in 1885 to the Bodleian Library in Oxford. A small part is in the Bavarian State Library, Munich.

4 A detailed description of these masks and their context was published by August Hermann Francke 1898 in the periodical *Globus*, Number 73.

5 Adolph Schlagintweit had been arrested in East Turkistan in 1857 as a supposed Chinese spy and was beheaded in Kashgar without trial.

6 The original appearance of the masks is shown in the illustrations of Francke's article in *Globus*. Their hair was made of animal hair, their collars and head coverings of cloth. An illustration of the mask of the deity Lha-mo is in Utzinger 1923: Fig. 14.

7 Bavarian State Library, Munich, Schlagintweitiana IV.6.1: Letter of thanks from 18 October 1858.

8 Bavarian Central State Archives, Munich: "Findbuch über Akten der zoologischen Staatssammlung VN 67, Abschrift Nr. 1182", Letter from Hermann and Robert Schlagintweit to the king from 4 February 1861.

9 See an article in the "St. Petersburger Nachrichten" from 26.10. and 7.11.1871 which Ernst von Destouches copied in his "Münchner Stadtchronik" 1871, p. 2001ff. under the title "Der neue Wintergarten auf der Königl. Residenz" (publ. in Schlim 2001: 47f.), also Mergenthaler 2010: 183–192.

10 Sheet no. 604 of the General Registers has been lost. From the watercolour a lithograph was made, however, which serves as plate no. 1 in the atlas accompanying the volumes with the scientific results by the Schlagintweit brothers.

11 Bavarian State Library, Munich, Schlagintweitiana VI.5.7.3: M. Wagner to E. Schlagintweit, 12.6.1884.

12 See Appel 2008: 27.

13 In Weigelt 2003, the trip of Scherman and his wife is described at length (pp. 116–150), also their stay in Darjeeling (p. 141).

14 More about Sonam Wangphal Laden-La in Rhodes & Rhodes 2006. Brief biographies are found in Hoffman & Lhalangpa 1983: 150 and Wikipedia (last accessed 7 June 2016).

15 It is possible that Count von Montgelas played a key role, as he was the personal adjutant of the Bavarian prince who was later designated crown prince.

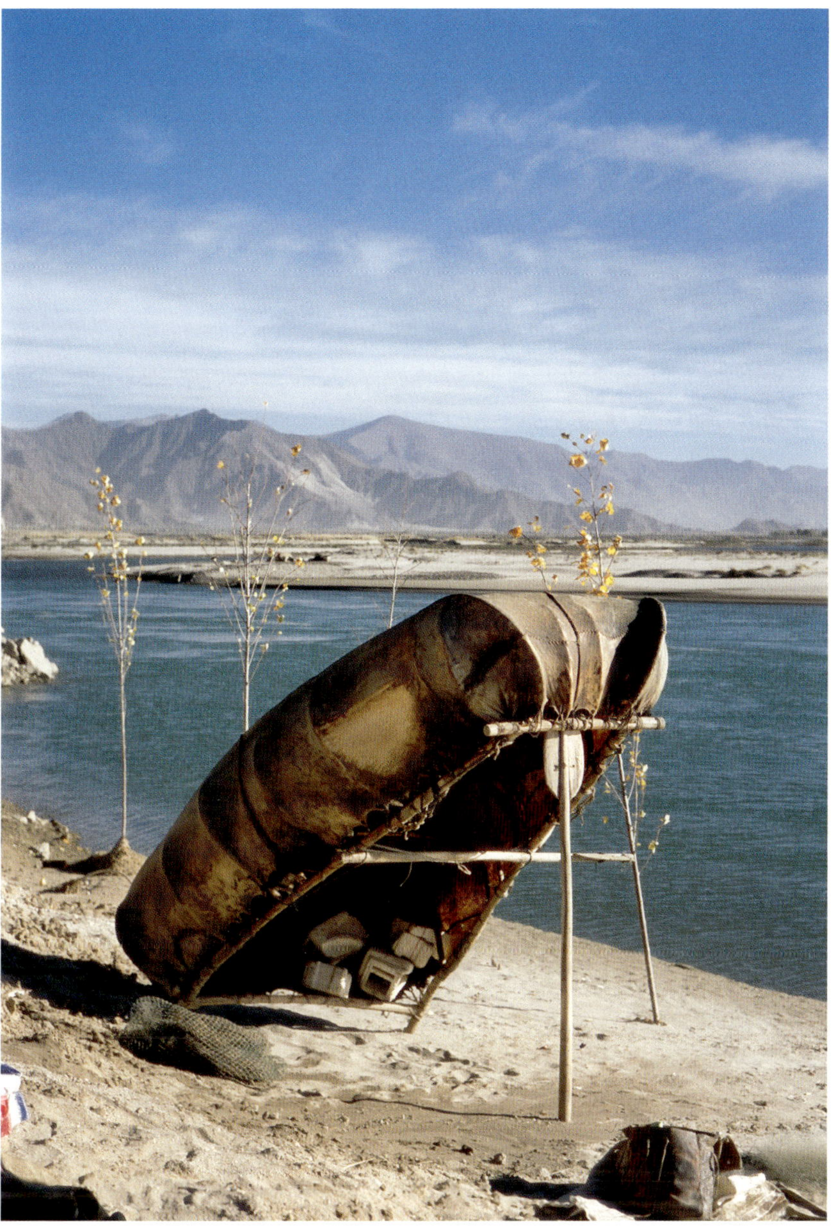

Fig. 8: A yak-hide boat (coracle) propped on a paddle to dry. Central Tibet, 1997

16 See [Aisin Gioro Pu Yi] 1983: 132–135. Thievery, smuggling and greed were also rampant in other institutions; see, e.g., the brief mention of corruption among Lamas in Peking in 1918 in the diary of the chemist Joseph Schedel (Holzammer 2003: 189). From Schedel's collection the museum received objects from Japan and China, but also 19 Tibetan cult figures and miniature paintings. See Walravens 2008 for more about Schedel.

17 About the trip, see Francke 1921. Scherman complained in a letter to Francke that in his publication he only referred to Hans Körber as "Mr. K."

18 See for this Gropp 1974.

19 See Richtsfeld 2010/11 with information on further literature.

20 See for this Engelhardt 2003: 189.

21 Of the many works about Schäfer and his Tibet Expedition, only these can be listed here: Kater 2006, Mierau 2006 and Engelhardt 2003, 2007. The interested reader will find references to further literature in these works. In a letter by Schäfer to Richtsfeld dated 25.2.1983, Schäfer describes the objective of the institute as follows: "I founded it under the greatest of difficulties in order to avoid political involvement. Its goal was to continue Humboldt's ideas and at the same time to anticipate the now modern ecological-biodynamic comprehensive approach. It included the fields of geophysics, geology, geography, special and applied botany (in an affiliated institute near Graz, the famous 'thirty-day barley' was bred from the collection of thousands of grain samples), entomology, ornithology, mammalogy, anthropology, and Tibetology. It was staffed with 8 outstanding young scientists, of whom 4 became full professors after the war. My own professorial dissertation 'Ecological and Bio-Geographical Study of Tibet', my venia legendi, inaugural lecture and resulting lectureship at Munich university are witness to the spirit of this comprehensive approach as applied to the 'Roof of the World'." It can be presumed that Schäfer oriented himself not only on Humboldt's ideas but also on the staffing and programme of the international Sino-Swedish Expedition of Sven Hedin, his role model. After a first publication in 1943, it was only after the war that Schäfer reported in detail about the expedition (Schäfer 1940 and 1950). In the abovementioned letter, he explained that his long silence was due to a ban on him publishing on the subject. As mentioned, however, in 1943 his first publication was printed by the Munich Bruckmann-Verlag. Beger published an extensive travel report in 1998.

22 Information from Hans Roth, Institut für Zentralasienkunde, Bonn University, also correspondence from Schäfer to Richtsfeld, 25.2.1983.

23 In his letter of 25.2.1983, Schäfer describes the situation as follows: "As the American troops were advancing on Munich at the end of April, I drove towards them and immediately surrendered. I was a long-standing associate and lifetime member of the Academy of Natural Sciences, Philadelphia. Hence, I was convinced that someone would help me prevent the plundering of Mittersill Castle. But instead of help came revenge and automatic arrest for 3 years. At my denazification in 1949, the decision of the tribunal read: 'Since Sch. repeatedly defied instructions from SS authorities and suffered reprimands, and helped racially persecuted persons and opponents of National Socialism, the panel with careful and just weighing of the incriminating and exonerating facts has come to the decision that the defiant and sometimes even adversarial acts of the accused outweigh his support of National Socialism, and he is exonerated and classified in Category V. Dr. Schäfer is exonerated.' The last information that I received in 1949 about my institute and my personal belongings was: 'Everything seized by the Americans and taken away.' I was ruined, the basis for my work destroyed. Out of pure worries about my existence, I followed a call to Venezuela at the end of 1949 for the establishment of a biological station in the national park. I worked for the ministry of agriculture and later was given a position at the university."

24 These statements were received by the author in many conversations between 1989 and 2001 with retired employees of the museum, especially those with Günter Bauer (restorer), Walter Scheidegg (carpenter) and Günter Sandner.

25 From Schäfer's own comments, he only learned through the exhibition that the collection from the expedition was located in the museum. It was his opinion that because the expedition had been independently financed and on the basis of contracts with its members the collection was his property (letter from Schäfer to Richtsfeld, 25.2.1983).

26 For life in the missionaries in Leh, see Appel & During & Huck 2014.

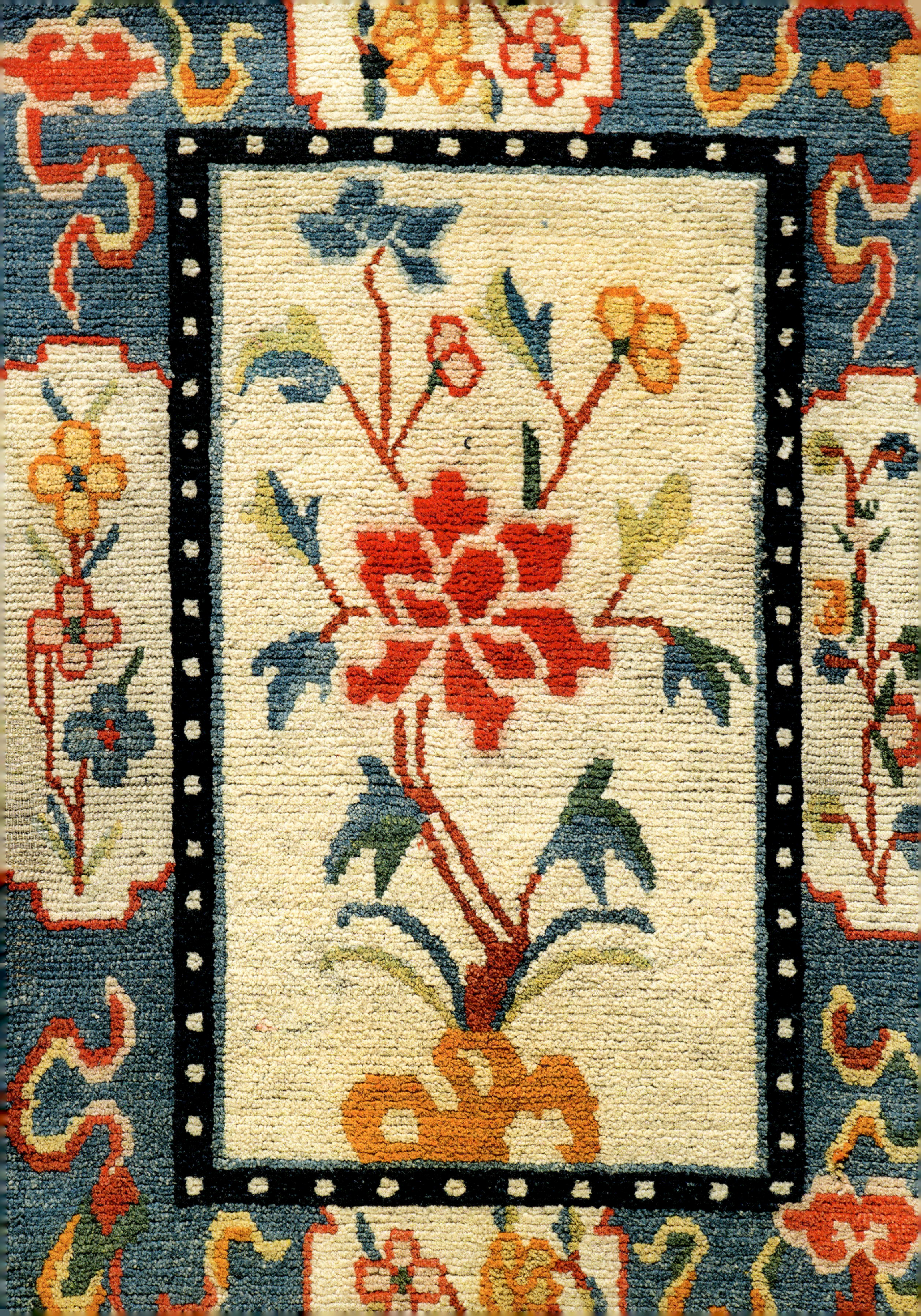

Michael Buddeberg

FASCINATION AND PASSION

On Collecting Tibetan Rugs and Textiles

20 YEARS OF COLLECTING

Detail of Fig. 20 in the contribution by Elena Tsareva

Tibetan rugs are not only a niche product that has little appeal to rug collectors and auctioneers; they have also never played any significant role as souvenirs for travellers to Tibet. The Barkhor in Lhasa, the middlemost street encircling the sacred Jokhang temple which is visited by Tibetan pilgrims, inhabitants of the city and tourists, is lined with the stalls of hundreds of travelling salespeople and it is where rug dealers naturally have their stands, too. However, with their new rugs, made either at home or in manufactories, they mainly address local buyers: pilgrims, nomads, and citizens of Lhasa – in short: Tibetans, for whom a rug is an everyday piece of furniture just as a chair is for Westerners.

No market for used – that is, old or ancient – rugs exists there, with the exception of a little less than a dozen antique shops scattered over the historic centre of Lhasa. Besides all kinds of more or less covetable artefacts, these usually have a small stack of dusty rugs in stock. However, those who stroll along the Barkhor with an expert eye may discover an old sitting rug, a knotted saddle blanket, or a *khaden* (the 160 × 80 cm standard rug of the Tibetans) hidden beneath a motley collection of everyday utensils, jewellery, receptacles, ritual objects, and other souvenirs mostly made in China or Nepal. This requires a bit of luck, though, as these objects, which are not very marketable, are usually not on display. They often remain stored in the carrier box, or are concealed by colourfully woven bags, shawls, and caps, or are simply used as seat padding. However, we have learned that it is possible to tip the odds in one's favour. A rolled-up old rug tucked visibly under one's arm is a clear signal to all vendors who screen the stream of passers-by for potential buyers of their merchandise. And lo and behold – all of a sudden, a rug is produced from a lower shelf of the stall or from some other previously hidden repository and bargaining can begin. This little trick brought many a piece to our collection; in addition, it led to encounters and experiences we would otherwise not have had.

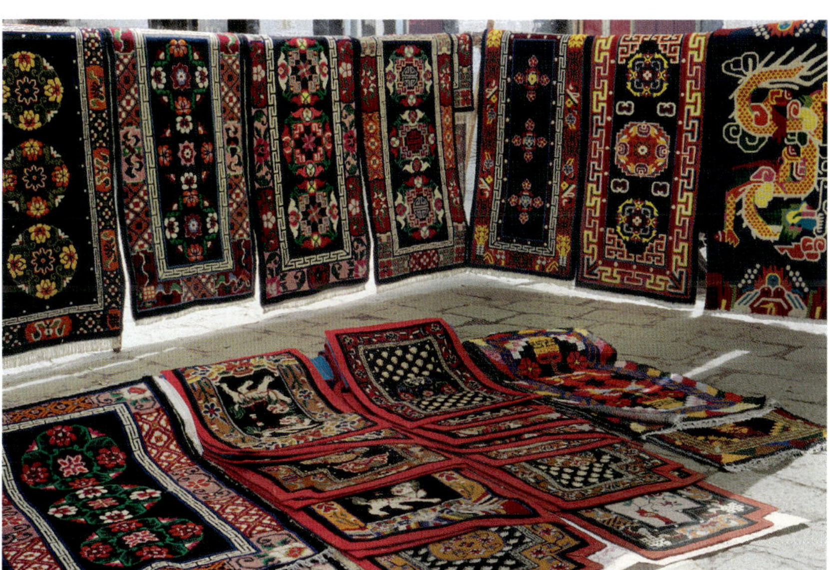

Fig. 1: Tibetan rugs of modern manufacture on the Barkhor. Lhasa, 1997

By revealing that trick I am already right in the middle of the story of how a collection of Tibetan rugs was compiled and enlarged, a story that actually began much, much earlier. I was probably born with the passion for collecting, that specific gene which was very pronounced in my father as well and that has enticed me, depending on age and opportunities, to compile the most varied collections. It began with pretty pebbles gathered on my way to school; after that, stamps were my favourites for many years, but I also amassed margarine collector cards. Still today, the pretty tin boxes used in the 1950s to promote and sell cigarette brands with evocative names such as "Effendi", "Kelim", "Prince of Wales", or "Simon Arzt" contain a collection of exotic coins, little presents brought back by my father from his business trips. The love for books – not only for their contents but also as objects of aesthetic design – marked the beginnings of a library, and has stayed with me until today.

Beautiful rugs in my parents' house, as well as a Qashqai presented to me by my father when I moved into my student's apartment in Munich, spawned a latent passion for rugs in me; however, it took many years for that passion to materialise. As a student, I intrepidly paid a visit to a renowned rug store in the 1960s, but the prices demanded for Caucasian rugs at the time prevented an early infection by the "rug virus". Eventually, however, as a young lawyer I fell in love with a Karabagh featuring animal-*göl* medallions at the preview of an auction. I succeeded in purchasing the rug with a modest bid and proudly carried it home. Before I went home I also bought my first book on rugs, *Kaukasische Teppiche* by Doris Eder. With that, the "maladie des tapis" had broken out which according to Martin Volkmann is a "sickness without any chance of being cured"; rugs of varied provenance were added to my collection, as well as more books. A time of learning began, my "rug horizon" broadened, a process that was aided by my visits to the annual Volkmann Meetings in Munich and the evening meetings of the "Münchner Teppichfreunde" ("Munich Rug Enthusiasts"), which were likewise organised by Martin Volkmann as irregular events held in the back room of an inn.

Subsequently the founding of the Pazyryk Society as an umbrella organisation of German circles of rug enthusiasts, my first participation in an international conference – the International Conference on Oriental Carpets (ICOC) held in Hamburg and Berlin in 1992 – and, last but not least, my appointment to the Executive Committee of the ICOC were milestones of a fascinating and lasting passion.

Along the way, Tibetan rugs at first did not play any role. They were viewed as exotic pieces, and what was known – and, rarely enough, seen – of them was generally believed not to be conducive to any deeper involvement with them: they featured strange patterns that differed considerably from the repertoire of patterns found in familiar collecting regions, bright and often synthetic colours, and a comparatively coarsely knotted structure. Hence, when Justyna and I were invited to join a privately organised trip, first to western China (Xinjiang) and then over land to Tibet in the early 1990s, it was not the rugs that attracted us but rather our general interest to see a part of Asia, a region that had long captivated our imagination.

In 1994 we set out for that big trip. Via Peking we flew to Urumqi, crossed marginal regions of the Gobi and Taklamakan deserts, visited the Turfan oasis (the archaeological site of the ancient city of Jiaohe/Yarkhoto), and the cave temples of Dunhuang. From Lanzhou we then proceeded to the Tibetan highlands. Tibet, the sceneries of the northern Changtang plateau, the Trans-Himalaya, and the Himalaya, the encounter with a fascinating civilisation and, last but not least, the amiable charms of the Tibetans and their profound spiritual devoutness left such a deep impression on us that we decided to return to the Roof of the World the following year. We ended up making 16 more or less extensive trips to Tibet, Nepal, Ladakh, Zanskar, Mustang, Bhutan and even Mongolia.

But let us return to Tibetan rugs. Needless to say we bought a small sitting rug in Lhasa during our very first visit. It was nothing special, as we did not have an expert eye yet. However, we had become enthusiastic about Tibet and its culture, and the review after our trip was intense. A completely new world opened up before us, including a new world of rugs; there were new contacts, new literature, and we had the opportunity to buy a few Tibetan rugs from the Teunis and Susanne Wollesen collection.[1] These seven rugs, chosen by intuition rather than expertise, became the basis of our collection. Besides the literature on the subject, which was scanty at the time, they were our first learning and contemplation material. From our second trip in 1995 – an adventuresome drive from Kashgar through the Kunlun Mountains and West Tibet to Lhasa – we brought back an additional number of rugs; together with a few "Tibetans" purchased in stores in Munich and Stuttgart, these already deserved the term "collection".

Viewed in retrospect, it was at that point in time that we began to systematically collect Tibetan rugs. In the "pre-Tibetan era" I had never collected selectively but merely bought what I liked – rugs that had "been waiting for me", as I like to say. Now Justyna and I had discovered a field of collecting that interested both of us and, due to its in many respects unusual diverseness, one that virtually cried out for enlargement. Delving into Tibetan rugs for a good year had opened our eyes to an amazing wealth of forms, to an unusual but as yet imperfectly understood aesthetic of rugs, an intriguing repertoire of diverse patterns and meanings, and the rug as a component of Tibet's material culture. We had learned that the Tibetans are a genuine "rug people", that every Tibetan is accompanied by at least one rug throughout his or her life and that rugs also play a significant role in the monastic life and temple rituals that are so important in Tibet. In short, our first trip to Tibet in 1994 spawned a passion that still continues today, and has resulted in a considerable collection both of Tibetan rugs and other Tibetan knotted objects which soon became complemented by Tibetan textiles and other items from Tibet's material culture. However, the heart of the continuously growing collection was, and still is, the rugs whose diversity never ceases to fascinate us. And even today, after almost

Fig. 2: Rare rug from the Wollesen collection featuring animals symbolising the "Four Dignities"

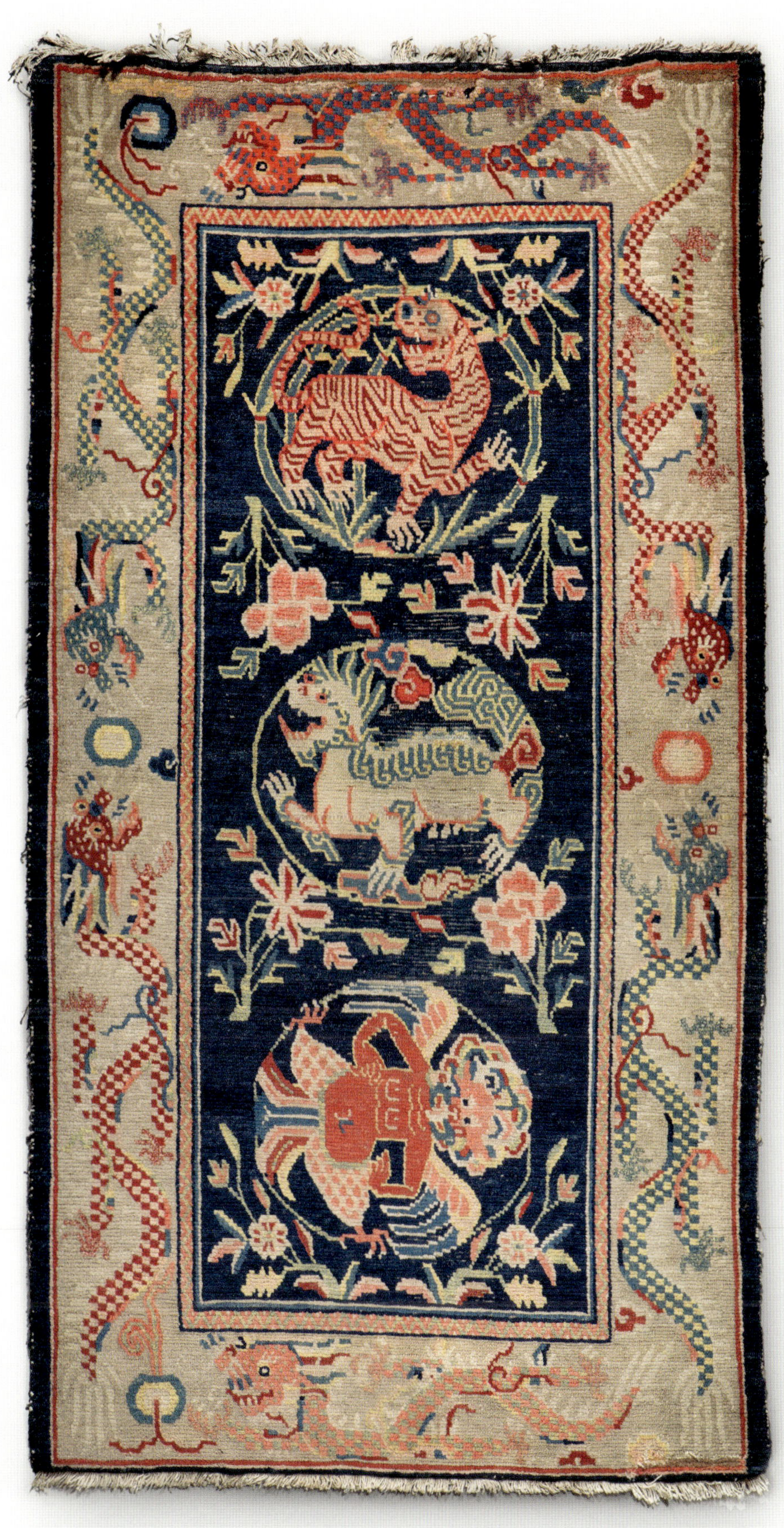

20 years of delving into the subject, after studying almost the entire literature on Tibetan rugs, and after having seen, touched, and memorised countless rugs in stores, at trade fairs, and at collectors' meetings, it still happens that we come across a Tibetan rug and have to realise, "We have never seen one like this before."

Our passion for collecting was kindled by various factors. There was our love for Tibet, our growing understanding of and closeness to the intriguing Buddhist civilisation as we visited Tibet again and again; the overwhelmingly beautiful and dramatic sceneries of the Tibetan plateau; and the amiability and openness of the people. But of course we also wished to expand our collection, we were curious about ever new aesthetic revelations and our passion for collecting was further fuelled by the obvious question as to the roots of that textile culture. The fact that we did not find any answers may have contributed to our curiosity. The typical questions of the rug enthusiast about how old the purchased piece is, when, where, by whom and for what purpose it was made, what material is it made of and which technique was used, are for no provenience as inadequately answered as for the Tibetan rug. It is interesting to investigate these questions further.

THE PERCEPTION OF TIBETAN RUGS IN THE WEST

Up to the 19th century, it was especially the natural barriers – deserts, rough mountainous regions, and the world's highest mountain ranges – that made the Tibetan plateau inaccessible for the western world. While some early travellers and Christian missionaries brought news from that foreign world, they never mentioned rugs. And while the few explorers who dared to venture into the Tibetan highlands in the late 19th and early 20th centuries – for example, Sven Hedin and Wilhelm Filchner – often mention having sat on soft rugs in tents, monasteries, or fortresses of their Tibetan hosts, their reports do not go into any detail. No descriptions, sketches, or photographs of rugs dating from that time exist. The small sitting rug brought back by the American private scholar and diplomat William Woodville Rockhill from an expedition to Tibet in the 1880s is the notable exception. It is edged in the traditional way with red wool cloth and features a simple medallion and a T-border on a blue background. Rockhill gave it to the National Museum of Natural History, Smithsonian Institution. It was practically unknown until it was published for the first time in 1984.[2]

In the context of the so-called "Great Game" over dominance in Central Asia, Tibet became a pawn in the conflict of interests between Great Britain, Russia, and China. For Tibet, that conflict culminated in the Younghusband Expedition of 1904/05, a British military intervention that led British soldiers and officers all the way to Lhasa in the wake of a cruel suppression of futile Tibetan resistance. Due to the ensuing British presence in Lhasa, some more information on Tibetan rugs reached the West; in addition, some original rugs found their way to the Royal Museum of Scotland in Edinburgh (Mauch 1987: 15–16). However, the most interesting information from that time is probably provided by Perceval Landon who accompanied Francis Younghusband as a correspondent of the *Times* and published a two-volume book entitled *Lhasa*. In it he gives an account of a rug manufactory outside Lhasa in which men and women were busy working at many looms, knotting diverse Tibetan rugs. Landon does not give any information on the type of rugs. However, he thought them interesting enough to recommend them for export to London (Landon 1905: 228f.). But the Great Game eventually resulted in an even more effective isolation of Tibet from the rest of the world. Only few select travellers (e.g., Ernst Schäfer) or bold adventurers (e.g., Alexandra David-Néel) made it to Lhasa. The British were again the exception in that era, and we owe the first original photographs of Tibetan rug manufacturing to Charles Bell, the long-time governor of the British trade mission in Lhasa.[3]

Even though such fragmentary information reached the outside world, Tibetan rugs remained almost unknown until the second half of the 20th century. One of the first experts and collectors of peasant and nomad rugs, Reinhard Hubel, whose large and diverse collection is today kept at the Museum Fünf Kontinente in Munich, wrote as late as 1965 in the first edition of his *Ullstein Teppichbuch* that no examples were known of knotted rugs made in Tibet (Hubel 1965: 279). The book appeared in print only a few years after the revolt of the Tibetan people against Chinese foreign rule, a revolution that was crushed with much bloodshed by Mao's People's Liberation Army in March 1959. Thousands of Tibetans, including noble families, high-ranking lamas, and monks followed the Dalai Lama to India where he still lives in exile. As they crossed the high, snow-covered mountain passes to India and Nepal, all they could take with them was their most precious and important belongings: jewellery, ritual objects and, of course, the most important article of daily use for sitting and sleeping – the rug.

Fig. 4: A small masterpiece of Tibetan knotting art

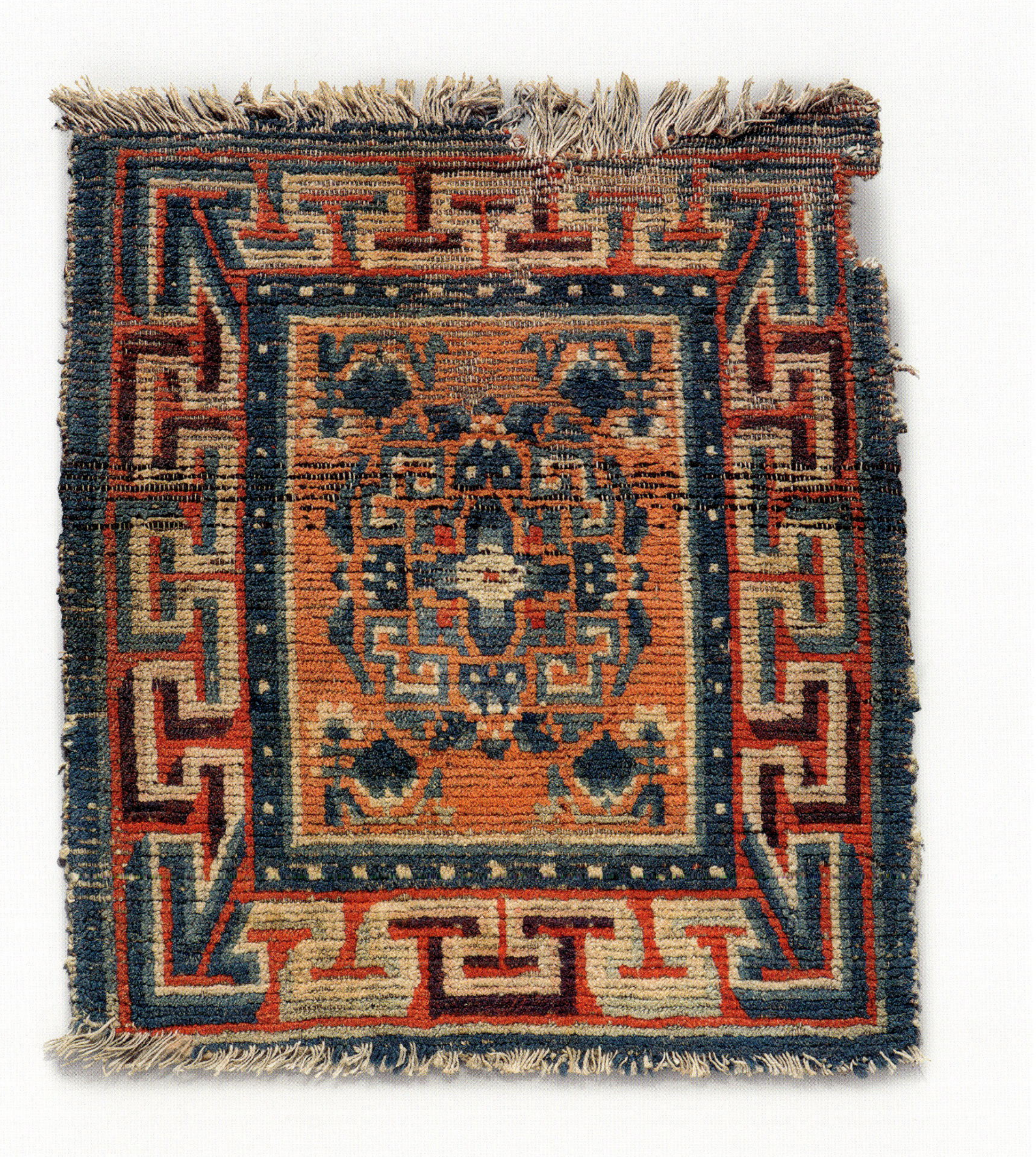

even if they are found on objects of everyday use. This has never before been stated as clearly in the literature on Tibetan rugs.

Thomas Wild is one of only a few experts on Tibetan rugs, and we met him – of course – in Tibet. He has been visiting Tibet every year for decades, not only to buy merchandise but also to record what knowledge still exists about the old ways of making rugs. Thomas has written down his thoughts on the development, techniques, and colours used in Tibetan rugs during the period of time represented by specimens from our collection. He, too, breaks new ground with his effort to relate a stylistic development of Tibetan rug patterns to the passage of time in history. The cautious opening of Tibet to the rest of the world, initiated by the 13th Dalai Lama at the beginning of the 20th century, in connection with the synthetic colours provided by European industry resulted in an almost revolutionary change in Tibetan rug patterns. The Dalai Lama's policy was meant to guide Tibet into the international community as an independent national subject, but his efforts were thwarted by the conservative clergy and the vast majority of the nobility.

A very important sphere of Tibetan knotted works is saddle rugs, horse blankets, and various other adornments for animals. This comes as no surprise given that no roads in the modern sense existed in Tibet prior to the early

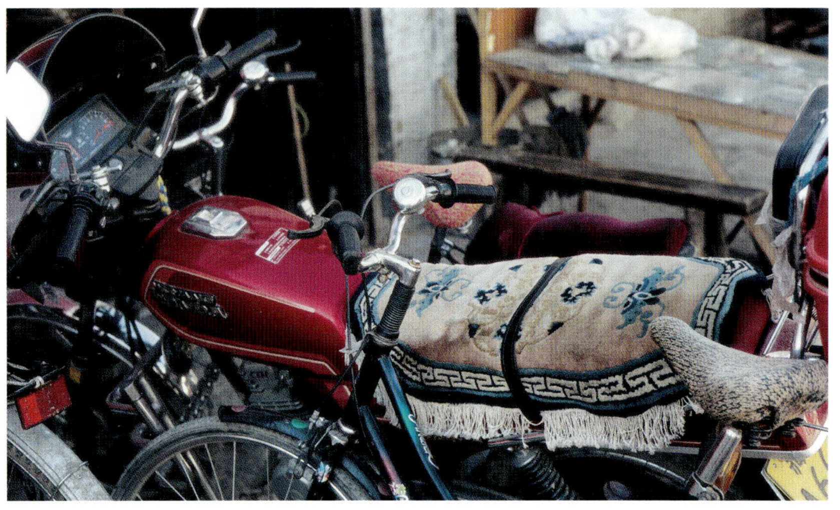

Fig. 5: The descendant of the saddle rug: a knotted piece for a motorcycle seat. Central Tibet, 1998

1950s, and that the horse was the most important means of transportation. Such works are amply represented in our collection. Apart from the saddle rugs used for the convenience of both the horse (rug under the saddle) and the rider (rug over the saddle), I would like to draw particular attention to the rare crupper rugs. In his book *Dragon & Horse* (2013), the Dutch art historian **Koos de Jong** has done pioneering work on horse equipment from China and the adjacent countries; his focus is on knotted works, including such from Tibet. We consider ourselves fortunate that he has studied that part of our collection and describes it in his contribution. The matter-of-factness with which equipment and adornments for horses were made in the knotting technique may hint at a very ancient tradition. And even though the horse has long lost its importance as a means of transportation, the knotted rugs used as slipcovers for car seats or as saddle rugs for the seats of motorcycles are nostalgic reminders of that tradition.

Karma Trinley Darchen, last but not least, is a colleague of Thomas Wild and the latter's fieldwork companion. He was one of the first experts to take note of the rustic *tsuktruks*, which are woven and knotted in narrow strips and then sewn together into rugs. It was also him who piqued the collectors' interest in these rugs. His thoughts on where and how these textiles were made are an important contribution complementing the unusual and ancient *tsuktruks* from our collection, which includes a little less than a dozen of them.

ALMOST UNKNOWN: TIBETAN TEXTILES

In variation of an old German proverb, one might say, "Take care of the textiles and the rugs will look after themselves". Looking back on almost 40 years of being part of the rug-collector scene, we can indeed note that textiles have come to play an increasingly important role. This development began in the 1970s with flat woven fabrics, particularly Anatolian *kilims*, and today comprises all types of textile works. The best example is the popularity of Central Asian *ikats* and *susani* embroideries.

Textiles from Tibet mainly comprise small and large fragments, garments, robes, banners, and flags made of old

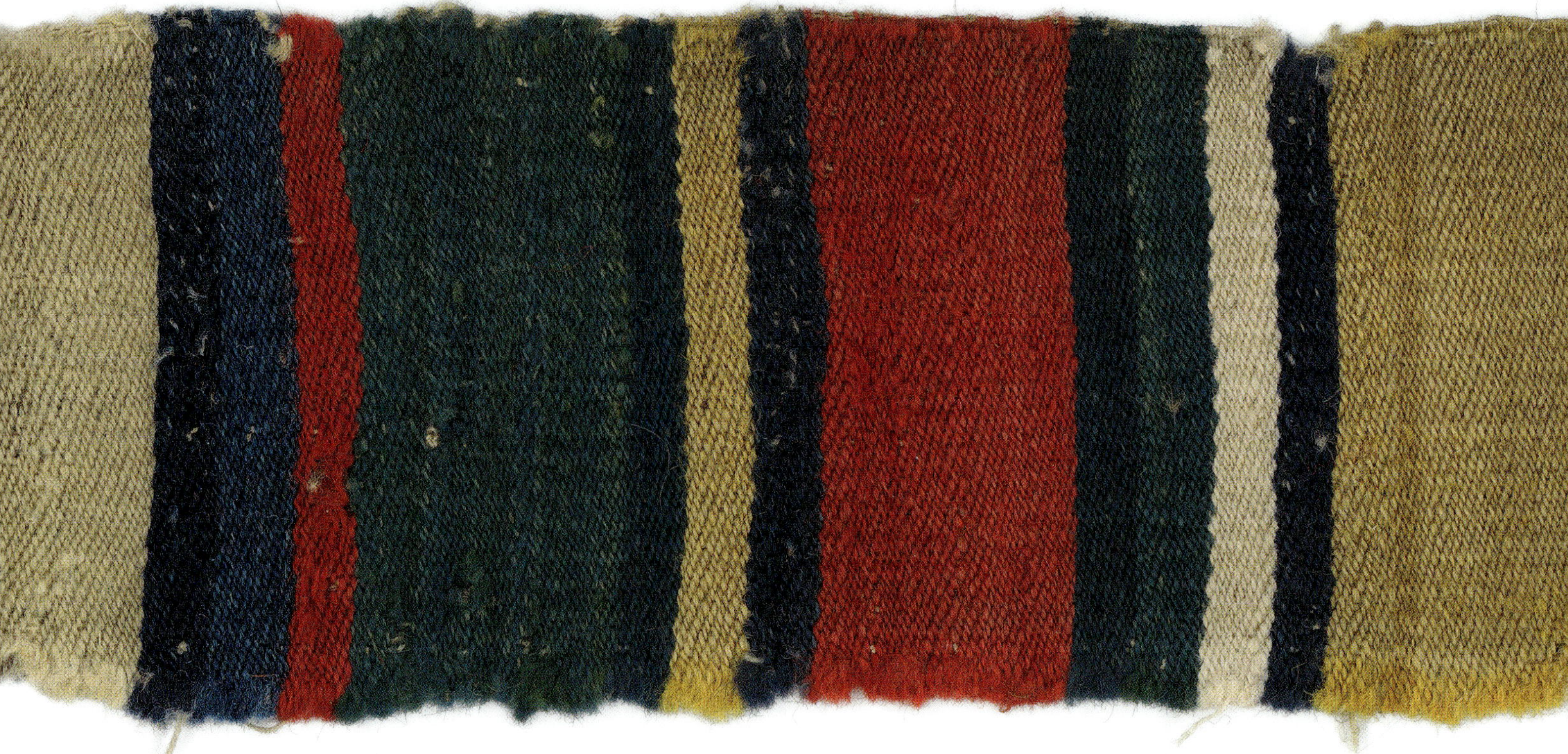

Chinese and Central Asian silk fabrics, all of which have made their way from monasteries, temples, and other places to the West from the early 1980s onward, that is, since the opening of Tibet. As a result, the history of silk weaving had to be rewritten. Chinese silk was present in Tibet at all times and in large quantities. Its role in monastic and secular life, in the clothing of nobility and clergy, and in the adornment of temples was so important that it can well be viewed as part of Tibet's material culture. We, too, were lucky enough to come across some Chinese brocade fragments, woven works, and embroideries that date back to the Ming era. In addition, our collection includes parts of temple hangings, baldachins, and the robe of a noblewoman made in Tibet of heavy Chinese silk. What, however, about textiles from Tibet itself? I daresay even less is known about them than about Tibetan rugs, and there are very few publications, such as those by Chris Buckley and Karma Trinley Darchen, in which they are even addressed.

The very first Tibetan textiles we brought home with us were something special: tablet-woven ribbons which, depending on their length and width, could be used either as belts, apron strings, or boot laces.[6] They were given to us as presents by a family of sedentary nomads from the Damchung region in northern Central Tibet – roughly the region where the endless Changtang plateau begins, which is inhabited exclusively by nomads. It was during our first trip that we met the family whose eight-year-old daughter, Palsang Tsomo, became our Tibetan godchild. We stayed in touch with her and supported her until she graduated from school in Lhasa. We would visit the family every year, and as guests were presented with yak jerky, rock-hard diced cheese, plaited herders' slingshots, and these more or less artfully woven ribbons. Two dozen tablet-woven ribbons thus make up a collection that has a big merit: their provenance is known. While they were not woven by the women of "our" family, we could watch women weaving on tablet looms in the neighbouring villages. The decoration of the ribbons ranges from simple ornamental designs to patterns not only derived from Buddhism, but also inspired by the local fauna such as antelope or even deer.[7]

The typical aprons, sewn together from several narrow panels of vertically striped fabric, are an indispensable component of married womens' clothing. They are very appealing collector's items so far neglected by research on textiles.

The wonderful colours of these aprons and the precise, very delicate weave suggest that Tibetan women bestowed great care on dyeing and weaving. After all, these aprons worn daily are not only evidence of their artisanal skills; they also guarantee the wellbeing of a woman's husband (Taring 1992: 144). It is also possible that the colours, their combination and the varying width of panels had a referential function indicating, for example, a family's origin, a clan, or the inhabitants of a specific valley. The way these aprons are worn varies from one region to another as well; in addition, they may be composed of three or more panels,

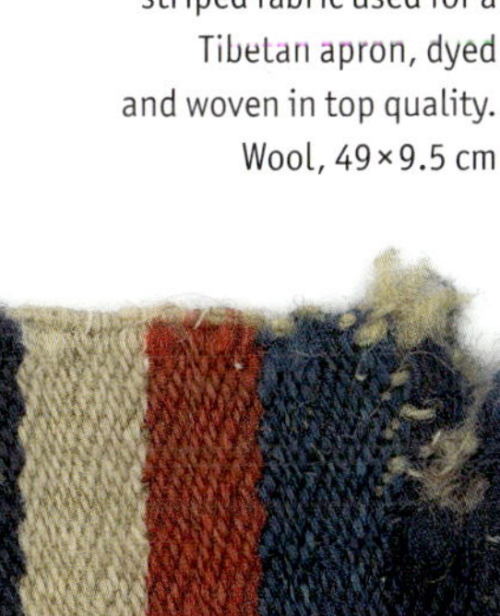

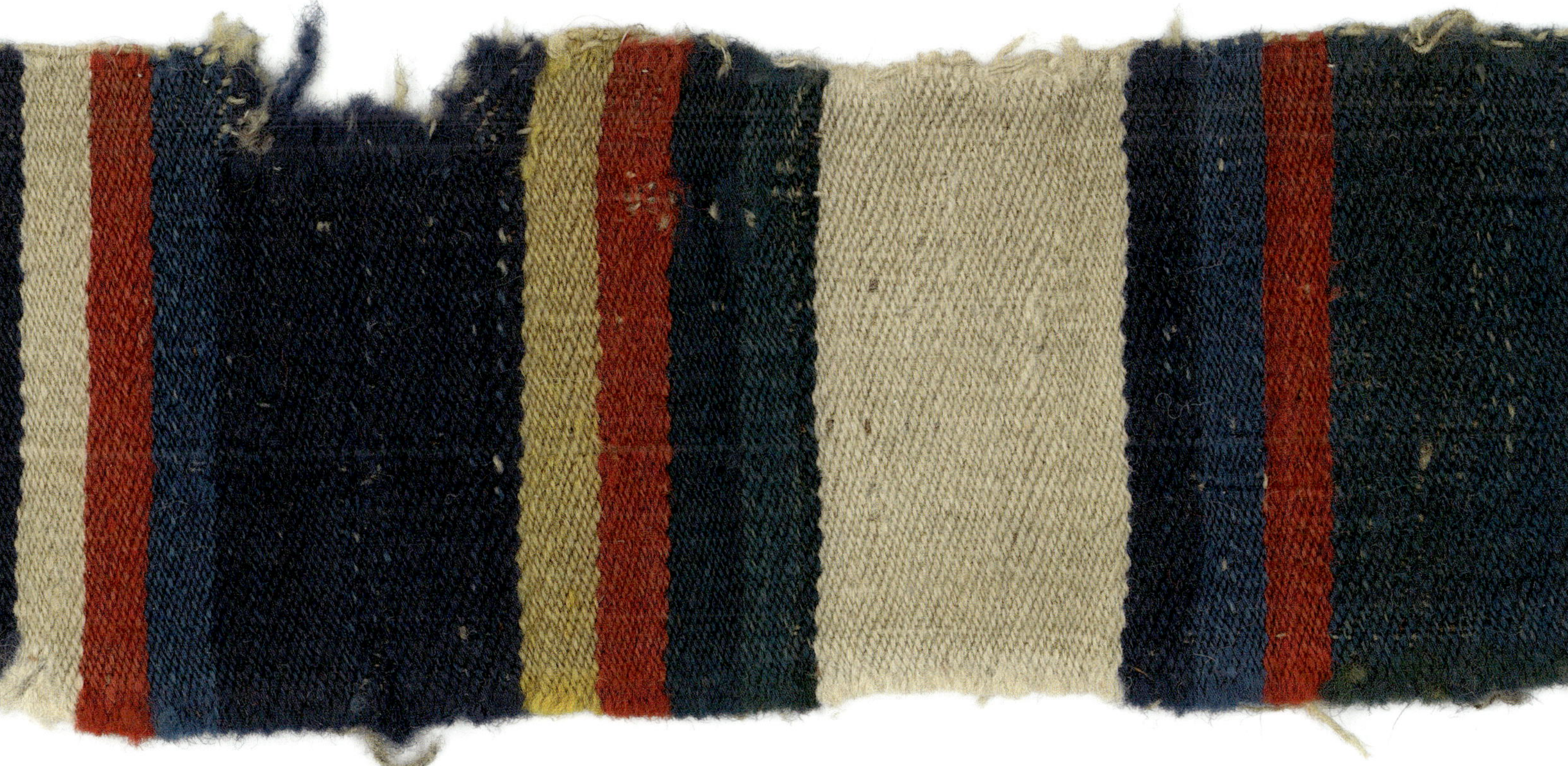

Fig 6: Fragment of striped fabric used for a Tibetan apron, dyed and woven in top quality. Wool, 49×9.5 cm

and they may be complemented by an apron worn on the back, as is common, for example, in Mustang. Beautiful specimens of these aprons have become a rare sight but are sometimes worn by pilgrim women who have come to Lhasa from remote nomad regions to visit the much revered Jokhang. In Central Tibet and in the towns, the cheap aprons made in China, featuring narrow stripes and muted colours, have completely replaced the beautiful hand-woven pieces.

The multi-purpose blankets, also made of up to eight sewn-together woven panels featuring stripe designs, are just as appealing as the aprons. Depending on their purpose and the material used (either wool or the hair of yaks or goats) they come in very diverse variants, ranging from coarse and heavy to fine and from bicoloured to multicoloured. Beautiful pieces with marvellous shades of colour were found on the Barkhor from the 1990s onward but became quite rare soon afterwards. The good dozen of such striped textiles we were able to buy from salesmen in Lhasa nicely illustrates this typically Tibetan production of textiles.

One of the motifs most appreciated by Tibetans on their textiles is the *tigma*, a cruciform symbol that comes in many variations and is created by a specific manner of binding off the fabric to be dyed. This pattern is found almost everywhere in the Tibetan cultural sphere: as a piping-like decoration of *chubas*, on belts and sashes, on *kiras* (the wrapped garments of Bhutanese women), on Ladakhian coats and back scarves, and on many other textiles. There are two beautiful specimens in the collection. One is a trapeze-shaped horse blanket sewn together from narrow panels decorated with stripes and *tigmas*, bought from an Austrian dealer at a textile fair in Berlin. The other is a textile cover for a long bench made of a fabric called *nambu* by the Tibetans. While it is only a fragment, it is nevertheless extraordinarily beautiful due to its combination of colours patinated by age.

Besides the abovementioned ribbons and herders' slingshots, aprons, striped textiles, and *nambus*, our collection – which has been compiled without any claim to completeness and dependent on the vicissitudes of supply – includes appliqué-work festive aprons, a sample of fabric used for nomad tents made of yak hair, woven belts, a plaited yak saddle blanket, and many other objects – a colourful kaleidoscope of a multitude of diverse textiles, witnesses to a rich and little known textile culture.

With regard to the torso of this collection of Tibetan textiles, we were also lucky to find an author who undertook the task of describing the use of textiles in the context of Tibetan history. In her contribution, the young Persian-Austrian Tibetologist **Christiane Kalantari** focuses mainly on depictions of the most varied textiles in early Tibetan painting, be it on *thangkas*, on temple walls, or on the wooden ceilings of temples. Her contribution, as well as the textile-technological analysis and description of some typical Tibetan textiles in the collection by **Britta Schwenck**, are intended as a stimulus for a comprehensive analysis of a much under-researched subject matter; such scholarly work promises to enrich our knowledge of Tibetan material culture.

Textiles and rugs (in those regions where rugs were made depending on climatic and other external circumstances) count among the earliest and most important objects of material culture. Hence, they are key testimonies of the material culture of Tibet, and we are happy to give glimpses into the little-known everyday culture of Tibetans by means of our collection, its exhibition, and the accompanying catalogue. While the part of Tibetan culture associated with religion and cult – painting, sculpture, and ritual objects – has been sufficiently appreciated and published about for more than 100 years, everyday culture has been largely neglected. An exception was the exhibition entitled "Der Weg zum Dach der Welt" in the Staatliches Museum für Völkerkunde Munich in 1982–83 and the accompanying catalogue of the same title edited by Claudius C. Müller and Walter Raunig. That exhibition was a milestone in terms of everyday culture but has unfortunately remained a singular event. By complementing the rugs and textiles with Tibetan furniture, a small selection of jewellery, and a very typical specialty of Tibetan metal craftsmen – the end caps for *thangka* rods, sometimes simply called *thangka* knobs – we attempt to somewhat broaden and complete the image of everyday Tibetan culture. The contribution by **Petra Maurer** serves the same purpose. Starting out from Tibetan material culture, she gives an account of the crafts and craftspeople in Tibetan society, both in old Tibet and in the present.

METAL OBJECTS, FURNITURE, JEWELLERY

The abovementioned collection of end caps for *thangka* rods has a history of its own. It is probably unique in the world; at any rate, no such collection has ever been published. During our first visit to Tibet in 1994, we had set out from Golmud, crossed the Kunlun Mountains – and thus our first pass higher than 5,000 metres – and arrived on the Tibetan plateau in northern Changtang. We were overwhelmed by

Fig. 7: At this booth, a few end caps for *thangka* rods are hidden amongst old and new metal objects. Barkhor, Lhasa, 1996

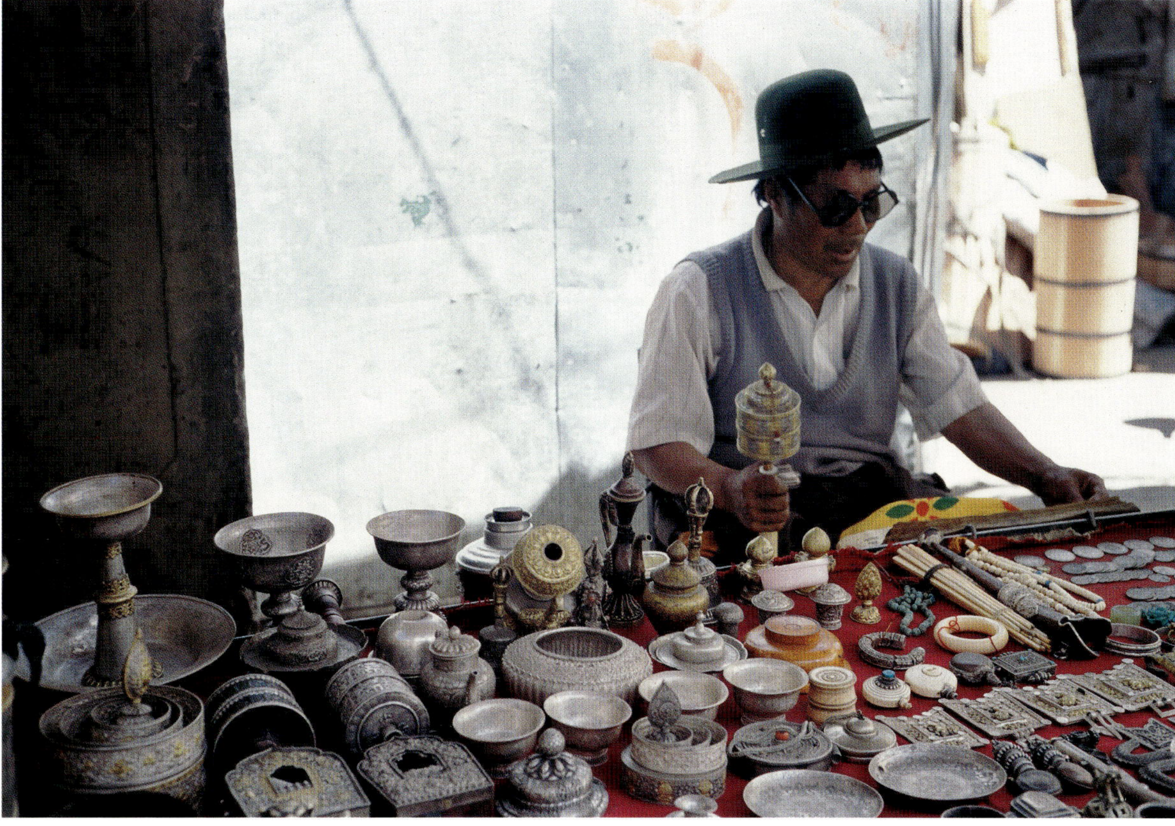

the grandiose landscape, and we looked askance at a very rugged road carved into the permafrost soil. Almost the entire trade in goods between China and Tibet was transacted via that road on overloaded trucks of limited roadworthiness. On our trip we had to suffer a couple of overnight stays in so-called "guesthouses", and thanks to the efforts of our enterprising travel organiser some Tibetans showed up late in the evening one day and produced rolled-up *thangkas* for sale from their *chubas*. The event, which was shrouded in an aura of mystery and secrecy, was staged in such a way that it was impossible not to buy the pictures which were old but not marketable due to their condition and quality. Of course, the *thangkas* we bought came complete with the rods needed to hang them and to roll them up, but the caps usually attached to the ends of the rods were missing. Hence, we wanted to complete the fragments we had purchased and, lo and behold!, we actually discovered such *thangka* caps on the Barkhor in Lhasa, hidden amongst all kinds of metal objects. Hence, a new collecting idea was born, as we soon realised that these caps not only differ in terms of size but also with regard to the material, processing technique, and ornamentation used. As we collected more and more such caps over the years – we had developed a special eye which enabled us to pick these caps from among the hodgepodge of objects – we became more and more convinced that the entire range of metallurgy techniques used in Tibet presents itself in these small objects.

This has been confirmed by **Friedrich Spuhler**, who over many years has compiled an exquisite collection of Tibetan metal fittings. He kindly agreed to use his expertise to write a contribution, and decided to study and describe exclusively these very special metal objects in our collection. It is the first monographic essay on end caps for *thangka* rods, on their diversity and on the metallurgy techniques used.

Like the rugs, furniture from Tibet is distinctive. While pieces of furniture are usually plain in terms of shape and material, they are lent almost irresistible appeal and charm by the way they are painted. At least we fell for their charm when our Tibetan hosts in Kathmandu, who knew about our passion for rugs, sent us to a young Italian rug dealer and his English wife who happened to live nearby. The couple were Luca and Camilla Corona, and it was in their shop that we first became aware of another little known part of Tibet's material culture. Besides beautiful carpets, a small selection of exquisite furniture was on display. As a result of this, as well as of the Coronas' expert advice and the assurance that furniture can be easily air-freighted, almost all our trips to Tibet ended with purchasing furniture from the

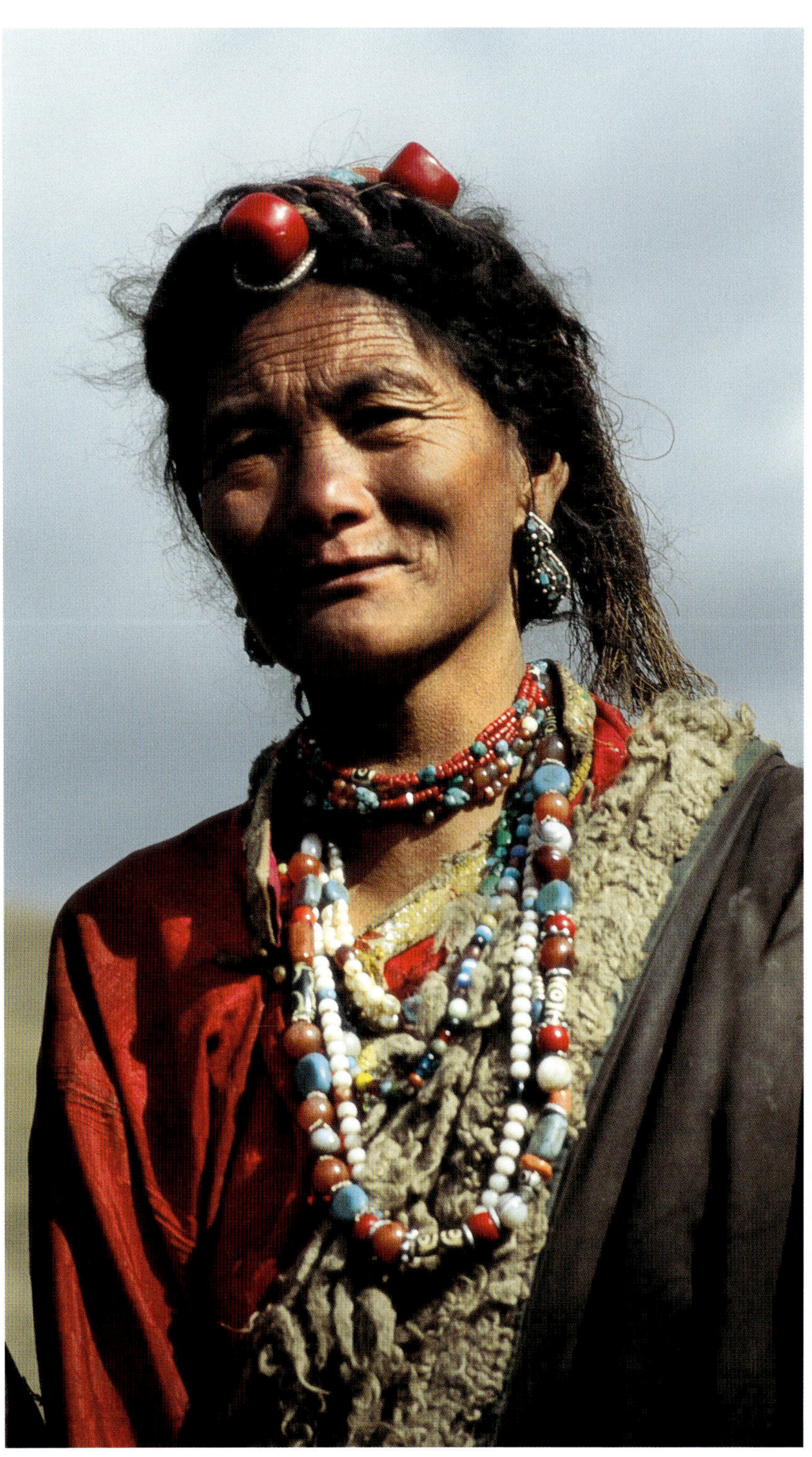

Fig. 8: Ngolok woman wearing her everyday jewellery. Near Jyekundo, north-eastern Tibet, 2002

Coronas, who later had a beautiful gallery in Bhouda. In no time, skilled Nepalese craftsmen built a stable carrier box around the piece of furniture; only a few days later and with minimal bureaucratic expenditure involved, we were able pick up our chest, *torgam*, or whatever else had caught our fancy, at Munich airport. Our collector friends **Heidi and Helmut Neumann** have described our pieces in their contribution, and classified them within the body of Tibetan furniture. It comes as no surprise that we met the Neumanns in Tibet, too. They have made an international name for themselves with their research on early Tibetan *thangka* and wall painting, and are owners of an excellent collection of Tibetan furniture.

Illustrated by important specimens from their own collection and from ours, that contribution is the first essay in German on Tibetan furniture, which is mainly distinguished by its high-quality painting.

Justyna would not be Justyna, and would not be a woman, if her collector's eye – schooled by rugs – had not been caught by various pieces of clothing and jewellery. Mention has already been made of the robe of a noblewoman, tailored in Tibetan style of elegant Chinese silk, which Justyna discovered at a stall on the Barkhor; the robe wanted cleaning but was in excellent condition. Thanks to Justyna, coral necklaces, earrings studded with turquoises, and saddle-shaped rings – which are typical of Tibet – found their way into our collection and into Justyna's jewellery case as well. However, our decision to add a chapter on jewellery to this catalogue was not inspired by these pieces but rather by some incidental and lucky purchases of extraordinary objects, as well as of amulet containers and reliquaries of various sizes. Used, high-quality specimens of all these objects have become rare. **Hans Weihreter** is the author of the contribution on that part of our collection. He first joined Tibetan nomads roaming the ravines and valleys of the Himalayas decades ago as a young man, and is second to none in his knowledge of the forms and – even more importantly – meanings of Tibetan jewellery, as well as of the materials and stones used.

I will now come to the conclusion of my introduction, which was intended to give first glimpses of our collection of Tibetan rugs and textiles as well as of some other spheres of Tibetan material culture, and to get you in the mood for what to expect in the catalogue accompanying the exhibition of our collection in the Museum Fünf Kontinente. This is usually the place for words of thanks. Please forgive me for expressing my gratitude briefly and somewhat sweepingly – there have just been too many people paving the way for us to Tibet and in Tibet, helping to compile and enlarge the collection as advisers, dealers, and friends, and helping to realise this book and the exhibition as authors or staff members. I am indebted to all of them with much gratitude forever. The only exception I would like to make from that sweeping address of thanks is my wife, Justyna. Without her and without her deep love for the Tibetans, their sphere of collecting, as well as our joint "hunting" for new objects never gave rise to any dissonances – on the contrary: it was always a pleasure. With Karl Steiner, we lost a dear friend, a highly regarded fellow collector, and an irreplaceable travel companion in June 2014. We dedicate this book to his memory.[8]

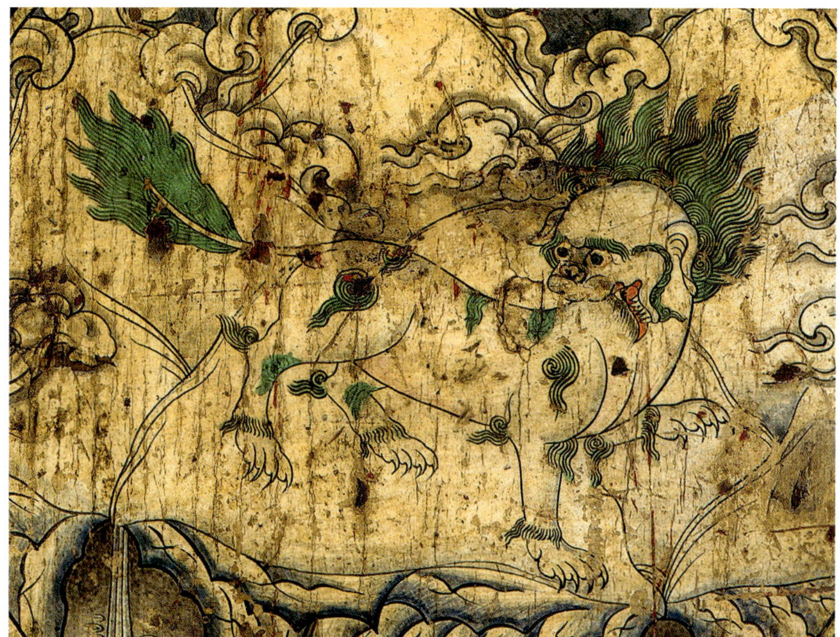

Fig. 9: Snow lion, one of the four mythical animals making up the "Four Dignities". Detail of Fig. 25 in the contribution by Heidi and Helmut Neumann

country, and their culture we would never have travelled to Tibet year after year; and without her love for this foolish collector of rugs she would never have shared and supported his passion, and we would never have joyfully realised that the two of us have actually compiled a collection of Tibetan material culture. As becomes apparent from Justyna's contribution on our travels in Tibet, it was not the rugs that brought us there but our increasing involvement with an initially foreign country and its culture – a process that lent a new quality to each visit; Tibetans became our friends, and to return home with a bagful of rugs and textiles after each visit seemed perfectly normal to us.

Last but not least I want to give a tribute to our late friend Karl Steiner. No one else has been so closely associated with our trips to Tibet and our Tibet collection. We met Karl – who was an out-and-out rug collector himself – in the early 1990s, and he was of the party as early as during our second trip to Tibet. With Karl we made eight extended trips to remote regions in Tibet, as well as to other countries in the Himalayas. His comprehensive classical education, his broad interest in music, literature, and the fine arts, his capacity for enthusiasm, his aesthetic judgement, and his readiness to help contributed significantly to making each of these journeys unforgettable. In the wake of our encounter with Tibet, the Buddhist-inspired material culture of that country became the focus of Karl's interest as a collector, in a similar way as it became our focus. In his case, too, it was the Tibetan rugs and textiles that appealed to his pronounced sense of formal and colour-related aesthetics. It is remarkable that our identical interest in that

NOTES

1 Part of the Teunis-Wollesen collection was exhibited and published by Taher Sabahi in Turin in 2001 (see Sabahi 2001).

2 Myers 1984: 15–16. The catalogue of an exhibition of Tibetan rugs in the Textile Museum, Washington D.C., includes a good compilation of places in early literature on Tibet where rugs are mentioned.

3 A number of these photographs by Charles Bell were published in 1974 by Philip Denwood in his book *The Tibetan Carpet*. The photos by Charles Bell are kept in the Pitt Rivers Museum in Oxford.

4 The book *Auspicious Carpets*, edited by Daniel Miller in 2009, pays tribute to these pioneer days and their protagonists.

5 Out of the altogether 197 knotted works in our collection – ranging from the small *takyab* (used to decorate horses' and donkeys' foreheads) to the *sabden* (the rare Tibetan floor rug) – Elena Tsareva has studied a representative cross-section of 120 pieces and made detailed technical analyses. These are printed in full length in the appendix.

6 As far as can be established, the only reference to women in southern Central Tibet using tablets for making ribbons in the German-language literature is by Veronika Ronge (see Ronge 2005).

7 Otfried Staudigel has given an account of the motifs on our tablet-woven ribbons from Tibet in his book *Gewebte Bilder – Enträtselte Motive. Doppelseitige Brettchengewebe aus Birma, Tibet und Tunesien* (2008).

8 After Karl Steiner had passed away, part of his collection of Tibetan rugs and textiles was presented as a donation to the Museum Fünf Kontinente by Karl and Barbara Steiner. Several pieces from his collection are shown in the exhibition and in this catalogue.

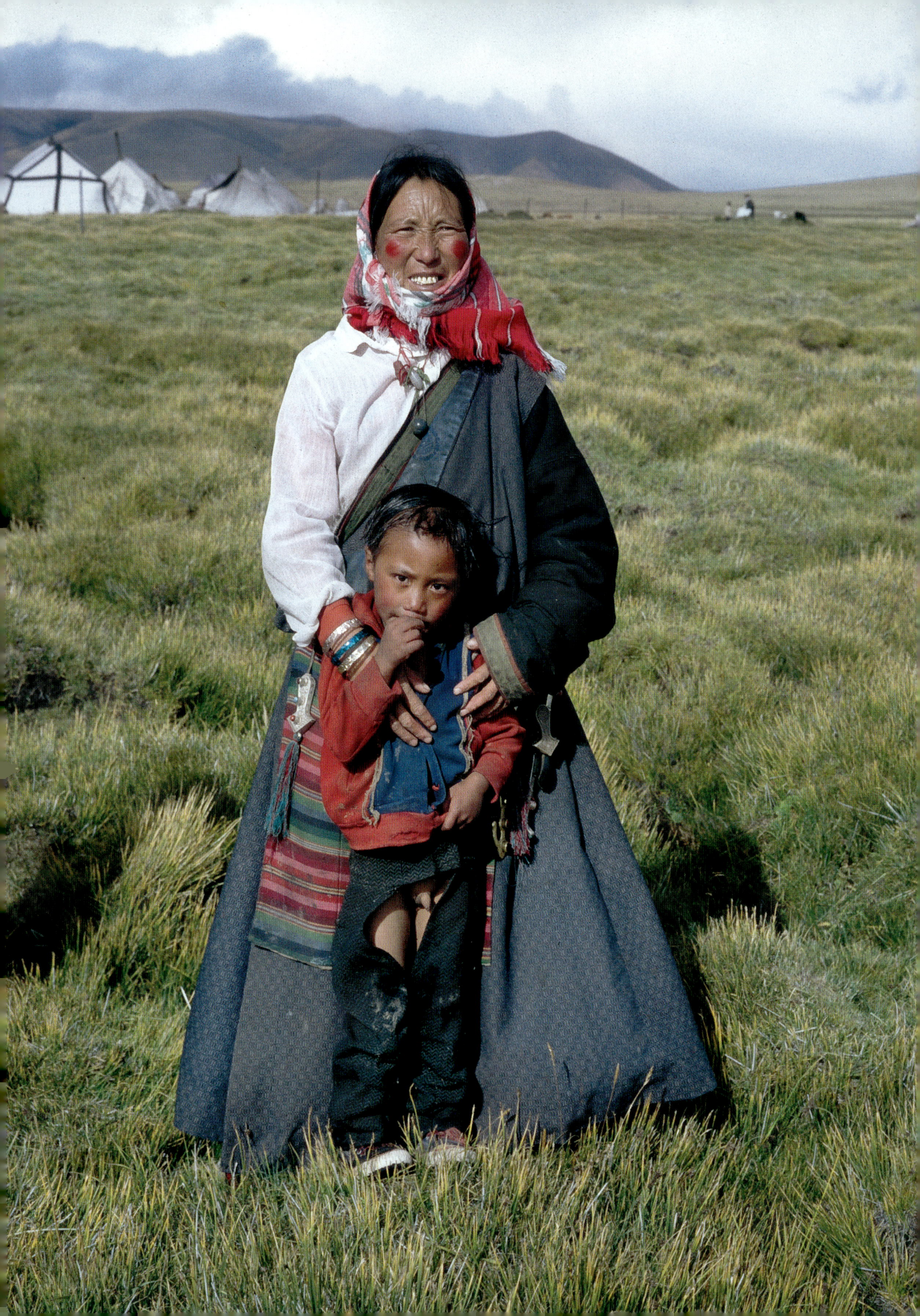

Justyna Buddeberg

3 OF 16

Our Travels in Tibet

HOW IT ALL BEGAN

Fig. 1: Tibetan woman and her son during grass harvest in a swamp at the foot of Mount Nyenchen Tanglha (7,162 m). Northern Central Tibet, 1997

We arrived in Tibet at Labrang monastery of all places, which is situated in the former Tibetan province of Amdo and visited by only few tourists. In 1994 we had joined a privately organised tour party that was to cross the Xinjiang province in western China and then to proceed in a southerly direction to Tibet, its capital Lhasa, and eventually to the Base Camp of Mount Everest. Our journey might be summarised by the motto: from one of the lowest places on Earth – the Turfan oasis is 150 metres below sea level – to the world's highest mountain. We saw mummies in Urumqi, the south-western end of the Great Wall of China in the sands of the Taklamakan Desert, early Buddhist murals in the Mogao Grottoes near Dunhuang, and the gracious Han-Dynasty bronze horse at the museum in Lanzhou. All these were profound impressions from a world that was still new to us at the time, and they were even to be surpassed by later adventures and images.

The first lasting impression was Labrang, a monastery founded at the beginning of the 18th century, that is, comparatively late. It is a monastery town of the Gelugpa order in which thousands of monks are living and studying again today. It is raining. The empty monastery road is steeped in diffuse light, and the reflections in the large puddles create the illusion of twice as many golden temple roofs. Some boys brave the weather and play soccer in their red monk's robes between two temples. They are a surprising contrast

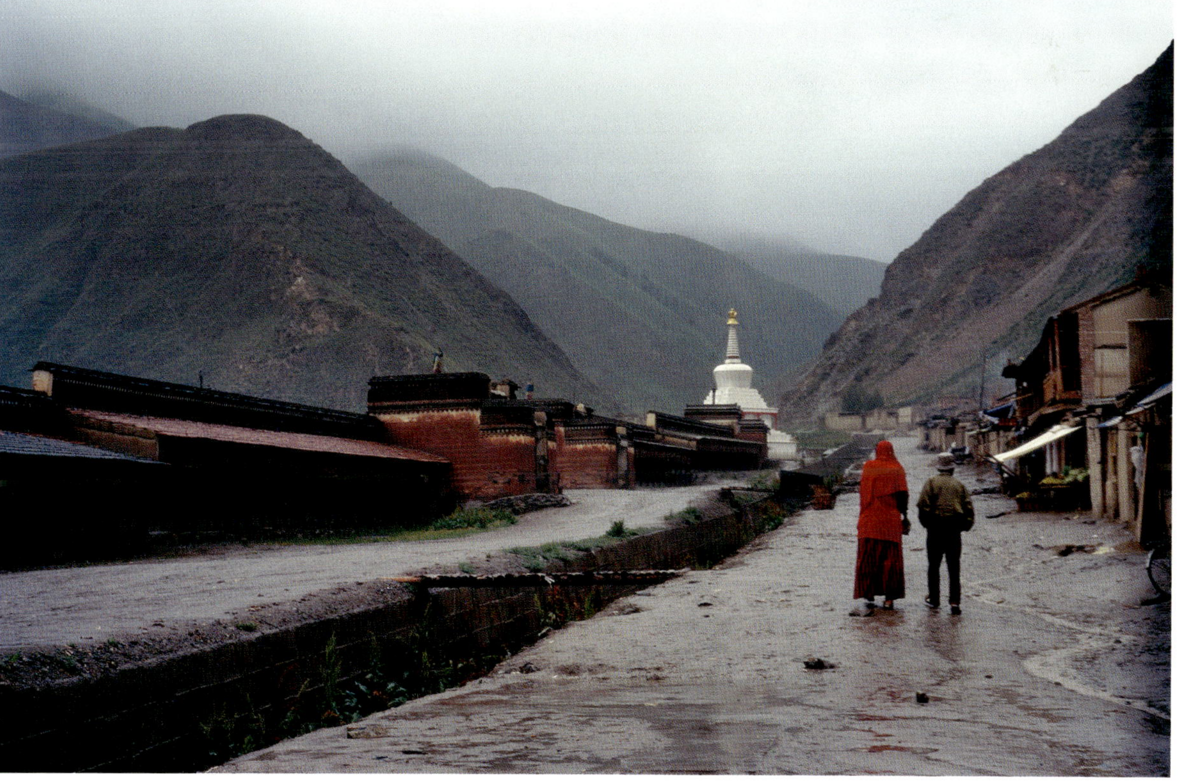

Fig. 2: A rainy day in Labrang, the monastery town in the former Tibetan province of Amdo (now Qinghai), 1994

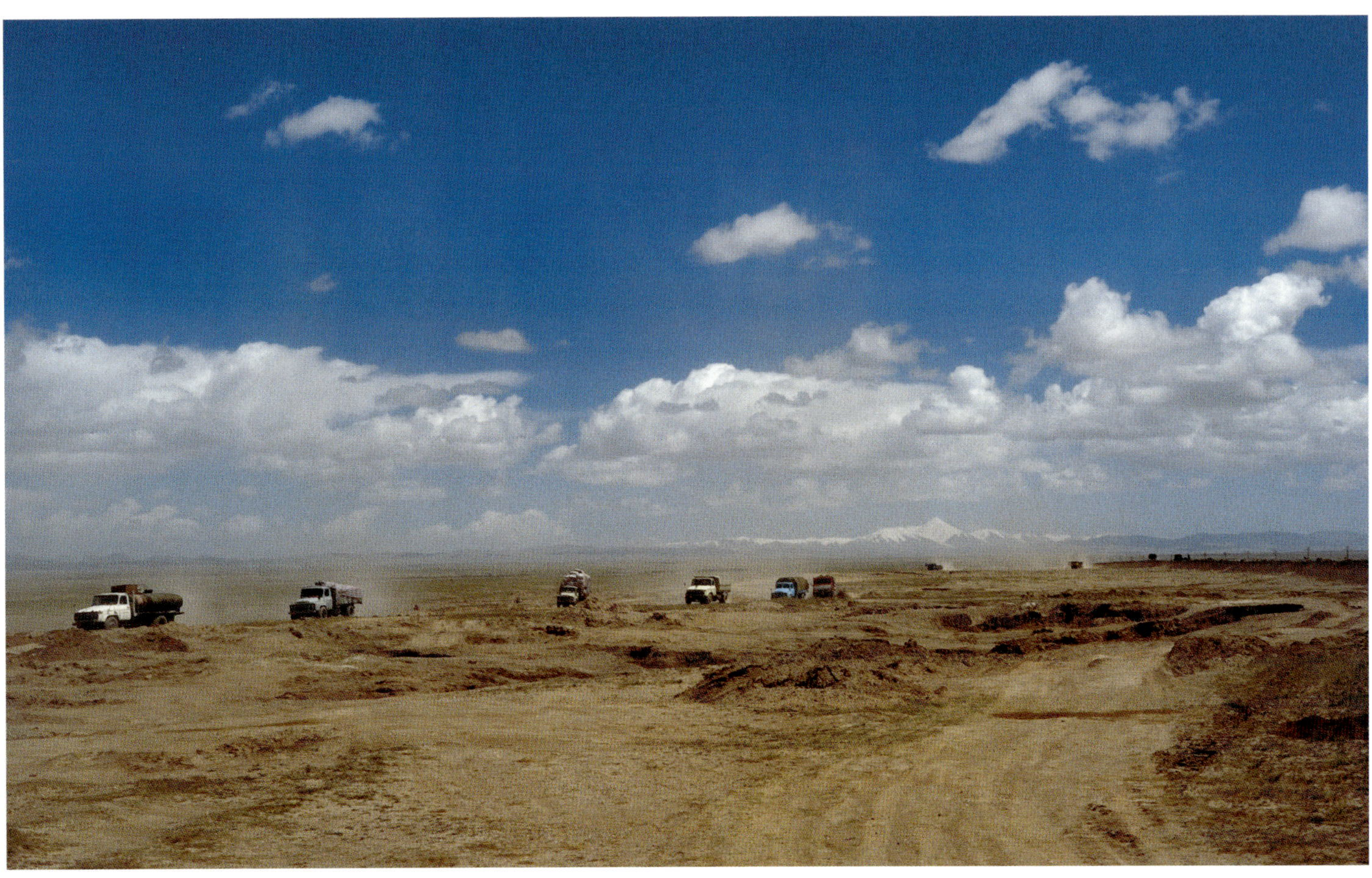

Fig. 3: The "Tibet-Qinghai Highway", a track through Changtang, the northern plateau of Tibet, 1994

to monastic life. At this time of the day, most monks are in the big assembly hall for worship, for a *puja*, and we have the opportunity to absorb the impressive atmosphere of a Tibetan temple ritual for the first time. Daylight falls in from above through narrow windows. Together with butter lamps that flicker like candles, it bathes the room, which is borne by towering columns, in a peculiar light and illuminates the victory banners of brocade woven with gold thread. They are the symbol of the Buddha's enlightenment, and of his victory over temptations. Many *thangkas* hang here as well, picture scrolls featuring Buddhist themes. On the low benches of the monks, narrow rugs are spread which look comfortable to sit on. In front of the benches are low tables with ritual paraphernalia and prayer books, the latter consisting of loose pages printed in block print enclosed in wooden covers with textile wrapping. All this we witness for the first time. The ritual is accompanied by the sound of small and large cymbals, shawms, and *radongs* (instruments resembling alphorns), and the chorus of the monks as they recite monotonous-sounding *mantras*. As all this is going on, we marvel not only at the Buddhas and *Bodhisattvas* that are opulently adorned with gold, precious stones, and valuable textiles, but also at the offerings made by devotees and pilgrims: banknotes and *khatags*, white silk shawls, which are deposited as an expression of veneration. Then the *puja* is over, and the novices bring in large copper vessels with freshly cooked food from the monastery kitchen. From the folds of his robe, each monk has conjured up an eating bowl, and the soup is served. The spiritual mood quickly gives way to an atmosphere that is taciturn yet relaxed. We, the foreigners, are welcome and well-liked. It was in Labrang that we first witnessed this simultaneity of spiritual contemplation and participation in everyday life, the saturation of the Tibetans' existence by their Buddhist attitude to life and their tolerance and open-mindedness. It is one of many reasons why we have visited that country over and over again.

After that day in the monastery town we set out for Lhasa. That is easily said, but back in 1994 it was quite time-consuming. It takes us three days to get to Golmud, the gateway to the Tibetan highlands. We are travelling in a region that in old Tibet was the province of Amdo, but which has been considered by the Chinese for a long time to be part of their territory. The province is now Chinese and called Qinghai. In fact, Chinese and Tibetans have lived here side by side more or less peacefully from time immemorial – the Chinese in the lower regions, the Tibetans in the higher elevations. This changed when Tibet was annexed under Mao Zedong; now China is omnipresent and Tibetans are becoming a minority, even in the higher altitudes. This, however, is the least of all evils.

Behind Golmud, the Kunlun Mountains tower in front of us. We cross three passes, each of them higher than the other: the Kunlun at 4,849 metres, then another at 5,010 metres, and finally the Tangula at 5,231 metres. After driving for many hours we arrive in Changtang, the sparsely populated plateau in the north of Tibet which has an average altitude of 4,700 metres. The air is thin and clear, the sky very close, and the clouds cast deep dark shadows. The horizon is lined with the snow-capped peaks of unnamed mountains, and we struggle along a hazardous road. In the early 1950s the Chinese built a road to Lhasa in this region, the first of its kind in Tibet, the so-called "Tibet-Qinghai Highway" (Fig. 3). The impact of that construction project, which was pushed on with no regard for land conservation and the environment, is still visible today: it left scars in a nature that has difficulty regenerating. Hardly anything is left of the road itself. The soil above the permafrost thaws only superficially in summer; hence, the road turns into a muddy track in many places. Particularly the ever increasing traffic creates a state of chaos: in the mid-1990s almost the entire transport of goods from China to Tibet was carried via the Golmud-Lhasa road: an endless stream of overloaded, not very roadworthy trucks whose drivers do what they can to handle the road conditions. The driver of our little tour bus does the same. The axes of the bus creak and squeak. Everywhere there are accidents and damaged vehicles, it is a veritable inferno. The dreariness of this landscape damaged by man is contrasted by the beauty of the plateau with the large herds of sheep, goats, and yaks, the primeval, shaggy "grunting cattle". In the distance we see Tibetan nomads' tents.

On the sixth day of this journey from Labrang to Lhasa, near the small town of Damchung – approximately at the border between Changtang and Central Tibet, the former province of U – our little group splits up for a few hours. Three people get on a truck and take a ride to Namtso Lake, while we just want to recover from the day's drive. We take a stroll in the scenery, have a picnic, and then visit the nearby village. All of a sudden, one of the village children takes my hand and signals unmistakably into which house my husband Michael and I should enter. We spend but a short time there and are entertained by the girl's mother. However, we learn much about each other by using gestures and other "aids". We have a small map of the world by "Doctors without Borders" which we carry with us and can show the girl and her mother where we come from. Palsang Tsomo – that is the girl's name – shows us her exercise book to let us know she attends the nearby school. Meeting that family established a much cherished link to Tibet. Palsang Tsomo was to become our Tibetan godchild with whom we stayed in touch and whom we supported for almost 20 years. We take photos, note the family's address, and soon have to board our little bus again so as to arrive in Lhasa by the evening. We could not forget that encounter. We sent letters – translated into Tibetan – and photos, but none of them reached their destination, as we learned when we visited Damchung again the next year. However, the little girl had dreamed (and thus knew!) that an important visit was ahead. One year later, thanks to contacts we had been able to make, we found a good school in Lhasa where Palsang Tsomo lived in a Tibetan house with a host family. Today we are still close friends with her, her parents, and the entire family.

But let us return to the year of 1994. The drive from Labrang to Lhasa takes six days. Our first encounter with the capital of Tibet is brief but very intense: the Jokhang temple, Potala Palace, the small old-town district. The inhabitants of Lhasa and the pilgrims leave a deep impression on us, too. The strange mixture of religion and commerce, which is typical of pilgrim centres all over the world, still has a completely different dimension in Lhasa, probably due to the omnipresence of Buddhist spirituality in everyday Tibetan life. Outside the old town, in contrast, Lhasa presents itself as a Chinese "Wild West" of sorts, with the typical sales booths lined up along both sides of the new streets.

The next destination on our itinerary is the Base Camp at Mount Everest. Hence we leave Lhasa after a sojourn of only two days. We stop in Gyantse, albeit too briefly, to admire the *stūpa*, or rather *Kumbum* which is arguably the most beautiful cult building in Tibet, and we are enraptured by the quality of the murals and sculptures dating from the middle of the 15th century. The last 100 kilometres we ride on the bed of a ramshackle truck. The sight of the world's highest mountain lit by the setting sun compensates us for all the exertions, and a chat with a team of Canadians preparing to climb Mount Everest puts us in an alpinist mood. The next day we enjoy a long walk on the Rongbuk glacier. By the afternoon we are already on the road again.

On our way back to Lhasa we visit the 13th-century monastery of Sakya, admire the porcelain brought 700 years ago from China as gifts by pilgrims, and stand in awe before the library of Tibetan manuscripts whose upper part wanes away in the lofty darkness of the tall assembly hall. But our stay is far too brief, our sightseeing dictated by the

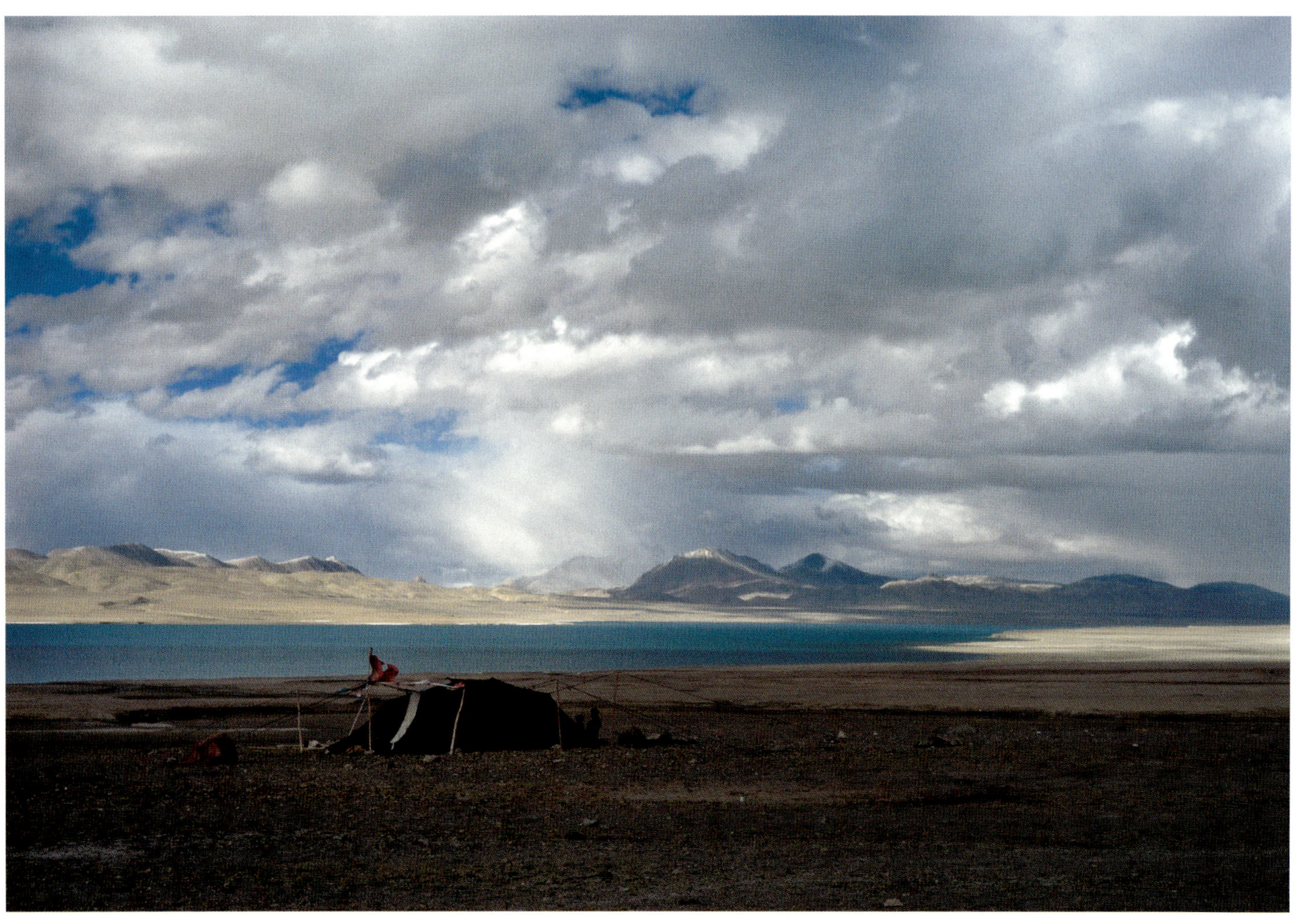

Fig. 4: First encounter with nomads in West Tibet at Lake Lungma Tso (4,970 m), 1995

schedule and circumstances of our trip. In Tashilhunpo, the famous residence of the Panchen Lama, we also have far too little time to see the monastery and its immeasurable treasures. At some point during these days and under the spell of what we have experienced and seen, we decide: we are coming back again next year!

IN THE KINGDOM OF GUGE

One year later we wanted to see those places in south-western Tibet that play an important role in religion and culture: the former Tibetan kingdom of Guge and the sacred Mount Kailash. At our hotel in Kashgar, the ancient metropolis on the Silk Road, we met our Chinese escort team: the drivers of the two off-road vehicles (we were a tourist group of seven people), the driver of the escort vehicle, and the young Chinese guide with English language skills. None of them had ever been in Tibet before. A day's drive from the Taklamakan desert to the dark, gruff northern slopes of the Kunlun Mountains brought us to Yecheng (Kargilik). After we had arrived at the hotel, our guide broke the bad news to us: there had been a huge landslide in the Kunlun Mountains, and the road to Tibet was buried for hundreds of metres, no way of getting through. He said that we needed to completely reschedule our trip. After endless discussions we put our feet down and said, "Let's go and have a look and see what it's like." We suspected that our Chinese crew actually had no intention of going to Tibet and were trying to sabotage the trip. This turned out later to be true: all four of them were afraid of the "dangerous Tibetans" and the scarcity of oxygen at high elevations; they literally feared for their lives.

The next day we continued with our journey. After several hours of driving through the foothills we came in a mountain landscape: narrow valleys, steep mountainsides, no bedrock but only debris, rubble, and sand. And then we came to a place where a landslide had completely buried the road under several metres of debris. People stood around with shovels next to the bulldozers doing nothing. The foreman was not available for questions. Our crew shrugged their shoulders, and we thought we had to bow to the inevitable. But then a miracle happened: two brand-new white Land

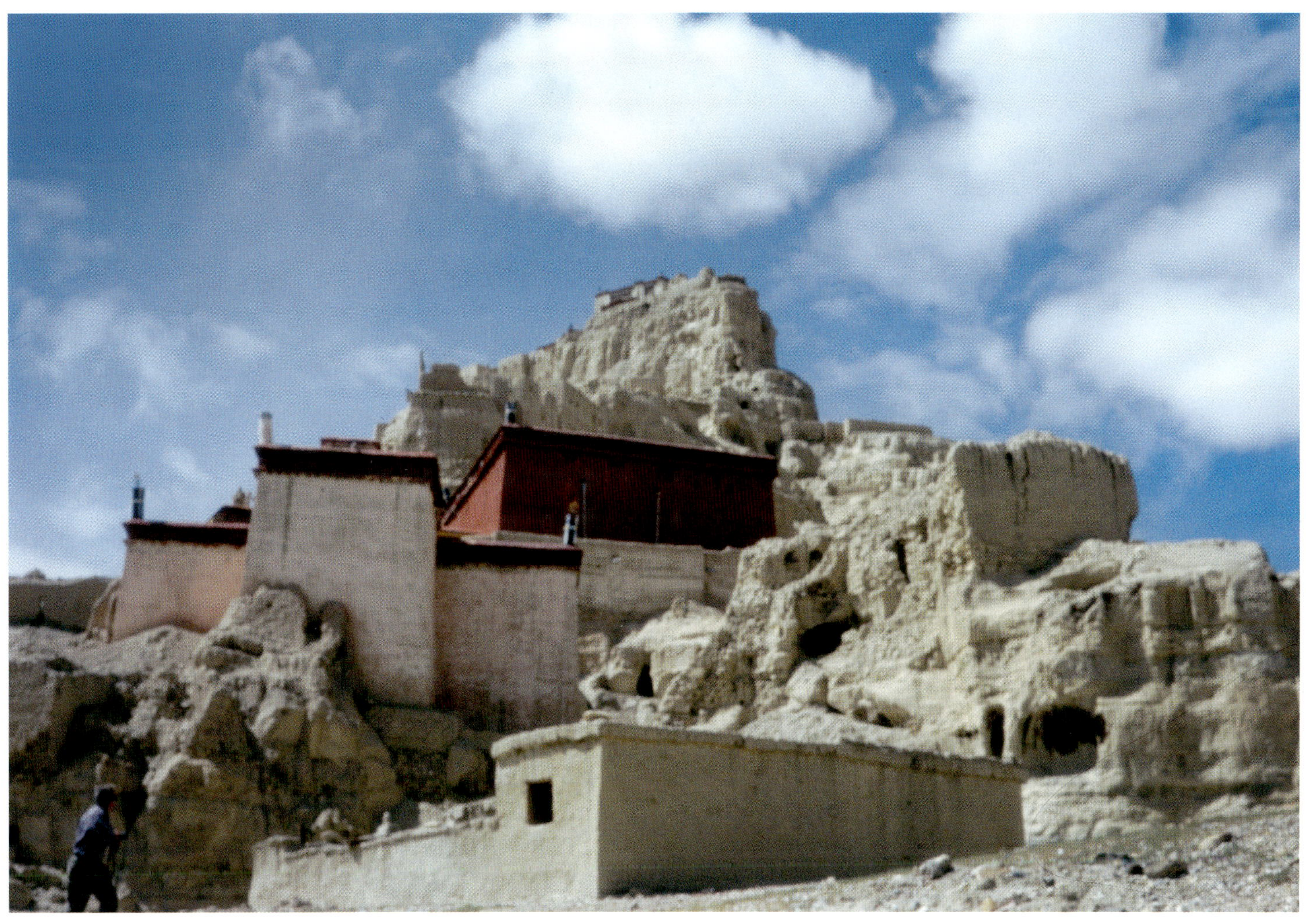

Fig. 5: Tsaparang, temple and ruins of the capital of the kingdom of Guge, which was deserted 300 years ago. West Tibet, 1995

Cruisers arrived with Chinese TV journalists inside. They were on their way to shoot a story on "Tibet – Unification with the Chinese Mother Country", commissioned by Chinese state television. They talked briefly to the foreman, and then the bulldozers started to plough a path through the chaos for the cars of the TV team. We joined those white heralds of a merciful fate, and were able to continue our trip in the desired direction.

We will never forget our first encounter with nomads. We met them south of the Kunlun Mountains after having reached the Tibetan plateau via the "Tibet-Xinjiang Highway". In a region that is claimed both by India and China but is geographically a part of Ladakh, India, a broad plain opens up behind a 5,400 metre-high pass, and a deep blue lake surrounded by snow-capped mountains comes into view. The sun and clouds paint a picture on the scenery which is speckled by flecks of light and the dark shadows of clouds (Fig. 4). In front of that magnificent backdrop are Tibetan prayer flags and a black nomad tent, secured against the winds with poles and ropes. In front of the tent stands a woman with two children. Heavy wind tousles her clothes and her black braid which flutters across her face. Rich jewellery with corals and turquoises and an apron with pink, green, and blue stripes turn her into an icon of Tibet. That image will always stick in our minds.

The first important destination on our trip is the former kingdom of Guge with its historical cities of Tholing and Tsaparang. They were founded in the late first millennium AD, at a time when the last king of the Yarlung Dynasty, Langdarma (ruled 836–842) had launched an unprecedented persecution of Buddhism which was gaining a foothold in the region. Back then, the scattered Buddhists retired to the world of the western Himalayas where communities emerged that quickly gained in importance, and the descendants of the Yarlung Dynasty founded new kingdoms, including the kingdom of Guge. Under the energetic king Yeshe-O (959–1040), who invited the translator and scribe Rinchen Sangpo and the Indian yogi and scholar Atisha to live at his court in Guge, Buddhism gained a foothold in Tibet again, and began to spread a second time. Yeshe-O later abdicated from the throne and became a monk. Atisha taught the "Great Vehicle", and Rinchen Sangpo is said to

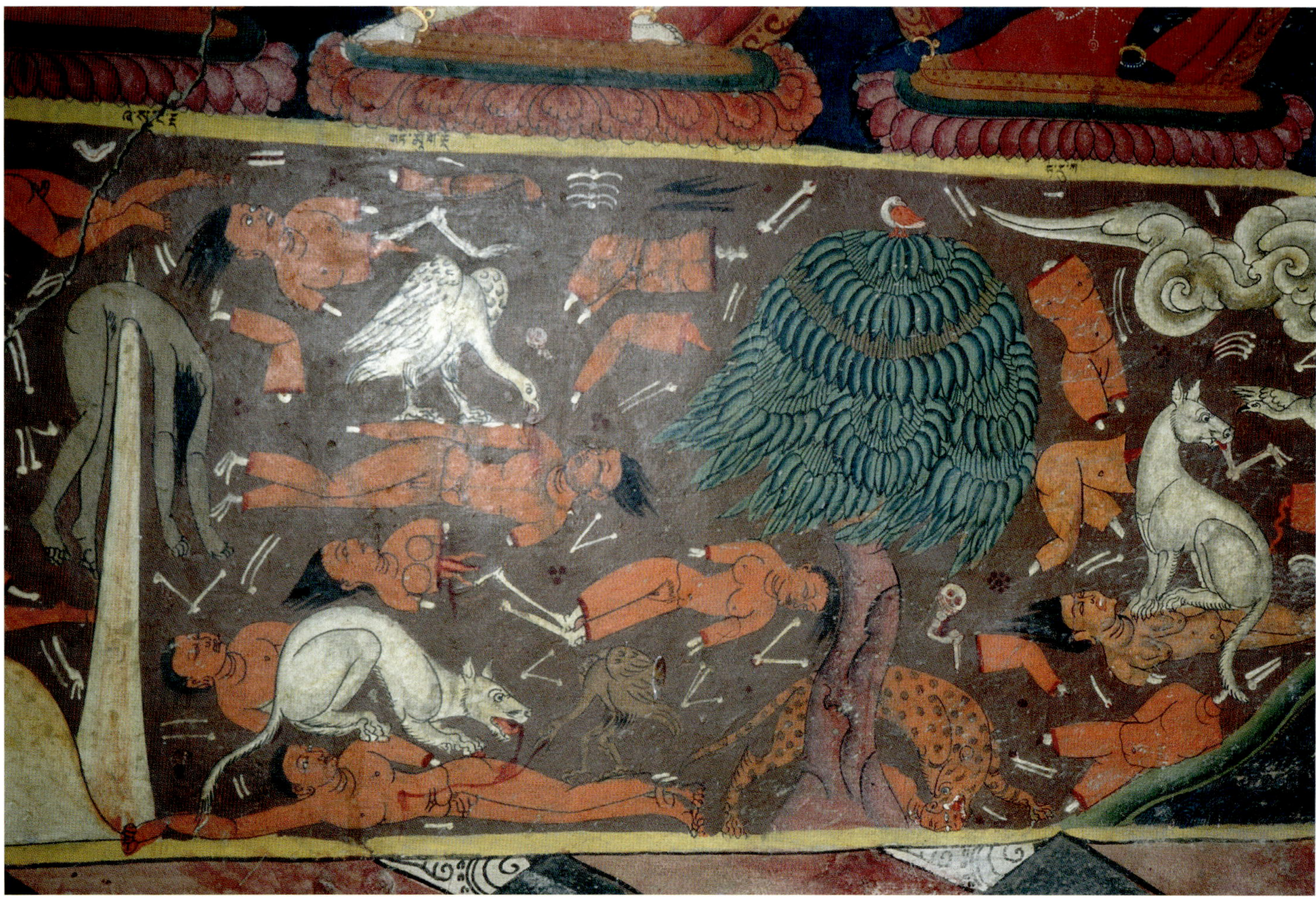

Fig. 6: Detail of the depiction of one of the Eight Charnel Grounds in the Mandala Temple (Tib. *Demchok*) in Tsaparang, mural, 15th century

have founded 100 monasteries. Buddhism was back, and became Tibet's religion – and is again in danger today.

We are on the road to the kingdom of Guge which was deserted in the 17th century, probably due to climate changes and wars. We now have to cross a mountain range with several passes at high elevations. After many breakdowns and repairs of the cars, night sets in. Several times we have to decide whether to take a left or a right turn at forks in the road. The only aid to orientation brought along by our Chinese crew is a "map" of western Tibet printed on a souvenir bandana. They refuse to use the travel atlases we have brought with us from Germany. Early in the morning at five o'clock, we arrive in Tholing and check in at the only local guesthouse. By this time we are already two days behind on our schedule. Instead of three days, as originally planned, we now only have one day for our visit to the two royal cities.

From Tholing it is only a few kilometres to Tsaparang. We drive in the valley of the Sutlej River which has washed a wide bed into the limestone over the course of millions of years. The steep bluffs, eroded by wind, water and extreme differences in temperature, look like fortresses with defence towers, or like the façades of fairytale palaces. Sheep and goats graze on green islands in the river. We pass by a small village, and after a short ride through a dried-up *wadi* where we meet a Yak caravan, we arrive in Tsaparang. The remains of the city, which was abandoned in the 17th century, sit on the slopes of a huge towering rock 200 metres in height. However, the scenery is still dominated by four temple buildings, picturesquely arranged in a staggered manner (Fig. 5). These are the White and the Red Lhakhang, the small Temple of the Scholars, and the Temple of the Guardian Gods. On top of the rock plateau, surrounded by the ruins of the former royal palace, is the small Mandala Temple which is our destination today. We follow the steep, narrow path inside the rock that rises almost vertically. This only access to the top of the rock had fallen into oblivion for a long time and was rediscovered by the Italian Tibetologist Giuseppe Tucci in the 1930s. Ten years later, the German lama Anagarika Govinda and his female companion Li Gotami came to this place to pray, do research, and document. Govinda describes the world of that kingdom and the path through the rock in his wonderful book *The Way of the White Clouds* ("Der Weg der weißen Wolken").

Then we are on the top, in bright sunshine, somehow removed from reality, surrounded by a bizarre, reddish brown and grey rocky landscape. Immediately in front of us is a small temple painted red, called *Demchok* by Buddhists because it was created as a three-dimensional mandala of Yidam Chakrasamvara (Tib. *Demchok*), a wrathful Tantric meditation deity. The sculptures once found in the interior have long been destroyed – gone even before Tucci visited the site – but the well-preserved 15th century murals count among the most beautiful works of art in Tibet. The kings of Guge invested huge amounts of money and gold. They summoned the best artists from Kashmir, Nepal, and Tibet who created scenes from heaven and earth. Hence, the pictures tell of the history of Guge and its historical protagonists in vivid, fresh colours, with much precision and overwhelming artistic expression. Above all, however, they feature the complete iconographic programme of one of the most important mandalas of Mahayana Buddhism: the five *Dhyani* Buddhas, fierce guardian deities, *Dakinis* engaged in coitus with *Herukas*, and many other manifestations and emanations.

Beneath, on a frieze that is about 40 centimetres high and covers all four walls of the room, we see pictures that are completely foreign to us: the Eight Charnel Grounds with dead bodies on which beasts of prey are feeding, eerie trees and white *stūpas*, vultures picking at dismembered bodies, demons, a river with *nāgas* (water spirits), skeletons, and bones scattered all over the ground (Fig. 6). The meaning of these pictures was not revealed to us until some years later, when a Buddhist friend explained that these Eight Charnel Grounds are an important component of any tantric *mandala*. In order to get to the centre of the *mandala* and to unite with the wrathful deity, the initiate has to stride through the various circles, beginning with the charnel grounds, so as to internalise the transience of earthly life. The initiate has to realise that everything is illusion on the way to understanding emptiness. This is "the teaching". Yet, is everything really an illusion? Our ascent of the Tsaparang rock, as we walked through the sun-lit mountain scenery and then up inside the heart of the mountain; then the sight of the bizarre rocky scenery and the snow-capped peaks in a distance – nothing but a phantom? But that is exactly what the charnel grounds tell us: concepts that we have are in a continuous process of dissolution.

For us, these hours spent in Tsaparang and in the Mandala Temple were an important encounter both with the Buddhist-Tantric religious world and with Tibetan art. Only little time in the evening was then left for our visit to Tholing and the *stūpa* of Yeshe-O, but in the light of the setting sun it was still a wonderful experience.

MOUNT KAILASH

We need two days and almost a whole night to drive to the Barga Plain, situated at an elevation of 4,800 metres, from which Mount Kailash rises. Car repairs, a miserable road sometimes hardly recognisable as such, and a mountain range with a high-elevation pass. In the dark, we count the rabbits fleeing from the beam of our headlights. We called this part of our trip the "rabbit rally". After sleeping a couple of hours in the car, we drive on and finally see the scenery broadening out into a plateau. We have arrived in the land of the nomads. Many herds of yaks, goats, and sheep liven up the grassland. There are black-and-brown nomad tents, prayer flags, and *chortens*. The latter are Buddhist sacred buildings (Sanskrit *stūpa*).

Compared to the giants among the Himalayan mountains, Mount Kailash is actually not that tall. However, with its 6,714 metres it is singular in the region, and lent magical appeal by its symmetrical, dome-shaped contour topped by a cap of eternal snow and ice. Not only the Buddhists but also the Bonpas, Hindus, and Jains view it as the centre of the universe, as the legendary Mount Meru, the visible axis of the cosmos. It is lent additional magic by the fact that the four great rivers of Asia have their sources in its immediate vicinity from where they flow in all four cardinal directions: the Yarlung Tsangpo, which is called the Brahmaputra in India, flows east; the Indus flows north; the Ganges, which in this region is called Karnali, flows south; and the Sutlej flows west. The Tibetans lovingly call Mount Kailash Kang Rinpoche, "Precious Snow Jewel".

The small village at the foot of Mount Kailash is called Darchen (altitude 4,650 metres). It is the starting point for the pilgrimage around the sacred mountain, the so-called *kora*. Some shrewd fellows from Tibet and China run a simple hostel in the village where we meet Tibetans, Indians, a group of Japanese, and a few Americans. We are helped in renting seven yaks to carry our baggage, tents, and other equipment during the circumambulation (about 55 kilometres) that usually takes three days. Rain sets in, and Mount Kailash hides itself in the clouds. We are told that it has been doing that for weeks, and that masses of snow lie up at Dolma La pass at an elevation of 5,700 metres. First of all, however, we have to prepare for a fitful night, as the roof of the hostel is leaky and we have to shift the beds to find dry spots. The dripping noise in the room is very unpleasant.

Fig. 7: The north face of Mount Kailash (6,714 m). West Tibet, 1995

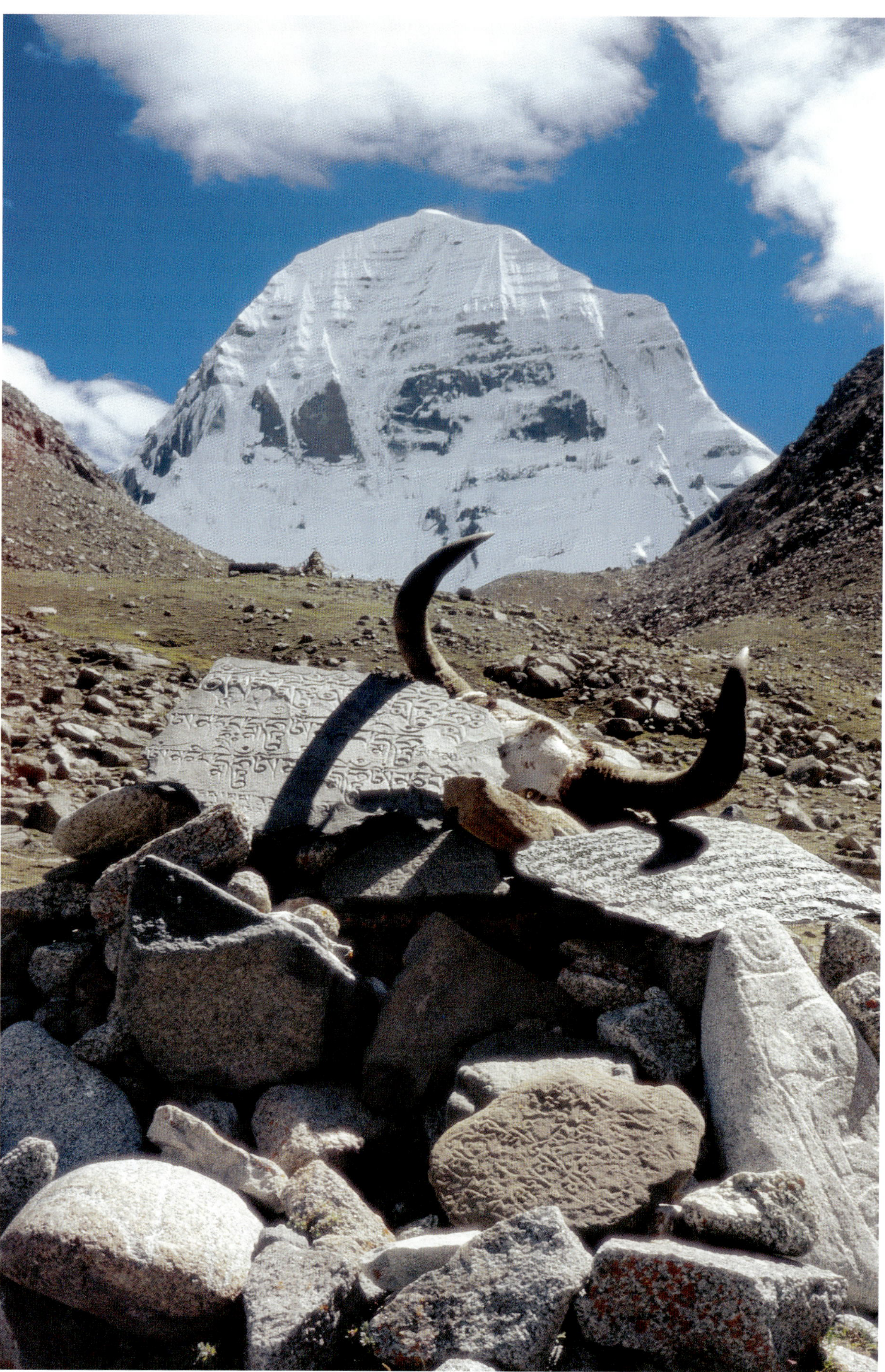

The morning surprises us with a bright, cloudless sky. The yaks and the three herders who lead them show up on time. Eight yaks are brought instead of the seven we ordered, eight being a sacred number and a good omen for the *kora*. Our circumambulation of Mount Kailash begins like a stroll on the edges of the Barga Plain. In the clear air we have a wonderful view of the peaks of the Himalayas to the south, the massive, glacier-covered Gurla Mandhata (7,730 metres) and the smaller of the two sacred lakes, the Rakastal. We follow the course of the Lha Chu ("divine river"). All along the *kora* are sacred sites and places: stone tablets bearing the Tibetan characters for the mantra of compassion, *Om Mani Padme Hum* – "Oh Jewel in the Lotus", *chortens*, thousands of prayer flags, and many monuments created by nature, where pilgrims perform specific rituals. At an elevation of about 5,200 metres, with a view of the impressive north face of Mount Kailash, we find a place to spend the night (Fig. 7).

The next day we are fortunate to join two Tibetan groups of pilgrims, and together we ascend to the highest place along the *kora*, to the Dolma La pass (5,723 metres). The two extended families have arrived at the final destination of their long pilgrimage, and they are in high spirits: boys and girls, women and men wearing traditional costumes and jewellery made of corals, turquoises, and amber, as well as amulet containers (called *ga'u*). A mother nurses her infant while walking, and children that are a little older are carried like backpacks on their mothers' backs. Behind the people trot the yaks laden with equipment for a long pilgrimage. While the Tibetans climb effortlessly and their children run playfully up and downhill covering twice the distance, we struggle to manage the last 200 metres in the altitude. The atmosphere at the sacred pass compensates us for that ordeal. The Tibetans are full of exuberant joy in which we wholeheartedly join. A large rock, which is a sanctuary dedicated to Tibet's guardian deity, Dolma (Tara), is being decorated with new prayer flags, and the Tibetans circumambulate it again and again. Silent prayers, prostrations, and happy faces express their joy at experiencing a very important moment in their lives. Tibetans believe that a new life begins at this place.

Circumambulating Mount Kailash is a very special experience for us and one of the big highlights of our travels in Tibet. We can only spare two days here, as our schedule, which we already have upset several times, urges us to drive on. The next day, we spend a couple of wonderful hours of

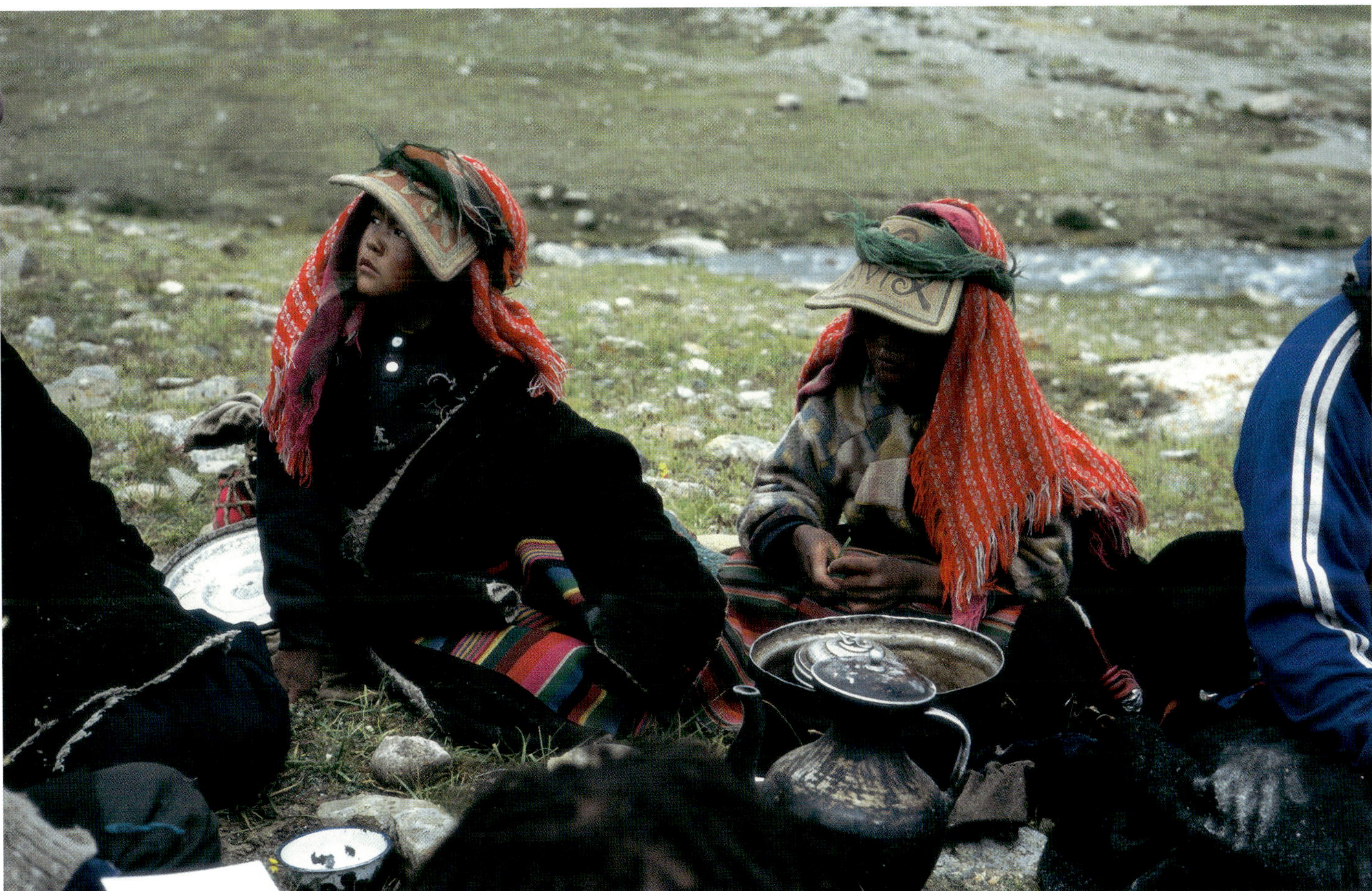

Fig. 8: Nomad children having a rest during the *kora* of Mount Kailash. West Tibet, 1995

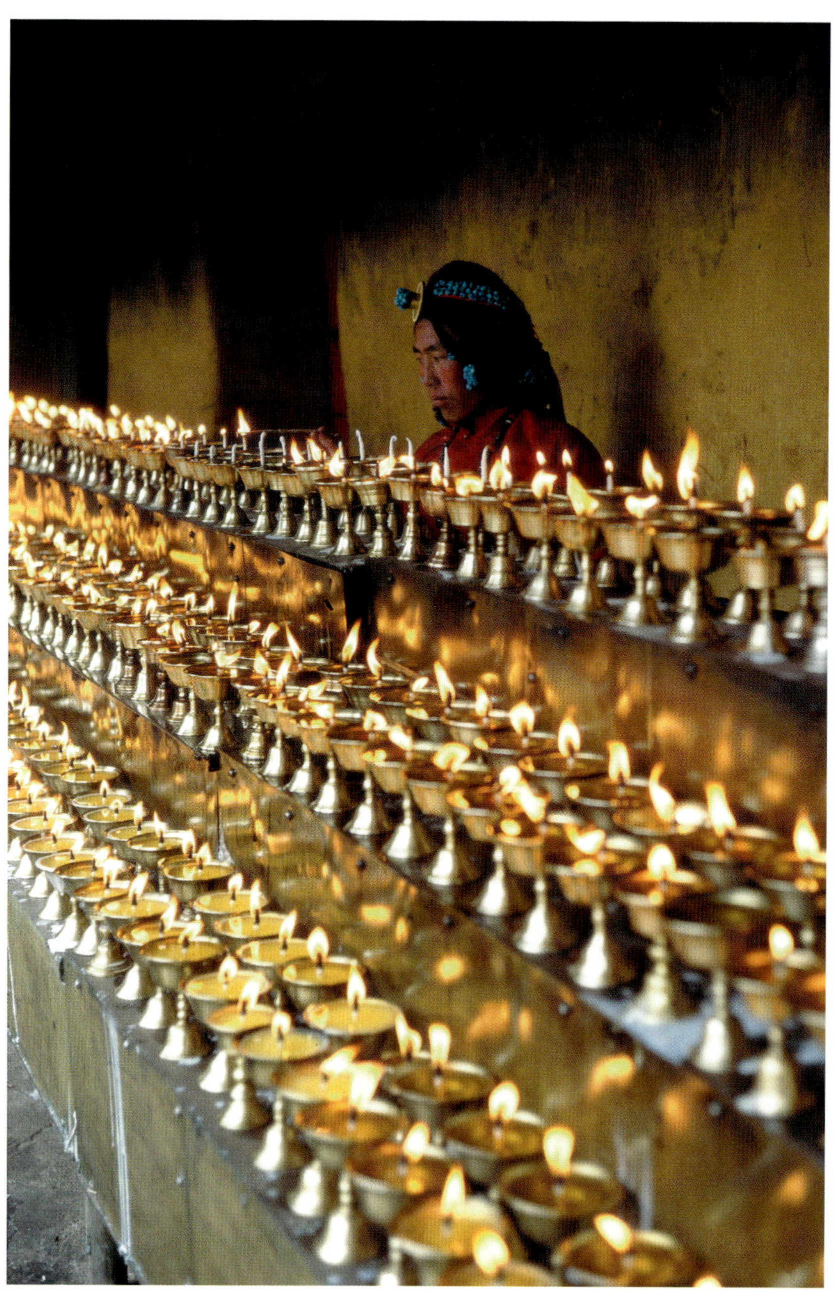

Fig. 9: Butter lamps in Jokhang temple in Lhasa, 1995

solitude at the sacred Manasarovar Lake and in a small temple situated on a cliff above the lake. From there we enjoy the magnificent unforgettable view of the deep blue water and the Gurla Mandhata with its elongated ridge and its five snow- and ice-capped peaks. Then we travel on eastbound, to Lhasa, where we should arrive in a week.

The scenery is absolutely beautiful here. Crossing the rivers, however, is only possible at fords as there are no bridges. Sand and dunes dominate the scenery in the vicinity of the rivers. One hour later the flat landscape of the steppe begins to alternate with stretches of mountains. The sky is very close, and in the thin and completely dust-free air white clouds cast dark shadows that wander over the land. And to the south we are accompanied by the Himalayas. We think we can spot the eight-thousanders Annapurna and Dhaulagiri in the distance. We drive through nomad country speckled with black tents, yaks, goats, and sheep. Everything breathes peace, beauty, and calmness. Only the so-called road continues to be so bad, that driving any faster than 20 kilometres per hour is impossible. Near Lhatse, we cross the Yarlung Tsangpo on a bridge and hit the Friendship Highway again. We make a little side trip to the monastery of Sakya which we had visited the year before. This time we are in less of a hurry, and we are once again impressed by that fortress-like structure whose outer walls are painted with vertical stripes in three colours: red, white, and black symbolising the *Bodhisattvas* Manjushri, Avalokiteshvara, and Vajrapani. In addition, the temples have all the features typical of Tibetan monastery buildings: the walls tapering at their upper ends, the dark red colouring, the brushwood top of the outer wall, and the use of textiles as part of the architecture.

This time we can also linger longer in Shigatse and Gyantse. Our perception has become sharpened by our engagement with Tibet. We are now able to recognise important historic figures in the murals, such as Padmasambhava or Milarepa, and to distinguish some deities and *Bodhisattvas* by their *mudras*, attributes, or colours. We are also developing a feeling for the antiquity and quality of Tibetan art. This, by the way, is a typically western perspective. As far as Tibetans are concerned, the only thing that counts is the spiritual content of sculptures and paintings. Hence, we repeatedly witnessed the repainting of pictures, which had become unsightly either due to ageing or the soot of butter lamps, with fresh, loud colours.

LHASA

One year later. This time, in 1996, we fly to Nepal and take a connecting flight from Kathmandu to Lhasa. It only takes an hour, and we have a fantastic view of Mount Everest and other mountain beauties. We will spend a few days in Lhasa and meet our goddaughter who now goes to school in the capital. We will also meet Tibetan friends and visit the places that by now have become familiar and dear to us, including the two large nearby monasteries, Drepung and Sera. The days spent in Lhasa (3,700 metres above sea level) also help us to acclimatise before we travel to our next destinations which are at elevations between 4,000 and 5,000 metres.

The first morning we want to visit the Jokhang temple. At this time of the day the old town is still sleepy. It is early, it feels like six o'clock or six-thirty, but the clocks here are not synchronised with the sun. China Standard Time is in effect throughout China, standardised according to time in the capital of Beijing. As in Beijing, it will soon be eight o'clock in Lhasa, and the gates of the Jokhang will open. The temple has official opening hours like a museum: from eight to eleven in the morning and from three to seven in the afternoon. The afternoons are exclusively reserved for tourists; Tibetan pilgrims are only allowed in the temple in the mornings. Since the early morning hours, armed policemen have "maintained" order in the queue of waiting devotees. The latter are nevertheless in a good mood – after all, the highlight of their pilgrimage is just a few steps away. They pray, chat, and laugh, the children would like to play around but are not allowed to run about – this is prohibited here by order of the police. On the small forecourt immediately in front of the temple gates that are still closed, some people are already performing their prostrations. Women and men, old and young raise their folded hands above their heads in a gesture of prayer; they touch their forehead, larynx, and heart, then fall to their knees and eventually prostrate themselves on the ground. They do this over and over again. Some of them wear strips of leather to protect their hands and knees. This indicates that they have been on the road for days or even months and have done the entire pilgrimage path prostrating, that is, measuring the whole distance with the length of their bodies: each new prostration began where the pilgrims' hands were stretched over their head during the previous one. Many pilgrims reach Lhasa on the beds of trucks that are either rented by the village community or provided by the respective neighbouring monastery. The nomads have donned their best clothes, and both women and men are richly bedecked with jewellery which protects them against spirits and demons. They wear coral necklaces around their necks and amber in their hair. Turquoises decorate the long golden and silver earrings or are carefully plaited into the elaborate hairdos consisting of 108 braids. The married women wear their hair in a bun to which they attach silver barrettes studded with corals and turquoises.

Residents of the city also briefly drop in at the Jokhang for a prayer and then go on with their daily tasks. Two girls carrying full school bags and wearing red pioneer scarves stop in front of the temple, whisper among themselves, and giggle. Then they pause, drop to their knees, bow deeply until their foreheads touch the ground, and pray. Then they whisper to each other again and run off to school. On the stroke of eight, the temple gates open, the Tibetans enter and we follow them. Before our marvelling eyes their piety and prayers transform the museum into a sacred temple.

Meanwhile, life awakes on the Barkhor. This pilgrims' path around the temple complex, is both a promenade and a market. It gives nomads the opportunity to supply themselves with all they need: clothing, fabrics, sewing needles, yarn, salt, pots, ropes, thermos cans, and the Chinese tea bricks needed to make butter tea. Shopping and bargaining is amazingly compatible with pilgrimage. People pray as they walk, always in a clockwise direction; they occasionally exchange glances with strangers or even engage in a conversation; or they agree terms with a vendor, tender the money, put their purchase into their bag, and then walk on completely immersed in their prayers. We have always admired the smooth switch from prayer to business and vice versa.

Let us briefly introduce the Tibetan national beverage. Butter tea is an emulsified mixture of hot tea, butter, and salt. A thermos can full of that tea must always be at hand, be it at home in the nomad tent, or on the road. If the butter used is fresh, the beverage is even palatable for Europeans as well, particularly if they do not just want tea but also crave a hearty, nourishing bouillon.

Lhasa is situated in a high valley on the Kyichu River that flows into the Yarlung Tsangpo 60 kilometres further south. The city is surrounded by snow-capped five-thousanders. There are three mountains in the city itself. The small Hare Mountain (Tib. *Bhamari*, 17 metres high) is today no longer visible among the multi-storey houses. Iron Mountain (Tib. *Chakpori*) is 100 metres high and still a very visible part of the cityscape. Up to its destruction by the Chinese armed forces in 1959 it was home to the Tibetan Medical College that had been founded in the 17th century. Today, only the transmission mast of Chinese broadcasting rises from its top. Opposite on Red Mountain (Tib. *Marpori*, 98 metres high) stands the Potala Palace. King Songtsen Gampo built a fortress at the same place as early as the 7th century. It was burned down 100 years later during the war between Tibet and China. However, a small part of the fortress must have survived back then because the palace built by order of the 5th Dalai Lama in the 17th century still features two rooms said to be from that time. Up to the mid-20th century, that is, for about 300 years, it was the seat of the religious and secular power in Tibet. Today, as decided by China, the Potala is only a museum. For the Tibetans, however, it continues to be an important religious centre.

We have joined the pilgrims and walked with them on Beijing Road, which traverses Lhasa from east to west, to the Potala. The magnificent white and red building is enthroned majestically above the city. Its whitewashed walls provide ample space for assembly halls, administrative facilities, and storage rooms, while the Red Palace harbours numerous chapels, state rooms, and the former living quarters of the Dalai Lama. Below the Potala the road broadens and becomes an eight-lane tangent which, together with space that has been added, is a perfect location for military parades and march-pasts. From here we proceed through the ruins of the former Tibetan government village called Zhol, and ascend a wide stone stairway up to the courtyard of the white six-storey building. The main gate to the Potala is on the front side of the building at the level of the first storey. Walking over a high, multi-step threshold and steep wooden stairs lined by massive handrails, we enter the palace jointly with the pilgrims. In the entrance hall, the Four Guardian Kings look at us from the murals, and the respect paid by the Tibetans to the guardians of the teachings is palpable. We pass the next murals with depictions of sacred buildings in Lhasa, and reach the roof of the White Palace over steep stairs. Sunlight and a blue sky beam at us. We enjoy the view of the city and its beautiful surroundings.

Now we come to the Red Palace, the halls and private rooms of the Dalai Lama which have not been used for their proper purpose since 1959. Our sightseeing of the central part of the Potala begins here, with the chapels adorned with precious Buddhist sacred objects and the two most ancient rooms, which according to tradition date from the time of Songtsen Gampo (who ruled from 617 until 649). One of them is said to have been the king's meditation chamber. The Tibetans' veneration for the precious figures, tombs, and sacred objects is deeply moving. We are very impressed by their devoutness.

This special atmosphere goes unnoticed by the tourists because the tour groups are guided through the Potala in the opposite direction. Minibuses arrive at the back entrance of the palace where local guides take charge of them. The guided tour begins in the large *Lhakhang* with the golden reliquary *stūpas* of the 10th and 12th Dalai Lamas (19th century) and the lavishly adorned great *stūpa* of the 5th Dalai Lama built in the 17th century. For the praying Tibetans, this *Lhakhang* is the last station of their pilgrimage.

Museums will often prescribe the direction to be taken by sightseeing groups due to reasons of organisation and museum education. In the Potala, the national sanctuary of Tibet which is under Chinese administration, the separation of tours taken by visitors has a political background. It aims at making the Tibetans' ties to the history of their nation and their devoutness to Buddhism invisible to foreign tourists. That way, at the historic seat of the Dalai Lama, the chance of encounters between tourists and Tibetan pilgrims is reduced to a minimum.

AT THE SACRED LAKE DRAKSUM LHATSO

A two-day drive in a Land Cruiser takes us from Lhasa in an eastward direction. First we travel along the Kyichu (Lhasa river), which becomes ever wilder, and pass a few villages. Then we drive on through nomad country, cross a pass at an elevation of 4,720 metres in a snow storm, and proceed along the still young Kongpo Nyangchu River. At about noon the second day we take a turn to the north, and our route now leads upstream along the turbulent Draksum Chu stream.

Late in the afternoon we arrive in the rain at the sacred Lake Draksum Lhatso which today is also called Basum Tso. It turns out that we are not allowed to camp here. Our guide has just learned why: a "recreation centre" was built here two years ago. While that building is empty and left to decay, there is a regulation stipulating that no tent may be put up if a hotel or guest house is available. So we have to move in there, much to the detriment of our travel funds.

The next morning begins with sunshine, but soon it starts raining again. With a raft we reach the island in the lake where there is a *Gompa*, a Buddhist temple. It was destroyed during the Cultural Revolution but was rebuilt by the people. Today, the whole island is still a much frequented sacred site (Fig. 10). Four monks are in charge of maintenance and worship at this peaceful place that features the insignia of faith (footprint of a saint, figures) and attracts a few pilgrims each day.

Our next task of the day is to go on the pilgrimage path that leads around the lake. It has rained a lot during the last few days; hence, the village street in Puru is completely drenched, we sink into mud that reaches up to our calves and knees. We need to make our way hand over hand along the fences, and set new records in long jump. Village children stand around barefoot in deep puddles, grinning at us. A man invites us into his house. Over a three-stepped threshold we first enter the vestibule; the entrance to the stables is from there because in Tibetan farmhouses the ground floor is always reserved for the animals; people live

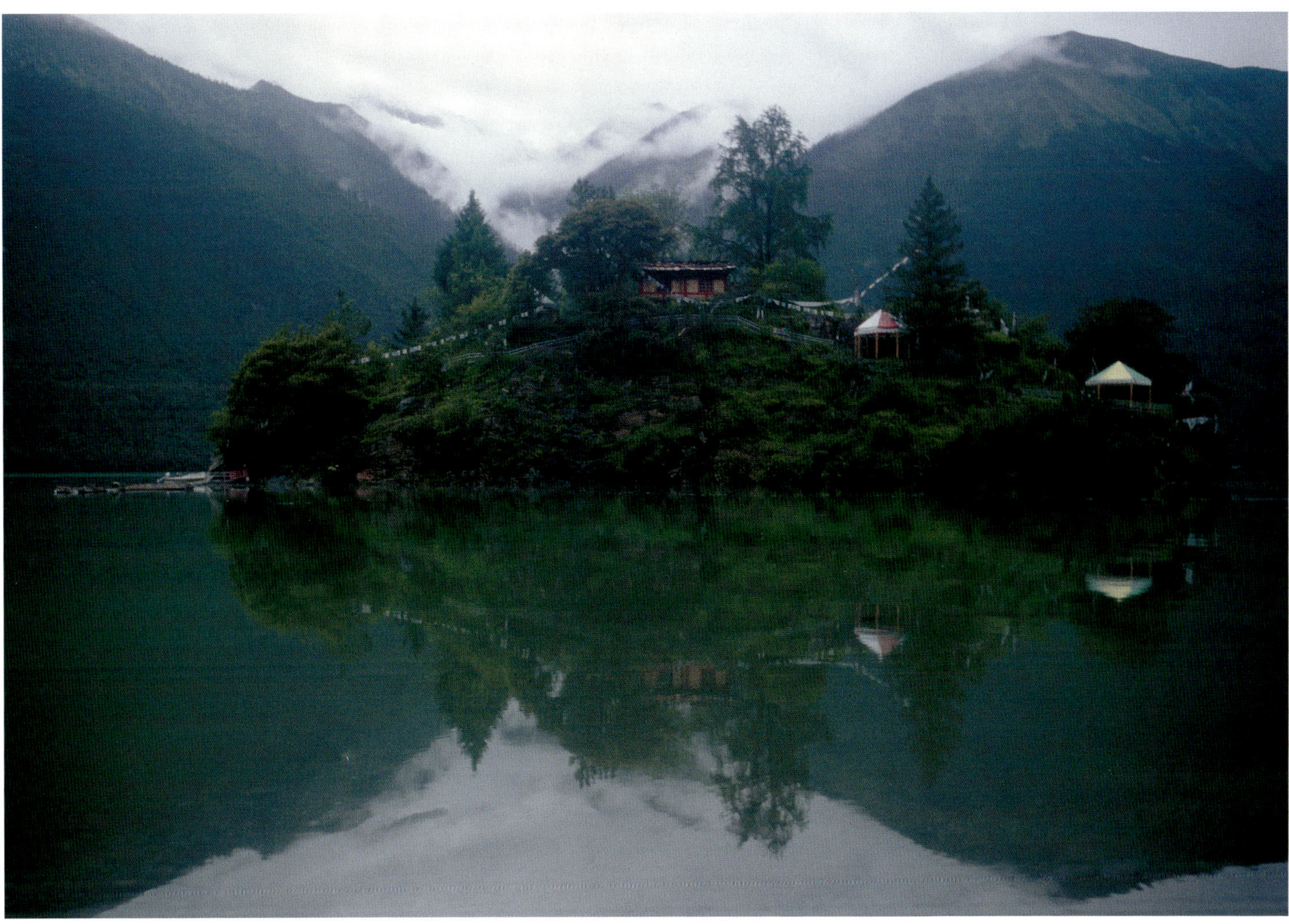

Fig. 10: The sacred Lake Draksum Lhatso. Eastern Central Tibet, 1996

on the first floor to which we now ascend on steep ladder-like steps. Before we go to the kitchen-cum-living-room, we are invited into the house chapel whose entrance is exactly opposite the kitchen door. The room is softly lit and fragrant with the smell of incense sticks. Butter lamps flicker in front of the Buddha figures and photos of venerable lamas. A wheel made of peacock feathers hangs on the wall. More pictures of saints are attached to a wooden column in the middle of the room. One of them is the faded, dusty portrait of a young Chinese man in uniform. We glance at it in amazement, and our guide translates our host's comment: the man is indeed Mao Zedong. The farmer nods and goes on to explain that the picture is very helpful. After all, Chinese from the municipal administration drop in at the farmstead every once in a while, as do assistant controllers.

We leave the house chapel and enter the living room which is also the kitchen. It measures approximately 40 or 45 square metres. The room is bright, with two windows in each of the south and east walls, and very cosy. Along the two windowed walls stretches a bench that is about 25 centimetres high and is covered with rugs and *kilims*. The lady of the house invites us in. Her little daughter clings to her skirt. A baby wrapped in nappies is sleeping on the bench. In the middle of the room stands a solid, brick-built kitchen oven; a wood fire is crackling under the kettle. We learn that food for the pigs is being cooked. The obligatory bowl of butter tea tastes delicious. We feel welcome for a number of reasons: the cosiness of the room, our hosts' relaxed amicability, and their unobtrusive curiosity about where we come from and what we are doing in Tibet. After a short visit, we have to be on our way again.

For a change it is not raining outside. We can even spot tiny specks of blue amidst the clouds, and we begin to believe that the sun and the snow-capped seven-thousanders really exist behind the blanket of clouds.

We follow the pilgrimage route along the lake. Prayer flags are fluttering in the wind, and the green tresses of moss hanging from the trees contribute to an atmosphere of enchantment. After a few kilometres the forest becomes sparser and gives way to colourful meadows full of flowers. Behind the hill we see barley fields and women working in them. Our path runs along the ridge of the little chain of hills between the lake and the fields. We reach a hamlet with a few farm houses, shingle-covered stone buildings, prayer flags, and a *chorten* (*stūpa*). A few children approach us; they are shy but curious. Apart from them there are only two young women and some old men in the village.

With his forthright manner, our guide helps to overcome the feeling of strangeness; we take Polaroid pictures and present them to the villagers. Most importantly, however, we have brought pictures of the Dalai Lama with us as welcome gifts. We answer questions as to where we come from, and learn that the men are on the upland pastures of the mountains with the yaks. We eventually buy 30 eggs which I carry the whole way back, carefully so that not one of them breaks. We are picked up at the bridge in Puru. We are completely soaked, as heavy rain has set in again. It's monsoon time.

PARADISE

After an overnight stay in Bayi we drive on south. It is raining again, sometimes heavily, sometimes less. To our right rushes a very swollen river that empties into the Yarlung Tsangpo 50 kilometres downstream. Our destination today is the Zangdok Pelri monastery near Lamaling village. After a two-hour drive we catch sight of the pagoda-shaped roofs half way up a wooded mountain slope. They shimmer in red, gold, and blue, and the monastery looks like a sparkling jewel displayed on green velvet. The monastery is still some distance away. How are we to get there? Our guide, Bulak, asks people working in a field but does not seem satisfied with the answer. We drive a bit further and then turn off onto a country lane where we stop to ask again. The uniform answer, as summarised by Bulak, is that Lamaling cannot be reached by car, everything is flooded. Nevertheless, we give it a try. After getting stuck in a mud hole we decide to proceed on foot. A two-hour march across the fields awaits us. In some places we need the agility of tightrope walkers to keep our balance on a foot-wide, slippery path between calf-deep mud and flooded land. For a while we follow a fast-running stream until we find a place where we can cross it barefoot, wading through knee-deep water. Mares and their foals feel at home on the wet pastures. Shepherd children warm up tea over a small fire. The scenery resounds with the songs of thousands of birds. The rushing, whispering and gurgling of water is omnipresent.

Our little path broadens and becomes a village street. Lamaling is situated in a depression between two hills, and parts of it are built into the slope leading to the monastery above. In the centre of the village stands a very old nut tree. A little bit down the road, thick logs of wood lie neatly stacked at the wall of a house. Three women have interrupted their chat and look at us full of curiosity. A couple of children do the same from a safe distance.

In this village, the whitewashed farm houses have red-and-blue latticed windows, and the ridges of their roofs are graced with prayer flags. The farmsteads are enclosed by mud walls and brushwood fences. Some of the handkerchief-sized barley fields are enclosed by small, low walls as well. A dog barks in the distance. A rooster crows. For some time the air is full of the cackling of a hen announcing that she has just laid an egg. Wood is being cut somewhere. The blows of the axe create rhythmic caesuras in the idyllic soundscape. We breathe the fragrant smell of log fires. Chinese language and music shrill from a radio in the village shop.

We ascend up to the temple. Bees are humming. The air is fragrant with the smell of roses, as a thousand roses are in blossom at the monastery. The attention of female pilgrims is torn between pious worship and curiosity about the foreigners. A lovely old lady does not want us to take her picture; she tells us she is not beautiful enough. When we present her with a picture of the Dalai Lama, however, she changes her mind (Fig. 11). We then follow her into the temple. It is magnificent and new, built in the traditional Tibetan style. It is muggy and cloudy, and there are intermittent rain showers. Never mind – that's just the way weather is in paradise today.

That was the third of our trips undertaken from 1994 onward. It was followed by thirteen more – eight to Tibet, one each to Mongolia and Bhutan, one to Mustang which is part of Nepal, and two to Ladakh and Zanskar in India. In all these places Tibetans have been living from time immemorial, and their culture has been an essential feature of these regions. On each of these trips we had new, extraordinary experiences day after day, of which only a few could be recounted here. When choosing the respective destinations, we were guided by our increasing interest in the life, history, and culture of that splendid nation, as well as by the love that had grown in us for the wonderful people who have given us so much with their open-mindedness, straightforwardness, and beauty.

Fig. 11: A Tibetan pilgrim at Zangdok Pelri monastery. Eastern Central Tibet, 1996

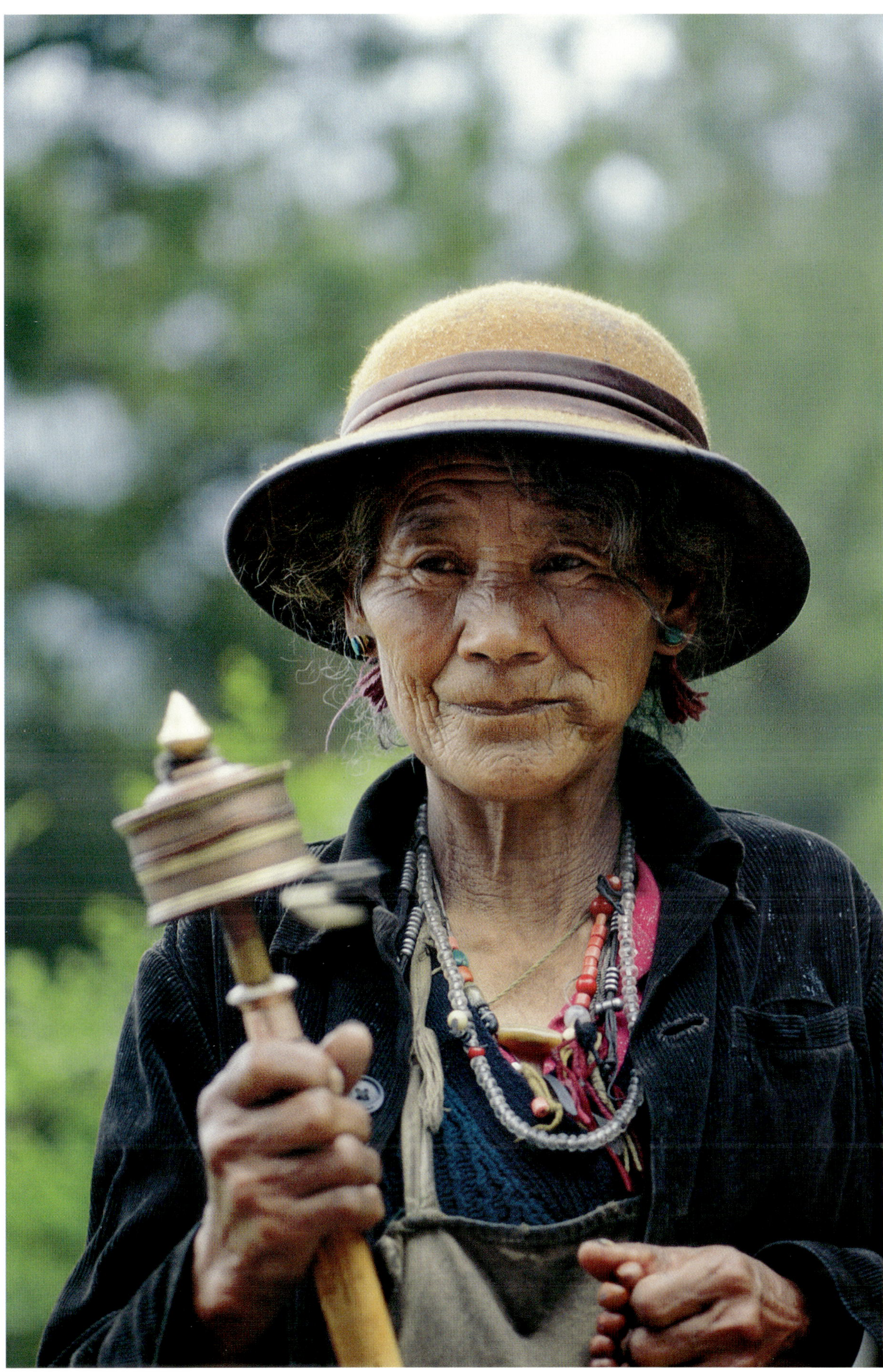

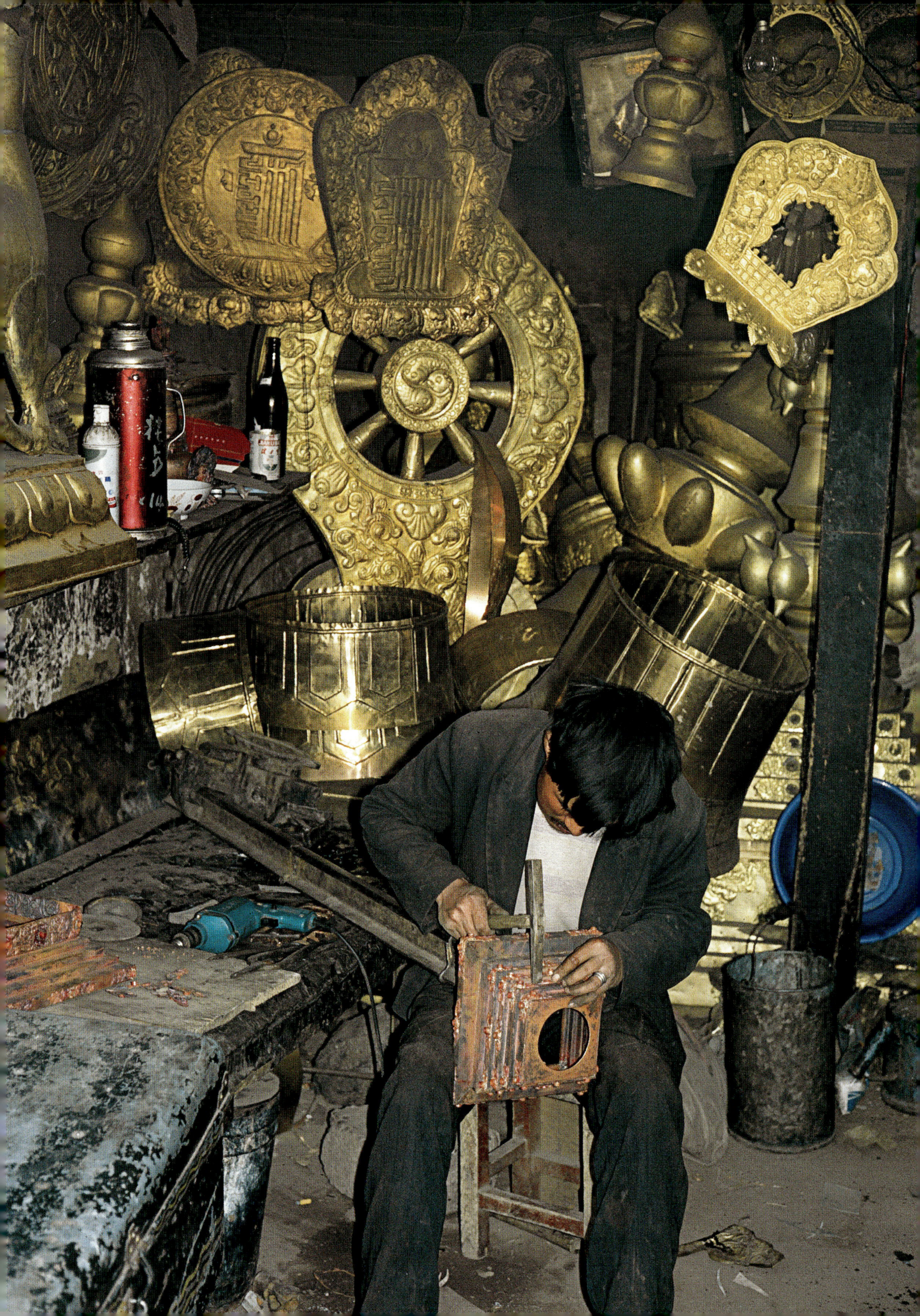

Petra Maurer

CRAFTSMANSHIP

The Material Culture of Tibet

INTRODUCTION

Fig. 1: Tinsmith's workshop in the old part of Lhasa, 1999

Material culture with its objects for use in daily life and religion permeates and defines all facets of human existence. They are a part of everyday activity and religious ceremony. The production and use of tools and implements is one of the most ancient activities of mankind. Material culture encompasses all the objects that a society produces and uses. They are a very significant identifying factor for recognizing different cultures and individual societies. The things which a person uses or enjoys contemplating are an expression of his culture. Without material culture, human life would be unthinkable.

The expression "material culture" immediately suggests questions about "immaterial culture" and considerations of how the two are related.

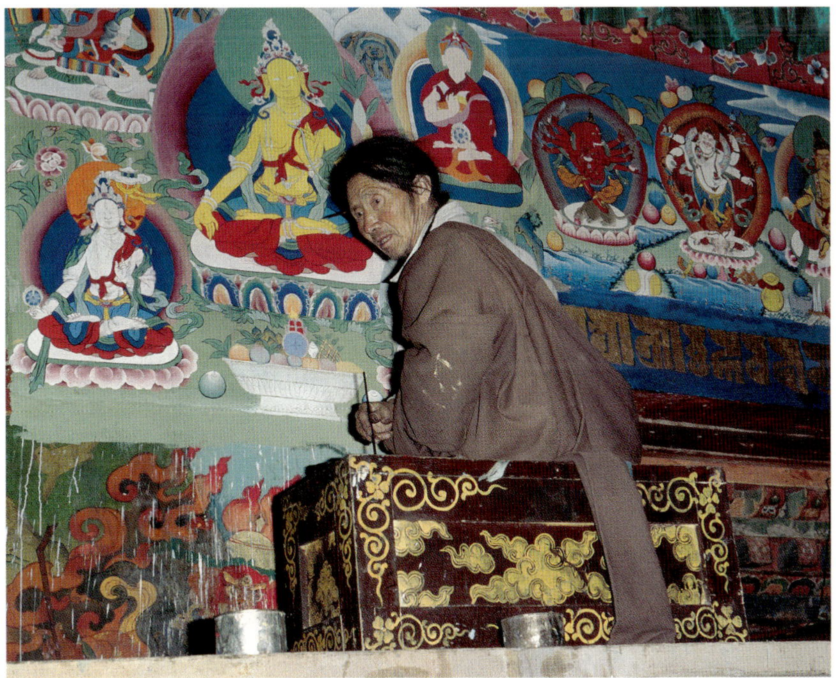

Fig. 2: When painting over an 18th century mural, such as here in Samye monastery, Tibetan fresco painters have no scruples; the only thing that counts is earning karma, 1997

THE SOCIAL POSITION OF CRAFTSMEN IN TIBET

Despite the great importance of the material culture, craftsmen (*lag shes bdag po* in Tibetan, "those who possess skilled hands") belonged to the lower social levels in traditional Tibetan society, consisting of the clergy, nobility, farmers, nomads, townspeople and craftsmen, and also "untouchables". The Tibetan expression *bdag po* (owner, master) implies that their skill and knowledge cannot be taken from them, a clear advantage over others in society: for example, the official could be relieved of his position or the tradesman could have his wares stolen. But the craftsman's skill was inseparable from his person.

Although he never belonged to a higher social level, the craftsman was respected according to the material he worked with and the objects he produced.

The painters of *thangkas* or frescoes (Fig. 2), sculptors of clay statues, those who made masks, and generally the more artistic practices or those who did "light and white work" (Tib. *dal dkar las*) had the highest respect. They were followed by those whose work required strength, "hard work" (Tib. *shugs las*); the wood carvers of the blocks for printing Tibetan books, texts for amulets, etc., also the carvers of furniture and the like. This also included the metal workers, smiths and founders of metal statues, as well as the gold, silver and copper smiths. The gold and silver smiths were sometimes suspected of dishonesty with the suspicion that they "did not use all the precious metal provided in their alloy" (Ronge 1978a: 31). This doubtful reputation was based on the belief that mining for metal in the earth disturbed *kLu* and *sa bdag*, the earth deities, and that could bring misfortune. Both groups completed commissions for monasteries and rich nobles and were well compensated.

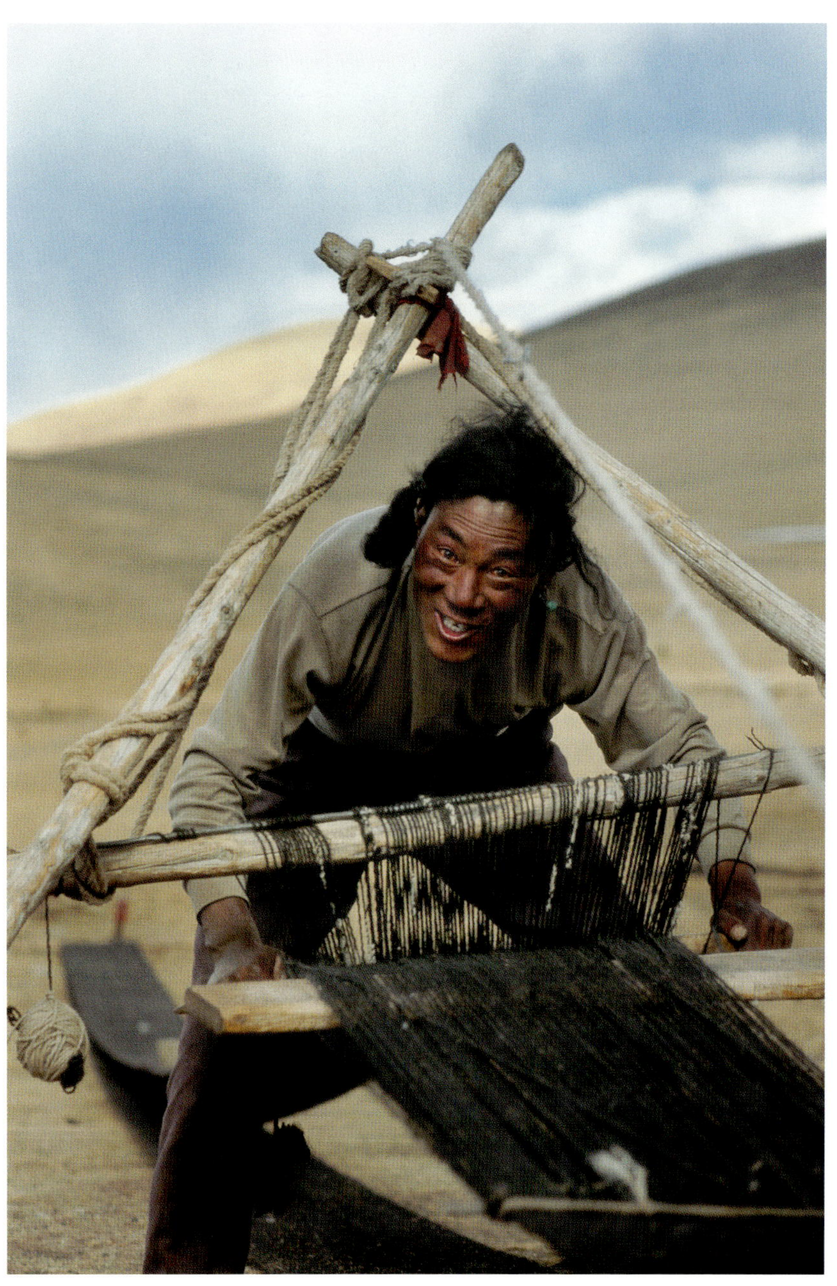

Fig. 3: Weaving black or black-brown panels of yak hair for nomads' tents is hard work which men do. In the region around Jyekundo, north-eastern Tibet, 2002

LEARNING A CRAFT AND LOCAL DISTRIBUTION

Traditional Tibetan art is exclusively religious and strictly formalised. *Thangka* painters and sculptors require a great knowledge of the iconography and the related religious texts.

Since crafts were usually handed down from father to son or sons, membership in the relative social level was often preordained by birth, especially in larger towns with many workshops.

In rural areas, nomads and farmers often learned specific crafts, or the landowner required the farmers on his property to learn a certain craft as a supplementary trade. The primary activity then often led to the craft that was learned and practised. Nomads, since they worked with animals, would learn tanning, spinning, weaving, felting, sewing tents and clothing, whereas farmers would learn carpentry, masonry, weaving and making clothing, or paper making (Ronge 1978a: 45–47).

On closer inspection, it is apparent that there is not only a differentiation between the material culture of everyday items and religious ones but also that the choice of the craft learned related to the living conditions and locally available raw materials. Prior to the influx of the Chinese, Tibet's economy was primarily rural.

Near the monasteries and larger settlements, crafts were independent professions. As a rule, craftsmen worked at craft centres whose products were delivered to the government and monastery administrations. For example, the gold, silver, copper and iron smiths in eastern Tibet enjoyed a high reputation throughout the country for their fine products, with the result that individual villages became specialised in one type of work.

Less respected was the heavier work of the iron and weapon smiths, known as "black work" (Tib. *las nag*), which was less well remunerated. At the lowest level were the dyers, cobblers, tinkers, tanners, potters and stone masons, also butchers, hunters and preparers of corpses, etc. (Ronge 1978a: 33–35).

This order of social ranking resulted among other factors from whether the work was directly or indirectly connected with killing a living being. A further criterion was a religious motivation for the craft, as in the case of *thangka* painters, sculptors of statues, and carvers of woodblocks for books, who were higher ranked. An exception to this were the stone masons, since they were itinerant workers and usually poor.

Rug Makers and Dyers

The workshops in Gyantse, Shigatse, Gampadzong, Tsethang and Lhoka were famous for their rugs and other woollen products; occasionally rugs were also made privately at home by farmers. In Lhasa, the craftsmen were more specialised in weaving wool.

It was usual that those who worked with wool, the rug makers, weavers or tailors, also dyed the wool themselves. The cloth dyed in Tsethang was famous for its use of the plangi technique (Tib. *thig ma*, which means "drops"), which produces cross-shaped motifs. Textiles with this motif were traded throughout Tibet and beyond. Because the motif was so popular, it was even knotted into rugs.

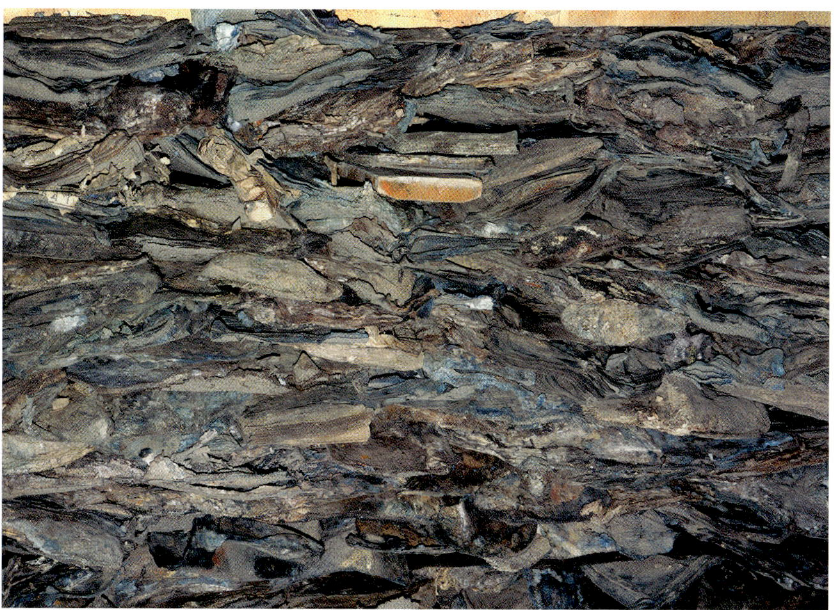

Fig. 4: The charred remains of the once famous manuscript library of Riwoche temple, 2002

In the south of Central Tibet there were centres in which knotted rugs were made. Centres for metalworking and painting were predominantly found in East and Central Tibet; wooden products and basketry, in South and Southeast Tibet. The woodblocks for printing books were carved near the major monasteries. Lhasa, as the administrative and religious centre, was an exception to this. All the different crafts were represented to assure that orders could be immediately fulfilled. The artisans and craftsmen were, however, not all Tibetans. The Newar from the Kathmandu valley were renowned as artists for their statues, the Chinese as tailors, and Indian Muslims as gunsmiths.

Metalworkers

Very significant were the workshops of those who made weapons such as swords and lances, but also household items such as teapots, knives and saddles, especially those in East Tibet, in Derge, Dagyab, Horpo and Pating.

From Poyul, a further centre for metalworking, weapons and jewellery were even exported to Assam and Kham in East Tibet. Derge and Riwoche were noted for high-quality bronze casting and Gartog for the statues produced there. Metal wares from Chamdo, where iron ore was found, were traded as far away as Sichuan in China. Also in the central provinces U and Tsang metal statues cast in bronze were made, e.g. in the central workshops in Lhasa.

Thangka Painters

The painting of *thangkas* was an especially traditional Tibetan art form practised in the monasteries, where in the course of time and through varying influences different styles evolved. The woodblocks for printing books were also carved in the monasteries, since Tibetan literature deals almost exclusively with religious themes. In Nyemo/Tsang about ten percent of the population were woodcarvers. The paper for the books came from the area around Gyantse. Near the famous monastery library in Derge paper was produced predominantly in farm workshops and supplied as a form of tax payment.

Woodcarvers

Wood from the extensive forests in East Tibet was important in everyday Tibetan life, not just for house construction but also for making vessels and bowls for the staples of tea, *tsampa* (roasted barley meal), butter and beer. Wooden bowls in all sizes from Southeast Tibet were popular and sold as far away as Nepal and India. Well-known workshops for carpentry and artistic woodcarving were also situated in the wooded south and east of Tibet, in Kham and Poyul. Carpenters from Lijiang in Yunnan were invited to Lhasa to make furniture for the Dalai Lama and design and carve the beams for his stalls (Ronge 1978a: 116–123).

DECLINE OF THE TRADITIONAL ARTS AND CRAFTS AND THEIR REVITALISATION

The traditional arts and crafts in Tibet were many and varied and were almost always of high quality. With the Chinese invasion in 1951, however, this all changed very quickly. Especially during the Culture Revolution, when the monasteries were plundered and destroyed, an enormous cultural treasure was lost. The pages of religious books were scattered to the winds (Fig. 4); their carved wooden covers were burnt or used as roof shingles or even as chopping boards. As a result, after the earthquake in 2010 in Jyekundo (Yushu) carved *mani* stones that had been used in construction were discovered and have now been restored to their original purpose. Statues were broken up and melted down; all types of items that represented the Tibetans' religious and everyday material culture were lost.

Refugees on their flight from Tibet took many artefacts with them to India, Nepal and Bhutan, where they had to sell some of them to support their families.

In Tibet, Chinese import goods flooded the markets. After the opening to tourists in 1980, many Tibetans saw the chance to offer some of their possessions for sale. The Chinese occupation brought modernization and technology that soon changed life on the Roof of the World.

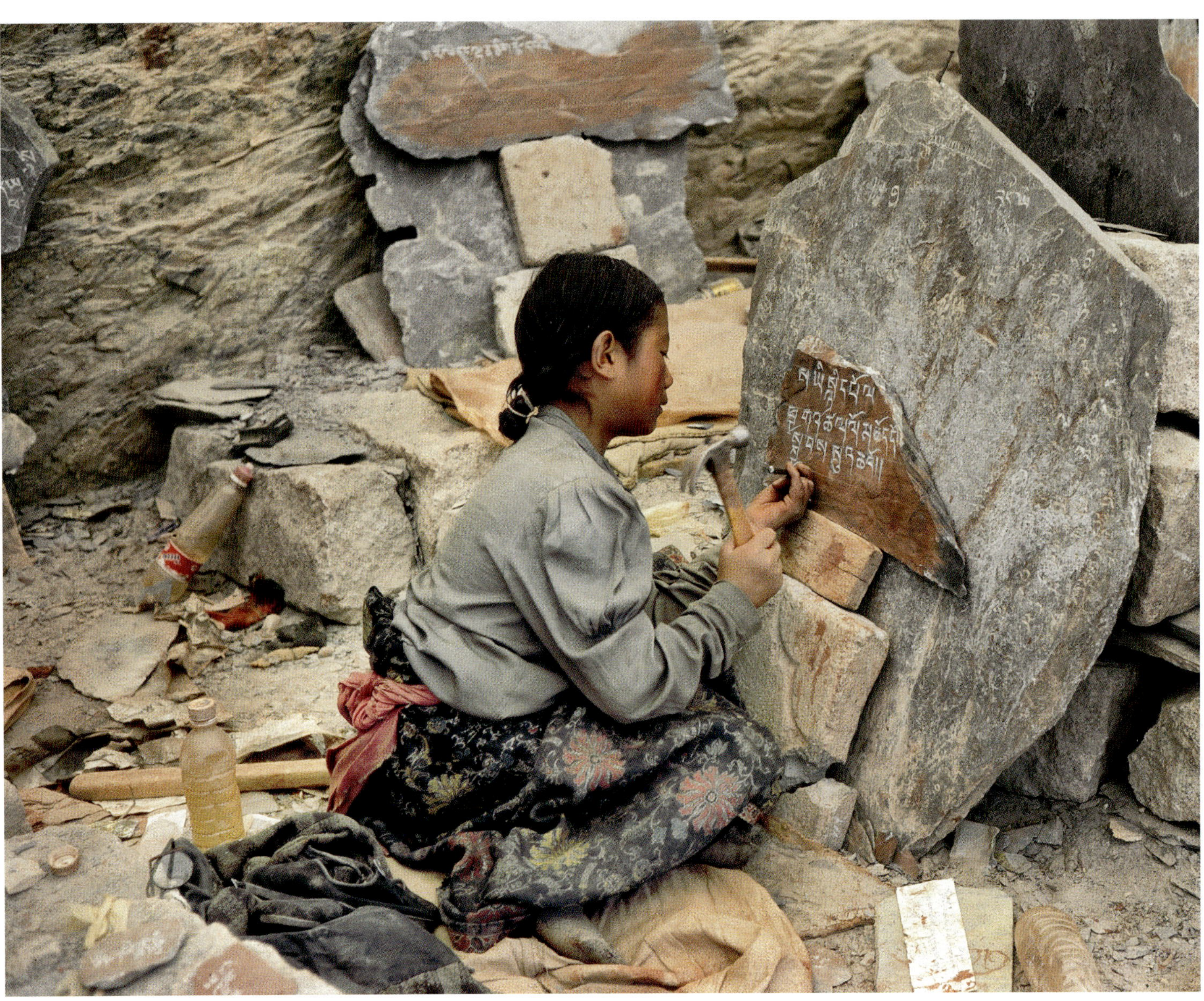

Fig. 5: "Practice makes perfect": a young girl engraving a stone tablet. Linkhor, Lhasa, 1999

The wooden churn was replaced by a plastic one or even by an electric mixer to make the traditional butter tea. This overwhelming and partly enforced change could be compared with a similar phenomenon in Germany during the "Economic Miracle" of the 1960s, when old ceramic kitchen containers were replaced by Tupperware.

With Hu Yaobang (20.11.1915–15.4.1989), the liberal Party chairman and later General Secretary of the Communist Party, the radical Chinese attitude towards Tibet changed around 1980, but only for a few years. The local, traditional culture received state support. The Tibetans founded cooperatives in which traditional craftsmen such as cobblers, hat makers or tailors could pursue their trades, and even renew contact with the historical craft organisations (Tib. *bzo las khang*). In the course of liberalisation, supported by private individuals but also by the Chinese state, monasteries began to be rebuilt. By the mid 1980s, many craftsmen could again resume their professions: carpenters, modellers of statues, fresco painters, as well as silver and goldsmiths. They were, however, primarily required to do restoration work. They not only re-established themselves, they also trained many, especially quite young apprentices in their crafts (Fig. 5). At that time in the markets in Central Tibet one could still find objects produced in the traditional way. The Chinese influence, however, with its influx of plastic goods, synthetic textiles and cheap metal imitations of everyday Tibetan household articles became ever more evident and visible. These imports were all produced in China, since the Tibetans did not have the technical know-how to work with these modern materials.

Containers for tea, water and beer, which once were made of wood or pottery, were now plastic or sheet metal.

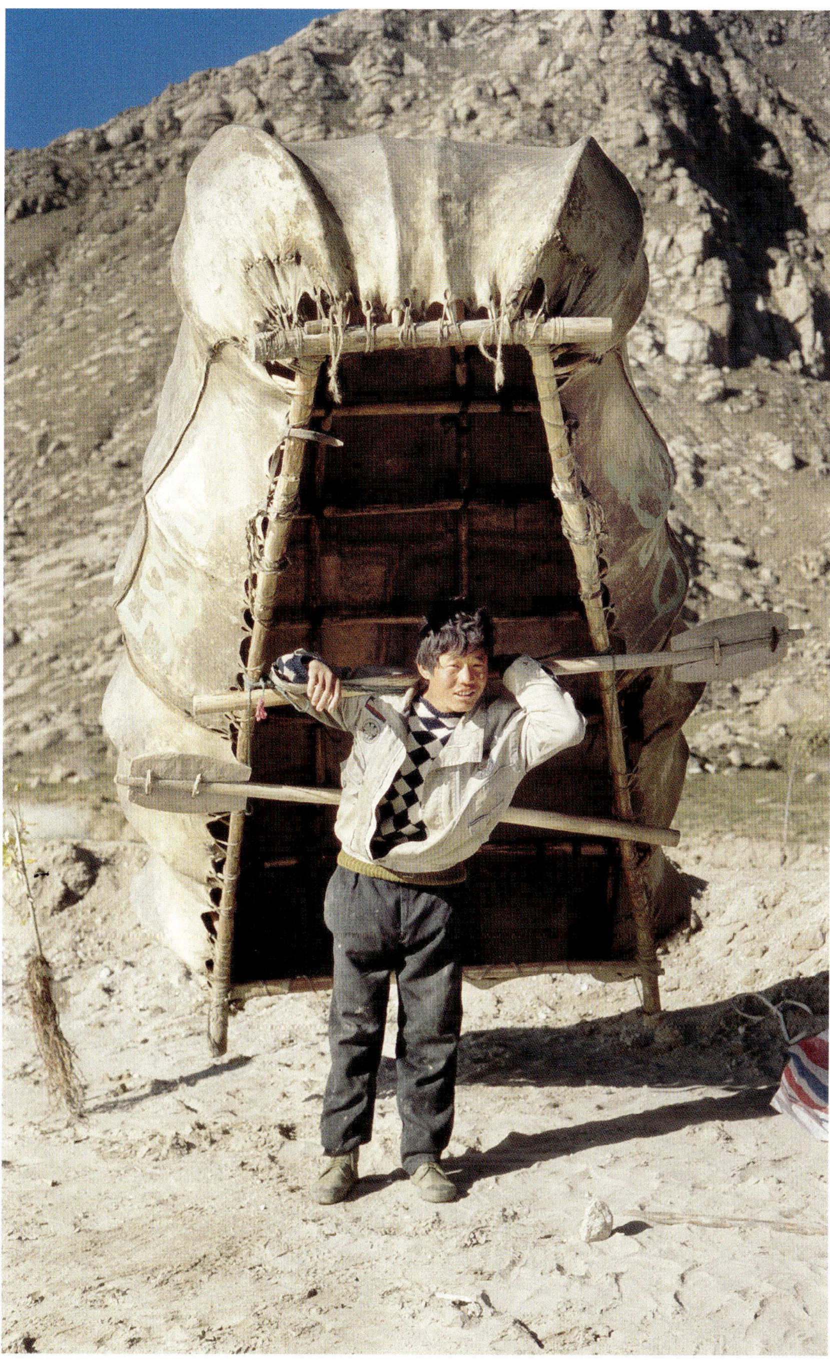

Fig. 6: Fishermen on the Kyichu river still use traditional yak-hide boats, 1998

The turned wooden snuffboxes so favoured by the Tibetans were replaced by plastic imitations; hats from the Amdo region once made of felt were now pressed from polystyrene.

Following the political disturbances in the late 1980s, the number of tourists again increased, which brought an increased demand for locally made products: works of art, antiques or simply traditional everyday objects. As a result, things which had only been made for local use were now produced for tourists. To some extent, the old crafts oriented themselves to serve this new market.

The pallet of products can now be compared with that in western souvenir shops for Tibetan items. Sacred, ritual and everyday items are widely available, and, depending on where they were made in Tibet, of very differing quality. One can find dolls in traditional costumes, miniature yaks of hide, cloth hand puppets – for example, dragons, tigers, and snow lions – miniature yak skin boats, stone slings, prayer wheels, bronze *vajra* and bells, bags, wooden and metal vessels in the style of the traditional tea, butter and *tsampa* bowls and vessels, carpets, painted wooden chests, woven textiles, felt boots, shoes and hats.

These items were apparently designed by non-Tibetans, since they are often only remotely related to the old, traditional Tibetan forms. Indeed, they sometimes seem to be caricatures of them. Since the 1990s, at the initiative of various organisations, workshops have been established to serve the tourist market, especially in and around Lhasa, and even complete crafts villages have emerged. Above the salesrooms in the old part of Lhasa are often workshops in which traditional and modern techniques are used. Now travellers can not only join a local tour of shops but can also order items via the Internet. Just two examples of these organisations are the Tibetan Village Project and the Dropenling Handicraft Development Center. Influential on product design are the international trade fairs and the favoured export to the United States (Lange 2012: 91ff.).

Jewellery, mostly costume jewellery, but also more fashionable knitted wear such as gloves, pullovers and shawls are generally imported from Nepal, as well as cast metal figures and new *thangkas*. The market for old, high-quality, authentic handicraft products in Tibet seems to have been swept clean. In the future the examples of Tibetan art and material culture to be found in museums and collections will be even more important for Tibetans in Tibet and those in exile around the world.

The Buddeberg Collection includes a surprising variety of materials and cultural artefacts from simple stone slings to metal fire steels, from end caps for *thangka* rods and *tsa tsa* to top-quality sculptures and *thangkas*. In the area of textiles it also includes a wide variety of rugs as well as horse ornaments such as saddle blankets and forehead decorations. It provides, therefore, an outstanding contribution to the documentation of the authentic material culture and traditional craftsmanship of Tibet.

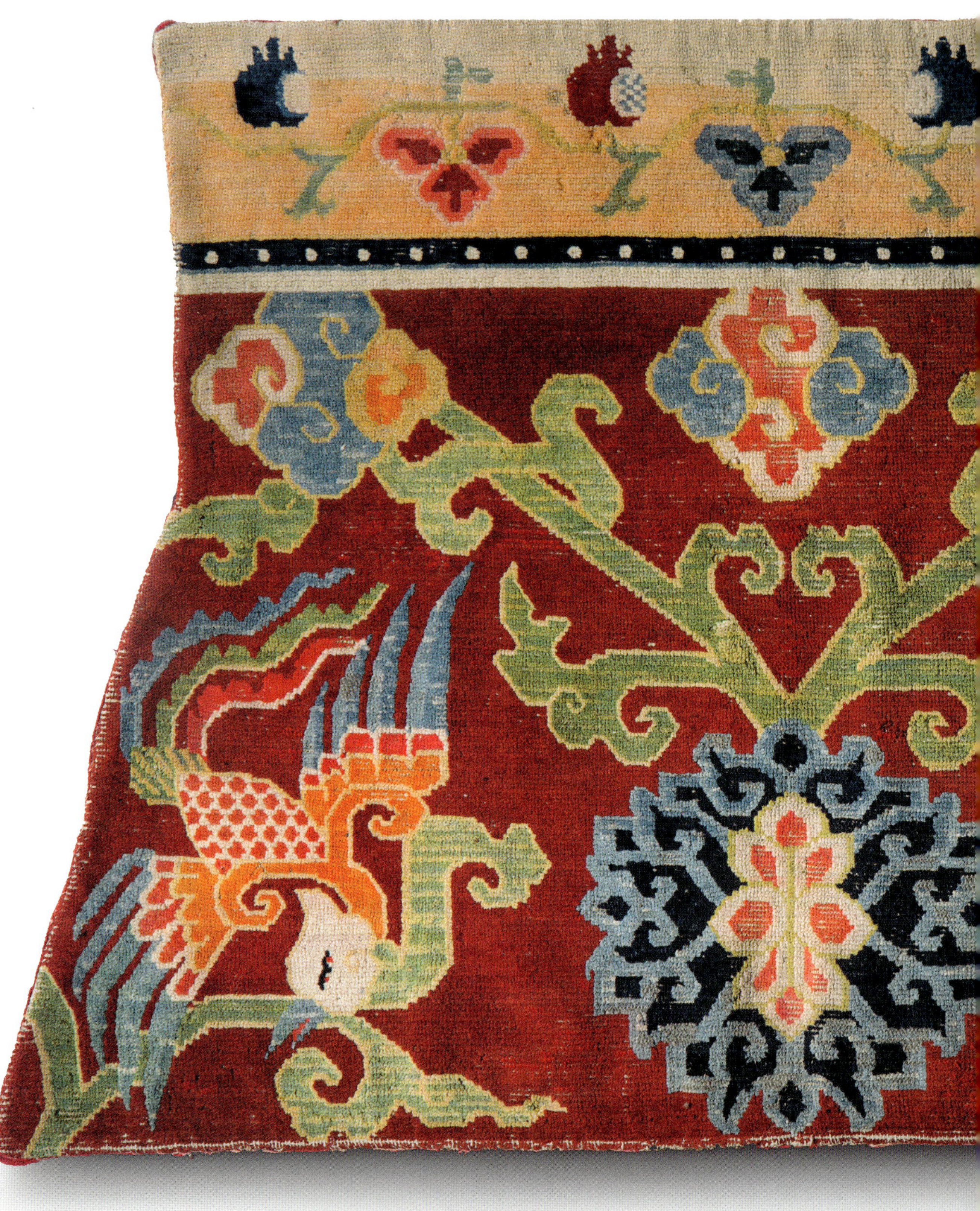

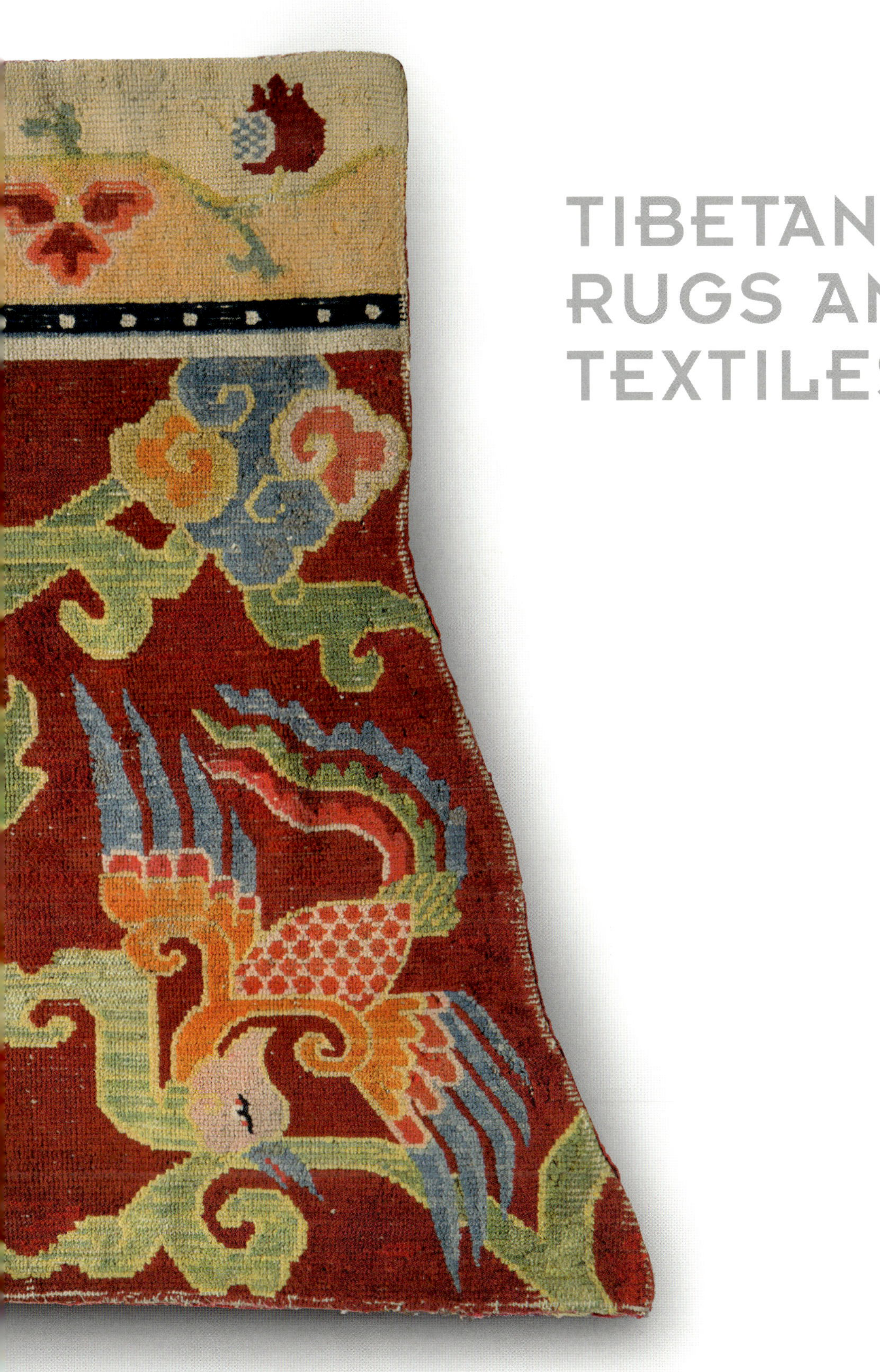

TIBETAN RUGS AND TEXTILES

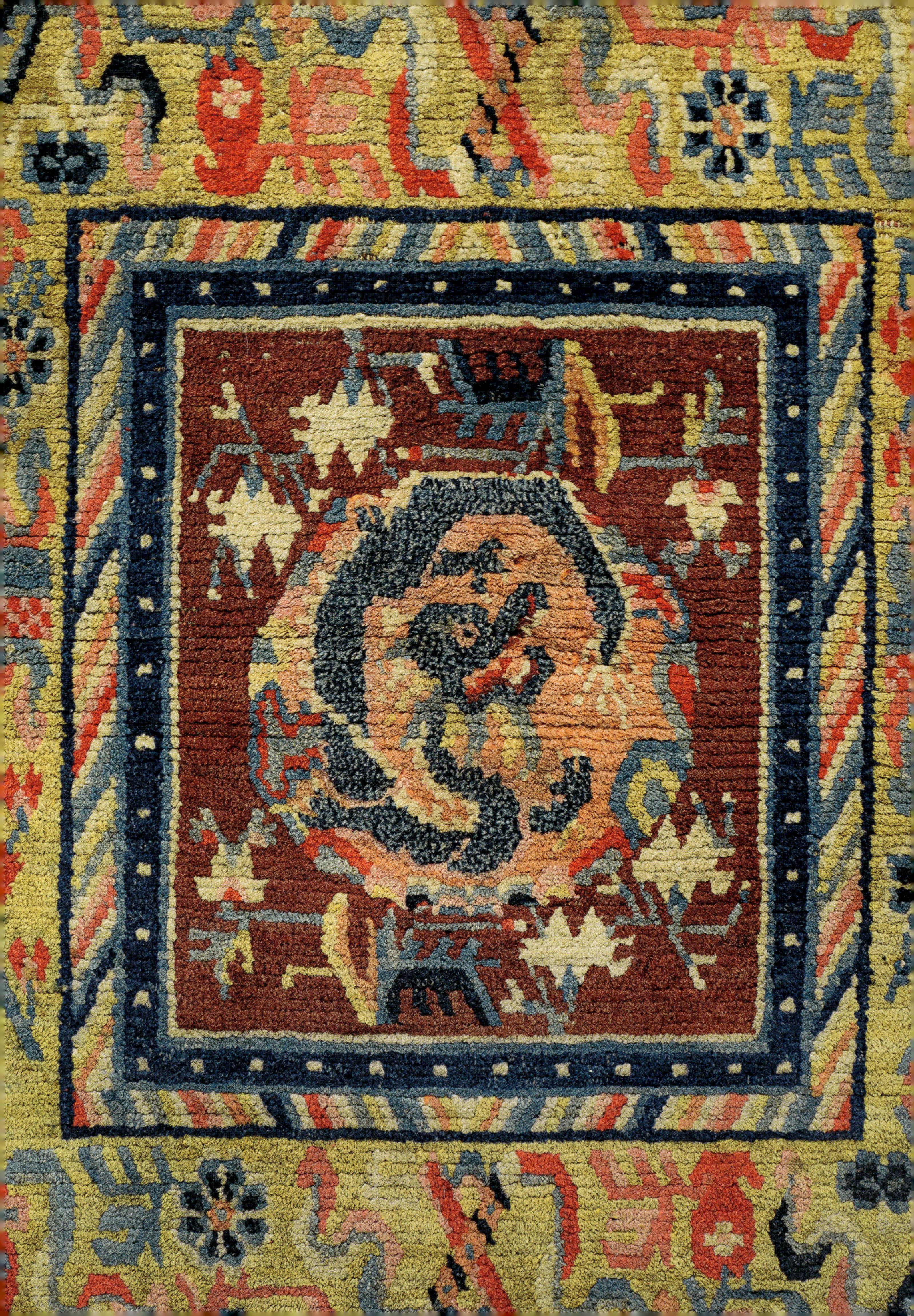

Elena Tsareva

WITH PERFECTION AND MANY TRICKS

Tibetan Rugs in the Context of the Eurasian Carpet-Weaving Tradition

Preceding double page: Horse blanket or "under-under-saddle rug"; see Fig. 11 in the contribution by De Jong

Left image: Detail of Fig. 5, C166

PREFACE

Generations of Russians saw Tibet as a harmonious, natural and mystical place as well as a subject of great interest and an inspiration for deep insight.

This comprehension went hand in hand with the desire of Russian academics, but also educated society and the general public, to understand the high spiritual ideas of Tibetans – both visionary and physical. This interest was initiated primarily by significant Buddhist populations in the Russian Empire, primarily the Buryats, Tuvinians and Kalmyks.[1] This explains to a major extent why the Romanovs welcomed Tibetan emissaries and missionaries in the 19th and early 20th centuries, whose activities culminated in the opening of the first Buddhist temple in Europe, in St. Petersburg in 1913.[2]

There are different ways to understand unknown lands and cultures. In many cases, people who strove to "decipher" messages of ancient civilisations and understand philosophical ideas of the past became geographers, archaeologists, historians, linguists, etc. For a person like me, with an interest in carpets as a historical source, it is only natural that my way to understand the rise of Eurasian civilisations came through the study of rugs. The origins of many characteristics of this art form are still cloaked in mystery, in which even the well-identified branches are still a labyrinth of patterns and methods of weaving, while others remain hidden from sight.

Good examples of Tibetan rugs are generally seldom and certainly poorly represented in Russian collections, which thus create a gap in our study of Eurasian rug weaving. A desire to fill this gap was awoken in 2008 when I became acquainted with the collection of Thomas Wild, Berlin, and was amazed by the richness and variety of this rug-weaving tradition. The desire took on concrete form in 2012 when Michael Buddeberg and I met during the Leipzig Symposium on Turkmen rugs. We discussed the subject and agreed to cooperate on a project which was not only going to be about Tibetan rugs and weaving.

We envisioned it as a series of articles by different knowledgeable authors in other fields of Tibetan arts and handicrafts, collected in a book, with an exhibition to be held in 2016 under the direction of the Ethnological Museum in Munich (today called the Museum Fünf Kontinente).

The project's goal was a multilateral examination of the material, with some elements concentrating on already discussed topics and others on never before – or only slightly – observed aspects of the subject. My part was to be based on the study of the large and unpublished collection of Justyna's and Michael Buddeberg's Tibetan pile weaves. I agreed immediately and I am extremely grateful to Justyna and Michael Buddeberg for their entrusting me with this extremely interesting and important undertaking. The time and enormous amount of work it took revealed that Michael and I had underestimated the project, which turned out to be a real challenge.

My task in the project did not include research on territorial, ethnic or ornamental peculiarities of Tibetan rugs, but covered other aspects of the project: identification and description of notable structures in Tibetan rugs with an attempt to identify these unique and hitherto undescribed elements and relate them to those of other rug-making societies in the context of the Eurasian textile tradition. It also included compiling a catalogue of the Buddeberg collection with precise descriptions of all parameters identified. The technical data of all the examined rugs are to be found in the appendix of the current volume in the index ordered according to collection numbers (C9 to C195). A large part of the research was dealing with a bulk of new and easily overseen details, in particular because some technical characteristics mentioned in earlier literature were not clearly defined. This called for new terminology, explained in a specially compiled glossary. To avoid any terminological misunderstandings, the glossary embraces not only new terminology but also other important terms for describing rugs, some of which are of Tibetan origin (names of objects, for example), while others are common in the carpet-weaving literature in general.

Similar to the study of other visual arts, understanding and describing rugs requires close recognition of their visual artistic (explicit) and their "hidden" technical (implicit) components.

Although my main goal in the project concerned identifying and defining structural details, these also related to the physical shape of an item and also to the design of a pattern, necessitating bringing these aspects into the discussion of the peculiarities of the structural details.

INTRODUCTION

The State of Research

Referring to the acknowledged literature on the subject, it should be emphasised that although Tibetan rugs are much less studied than related Chinese, Central Asian or Near Eastern examples, there are quite a number of books and articles in this field. Some contain short but very important notes: a good example is in the book on Chinese carpets and rugs by Adolf Hackmack (Hackmack 1924), and the famous research of Hans Bidder on carpets of Eastern Turkestan (Bidder 1979). Other editions deal intensely with Tibetan rugs, such as the chapter on Tibetan rugs in Murray L. Eiland's book *Chinese and Exotic Rugs* (Eiland 1979: 74–100), the publication of Robert P. Piccus's impressive collection (Piccus 2011), and the uniquely beautiful book *Dragon & Horse* by Koos de Jong (De Jong 2013). Valuable data can also be learned from a series of articles published from 1990 to 2011 by Tom Cole (Cole 1990a, 1990b, 2003, 2004, 2011). Additionally there are a number of monographic catalogues of Tibetan rug exhibitions and collections, such as *Temple, Household, Horseback. Rugs of the Tibetan Plateau* for an exhibition at the Textile Museum in Washington, D.C., with texts by Diana K. Myers, Arthur A. Leeper and Valrae Reynolds (Myers 1984); *The Woven Mystery. Old Tibetan Rugs* by John and Serina Page (Page 1990); *Woven Jewels. Tibetan Rugs from Southern Californian Collections* with articles by Tom Rutherford, Murray L. Eiland, Deepak Shimkhada and Nicholas H. Wright (Pearce 1992); and finally the small, intriguing catalogue *Wangden Style* of the Sam Coad collection with a preface by Thomas Wild (Wild 2014a). These and other unmentioned works provide fantastic images of Tibetan rugs and are rich in data on their shapes, ornamentation and ideas concerning their use and place in Tibetan society. They also unanimously mention the special character of the Tibetan method of rug weaving, although with no or very little data on precise structural details.

The pioneering and most special place in this list belongs to an encyclopaedic monograph *The Tibetan Carpet* by Philip Denwood (Denwood 1974). This really fundamental work gives precise information on many aspects of the rug-making craft. But also, and of special importance for my goals, it provides invaluable information on the process of the making and structural peculiarities of Tibetan rugs, often supported with photographs and schematic drawings. The ones that show the use of the Tibetan weavers' pile-forming gauge rods (Fig. 2) and a table with an "Analysis of the knotting of the segment of rug" (Fig. 3) should be accepted as an "Ariadne's thread" in the Tibetan labyrinth of looped structures. "Looped structure" is a generally accepted term in rug-weaving literature to differentiate knotted and "looped" textiles.

Being aware of the contradictions, and trying not to be influenced by other authors' opinions, I referred to the technical descriptions in the acknowledged works only after I had finished examining individual rugs and had come to conclusions on the character of the identified structures. It was a great relief to realise that in general our opinions coincided, although none of the quoted works provided a fully adequate description of the structure of Tibetan weavings. (It should be noted here that there are several, with variants, sub-variants, and what are possibly "errors"). Nevertheless, the hard work and incomparable value and interest of the pioneering work by the pathfinders in the field earn my deep respect and admiration. The only reason for my above remark about the not quite adequate definitions of the earlier researchers is to explain why some of my drawings and observations are partly different from those in the quoted publications.

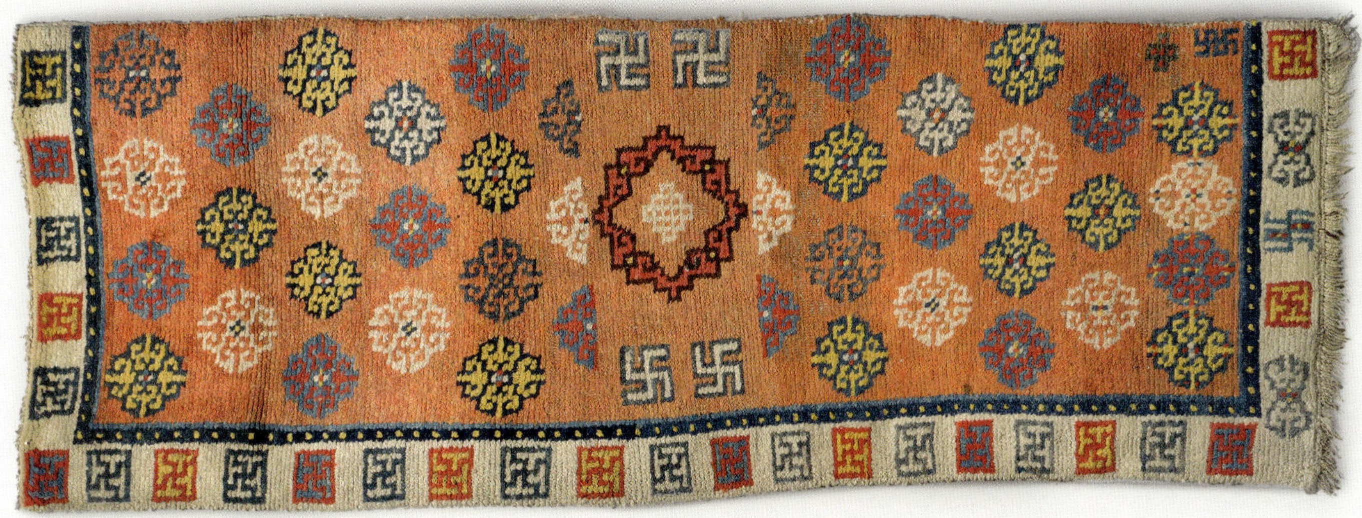

Fig. 1: C60. Fragment of a *sabden* (or antependium?). Mid-19th c. (?), 192 × 72 cm

It is appropriate here to include some notes on the scale of the Tibetan rug industry and trade and its influence on collecting and study of the craft.

Tibetan rugs became an object of active collecting in the second half of the 20th century and have been extensively published since the 1970s. This late coming of the group to the interest of collectors and historians of textile arts is reflected in our insufficient knowledge of the type. Today we are still unable to attribute them their correct time, place and producer within Tibetan society or trace their origin and explain the specific character and diversity of structural and, although to a lesser extent, artistic features. Evidently the main reasons for the situation were caused by a number of circumstances. The first to mention is that for hundreds of years Europeans were excluded from the country. This wilful isolation of the Land of Snow was reinforced by the natural geographical inaccessibility of the plateau and the extremely hard climatic conditions of the country.

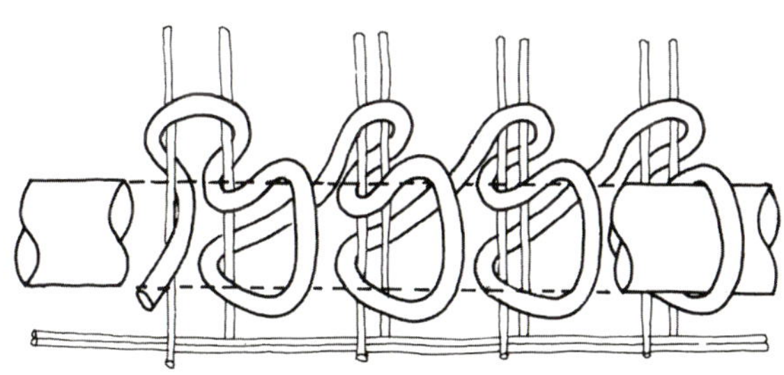

Fig. 2: Drawing by Denwood (Denwood 1974: Fig. 46) shows how the pile thread is led around the gauge rod in relation to warp and weft before it is cut

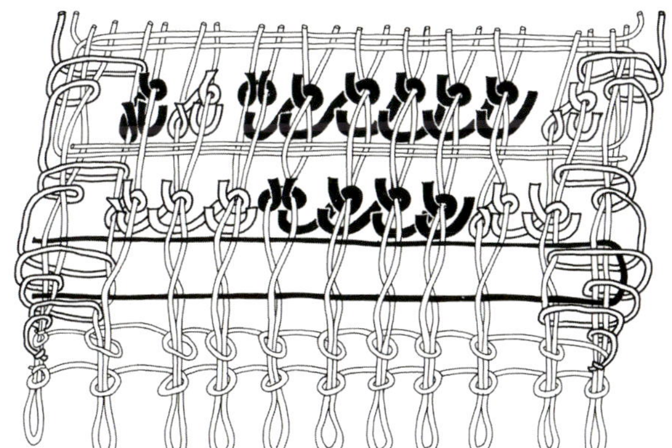

Fig. 3: The structure of a Tibetan pile weaving with warp and weft and knots (loops) in different colours as well as the finish (Denwood 1974: Fig. 53)

In addition, our insufficient knowledge of Tibetan rugs results from the limited production of local rug weavers. The population is very small, thus there were relatively few people making rugs, and many of them worked only for the needs of monasteries and their own families. These products were and are still strongly affiliated to local culture and way of life: thick, long-pile sitting and sleeping rugs, small individual and long monastic meditating rugs, all with mostly simple, archaic patterns. Still others with finer patterns and structures, saddle and under-saddle horse trappings and cushion covers were produced for high-ranking lamas and for export. Even though these are well represented in foreign collections, they still only make up a small percentage of the total output.

As a result, the circle of users of Tibetan rugs was limited to the Tibetans themselves and the Buddhist populations in neighbouring highland countries lying to the south and west of Tibet and those in the coldest zones of the Mongolian

Fig. 4: C142. Tantric rug in *khaden* format. Tibet, China or Central Asia (?), 19th/20th c. (?), 126×77 cm

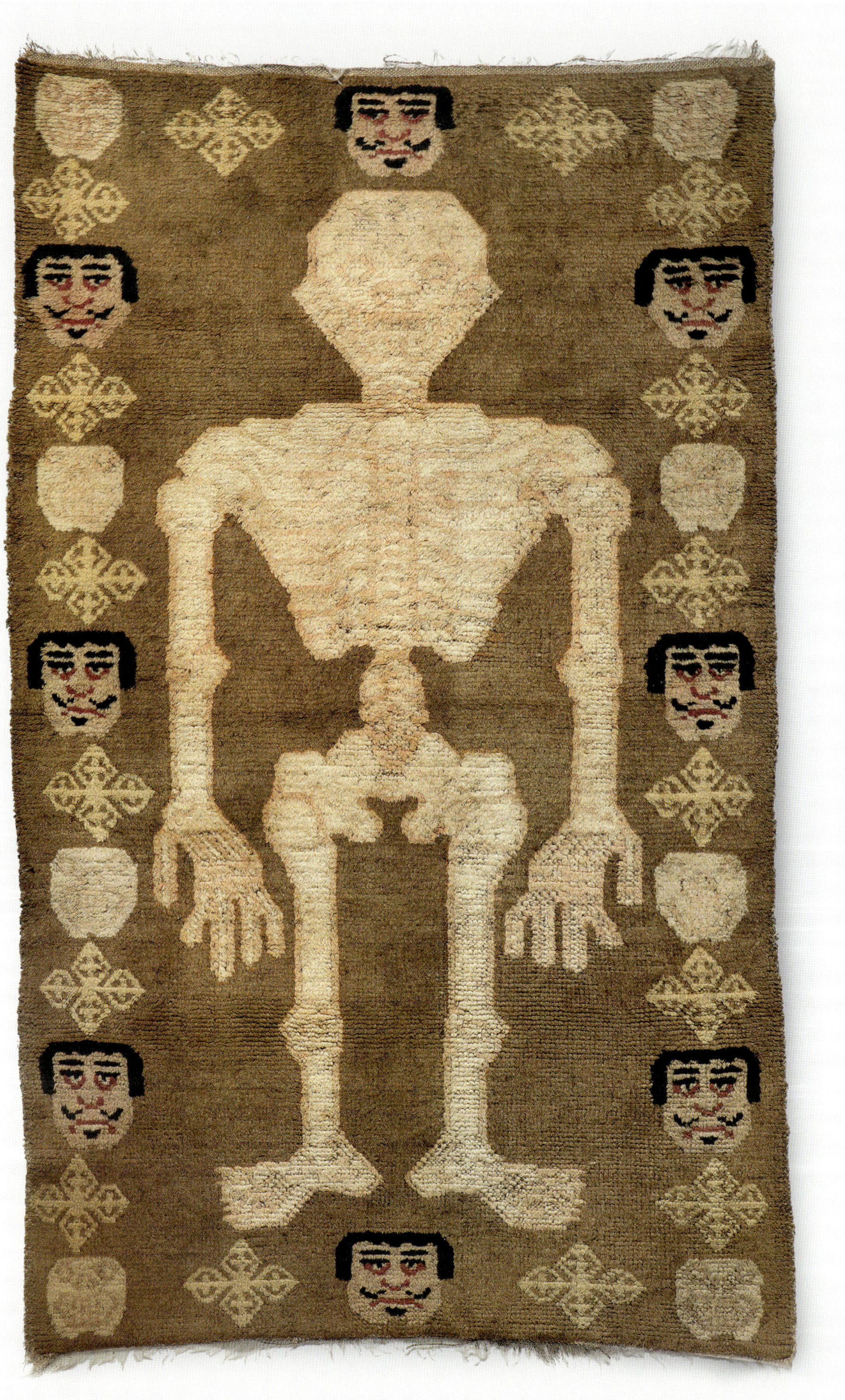

and Xinjiang steppes and deserts. Notable to mention is also the fact that the low productivity of the local rug-weaving craft was caused by the comparatively small volume of wool produced in the country, as the thickness of yarn and the length of pile of even small Tibetan-type sitting rugs needed several kilograms of wool (for more detailed information see the section "Materials" in the chapter "Materials, Composition of Yarns and Their Use").

Tibetan pile weavings were not only almost unknown in the West, they also did not find a place in the world-famous private and museum carpet and textile collections, which were initially compiled to preserve what were once purely decorative textile furnishings used to adorn wealthy houses and royal palaces of both the East and the West. Luxurious Oriental and European pile weavings were mostly of large size, fine in weave and had rich, mainly floral ornamentation. In contrast, the small, very thick texture of Tibetan weavings, also their use-specific shapes and modest design, were inappropriate for furnishing European and Oriental official and private interiors, and thus were of no interest to carpet dealers.

Even if people with ethnographic and historic interests found Tibetan rugs attractive, the decision to bring home traditional Tibetan rugs meant introducing into one's house a lot of sand and greasy wool, along with its quite alien and sometimes even scary ornamentation, in particular in the case of ritual rugs with tantric images (Fig. 4, C142).[3]

Notwithstanding this general picture, there were all kinds of inevitable exceptions, beginning with the earliest known 19th-century acquisitions (Myers 1984: 21). A good story to read about the process of the growth of interest in Tibetan rugs is published by Sam Coad in his *Wangden Style* catalogue of a small exhibition of long-pile rugs. It points to a period of the initial rise of enthusiasts' attention to Tibetan pile rugs, which also coincides with the Tibetans' exodus from their homeland in 1959 and the 1980s. Saving themselves from imprisonment or worse, the escapees, monks in particular, brought their Buddhist treasures and ritual objects to Nepal, Bhutan and India and beyond, with rugs making up quite a part of the saved items. These rugs, heretofore never seen by most foreign collectors, attracted the attention of rug connoisseurs and gave birth to a new trend in the study of pile weavings.

For collectors and scholars, the initial stage of exploration of any new branch of arts and crafts is devoted to a search for all kinds of information on the types of objects, their ornamentation and corresponding terminology, as well as gradually on the history of the trade. The next, so to say, "traditional" step is publication of the obtained material and images of items. Quite logically, some aspects of the skills, their historical roots in particular, remain veiled in mystery for a long time. Information which for decades was unclear, sometimes mistakenly given by the dealers to satisfy buyers' curiosity, is now well known and described in detail. This is typical of the study of tribal rugs elsewhere, and the research of Tibetan rugs is no exception, as there was no data to prove time, place, origin and rise and development of their manufacture.

The process of developing methods to study rugs as a phenomenon was neither easy nor short. Decades of thorough work by hundreds of scholars and connoisseurs in the field of pile-weaving research resulted in the development of a descriptive model which helps to describe any kind of rug in all the details of its implicit and explicit components. When complete, the obtained data allows classification of the items under research, their arrangement according to types and groups whose technical features often correlate with definite patterns. The final stage is the introduction of the group into the cultural-historical contexts, which is possible if we can draw upon enough comparative ethnographic and archaeological material.

This system gave excellent results, as many of the earlier unidentified or "suspended" types and groups within them, Central Asian Turkmen, for example, are now well attributed and traced to the roots of earlier traditions (Tsareva 2011, 2016). Now the system has been used on Tibetan rugs. Hopefully with the publication of this monograph we have resolved the problem of identification of the Tibetan pile-making systems, made a large step forward in singling out the main types, variants and sub-variants of their pile structures, and have come to a better understanding of the origin of the craft and its significance for those who practise it.

General Reflections on the Study of Tibetan Piled Rugs

Love and understanding of rugs is a kind of talent, and, similar to other gifts of God, it can be more pronounced in some people. While some admire the history of the craft, others are passionate about the well-known flat-woven and pile weavings of Iran, Asia Minor, or Turkmenistan or later arrivals to the field such as the knotted rugs of China and Morocco. Tibetan rugs gave rise to a new line of quickly

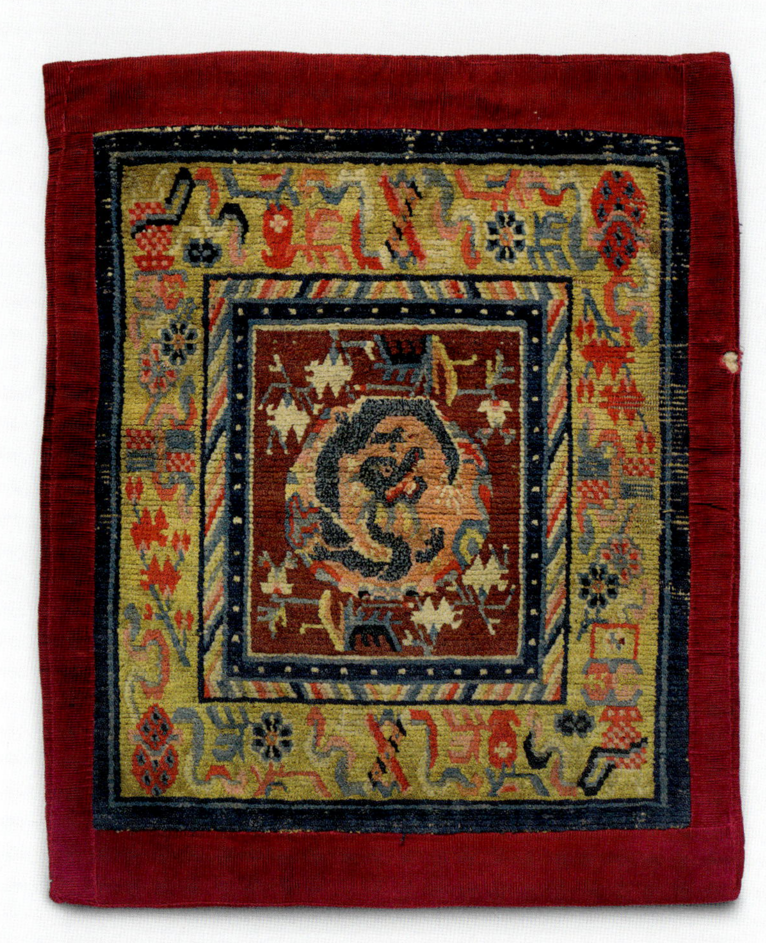

growing interest. The reasons that attract collectors and scholars are the novelty of the type, their rarity, peculiar structures and patterns, but also the feeling of archaism, magic and mystery radiated by those strange objects (Fig. 5, C166).

Archaism, magic and mystery are responsible for the aura of Tibetan rugs and will possibly remain a mystery forever, while their "body" – in other words their structures – can be recognised when studied with passion and patience. To do this, ideally one should visit the country and observe *in situ* the Tibetan craftsmen and craftswomen at their work. Not being able to make such a trip, in my attempts to understand the phenomenological part of the process of making rugs in the Land of Snow, I used narrations of luckier authors, especially the extremely informative work of Philip Denwood (Denwood 1974). In Chapter Four, "Making a Carpet", the great expert in the field describes the typical Tibetan vertical loom and explains in numerous details the manner employed by the local weavers' pile-making tradition. Their main technical peculiarity consists of the looping technique which is carried out with the help of a gauge rod. His extremely helpful drawing (Fig. 2) and the one in the article by Murray L. Eiland (Eiland 1979: 83, Fig. 6) were guides in my attempts to connect what I saw with the variety of structural forms identified by my closer analysis of individual Tibetan pile weavings.

Fig. 5: C166. Over-saddle rug (*masho*) with dragon motif. 19th c., 64×55 cm

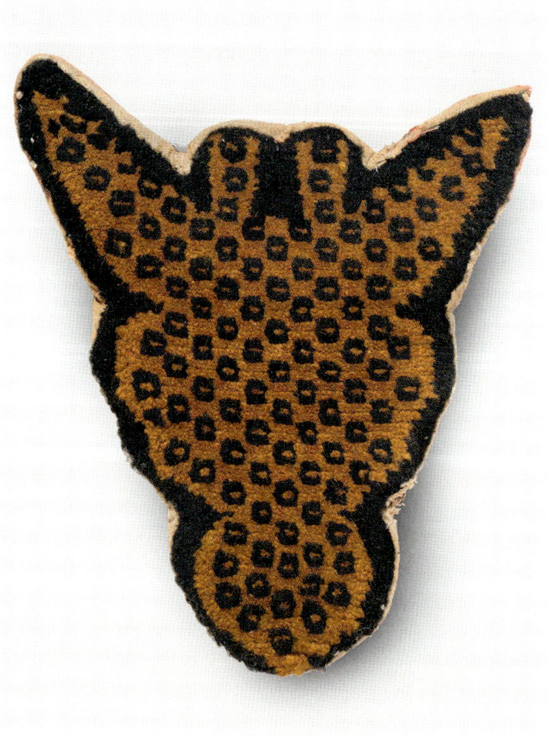

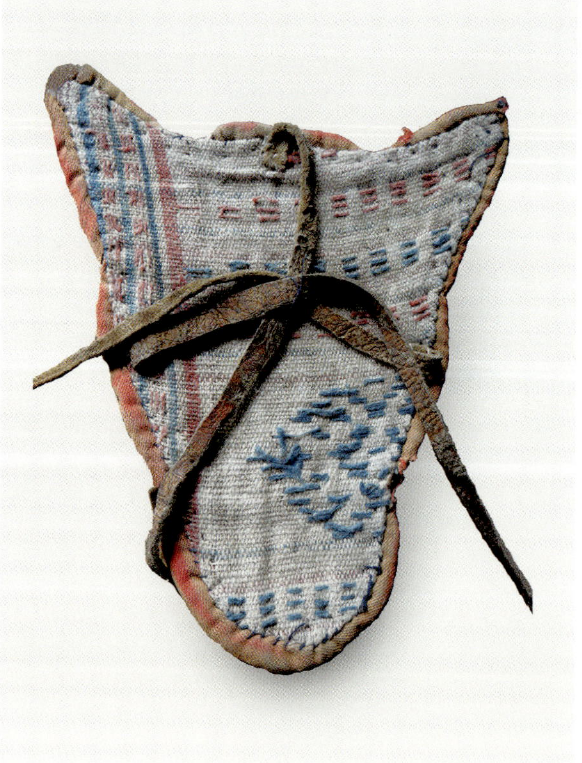

Fig. 6: C184. Horse ornament: front and back sides, latter lined with cloth from Bhutan. 19th c., 25×22 cm

It took me some time before I realised how the pile yarns move when wrapped around the gauge rod and how they manage to produce – when cut – a progression of small and large, long-leg and regular loops of different configurations and combinations. It was only later that I managed to represent numerous variants of these in graphic drawings. These result exclusively from own my observations and conclusions and, I hope, are detailed enough to give a picture of the structural schemes regularly used by Tibetan weavers, plus a number of peculiar variations.

I still consider them nevertheless incomplete. Firstly, despite the fact that the structure of every object under examination is painstakingly fixed and described in the catalogue, some elements of the process remain unclear, despite Philip Denwood's precise descriptions. Secondly, a complete analysis of every item in the collection was hampered by the fact that many of them have solid lining on the back and trimming on the sides (Fig. 6, C184). Consequently, this leaves questions with no answers. This suggests the possibility of other, still to be identified structural details. In the catalogue, question marks in brackets indicate where this could be the case. And the third point concerns the items under research, because material from only one – albeit excellent collection of Justyna and Michael Buddeberg – is not enough to give a complete panorama of this extremely complicated and illusionistic weaving tradition.

It is important to understand that the pile-weaving tradition in Tibet combines two clearly identified lines, known in the literature as "domestic" or "nomadic" and "monastic". This distinction is correct, but we must also recognise that the picture is much more varied. The items produced in rural areas originate from different territories and could be made for family use or for sale, and thus can vary significantly in shape, materials and structural and artistic peculiarities. The workshops which belonged to or depended on the monasteries produced different pile weavings specifically for use in that monastery.

As far as I know, such enterprises, usually located in temples' vicinities, produced rugs made to order for lamas' and monks' monastic needs and for sale, and functioned under strict control of specially appointed supervisors. From what we read about Tibetan society, monks could originate from every strata of the population. Thus, when either a nomad or someone from a town came to a monastery he would bring with him not only his personal *khaden, khagangma* and other necessary rugs, but also an understanding of the peculiarities of his region's art of weaving.[4] Observations suggest that rugs ordered from the monastic workshops could belong to different traditions or at least have traces of them. Examples demonstrate this, such as the so-called *single-level* rugs (either *plain*, or in the *warp-faced* technique, for comparison see the section "Single-Level Looping Techniques" in the chapter "Basic Structures and Structural Peculiarities of Tibetan Rugs"), but also the most refined *double-level* (otherwise *two-level*) weavings with their weave and pattern, many with evident Chinese iconographic borrowings. To identify the varieties in the catalogue, I make very general references: "monastic", "rural", "nomadic", "made to order".

Another significant matter concerns the terminology used. It is well known that the structure of Tibetan rugs is made not with knots, but with cut loops. Earlier publications in the field follow the generally accepted tradition and use the terms *knot* and *knotting* when they describe this. To clarify this confusion, I made an uneasy decision to rehabilitate "historical equitableness" and define the technique with the terms *loops* and *looping*.

There is another, but generally very important peculiarity of Tibetan pile weavings that is usually not mentioned. Unlike Persian rugs with their all-over *asymmetric knot structure,* or Turkish rugs with their *symmetric knots*, Tibetan rugs do not use one basic pile-making element, but use a system of specifically arranged *asymmetric* and *symmetric open* and *closed loops*.[5]

To make this intricate subject clearer and facilitate perception of long and complicated narratives, I have supplemented the descriptions with coloured drawings and quite a number of macro and general photos. References to rugs in the collection are intended to illustrate my explanations.

BASIC STRUCTURES AND STRUCTURAL PECULIARITIES OF TIBETAN RUGS

The Structural Variety of the Tibetan Pile-Making System

Reviewing of technical parameters of whichever particular group of rugs traditionally begins with data on the characteristic materials and structural indices distinctive for the particular type. Yet the peculiar features specific for Tibetan rugs necessitate observation of their "anatomy", of the pile-making segment, whose precise portrayal considers a number of innovative factors and elaborations of their different genesis.

Fig. 7: C79. Sitting and sleeping rug (*khaden*) with an archaic design. 19th c. (?), 121×71 cm

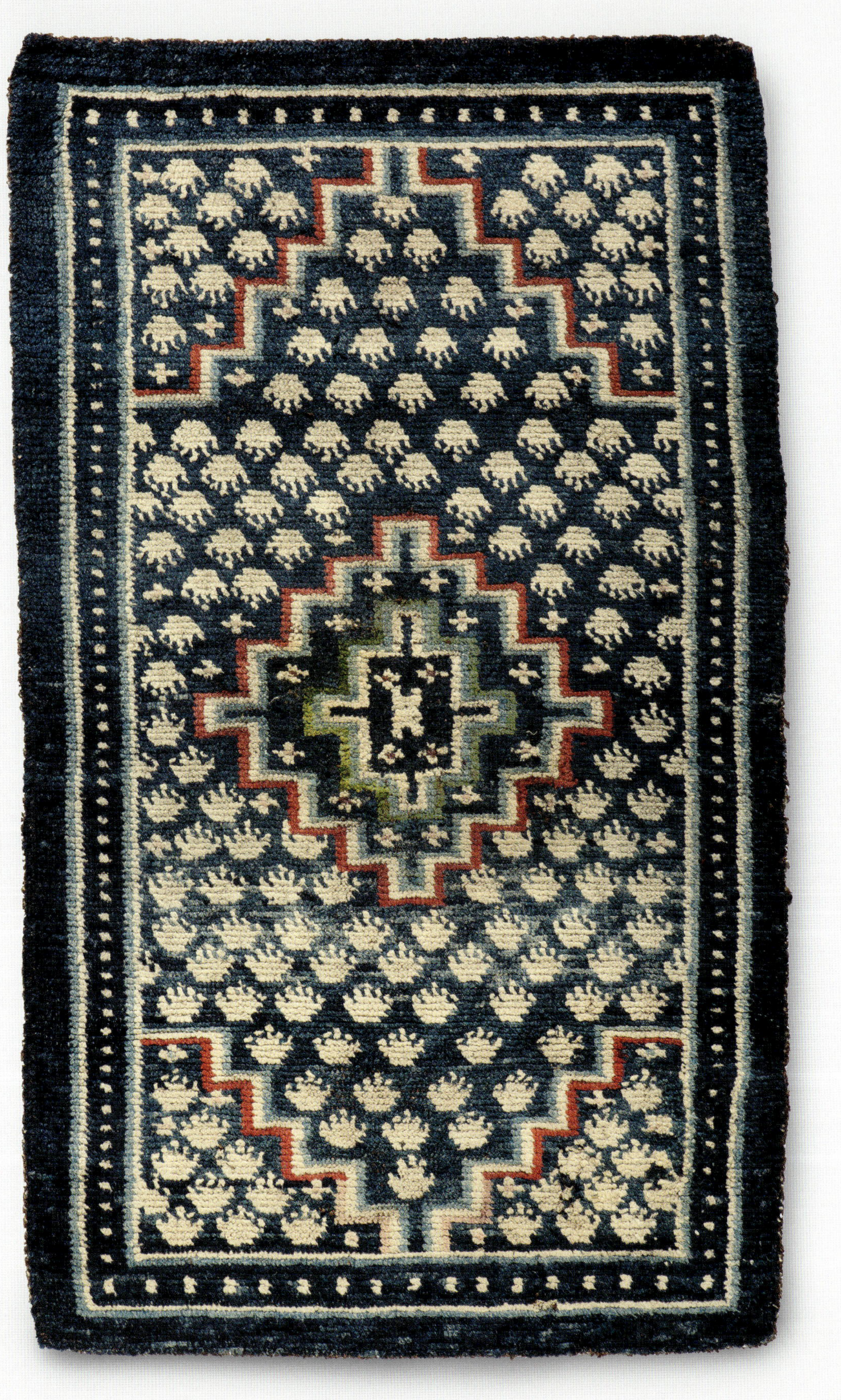

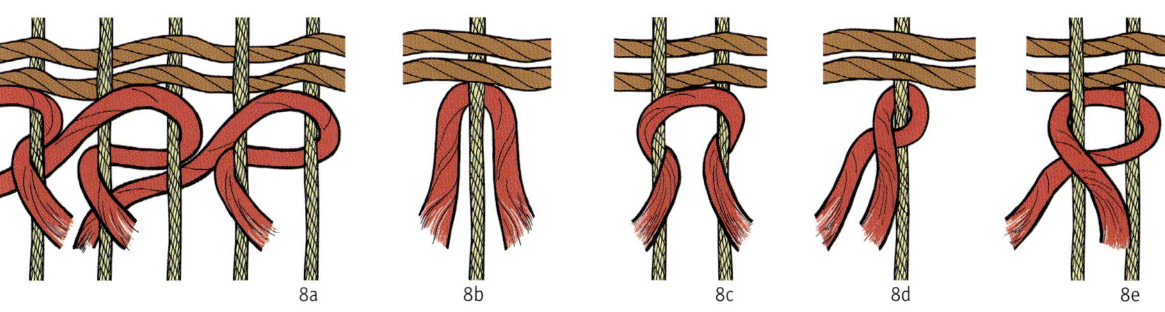

Figs. 8a to 8e: Main types of basic pile-making elements for Tibetan rugs: a) asymmetric open left long-leg loops, b) symmetric loop on one warp (open loop), c) symmetric loop on two warps (closed loop), d) regular asymmetric loop on one warp, e) regular asymmetric loop on two warps

As mentioned in the catalogue, 113 of the 120 examined items are genuine Tibetan works.[6] Only the examination results of this group are the basis for further conclusions expressed on the character of the Tibetan pile weavings (Fig. 7, C79).

One of the main outcomes of this study confirms the abovementioned and generally known data that Tibetan pile rugs demonstrate two different structural groups, namely double/two-level and single-level warp structures. The double-level group in the collection consists of 95 items, which make up 86 percent of the examined rugs. The other 18 items belong to the single-level group.

Starting with the first group, we will observe the technical peculiarities of rugs with double-level warps. The initial thing to discuss is the variety of *basic pile-making elements* applied by Tibetan weavers, their typical combinations and systematic irregularities.

Two-Level Weavings

First, basic for this pile-making element is the *asymmetric open left long-leg loop*, on four (sometimes on three) warps (in the following termed *basic asymmetric long-leg loops* or simply *long-leg loops*) (Fig. 8a). The term *long-leg* is not accidental but specific to loops of this kind, whose left-side end, as you see on this and other drawings, is much longer than the right one. The reason for this is due to the Tibetan weavers' scheme of looping, when long leg comes as a continuation of the previous left loop (Fig. 8c), both formed after the weaver cuts all loops wrapped over the gauge rod with a knife.[7]

Second, inherent and basic for this type of pile-making component are *regular loops* of two sorts: *symmetric*, and the other – less frequent – *asymmetric open left*. The symmetric kind makes loops either on one warp (in the following *open loops*) (Fig. 8b), or on two warps (in the following *symmetric loop on two warps*) (Fig. 8c). The *regular asymmetric* kind can also "sit" on one or two warps, but because of their rarity both are fully described in the catalogue: the *regular asymmetric loop on one warp* and the *regular asymmetric loop on two warps* (Figs. 8d and 8e). By "regular" I mean that loops of this type have equal length ends and are similar to symmetric and asymmetric knots, which are otherwise familiar to us as Turkish and Persian knots.

These structure-forming long-leg and regular pile-making elements, which are basic for the group, can be arranged in a number of assemblages; the three most frequent variants are named in the catalogue as *single, doubled* and *long rows* ("lines" in Denwood's terminology). As the terms suggest, they define the number of loops: either one (Fig. 9a), two (Fig. 9b), or from three to dozens, whereby the number depends on the length of the depicted details of a pattern (Fig. 9c; see also Fig. 9d and Fig. 10, C145).

These divisions explain a peculiarity crucial for Tibetan rug weaving. Each of the sequences we find (single – double – long row) corresponds to an assemblage of elements in the same colour, regardless of the number of loops in a row. Each time the pattern calls for a change of colour, the process is accompanied with an alteration of the final loop of the current row and the initial element of the next row's basic loop in a different colour. In other words, each group of monochrome loops has a distinctive structure with systematic initial, middle and terminal elements. To nominate those specific to the Tibetan tradition of one-colour sequences, I introduce the term *unit of loops* or *colour unit*.

Here it is also time to add that, besides the long-leg and regular elements, each *unit of loops* contains yet a third pile-making element. What I mean are small and seemingly additional loops to the basic structure, which in reality are "equal in rights" to the basic components. They are mandatory at the end, but we also often find them at the beginning of each colour unit, as represented on each of the three illustrations in Figs. 9a to 9c. Although first mentioned here, their place in structure and corresponding terminology will be discussed below, in the sections on packing and variants of loop sequences in one or several units.

Figs. 9a to 9d: Variants of typical double-level looping units for Tibetan rugs: a) single, b) double, c) long row, d) detail of C145 with geometric pattern and clearly visible *double* and *long row looping units*

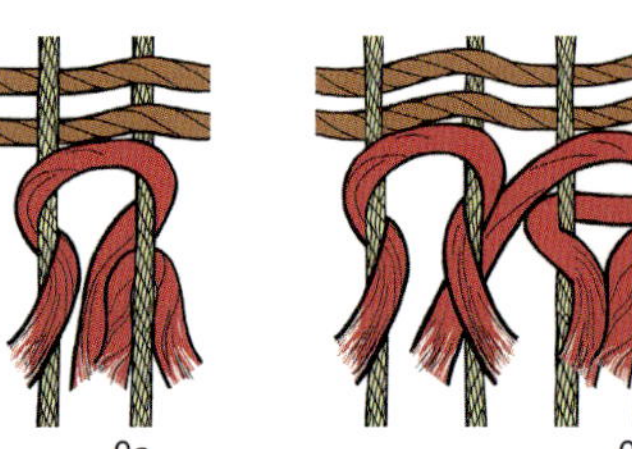

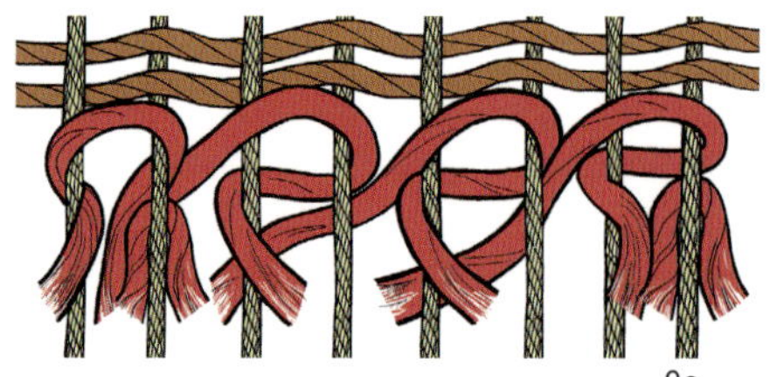

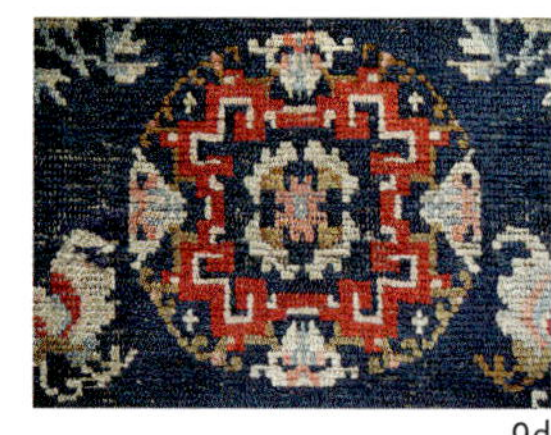

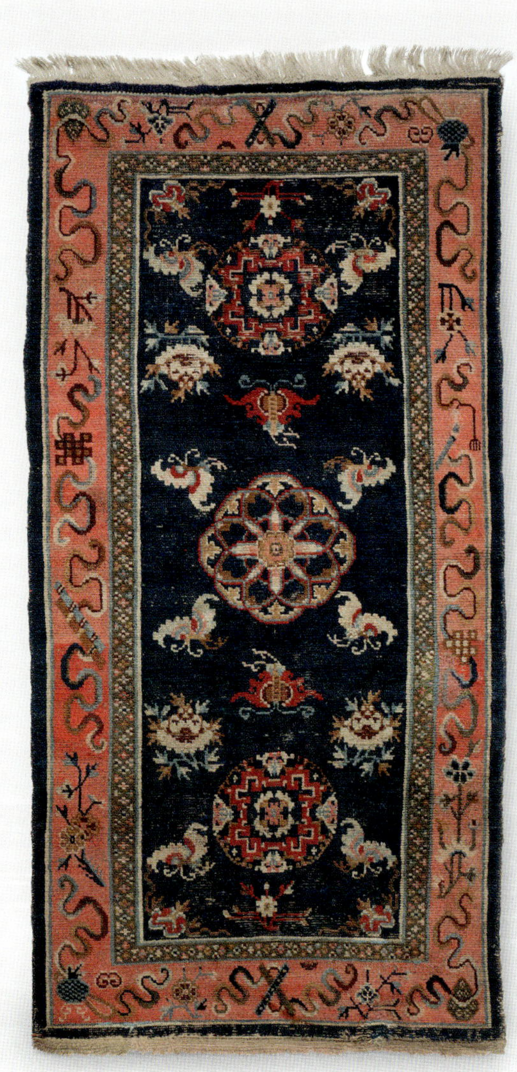

Fig. 10: C145. Sitting and sleeping rug (*khaden*). Late 19th c., 165×80 cm

The most precise step-by-step description of the general process of looping can be found in *The Tibetan Carpet* by Philip Denwood (Denwood 1974: 44–46). In the notes I quote page 44 of this Denwood text[8] and I recommend trying to read it together with the drawings (Figs. 2 and 3). Even though these are just as difficult to comprehend as the weavers' operations, the narration helps to understand the process, while the drawings make it easier to follow Denwood's written description.

Main Regular and Irregular Structural Peculiarities

With continued acquaintance with the variations of Tibetan pile rugs' looping system, we see that besides the basic long-leg and regular asymmetric and symmetric loops the structure demonstrates a number of other, quite peculiar forms, which we now know under the names of *sharing, offsetting, packing, eccentric weave*, etc. Some were identified by Lesley Pinner with regard to Chinese rugs (Pinner 1983), others were described in detail in 1999 for Turkmen knottings (Tsareva 2008) and have since been designated in the literature as *structural irregularities* (otherwise *irregular devices, methods* and *tricks of weaving*), regardless of whether one is speaking about knotting or looping textures. While these methods can be quite clearly denoted as irregularities with regards to the form and function of Turkmen or Chinese rug structures, most of the tricks in Tibetan pile weavings, in particular sharing and offsetting, cannot be classified as purely irregular devices, since their role is determined as integral for the Tibetan manner of looping.

The special technique of **packing** can be described as using more than one elementary loop between two *units of wefts*. This method can be applied both for single and for multiple loops in a row; not only for loops in a single colour but equally for elements that differ in colour (Figs. 11a and 11b). Initially identified and described by Lesley Pinner with regard to Chinese rugs (Pinner 1983), the device was later identified in Turkmen and several other archaeological and ethnographical Eurasian traditions (Tsareva 2005: 190–191; 2008; 2011). Acknowledged as very specific, with

Figs. 11a to 11d: Packing device variants: a) single-pack variant in same colour as basic loop, b) single-pack variant in colour different to basic loop, c) detail of the reverse of C32 with rows of packing loops in identical and different colours, d) macro detail of the reverse of C15 with different colours in single-pack element (small round central element)

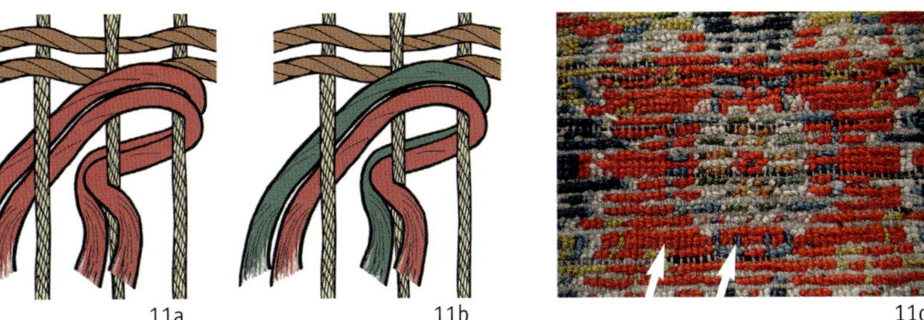

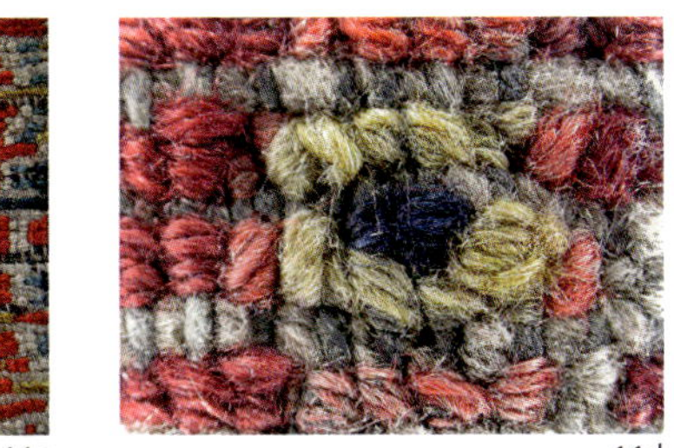

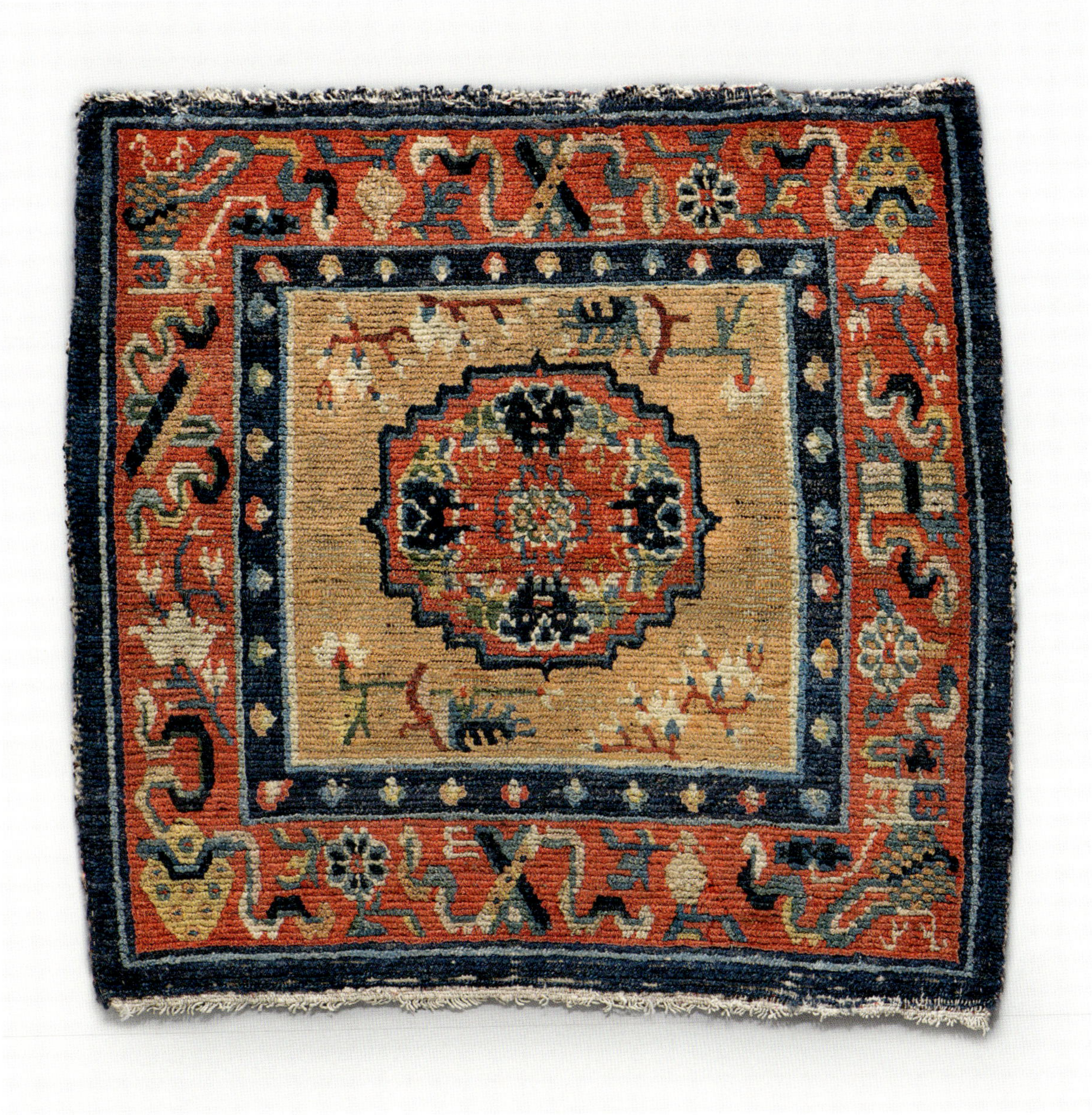

Fig. 12: C32. Sitting rug (*khagangma*). Late 19th c., 65×66 cm

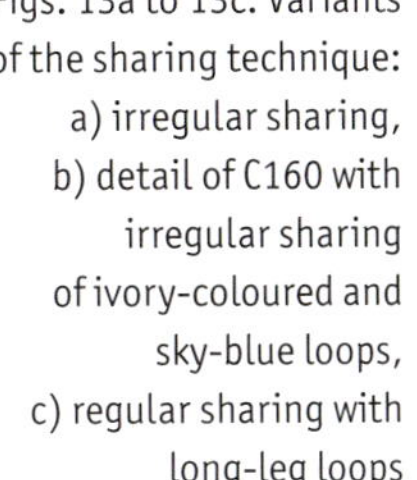

Figs. 13a to 13c: Variants of the sharing technique: a) irregular sharing, b) detail of C160 with irregular sharing of ivory-coloured and sky-blue loops, c) regular sharing with long-leg loops

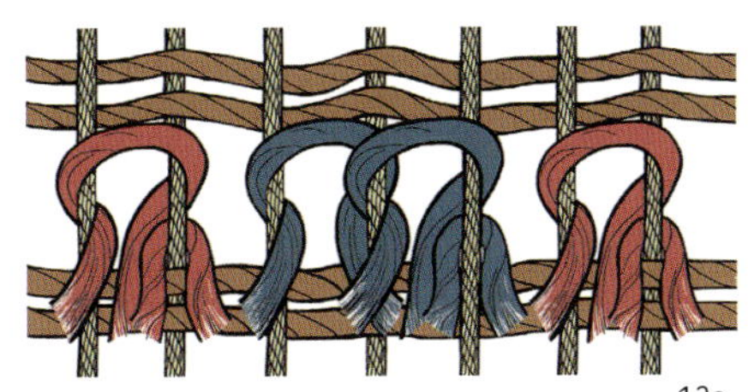

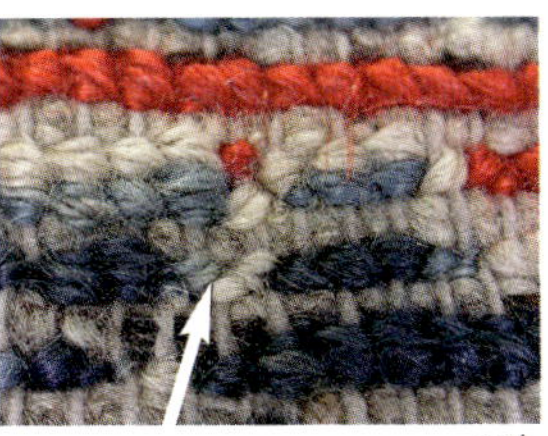

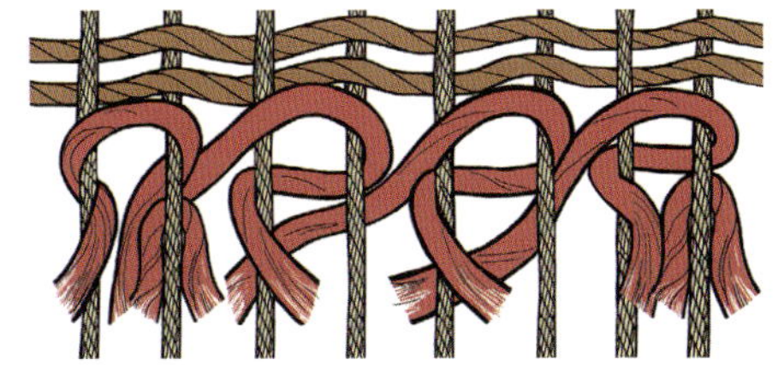

unique peculiarities, in Tibetan rugs this method demonstrates two forms different in shape, and used for different reasons. One is identical to the Turkmen and Chinese arrangement and application, and can be attributed as an irregular packing trick. The purpose of its insertion seems to be totally artistic in order to form tiny details of the pattern (Fig. 11d; see also Fig. 2 in the contribution by Michael Buddeberg), also curvilinear lines, as well as a denser filling of motifs in the central pattern (Figs. 11c and 12).

A second variant of packing is an inherent part of the Tibetans' process of looping. It is unavoidably involved in the sequences of long-leg elements basic for the structure, whose long left-side ends make packs with the previous (left-side) basic loops of the structure (Figs. 9b and 9c). Being an integral element of all double-level and *drumze* Tibetan weavings, this packing device can automatically be classified as a *regular trick*, or rather *technique*. The same can be said for the small one-warp or two-warp loops, which we find at the beginning and at the end of each colour unit. Depending on their place in a unit, in the catalogue they are named either "bottom-packing loop" or "top-packing loop".

Equally inherent in Tibetan rugs is the device of **sharing** loops. At present a term broadly known for pile weavings, it was adopted from the tapestry glossary in order to designate the arrangement of two adjacent knots, or loops, or only the common parts in both elements' warp. Similar to packing in Tibetan rugs, sharing also has two forms. In one case the neighbouring loops interlink with each other and around a shared warp (Figs. 13a and 13b). This kind is also typical for some Eurasian knottings, including Chinese (Pinner 1983; Tsareva 2005), Turkmen (Tsareva 2008), and a number of archaeological rugs (Tsareva 2015). In all types mentioned, this form is ascribed to the group of irregularities.

A second variation is only known in Tibetan rug weaving. It comes from the long-leg loops, to be exact from the arrangement of these long ends. Making a pack with the neighbouring elements to the left, these ends automatically share the left-side warp for both elements, and as such belong to the class of regular devices (Fig. 13c). When conjunctions of this type make up an integral part of all doubled and long-row units, the device is presumed to be present and is not mentioned in the catalogue structural descriptions.

Another actively used trick specific to Tibetan weavings is **offset** and visually (although not technically) close to its **offset effect**. Proper offset comes as a result of a one-warp shift of basic loops in a rug's texture. To gain this shift Tibetan weavers used sharing (Figs. 15a to 15d and Figs. 16a to 16c), which is inserting basic loops on 1 or on 3 warps, the *missed warp technique* (Fig. 15a), and probably a number of other, unidentified variants. The main artistic goal of application of the method was the formation of beautiful and smooth diagonal and curvilinear lines, which we see in many Tibetan rugs, in monastic work in particular. In addition, this technique prevents formation of slits in a rug's texture, thus strengthening the fabric and making it more durable. For this reason the *offset technique* can also be included in the group of technical elements.

The formation of the *offset effect* is mainly conditioned by the shape of small open loops, which are packed with the last element for a monochrome unit's right-side basic loop (or also with the initial, left-side). Viz.: as soon as the right end of this small loop comes between two different colour units of pile (in our case green and rose), its fibres mix with yarns of an initial element of the unit to the right to produce an offset effect. In the case of a geometric pattern, when colour lines change vertically, the effect is not so obvious, but it is clearly seen in the curving lines (Figs. 16a and 16b) of animal and floral images, with diagonal change of rows of differently coloured loops (Fig. 16c).

These technical details and those still to be discussed reveal that the methods of weaving used by Tibetans demonstrate a long and elaborate pile-making tradition. When studied from different angles, structural elements of this lore suggest information which helps to trace the roots of the Tibetan pile-making method and introduce it into the context of the Eurasian carpet weaving practice. This conclusion is evidenced by comparison with archaeological materials and archaic methods, many of which were used by local rug weavers in the Bronze Age, yet later were either forgotten or substituted by easier tricks. They have only survived and been preserved in remote areas or from a special devotion to ancient, ritual techniques of the craft, as in Tibet in particular.

One such technically difficult and artistically refined structural method is **eccentric wefts weave**. This intricate trick is made by inserting additional wefts which curve to allow additional loops and so make small lozenges or circular details of a pattern (dragon's eye, flower petal, etc.) (Figs. 17a to 17c). Used for millennia in tapestry weavings, with regard to pile structures the term was first used in my Liestal symposium lecture in 1999 and then in an article on

Fig. 14: C141. Sitting rug (*khagangma*). Around 1900, 63×73 cm

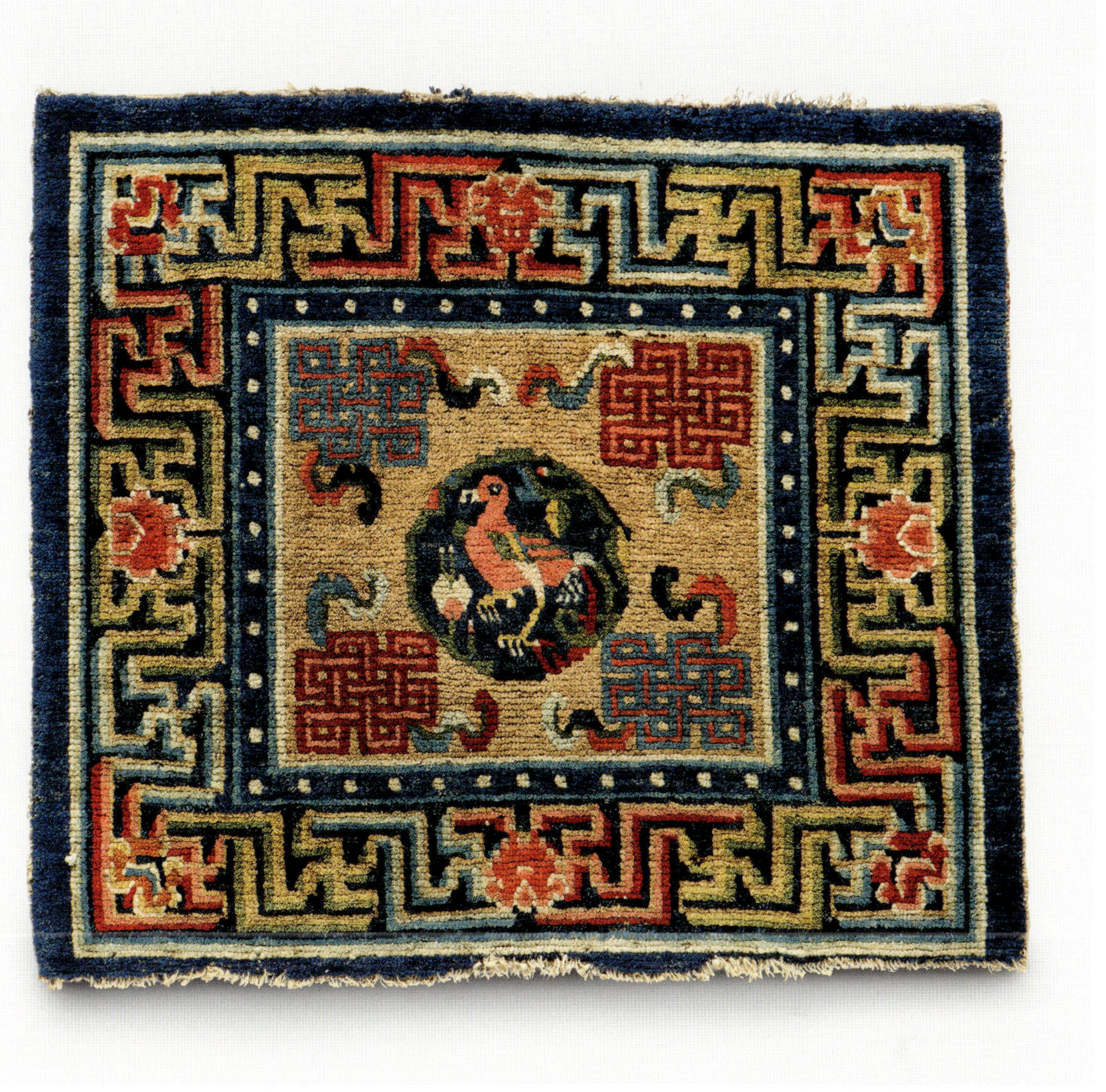

Figs. 15a to 15d: Offset device: a) offset trick, by missed warp method, b) offset trick, by loop on one warp method, c) and d) details of C20 (both sides, see Fig. 4 in the contribution by De Jong)

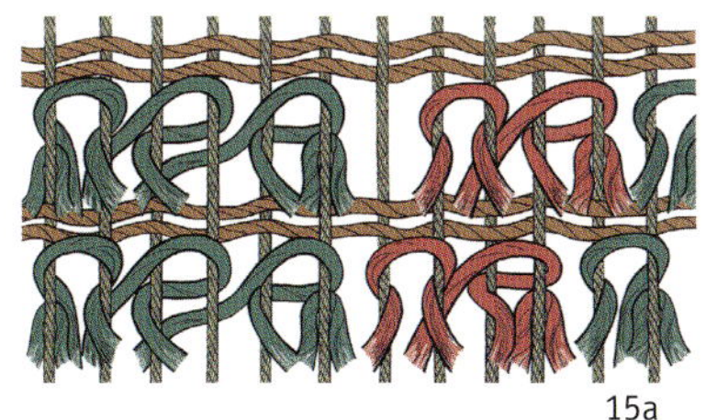

15a

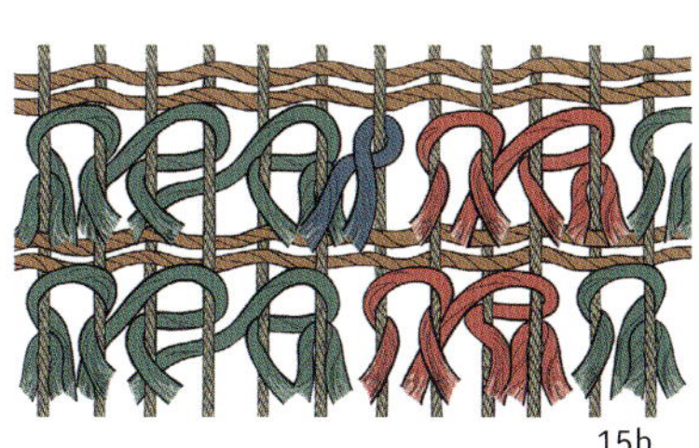

15b

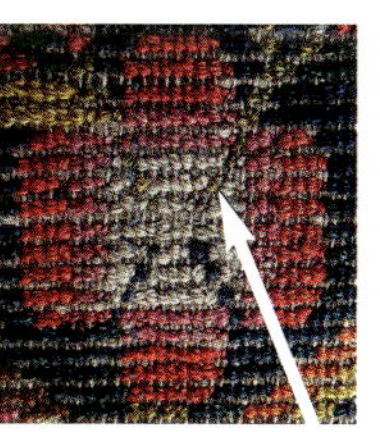

15c

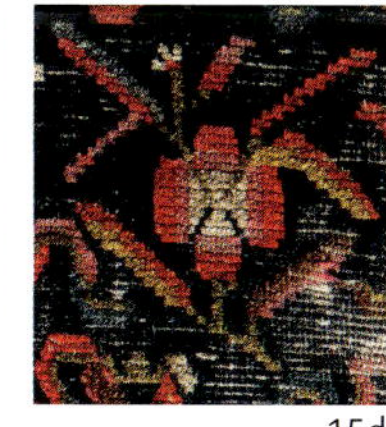

15d

Figs. 16a to 16c: Macro and detail photographs clearly showing the offset effect

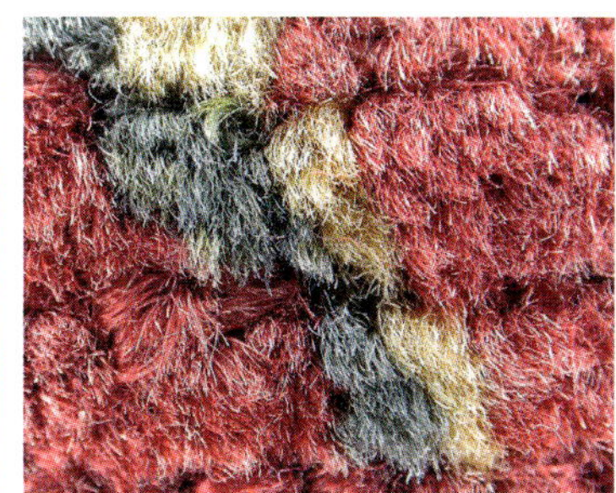

16a

16b

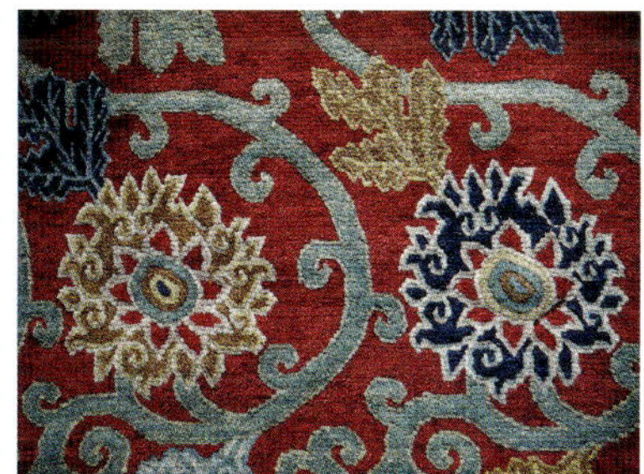

16c

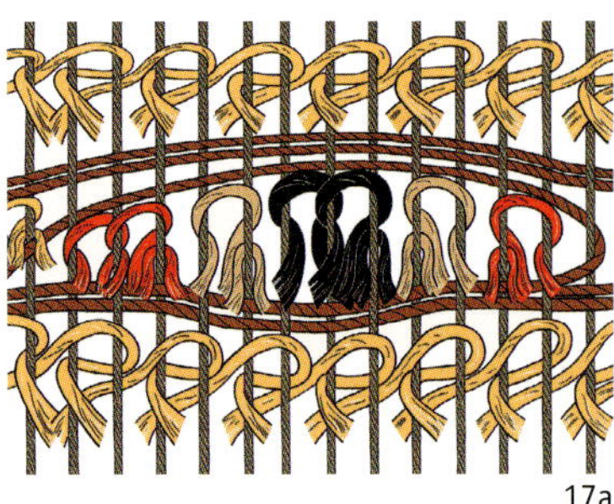

17a

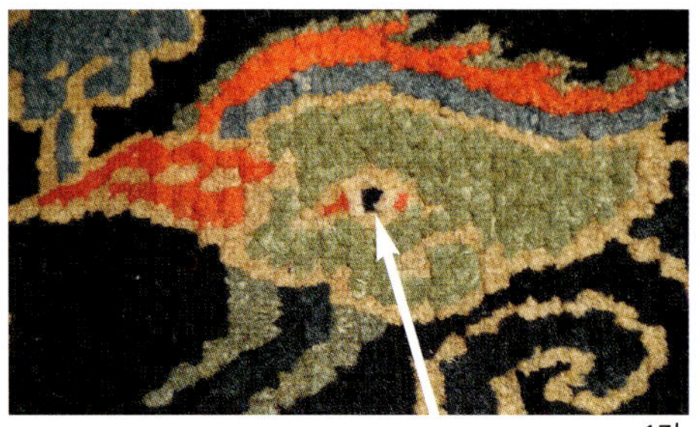

17b

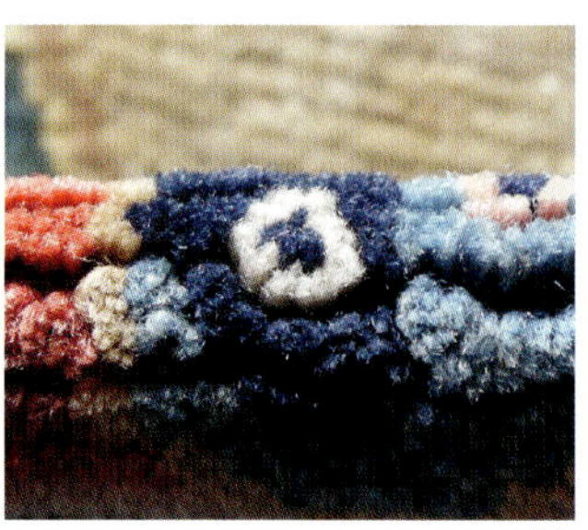

17c

Figs. 17a to 17c: Variants of eccentric weft weave device: a) small round-shaped eccentrically woven element, b) detail of C131 with eccentrically woven phoenix's eye (see Fig. 15 in the contribution by Wild), c) eccentrically woven detail of Yin and Yang symbol on C73 (see Fig. 2 in the contribution by Montigel)

carbon-dated Turkmen carpets (Tsareva 2008). Later it was identified as typical for some groups of Turkmen as well as for knotted archaeological objects of Eurasia (Tsareva 2011, 2015, 2016).

What amazed me was the principle similarity with a technique which we call *eccentric warps*, even if the involved elements are different. The method involves inserting warps additionally to the main structure as well as triangles of warps and loops applied to widen the weaving's format (Figs. 19a to 19b). Never mentioned before, it was identified in an under-saddle rug (Fig. 18, C87) of complicated shape: two symmetrically arranged oval-shaped parts, wide at the ends and narrowing to the centre. Although in principle identical with the eccentric wefts technique, these two methods have different purposes: an artistic one in the sitting and sleeping rugs C73 (Fig. 17c) and C131 (Fig. 17b), and a technical one in the case of the under-saddle rug in Fig. 18. With this rug, as far as it was possible to identify, the weaver was adding warps where he needed to widen the surface of the rug, and then dropped them when it was narrowing.

Another very special technical trick appears in a group of especially masterful small Tibetan rugs with perfectly executed floral patterns (Fig. 20, C89). It is also mentioned by Denwood (1974). Additionally to the main structure, short lengths of warps are introduced which makes it possible to make especially complicated curvilinear motifs (Figs. 21a to 21c). In Tibetan practice, the method is combined with substantial change in the arrangement of warps, together producing an all-over offset structure and an unusual interplay of warps and loops. The extremely specific character of this method made it possible to name it the *dancing warp trick* (Figs. 28c and 28d). This trick is also known in Central Asian carpet weaving, in Turkmen knotted weaves, for example, but as a much simpler variant, although with the same artistic purpose.

In addition to these regular and irregular devices with known foreign parallels, several other structural tricks peculiar to Tibet were first found in local weavings. One was identified in a charming early *khagangma* (Fig. 22, C116), comparable in difficulty and purpose with the above discussed "additional warps" method, with the only difference that in this case we find these inserted between one or two loops and the main weft unit below *additional* short (one or two loop length) *bits of weft* yarns.[9]

Another specifically Tibetan device got the name of *over-the-weft loop*, a term that does not sound felicitous but is easy to understand. To make an element of this kind, the weaver attaches a loop (or several loops) to front shed warps over the weft (Fig. 23a and Fig. 30, middle of the central row). Loops of this kind are added to the upper plane of warps and "sit" above the wefts, hence the term described above. We see these loops only from the front, but never from the back, thus they are rather difficult to find on the thousands of square centimetres of surface on even small items, not to mention on large carpets. In spite of this, the number of items with the *over-the-weft loop* technique in the collection is quite impressive, which speaks for the popularity of the trick among Tibetan weavers.

All the abovementioned techniques are mostly – if not entirely – intended to add smoothness to curving lines and are mainly found in rugs with animal and floral patterns (Figs. 24a and 24b, also Fig. 25, C153). Correct identification of the structural elements that shape curvilinear images is difficult. Although I name the over-the-weft elements "loops", from what we see when studying a rug is that it is not possible to say if we are dealing with a loop or with an additionally inserted knot (Fig. 23a). This is why I wish I could have seen the process of Tibetan pile-making with my own eyes, and that is also the reason why in the catalogue cases of an unclear origin are tagged with question marks in brackets.

Another typical and traditional irregularity practised by Tibetan weavers is also known from the Imperial Chinese group of tricks, namely very large loops (Tsareva 2005: Fig. 58). In most identified cases, they perform the function of

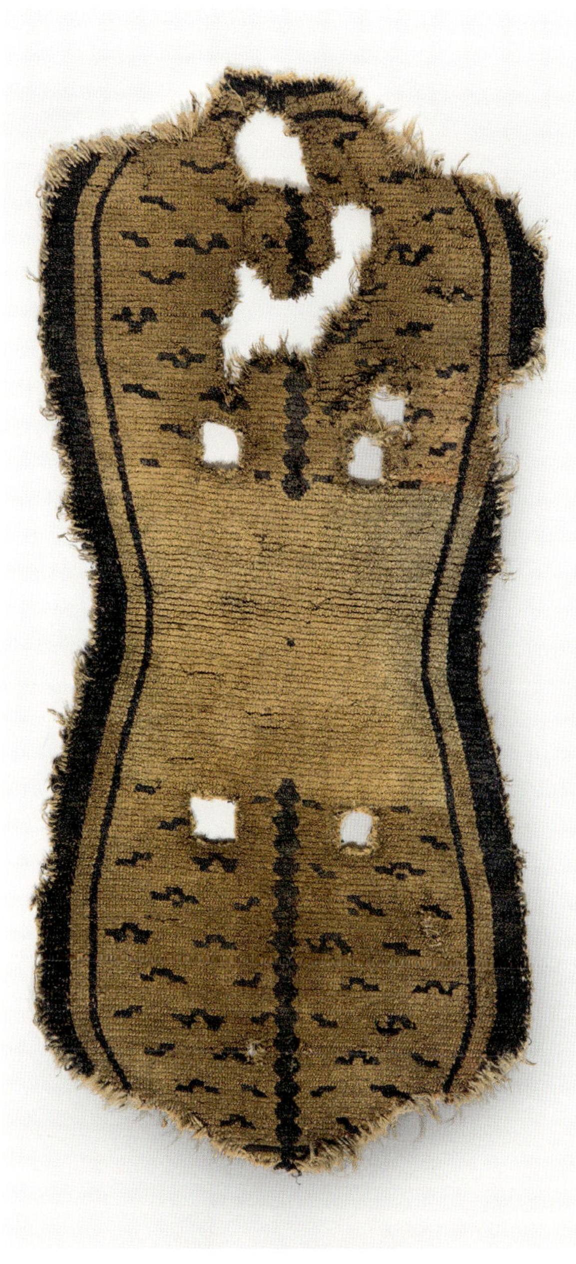

Fig. 18: C87. Under-saddle rug (*makden*), early oval shape. 19th c. (?), 122×58 cm

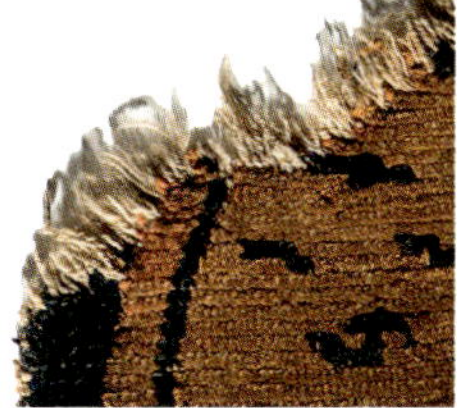

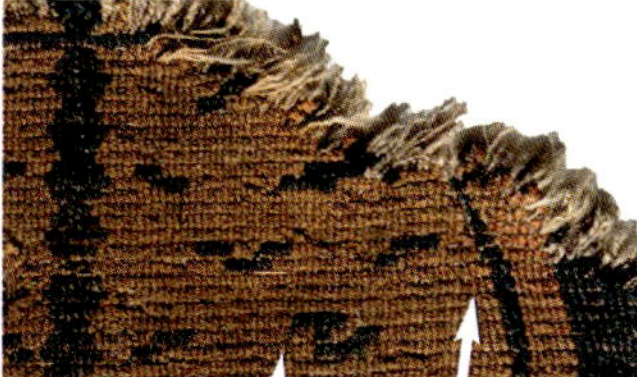

19a 19b

Figs. 19a and 19b: Details of both sides of rug C87 with eccentric warp weave

pushing elements, and participate in this capacity in the formation of diagonal loops (read curvilinear lines) and beyond (Figs. 26a and 26b, Fig. 27).

One of the most progressive carpet-weaving methods we know to help form diagonal and curvilinear lines is depression of warps, which automatically calls for depression of loops (Figs. 28a to 28d). The device will be discussed below in the section "Warps" in the chapter "Materials, Composition of Yarns and Their Use". Here I just want to underline that depression of warps should be regarded as one of the most characteristic for the Tibetan weavings' structure, so highly developed we should name craftsmen and craftswomen of the Land of Snow "masters of the depression trick". The easiest way to identify depression is to check the back side of a rug, as depression shifts the warps, producing ribbing. This makes it possible to reproduce any pattern without the use of other devices and is intrinsic in the products by users of the asymmetrical open left knot (Iranians, Salor Turkmen, Chinese, etc.).

In contrast with their very regular and even depression, the angle of shift in Tibetan rugs can vary from very small to very deep, depending on the character of the pattern. The most complicated examples of this were identified in the above-discussed items with the "additional warps" device, whose extremely specific character made it possible to name them the "dancing warps' method", although in reality the picture we find is formed not by a single, but by a combination of two tricks, one of which is depression proper, while the second, and in this case even more importantly, is the "additional warps" device (Figs. 21a to 21c).

A final structural device to discuss is a trick used in all carpet-making lands in which trapezoid animal trappings are made. In the collection under research, this form is represented by the rug C120 (see Fig. 6 in the contribution by Montigel). Exemplary for this device is this horse blanket, whose width narrows from bottom to top with every row of loops. As a result, one by one warp yarns become superfluous. Unlike other trapezoid trappings, however (compare C36; see Fig. 11 in the contribution by De Jong), the released warps are not cut but swing 90 degrees to function as wefts. The method automatically produces stable offset, suggesting the use of patterns with all-over diagonal lines, as we see on this horse blanket: a purely diagonal geometric motif of linked *swastikas*.

Although irregular devices used by the Tibetan weavers have "relatives" in other pile-making practices in Eurasia, the discussed methods are so individual that one should

Fig. 20: C89. Over-saddle rug (*masho*). Late 19th c. (?), 80×58 cm

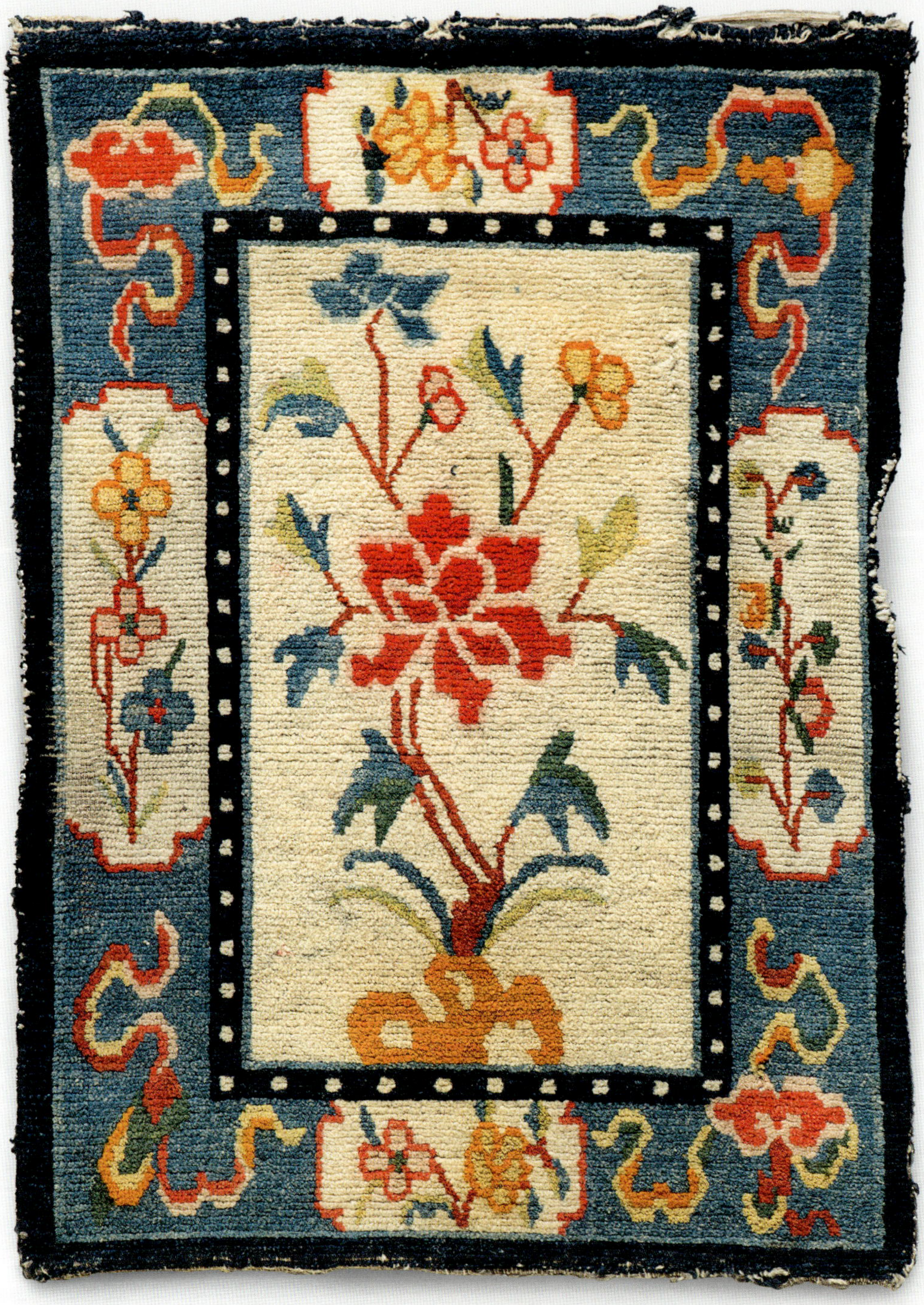

Figs. 21a to 21c: Details of rug C89 with additional warp lengths and warp depression: a) and b) details of the reverse in different enlargements, c) large detail of the front

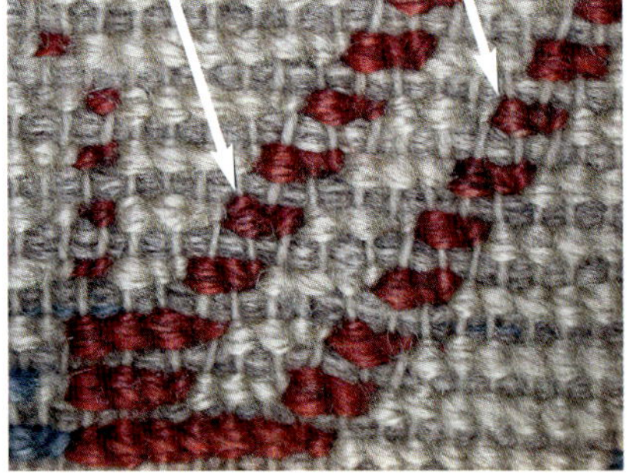

21a

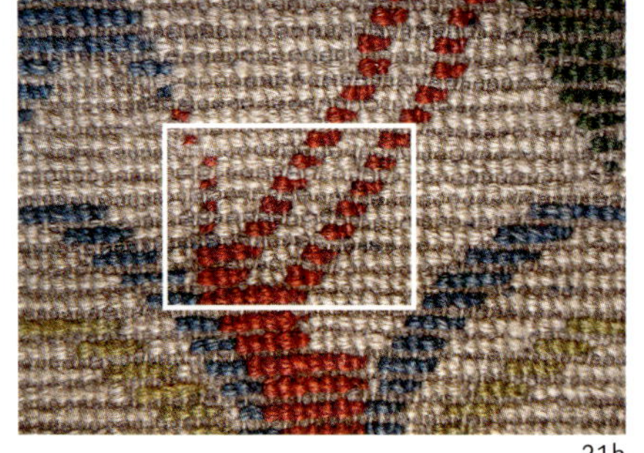

21b

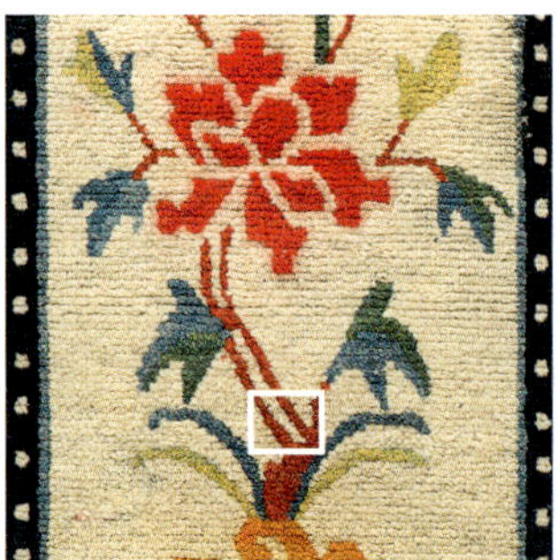

21c

Fig. 22: C116.
Sitting rug (*khagangma*).
19th c., 76×78 cm

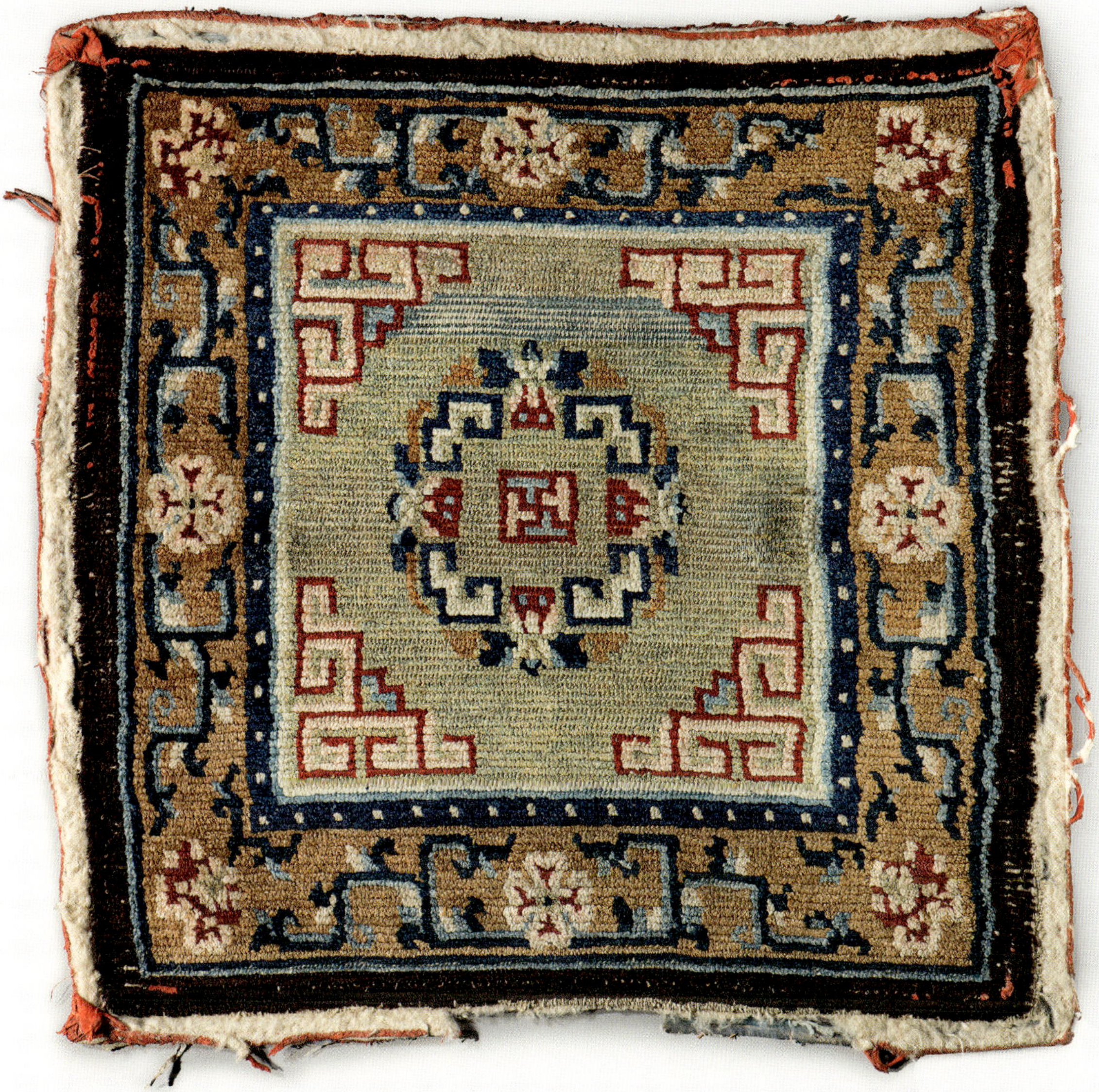

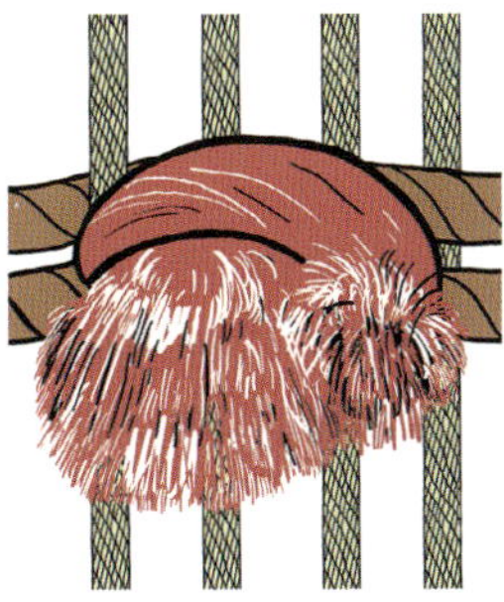

23a

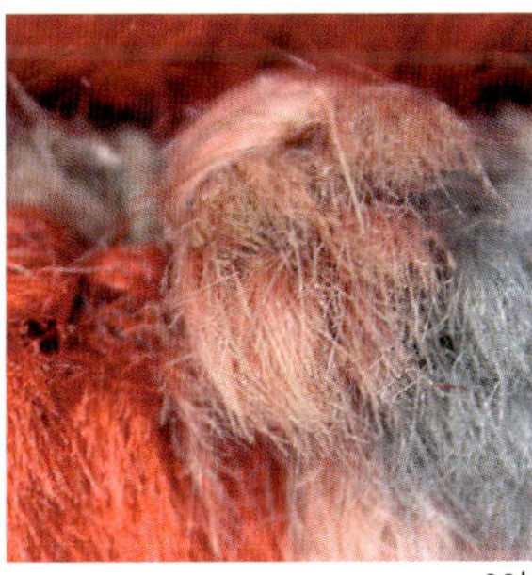

23b

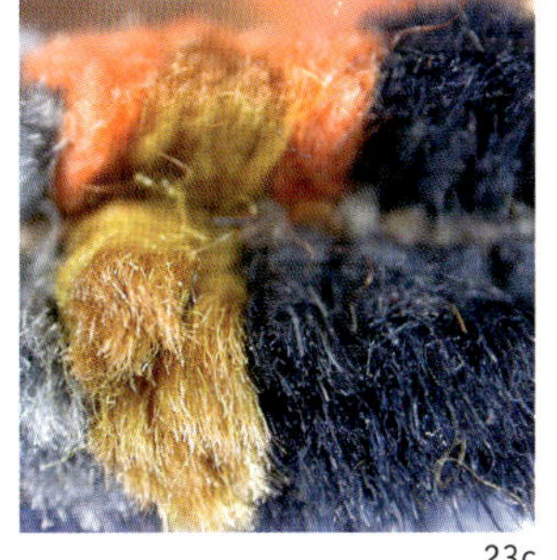

23c

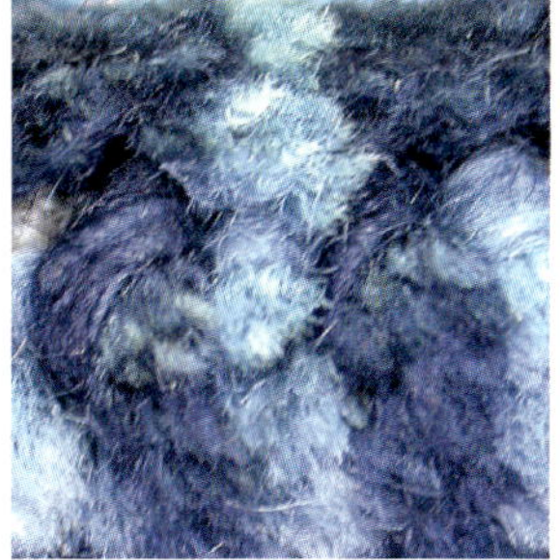

23d

Figs. 23a to 23d: Variants of over-the-weft-loop device: a) drawing, b) and c) macro details of individual over-the-weft-loop device (C69 and C127), d) macro detail of a group of loops knotted over the weft loop

Figs. 24a and 24b: Examples for animals and flowers in designs: a) detail of C12 with skilful representation of a bat, b) detail of C153 (see Fig. 25) with the masterfully executed lotus and serrated leaves

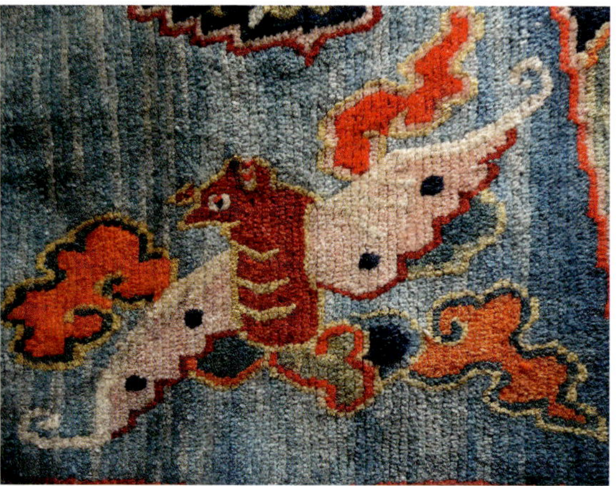

24a

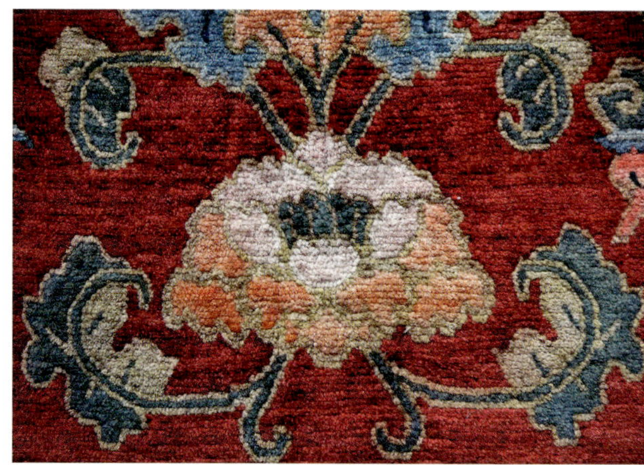

24b

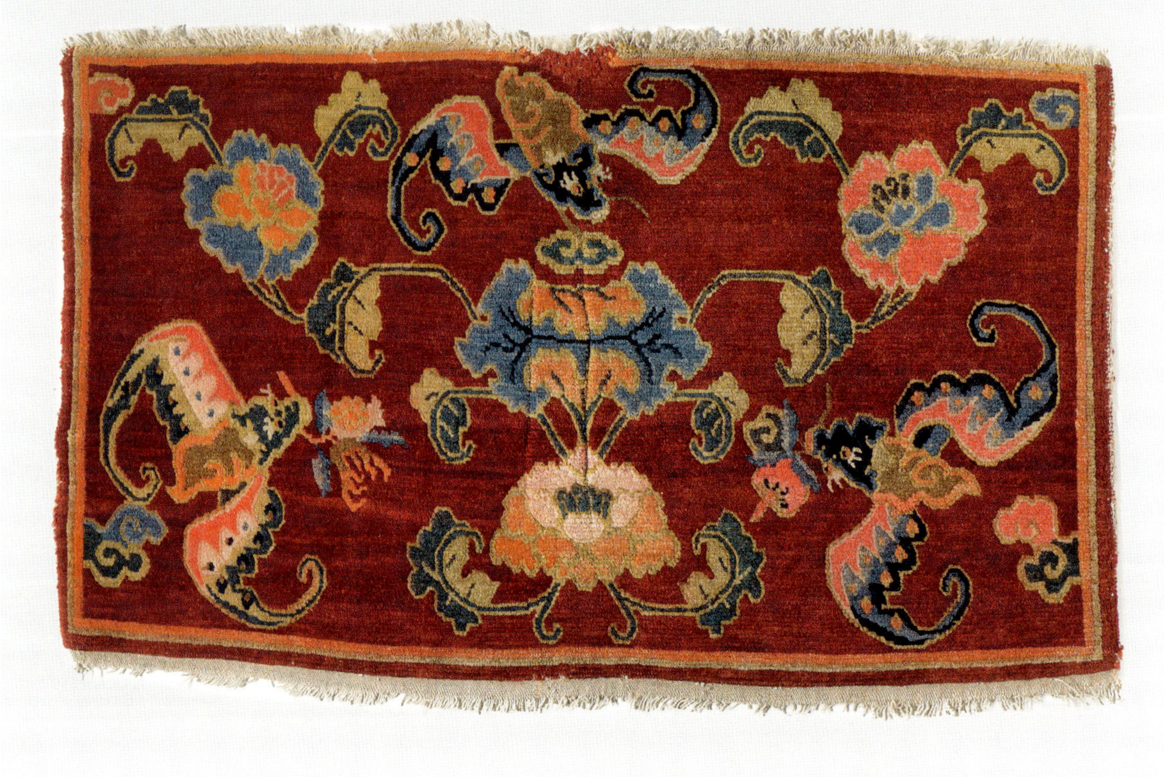

Fig. 25: C153. Large, oblong sitting rug (*khagangma*) with lotuses and bats. Early 20th c., 52×93 cm

Figs. 26a and 26b: Large and diagonal loops devices: a) macro detail with large loops (C79, see Fig. 7), b) detail of diagonal loops shoved through a large loop (C48, see Fig. 27)

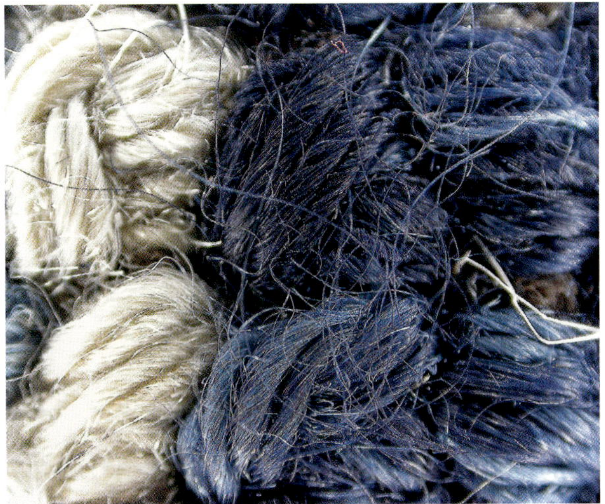

26a

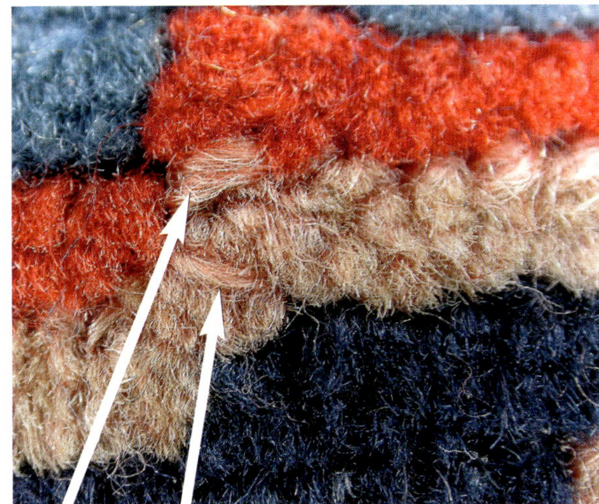

26b

Fig. 27: C48. Horizontally woven over-saddle rug (?). 1st quarter 20th c., 54×91 cm

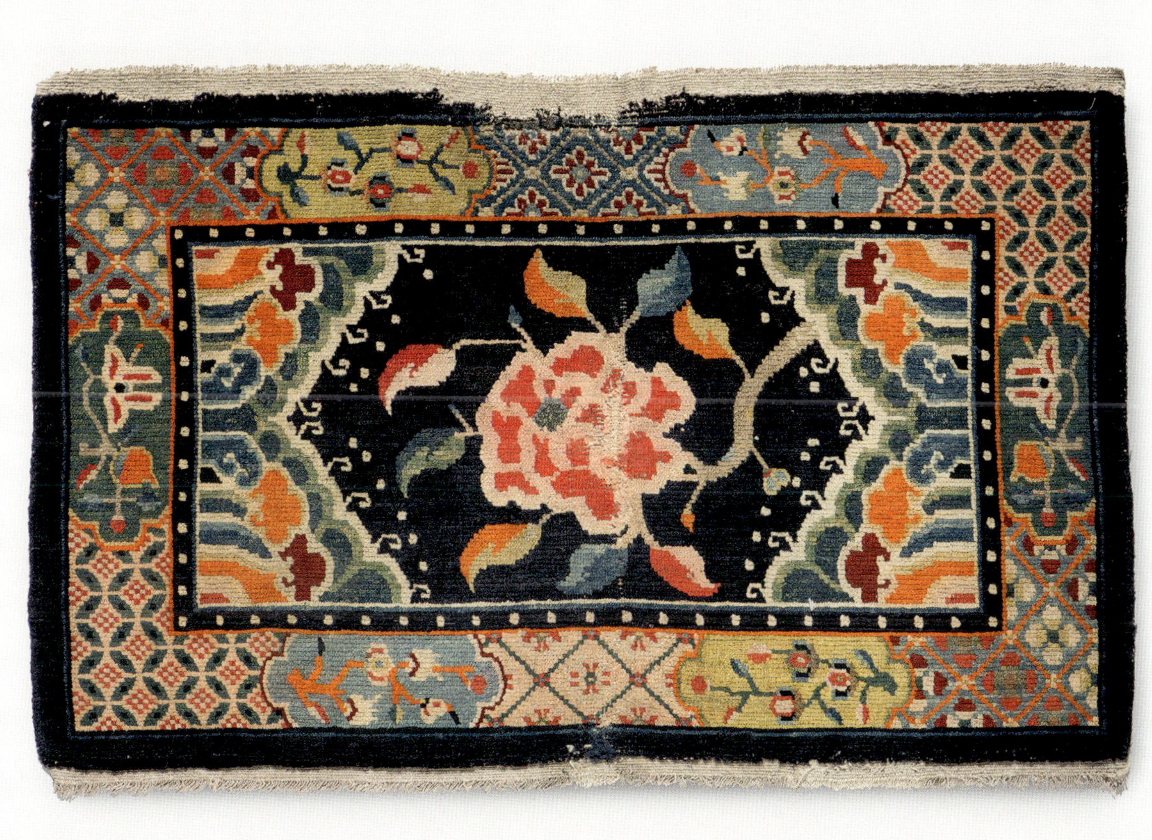

Figs. 28a to 28d: Variants of depression device: a) drawing, b) detail of rug C103 with depression, c) and d) details of rug C36 with depressed dancing warps structure (see Fig. 11 in the contribution by De Jong)

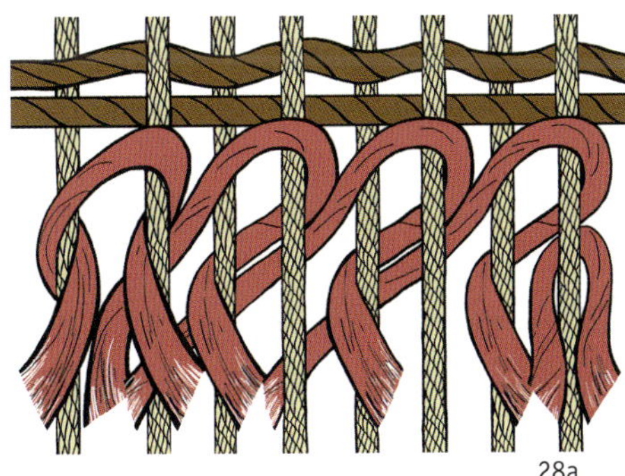

28a

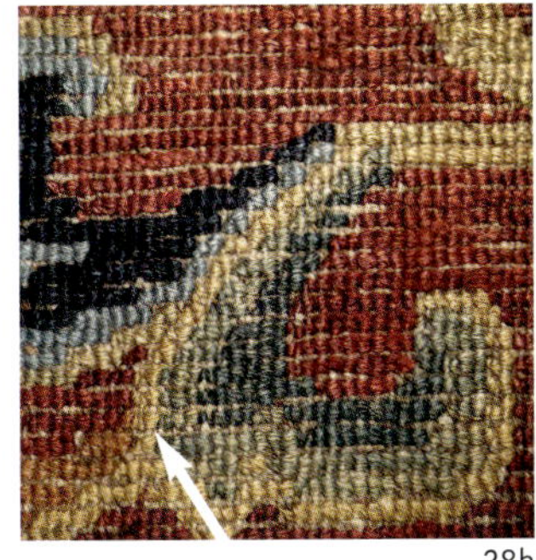

28b

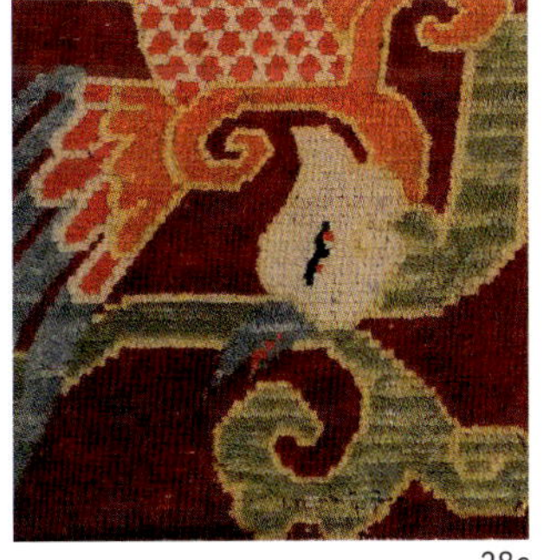

28c

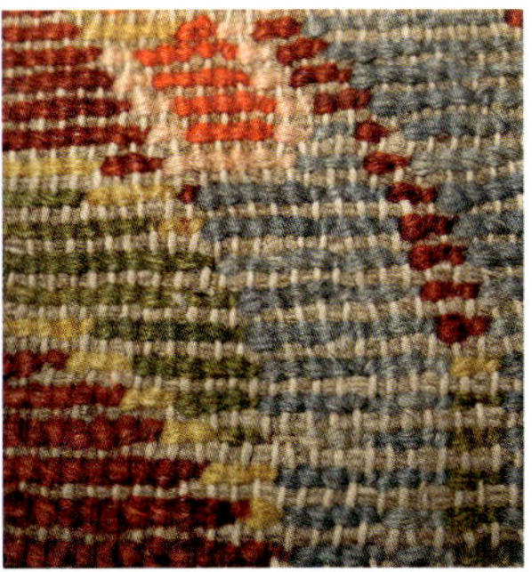

28d

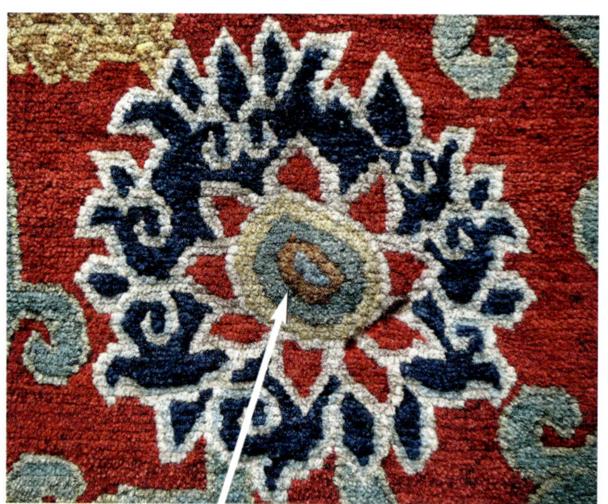

29a

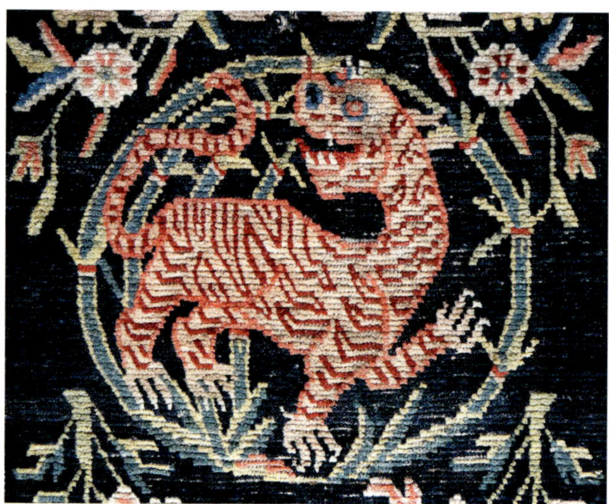

29b

Figs. 29a and 29b: Carving device (sculpturing) and carving effect: a) detail of a rug with modestly carved central part of a lotus flower (C24, see Fig. 16 in the contribution by Wild), b) detail of rug, with red and light rose tiger stripes with carving effect (C15, see Fig. 2 in the contribution by Michael Buddeberg)

not interpret them as borrowing, but rather they suggest a continuum from common prototypes. The technique of *sculpturing* (also *carving*, see below) is different and most probably should be considered a comparatively late borrowing from China (Tsareva 2005: Fig. 72).

The well-known term *sculpturing* describes when the lines between different coloured details of a rug's pattern are trimmed in half-relief, executed by skilful, step-by-step cutting of looping yarns, usually with 2 mm difference in height. Used after the end of the process of looping, then followed by cutting and trimming, the device needs special training and represents a rare and so to say "seldom guest" on Tibetan rugs. I say "seldom guest" because in the Buddebergs' collection it was identified only in the most picturesque floral details of exclusively manufactured items of highly professional work (Fig. 29a, central detail).

Visually similar to *sculpturing* is the *carving effect* (relief effect), which, however, results from uneven wear of pile dyed in different colours and of different types of fibres (Fig. 29b). Looking at both variants from the historical point of view, one can suppose that the time-consuming and laborious "artificial" *sculpturing* developed to mimic the natural pile wear *carving effect*. For hundreds or perhaps thousands of years, this effect was observed by weavers and then copied manually either by weavers or at the instigation of rug designers – as a mark of supreme quality and exclusive value of the most refined pile weavings.

The *carving effect* appears primarily when the weaver uses yarns of different quality; first-rate fibres withstand wear better. This was observed mostly on professional, monastic weavings, while home-made items are regularly manufactured from wool identical in quality (except for camel and yak hair). Another factor that causes uneven wear of pile is the destructive influence of mordents and whiteners, when for lack of wool with shades of ivory the weavers were forced to bleach light grey or brown yarns before dyeing them into pale tints. This is the case, for example, with Fig. 29b, where the cherry red tiger stripes have a height of three millimetres, whereas the light rose stripes were worn down to two millimetres, definitely as a result of mordents before dying. An easy way to differentiate the carving effect from proper carving is to check the difference in the height of the pile. For pile in one colour, it will be equal in the case of the sculpturing effect, but gradual if in specially formed half-relief shape.

With this understanding of the regular and irregular pile-making devices (elements) used by the Tibetan masters and the idea of "loop" units, we can explore their arrangement in the double-level structured textures. An important point for recognising the formation of **variants of loop sequences in one or several units** is first mentioned in note 8, quoted from Philip Denwood (Denwood 1974: 44), which explains that the Tibetan pile-making process proceeds from left to right. My descriptions in the catalogue follow the same sequence.[10]

As shown by Fig. 30 and previous drawings, any type of unit (I repeat, that this is a group of identically coloured loops) begins on the left side, and regularly starts with a two-warp symmetric or asymmetric loop. In either case, this initial element can be packed with an additional loop, sometimes on two warps, but mostly on one, in the latter case inserted either from the bottom (in the following *bottom loop*) or from the top (in the following *top loop*). With long sequences of loops, the weave generally continues

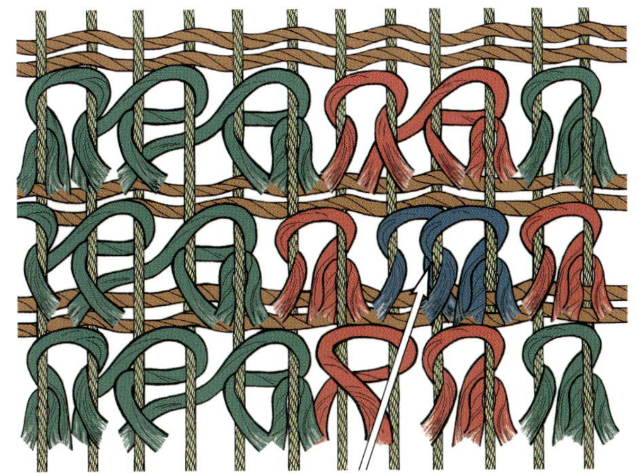

Fig. 30: Variants of looping units with differently formed, arranged and coloured elements. Typical for the formation of circle motifs is the arrangement of crimson-coloured regular and packing bottom loops. Top row, from left to right: long row unit (green) – doubled unit (red) – single (green); central row: detail of long row (green) – single (red) – pair of sharing loops (blue) – single (red); bottom row: long row unit (green) – doubled loop (red) – single (green)

with a number of basic long-leg loops, whose long left-side ends make bottom packs with the preceding pile-making elements. In all identified cases, the final element of a unit is packed with an additional open (viz.: one-warp) bottom element.[11]

As discussed above, with a textile's "body" the extended ends of all long-leg loops always pack the neighbouring elements to the left, whether a symmetric, asymmetric, regular or identical long-leg component. Of the variety of possible combinations, the drawing in Fig. 30 represents those that are found most often. (All depicted sequences and conjunctions are commented in detail in the annotation to the drawing in Fig. 30. Note the dark-blue sharing loops and rose-coloured diagonal as well as the "over-the-weft" loops, a combination used with circular motifs.)

Another essential feature of Tibetan rug weaving is the unrestricted application – within the framework of local tradition – of methods of weaving. Although in general we deal with a stable system, there are numerous variations within the sequence of elements and their arrangement in a unit. Viz.: we find packing loops on two warps, or lack of a packing bottom loop at the beginning of a unit; besides, those packing loops can "sit" on one or two warps, etc. The variations depend mostly on the character of the pattern, whose most representative variants are either strictly geometric, or rich in curving lines with floral and animal images. (An exceptional case is the rug C108, Fig. 31, with a refined combination of motifs in both styles.)

From the variety of systematic and accidental features observed in Tibetan pile rugs, we can recognise recurring traditional ones, but we also discover ones peculiar to an individual weaver or type of weaving – or both. These are methods to form details in the conceived pattern as well as secondary, accidental and individual features for the classification of Tibetan rugs. This will be addressed below in the section "Possible Reasons for Irregularities" and in the descriptions in the catalogue.

Another difficult technical parameter in describing Tibetan rugs is identifying their "density", the number of knots/loops per square decimetre, a standard parameter when analysing pile weavings. It is relatively easy to accurately count the knots per decimetre vertically and horizontally on regularly knotted structures, but not on Tibetan rugs with their numerous shared, missed warps, knots on one or three warps, etc. In the case of the Tibetan looping system and its irregularities, this method does not work. All we can do to tell the weaving structure density is to calculate the number of warps in the horizontal direction and the units of wefts vertically, as recorded in the catalogue. Nonetheless, following carpet books' manner of describing pile structures, I will discuss "density". Although the figures rely on the number of warps and wefts and are in no way precise, it allows a rough comparison of the items in the collection.

Single-Level Looping Techniques

In contrast to the two-level technique in which the loops bind together warps on both sides of the wefts, in the "single-level" technique the pile-making elements only interlace with the warps on the front plane of the shed ("active warps" in textile terminology), while the back plane – "passive warps" – are only bound into the texture of the rug by the wefts. This technique is also common in Tibetan rug weaving (Fig. 33, C164).

In Tibetan tradition, the group is represented by two different types. One is known to us under the name of *drumze*,[12] with a *warp-faced* structure (Figs. 34a and 34b, Figs. 35a to 35c). The other one is called *tsuktruk*, and should be attributed to the *plain single-level* type (Figs. 36a and 36b, Figs. 37a to 37c). In the Buddebergs' collection, the group is represented by eighteen pieces (15 per cent of the collection), seven are made in *drumze* and eleven in *tsuktruk* technique. Because of their long pile, loose structure and stylistically close patterns, the distinction between these types is not evident when looking at them from the front. It can be clearly seen, however, when one compares their back sides.

With *drumze*, almost identical with two-level rugs, we see colour units with dominating asymmetric long-leg loops, and open and closed packing and sharing elements (Fig. 34a, Figs. 35a and 35b), but only with the single-level

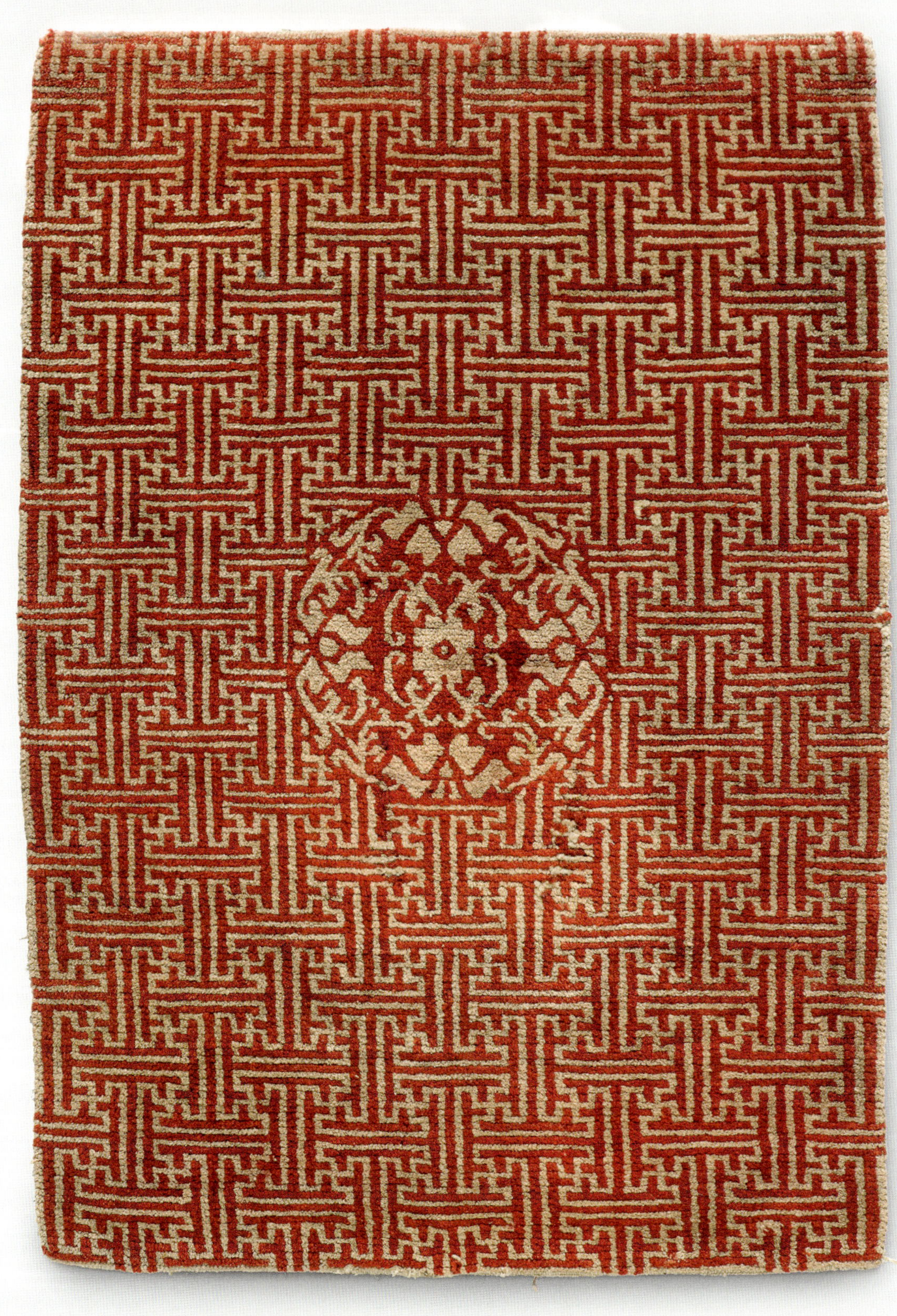

Fig. 31: C108.
Sitting rug (*khagangma*) with the combination of a medallion following a brocade pattern and a *swastika* lattice.
19th c., 82 × 58 cm

Detail of Fig. 31

Detail of Fig. 32

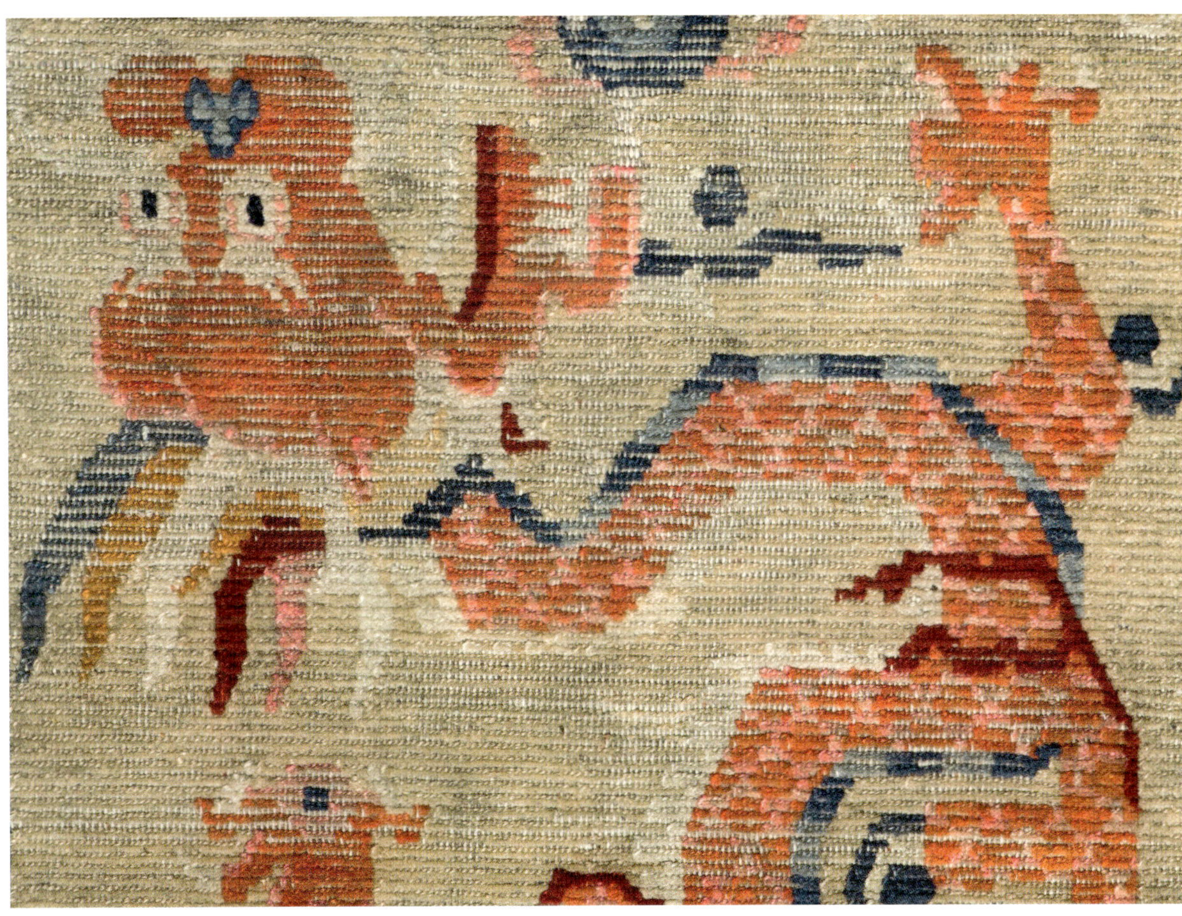

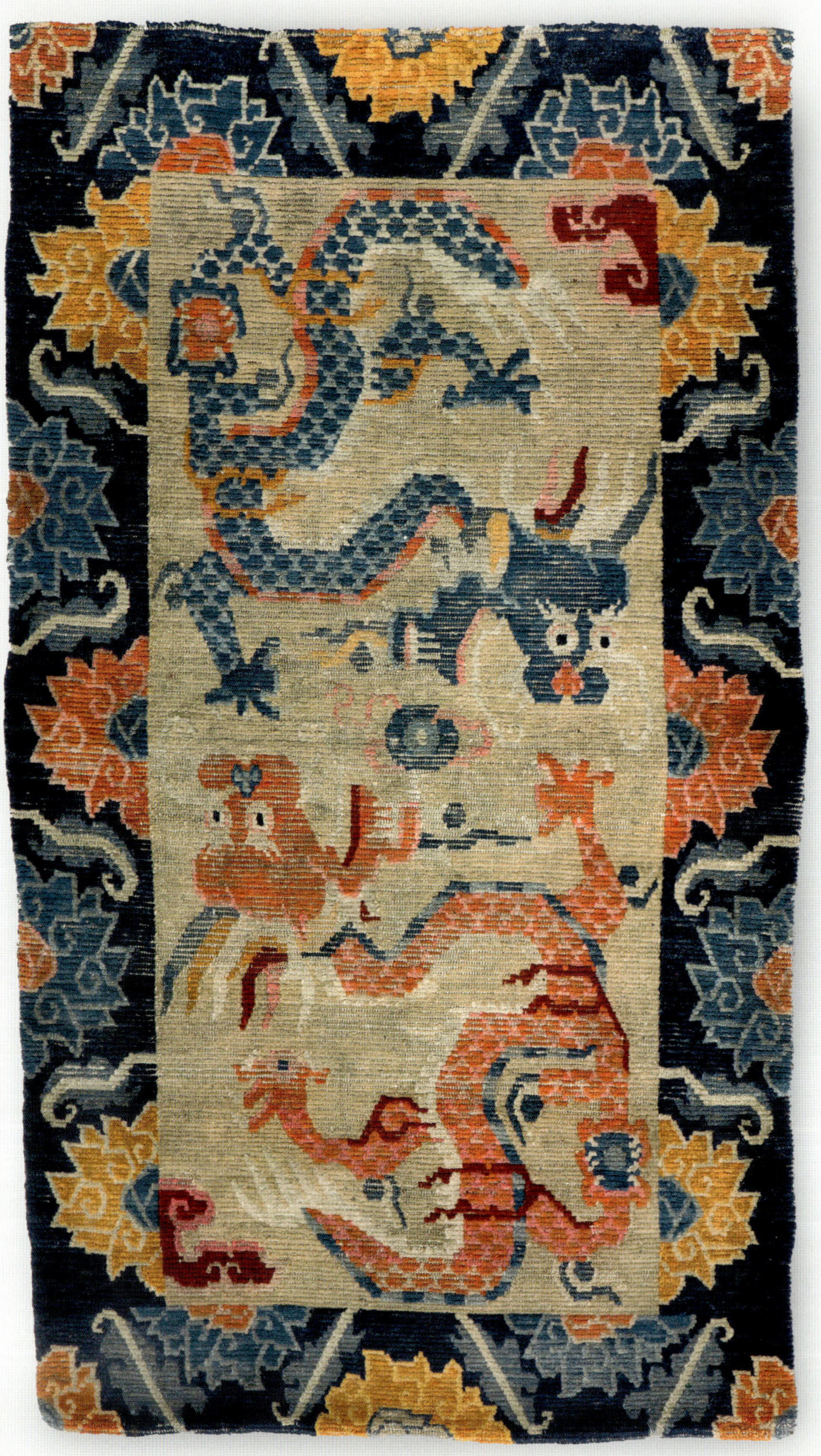

Fig. 32: C26. Sitting and sleeping rug (*khaden*) with two dragons and a border of half lotus flowers. Around 1900, 156×90 cm

Fig. 33: C164. Wangden *drumze* rug with *swastikas* in different colours on a yellow field. 19th c., 147 × 62 cm

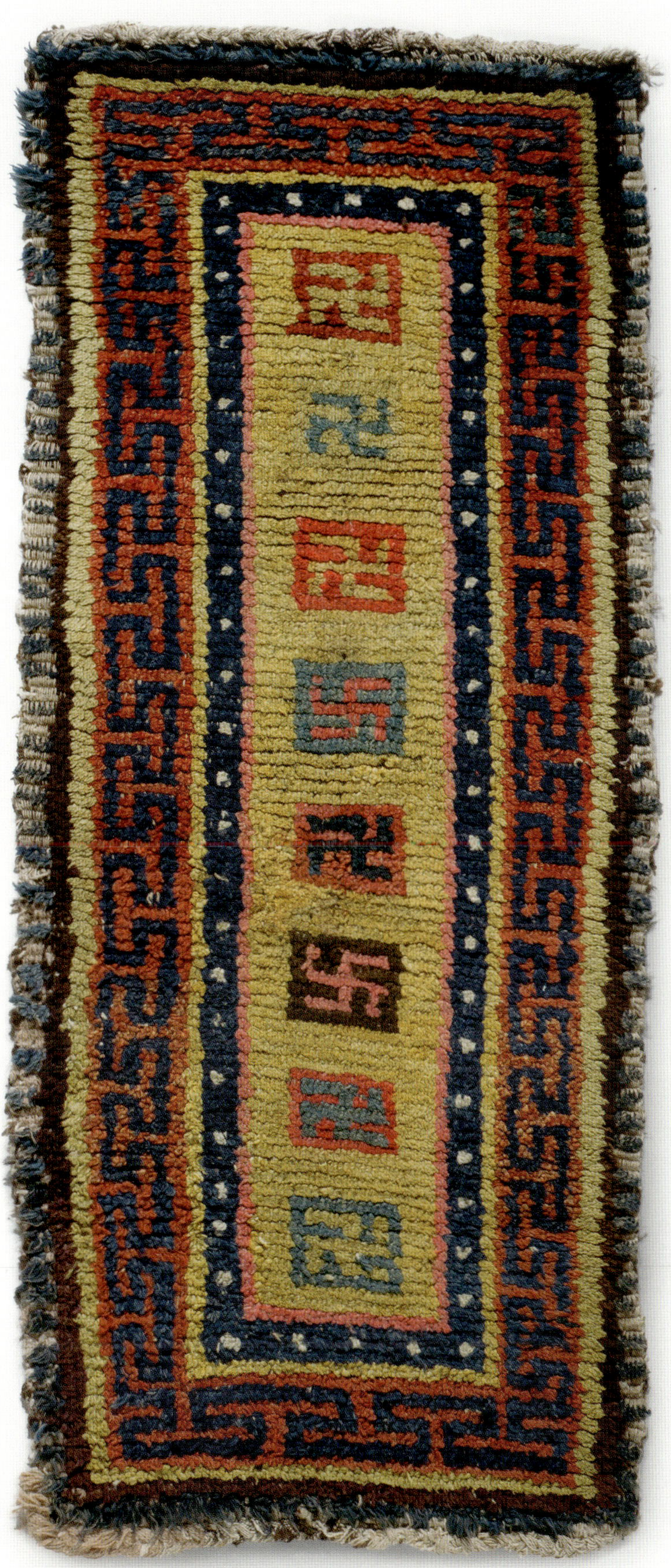

Figs. 34a and 34b: C164. Single-level warp-faced Wangden *drumze*: a) detail of the front (see Fig. 33), b) detail of the back

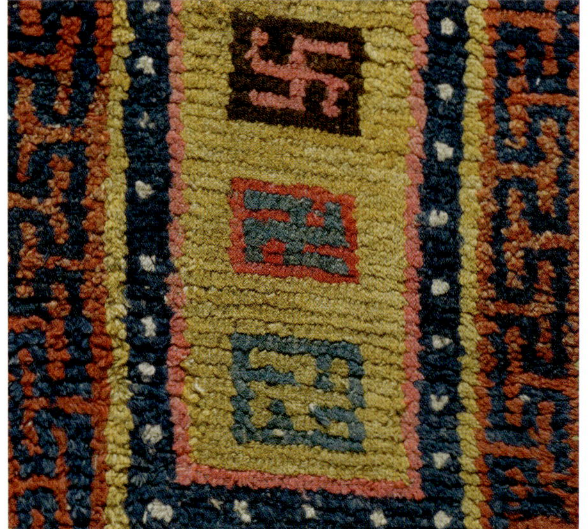

34a

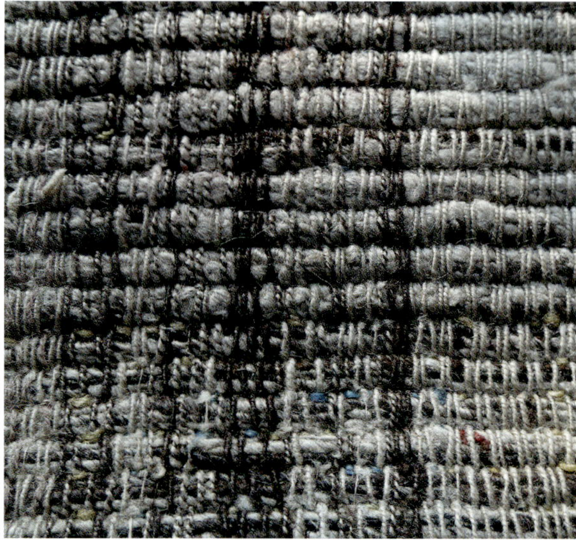

34b

Fig. 35: Structural elements of *drumze* rugs: a) schematic drawing of *drumze*-type looping system, b) detail of the front of C164 with floating pile yarns, c) detail of the back of C164 showing yak hair wefts of black-brown and ivory that were spun without the use of a spindle, two to three shoots in a unit

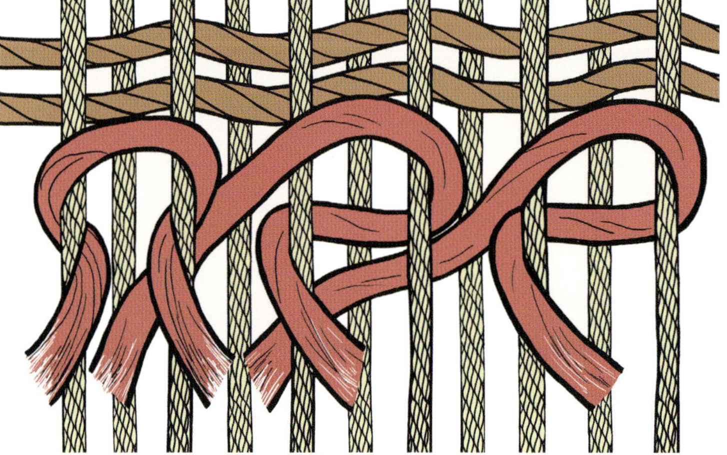

35a

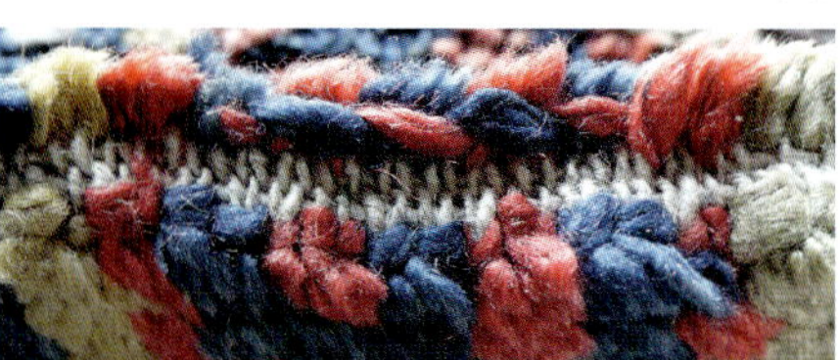

35b

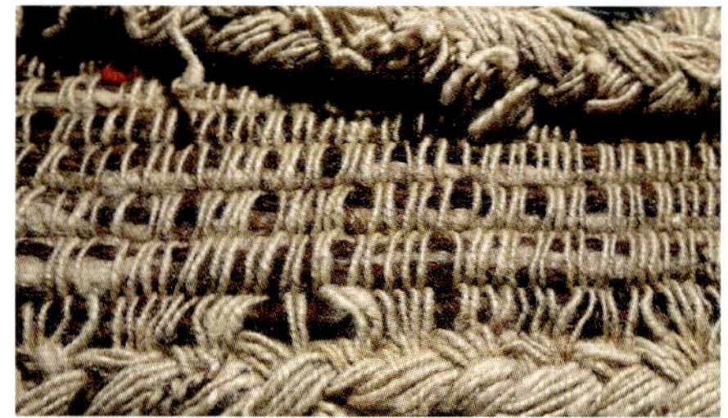

35c

structure. The feature which justifies identifying *drumze* as a type can only be seen on the back (Figs. 34b and 35c).

The rugs have fine warps and extremely thick and loose wefts, whose amazing contrast can reach a ratio of 1:16, which adds to the generation of the warp-faced structure as a phenomenon. Another factor which seems characteristic for *drumze* is their unusually low density of looping with 105 to 195 loops per decimetre and their long, up to 20 mm pile, whose loose texture allows weavers to apply a unique pile weaving trick – *floating pile yarns* – which stretch from one group of loops in a particular colour to the colour's next use without being cut, hidden within the intervening pile. A splendid example is C164 (Figs. 34a and 35b).

Although discussed in more detail below, it should be noted that all *drumze* rugs in the collection use precious yak hair in warps and sometimes also in wefts and pile yarns. Another unique feature is that the loose, thick and uneven weft yarns are hand spun, without the use of a spindle (Fig. 35c), as discussed in the section "Thread-Making System" in the chapter "Material, Composition of Yarns and Their Use".

The *drumze* technique is used for the production of a limited variety of items, including nearly square individual *khagangma* and long meditation rugs which seat several monks. Besides, we find *khaden* sitting and sleeping rugs of rectangular shape, and sometimes *masho* saddle rugs (just one in the Buddebergs' collection, C77, see Fig. 8 in the contribution by Wild). Typical for *drumze*, all of these items have very long fringes which can be regarded as a kind of hallmark for items of this kind (except for the *masho* rug C77, although this item most probably lost its fringe during restoration).

Figs. 36a and 36b: C61. *Tsuktruk* rug, single-level open-loop weave: a) detail of the front (see Fig. 4 in the contribution by Darchen), b) detail of the back

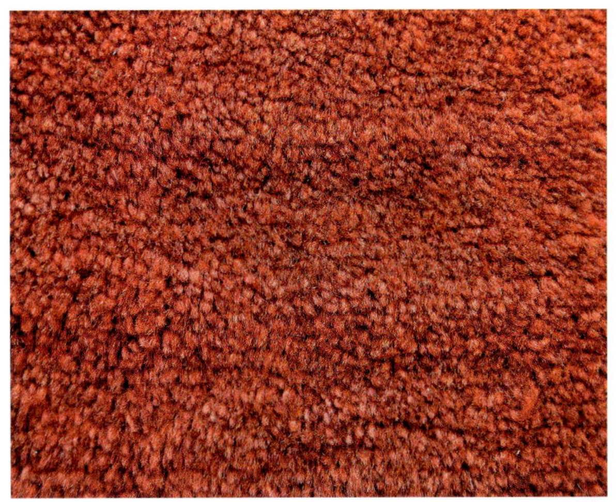

36a

36b

Figs. 37a to 37c: a) Variants of *tsuktruk* structure. Upper row: alternating *active* and *passive* warps (1:1:1), bottom row: loops on two active and one passive warp, b) detail of the front of C93, c) detail of *tsuktruk* rug with many shoots of wefts (C122, see Fig. 7 in the contribution by Darchen)

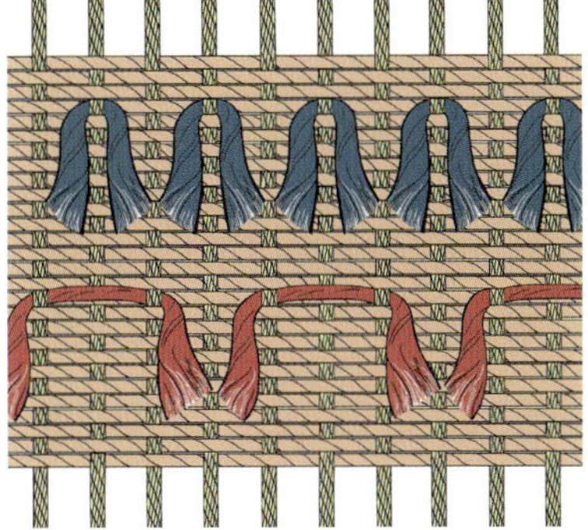

37a

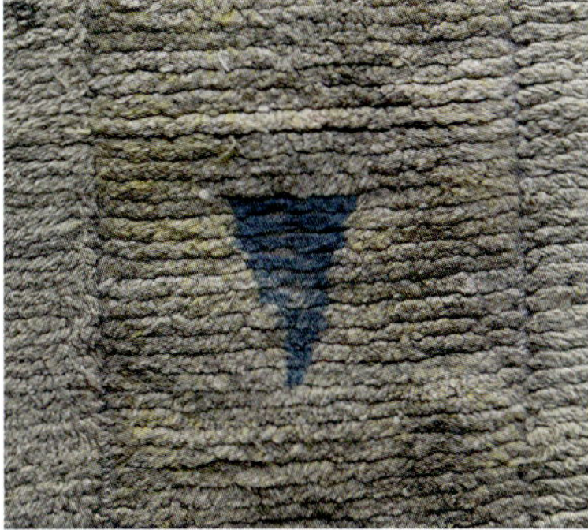

37b

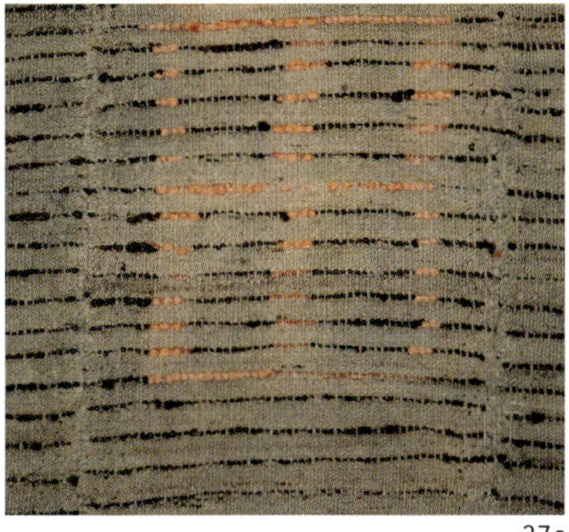

37c

An interesting observation is that if we compare *drumze* and the classic Tibetan two-level weavings with single-level and classic two-level symmetrical knottings of Central Asia, we see a partly identical picture in that both lines follow solid ancestral traditions, suggesting two-level variants as derivations from the single-level pile-making systems.

As to the *tsuktruk* type rugs, at first glance their back side gives an impression of a regular double-level weave, but a second glance reveals that this is not the case. One can recognise their very loose structure, uneven thickness of pile and weft threads and, of course, the manner of making large items by stitching together several narrow panels. In objects of this kind, pile is formed by supplementary wefts (additional to the basic structural wefts, which go over and under each warp). These wefts are looped around the gauge rod and then cut, creating different length and arrangement in the pile, so called weft-loop pile. The Buddebergs' collection has pieces in both uniform and non-uniform structure. Most frequently, these wefts followed a 1:1:1 sequence (one active warp between two passive); 1:3:1 and 2:2:2 sequence (with different alteration of active and passive warps) (Fig. 37a). In other literature this is called "non-structural 'tufts'" (Emery 1980: 149).

Another peculiar feature of the *tsuktruk* is the variety of number of wefts in a unit (space between the rows of pile loops). In some cases we find only one to two wefts per unit (Fig. 36b, C61), while in others there can be as many as 56 wefts or more between the rows of loops (Fig. 37c, C122).

The absolute majority of weavings in the collection demonstrate a Z-spinning structure of elementary threads which is common for Tibet and for Eurasia in general. In contrast to this, in four *tsuktruk* items the use of S-spun warps and wefts was identified (Fig. 62a), which is quite unique for this craft. Of special interest is also the Tibetan masters' manner of making weft yarns by hand, without a spindle (Fig. 68f). Both exceptional devices will be discussed in the section "Thread-Making System" in the chapter "Material, Composition of Threads and Their Use".

In weavings of this kind, pile height depends solely on the length of wefts' floats, but in the Tibetan tradition it is limited by the diameter of the gauge rod. A technically and historically important point is the application of the

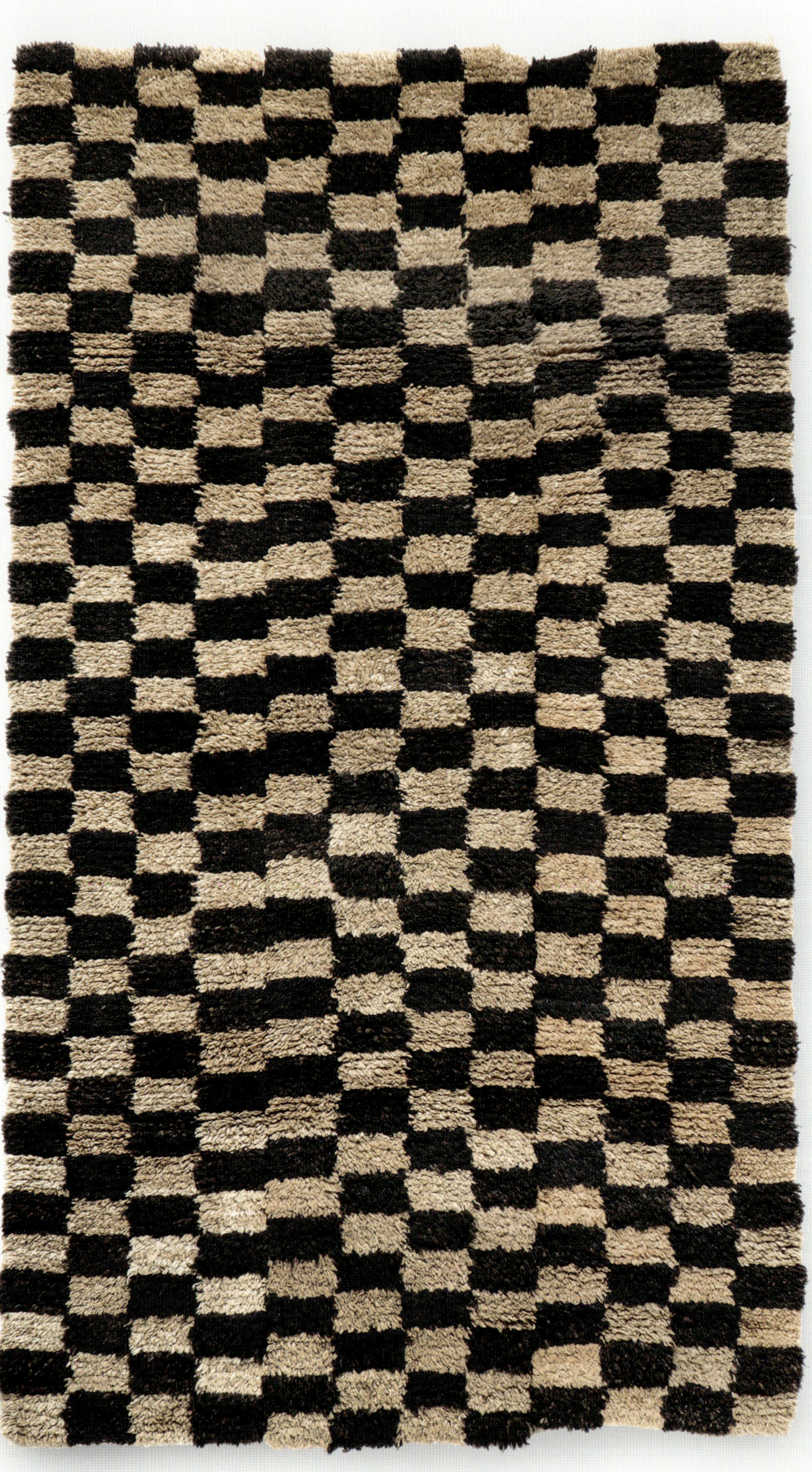

Fig. 38: C163. *Tsuktruk* rug with three panels and a chessboard pattern. 20th c. (?), 139×80 cm

symmetrical (Ghiordes) shape of *tsuktruk* loops, which points to an original adaptation of this technique. The same applies to the rather narrow width of these panels, from 16.5 centimetres (C86) to 31 centimetres (C85), whereby several panels are stitched together to make a large-format piece. This peculiarity suggests use of a narrow, most probably backstrap type of weaving loom which is still in use in Tibet (Fig. 39) and among the heirs of other archaic weaving traditions both in the eastern and western parts of Eurasia.

The archaic character of the *tsuktruk* type structure is evidenced by a long history of pieces with similar structure. The earliest are from the 12th century BC and territorially close examples have been found in the Tarim Basin, followed by the Pazyryk rug found in a grave in the Altai Mountains (6th to 3rd century BC; tombs no. 2, 3, 5) as well as the Bashadar findings (Tsareva 2006: 250–255). Among the modern variants, the closest in shape and structure are the so-called *dzulkhyr* rugs, still produced in Tadjikistan, Uzbekistan and Central Asia and by Arabs in Afghanistan (Tsareva 2015).

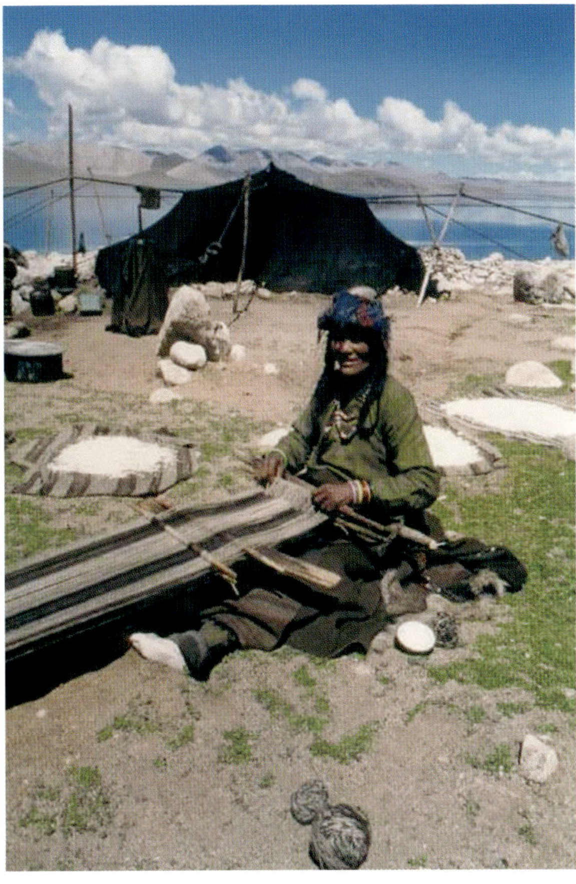

Fig. 39: Tibetan nomadic woman with a typical backstrap loom. Western Central Tibet at Lake Mun Tso

Possible Reasons for Irregularities

As mentioned earlier, general for the Tibetan rug's structural features is an unrestricted – within the framework of local tradition – application of methods of weaving. Thus on the one hand we are dealing with a clear and stable tradition and on the other with the weaver's individual choice of tricks to realise the artistic pattern in the rug. We also find some very strange irregularities, rather clumsy structural details within otherwise masterly executed weavings.

It has to be noted that I did not find any cases of this kind among monastic or supposedly professional commercial works, but in domestic products only. Items of this type really raised questions with no answers because there was no logical or technical need for such strange details which varied in quality to the otherwise very well manufactured textiles. An important piece of information to explain the origin of those irrational structural irregularities was given to me by Tatyana Taushan, an art historian and parapsychologist, who visited Tibet in the early 1970s with a group of specialists to study the use of medicinal plants and minerals in Tibetan medicine. A person with broad interests, she paid attention to some specific rituals and conditions of rug making. One of her observations tells us that the reason for such odd irregularities is very simple and should be explained not by technical but by other peculiarities specific to Tibetan culture. Viz.: in this particular case it lies in the traditional belief of Tibetan women that when started, no rug should be left without a weaver even for a second, as that second can be enough for the penetration of evil forces into an unfinished textile. To avoid such a misfortune, a women would ask another, unoccupied weaver or even a passing child to take her place in case she needed to go away for a while. It is clear that small children cannot weave properly and that many, if not all, of those strange and useless irregularities came as the result of children's eager, yet unskilful attempts to help their mothers, aunts or elder sisters. Besides such accidents supposedly made by children, we find items that are clearly the work of a beginner, i.e., numerous small technical and artistic slips. The most representative example of the kind is a saddle rug (Fig. 41, C157).

MATERIALS, COMPOSITION OF YARNS AND THEIR USE

Not being able to trace all of the links mentioned, wherever possible I try to clearly specify instances to show the multilevel, polyphonic essence of Tibetan rug weaving as a

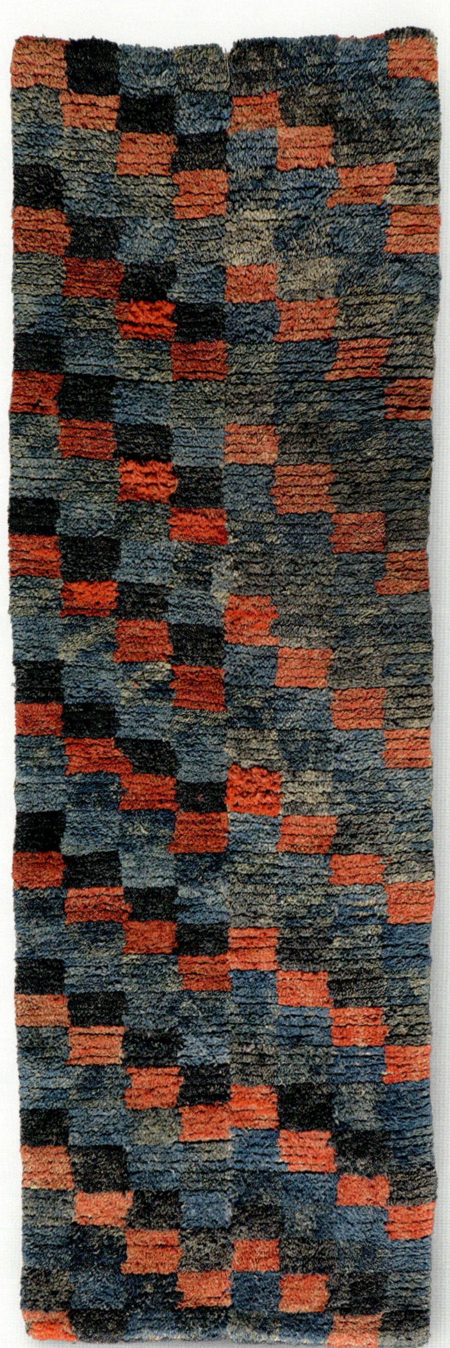

Fig. 40: C124. *Tsuktruk* rug made of two panels with chessboard pattern (not in catalogue)

phenomenon. I want to underline that the main source for my data are the 120 textiles studied in the collection, thus my results can differ dramatically from information given by other authors.

Materials

Study of the 120 items in the collection shows that the basic rug-weaving material of Tibet is sheep wool. The fleece is mainly obtained, according to the literature, from the flocks shepherded on the Qinghai upland region pastures, the grazing lands of which are one of the world's greatest grassland ecosystems, most of which is over 4,000 metres above sea level. Broadly known as Xining fleece, this wool is famous for its strong, long, thick and lustrous fibres, with special qualities due to the high percentage of lanolin (Fig. 42). Historically, sheep as a species is not native to the plateau but were brought to the territory approximately four thousand years ago from more western areas where sheep were already being bred. Important for the quality of the fleece of Tibetan sheep is its natural ivory-tint which allows for clean and bright colouration when dyed, light shades in particular.

Also popular among Tibetan weavers is the very fine, silky and soft downy winter undercoat of a species of goat that also lives on the Qinghai plateau (Fig. 43).[13] Commonly known as cashmere wool, more technically correct is the term "hair", the undercoat being tremendously different from the goat's course outer coat. The high value of this fibre is determined by its high technical qualities (including light weight) and also by the fact that one animal provides only 110–170 grams of the precious down per year.

It is evident that both sheep wool and cashmere hair were used by producers of all types of Tibetan rugs, both in the warps and wefts, but especially in the pile yarns. It is impossible without a microscope to differentiate precisely between finer sheep wool and cashmere hair. Therefore, I can only make the logical supposition that objects with very fine, silky and soft pile must have been made with goat down pile, while pile of a slightly less silky and smooth surface is made of wool or other fibres, but not cashmere fibres (C119, Figs. 45a and 46; C145, Figs. 45b and 10). Accordingly, in the catalogue both fibres are called wool.

Cashmere fibres were also found in warps and wefts, primarily in the latter. It seems unlikely that the Tibetans would use expensive cashmere in the warps of their rather coarse rugs, where its special qualities would be wasted.[14]

Yak and camel hair are also found in Tibetan rugs, but in fewer instances. Domesticated in antiquity by the Tibetans

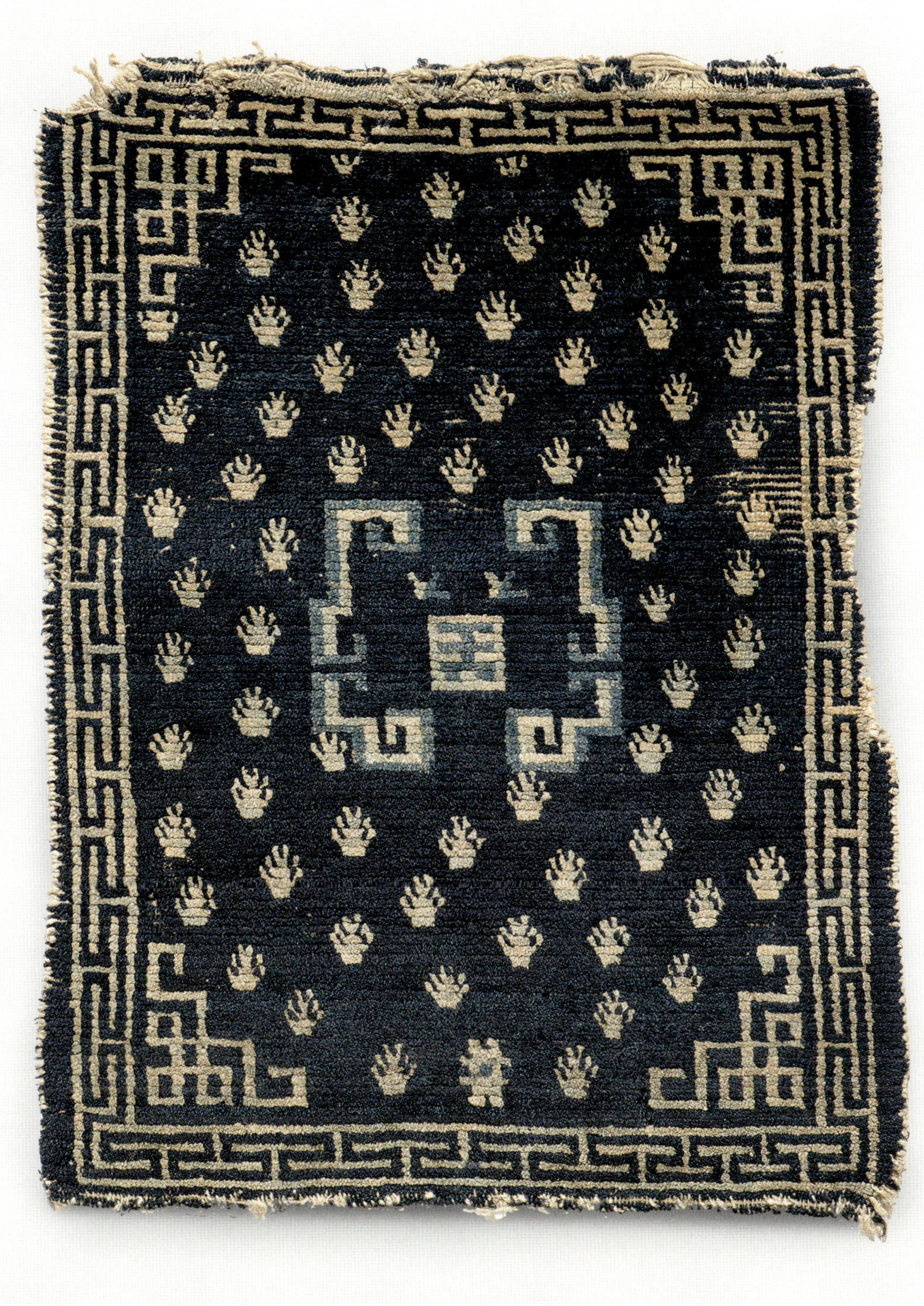

Fig. 41: C157. Sitting rug (*khagangma*) or over-saddle rug (*masho*). 20th c., 70×54 cm

Fig. 42: Herd of sheep in southern Central Tibet, 2004

Fig 43: Kashmir goats in eastern Central Tibet, 2002

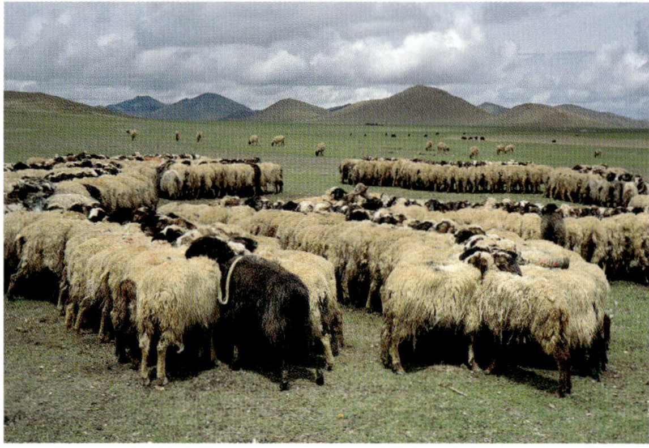

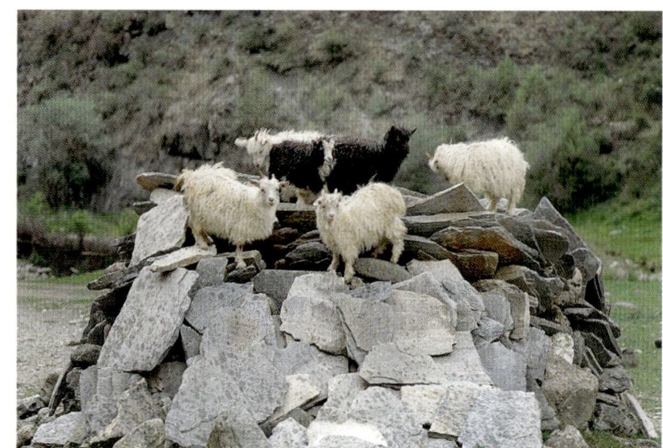

Fig. 44: C127. Over-saddle rug (*masho*) with lotus flowers. 19th c., 64 × 57 cm

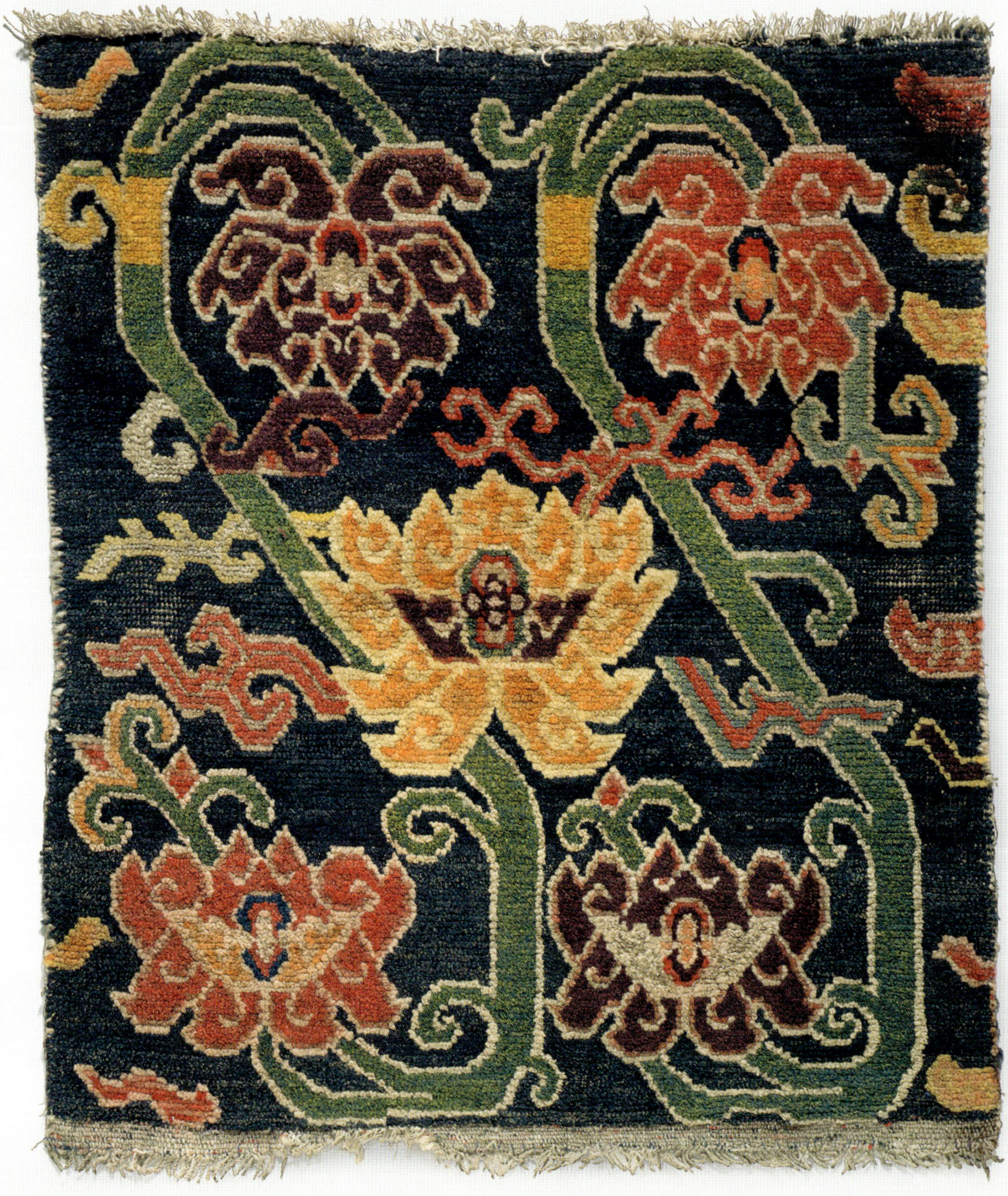

Figs. 45a and 45b: a) Detail of horse crupper rug (C119, see Fig. 46) with wool and camel hair pile, b) detail of a sitting and sleeping rug with extremely soft and silky pile, presumably cashmere fibre (C145, see also Fig.10)

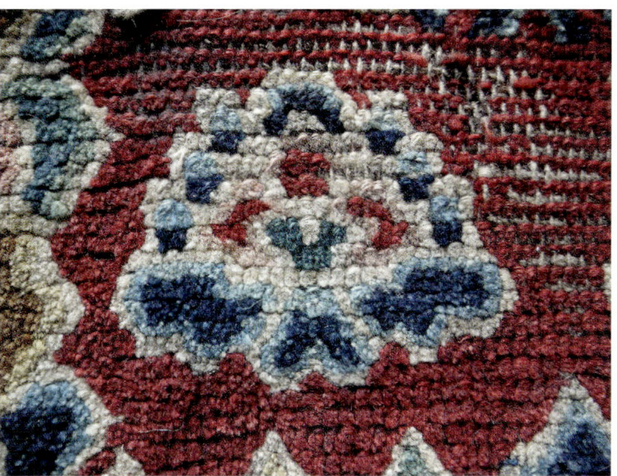

45a

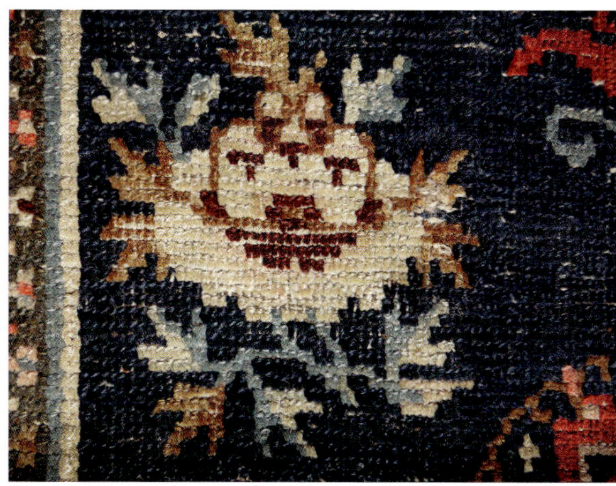

45b

Fig. 46: C119. Crupper rug. 19th c., 49 × 52 cm

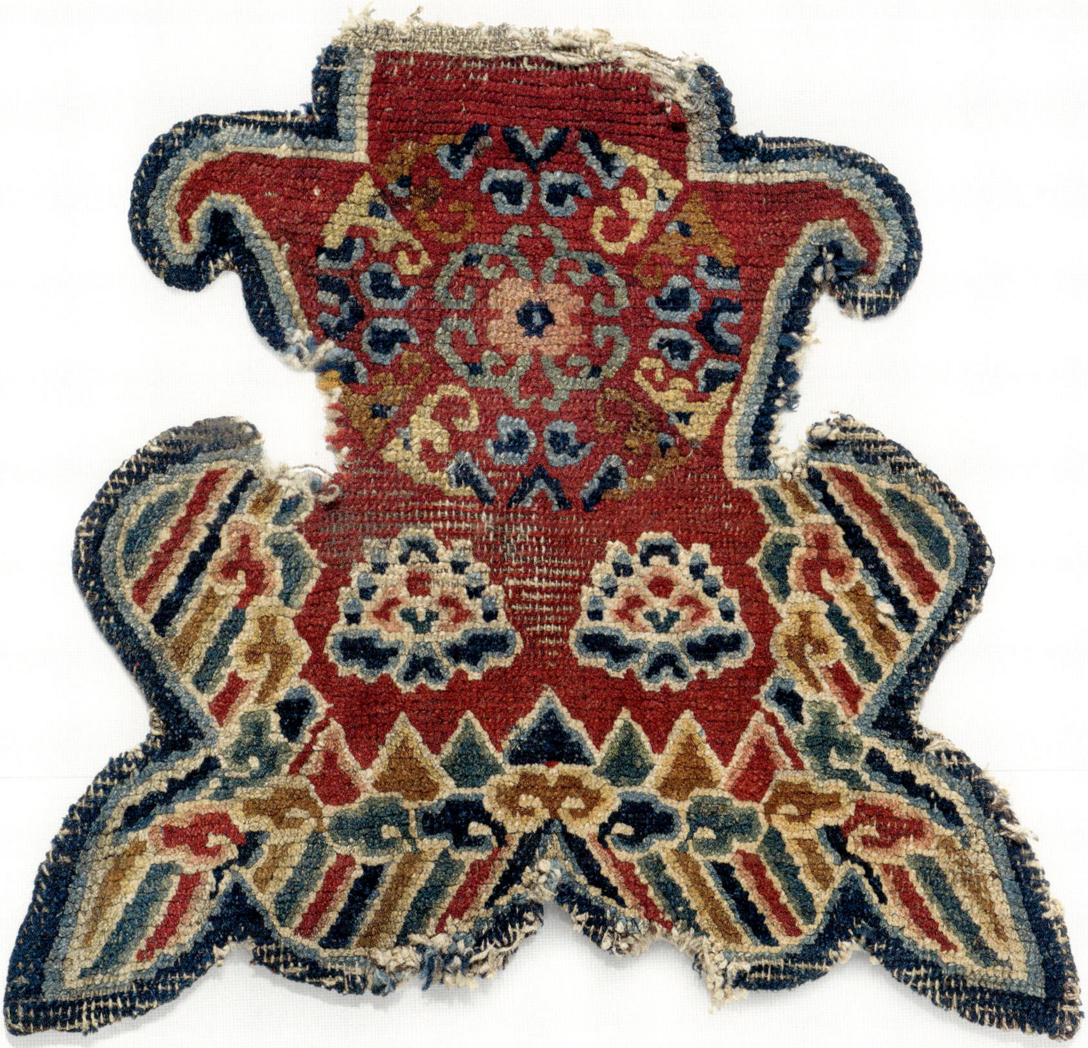

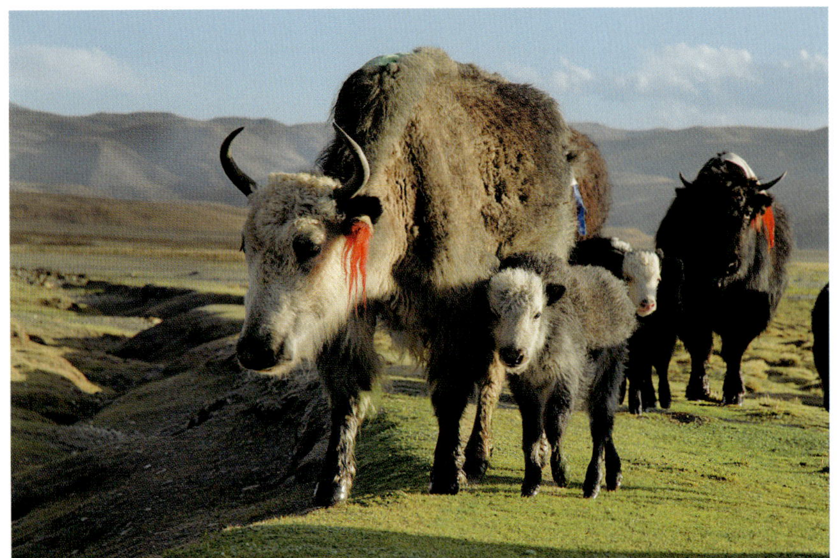

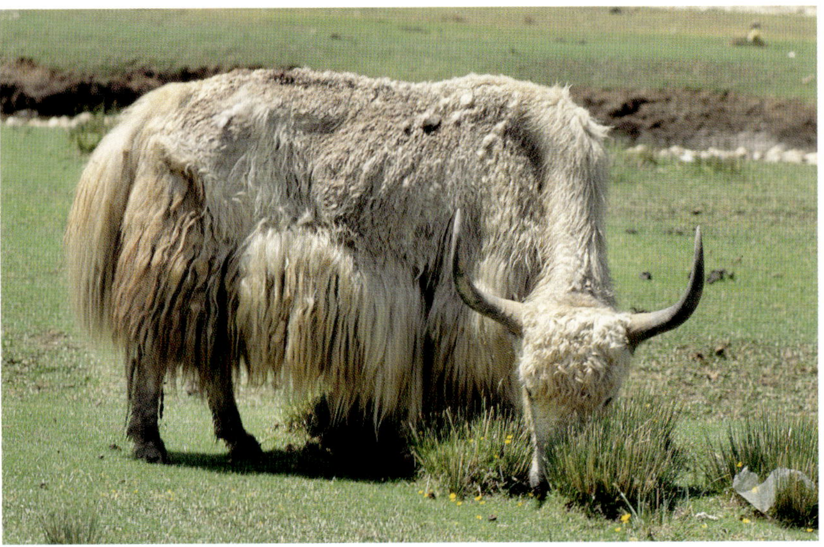

Fig. 47: Brown female yak (Tib. *'bri*) with calf, 2009

Fig. 48: White yak, 2004

(according to sources from the 1st millennium BC), yaks (*Bos mutus* or *Bos grunniens*) are native inhabitants of the over 4,000-metre Tibetan plateau (Figs. 47 and 48). Similar to goat fleece used in the textile industry, yak down is produced by the animal during the winter season and has to be collected the same way, by hand-combing (each yak individually), once a year, before the down is shed by the animal during late spring to early summer.

The coat of the yak is composed of three different types of fibre which vary greatly in appearance and technical characteristics. The top-rate undercoat is amazingly different in quality to the long coarse outer coat hairs, which give the yak its shaggy appearance. In between are the still strong and much longer fibres than the down mid-type heterotypical fibres, with a diameter size of between 20 and 50 microns.

Yarn made from yak down is now known as one of the most luxurious textile materials in the world, characteristic for comparatively long (3.4 to 3.5 cm) elastic and silky hair, and close in fineness and softness to cashmere (yak down: 16 to 24 microns; cashmere fibre: less than 18.5 microns). Different to the dark-coloured wild yaks, domesticated yaks have a wide range of coat shades, with some individuals being white or grey, some brown, roan or piebald.

The visual and tactile impression of yak fleece is confirmed by scientific research of the properties of yak fibres, which directly result from their special histological structures. One of these properties makes yak's undercoat fibres much lighter in weight than sheep wool, which explains the use of wild yak fleece for the production of long-pile rugs made with dense, thick yarn. If made from sheep wool, these yarns would be much heavier and thus more difficult to manage.

From the material in the collection we can conclude that yak fleece was mainly used – either pure or mixed with upper coat and/or wool – in all single-level *drumze* rugs: in warp yarns (C35, see Fig. 3 in the contribution by Wild; C49, see Fig. 5 in the contribution by Wild as well as Fig. 50b in this contribution; C77, see Fig. 8 in the contribution by Wild; C78, Fig. 49; C164, Fig. 33), but also as pure downy fibre in wefts (C77, C164) and in pile (C78). In the *tsuktruk* rugs, I only identified one item with yak down, notably in pile yarns used only for brown elements in the pattern (C163, Fig. 38).

Items in two-level structure occasionally show wild yak fibre in wefts (C82, see Fig. 5 in the contribution by De Jong; C102, Fig. 52; C117, see Fig. 4 in the contribution by Michael Buddeberg) and – rather often – in pile yarns, of mostly dark brown shades (C21, C34, C39, C46, C65, also C67, see Fig. 9 in the contribution by Wild). Yak fleece is mainly found in rural items, many with designs of exceptional artistic quality. One *khaden* (C154, Fig. 51) is an example of this: a minimalistic "cross and *swastika*" pattern with a very high quality weave, which is plain, so to speak honest, without any over-elaborated tricks in its structure (Fig. 50c). In numerous other cases, yak fibre is used mostly in non-ornamented outer stripes and as the background for inner "pearl" borders, which is of special importance for many cultures of both East and West.

Hopefully in the future, when investigated by improved, more precise technical methods, the number of rugs with colours other than brown-coloured yak fleece will be identified. Sheep wool as well as goat and yak down have an almost exactly identical natural colouring which makes it

Fig. 49: C78.
Wangden *drumze* rug
with *swastika* pattern.
Late 19th c. (?), 69×60 cm

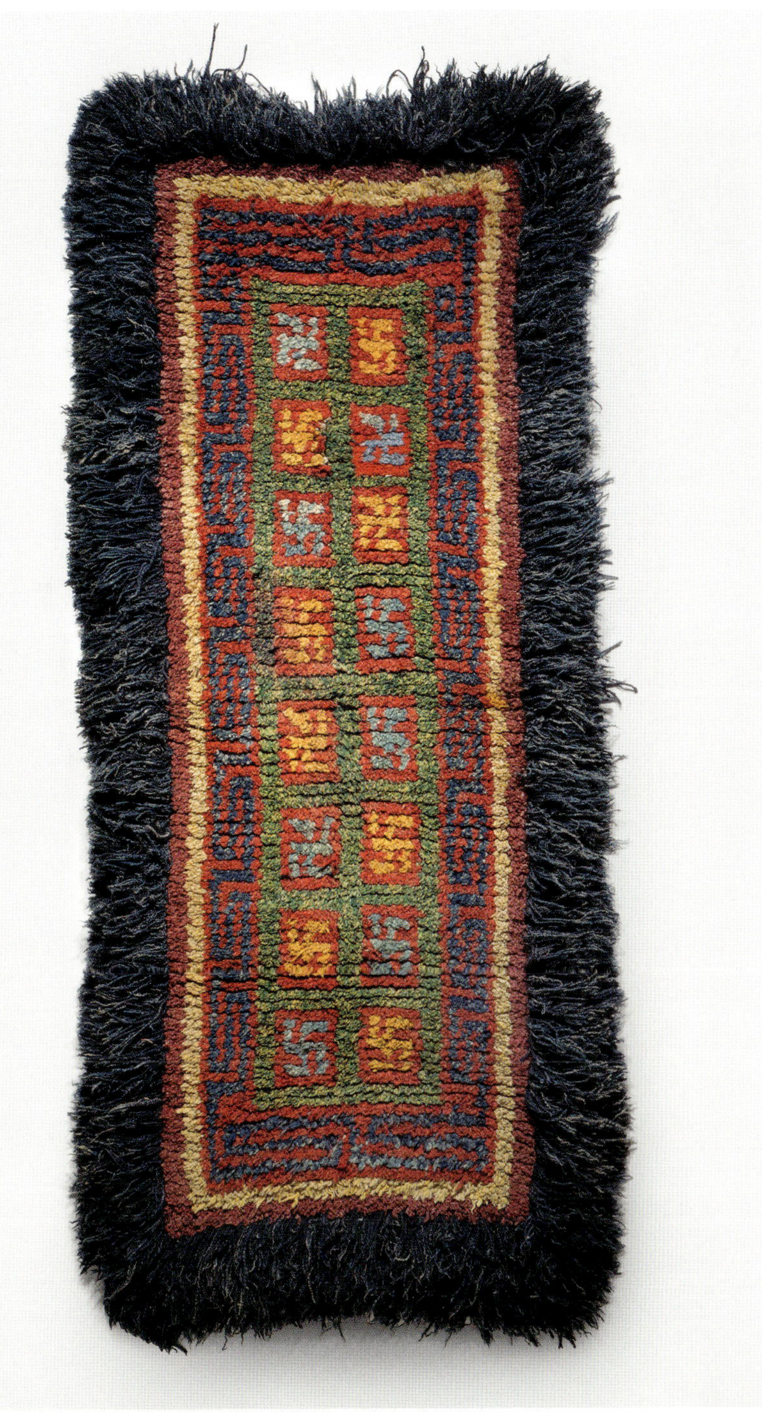

Figs. 50a to 50c:
a) and b) front and back of a *drumze* rug with warp yarns made from a mixture of yak middle and outer coat fibres (C49, see also Fig. 5 in the contribution by Wild), c) detail of a rug with yak hair pile (C154, see also Fig. 51)

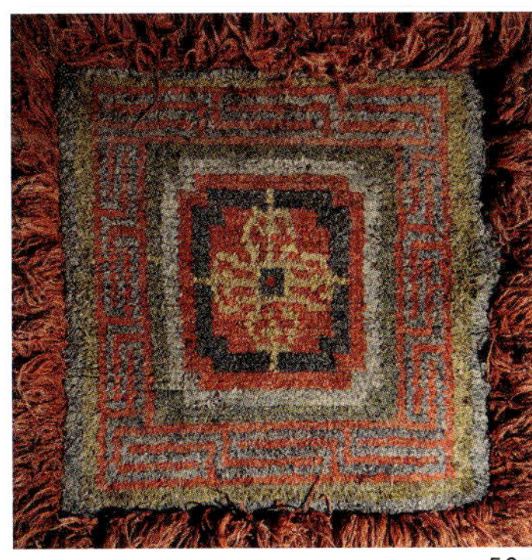

50a

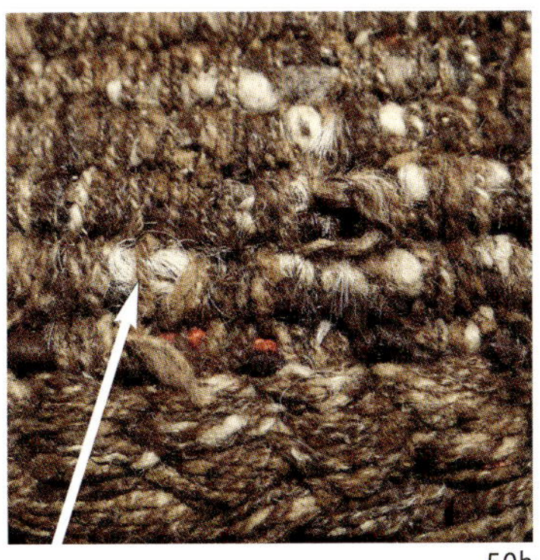

50b

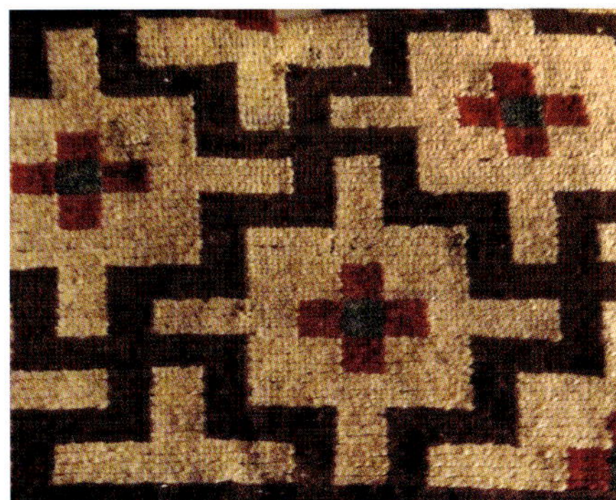

50c

Fig. 51: C154.
Sitting and sleeping rug (*khaden*) with a geometric pattern of crosses (*tigma*) in a *swastika* lattice.
Mid-19th c. (?),
140×87 cm

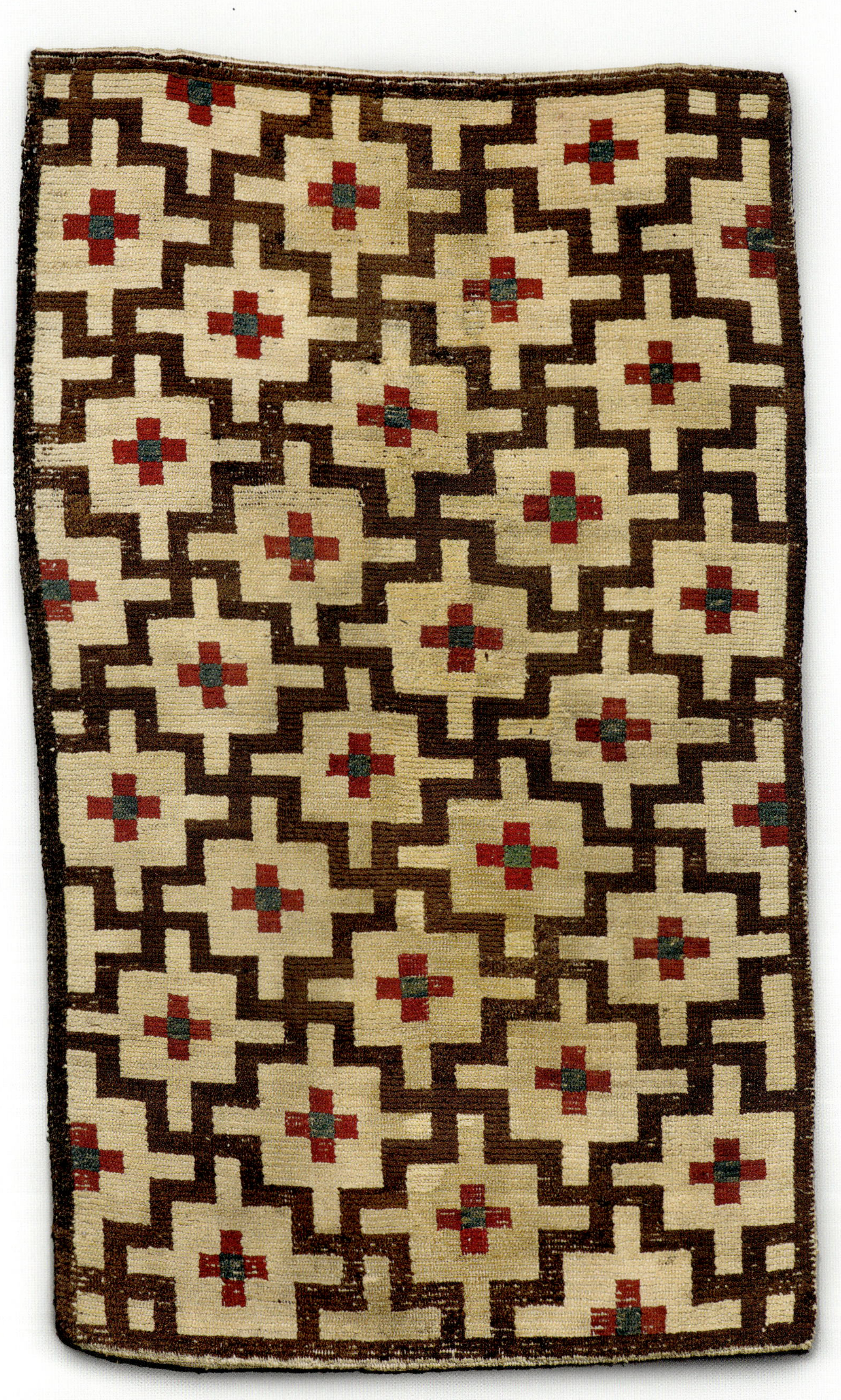

Fig. 52: C102.
Sitting rug (*khagangma*).
Around 1900, 68×54 cm

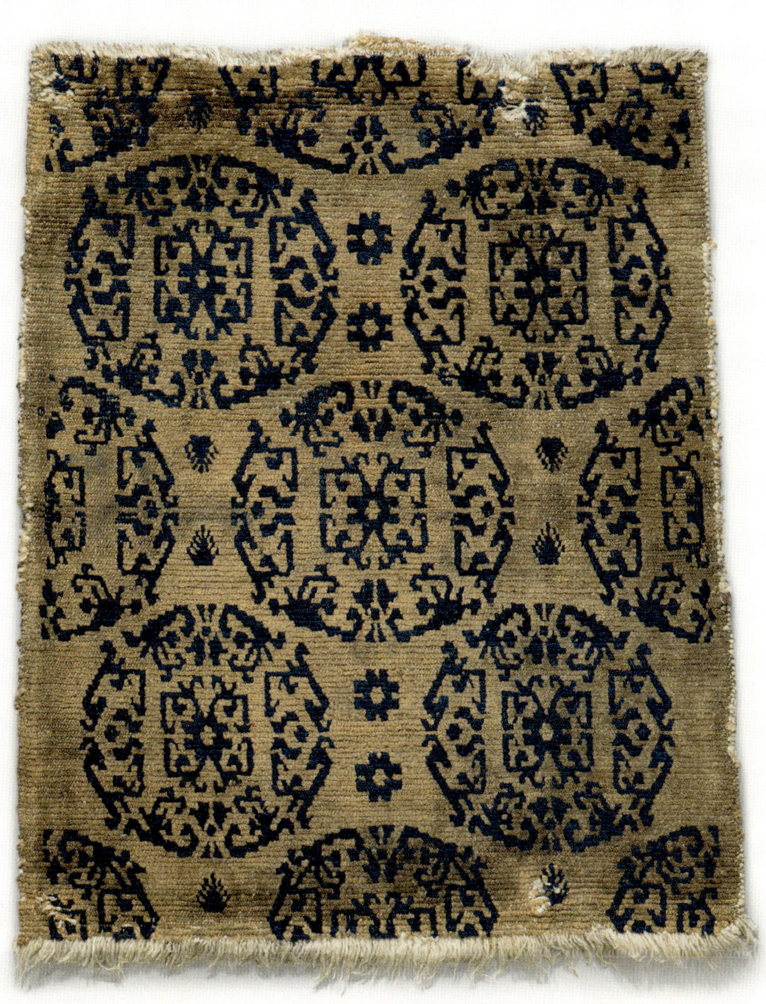

Fig. 53: C21.
Sitting or sleeping rug (*khaden*) with chessboard pattern.
Early 20th c., 149×81 cm

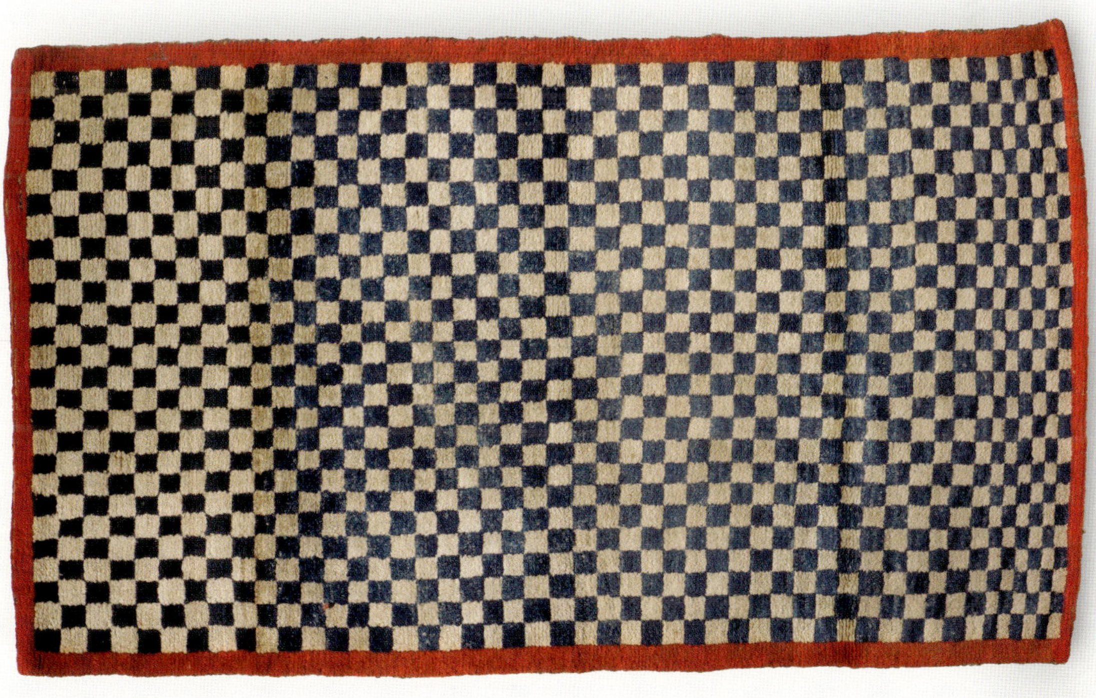

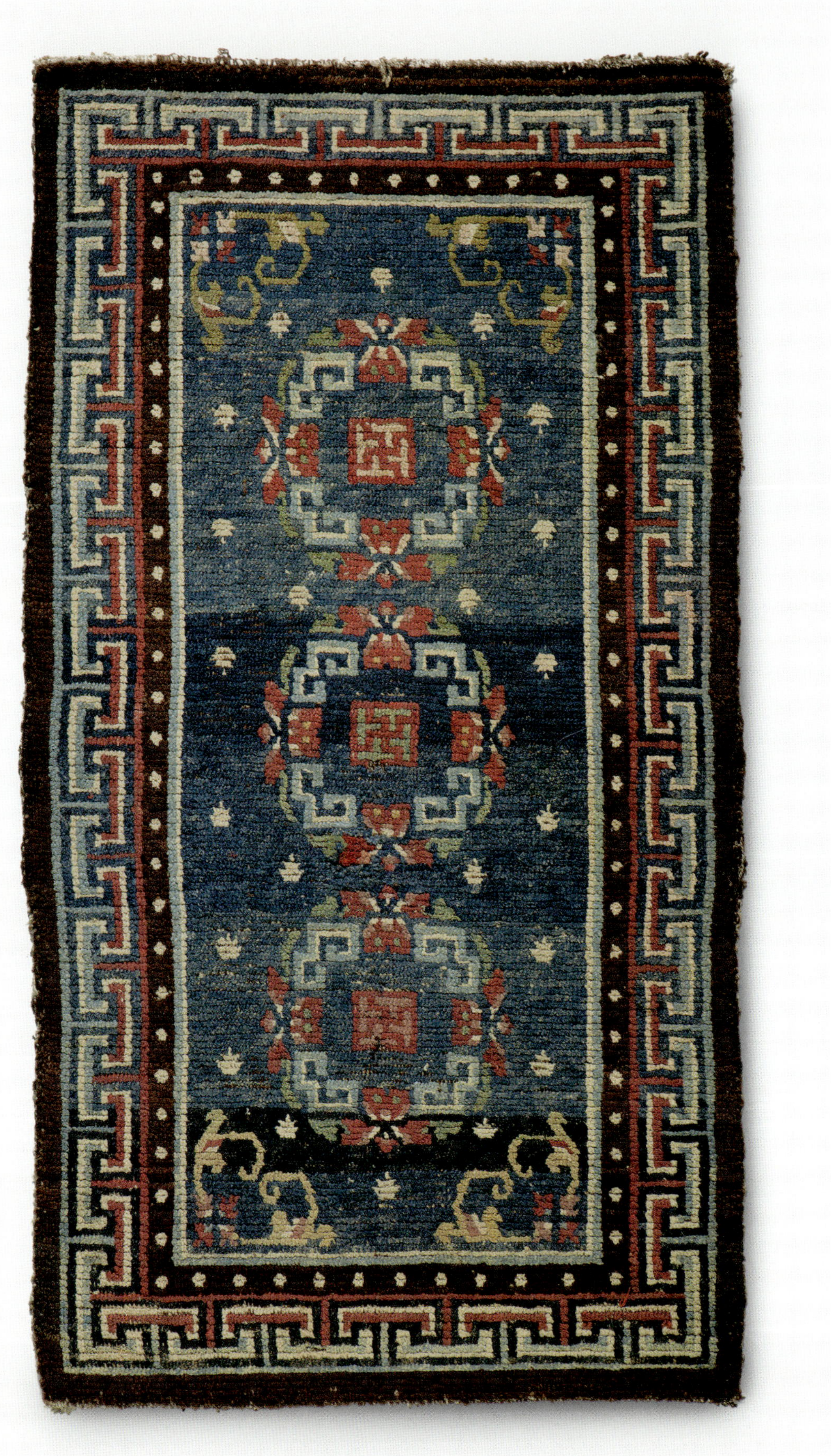

Fig. 54: C46.
Sitting and sleeping rug (*khaden*) with a classic field and border design. Mid-19th c. (?), 131×71 cm

Fig. 55: C65.
Sitting and sleeping rug (*khaden*). 2nd half 19th c., 110×66 cm

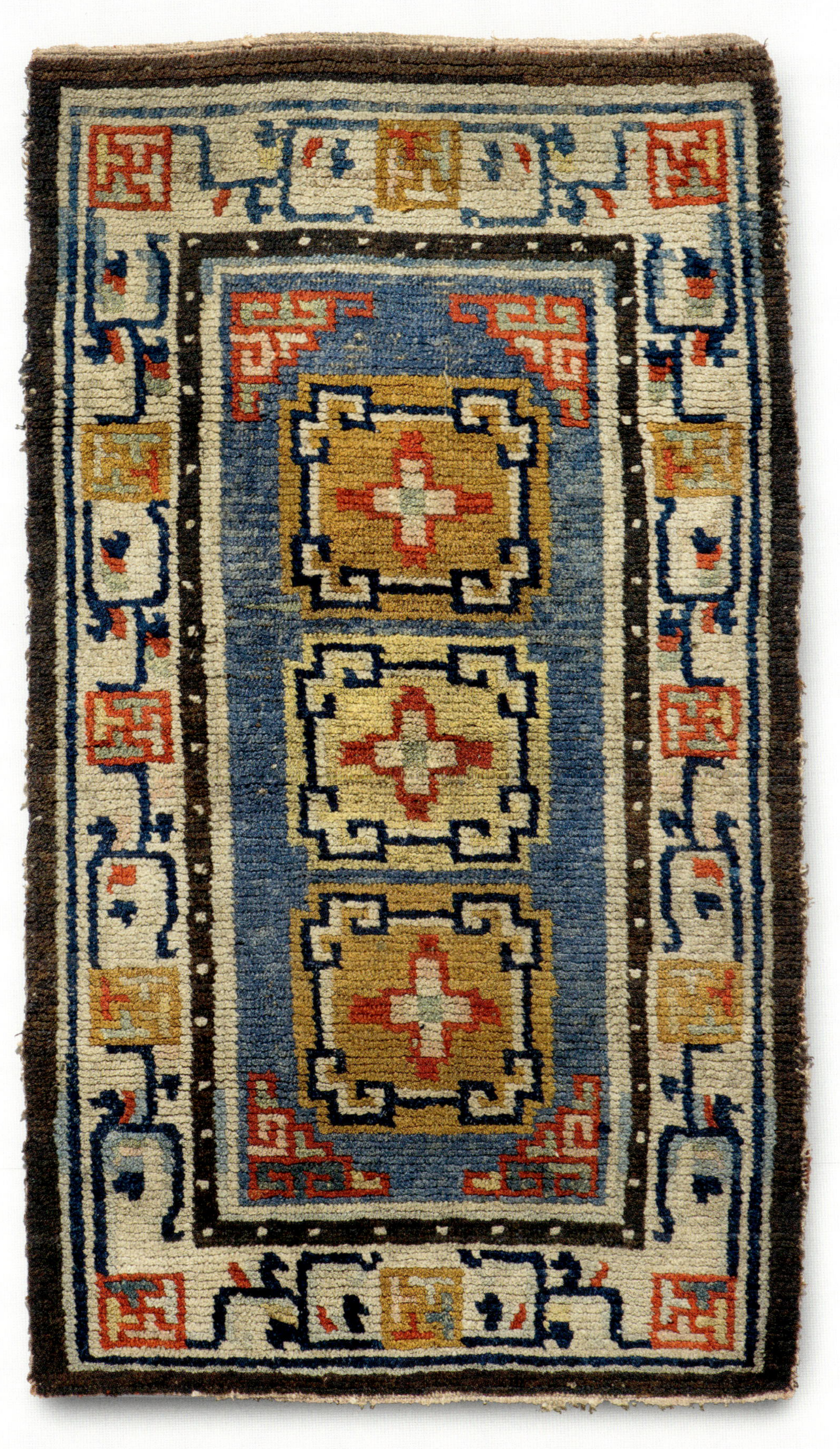

Figs. 56a to 56c:
a) Bactrian camel (*Camelus bactrianus* or *Camelus ferus*),
b) and c) crupper rug (C119, see Fig. 46) made of sheep wool in various shades of camel-down pile yarns

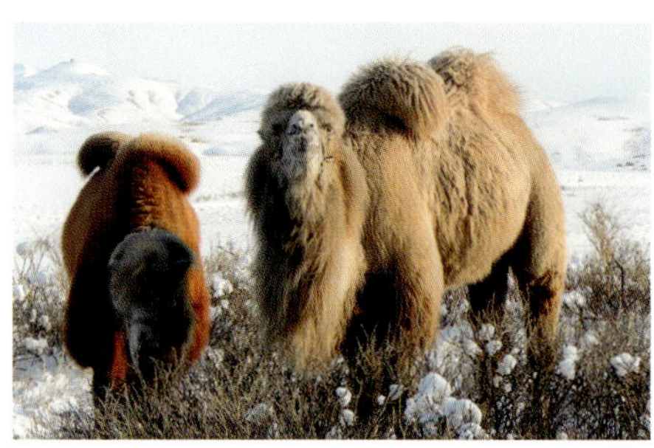
56a

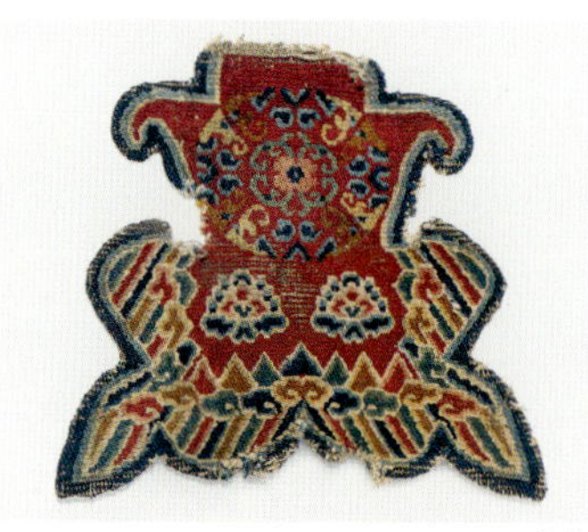
56b

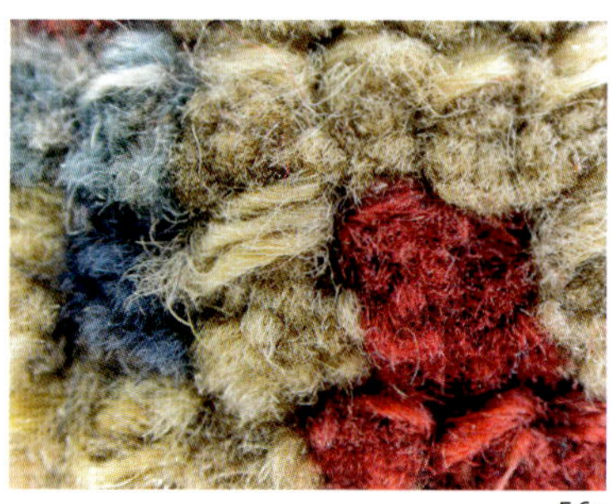
56c

difficult at the moment to identify them exactly, and the materials used in many questionable cases can only be named with the unspecific term "wool". Even taking special account of this fact, I assume that wild yak (*Bos mutus*) down was somehow avoided by regional rug weavers despite the quite amazing technical, artistic and ecological qualities of the fibre, and thus a substantial amount of fleece produced by the animals was never used.

The fourth animal fibre used in Tibetan rugs is camel hair from the Bactrian camel, which lives on the plateau and was domesticated in Central Asia around 2500 BC (Fig. 56a). Just as with goats and yaks, camels produce fibres of different natural shades from brown-black to ivory, and of different qualities. The most valuable undercoat is comparable in fineness to cashmere and yak down. What is different, however, is the volume of fleece produced. The undercoat makes 80 to 85 percent of the total volume produced by the animal and reaches four to nine kilograms of fibres annually per animal, potentially a lot of top-quality rug weaving material. Camels are not, however, generally domesticated in Tibet; hence I found rather few items with camel fibres in the collection.

I did identify camel hair for making wefts, sometimes in combination with wool (C78, Fig. 49). In other cases it makes the pile yarns of some exceptionally beautiful items, of special purpose, with three to five shades of soft naturally coloured camel hair adding charm to complicated eloquent patterns (Figs. 56b and 56c).

The only plant fibre native to the Tibetan plateau that I found in rugs was hemp, one of the most archaic and still used textile materials wherever it is grown (Fig. 57a). In the collection it was identified in two items. The first is an early *khagangma* (C39), notable for Z2S plied warp and weft yarns of hemp and ivory-coloured wool (Figs. 57b and 58). The second, a *makden* (C87) of a very special type, has identical Z2S structures of pure hemp wefts (Fig. 57C; see also Fig. 18). Thanks to some early representations of identical oval-shaped items with tiger-skin pattern, the piece makes one of the most interesting rugs in the collection; with hemp fibre wefts adding to its historical importance.

Cotton (Fig. 59a) is the other plant fibre found in the collection's pile weavings, indeed, in forty-one (more than one third) of the two-level items (Fig. 61, C160), but in only one single-level item (*tsuktruk*, Fig. 64, C85). Cotton (*Gossypium*), unlike hemp, is not native to Tibet and was only introduced thousands of years later. The plant is supposed to be a traditionally cultivated crop in southern Tibet where the climate is warm enough to grow not only cotton but also rice. Although cotton is grown in all of Tibet's neighbouring countries, it seems most logical that, like Buddhism, it was introduced from India.

The often expressed opinion is that Tibetan rug makers started to use cotton fibres in the late 19th century. I have doubts about this statement, considering it is only correct for single-level weavings. My doubts come from the observation that I found cotton in only one of the eighteen *drumze* and *tsuktruk* items in the collection, namely in the warps of the very late *tsuktruk* C85. On the other hand, cotton was identified in the warps of several supposedly early 19th-century pieces (C12 and C41) and many mid-century items.

Summarising, it is possible to say that in general animal fibres were preferred – quite expectedly – both by the rural and urban populations of the country, especially concerning weavers in the eastern and northern parts of the country, and for all producers of single-level rugs, no matter whether of domestic or monastic manufacture. Another observation evidences that professional workshops started to use cotton for warps rather early (we can definitely speak about the beginning of the 19th century, latest). Also, it is quite possible to assume that otherwise excellent hemp fibre was substituted with time by easier to process cotton, although this last supposition is pure speculation, based only on recognition of the historical role of hemp in the development of textile technologies of the Asian continent and beyond.

Figs. 57a to 57c:
a) Wild hemp,
b) detail of sitting rug C39 with warps on wefts of plied threads of hemp and wool fibres,
c) macro photograph of hemp-made weft yarns (C87, see Fig. 18)

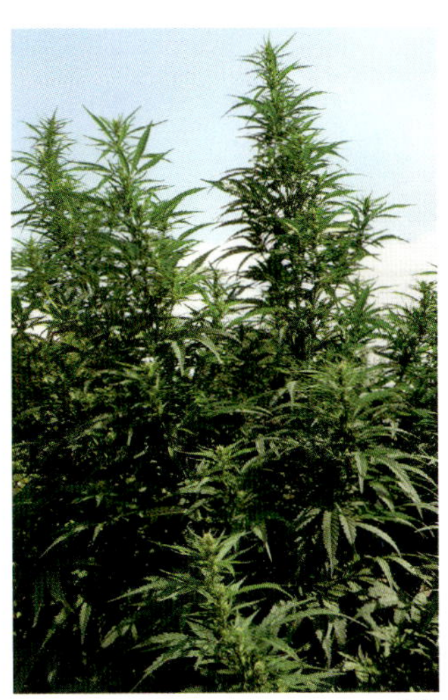

57a

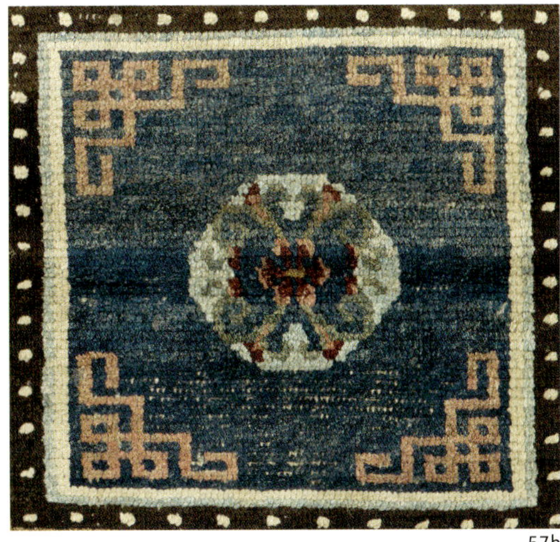

57b

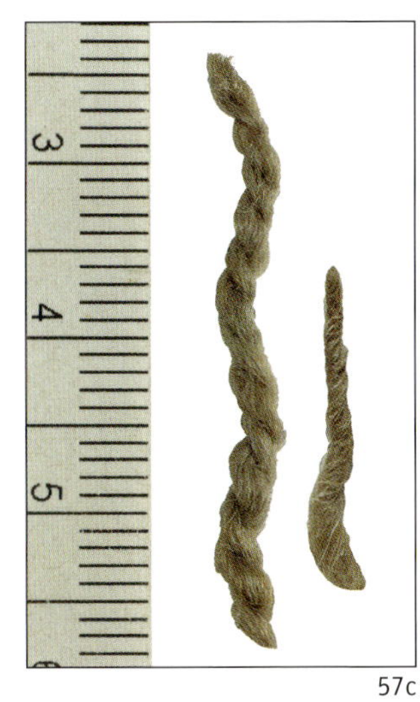

57c

Fig. 58: C39.
Sitting rug (*khagangma*).
19th c., 67.5×72.5 cm

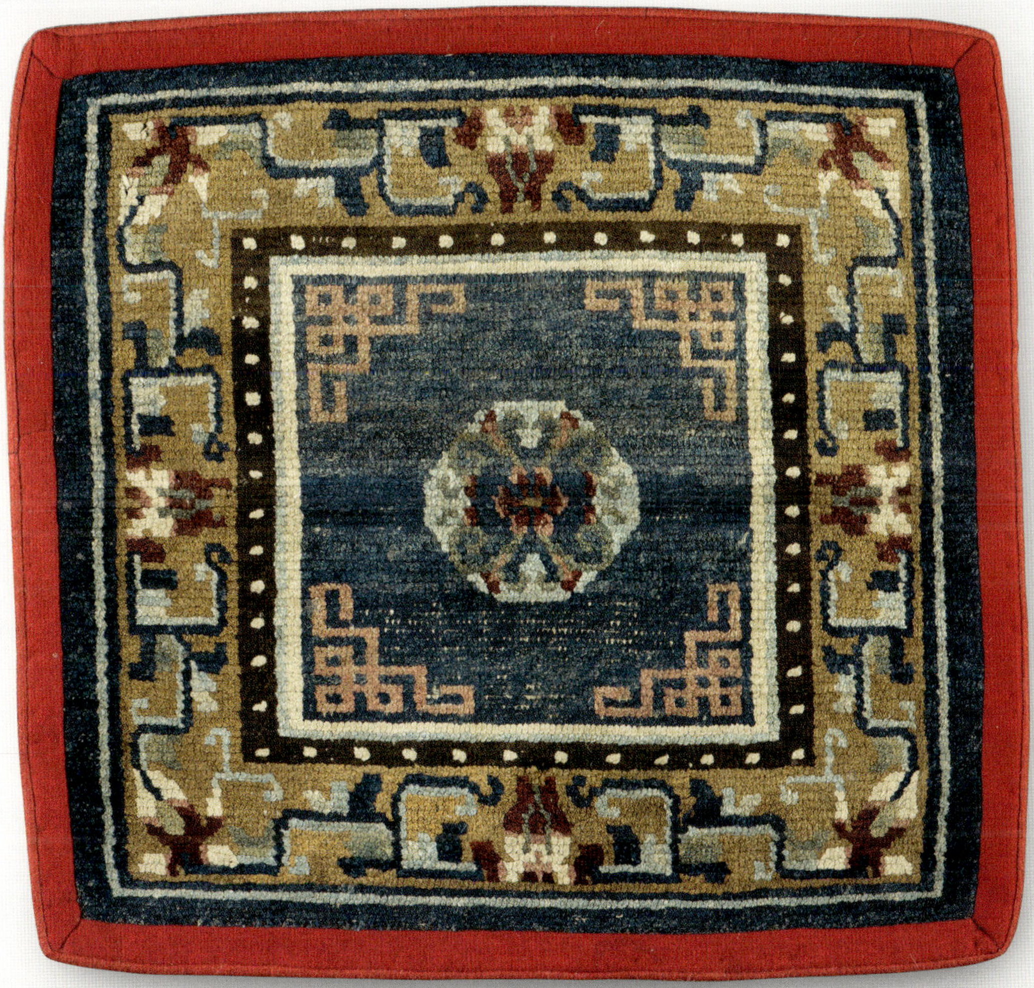

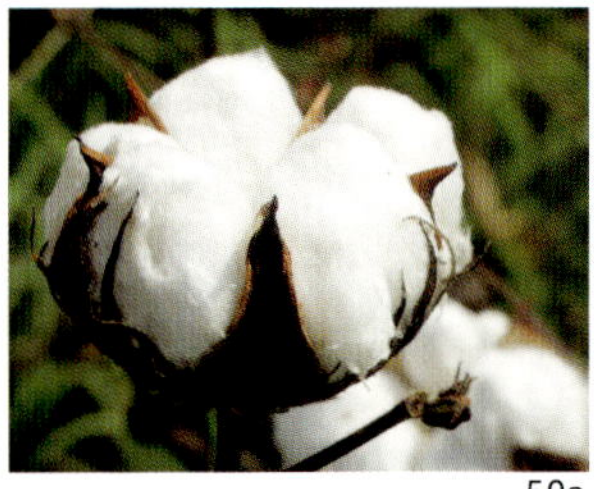
59a

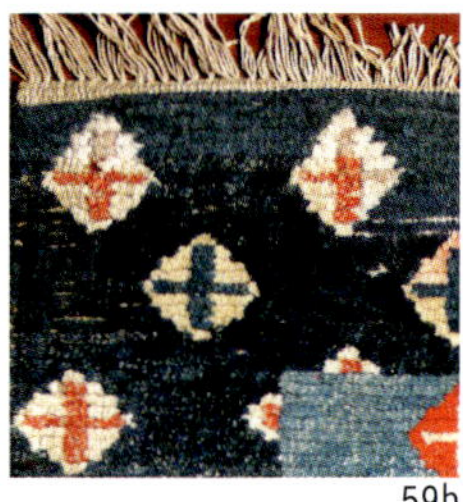
59b

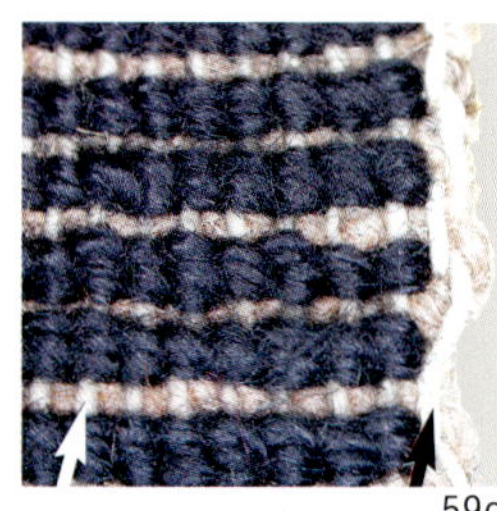
59c

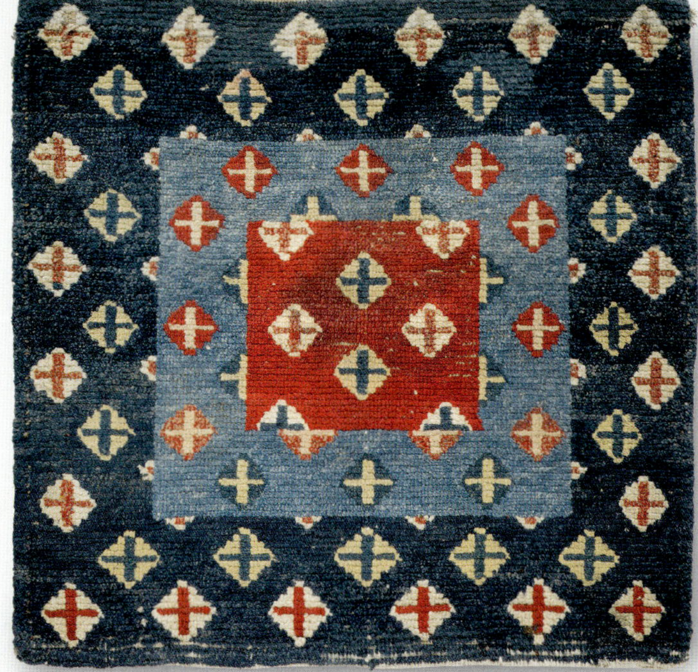

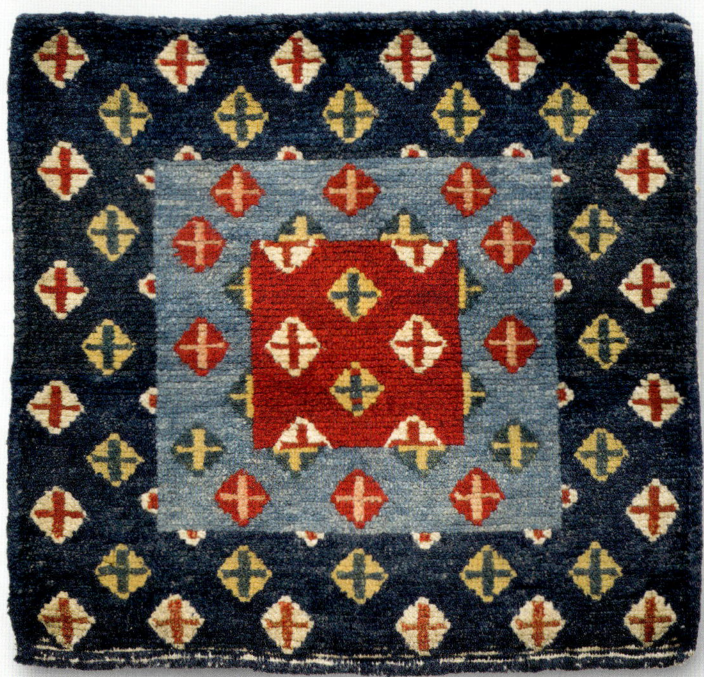

Thread-Making System

Pile weavings from the collection of Justyna and Michael Buddeberg demonstrate that Tibetans consistently prefer the spinning method that produces elementary Z-spun threads (Fig. 62b). In case of technical need, this primary form is followed either by combining several elementary threads (Z2, Z3, Z4, etc.) or their plying (Z2S, Z3S, Z2S2, etc.: Fig. 62c). In any case, the preferred method works independently of the yarns' material and their location in rugs' structures. Exceptions to this Tibetan tradition are the thick and loose threads which are twisted just with fingers, without a spindle, and also intriguing examples of S-spun yarns.

S-spinning (Fig. 62a) is not unique for textile industries of the modern world; it is enough to remember the millennia-long Egyptian/Coptic tradition, for example. Still the manner is a rare guest on the spaces of Eurasia. In territories geographically close to the Tibetan plateau, for instance, we find it in archaeological rugs of the Tarim Basin,[15] in the Imperial carpets' group of China (Tsareva 2005: 194–195), and in early piled rugs and tapestries of supposedly Uyghur origin (Gonick 2015: 141, Fig. 119) which demonstrate peculiarities in style and technique. The question of tracing the roots of this practice on Central Asian soil is still open, and despite the extremely precise and interesting investigation of Gloria Gonick, there is still no chance that we will be able to find a reliably proven connection in the near future, although from what we see it is clear that there should be a relation.

Seen historically, the very loose handmade yarns are likely to have come from the earliest use of animal fibres from the "pre-spindle" era. As soon as spindle whorls evidence the presence of spindles in the Near East and South Turkmenistan in the late Neolithic, the "pre-spindle" era should stretch into the Upper Palaeolithic time at least.[16] An amazing fact that illustrates the near immortality of textile technique is that the method was discovered in the Bronze Age (Sumer, Elam and others of the Bactria-Margiana Archaeological Complex [BMAC] of Southern Turkmenistan and Uzbekistan) for making pile yarns.[17] The structure was very exactly named by Mary Houston "tufted material" (Houston 1920: 110, Figs. 111 and 112), suggesting the "tufted" yarns have no or only very loose twist.

In geographically close territories, we identify these kinds of yarns in a number of the Tarim Basin archaeological findings, both as wefts and *padding loops* (Fig. 62d). At present, the technique is still used by some shepherding

Figs. 59a to 59c
(see page 102):
a) Cotton bolls,
b) cotton fibre warp yarn loops of the bottom end of a rug, detail of C33 (see Fig. 60),
c) cotton fibre warps and side finish yarns, detail of C96

Fig. 60 (see page 102):
C33 and C126.
Pair of sitting rugs (*khagangma*) with *tigma* motifs on three different-coloured backgrounds. 19th c., 62 × 65 and 61 × 64 cm

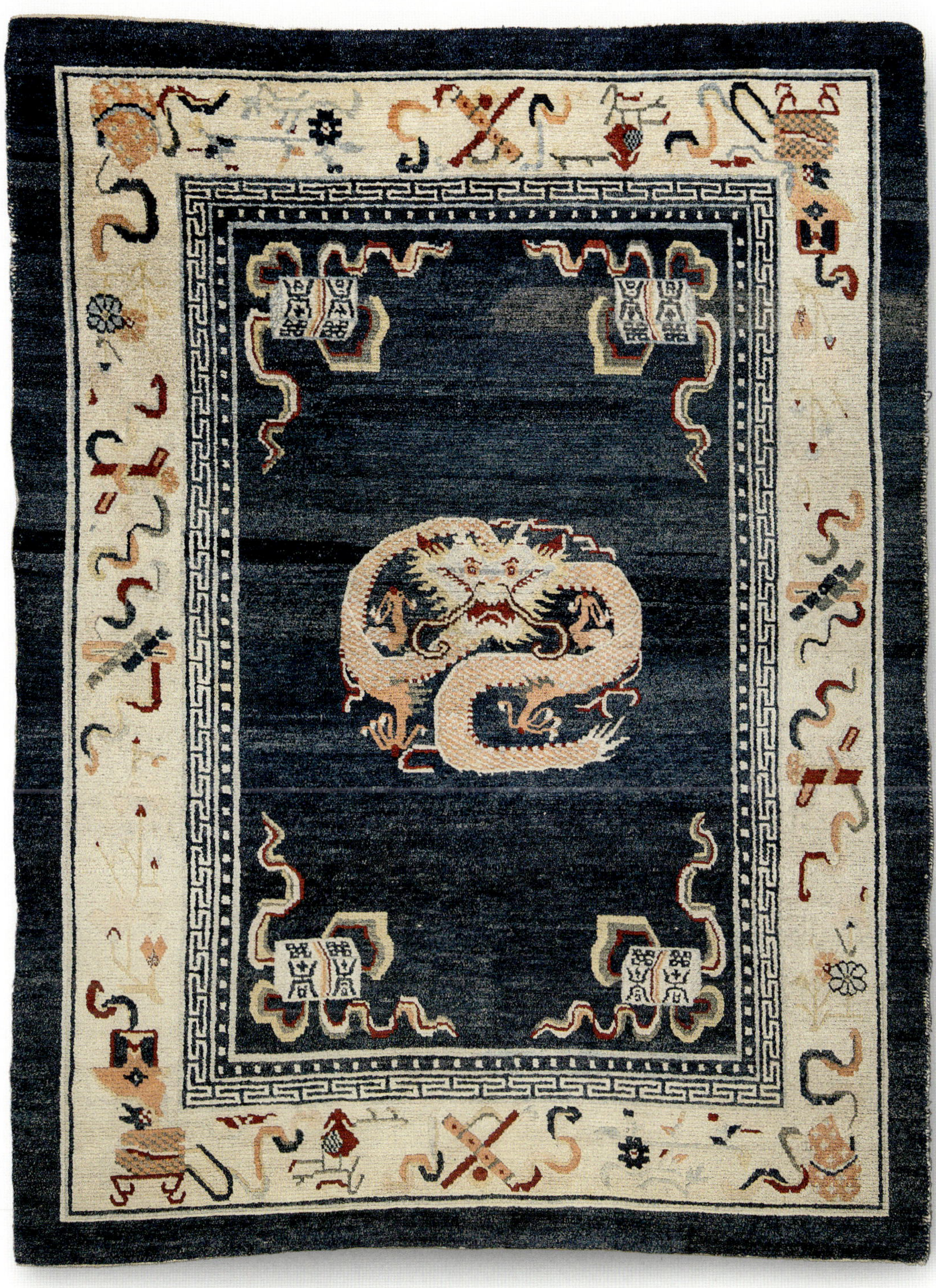

Fig. 61: C160.
Floor rug (*sabden*) with unusual dragon medallion.
Around 1900, 242 × 180 cm

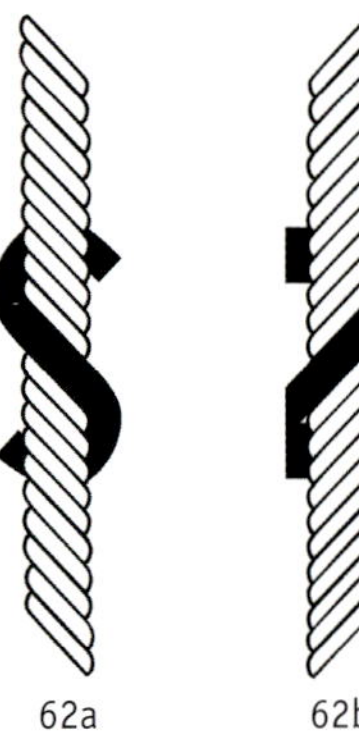

62a

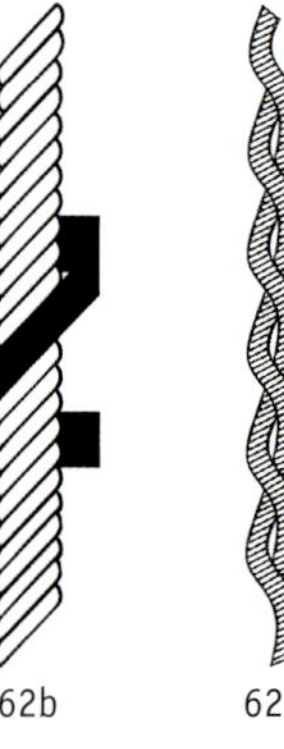

62b

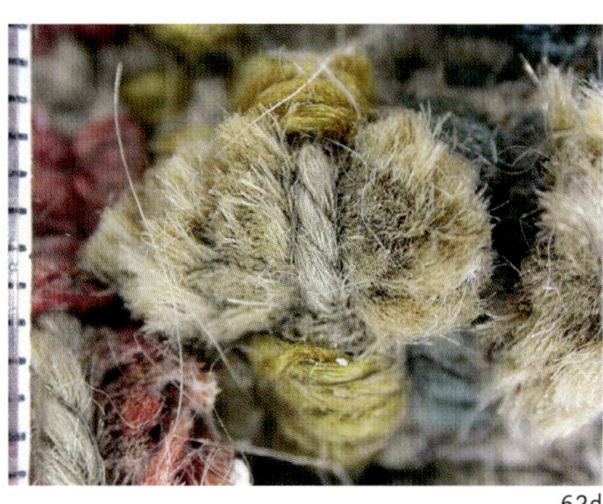

62c

62d

Figs. 62a to 62d: Different types of spinning and plying methods used by Tibetans: a) S-spun yarn, b) Z-spun yarn, c) Z2S plied yarn, d) detail of Tarim Basin rug. China, Han Dynasty

cultures of the Balkans and Carpathian region, Asia Minor, and some once purely nomadic populations in the Eurasian Steppe Corridor, and beyond.

My friend Tatyana Taushan[18] described to me the technique she observed at a spinning workshop in the vicinity of one of the Lhasa-area monasteries. The whole process looked like a precisely developed ritual, performed by two groups of spinners: some sitting, others standing. A group of fibres was twisted between the palms of the first participant, who passed it to the second person in the line to repeat the motion, and so on back and forth until the yarn was ready.

Warps

The warps of Tibetan pile weavings, like those everywhere else, experience tension and the strain of the weft- and pile-making, and hence must be hard-wearing. As a rule, Tibetan warps are spun yarns reinforced by plying, less often by summation, and are made of strong durable materials. The latter, as mentioned, firstly include sheep wool and cotton, other variants are represented by yak down, hemp, and their combinations, with animal fibres of preferably a natural ivory colour or a mix of materials in light shades (including dirty blue C89, Fig. 20).

The warps of two-level rugs are almost always a Z2S construction of animal and hemp fibres, but we also find Z3S plying (Fig. 63, C115). Cotton warps show much greater variety in Z?S structure, the question mark pointing to an unrecognised number of elementary Z-spun threads in the final plied product. Also found were single instances of Z2, Z3, Z4 and Z4S warps. In weavings with the "additional warp" trick, these are always identical to the basic warps (C20, see Fig. 4 in the contribution by De Jong; C36, see Fig. 11 in the contribution by De Jong; C89, Fig. 20; C101), as clearly displayed in Fig. 21a (C89).

The differences between the *drumze* and the *tsuktruk* single-level methods of looping and their materials was explained in the section "Single-Level Looping Techniques" in the chapter "Basic Structures and Structural Peculiarities of Tibetan Rugs". This difference is also evident in their wefts. The *drumze* type of wool and yak fibre warps show preference for the Z2S tradition. Two sub-variants, with Z2S2 (C49, see Fig. 5 in the contribution by Wild) and Z4 (C77, see Fig. 8 in the contribution by Wild) both follow the Z-spinning trend and are in the framework of the thread-making tradition common to the country.

Producers of the loosely woven and elastic *tsuktruk* rugs developed more exotic and less uniform devices. The minority of studied items follow the inherent for Tibet Z2 and Z2S spin and ply (C61, see Fig. 4 in the contribution by Darchen; C85, Fig. 64; C93, see Fig. 5 in the contribution by Darchen; C100, Fig. 65), whereas the majority (82 percent) give preference to S1–S2, and S10 and S2Z structures.

Cotton, much finer and less elastic than wool, when used for making warps of natural white/ivory colour, usually gets multiple plying; with so numerous and tightly Z-spun elementary yarns one cannot identify the number in the thick structure of Tibetan rugs, especially when the back is covered by trimming and lining. In such items, it was only possible to identify Z-spinning and S-plying, marked in the catalogue as Z?S. In rugs without trimming, warp threads show clearly Z2S (C126, Fig. 60), Z3S (C59, Fig. 66; C83, see Fig. 7 in the contribution by De Jong), or Z4S construction (C117, C124).

Variation in the strength of warps as a load-bearing element of a rug's "anatomy" is determined by the structure and density of items, which depend on a variety of implicit and explicit features. Thus items with simple large-format patterns usually have long pile and heavy texture, which calls for strong, thick warps. On the other hand, pieces with elaborated and delicate décor require fine structure and, inevitably, thin and smooth warp yarns.

The difficulty of defining the density of Tibetan pile weavings has been explained, so that instead of trying to count loops, many of which overlap, the number of warps and wefts per decimetre is given.

In two-level Tibetan rugs, the highest warp density (both for cotton and woollen yarns) is 90 to 100 warps per decimetre. This high density is found in professionally woven late 19th to early 20th century items, while in rural works of the same age it seldom exceeds 60 warps per decimetre. Older rugs tend to have lower densities, even those from exclusive monastic workshops, which seldom exceed 80 to 90 warps per decimetre. Generally it could be observed that the larger an item is, the lower its density is (although, as always, there are exceptions).

In single-level *drumze* the range of warp density is even higher: from 44 warps/decimetre in a 19th-century *khagang-ma* of nomadic work (C35, see Fig. 3 in the contribution by Wild) to 123 to 124 warps/decimetre in a made-to-order and younger *masho* over-saddle rug (C77, see Fig. 8 in the contribution by Wild). Quite expectedly, the middle figures lie between 56 to 68 warps/decimetre. The situation is similar with the *tsuktruks*, with 24 (C95, Fig. 67) and 61 warps/decimetre (C86) as the extreme figures, and 41 to 56 warps/decimetre (C163, Fig. 38; C123, see Fig. 8 in the contribution by Darchen) as average numbers. As with the items with two-level warps, the warp densities of both groups with single-level warps seem to vary with age, origin and size of the items.

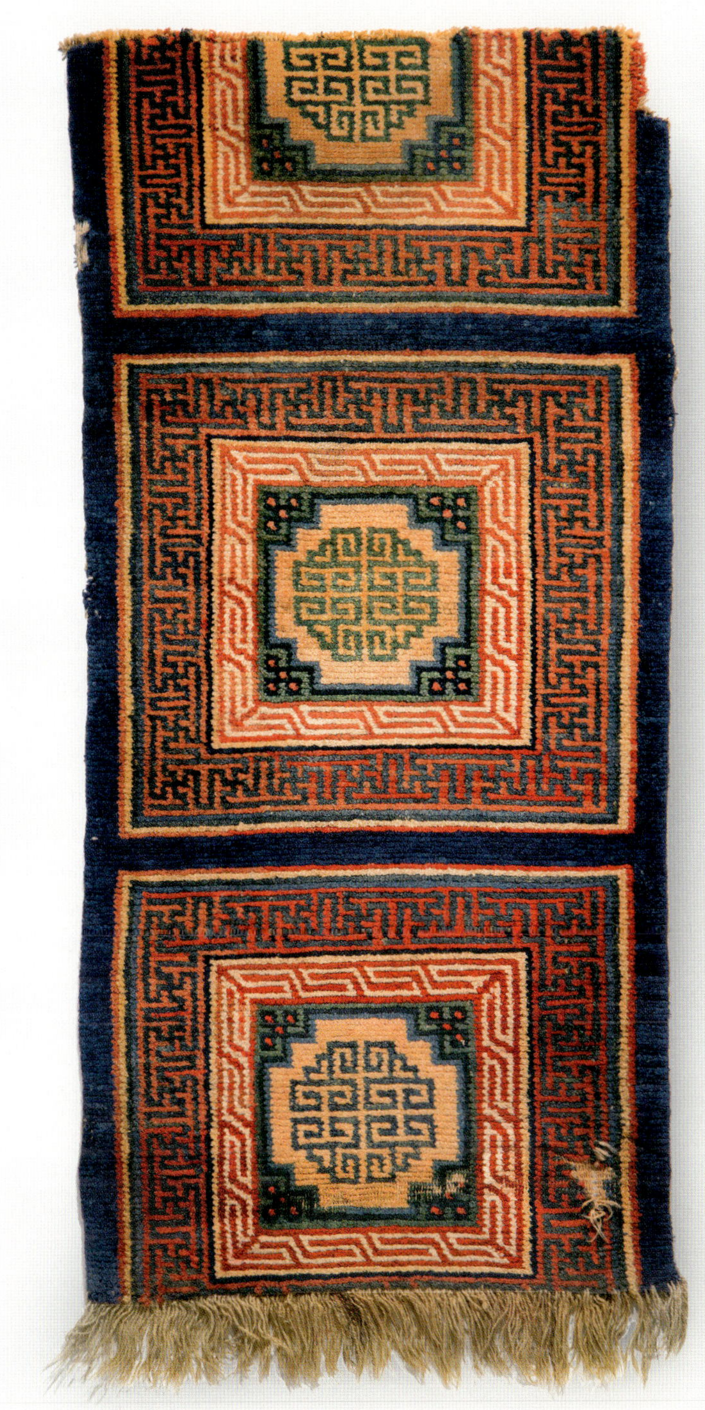

Fig. 63: C115. Fragment of a multi-part temple seat with geometric pattern. Early 20th c. (?), 165×77 cm

Wefts

Wefts interweave with the warps to form the fabric of every woven textile. In pile weavings they also function to lock the loops/knots into the texture of the item. In Tibetan rugs with the *eccentric-weft* trick, they also supplement the pile, also – special for Tibet – the very short one. Both devices are discussed in the sections "Two-Level Weavings" and "Main Regular and Irregular Structural Peculiarities" in the chapter "Basic Structures and Structural Peculiarities of Tibetan Rugs".

As shown by the details of rugs (Figs. 68a to 68f), there is no strict rule to limit the colour, material and even the number of shoots of wefts in one and the same item. Although undyed wool in all its shades is by far the most common material, the wefts of other pieces also included bits of dyed yarns, as well as plied wefts combining one thread of sheep wool and one of yak fleece (C32, Fig. 12). In the catalogue, this is defined for individual items (e.g., C113, C125, and C148).

In the great majority of items under study, including two-level rugs and single-level *drumze*, we see two *parallel wefts* in a unit interlaced through an unchanged warp shed. Some weavers were consistent in using only one shoot of weft, others even using three shoots in a unit, while a very few did not follow any consistent system, using from one to four shoots in a unit in the weaving of a single item (C87, Fig. 18; C102, Fig. 52). Items of exclusive quality and décor do generally show a single weft, more so in pieces with a

Fig. 64: C85.
Tsuktruk rug made of
two panels with
a tiger-skin design.
20th c., 141×61.5 cm

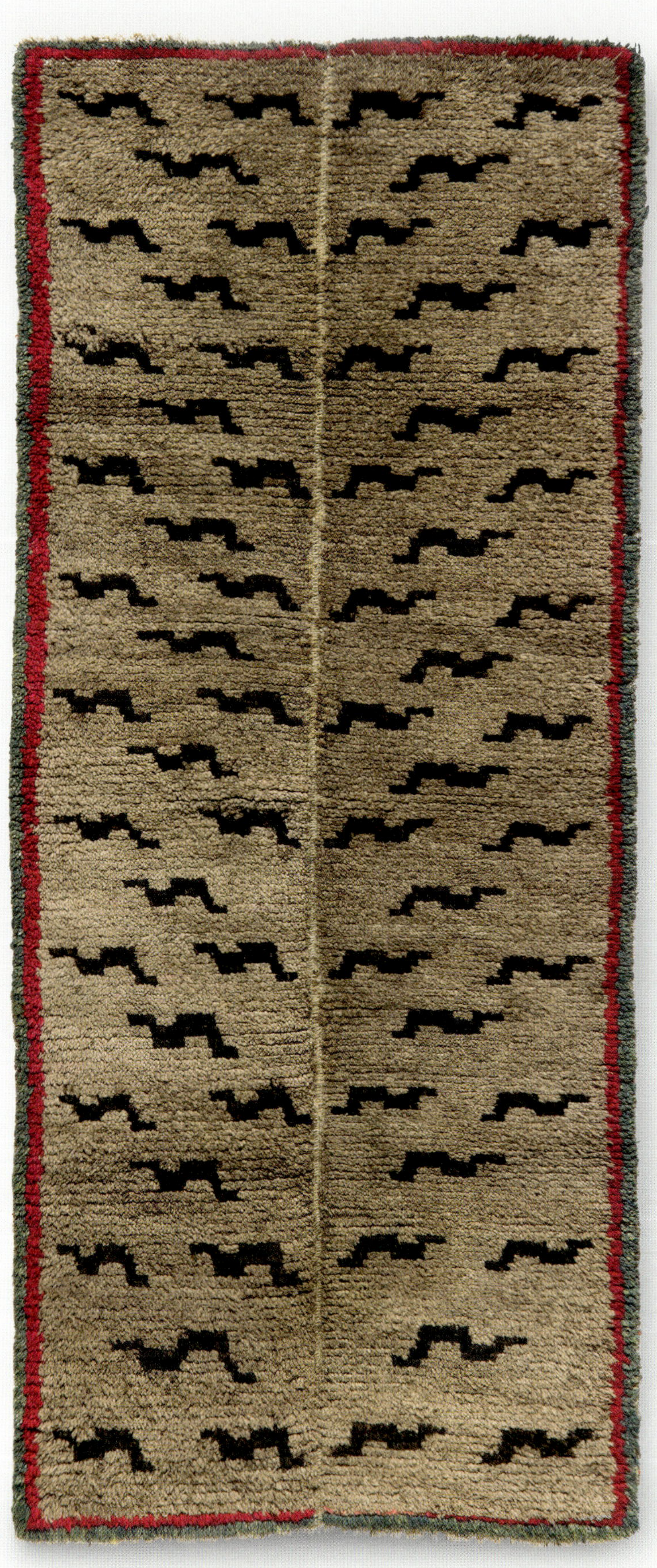

Fig. 65: C100.
Tsuktruk rug made of three panels with chessboard pattern. Late 19th/ early 20th c., 179×74 cm

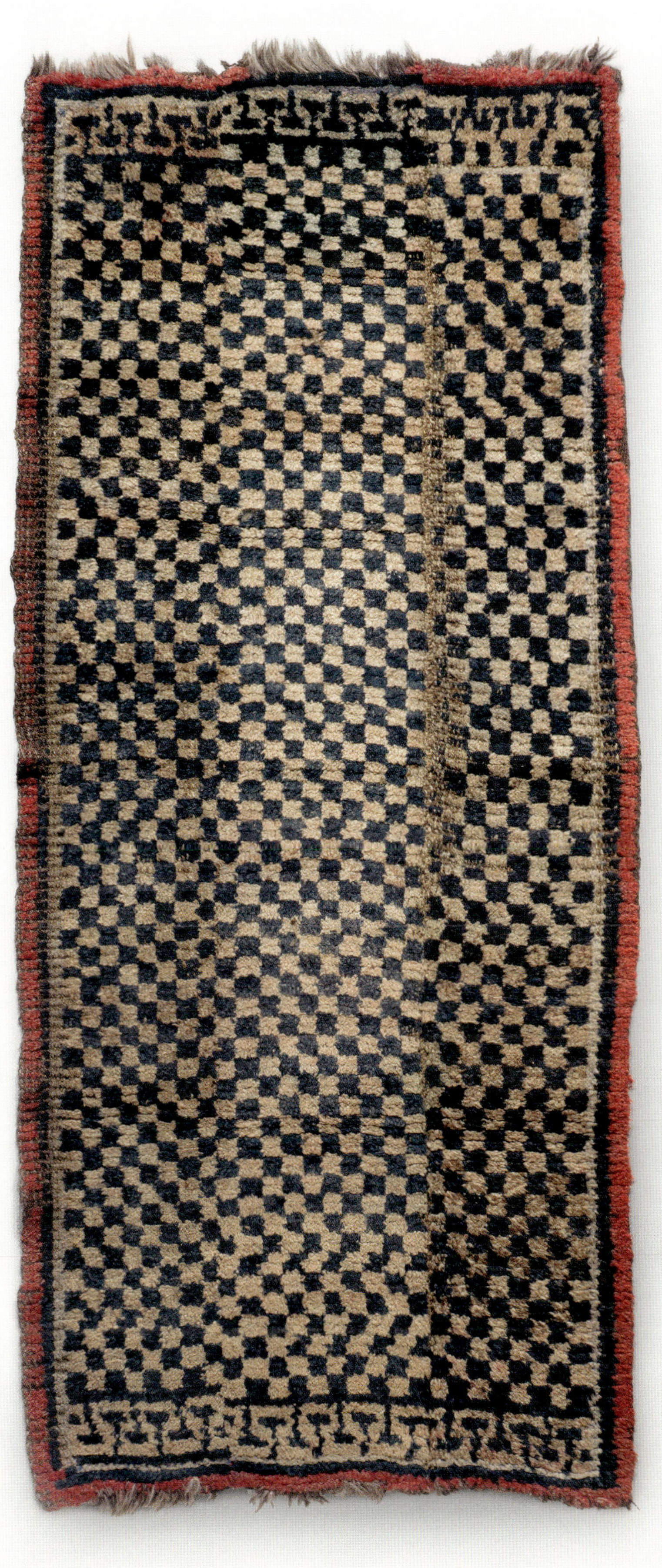

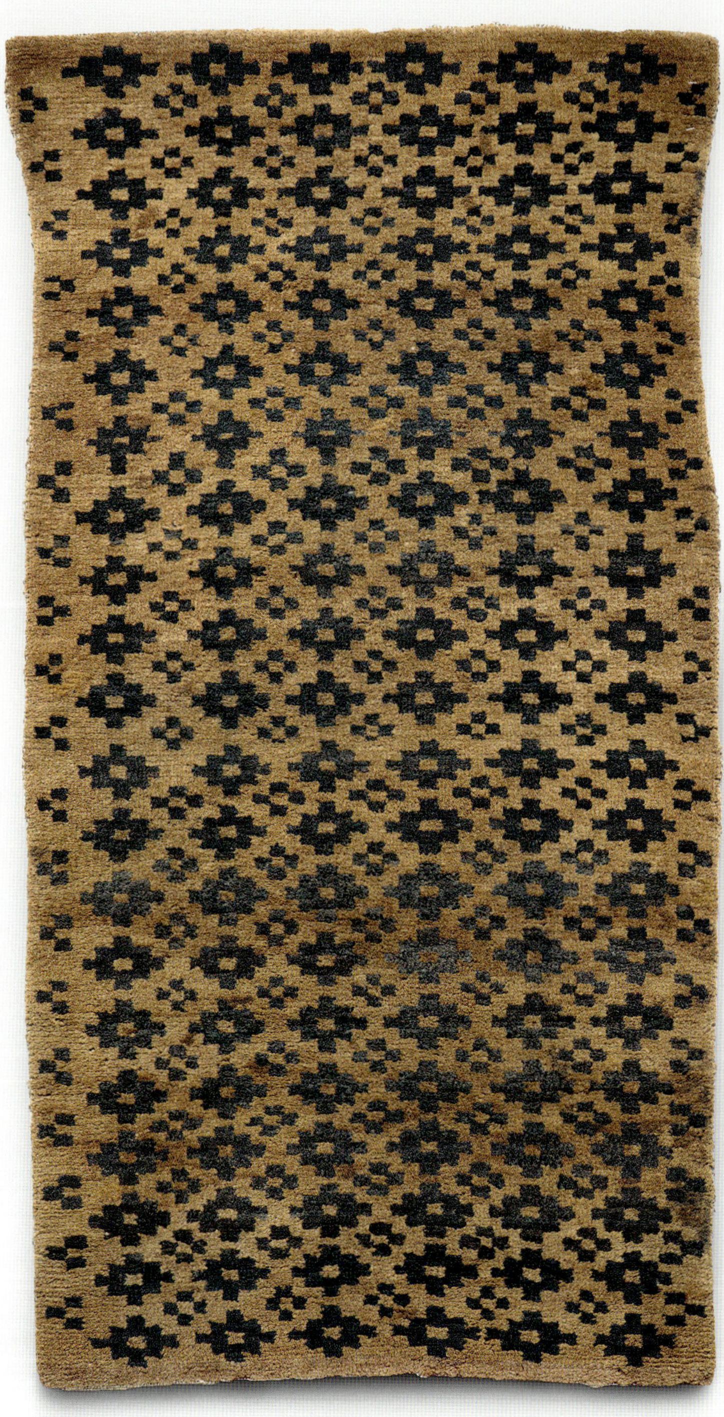

Fig. 66: C59.
Sitting and sleeping rug (*khaden*) with a decorative adaptation of the cross (*tigma*) pattern.
Around 1900, 149 × 76 cm

coarser texture, but with the usual exceptions. The *masho* C20 (see Fig. 4 in the contribution by De Jong) with three shoots of weft in a unit belongs to items with exclusive weave and pattern, whereas the *khaden* C21 (Fig. 53), a rurally woven sitting or sleeping rug, has just single wefts, like the model masterpiece C58 (see Fig. 12 in the contribution by Wild).

Weavers of *tsuktruk* rugs consistently use only single wefts of their loosely spun weft yarn, always changing the warp shed between each shoot of weft, almost alien to the structure of other Tibetan pile weavings. The several to many wefts (max. 32 shoots in C86) between rows of pile loops in *tsuktruk* rugs makes this necessary to bind the warps together, a regular tabby structure between the rows of pile (C122, see Fig. 7 in the contribution by Darchen), common to the wefting practice of other Eurasian populations.

Weft density (number of wefts/decimetre) in the items in the collection ranged from 14 to 45. It does not always have the expected relationship to the number of warps. A *masho* (C10, see Fig. 2b in the contribution by De Jong) with 90 warps/decimetre survives happily with only 18 wefts/decimetre. One of the most splendid rugs in the collection (C153, Fig. 25) has 94 warps and 36 wefts, and the finely made *takyab* (C176, see Fig. 19 in the contribution by De Jong) has 100 warps and 45 wefts. The density of the items in the collection is given in the catalogue.

The amazing diversity of variations we see tells us that to make a rug of definite shape and pattern the weaver had to keep in mind precise accounting of all the necessary implicit characteristics, including thickness of warp, weft, and pile; an exact number of warps and wefts; the exact degree of warp depression, etc. The level of skill to produce such seemingly "free of any rules" masterworks suggests an almost genetically inherited ability formed by a long-refined tradition and aesthetic feeling, both of which would have crystallised in the process of a weaver's training.

The single-level *drumze* and *tsuktruk* weavings show a somewhat broader variety of weft density with individual priorities for each of the groups, as detailed in the catalogue.

Pile Yarns

The art of pile weaving can be seen as an inventive alternative to using sheep wool by animal breeders, no longer sacrificing the sheep, just shearing them and using their wool. This in turn allowed the wool to be dyed, allowing

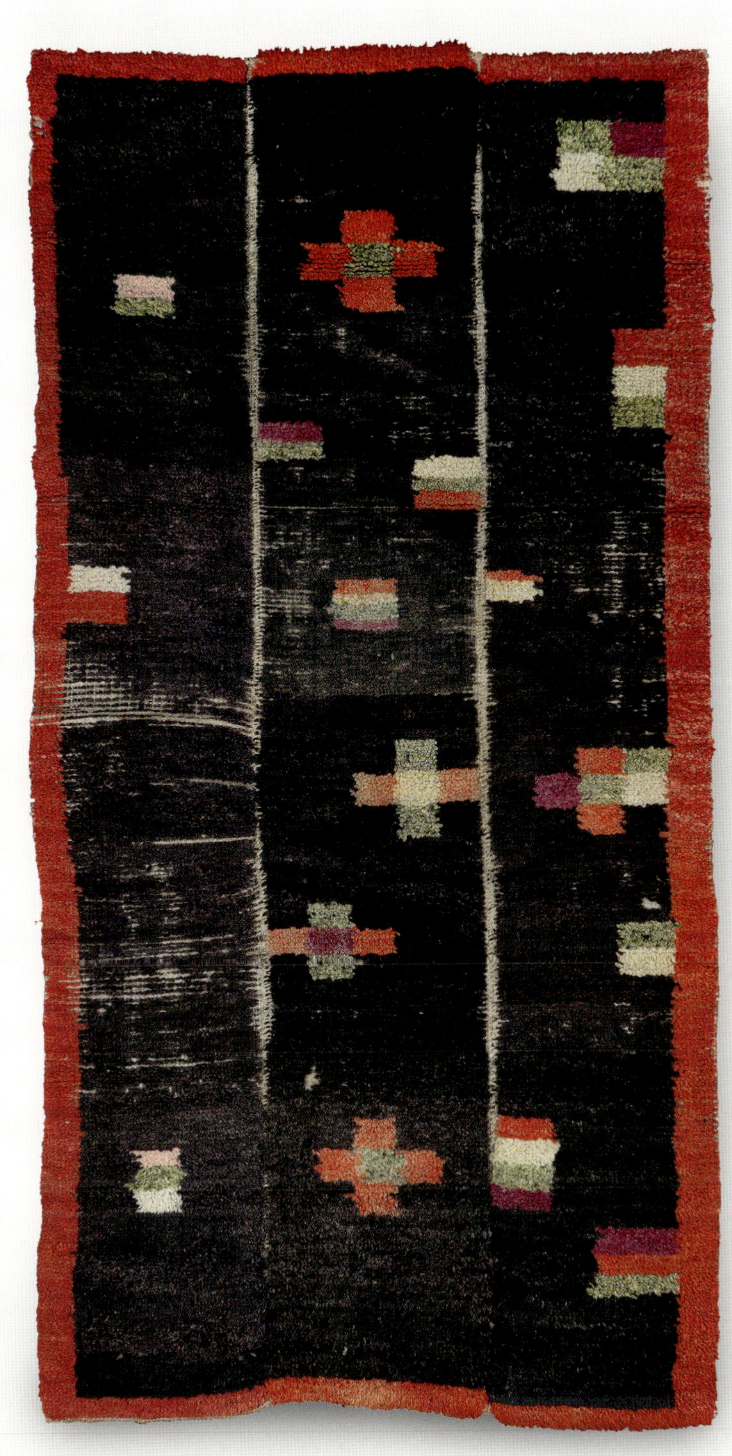

Fig. 67: C95.
Tsuktruk rug made of three panels with *tigma* pattern.
20th c., 144×73 cm

and stimulating decorative pile weaving. Plant fibres – hemp, linen, cotton – were less suited for pile and used mainly in the warps and wefts, with exceptions, of course: linen in Egypt and silk in China as the extreme examples.

The Tibetan pile-making tradition clearly reflects the situation on the plateau, as we see pile made only of animal fibres, with cotton (in ancient times also hemp) used in the rug's foundation. Although cotton is actively used for making wefts and warps, we neither find it in rugs' pile, nor in silk, so popular among the neighbouring carpet-weaving cultures both to the east, west, north, and south of Tibet.

It is apparent that in most animal-breeding cultures the inclusion of non-wool fibres in the foundation is typical for professional made-to-order or weavings for sale, while rugs with a purely woollen foundation and pile point to rural production or specially made pieces of a ritual character.

It appears there were no special regulations concerning the choice of materials, thus weavers used whichever fibre was the best for their purposes or for the client they worked for. As a result we see that yarns' quality varies not only from item to item, which is a natural circumstance, but even from one shade to another inside one and the same weaving. The difference is so clear it can be identified with the naked eye, with ivory and cold red tints especially evident in illustrated cases (Figs. 68a to 68f and Figs. 69a to 69g). Although there are no strict rules, observation tells us that those items that are best in quality and most rich in colour are those made in the monastic workshops; while those of rural manufacture demonstrate the limited resources accessible to weavers in remote areas. The Tibetan tradition is no different to textile production elsewhere in the world.

Rugs from the Buddeberg collection represent a variety of pile yarn structures, whose working elements can be either only spun, spun and combined, or spun and plied. The largest group identified points to the Z2 and Z3 constructions; less frequent are the Z1 and Z4 variants, while Z5 and Z6 come as exceptionally rare forms. In the spun-and-plied group, the majority is Z2S and Z3S variants. Other alternatives show Z2S2, Z5S and Z6S construction. The more numerous the elementary components is, those plied in particular, the thicker are the resulting working yarns and thus the quicker should also be the process of making a rug, although to keep the pattern in balance the weaver has to keep the situation under strict control, which is not easy. Examining the identified examples, we come to the conclusion that in most cases the reason for the use of differently plied pile yarns was caused by a manufacturing necessity.

Figs. 68a to 68f: Collage showing a variety of wefts in different colours and their combinations

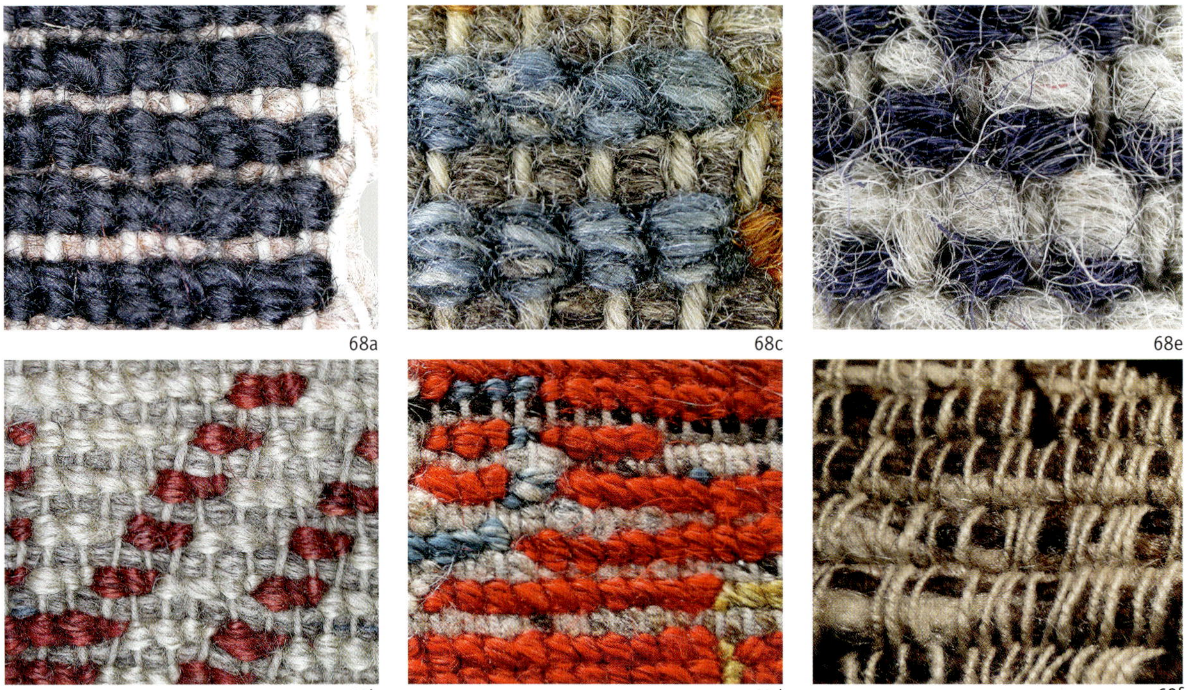

68a 68c 68e

68b 68d 68f

Figs. 69a to 69g: Collage of the different qualities of pile yarns

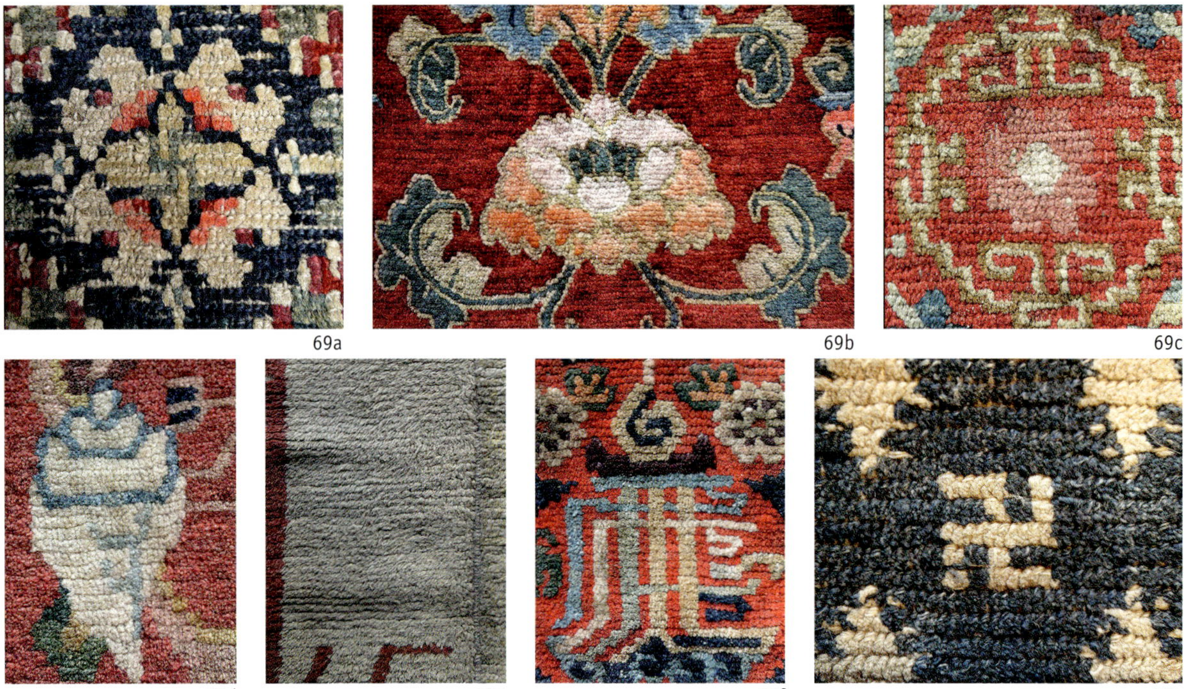

69a 69b 69c

69d 69e 69f 69g

Figs. 70a and 70b: Yarns of different structure and thickness

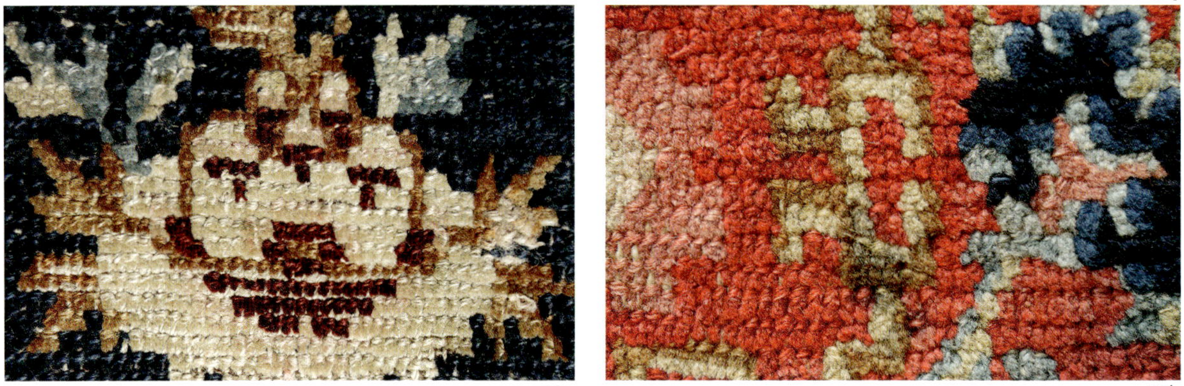

70a 70b

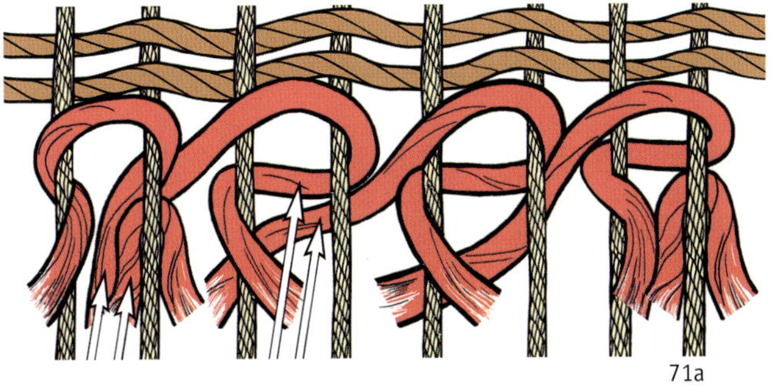

71a

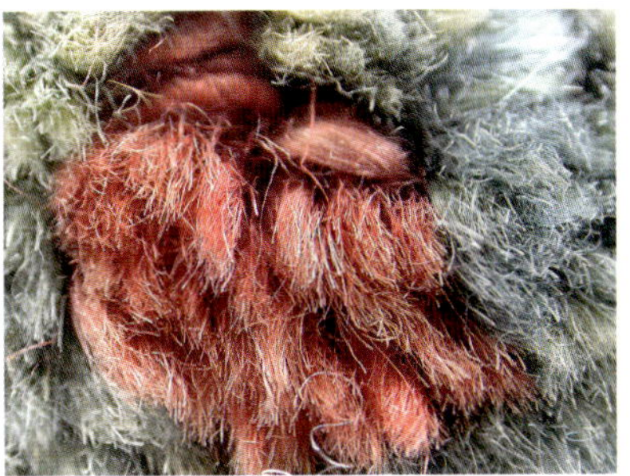

71b

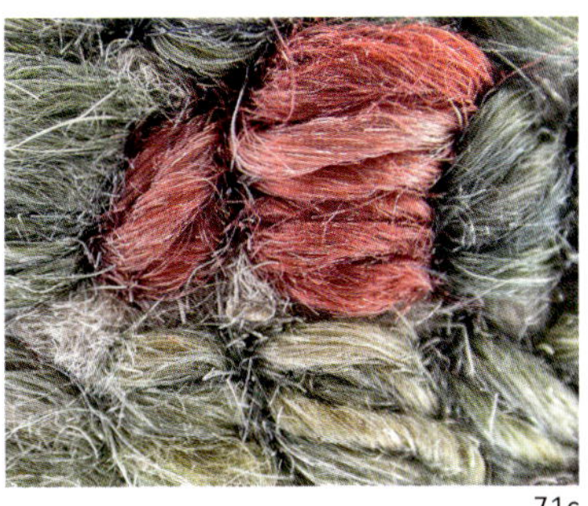

71c

Figs. 71a to 71c: Z4 = Z2x2 and Z6 = Z3x2

Quite logically, we find that producers of thick textures prefer thick threads. In Tibet these are *sabden*, *khaden* (*drumze* variant in particular) and small head and crupper horse trappings. This relationship is not exact, however; we find thick long-pile single-level *tsuktruks* with Z1, Z2 pile yarns and two-level delicate *khagangma* rugs with Z3, Z3S pile building.

As mentioned, typical for Tibetan rugs is the situation when the pile yarns in a single item demonstrate a diversity of structures (Figs. 69a to 69f as well as Figs. 70a and 70b). Model examples are the *khaden* rugs (C145, Fig. 10) with Z2, Z3, Z4 or Z6 structure as well as with Z3, Z3S and Z2S yarns in their pile construction (C58, see Fig. 12 in the contribution by Wild). The reason for diversity in these two cases looks different. In C145, the Z4 threads are used to make extra large loops (Fig. 70a) which are sometimes used to enlarge individual single loops, sometimes also to produce pushing loops (see Figs. 26a and 26b).

In C58 (see Fig. 12 in the contribution by Wild), the weaver used initial (before plying) elementary threads of different thickness. The basic variant is Z2S (7 of the 11 colours), while others, most probably purchased yarns, have dissimilar texture but are Z2S plied, similar to the weaver's own Z3S cherry-red yarns and Z3 yarns combining elementary threads of old rose, rust (faded to olive-brown) and sky blue (Fig. 70b).

Three variants of pile structure in this early and elegantly woven rug speak for three sources of elementary yarns, while the very specific texture of ivory-coloured fibre adds a fourth. The asserted monastic-workshop manufacture of the piece does not contradict this observation. Intended for a high-ranking lama, the piece was made to special order, thus the weaver was able to choose yarns of the colours and quality needed.

And last but not least to clarify the problem of identification and definition of the Tibetan pile thread structure: In the literature we often find the opinion that pile yarns used by Tibetan weavers have Z4 and Z6 construction. Although it is true and we did recognise this Z4 and Z6 description in the majority of the items, the Z4 and Z6 is the result of seeing the pile ends of either two Z2 or Z3 yarns of a basic loop and the long-leg end of the next adjacent loop as a single Z4 or Z6 yarn, whose ends can be categorised as packing (Fig. 71a); or – alternatively – the ends of the basic loop and its packing bottom element, with the same structure (Figs. 71b and 71c). Derived pictures cause practically identical results giving Tibetan rugs thick texture and solidity; still it is better to identify the actual structure of the items under study, be they Z2, Z3 or Z4, Z6.

Colouration of Pile Threads

A matter of special interest is represented by the Tibetan masters' system of creating colourful patterns, which can be bright and include up to 16 tints, but otherwise limited to two or even one shade only. General observation shows that typical for the Eurasian artistic textiles in general, items with few colours belong to rural works, while those with a rich, diverse scale predominately to professional, refined products.

With Tibetan rugs the situation is exactly the same, and quite naturally the extremes appertain on the one hand to single-level *khaden* in *tsuktruk* technique (C61, see Fig. 4 in the contribution by Wild) which are archaic in design, have only one colour, but are still gorgeous, and on the other hand in contrast to those structurally and artistically refined pieces of monastic work, especially those with Chinese iconographic elements (for example, C103, Fig. 72; C137, see Fig. 14 in the contribution by Wild). Even so, in the *tsuktruk* group, there are items with as many as nine colours (C95, Fig. 67), and some breathtakingly beautiful monastic works, those created for high-ranking lamas, which only have two colours and two motifs (C108, Fig. 31; C114, Fig. 73).

Fig. 72: C103.
Sitting and sleeping rug (*khaden*).
20th c., 156×78 cm

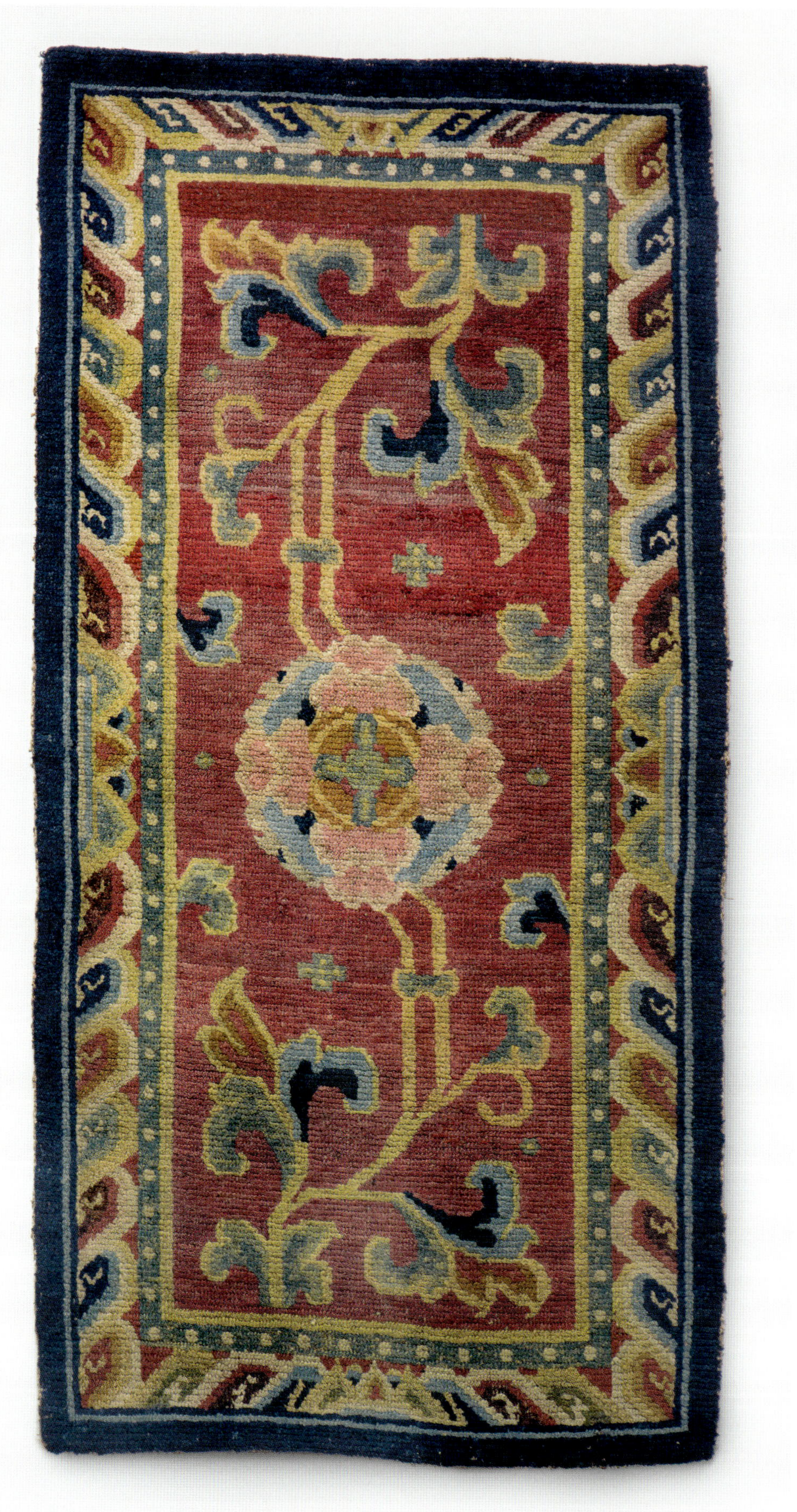

Fig. 73: C114.
Over-saddle rug (*masho*)
with exquisite colours.
19th c., 82 × 60 cm

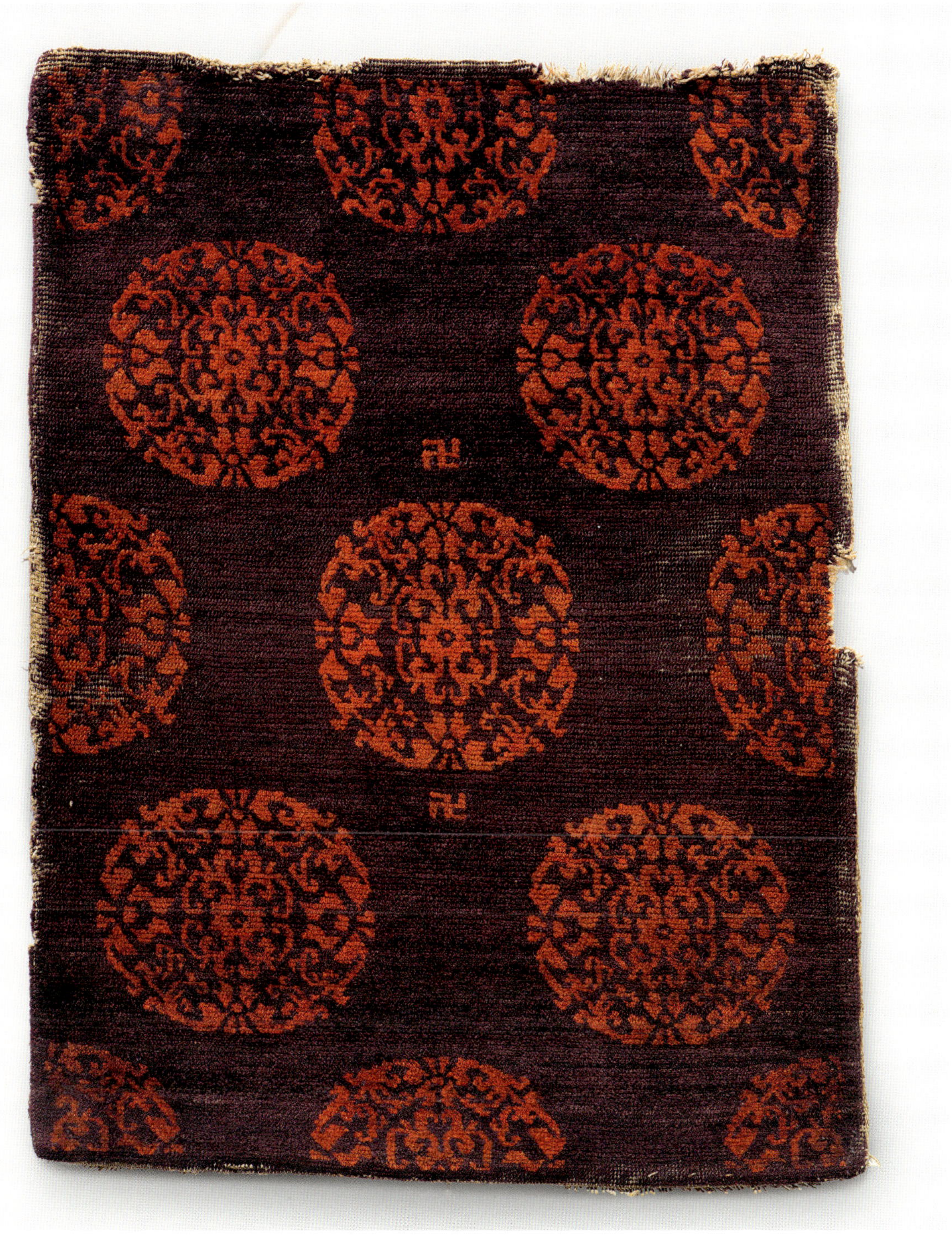

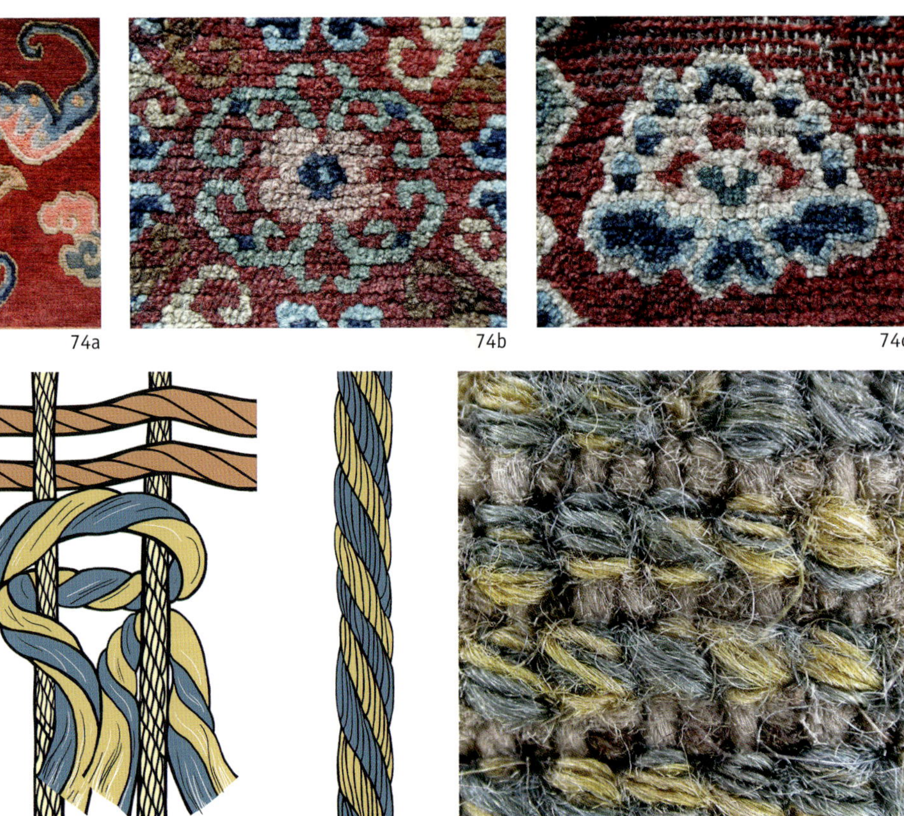
74a 74b 74c 75a 75b 75c

Figs. 74a to 74c: Red and blue tones created by using three vats in different shades of the same colour: a) detail of C153 with burgundy red, rose and light rose tones, also dark marine blue, b) and c) details of C119 with dark cherry red, strong rose and light rose as well as dark and sky-blue

Figs. 75a to 75c: a) and b) variants of Z2S plying of strands dyed with different colours, c) detail of C40 (see Fig. 76)

It is interesting and important to note the Tibetan tradition of using animal fibres of different natural colours in the pile to achieve the desired design. This is almost unique and unknown in other Eurasian areas. The colours can vary from ivory to shades of grey and broad gradations of brown tints, including black-brown. A model example of the kind is the *takyab* horse ornament (C119, Figs. 46 and 45a), whose pile includes camel down in ivory, very light olive-brown, light grey and two shades of soft brown, combined with sheep wool and other dyed animal fibres yarns in dark claret, dark rose, rose, light rose, light yellow, light emerald-green, sky-green, turquoise, light turquoise, deep blue and sky blue colours. This is practised by all groups of Tibetan rug weavers including nomadic, rural domestic and both rural and monastic professional commercial weavers, and gives really fantastic results when natural-coloured pile yarns are combined with other, deep and bright shades (Fig. 59b and Figs. 74a to 74c).

To identify one group from another regarding the colouring, firstly we have to pay attention to the quality of dying and the range of colours used by a weaver. The more solid the shades are and the broader their variety, the more likely it is that we are dealing with made-to-order professional monastic work. A brilliant example is Fig. 74a, a detail of *khagangma* rug C153. On the contrary, the more abrash shades we find and the more limited the colour scale, the stronger can be the assumption that we are dealing with rural work, whether domestic or professional. Even so, it should be clearly understood that "rural" does not mean poor in quality, and quite a number of artistically charming items full of high spiritual content in the collection belong to the rural works' category (for example C49, see Fig. 5 in the contribution by Wild, and C154, Fig. 51).

A marker to distinguish professional monastic works from domestic products is the quality of dying, blue in particular. There are two aspects to discuss in this respect.

The first aspect is that the fibres can be dyed either prior to being spun and plied or after they have been. In the first case, the mordent and dyestuff have even access to the fibres and the subsequently spun and plied pile yarns have strong and clear shades. If they are dyed after spinning and plying, the colour can be uneven and accordingly motley (see Figs. 69b and 69g).

The second aspect is the choice of accessible dyestuffs, especially those producing blue, the most evident problem for weavers of other Eurasian highlands and steppe zones. The best blue dye-stuff is indigo (*Indigofera tinctoria*), a member of the group of dye-stuffs which do not grow in Tibet. According to the literature, indigo is thus unfamiliar to local dyers and considered to be the most difficult of natural dyes to use successfully in Tibet. Although it is mentioned in the literature as a typical pigment in Tibet, we should assume that local craftsmen used either imported natural or chemical indigo. The alternative for indigo and a very reasonable assumption that they were used would be locally wide-spread woad (*Isatis tinctoria*) and other indigoids.

As already mentioned, the Tibetans are skilled at combining/plying two different coloured threads in pile yarns, either giving a beautiful gradation of closely coloured threads or by combining threads of contrasting colours (Figs. 75a to 75c). This technique is common elsewhere in Eurasia and evidenced in the Bronze Age and later at archaeological findings. The Tibetans also use another widely practised dyeing technique, repeated use of the dye vat. The first dye batch has a strong and deep colour, subsequent ones then lighter shades, as we find in many rugs, as the examples in Figs. 74a to 74c (C153 and C119) and Fig. 76 (C40) show.

CONCLUSIONS

My study of Justyna and Michael Buddeberg's fantastic collection concludes with a summary of the results of our long journey into the amazing world of Tibetan rugs, whose "texts" are "narrated" in the language of threads which is specific for Eurasian weaving cultures. Devoted companions of mankind in the long and hard process of formation and survival of Homo sapiens as a species, threads and the textiles created with them helped people exist in the most unbearable natural conditions and brought warmth and beauty to the uneasy life of our ancestors. In this way they added to the rise of the ideas of humanity, spirituality and self-expression of their creators.

Similar to other yarn-made artefacts, rugs represent a complicated multi-layer structure, with partly visible and partly hidden components. Those explicit, artistic elements express the copious spiritual ideas of their makers, while implicit, or technical units, fulfil the task of bearing the artistic layer and at the same time making up each rug's "body".

When one studies textile artefacts it becomes clear that external beauty can only be achieved with the perfect execution of all internal components. This is exactly the case with piled rugs: when masterly fulfilled, they stir up admiration with depictions of phenomenological and fantastic images from the surrounding world. Besides, superbly woven rugs live a long and happy life, with age only adding to their brilliance (Figs. 74a to 74c).

The "language of threads" has, however, yet another important quality: child of one of the most ancient skills of mankind, threads were invented in the Upper Palaeolithic period at least, as evidenced by over 71,000-year-old needles from Sibudu Cave, South Africa. Were one to compare the history of the invention and development of the art of thread-making with the formation and development of Homo sapiens, one could say that yarns' structures carry evidence of their formation on the level of "genetic memory", thus can be arranged according to specific "textile haplotypes". When identified, these "textile genes" help to trace the roots and routes of the formation of individual branches of the tree of carpet weaving, in other words, the processes of cultural phylogenesis of the craft.

It is similar with the components of all knotted and looped pile-making techniques. This trend in rug study actively developed during the last few decades and has finally shaped into a special branch of research, whereby the archaeological finds in the Tarim Basin and in other Central Asian regions are particularly helpful as guidelines.

As explained in the beginning of this article, the special goal of this research concerned tracing the roots of the Tibetan pile weaving practices. The first step in this direction aimed at identification of the structural parameters of the tradition; second, the search for comparable, related ethnographic and archaeological material; and third, reviewing data on history, biology, geography, linguistics and other related subjects in order to detect the cultural background of the tradition.

Quite predictably, study of supposedly related segments of textile practices brought us to pile weavings of other Eurasian groups, especially to a number of Central Asian groups, and even more precisely, to the Saka-Bactrian line of the craft and its rather late Chinese offspring. I have attempted to present the newly-won knowledge of the structural details of Tibetan pile rugs in a cogent manner in the respective sections of this contribution. As a reminder, the most significant ethnographic and archaeological material concerns such complicated methods of weaving such as packing, offset, eccentric weave and other irregular methods of knotting and looping specific to the Tibetan and Saka-Bactrian schools of rug weaving and their derivations, Turkmen and Chinese lines in particular.[19]

When studied precisely, we see that three selective lines of Tibetan rugs have different relatives inside the Eurasian family. The richest in kinfolk is *tsuktruk*, with numerous published "natural relatives", including the Pazyryk looped rugs. This group is well-studied, thus it is not problematic to trace and find its place in the Eurasian carpet-weaving tradition.

Two other complicated looped structures, namely the single-level *drumze* and the more numerous two-level group, were more difficult to trace back to their roots, although in different ways.

In the case of *drumze*, we find a distant relative to two techniques still practised in Central Asia, even though this is a knotting technique. One, known as *dzulhkyr*, is used by the ancient Iranian-speaking populations of Central Asia, with Tadjiks as supposed initial bearers of the tradition in the territories of modern Tadjikistan and South Uzbekistan. Another single-level type is used in a variety of combined-technique tent bands, all made by Turkic-speaking animal-breeding populations of the region, mainly Turkmen, Karakalpaks, Kazakhs and once nomadic Uzbeks. Both lines are so ancient that we do not have data to even suppose the time of their formation as individual techniques. The only thing to suggest is that they originated from an unknown archaic prototype, separating at some time in the distant past to make knotted and looped variants of Central Asian piled weavings.

A member of the same family and a child of the early nomadic textile culture in Eurasia,[20] the main group of Tibetan rugs shows a direct kinship with very early items in the al-Sabah Collection at the Dar al-Athar al-Islamiyyah museum, Kuwait. Found in one of north Afghanistan's Samangan Province caves and dated to the 6th to 7th century AD, are three of five registered fragments under one number (coll. No. 48R [A]), structurally very closely related to the predominating Tibetan rugs' two-level loopings. All were published by Friedrich Spuhler in *Pre-Islamic Carpets and Textiles from the Eastern Lands* (2014), regrettably with no exact structural descriptions. Fortunately I had a chance to study them, if only briefly, when visiting the museum at the invitation of Michael Franses. Checking my notes I found exact analogues with the Tibetan weavings. Earlier studies of the al-Sabah fragments made it possible to identify them as clearly belonging to the Saka-Bactrian group with its numerous branches spread all over the Tarim Basin and beyond.

Discovery of textiles in the Tarim Basin started with the expeditions of Sven Hedin, Sir Aurel Stein and Albert von Le Coq, all of whose findings were published in special books and articles. In our day expeditions continue, with some unearthed artefacts presented in exhibitions and printed works, although many in Chinese, so that the majority of items remains unknown to a broader public. These were supposed to be studied in the framework of publications and exhibitions in the course of the project "Birth of the Carpet" planned for 2017 and shown en masse. Alas! The project was cancelled in February 2016. Without exaggeration, this is a tragedy for historic carpet research, as an enormous volume of valuable material may now remain unknown for years or even decades to those researchers who do not read Chinese.

Thus we see that all branches of the Tibetan pile techniques link them to the vast world of the Eurasian textile tradition. Most probably they have their roots in the Saka-Bactrian methods of weaving, most fully revealed by archaeological discoveries in the Tarim Basin and ancient Bactria proper. At the same time, especially the Tibetans' "language" of pile votes for an individual line of development of the craft and continuation of probably the most archaic pile techniques that have survived, as if frozen in the bitterly cold and dry air of the Land of Snow.

Justyna and Michael Buddeberg initiated a project on the study of the art of Tibetan rugs that has greatly added to the knowledge of the field. It has been my pleasure to be a member of the small team of authors on this subject in the book. It is clear, however, that there is still a lot to do to shed more light on the amazing world of the pile creations by the dwellers of the Land of Snow and to further understanding of their place in the context of Eurasian pile-making traditions. Hopefully, we will see this research continued.

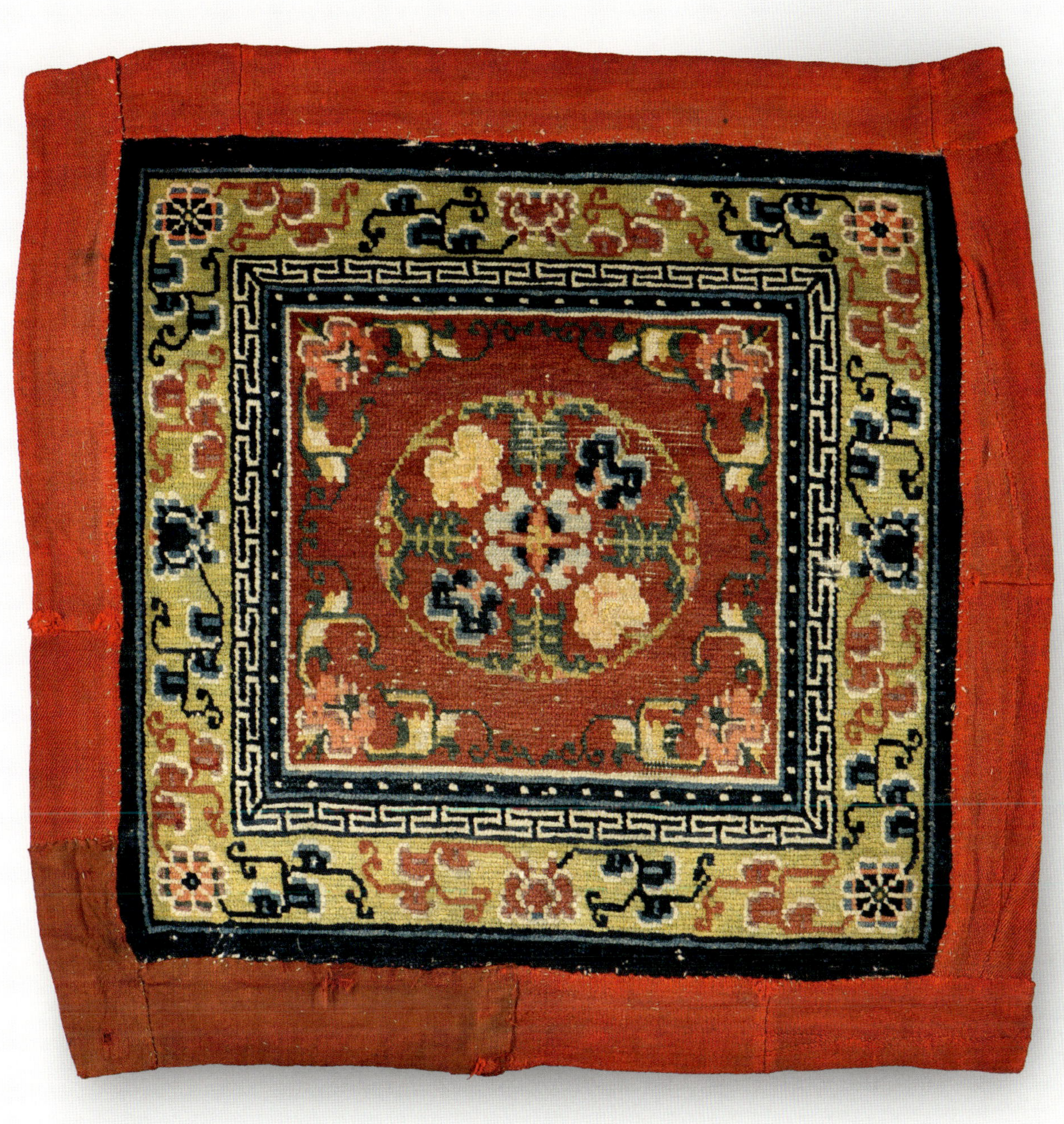

Fig. 76: C40. Sitting rug (*khagangma*). 2nd half 19th c. or early 20th c., 64 × 66 cm

NOTES

1 Buddhism appeared in the territories of modern Russia as early as the late 16th century with the coming of the Kalmyks. In 1764 it was officially accepted as one of the state religions. The 1993 Constitution of the Russian Federation recognises Buddhism as one of the beliefs native to Russian soil (1 percent of the population), along with Islam, Judaism, and Orthodox Christianity.

2 In 1909 Agvan Lobsan Dorzhiev, a Buryat in origin, study partner and close associate of the 13th Dalai Lama, a minister of his government and his diplomatic link with the Russian Empire, received permission from Nicholas II for the construction of a Buddhist temple in St. Petersburg, the *Datsan Gunzechoinei*, or "The Source of the Buddha's Religious Teaching that has Deep Compassion for All Beings". Construction started in 1909 and was completed by 1915, although the first service was held in 1913.

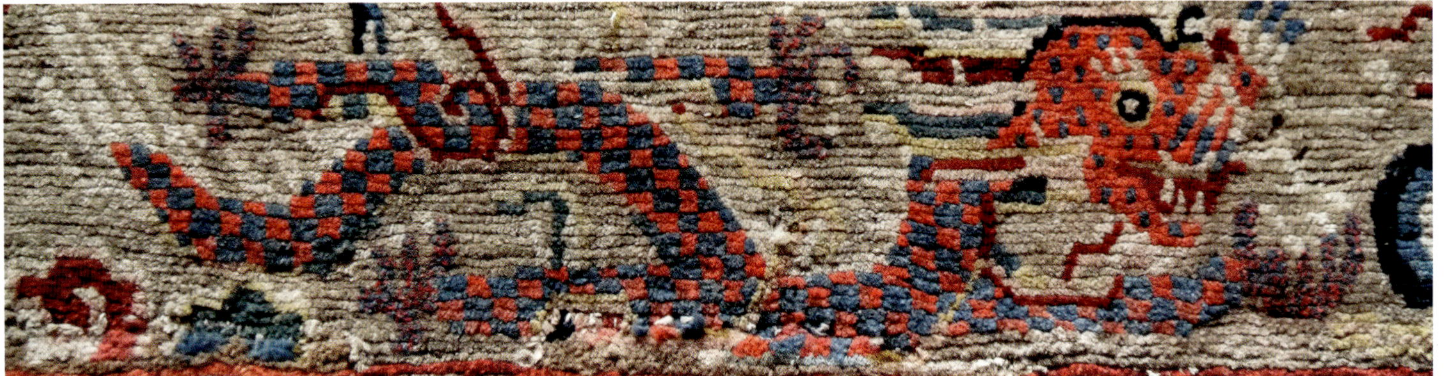

Fig. 77: Detail of C15: dragon

3 It is important to note that the only tantric rug in the collection has a different structure from that of typical Tibetan rugs. It has a cotton foundation with pure pashmina pile, rare for Tibetan rugs. Its all-over asymmetric open left knotted structure, however, does not question its Tibetan origin.

4 The situation is much more complicated, here I mention only one peculiarity of the monastic weaving tradition.

5 From the point of variety of the applied pile-making elements, the closest to the Tibetan tradition is the Gassan-Kuli Turkmen group, notable for use of both asymmetric open left, asymmetric open right and symmetric main knots (Tsareva 2011: note 17).

6 Seven items of Chinese and Central Asian manufacture were included for comparison.

7 The term chisel is used here by Denwood (Denwood 1974: 45).

8 "When beginning a line (and when starting a new colour within a line) a special sort of knot is usually tied. The loose end of a ball of the pile yarn is taken from left to right behind the third warp thread from the left hand edge, then pulled forwards to the right of it either above or below the gauge-rod, which is hung or held to the left, its right hand end level with the knot being tied. The continuation of the yarn towards the ball is then taken to the right in front of the third and fourth warp threads, and pushed back leftwards behind the fourth thread in a loop which is pulled forwards between the two warp threads (below itself) and slipped over the end of the gauge-rod. (All references to left and right are from the point of view of the weaver.) The continuation of the yarn can then be pulled lightly so that the knot grips the threads and the rod.
For the next knot, and all subsequent knots of the same colour, the continuation of the yarn is led up behind the gauge-rod, rightwards in front of the next rightward pair of warp threads (the first of which should be odd, the second even), then leftwards behind them both and forwards (below itself) to the left of both of them in a loop as before. The gauge-rod is pushed progressively towards the right as the loops are slipped over it. The last knot of a particular colour of yarn may be finished by leaving the continuation of the yarn either above or below the gauge-rod, and likewise the first knot of a subsequent colour may be started with the projecting end either above or below the rod. [...]
All Tibetan weavers I have seen tie the knots successively from left to right, changing colour as and when demanded by the pattern [...] When two weavers work on the same carpet, one will start from the left edge, the other from the centre, both working with her own rod." (Denwood 1974: 44).

9 Similar to many other cases, lining prevented photographing the back.

10 Perhaps not so important for the historical aspects of the subject, although definitely interesting as a fact, is my observation that all modern rug weaving practices of Eurasia use the same direction, viz.: knotting/looping is always executed from left to right.

11 I repeat again, that although I name those small packing loops "additional", in reality they are integral for the Tibetan manner of weaving, thus the term "additional" is used only to describe that they are supplementary to the main loop position in the structure.

12 The term is used for both the technique and the rugs in this structure.

13 Although the name "cashmere" comes from Kashmir, the wild and mountainous area of India and Pakistan, initially the animal was domesticated by the Tibetans.

14 This supposition comes from data on other rug weaving traditions of Eurasia which show that silk or very smooth camel hair is used regularly in items with exclusively dense structures; among most rare exceptions are rather loose Chinese rugs of the Imperial group, which is understandable if one takes China's devotion to silk into consideration (Tsareva 2005: 194f.).

15 Unpublished personal data.

16 Although we know that the initial methods of making long strands was twisting and tying the ends of split plant fibres, the creative early Homo sapiens began to collect and use soft and warm rabbit or goats' undercoat fibres.

17 It should be noted that similar to Tibetan weavings, in all listed Asian cases this type of spinning makes up only a small percentage.

18 See the section "Possible Reasons for Irregularities".

19 Some details of the Imperial (Beijing) group of Chinese knotted rugs with irregular structural details tell us that this practice is later in age than that in Tibet. This is quite understandable, considering China's attitude to wool as a "barbarian's" material. As to the pure silk rugs of the Middle Kingdom, they are made entirely with deeply depressed asymmetric knots.

20 Common name for Saka and other shepherding populations of Central Asia, also for the Xiongnu nomads.

Fig. 78: C57.
Over-saddle rug (*masho*) with snow lion, phoenix and dragon.
19th c., 71 × 57 cm

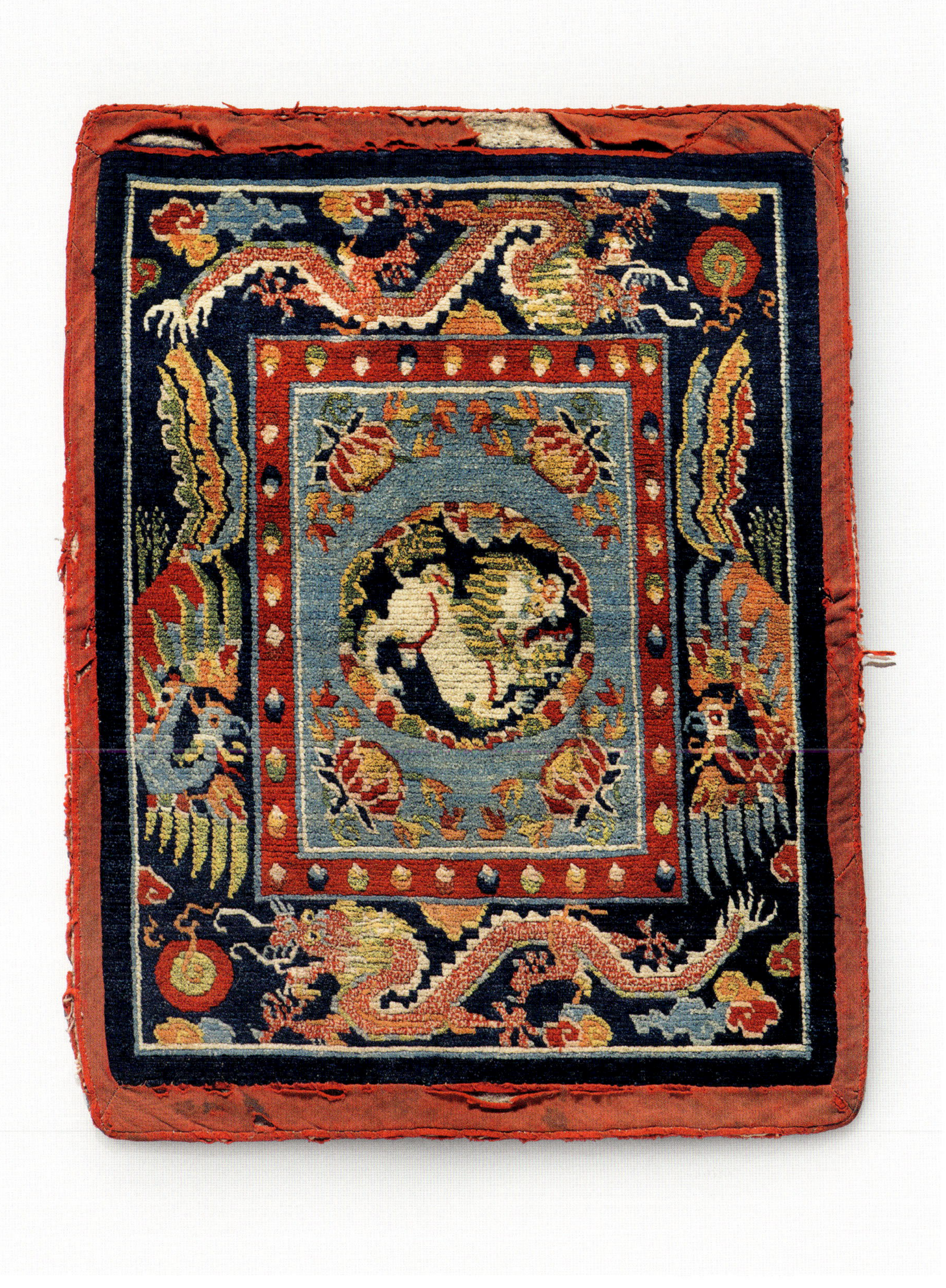

GLOSSARY

Active warps
Warps on top of the shed in single-level structure in which the pile yarns are only looped around these warps.

Additional bottom packing loop
(Additional) packing element put under the basic loop of a horizontal unit of loops. Can be either open, on one warp, or closed, on two warps.

Additional loop
Any compliment to basic loop; see also *top-packing loop* and *bottom-packing loop*.

Additional warp
Additionally inserted short warp lengths used to make intricate floral images (see Figs. 21a to 21c).

Additional/supporting weft-bits
Additional short (loop length) bits of weft yarn, inserted between one or two loops and the main lower weft unit.

Additional weft
Additional, complimentary to basic structure weft, applied in *tsuktruk* to form pile loops.

Asymmetric long-leg loop
Also: long-leg loop. See *asymmetric open left long-leg loop*.

Asymmetric loop
See *asymmetric open left long-leg loop; regular asymmetric loop*.

Asymmetric open left long-leg loop
Basic element of Tibetan rugs. With asymmetric open left loops, the left-side end is much longer than the right-side; its structure is made of four warps (sometimes three), so that the "body" of the loop and its short end twist around two right-side warps, while the left-side long end goes under the third and fourth neighbouring warps to the left, which at the same time works as the first working warp of the previous loop, no matter asymmetric or symmetric. In texts it is also named basic asymmetric long-leg loops or simply long-leg loops (see Fig. 8a).

Backstrap weaving device
Also: backstrap (weaving) loom. Simple horizontal ground loom, the tension on the warps provided by a strap around the back of the weaver.

Basic element
Most typical structure-forming element.

Basic loops
Cluster of Tibetan pile-making elements including asymmetric open left long-leg loops, symmetric loops and open packing loops.

Basic pile-making element
See *basic loops*.

Bottom-packing loop
Usually open, single-warp loop put under the right-side warp of initial and terminal basic elements of each loops' unit (see Figs. 11a to 11d).

Carving
Also: sculpturing. The edges of the pile along the lines between different colours are trimmed down, ca. 2 mm to accentuate the pattern (see Fig. 29a).

Carving effect
A visual effect similar to proper carving (sculpuring), in this case resulting from pile of different colours or materials wearing differently (see Fig. 29b).

Closed loops
Symmetric loops in Tibetan rugs on two warps (see Fig. 8c).

Colour unit
See *unit of loops*.

Dancing warps
With additional warp lengths which change the degree/angle of warp depression, which can alternate from very small to very deep causing overlapping of neighbouring warps when they are seen at the back (see Fig. 21a).

Density
In piled rugs the number of horizontal and vertical knots/loops in square decimetres. In Tibetan rugs only calculated approximately because of a specific character of looping. To give an exact figure in structural descriptions the number of warps and wefts per decimetre has been counted.

Depression of warps
Shift (offsetting) of warps which is caused by difference in wefts' tension and calls for depression of loops; in structure it produces formation of back-side ribbing (see Figs. 21a to 21c and 28a to 28d). See also *dancing warps*.

Diagonal loops
Also: diagonal weaving technique. Method of weaving to allow formation of curving floral and animal motifs.

Double-level structure
Also: two-level technique or weaving. See *two-level structure*.

Doubled loops
Unit of loops consisting of two basic elements (Figs. 9b and 9d).

***drumze* (Tib.)**
Also: *drumtze* or *dromtse*: 1) long-pile rug, 2) type of *single-level warp-faced technique*, with dominating *asymmetric long-leg loop* weaving structure (Figs. 34 and 35).

dzulkhyr
Name used in Tadjikistan and Uzbekistan for weaving structures similar to the *tsuktruk*, as well as for rugs made in the technique of stitching panels together.

Eccentric warp weave
Structural device of inserting additional short warps to allow additional loops to create a more detailed portion of the design (Figs. 19a and 19b).

Eccentric weft weave
Similar to eccentric warps: the insertion of additional short wefts to allow additional loops to create a more detailed portion of the pattern (see Fig. 17a).

Edge loop
See *end loop*.

Fig. 79: C50.
Sitting and sleeping rug (*khaden*) with multi-coloured chessboard pattern.
Around 1900, 163×80 cm
(not in catalogue)

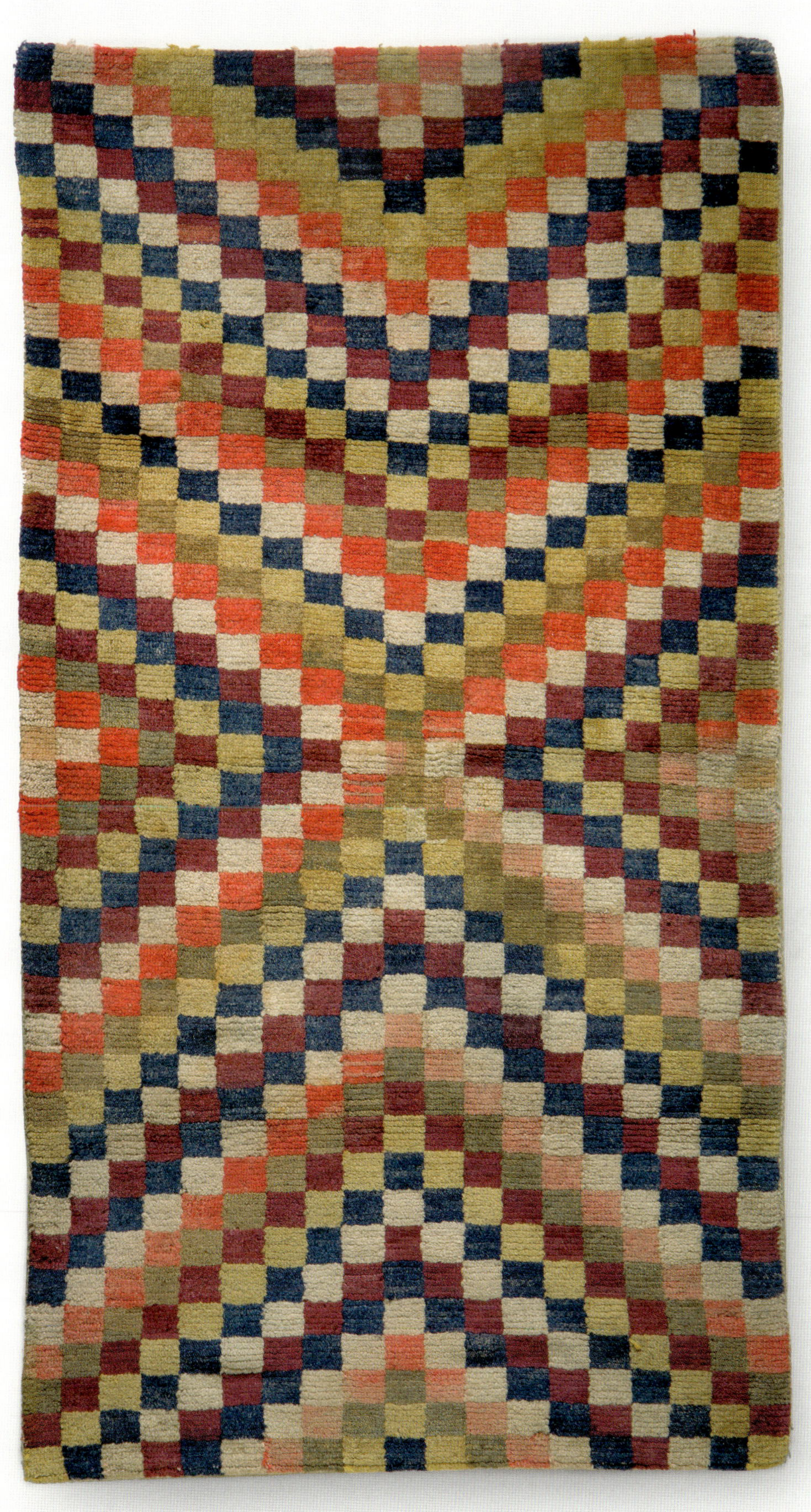

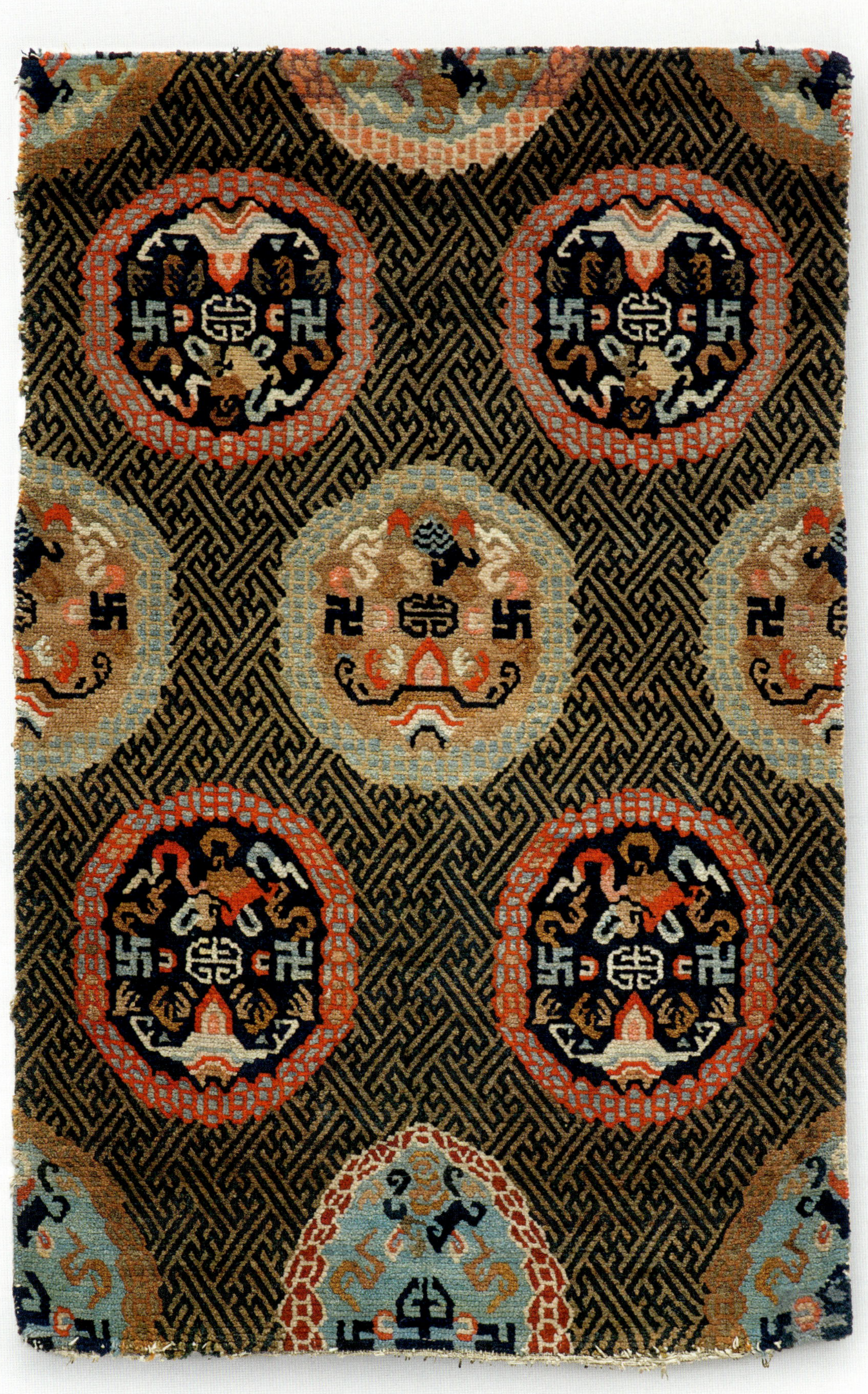

Fig. 80: C13.
Sitting rug
(*khagangma*) or
over-saddle rug
(*masho*).
19th c., 86×56 cm

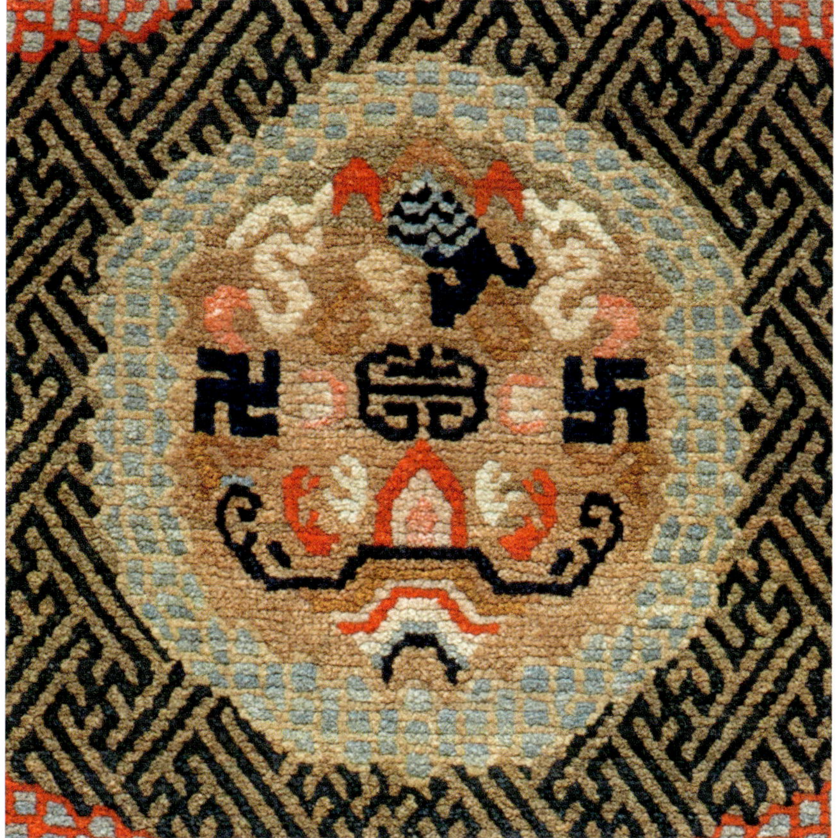

Detail of Fig. 80

End loop
Initial (left end) or final (right end) loop in a long row of loops in Tibetan piled weavings.

Horizontal end
Asymmetric loop with left end arranged parallel to wefts.

Irregular device
Also: irregular methods or tricks of weaving. Other than regular methods of weaving and arranging loops in textile structure (see also *sharing, offsetting, packing, loop over the weft*).

khaden **(Tib.)**
Rug used for sitting or sleeping.

khagangma **(Tib.)**
Sitting rug in square or almost square form.

Large loops
Also: pushing loops. Loops of unusually large size (mainly Z2S2, Z2S3) used to push neighbouring elements to give them diagonal direction (see Fig. 26).

Level
The two levels of the warps separated by the shed which alternate after the weft has been inserted. See *single-level* and *two-level structure*.

Long leg
Also: long-leg loop. See *asymmetric open left long-leg loop*.

Long row
Sequence or unit of horizontal pile-making elements of three and more loops (see Fig. 9c).

Loop
Main pile-making element of Tibetan rugs. For the variants of loops see:
- *asymmetric open left long-leg loop* (also basic loop);
- *long leg;*
- *open loop*, on one warp (can be asymmetric and symmetric);
- *closed loop*, on two warps;
- *bottom-packing loop*, packed with the basic loop from the bottom additional open or closed loop;
- *top-packing loop*, packed with the basic loop from the top additional open or closed loop.

Looping
Loop-making method by means of loops.

Loop over the weft
Additional to basic structure *loop* or knot, one knotted to the warps directly over the front surface yarns of the weft unit, a trick used to achieve complicated floral or animal images (see Figs. 23 and 30, on the right and above).

Loop sequence
Also: unit of loops. The sequence of loops in the same colour made with one pile yarn. See Figs. 9a to 9c: a) single loop, b) two loops, c) a longer series of loops.

makden **(Tib.)**
Under-saddle rug.

masho **(Tib.)**
Over-saddle rug.

Missed warp trick
A warp thread not involved in a looping sequence.

Offset effect
Visual effect of offset method, conditioned by shape of open bottom loops, packed with terminal for the monochrome-colour unit right-side basic loop (see Figs. 15a and 15b).

Offsetting
Also: offset, offset technique. Special trick causing a one-warp shift of basic loops; can be also be achieved by sharing, the missed warp trick, insertion of basic loops on four warps, etc. (see Figs. 15a and 15b).

Open loop
In Tibetan rugs regular symmetric loops on one warp, often identified as packing (see Figs. 8b, 9b, and 9c).

Pack
Two and more knots/loops put one over the other between two shoots of wefts (see Figs. 11a to 11b).

Packing
Also: packing method. See *pack*.

Padding loop
Loop of very loosely spun pile yarn on the reverse of a knotted rug (see Fig. 62d).

Paired loops
Also: double loops. In the catalogue two loops of one colour, different in colour to the neighbouring looping elements to the left and to the right of the pair (see Fig. 9b).

Passive warps
In single-level piled structures warps which interweave with wefts but not with pile yarns (Figs. 35a and 37a).

Plain single-level piled rug
See *tsuktruk*.

Pushing loops
See *large loops*.

Regular asymmetric open left loop
In Tibetan rugs asymmetric open left loop with ends equal in length (Figs. 8d and 8e).

Regular elements
Also: regular tricks or methods. In case not specially defined (asymmetric open left loop, for example), the term concerns weaving structural peculiarities characteristic to the Tibetan system.

Regular loops
See *asymmetric* and *symmetric loops*.

Regular symmetric loop
Symmetric loops in Tibetan rugs with equal ends, either on one (also open loop, see Fig. 8b), or on two warps (also closed loop, see Fig. 8c).

Released warp yarns
Warp yarns released in the process of weaving of trapezoid- and oval-shaped objects, with released ends used as wefts.

sabden **(Tib.)**
Large ground rug.

Sharing
Arrangement of two adjacent knots, or loops, or their parts on a warp used for both elements (Figs. 13a to 13c).

Shoot of weft
A single-weft passage through a warp shed.

Single-level structure
Also: single-level weaving or technique. Type of structure, with loops made on front/upper plane of warps' shed, with back plane bound by wefts only; see also *drumze* and *tsuktruk*.

Structural irregularities
See *irregular device*.

takyab **(Tib.)**
Also: *takheb* or *tekheb*. Riding animal trapping, specifically a small forehead cover of complicated shape.[1]

Top-packing loop
Packing element in Tibetan rugs added from the top to loops basic for the structure. Can be either open, one warp, or closed, two warps. Characteristic for the structure although not obligatory.

tsuktruk **(Tib.)**
1) Thick long-piled sleeping rug, or blanket, or both, made of two to four narrow panels stitched together, 2) Type of single-level technique used only for loops made on front-side plane of warps shed (see Fig. 37a).

Tufts
Also: tufted loops. Loops whose threads have no or only very loose twist.

Two-level structure
Also: two-level weaving or technique. Most common for Eurasia *looping* and knotting type of structure, with loops woven on both upper and lower planes of warp shed.

Unit of loops
If not defined specifically, the smallest one-colour unit of Tibetan looped structure, namely one *basic long-leg loop*, regularly *packed* from the bottom with an additional *open symmetric loop*. See *paired loops* and *long row*.

Unit of wefts
More than one weft between rows of loops.

Wangden *drumze*
See *drumze*.

Warp-faced type
See *single-level structure/technique*.

Weft loop pile
Characteristic for Eurasia, including the typical pile for Tibetan *tsuktruk* rugs formed by means of insertion of loosely floating supplementary wefts.

NOTE

1 Editors' note: The terms above can be used differently in the literature, not only those for forehead trappings but also for knotted works used on riding and working animals.

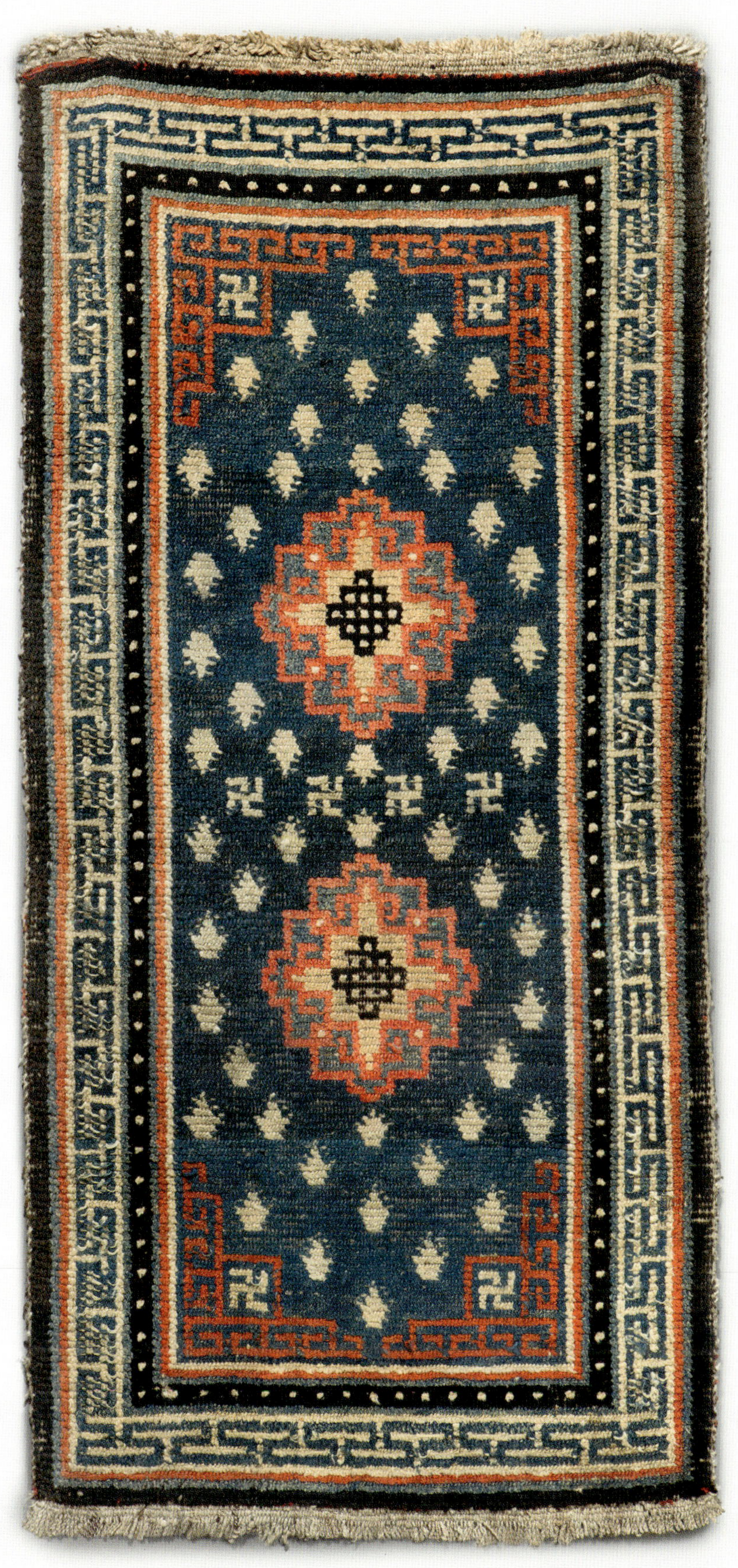

Fig. 81: C129.
Sitting and sleeping rug (*khaden*) in *khamdrum* style.
Mid-19th c., 130×66 cm

Fig. 82: C55.
Sitting and sleeping rug (*khaden*) with classic design. Mid-19th c., 130×73 cm

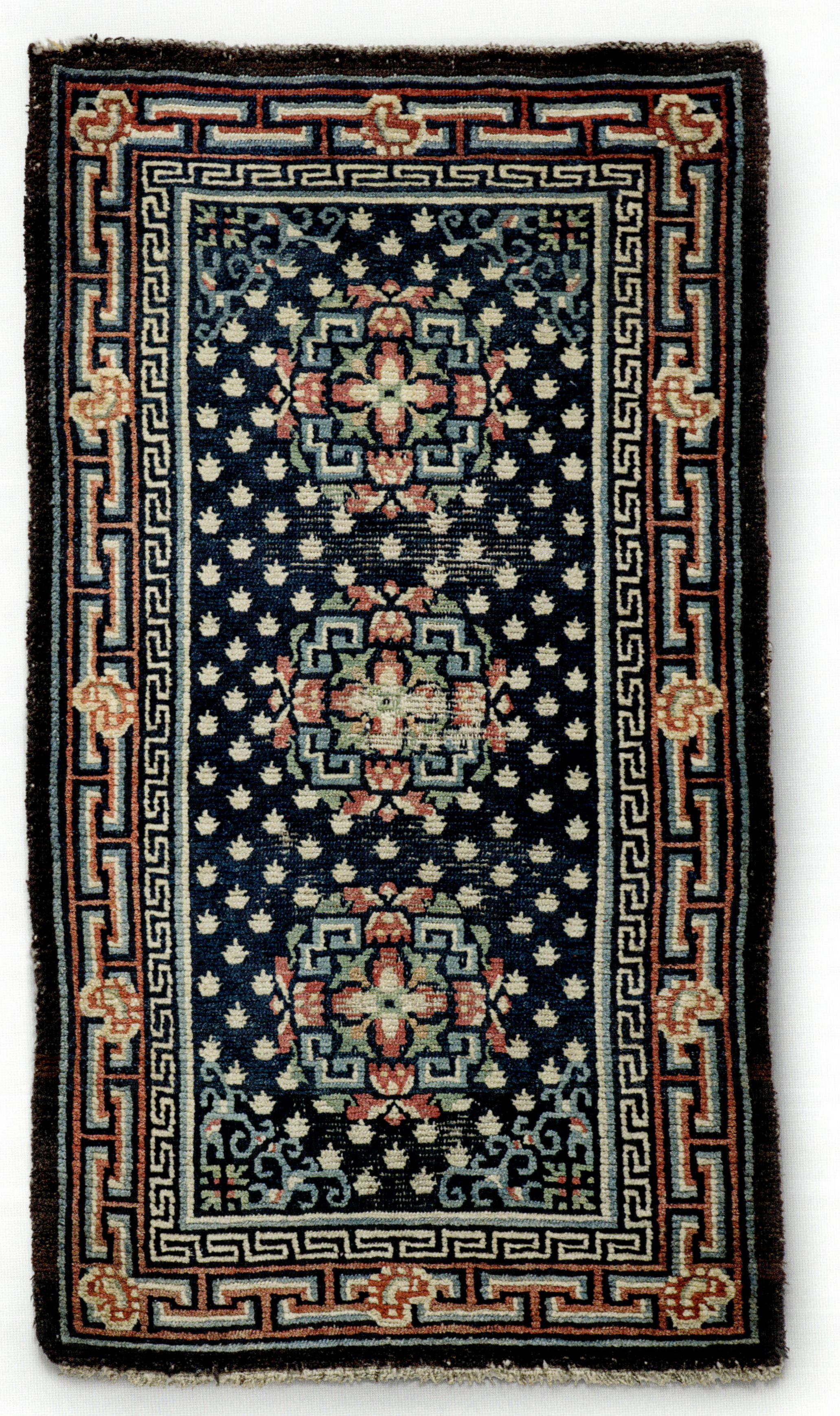

Fig. 83: C165.
Sitting rug (*khagangma*) with an unusual geometric pattern. Early 19th c. (?), 63×68 cm

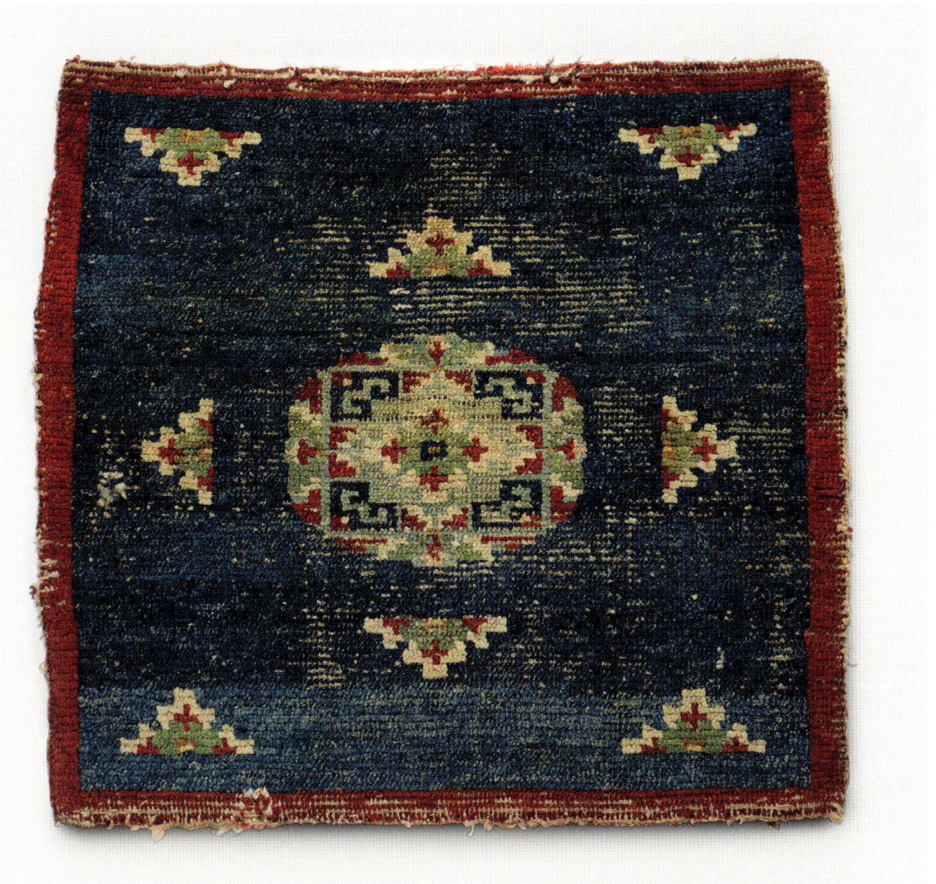

Fig. 84: C76.
Sitting rug (*khagangma*), classic medallion design with 3-D border. 3rd quarter 19th c., 78×70 cm

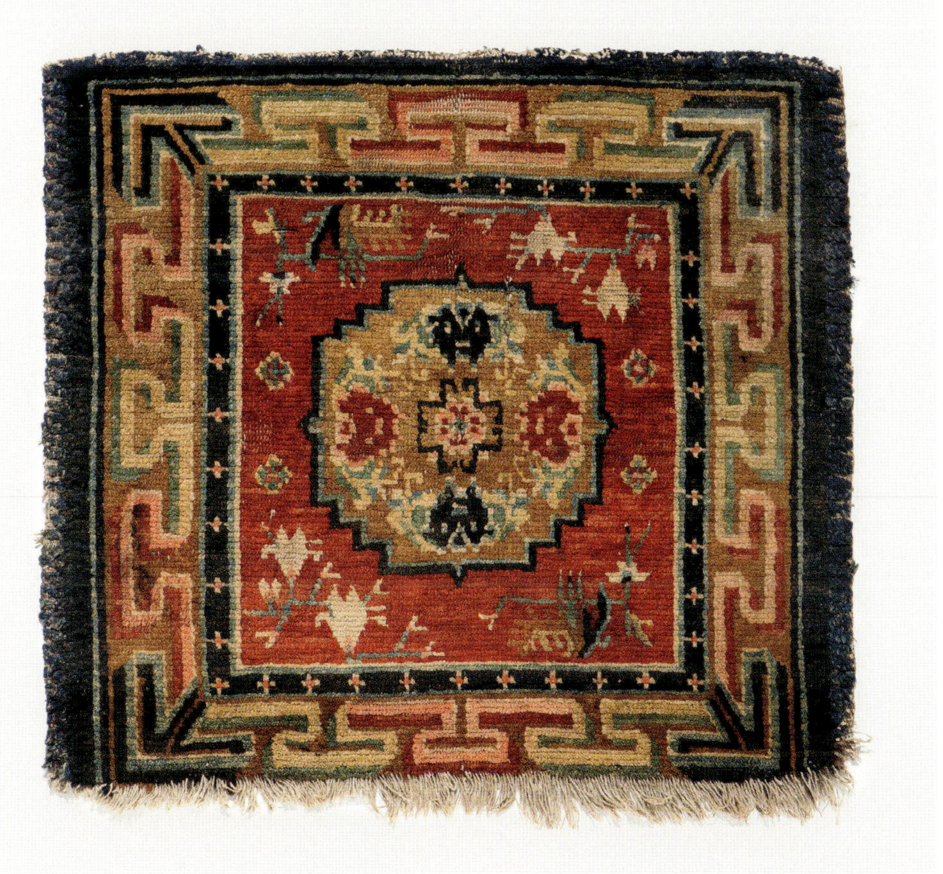

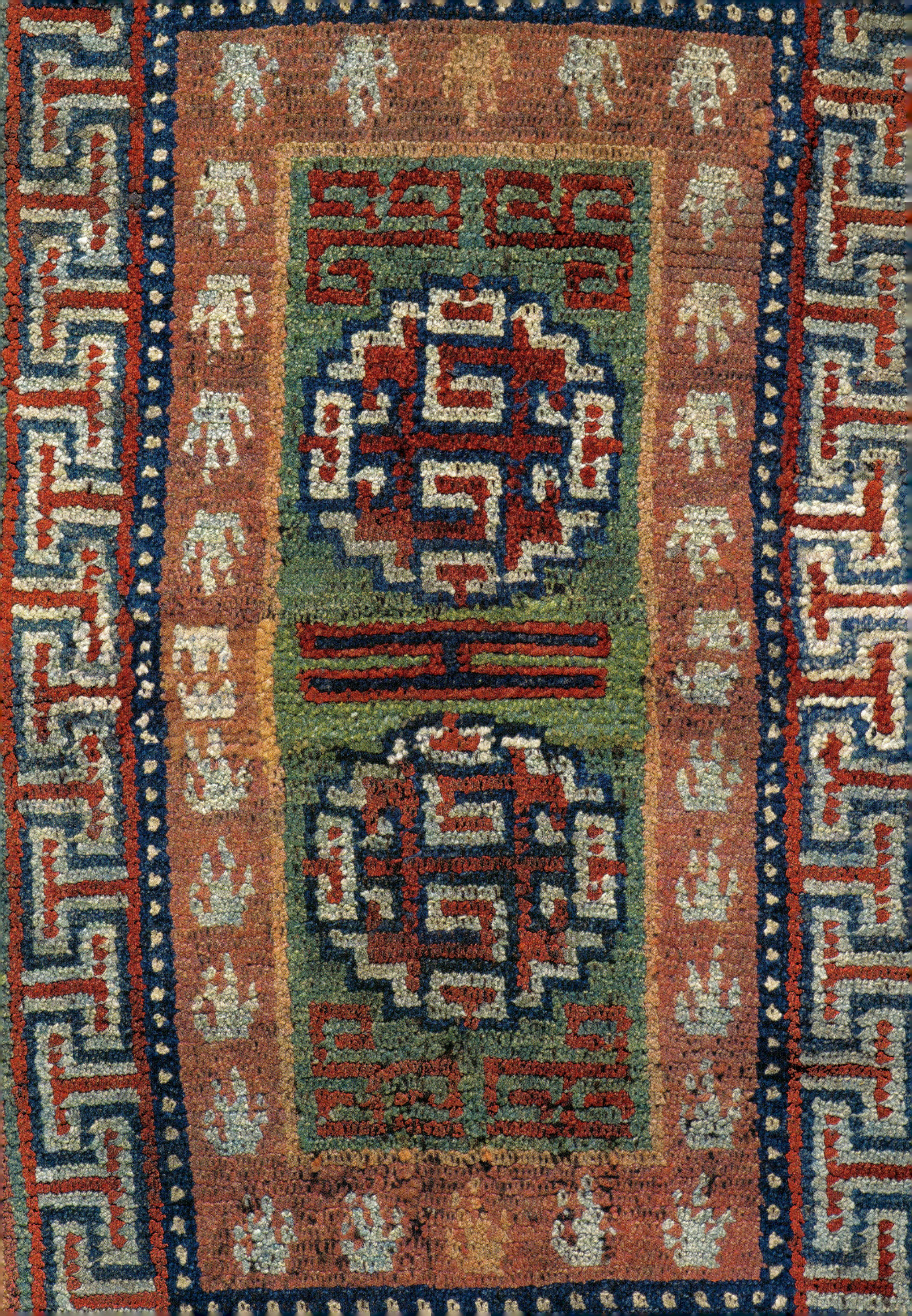

Thomas Wild

IN STYLE AND TIME

The History of the Development of Central Asian Rugs

INTRODUCTION

Detail of Fig. 8

A unique culture has survived on the Tibetan plateau, one in which different traditions have flowed together, intermingled and enriched each other. Their rich inheritance is still today evidence of a Central Asian world dominated by Buddhism which once included a large part of Eurasia along the Silk Road. Adapted to the concepts and requirements of the Tibetan people, this world manifested itself in the material culture of the region. Within this framework, the rug-making art of the Tibetans established its own rules and allows recognition of only slight influence by the subsequent Islamic culture in Central Asia. The arabesque was not accepted in their style book (Ford & Ford 1989: 159) and only seldom do Tibetan rugs appear cryptic or to have hidden symbolism, as those do. The language of their designs is legible, direct and demonstrates this in bold and wilful compositions of colour which often include figures and are graphically strong.

It can be quite a challenge to understand Tibetan rugs in their historical and stylistic development. At first glance, they can appear to be a confusing, too colourful conglomeration of mythical figures, flowers and symbols. Other rugs are minimalistic with only one colour or two, or have a design with a border and medallions reminiscent of classic rugs. Sometimes all these style elements are combined, so that for the outsider it appears to be an entirely haphazard product. On further inspection, however, the use of these rugs and their stylistic, historical development can be identified. Rugs that are used only in a religious context within a monastery can be differentiated from those used in secular environments. Both follow to some extent a common, traditional design canon but also demonstrate great individual variety (Van Grevenbroek & Gay 2009: 133–145).

Although source material about the history of Tibetan rugs is sparse with large gaps between the historical sources making it difficult to develop a coherent picture out of the individual pieces of the puzzle, I will attempt a sort of "tour de force", to at least provide an outline of the different stylistic currents, concentrating on rugs from Central Tibet. The areas along the Tsangpo (Brahmaputra) and the adjacent valleys are very fertile and consequently densely populated. In addition to the nomadic herders and sedentary farmers, there were enough people who could make rugs. Especially the Nyang area in Tsang Province was a centre of rug-making (Denwood 1974: 15).

PROTOHISTORIC PERIOD

The earliest written record for the use of a rug in Tibet documents that in the 8th century AD in the audience hall of the royal palace in Tibet an "excellent" rug was displayed (Stein 1972: 61).[1] One may assume, however, from the geographical conditions in Tibet that rugs were used before the first historical information about the country in the first half of the 7th century (Leeper 1984: 21–25; Miller 2009: 75–78). The open ranges on the plateau are ideal for raising sheep. The great elevation and with it the freezing temperatures virtually demand the production of rugs. How these early rugs looked must remain unknown.

There is evidence, however, that suggests that these rugs were made in a manner which is still practised in Tibet today, as an interesting archaeological find in the Tarim basin, which borders Tibet to the north, demonstrates (Zhang He 2010). In a grave in Shanpula near the southern Silk Road a group of rugs from the 4th to 6th century were found. When one compares the back of one of the Khotan grave rugs with that of a Tibetan style rug, the technical relationship is obvious (Fig. 1). On the back of both rugs the

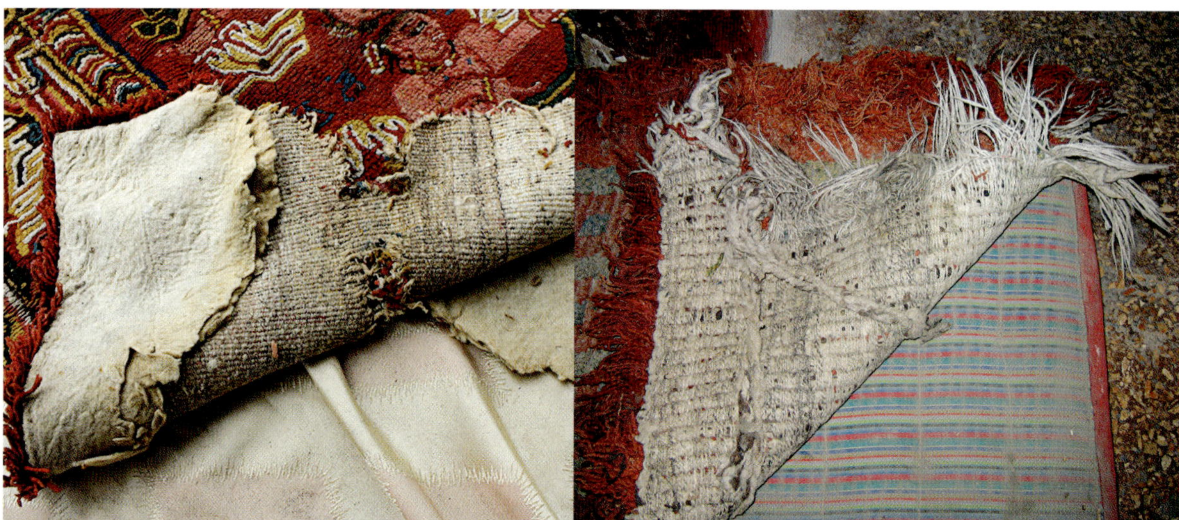

Fig. 1: Technical comparison. Left: reverse of a Khotanese grave rug. Shanpula, 4th–6th c. Right: reverse of a Wangden *drumze*. Pelkhor Chode Monastery, Gyantse, Tsang Province, Central Tibet, 19th c.

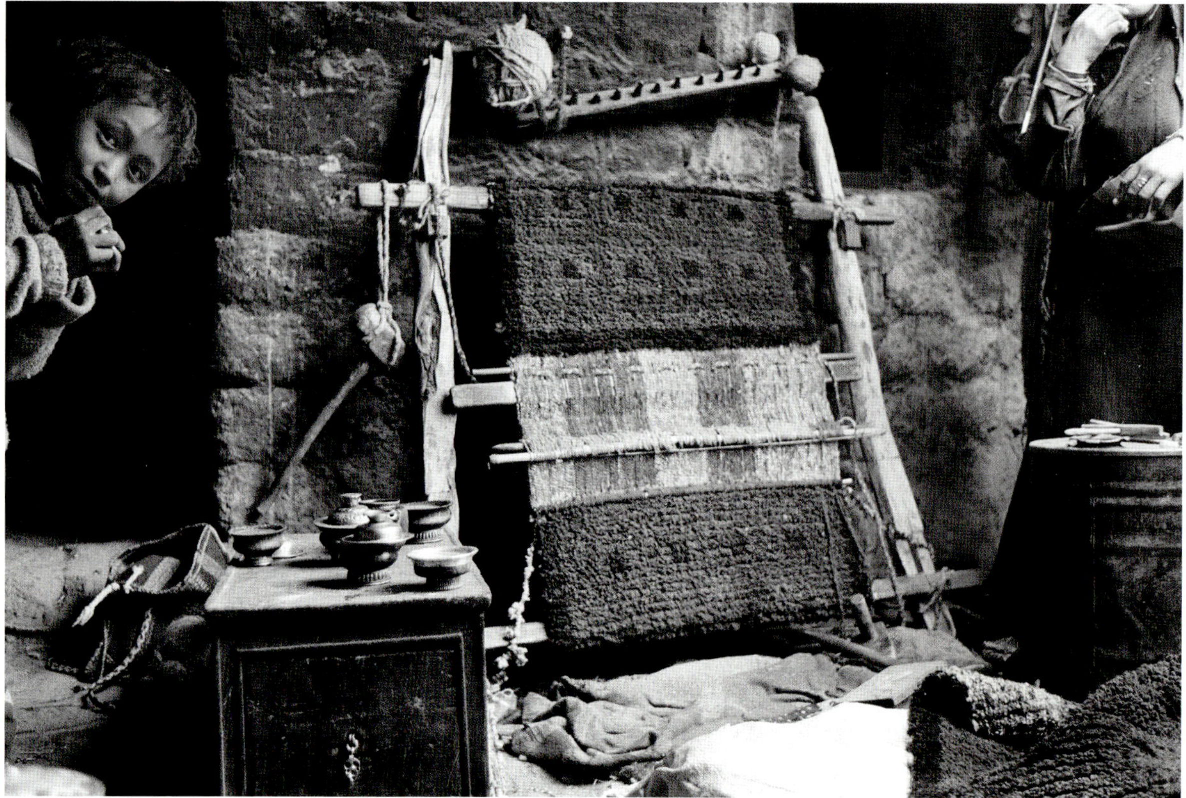

Fig. 2: A Wangden *drumze* being made in the village of Gabu. Wangden region, Tsang Province, Central Tibet, 1996

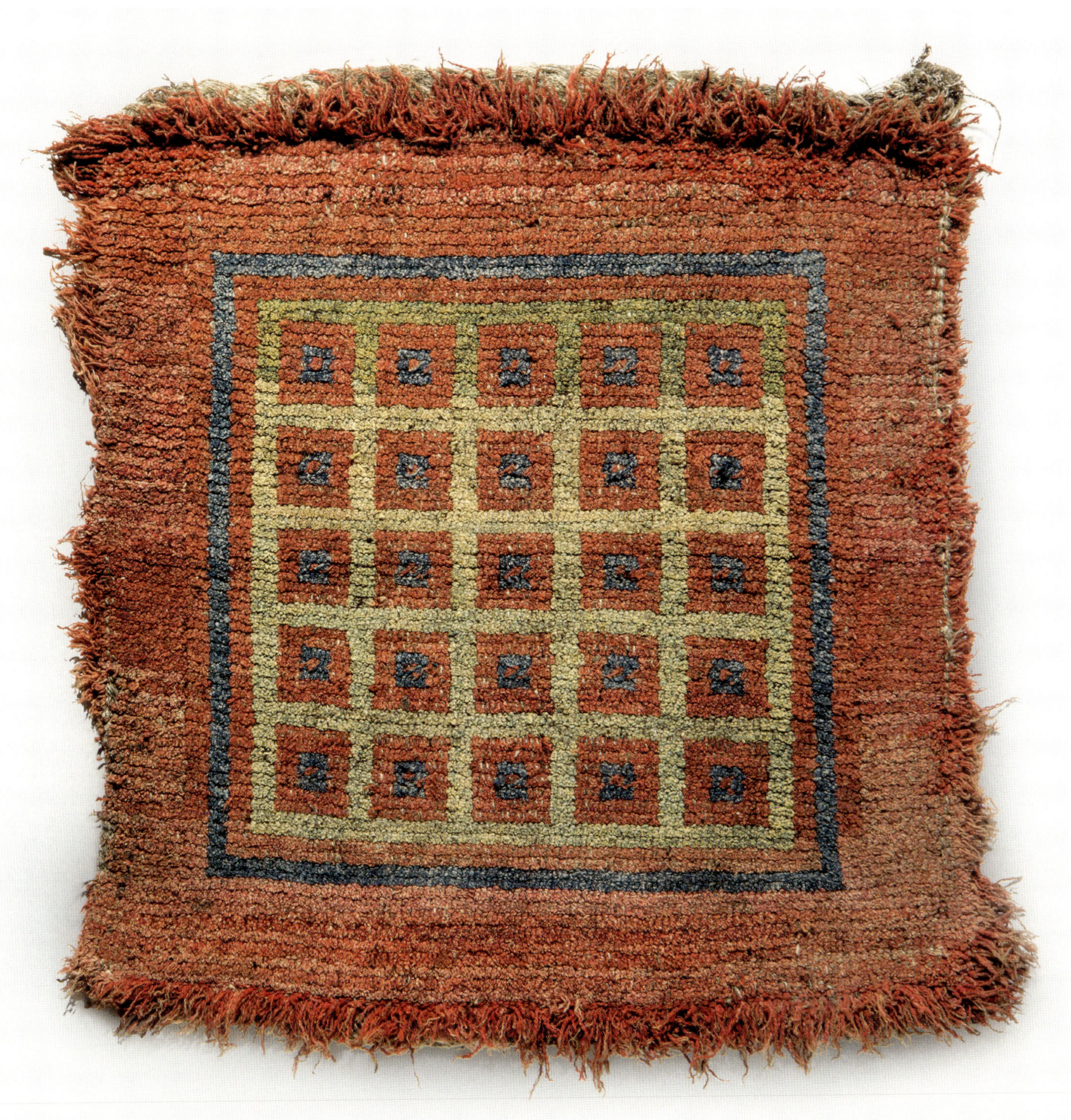

Fig. 3: Monastic throne seat, Wangden *drumze*. Wangden region, Tsang Province, Central Tibet, 19th c., 98×99 cm

Fig. 4: Wangden *drumze* on temple seating in Pelkhor Chode Monastery. Gyantse, Tsang Province, Central Tibet, 2006

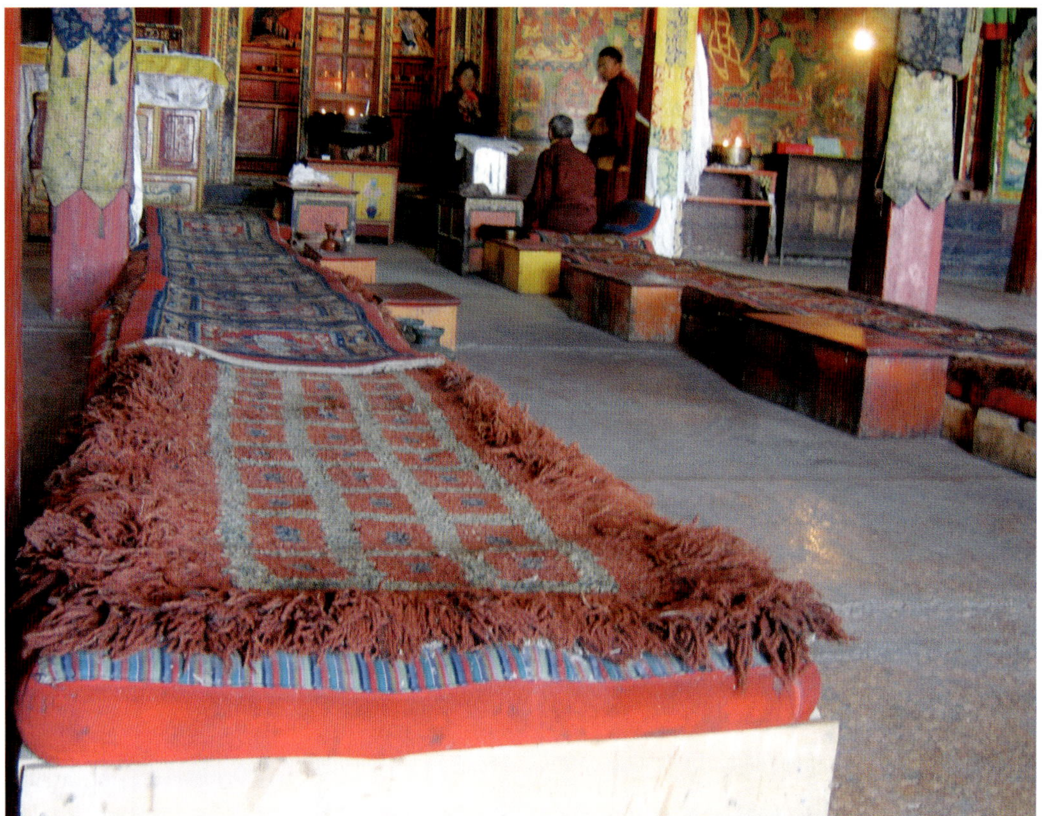

Fig. 5: Monastic throne seat, Wangden *drumze*. Wangden region, Tsang Province, Central Tibet, 19th c., 72 × 76 cm

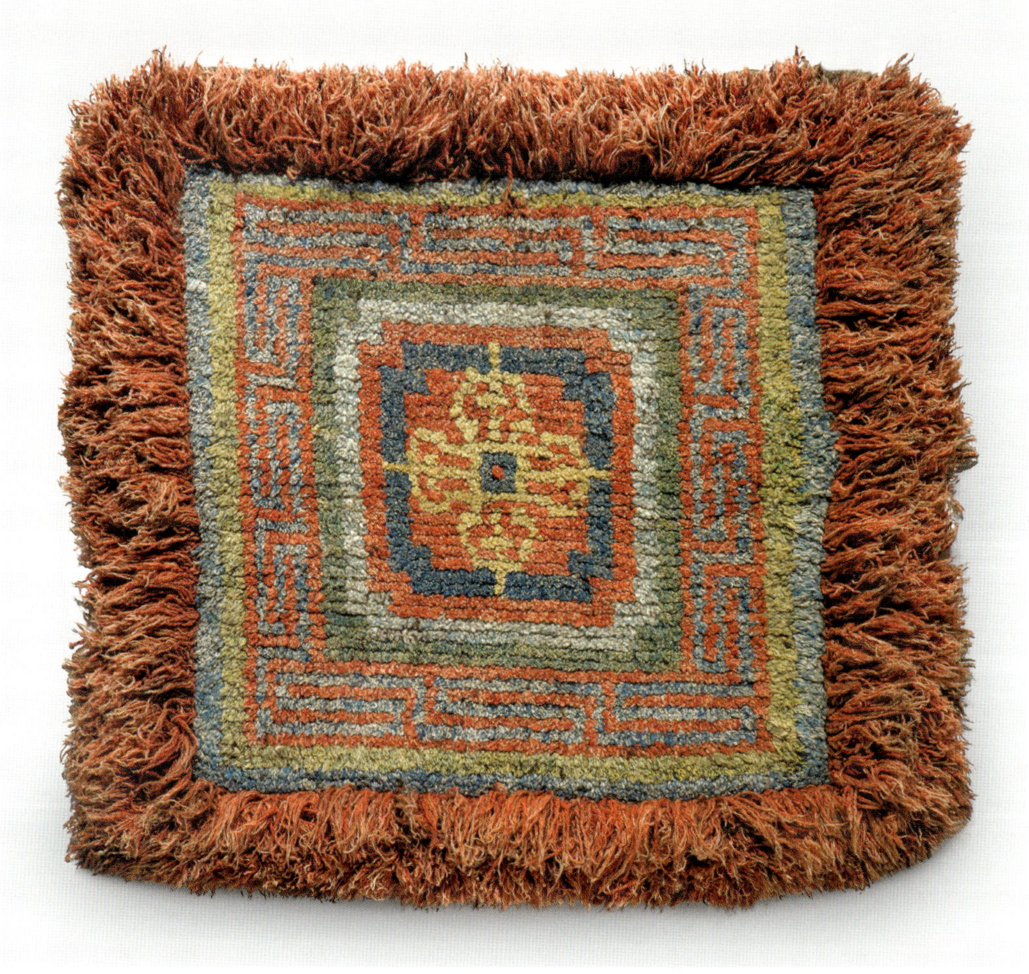

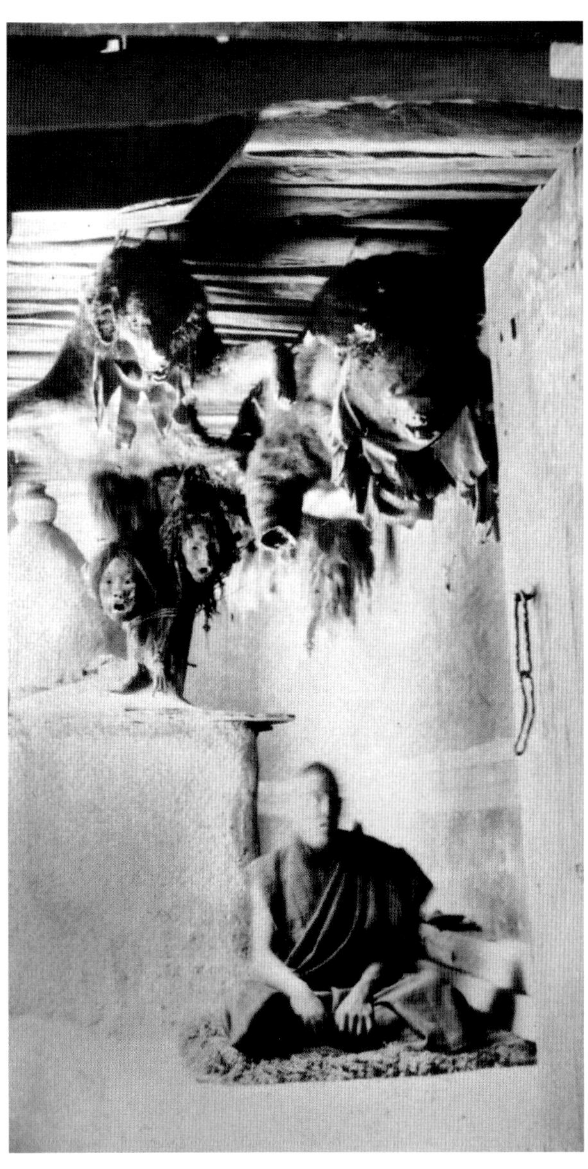

Fig. 6: A monk in a Bon monastery sitting on a Wangden *drumze*. Tangna, Tsang Province, Central Tibet, around 1930

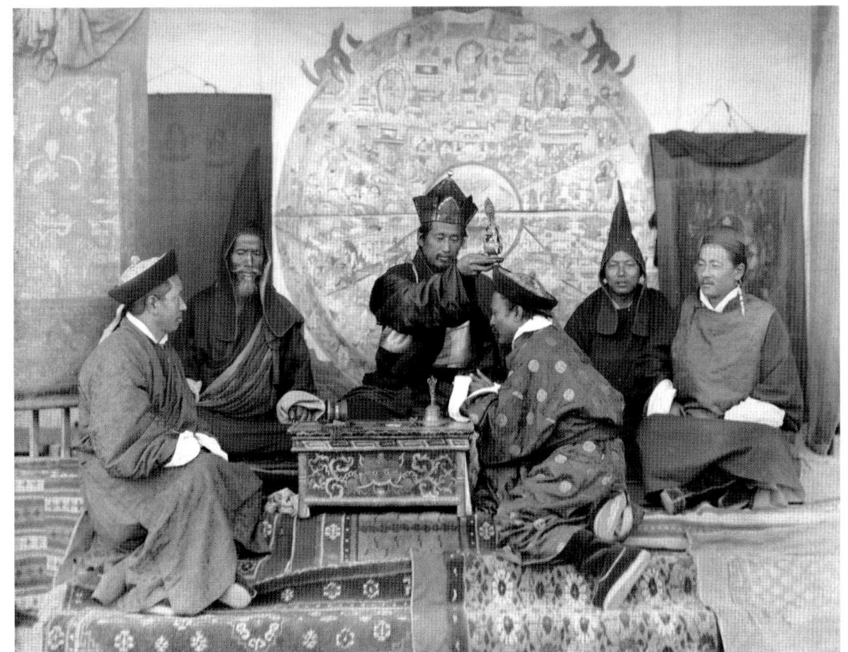

Fig. 7: Audience with a high lama. In the foreground three rugs in *khamdrum* style. Drongtse Monastery, Gyantse region, Tsang Province, Central Tibet, 1882 (?)

warps are visible and the fringing at the edges is nearly identical. The significance that rugs were included in the grave and that in Tibet they are valued in the religion allows the assumption of a protohistoric cultural connection (Wild 2009: 66).

In Tibet, this type of rug is called "Wangden *drumze*", which means a rug from Wangden (Fig. 2), even though the piece must not actually come for the Wangden valley in south Central Tibet. Most of these – like the Shanpula rugs – have a high pile and bushy fringes on all edges, and are of a thick and coarse structure, which does not agree with the expected appearance of an Oriental rug. They are seldom more than one metre wide and square (Fig. 3), but can, however, be up to ten metres long (Wild 2014a: 7).

MONASTIC RUGS

In a visit to a monastery in Central Tibet, we can understand why this is like that. Wangden rugs are laid out on the seats for monks in temples and monasteries, for the raised throne seat and the rows of benches (Fig. 4). The design motifs are limited to a small canon and appear exotic – centred, and yet simple, expressing strength rather than decoration. Except for the double "thunderbolt" (*vajra*) motif, which is found predominantly on *drumze* for throne seats (Fig. 5), all other patterns follow the principle of repetition. The motifs are supposed to give the monk strength during his participation in the rites. The unusually thick material of the rug warms him during the long assemblies, meditation and ceremonies.

Such rugs are used in all Buddhist schools of faith as well as in the pre-Buddhist Bon schools (Fig. 6; Wild 2009: 66). One rug, whose style and feel suggested it could be very old, was tested by the C14 method and dated to the 15th to 17th century (Wild 2009: 66, Rudi Molacek collection).

Two other types of religious rugs need to be mentioned: the group of rugs with a tiger-skin imitation and the so-called "tantric" rugs. Originally, Tibetan yogis wore tiger skin and meditated sitting on them. They hoped that the strength of the tiger would be thereby transferred to them. The tiger skin – or its more or less abstract imitation as a rug – was often used in ritual dances and was also popular as decoration to underline power both in the monastic and profane civilian sectors (Fig. 7; Lipton 1989: 9–16).

The small group of "tantric" rugs found use exclusively in a religious context. Their motifs include human skulls and skeletons, often shown dancing. Chained demons with naked human bodies can also dominate the field of such

Fig. 8: Over-saddle rug (*masho*), secular Wangden *drumze*. Wangden region, Tsang Province, Central Tibet, 19th c., 101×67 cm

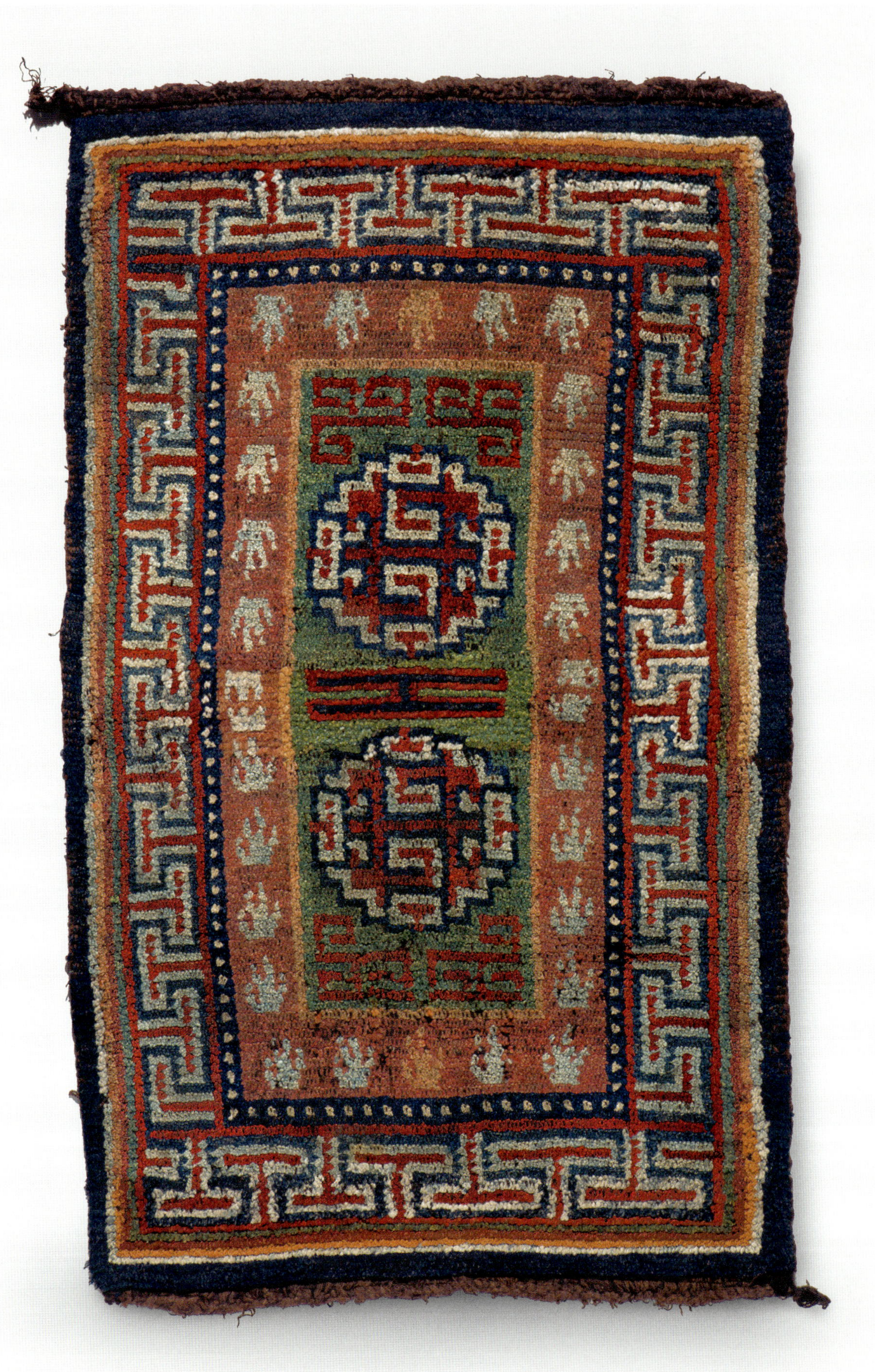

rugs. These are part of the interior decoration of the so-called *Gonkhang*, a room dedicated to guardian deities and effigies related to esoteric rituals performed with annual frequency (Casey 2008).[2]

SECULAR RUGS

In the home, Tibetan rugs were used primarily to cover the raised beds and seats. This is reflected in both their size and proportions as well as in the type of design. With the exception of larger rugs (Tib. *sabden*) that were mostly made for use on the floor for audiences, one rarely finds rugs in Tibetan culture that are more than one metre wide. These relatively narrow pieces were never intended for use on the floor and the choice of designs and motifs shows this in their easy verve, in contrast to the designs on floor rugs.

Different from the interiors in temples and monasteries, where stylistic change came only slowly over the centuries, in the secular environment material culture reacted faster and more directly to trends and taste. It is thus only possible to make rudimentary conclusions about the appearance of much earlier rugs on the basis of those now available. The fact that such "early" rugs existed and that they were sold is, however, documented, as evidenced by the first references to trade in rugs in the Nyang area in the lower part of the Wangden valley between Gyantse and Shigatse. For example, the chronicler Jonangpa Tharanata (1575–1635) mentions two markets for rugs in this region, Duchung and Thugo. Thugo was a market place in "earlier" times (Tucci 1941: 50), whereby Tibetans use the expression often to refer to the imperial era, ca. 7th to 9th centuries. Thus it is not surprising that just in the area of the Wangden and adjoining valleys rugs with seemingly old designs are still made to this day for everyday use, as the author's field research in Khikar valley in Nyangbar showed (September 2006).

An over-saddle rug in the Buddeberg collection is a nice example of this small group of rugs, as it shows in addition to the usual "T-border" a seldom and well-nigh "archaic" border with the repeated motif that is commonly called "frog foot" or "burning jewel" (Fig. 8). In the rug world, this border variant is one of the older known borders. It is comparable with that of the so-called Shanpula rug (probably 2nd to 3rd century), which was found in another grave in the Taklamakan region (Bunker 2001: 37). In addition, this rug has two medallions in the field that the locals call a "coin medallion" (Tib. *thranka*) (Wild 1998: 152). This motif, which can generally be assigned to the canon of monastic motifs in the Wangden valley, has found its ways into profane use. The medallions in this form and the use of the finest Wangden knotting technique are the prominent feature of this small group of rugs, which are characterised by their strict adherence to the design, which often fills the whole area.[3] From a stylistic point of view, the transition to *khamdrum* rugs can be said to flow.

If it was difficult elsewhere to identify Tibetan rugs made for everyday use on the basis of symbols and other markings as belonging to a specific region or clan, for this small group this is possible based on the similarity of the knotting technique and on the characteristic choice of design elements, as discussed with the coin medallions. The origin of the coin medallions is unknown. Since it stands out as a regional symbol, it can be tentatively suggested here that it is a very old, perhaps a clan-identifying symbol, perhaps similar to the concept of the *göls* on Turkmen rugs.

Khampa Dzong is situated further south and close to the Nyang region on the edge of the Tibetan plateau at the foot of the eight-thousand-metre Kanchenjunga. This market town on the border to Sikkim is apparently the source for the name *khamdrum* for these rugs, whose style in view of quality and quantity were the fundament of pre-industrial Tibetan rugs (Myers 1984: 34; Wild 2014b). These rugs have a strict basic design of border medallion on a usually indigo field with corner motifs (Figs. 9 and 10). Next to stylised flowers variations, the main border is most often one related to the Greek style; a pearl border is favoured in the secondary border. The corners of the field have geometric or organic motifs. Most usual are three medallions on the field, the centre one often more dominant. Stylised flowers, frog foot and cloud variations can be scattered motifs on the field. Besides the three-medallion type of these sitting and sleeping rugs, there are rugs with two or just one medallion, but also designs without a medallion are common.[4] The meaning of these medallions is still not adequately clarified.

It is worthy of note, however, that seen from above these medallions have a quadratic form with a centre, recalling the Tibetan cosmic model: the mythical Mount Meru is the centre of the world; four rivers flow from it, indicating the four cardinal points, thus forming a square around the central, primal *mandala* (Krotkov 1991).

When this classical type established itself stylistically remains speculation. If one assumes that the primary factor for the development of a style is a certain measure of demand or market for it, then social stability and economic prosperity are a precondition. The unification of Tibet and

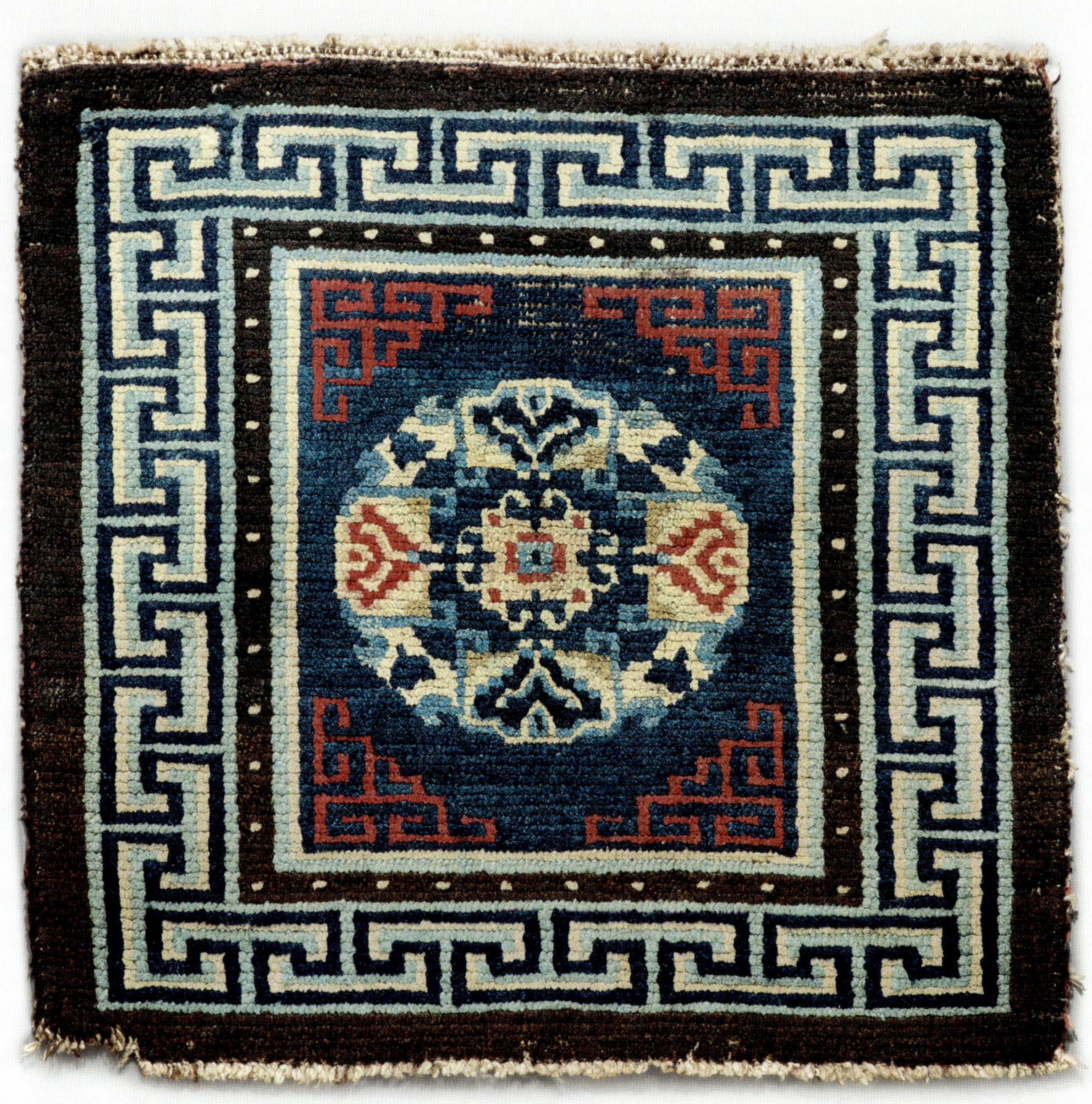

Fig. 9: Sitting rug (*khagangma*), *khamdrum*. Tsang Province, Central Tibet, possibly 1st half 19th c., 67 × 72 cm

Fig. 10: Sitting and sleeping rug (*khaden*), *khamdrum*. Tsang Province, Central Tibet, possibly 2nd half 19th c., 129 × 72 cm

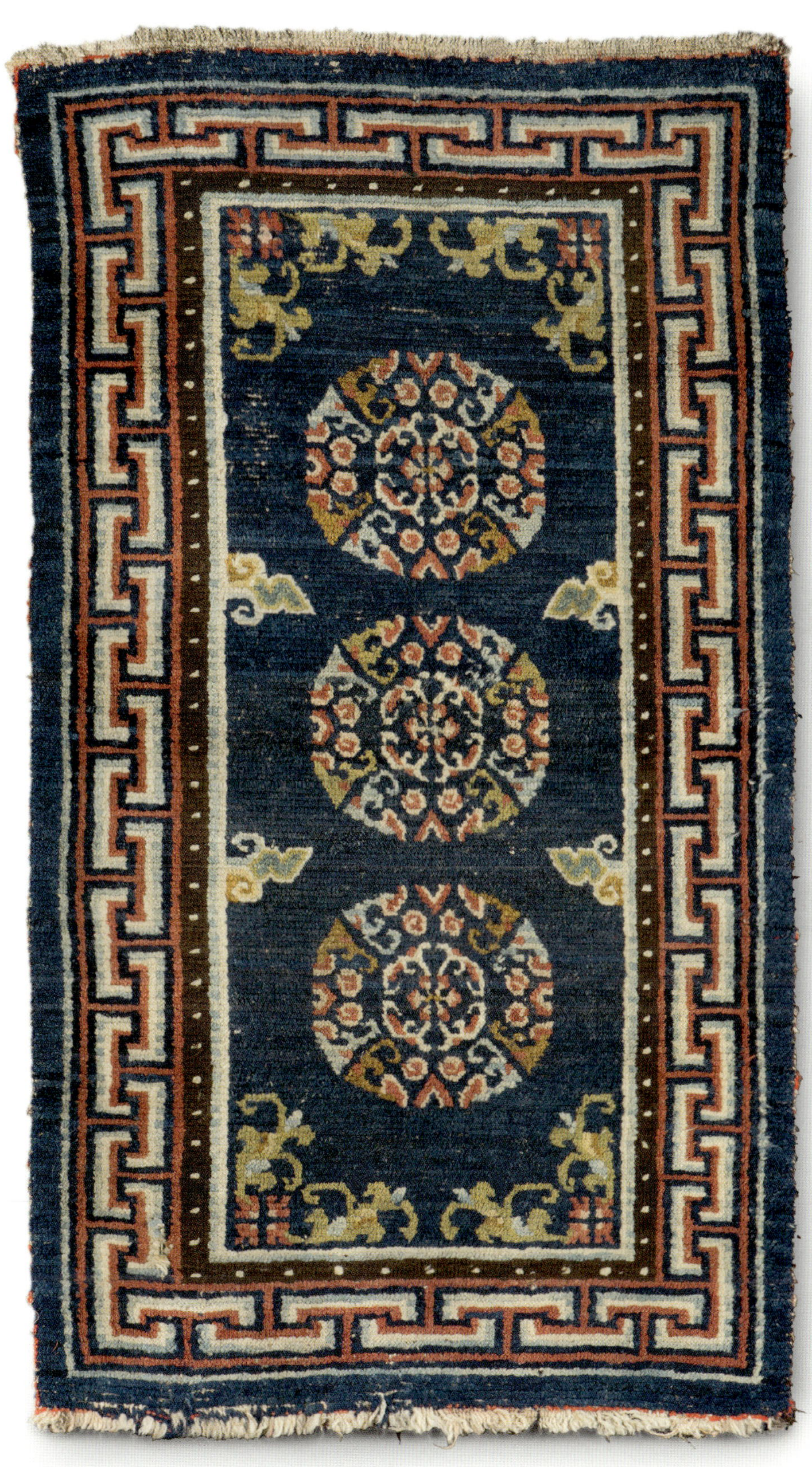

resulting inner political stability, which the fifth Dalai Lama, Ngawang Lobsang Gyatsho (1617–1682), achieved during his long reign were undoubtedly favourable for trade in rugs throughout the entire Tibetan cultural area. The new situation would have generated an increased demand for rugs and could have led to the fixation of the style of the *khamdrums* in the form that is shown here. In any case, the earliest photographs and datable purchases for the 1880s show only this type of rug. Fig. 7 shows an audience with a high lama. In the foreground are three rugs in *khamdrum* style, recognisable by the six-petalled flower border. The *khamdrum* with the tiger-skin design under the table serves to underline the lama's authority. This photograph is to date the oldest known picture of a Tibetan rug (Wild 2014b: 65–73).

FREELY DESIGNED CARPETS

The majority of pre-industrial Tibetan rugs do not follow the border-medallion scheme. The makers had apparently no qualms about creating a design freely to their own taste. Their independent approach is seen in differing borderless variations in which a constantly repeated design shows the maker's playing with her expression of the concept of infinity.

These are often polychrome, but usually with only two colours. We find rugs with a chessboard design, medallions, tiger, *mandala*, *swastika*, flower, cloud motifs (Figs. 11 and 12)[5], but also monochrome rugs with strong abrash belong in this group. The popularity of these rugs and their often outstanding quality indicates that they were also produced in large workshops. This leads us to the area around Gyantse in the upper Nyang valley in the Tsang province. In the course of time, it became the largest market place in Tibet for rugs.[6] Thus Sarat Chandra Das (1849–1917), an Indian pandit, who made several research trips through Central Tibet for the British-Indian government (Raj) between 1879 and 1882, reports in his travelogue *Journey To Lhasa and Central Tibet* that there were manufactories employing as many as 90 women in making rugs (Fig. 13;[7] Das 1902: 213). In his report, he differentiates between "Khampa rugs" and "Gyantse rugs", which were probably both made in one manufactory (Das 1902: 96–103). He does not, however, mention stylistic differences.

Whereas the Khampa rugs, commonly known as *khamdrum* rugs, retained their traditional design, it is quite possible that designs of the Gyantse rugs followed trends and responded to current demand in the inner Tibetan market.[8] Whether and how such "Gyantse rugs" can be understood in their completeness has to be determined. It could be that

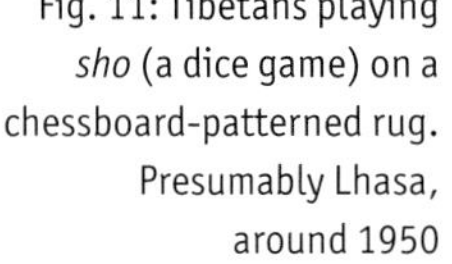

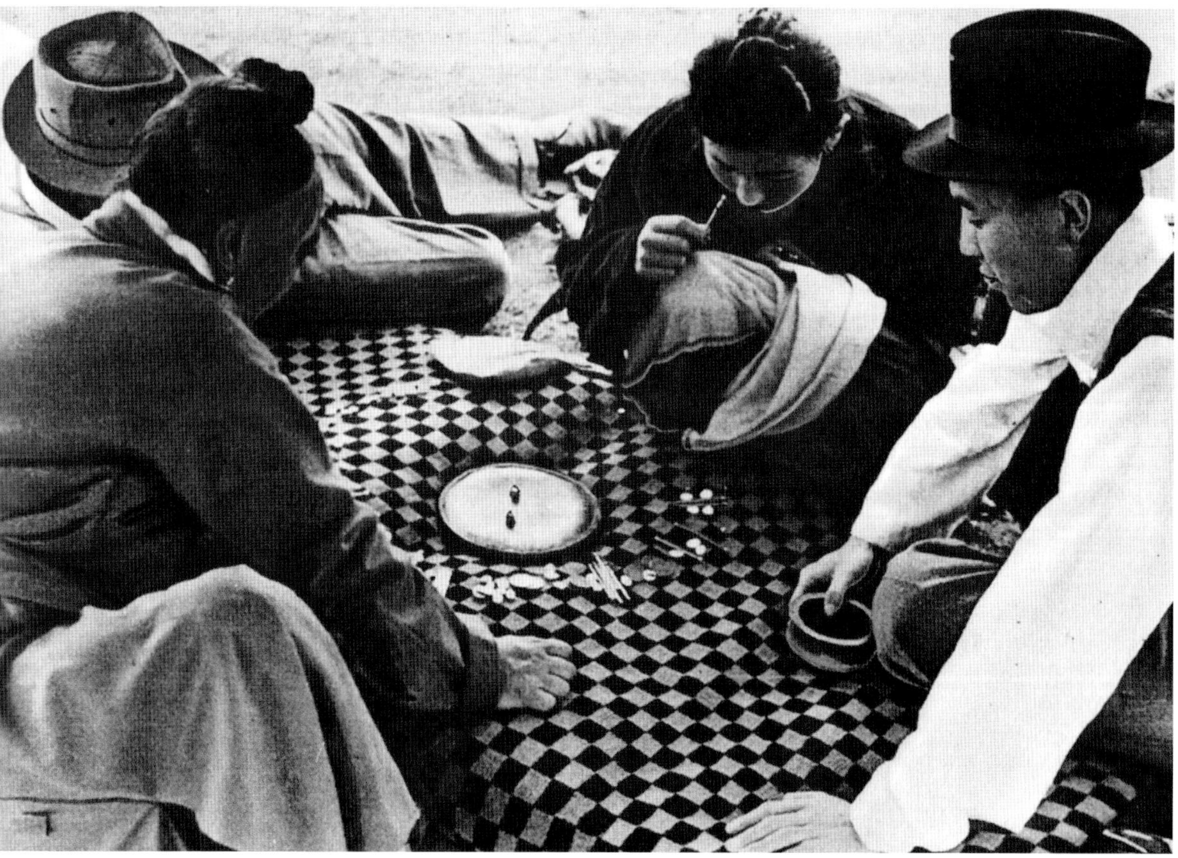

Fig. 11: Tibetans playing *sho* (a dice game) on a chessboard-patterned rug. Presumably Lhasa, around 1950

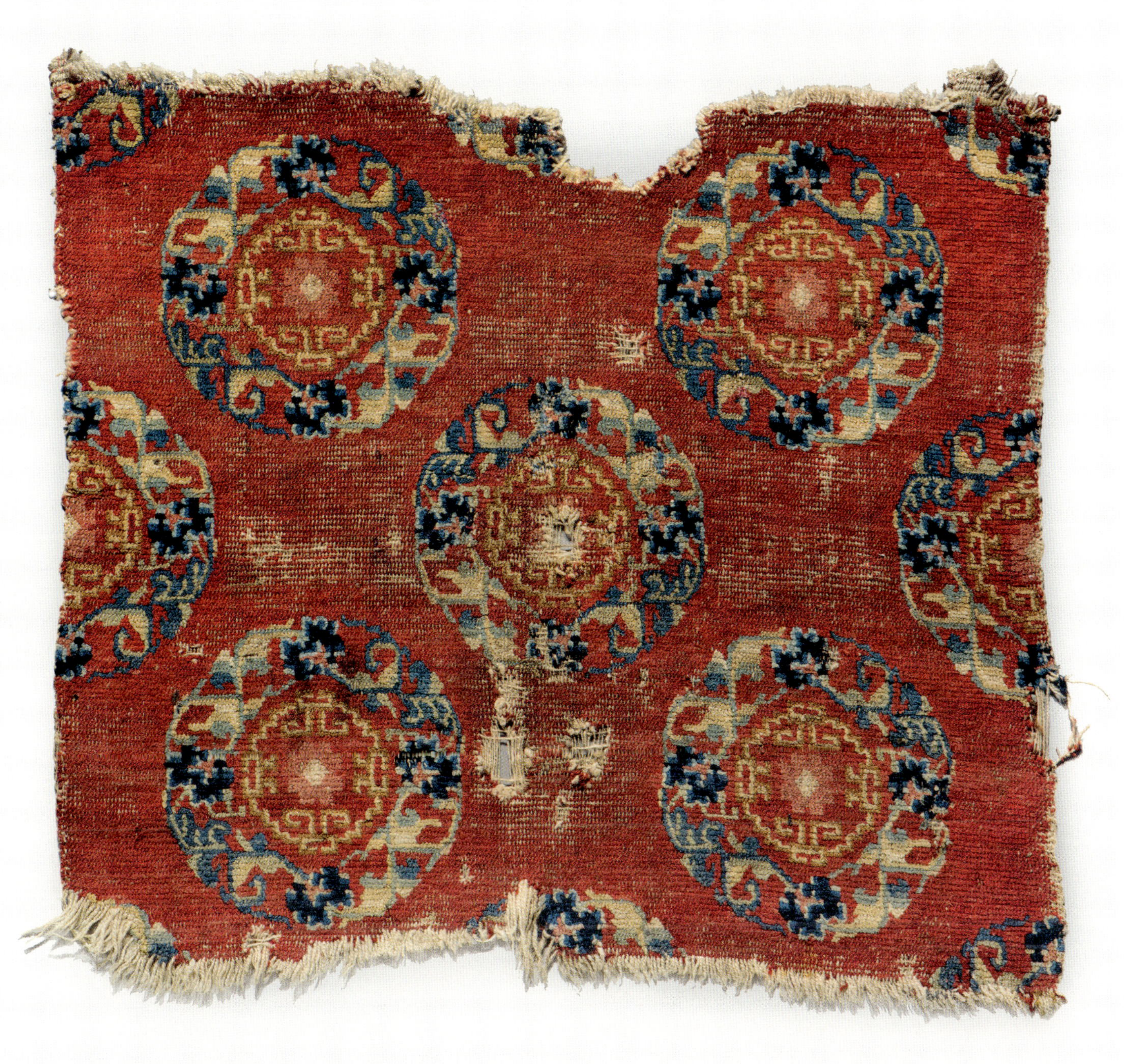

Fig. 12: Sitting or sleeping rug (*khaden*) (?). Fragment of a medallion design in endless rapport. Following a silk textile in Mongolian style. Possibly Gyantse region, Tsang Province, Central Tibet, possibly 1st half 19th c., 70×80 cm

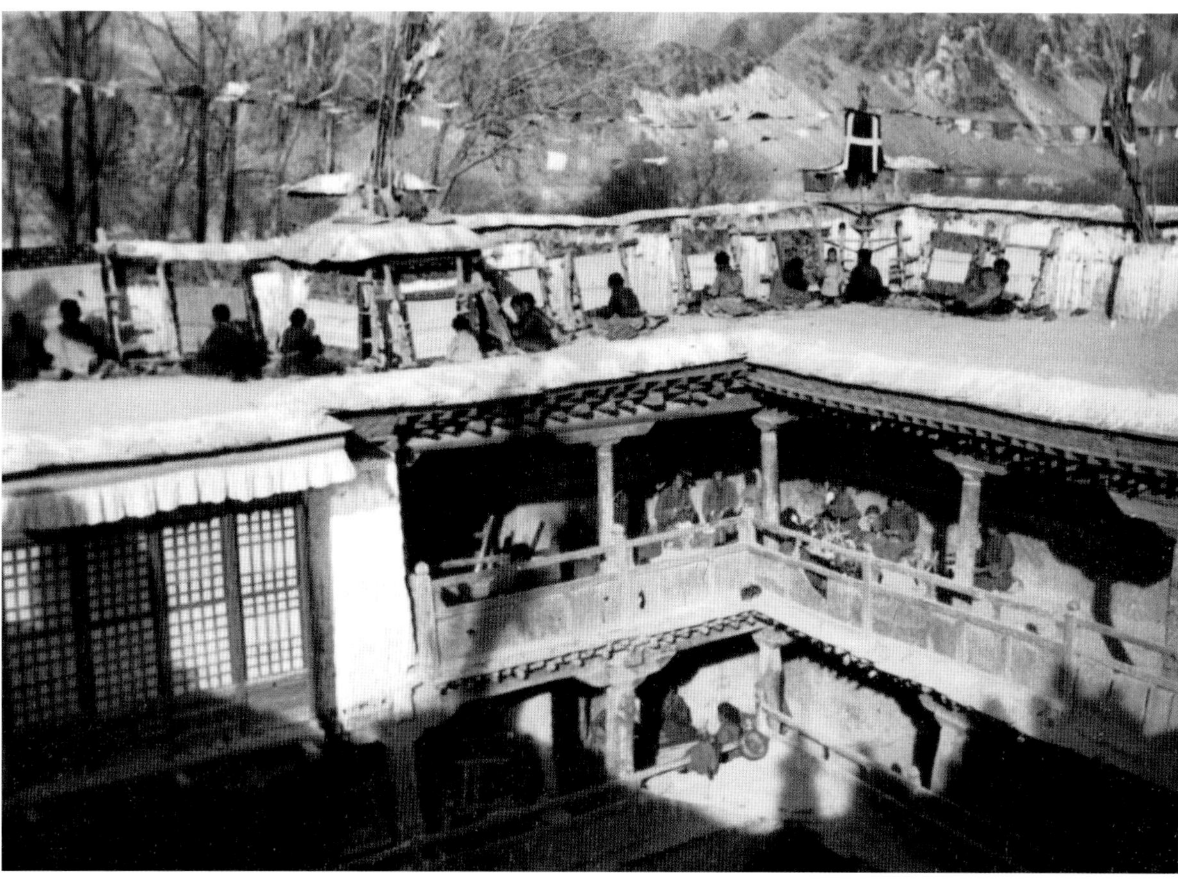

Fig. 13: Rug manufactory on the property of the Doring family. Gyantse, Tsang Province, Central Tibet, between January and July 1940

Sarat Chandra Das used the expression to describe these borderless or freely designed rugs.

Although the question of how far back in history this tradition of individually designed rugs goes must remained unanswered, one can suppose that it is just as old as the tradition of the classical rugs. In my opinion, there are two independent and very old traditions, each with its own basic concept of design.

RUGS WITH CHEMICAL DYES

A wave of stylistic changes came when at the end of the 19th century the first chemical dyes found their way to Tibet. The dyeing process was simpler, and it was possible to experiment with colours in a way that could not be done previously. The types of rugs anchored in old tradition suffered a slow degeneration, whereas the freely designed rugs experienced a new impetus (Lorentz 1975: 150; Pallis 2004: 362–354). In no other Central Asian rug-making tradition did the introduction of chemical dyes give rise to a completely new artistic development as it did in Tibet. The designs seemed to know no restrictions and the whole world of Tibetan fables and motifs were able to find representation on rugs.

How could it happen that design formats that had grown and been fixed over centuries were given up so quickly and replaced by completely new paradigms? And why in just the eastern Central Asian region to this extent? In the western traditions of the Eurasian area, chemical dyes also replaced natural dyes but the traditional patterns remained unchanged, even though the western market demand did have a permanent influence on size, choice of design and quality. The current literature has no explanations for the source of this significant style change. A glance at the neighbouring Chinese rug production could suggest an explanation. Early in the 20th century the production of rugs for the western market, predominantly the American market, began and increased after World War I. Inspired by Art Deco, in Beijing and mainly in Tianjin so-called area rugs (rugs for large rooms) were produced in great numbers. At the wish of their customers, western producers such as the American Walter Nichols adapted their own designs and followed the trend. Thus from the traditional Chinese rugs developed the first designer rugs, also called "New Chinese Style" (Lorentz 1975: 150–152, Anonymus n.d.). This massive change in traditional rug production apparently did not go unnoticed in the wider field of the industry. On the contrary, it may have opened a new and even welcome view

Fig. 14: Sitting or sleeping rug (*khaden*), so-called "Kapsho Pesar". Central Tibet, around 1900, 170×93 cm

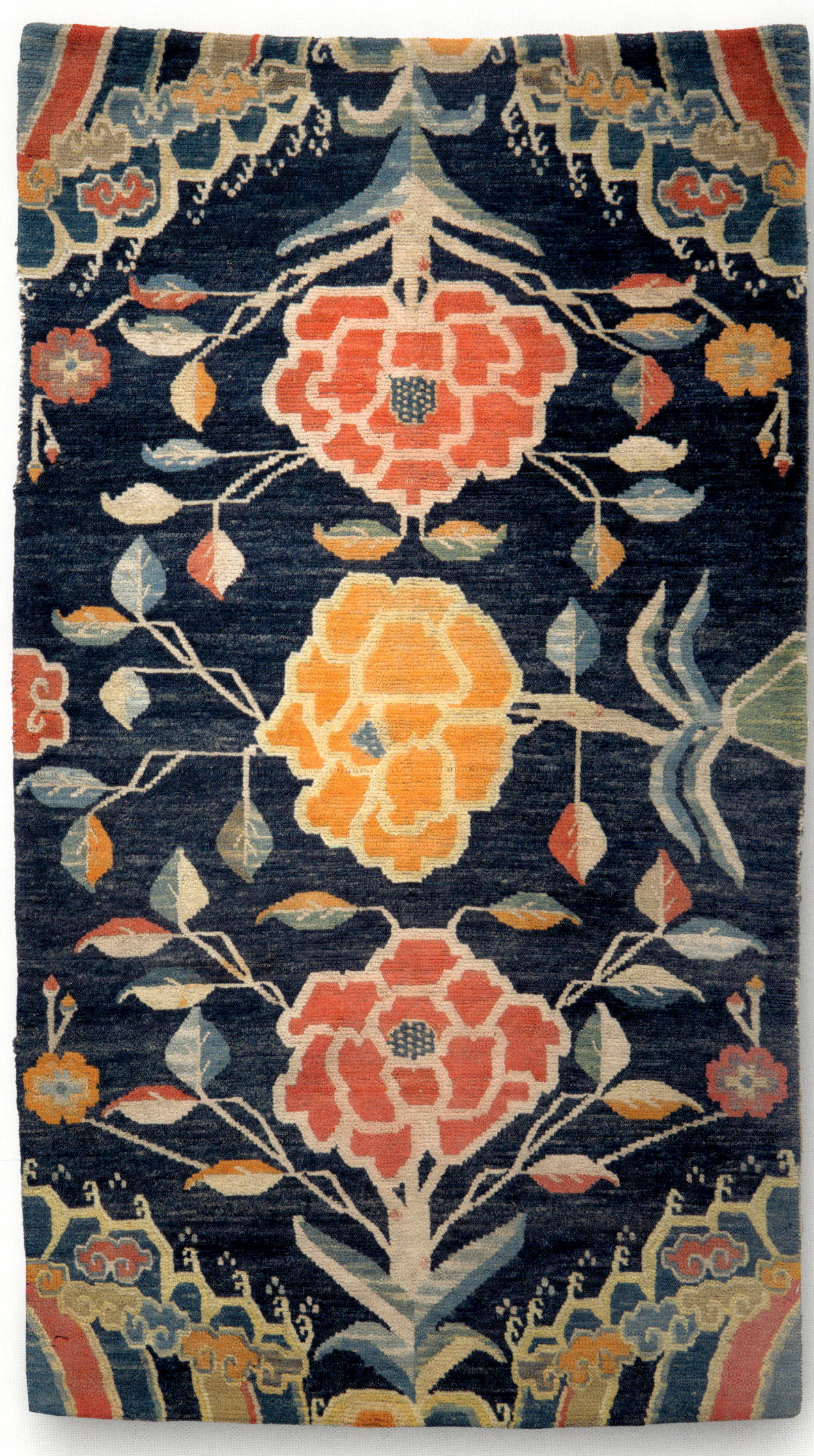

Detail of Fig. 14

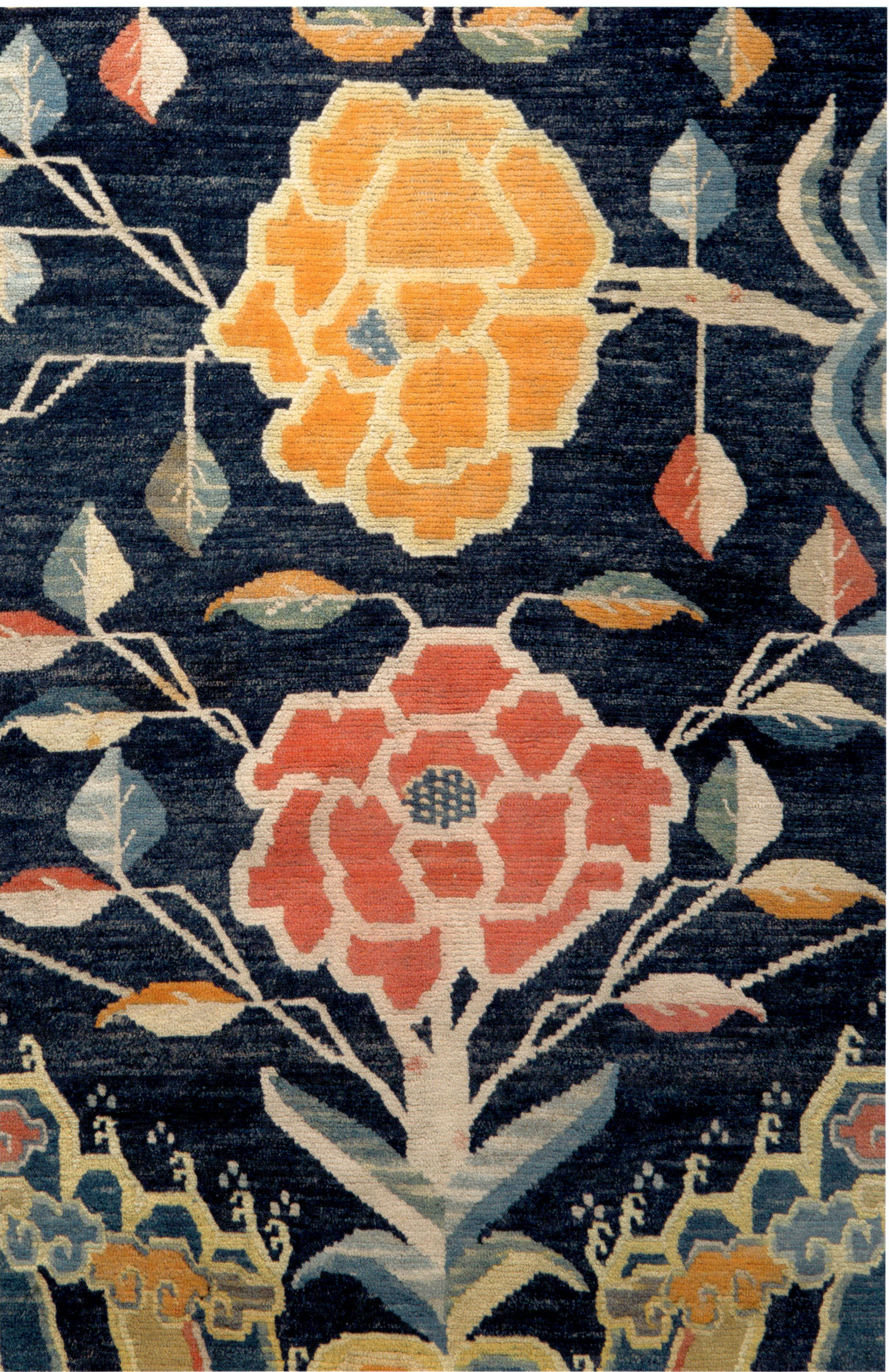

Detail of Fig. 15

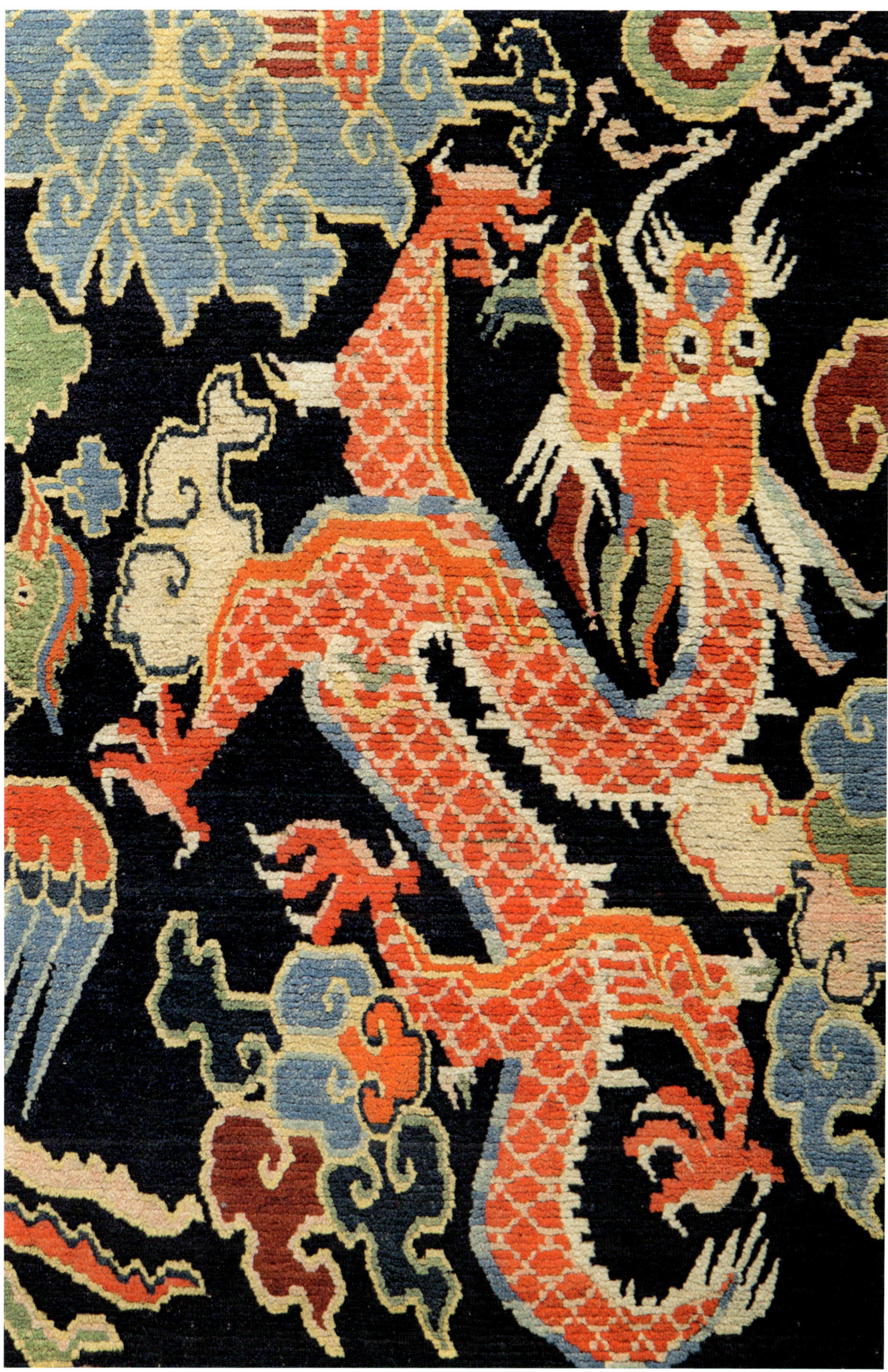

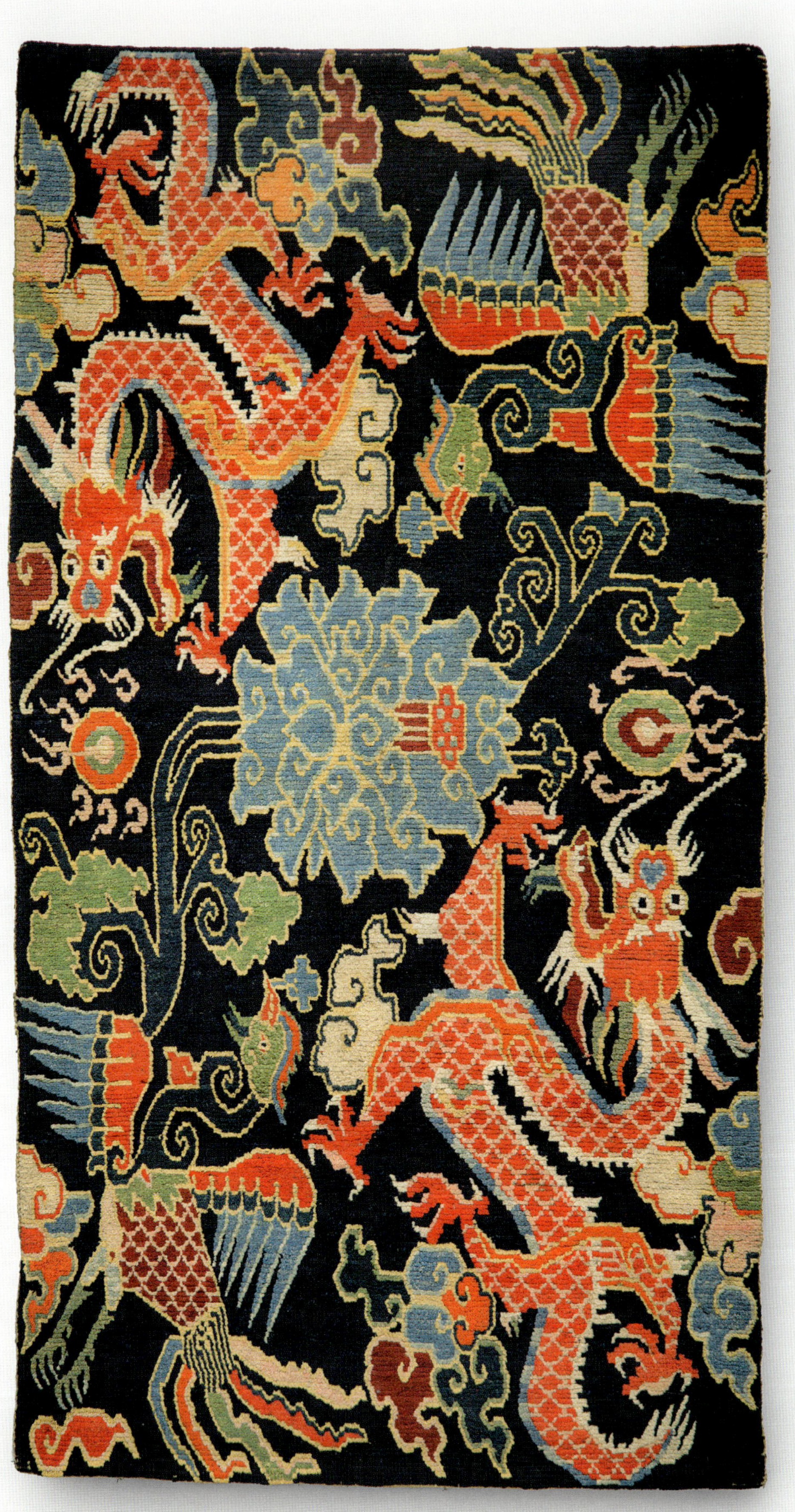

Fig. 15: Sitting or sleeping rug (*khaden*) with dragon and phoenix motif with a central lotus flower. Central Tibet, around 1920, 160×86 cm

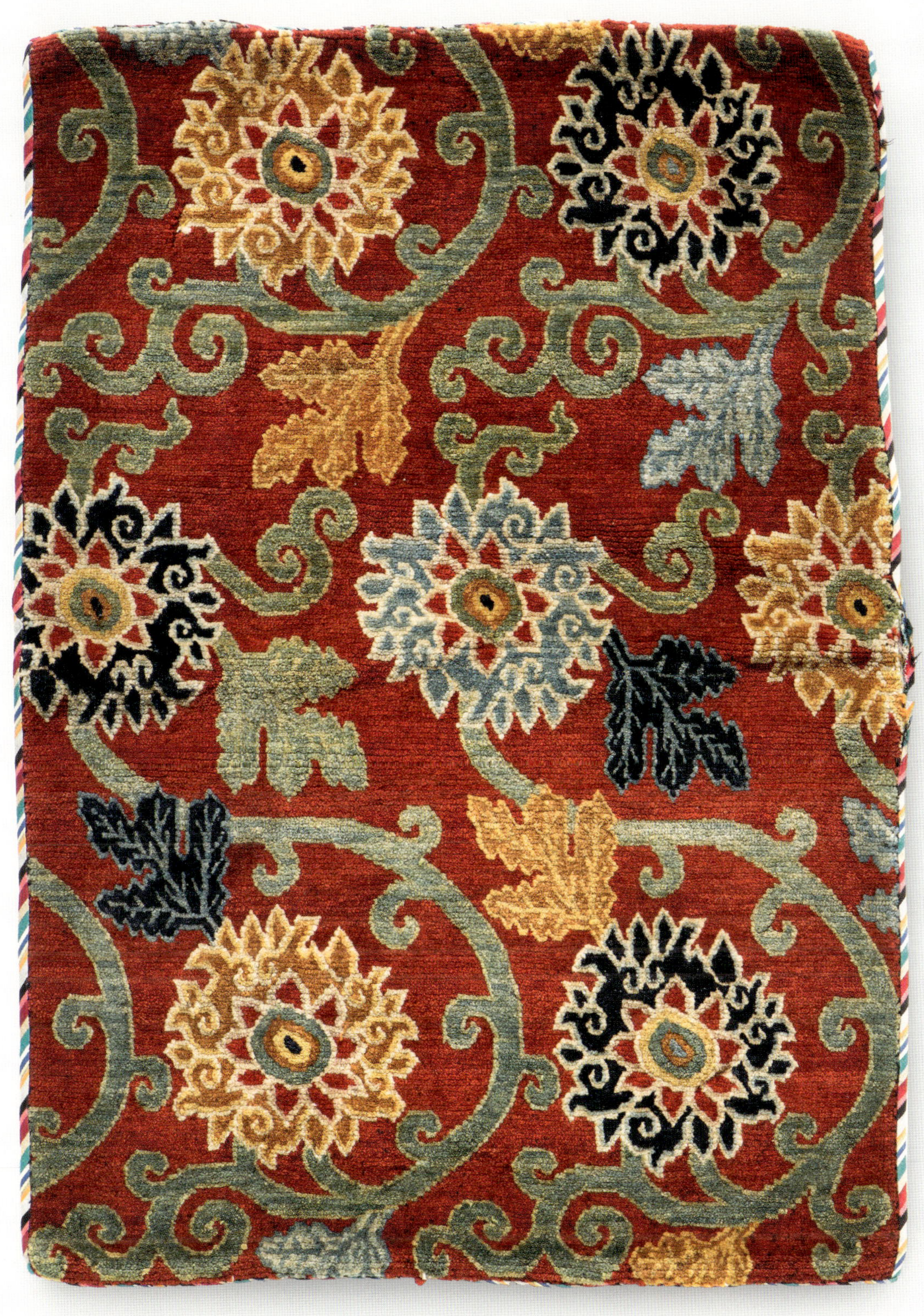

Fig. 16: Sitting rug (*khagangma*), so-called "Twelve-Lotus rug". Central Tibet, around 1920, 81×58 cm

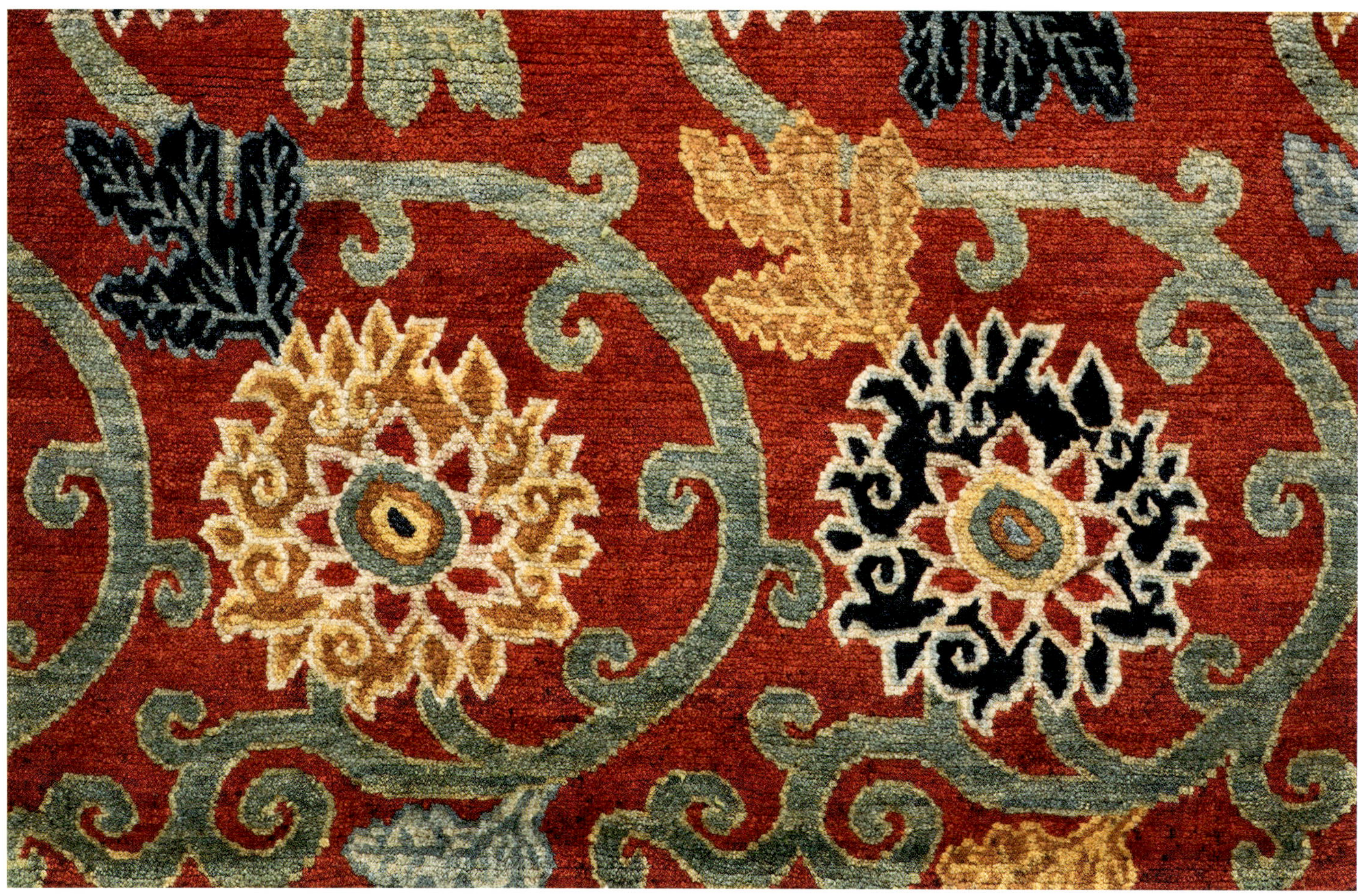

Detail of Fig. 16

of the old handicraft. The wool for the major Chinese producers came solely from the western, traditional rug regions such as Xinjiang, Inner Mongolia, and Tibet. Tibet with its high quality "Sining" wool was the major provider.[9] One can imagine that the inquisitive Tibetan wool dealers learned firsthand about the innovative way to create rugs and told about it back home. Admittedly, in Tibetan rugs no copying of the Chinese designs intended for the western market can be identified. Instead, the impulse from outside inspired the Tibetans to experiment with the new chemical dyes to make new but still original Tibetan rugs for the domestic market. These new designs are to some extent inspired by motifs from silk cloths, which were used to make clothing in Tibet, also to decorate entire interiors, but also from porcelain and non-Tibetan rugs. In the group of freely designed pre-industrial rugs, which seldom had figures as motifs, now with the chemical dyes suddenly fabled beings and animals appear: dragon, phoenix, tiger, snow lion, crane and bat, just to name the most common ones. These allowed fanciful and manifold variations, some even similar to comics. But also magnificent lotuses and peonies were generously depicted. The mostly aristocratic customers competed to outdo each other by designing such pieces and bragging about the skill of their best rug-makers. To mention one of these, Kapshopa, a minister in the Tibetan cabinet, was known for his "flower rugs". An often copied example with three flowers in the field was sold with his name as *Kapsho Pesar* (Kapsho's new design) (Fig. 14; Chodrak & Tashi 2000: 98; also oral information from Ted Worcester 1996). Especially favoured was a dragon-phoenix composition with a flower in the centre (Fig. 15) as well as a so-called twelve-lotus variation (Tib. *pema chuni*)[10] with curving stems and tendrils (Fig. 16). All these were produced in great numbers and generally in the manufactories. It is unknown how the prototypes of these individual designs might have looked. The templates for the design was probably repeatedly copied, varied, further developed and soon became a part of the general design canon, which then eventually became established as the dominant style of Tibetan rugs in the first half of the 20th century (Fig. 17).

With the demise of the lamaist ruling system and the Chinese Cultural Revolution in the 1960s and 1970s, the cultural and economic life of old Tibet in its traditional form was irretrievably gone. Rugs were now made in government-

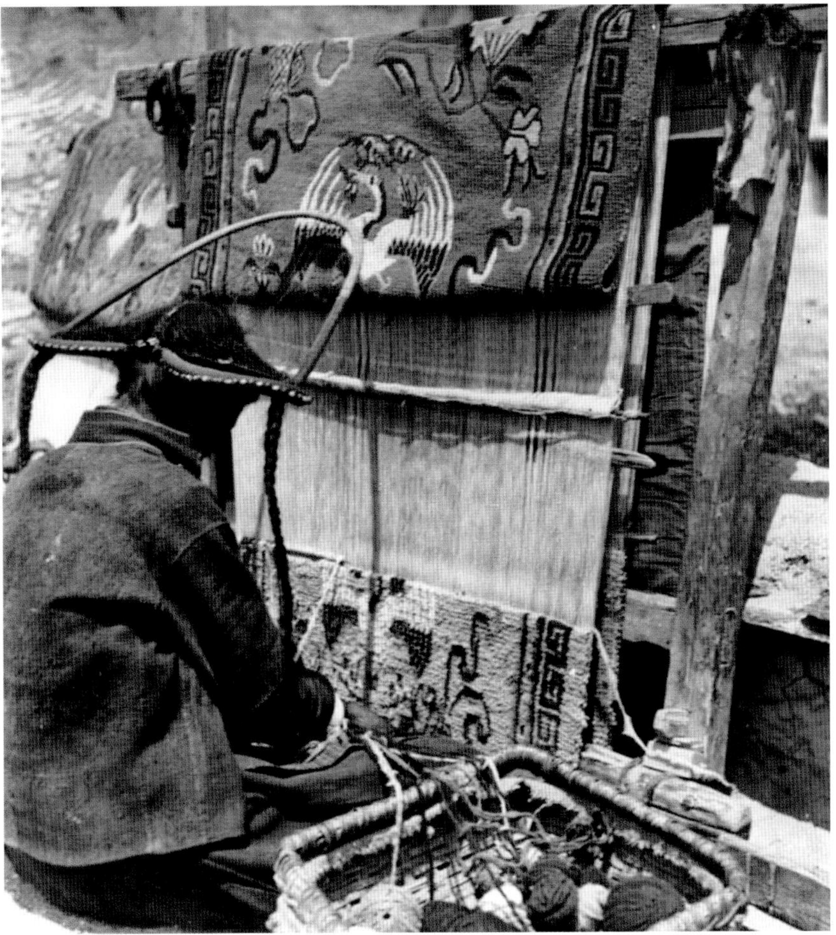

Fig. 17: Female rug-maker with the typical headpiece of Tsang Province, making a rug in the "new style". Rug workshop of the Phala family, Gyantse, Tsang Province, Central Tibet, 1938

owned workshops in quantity and in relatively negligible quality and lack of stylistic innovation. During this period, a few Tibetans in exile – first in Nepal and India, but then increasingly in Tibet itself – discovered the potential for Tibetan rugs on the world market (Ford 1987; Zhang 2009). The producers benefited from the traditional liberal understanding of rug design, encouraging continued innovation. Designer rugs produced in Tibet are now the basis of one of the largest branches of rug-making today. Rugs designed by Tibetans and non-Tibetans now decorate the homes of the fashion-oriented around the world, but they are still Tibetan rugs from their structure and how they are made.

SUMMARY

From a review of the Tibetan rug over the course of time, it is evident that it represents a very old and unique rug-making art extending long way back before the 19th century.

Although wool is Tibet's most important export, the rugs were made almost entirely for the domestic market and seldom found their way outside the country. They were, therefore, free from all the demands of an export market and were allowed to please themselves stylistically, and to please those of Tibetan culture. The overriding motivation of Tibetan rug art shows itself less in the mere continuation of standardised or traditional styles, but points much more strongly to the needs of the people, namely people living in extreme climatic conditions on the Roof of the World and for whom rugs with their strength and auspicious designs and motifs first and foremost make house and tent a comfortable environment and exude a positive atmosphere (Worcester 2009).

NOTES

1 Unfortunately, a source for this statement is missing in Stein's work.

2 Only a few tantric rugs have been published which can definitively be identified as Central Tibetan rugs (Rossi & Rossi 2008: no. 8, 9, 10; Piccus 2011: 70, pl. 30).

3 Further rugs from this group are published in Piccus 2011: pl. 144, 151, 152, 153, 155, 156, 161 and 162.

4 A selection of *khamdrums* is published in Wild 2014b. Disregarding size and choice of colours, one finds this schematic pattern in similar form in the neighbouring regions to the north and northeast, especially in rugs from the Khotan oasis and the Ningxia area. This underlines the cultural connection via the Silk Road.

5 In the Robert P. Piccus collection some of these borderless variations are published (Piccus 2011: 140–189).

6 Taranatha (Tucci 1941: 49) mentions around 1600 AD markets for rugs in the lower Wangden valley (Nyangbar), but only hats, drums and woollen cloth as products of the Gyantse area (Nyangstod). Lu Hongqi describes the shift in trade from Wangden to Gyantse (Lu 2003: 8).

7 This photograph allows an insight into a rug manufactory. On the flat roof are looms, on the floor below wool is carded and spun.

8 Marco Pallis (1895–1989), the Tibetan rug informant for Lorentz, also describes around 1940 – about 60 years after the report by Das in 1880 – a differentiation between Khampa (*khamdrum*) rugs and those in Gyantse style. By this he reinforces the assumption that Khampa rugs were traditional and Gyantse ones followed the trend. Lorentz describes both types as "Central Tibetan style" (Lorentz 1975: 215).

9 The "Sining" wool is named after the city Xining (earlier transcription: Sining) in the Chinese province Qinghai, once the trading place for Tibetan wool that was sold to China (Lorentz 1975: 161).

10 Among Tibetan rug dealers, this variant is still called a Twelve-Lotus rug (Tib. *pema chuni*), even if there are not always 12 flowers (Chodrak & Tashi 2000: 107).

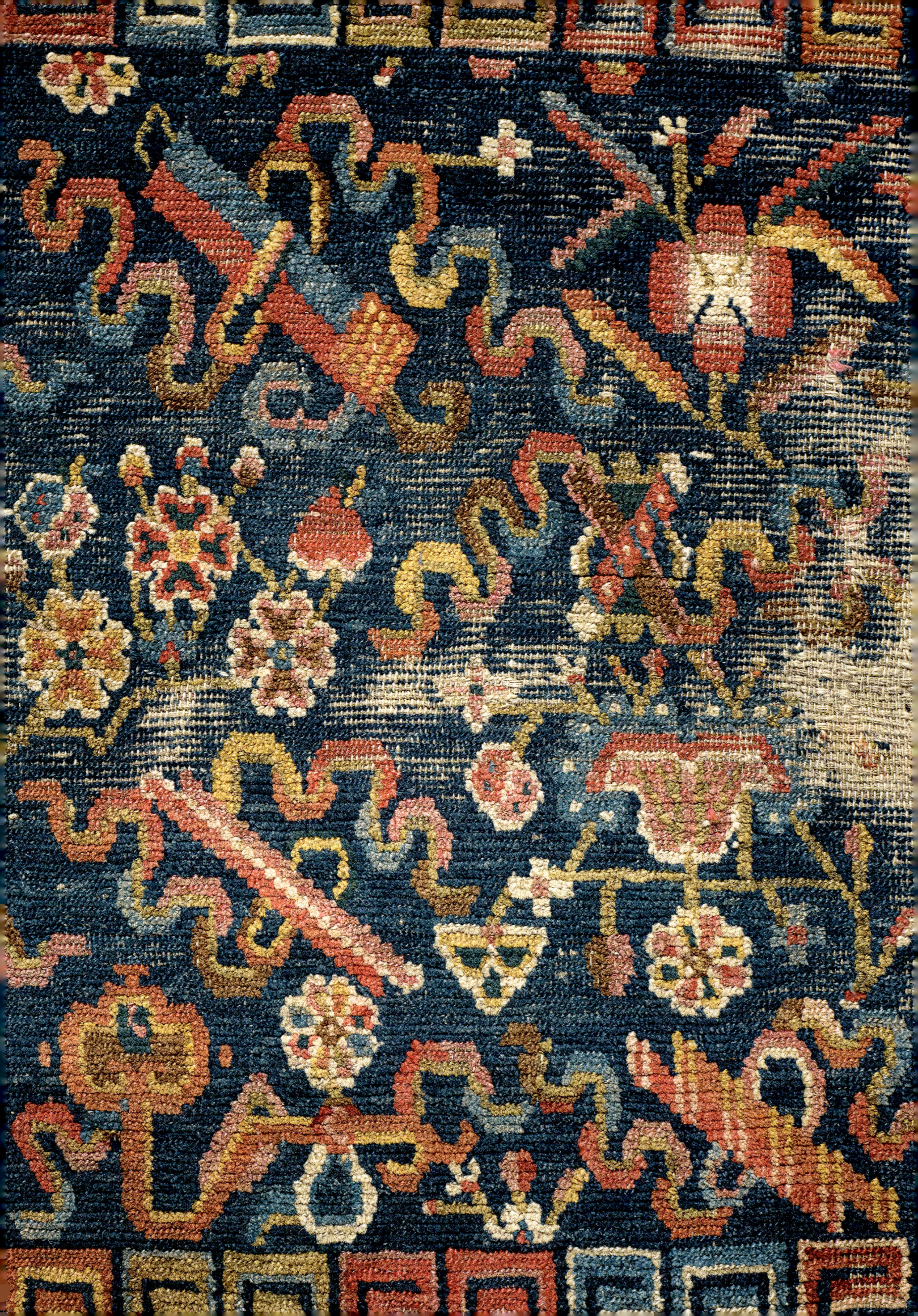

Koos de Jong

DRAGONS AND HORSES

Pile-Woven Horse Trappings

INTRODUCTION

Detail of Fig. 4

I concluded my latest book, *Dragon & Horse*, as follows: "I do expect a lot of further research, in particular by Chinese [and Tibetan!] researchers themselves. This applies especially to archaeological and archival research. I am convinced that these sources will provide much more useful information. The same goes for ethnographic research, which could be of great help regarding the saddle rugs from Gansu, Inner Mongolia, Xinjiang, and Tibet. [...] It is of the utmost importance that this typology, as the outcome of my research, is tested by technical research of the saddle rugs themselves, whether in public or private collections, and that these results are published" (De Jong 2012: 163).

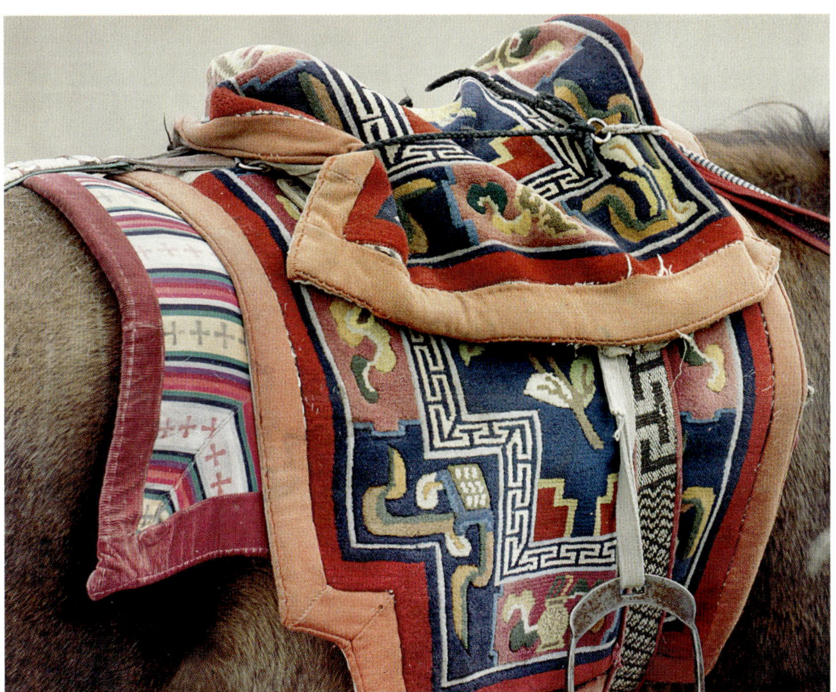

Fig. 1: A set of over- and under-saddle rugs as well as a horse blanket of *nambu* fabric with *tigma* motif, here used as "under-under-saddle rug". Shigatse, Central Tibet, 1995

Hence, the reader will understand my delight when I was invited to study the collection of Justyna and Michael Buddeberg, and my eagerness to focus on the technical aspects. What I had hoped for, and secretly expected, came true. Our knowledge of Tibetan rugs is still so limited, that a close look at any unpublished or only superficially published rug will yield new results. That's how scholarly research works: progress is gained by patiently collecting small bits of evidence until, after careful analysis and synthesis, a reliable general picture emerges. Progress is not achieved by presenting long-known results over and over again, as is done so often.

However, I do not intend to reiterate new results, either, because these are presented in length in the chapter on Tibetan horse tack in my book. Instead, I will confine myself to a description of how my study of the horse tack in the Buddeberg collection augments or corrects our existing knowledge.

Knotted horse tack makes up a considerable part of the collection. Hence, I was able to study two complete sets of saddle rugs, seven separate over-saddle rugs (Tib. *masho*), eight under-saddle rugs (Tib. *makden*), four horse blankets[1], one yak-saddle rug, four crupper rugs, seventeen forehead decorations and three other trappings. They will be discussed in that order below.

My technical description will be most detailed in those cases where rugs are rare and not well published. This applies, for example, to the *takyab*, that is, all horse trappings not associated with the saddle, and the yak-saddle rug. We know so little that any detail can give us useful clues, either now or at some later point in time.

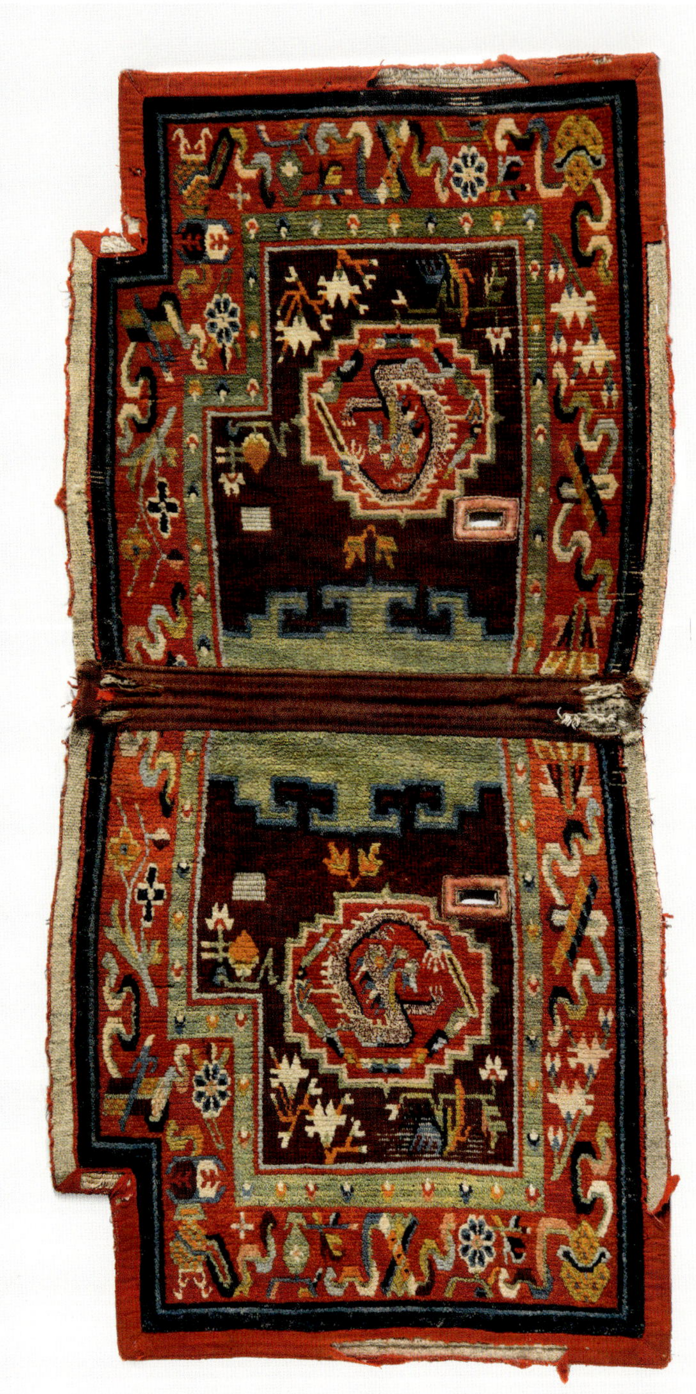

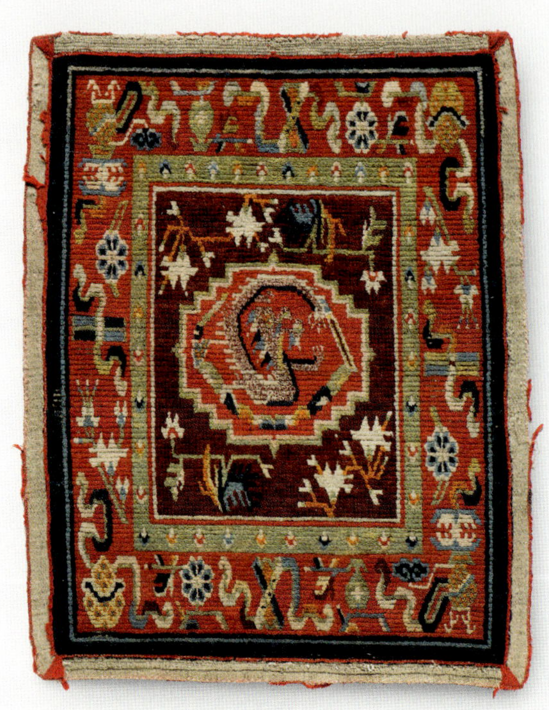

Figs. 2b and 2a: Under- and over-saddle rug (*makden* and *masho*), traditional dragon-medallion design and secondary border with jewels. Late 19th c., 72×55 cm and 125×59 cm

COMPLETE SETS OF SADDLE RUGS

The Buddeberg collection includes three complete sets, or rather pairs, consisting of an over-saddle rug (Tib. *masho*) and an under-saddle rug (Tib. *makden*). I have analysed two of these sets (Figs. 2a and 2b, and 3a and 3b). Although a few sets from Ningxia in China have survived[2], the majority is of Tibetan origin. The reason for this is not yet clear. Maybe the Chinese preferred small rectangular over-saddle rugs to oval pieces. If a set has been separated for commercial reasons, a rectangular over-saddle rug becomes difficult to identify as such. As the sets do not differ from separate under- and over-saddle rugs, I will discuss them in the respective chapters.

OVER-SADDLE RUGS

Besides providing comfort for the rider, the function of an over-saddle rug is to cover the unevenness of the straps and girths of the saddle and the stirrups. There are both oval (Figs. 5 and 6) and rectangular (Figs. 2a and 3a of the sets, and Figs. 4 and 7) over-saddle rugs. However, an over-saddle rug that has been separated from its matching under-saddle rug may be difficult to identify as such. As I point out in my book (De Jong 2013: 135), some small rec-

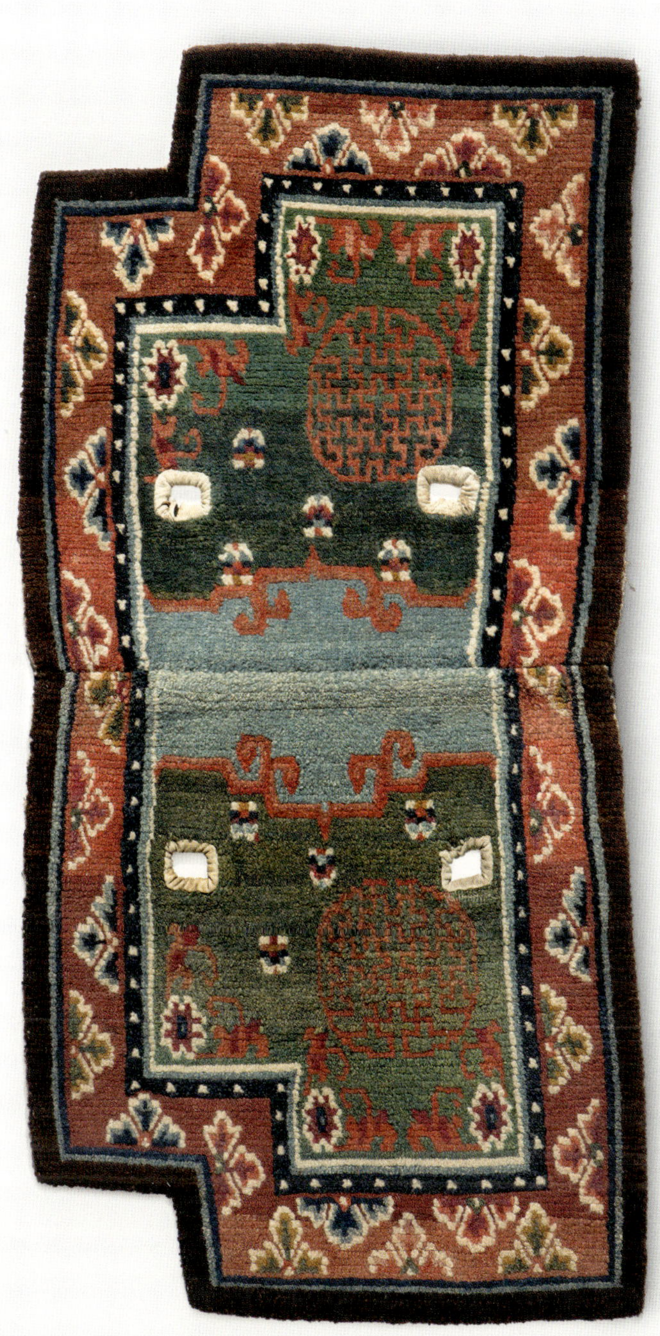

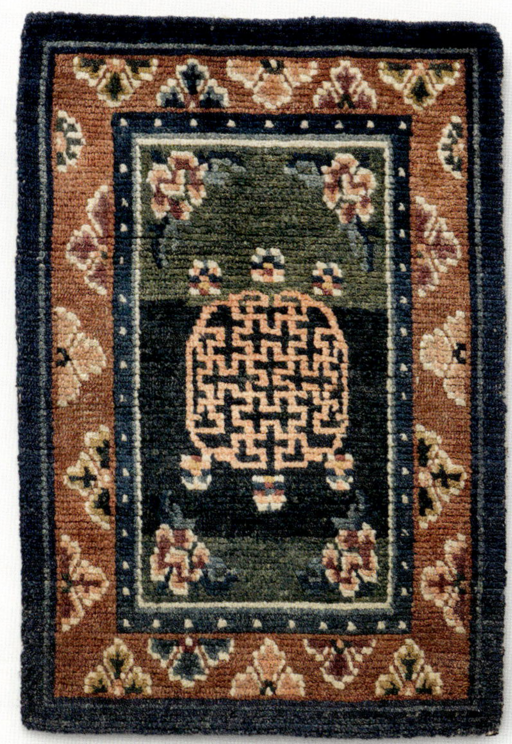

tangular rugs were multi-functional. For example, rectangular sitting rugs (Tib. *khagangma*) and cushion covers (Tib. *gabny*) could also be used as over-saddle rugs. If they look worn in their middle, this indicates long use as an over-saddle rug. In some cases part of the rug is cut out to accommodate the rising pommel and the cantle (Fig. 4, see also C118 and C157 in the catalogue in the appendix). The oval-shaped specimens, in contrast, can be identified as over-saddle rugs without any problem (Figs. 5 and 6). Although Fig. 7 is rectangular, it is an over-saddle rug, too. It once belonged to a set, now separated, of which the under-saddle rug has been published (Darchen 2012: 101).

If we look at the structure of these over-saddle rugs, we see that most 19th century pieces have undyed woollen warps and two or three shoots of natural-coloured or grey woollen wefts (e.g., Fig. 3a). Late 19th- or early 20th-century pieces, in contrast, have either cotton warps and wefts or cotton warps and wool wefts, although some (made by nomads?) are still completely of wool. For example, C118 in the catalogue in the appendix has machine-spun cotton warps and two cotton wefts. In addition, some of the dyes are synthetic, so I date this rug to the first quarter of the 20th century. The rug in Fig. 8 has a very unusual structure: a plain weave of natural wool warps and two natural-coloured wool wefts with burls made in the so-called "back-stitching looped" technique. This technique is said to have

Figs. 3b and 3a:
Under- and over-saddle rug (*makden* and *masho*) with *Shou* medallion and cross-blossom border. Around 1900, 78×55 cm and 124×65 cm

Fig. 4: Over-saddle rug (*masho*). 19th c., 72×59 cm

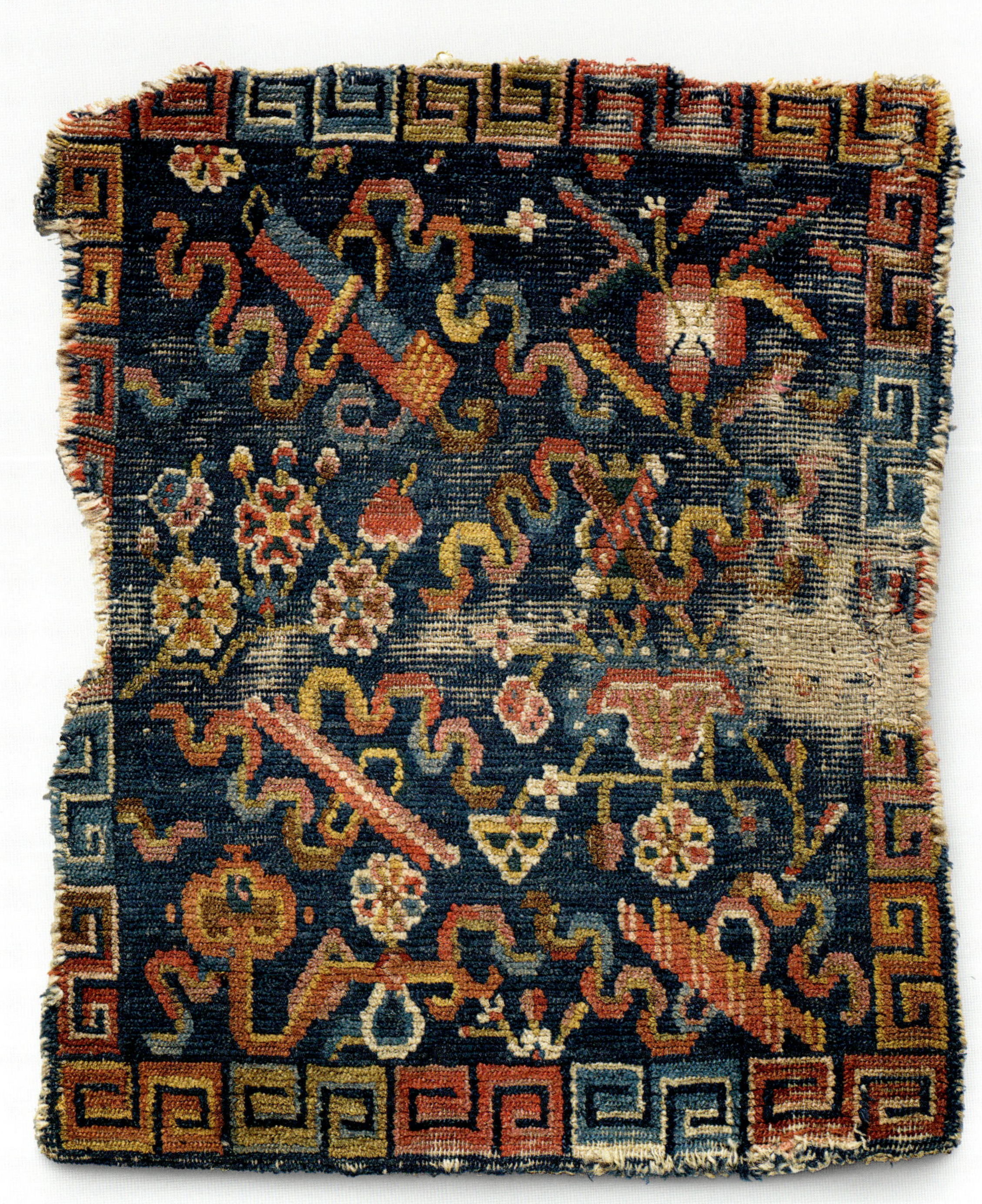

Fig. 5: Over-saddle rug (*masho*), oval shape. 19th c. or earlier, 79×56 cm

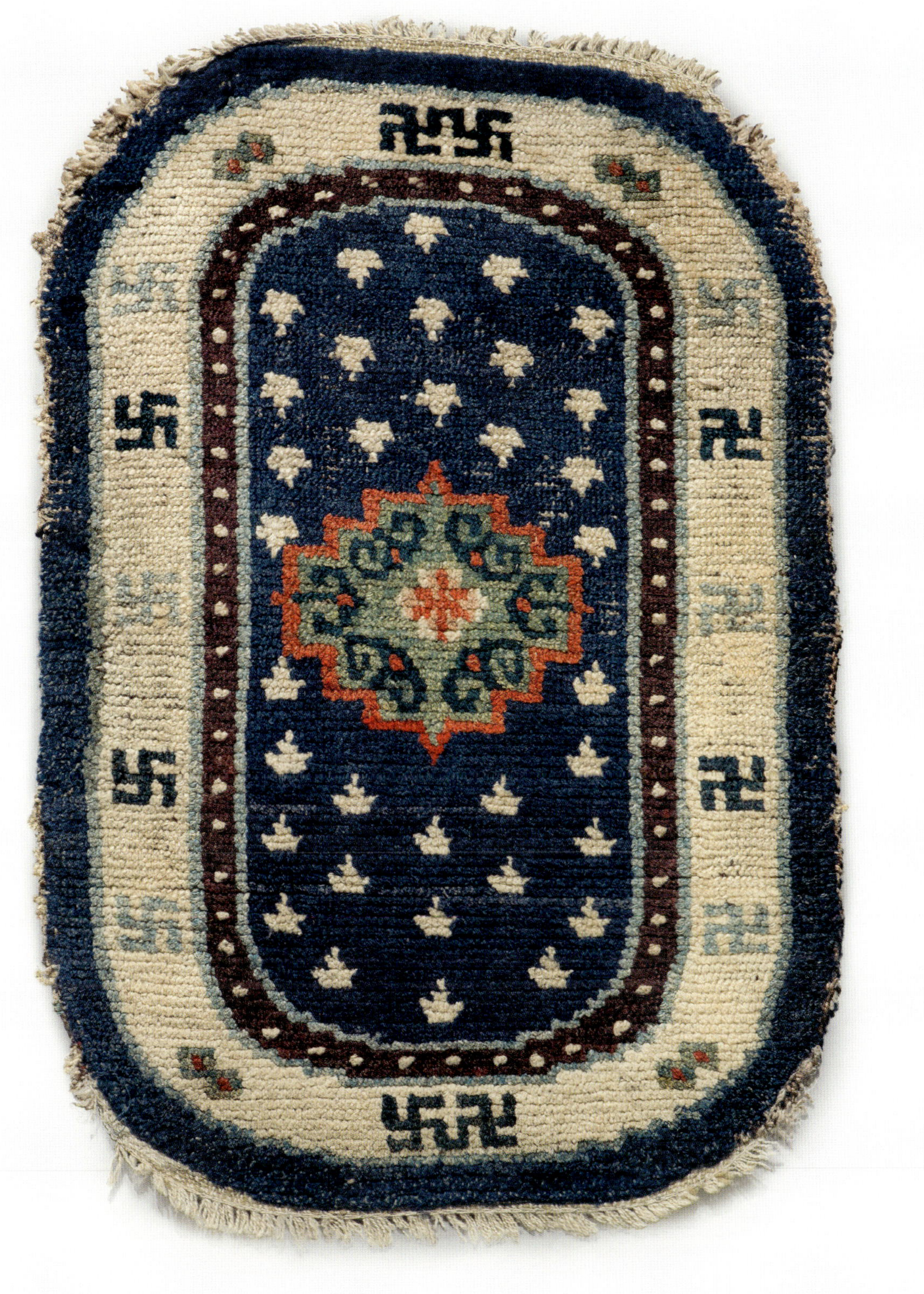

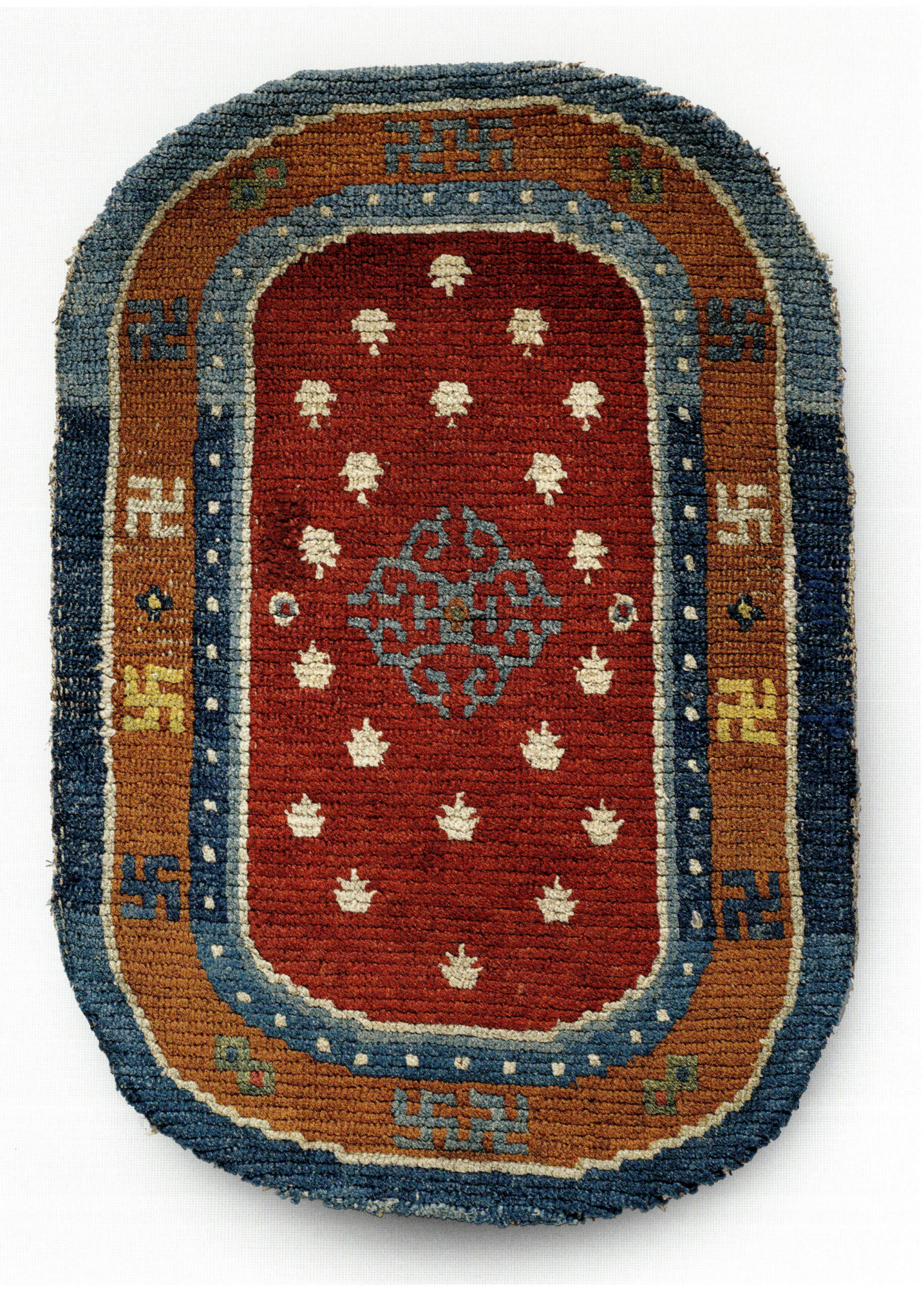

Fig. 6: Over-saddle rug (*masho*), oval shape. 2nd half 19th c., 79 × 55 cm

Fig. 7: Over-saddle rug (*masho*). Around 1900, 63×56 cm

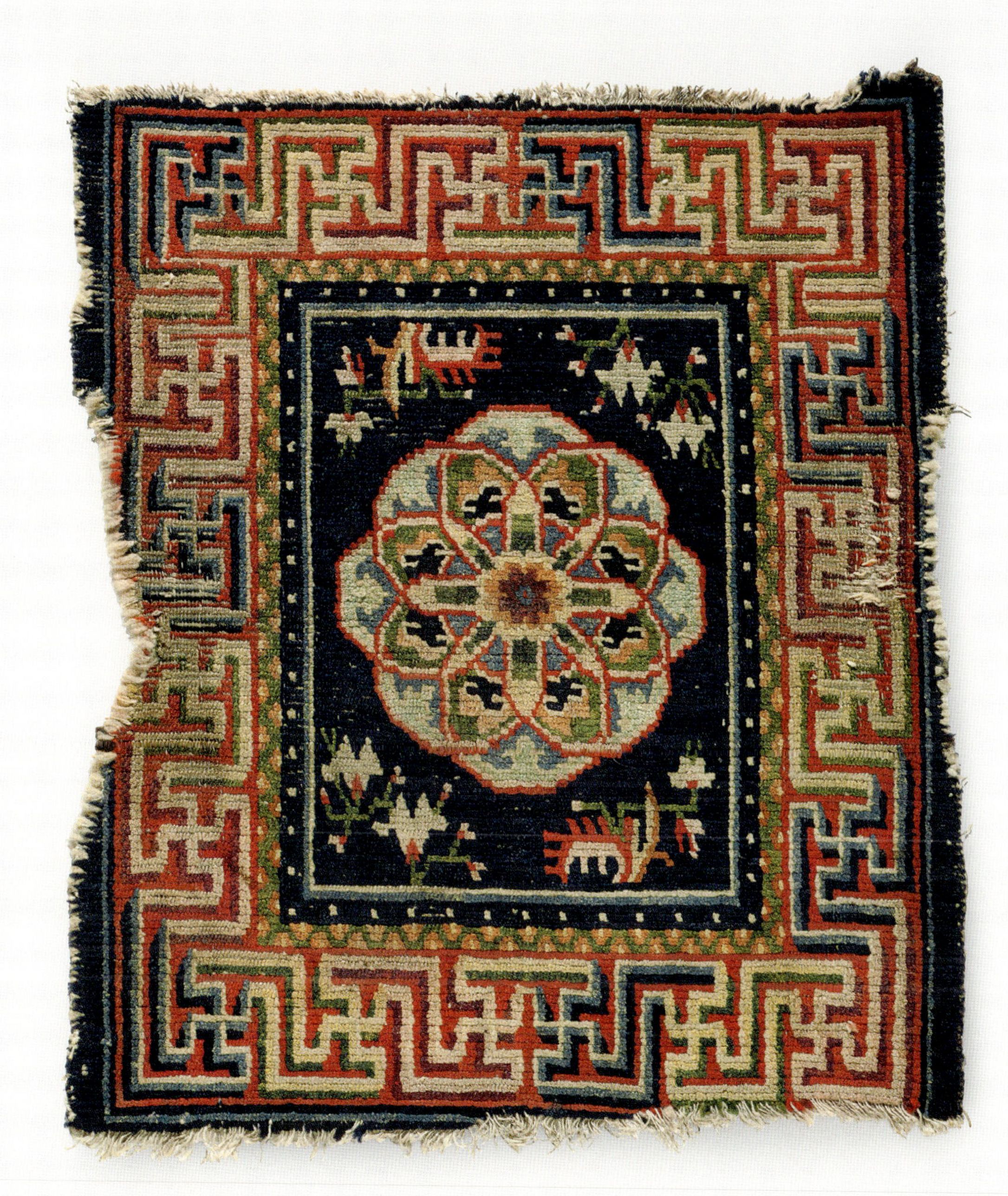

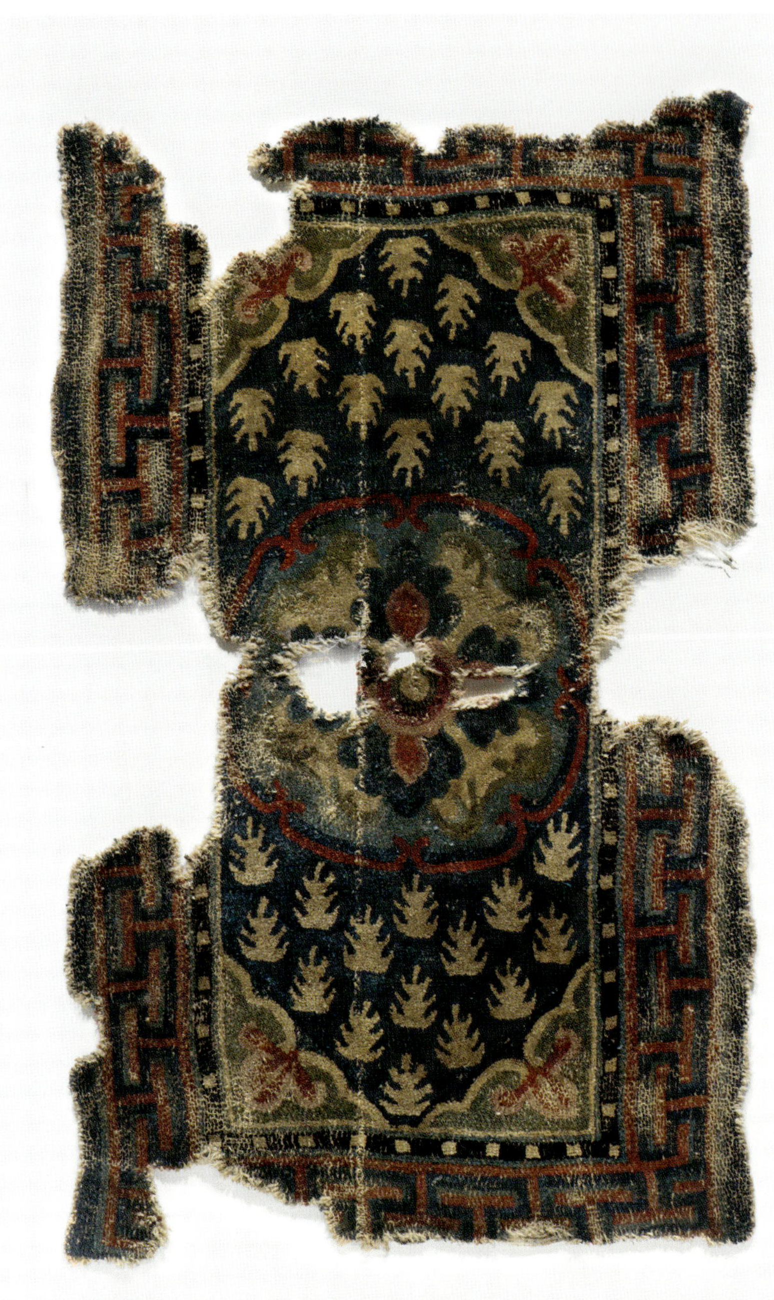

Fig. 8: Fragment of an over-saddle rug (*masho*) in rare embroidery technique. 19th c. or earlier, 89×55 cm

originated in Kashmir (De Jong 2013: 134; see also Piccus 2011: 199 and Darchen 2012: 107).

The design of the field varies. It may feature a central dragon medallion (Figs. 21 and 2b), various Buddhist symbols enclosed by long curling ribbons and combined with scattered blossoms[3] (Fig. 4 and C118 in the catalogue), or the so-called "frog-foot" pattern[4] (Figs. 5, 6 and 8, also C157 in the catalogue), which is either surrounded by an openwork medallion consisting of a double *vajra* (Tib. *dorje*), a cloud-band or flower medallion, or a *mandala*- or lotus-shaped medallion (see Fig. 7). Another rug is decorated with a grid-like medallion composed of *Shou* symbols and *swastikas* (see Figs. 3a and 3b). The central "medallion" of rug C157 is more difficult to interpret: it consists of two different pairs of cloud symbols or ram heads (Tib. *kotchaks*); between them is either the Chinese character for king (Chin. *wang*) or the much stylised version of the character of longevity (Chin. *shou*), combined with two arrowheads. At first sight this central medallion with its "brackets" does not look skilfully made. However, the weaver succeeded in knotting a very complicated T-meander border design with perfect corner solutions, so the asymmetry of the "brackets" must be intentional. As to the reason, I have not yet found an explanation.

The various main borders show a meander (see Fig. 4), a design of half blossoms (see Figs. 3a and 3b), a combination of flowers, Buddhist symbols and *swastikas* (see Figs. 5 and 6), an all-round *swastika*-meander, once more with a perfect corner solution (see Fig. 7), and an alternating T-meander (see Fig. 8 and C157 in the catalogue).

The combination of two *swastikas* forming a cross (see Figs. 5 and 6) most probably symbolises a happy marriage. Saddle rugs decorated with this symbol may have been appropriate bridal gifts. Some over-saddle rugs have no border at all (e.g., C118 in the catalogue).

Some secondary borders show small half blossoms, pearl borders (see Figs. 7 and 8, also 3a and 3b), the typical Tibetan multi-coloured jewels (see Fig. 2a), or just different stripes.

UNDER-SADDLE RUGS

The function of an under-saddle rug is to protect the horse against the chafing of the saddle. The shape of (half) a Tibetan *makden* corresponds to that of a Chinese saddle rug from Ningxia, Gansu, Inner Mongolia or Xinjiang: oval, rectangular or square, with or without notched corners at the rear. Typically Tibetan is the so-called butterfly shape (Fig.

Fig. 9: Under-saddle rug in butterfly shape. Early 20th c., 122×75 cm

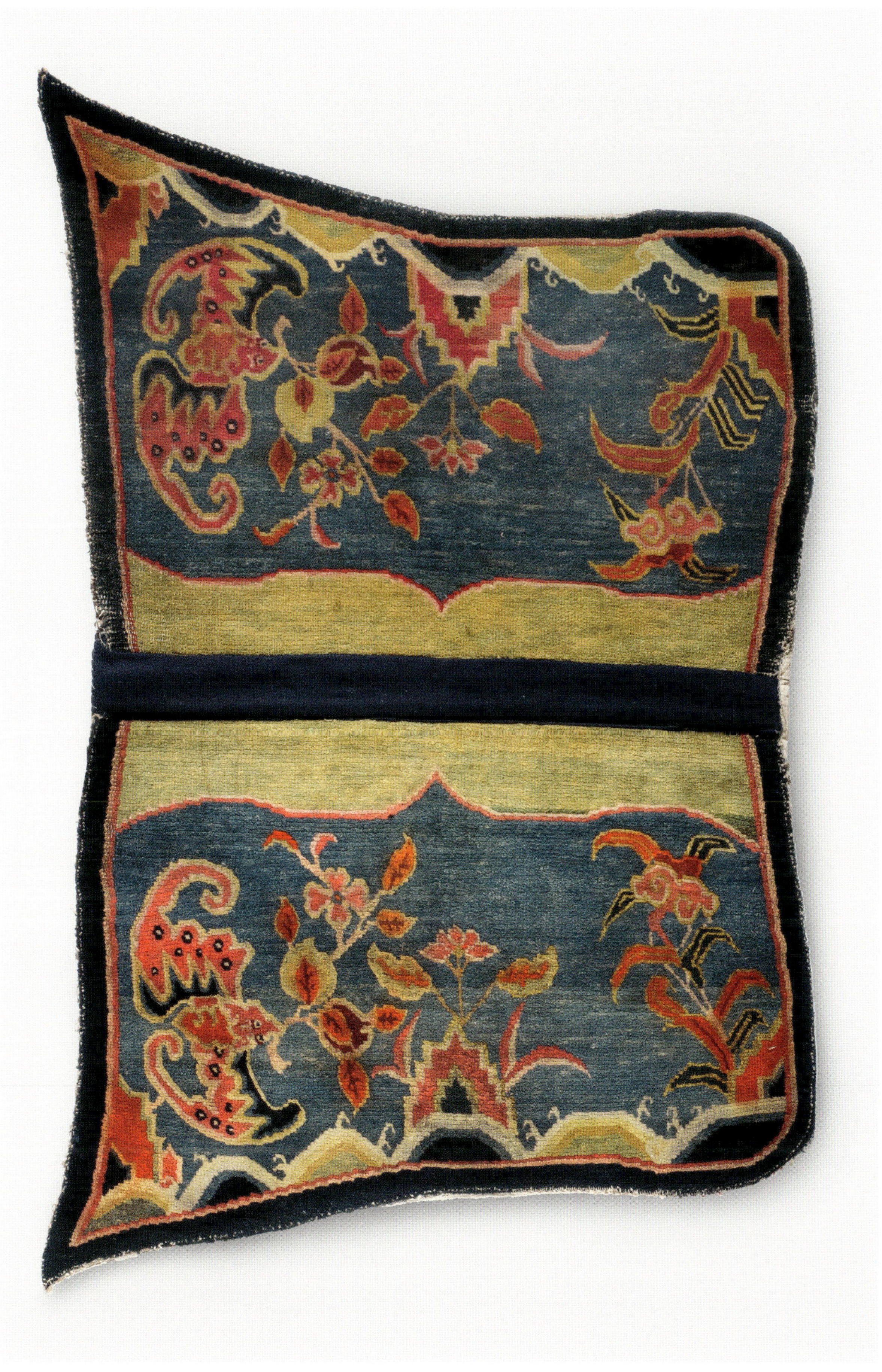

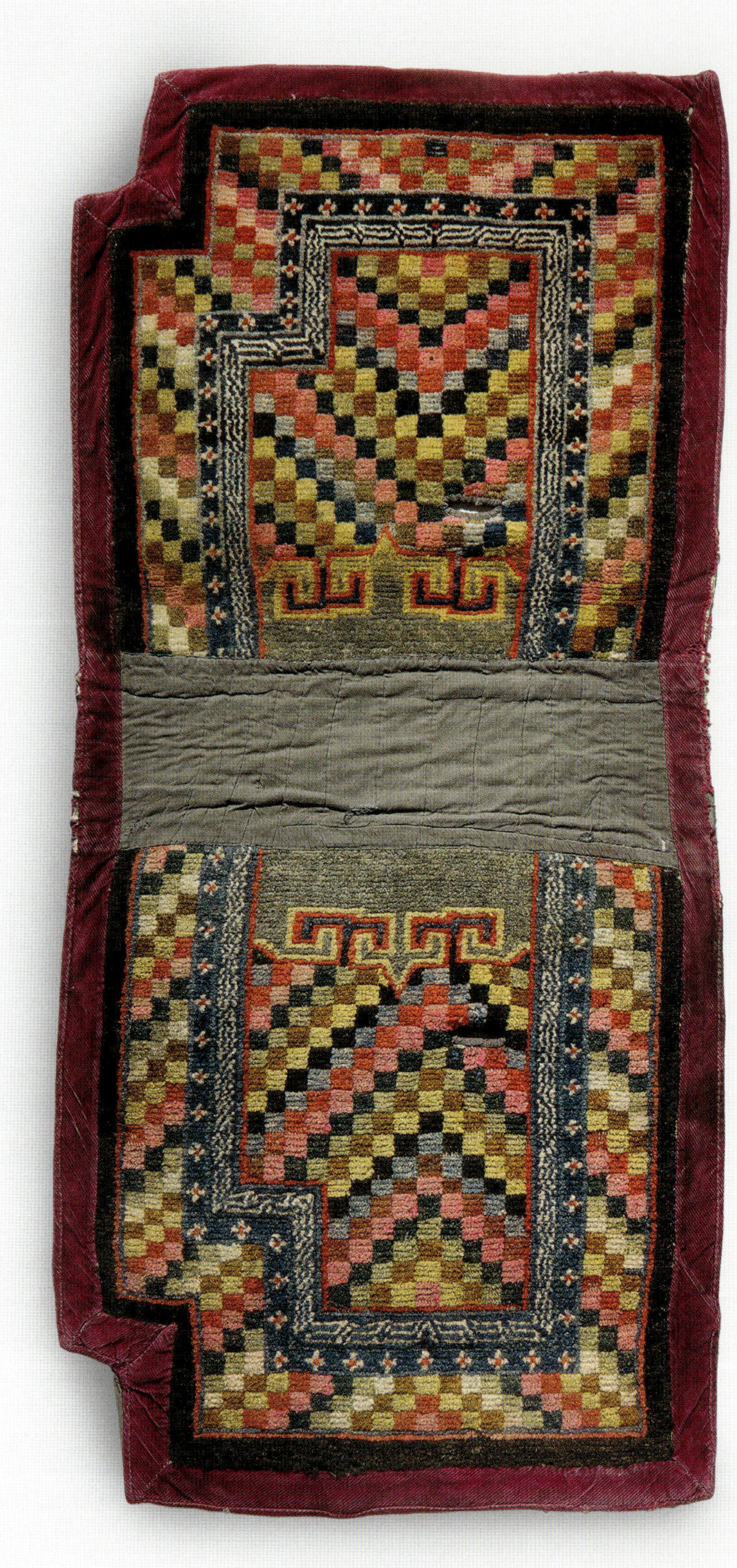

Fig. 10: Under-saddle rug with multi-coloured checkerboard design. Around 1900, 143.5×68.5 cm, Karl Steiner collection no. 4, MFK inv. no. 2015-80-2

9, also C12 in the catalogue). However, that shape emerged as late as in 1904 (De Jong 2013: 136). As is to be expected, the structure and design of the under-saddle rugs is more or less the same as that of the over-saddle rugs; this is due, among other things, to the fact that the former "mirror" the patterns of the latter for obvious reasons.

Besides the three complete sets, the Buddeberg collection includes eight separate under-saddle rugs.

An unusual and aesthetically very appealing under-saddle rug with a many-coloured checkerboard design is from the collection of Karl Steiner (Fig. 10).

Two under-saddle rugs in the collection were produced in Ningxia and Suiyuan-Baotou, respectively, and have the typical asymmetrical knots open to the left. All Tibetan *makden*, in contrast, have a wool pile made in the Tibetan technique of knotting. However, the underlying fabric differs and in some cases can be helpful for dating: most early pieces have a underlying fabric of wool (see Fig. 3b, also Fig. 18 in the contribution by Tsareva), while the underlying fabric of most later pieces is either of cotton (see Fig. 9, also C12 in the catalogue) or of mixed cotton warps and wool wefts (see Fig. 2b). Still, one has to be careful, as there are many exceptions to this rule. In contrast to Chinese under-saddle rugs, the halves of the Tibetan specimens are often connected in the middle by a strip of woven cotton or woollen cloth. This cloth can be either plain (see Fig. 2b) or decorated with a design of small crosses (Tib. *thig ma*) in the tie-dye technique. To protect the rug against sweat and wear, *makden* were originally lined with blue cotton (see Fig. 2b and rug C12 in the catalogue), and the selvedges were finished with woven plain red (see Fig. 2b) or plain blue cloth (see Fig. 9) or felt. However, in most cases this trimming is gone or has been replaced by other material.

Most *makden* are provided with two or four rectangular holes for the saddle straps. In the older pieces the strap holes are finished with natural leather, which is sewn around the edges and lined with cotton on the backside. In some cases this leather finishing is stuffed with horsehair, which lends it a raised appearance (see Fig. 3b). In later pieces the strap holes are reinforced with patches of leather sewn flatly on the front and back. Sometimes the two notches at the back are unopened (see Fig. 2b), and the underlying fabric is visible. Another unusual feature of this under-saddle rug is the red-dyed leather finishing of the holes for the saddle straps, which suggest Inner Mongolian influence. The (half-)round strap holes of a *makden* in the collection, which is not shown here, reveal Inner Mongolian influence as well.

Fig. 11: Horse blanket or "under-under-saddle rug". Early 20th c., 105 × 120/157 cm

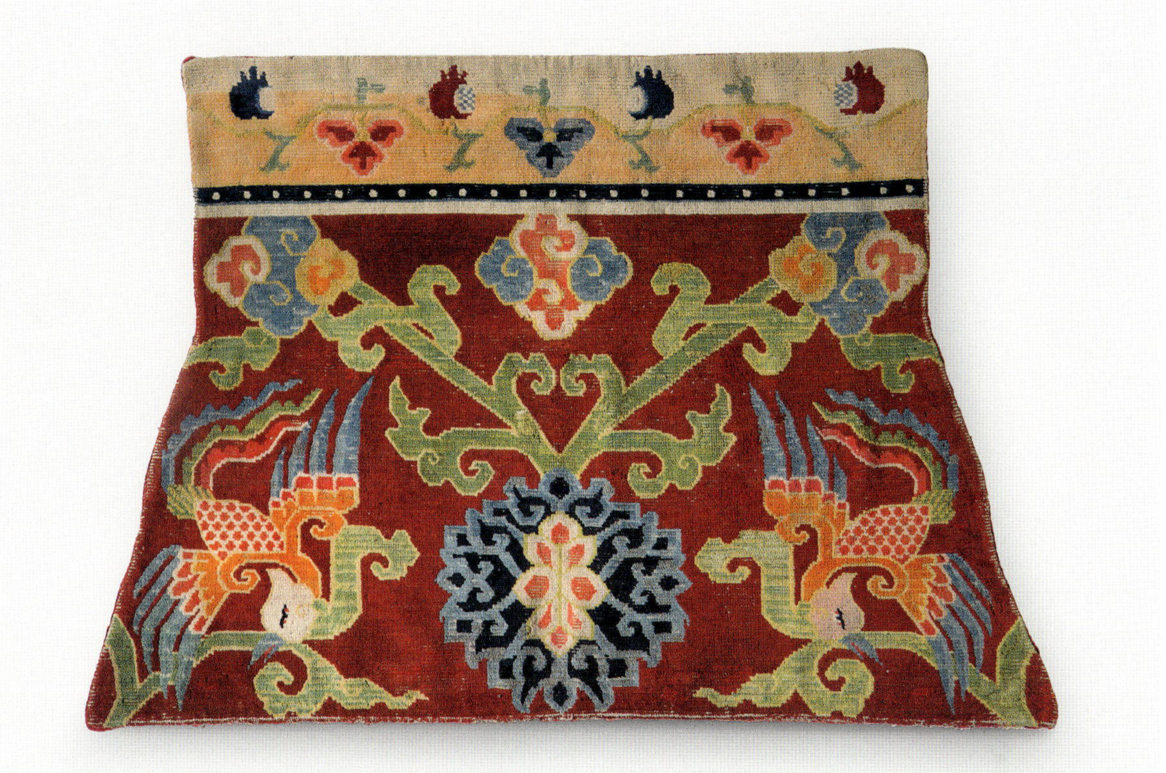

Only rarely are worn parts patched up with leather or with cloth, as in a Ningxia saddle rug in the collection (not shown here). The patches of that rug are made of cloth decorated in the tie-dye technique. Strangely enough the strap-holes are patched up with lambskin. The tie-dyed cloth, reinforced with strips of natural wool felt, was also used for the trimming of the selvedges. The finishing of both ends is provided with long fringes, which is typical for Ladakh.

The field of these *makdens* may be decorated with the following elements: a combination of bat, lotus flower, peach blossom, and the sea-mountain-clouds motif (Chin. *haishanyun*) at both ends (see Fig. 9); a bat flying between clouds (C12 in the catalogue); a tiger-skin pattern (see Fig. 18 in the contribution by Tsareva); on *makdens* in the collection that are not shown here, a "frog-foot" pattern in combination with a central lotus flower medallion; strewn flowers and peach blossoms in the corners; a central medallion with a grid of flowers and quarters of flowers in the corners; and, last but not least, a snow lion.

In most cases the seating surface in the middle of the rug is monochrome with cloud-head borders (see Figs. 2b and 9). In the case of the under-saddle rug with the tiger pattern, the seat is not indicated as such, but the middle of the rug is accentuated by a single dark blue spot (see Fig. 18 in the contribution by Tsareva).

The main borders may be simply striped (Figs. 9 and 18 in the contribution by Tsareva) or decorated with green cartouches and grids filled with lotus flowers (C12 in the catalogue), an all-around *swastika*-meander, flower and coin medallions with flowering branches, dragons and phoenixes chasing the flaming pearl amidst clouds, or a diagonal brocade pattern.

The secondary borders usually consist of various stripes, half-blossoms, a T-meander or a pearl border. Large and rather crude white pearls on a red-brown or mid-blue ground of the inner secondary border, like those in the two over-saddle rugs (see Figs. 5 and 6), suggest a dating to the second half of the 19th century, while smaller and more even pearls on a dark blue background indicate that the respective rugs were made in the late 19th or early 20th centuries (Fig. 3b). An important exception is a dark blue broad main outer stripe "mirrored" by a thin dark blue stripe inside the field (see Fig. 18 in the contribution by Tsareva). The fact that this particular feature is very similar to the famous Ming Dynasty under-saddle rug in the McMullan collection supports an early dating (De Jong 2013: 61).

Fig. 12: Horse with a crupper rug. Gyantse, 1995

Fig. 13: Crupper rug. 19th c., 59×59 cm (not in catalogue)

Fig. 14: Crupper rug. Around 1900, 43×60 cm

Fig. 15: Crupper rug. Around 1920, 36×53 cm

Fig. 16: Forehead ornament in use. Shigatse, Central Tibet, 1995

Horse Blankets

It took me a long time to figure out the function of these mysterious rugs. Some photographs eventually taught me that they were, and still are, used as horse blankets (see note 1) or sweat blankets (De Jong 2013: 148ff.). Some riders use up to three or even more rugs and textiles on top of each other. Although the structure and design are very different, the trapezoid shape of these Tibetan horse blankets is similar to Central Asian specimens, particularly the embroidered horse covers from Uzbekistan and the embroidered felt rugs from Kyrgyzstan.

The Buddeberg collection includes three Tibetan horse blankets or "under-under-saddle rugs" (see note 1). The structure of the rug in Fig. 11 is not much different from that of the saddle rugs described above. The warps are of cotton. Of the two wefts one is cotton, the other dark-grey wool. The woollen pile is knotted in the Tibetan technique. The backside of the upper border is lined with a broad strip of natural cotton, the rest of the border with a strip of blue cotton. Between the selvedges of the actual rug and the natural and blue cotton lining strips, a narrow strip of red ripcord provides for extra strength. The structure of another horse blanket (C111 in the catalogue) is more or less the same; however, both its wefts are of wool. For reinforcement, the upper end has simply been plied back around a strip of machine-woven natural cotton plain weave. Most colours are natural, except for the pink. That is why I date this piece to the first quarter of the 20th century. The underlying fabric of the horse blanket C120 (see Fig. 6 in the contribution by Montigel) is all wool. The pile is wool, too, with Tibetan knotting. The top and bottom *kilim* ends are plied back over a width of 2.5 to 3 centimetres.

The typical trapezoid field of the horse blanket in Fig. 11 is decorated with a large central peony. Two branches rise from the bottom on both sides. Phoenixes grace the lower corners, clusters of clouds the top end of the field. The field of the horse blanket C111 (see catalogue) has an all-over pattern of multi-coloured flowers and a very appealing wavy pattern in the lower corners, presumably a stylised version of the *haishanyun* pattern. At both sides a triangle imitates the leather applications, used for the attachment of ropes, of the earlier specimens. The larger triangle the middle of the lower end is inspired by such applications as well. The horse blanket in Fig. 6 in Montigel's contribution has continuous, diagonally arranged *swastikas* which meander in black on a yellow-ochre background, and triangles similar to those in the previous example.

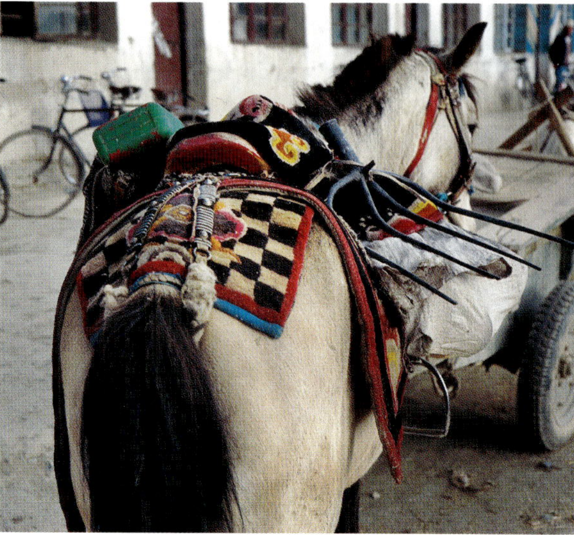

All "under-under-saddle rugs" have a peculiar feature in common: they have only a border at the top of the field, not a border running around. This main upper border may be decorated with a pomegranate branch and blossoms (see Fig. 11), a multi-coloured alternating T-meander (C111 in the catalogue), or multi-coloured dotted stripes (Fig. 6 in the contribution by Montigel). The inner secondary border consists of a pearl border and stripes (see Fig. 11, also Fig. 6 in the contribution by Montigel).

YAK-SADDLE RUG

The Buddeberg collection includes a singular specimen, which I suspect to be a yak-saddle rug. However, some caution is advised: one might be tempted to classify all square saddle rugs, both knotted and plain woven, as yak-saddle rugs. I am still not sure whether square pile-knotted wool rugs ever graced the backs of yaks, because such rugs were simply too expensive to be used for that purpose. The few existing photographs show yaks with covers of simple woven textile or felt (Bunn 2010: 77). The Buddeberg piece (shown as Fig. 27 in the contribution by Kalantari) falls into that latter category.

The rug is of a rectangular shape, and the field is decorated with a pattern in dark blue, yellow and red. That pattern was not made on a loom. The flat-woven border is 18 centimetres wide and consists of grey wool warps and natural white, natural brown, yellow, red, and mid-blue wefts. It has diagonal seams at the corners. The back of one of the long sides is reinforced by a centred rectangular piece of natural leather measuring 12.5×16.5 centimetres, which has been sewn on with black wool thread.

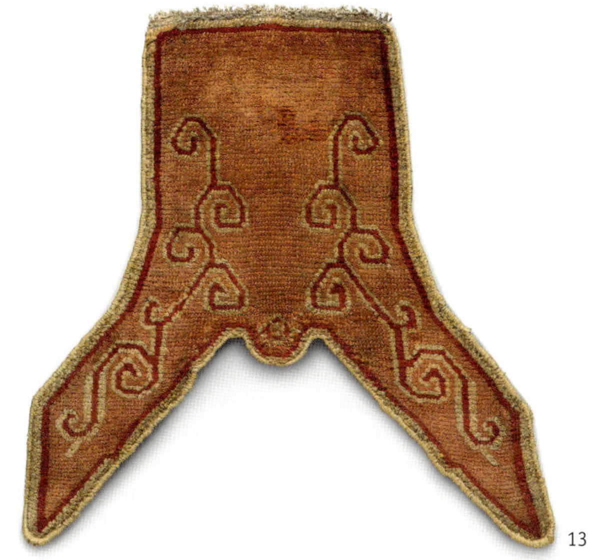

13

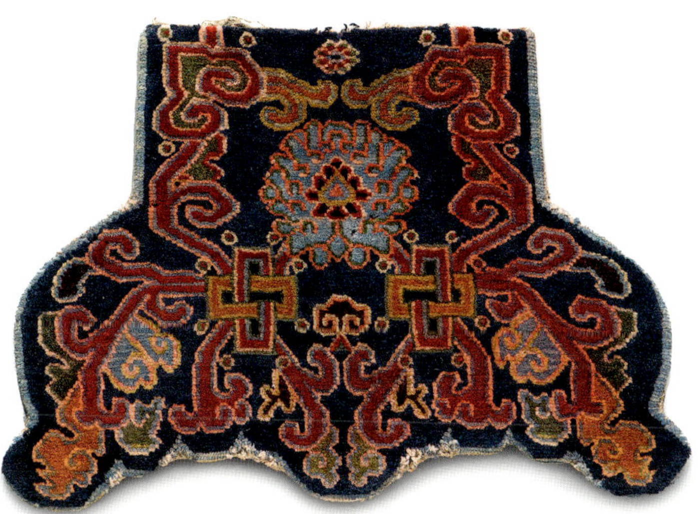

14

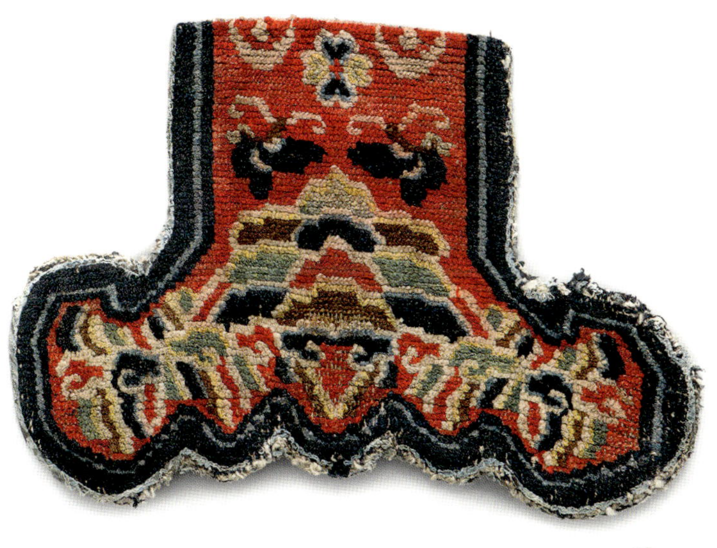

15

The field is decorated with a continuous zigzag pattern which at the top and bottom ends in a finer pattern of zigzags combined with a blossom-like pattern.

The border consists of a broad stripe as well as several horizontal and vertical narrow stripes. At both ends of the inner brown (first) stripe are small loops made of black wool. All around the back side of the last broad brown stripe, at the corners and in the middle, the ends of black and grey wool threads are sticking out, alternating with a few loops.

TAKYAB

The so-called *takyab* (De Jong 2013: 151f.) constitute a particular kind of horse tack which is only found in the Sino-Tibetan context but shows some interesting similarities with the nomadic horse tack from Persia and Central Asia. The Tibetan term comprises various horse trappings, like the crupper rug, the forehead ornament, and various decorated bands and straps with or without tassels and bells. They are made of leather or felt, and may be braided, embroidered or of pile-knotted wool.

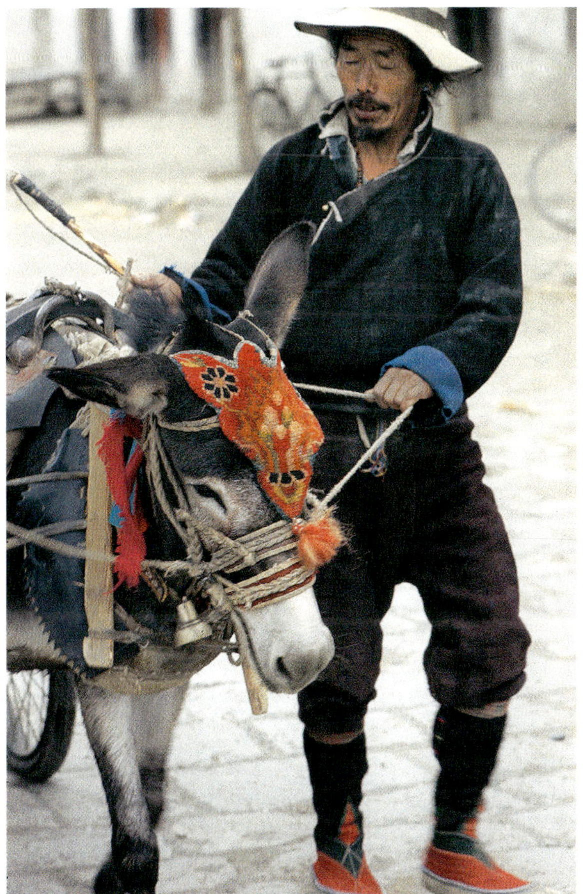

Fig. 17: Forehead ornament with the good fortune symbol "fishes". 20th c., 25.5×23 cm

Fig. 18: Forehead ornament, "vase with jewels". 20th c., 24×21 cm

Fig. 19: Forehead ornament, "lotus flower". 19th/20th c., 25.5×25 cm

Fig. 20: Forehead ornament, "checkerboard pattern". 19th/20th c., 23×21 cm

Fig. 21: Forehead ornament, "peony". 19th/20th c., 26×24.5 cm

Fig. 22: Forehead ornament, "vase with lotus flower". 20th c., 24.5×23 cm

Fig. 23: Forehead ornament, "large lotus". 20th c., 19.5×20 cm

Fig. 24: Forehead ornament, "leopard pattern". 19th c. (?), 25×22 cm

Fig. 25: Forehead ornament, "*kalachakra*". 20th c., 24×21.5 cm

Fig. 26: Forehead ornament, "flaming jewel". 20th c., 29 x 28 cm

Fig. 27: Forehead ornament, "*Garuda*" (1). 20th c., 21.5×18.5 cm, Karl Steiner collection no. 45, MFK inv. no. 2015-80-20

Fig. 28: Forehead ornament, "*Garuda*" (2). 20th c., 24 x 27.5 cm, Karl Steiner collection no. 48, MFK inv. no. 2015-80-22

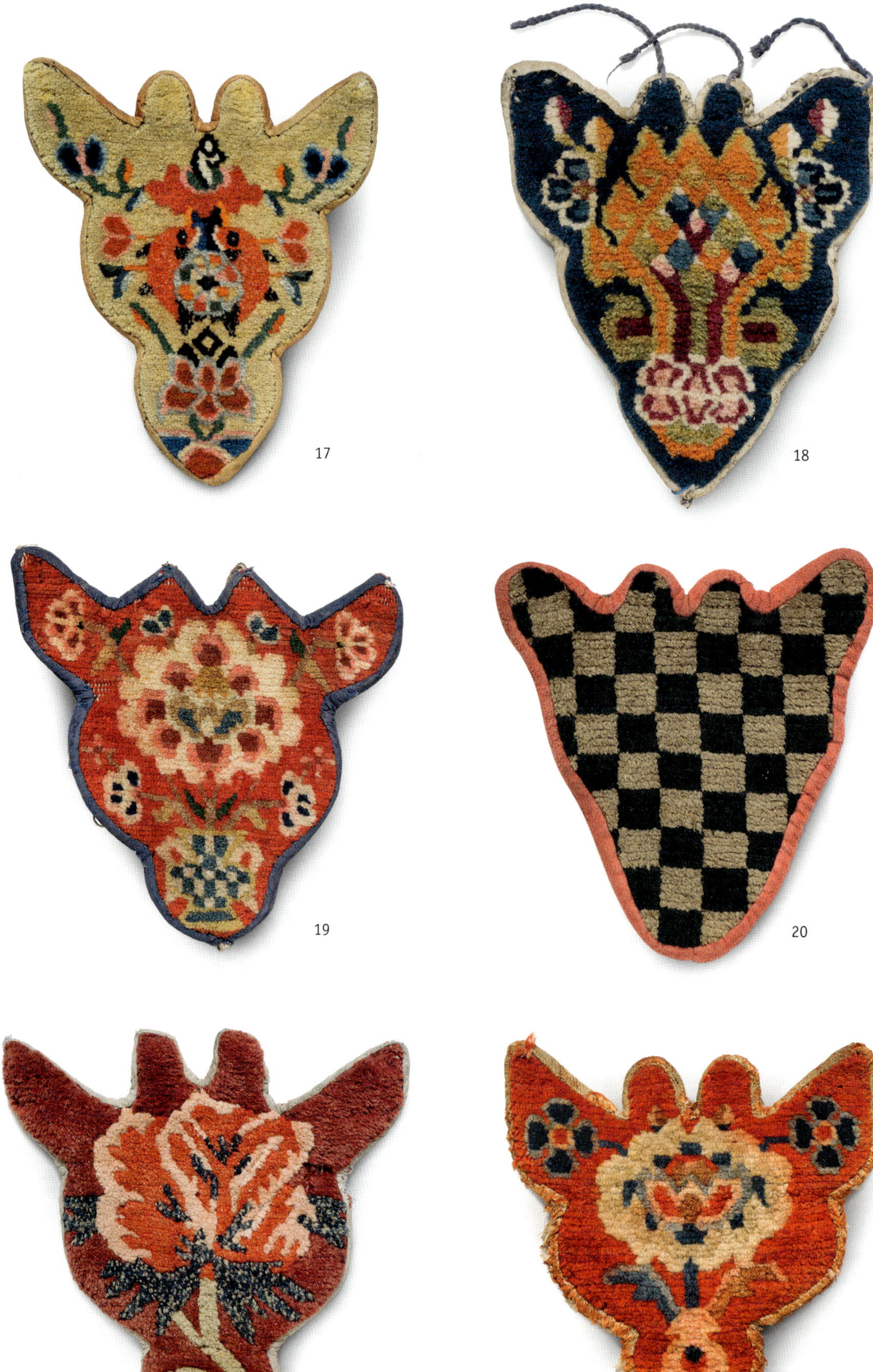

17 18 19 20 21 22

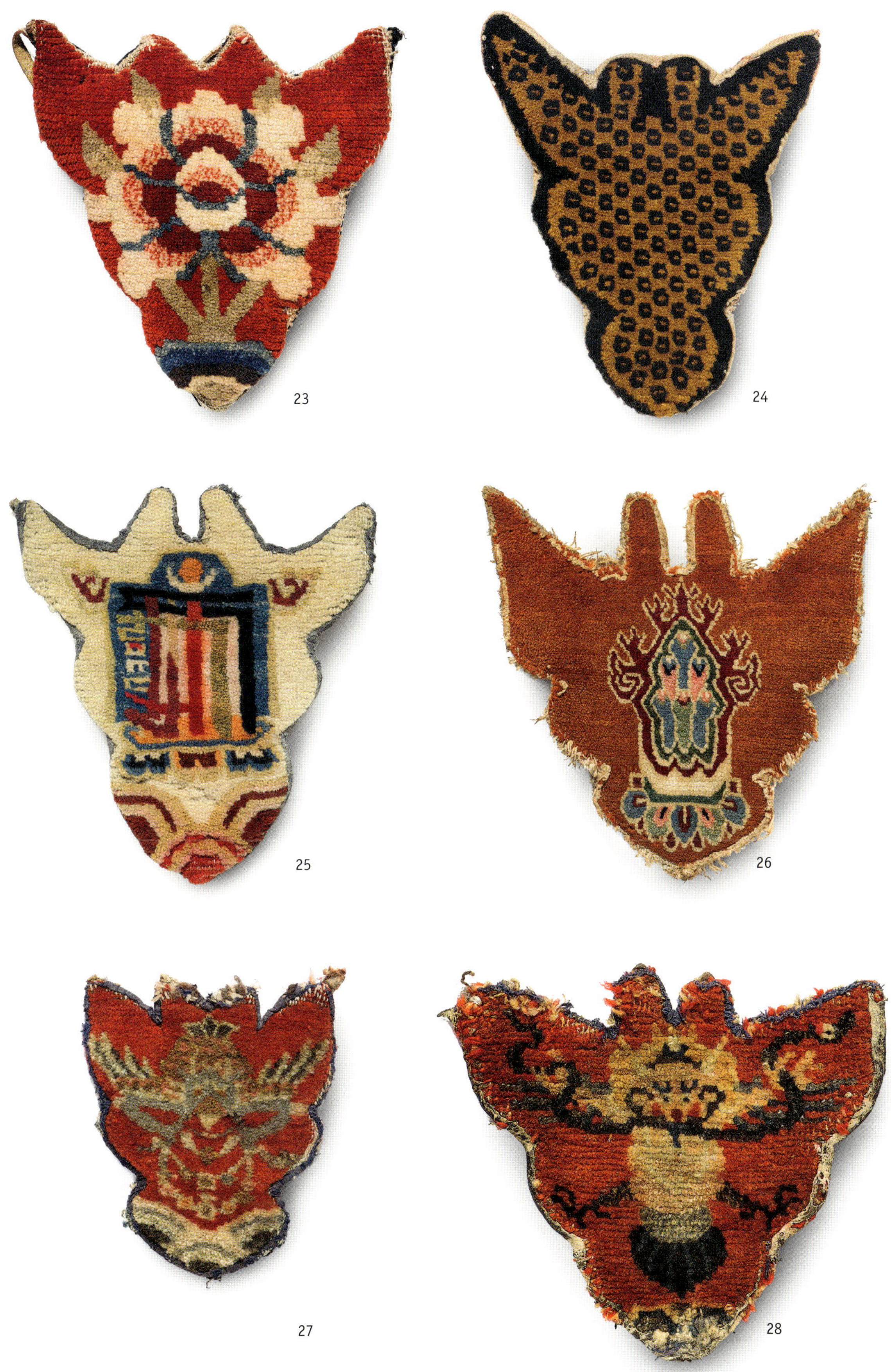

23

24

25

26

27

28

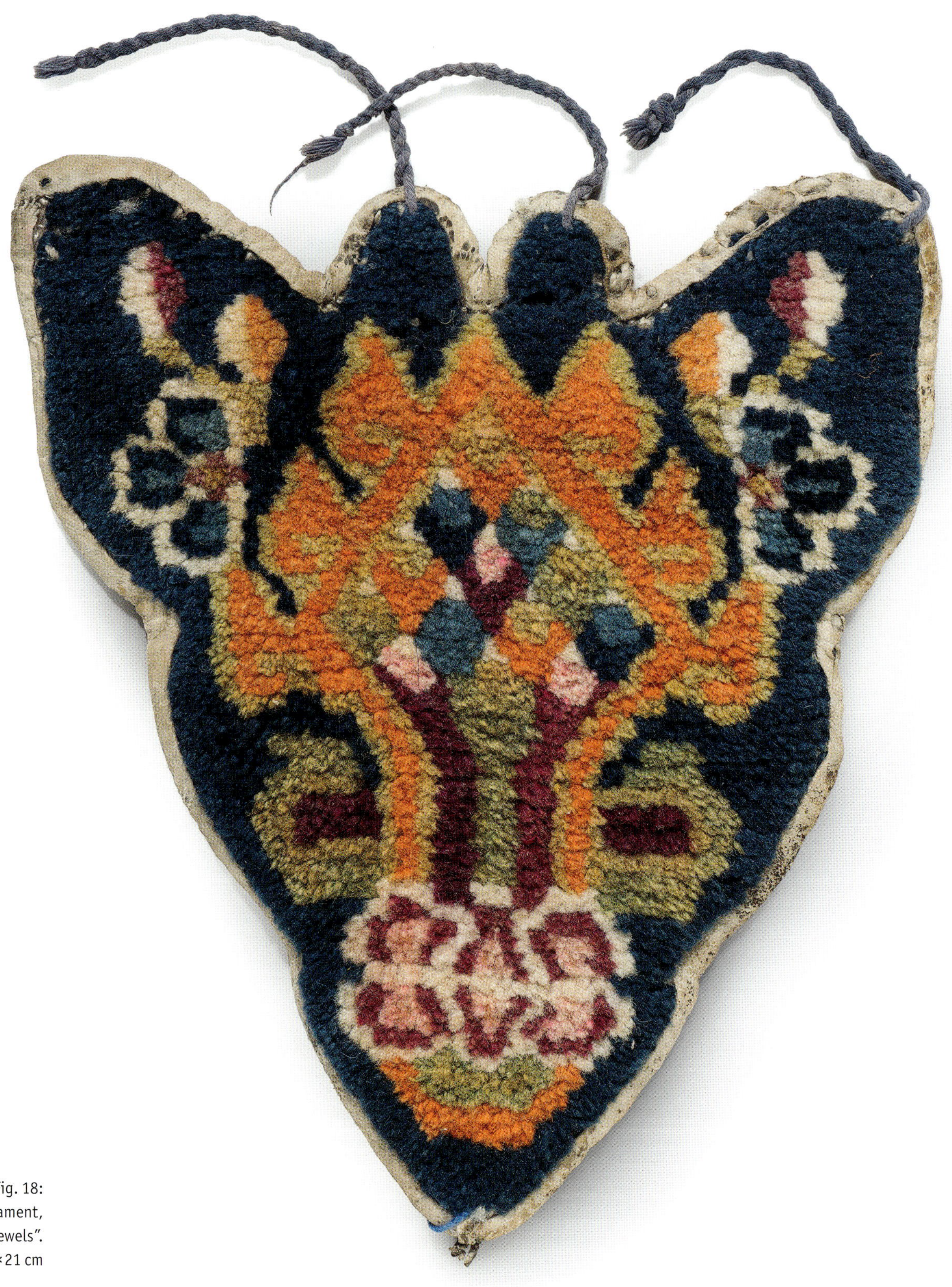

Fig. 18:
Forehead ornament,
"vase with jewels".
20th c., 24×21 cm

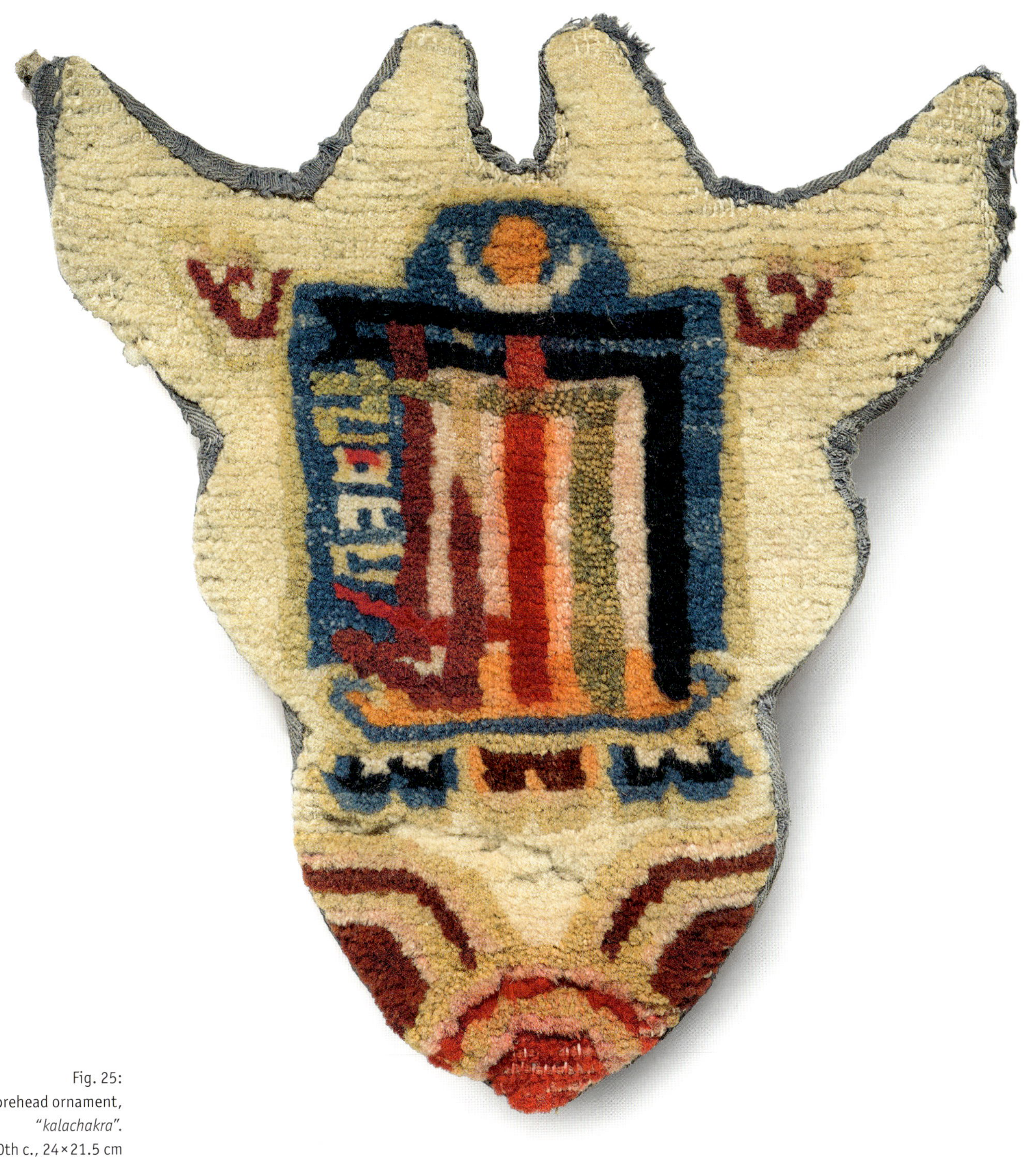

Fig. 25:
Forehead ornament,
"*kalachakra*".
20th c., 24×21.5 cm

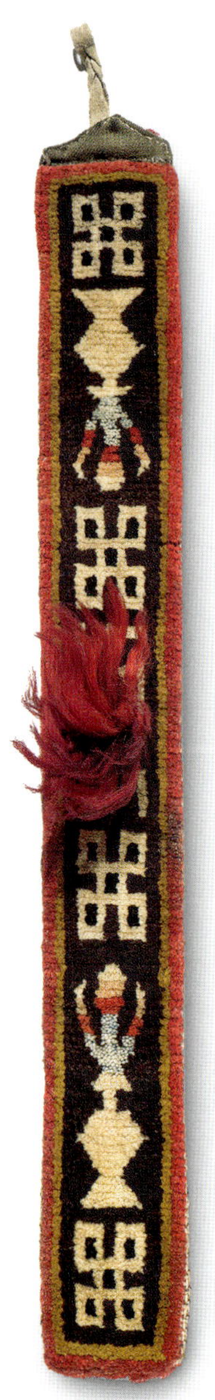
Fig. 29: Animal collar (1). 20th c., 74×9 cm

Crupper Rugs

Crupper rugs (see Fig. 12) underlay the crupper straps by which the backside of the saddle (cantle) is secured. Most crupper rugs have a trapezoid or triangular shape with contoured sides. The underlying fabric of the four crupper rugs in the Buddeberg collection is all wool (Fig. 13, 14 and 15, also Fig. 46 in the contribution by Tsareva). They have a wool pile and the knotting is Tibetan.

The field shows cloud bands (see Fig. 13), a flower medallion (see Fig. 46 in the contribution by Tsareva), a peony medallion in combination with endless knots and blooming branches (see Fig. 14), and a combination of two half-eyes (?), a small flower, two butterflies and the *haishanyun* pattern (see Fig. 15). The border consists of several stripes.

Forehead Ornaments

The charming forehead ornaments are called *takyab* by the Tibetans. Others call them "horse jewels" (Kuloy 1996: 217) or "horse faces", according to personal information from Zang Hanzhai. They have inspired various kinds of romantic lore. It is said that these *takyab* graced the forehead of the leading horse, mule or donkey of a pack train. However, since it is highly improbable that horses were used as pack animals, it seems much more likely that the *takyab* were part of the tack of all kinds of mounts.[5]

Shaped to fit the animal's forehead, they are all triangular with four protrusions at the top. According to some, these protrusions originally represented the ears and horns of a mythical animal, such as the dragon. The *takyab* are made of pile-knotted wool; in rare cases they are decorated with embroidery. They are fastened to the animal's head with three or five leather or plain cotton strings. Like most saddle rugs, the backside and the edges are finished and lined with plain blue or red woven fabric.

The Buddeberg collection includes no less than twenty-two *takyab*. They all have the usual four "ears and horns" at their upper end, with one exception, a forehead ornament ending in three instead of four "ears and horns". They all show more or less the same structure: warps of hand-spun cotton (Figs. 17, 20 to 26) or wool (Fig. 18) with one (see Figs. 17, 24 to 26), two (see Figs. 18, 20 to 23) or even three wefts of wool. All were made in the Tibetan knotting technique to create their thick wool pile. Although most colours are from natural dyes, pink and orange are synthetic which supports a dating to the first quarter of the 20th century, if not later. The edges of a few forehead ornaments are made of leather (see Fig. 17), which is unusual.

The designs of the forehead ornaments from the Buddeberg collection are very similar to those described in my book. By far the most popular design is the "Ten Combined Tibetan Characters" (Sanskrit *kalachakra*)[6] above a lotus flower rising either from a vase decorated with the wish-fulfilling jewels (see Fig. 26) or above the sea (see Fig. 25). Another popular design is a lotus flower rising from the water (see Figs. 21 and 23) or from the jewelled vase (Figs. 19 and 22). The same goes for the peony[7] and the Flaming Jewel in combination with a lotus flower (see Fig. 18) rising from a jewelled vase or above the sea/water symbol. In rare cases, *takyab* are decorated with two well-known Buddhist symbols which appear in the forehead ornament in Fig. 17: the Two Fishes, a charm to avert evil, in this case in combination with what looks like the Wheel of the Law (Sanskrit *dharmachakra*). Even rarer are the checkerboard pattern (Tib. *shotima*) represented in Fig. 20, the "eyes" in combination with two cloud bands in Fig. 13, and the leopard spots in Fig. 24. These designs demonstrate that most, if not all, forehead ornaments have a magical, i.e., protective function.

The Karl Steiner collection includes two head ornaments with the very rare depiction of a *Garuda* (Figs. 27 and 28).

Bands and Straps

While gilded copper forehead ornaments and bell or talisman collars (Tib. *dom*) were probably reserved for the mounts of high-ranking lamas or officials, all kinds of trappings made of pile-knotted wool, flat-woven or embroidered fabric, or coloured and ornamented leather were used by other Tibetans to decorate their horses, mules, donkeys and yaks. Collars with bells and spice bags are particularly charming (De Jong 2013: 153). Quite understandably, they evoke all kinds of romantic stories. We are made believe that the leader of a pack train, be it a camel, yak, mule or donkey, could guide the other animals during the night by means of the sound of the bells or the aroma of the spice bag. I myself am inclined to agree with Sjoerd de Vries, who says that this kind of talisman simply had a danger-averting function. These trappings are strikingly similar to the nomadic animal trappings from Persia and Central Asia (Tanavoli 1998: 70–73). This shows that Tibetan society was much more open to foreign influences than is often believed.

The Buddeberg collection includes a pair of collars and two individual specimens, which will be described in the following. Much more extensive is the collection of tablet-

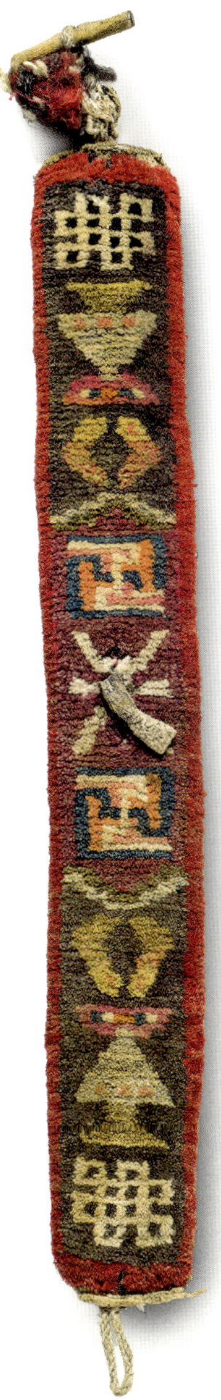

Fig. 30: Animal collar (2). 20th c., 63×8.5 cm

woven bands and plaited herders' slingshots, whose discussion is beyond the scope of this contribution (see, however, the contribution by Kalantari).

The underlying fabric of these collars consists of wool (see C190 in the catalogue) or cotton warps (Figs. 29 and 30) with either two shoots of wool weft or one cotton and one wool weft (see Fig. 29). The wool pile is made in the Tibetan knotting technique. The selvedges are either plain (see Figs. 29 and 30) or finished with red cotton (C190 in the catalogue). The backs of the collars are lined with blue, red or black cotton. In the middle of the collar C190 is a square strap hole reinforced with natural leather for attaching a tassel or bell, now lost. In one of the pair (C190 in the catalogue) the short leather strap, which originally formed a loop for attaching a bell or tassel, has survived. It is now loose on one side. In the collar shown in Fig. 29, one of the *kilim* ends is folded up by two centimetres and stitched down at the back of the collar. The other end is reinforced with a triangular piece of woollen plain weave and hemmed with red cotton. A perforated natural leather strap measuring 20 centimetres in length is sewn on the back of one end. The other, reinforced end is provided with a similar loop strap. A short tassel of red dyed yak hair is attached to the middle of this trapping. The collar shown in Fig. 30 displays another interesting feature: a cord about six centimetres in width, made of plaited natural, black and red wool threads, is sewn on one of the *kilim* ends. It is tied around a wooden toggle which is seven centimetres in length. Sewn on the other end is a similar but looped cord, five centimetres in length and of undyed wool. A short, originally looped natural leather strap, now loose on one side, served to attach a bell or tassel.

Although the structure is very different, the design is quite similar to that of the tablet-woven bands. The field is decorated with a combination of endless knots, *swastikas*, flower vases, fishes, or a star. All borders are simply striped.

CONCLUSION AND OUTLOOK

So far my discussion of the Buddeberg collection of horse tack. As I said: almost every piece is providing us with new information, particularly when we take the trouble to look at the details. And what is more important: this is only the beginning. I sincerely hope that other private collectors or museum curators will follow my example.

NOTES

1 Editor's note: De Jong uses the term "under-under-saddle rug" based on his observation that these trapezoidal pieces are used in addition to the saddle rug pair (*masho* and *makden*). In the previous literature, these are called "horse blanket" or "horse cover" (Tib. *takyab*). In a German publication on decorative horse blankets of varied provenance, these Tibetan pieces are called "Schabracken" (caparisons).

2 To date, only two complete sets of Ningxia saddle rugs have been published (Eiland & Eiland 1998: 315, Fig. 31; De Jong 2013: 77, Fig 6.08).

3 This design is derived from the classical leaf pattern (De Jong 2013: 94f.).

4 Editor's note: the expression "frog feet" or "frog foot" was most probably coined by dealers and has nothing to do with the origin or any possible meaning of the motif. Much more likely is that it is a simplified representation of the wish-fulfilling jewel in a bowl.

5 Oral information from the Tibetologist Sjoerd de Vries, owner of the Astamangala Gallery in Amsterdam.

6 Oral information from the Tibetologist Sjoerd de Vries, June 2012. These refer to seven different Tibetan symbols, plus sun, moon, and flame.

7 The representations of the lotus flower and peony are often so similar in iconography that it is difficult to decide which flower is meant.

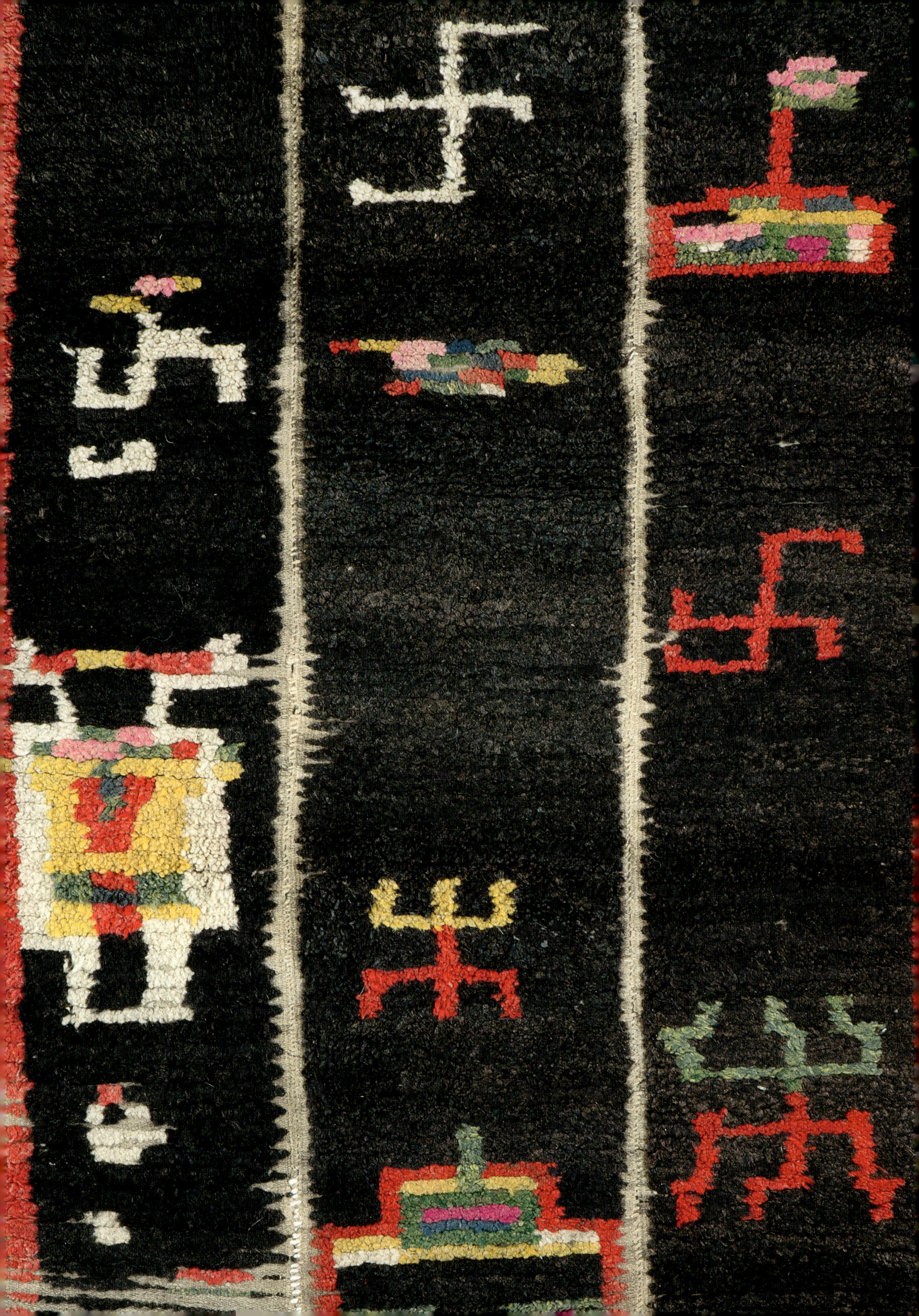

Karma Trinley Darchen

A REMINISCENCE ABOUT OLD TIMES

Tsuktruk Looped Pile Textiles

Detail of Fig. 6

In antiquity Tibet was more influenced by the Shang Shung (Tib. *zhang zhung*) Dynasty to the west than by Central Asian nomadism. Hence before Buddhism and Lamaism, during which we assume the Bon religion was practised, there existed a formal culture with kings as rulers and aristocratic households.

The Tibetan language shares its roots with Burmese rather than Chinese, and trade influences, ancient migration patterns and genetic characteristics also come from that direction as well as from the west.

There are also connections between Burma and Tibet with regards to textiles.

The Rawang tribe in present-day Burma makes looped pile cotton blankets in strips which look surprisingly like the looped pile woollen *tsuktruk* blankets made in Tibetan households as well as by nomads. I assume they do not use the Tibetan wooden horizontal loom for these pieces.

The horizontal or *trikja* loom (Fig. 1) is so ancient that we can assume something similar may have been used in antiquity. This was confirmed in an interview during my fieldwork with the Gabu villagers of the Wangden valley, who said this loom was in use prior to the making of the Wangden Valley style warp-faced knotted pile carpets. One of these rugs was recently carbon tested and proven to come from the time between the 14th and 16th centuries. *Tsuktruks*, being made for everyday use, have not been preserved for hundreds of years in monasteries like the warp faced carpets. Figure 2, however, which shows an unusually well-saturated madder dye and a frog-foot motif used on knotted pile rugs of unusual age, is an outstandingly old version of *tsuktruk* looped-pile weaving. As it has a border of a similar scale and design to ancient Ningxia rugs, it may be an early prototype given by a Lama to the weavers of Ningxia to reproduce for Tibetan monasteries. Hence this *tsuktruk* possibly comes from the 17th century, but only a radiocarbon test would give an exact date.

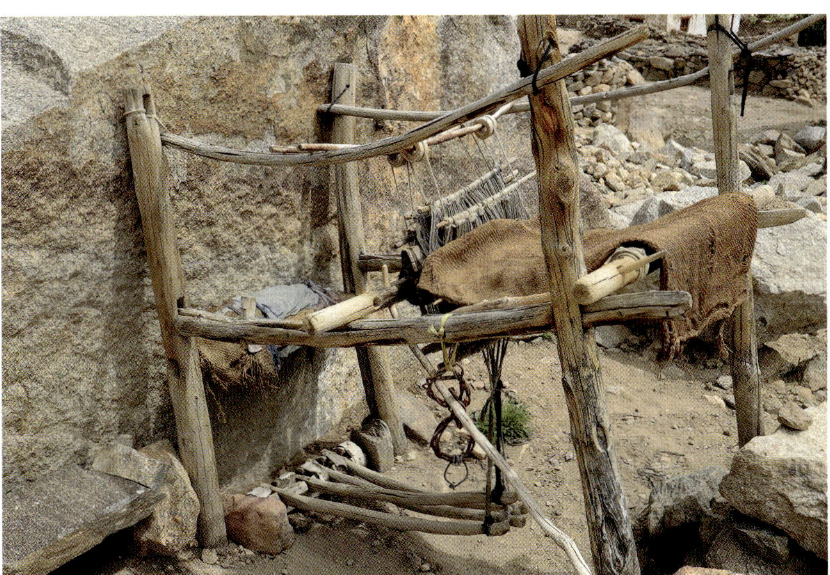

Fig. 1: Pedal loom in Reru village. Zanskar, Himachal Pradesh, India

I was lucky to be shown a piece of great antiquity which had been carbon-tested to the Han period (1st–2nd century AD) and was very likely excavated in a Silk Road oasis area. This had a chequered design and was made in three strips with looped pile identical to the other existing pieces. In the book *Tibet: Caught in Time* (Clarke 1997: 69) is a photograph by Charles Bell of a lady weaving on a *trikja* loom, although the textile she is making is not easily visible. It is captioned: "Woman weaving woollen cloth on a horizontal frame loom operated by foot treadles. The warp is wound around rods laid parallel to the ground and the weft inserted by means of a bobbin. This type of loom, used mainly for cloth weaving in Tibet, was introduced into Bhutan in the 1930s, where it is still in use." This statement has brought about two misconceptions: firstly, that since the loom was introduced to Bhutan so recently it might also have been a recent introduction to Tibet; second, that looped pile *tsuktruk* rugs and blankets are the predominant textiles made on this loom.[1]

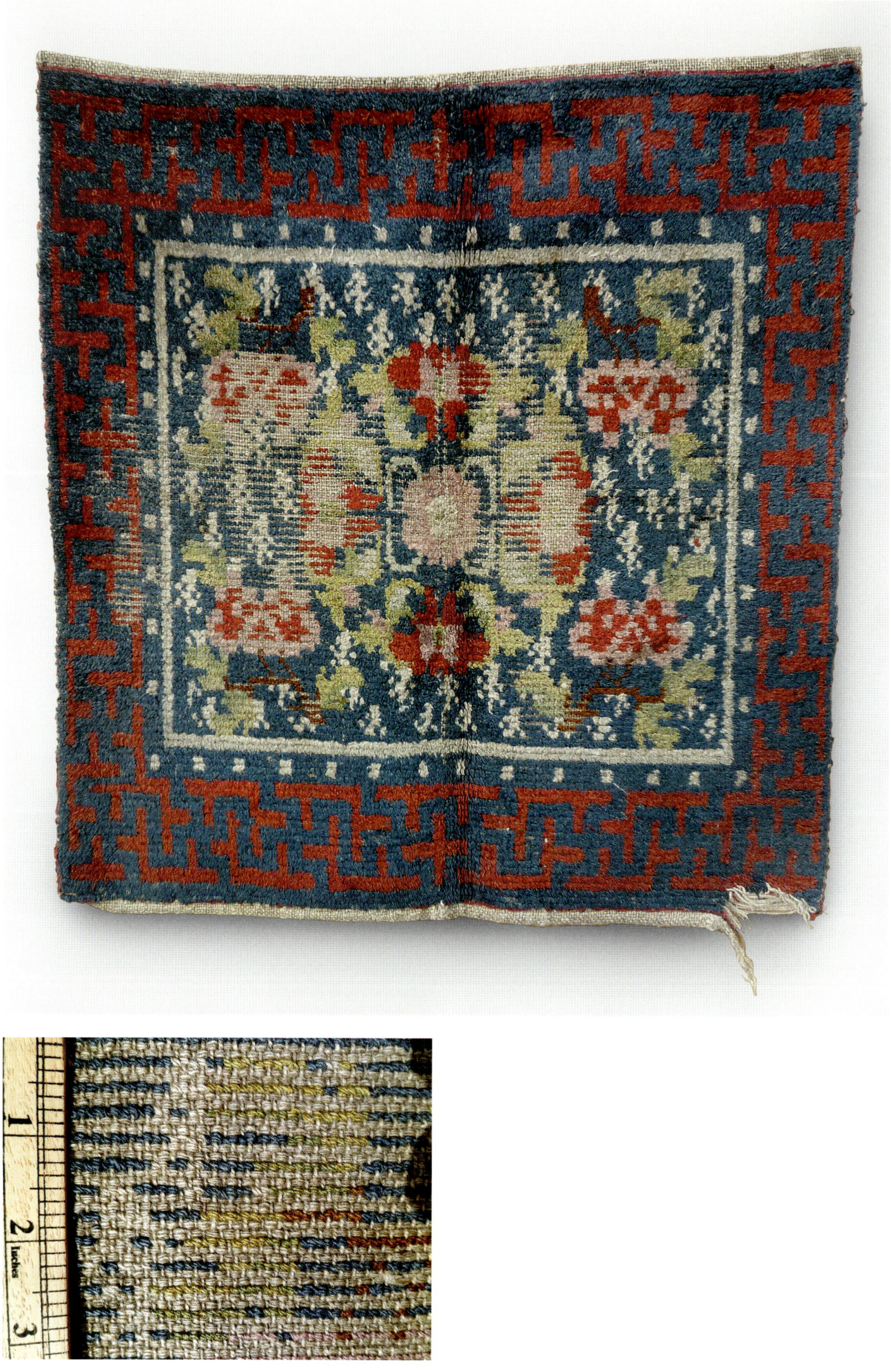

Fig. 2: Sitting rug (*khagangma*) in *tsuktruk* looping technique with detail of the reverse side. 19th c. or earlier

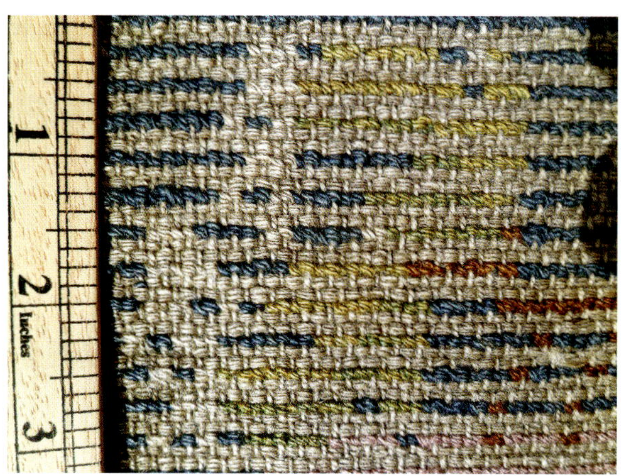

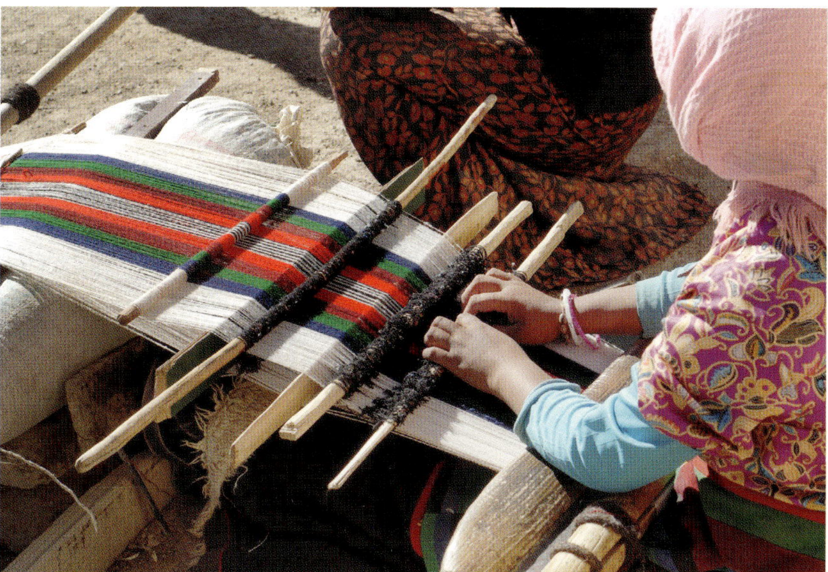

Fig. 3: Backstrap loom. Nyima region in southern Changtang

Almost everything about Tibetan weaving is different from that of its Central Asian neighbours. If one has not been there many times, it is easy to assume that things are done in similar ways to other nomadic cultures. Tibet is not only a nomadic culture, it is also monastic and has been for more than thirteen hundred years. Lamas design and order most textiles and nomads make similar pieces, albeit inferior. These lamas are the real artists, not the nomadic people. The nomads are heavily influenced by the teachings of the Buddha, as conveyed by the lamas. At all times these teachings have been in the peoples' minds, rather than the ancient influences of shamanism, animism or prehistoric rock art. All people in Tibet believe in what the Buddha taught and perpetuate the symbolism which helps to preserve these sacred beliefs. Bed-sized *tsuktruks* are made by a mother for her sons when they go to a monastery, so high quality wool and dyes are used. Whether they weave to sell, for their own use or to give to a monastery, the women are proud to preserve these sacred ideas and give them expression in their craft which is a life-saving resource and an absolute necessity in this inhospitable environment.

The long loom used to make strips of yak hair flat weave for making nomad tents is not a backstrap loom. The only backstrap loom (Tib. *pang thag*) I have ever seen in Tibet was in Gabu. We arrived one day in the village of Gabu and I photographed a girl with warps strung apparently for the making of *liu* type material, though it was a wider type than the old pieces which we can assume were also made on a backstrap loom (Fig. 3). However, none of the other flat weaves or piled textiles from Tibet are made on a backstrap loom. The *trikja* all-purpose loom is responsible for *nambu* flat weaves, aprons[2] (Tib. *pang gdan*), *tsuktruk* blankets and *tsukden* as found in the Buddeberg collection (Figs. 4–8). Hence none of these can be considered exclusively nomadic. Nomads with their herds of yak and sheep that produce milk and butter, as well as wool and hair for sale and trade, buy saddle carpets for their horses and *nambu* flat weave for clothing from villagers or at festivals and town bazaars. The finest *nambu* – called *sherma* – is traditionally produced in Chetishol, and orders are taken for various lengths to make special New Year dresses and coats. Heavy coats also known as *chubas* are made from sheep skin with the wool on the inside. Nomads on pilgrimage to Lhasa can often be seen with them.

All these traditional techniques for diverse uses are still practised to this day and over many centuries have influenced Tibet's neighbours in all the surrounding areas, those who have let themselves be inspired by them. An unusual example is an Uzbek rug which copies the tie-dyed, cross-shaped motif (Tib. *thig ma*) often found on *nambu* edging of Tibetan rugs.

With projects in Wangden Valley (Fig. 9; see also www.wangdenrugs.com), Lhasa itself and Boudha in the Kathmandu valley, these techniques of weaving and dying are all still practised. We hope for help with their financial support in the future as they preserve the real secrets of Tibet. Sponsorship for the production of items to be donated to Buddhist monasteries is the first step on the path to enlightenment!

NOTES

1 Editors' note: Such horizontal pedal looms (see Fig. 1) are still used throughout the Tibetan cultural area, not only by rural villagers, but also by professional weavers. They can often be dismantled for transport.

2 Editors' note: Examples of *nambu* and striped textiles, which are used to make aprons and covers, are illustrated and described in the article by Christiane Kalantari.

Fig. 4: *Tsuktruk* rug. The velvety pile and unusually fine structure of the five panels suggests that it was made for a high lama. 3rd quarter 19th c., 156×77 cm

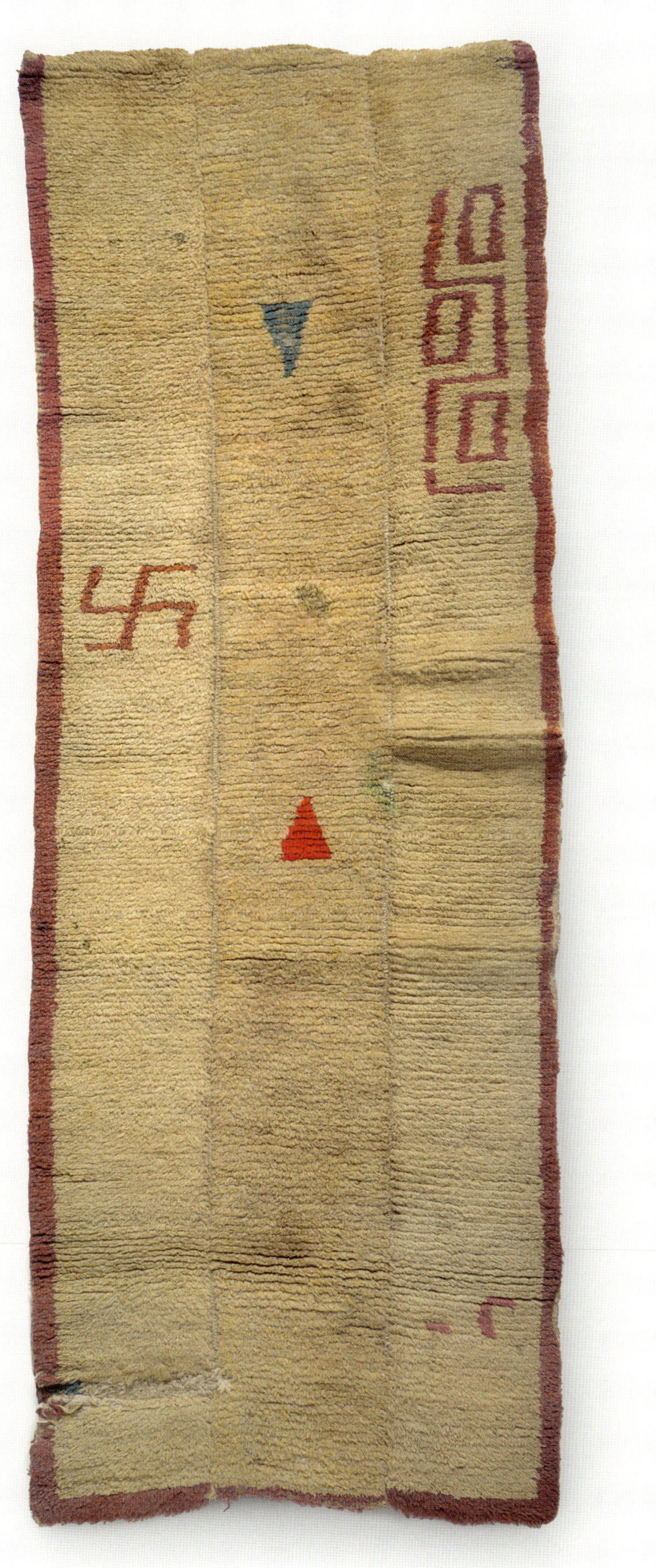

Fig. 5: *Tsuktruk* rug.
A rustic example made as a donation to a monastery. The border suggests similarity with the design of a Wangden *drumze* rug.
Around 1900, 200×70 cm

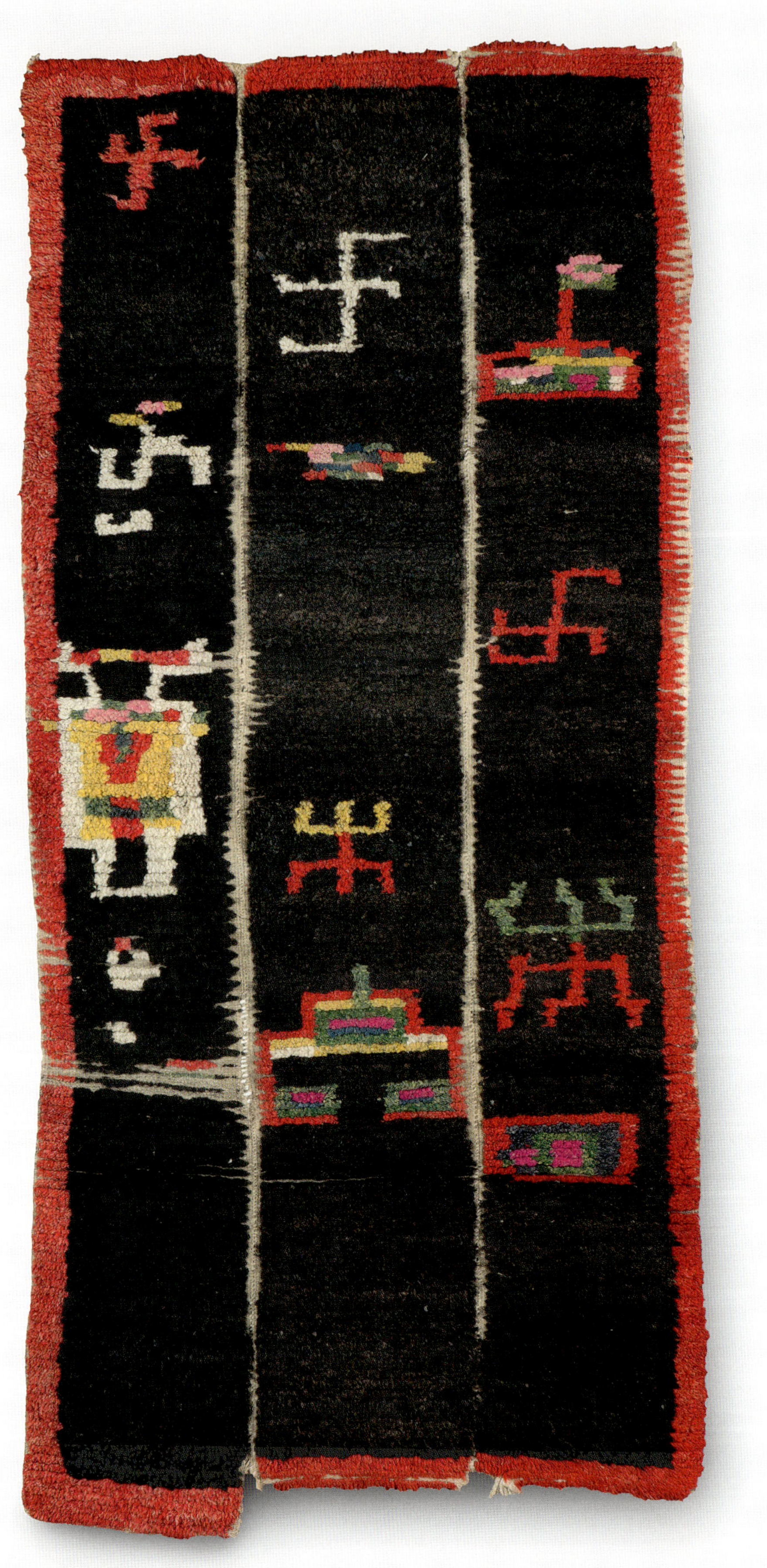

Fig. 6: *Tsuktruk* rug. The design shows among other things a nomadic tent and a *stūpa*. Perhaps the donation by a nomadic family to a monastery. Early 20th c., 151 × 68 cm

Fig. 7: *Tsuktruk* rug.
Tigma design and the view through a window.
Early 20th c., 139 × 65 cm

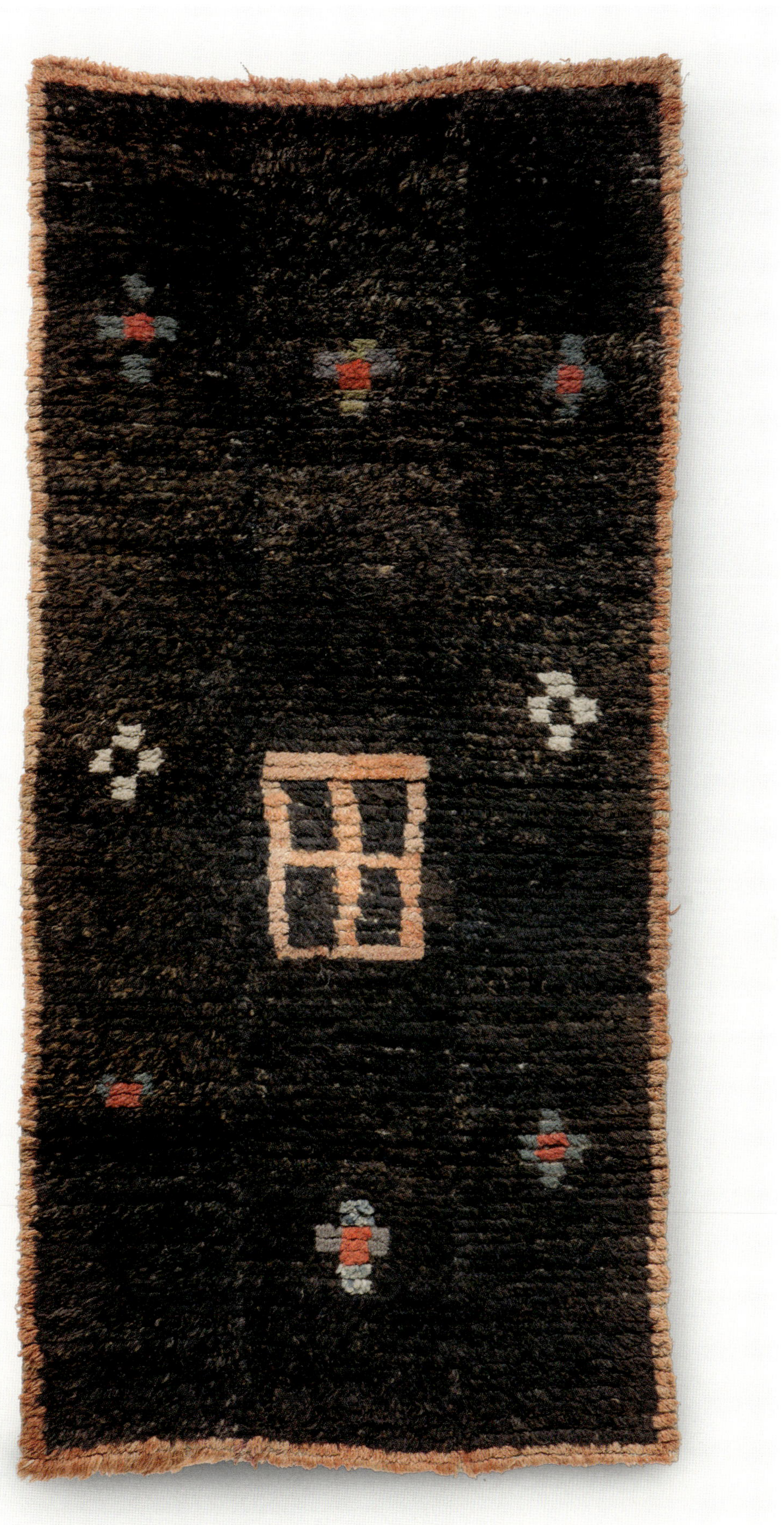

Fig. 8: *Tsuktruk* rug. Fine and carefully made rug with four panels, perhaps for the doorway to a lama's reception room. 20th c., 155×74 cm

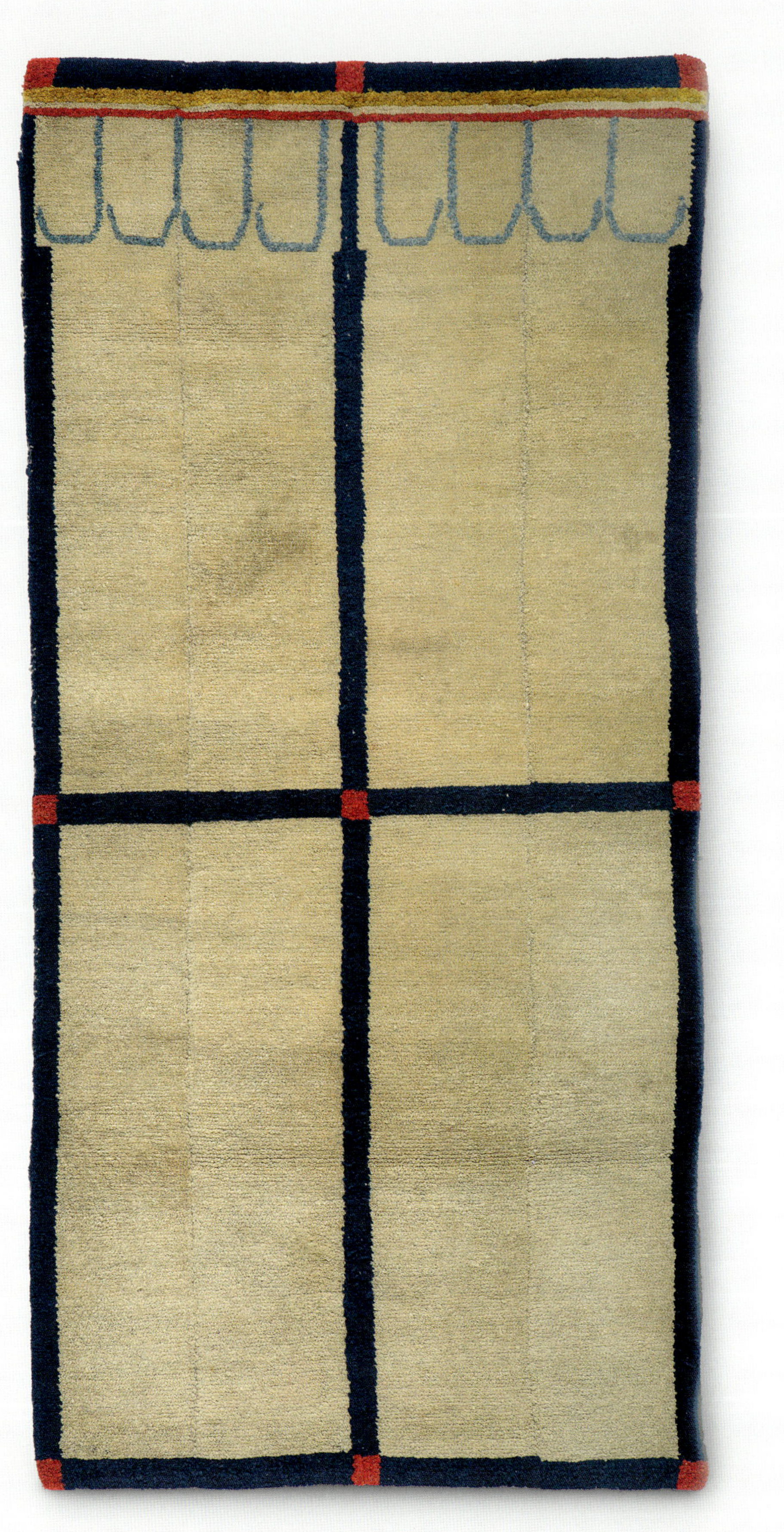

Fig. 9: Wangden *drumze* rug made in the current production initiated by Rupert Smith and Thomas Wild. Gabu village. 164×74 cm

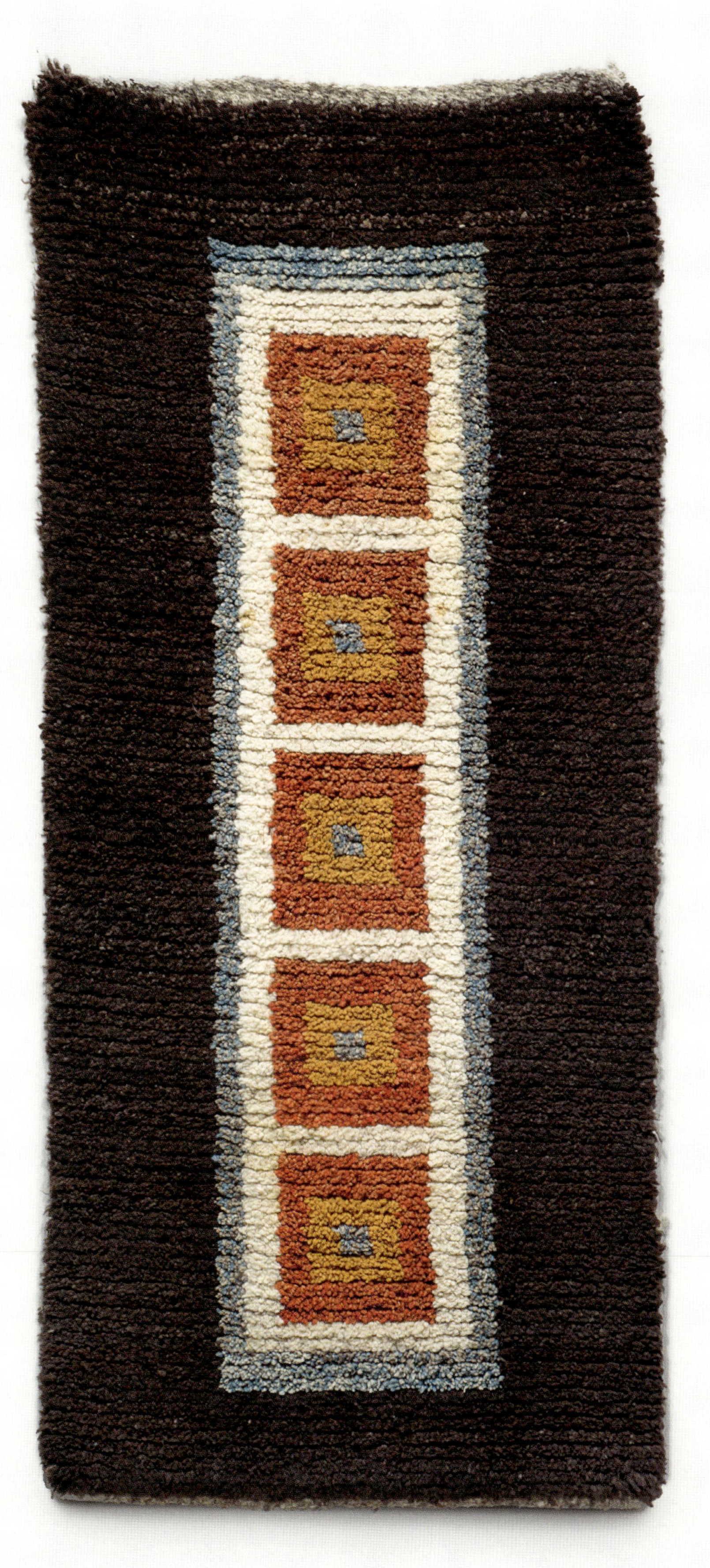

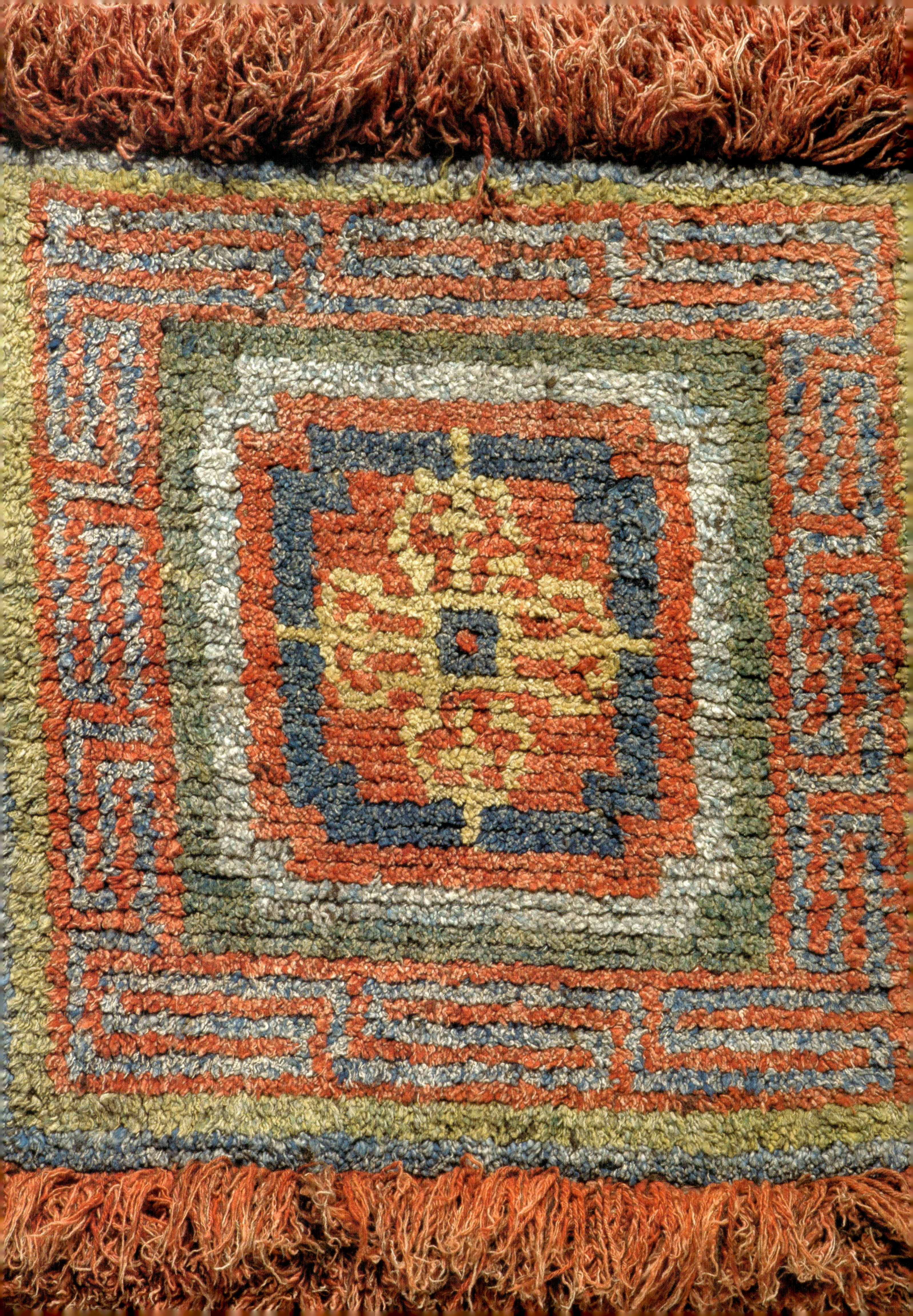

Ulrike Montigel

THE ENLIGHTENED DRAGON

Chinese and Tibetan Symbols

INTRODUCTION

Detail of Fig. 8

Human beings have always attempted to influence their fate in many ways and in every area of their lives. Whether it is through magic practices, religious rituals, through prayer or magic formulas, or the wearing of amulets or objects to protect them from the "evil eye", the idea is prevalent that there is something we can do to make our path in life easier and more successful.

I cannot think of a culture that has entirely stayed away from the effort to achieve good fortune by the above-mentioned means, however, the tools used to this end differ from culture to culture.

At first glance there seems little difference between Chinese and Tibetan symbolism. Chinese popular symbolism focuses around three wishes: creating wealth and professional success, ensuring good health and longevity, and perpetuating the family through marital happiness and children (preferably boys) (Bartholomew 2006: 17).

We find the symbols expressing these wishes everywhere in Chinese life and material culture. Being surrounded by auspicious symbols is believed to bring about what they signify. For example, peonies are said to help accumulate riches; pomegranates and grapes are believed to provide for the procreation of sons; and the peach and the crane are thought to ensure a long life.

The iconography of Chinese symbolism is also characterised by the love of "rebus", picture puzzles in which "seemingly unrelated objects whose names share the same sounds as the words in the sayings" (Bartholomew 2006: 16). The most quoted instance for the use of homophones (same-sounding words) in Chinese symbols is "bat", which is pronounced *Fu* in Chinese. But *Fu* is also the most general word for "blessings". *Lu* means professional success and wealth, and *Shou* longevity. An abundance of images taken from nature represent these three basic desires, birds, flowers, fruits and animals express these wishes. Because the Chinese use so many different characters for basically the same few wishes, fine shades of meaning can be achieved through using groups or sequences of characters. Thus the Chinese have a "flowery language" at their command and even lengthy blessings can be expressed figuratively.

TIBETAN SYMBOLISM

What makes Tibetan symbolism so special is that it is deeply influenced by Tibetan Buddhism. Whereas *Fu*, *Lu* and *Shou* describe what the Chinese most desire and strive to make happen, enlightenment is high on the Tibetan wish list.

Certainly Tibetans want a good life, health and a happy family just as much as the Chinese, but their culture has a spiritual dimension that we do not find as widely spread in China.

"For more than a thousand years Tibetan culture has been imbued with and characterised by a powerful spirituality in which Buddhist studies and profound philosophical insight, intensive meditation practice and simple superstition, have peacefully coexisted side by side. Religious practice extended to nearly all areas of private and public life, and it was by no means only to be found in monasteries, but also in the houses of farmers and traders as well as in the tents of nomads. In Tibet a nearly indescribable unique atmosphere was prevalent, a special spiritual climate, which was hardly perceived consciously by us Tibetans" (Dagyab Rinpoche 1992: 7).

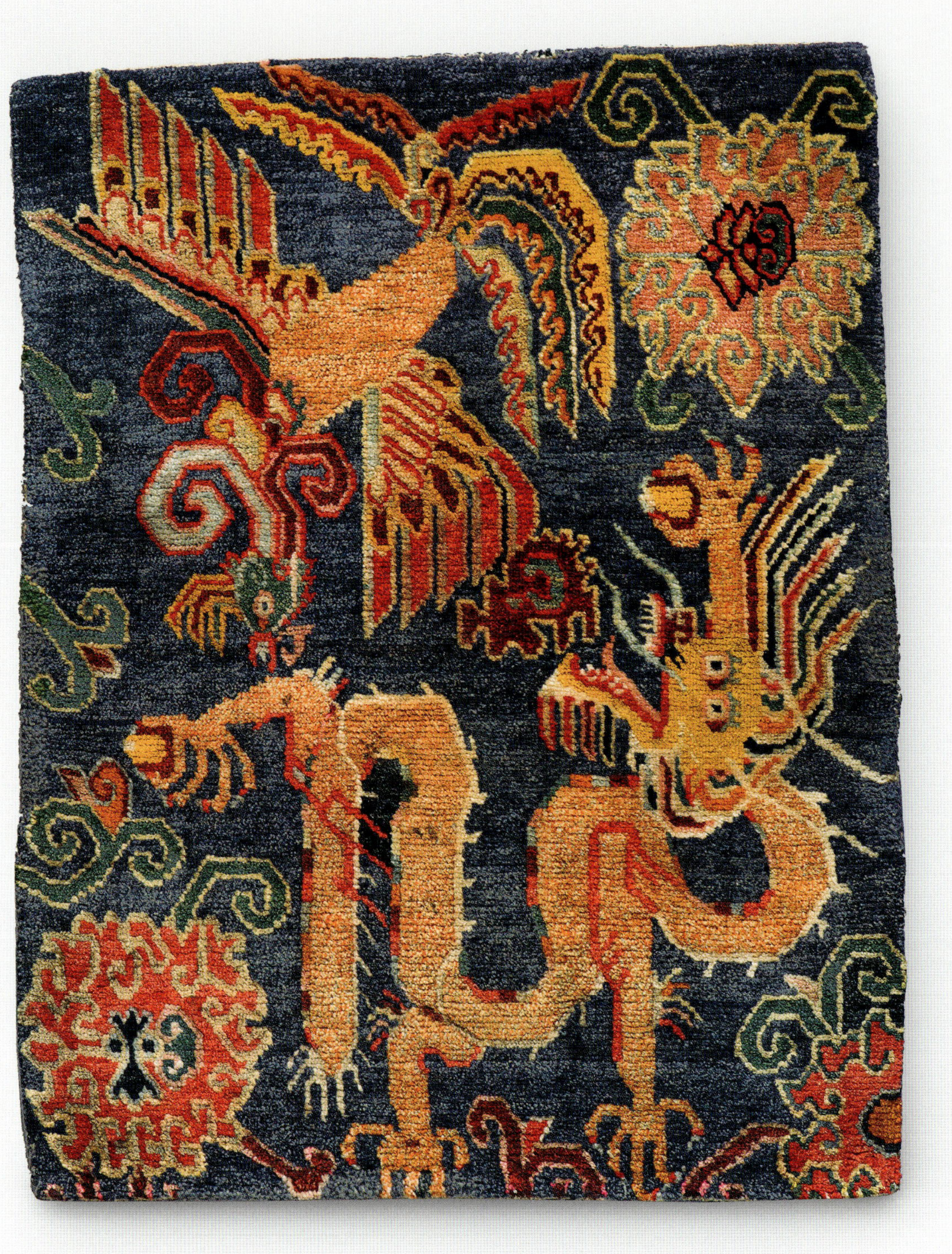

Fig. 1: Sitting or saddle rug (*khagangma* or *masho*). Tibet, early 20th c., 75×59 cm

Buddhist teachings have been part of the culture in Tibet for centuries – many families had sons and daughters in monasteries and daily life was accompanied by Buddhist rituals and symbols.

Buddhist philosophy developed a symbol concept which Dagyab Rinpoche has made available to us in the West (Dagyab Rinpoche 1992: 9ff.). In this concept of symbols, the principal Buddhist understanding of reality – the emptiness and limited existence of our reality – is countered by the concept of *chu* (Tib. *bcud*), a force, energy or quality that permeates all phenomena.[1] *Chu* is understood to be the active force in Tibetan symbols and rituals. "Those who are in command of this language are naturally able to draw from the pool and set strong forces free." (Dagyab Rinpoche 1992: 26). That means that *chu* is manipulable, that specially trained practitioners can enrich it and make an instrument of it. Thus magical practices and a strong faith in their effectiveness are part of the culture of Tibet and the beliefs and experiences of Tibetans.[2]

As far as the images of symbols are concerned, Tibetans use many Chinese characters. They can be found everywhere on items of everyday life as well as on ritual objects. But in the transfer from China to Tibet their meaning shifted under the influence of the concept of *chu*, as described above. This different and deeper meaning can also be found again in the symbols.

For example, the Eight Auspicious Buddhist Symbols are used very often in both cultures, but their meaning is different. This shift in meaning sometimes, but not always, rises to the surface of the image and creates the small changes which I shall describe below.

Bartholomew says of the lotus flower (one of the eight symbols) that it symbolises purity (Bartholomew 2006: 47, 185), whereas the Tibetan understanding is decidedly more complex. Here the lotus stands for the process of purification through which the person meditating figuratively works through and cleanses the dark and muddy waters of his mind. The lotus flower thus stands for the result of a long and deep meditation. The tantric Buddhism of the Tibetans is about processing the energies connecting the inside and the outside, the cosmos and the inner energy channels of the person, and it is about the *chu* that flows through all things.

This short contribution on the Buddeberg collection is not, however, the place to go into detail about Tibetan Buddhism; it is sufficient for our purposes to state here what Tibetan symbolism refers to – transformative experiences through the skilful use of spiritual energies.

Apart from the Chinese tradition in the iconography of Tibetan symbolism we also find the discrete Tibetan iconography which comes from the original nomadic culture of Tibet and the Bon religion.

The Buddeberg collection was not formed with tantric symbolism in mind, in its exhibits we actually find a predominance of Chinese iconography; there is, however, enough material to illustrate some of the main features of Tibetan symbolism. My comments in this article are based on the rug and textile segments of the Buddeberg collection, the only areas I feel I can discuss with any confidence.

The design and colours of Tibetan rugs and textiles differ greatly from Chinese. To me they are more original and more exciting. They exude a marvellous, happy mood, great vitality and playfulness.

Figs. 1, 2 and 3 show rugs whose iconography is in the Chinese tradition, but there is a large amount of artistic freedom in their drawing that is very appealing. The first rug (Fig. 1) has a dragon, phoenix and lotus flower design that takes us right into the midst of our discussion: in China, the dragon and phoenix represent the emperor and empress; in Tibet, the dragon and phoenix symbolise the male and female principles as creatively charged energy.

One of the most basic tenets of Tibetan Buddhism is that this polarity has an energising charge, which one can use during meditation on the way to freeing the mind. In Tibetan medicine, the human body is perceived as having energy channels. These need to be cleansed and purified through meditative practices in order to be able to physically absorb the highly transformative energy of enlightenment. This enlightenment causes changes to the human body which becomes more receptive to higher vibrations and thus goes through a process of change from a thicker to a finer materiality. Since this is a very long process, Tibetan Buddhism has developed a number of meditations to this end.

The rug in Fig. 1 depicts the most desirable result – the dragon is no longer chasing the pearl of enlightenment as he habitually does in Chinese iconography, he already has it in his talons; he has reached his goal and is therefore an enlightened dragon.

Fig. 2 also shows the dragon in possession of the pearl. He has no female counterpole for his joyful sky dance. The borders of the rug show the Eight Auspicious Symbols of Buddhism – the lotus, the conch, the vase, the wheel, the parasol, the endless knot, the fishes, the standard of victory, as well as four yin and yang symbols and four *swastikas*, two turning to the right, two to the left. We will get

Detail of Fig. 1

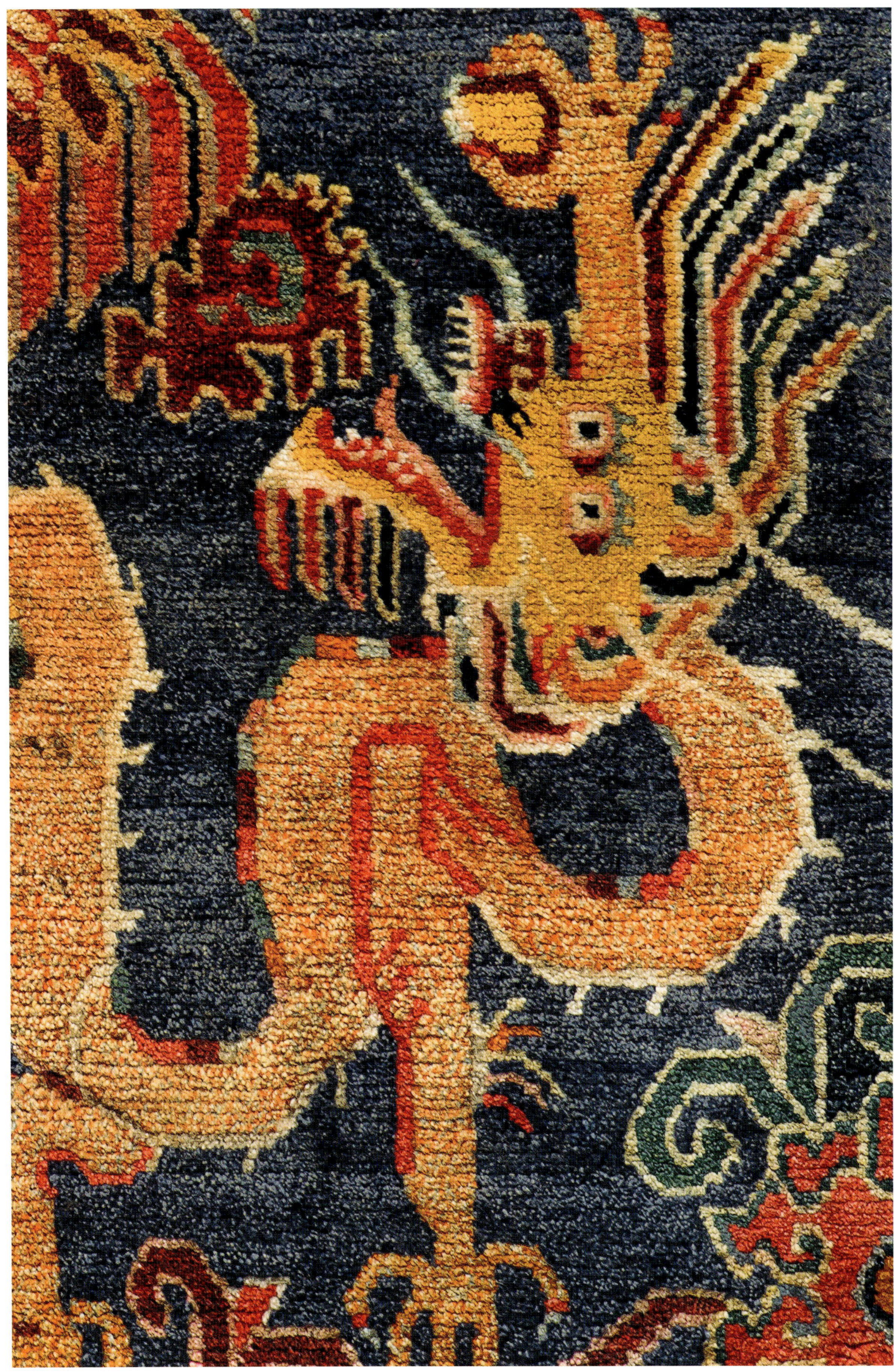

Detail of Fig. 3

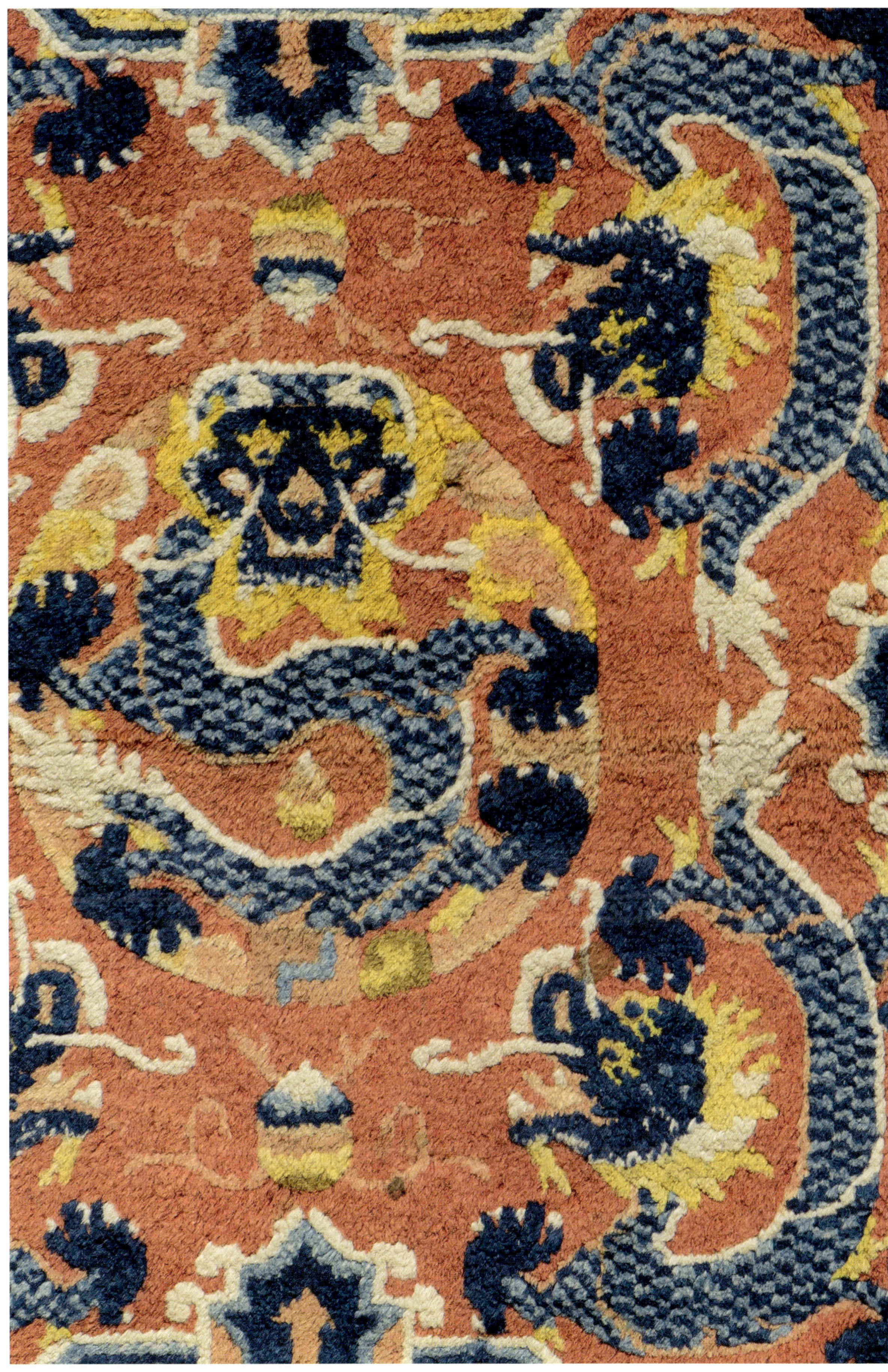

Fig. 2: Sitting or sleeping rug (*khaden*) with dragon and rich in Tibetan symbolism. Tibet, early 20th c., 160×87 cm

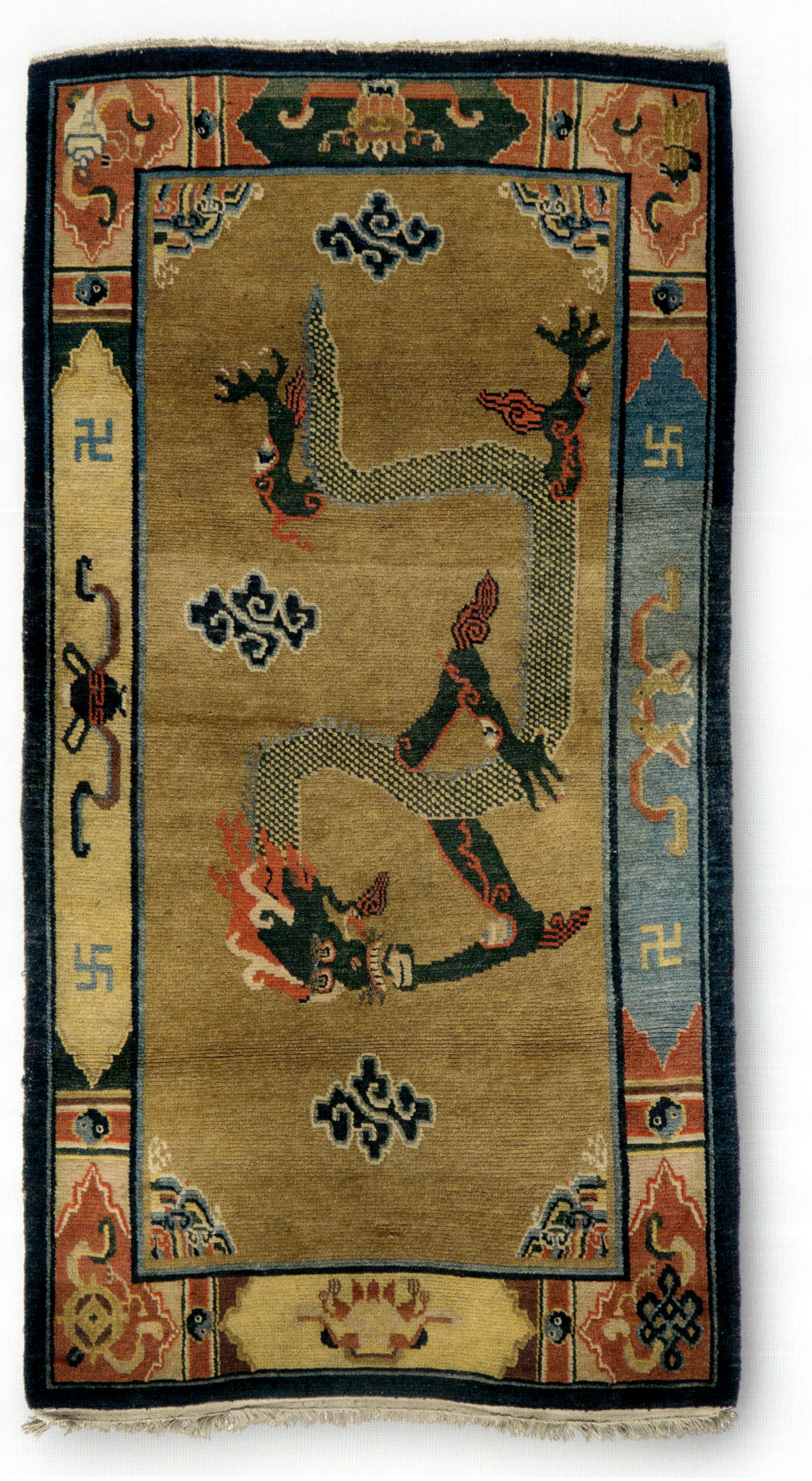

Fig. 3: Sitting rug (*khagangma*), in five-dragon design for the Tibetan market. Ningxia Province, China, 19th c., 67 × 67 cm

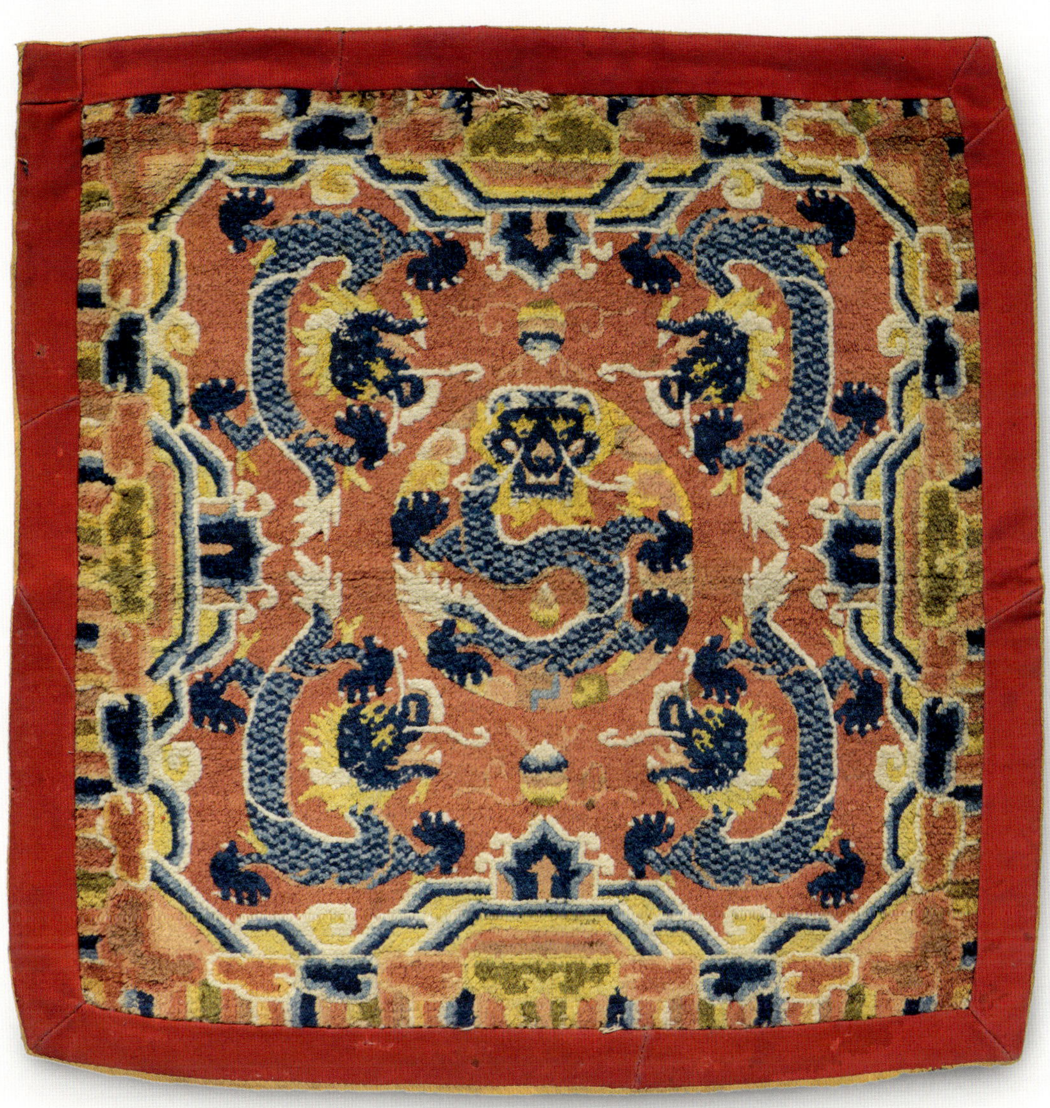

to the meaning of the *swastika* later. The yin and yang symbols in the border imply the polarity of the male and female principles thus complementing the female aspect that is missing in the centre of the rug.

There is a message in the design of this rug, namely, the answer to the question: how can the *chu* be enriched, the energy one needs for the path to enlightenment? The answer lies in the agency of the symbols, in the yin and yang, the *swastikas* and the Eight Auspicious Symbols. The traditional Chinese symbols for good fortune thus gain a deeper significance in that they are seen to contribute to the increase of *chu*.

Sometimes the symbols representing Buddhist teachings in Tibetan rugs are very inconspicuous. Take Fig. 3 as an example: the design of the rug shows a classic Chinese dragon and along the border the very popular motif of "Mount Meru". It is the thin outermost part of the border, however, that carries the typical Tibetan iconography: the coloured stripes represent the "rainbow light" that one can also see on *thangkas* and that often emanates from enlightened teachers. It refers to the transformation of the "coarse" physical body into a "more vibrant" light manifestation.

The rainbow colours are to be found almost everywhere in Tibetan culture, on rugs and ritual objects as well as on representations of high lamas who are said to have dissolved into rainbow light at the moment of their death.

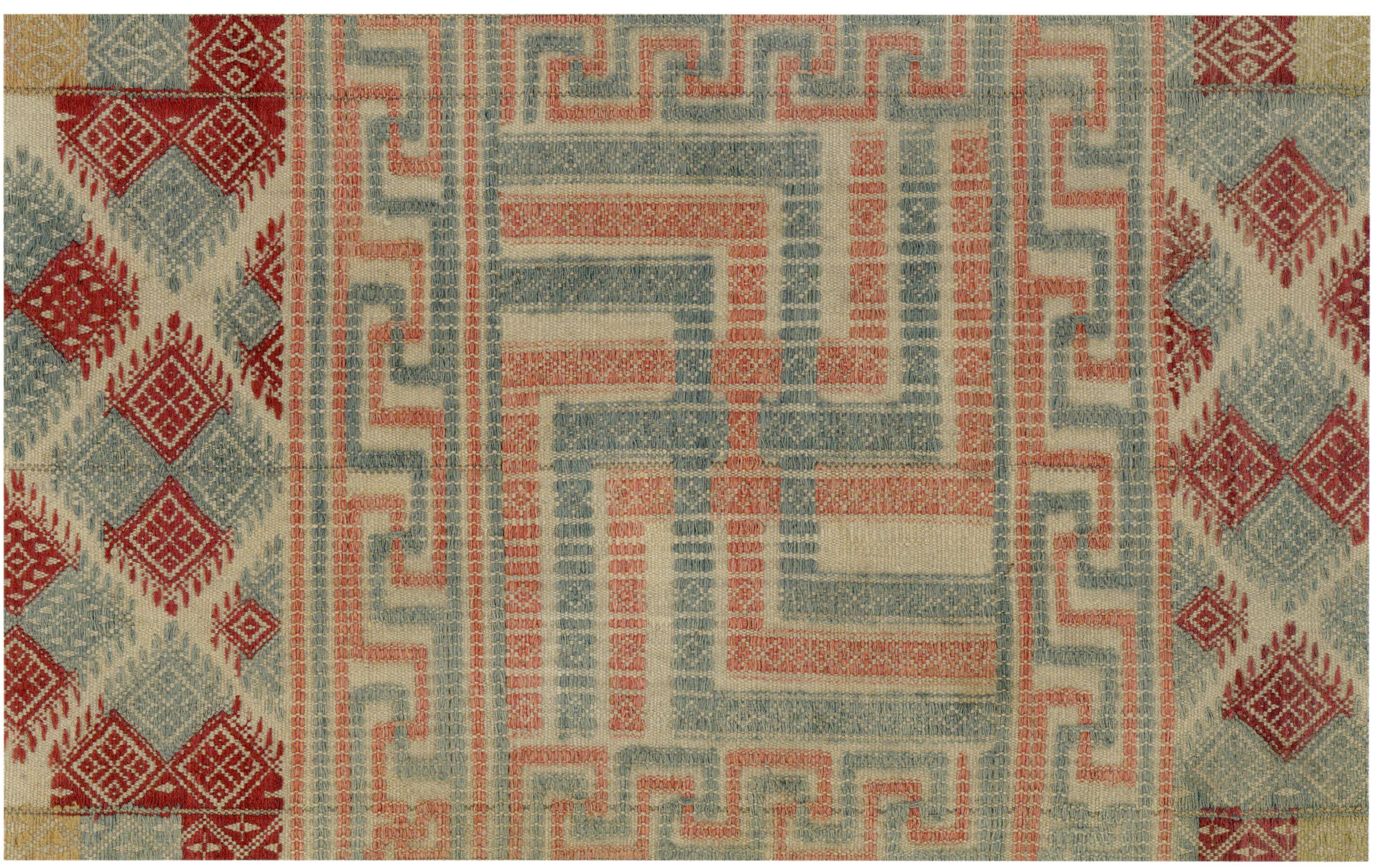

Fig. 4: Detail of a woven textile for a bag (*phechu*). North or Central Bhutan, 1st half 20th c., cotton and wild silk, 260×28 cm

Those who do not know the connections will also not understand the real meaning of the colourful outer borders that so many Tibetan rugs have, and will probably only see them as simple decorations.

THE SWASTIKA

Bartholomew writes: "The *swastika* was a good-luck symbol introduced to China from India with Buddhism. In 693 Empress Wu recognized the *swastika* as the source of all auspiciousness, and it was given the pronunciation *wan* – a homophone of the Chinese word for 'ten thousand' or 'infinity' [...]" (Bartholomew 2006: 263).

For Tibetans the *swastika* is a symbol of dynamic energies or *chu*. In Fig. 2 we see a right- and a left-turning *swastika*. Williams mentions the wide proliferation of the sign in the cultures of Northern Europe, India as well as ancient Peru and associates it with the sun and the making of fire (Williams 1941: 381).

In Tibet not only Buddhism adopted the *swastika*, but also the earlier folk religion of Bon, so that the right- and the left-turning *swastikas* also stand for the assimilation and integration of Bon rituals and practices into Buddhism.

How important the *swastika* is in Tibet is illustrated on Tibetan statues of the Buddha which often carry the symbol at the height of the heart *chakra*. For the meditator the right- and left-turning *swastikas* stand for the energies of the earth and the sky. At the heart *chakra* the energies coming up from the earth and those coming down from the universe meet and thus advance the transformation on the way to enlightenment. The Buddeberg collection has wonderful examples of Bhutanese weavings with the *swastika* (Fig. 4 and Fig. 5).

The *swastika* appears also in a design with an unending pattern (Fig. 6). This design is common to the Chinese and Tibetan design pool. In Tibet is serves to signify the interrelated nature of reality, *samsara*, which is the veil that keeps us from understanding the true nature of things. It is the veil that needs to be torn aside in order to finally "see".

The knotted protective amulet (Fig. 7) shows the *kalachakra* mantra. This is also called the Ten Syllable Mantra and includes the following syllables: *Om, Hang, Tscha, Ma, La, Wa, Ra, Ja, So, and Ha*. It is intended to protect the horses and yaks from the dangers of a journey in the Himalayas. For the Tibetans the *kalachakra* is very important and meaningful. At the same time it is a form of high Tantric medita-

Fig. 5: All-purpose sling (*bhindi*). Bhutan, early 20th c. (?), cotton and wild silk, 131×21 cm

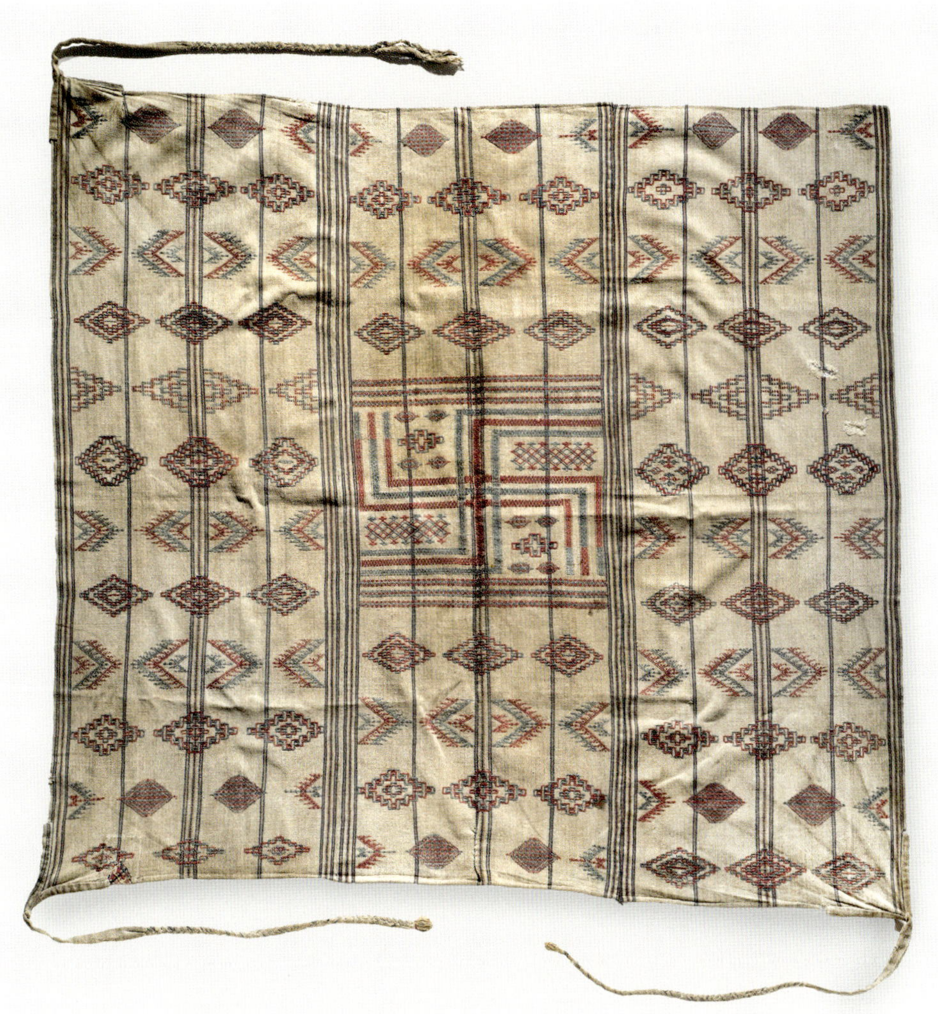

Fig. 6: Horse blanket (*masho*) with *swastika* pattern. Tibet, 19th or early 20th c., 102×95/141 cm

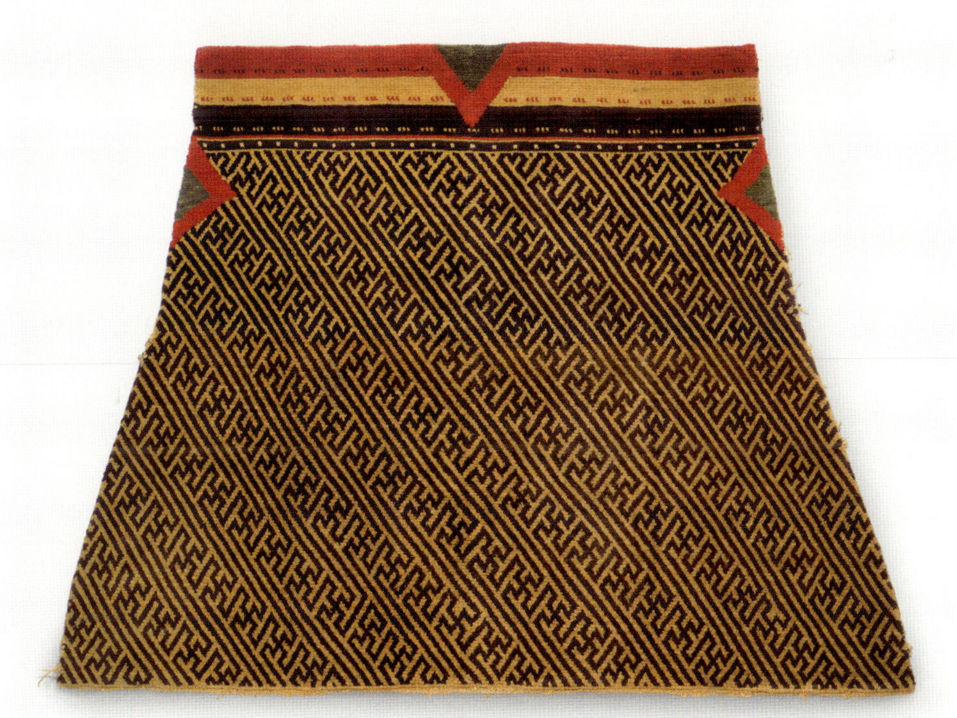

Fig. 7: Forehead decoration for a horse or mule (*takyab*) with *kalachakra* motif. Tibet, 20th c., 28×26 cm

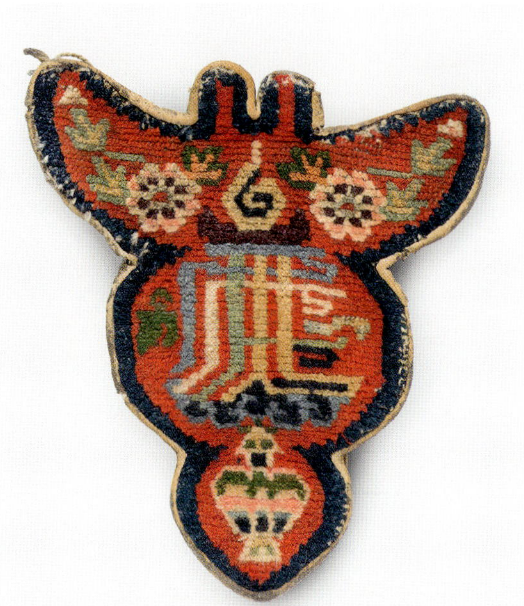

tion for which an initiation ceremony lasting several days has to be held (Dalai Lama & Hopkins 2002). For centuries a secret and only accessible to a few monks, the ceremony has become more widespread in recent times. Whenever the present Dalai Lama has given the initiation – 34 times to date – into the *kalachakra* (also called the "Wheel of Time"), as many as 200,000 Tibetans have flocked to receive it. Tibetans believe that the Dalai Lama and a few other high lamas now give this initiation more often because we live in difficult times and they want to protect future generations through this ceremony. The promise of the *kalachakra* initiation is to ensure a rebirth that is conducive to helping bring about freedom for many people and protect the political and spiritual freedoms that we enjoy.

Fig. 8: Wangden *drumze* with double *vajra*. Tibet, 19th/20th c., 72×76 cm

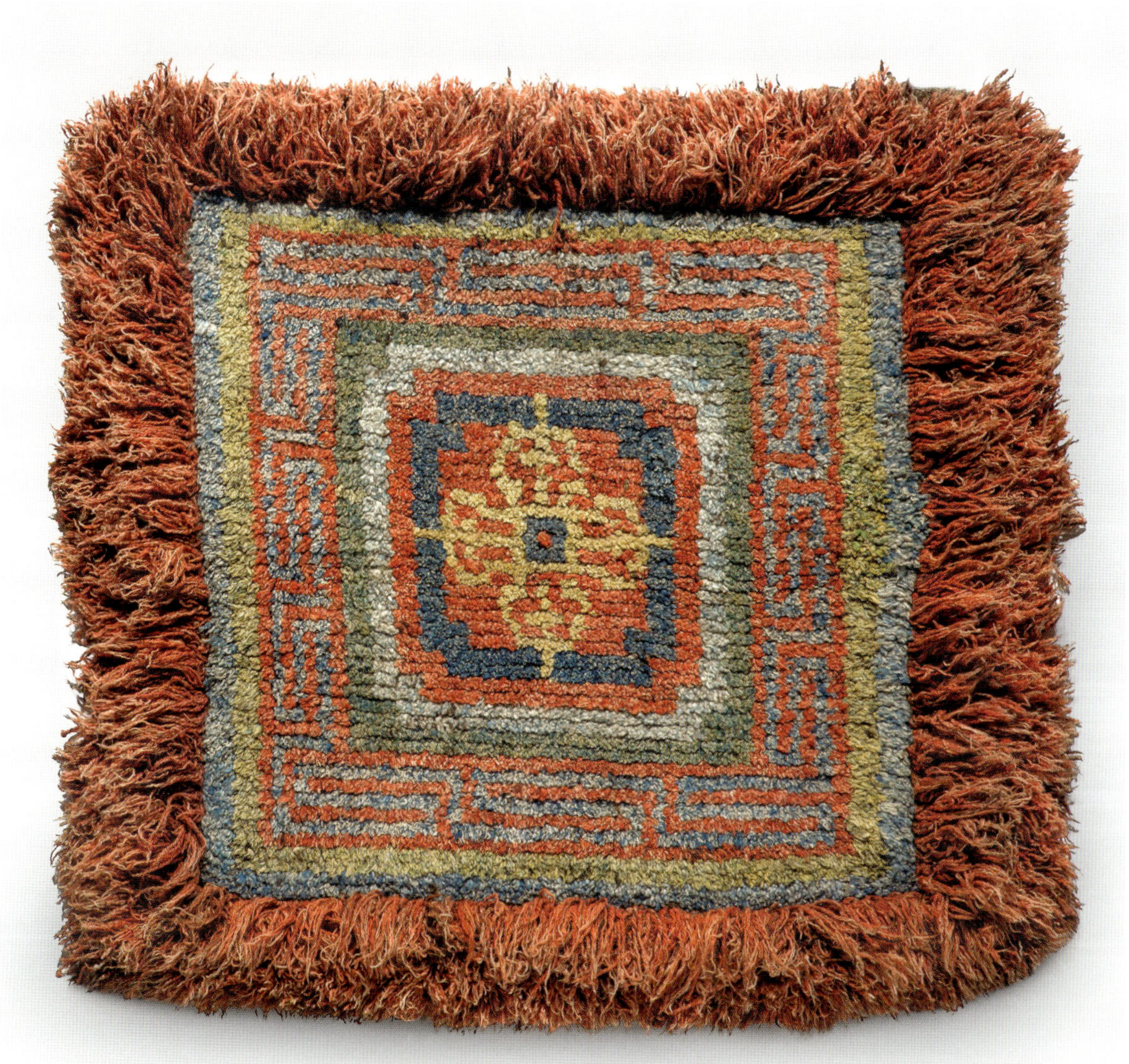

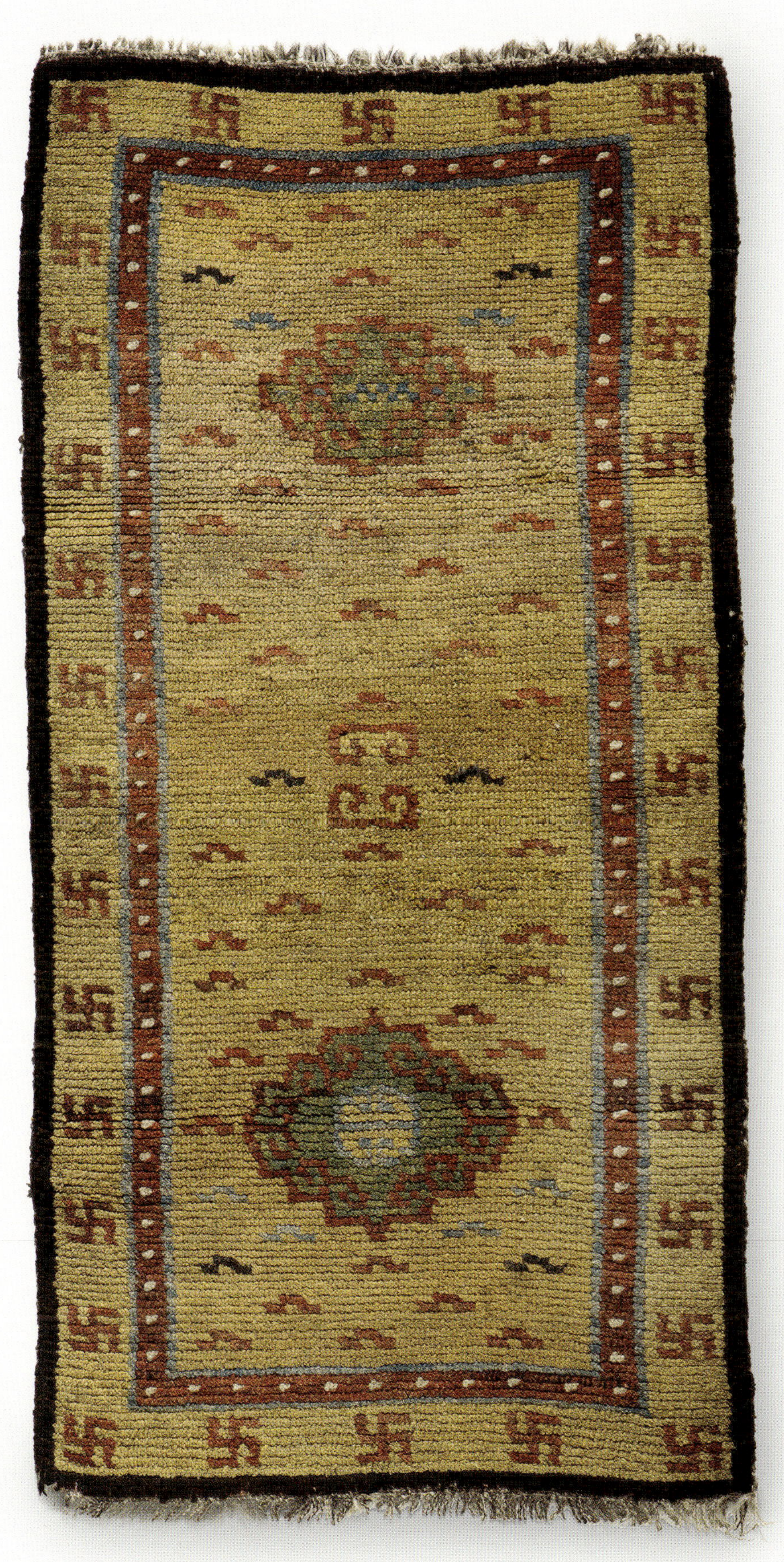

Fig. 9: Sitting or sleeping rug (*khaden*) with tiger motif. Tibet, early/mid 19th c., 136×70 cm, Karl Steiner collection no. 31, MFK inv. no. 2015-80-17

But Tibetans are also practical; the Wangden *drumze* rugs in the Buddeberg collection bear witness that the monks could sit comfortably during their long meditations.

Fig. 8 shows a Wangden with a double *dorje* in the middle. In Tibetan rituals, the lama will hold a bell in one hand, the female symbol, and a *vajra*, the male symbol, in the other. With the gesture of crossing his arms over his chest, he displays the union of male and female energies.

The pattern on the Wangden shows the union of both symbols, whereby four bells are hidden in the pattern of the double *dorje*.

The most famous meditation rugs from Tibet most desired by collectors are tiger rugs (Fig. 9). In Tibet we find the tiger symbolism has a deeper, very powerful meaning.[3] One can often read that the meditator uses the tiger's energies for his meditation. This is not quite correct, as the tiger actually symbolises our own animal nature. In tantric meditation this animal nature is not renounced as in asceticism, but is acknowledged and used to purify the strong animal energies and put it in the service of transformation. In this meditation the enrichment of *chu* takes place on a very high spiritual level.

Fig. 10 illustrates this very clearly: here we find the tiger motif in the border and a large *swastika* in the centre of the field. This meditation rug portrays a programme – the abovementioned charging of *chu* with a purifying transformation in the energy channels of the meditator.

Fig. 11 shows the wonderful Ming silk fragment of the Buddeberg collection with a camel, the endless knot and an inscription in *Uchen* (*dbu can*) script on it. The inscription is

Fig. 10: Sitting rug (*khagangma*). Tibet, 19th c., silk, 60×64 cm

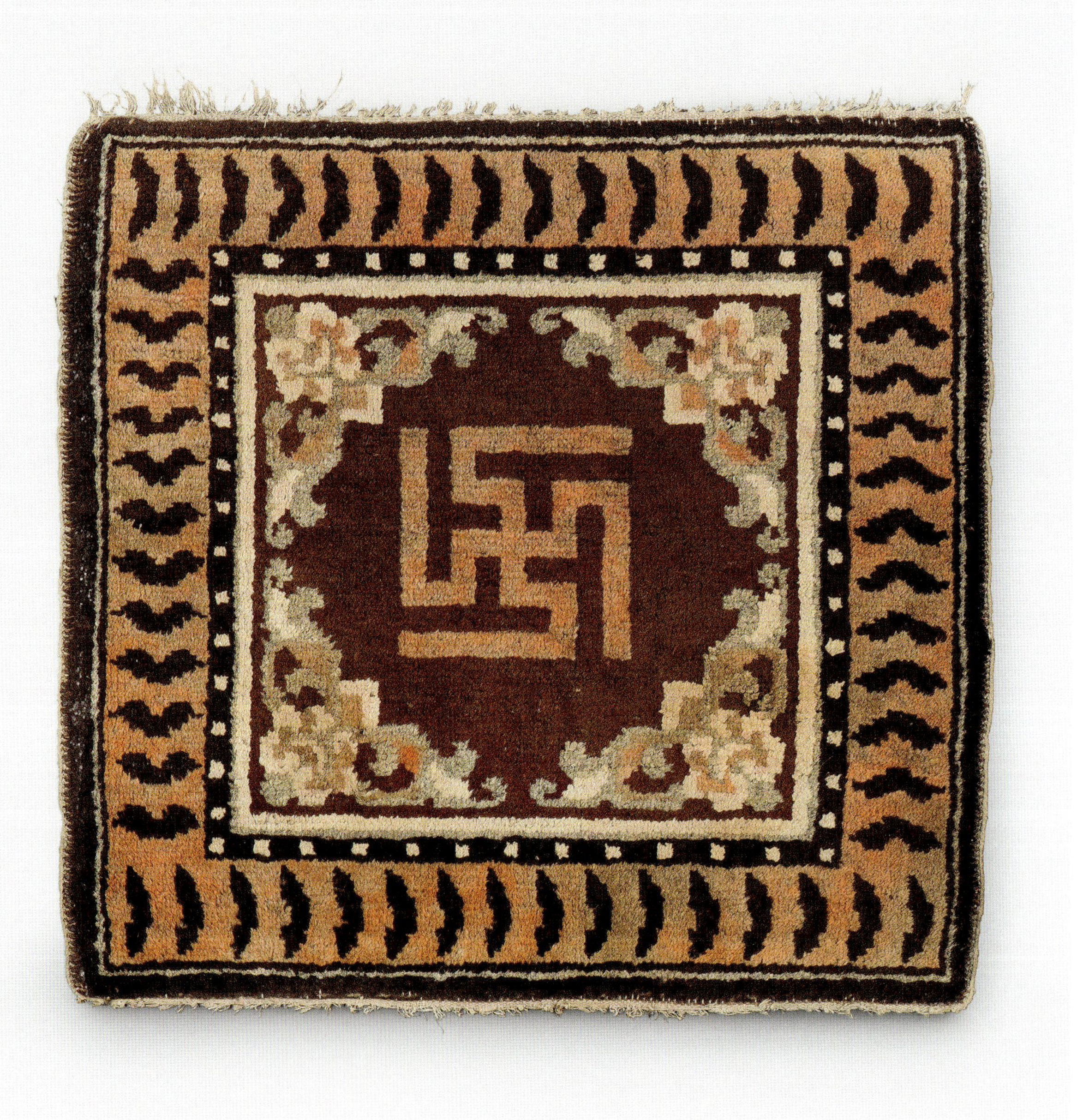

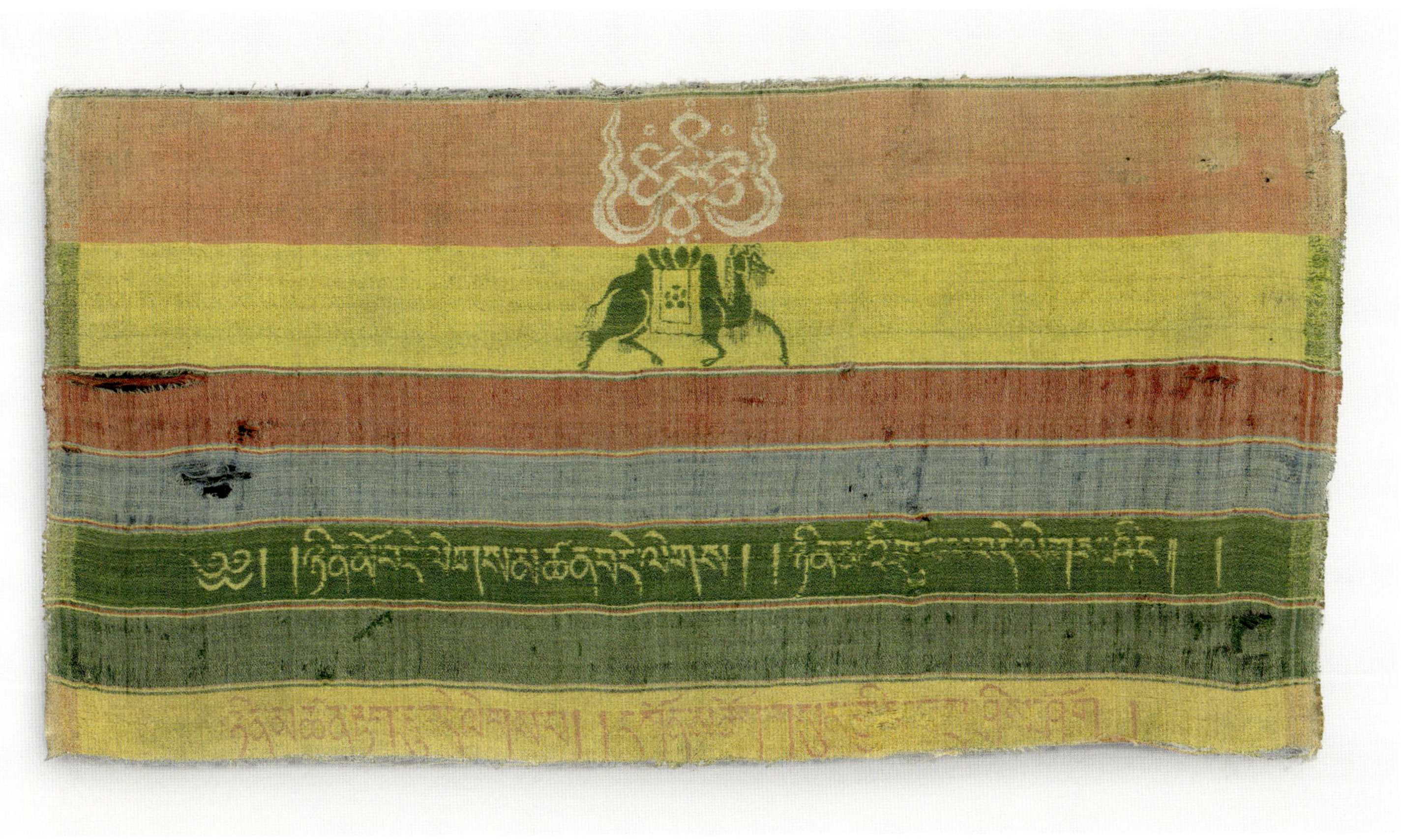

Fig. 11: Fragment of a ceremonial shawl (*khatag*). China, 15th/16th c., 29×56 cm

a blessing: "Wishing happiness in the morning, at midday and in the night, may the blessing of The Three Jewels be ever present." The three jewels refer to the teacher (Buddha), the law (*dharma*) and the order of monks (*sangha*).

This fragment points to a characteristic trait of Tibetan Buddhism that defines itself as the union of compassion and wisdom: the good energies of *chu* will be shared with everyone.

Happiness, good *karma* and good meditation results are not miserly kept for oneself, but shared with all the world. That also shows itself in everyday life, just think about all the prayer wheels and prayer flags and rainbow banners fluttering everywhere, for example.

Spreading the benefits and including others in one's own spiritual progress is the final wish expressed at the end of many Tibetan Buddhist meditations: "May the precious spirit of enlightenment arise in those who have not yet started to develop it. May it never decrease, but increase and strengthen in those who have developed it. May merit and good fortune spread far" (Anonymus 1987: n.p.).

NOTES

1 Western semiotics has great difficulty differentiating between symbols and signs. The relationship between the sign and its meaning is described as "empty", see Eco 1972: 86: "This relationship between signifier and that signified is almost empty. The borders of the signified are drawn by the signifier." The symbol in such a dyad of signified and signifier cannot be determined. On the other hand, the semioticians Jean Piaget and Charles W. Morris have been able to explain the symbol as a sign by including the aspect of the recipient. A sign first becomes a symbol through the "perception" of the recipient. The meaning of the sign becomes an "active effective perception" in the symbol (Piaget 1973: 101). Both semioticians have expanded the dyad of signifier and signified for the sign to a communication triangle.

2 Dagyab Rinpoche 1992: 21: "The connection between the Buddhist teaching of a reality characterized by emptiness and the recognition and intensification of pure quality in all phenomena is among Tibetans, however, only to a minor extent known in this way."

3 Williams 1941: 399: "The tiger is called by the Chinese the king of the wild beasts, and its real or imaginary qualities afford them matter for more metaphors than any other wild animal." In this connection, I owe thanks to Thomas Wild, Berlin, for an important recognition: he assigns the Wanden *drumze* rugs to Rinpoches in the monasteries, and the tiger rugs and meditation mats to yogis living in the wild.

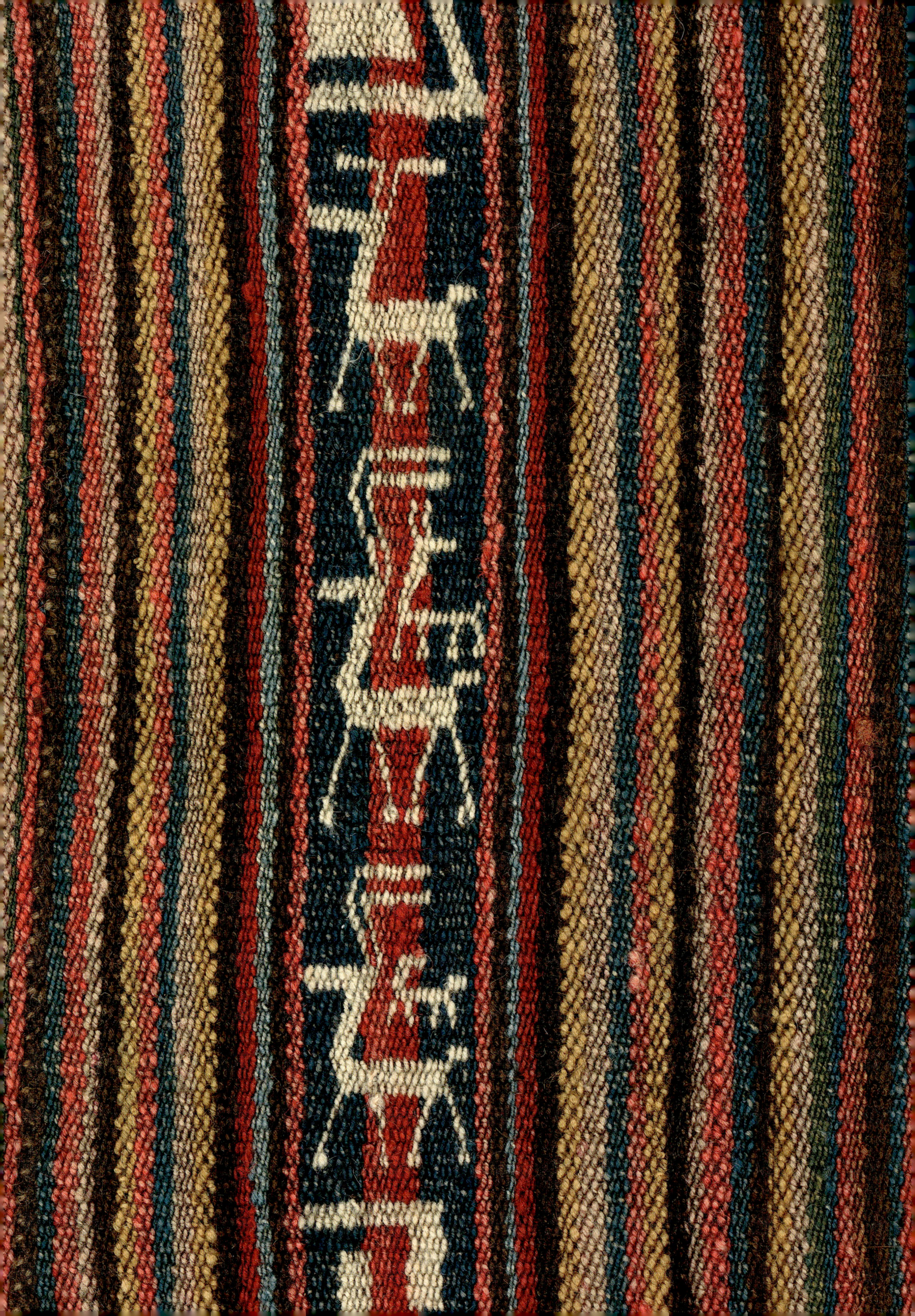

Christiane Kalantari

WOVEN WORLD ORDER

The Textile Arts of Tibet between Buddhism and Protective Magic

Detail of Fig. 29

"See the loom as precious, that is good. [...] See the parts of the loom as a mother with her twelve children, [...] the loom as a Buddhist shrine, that is good. Consider the heddles of the loom to be the wooden covers of a holy book, and you will blossom."[1]

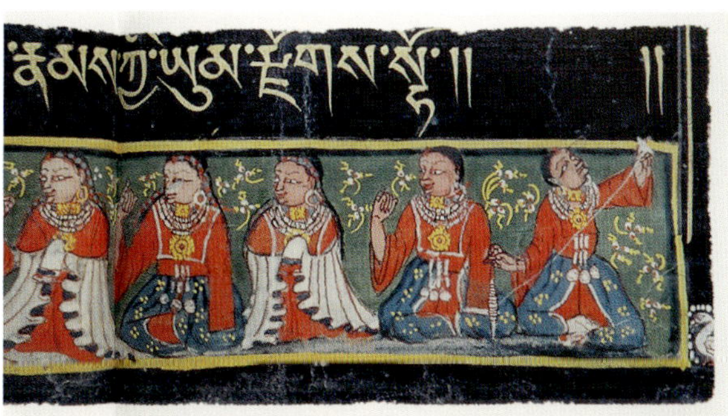

Fig. 1: Image of founders. Detail of the title page of a Tibetan manuscript (Prajnaparamita, Tib. *Yum chen mo*). Dolpo, Nepal, ca. 12th c., gold lettering and coloured illumination on blue paper

THE TEXTILE ARTS[2]

This article is not intended to be a history of Tibetan textile arts but rather a first description of examples of specific textiles from the Tibet collection of Justyna and Michael Buddeberg. It includes such diverse items as colourful flat-woven blankets for use in the house or tent; single-coloured wool materials for use in monasteries and for religious garments; and also striped textiles in wool and yak hair for clothing, e.g., for aprons (Tib. *pang gdan*, pronounced *pangden*). The methods of decorating the textiles include tie-dyeing (Tib. *thig ma*) for textiles and textile stripes used to make cushions, under-saddle blankets and traditional capes. Another method is elaborate appliqué work to decorate the aprons women wear on festive occasions. The collection has a large number of plaited articles, such as slingshots as well as richly patterned tablet-woven bands. The description of the pieces should always have an eye to the aspect of Tibetan material culture in its religious environment. Despite the "secular" character of Tibetan textiles, they are always an expression of a consciousness of the spiritual rhythms of life (Reynolds 1999: 47).[3]

The close economic and spiritual connection between the Tibetan population and the geography of the country's plateau is expressed in the lifestyles of the village residents and nomads. The myths about creation centre on the plateau as a sacred realm, thereby ascribing it animistic powers, i.e., the belief in the inherent powers of natural phenomena. With the introduction of Buddhism, belief in many of these powers was "tamed" or they were incorporated into the new religion. For these folk-religious traditions, it was important to carefully propitiate the powers of the earth and spirits to assure protection from negative influences, illness and misfortune. One finds, therefore, ornamentation and amulets on all daily objects and clothing, so that a person is surrounded by "empowered" objects that are intended to assure the continuing safety and well-being of the user (Reynolds 1999: 47).

WOOL AND WEAVING IN TIBET

Mythical tradition tells that Princess Wencheng introduced the art of weaving into Tibet. She was the Chinese and Buddhist wife of King Songtsen Gampo (*Srong btsan sgam po*, 7th century), founder of the Tibetan empire. It can be assumed, however, that a culture of textile techniques in Tibet existed much earlier, since they are so much a part of the nomadic lifestyle in the region. The Tibetan plateau, 4,000 to 5,000 metres altitude with its harsh climate, offers only limited forms of livelihood. By far the leading one is pastoralism, the production of wool for ropes, tents, clothing and other textiles having great importance. The climatic conditions in Tibet are most favourable for wool, indeed, account for Tibet's textile tradition. The hardy Tibetan yaks (*Bos mutus*; Tib. *gyag* for the male, *'bri* for the female), goats

Fig. 2: Stretched warps of a backstrap loom in a nomad's camp. Kailash region, Tibet, 1995

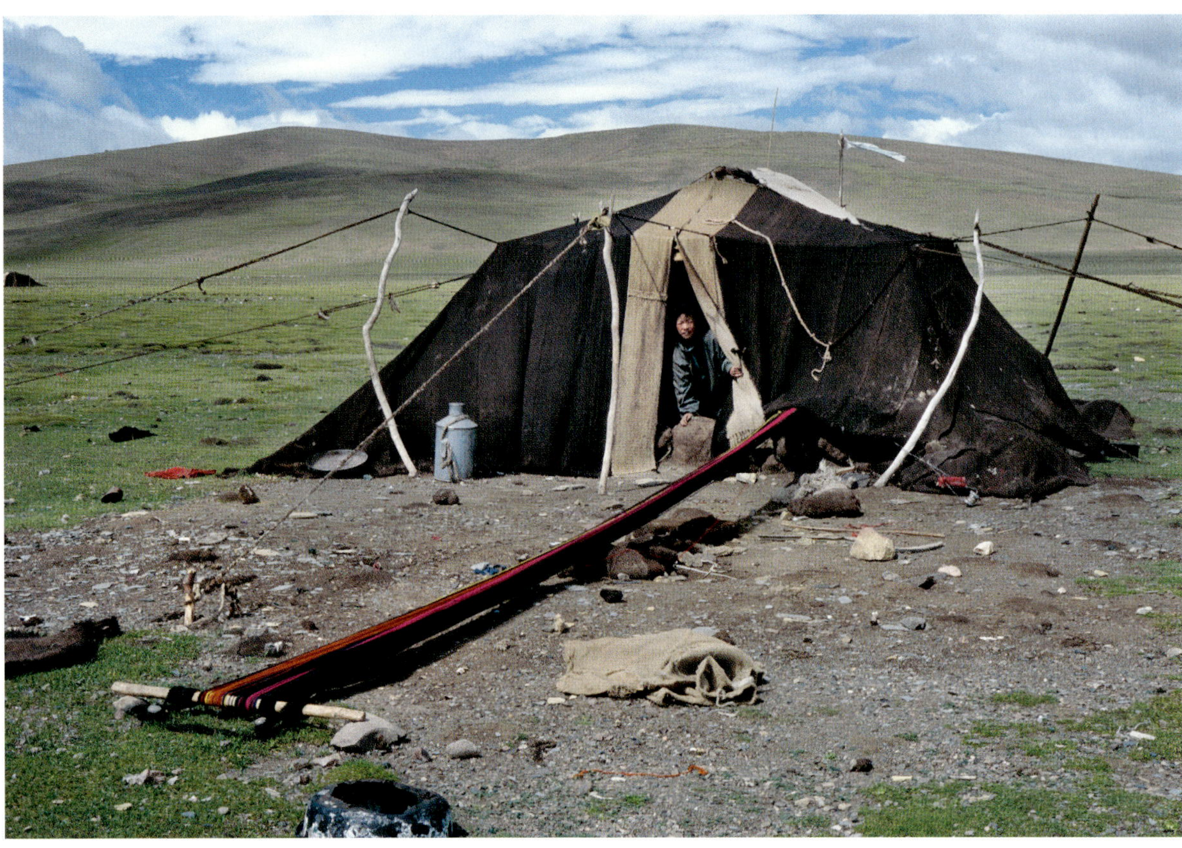

Fig. 3: Tibetan herder spinning. Puma Tso, South Tibet, 2000

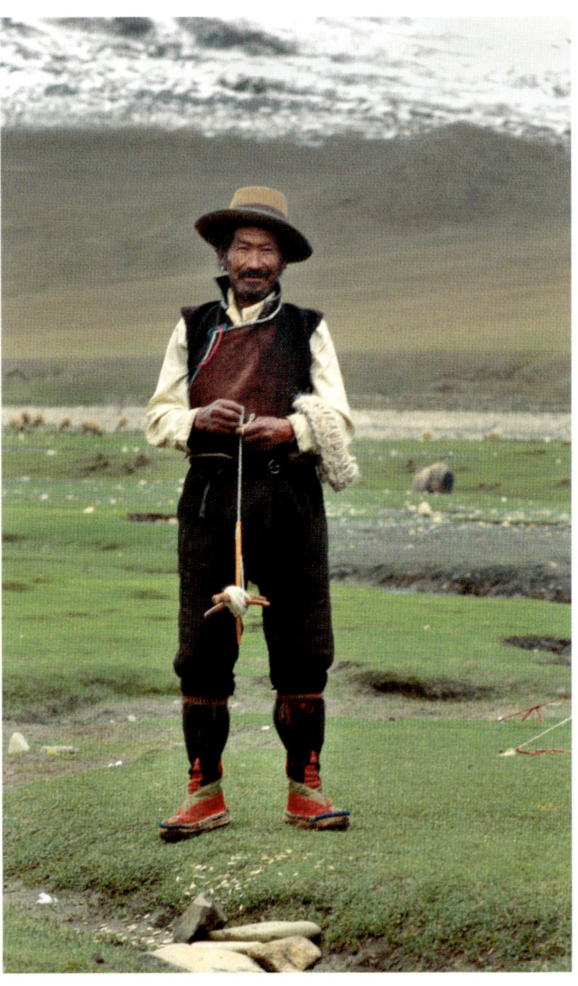

and sheep produce especially fine wool, whose outstanding quality is especially sought after. It is traded within Tibet and exported around the world. Even today, Tibetan woollen textiles are packed in bales and transported over the old caravan routes to Nepal and India.

The yak has a special place for those living on the Central Asian plateau on account of its complete adaptation to the harsh climate. The yak provides not only wool and hair, but also milk and meat, and its dung is the most important fuel for stoves. It is also ridden and used as a pack animal.

The most important fibres for yarn are the soft yak wool (Tib. *ku lu*), the coarse and stronger yak hair (Tib. *rtsid pa*, pronounced *tsiba*), goat hair (Tib. *rebu*) and various qualities of sheep wool (Tib. *bal/beh*). The nomads both market the different types of wool and use them themselves with all the various techniques: felting, knitting (for socks and hats), plaiting and weaving. Weaving is most often done on transportable looms, producing narrow rugs and patterned flat weaves. Still today in Tibetan villages nearly every family has a loom and uses it to make things for the family's own use (Figs. 2 and 5). Some nomads in western Tibet specialise in collecting the long, very fine shiny hair, which grows on the neck and under the stomach of a species of goats (Tib. *le na*) that only lives above a certain altitude. The nomads sell this in certain market places in the Himalayas, much of which is bought by Muslim dealers from Kashmir where it is then used to produce the famous Pashmina (from the Persian word for wool *pashm*), which is then sold internationally. Pashmina shawls were sold in Vienna and Paris from quite early on, and Viennese manufacturers of fine cloth attempted to copy the techniques and designs early in the 19th century. Indeed, fine shawls with somewhat oriental patterns became part of the traditional Austrian costume, e.g., in Linz, Upper Austria.

TECHNIQUES AND MATERIALS

In Tibet, no distinction is made between artists and craftsmen. The objects which they produce are ranked, however, the greatest recognition being given those which have a religious content, that is, those which require an exact understanding of the rules of iconography and iconometry to be ritually effective. Religious objects represent the body (painting and sculpture), the speech (Buddhist texts) and the spirit (Sanskrit *stūpa*; Tib. *mchod rten*, pronounced *chorten*) of Buddha. Religious rituals consecrate these objects, giving them divine energy. Weaving and tailoring have less prestige, but are ranked above metalworking, which is done by socially lower classes. Religious craftsmanship is an activity of monks in the monasteries who earn great merit with their service. The monks' clothing and that for cult statues are also often made in the monasteries, whereby nuns weave, while monks do this only as an exception (Ahmed 2002: 92). Since the 17th century in Lhasa, master tailors, who were organised in special ateliers and had a high official status, were entrusted with making the robes for the Dalai Lamas and the liturgical drapes of imported silk brocade used to decorate the Jokhang, Tibet's most holy shrine (Ronge 2005: 534).

In private households, textile techniques are closely bound with the complex Tibetan world order. They also reflect the relationships between genders. The shorn wool is washed, teased and carded by the women, while both men and women then spin (Tib. *khals cis*) and twine (Tib. *yog cis*) the yarn. In Rupshu, Ladakh, spinning is done solely by women, while the plying is predominantly the responsibility of men (Ahmed 2002: 71). Throughout Tibet, one can see men plying yarn with a hand spindle (Tib. *skor ru*, pronounced *kor ru*) whenever the situation allows it, for example while herding the sheep (Fig. 3). Monisha Ahmed, in her book *Living Fabric* (2002), explains that in Ladakh the looms clearly reflect the complementary but separate spheres for men and women. In certain nomadic areas, the women only use a backstrap loom (Tib. *sked 'thags*) sitting, not standing. The men weave on a heddle loom (Tib. *sa 'thags*), kneeling. The "female" backstrap loom symbolises fertility and the flow of life: the warp (Tib. *sna rgyu*) is the mother and the weft is the child which is growing in her womb (Ahmed 2002: 91). Furthermore, the "female" loom is thought to be connected with Buddhist spirituality and the possibility – even the obligation – to amass religious merit. This is not the case for the "male" heddle loom. This gender differentiation is also reflected in what they produce: as a rule, women produce undyed material for clothing or striped weaves for aprons, blankets, bags, floor mats and tent blankets. The men weave heavier material, such as yak or goat hair for saddle blankets and tents. They sew the yak hair panels together to make large tents (Müller & Raunig 1982: 143; Ahmed 2002: 76). The historian Tsering Gyalpo, who grew up as a nomad, has explained that this is the same in Ngari, West Tibet.

Most textiles are woven in small widths of 30 to 40 centimetres and ca. 10 metres in length, and are subsequently handled in different ways. For garments several panels are put together to create larger pieces of cloth. The long pieces are made for use within the family or they are rolled up in bolts which are sold, for example, in the market next to the Jokhang in Lhasa. One differentiates between the types of textiles called *nambu* and *sherma*. *Nambu* (Tib. *snam bu*) is a strong, wear-resistant weave, often a mixture of sheep and lamb wool, which combines the strength, softness and warmth of both fibres. It is produced in undyed, monochrome lengths, which are often dyed after being woven. *Nambu* is primarily used for everyday garments (black for laypersons, red for nuns and monks). It is also used for transport bags, saddle blankets and the shafts of boots. Pieces with narrow stripes (Tib. *num ba*) are used to make panels for tents (Tib. *phug shar*) and blankets. *Sherma* is a finer, striped textile of softer yarn (often the finer, shiny wool from the neck of the sheep), which is tightly woven to make outdoor clothing which is water- and wind-proof (Buckley 2011: 31). Three panels of *sherma* sewn together make an apron (Tib. *pang gdan*). Today, these narrow lengths of *sherma* are often produced in Lhasa and sold throughout Tibet (Fig. 4).

The backstrap loom (Tib. *sked 'thags*, pronounced *ketha*) is the simplest type and commonly used by nomads because of its easy transportability. The end of the loom are fastened in the ground or on a frame. The other end is kept taught by the weaver's back (Fig. 5). With this loom, nomads weave plain long strips of cloth (Tib. *liu*) and flat weaves with

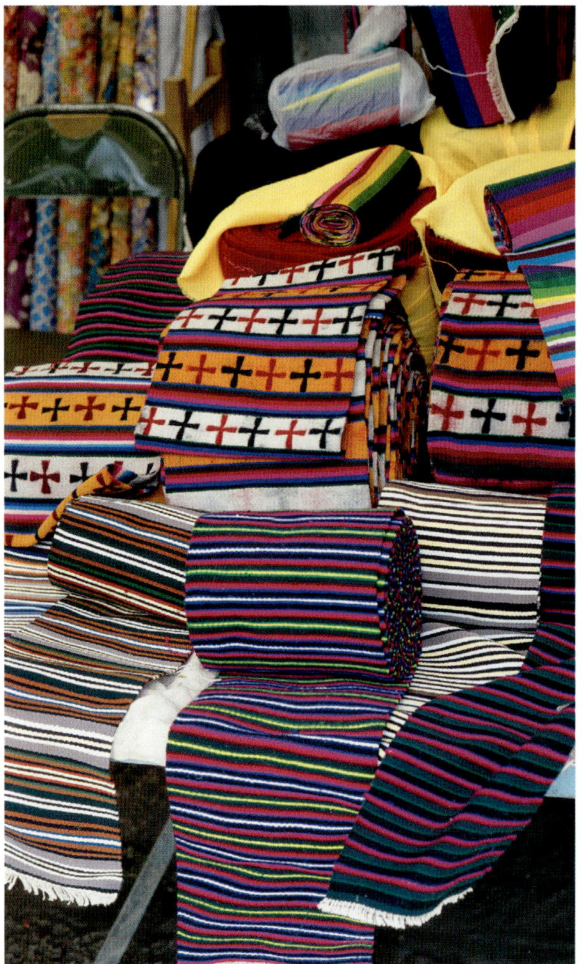

Fig. 4: *Nambu* cloth. Lhasa, Tibet, 1996

simple stripes, as well as stepped decoration. These are used to make blankets and bags of every type (for a description of this type of textile, see Ahmed 2002: 84). The heddle loom has a fixed frame (Tib. *sa 'thags*, pronounced *sata*) and is used by men of the Changthang plateau in Ladakh (Ahmed 2002: 15). These are various types of simple looms with heddles that rise and lower to form the shed. Throughout Tibet the more complicated heddle looms (Tib. *'thags cha*) are used, whereby the weaver uses pedals to raise and lower the heddles.

Many types of natural dyestuffs are found in Tibet and extracted from various local plants: dark yellow from rhubarb, light yellow from the root of the barberry, and red from mader root (Tib. *tso*) which grows on the Himalayan slopes; brown is dyed with walnut shells. Indigo must be imported from India. Dyeing is done either by the family itself or by specialists (Tib. *thos mkan*). In Lhasa, the Nepalese have a good reputation as dyers. Buckley (2014) gives an overview of the dyestuffs for aprons in Lhasa, and Ahmed (2002: 105ff.) describes in detail the methods of dyeing in Ladakh. Generally speaking, the colour for clothing is not a personal preference but reflects the status of the person. Men in Ladakh still often wear white *nambu*, the women natural wool in brown and black. Clothing in colours was a privilege of the nobility and clergy because the dyeing was expensive and time-consuming.

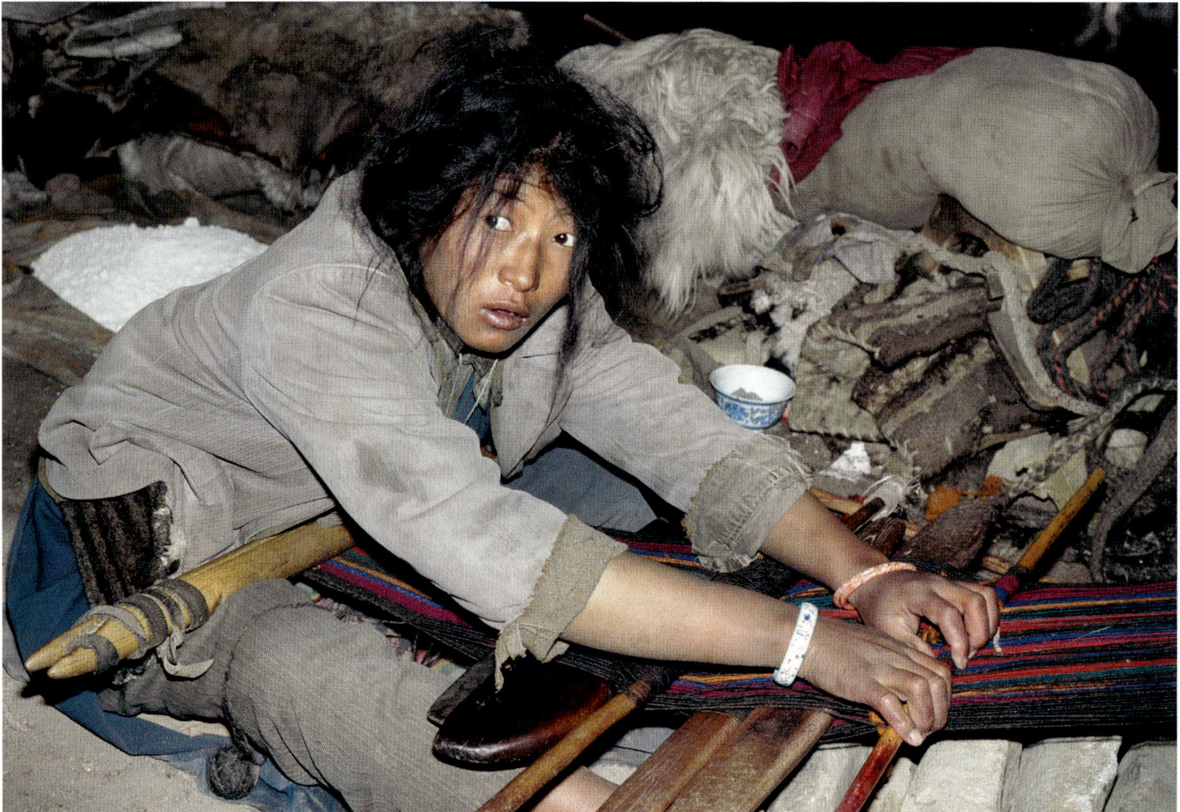

Fig. 5: The other end of the loom in Fig 2: Woman with backstrap loom. Kailash region, Tibet, 1995

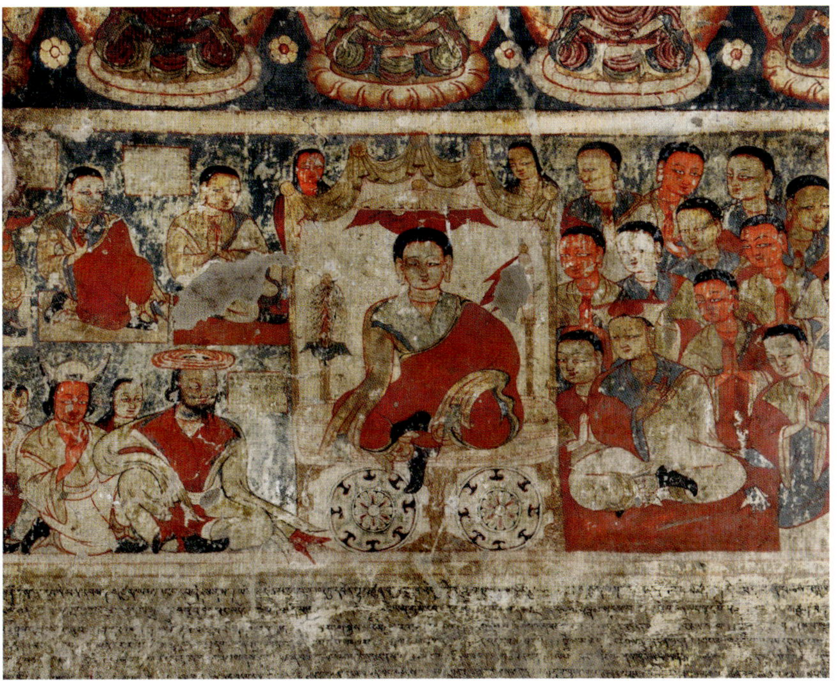

Fig. 6: Picture of an assembly, mural in the Dukhang of Tabo monastery. Himachal Pradesh, India

In the Tibetan world of symbolism, the combinations of primary colours are a leitmotif. This relates to the Tibetan concept of a world order of a vertical arrangement of the universe and represents the elements: white for air, blue for the sky, red for fire, yellow for the earth, and green for the underworld and water. The colours also represent the directions in the cosmos. The prayer flags (Tib. *rlung rta*, pronounced *lungta*, "wind horses"), which are printed with sacred texts, are also a series of the five colours. Strings of these flags are hung from masts (Tib. *dar lcog*, pronounced *tarchen*) in the centre of monastery courtyards, from house roofs and tents, and also displayed at mountain passes and on bridges, thereby spreading beneficial energy in all directions. The tradition of prayer flags in Tibet is considered to be from pre-Buddhist cult practices (generally assumed to be connected with the Bon religion), namely the offering of wool by nomads who would fasten it to something and thereby secure fulfilment of wishes and prayers.[4] Horizontal bands of the colours also decorate the lower part of walls in the rooms of private houses. This is not only considered by the residents to be decorative but also that it has a protective symbolism. One also finds the colours in similar striped pattern on clothing, for example, on aprons and ribbons, thus letting the wearer feel enveloped by the protective world order.

An old, widespread dyeing technique produces a typical cross-shaped motif (Tib. *thig ma*), which was originally a privilege of the nobility. It results from a combination of reserve dyeing techniques: tie-dyeing (plangi or batik, both Indonesian expressions) and a unique Tibetan method of dyeing. The bound up points of the cloth are drawn through the holes in the bottom of a large tub and dipped in the dye. Fabrics dyed with the motif were used to make coats (Tib. *chuba*) or hats, also covers for cushions to sit on and for decorated horse and saddle blankets. Today, this type of cloth is sold from Central Tibet to all areas of the country. A textile-technical analysis by Britta Schwenck of some selected items in the collection can be found in the appendix, "Textile-Technical Analysis of Nine Tibetan Textiles".

TEXTILE, RITUAL AND TEMPLE

Woven textiles and knotted rugs are not only functional; they have always had a significant place in the rituals and status culture of Tibet. Textile traditions and a luxury culture, both amongst the ruling class and also within the religious world, were closely related since the earliest era, since the time of the cosmopolitan, great Tibetan Empire in Central Asia. Their prestige and aura complemented each other. The floor cushions as seats for honoured secular and religious dignitaries were from earliest times covered with both knotted and woven material. Historical wall and ceiling paintings in monasteries are an important source of information about textiles, the traditional styles of clothing and transportable dwellings in Tibet. In Tabo (Spiti, Himachal Pradesh, India), one of the oldest still active monasteries in an area which was once part of West Tibet, above the inscription about its renovation, the royal lama Changchub-O is shown as ruler enthroned under a parasol in a tent (Fig. 6). The figures at the sides represent donors (Tib. *yon bdag*, pronounced *yondag*) from the most important clans in the region, who were very instrumental in establishing the Buddhist kingdom in West Tibet. Clothed in fine robes and hats, they sit according to rank on carpets and pay homage to the ruler, who, in recognition of his deified status, is seated in the centre and shown larger than the others. This demonstrates that in the 11th century or earlier carpets and seat cushions were used in Tibet, or were even produced there. It is also evident that non-permanent architecture and transportable housing made of textiles, especially tents, were not only part of the nomadic world but also a residence with a status appropriate for the all-so important noble donors who – together with the great translator Rinchen Zangpo (958–1055) – initiated from West Tibet the second wave of expansion of Buddhism in the 10th century.

Carpets and wall hangings can also have specific ritual functions and blessings can emanate from them, as is

Fig. 7: Meme Buchen performance. Pin Valley, Himachal Pradesh, India, 2009

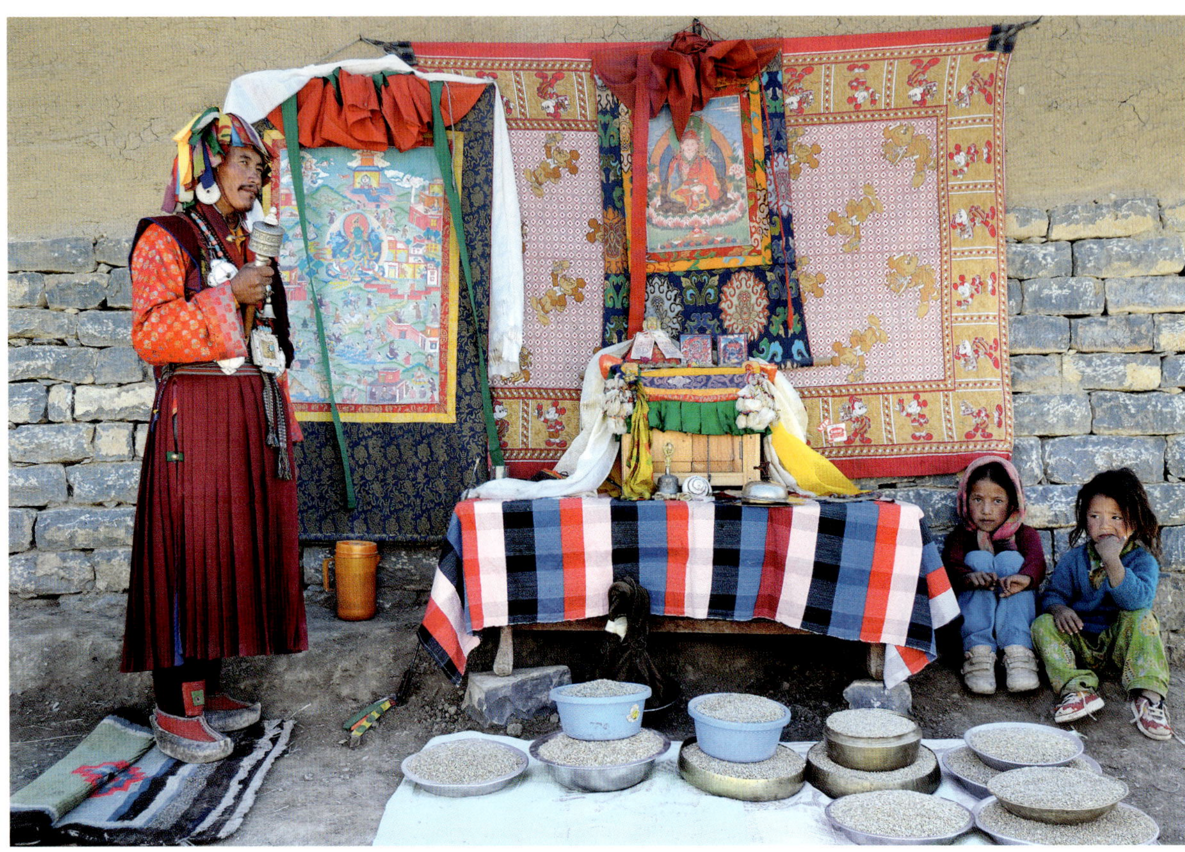

Fig. 8: Meme Buchen, 2009

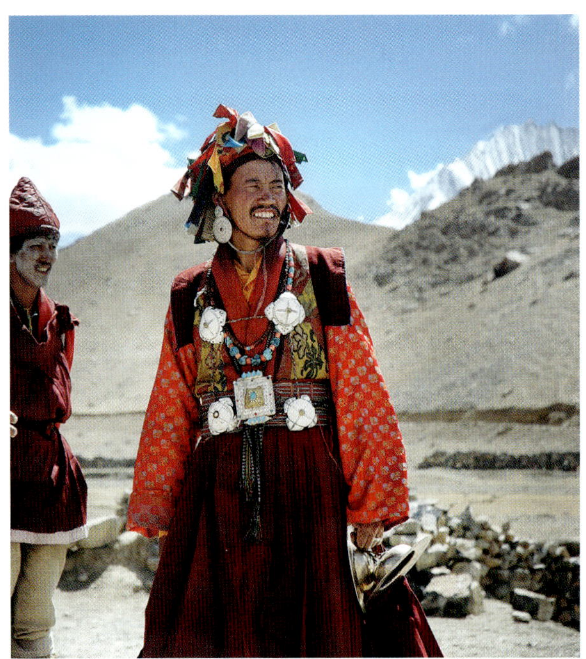

believed they do from the Buchen wandering performers in western Tibet when they present traditional stories from moral texts (Tib. *rnam thar*, pronounced *namtar*) and perform as actors in Buddhist plays (Fig. 7). In a song during such a performance in Khar (Pin Valley, Himachal Pradesh, India), we are told that the backdrop cloth (once silk brocade) was to be seen as a "tent," that is, as a heavenly space for the *Dakinis*. It recalls the function of the drape that is usually hung on the back wall of tents. The carpet called lotus (Sanskrit *padma*), on which the lead character in this play stands, the Meme Buchen, represents an ephemeral area for rituals. In this religious-aesthetical space – as defined by Jürgen Wasim Frembgen – Buddhist stories can unfold. When Meme Buchen recites and rotates as he dances the 108 pleats of his robe of red, fine woollen plissé garment (which was woven in the area) flare out and thereby disseminate the teachings and the divine power of the clothing which is seen as the robe of Avalokitesvara (Fig. 8).

The sacred inner room of the assembly hall in monasteries is usually made up of the area around the altar or the cult niche on the back wall of the hall, which is often ritually circumambulated (Fig. 9). The front area is the space for the rituals performed by the monks who sit along the length of both sides of the cult room. Their seats are made of thin cushions and low tables for the ritual articles; during the

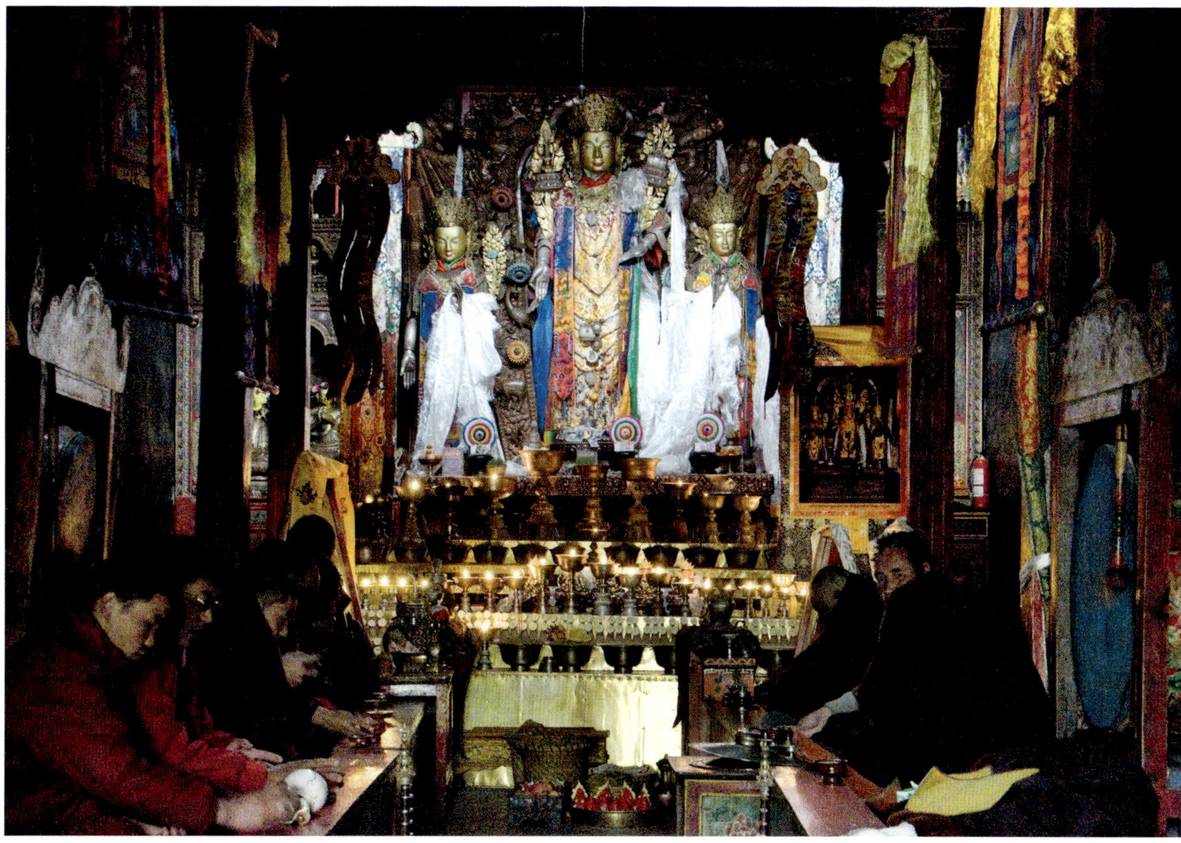

Fig. 9: Ceremony in Jokhang temple of Khorchag monastery. West Tibet, 2010

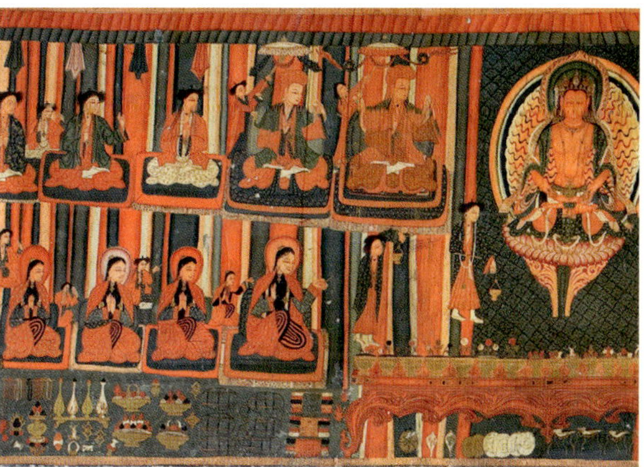

Fig. 10: Founders with offerings, including wool and silk. Red Temple, Tholing, West Tibet, 2009

ceremonies the monks sit in a predetermined order opposite each other. The abbot sits furthest back at the end of the row of seats in the most prestigious position directly to the right of the statue.

The visual richness of the insides of temples is essentially created by silk brocades (Tib. *gya ser*) and the richly patterned silk materials embossed with silver and gold thread. They also play an important role in the magnificent furnishings, for example in the hangings around the altar and columns and baldachins in the sacred rooms as well as in the precious robes and ceremonial garments of the high lamas and noblemen with their felt hats. Donating precious textiles has always belonged to religious practice as a way of earning merit (Fig. 10). The abbot of Tabo, a monastery founded in the Spiti Valley in Himachal Pradesh in the year 996, informed our research team[5] that materials such as these have been bought for his monastery for over 100 years in Varanasi in India where they are made by the famous Muslim silk-weaving family Kasim.

Traditional Tibetan monk's clothing consists of several layers: an undergarment, a robe and an outer shawl. The individual pieces can be made of different, sometimes very valuable, material. In West Tibet the robe is often a variation of the Tibetan woollen coat called *chuba* which is made of woven panels of wool sewn together. Over that the long square shawl (Tib. *chos gos*, pronounced *chogu*; the shawl for sitting is called *zla gam*) is worn draped around the body and shoulders and is often red-brown or saffron yellow; this goes back to the Buddha's garment (Sanskrit *kāṣāya*) whose shawl, following his vow of poverty, was sewn together from old thrown-away pieces of cloth from which the typical patchwork pattern of this clothing is derived. Together they make up the "Triple Robe" or *tricīvara*.

Seat Cushion Cover (Fig. 11)

The brightly coloured surface of this rectangular seat cushion for use in the monastery is made up of strips of light *nambu* in red and green, which frame a yellow centre strip.

Fig. 11: Sitting cushion, *nambu* cloth. 19th/20th c., 232×86 cm

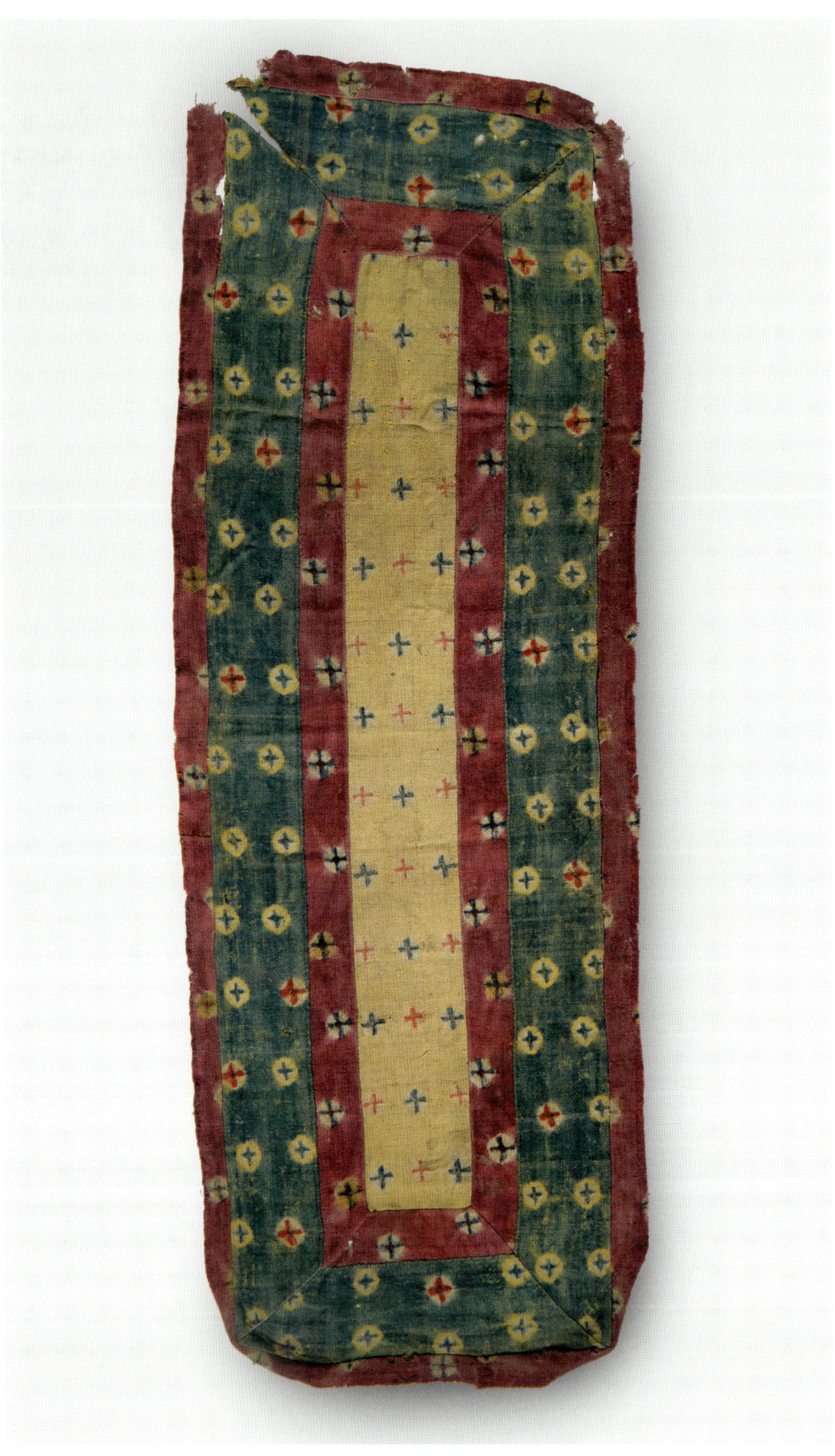

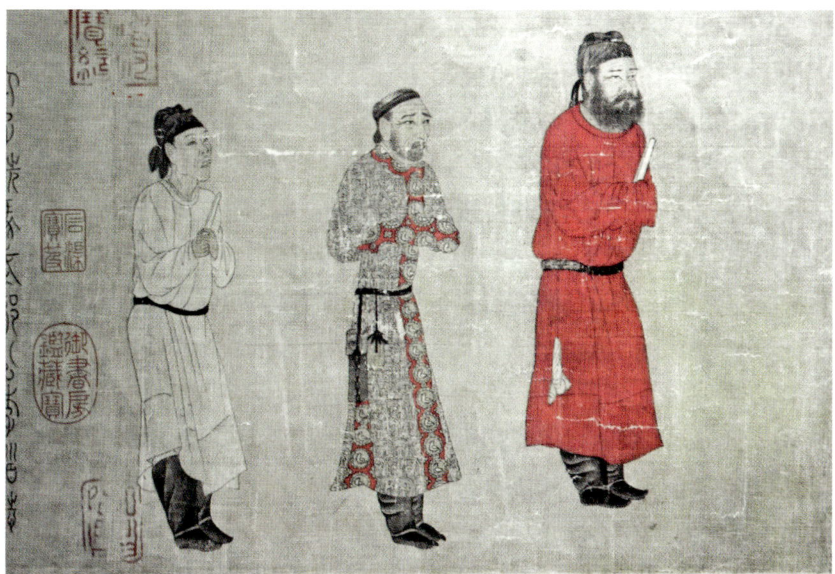

Fig. 12: Tibetan minister M'Gar (middle) at the Tang court in Chang'an, China. National Museum, Lhasa, ca. 7th c., painting on paper

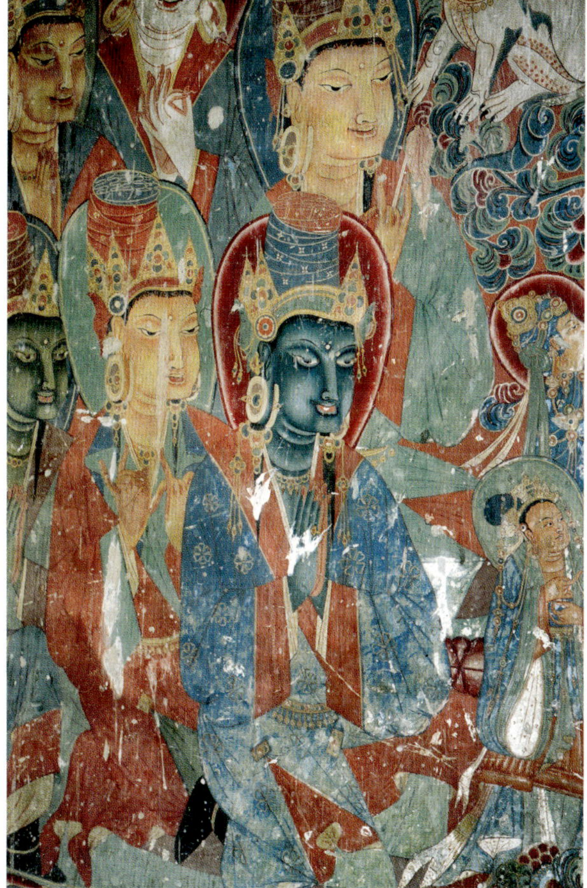

Fig. 13: Founders in a Buddhist assembly in Tibetan robes. Drathang, Central Tibet, 11th c.

This centre strip has been dye-stamped with the cross-form motif (three in each row, alternating blue and red) which copies the same tie-dyed motifs (Tib. *thig ma*) on all the other pieces, consisting of red and blue cross motifs on the green strips (two in each row) and an single row of blue crosses on white medallions on red strips. The additional strips are to fasten the cover to the cushion.

FORMS OF CLOTHING IN THE SECULAR SPHERE

Clothes in Tibet are far from just being functional and attractive; they are always an expression of social rank, the home region, and also reflect their Buddhist world order. The wearing of traditional decorative robes also is a form of showing religious respect. In the *shon glu* (pronounced *shonlu*) type of dance song from the village of Shey in Ladakh, individual pieces of clothing are mentioned whose wearing honours the local deity, Dorje Chenmo, who in the 10th century was venerated as protector of various monasteries in West Tibet: "By wearing the golden headdress – O Mother – we come to salute [protectress] Mother Dorje Chenmo. [...] By holding woolen scarfs, we come to salute Mother Dorje Chenmo, [...] we villagers of Shey dance shon. O Mother, wearing brocades of soft fabric, [...] wearing belts made of silk, [...] we come to salute Mother Dorje Chenmo!" (Nawang Tsering Shakspo 2008: 67ff.).

Tibet's impressive robes and articles of jewellery are in the tradition of the luxurious textiles and the status culture of the dignitaries in the period of the great old Tibetan Empire in Central Asia from the 7th to 9th centuries (Fig. 12; for examples, see also Watt & Wardwell 1997: 34ff.). The styles from that time continued in the culture of the Central Tibetan nobility and leading civil officials. The paintings of a Buddhist assembly in Drathang, Central Tibet, from the 11th century (Fig. 13) show the royal founders as *Bodhisattvas* in Tibetan robes. For generations, such costly attire was passed down and worn especially for festive occasions such as pilgrimages to Lhasa to the central temple, the Jokhang, where the time-honoured Jowo statue of Buddha Sakyamuni would be venerated. In Tibet, pilgrimage is central to the religion, whereby the pilgrim walks clockwise around the representation of the venerated deity. The person not only identifies him- or herself with the qualities characteristic of the deity but also believes to be in direct contact with its consecrating energy. In this manner, the pilgrim earns merit for the attainment of a better reincarnation and eventually even enlightenment. Well-to-do pilgrims donate in the

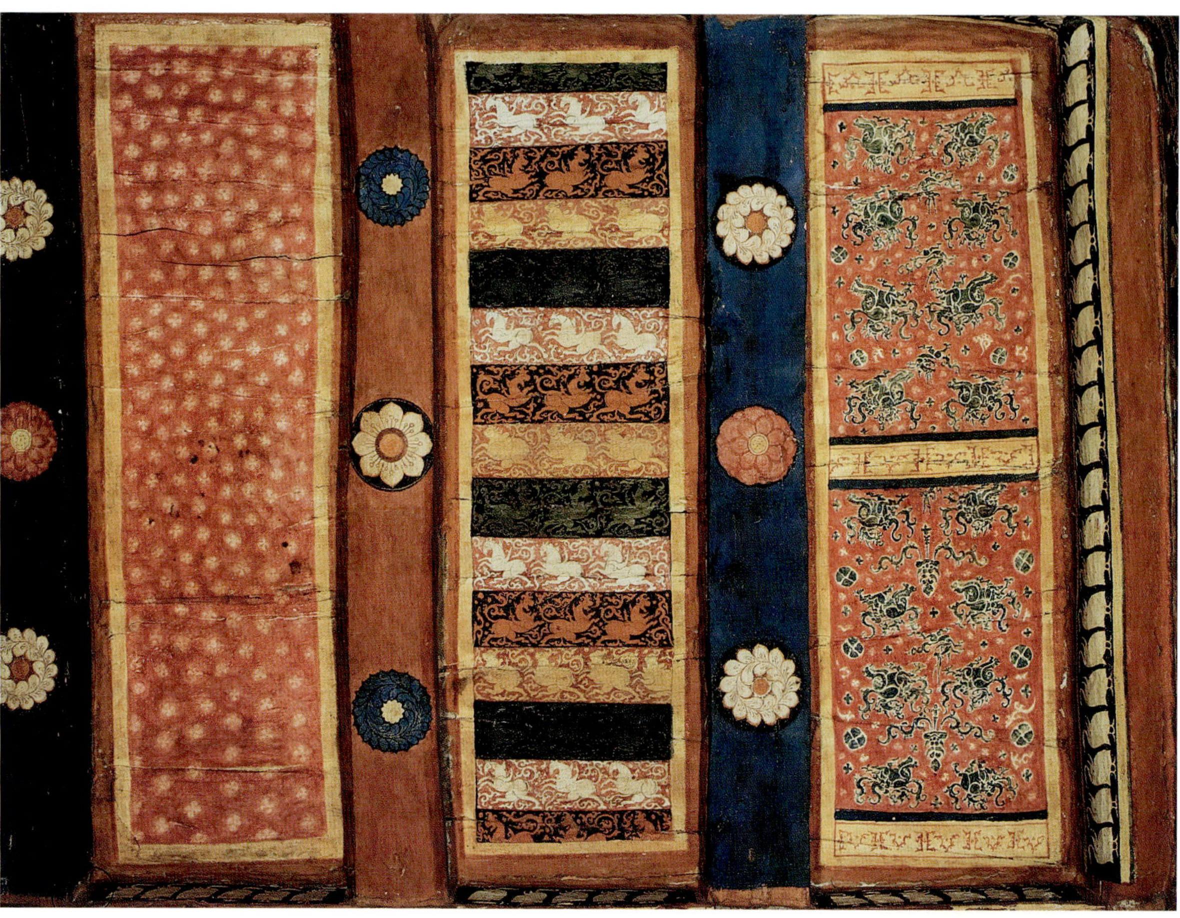

Fig. 14: Ceiling painting in the Sumtsek. Alchi, Ladakh, India, around 1220

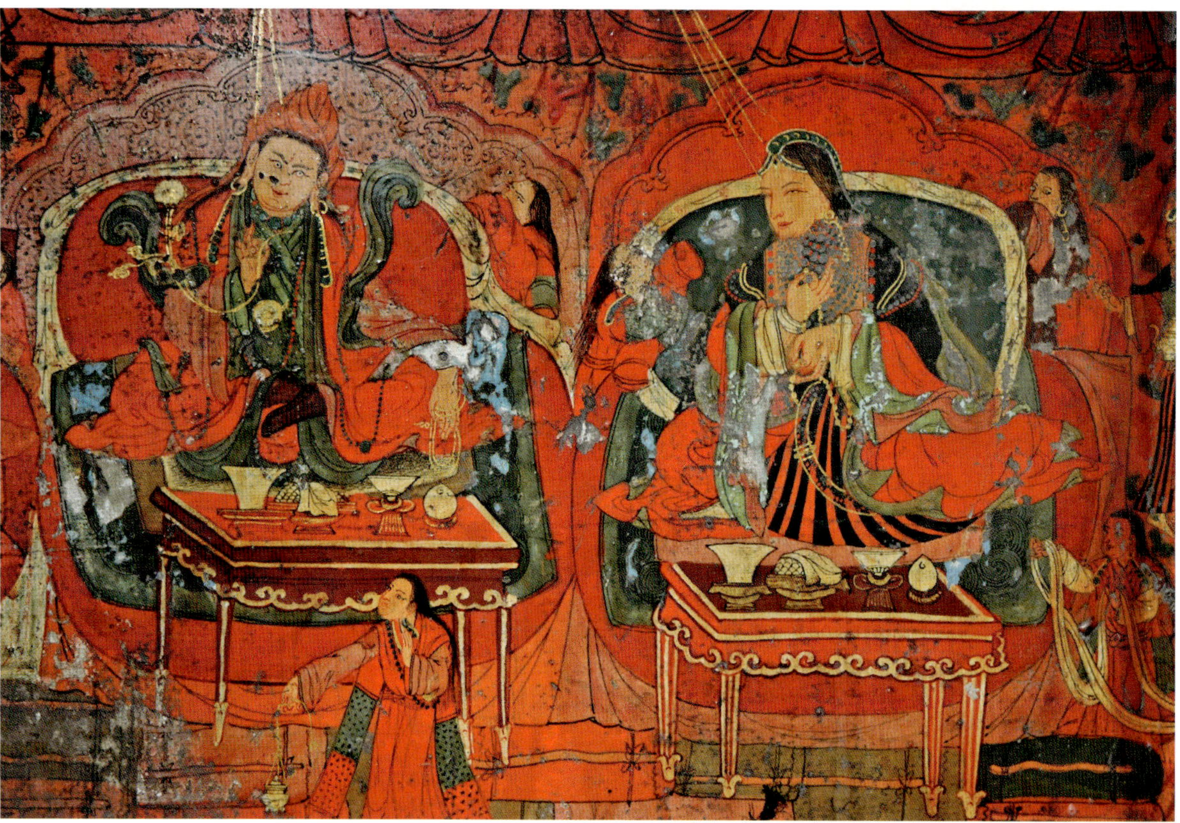

Fig. 15: Royal founders, mural in the Red Temple. Tholing, West Tibet

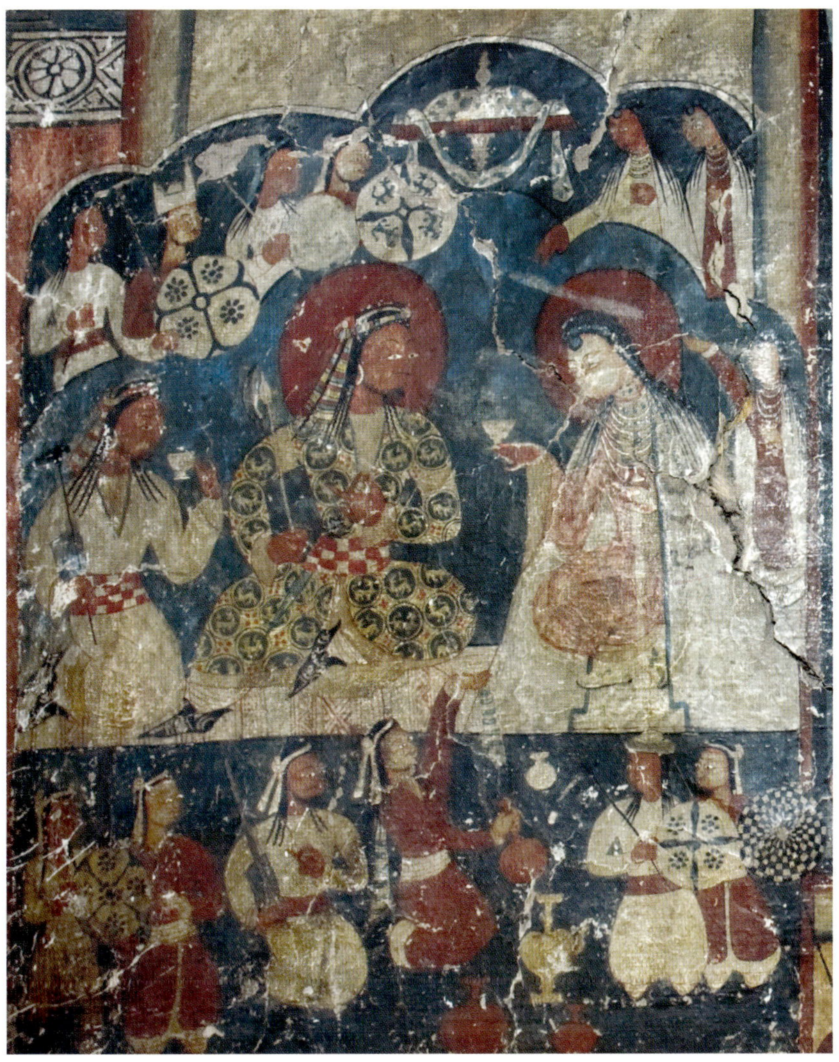

Fig. 16: Founders in the Dukhang. Alchi, Ladakh, India, 2009

Jokhang not only white ceremonial shawls (Tib. *kha btags*, pronounced *khatag*) but also costly textiles, such a silk brocades (Ladakh: *gos chen*, Tib. *gya ser*) for the apparel of the cult statues. In return, these persons are given fragments of older textiles from the Jowo (Tib. *namze*) which have the consecrating energy of the deity (Tib. *byin rlabs*, pronounced *chinlab*) and are placed in amulets. The ceiling paintings in the oldest Buddhist temple complex in Ladakh, the Alchi Sumtsek (Fig. 14), show textiles which are still imitated today. The paintings also reflect the importance of valuable textiles as offerings, as a sign of veneration, and also as a demonstration of the elite cosmopolitan culture of that era and its expression in the religious context (Kalantari & Gyalpo 2011; Papa-Kalantari 2000, 2002). The paintings also show the simpler tie-dye technique (plangi; Tib. *thig ma*) which is still common in Ladakh. They are important evidence that from earliest times locally made textiles were supplemented by those from an intense trade in imported luxury textiles from Iran and China, or fine cotton from India. Roger Goepper and Jaroslav Poncar (1996) and Finbarr B. Flood (2009) were the first to point this out.

In traditional Tibetan society, men wear the kaftan-like *chuba* (Tib. *phyu pa*), a long, lined coat sewn together from the narrow widths of locally woven heavy wool (it can also be made of sheep fleece). Their traditional footwear are boots (Tib. *lham*) of yak leather with a calf-high shafts, which are often trimmed with *sherma* cloth. The front of the *chuba* is overlapped and held together with a sash. It typically has sleeves that cover the hand and is the equivalent of the *go* in Ladakh (Tib. *gos*), which is somewhat differently cut and has buttons on the shoulders (see also Ahmed 2002: 117). The generously cut front of the *chuba* can be pulled up through the sash, creating a sort of pocket (Tib. *ambag*) in which traditionally men keep frequently used items, for example, an eating bowl or a pouch of *tsampa* (a staple made of roasted barley flour). During festivals in West Tibet the men also wear splendid long coats of imported silk brocade (Tib. *gos chen*) with a sash from which can hang on display such things as a container for ink, a fountain pen, a sheath for eating utensils, or an elaborately embroidered brocade pouch for tobacco or spices. A 16th century mural in the Red Temple in Tholing, West Tibet, shows a royal couple with the woman donor whose robe is made up of different coloured pieces of woollen cloth in narrowly woven panels. On top of this she is wearing a shawl or cape for additional warmth, a style of clothing that is still traditional today (Fig. 15). This square piece[6] worn over the women's *chuba* or *sulma*, as it is called in Ladakh and Spiti, is made of different materials, according to the season and region: woven wool, felt or fleece. Another wrap (Tib. *rkyed log*, *rked slog*), which hangs at the back over the hips and is held in place around the waist by a belt or decorative clasp, serves to protect and warm the small of the back and kidneys (Fig. 16). Historical paintings in Tholing and Alchi show noblewomen wearing headdresses (Tib. *pad rag*, pronounced *perag*) decorated with turquoises. These impressive exhibits of family jewellery in the form of long headdresses richly decorated with turquoises and amulets (Tib. *ga'u*) are worn by the women of upper class families in West Tibet over their many long braids of hair at religious festivals (Tib. *cham*). In the 1980s, the Chinese ideologists circumspectly allowed demonstration of tolerated cultural diversity. In response, the government of the autonomous region of Tibet propagated national costume celebrations, with the result that the clothing and accessories now seen at traditional festivals throughout Tibet no longer are consistent with the "original" local styles.

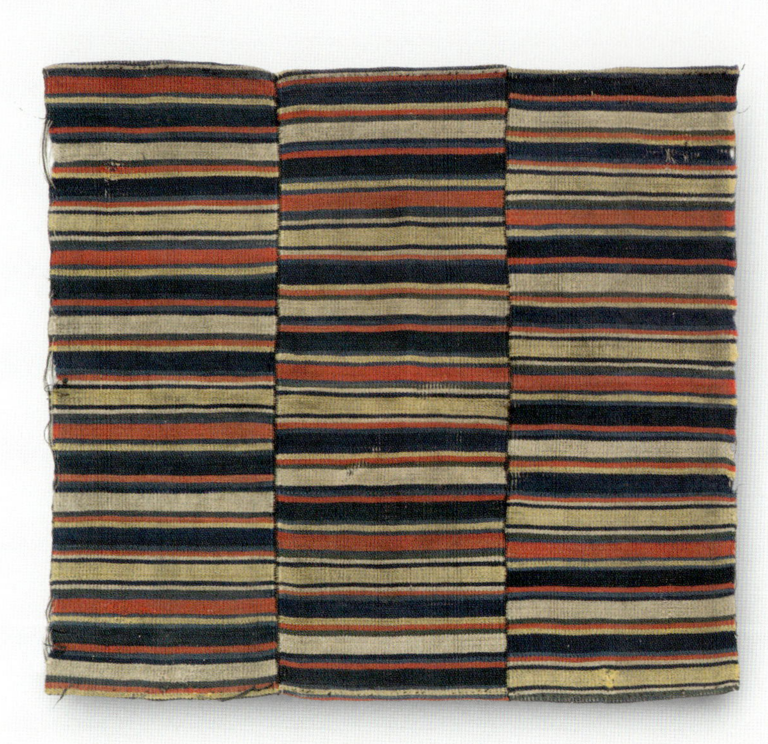

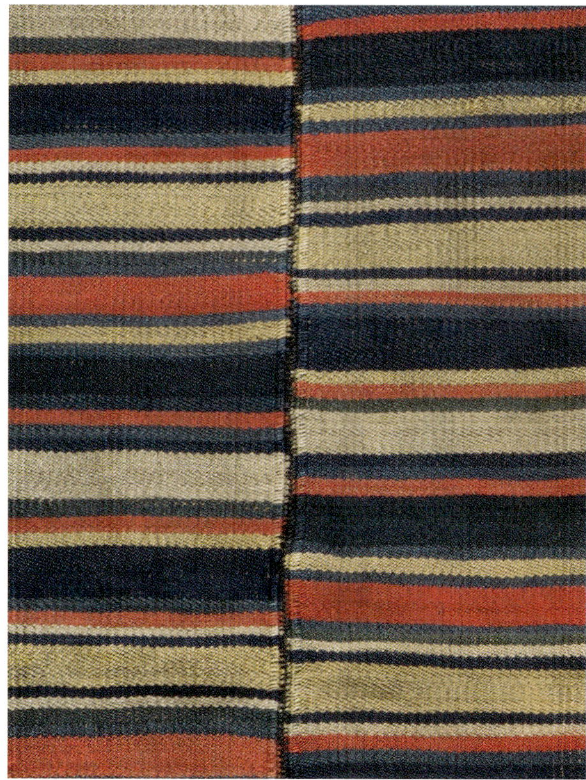

Fig. 17: Apron. Early 20th c., wool, 62×68 cm

Detail of Fig. 17

The women in Tibet generally now wear the popular floor-length sleeveless woollen dress, which has deep pleats at the back, and under it a wide-sleeved silk blouse. In addition, if they are married they wear a hand- or machine-woven woollen apron (Tib. *pang gdan*), which has become a mark of Tibetan identity. Aprons are often now worn by women before their marriage. The aprons are traditionally woven of relatively soft, finer wool and closely woven, which is why new textiles are fairly stiff. They are known for their stripes in especially attractive colours which are characteristic for certain regions. Not infrequently, individual households have their own order of colours. The women's aprons consist of three or more panels of the narrow, striped cloth from the same swath of material which are always sewn together so that a lively effect is produced. Women in Lhasa often prefer newer, brighter colours in the stripes from different yarns, also synthetic ones. In contrast, among the Tibetan elite in China (e.g., Beijing), a "revival for the authentic material" for aprons can be observed, in other words to put the material centrepiece in an attempt to strengthen the identification with Tibet (Harris 2013).

Woollen Apron[7] (Fig. 17)

This apron consists of three pieces of the same narrow cloth, the selvedges sewn together with black thread. The aesthetic appeal of this type of apron comes from the cheerful combination of colours in random stripes on the three panels. With this piece the colours must have originally been brighter and more intense. The repeating broader stripes in blue, white, yellow and red are separated by three or four narrow stripes in the same colours, plus dark green. Chris Buckley (2011: 32) indicates that such combinations of these colours are common in Lhasa and Shigatse, whereas in the border area between Tibet and Nepal more muted colours are preferred, such as green, enlivened with fine stripes of red and pink.

Woollen Apron (Fig. 18)

This apron was the gift of a nomadic family from the region around Damchung. It is very finely made in appliqué technique using many pieces of machine-woven, flannel type wool. The middle section has horizontal pieces. The bordering sides are vertical pieces on which ornamental stripes have been appliquéd with fine stitches. The motifs were glued to the underlying fabric and then a white band was sewn around them. The side panels each show the typical vase of life (Tib. *bumpa*) with a vine growing out of it, one of the eight Tibetan auspicious symbols which are repeated in the horizontal strips. In addition, the apron is decorated with leaves and a stylised *dorje* (diamond sceptre) and a *swastika* band, both on a red background, and also a leaf twig on a green background. These elements are crowned

Fig. 18: Apron in appliqué technique. Damchung region, 20th c., wool, 70×45–60 cm

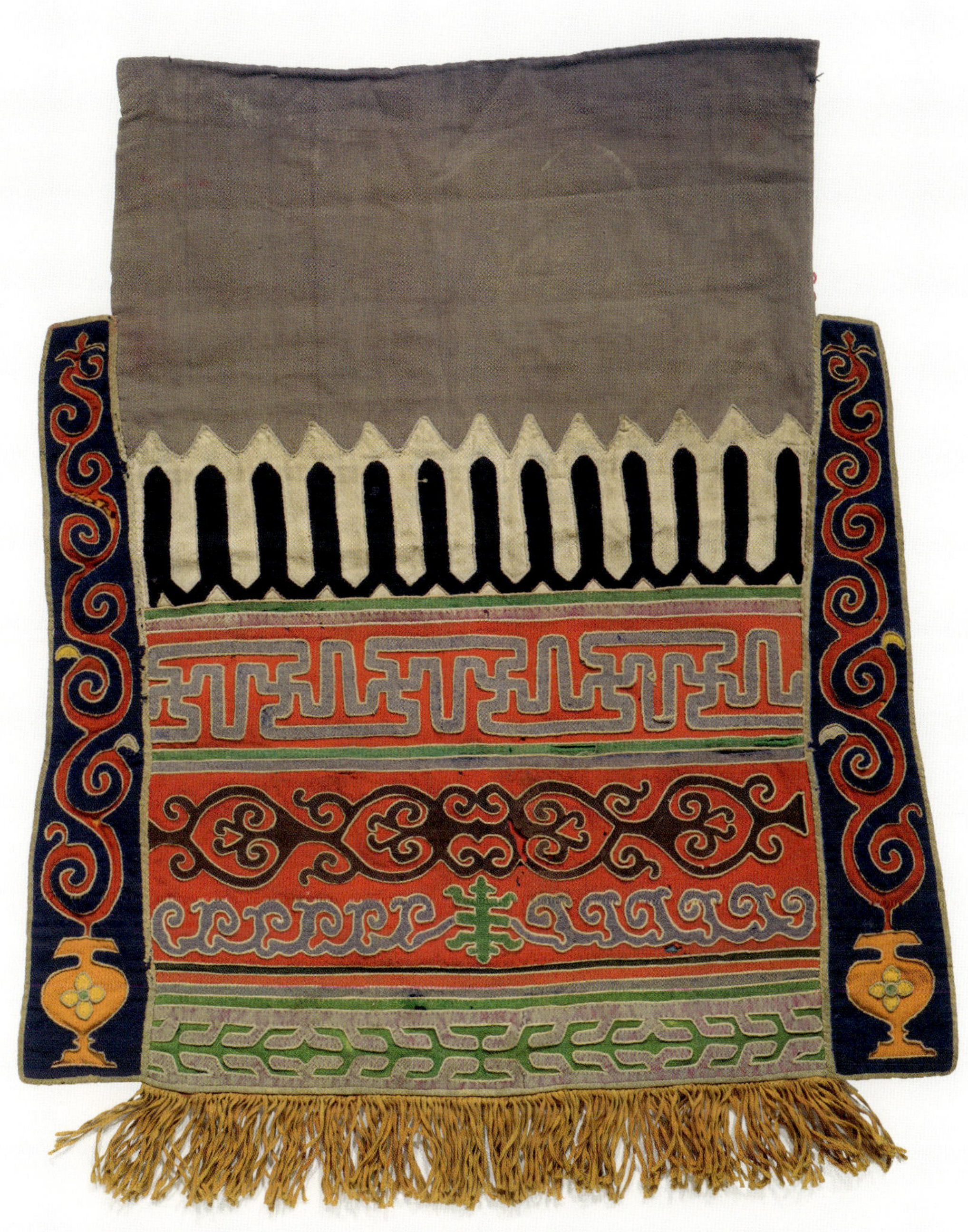

by a crenelated blue strip on a white background. The upper grey third of the apron is unadorned. At the bottom edge there is a saffron yellow strip with fringes. The play between the motifs in the centre and those with "negative form" at the sides, where the appliquéd elements slip into the background, gives a subtle visual effect with a certain plasticity.

This technical refinement is an example of the importance of this technique in many areas of Tibetan artwork, particularly that of religious images on special silk *thangkas*, as well as those made by appliquéing silk pieces together. These are primarily pieces of silk brocade that have been donated to the monastery or are remnants of the robes of venerated lamas. This elaborate technique can be described as "needlework painting" (for examples, see Reynolds 1999: 186). Such silk *thangkas* can be extremely large and are only temporarily unrolled and hung on special walls in the monastery for veneration by the religious community (Reynolds 1999: 187).

This same technique is also used to decorate other religious textiles, wall hangings, ritual costumes and aprons (Tib. *pang khebs*) for the *cham* dances. Appliqué work is also used to decorate door-hangings, summer tents and the

Detail of Fig. 18

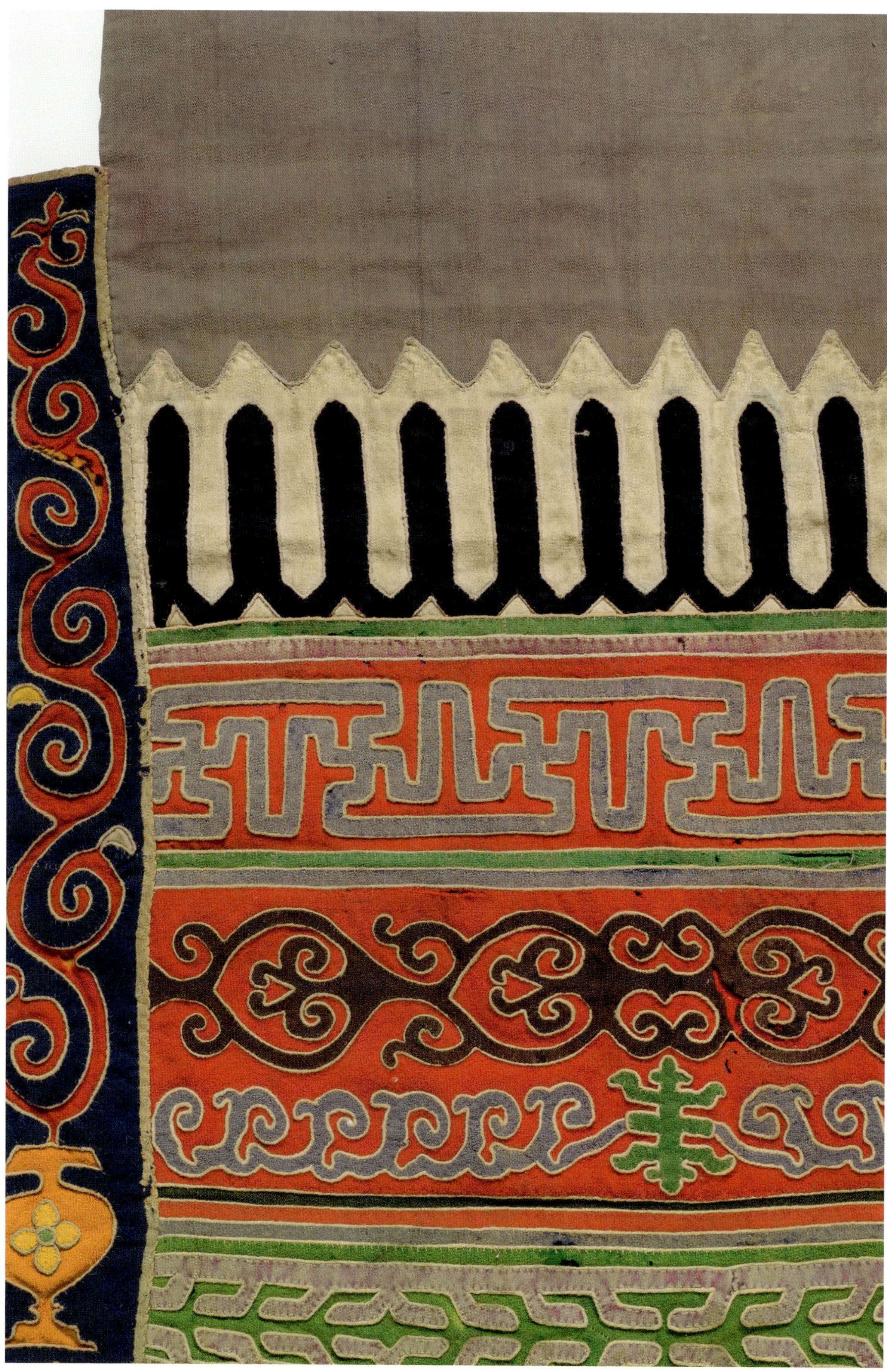

Detail of Fig. 19

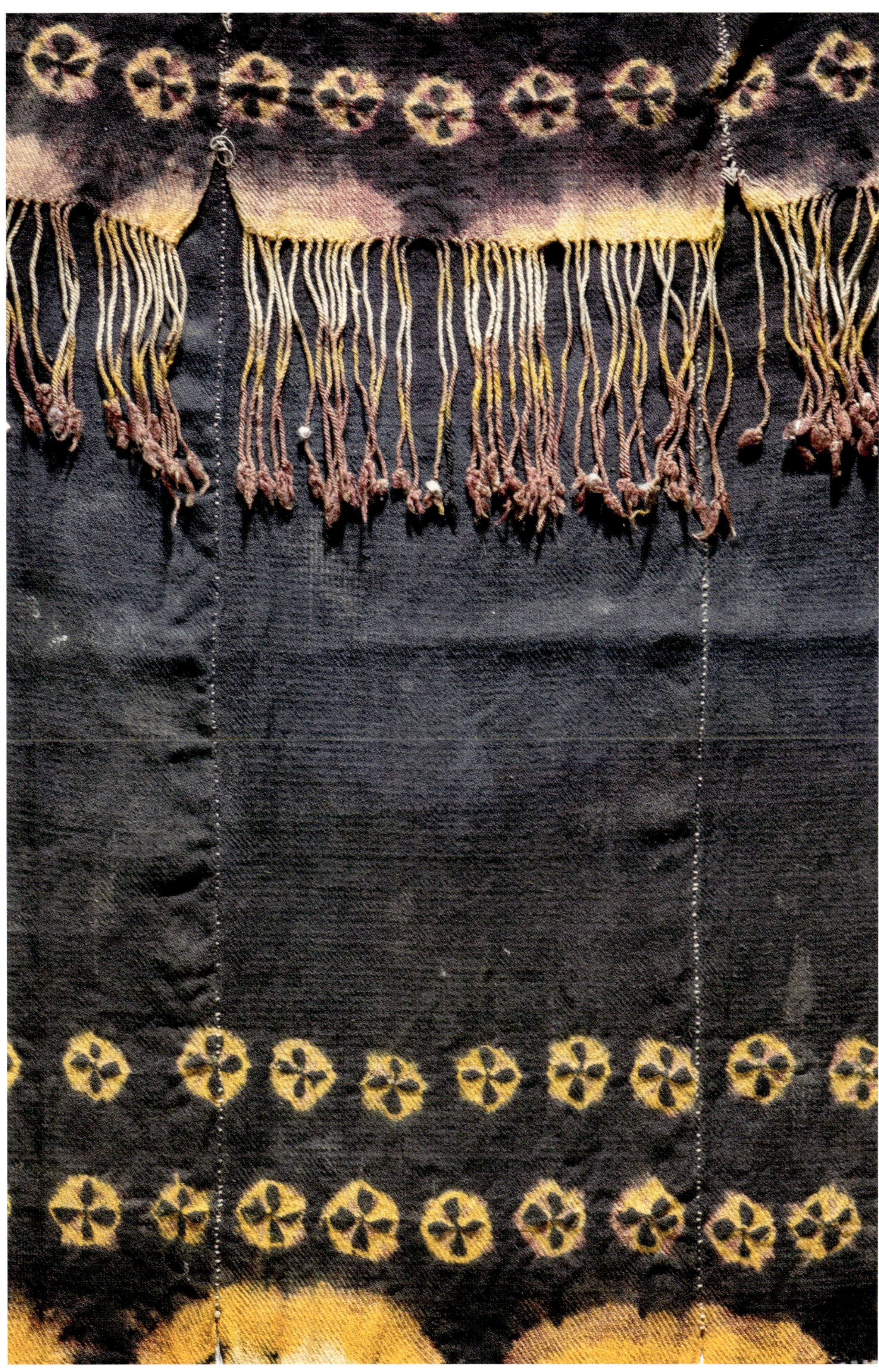

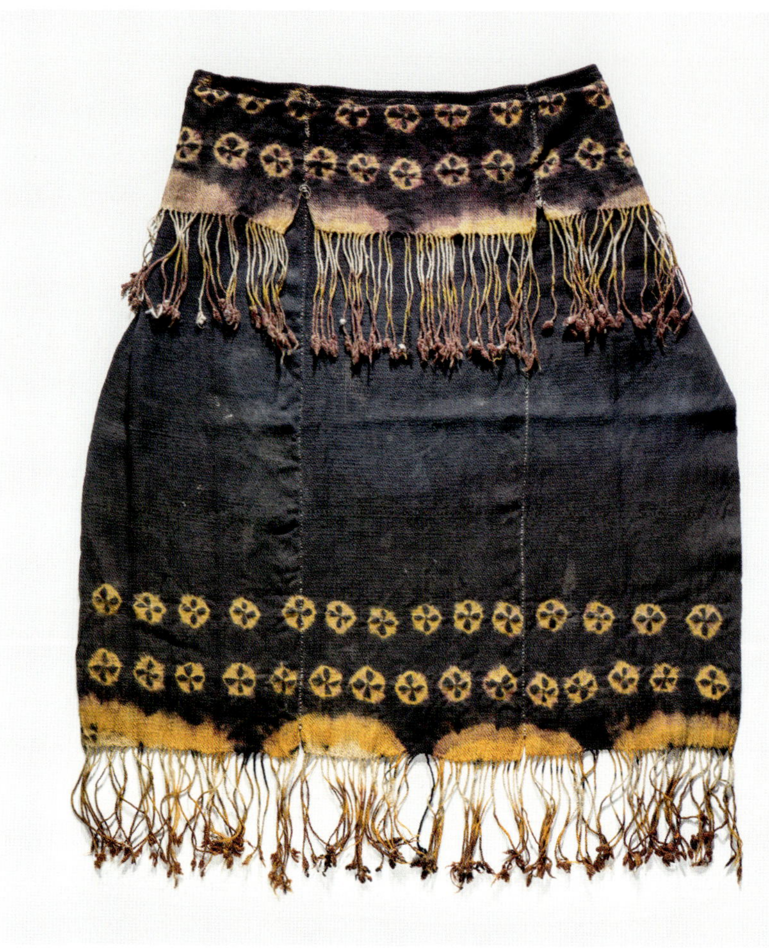

Fig. 19: Shoulder cloth of a woman's festive costume. Rangdum Gompa, Zanskar, India, 20th c., wool, 90×86 cm

baldachins over deities in temples. The motifs and their arrangement on the horizontal and vertical panels of this apron relate to the principles of the composition of *thangkas*. They suggest the appearance of a throne with a central element – here a horizontal double *vajra* from which tendrils extend at both ends. These refer to the lotus as the seat of Buddha on the cosmic lake. *Swastikas* on the throne are a symbol of good fortune, while the vases recall the bases of the lotus columns for deities. Aprons of this type not only have high symbolism but also reflect the prosperity of the owner.

Woman's Shawl (Fig. 19)

In Ladakh the expression for the light, colourful summer shawl is *sbog* (pronounced *bog*), that for the warmer winter shawl is *rgyab sle* (pronounced *gyeble*) The almost square shawl is made of three panels of *nambu* (*snam bu*) with long fringes, the main colour being black. The edges of two sides are decorated with tie-dyed medallions, then with red, yellow and white fiery stripes, which also end in fringes. When worn, the fringed side at the shoulders is folded back so that both rows of fringes are displayed. The corners are trimmed with embroidered triangles (Tib. *rog sden*, pronounced *rogden*) and have bands to allow the shawl to be fastened in front. The embroidering shows the wish-fulfilling jewel (Tib. *yid bzhin nor bu*, pronounced *yishi norbu*) which represents the "Three Jewels": the Buddha, his teachings, and the community of monks. The relatively simple tie-dye technique (Tib. *thig ma*) is still used in Ladakh. Shawls of this type are not just worn for warmth but also are used to carry burdens and small children.

Originally the *tigma* design was reserved for nobility and higher officials. Later, persons of lower status began to wear clothes decorated with it (Ahmed 2002:106ff.; for a similar example, see Müller & Raunig 1982: 163).

Apron or Back Cloth (Fig. 20)

The virtually square back cloth made of cloth stripes for the lower part of the body consists of four full-width panels of *sherma* cloth in the same size. The rich colour contrast of the striped pattern is in yellow, red, light and dark blue, green and white. It is worn over the woman's *chuba* or *sulma* (Tib. *sul ma*), held around the waist by a belt, sash or a clasp. Called *rked log* in Ladakh, it is worn by married women after the birth of their first child (Ahmed 2002: 116). According to Tsering Gyalpo, it can also be used as shawl, the ends held together in the front by a brooch (Tib. *tigra*). This is usual for unmarried women, whereas those married fasten their shawls with bands attached to trimming on the shawl (Tib. *rog sden*).

Sash (Fig. 21)

Men use sashes of this type in Ladakh to hold together their coats. In West Tibet, the shafts of boots are often decorated with this patterned material. The hand-woven narrow band of finest *sherma* wool from the neck of the sheep has a black background with alternating rows of *tigma* medallions and sets of three or four weft stripes of indigo blue, separated by thin lines of black weft. The medallions have an indigo centre surrounded by a ring combining red, white and blue, which contrasts with the black background. The tie-dye technique and the dyeing in different colours results in almost limitless variations and the typical flaming colours. Textiles with this kind of woven pattern and decoration applied after weaving are called *rgy khra snam bu* (Müller & Raunig 1982: 165).

Fig. 20: Apron or back cloth bought from a nomadic family. Tingri, South Tibet, early 20th c., wool, 84×85 cm

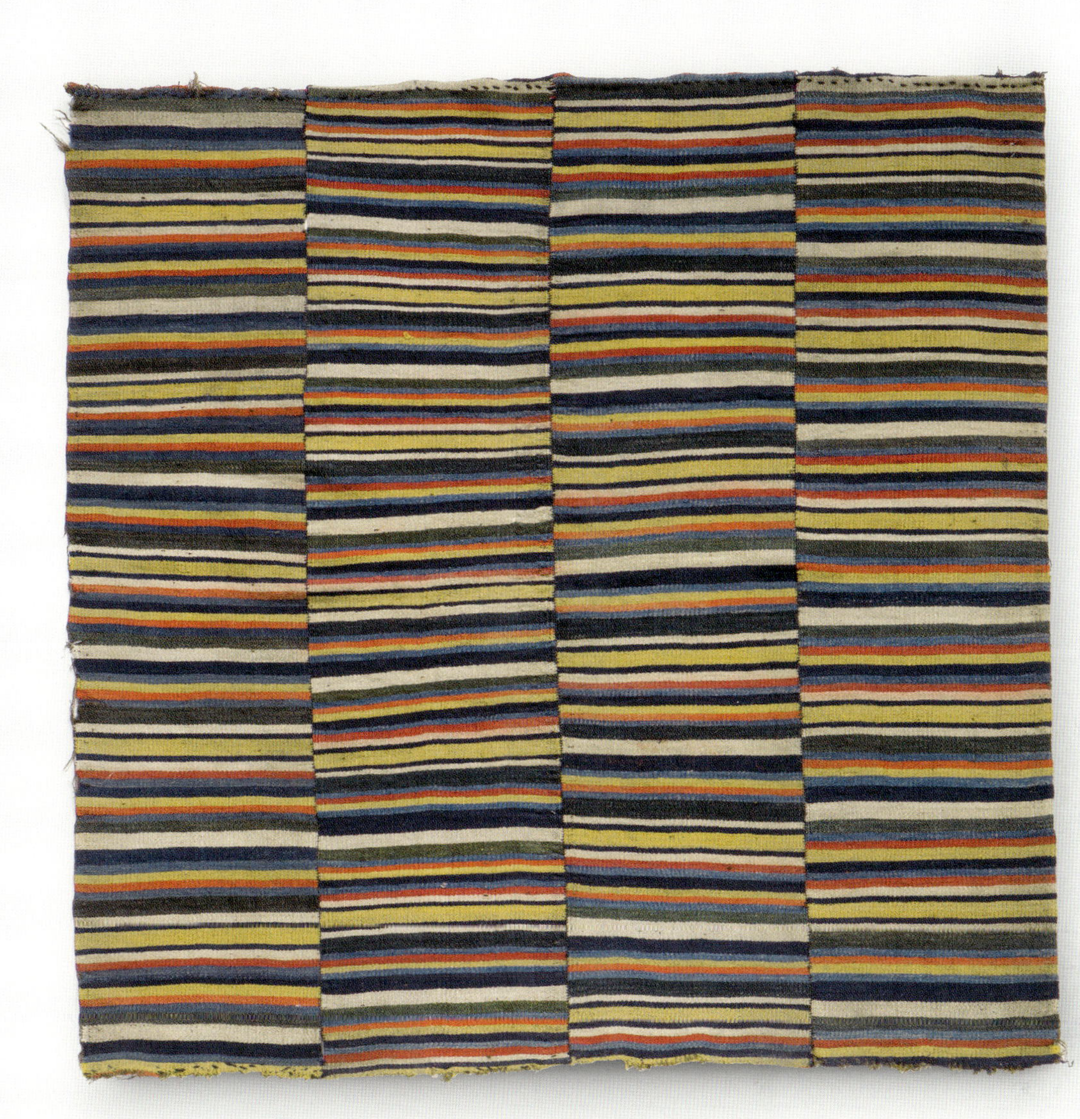

Fig 21: Detail of sash. End 19th c., wool, 320×16 cm

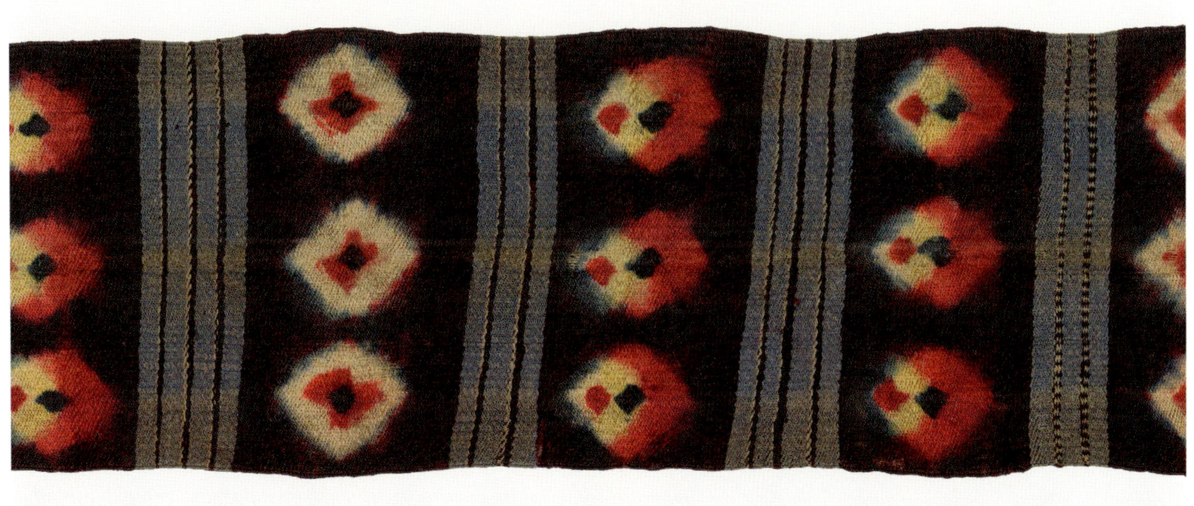

Fig. 22: Pannier. Gift from nomads. South Tibet, 20th c., yak or goat hair, 54×41 cm

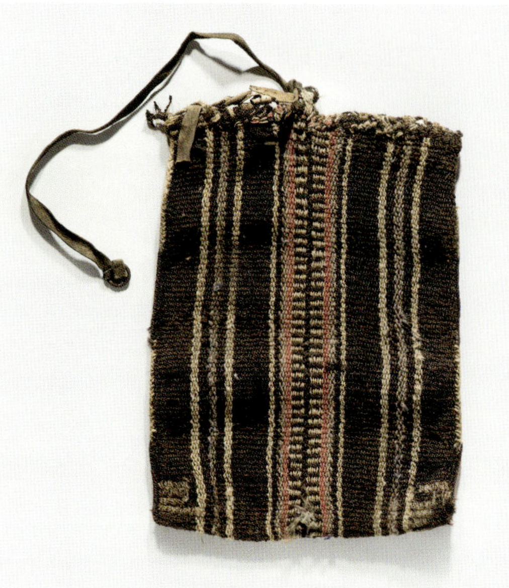

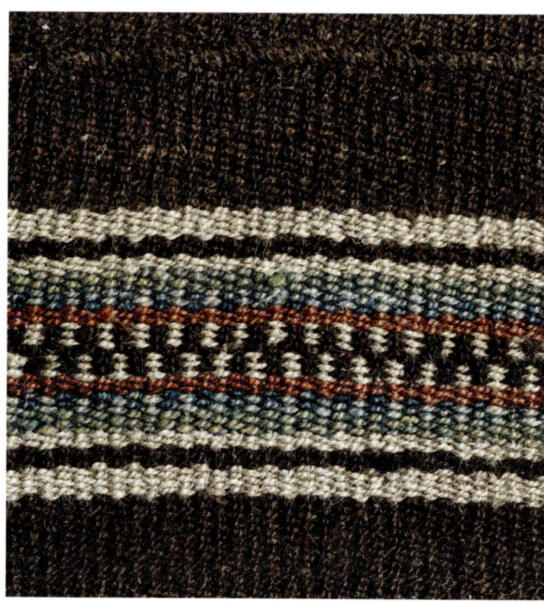

Detail of Fig. 23

Fig. 23: Heavy blanket. 19th/20th c., yak or goat hair (?), ca. 145×143 cm

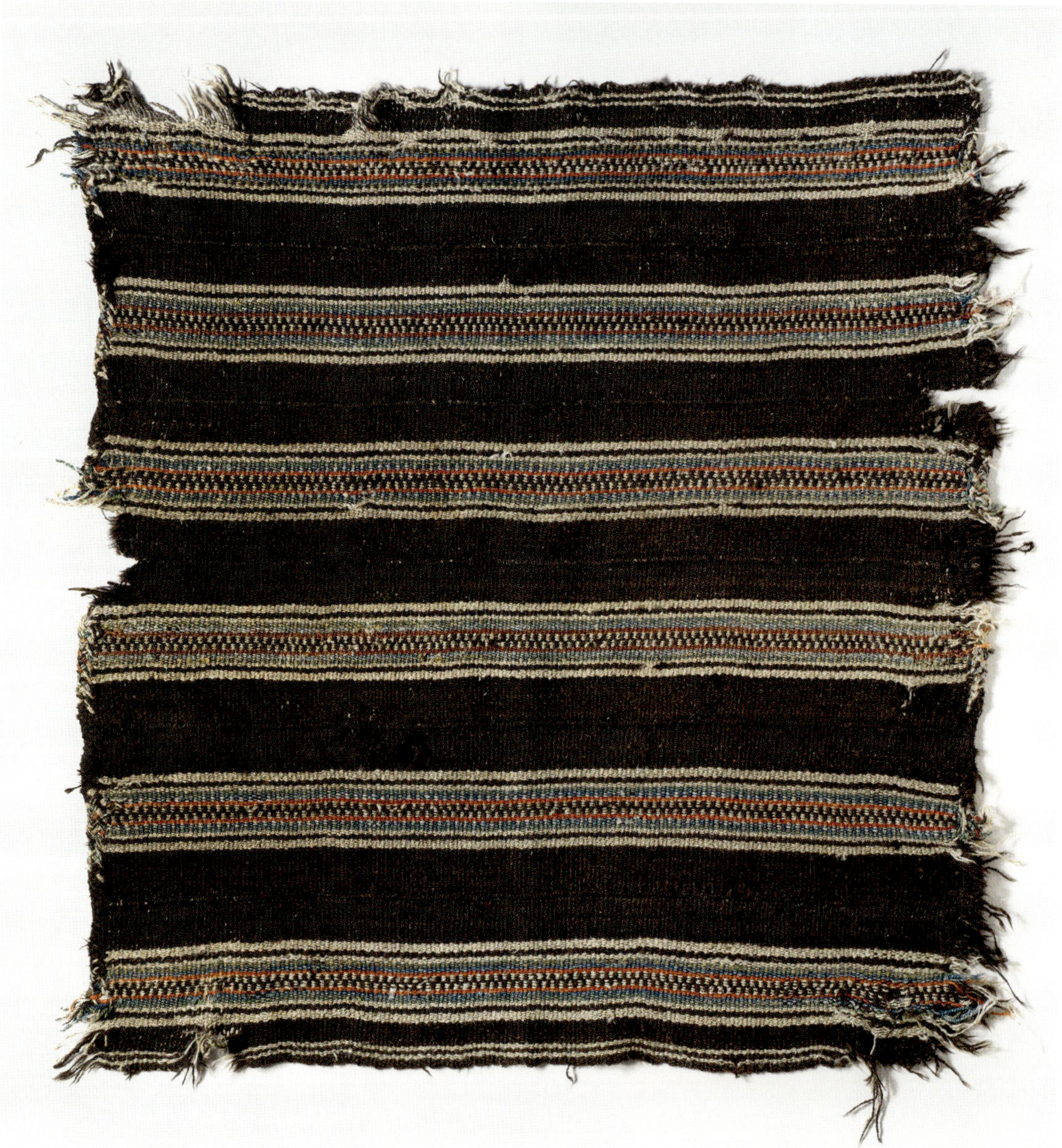

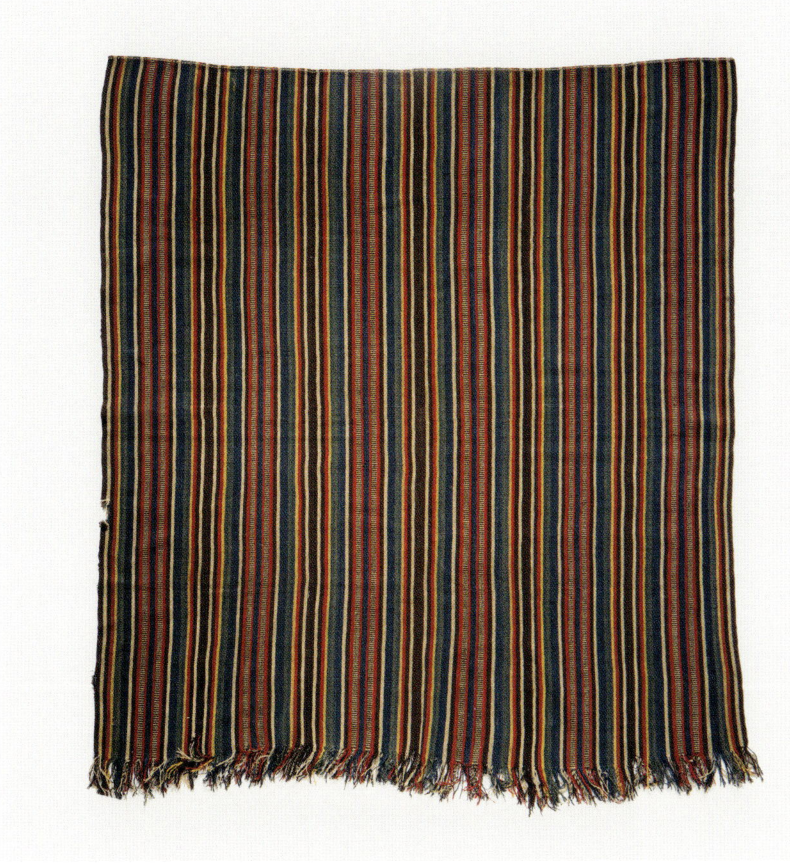

Fig. 24: Striped multi-purpose textile. 19th/20th c., wool, 149 × 133 cm

THE TIBETAN NOMAD'S TENT

The traditional portable dwelling of nomadic herders (Tib. *'brog pa*, pronounced *drogba*) in Tibet is a black tent. The general Tibetan name for tents made of yak hair is *dranak* (*sbra nag*), which also encompasses tents made of yak hair combined with other fibres. In West Tibet, however, the typical tent is only ever made of panels of yak hair (Tib. *tsiba*). Due to its fat content and swelling and thickening when wet, it provides good protection against wind and water, although not always entirely. Within the tent, knotted rugs and flat-woven covers and wraps protect against the cold. The seating order is in accordance with hierarchically structured society and its separation of men's and women's realms. From the entrance, the women's side is to the left, that of the men to the right. The utensils in the tent are also kept on the side of those who would use them. Yak hair sacks filled with provisions and clothing serve as "furniture" in the tent. Along the sides of the tent items such as rolls of hand-woven cloth, saddles, pots and the butter churn are stored. In the centre of the tent is a hearth of stone, today usually an iron stove, which is under the opening in the tent for the smoke. Opposite the entrance at the back wall of the tent is the altar. Behind it, fastened to the tent, is usually a striped textile (Tib. *num ba*), which protects the holy area and symbolically reinforces it. Similar textiles showing respect are seen in the murals in West Tibet draped behind the deities and revered religious leaders (see Fig. 6).

Pannier (Fig. 22)
This pannier is constructed from one piece of striped cloth, doubled back and the selvedges sewn together. In the middle of the piece is woven a stepped design flanked on each side by narrower stripes of a different width. The handle is made of leather. A leather strap with an iron ring serves to close the sack. Nomads normally transport provisions such as grain, sugar or dry cheese in such sacks.

Heavy Blanket (Fig. 23)
This type of cloth is usually woven by men. The six panels (23 to 24 centimetres in width) are woven with goat or yak hair. The background colour is brown with characteristic warp stripes in white, blue and red with a stepped design in the middle, where black and white warps alternate. Both panels at the sides are decorated with two white stripes; these recall the "weaver's mark" (Tib. *yud*), which in Ladakh identifies the owner, as explained by Ahmed (2002: 147ff.).[8]

Striped Textile (Fig. 24)
This blanket (Tib. *sug dul*) is made up of six panels (22 centimetres each) of warp-striped material. The stripes are symmetrically arranged on both sides of a middle stripe in reddish-brown, narrow stripes of red, brown, twice white, blue, yellow, red, brown, white and then brown. Such blankets can have many different functions, not only as a warm shawl or baby carrier. This example has fringes on one side, which could indicate that it was used to cover things placed along the wall of the tent, showing the side decorated with borders and the fringes hanging down.

Striped Textile, Multi-Purpose Blanket with an Appliquéd Amulet (Fig. 25)
This textile has striped warps and is made of eight panels each 22 centimetres. Similar to the previously described blanket, the textile is in muted colours with dark red and blue dominating. In the middle of the longer side, two squares have been sewn on to each other; the larger one underneath is red at the corners with a smaller green square appliquéd diagonally at 45 degrees on it, both sewn on with

Detail of Fig. 24

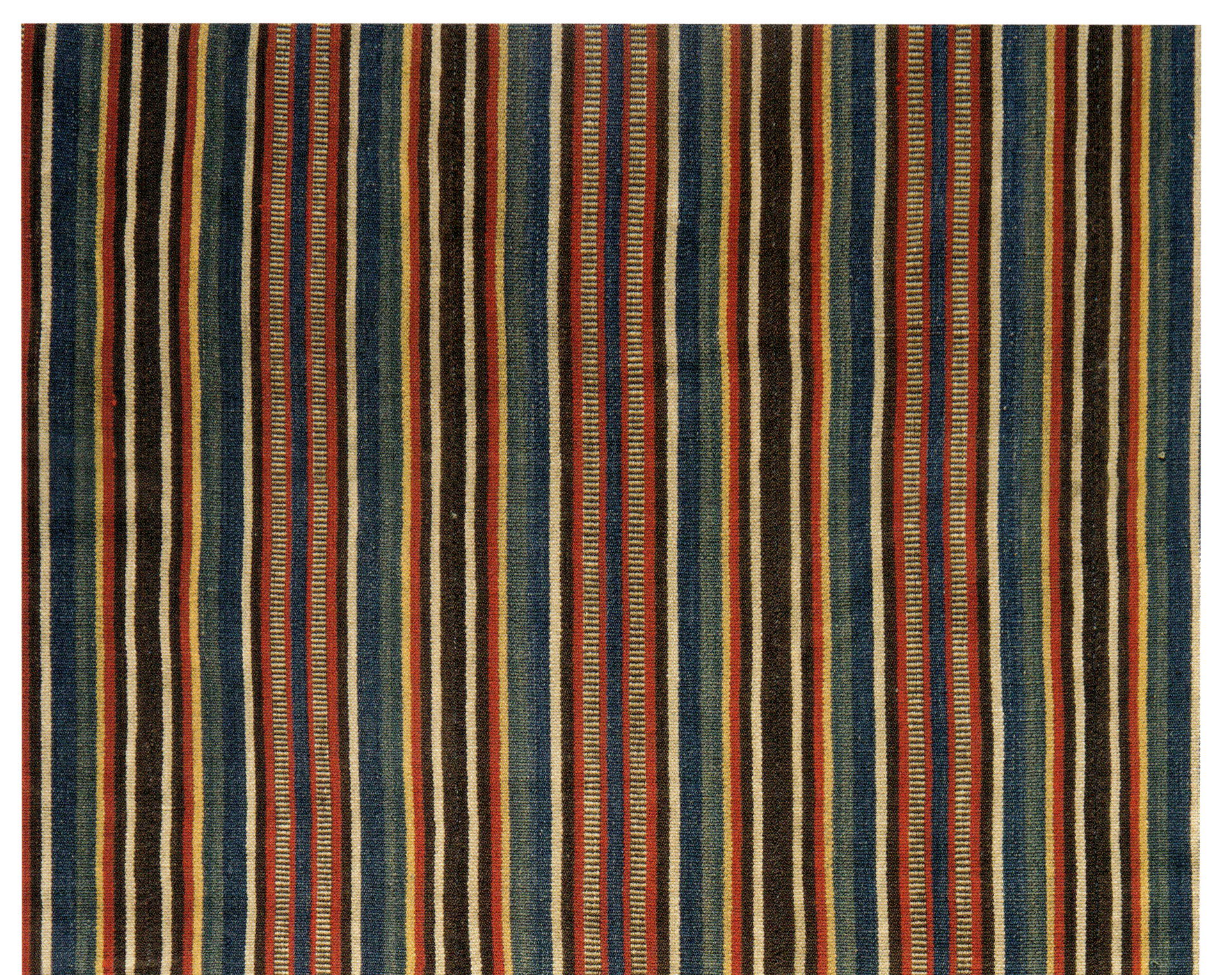

Detail of Fig. 25

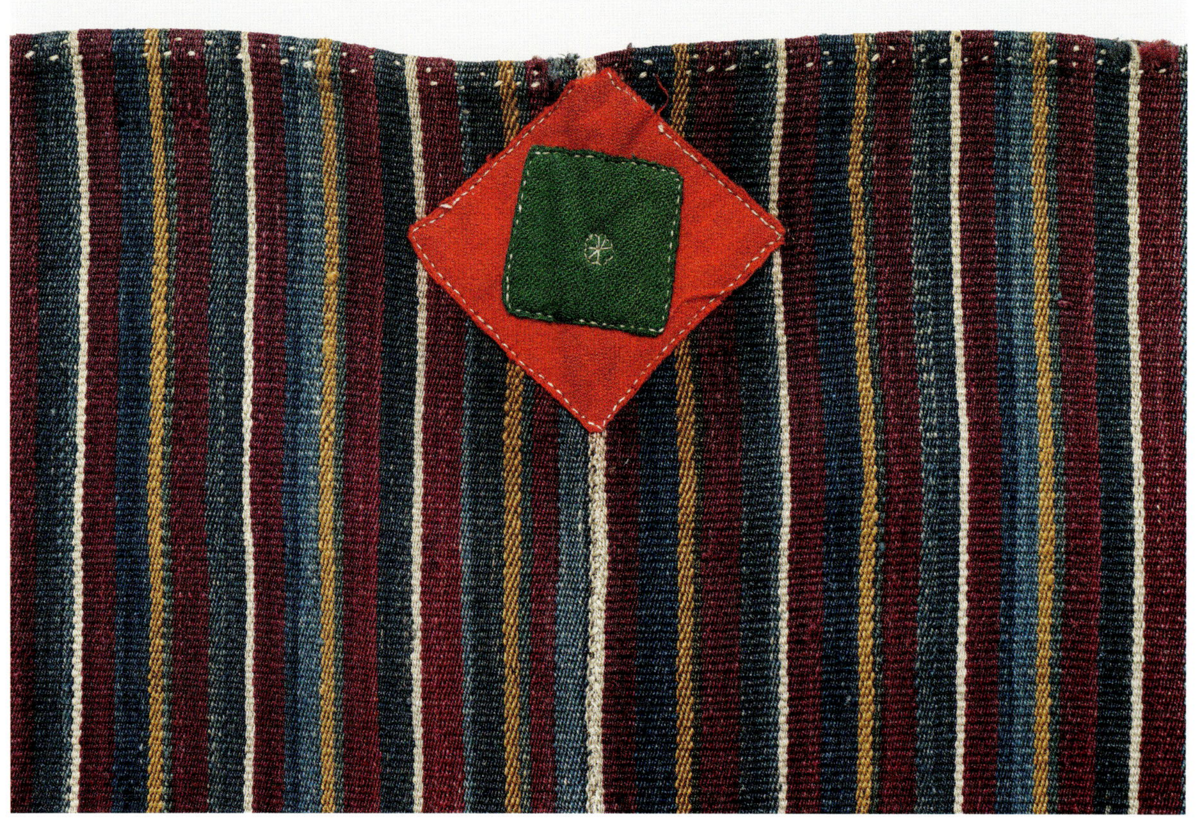

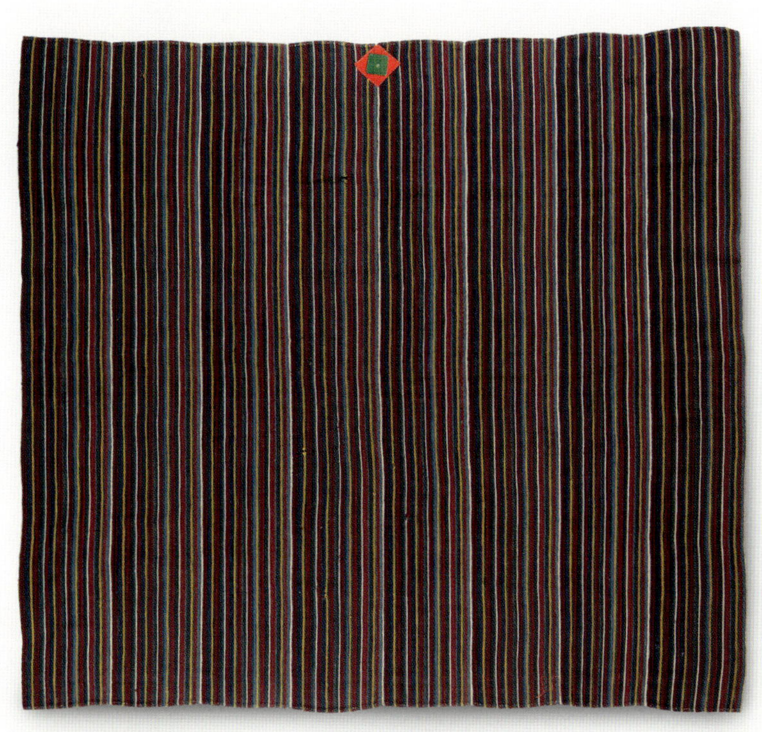

Fig. 25: Striped multi-purpose textile with appliquéd amulet. 20th c., wool, 167×178 cm

white thread. In addition, an eight-petalled (lotus) rosette has been embroidered additionally in the middle (for a similar piece see Ahmed 2002: 121). According to Tsering Gyalpo, this has both a decorative and practical function: such blankets are often folded parallel with the longer sides and used as the uppermost bed blanket, the decoration indicating which end belonged at the head of the bed.

NOMADISM, ANIMAL SYMBOLISM AND FOLK TRADITIONS

Buddhism and traditional religious beliefs in Tibet cannot be separated. In contrast to Buddhism which is practised by a relatively small elite who use sacred texts and secretly transmitted oral traditions to gain inner enlightenment, the religious beliefs of the greater populace are more about protection from misfortune and achieving a better life in this world. In their animistic concept of the world and cosmos there is an established order of latent powers (demons and spirits) that are closely connected to humans and which must be shown respect, appeased and propitiated (Brauen 1980: 101; Brauen 1982: 245). The divine power of local guardian deities, who are believed to reside on hills and fields and in mountain passes, can counter such malevolent influences. To assure this protection, there are various rituals to appeal to these deities and make offerings to them (including symbolic animal sacrifices, primarily of sheep but also of horses and yaks). In addition, in everyday life people surround themselves with objects and clothing with auspicious and appeasing symbols, as well as amulets (Tib. *srung wa*) with protective power.

The representation of animals on textiles reflects the natural environment of the Tibetan nomads on the plateau and the importance to the nomads of the yak, *dzo* (crossbreed of cattle and yak), goat, wild donkey, antelope, Tibetan wild sheep and other animals. In their predominantly pastoral way of life, the animals are considered important media between the people and deities (Ahmed 2002: 49). Special influences are ascribed to them in the animistic concept of their natural surroundings. Accordingly, animal symbolism is significant in the Tibetan pantheon. Prosperity and good fortune are dependent on animals; this good fortune is in turn ensured by appeasing the deities of this hierarchical pantheon by the symbolic sacrifice of animals to the guardian deities on certain feast days, offering butter and *tsampa* instead. This is also depicted on special roll-pictures, *gangdze* ("objects for satisfaction"), which are displayed in the monastery during the performance of certain rituals. These also show the deity's mount and his or her personal attributes and ornaments, thereby symbolically evoking the presence of the deity.

Animals are also found accompanying certain deities to whom they are consecrated. In Khorchag monastery, for example, the warlike guardian deity Dabla, who also protects private households, is accompanied by animals. In the form of stuffed wild animals displayed in the entrance hall these have the function of repelling harmful and malicious elements (Gyalpo et al. 2012).

According to legend, the local female deity Dorje Chenmo came to protect the earliest temples in West Tibet, riding first on a stag and then on a horse. She may originate from local pre-Buddhist traditions. She became a powerful ally of the religious rulers in the 11th century. At performances in her honour during religious festivals at Korchag monastery, which together with Tholing and Nyarma is one of the three great monasteries founded by the kings of Purang and Guge in West Tibet, pilgrims come from all levels of society to come into contact with her when she is sitting (in the form of a statue) on a stuffed toy horse in front of the monastery. Nomads used to travel there on richly decorated horses, today they arrive on motorbikes which are decorated with a knotted blanket when they visit the monastery.

Fig. 26: Decoration for the back. East Tibet, 19th/20th c., wool, silk, metal thread embroidery, 104/106 × 10 cm

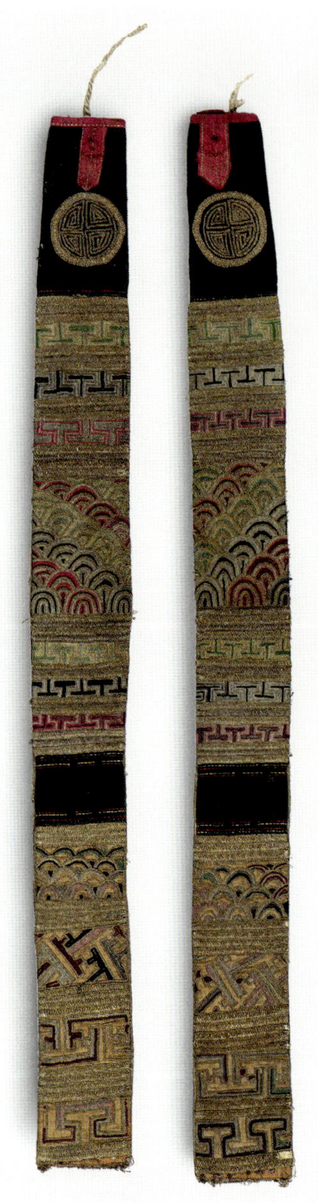

Animals shown in rock paintings in the Indus valley and in West Tibet, which bring to mind motifs on decorative bands, demonstrate their close economic and spiritual importance for those living on the Tibetan plateau. The power, strength and aura of the animals and their guardian function led to the animals being included in representations of local guardian deities, and also to the many and varied use of animals to decorate textiles. Their appearance on tablet-woven bands brings to life the strength and influence imputed to them in the Tibetans' animistic world.

Decoration for the Back from East Tibet (Fig. 26)

This pair of decorative bands for a woman is richly embroidered with typically Chinese motifs: meander, mountain or overlapping scales design, braided bands, connected with gold-coloured bars. In the middle and at one end are strips of cloth (similar to corduroy). The latter is decorated with golden medallions which recall the Chinese *Lu* symbol for prosperity. The overall design with three bands separating the ornamental fields could represent the Chinese "trigram", whereby the three undecorated lines would represent heaven.

Under-Saddle Blanket (Fig. 27)

The pride of the nomad is his horse (Tib. *rta*, pronounced *ta*, or as an honorary title *chibs* for a riding horse). As a consequence, blankets, saddle, bridle and decorative bands are of the highest quality and richly decorated with designs and auspicious Buddhist symbols.

The use of a Tibetan saddle (Tib. *sga*) includes woven and felt saddle blankets and also knotted rugs, which are laid both under the saddle to protect the horse from the wooden saddle and over it for the comfort of the rider. This woven goat hair blanket could have been placed first, directly on the horse. The border is the full width of the brown, yellow, and red striped textile, with a black and white interlocking stripe. The middle section of the blanket is in a technique used especially for under-blankets and the collars for horses and yaks. This unwoven midsection consists of a bundle of variously coloured cords which are sewn together.[9] In the middle of one long side is leather trim as reinforcement for the area of the tail.

Horse Blanket (Fig. 28)

The Tibetan term for this type of decorated blanket is *meden*, when the blankets, as here, are elaborately decorated; for that of plainer blankets is *taden*. The white material printed with crosses (combined with striped patterns which are woven) imitate in the decoration the typical tie-dyeing process (Tib. *thig ma*). On the narrower end, red reinforcement and triangular pieces are sewn on; on to the latter are bands for fixing the blanket onto the horse's back.

Striped Textile (Fig. 29)

This piece consists of single 26-centimetre panels woven with thick yarn of yak or goat hair. The panels have narrow woven stripes in the middle and at both sides interrupted

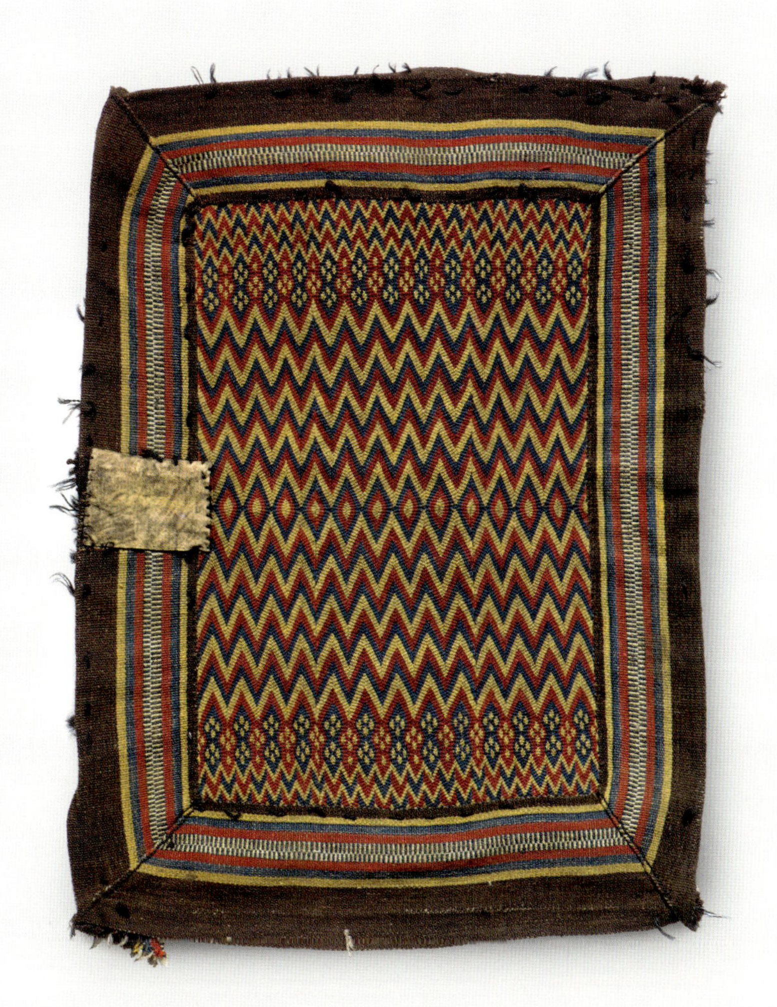

Fig. 27: Under-saddle blanket, presumably for a yak's pannier. 19th/20th c., goat hair (?), 112 × 80 cm

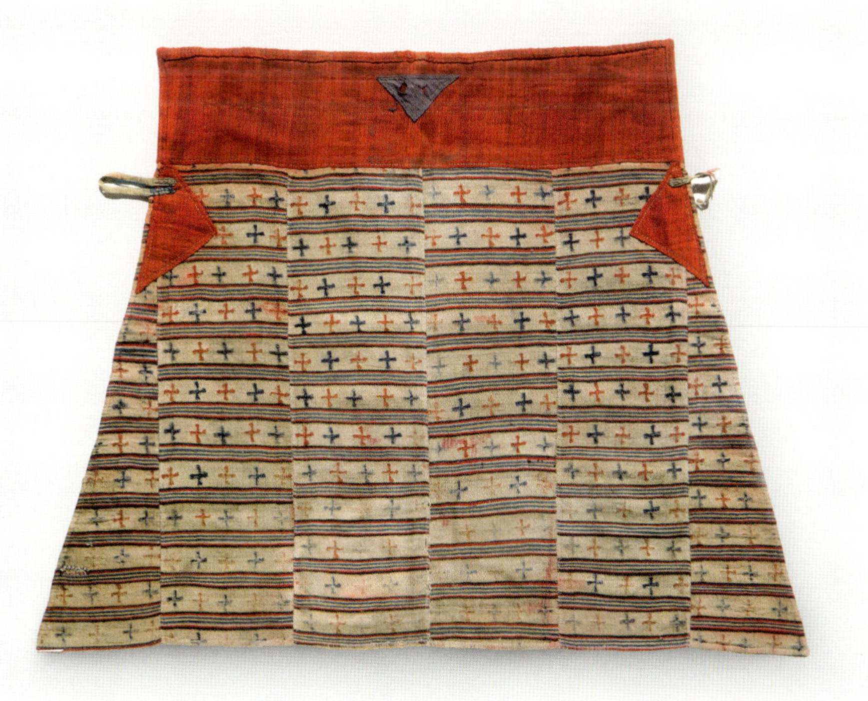

Fig. 28: Horse blanket. 19th/20th c., wool, 101 × 89/133 cm

Detail of Fig. 27

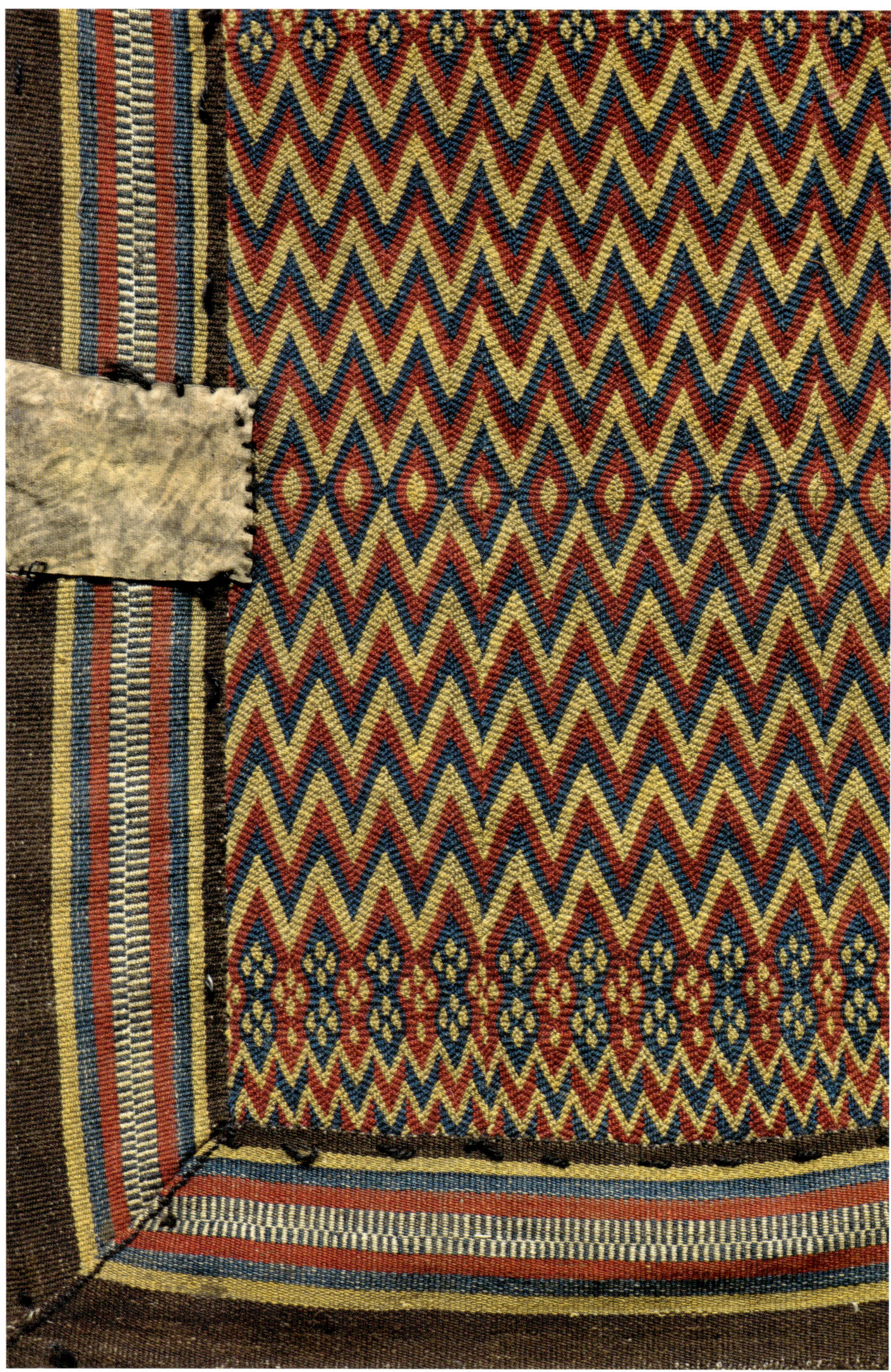

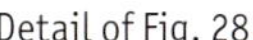

Detail of Fig. 28

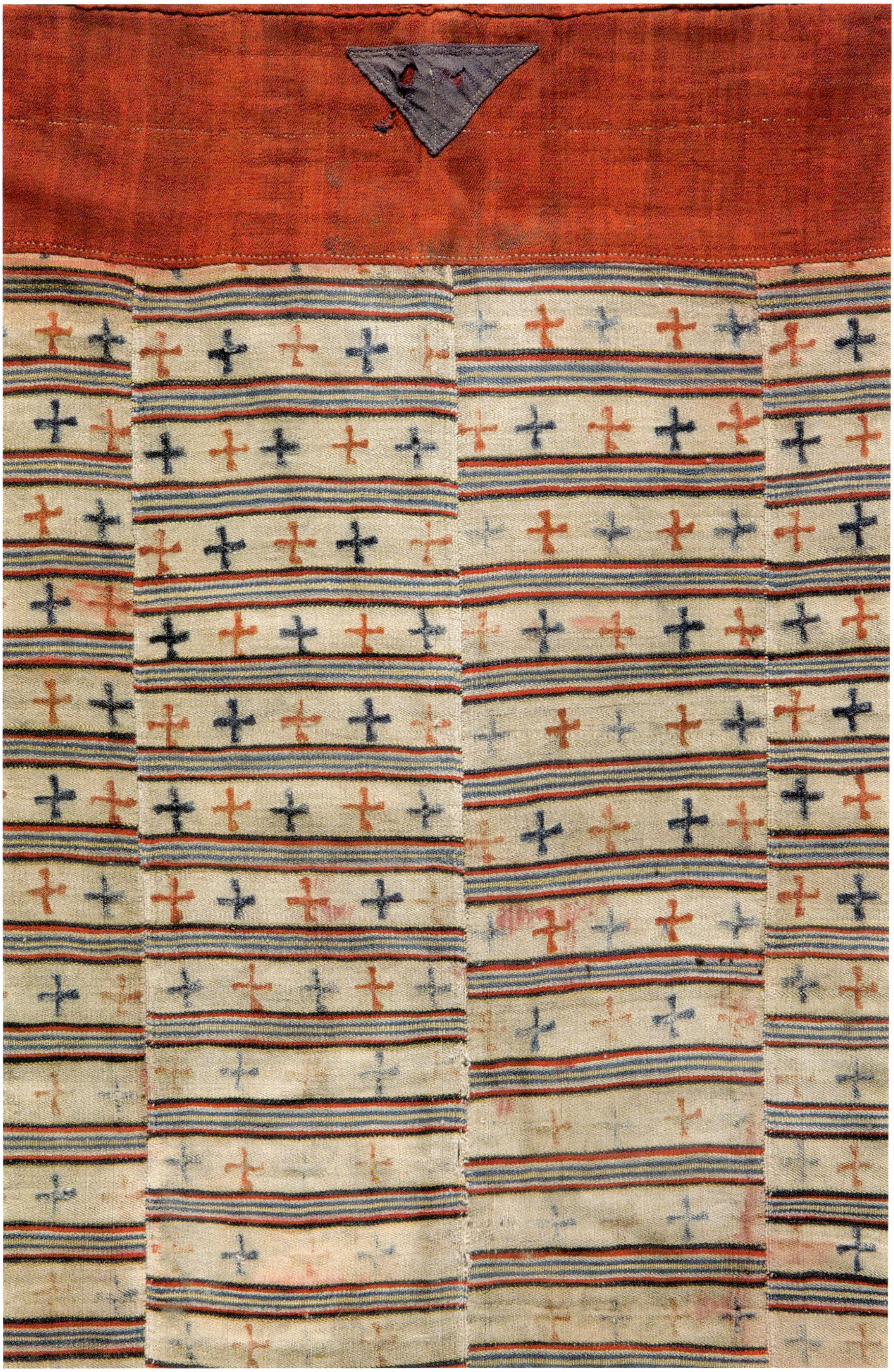

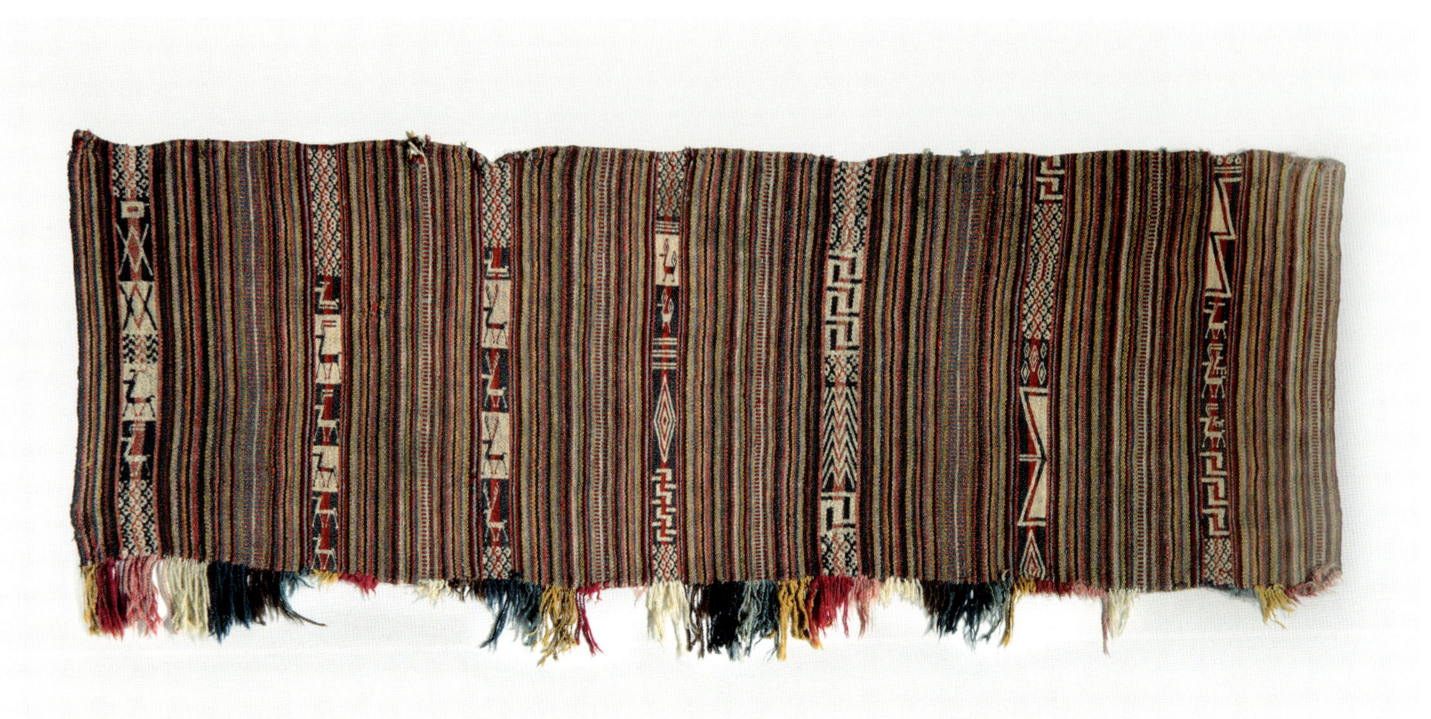

Fig. 29: Striped cloth with woven motifs. 19th/20th c., wool with yak or goat hair (?), 75 × 204 cm

stripes and a broad ornamental stripe. On one long side of the panel are sewn fringes in the colours of the stripes which were added later. The complex design of the ornamental stripes recalls that of tablet-woven bands and sashes and shows antelope, deer, stags and geometrical motifs such as meander, zigzag and rhomboids. An almost identical piece is illustrated in Buckley (2011: 26). Professor Tsering Gyalpo has explained that textiles like this are used to cover objects along the back side of the tent, the fringes hanging down. Folded to half its length, it could also be used as an under-saddle blanket.

STONE SLINGS

Stone slings (Tib. *'ur rdo* or *sgu rdo*, pronounced *urdo*) are one of the nomad's most useful implements. He uses it to keep the herd together and guide it, as well as to drive wolves away from the campsite or herd. Slings used by women are usually smaller than those of men. At about the age of eight years, children can already use a sling. At one end of the sling is a thumb-loop, in the middle a pouch for the stone; the loose end is held between thumb and fingers. The sling is then swung over the head and the loose end released.[10] In May 2015, Tsering Gyalpo demonstrated for me another important use of a sling, as a noise maker. One end is pulled through the thumb-loop; the large loop is held while the yak-hair other end is whipped down on a flat stone on the ground, making a sound like a pistol shot. This is done to call the grazing animals back. The slinging of small stones is used to drive the animals forward. One also whips it on a stone in front of the tent in the evening to drive away supposedly evil spirits. As a weapon, it can be used to drive off intruders or wild animals. This function is symbolically indicated, when a sling is hung on the rear view mirror of an automobile in Lhasa.

Herders' slings are not only complex in the techniques of their fabrication and combination of materials (wool, goat and yak hair). The examples in the collections are also colourful and elaborately made. Slings also have a symbolic character; one often finds an interesting agreement with the patterns seen on the *dzi* or *gzi* stones made of agate, which are greatly valued in Tibet with their dark brown and white markings, and which are believed to have a protective influence (Desrosiers 1982: 177; Jones 1996: 167). This button-like pattern is called *chu mig dgu sgril*, "nine-eye," or more precisely, "nine-fold turned water-eye." Similar "eyes" on a sling and those on the *dzi* stones are called *chu mig*. Other patterns of the markings have other names, such as "small spotted" or "striped calf".[11] Slings are plaited by men and women, who are both equally skilled at using them. It is typical that every nomad always has a sling with him, tucked through his belt.

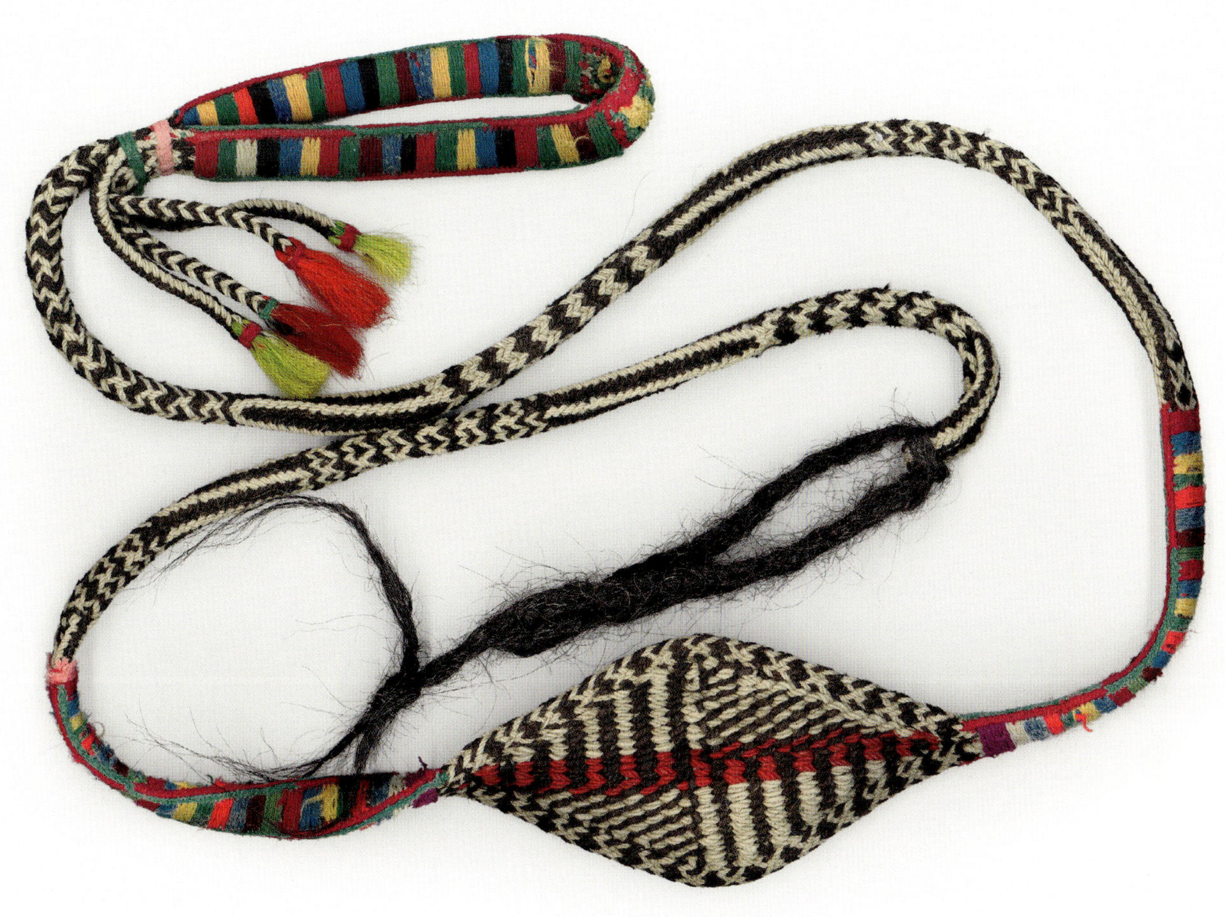

Fig. 30: Sling. Damchung region, southern Changtang, 20th c., yak wool and hair, wool, total length 208 cm

Sling (Fig. 30)

This sling is braided with black and undyed yak wool, also yak hair and dyed wool, with additional coloured embroidery. It consists of three parts: the pouch for the stone, the plaited band with the thumb-loop and the other, whip end of yak hair, which is knotted with a cord. The total length is 205 centimetres, the width of the pouch is 8.5 centimetres; the pouch is woven with wefts of alternating white and black, in the middle with supplementary red wefts. The ends of the warps are plaited in two flat bands, which are wrapped with rainbow-coloured threads and sewn onto the borders. One of them – the part on the whip end – serves to roll the stone from where it sits when it is let go. Attached to them is the round braided section whose spiralling and zigzag pattern suggests the so-called "eyes" and the three-piece, loosely braided black yak hair whip end.

The other side of the pouch is fastened around braided strip that ends in a flat braided loop. This colourfully striped piece has knotted strengthening in the loop and ends in four braided fringes.

TABLET-WOVEN BANDS

Tablet-woven bands are considered the most highly refined form of Tibetan textile art, one full of symbolism. Using the tablet-weaving device (Tib. *ko 'thag*), patterned bands of various widths are woven, whereby the shed is created by twisting the square leather tablets with holes through which the warps have been threaded. Wool is the principal material, but also silk and imported cotton are used. Veronika Ronge (1978b) has prepared technical analyses (for other examples, see also Köpke & Schmelz 2005: 869). Since the technique is described in detail in those works, I will concentrate on the motifs, using to some extent examples from the Buddeberg collection. These were gifts from Palsang Tsomo in the years 1996 to ca. 2009, who comes from a semi-nomadic family in Damchung, Changthang. They provide a remarkable impression of the visual richness of the technique and show animals and other symbolic motifs in clear, stylised forms. Tablet-woven bands are used for a multitude of purposes: to fasten the shaft of boots to

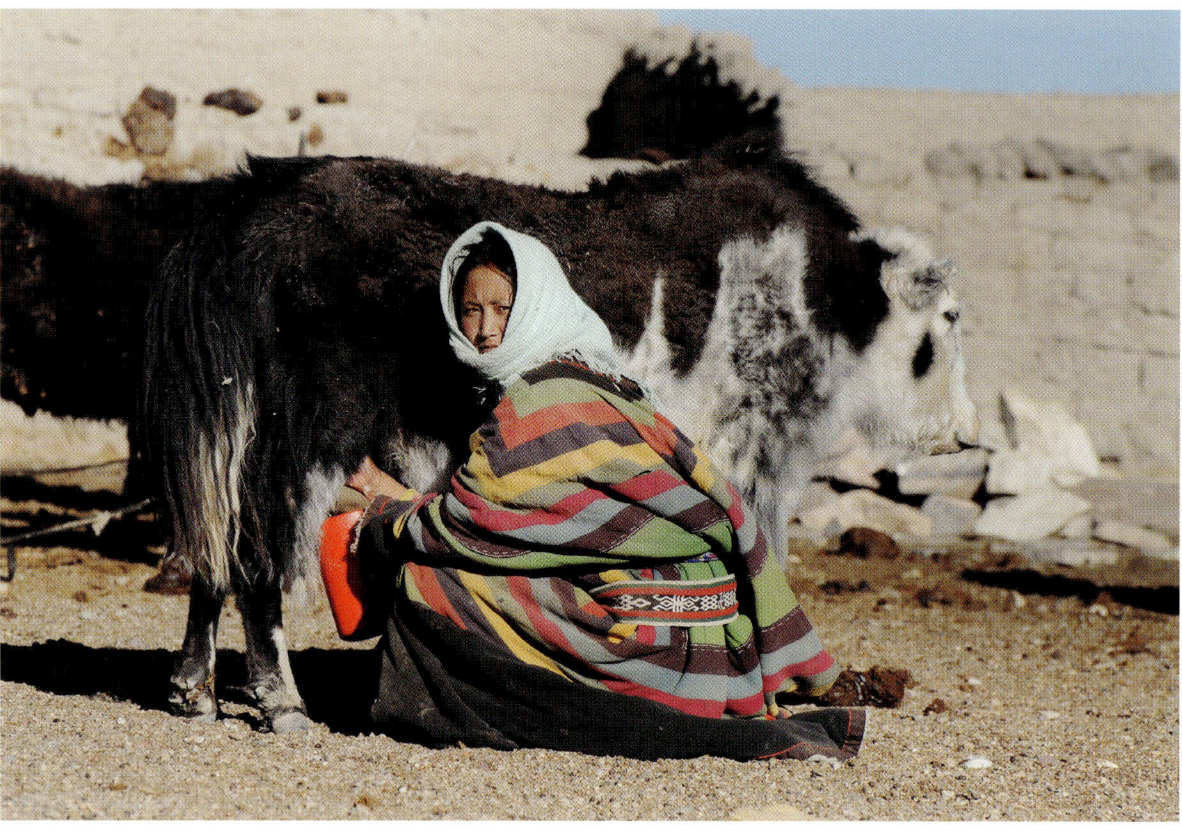

Fig. 31: Nomad woman milking a *dri*. Near the Bangra Tso, southern Changtang, 2002

the leg; as apron bands (Tib. *spang sgrog*) and shoulder straps to hold amulet containers (Tib. *ga lung*); also as a woman's belt (Tib. *sked rags*, pronounced *ke rag*) (Fig. 31). They may occasionally be used in bridles, and are used to bind up the loose-leaf sacred books (information from Tsering Gyalpo). Bands used as a sash around the *chuba* were an item of prestige and decoration. Often decoratively embellished, useful accessories are hung from it: a purse (Tib. *baghu*), a small case for the fire steel (Tib. *me lcag*), a needle case (Tib. *khabung*), or a short sword in a silver sheath set with stones, which can also be carried by women.

Corresponding with the bands' important practical and also decorative functions, their woven designs are full of symbolism. Often found are Buddhist motifs: *swastika*, vase of life with sacred water, butter lamp and bell, also the Chinese *Shou* symbol for longevity. These motifs are woven in the band with the wish that they convey and secure beneficial influence to the wearer. A constant element is the rainbow-coloured outer stripes which reflect the Tibetan concept of the hierarchically structured world, which is represented by the colours. In this way, the wearer of the band is included in this sacred order. In no other medium of Tibetan textile art is the definition of symbols by Mircea Eliade (1987: 137) realised so meaningfully: "They are manifestations of the sacred that connects us to ultimate structures of realities of man and cosmos". The different widths of tablet-woven bands correlates with their intended use (Ronge 1978b: 238). Bands for aprons and boots are 1 to 2 centimetres wide (Figs. 34a and 34b). For shoulder bands, 3 to 4 centimetres is usual, and the broadest bands shown here are 5 centimetres and more (Figs. 32 and 33), and could, therefore, have been used as a sash, which was usually wrapped twice around the waist. Ronge has recognised a certain concept in the order and distribution of motifs on sashes which relates to their length. On one band, it can be observed that on the end of the band that is first wrapped around the body there is a simple design, since this part cannot be seen. Then there are individual motifs separated by horizontal lines. On the last portion, which is most visible, the most complicated figures have been woven.

MOTIFS

In the motifs in the middle section the length of the bands is consistently in the colours black and white, and white and black on the reverse side of the band, which can usually be worn with either side exposed. On wider bands (see Fig. 36), red and blue stripes can separate the stripes of black and white. Often the patterned area of the band is bordered at the edge with the aforementioned rainbow-coloured lines (cloud-rainbow), to be seen almost everywhere in red, green, yellow and blue. If available, bright pink, violet or orange may be included.

The individual motifs that decorate the bands can vary greatly in their ornamental style, from naturalistic to an abstract, stylised form for the same motif. The combinations of the motifs produce complex compositions that reflect the weaver's surroundings, family economy and religion. The bands allow a unique insight into a complex cultural inheritance that cross-culturally brings together the panoply of symbols from pre-Buddhist civilisation with those from Buddhism and China.

Often animal motifs are found that relate to "Eurasian animal style art," such as the native grazing and hoofed animals: stags, ibex, antelope (see Figs. 34 to 36). The presence of these animals indicates their importance as grazing animals and as game for the nomadic population in the region, who depend on them for sustenance. Another band shows a great variety of animals: in addition to horses and stags, also donkeys and sheep or rams. The stag, which dominates on many bands, can be immediately recognised by his impressive antlers. The prominent representation of hoofed animals recalls their significance as mounts for different local deities, such as Dorje Chenmo, who is especially venerated in West Tibet. On the earliest murals in Tabo monastery (Spiti, early 11th century), she is shown riding on a stag. A recently found illustrated manuscript for the death cult, which seems to be from the Bon tradition, underlines the significance of various animals – especially the stag – in local pre-Buddhist traditions (Bellezza 2013).

On some bands, animals are shown in pairs, often suggesting a mother and her young. Very surprisingly, the yak – so important economically – is not shown on the bands. Birds are found only on one band (see Figs. 34a and 34b), although they are very frequently found in rock paintings. Anthropomorphic figures are also common. They are often quite geometricised and sometimes have hybrid, zoomorphic characters (see the frog-like creature in Fig. 32). In one case human figures have been very naturalistically woven (see Fig. 35). Animal-human hybrids are often found on Tibetan petroglyphs. Questions about what they represent and their meaning have not been finally clarified, since there are no written sources, as there are for the institutionalised religious traditions. Often the weaver apparently wanted to show a large variety of different motifs to create a particularly rich visual impression and to increase the decorative value of the piece.

The panoply of animal motifs with their succinct stylisation is the result of a long history of development and recalls the "Eurasian animal style art". They are comparable with the petroglyphs and rock paintings left by early nomadic groups in North and West Tibet. John Vincent Bellezza has documented (Bellezza 2000) ca. 100 such findings on the Tibetan plateau known as Changthang and *tod* (pronounced *to*). They cover a long time span of more than 3,000 years and document the long cultural constancy of the motifs. The permanence of the medium and the location on important routes could allow this "image portfolio" of rock art to serve as models for other genres, even to the present day. Similar motifs are found in rock art in the Indus valley, which were discovered for the West by Jettmar (Jettmar & Thewalt 1985), for example in Thalpan, where a branch of trade routes connects Central Asia with Tibet and India.

Among the non-representational motifs on bands, the *swastika* is found – as in the rock art. The *swastika* is a key symbol both in different religious traditions and in the cosmological concepts in the region. It occurs both with the ends pointing counter-clockwise, which is a symbol of the Bon religion, or with the ends pointing clockwise, which in Buddhist symbolism signifies the indestructibility of the Buddhist path (Beer 2003: 98). Another frequently found symbol is the endless knot, which in Tibetan Buddhism is considered one of the Eight Auspicious Symbols (Sanskrit *Aṣṭamaṅgala*, Tib. *bkra shis rtags brgyad*, pronounced *tashi tagye*). It is also a symbol that represents the intertwining of wisdom and compassion. A motif could also represent religious paraphernalia, such as the highly stylised butter lamp (Tib. *mar me*) (Fig. 31) as is often seen on bands.

Another motif is a sort of double trident that represents the Chinese *Shou* symbol for longevity (see Fig. 33). It is an adaptation of the Chinese character with that meaning and is a very frequently used symbol in Tibet, where it can be a medallion or in angular form, as on the bands. In Tibet it is considered a symbol for good fortune in general (Jones 1996: 439; Ronge 1978b: Fig. 3). Repeating patterns on bands are often meanders that recall Chinese ornamentation, also motifs that are called "Chinese wall" or "iron fence with column-heads" (Band no. 20; Ronge 1978b: Figs. 1d to 1f). There also occur staggered T-motifs and interlinked *swastikas* as a continuous pattern, like those often seen on the Chinese silk brocades of magnificent Tibetan religious robes.

Fig. 32: Details of both sides of a tablet-woven sash. Damchung region, 20th c., 5×229 cm

Fig. 33: Detail of a tablet-woven sash. Damchung region, 20th c., 5.4×88 cm

Figs. 34a and 34b: Details of a pair of tablet-woven bands for fastening boots. Damchung region, 20th c., 2.8×103 and 2.8×102 cm

Fig. 35: Details of both sides of a tablet-woven sash or shoulder band. Damchung region, 20th c., 2×208 cm

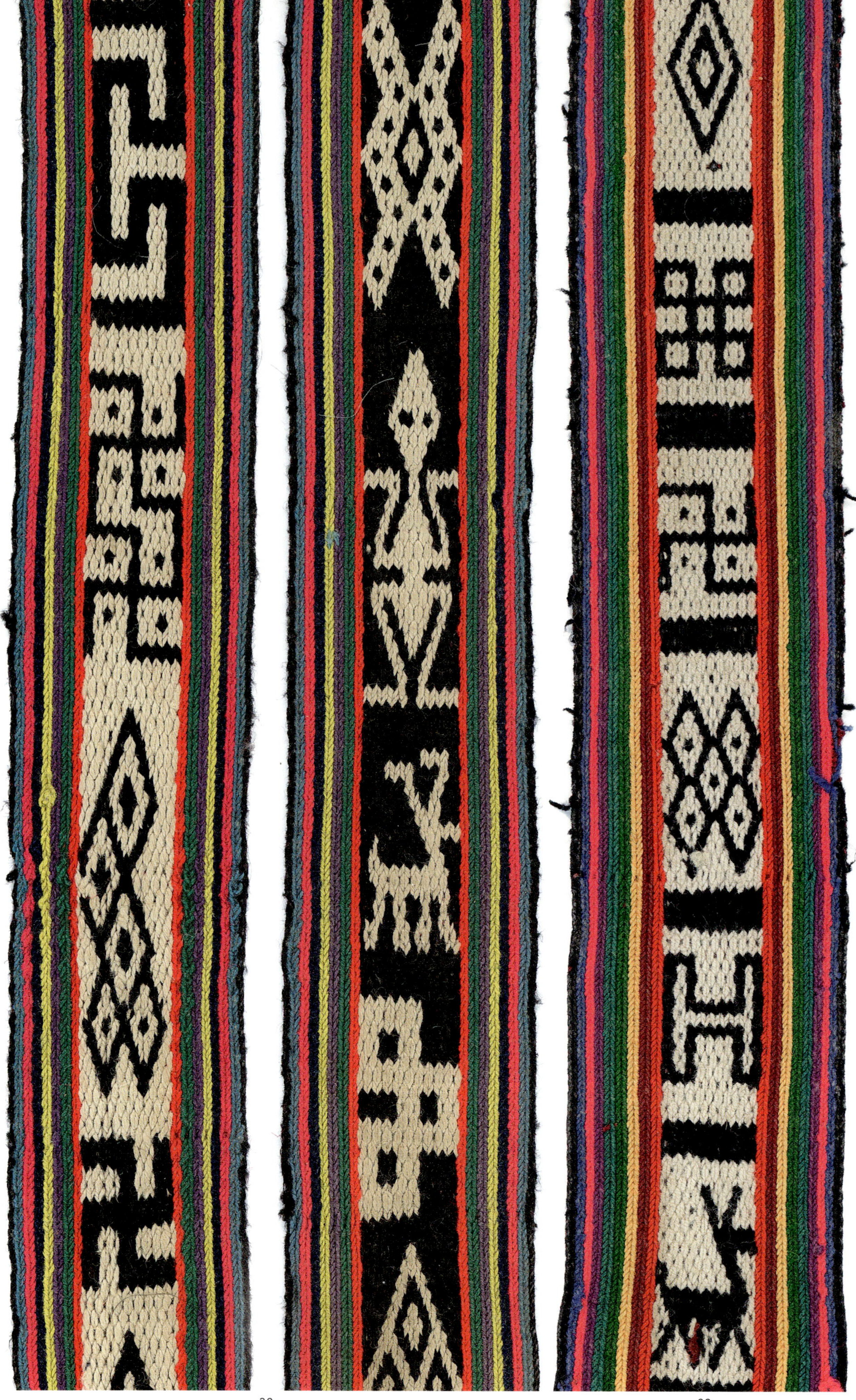

32

33

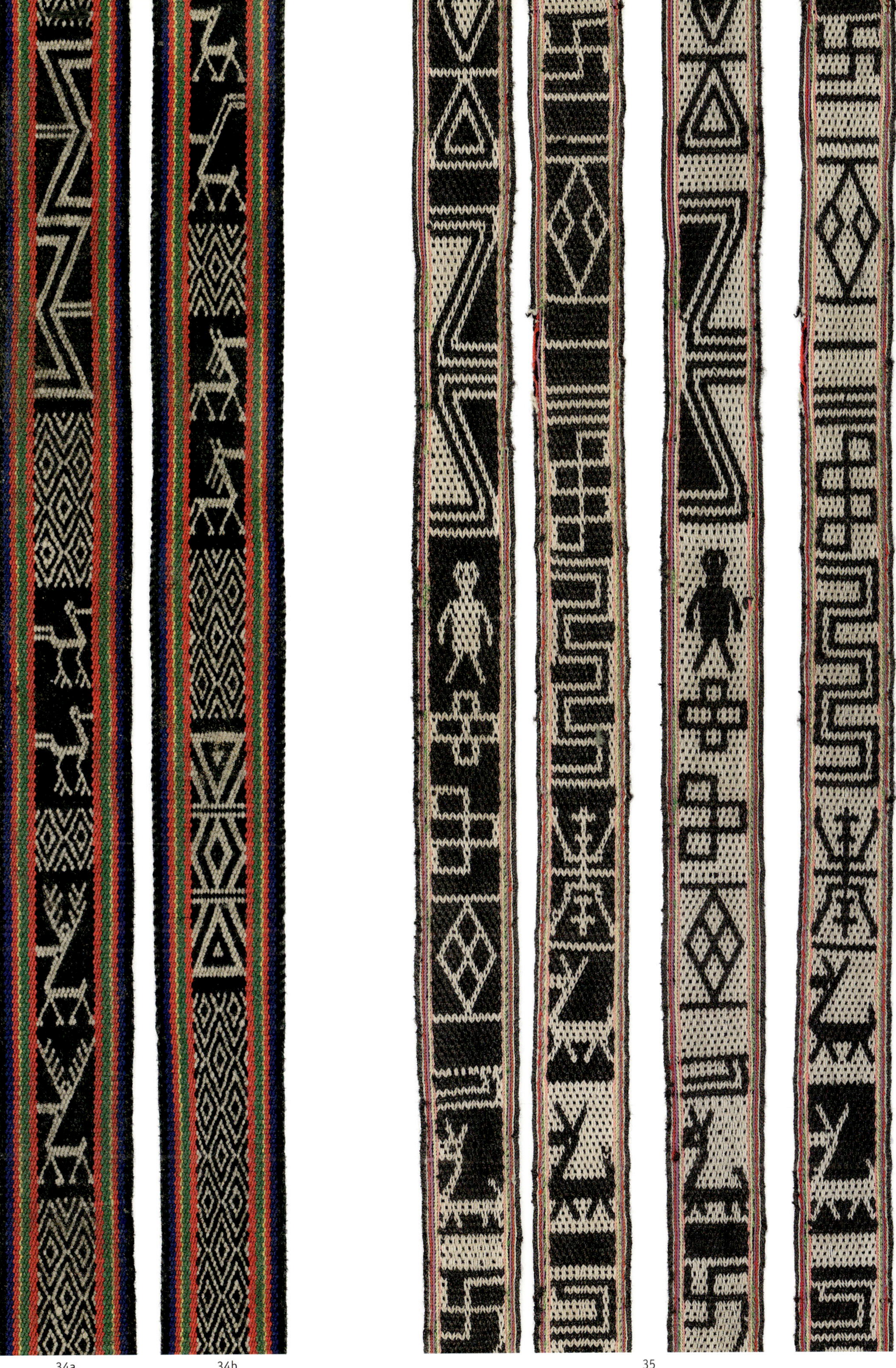

34a 34b 35

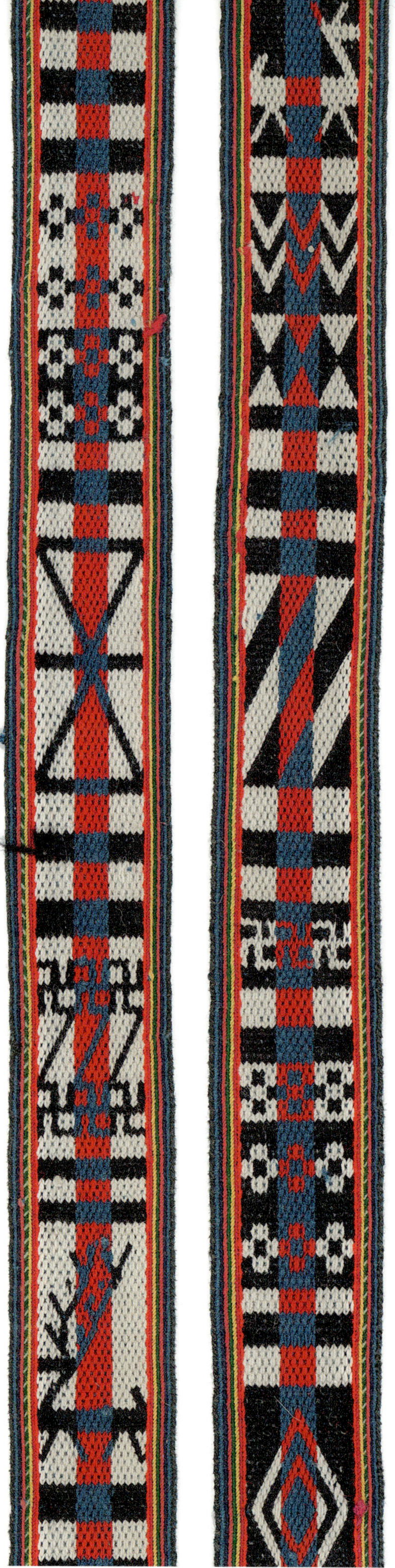

Fig. 36: Details of both sides of a tablet-woven sash or shoulder band. Damchung region, 20th c., 3 × 193 cm

Often other ornamental motifs are plaited elements, such as the often-seen rhomboids, which create an interlocking design. These designs can be interpreted either as purely ornamental/decorative, or they relate to the "thread-cross" (Tib. *mdos*), which has a protective function (see Beer 2003: 214). Other popular designs are a chessboard and diagonal checkered pattern. Ahmed associated the latter with Ladakhi board games. Herringbone designs, which are also called "beak of a small bird" (Tib. *byi phrug kha*; Ronge 1978b: 240), are also often found.

Other repeating patterns are rhomboids, zigzags, waves and lattices. In many of these patterns one could also see eyes, as they are found on *gzi* stones and incorporated in the decoration of slings, where they are intended as protective amulets.

In summary, it should be noted that the décor motifs on these bands relate to the folk religious traditions of the nomads and semi-nomads in their natural environment and to the animals as their economic basis, with a focus on them as symbols of affluence and life force. Symbols such as the knot, *swastika* and Chinese characters for good fortune are not only key symbols of different religious cultural traditions. On the everyday religious level, the wearer of the objects "empowered" by these symbols combines the wish to propitiate supernatural forces and secure continued well-being and prosperity.

We find, therefore, a symbolism of pre-Buddhist animal style art spanning the cultures with Buddhist emblems which originated in India and elements from the sphere of fortuitous Chinese symbolism. The textiles and bands in the collection provide an excellent overview of the processes of an intercultural and inter-religious dialogue as part of the exchange in Central Asia.

From the rich treasure of more than two dozen tablet-woven bands in the Buddeberg collection and their many more motifs, only a few can be seen here, and those only partially:

Sash (Figs. 32 and 33)

Mainly black and white, with multi-coloured border stripes and many different motifs: animal, *swastika*, reptile (?). One end is finished with careful plaiting. As a man's sash, it would be wrapped twice around the waist and joined at the front with the fringes decoratively hanging down. Tsering Gyalpo has explained another use in the privacy of polyandrous families (brothers married to one woman, in West

Tibet an historical and still existing practice). There it is usual that before going to bed, the sash of the brother who is to spend the night with the wife is hung on the door.

Pair of Bands for Boots (Figs. 34a and 34b)

These are a pair of very finely woven bands, which the local informant in Damchung explained were used to fasten shoes, which agrees with their dimensions: 103 × 2.8 and 102 × 2.8 centimetres. Remarkable are the floating warps on the reverse sides of the bands.

Sash or Shoulder Band (Fig. 35)

An extremely finely woven band, mainly black and white with narrow, varicoloured borders. The ends differ, having a longer and a shorter section with a simple pattern. This could suggest its use as a decorative sash with the more decorative end being exposed. Bands of this type could also be used to bind up Tibetan books, after they had been wrapped in cloth.

Sash or Shoulder Band (Fig. 36)

Mainly black and white with a centre stripe in blue and red. It is very finely woven with decorative, geometrical figures, animals and *swastikas*. Here also the asymmetrical distribution of the motifs is seen. The end of the sash with the more complex motifs, ending with long fringes, would cover the other end with its simple pattern of rhomboids.

NOTES

1 This is an excerpt from a song that women in Ladakh sing annually at the start of the weaving season (Ahmed 2002: 94; translated by the author).

2 My thanks go to Prof. Dr. Jürgen Wasim Frembgen, Museum Fünf Kontinente, Munich, for his inspiring ideas, his manifold assistance and his interest in my work. Special thanks go to my admired research colleague and dear friend Professor Tsering Gyalpo, Tibetan Academy of Social Sciences (TASS, Lhasa), the expedition leader of many joint undertakings in West and Central Tibet, who provided important information about the use of textiles in this article. My work is dedicated to the memory of Guge Tsering Gyalpo and his family in Lhasa and Ngari. The structural analyses of several of the textiles discussed was made by Britta Schwenck, restorer of textiles, Schönbrunn Palace, Vienna. These are published in the appendix.

3 The analyses are the results of research from some projects together with and under the leadership of Dr. Christian Jahoda and Prof. Tsering Gyalpo: P21806-G19 "Society, power and religion in premodern Western Tibet: Interaction, conflict and integration" and P20637-G15 "Oral and Festival Traditions", both led by Christian Jahoda, Institute for Social Anthropology (ISA), Austrian Academy of Sciences, Vienna. The projects were financed by the Austrian Science Research Fund (FWF).

4 Prof. Charles Ramble, Oxford University, oral information, May 2006.

5 The research work in Tabo was conducted in cooperation with and under the leadership of Dr. Christian Jahoda in the context of the FWF research project P20637-G15 "Oral and Festival Traditions" of the Institute for Social Anthropology (ISA), Austrian Academy of Sciences, Vienna.

6 *bog* in Ladakh; another term is *rgyab sle*: see Müller & Raunig 1982: 163.

7 The provenience of this apron is uncertain due to lack of data; it will be a subject for further research.

8 For similar pieces, see Ahmed 2002: 152.

9 For a similar example from Central Tibet, see Buckley 2011: 36–37.

10 A detailed, illustrated analysis of this instrument can be looked up in Sophie Desrosiers' "Beschreibung einer tibetischen Schleuder" (1982: 177). LaRocca (2006: 277, 280) has assembled a glossary of Tibetan terms and in Jones (1996: 166–167) the use by nomads is described (for similar pieces, see Hummel 1956/57).

11 Müller & Raunig 1982: 144; for an example, see also Köpke & Schmelz 2005: 851.

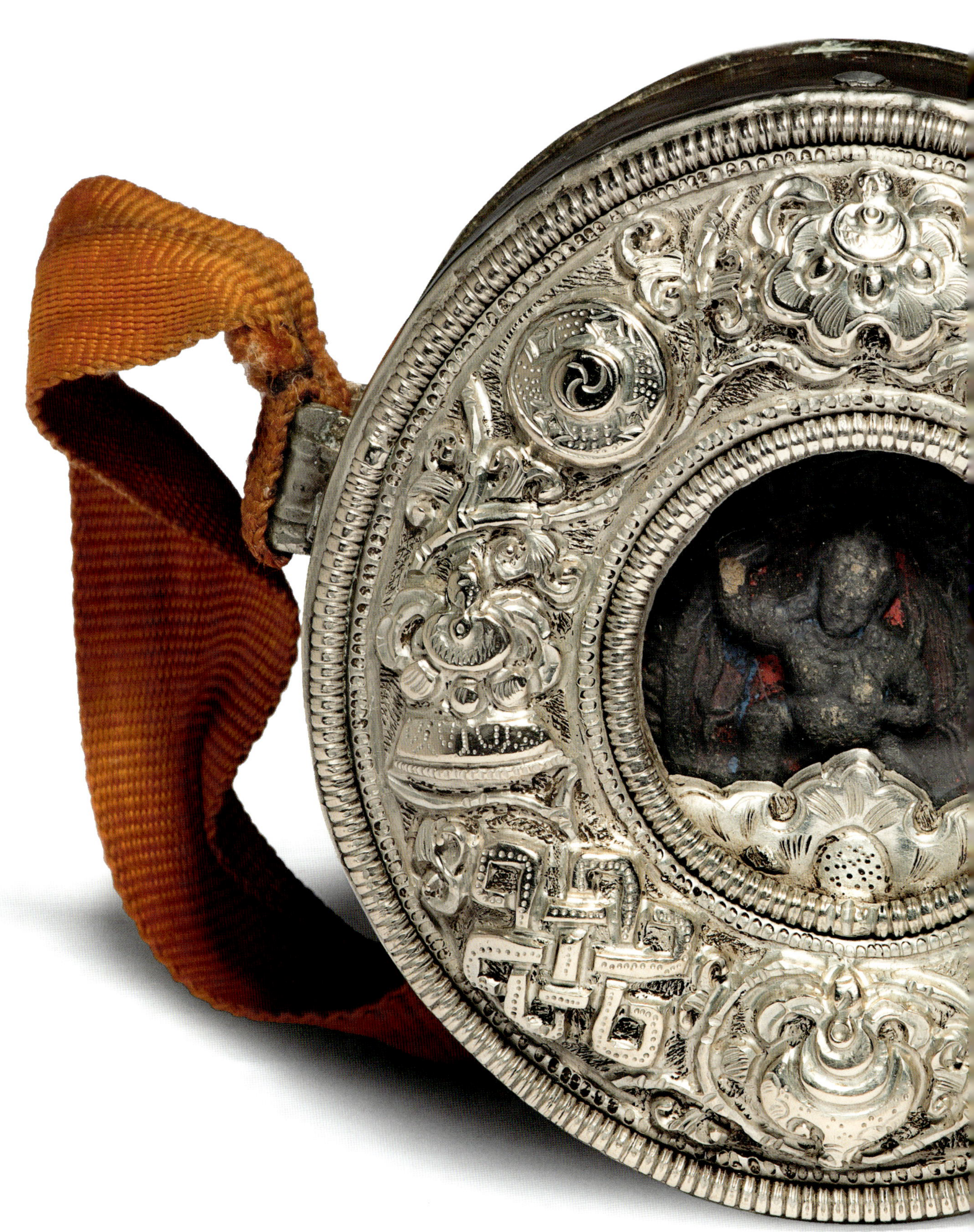

METALWORK AND JEWELLERY

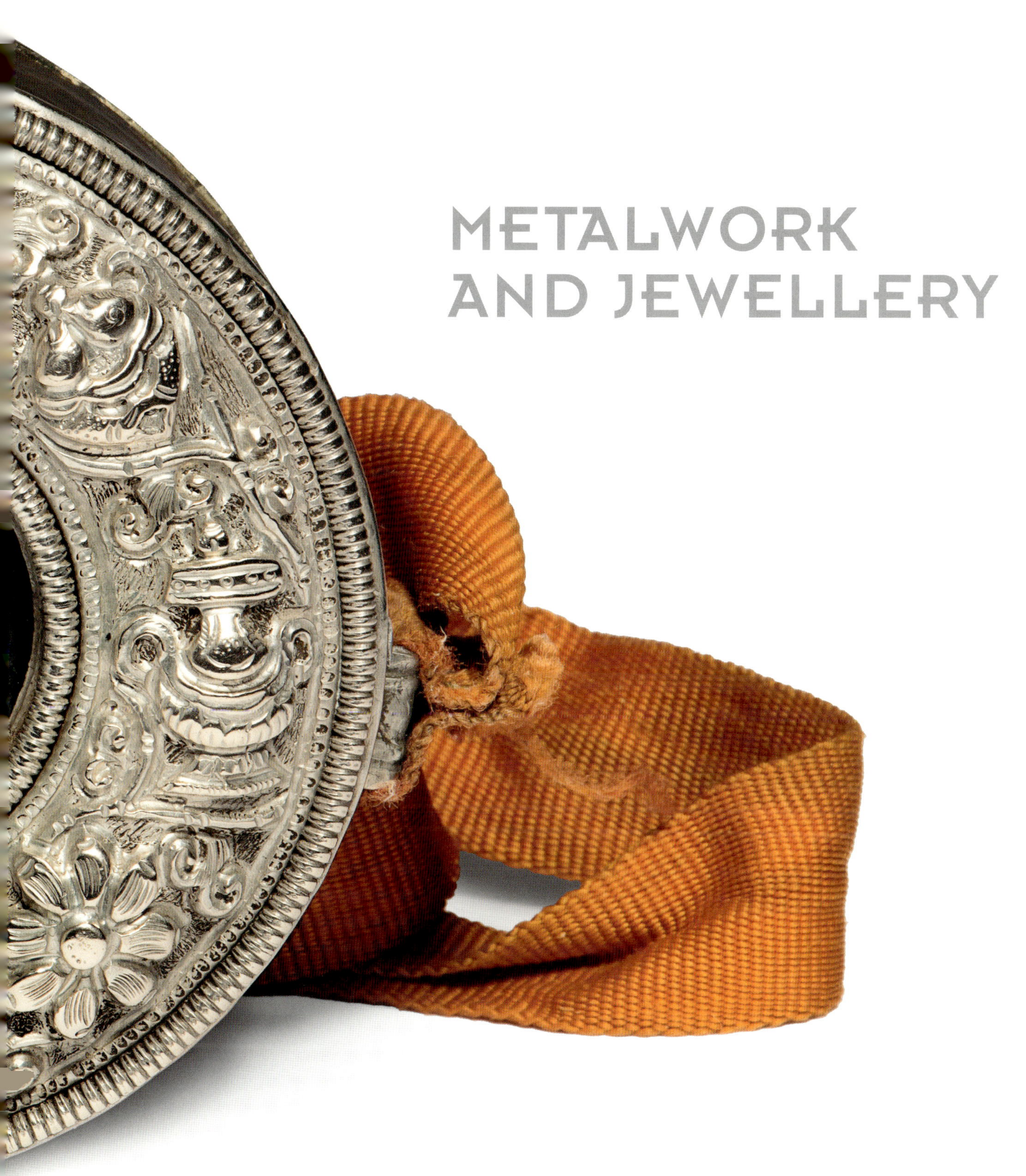

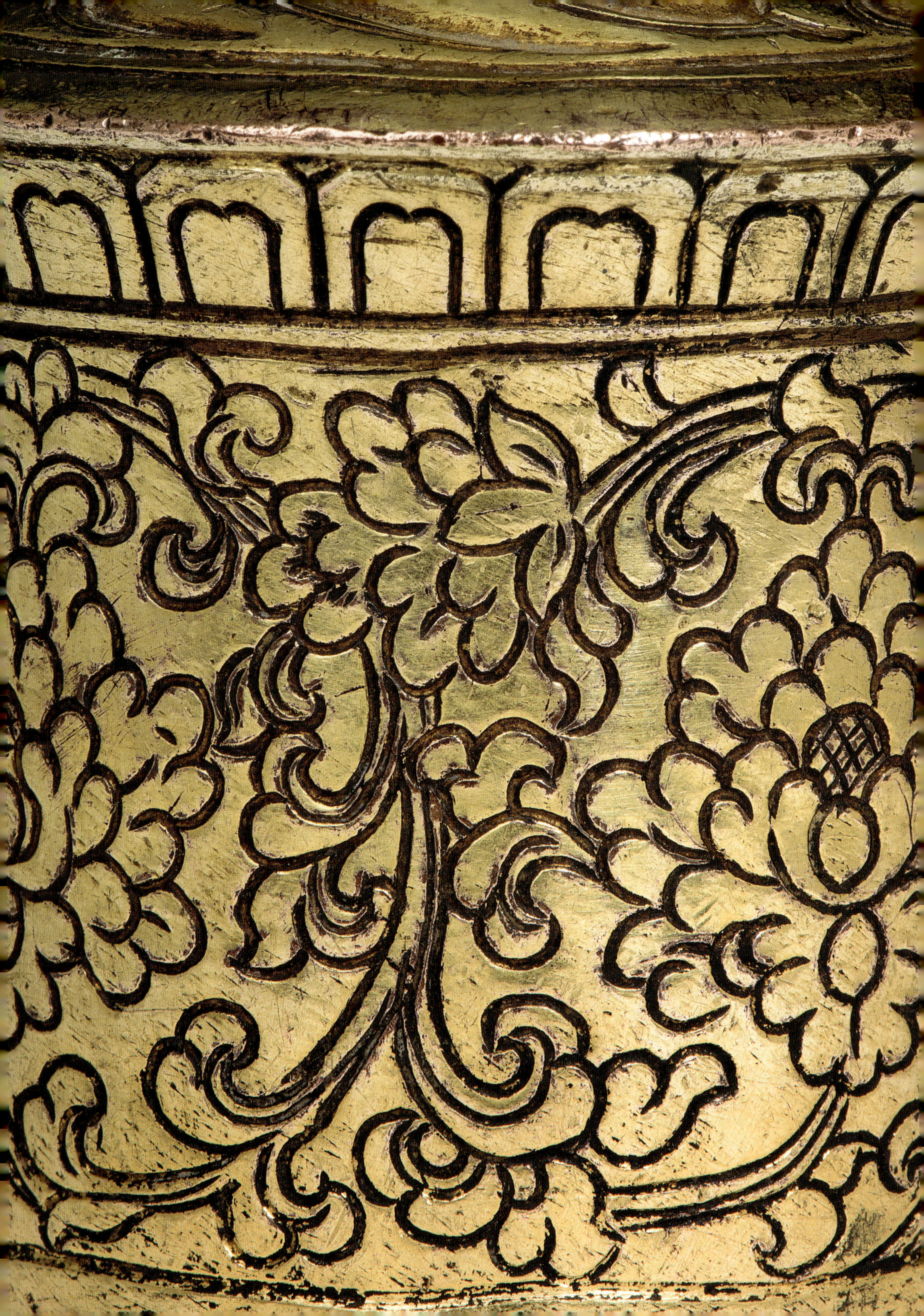

Friedrich Spuhler

END CAPS FOR THANGKA RODS

A Special Group of Sino-Tibetan Metal Objects

Preceding double page: amulet container or reliquary; see Fig. 14 in the contribution by Weihreter

Left page: Detail of Fig. 27

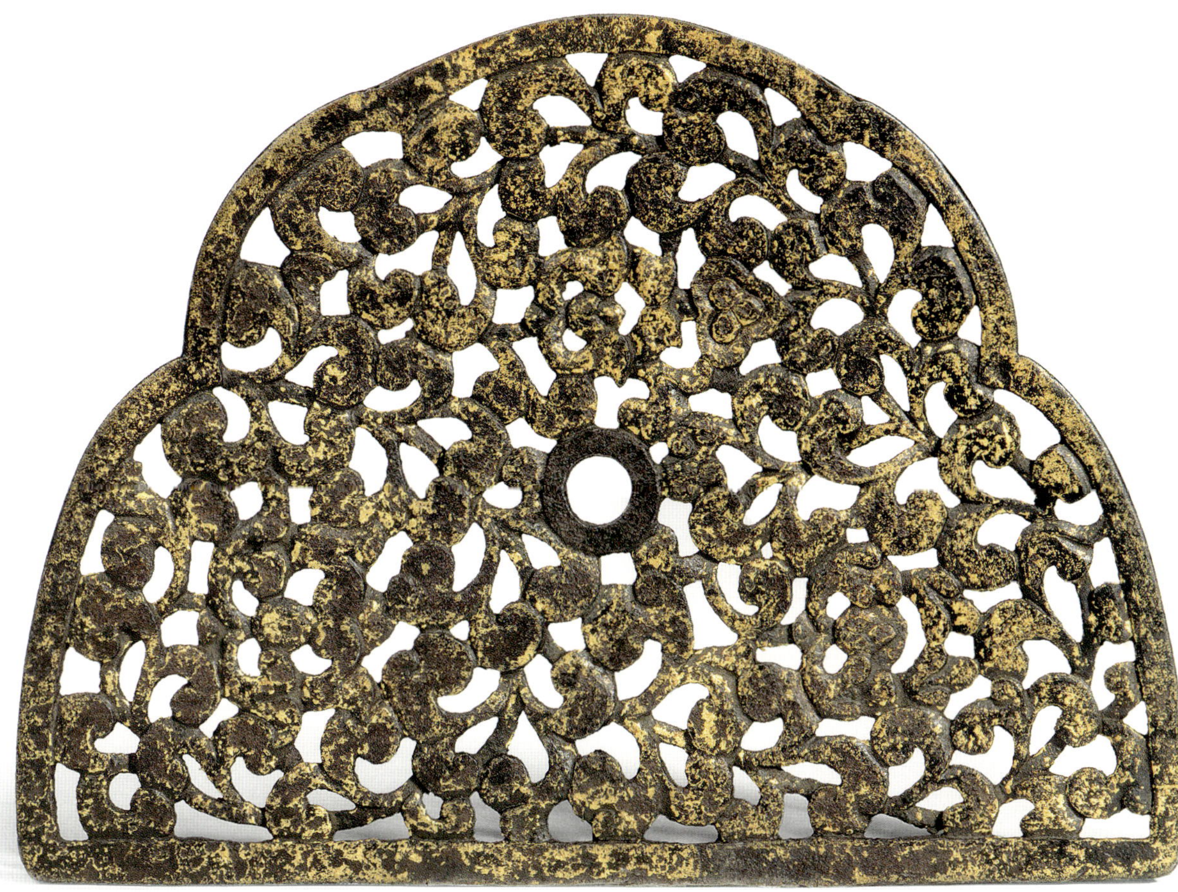

Fig. 1: End piece of door hinge, openwork iron with traces of gilding. Tibet, 17th c., H. 13.8 cm, B. 19.1 cm, WT. 4 mm, Wt. 350 g

INTRODUCTION

The Tibetan-Nepalese cultural sphere is unique in its almost inexhaustible variety of iron artefacts, including tools and other implements as well as decorative and ritual objects. Iron hinges and other fittings are indispensable features on the doors of every monastery. Iron is used for many things, from the decoration of saddles and harnesses, to the manufacture of weapons. It is present in everything, from plain functional items to elaborately decorated objects. There is almost no other culture throughout all historical epochs in which iron has been used in so many ways. The existing overviews of Tibetan-Nepalese art, most of which are of a "general" nature, invariably identify Derge in East Tibet as the original geographical source for such ironwork. It is doubtful, however, whether this sweeping generalisation provides an accurate explanation for the great diversity of these works, in terms of either place or time.

For decades, monographs on the history of Tibetan art have focused on Buddha statues and *thangka* paintings. Only recently have two new approaches been developed which offer a more nuanced representation. One is Günter

Grünbold's catalogue of the collection of wooden book covers held in Munich by the Bavarian State Library (1991). The other is Donald LaRocca's collection of articles about "Warriors of the Himalayas" (2006), which accompanied a remarkably comprehensive special exhibition at the Metropolitan Museum of Art in New York. I would like to propose John Clarke's article, "A History of Ironworking in Tibet. Centers of Production, Styles and Techniques" (2006), as a basic classification of the many diverse types of utensils and implements: we can differentiate between massive iron objects with polished silver- and gilded ornamentation, and a second more open type. In the case of the latter, a pattern consisting of several levels of intertwining tendrils is cut into a comparatively thick layer of iron. The surface is then polished and often further decorated with threads of gold and silver.

Large sheets of iron are used whenever stability is particularly important. Door hinges, which often have to support considerable weight, are a prime example (Fig. 1). Locks need to be robust as well. Where iron strips are used as a decorative trim, they are generally in delicate filigree, as seen on most saddles. In this context they may be regarded as purely ornamental, since they have no other function.

The highpoint of this perfect craftsmanship is represented by massive thick iron pieces featuring up to three levels of horizontal interlacing tendrils. Their surface is polished and usually embellished with gold and silver. They are most commonly found on horse harnesses. It is still to be investigated whether the differences in techniques can be related to individual workshops or regions.

According to Clarke's research (LaRocca 2006: 21), which focuses on what is doubtless the main area of metalwork – weaponry – metallurgy techniques were already well-developed among the Sasanians and Sogdians, and already known in Tibet by the 7th or 8th century at the latest. He states that the art of metalwork reached its pinnacle during the reign of Emperor Yongle (1403 to 1424), when contacts between Tibet and China were particularly intense.

The establishment of monasteries boomed throughout Tibet from the 13th to the 17th century. One may assume that every large monastery construction site also contained workshops for metallurgy and carpentry. This suggests the existence of local variations in style. To my knowledge, no research has yet been published in this field. A prerequisite for such research, which ought to proceed from an assumption of stylistic differences, would be groups of metal objects known to be connected to significant monasteries. With some luck, historical data contained in construction records should yield information on the scope of the building projects and the associated tasks involved, as well as about individual groups of craftsmen and the regions from whence they came. Existing attempts to classify items are based on the differences in their appearance, and as signatures are rarely found there is no basis for establishing their age and place of origin. An exception would be some rare engravings referring to Emperor Yongle.

At present, consulting the building records, and where possible tax and trade records, seems the only method which might promise better results.

Whenever different ages are suggested for various objects in the following text, they are based on the development from complex and aesthetically highly refined work in the 15th to 17th centuries to the simplification and less precise workmanship of the 19th century. This dating is guided by western concepts of art history, however, whose application may be questionable in relation to craftsmanship in the Far East.

END CAPS FOR THANGKA RODS

The cloth on which a *thangka* is painted is rolled up on a wooden rod, which is usually 2 to 3 centimetres in diameter. The ends of the rod are covered by metal caps, which are held in both hands when the *thangka* is being rolled up. Nowadays *thangkas* are only rarely found with their original coverings. When they arrived in western museums and collections, they were unfortunately adapted to the European notion of painting: the cloth borders were removed, as well as the "veil" that usually covered the picture scroll in the monastery, and the *thangkas* were displayed in European-style frames. In this way their ritualistic nature was lost.

As the component parts of the end caps are the same in all specimens, I have chosen to apply the term "cylinder" to the part of the end cap which sits on both ends of the wooden rod and which features the primary decoration. As for the shape of the round cover on top of the cylinder, I will distinguish between "flat" and "convex". Measurements are always given in the same sequence: height (H.); greatest breadth, usually the diameter of the top cover (B.); wall thickness (WT. or WT. n.g., "not given", for example where no measurement has been made, perhaps because of irregularities in the shape of the edge); and weight (Wt.).

End Cap (Fig. 2)

This end cap is one of the most exquisite in the collection. Between two horizontal rings is an openwork carved relief with at least two layers. The slender, spotted serpentine

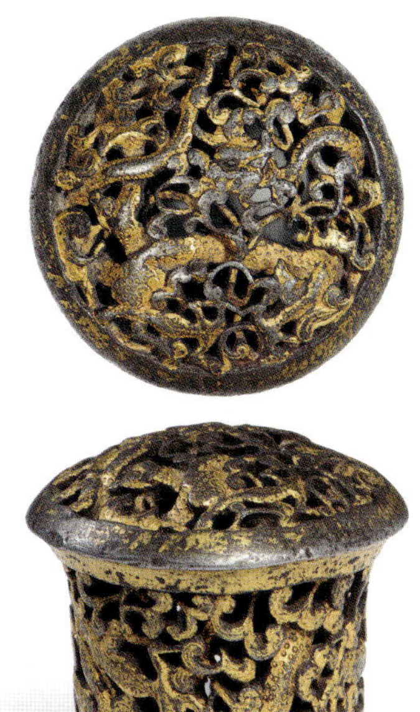

body of a dragon with the head of a *Makara* slithers through a tangle of tendrils, which typically end in pairs of leaves curving away from each other. This can be regarded as the classic tendril design to be found on rosettes (Fig. 51) and other decorations for harnesses and saddles (Fig. 50), as well as on porcelain bowl holders (LaRocca 2006: 20). It had become a regular feature in the ornamentation of Tibetan ironwork by the 16th century at the latest. The slightly convex top of the end cap is decorated with the same tendrils and dragon motif (similar pieces for comparison in LaRocca 2006: 220, pl. 113; 221, pl. 114).

Fig. 2: Iron, openwork, surface polished and gilded. 15th/16th c., H. 4.4 cm, B. 4.4 cm, WT. 0.6 cm, Wt. 115 g

Detail of Fig. 2

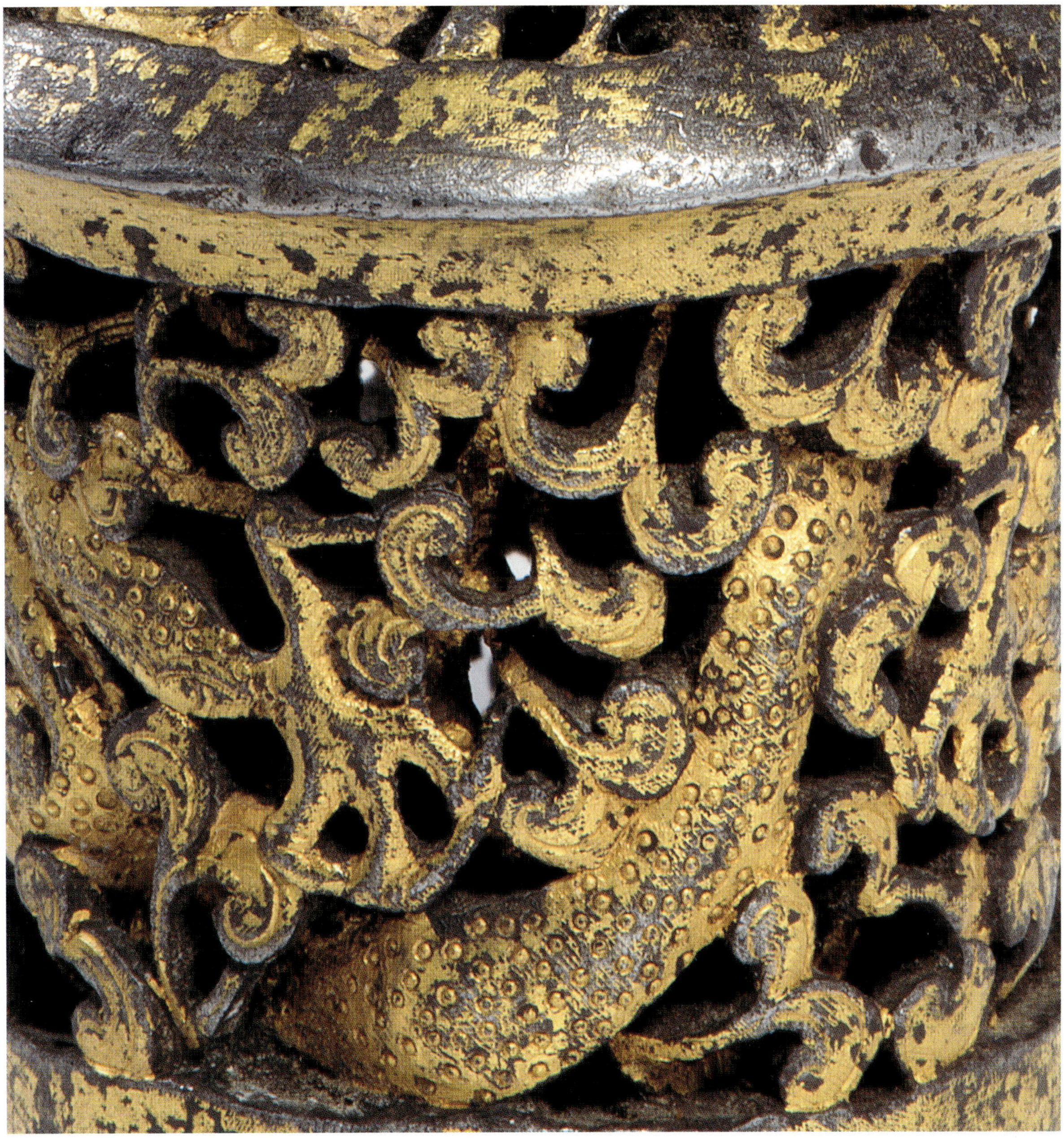

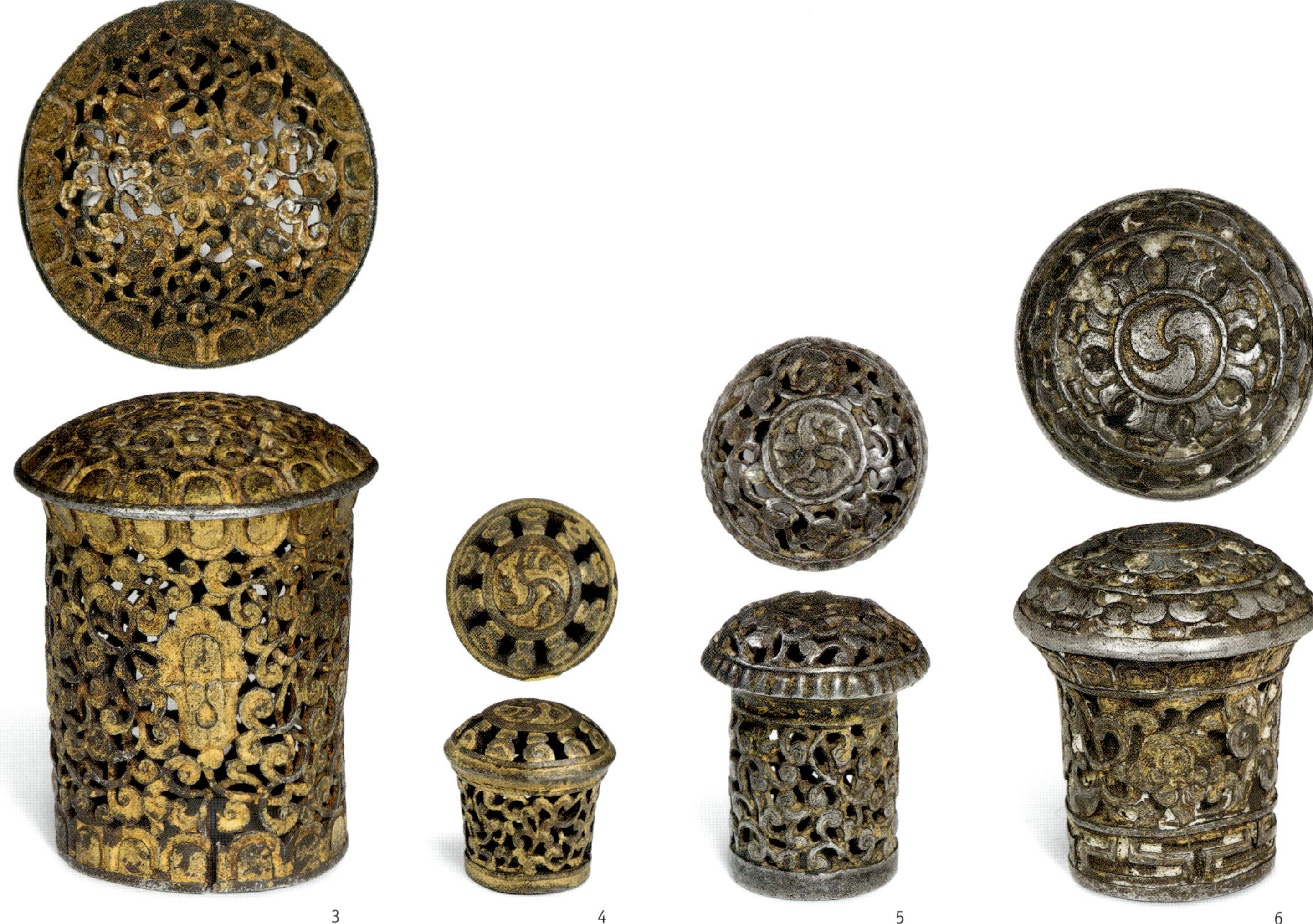

Fig. 3: Iron, openwork, surface polished and gilded. 15th/16th c., H. 7.2 cm, B. 5.8 cm, WT. 0.3 cm, Wt. 119 g

Fig. 4: Iron, openwork, surface gilded. 16th c., H. 2.95 cm, B. 3 cm, WT. 0.3 cm, Wt. 29 g

Fig. 5: Iron, openwork and gilded. 16th c., H. 4.45 cm, B. 3.85 cm, WT. 0.2 cm, Wt. 40 g

Fig. 6: Iron, openwork tendril motif, solid top. 16th c., H. 5.6 cm, B. 5.05 cm, WT. 0.5 cm, Wt. 145 g

End Cap (Fig. 3)

The cylinder segment consists of a perfectly designed double-layered pattern of intertwining tendrils. They end in a multitude of harmonious scrolls, each of which tapers gently towards the centre, suggesting an analogy with the scroll at the head of a violin's neck. Half way up the cylinder is a sort of palmette rising from a flower calyx. This is most probably a reference to the subject of a specific *thangka*. Both ends of the cylinder segment end with a row of scales. This is repeated along the edge of the convex top as the basic design for the pattern of tendrils which grow towards the centre. From the 14th century onward, this flawlessly executed tendril motif is generally ascribed to Chinese craftsmanship (LaRocca 2006: 221, pl. 114; 248, pl. 134, and Spuhler 2007: 252, Fig. 1).

End Cap (Fig. 4)

The horizontal panel features densely intertwined tendrils in the usual stylised manner. The convex top consists of an inner solid disk segmented by windmill-like arms. The central disk is connected to the rim of the cylinder by rows of scrolls. The interlaced tendrils correspond to the classic style of the 16th century.

End Cap (Fig. 5)

The cylinder is made up of intertwined openwork tendrils, ending in the familiar rolled-up "buds" and hinting at traces of the original gilding. The same pattern appears on the convex top, whose edge has a solid serrated rim. This piece can be dated to the same classic period as the previous one.

End Cap (Fig. 6)

A double base consisting of longish horizontal openings supports a relatively short cylinder featuring a pattern of intertwining tendrils. Traces of the original gilding have survived on the surface. The top is solid, showing grooves from the original damascene work. Its concentric bands are decorated with rows of paired petals, which can be interpreted as the beginnings of a row of blossoms.

Detail of Fig. 4

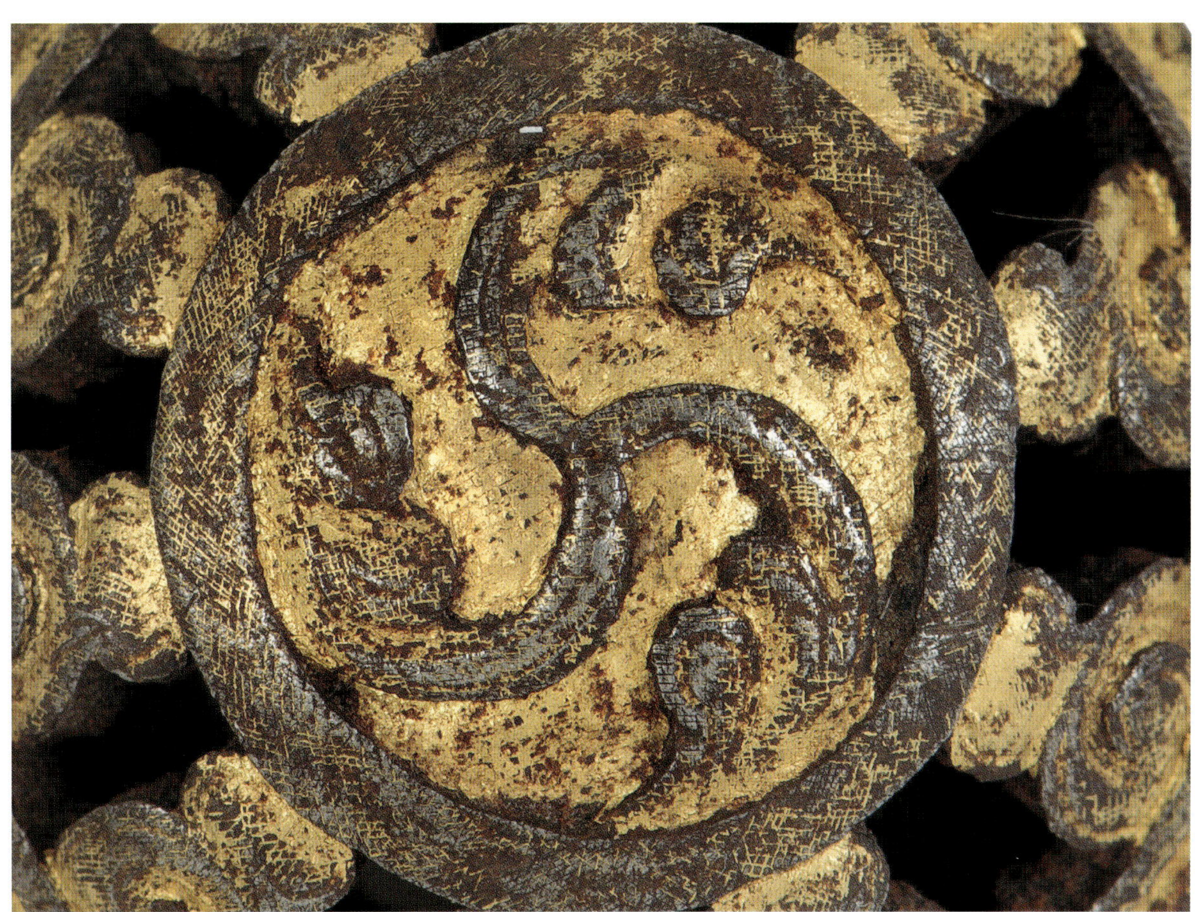

Detail of Fig. 6

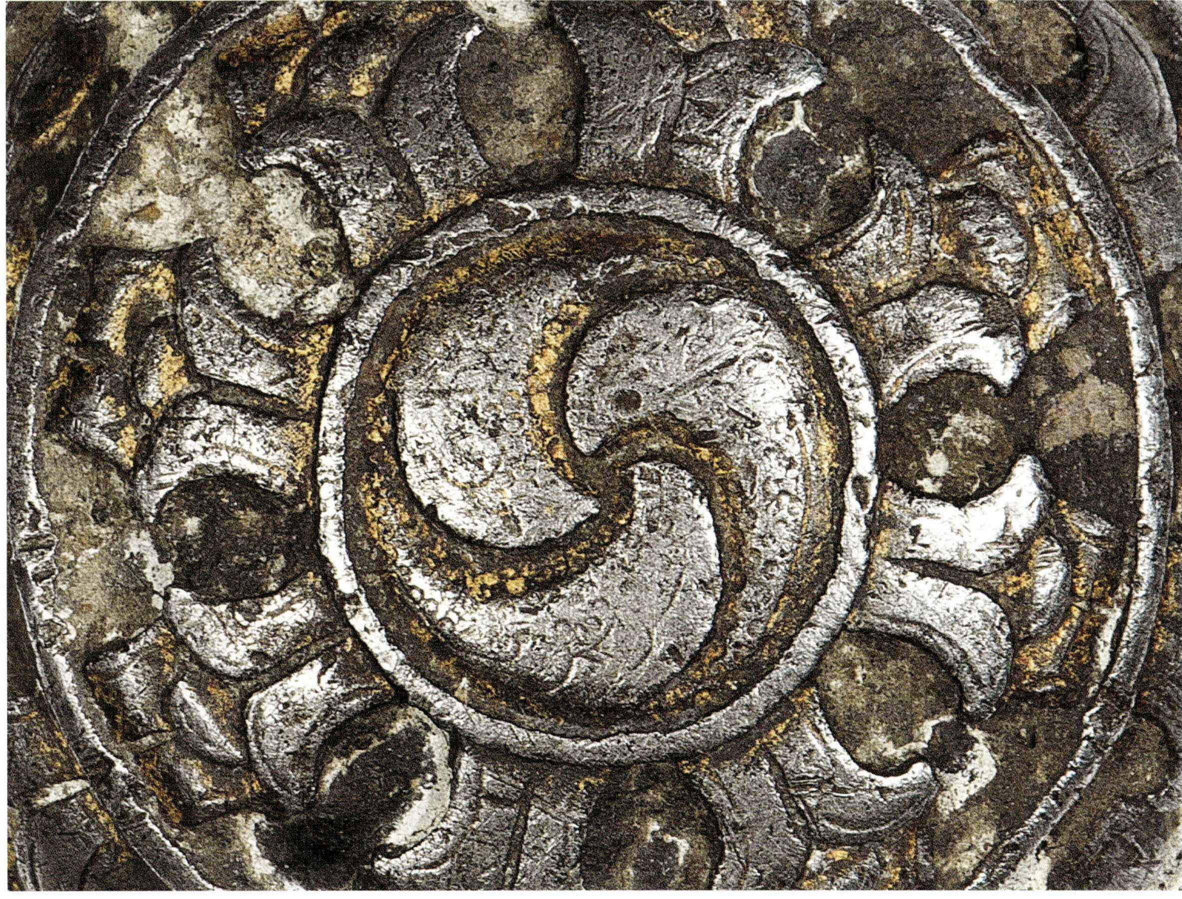

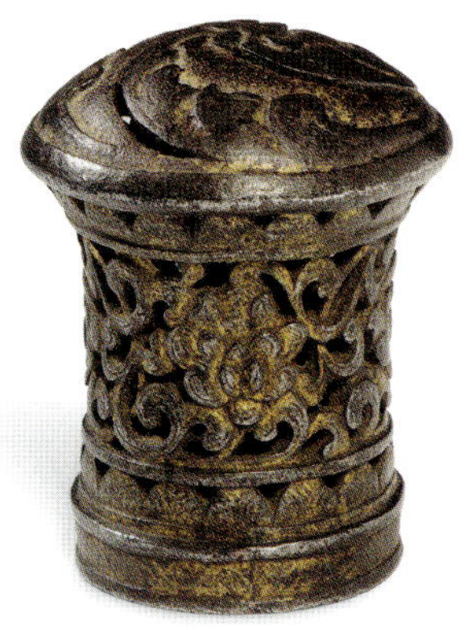
7

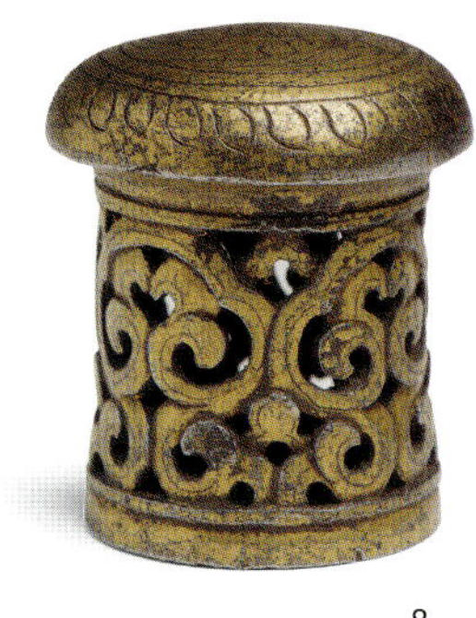
8

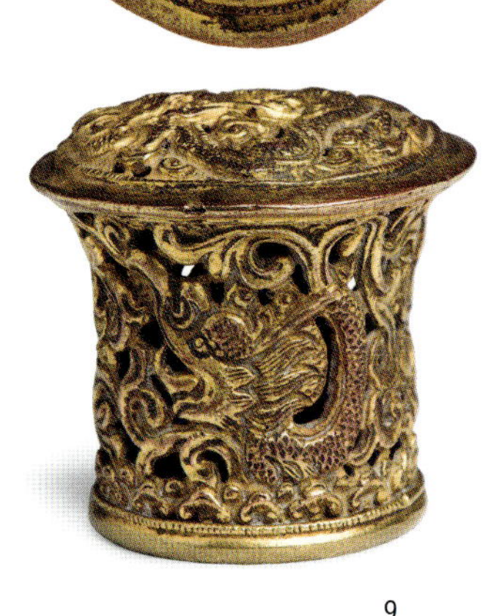
9

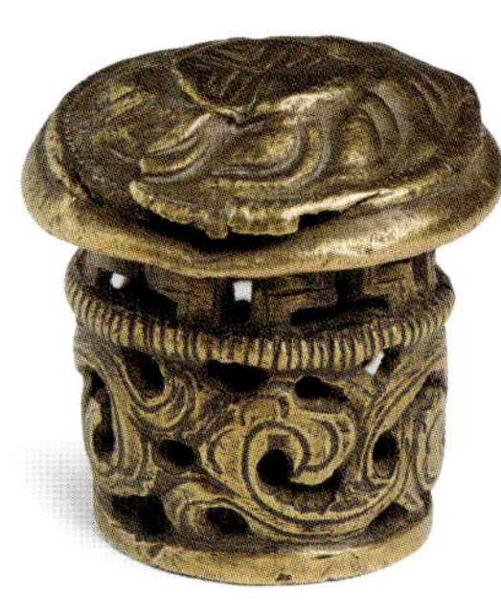
10

Fig. 7: Iron, tendrils on solid background. 16th c., H. 4.85 cm, B. 4.8 cm, WT. 0.3 cm, Wt. 65 g

Fig. 8: Iron, openwork ornamentation. 17th c., H. 3.95 cm, B. 3.5 cm, WT. 0.3 cm, Wt. 59 g

Fig. 9: Embossed brass sheet, partially openwork. 18th/19th c., H. 4.2 cm, B. 4.4 cm, WT. n.g., Wt. 29 g

Fig. 10: Brass, cast (?) and openwork. 18th c., H. 3.85 cm, B. 3.5 cm, WT. n.g., Wt. 37 g

Fig. 11: Solid iron, gold and silver damascene. 16th/17th c., H. 6.4 cm, B. 5.62 cm, WT. 0.3 cm, Wt. 230 g

End Cap (Fig. 7)

The base of this cap consists of two different rings: one with engraved diagonal lines in a trellis motif, above it a ring of striped leaf-ends. The intertwining pattern with the small palmette is typical of this style of decoration as well. The solid top is covered with ornamental swirling clouds. It shows considerable signs of wear and has a curved fissure for which an explanation is still to be found.

End Cap (Fig. 8)

The decoration of the cylinder segment is like a relief scroll. Its pattern repeated four times is similar to the mushroom- or cloud-shaped end plates on the Ruyi sceptre (Williams 1941: 158) of Chinese iconography (Spuhler 1987: 83, Fig. catalogue no. 81). Compared to the decoration of the cylinder, that of the top is strikingly plain. The irregular, engraved garland of petal-shaped elements may possibly be interpreted as a later embellishment.

End Cap (Fig. 9)

The cylinder, parts of which are in openwork, is graced by a wriggling dragon with a wide open mouth. This motif is repeated on the top, whose openwork is quite irregular. Due to the shift from solid openwork iron to sheet iron and the

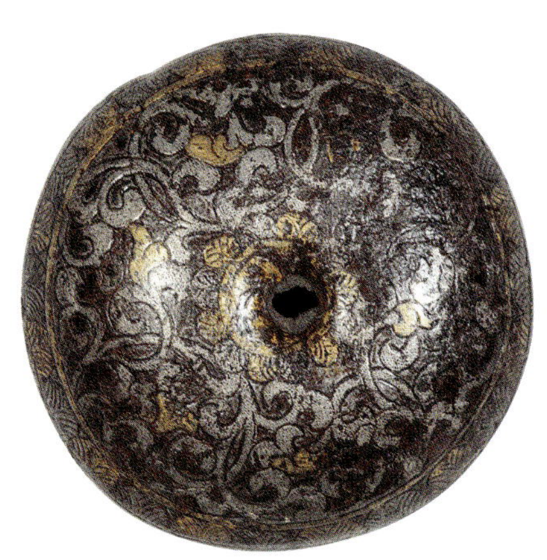

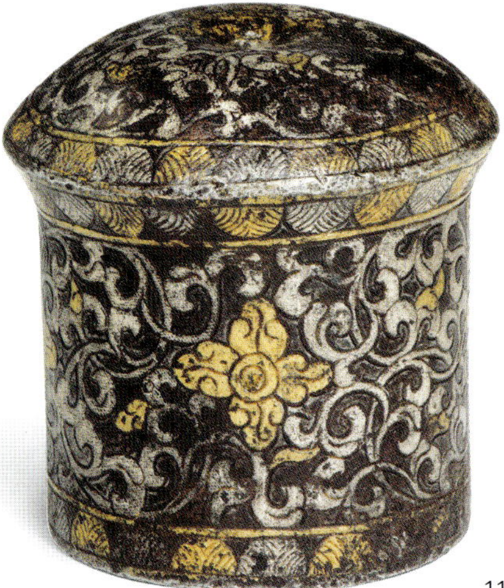
11

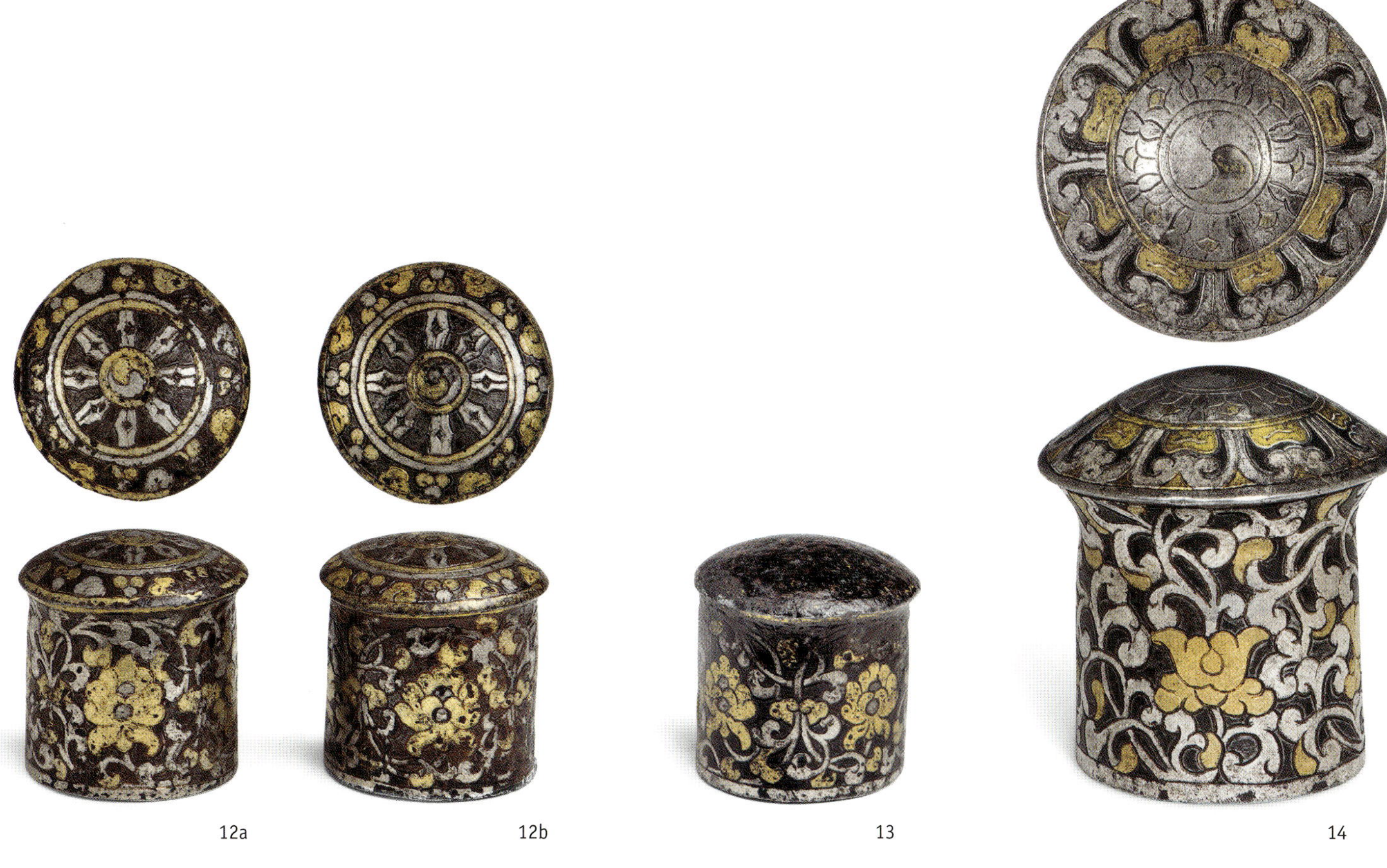

12a 12b 13 14

Figs. 12a and 12b: Solid iron, gold and silver damascene. 17th c., H. 3.8/3.8 cm, B. 3.8/3.7 cm, WT. 0.2/0.2 cm, Wt. 60/62 g

Fig. 13: Iron, gilded and silver-plated, surface corroded. 17th c., H. 3.7 cm, B. 3.7 cm, WT. 0.2 cm, Wt. 60 g

Fig. 14: Iron, gilded and silver-plated. 17th/18th c., H. 5.9 cm, B. 5.5 cm, WT. 0.2 cm, Wt. 128 g

comparatively careless design, this piece has been dated as late as the 18th/19th century.

End Cap (Fig. 10)

The cylinder is divided into two panels. The lower portion has a repeating pattern of swirling and self-dividing tendrils. Above a notched ring, rectangular openwork bands support the heavily worn top, which shows traces of a border formed by slanting sickle-shaped leaves.

End Cap (Fig. 11)

Spiralling tendrils of silver damascene are overlaid in the middle of the cylinder with golden quatrefoil flowers. Randomly chosen nodes of the silver tendrils have been fancifully finished in gold, discreetly enlivening the effect. The base of the cylinder and its widened lid, as well as the border of the top, are decorated with alternating gold and silver semicircles consisting of divergent parallel lines. The depression in the convex top was created by a nail being driven into it at some later point in time.

Pair of End Caps (Figs. 12a and 12b)

Pairs such as these are a rarity. The cylinder is damascened with alternating silver tendrils and small leaves in gold. An outer band of alternating cloud shape and three-ball ornaments (Sanskrit *cintāmaṇi*) decorate the convex top, whose centre is filled by the Buddhist Wheel of Teaching with silver spokes.

End Cap (Fig. 13)

Silver tendrils ending with leaves cover the surface of the cylinder. Palmettes with mostly round petals divide the surface into four parts. As with the previous very similar pair (Figs. 12a and 12b), individual gold leaves enliven the pattern. The top is so corroded that its decoration cannot be described.

End Cap (Fig. 14)

The basic similarity with the two previous examples is obvious. Differences become apparent in the decoration of the cylinder panel with its somewhat simpler arabesques and smaller, much less dominant palmettes. These imperfections have led us to suggest a slightly later dating. The stylistic observations also apply to the top with its central "wheel" and the repeating curved scale-shaped elements which surround it.

Fig. 15: Iron, gilded and silver-plated, silver-wire damascening (base ring).17th/18th c., H. 6.7 cm, B. 5.35 cm, WT. 0.25 cm, Wt. 140 g

Fig. 16: Iron with traces of gilding. 17th c., H. 4.1 cm, B. 3.6 cm, WT. 0.2 cm, Wt. 47 g

Fig. 17: Iron, gilded. 17th c., H. 4.7 cm, B. 4.55 cm, WT. 0.3 cm, Wt. 88 g

Fig. 18: Iron, blackened, design in gold. 18th c., H. 4.2 cm, B. 3.1 cm, WT. 0.1 cm, Wt. 23 g

Fig. 19: Iron with traces of gilding. 17th c., H. 5.5 cm, B. 4.7 cm, WT. 0.3 cm, Wt. 115 g

Fig. 20: Iron, gilded and silver-plated. 19th c., H. 4.35 cm, B. 4.05 cm, WT. 0.15 cm, Wt. 44 g

Figs. 21a and 21b: Solid iron, damascened image, traces of gold and silver. 17th c., left end cap: H. 4.5 cm, B. 3.6 cm, WT. 0.2 cm, Wt. 52 g, right end cap: H. 4.4 cm, B. 3.7 cm, WT. 0.2 cm, Wt. 58 g

Fig. 22: Iron, gilded. 18th c., H. 7.5 cm, B. 4.7 cm, WT. 0.15 cm, Wt. 97 g

End Cap (Fig. 15)

The upper rim of the cylinder is embellished with a garland of gold tendril ends with leaves. The forked tendrils, most of which are of silver, are comparatively wide, with the result that the familiar palmettes appear smaller. The decoration of the base ring is unusual, executed in thin silver wire in a somewhat uneven wave pattern. The centre of the top has a yin and yang motif, which is surrounded by a similar garland.

End Cap (Fig. 16)

The cylinder is heavily corroded, making it difficult to identify its gold tendril design and also the extensive gilding on the top. Nonetheless, what is still visible of the pattern allows a dating in the 17th century. The shape of the iron cast, especially the perfect concave form of the top, testifies to the craftsmanship of a superior workshop.

End Cap (Fig. 17)

Both the slight conical widening of the cylinder towards the top and the "support ring" at its base are unusual formal particularities. A perfect repeating pattern of offset oval wreaths in broad gold strips frames each palmette. The top is graced by a broad band with centrifugal "spokes", each of which is flanked by a forked tendril. The perfect state of preservation further enhances the impressive balance between the gold design and the untreated dark background.

End Cap (Fig. 18)

Generously proportioned tendrils spread over the cylinder, ending with the familiar paired leaves. Plain wide gold stripes encircle both the base and the rim of the top, which is decorated with a similarly large-size double *vajra* rosette. This stylistically perfect work shows that excellent designs were still created as late as the 18th century.

End Cap (Fig. 19)

Between a lower band of diagonally alternating "leaf-shaped" elements or "rice grains" and the band below the rim of the top, which is decorated with a series of pointed tendril leaf ends that swing out, is the frieze. The irregular contours of some tendrils give a somewhat confused impression of the primary design on the cylinder. The convex surface of the top is corroded but allows identification of a six-leaved rosette.

End Cap (Fig. 20)

The decline of traditional artistry and craftsmanship is obvious if we compare the elegant tendrils enclosing the central palmette of the end cap above (Fig. 3) with the similar but unskilful and simplified design on this end cap. Another possibility is that this piece was made in a provincial workshop.

Pair of End Caps (Figs. 21a and 21b)

It is very likely that these two end caps are a pair, despite slight differences in their decoration. The left cap has large spiralling tendrils with abundant end leaves and traces of silver in the spaces between the four *Shou* motifs – the stylised Chinese character for long life – which make up the structure of the medallions. There are differences in the bottom bands of the cylinders. The band of the left end cap is clearly composed of oval four-leafed flowers. The relative designs of the cap tops show the biggest difference: the left cap has traces of a circular rotating four-leafed ornament (see end cap Fig. 22), whereas closer scrutiny of the right cap reveals a ring of tendrils separated by "wheel spokes".

End Cap (Fig. 22)

The cylinder of this end cap is divided into four distinctive horizontal panels. At the bottom is a meander. Like the circles of four-petalled flowers on the third panel, it is still used in Chinese ornamentation today (e.g., on porcelain). Between these is the most important panel, featuring spiralling tendrils and leaves, and dominated by an elegant footed bowl of round fruits – a previously unknown motif. The elegantly curved and overhanging top is decorated with four quite voluminous and slightly spiralling leaves.

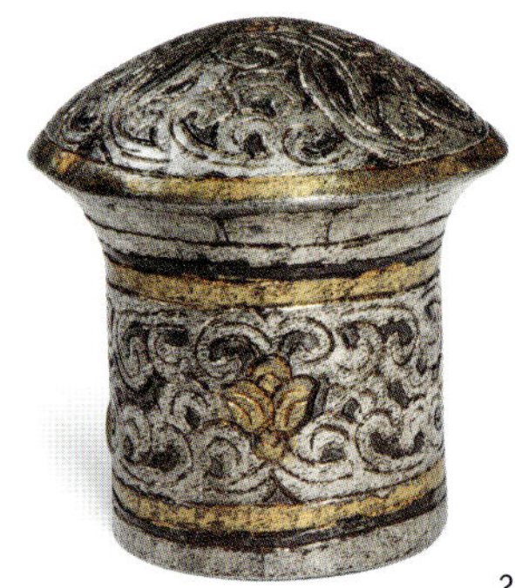

20

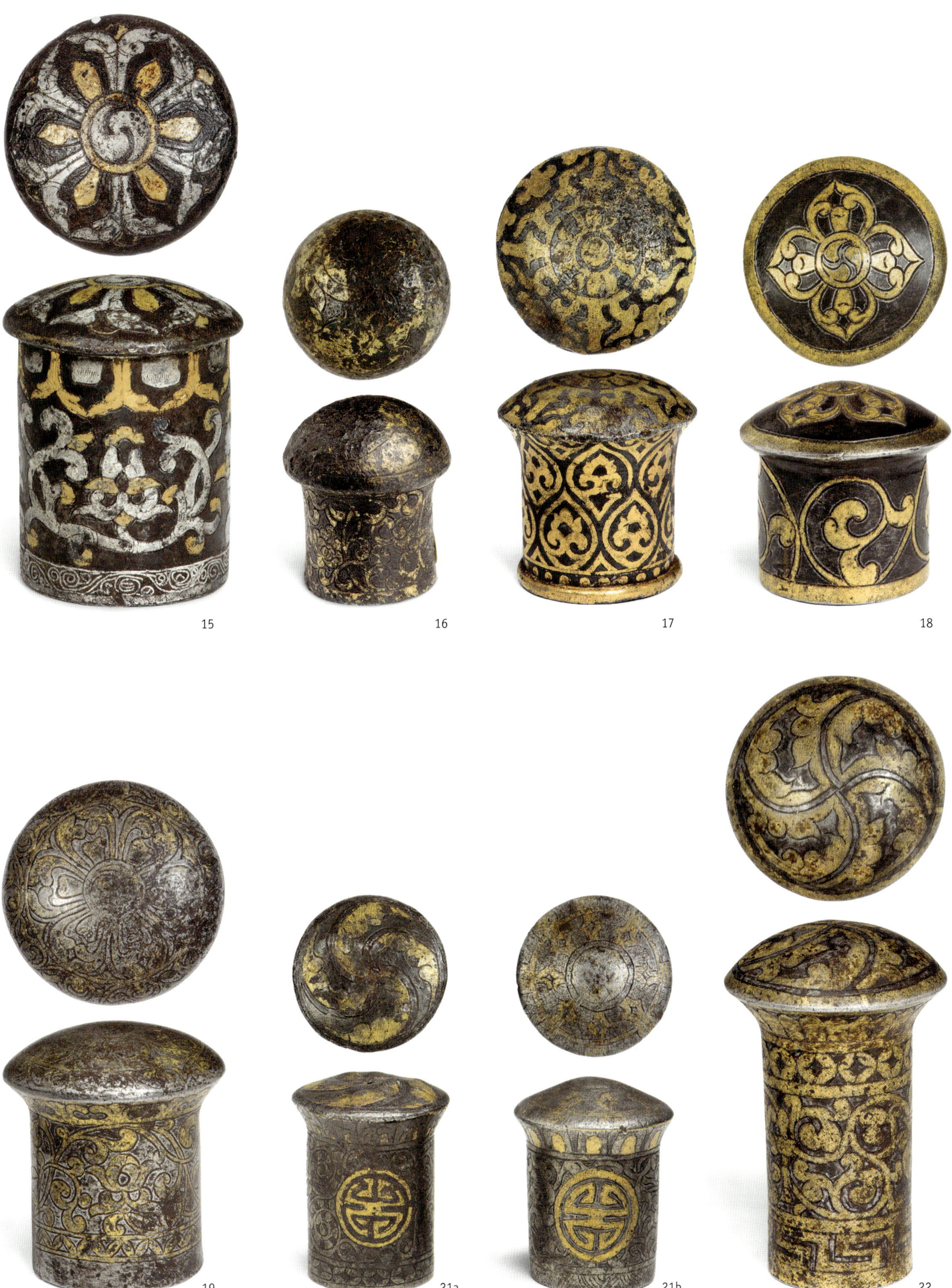
15 16 17 18

19 21a 21b 22

Detail of Fig. 18

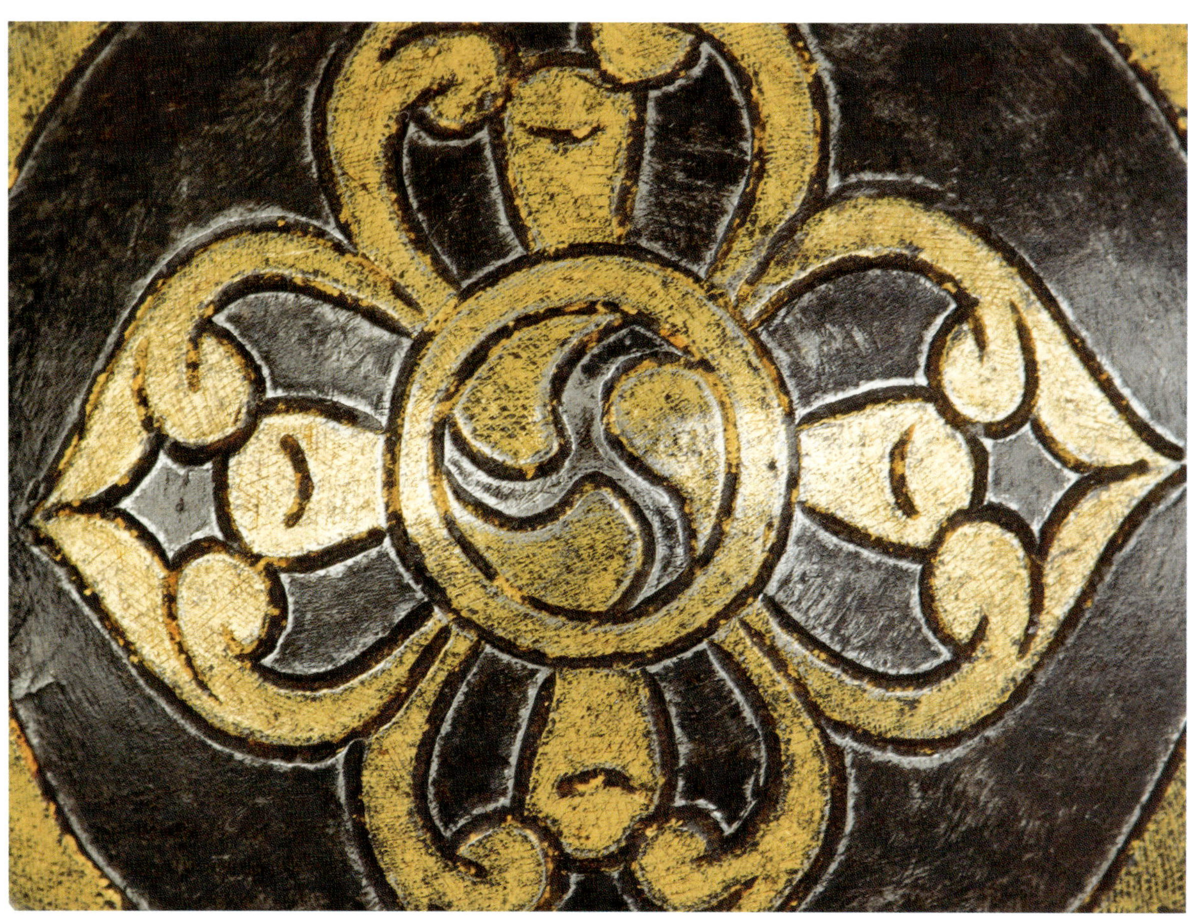

Detail of Fig. 22

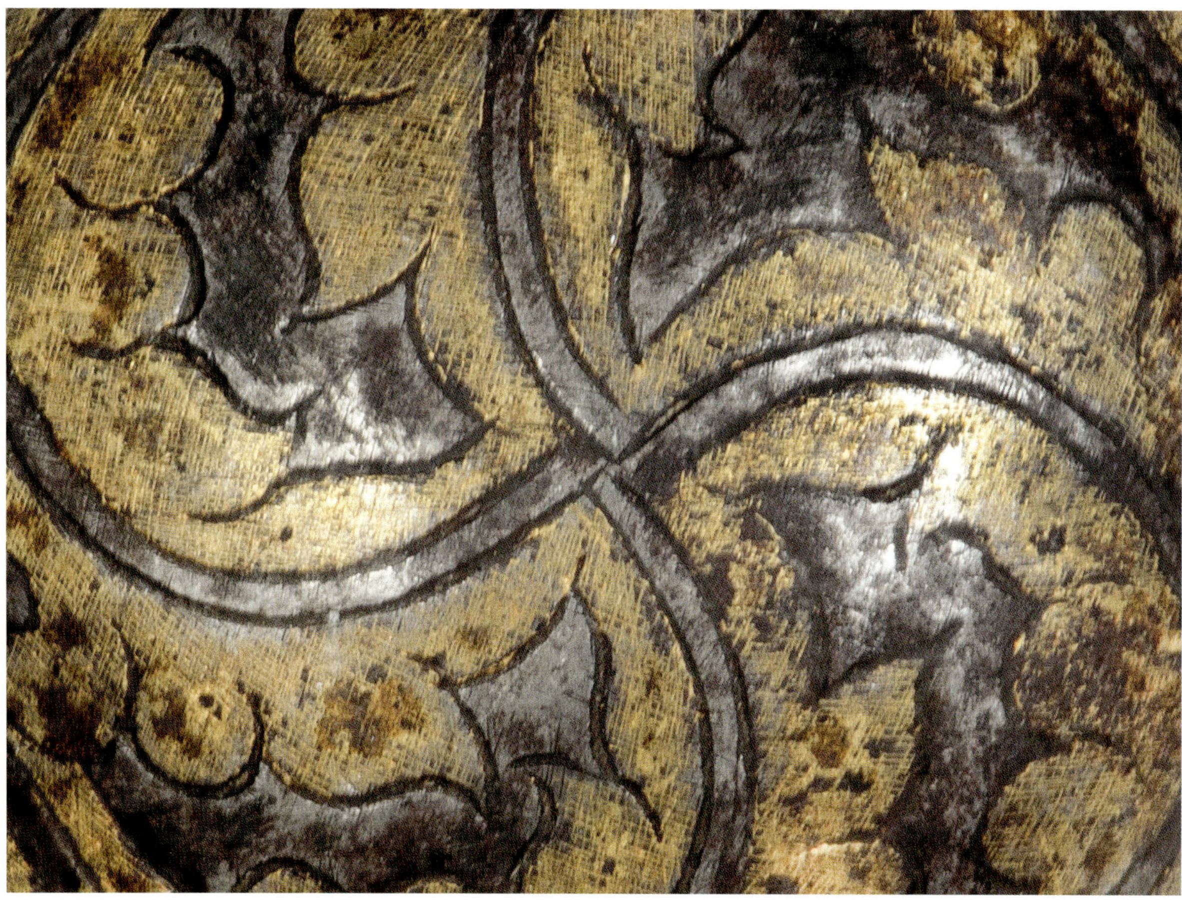

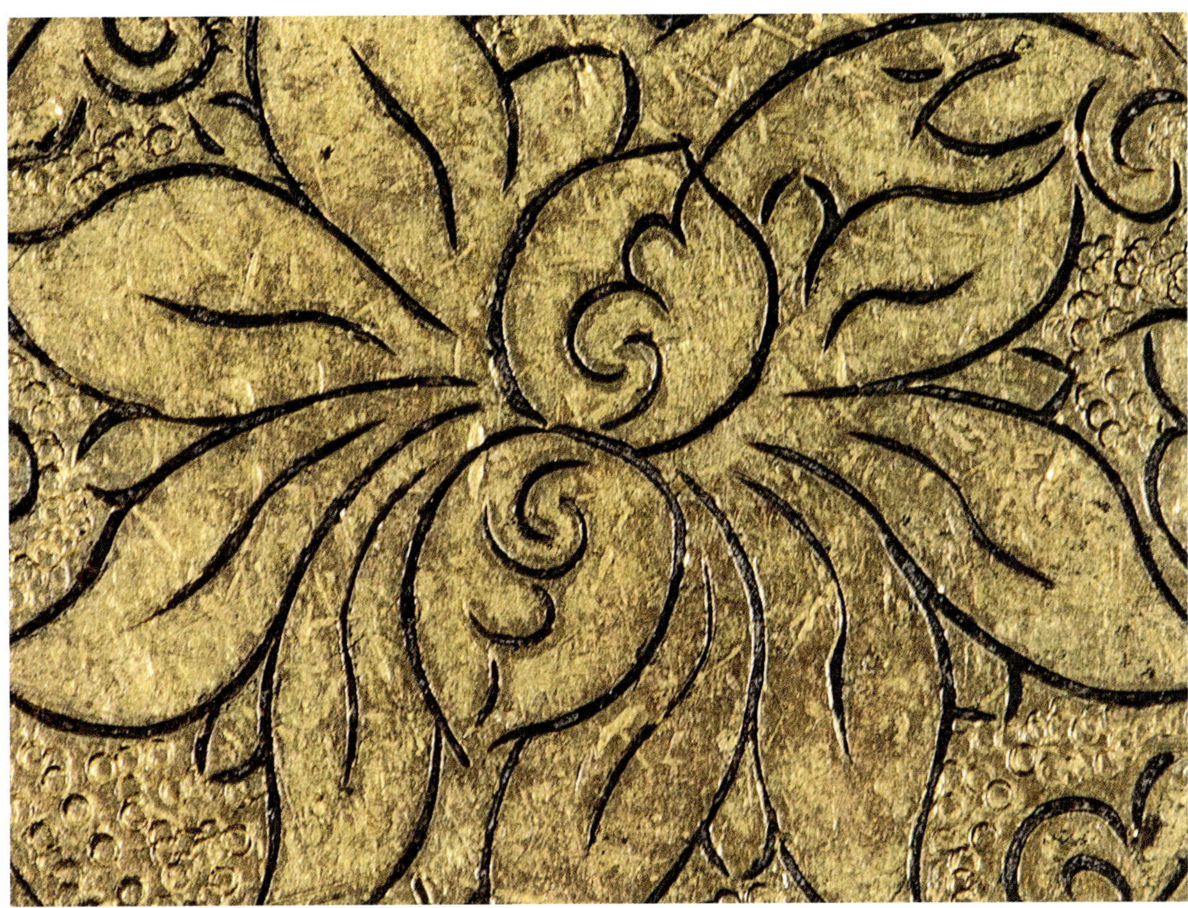
Detail of Fig. 28

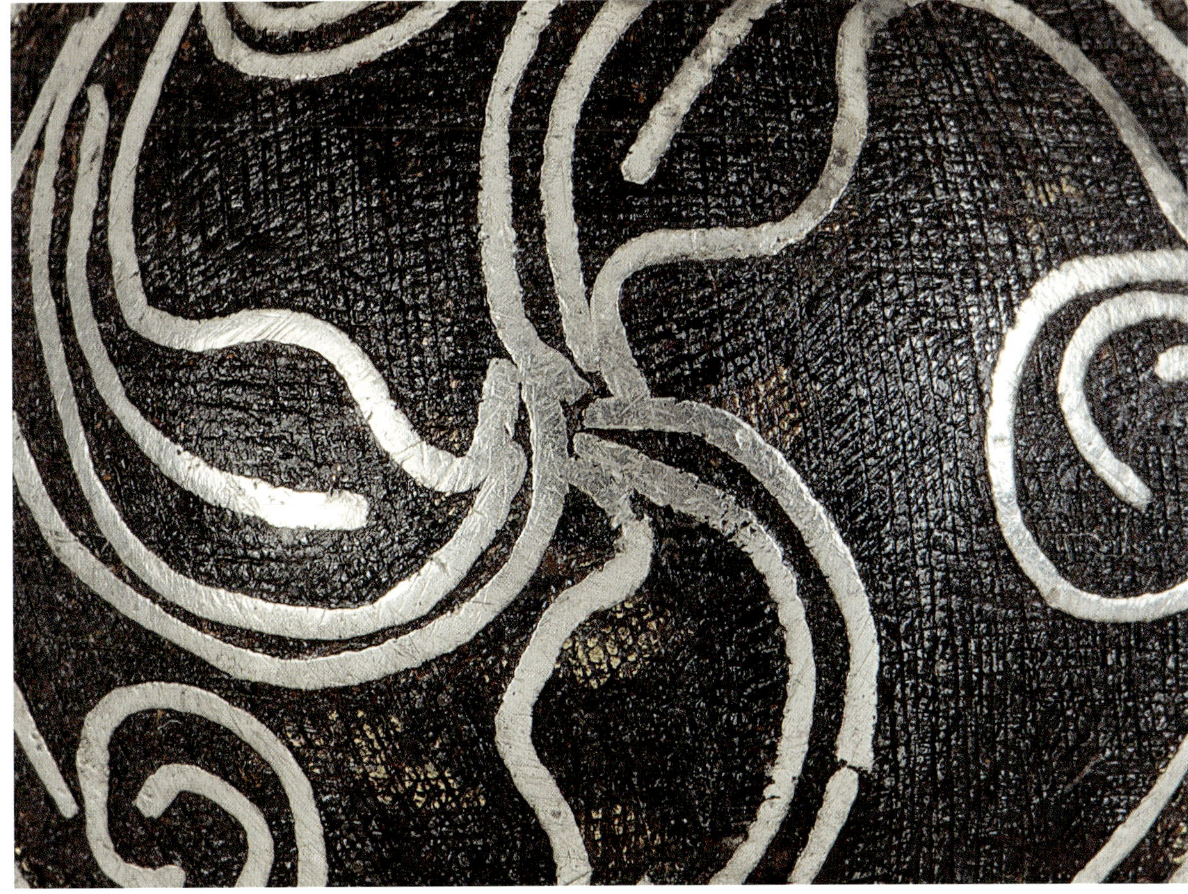
Detail of Fig. 29

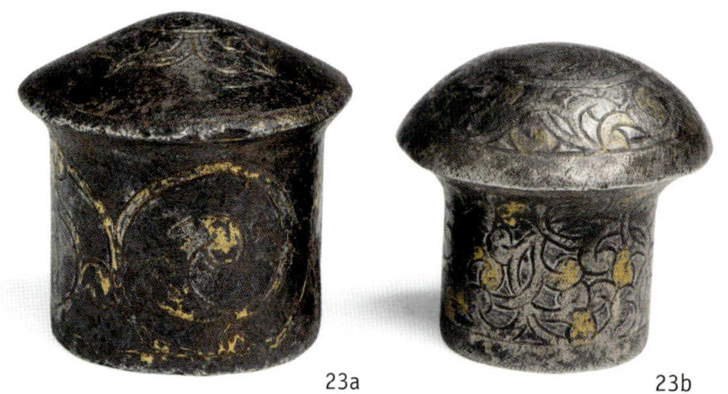

23a 23b

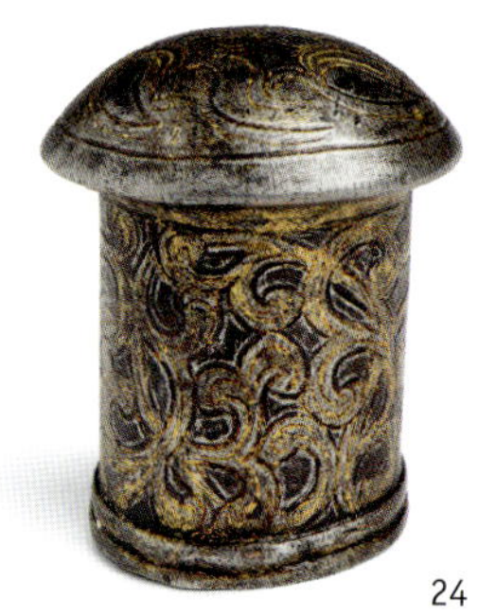

24

Figs. 23a and 23 b: Solid iron, traces of gold and silver damascene. 17th/18th c., left end cap: H. 4 cm, B. 4.2 cm, WT. 0.2 cm, Wt. 65 g, right end cap: H. 3.6 cm, B. 3.9 cm, WT. 0.15 cm, Wt. 32 g

Fig. 24: Iron, damascened and partially gilded. 17th/18th c., H. 4 cm, B. 3.3 cm, WT. 0.25 cm (with a ring), Wt. 45 g

Figs. 25a and 25b: Silver alloy or brass. Around 1800, H. 3.6/3.5 cm, B. 3.9/3.65 cm, WT. 0.15/1.15 cm, Wt. 53/42 g

Fig. 26: Iron, gilded and silver-plated. 18th/19th c., H. 3 cm, B. 2.3 cm, WT. 0.2 cm (with a ring), Wt. 12 g

Fig. 27: Copper/Iron, gilded all over. 17th/18th c., H. 6.35 cm, B. 6.65 cm, WT. 0.15 cm, Wt. 142 g

Fig. 28: Solid brass, engraved design. 18th/19th c., H. 4 cm, B. 4 cm, WT. 0.35 cm, Wt. 119 g

Fig. 29: Iron, silver damascene. 18th/19th c., H. 4.2 cm, B. 3.1 cm, WT. 0.1 cm, Wt. 23 g

Figs. 30a and 30b: Iron, engraved and gilded. 16th/17th c., H. 5.55/5.56 cm, B. 7.85/7.9 cm, WT. 0.25/0.3 cm, Wt. 85/88 g

End Caps (Figs. 23a and 23b)

These two end caps are not a pair but are shown to illustrate the striking contrasts that exist in artistic quality. Both the large spiral with golden end leaves (left end cap) and the tendrils on the right end cap stand in the classic tradition of the 17th century. Their poor craftsmanship, however, reflects the great differences in quality depending on the workshop. In places where there was great demand for *thangkas*, provincial craftsmen were employed alongside equally provincial painters.

End Cap (Fig. 24)

A web of relatively short tendrils and leaves – but with no medallion – surrounds the cylinder. The top is decorated with rotating leaves, whose gilding has been heavily worn.

Pair of End Caps (Figs. 25a and 25b)

This cylinder has a very unusual design, being divided into vertical fields with different patterns. The first decorative element is a pair of fish flanking a vertical flower stem. Next to this is a bulbous porcelain vase on a wooden stand, then a peony with large petals. The style of this unusually late and Chinese design suggests a dating of 1800 or later. Were these end caps intended for export to China? Stylistically, the pattern of leaves on the top matches that on the cylinder. The centre of each is a simple engraved drawing of the *Shou* motif.

End Cap (Fig. 26)

The decoration of the cylinder begins with a gilded meander border above the "support" ring. The broad main panel shows variegated flowers in gold between opposing leaves. The upper band has scaled lobes before it meets the top, which features the familiar rotating wheel of leaves.

End Cap (Fig. 27)

A large tendril with a many-petalled peony has been punched into the golden surface of the cylinder. The frieze of tendrils is densely arranged and looks very elegant. Together with the ring of scales and the four-leaf rosette on the top, it makes this end cap very impressive. A short text is engraved in the ring at the base which has been translated as "Year of the Fire Rabbit". At present I cannot give an interpretation.

End Cap (Fig. 28)

The perfectly round cylinder and the flat top suggest that this piece may have been lathed. Elegantly swinging tendrils with leaves stand out against the punched background of the frieze. The flat surface of the top is covered with an elegantly drawn peony. Horizontal traces of lathe work are unlikely to be found on pieces made prior to 1800 (see the brass end caps Figs. 46a to 46d and 47).

End Cap (Fig. 29)

The lines of the silver damascene interlacing *swastika* design, which is known from many examples in Chinese and Central Asian art, stand out against the blackened iron surface of the cylinder. The top is decorated with the familiar trefoil of swirling leaves made using the same technique. The entire décor, including the meander-like pattern at the base, is rooted in tradition, but the sloppy workmanship would be unthinkable before the 19th century.

Pair of End Caps (Figs. 30a and 30b)

We have already encountered the skill for multi-layered relief décor at the beginning of the present description of end caps. Examples include end caps of solid iron with openwork spaces between the tendrils, resulting in multiple layers that lend the design a netlike character (e.g. Figs. 2, 3 and 4). In this pair, the net of tendrils covers the cylinder and top without any spaces in between. The style of the tendrils, with pairs of leaves at their ends, can be regarded as classical. The harmonious crenellated bands on the cylinder underline the exceptional beauty of this pair of end caps. The decoration of the tops is dominated by a writhing dragon. The complete gilding adds to the magnificent overall impression.

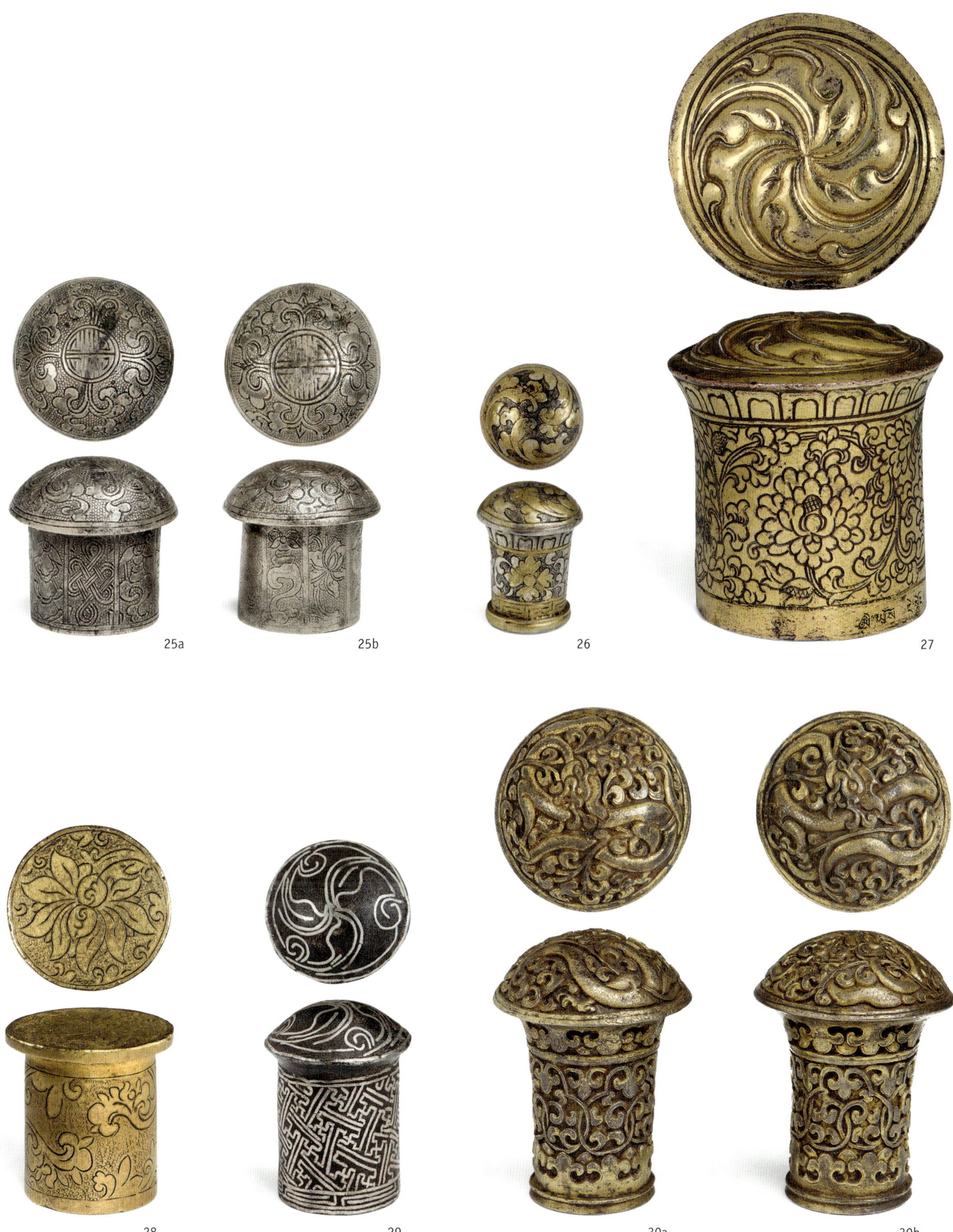
25a 25b 26 27
28 29 30a 30b

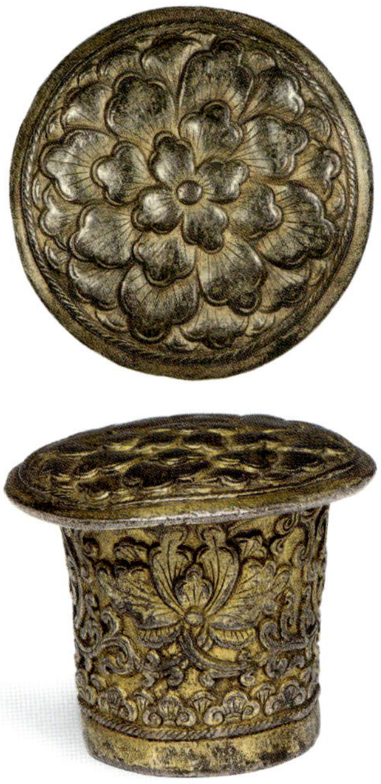

31 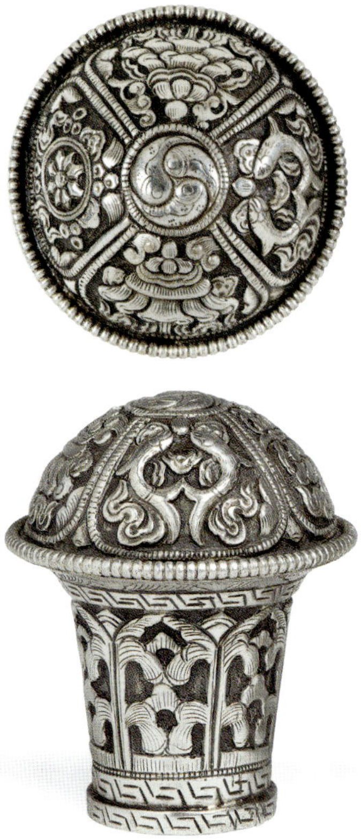 32a 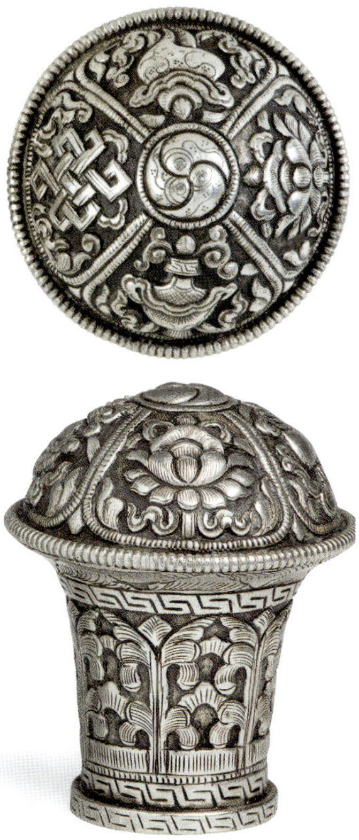 32b 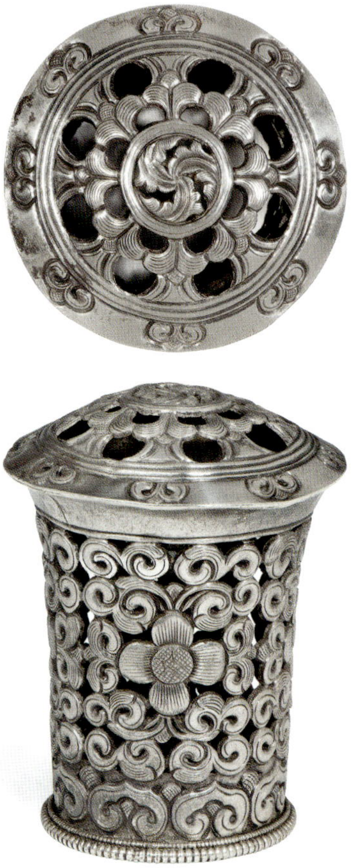 33

Fig. 31: Iron, completely gilded.17th c., H. 3.9 cm, B. 4.65 cm, WT. 0.3 cm, Wt. 61 g

Figs. 32a and 32b: Embossed sheet silver. 18th c., H. 5.45/5.5 cm, B. 6.5/6.45 cm, WT. n.g./n.g., Wt. 60/50 g

Fig. 33: Embossed sheet silver. 18th c., H. 6.4 cm, B. 8.3 cm, WT. n.g., Wt. 85 g

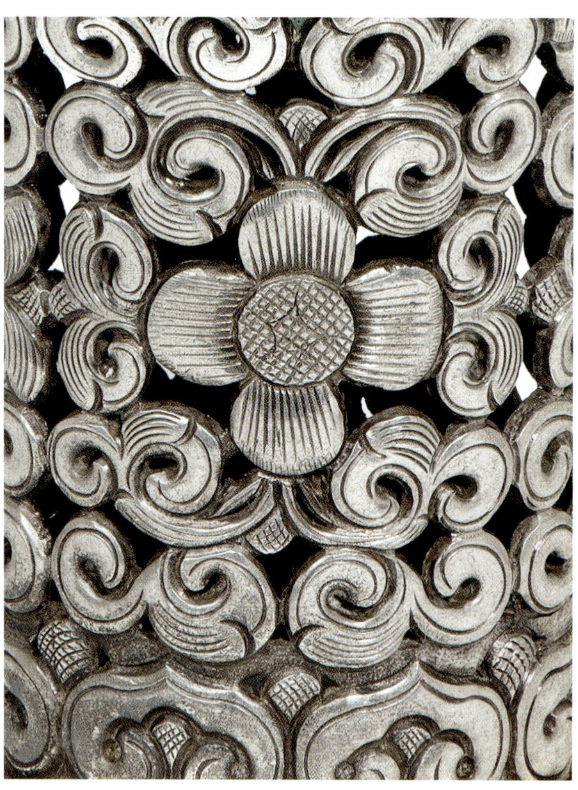

Detail of Fig. 33

End Cap (Fig. 31)

Lively tendrils surround large-petalled flowers on a panel bordered by a crenellated band at the base of the cylinder. The lack of strictness of style in the detail of the tendrils suggest a slightly later dating. However, the gorgeous flower on the top reconciles the viewer with the shortcomings of the décor on the cylinder.

Pair of End Caps (Figs. 32a and 32b)

The relatively slim and slightly conical cylinder features repeating vertical flower stems. The top protrudes considerably over the cylinder and is the dominant feature. Each top is divided into four segments, with a different Buddhist symbol in each of the eight fields. The silver sheet was most probably pressed or hammered into a negative form, the details then being worked on the outside. Top and cylinder were then connected with a silver beaded ring. This type of metalworking enabled repetition of the same décor and thus serial reproduction. It is unclear when this technique

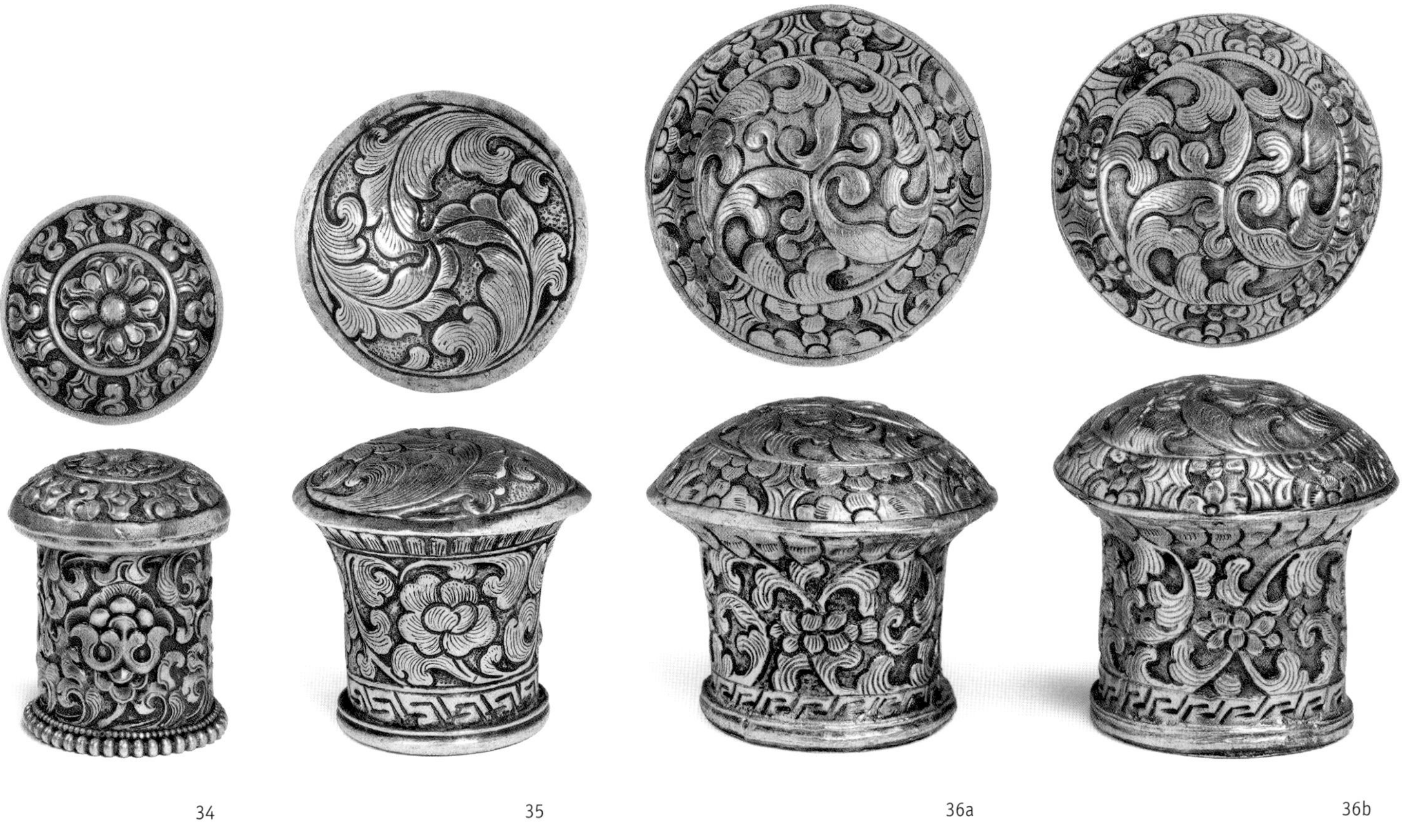

34 35 36a 36b

Fig. 34: Embossed sheet silver. 17th/18th c., H. 4.1 cm, B. 3.2 cm, WT. n.g., Wt. 20 g

Fig. 35: Embossed sheet silver, protruding top. 17th/18th c., H. 4.5 cm, B. 4.6 cm, WT. n.g., Wt. 35 g

Figs. 36a and 36b: Embossed sheet silver, protruding top. 18th c., H. 4.65/5.1 cm, B. 5.3/5 cm, WT. n.g./n.g., Wt. 38/34 g

began, but it would be hardly imaginable before the 18th century. It is also possible that it was only used in a specific region.

End Cap (Fig. 33)

This cylinder was probably also made using a cast. Symmetrically placed tendrils with end leaves surround a simple four-petalled central rosette. The top is made in generous openwork, and its solid outer ring is decorated with small crenellations, larger variants of which are aligned towards the centre.

End Cap (Fig. 34)

The lush tendrils on the cylinder are still in the tradition of those fashioned from solid iron (see Figs. 5 and 6). The top, however, has a much simpler decoration with a circle of tendrils directed spoke-like towards the centre. A striking feature of the sheet-silver caps discussed above is the beaded ring at the base, which neatly conceals the unfinished edge of the thin silver sheet (Figs. 32a and 32b; Fig. 33).

End Cap (Fig. 35)

In comparison with the previous end cap (Fig. 34), the tendrils, which end with paired leaves, are given more generous space. The three leaves spiralling on the top are on the same scale, thereby making the two parts into a harmonious whole.

Pair of End Caps (Figs. 36a and 36b)

Spiralling tendrils with double-leaf ends and flat peony petals coil around the cylinder. The most impressive feature of this pair, however, is the decoration of the tops. Flat-ribbed leaves float around the centre in the usual rotating manner. On the border surrounding them are the popular leaf quatrefoils and quatrefoil half-rosette. A tendency towards stereotyped ornamentation should not be overlooked in this pair, and is probably typical of specimens from the 18th and especially the 19th century.

Detail of Fig. 31

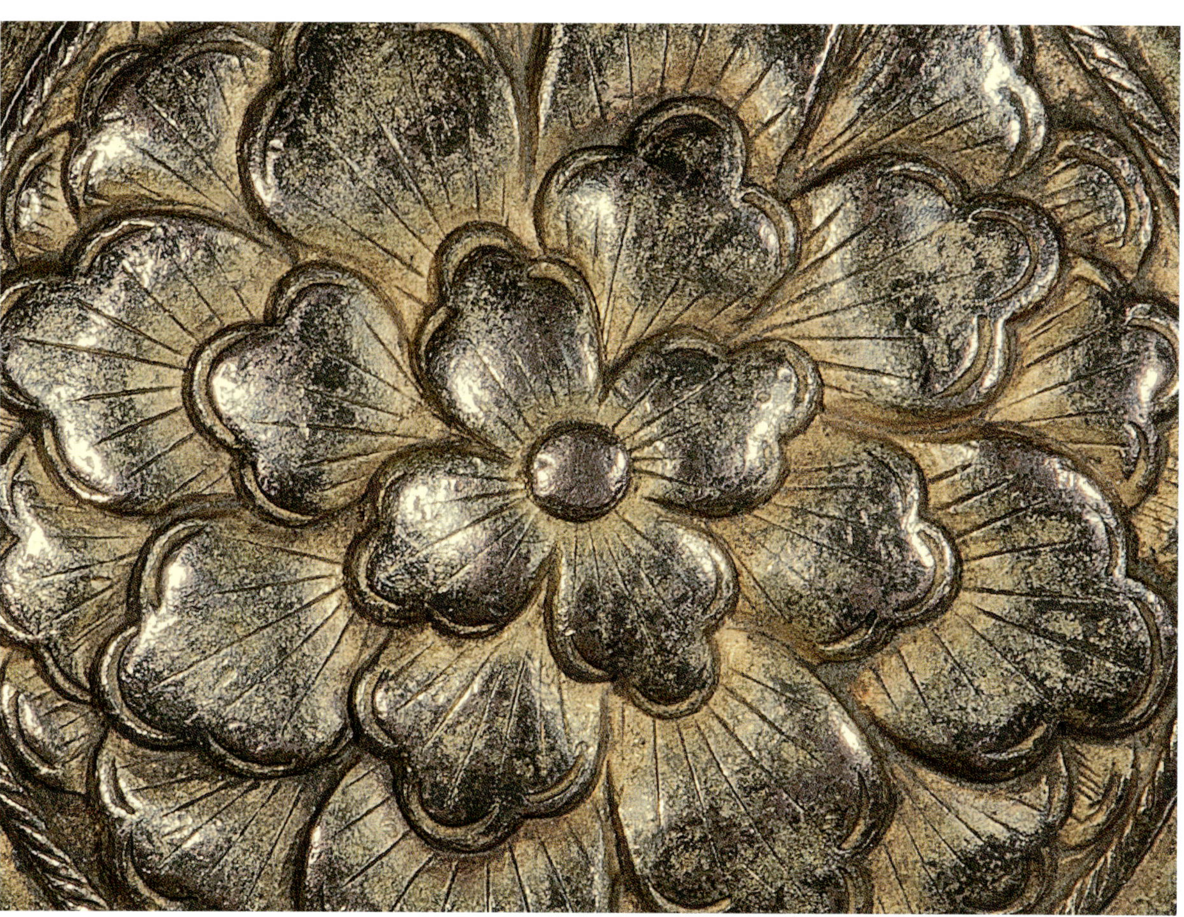

Detail of Fig. 32

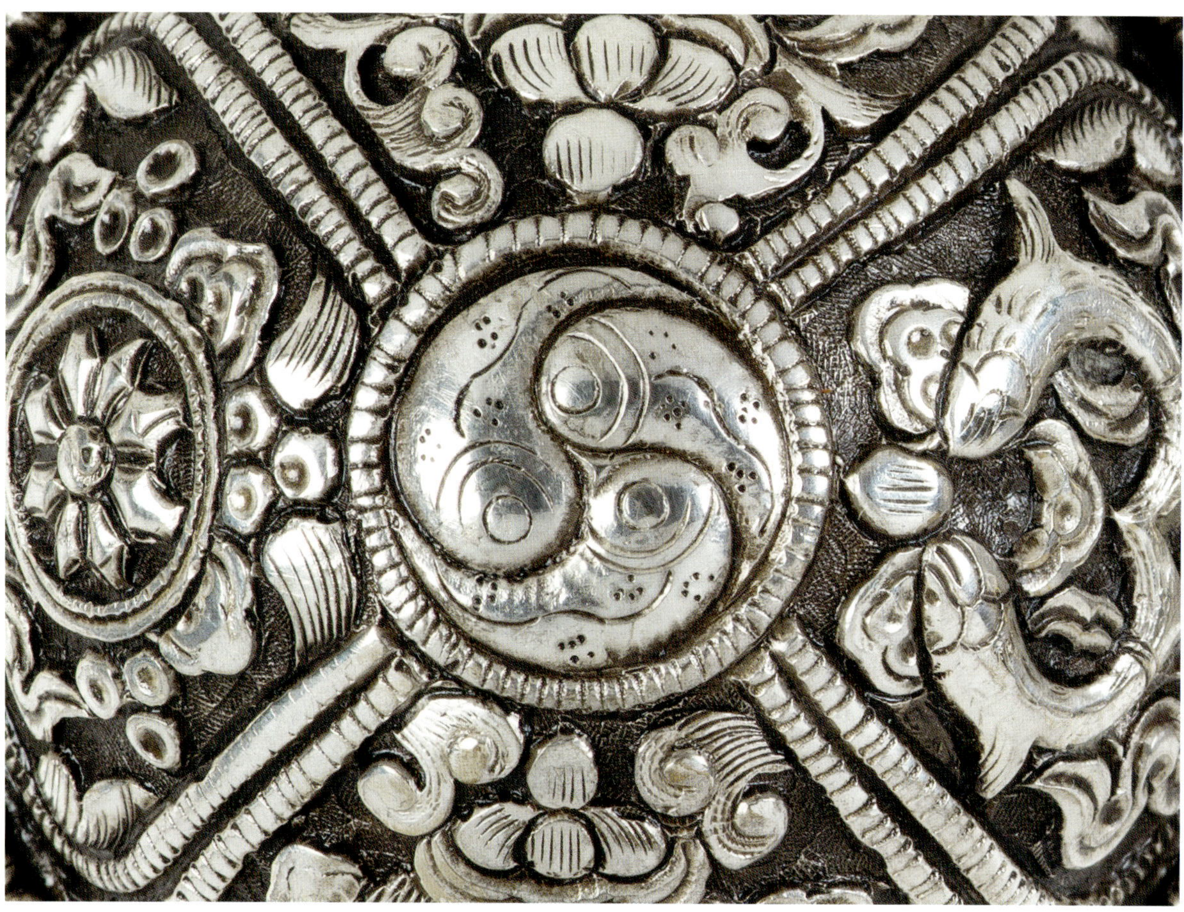

Detail of Fig. 39

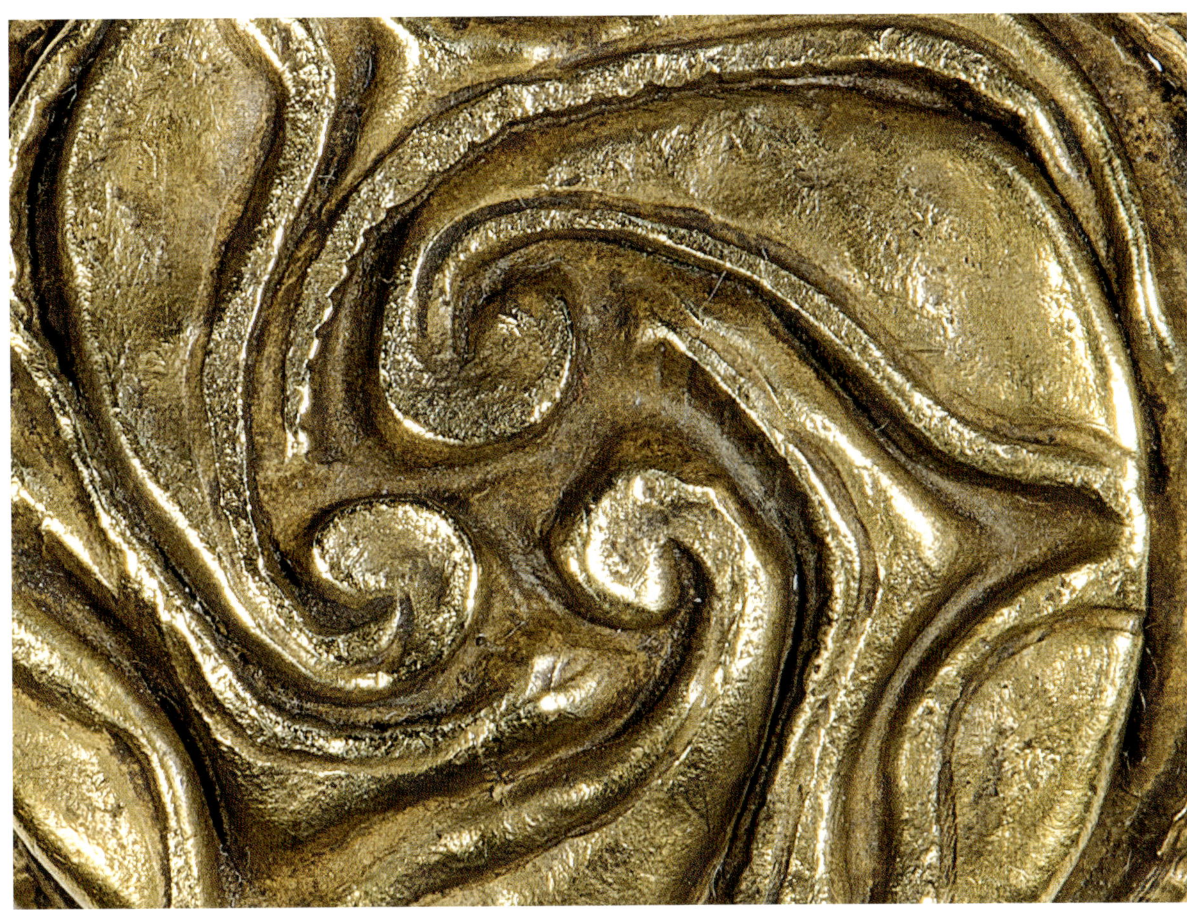

Detail of Fig. 43

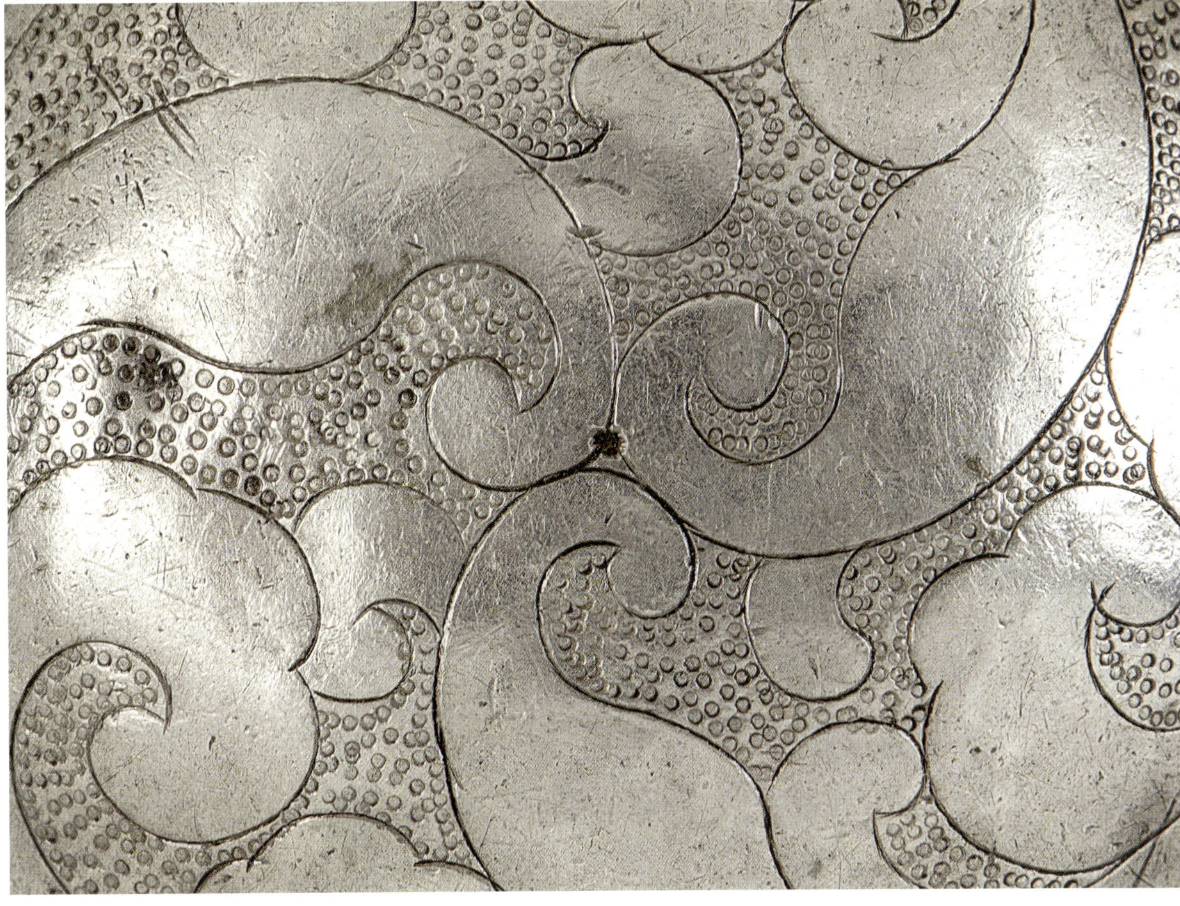

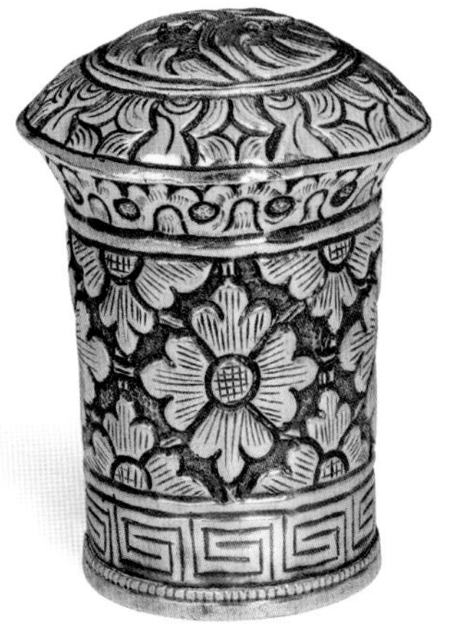

37

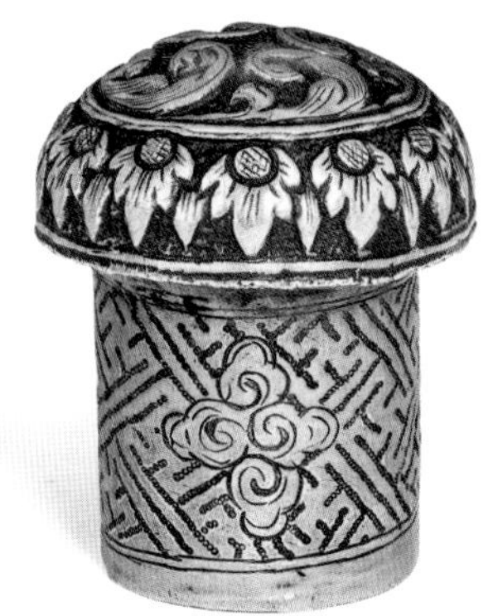

38

Fig. 37: Embossed sheet silver. 19th c., H. 5.55 cm, B. 4.1 cm, WT. n.g., Wt. 32 g

Fig. 38: Embossed sheet silver, pressed cylinder ring, protruding top. 19th c., H. 4.8 cm, B. 4 cm, WT. n.g., Wt. 22 g

Fig. 39: Sheet brass. 17th c. (?), H. 4.5 cm, B. 3.7 cm, WT. n.g., Wt. 27 g

Fig. 40: Embossed sheet brass. 18th c. (?), H. 7.5 cm, B. 4.9 cm, WT. n.g., Wt. 58 g

Fig. 41: Sheet brass. 18th/19th c., H. 3.7 cm, B. 3.8 cm, WT. n.g., Wt. 9 g

Fig. 42: Embossed sheet copper. 18th c. (?), H. 5.75 cm, B. 4.6 cm, WT. n.g., Wt. 40 g

Fig. 43: Sheet silver. 18th c., H. 3.6 cm, B. 3.5 cm, WT. n.g., Wt. 18 g

Figs. 44/1, 44/2 and 44/3: Iron, silver-plated, traces of gilding. 17th/18th c., H. 3.9 cm, B. 3.5 cm, WT. n.g., Wt. 27 g

End Cap (Fig. 37)

The main portion of the cylinder features a segment of an endlessly repeatable pattern of large diagonally arranged four-petalled flowers. The border around the top is decorated with somewhat uninspired quatrefoils alternating with spiralling leaves cut off at their tops. This is doubtlessly a fairly monotonous piece.

End Cap (Fig. 38)

A similar design with inlaid iron *swastikas* has already been described and illustrated above (Fig. 29). The familiar spiralling leaves in the centre of the top are surrounded by a border of round inflorescences with hanging petals.

End Cap (Fig. 39)

Even upon close examination, the archaic décor of this cylinder remains puzzling. For one, I wonder whether the top is in its original position or whether it was originally attached to the other end of the cylinder. In the latter case, two thick stems each ending in a leaf would divide the cylinder into four upright rectangular "scales". Each individual "scale" in turn is decorated with a pair of stems with scroll-shaped rolled-up ends, beneath which is a phallic-like element. The condition of the end cap, particularly of its flat top, suggests frequent use. Hence, it may well have been attached to the other end of the cylinder.

End Cap (Fig. 40)

This much larger end cap shows a décor resembling that of Fig. 39 and also defies interpretation. The top shows a rudimentary suggestion of spiralling leaves. Attempts to find similar parallels on Tibetan and Nepalese book covers have not yielded any results. The dating remains uncertain.

End Cap (Fig. 41)

The cylinder of this rather short brass cap is decorated with four stylised flowers whose inflorescences are plump and pointed. The centre is dominated by the *Shou* motif and surrounded by a simple band of tendrils.

End Cap (Fig. 42)

The cylinder and top are of thin metal sheet worked in repoussé. The design of the cylinder is dominated by the spotted and wildly writhing body of a dragon with a rather large head. Its two long chin barbells extend towards the rolled-in edge which is decorated with a cloud pattern. A similar dragon appears on the top. This unskilful piece of work defies dating.

End Cap (Fig. 43)

Rolled-in leaves resembling clouds stand out against the dotted background. The harmonious composition of rounded leaves and dotted background testify to the silversmith's high sense of quality.

End Cap (Figs. 44/1, 44/2 and 44/3)

The cylinder bears symbols from the group of the eight "treasures" (Lorentz 1972: 59). We can identify the "stone chime" which is the source of expanding waves of sound; the "rhinoceros horn cups"; and possibly the "books". I was not able to interpret a further symbol: opposing trefoils that are tapered at their junction. The division into four sections on the cylinder is repeated on the top, which features smaller images of the same symbols.

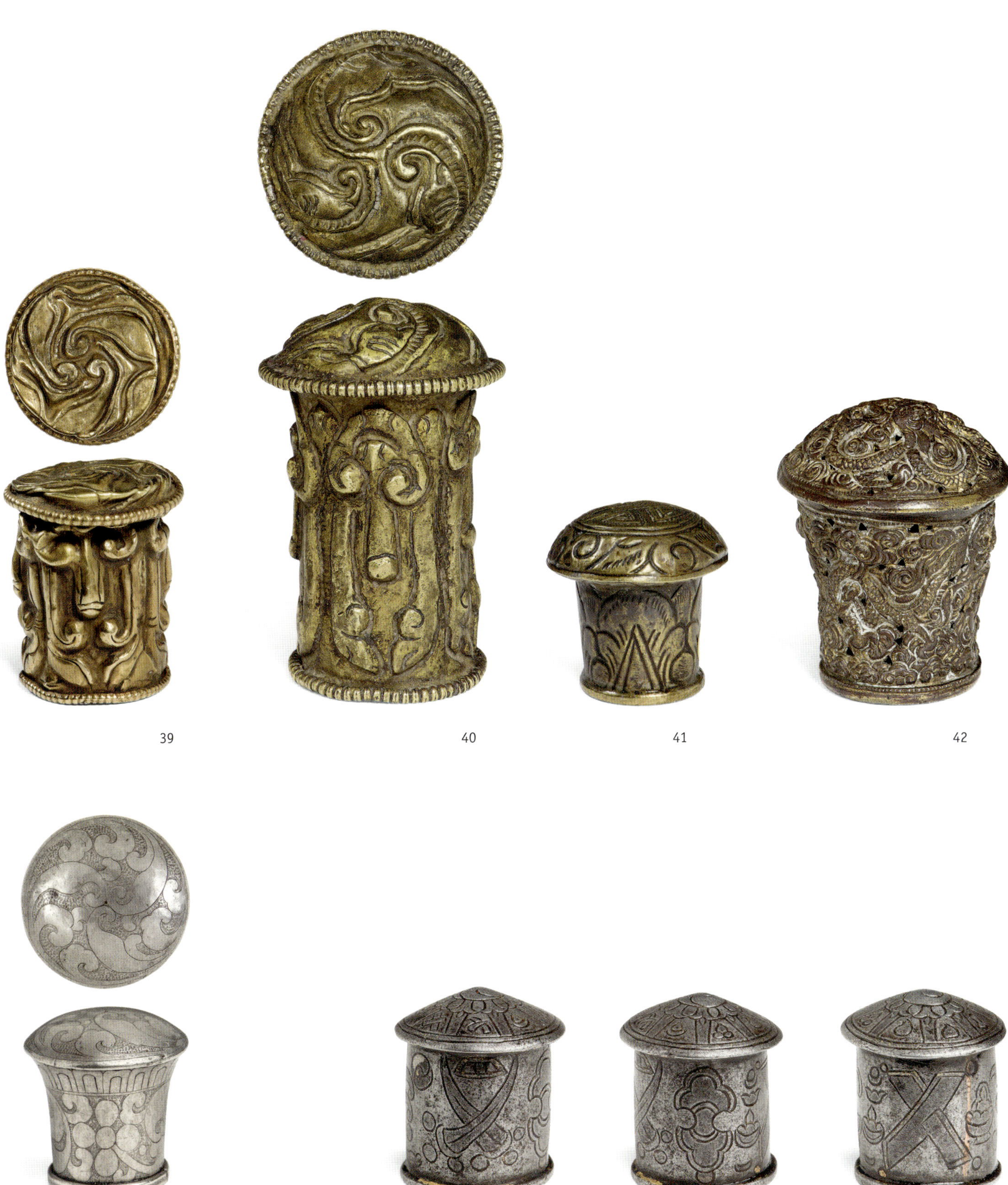
39 40 41 42
43 44/1 44/2 44/3

Detail of Fig. 39

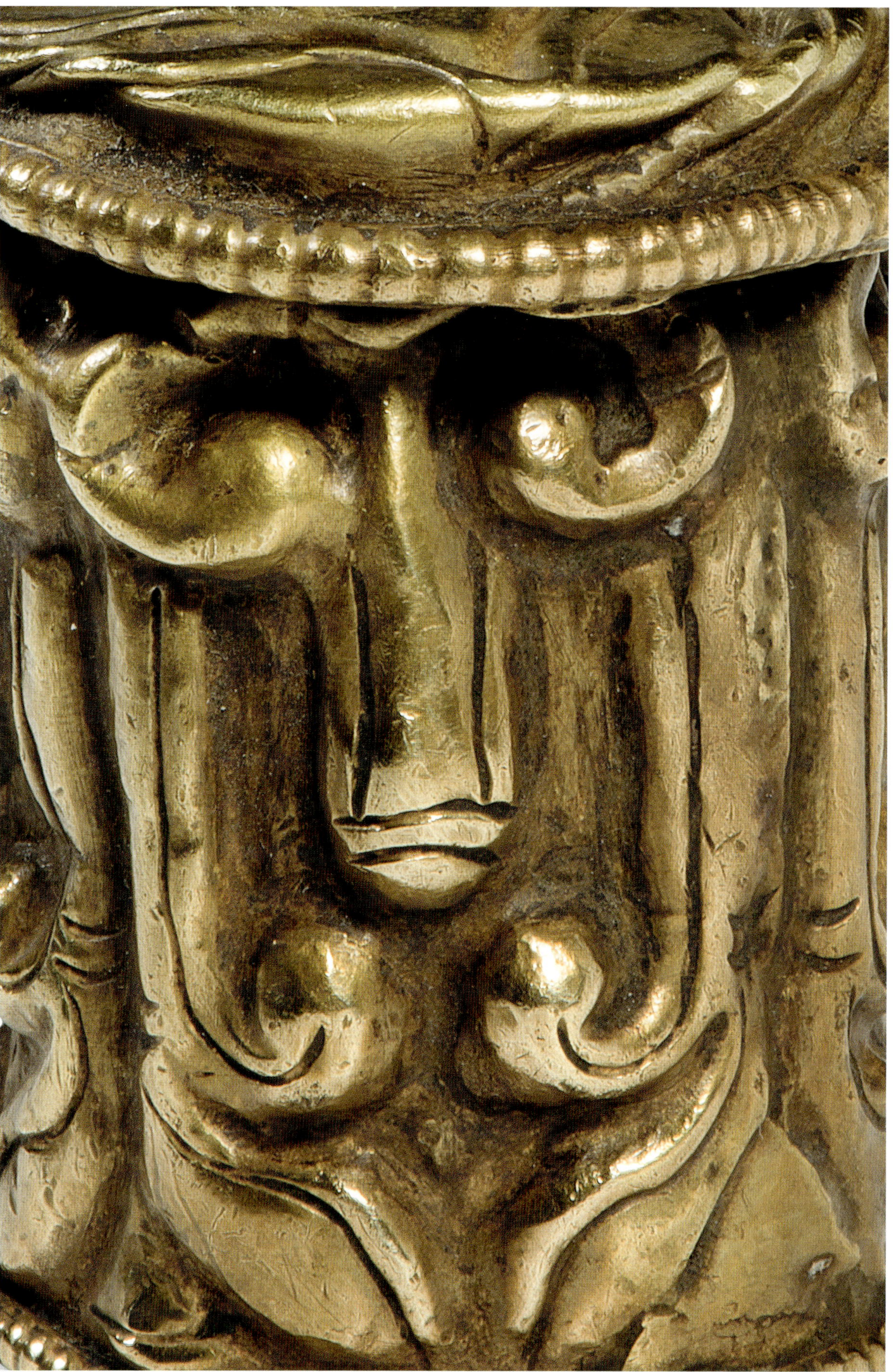

Detail of Fig. 49

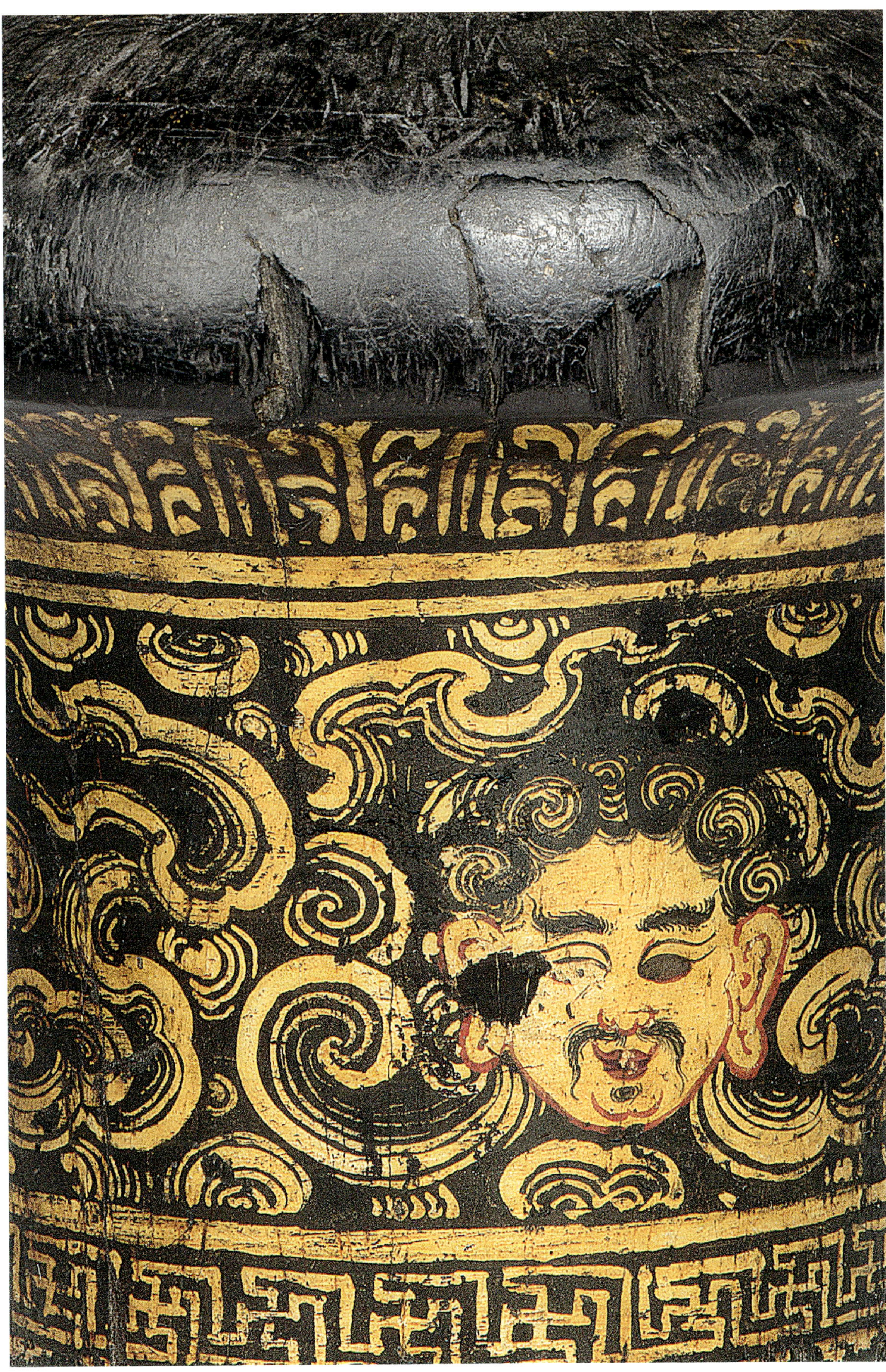

Figs. 45/1 and 45/2: Embossed sheet silver, top connected to cylinder. 18th/19th c., H. 5 cm, B. 3.8 cm, WT. n.g., Wt. 27 g

Figs. 46a, 46b, 46c and 46d: Solid brass. 18th/20th c., H. 3 to 4 cm

Fig. 47: Bone, turned. 18th to 20th c., H. 3.6 cm, B. 3 cm, WT. 0.35 cm, Wt. 23 g

Fig. 48: Porcelain, blue underglaze. 18th to 20th c., H. 4.1 cm, B. 4 cm, WT. 0.6 cm, Wt. 51 g

Fig. 49: Fragment, wood, lacquered with gold painting. 16th/18th c., H. 8.8 cm

Fig. 50: Decoration for a saddle or horse harness, iron, openwork, gilded and silver-plated, movable dragons. 14th to 16th c., 4.35 x 16.6 cm, Wt. 116 g

Fig. 51: Rosette from a small monastery cabinet, iron, openwork, gilded. 16th/17th c., diameter 6.75 cm, Wt. 75 g

End Cap (Figs. 45/1 and 45/2)

This end cap, whose cylinder elegantly broadens towards the top, is engraved with various Taoist symbols: the bamboo organ, the castanets, and a hitherto unexplained symbol that looks like a sheet of paper whose corners have been folded. The ribbons floating around the symbols epitomise the elegant style of the 18th century.

End Caps (Figs. 46a, 46b, 46c and 46d)

By 1800 there was a tendency towards simplification, as becomes apparent from the silver-sheet repoussé end caps which first appeared at that time. These undecorated end caps of turned brass represent the climax of that development. While they are not without elegance, they are nevertheless mass products and no longer comparable to earlier individually designed *thangkas*. In the collection, there are at least eight such almost identical end caps.

End Caps (Figs. 47, 48 and 49)

To complete the picture of end caps, the collectors have included these three specimens made of different materials. The end cap in Fig. 47 is made from turned bone, and its only embellishment is the milled double line. The porcelain end cap (Fig. 48) with blue underglaze painting can be dated to the 18th to 20th century. Only half of the end cap shown in Fig. 49 has survived. It was made from turned hard wood and lacquered in black, then decorated with gold painting. In the middle of this very appealing painting is a sort of mask with a moustache in the popular Chinese style with long drooping ends, framed by a lively border of clouds. A comparison with Tibetan book covers suggests a dating from a relatively long period prior to the 18th century.

SUMMARY

It is amazing that that there is not a single mention of end caps in the recent literature about Tibetan art, let alone an illustration. This, too, is part of the regrettable loss of religious aura suffered by *thangka* paintings when they arrived in western collections and museums where they became just pictures in frames.

The earlier end caps are complex compositions of multilayered tendrils carved out of a piece of iron by craftsmen who had a pronounced sense of three-dimensionality. The most outstanding example of this in the Buddeberg collection is a long rectangular ornamental piece for a horse harness or saddle (Fig. 50). In a design of intertwining tendrils, two symmetrical dragons face a central mountain.

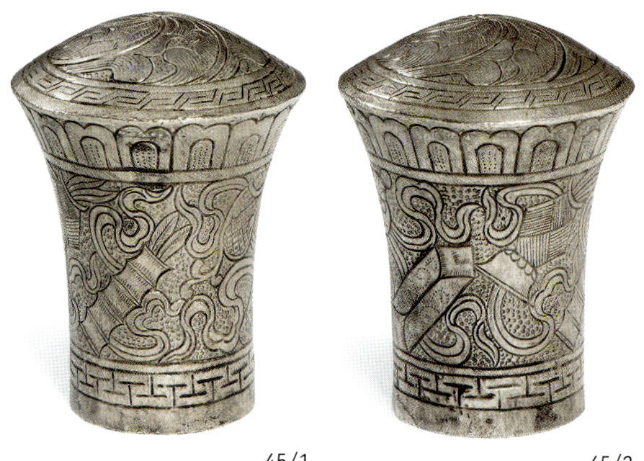

45/1 45/2

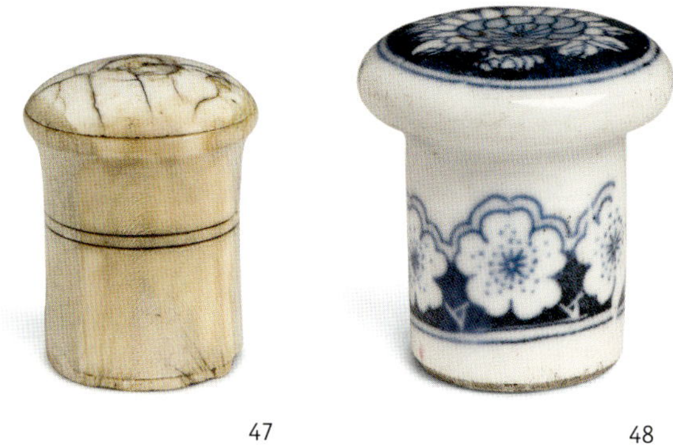

47 48

They were made separately, so that their slender bodies are moveable. This stylistic period is usually dated to the 14th to 16th centuries.

A further stylistic development is represented by end caps which are likewise openwork, whose uppermost level is a dense net of intertwining tendrils with pairs of leaves. These elements form a gilded layer. The most luxuriant examples are dated to the 16th and early 17th centuries. The relatively small rosette (Fig. 51) is typical of this stylistic period.

Solid iron objects without openwork form another genre. Their ornamental decoration consists of gold and silver damascene work (Figs. 16 and 21a). They were made from the 16th to the 18th century, that is, over a relatively long period of time. Dating within that period depends on the finesse of the work and the vividness of design.

The end caps made of sheet silver suggest that serial production began in the 18th century or earlier (Figs. 34 and 38).

The final period is represented by turned brass end caps (Figs. 46a to 46d) which are devoid of decoration. Some degree of structure is only provided by the rings resulting from the process of turning. This simplification began before or at the beginning of the 19th century.

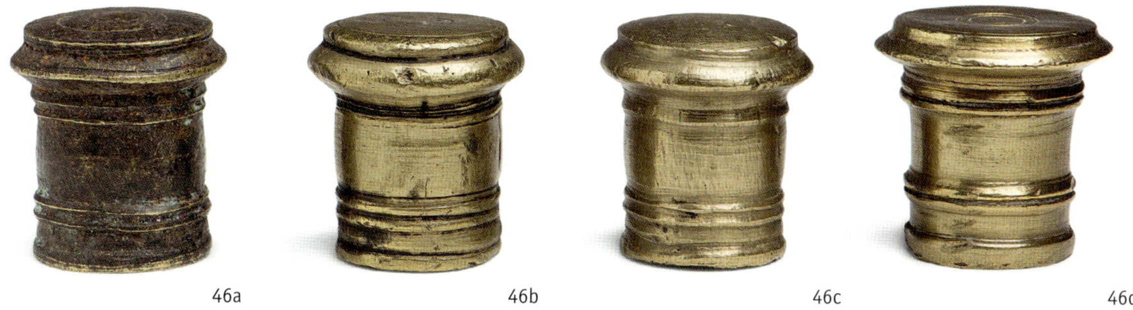
46a 46b 46c 46d

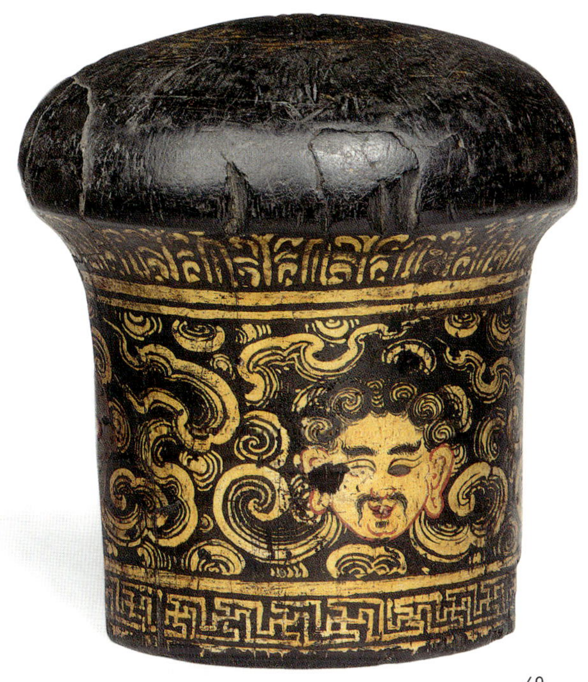
49

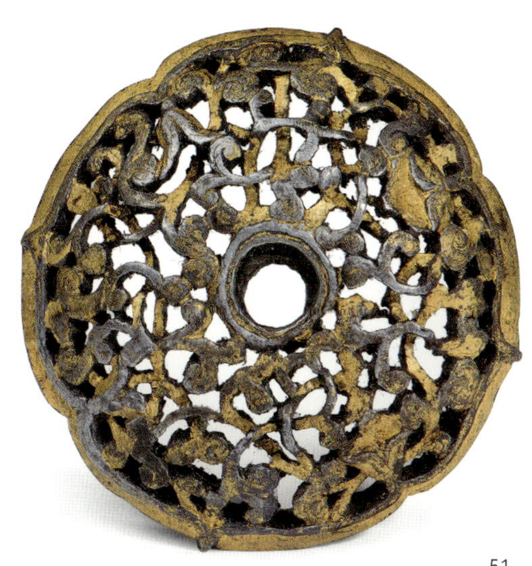
51

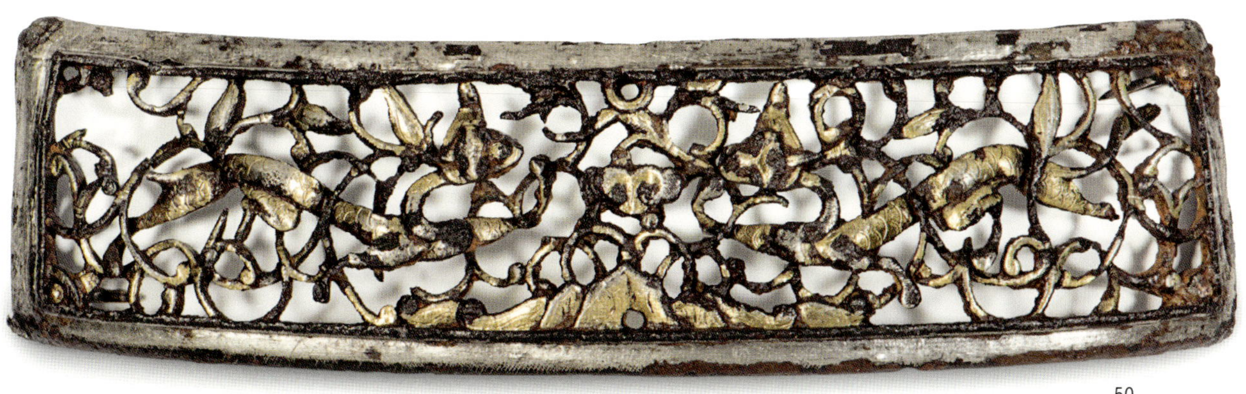
50

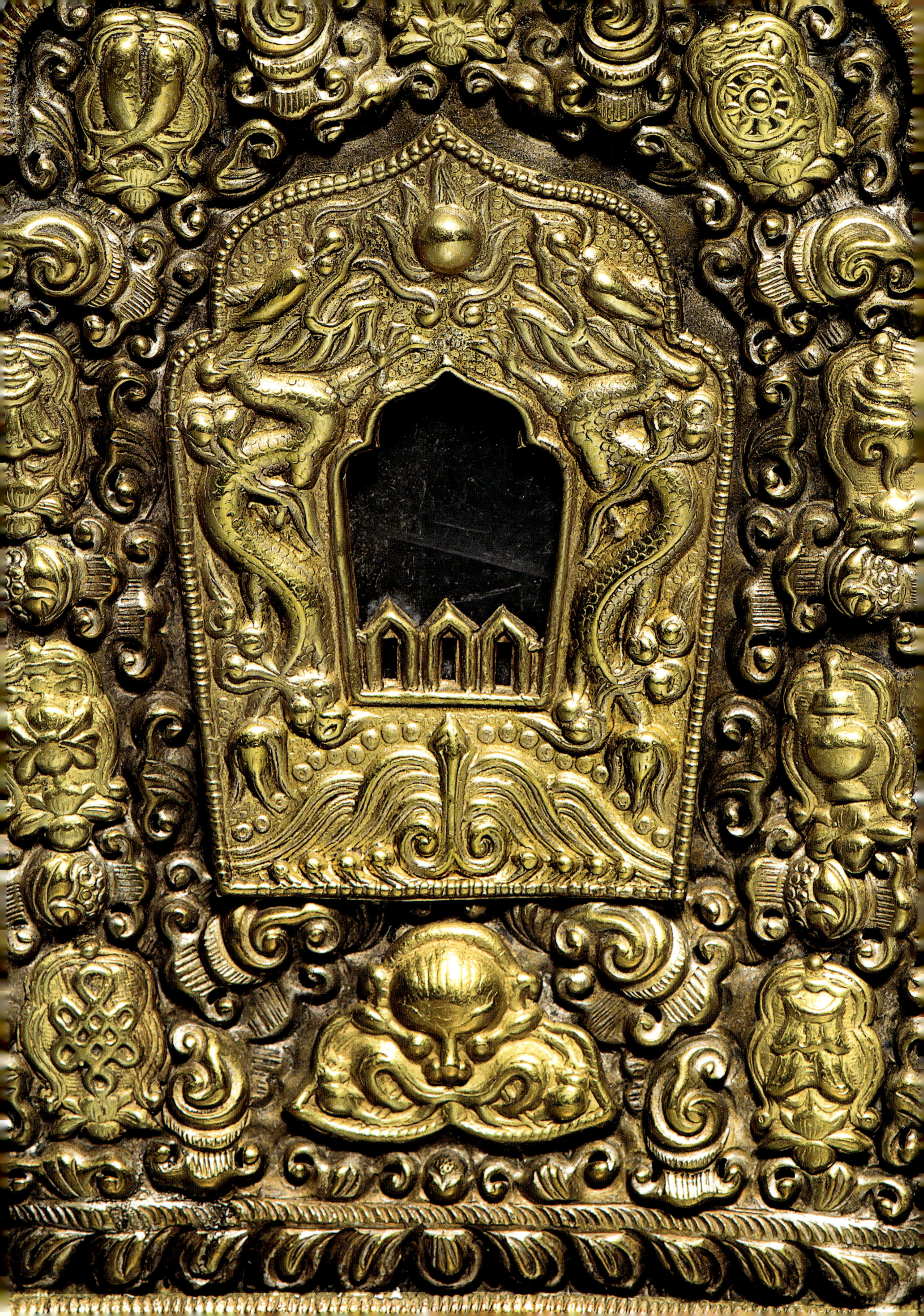

Hans Weihreter

THE BLESSINGS OF SACRED SIGNS

Jewellery in the Tibetan Cultural Sphere

THE ESSENCE OF TIBETAN JEWELLERY

Detail of Fig. 12

In the Tibetan cultural sphere, jewellery is said have an effect beyond the merely decorative. The primary aim is to protect those who wear such jewellery against the uncounted dangers which lurk all around, through the materials from which the jewellery is made and in its depiction of sacred characters. To provide the widest and most magical level of protection, it is also imperative to adorn animals with protective jewellery. Bridles are richly decorated with powerful symbols and amulets are specially made for animals in order to serve this important purpose, as well as the desire to demonstrate the social rank and dignity of their owners.

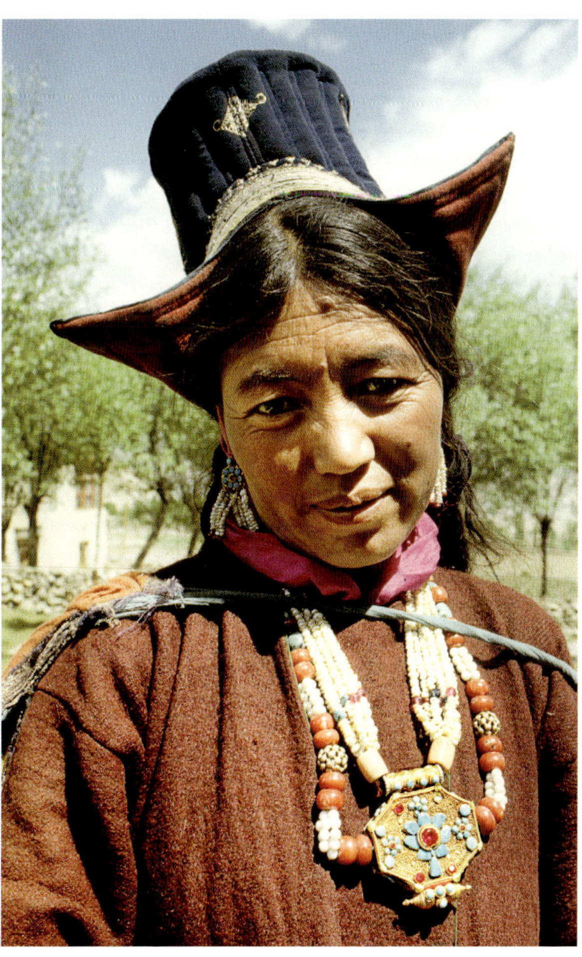

Fig. 1: Woman from Ladakh with typical golden *ga'u*

In the eyes of people living in the Tibetan cultural sphere, a panoply of magnificently crafted everyday objects should not only provide decoration and a display of material wealth, but also exercise a decidedly magical form of protection. It would be presumptuous to offer a comprehensive overview of the complexities of "jewellery in the Tibetan cultural sphere" within the framework of this article. Nevertheless its basic features can be outlined with reference to examples of typical Tibetan jewellery.

AMULET CONTAINERS, RELIQUARIES, PORTABLE AND HOME ALTARS: THE GA'U

The objects known as *ga'u* in the Tibetan cultural sphere form a complex group of items, bringing together concepts such as jewellery, amulets, reliquaries, home shrines and temple offerings. The literal meaning of the word *ga'u* is simply "box" or "container". However, for Buddhists in the Tibetan cultural sphere, objects labelled as *ga'u* are connected with many diverse aspects of their religious life.

Even with small amulet containers, the decorative character of a *ga'u* can be seen quite clearly. In this form, a *ga'u* is usually worn on the chest from a necklace of coral and turquoise (e.g., see Figs. 7 to 11). If the wearer is a woman, a pearl necklace might also carry the amulet container. This woman from Sabu (Ladakh) was photographed in 1982 (Fig. 1). She was wearing a *ga'u* of gold, turquoise and red glass beads. A necklace of magnificent coral, pearls and gold beads confirms the high social rank of the lady. This style of *ga'u* is typical of production in Ladakh during the second

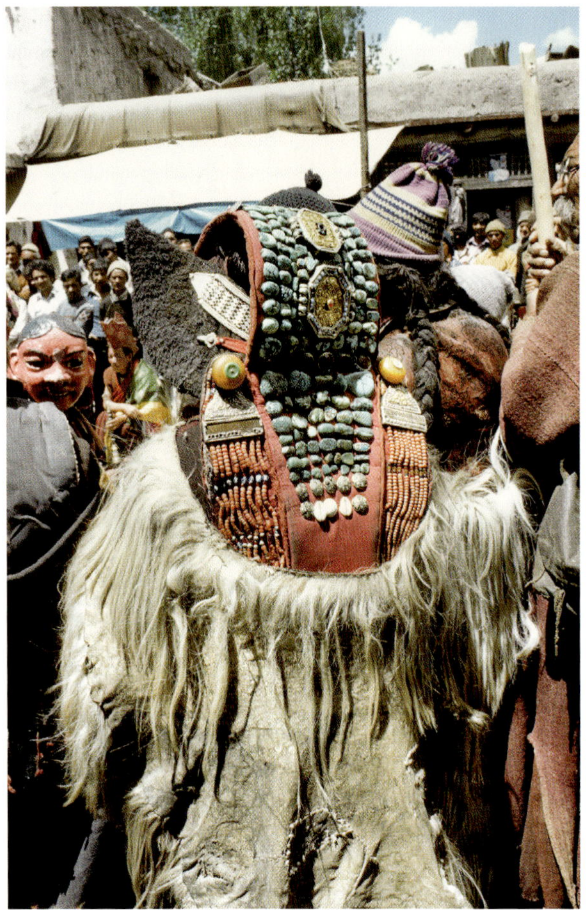

Fig. 2: Festively attired woman with *perag* and *perag-ga'u*, photograph taken in Leh

half of the 20th century (Weihreter 1988: 104, 108). It shows a floral stylised "Tree of Life" made of eight turquoises and a single red glass stone, on a base of fine filigree wire. A *ga'u* for men would never use pearls to form a necklace, since the wearing of pearls is reserved solely for women. There are different basic forms for this kind of amulet container, specifically for men and for women (Weihreter 1988: 109). In addition, in some areas of the Tibetan cultural area, amulet containers also known as *ga'u* are specially made for the monumental headdresses worn by women. Prime examples are the *ga'u* which often adorn the splendid turquoise-embellished headgear (*perag* in Ladakhi and Zanskari) of women in Ladakh and Zanskar (Weihreter 1988: 85–87, Figs. 29, 30, 33, 35, and Weihreter 2010: 162-165). For example two *ga'u* can be seen (Fig. 2) stitched onto the *perag* of this festively attired woman in Leh (Ladakh). They differ from the *ga'u* worn on a necklace in that they have two wide eyelets which allow them to be sewn onto a textile background. These amulet containers were made in Ladakh specifically for the turquoise headdresses known as *perag*.

With *ga'u* made in the style of jewellery, the features which are regarded as having magical properties remain for the most part hidden inside the amulet container. It could be a holy scripture consecrated by a lama, perhaps sewn into a cloth bag or preserved in a *ga'u* worn by animals and humans. Woollen threads form the shape of a strictly stylised *mandala*. Holy *mantras* and magical texts are written on carefully folded paper, invisible from the outside. This is often done by a qualified lama, carefully matched to the client's need for protection (Weihreter 1988: 174–175). Often the five correct iconographic colours of the five transcendent Buddhas (Sanskrit *Dhyani* Buddhas) are used for the different coloured woollen threads, underlining the *mandala*-like character of the amulet (Fig. 3).

Soil from a place of pilgrimage, magic stones regarded as holding special powers, consecrated rice grains or a contact relic of a holy person are also kept in a *ga'u* of this kind. Small scraps of cloth from a holy man's garment are regarded as having a very beneficial effect.[1] A *ga'u* carrying a pebble from holy Mount Kailash or from sacred Lake Manasarovar (in West Tibet) is considered especially propitious. Often the contents of a *ga'u* are collected by a recognised lama specifically for the wearer or the bearer. A little window can be seen on the front of a few of the smaller amulet containers of the type worn on a necklace as jewellery. Such pieces are closely related to the often very large *ga'u* shrines found mainly on the home altar of residential families or on the altar in a nomad's tent. This view inside a tent in West Tibet (Fig. 4) was taken near holy Mount Kailash. In the background is the home altar of the family. It consists of two collapsible wooden tables (Tib. *tschoktsche*), on which can be seen some metal ritual vessels and a holy book, with a picture for meditation (Tib. *thangka*) hanging above. On altars of this kind, small-format *thangkas* (Tib. *gzagli*) are often found in handsome box-shaped *ga'u* (e.g., see Fig. 17).

In a *ga'u* with windows, small paintings are kept which depict deities or a holy person. These miniature *thangkas* are called *gzagli*. They are painted by expert lamas under the same strict rules and purity laws as also observed when painting the large *thangkas* (Weihreter 1988: 102).

Sometimes a small idol, made of loam from a metal cast and then dried in the sun (see Figs. 14 and 15), is clearly visible in this kind of *ga'u*. Now and again some of the ashes of a deceased holy man could be mixed into the loam used to make these idols. Such clay figurines were thus turned into relics. These idols are called *tsa tsa*. Only very rarely is a *tsa tsa* made of fired clay. *Tsa tsa* could also be used as votive offerings in temples and *chorten* (Tib. *mchod rten*; Sanskrit *stūpa*). Many *tsa tsa* emerged from the wanton destruction of a *chorten* at Tholing in West Tibet, dating

Fig. 3: Contents of a *ga'u* made from paper and woollen threads

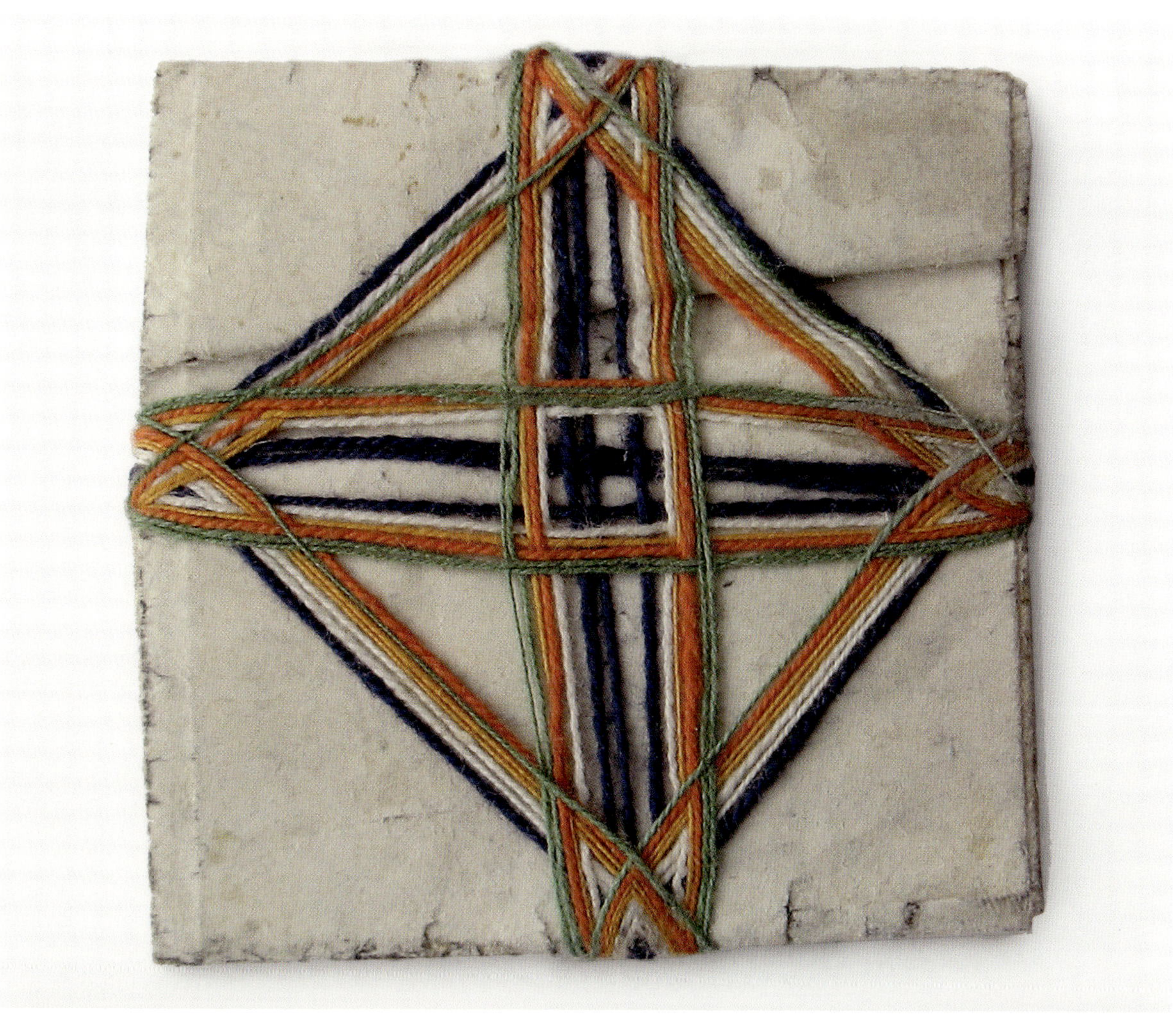

Fig. 4: Nomad tent with home altar in West Tibet

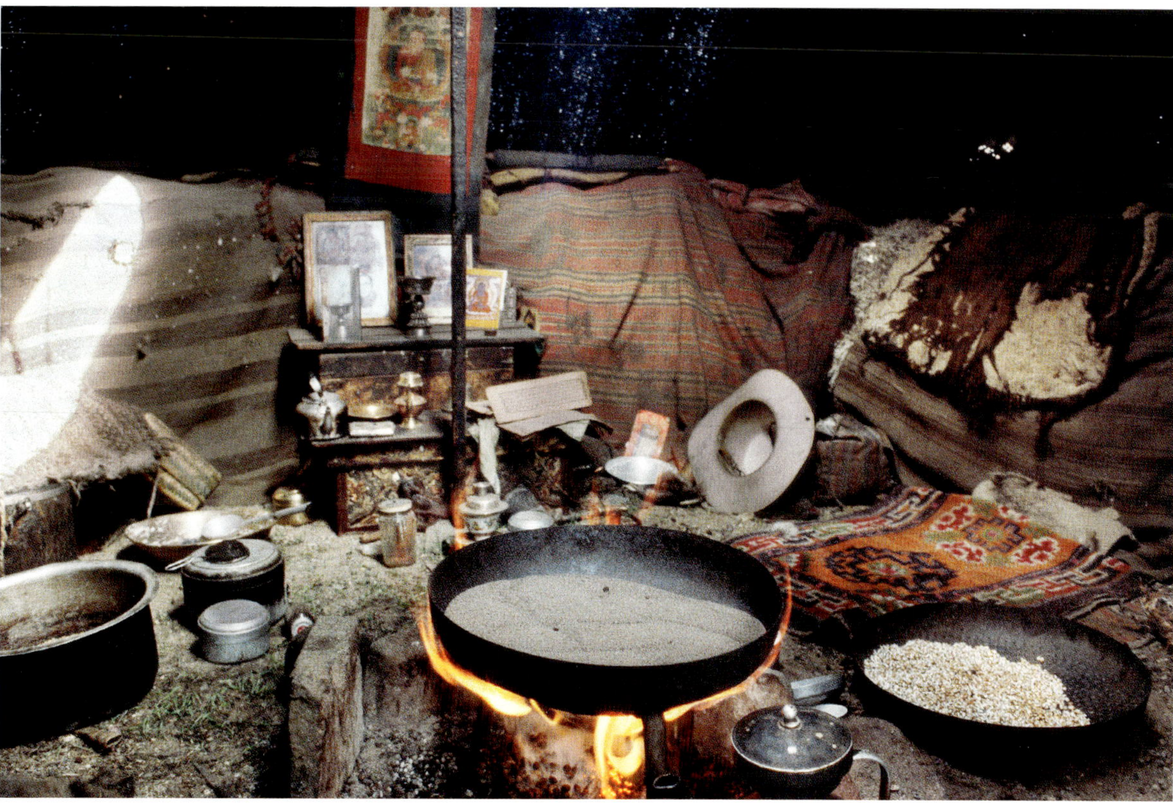

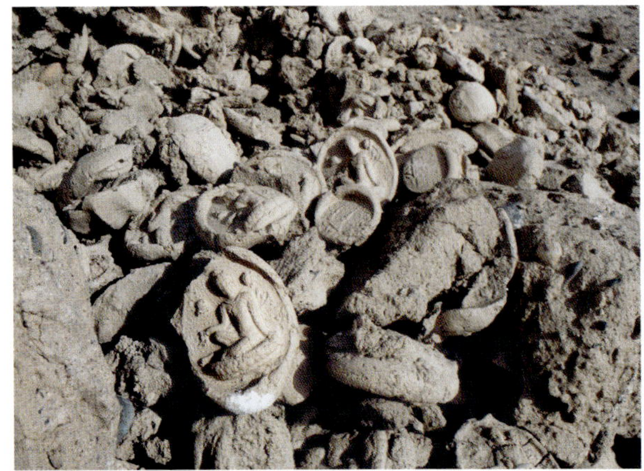

Fig. 5: *Tsa tsa* in a ruined *chorten* at Tholing, West Tibet

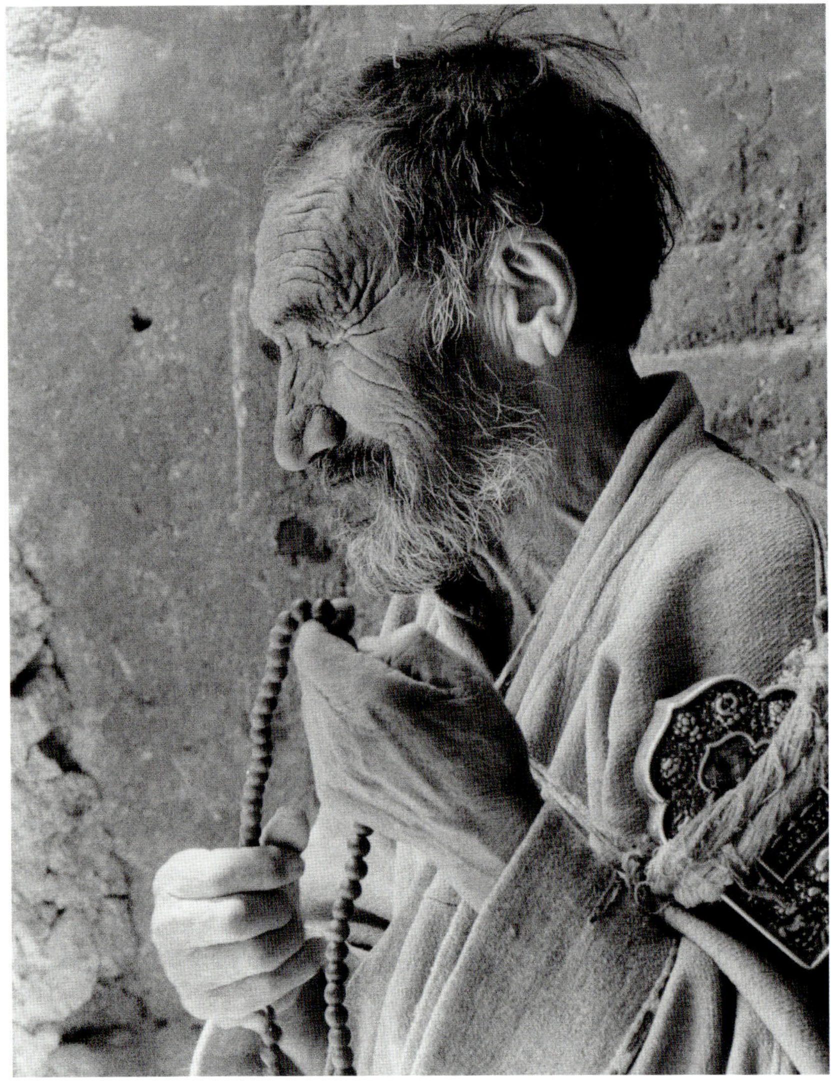

Fig. 6: Pilgrim in Ladakh with large box-style *ga'u*

back to the 10th and 11th centuries. On the nearest *tsa tsa* can be seen the image of an elegant *Bodhisattva* (Fig. 5). Every Tibetan believer would consider himself most fortunate to carry a *tsa tsa* of this type in his *ga'u*. However, a Buddhist would never steal an object from a *chorten*, not even if it were damaged, for fear of unleashing some kind of great calamity.

Occasionally one might find images of a deity made from metal (see Fig. 18) being used in a *ga'u* with window. This would happen above all in the large-format portable *ga'u* shrines used predominantly on the altars of monasteries, the home altars of wealthy families and in the tents of nomads.

Pilgrims sometimes tie a large *ga'u* shrine to their body, and so carry it with them on their journey. This pilgrim (Fig. 6) was praying in the monastery at Zerskamo (Ladakh). He was carrying a large box-type *ga'u* with a *gzagli* on his left upper arm (Weihreter 1988: 220–223).

If someone was going on a long, perilous caravan journey, he would be happy to take with him a shrine featuring the image of a deity or a saint in order to occasionally meditate in front of it. The contemplation of a sacred image or a god figure should, according to Buddhists in the Tibetan cultural sphere, enable the achievement of a lofty goal in meditation, namely "liberation through seeing"!

It was considered a very great happiness to carry round a small metal figure from a bygone period in one's *ga'u* shrine. Tibetans still devote high veneration to medieval cult figures today (see Fig. 18), especially those made from precious metal alloys. In this way numerous works of art from long defunct empires, e.g., from the Buddhist-Hindu Kashmir of the Middle Ages, the West Tibetan kingdom of Guge-Purang and the Empire of the Pala kings in Bengal, have survived through stormy times in a carefully guarded family treasure chest. Even the enigmatic ancient metal objects known as *thog lcags* in Tibet (Weihreter 2002: 89–98) have sometimes been carried in a *ga'u* (see Figs. 18–20). It has also happened occasionally that a *ga'u* has been custom built in the necessary form for a *thog lcag*, because of its perceived effectiveness as a particularly magical alloy and its advanced age.

Amulet Container and Reliquary *ga'u* (Fig. 7)

This type of amulet container was only carried by women in the Tibetan cultural sphere (Weihreter 1988: 109). The specimen shown here has a silver body. The reverse side is closed by an iron cover. The wide eyelet mount was stabilised with copper leaf.

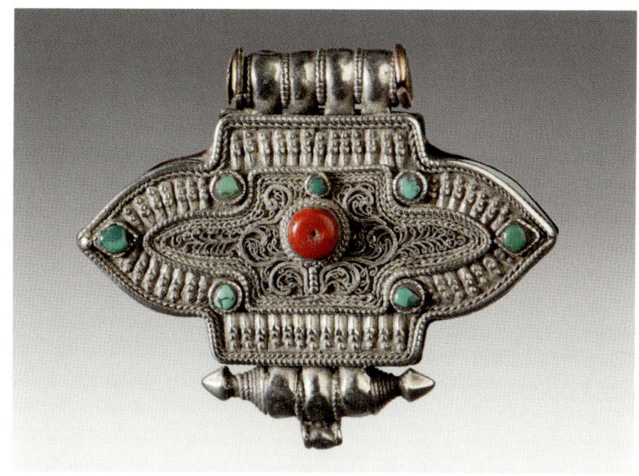

Fig. 7: Amulet container and reliquary. Tibetan cultural sphere, 1st half 20th c., silver, copper, iron, turquoise, coral, 10.1×8.2 cm, 80 g

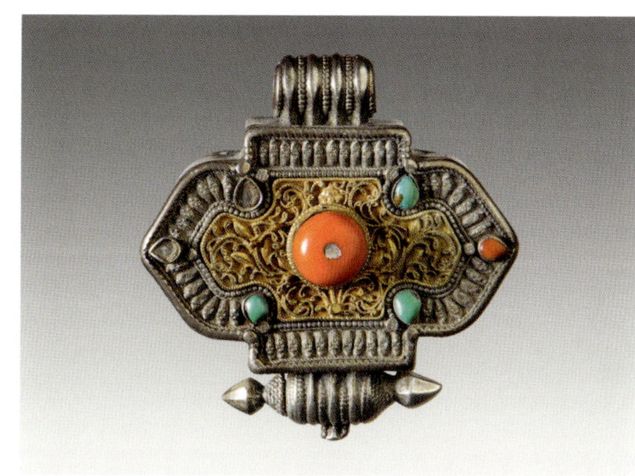

Fig. 8: Amulet container and reliquary. Tibetan cultural sphere, 1st half 20th c., silver, partly gilded, turquoise, coral, copper, 7.8×8.1×2.1 cm, 100 g

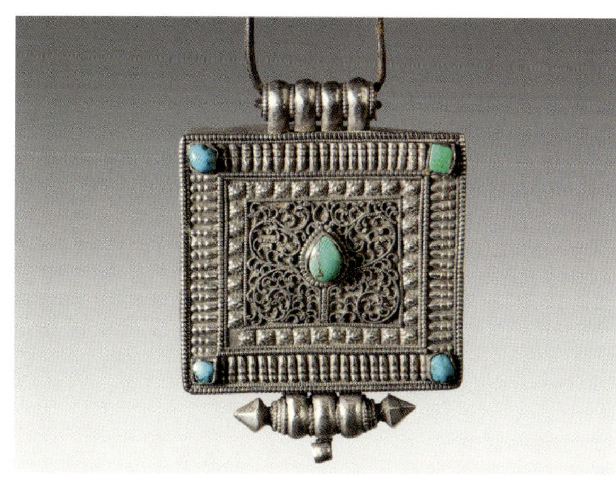

Fig. 9: Amulet container and reliquary. Tibetan cultural sphere, 1st half 20th c., silver, copper, turquoise, 6.3×8.8×1.5 cm, 70 g

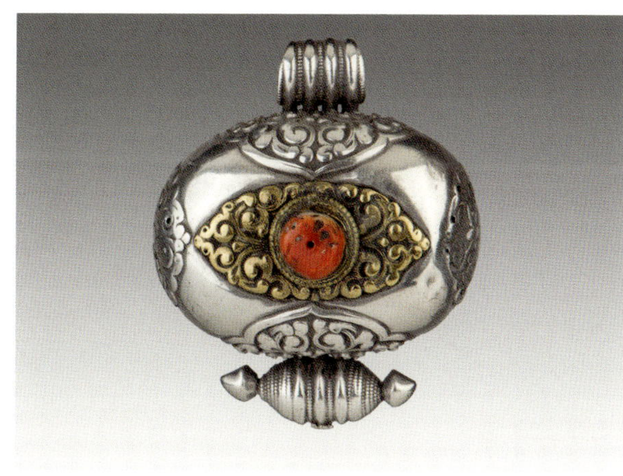

Fig. 10: Amulet container and reliquary. Tibet, early 20th c., silver, yellowish metal alloy, coral, 6.6×7.6 cm, 90 g

This kind of *ga'u* would be worn on the chest from necklaces of turquoise and coral, occasionally also of pearl. On its front is an extremely stylised world tree of silver filigree. This symbol appears often on Tibetan jewellery, because it is connected in Tibetan culture with very complex ideas and should offer very wide-ranging protection (Weihreter 1988: 62). At the centre of the world tree is a resplendent deep red coral, over which a small turquoise appears at the top of the tree motif. Six more turquoises are fixed in a wide and ornately embossed border. The bottom is formed by an extremely stylised *vajra* (Tib. *rdo rje*) and a small eyelet, to which an additional chain could be hooked.

Holy scriptures were sometimes kept in such *ga'u* (see Fig. 3), perhaps also a small stone from a place of pilgrimage or the contact relic of a saint.

Amulet Container and Reliquary *ga'u* (Fig. 8)

This *ga'u* was worn by women and belongs to the same type as that shown in Fig. 7. It consists of a silver body, the centre of which is gilded. The reverse side is closed with a copper lid.

On the front is an extremely stylised world tree of silver filigree. The centre of the world tree is resplendent with a bright red coral. Four additional turquoises and two pieces of coral would originally have been set in a wide and ornately embossed border. One turquoise and a piece of coral are missing. The decorative plate and world tree motif were gilded. Obviously the wearer of this jewellery also wanted to enjoy the magical protection of the sun metal, gold (Tib. *gser*). The bottom is formed by a stylised *vajra* (Tib. *rdo rje*) and the remains of a small eyelet.

Amulet Container and Reliquary *ga'u* (Fig. 9)

This rectangular *ga'u* has a body made of silver. The reverse side is closed with a copper lid. On the front is a stylised world tree of silver filigree. A turquoise is fixed in the centre of the world tree. Four additional turquoises feature in a wide and ornately embossed border. One of them is presumably a replacement for the original. Between the wide outer border and the world tree motif runs a narrow margin of extremely stylised floral motifs, made using the dapping technique. The bottom is formed by an extremely stylised *vajra* and the remains of an eyelet.

Amulet Container and Reliquary *ga'u* (Fig. 10)

This type of oval *ga'u* was only worn by women (Weihreter 1988: 109). The example shown here has a silver body. The reverse side is closed with a lid made of a yellowish metal alloy.

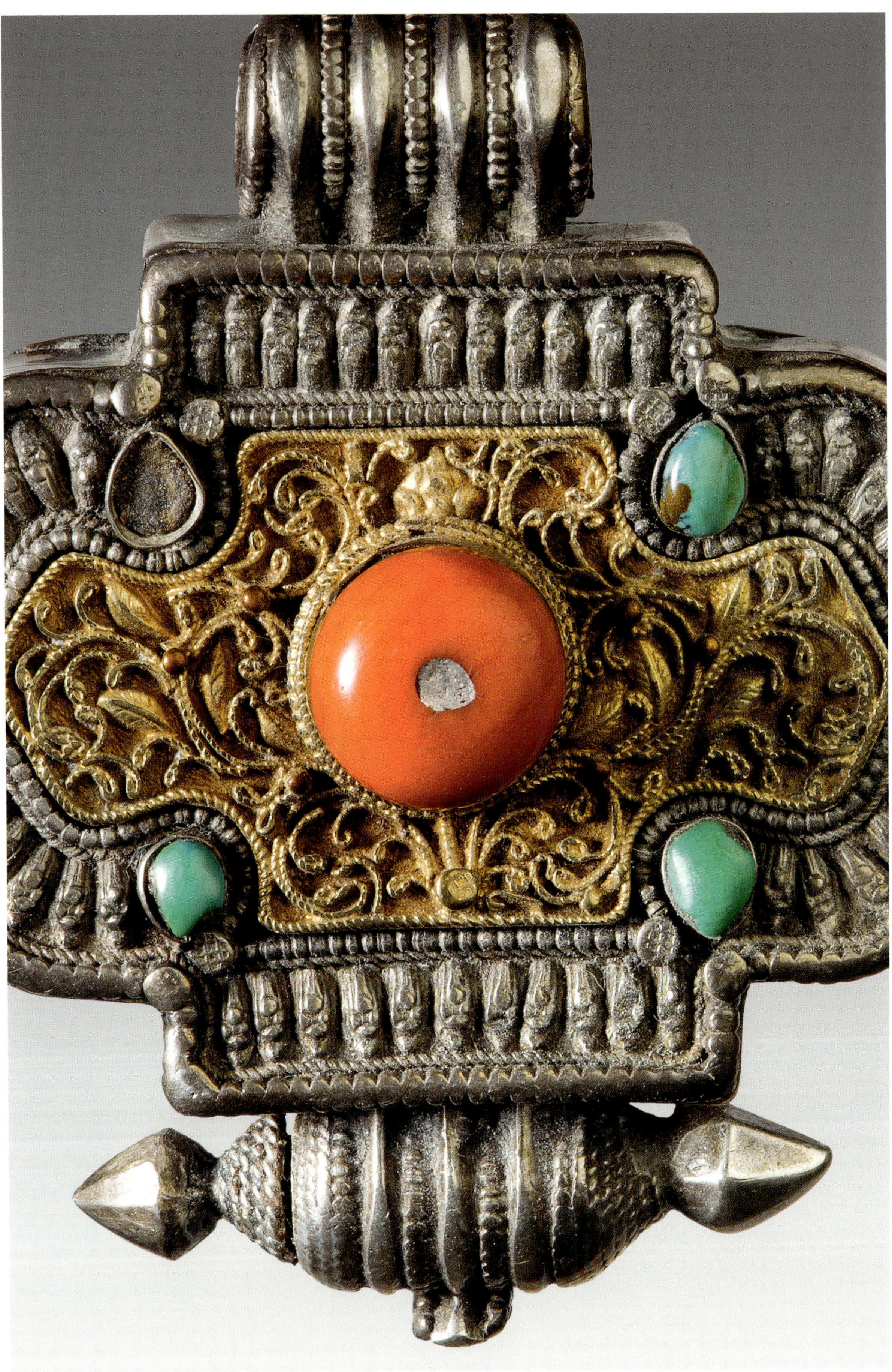

Detail of Fig. 8

Detail of Fig. 11

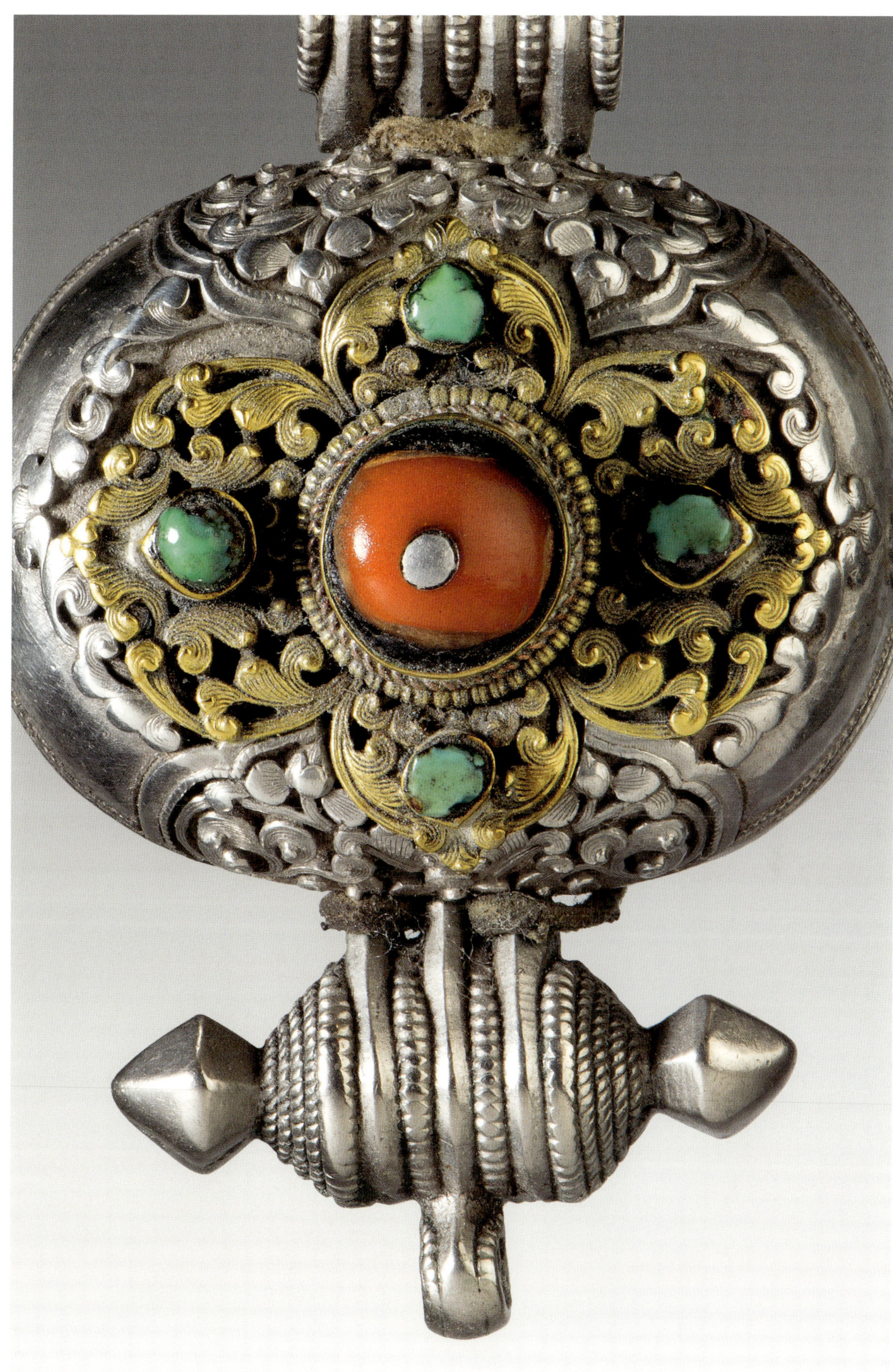

Such *ga'u* were worn on the chest, hanging from necklaces of turquoise and coral or pearls. The front shows stylised floral motifs created using embossing and engraving techniques. The centre of the *ga'u* is dominated by an embossed ornamental plate of gilded silver or a yellowish metal alloy, in which a piece of deep red coral is fixed. The bottom is formed by an extremely stylised *vajra*.

A *ga'u* of this kind might contain sacred writings (see Fig. 3), sometimes perhaps also a small stone from a pilgrimage site or the contact relic of a saint.

Amulet Container and Reliquary *ga'u* (Fig. 11)

This oval *ga'u* has a body of silver. The reverse side is covered with a silver lid. On the front are stylised floral motifs created by embossing and engraving techniques. The centre of the *ga'u* is dominated by a decorative panel of a yellowish metal alloy in a floral design, into which a deep red coral piece and four turquoises are set. The depth of the embossed work and the elegant curve of the floral motifs suggest a slightly older age than the similar *ga'u* shown in Fig. 10. The bottom is formed by an extremely stylised *vajra* and a small eyelet into which another chain could be hooked occasionally.

Amulet Container and Reliquary *ga'u* (Fig. 12)

This *ga'u* has a body made of copper. Its front is formed by an ornately embossed brass plate. The middle part of the brass plate and the ten small metal plates with religious symbols were made separately, and attached to the front panel with metal clasps. One of the original four eyelets for attaching the carrying strap on the sides of the *ga'u* is missing.

The following symbols are represented: at the top is a six-piece jewel (Sanskrit *ratna*, Tib. *nor bu*). Left and right of the window appear the Eight Auspicious Symbols (Sanskrit *Aṣṭamaṅgala*, Tib. *bkra shis rtags brgyad*). The window is flanked by two dragons (Tib. *'brug*), with the sun appearing lit up by flames between the dragons' mouths. Just

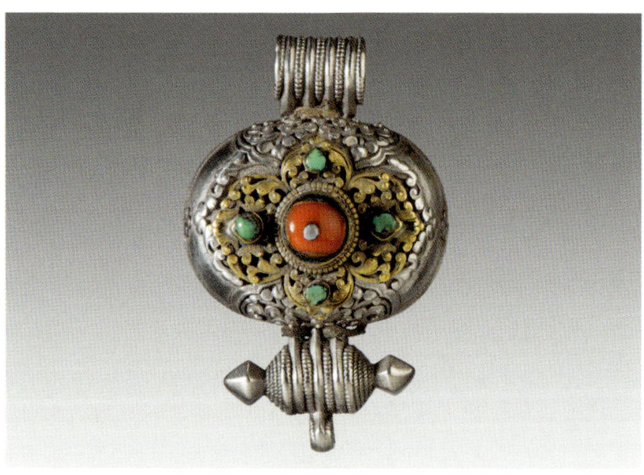

Fig. 11: Amulet container and reliquary. Tibet, presumably 19th c., silver, yellowish metal alloy, coral, turquoise, 5.6×8.4 cm, 88 g

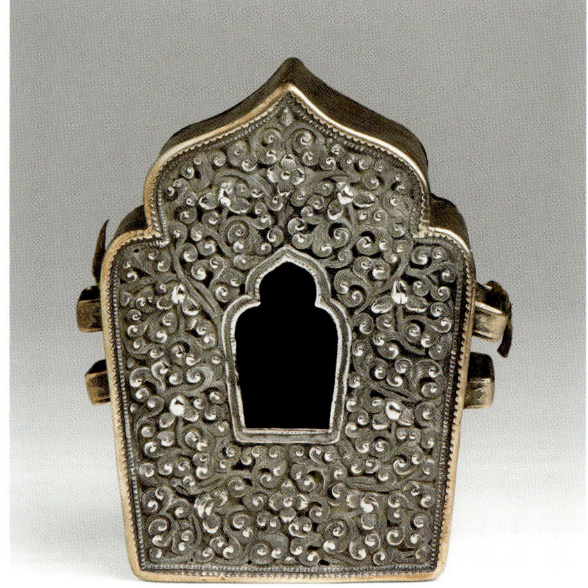

Fig. 12: Amulet container and reliquary. East Tibet, 1st half 20th c., copper, brass, glass, 11.9×9.2 (without lateral eyelets) ×3.9 cm, 155 g

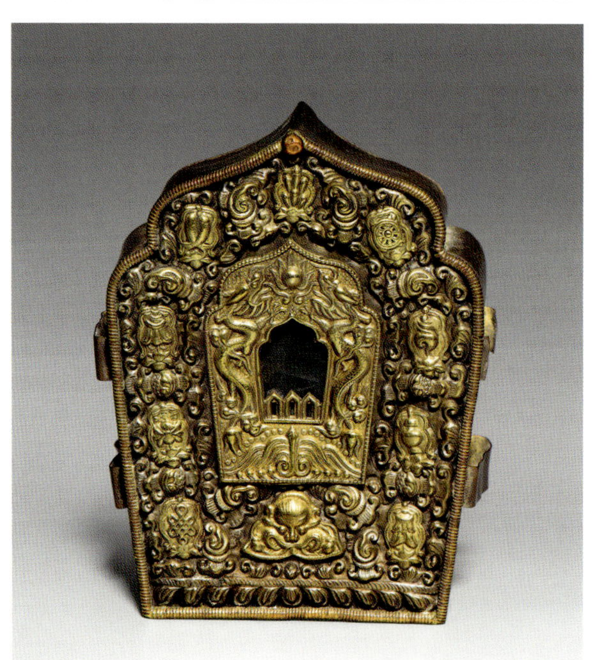

Fig. 13: Amulet container and reliquary. Tibet, 1st half 20th c., silver, silver-plated copper, 10.7×8.1 (without lateral eyelets) ×4 cm, 165 g

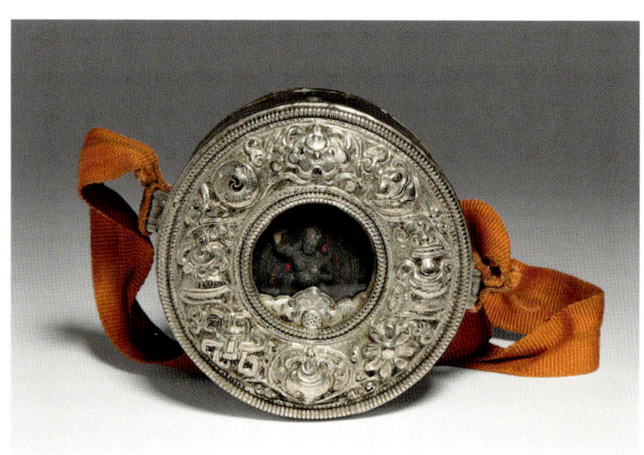

Fig. 14: Amulet container and reliquary. Tibetan cultural sphere, 20th c., silver, copper, fabric ribbon, enclosed a *tsa tsa* made of clay, diameter 9.8 cm (without lateral eyelets), height 5.2 cm, 200 g without contents

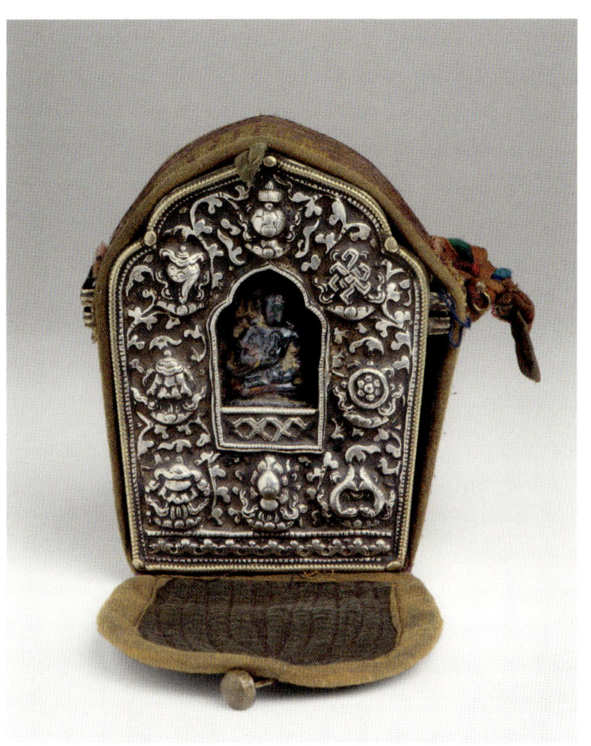

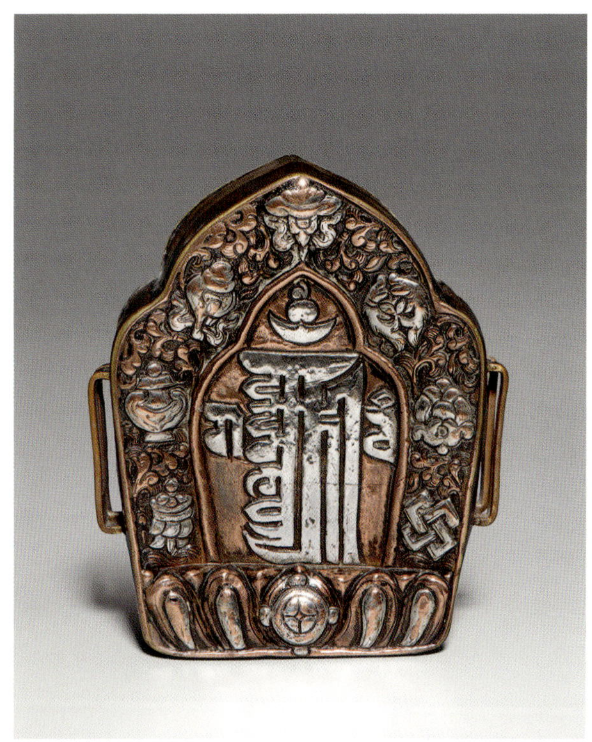

Fig. 15: Amulet container and reliquary. Tibetan cultural sphere, date uncertain, copper, silver, glass, textile, enclosed a *tsa tsa* made of (fired?) clay, 11.2×8.6 (without lateral eyelets) ×5.1 cm, 300 g (with textile covering)

Fig. 16: Amulet container and reliquary. Ladakh, 19th c., copper, partially silver-plated, silver-plating in the centre, 13.3×9.8×3.6 cm, 205 g

below the window one can recognise water symbols and an extremely stylised mountain icon, probably the world mountain Meru. Below Mount Meru, an expressively styled "Glorious Face" (Sanskrit *kīrtimukha*, Tib. *ci mi 'dra* or *gzi gdon*) provides magical protection. The bottom edge of this highly ornate front plate is formed by a stylised lotus base, which may suggest that the *ga'u* was occasionally used on a home altar, with dedications and a meditation image (Tib. *gzagli*). The style of work has Chinese elements, which clearly indicate an origin in East Tibet before the 1950s.

Amulet Container and Reliquary *ga'u* (Fig. 13)

An embossed and partially broken front plate with fine silver engraving graces this *ga'u*. The stylised floral motifs point to manufacture before 1950 in Central Tibet. The body of the *ga'u* is made of silver-plated copper and has floral decoration.

Amulet Container and Reliquary *ga'u* (Fig. 14)

The front of this *ga'u* displays the Eight Auspicious Symbols in embossed work. This is a very rough but also charming work from a provincial workshop. Inside is a clay *tsa tsa*, representing the *Bodhisattva* Vajrapani. The *tsa tsa* could be considerably older than the *ga'u*, although maybe it was just produced using an old model. A more recent textile ribbon proves that this *ga'u* was in use until just a few years ago.

Amulet Container and Reliquary *ga'u* (Fig. 15)

The front of this *ga'u* displays the Eight Auspicious Symbols in embossed work. It comes from a provincial workshop, and so it is not possible to establish the exact date of origin. However, production in the 19th century would seem very likely. This is suggested in particular by the remains of very fine engravings in which the auspicious symbols can be seen. The *ga'u* has obviously been used by travelling pilgrims. The original has been completely preserved, with its very elaborate casing made of quilted brocade. It could be sealed using a protective textile flap and a toggle closure, so that the front of the *ga'u* was well protected while travelling. The textile strap is made from a typical Bhutanese fabric. According to its previous owner this *ga'u* was used in Bhutan, where it was also acquired.

Inside the *ga'u*, a *tsa tsa* is visible in the image of the *Bodhisattva* Vajrasattva. This *tsa tsa* is very likely a much older work. Nevertheless an exact dating is not possible, since the metal casts for producing the *tsa tsa* were often used over a very long period of time.

Amulet Container and Reliquary *ga'u* (Fig. 16)

This *ga'u* is a classic representation of metal work from the ancient kingdom of Ladakh. Shown in embossed work on its front is the sign of the Ten Powerful Truths (Sanskrit *daśākāro vaśī*; Tib. *rnam bcu dbaṅ ldan*). This is one of the most complex symbols in Tibetan Buddhism (Weihreter

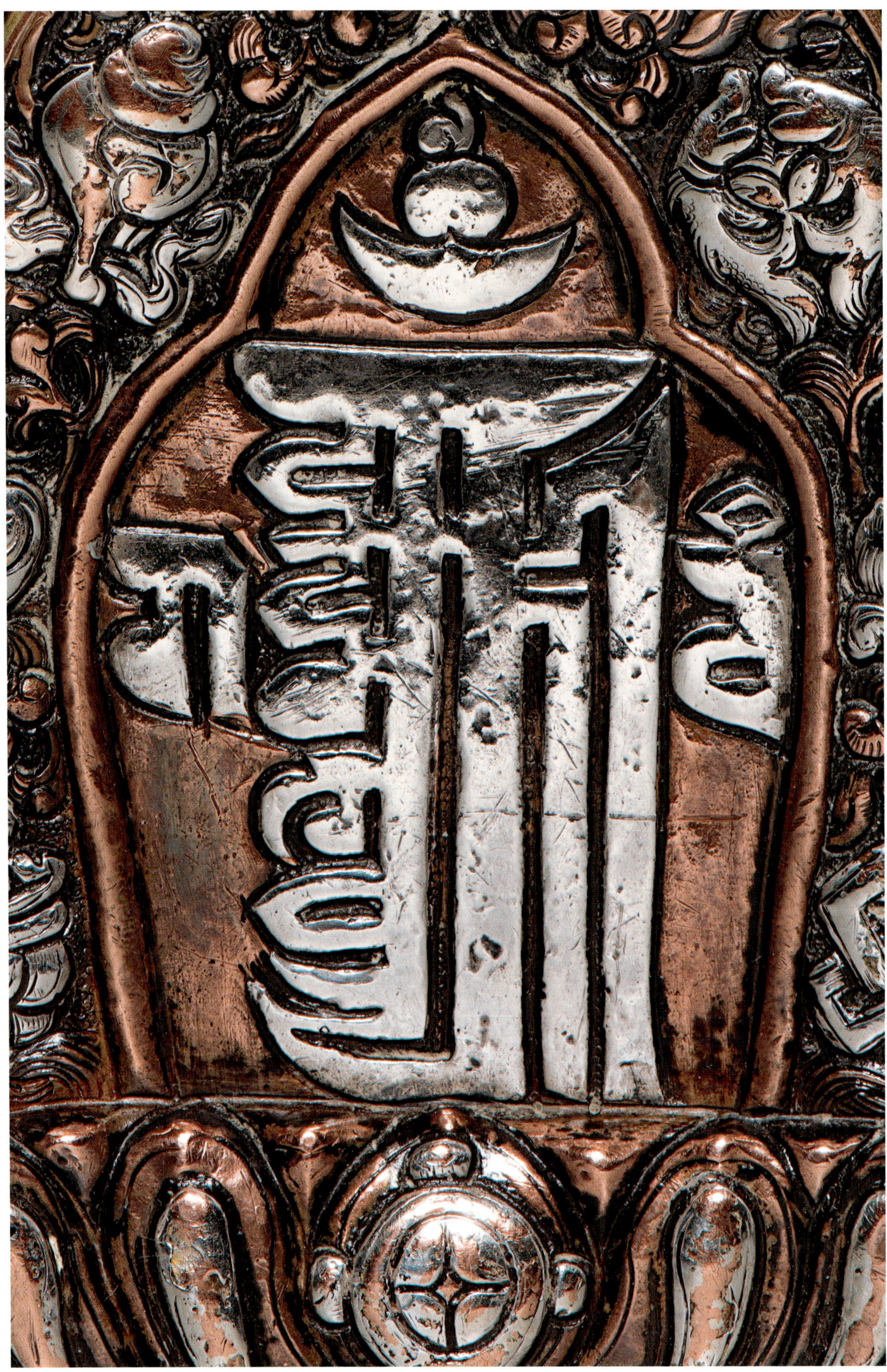
Detail of Fig. 16

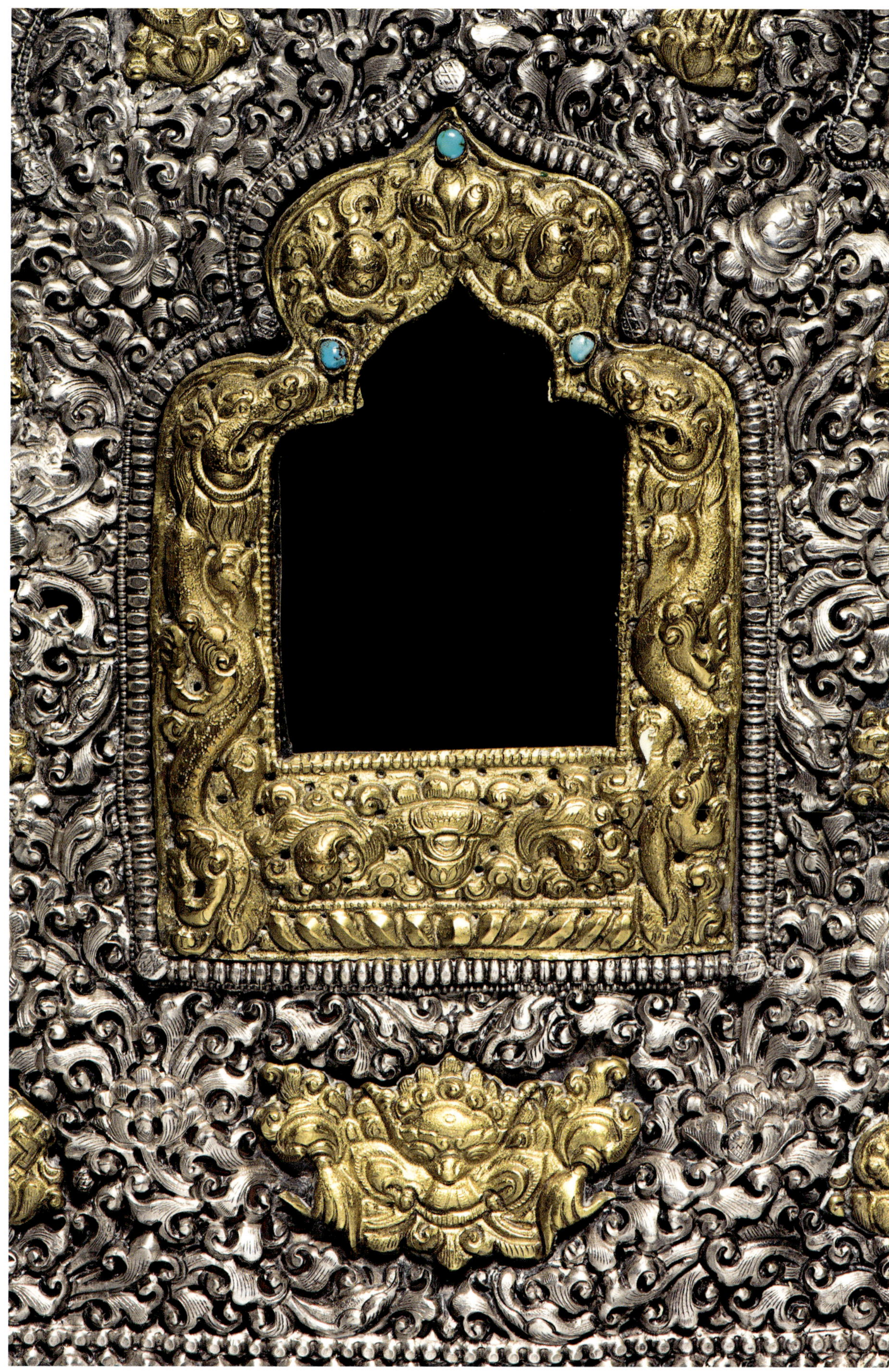
Detail of Fig. 17

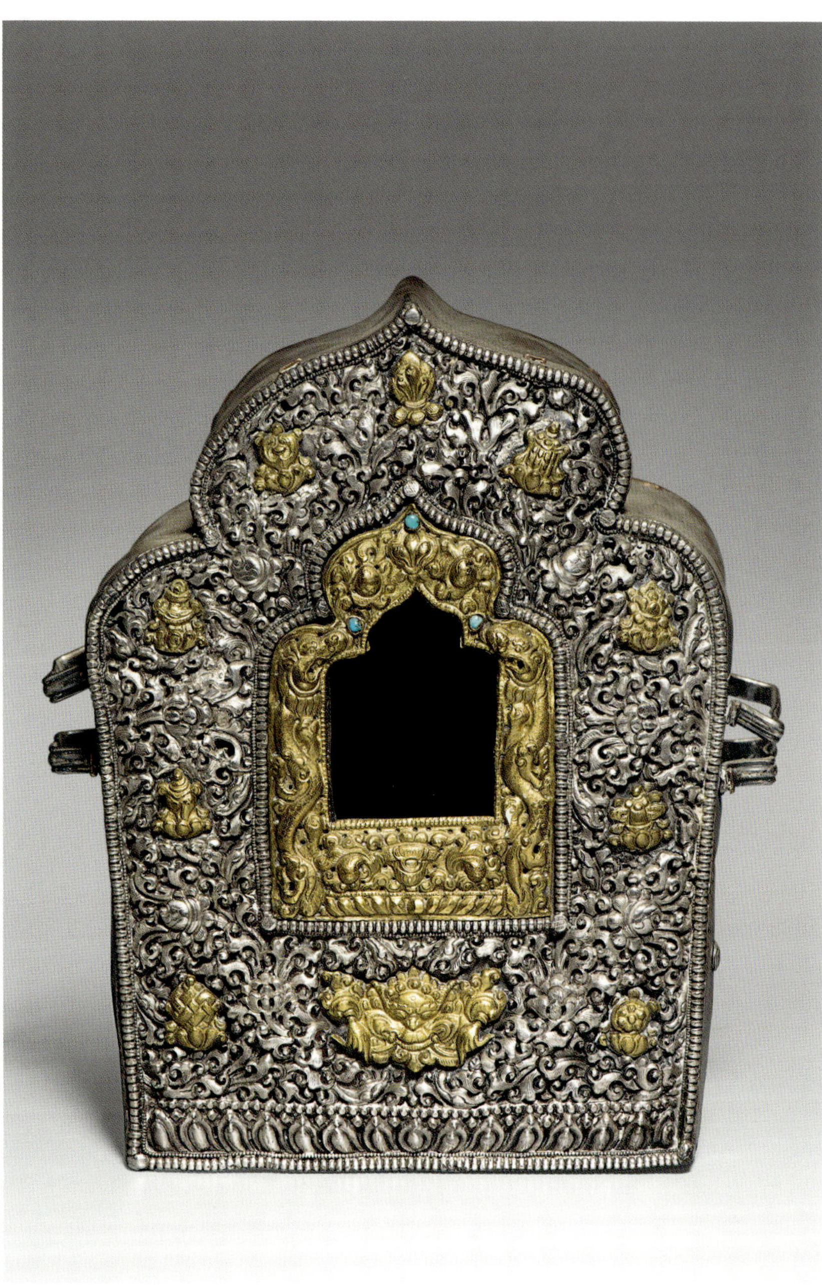

Fig. 17: Amulet container and reliquary. Tibet, 19th c., silver, yellowish metal alloy, copper, turquoise, glass, 20×14.9×9.9 cm, 860 g

1988: 72). It is surrounded by the Eight Auspicious Symbols. These representations rest on four stylised lotus leaves. All of the symbols show the remains of silver plating. The construction of this *ga'u* has an unusual feature: normally a *ga'u* is closed on its reverse side with a simple metal cover – this *ga'u*, however, is made of two components which are pushed into each other in order to create a box. Two eyelets are soldered onto each component, so that the *ga'u* has four of these in total. One could therefore keep it safely closed, which was very important for the protection of the sacred contents during long caravan journeys.

The original content is still inside this *ga'u*, namely some sand (perhaps from a place of pilgrimage) and a few seeds from a plant believed to have beneficial properties. These substances are held in a little plastic bag, which proves that the *ga'u* was still being used as an amulet container well into the 20th century.

Amulet Container and Reliquary *ga'u* (Fig. 17)

This *ga'u* has a copper body. On the front a richly embossed and decorated silver plate is fastened with metal clips, its edge overlapping the body of the *ga'u*. The central decorative panel with the window and all of the religious symbols were made separately from a yellowish metal alloy, and also secured to the front panel of the *ga'u* with metal clasps. The style of the work suggests a date of origin in the 19th century in Central Tibet.

The following symbols are represented: at the top is a three-piece jewel. Left and right of the window appear the Eight Auspicious Symbols. The window is flanked by two dragons (Tib. *'brug*), floral symbols and three turquoises appear between the dragons' mouths; just below the window is a holy book. A "Glorious Face" in the lower middle section provides magical protection. The lower border of this ornate front plate is formed by a stylised lotus base, which suggests that the *ga'u* may have been used occasionally on a home altar, with dedications and a meditation image (Tib. *gzagli*).

Amulet *thog lcags* (Fig. 18)

Ancient metal artefacts which were found by chance in the soil are known as "first iron" (Tib. *thog lcags*) in the Tibetan cultural sphere. Such objects are believed to have fallen from heaven, and are thus gifts direct from the gods. Ancient Buddhist figures are not referred to by all Tibetans as *thog lcags*. However, they are said to provide great magical protection (Weihreter 2002: 10). Despite strong signs of wear, elements of the Pala style can still be seen on this amulet. It originated either in North India (Bengal) or in Tibet in the 12th century or even earlier.

The iconography is no longer recognisable because of the strong signs of wear. Possibly it is an early form of the wrathful deity Vighnantaka (Tib. *bgegs mthar byed*).[2] Small antique figurines, such as the one shown here, were often kept in a *ga'u* in and venerated (see Fig. 12 to 15).

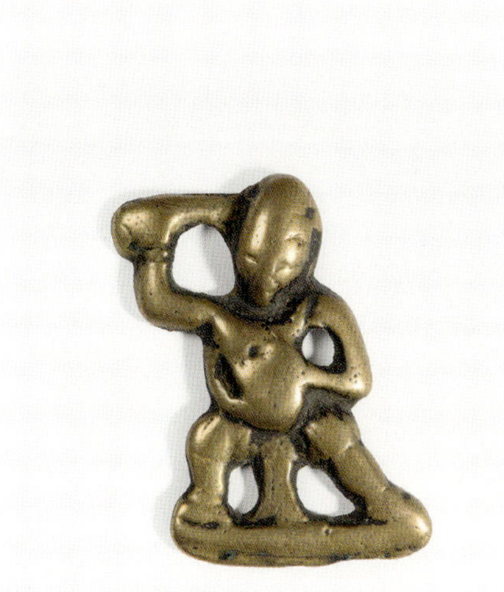

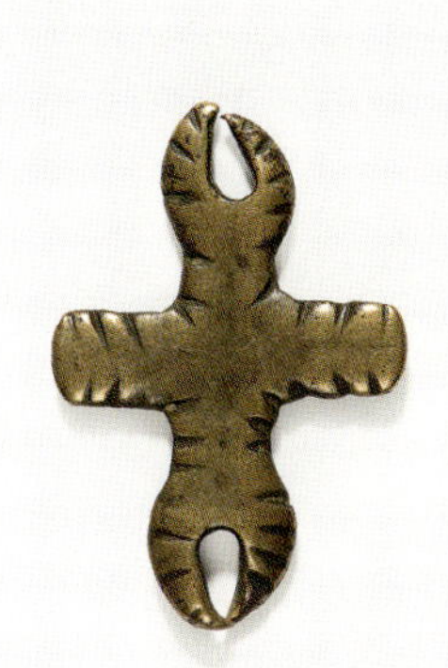

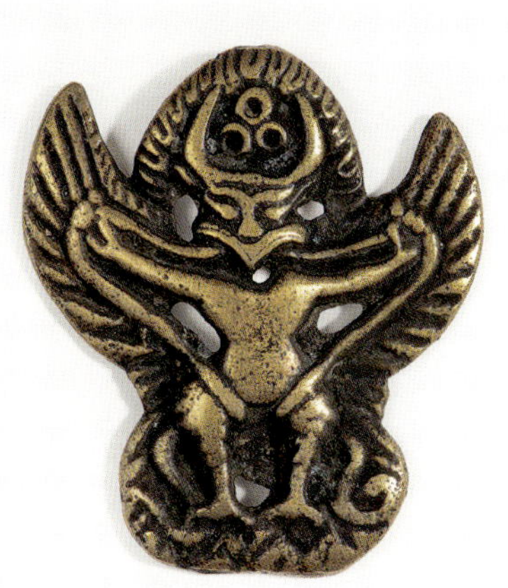

Fig. 18: Amulet. Bengal or Tibet, 12th c. or earlier, yellowish metal alloy, 4.2×3.6 cm, 13 g

Fig. 19: Amulet. Tibetan cultural sphere, date uncertain, yellowish metal alloy, 3.7×2.5 cm, 6 g

Fig. 20: Amulet. Tibetan cultural sphere, ca. 13th/14th c., yellowish metal alloy, 5.1×4.6 cm, 22 g

Amulet (Fig. 19)

This metal object is clearly a *thog lcags* according to Tibetan perceptions. People wore such objects because of their anticipated magical protective force, as a pendant or sewn onto a garment, or occasionally kept in a *ga'u*. Neither the exact age nor the original purpose of this item are known, but it is certainly a very old object.

Amulet (Fig. 20)

This amulet represents the form of the mythical bird-like creature known in the Tibetan cultural sphere as *Khyuṅ*. Although the Tibetan *Khyuṅ* is related to the Indian *Garuda*, it has much older Tibetan roots. It symbolises the masculine sky energies and stands in opposition but also as the necessary counterpoint to the feminine earth forces symbolised by snakes (Tib. *kLu*). Consequentially on this amulet he is also holding a stylised snake to his beak in his hands (in great detail in Weihreter 2002a: 71–85). People wore such *Khyuṅ* amulets either sewn onto a garment, as a pendant or as a precious protective figure in a *ga'u*.

TINDER POUCHES (ME LCAGS) AND PURSES ('BA 'KHUG)

In the Tibetan cultural area, utensils and jewellery are often one and the same thing. This is particularly evident in two everyday objects commonly used by both men and women, namely purses (Tib. *'ba 'khug*) and tinder pouches (Tib. *me lcags*). *'Ba 'khug* refers to a small leather bag which can be used as a purse. They are worn clearly visible hanging from a metal loop on one's belt.

Me lcags are also small bags of leather, in which some tinder and a small flint (usually silex) are kept. These tinder pouches are sealed underneath by a solid forged iron clasp. To make a fire, one takes the silex and some tinder out of the bag and hits the silex with the iron clasp so as to cause sparks and make the tinder glow. Admittedly this is a very laborious process which, however, in countries where the next box of matches is often in a small bazaar several days' walk away, can occasionally be very useful and even life-saving.

Both *'ba 'khug* and *me lcags* were often decorated on both sides with lavish ornamentation in different metals, often silver, and various precious stones. The eyelet mounts usually show some form of symbolic representation. Through such decoration everyday objects become similar to jewellery, since they can assume some of the important functions of jewellery in addition to their practical function: they provide a highly visible display of the wealth and social rank of the wearer. To a certain extent they also provide a means for capital investment. Above all, however, they are intended to provide magical protection through the materials of which they are made and the symbols shown on them.

Fig. 21a: Purse (front). Tibet, 19th/20th c., leather, silver, yellowish metal alloy, coral, 9.1 (up to the eyelet mount) × 12 × 4 cm, 165 g

Fig. 21b: Reverse side of the purse shown in Fig. 21a

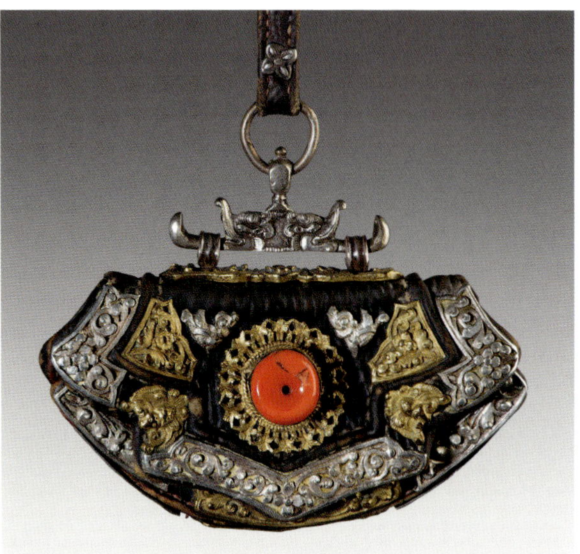

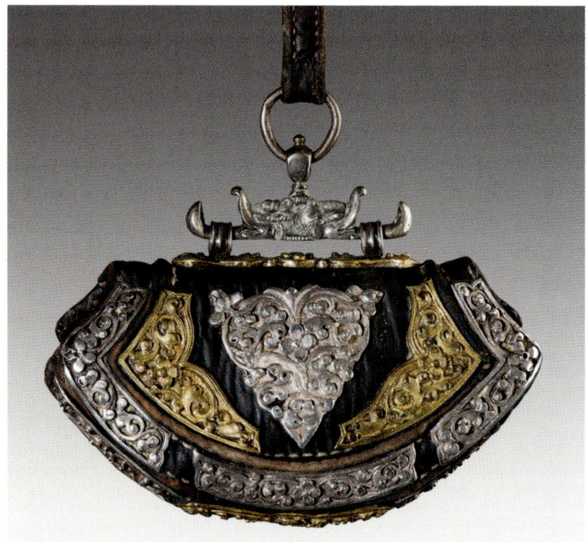

Fig. 22a: Purse (front). Tibet, presumably 19th century, iron ring (added later), leather, silver, yellowish metal alloy, iron, coral, 8.2 (without iron ring) × 11.4 × 3.6 cm, 170 g

Fig. 22b: Reverse side of the purse shown in Fig. 22a

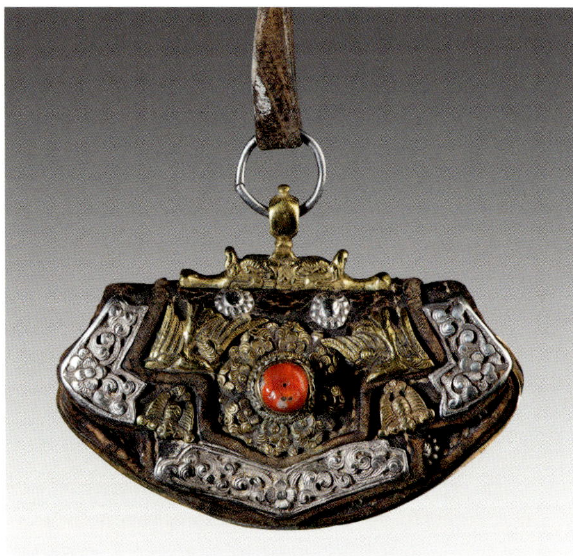

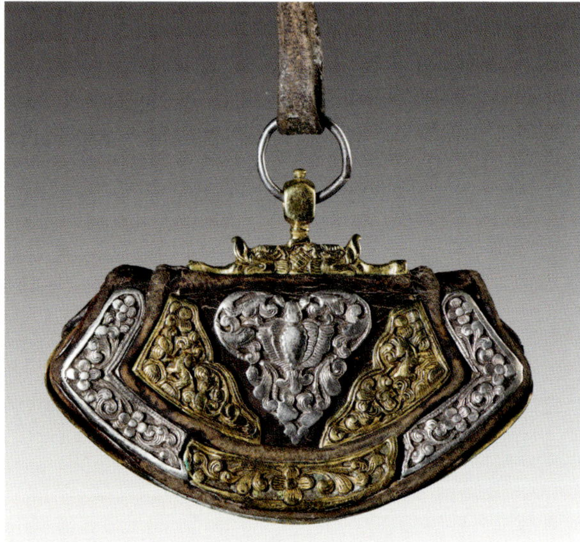

Fig. 23a: Purse (front). Tibet, 19th c., iron ring (added later), leather, silver, yellowish metal alloy, iron, turquoise, 8.2 × 11 × 4.3 cm, 165 g

Fig. 23b: Reverse side of the purse shown in Fig. 23a

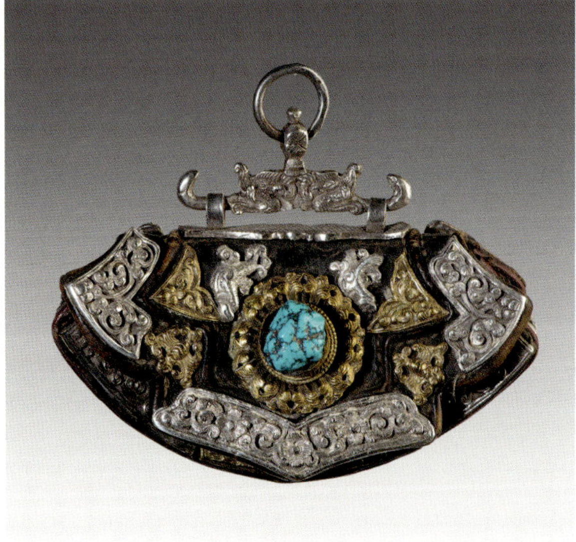

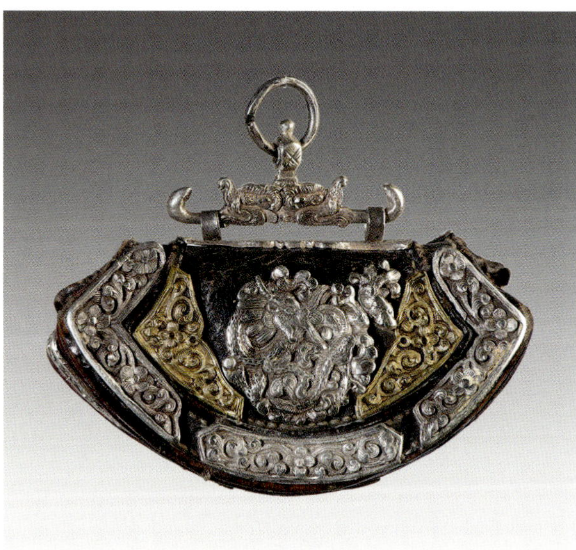

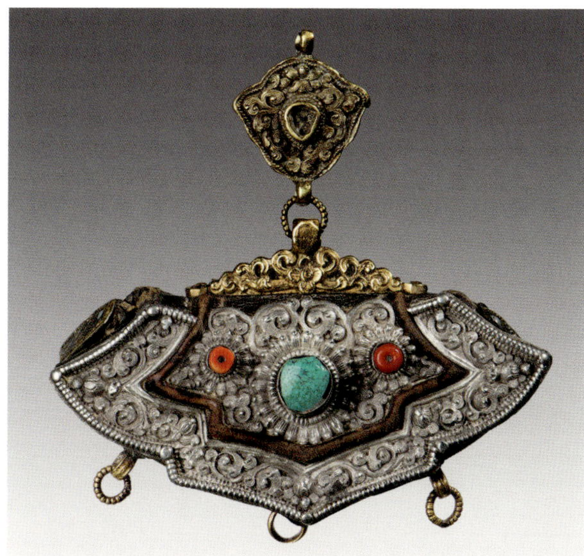

Fig. 24: Purse. Tibet, presumably around 1900, leather, silver, yellowish metal alloy, coral, turquoise, 8.5 (without ornamental plate over the eyelet mount) ×13.2×5.2 cm, 205 g

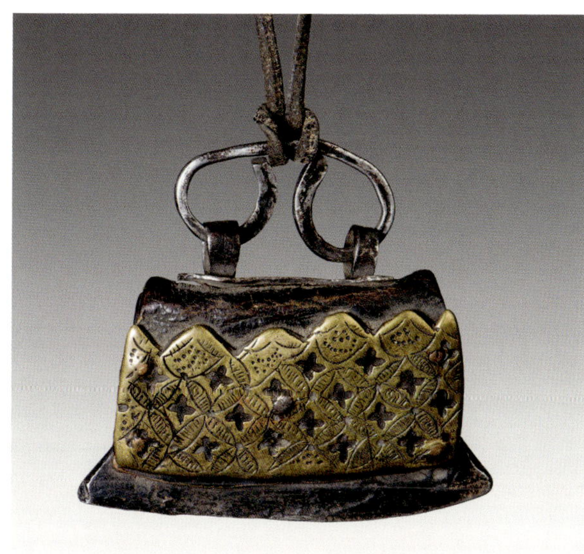

Fig. 25: Tinder pouch. Ladakh, presumably 19th c., leather, iron, yellowish metal alloy, copper, 7.2 (including eyelet mounts) ×9.6×1.9 cm, 140 g

Purse *'ba 'khug* (Figs. 21a and 21b)
The front cover of this purse is decorated with embossed decorative fittings of silver and a yellowish alloy. In addition to stylised floral motifs, one can also recognise two tiny mythical creatures which resemble fish and two stylised insects (Tib. *'bu*). The bearer would want the *'bu* to deliver effective magical protection against attacks by earth demons (Tib./Ladakhi *sa bdag*; Weihreter 1988: 59). The eyelet mount displays two tiny heads of the *Makara* (Tib. *chu srin*). A piece of coral provides a colourful accent. The reverse and the bottom sides of this *'ba 'khug* are decorated with fittings of yellowish metal and silver in a theme of floral motifs.

Purse *'ba 'khug* (Figs. 22a and 22b)
The front of this *'ba 'khug* is decorated with embossed fittings of silver and a yellowish metal alloy. In addition to the stylised floral motifs, two birds and two stylised insects are also represented to provide magical protection against attack by earth demons. The eyelet mount displays two tiny heads of the *Makara*. A piece of coral provides a colourful accent (Fig. 22a).

On the reverse side were mounted fittings of silver and a yellow metal. Two tiny antelopes can be seen between the elegant floral motifs. A large insect provides the symbolic theme (Fig. 22b).

The bottom of the *'ba 'khug* has been reinforced with a brass band and fastened to the leather by two ornate silver rivets.

Purse *'ba 'khug* (Figs. 23a and 23b)
The front of this *'ba 'khug* is decorated with embossed fittings of silver and a yellowish metal alloy. In addition to the stylised floral motifs, two fish and two stylised insects are visible. The silver eyelet mount is decorated with two tiny heads of the *Makara*. A turquoise provides a colourful accent (Fig. 23a).

On the reverse and bottom sides, fittings were mounted in silver and yellow metal. Elegant floral motifs and a playful dragon amidst the intertwining tendrils provide the symbolic theme. To the right of the dragon is a small stylised fish. A second fish is obviously missing on the left (Fig. 23b).

Purse *'ba 'khug* (Fig. 24)
The front of this *'ba 'khug* is decorated with embossed silver fittings. The design is purely floral. Above the eyelet mount is a richly designed ornamental plate, fitted with a stone setting. The gemstone is missing.

The reverse side is also richly decorated with embossed floral silver patterns. Formerly a jewel (coral or turquoise) would have been set here, but it is missing today. Nevertheless one can still detect the residue of bitumen from the old adhesive fixture. This is definitely an unusual design for a purse. Presumably the gemstone on the reverse was lost because it was subjected to greater exposure.

Tinder Pouch *me lcags* (Fig. 25)
The metal fitting on the front of this *me lcags* has its origins in Ladakh. One can clearly recognise the influences of Islamic ornamentation from Central Asia in the use of geometry, as can often be found in the folk art of Ladakh. The reverse side has been reinforced with copper bands. An additional iron bracket was fixed to the two fastening eyelets, allowing a more flexible attachment to one's belt.

Detail of Fig. 21a

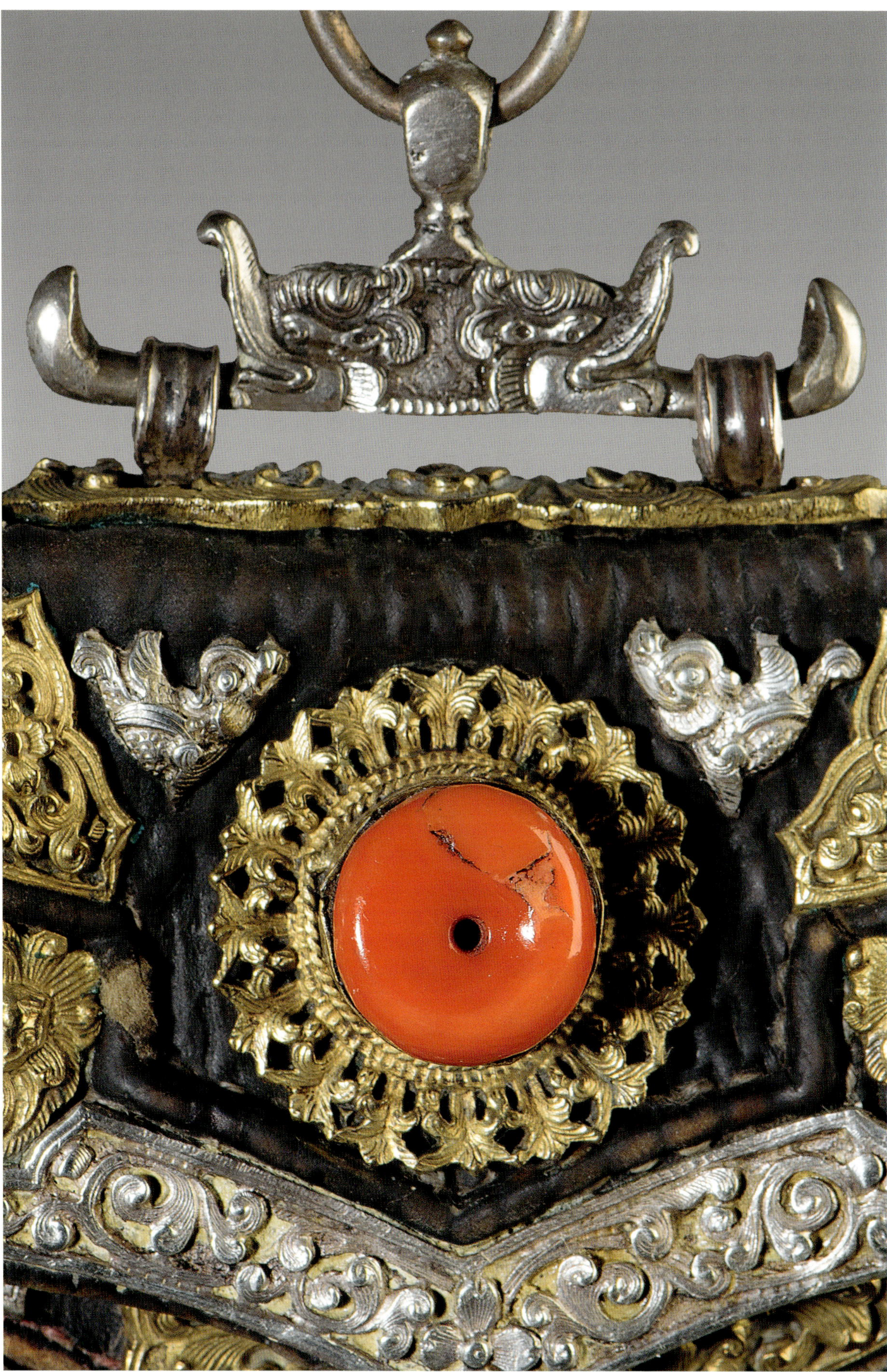

Detail of Fig. 25

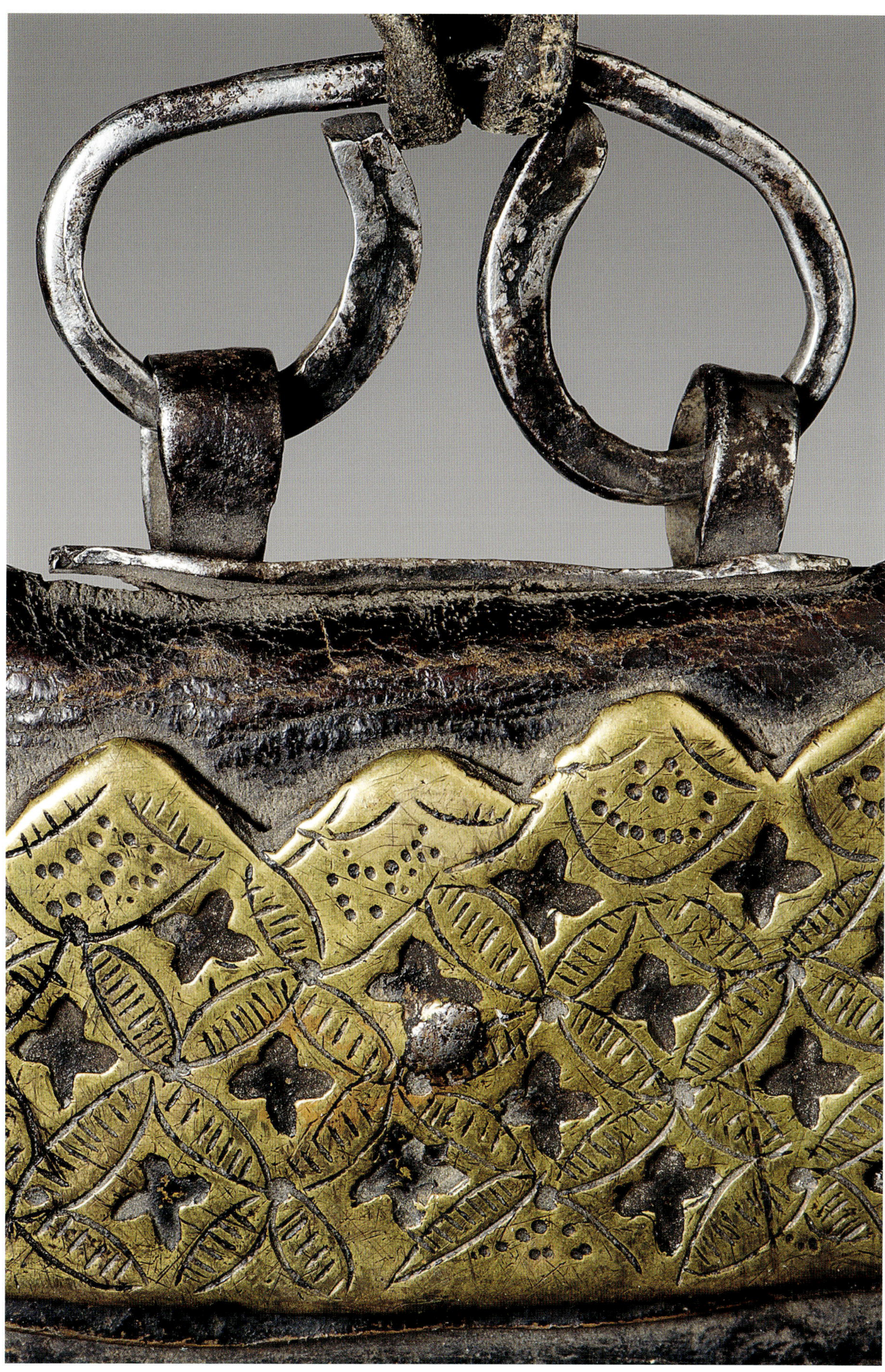

Fig. 26: Tinder pouch. Tibetan cultural sphere, 1st half 20th c., leather, iron, silver, yellowish metal alloy, copper, turquoise, flints also enclosed, 8.1×13.1×3.2 cm, 200 g

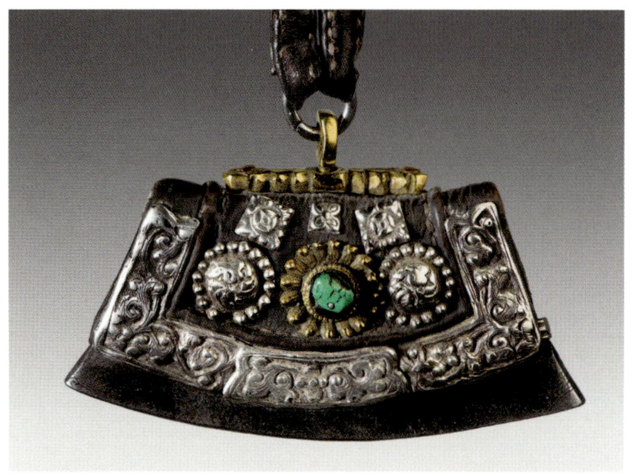

Fig. 27: Tinder pouch. Tibet, 1st half 20th c., leather, iron, silver, yellowish metal alloy, coral, flints also enclosed, 8.5×14.3×3.3 cm, 190 g

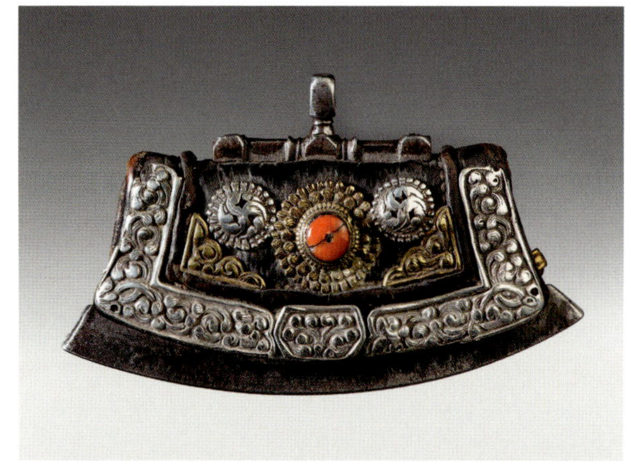

Fig. 28: Tinder pouch. Tibetan cultural sphere, 1st half 20th c., leather, iron, silver, yellowish metal alloy, turquoise, flints also enclosed, 7.3×10.4×3.2 cm, 135 g

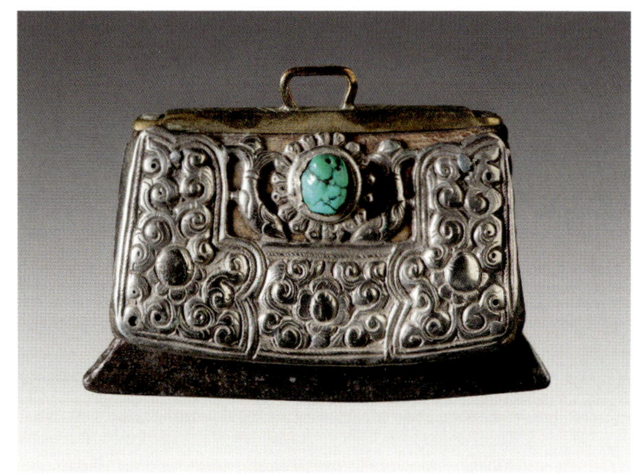

Tinder Pouch *me lcags* (Fig. 26)

The silver fitting on the front of this *me lcags* has its origins in the Tibetan cultural sphere. A more precise geographical identification of this folk art object is not possible. The bronze eyelet mount is secured with copper rivets. The stylised flower surrounding the turquoise inlay could be a lotus symbol. On the reverse side one can see that the fire steel was fixed to the leather pouch with copper rivets and a silver band. Additional balance is provided by twelve curved silver-plated copper studs.

Tinder Pouch *me lcags* (Fig. 27)

The silver and bronze fittings on the front of this *me lcags* demonstrate its origins in Central Tibet. The simply decorated eyelet mount is made of iron. The stylised flower surrounding the coral inlay could be a lotus symbol. In the two silver discs can be seen a faint motif resembling a Triskelion. In the Himalayan cultural sphere this symbolises the three phases of the moon, namely waxing, waning and the new moon.[3]

The reverse side was originally reinforced with eight metal arches (one missing). Seven of them can still be seen even if heavily scuffed. The fire steel was attached to the leather bag by a metal strip and iron rivets.

Tinder Pouch *me lcags* (Fig. 28)

The silver fitting on the front of this *me lcags* has its origins in the Tibetan cultural sphere. A precise geographical identification is not possible with this object of folk art. The eyelet mount is made from a yellowish alloy with a soldered copper eyelet. The stylised flower surrounding the turquoise inlay could be a lotus symbol. Two fish flank the turquoise.

The reverse side is made of heavily worn leather. An iron band and two iron rivets connect the fire steel to the pouch.

ADDITIONAL JEWELLERY PIECES

The presentation of the other Tibetan jewellery types will be limited to a few particularly significant objects.

Rear-Head Decoration *the kyo* (Fig. 29)

In Tibet married women would sometimes wear enormous silver discs mounted in their hair on the back of the head. This disc shown here is a fine example of this type of jewellery, which is very rarely seen today. The original silver disc curved upwards and was partially decorated with embossed patterns and stylised flowers. Two rows of beads provide additional geometric features. Five turquoises and two pieces of corals are not only for decoration, but also to give magical protection to the wearer of the jewellery. The inside of the disc is filled with bitumen for balance. The bottom consists of an iron plate.

Bracelet (Fig. 30)

Large bracelets finished with animal-head ends were widespread between Afghanistan and China. This example is typical of the time when the form of the animal head

Fig. 29: Rear-head decoration. Tibet, presumably 19th c., silver, turquoise, coral, bitumen, iron, 12 × 10.8 cm, 102 g

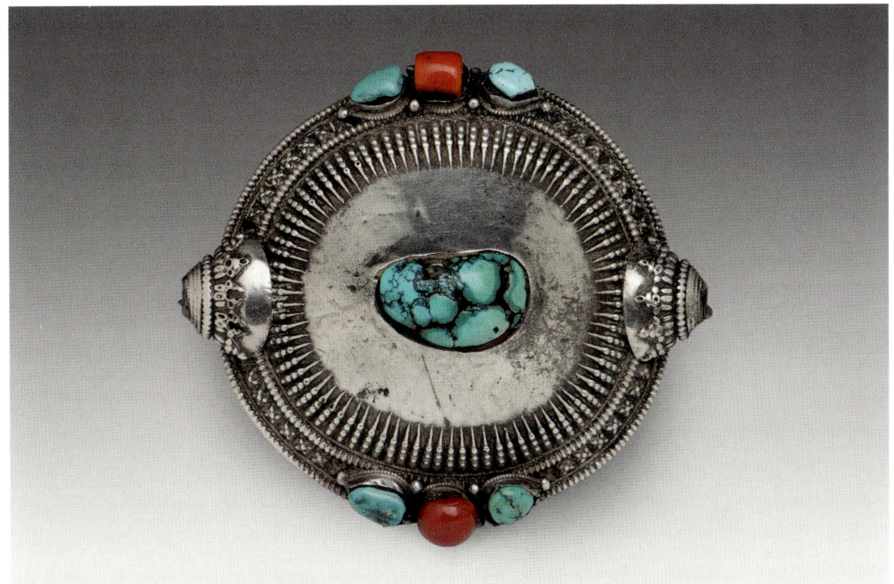

Fig. 30: Bracelet. Tibetan cultural sphere, 1st half 20th c., alloy containing silver, maximum width 8.7 cm, opening between the two animal heads 2 cm, 182 g

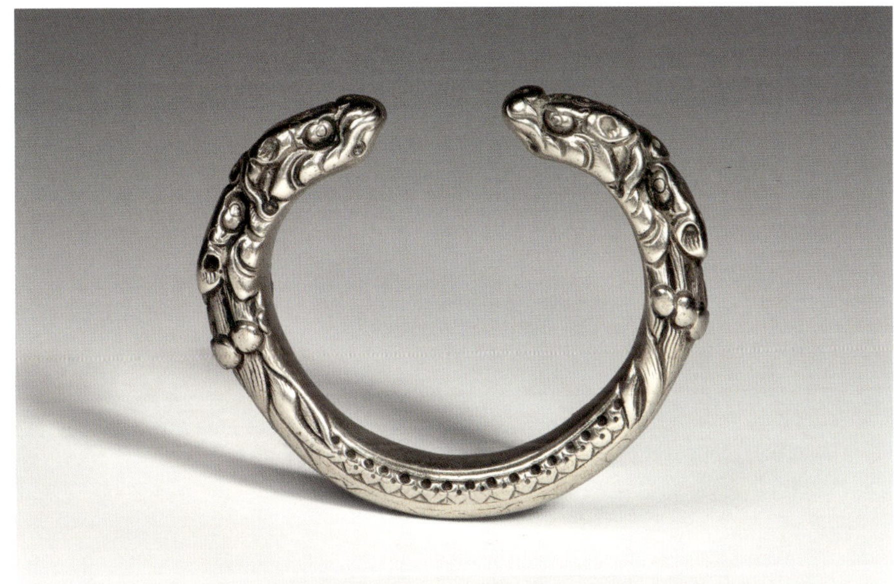

Fig. 31: Ornamental plate, belt attachment. Tibet, 1st half 20th c., silver, yellowish metal alloy, turquoise, 14 × 10.7 cm, 100 g

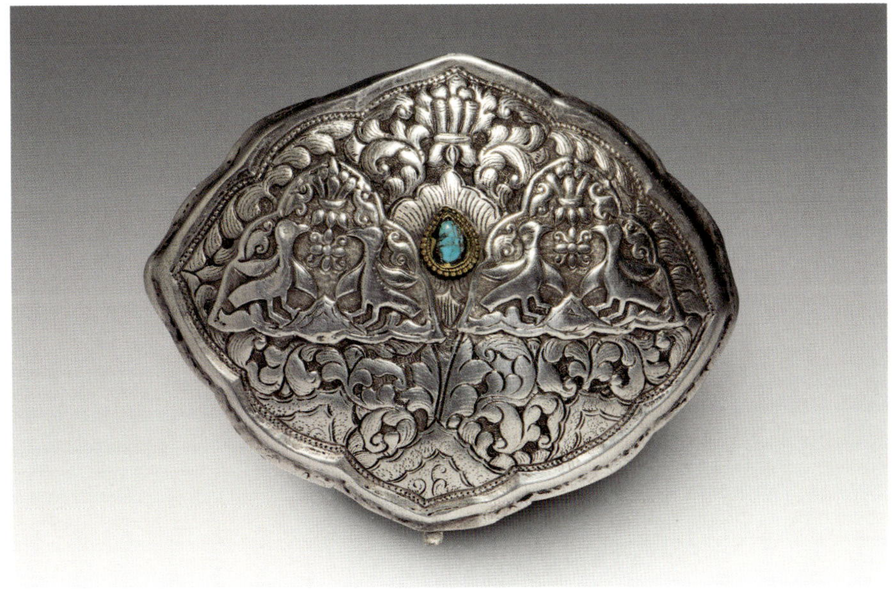

Detail of Fig. 27

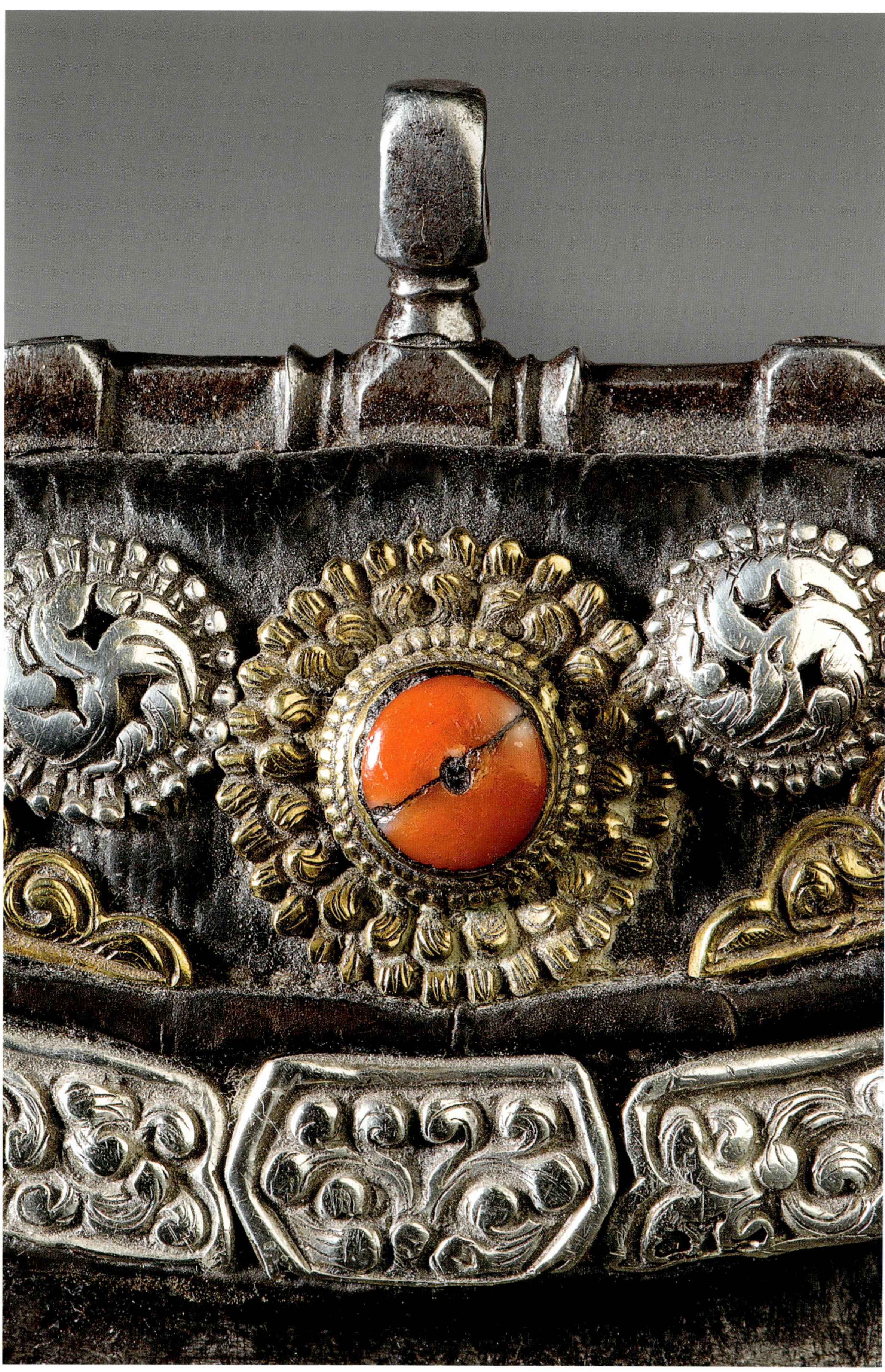

Detail of Fig. 28

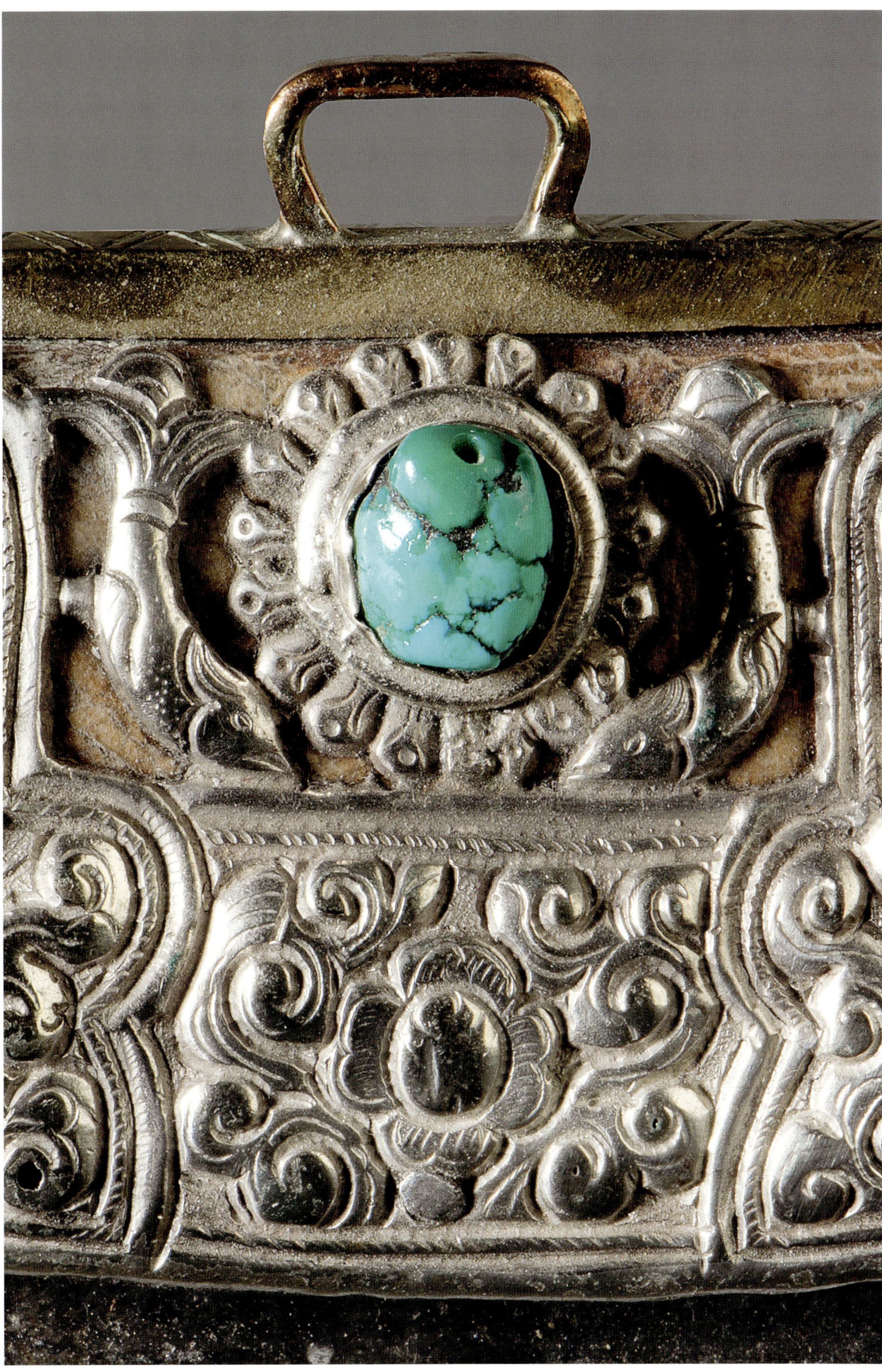

Fig. 32: Tibetan woman in West Tibet with a belt plate

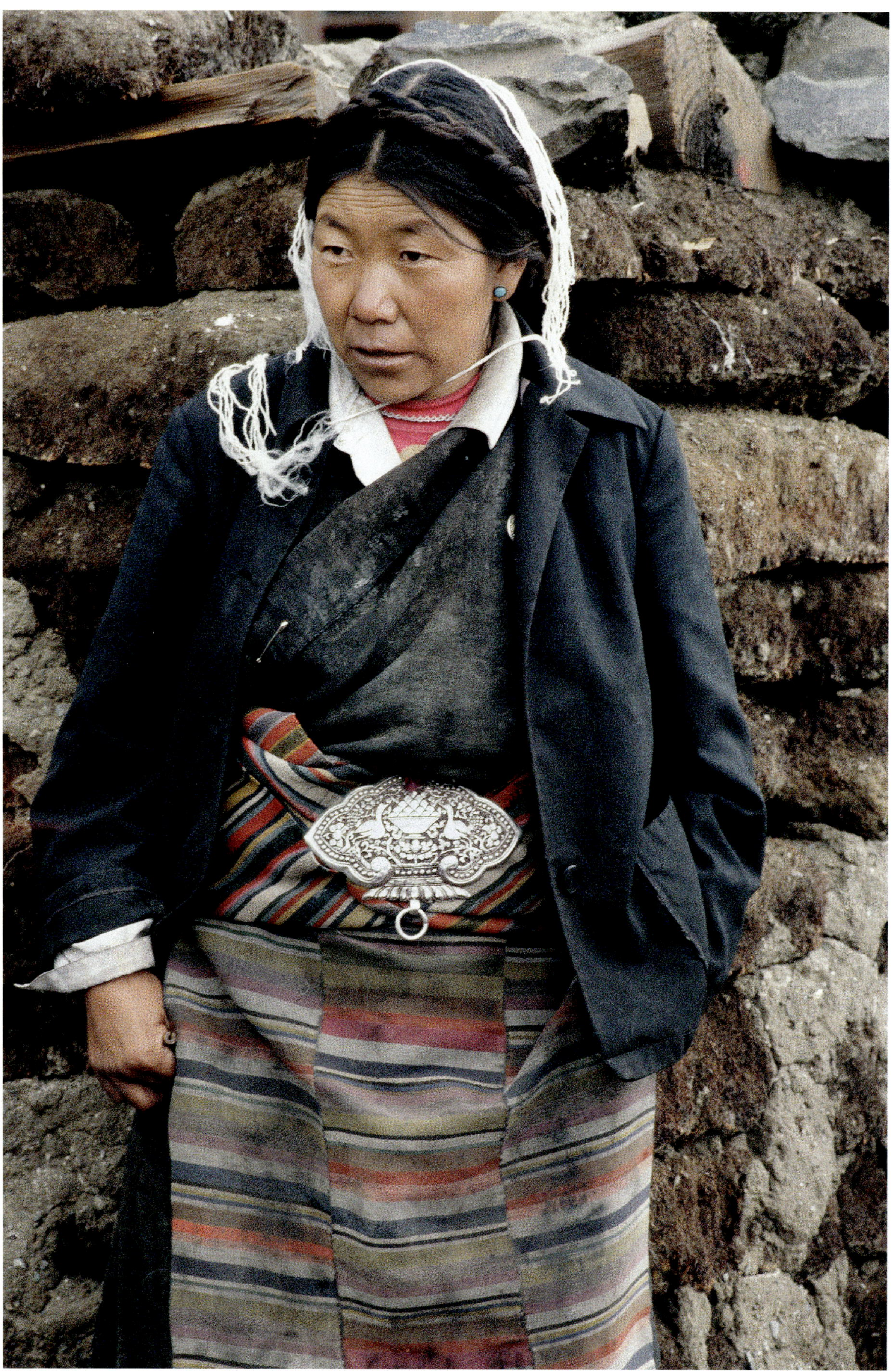

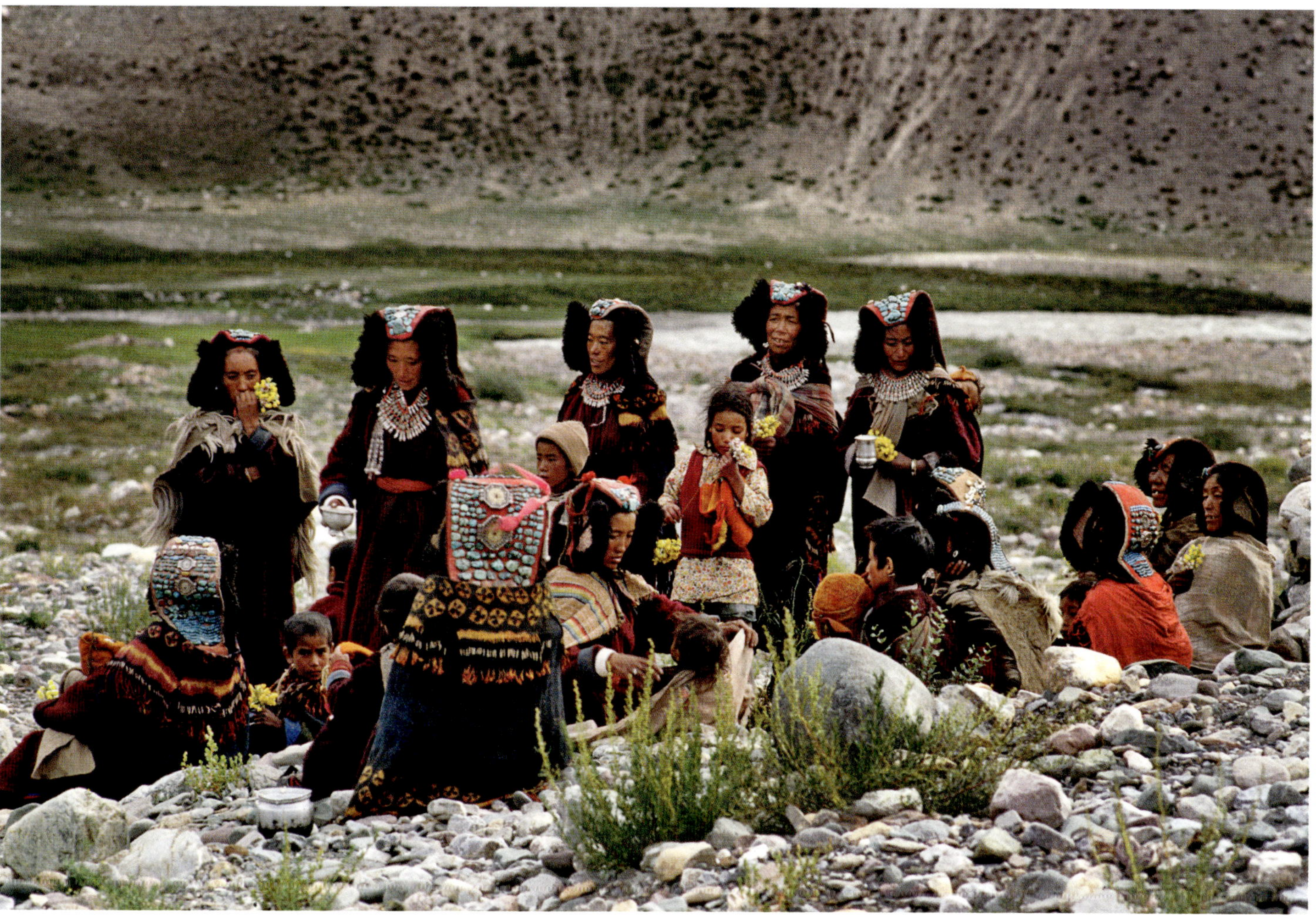

Fig. 33: Women in Zanskar waiting for the visit of a holy man

underwent a stylistic change from a lion's head to that of a dragon. This points to an origin in southern Tibet or in neighbouring Bhutan (Weihreter 1988: 208–209, 300–303).

Decorative Plate, Belt Attachment (Fig. 31)

Women in Tibet often wore magnificently decorated silver plates attached to a broad textile belt. In the centre of the present example, a turquoise was set in yellowish metal. The gemstone is framed to the sides by two pairs of birds. Above each of the pairs is a stylised wish-fulfilling jewel (Sanskrit *cintāmani*). Flower symbols and a stylised mountain symbol can also be seen between the birds. Three further mountain symbols appear above the lower border of the plate. Lush floral motifs rise up from these and spread over the whole disc to frame another stylised wish-fulfilling jewel at its upper end. This is very similar to the magnificent silver plate worn by a woman in Guge (West Tibet) on her textile belt (see Fig. 32). This shows two birds flanking an offering bowl. Under the bowl can be seen a stylised lotus base.

We end our little excursion into the world of Tibetan jewellery with this picture (Fig. 33), which offers impressive testimony to the splendour of Tibetan jewellery. It shows women in the south of Zanskar who are dressed in readiness for festivities. They were waiting for the visit of a high lama who was already worshipped as a saint during his lifetime. The fantastic wealth and beauty of jewellery in those barren highlands counts among the most impressive in the whole of Asia.

NOTES

1 For this comment I am grateful to Dscho Tsering rDorje, Guskyar, Bara-Lahoul, Himachal Pradesh, India.

2 For *thog lcags* with Buddhist themes and style see Weihreter 2002: 103ff.

3 For this information I am grateful to Dscho Tsering rDorje. See Note 1.

Detail of Fig. 29

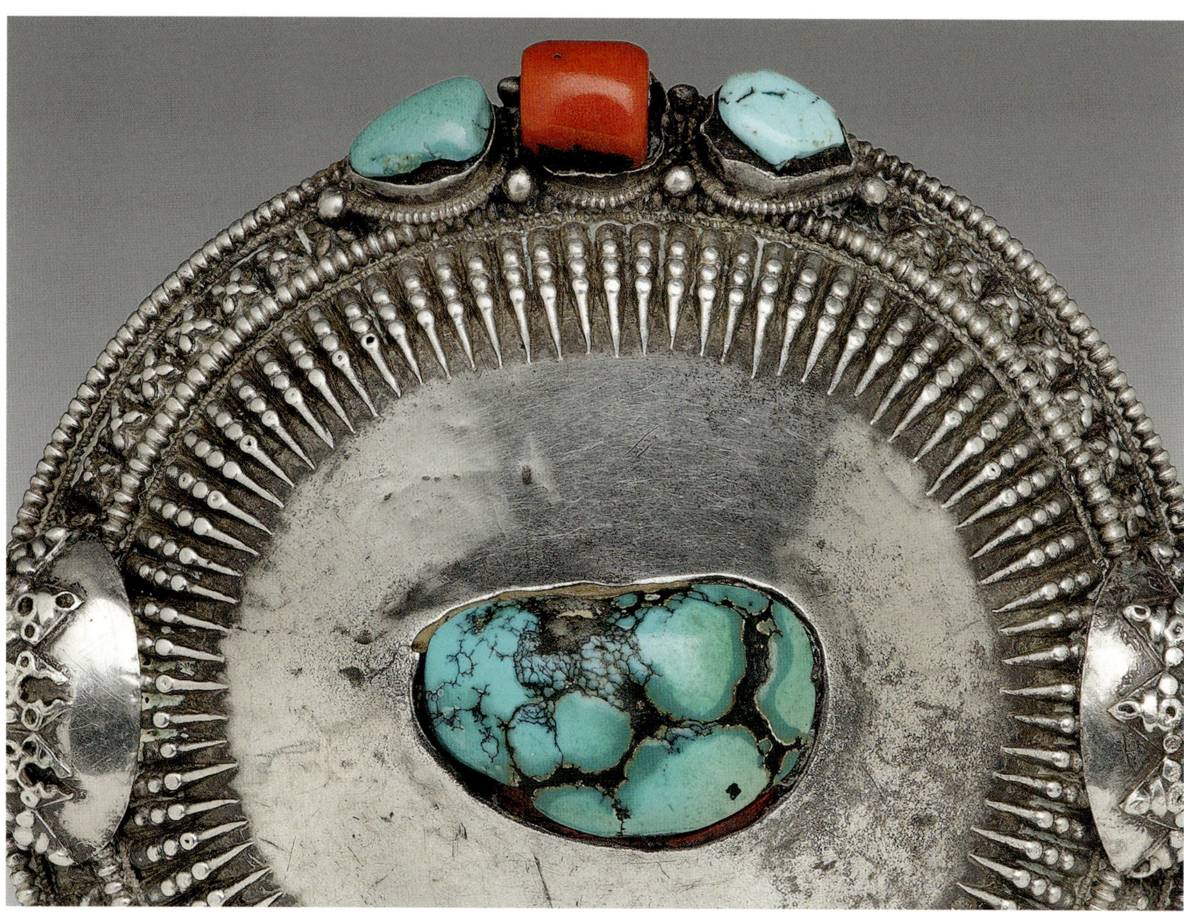

Detail of Fig. 31

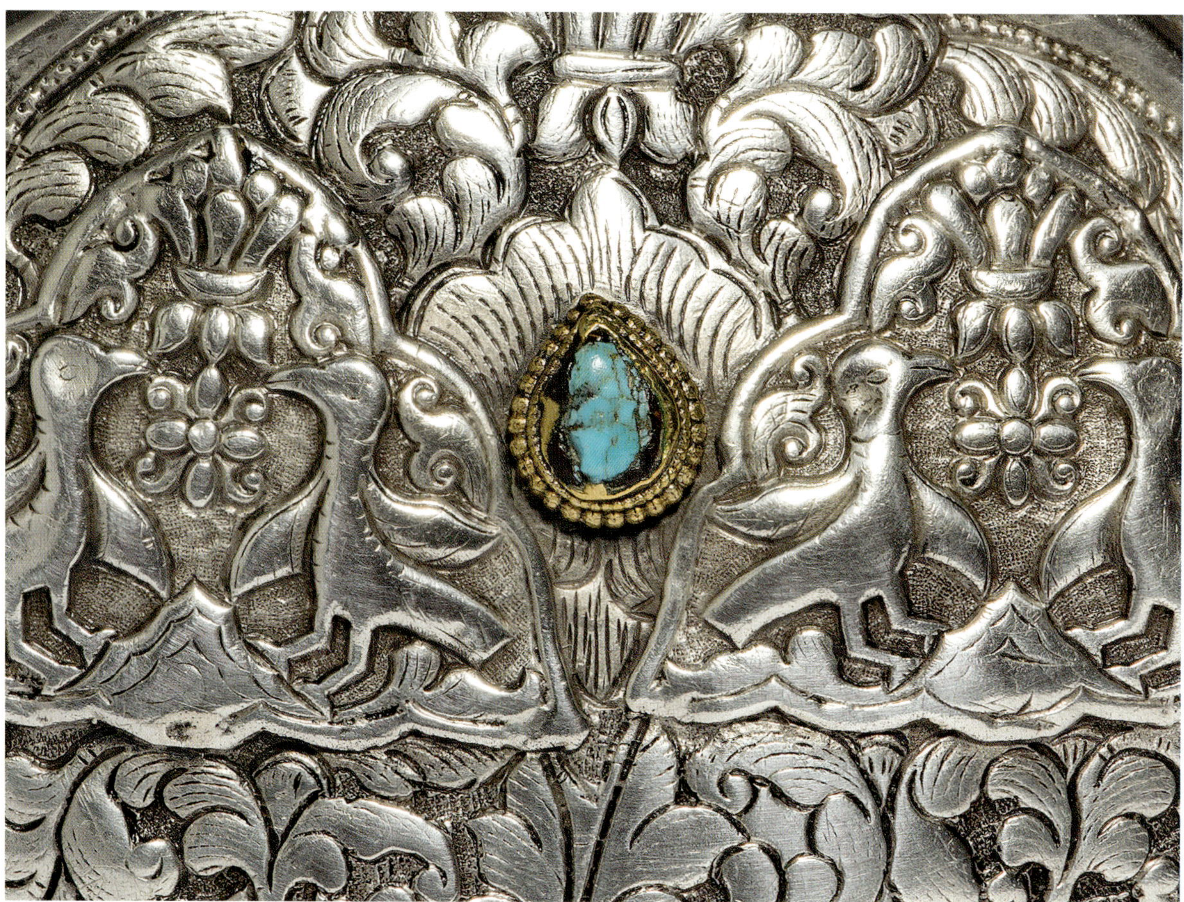

GLOSSARY

Aṣṭamaṅgala
Sanskrit word for the Eight Auspicious Symbols (see also *bkra shis rtags brgyad*).

'ba 'khug
Tibetan word for a purse worn on the belt.

'bu
Tibetan word for insects. They are occasionally depicted on jewellery to exercise a kind of negative magic for the benefit of the carrier.

bkra shis rtags brgyad
Tibetan word for the Eight Auspicious Symbols, pronounced: *tashitaghe* (see also *aṣṭamaṅgala*).

chu srin
Mythical creature, Tibetan name for the Indian *Makara*. It is considered to be an emblem of the god of love, Kāmadeva (see *Makara*).

daśākāro vaśī
Sanskrit word for the symbol of the "Ten Powerful Truths". It often appears on amulet containers. In Tibetan it is known as *namdshuwandan* (*rnam bcu dbaṅ ldan*).

Garuda
Winged deity of Indian mythology, Lord Vishnu's mount, opponent of snakes, related to the Tibetan *Khyuṅ*.

ga'u
Tibetan word for certain types of amulet containers and reliquaries, as well as portable box-shaped travel altars.

Khyuṅ
Winged deity of Tibetan mythology, opponent of the snakes (Tib. *kLu*), related to the Indian *Garuda*.

Kīrtimukha
Literally "Glorious Face", mythical creature in India and Tibet (Tib. *ci mi 'dra* or *gzi gdon*) which wards off mischief.

kLu
Tibetan word for snake, pronounced: *Lu*.

Makara
Mythical creature, considered in India as the emblem of the god of love, Kāmadeva (see *chu srin*).

mchod rten
Tibetan name for a *stūpa*, pronounced: *chorten* (see also *stūpa*).

me lcags
Tibetan for a tinder pouch worn on the belt, pronounced: *metshak*.

nor bu
Tibetan word for "jewel" (see *ratna*).

pad ma
Tibetan word for lotus.

ratna
Sanskrit word for "jewel" (see *nor bu*).

rdo rje
Tibetan word for thunderbolt (Sanskrit *vajra*), pronounced: *dorje*.

sa bdag
Name in Tibetan culture for dangerous earth demons which can be incarnated in the bodies of insects. They are the reason why bee-keeping is not practised in the Tibetan cultural sphere, unlike in the Hindu Himalayas. They can be fought with magic rituals (Ladakhi *do*, Tib. *mdos*) using ghost traps (Tib. *nam mkha*) as well as representations of insects on jewellery (see *'bu*).

stūpa
Sanskrit term for Buddhist religious buildings which date their evolution back to ancient tombs and symbolise the Buddha and the *Dharma*. In the Tibetan cultural sphere significant holy men were also occasionally buried in a *stūpa* after death (see also *mchod rten*).

thog lcags
"First iron" (pronounced *togchak*) is the name for metal objects found in the soil which are considered to have a magical effect. Other names are "fallen from heaven" (Tib. *thog rdeu*, pronounced *togde*) and "soaring thunderstone" (Tib. *mtho ldin*, pronounced *toding*).

tsa tsa
Tibetan word for votive offerings of sun-dried loam, more unusually of fired clay. Now and again some of the ashes of holy men might be mixed into the clay. *Tsa tsa* are kept in a *stūpa* (Tib. *mchod rten*), but also sometimes in a *ga'u*.

vajra
Sanskrit term for "hard" or "powerful", as well as for ceremonial objects whose "diamond hardness" reflects the absolute spirit and the male principle (see *rdo rje*).

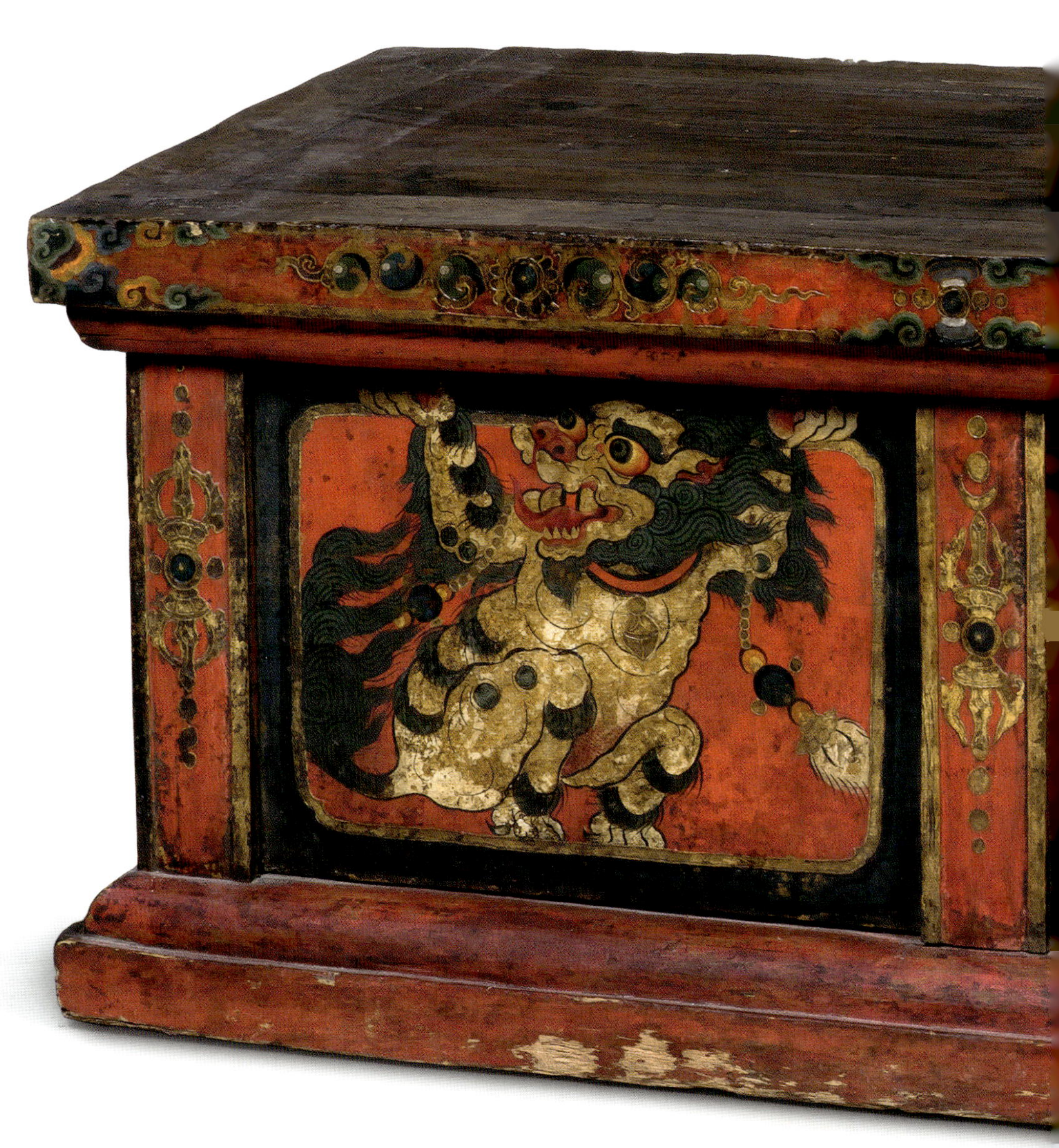

TIBETAN FURNITURE

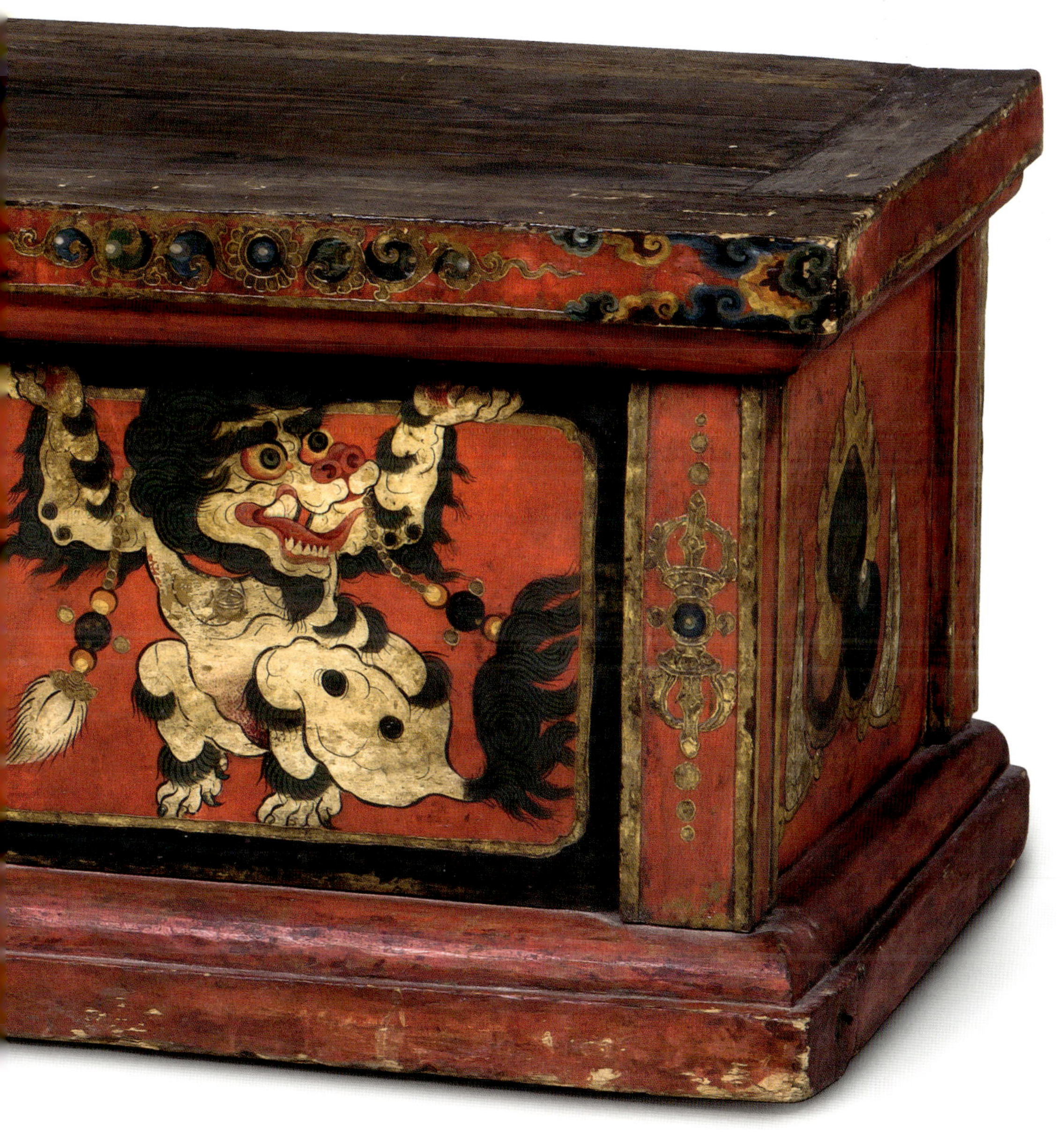

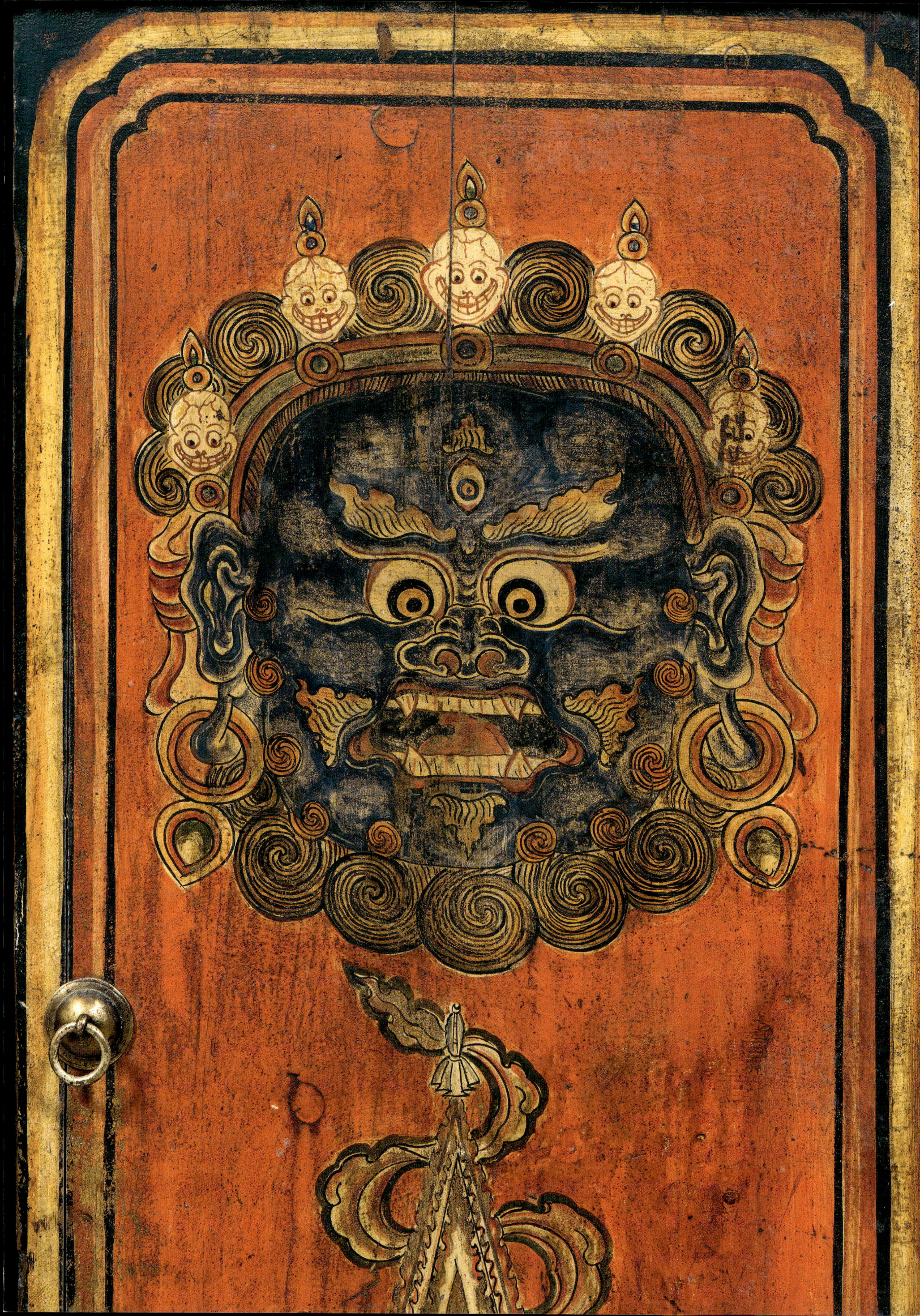

Helmut F. Neumann and Heidi A. Neumann

DRAGONS AND TIGERS, SNOW LIONS AND FLOWERS

Tibetan Tables, Chests and Cabinets

Preceding double page: Stand for an altar figure; see Fig. 27

Left image: Detail of Fig. 21

The varied and unique characteristics of Tibetan furniture are a direct reflection of the rich culture of Tibet. Their uses are manifold and relate to all facets of the culture: ritual, monastic and secular life, in the monastery, at home and when travelling. They owe their forms, construction and decoration to a variety of craftsmen, primarily carpenters, artists, metalworkers and leather craftsmen, as well as those who provide the raw material.

In the accounts of researchers and travellers, Tibetan furniture finds little mention and is also neglected in Tibetan texts, which only rarely report who the artisans were, who made the bronzes and paintings in the temples. The few non-religious texts deal with historic events, but the predominant body of texts belongs to the canon of Tibetan Buddhism.

Interest in Tibetan furniture has, therefore, only arisen in recent decades, when an increasing number of pieces came on the market, at first in Kathmandu and Hong Kong. These items came primarily out of hiding where they had been kept safe from the Cultural Revolution. The increasing interest resulting in higher prices opened new sources to dealers, but also many Tibetans unfortunately sold family heirlooms. Only in recent years, thanks to greater prosperity, have a few old pieces returned to Tibet.

In response to the growing interest in Tibetan furniture, first articles specifically dealing with the subject appeared at the end of the 20th century (Anninos 1997; Anninos 2000). The first major exhibition of Tibetan furniture was held in the Pacific Asia Museum, Pasadena, in 2004, "Wooden Wonders", which exhibited outstanding examples from public and private collections on the West Coast of the United States. The director of the museum and curator of the exhibition, David Kamansky, asked a few renowned researchers and specialists to analyse specific aspects of Tibetan furniture in individual monographs for the comprehensive catalogue (Kamansky [ed.] 2004).

One article in this book providing a well-founded introduction to Tibetan furniture was written by Luca Corona and Camilla Hulse Corona (2004), from whom Michael and Justyna Buddeberg purchased a major part of their collection.

The eleven Tibetan pieces in the Buddeberg collection represent five major categories of Tibetan furniture:

- Tables (1)
- Chests (4)
- Shallow Cabinets (4)
- Altar Cabinets (1)
- Stands for Statues (1)

In order to give a broader overview of the two most important and presumably oldest categories of Tibetan furniture, tables and chests, reference to examples from the authors' collection ("H2N collection") will be included.

Furniture is adapted to the lifestyle of its users. Traditionally in Tibet there are no chairs; one sits on carpets or flat cushions, either on the floor or on a dais. In Central and West Tibet at an altitude of 3,600 to 5,000 metres (11,800–16,400 feet) with little precipitation, breeding livestock is the only livelihood, predominantly that of yak and sheep. Only in lower areas, in valleys that cut through the plateau, is it possible to grow grain. In the virtually treeless terrain, wood is rare and expensive. This is why most Tibetan furniture is made of thin wooden slabs. There once were, centuries ago, small forests in climatically favourable lower areas, but these have been felled leaving no traces, since even the roots were in demand as firewood. Along the waterways in the valleys, fast-growing poplars are now being planted. Their thin trunks are used primarily to support the roofs of houses made of stamped and oiled clay. Their wood,

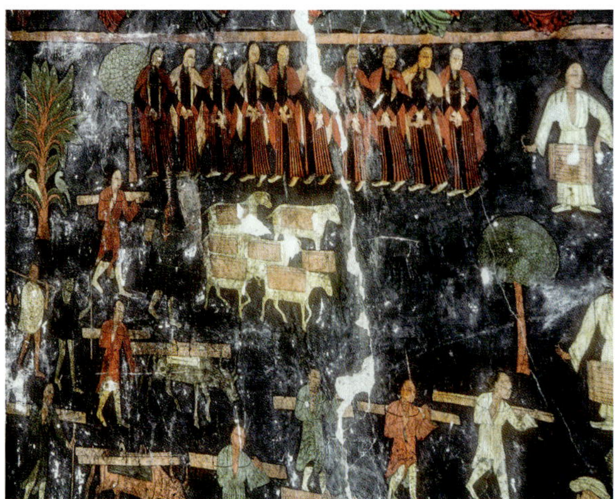

Fig. 1: Transport of wood, mural. Lhakhang Marpo (Tib. *lha khang dmar po*), Tsaparang, West Tibet, 15th c.

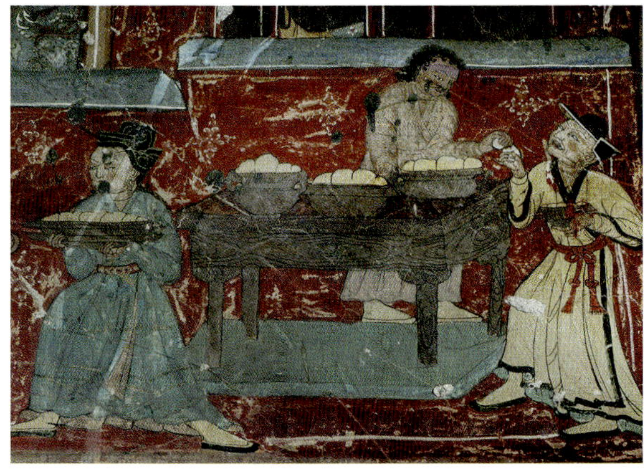

Fig. 2: Table on mural, circumambulation corridor (Tib. *khor lam*). Shalu monastery (Tib. *zha lu dgon pa*), Central Tibet, 14th c.

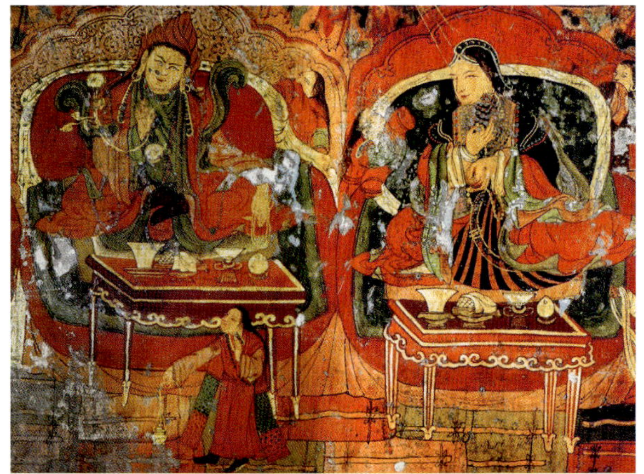

Fig. 3: Tables on mural, Temple of the Prefect. Tsaparang, West Tibet, 15th c.

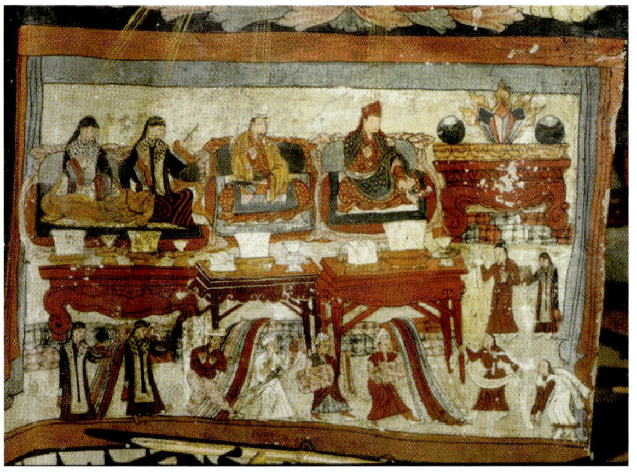

Fig. 4: Tables on mural, House of Spears. Tsaparang, West Tibet, 15th c.

though, is not suitable for the construction of furniture. For this, boards of fir, cedar and pine had to be used, which were transported to Central Tibet from the southern province Lhoka. Since the wood had to be carried over the mountain ridges by pack animals (Fig. 1), it was a valuable material and was therefore used sparingly.

TABLES

Tables are probably the oldest type of Tibetan furniture. In the past, the majority of Tibetans were nomadic herders. Small tables are the only furniture in their tents. They can easily be transported by pack animals. Radiocarbon dating has shown that a few small tables are the oldest extant Tibetan furniture. One finds tables on older wall paintings in Tibetan temples more often than any other type of furniture. The earliest representation of a Tibetan table known to us is found on the murals in the great *khorlam* (circumambulatory) of the *Serkhang* (main temple room) in Shalu monastery. It is documented that the painting was made at the direction of the third Karmapa after 1306 AD (Fig. 2). The massive table bears three bowls of offering cakes. The next two illustrations from murals in Tsaparang, residence of the western Tibetan kings in the 15th and 16th centuries, show a much more typical use of tables. Fig. 3 from the Temple of the Prefect shows two tables with drinking vessels for the royal couple seated behind them.

In a similar scene in the House of Spears, three tables serve the same purpose (Fig. 4). The two tables in front of the lamas have straight legs with diagonal braces adding stability. The two noble ladies share a table with S-formed legs, referred to in Tibetan as *khyisu* ("dog-legged"). A similar, larger table is shown in the upper right of the illustration, next to the thrones of the monks. Unlike European tables, which often just have the table top supported by legs, the table top of Tibetan tables is always supported by a substructure of varying size. The complex form and richly decorated front of the substructure is the main element of the table. It is usually larger than the side elements. The backside is often undecorated or entirely absent.

This special feature of Tibetan tables is explained by their function: one does not sit around the table, as in Europe, tables are used in a ritual context, as seen in Figs. 3 and 4. Lamas sit at individual tables with ritual implements, cups for tea and *tsampa* and the pages of a book within easy reach. For participants in the ritual, the front of the table is visible which is why its decoration is given special attention.

Fig. 5: Table for monastic use (Tib. *lchog tse*), wood, front side richly carved and painted with auspicious *zipak*. Central Tibet, 15th–17th c., 41 × 79 × 30.5 cm

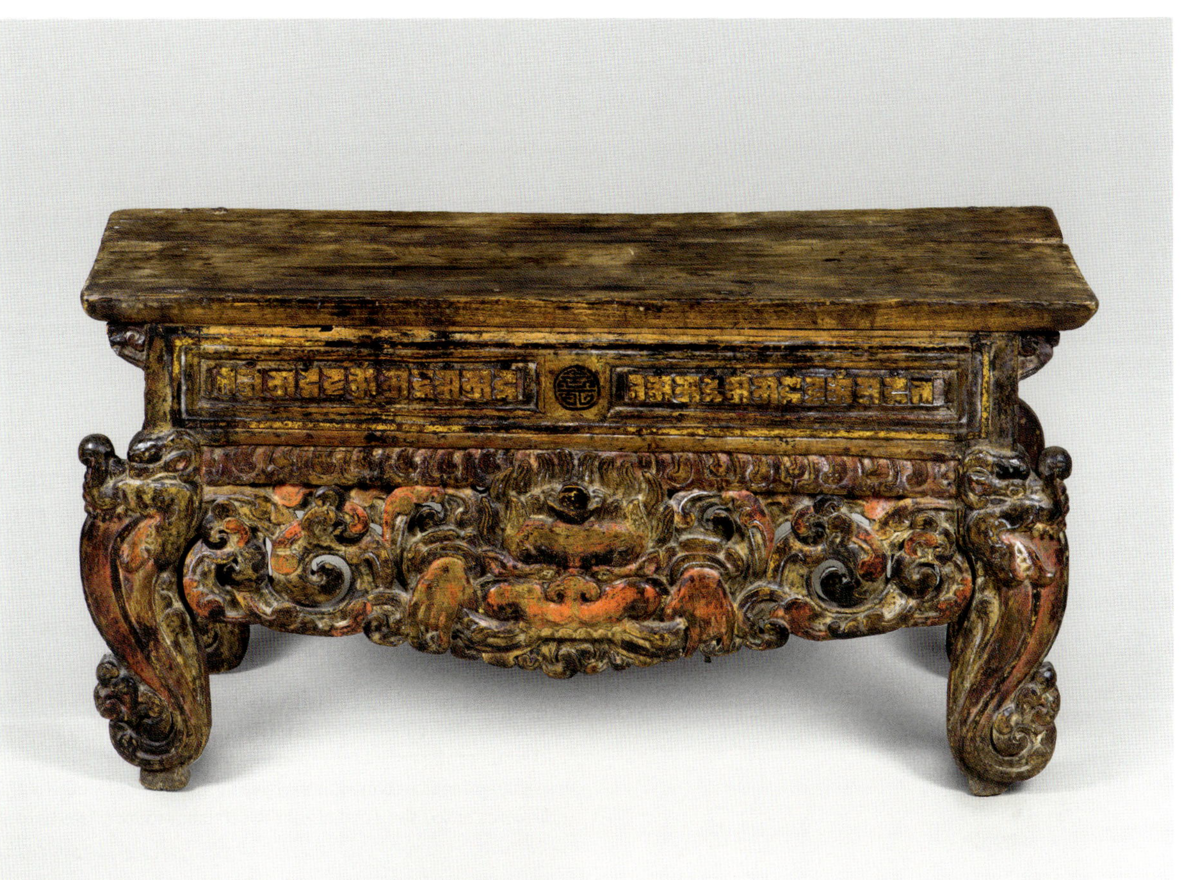

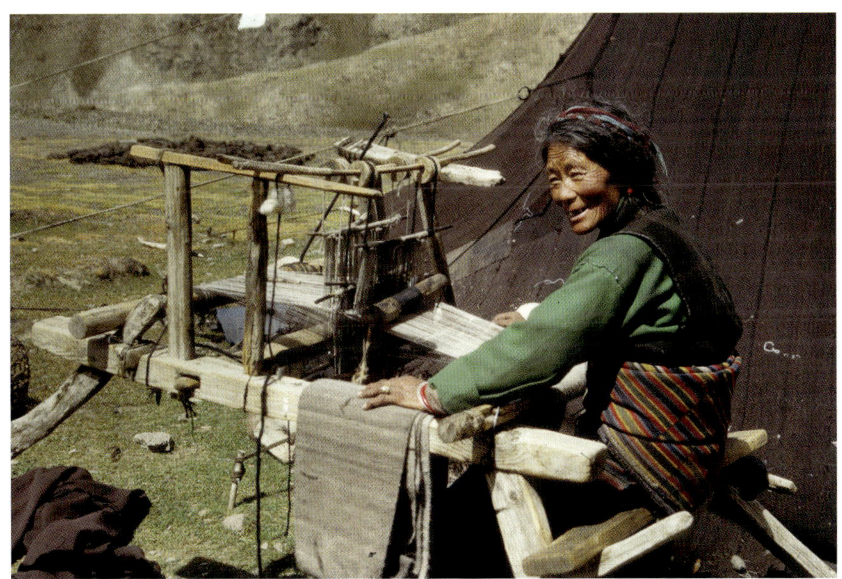

Fig. 6: Ngawan Choltum at her loom. Near Riwoche, Central Tibet, 1995

The two "dog-legged" tables in Fig. 4 could be seen as precursors of the table in the Buddeberg collection (Fig. 5). It belongs to a small group of relatively early tables with a very prominently decorated front, the upper part of which bears the mantra *Om mani padme hum*, carved and painted in *Lantsa* script in two framed fields. The lower part, often referred to as the apron, is dominated in the middle by a *zipak*, a symbol for good fortune derived from the Indian *kīrtimukha*, a mythological figure with a pig's snout, sun and moon symbols between curved horns, and two hands holding the foliage emerging from the pig's mouth. Foliage also covers the front legs of the table, growing out of the *Makara* heads.

A table in an American private collection similar in all formal details has been dated to the period 15th–17th century (Kamansky [ed.] 2004: 190f.). Taking this table as an example, a characteristic of Tibetan furniture can be explained: they are painted and exemplify the Tibetans' preference for bright colours, despite the fact that in the present condition their brilliance is dimmed, darkened by the grime from butter lamps.

Lamas most often used tables similar to the one in the Buddeberg collection during the daily religious ceremonies in the temple. They were made in different heights, appropriate to that of the dais on which the lama sat.

Small folding tables (Tib. *lteb lchog*) were developed for use in ceremonies in the open or in a distant nomadic encampment. These were easier to transport, like the loom in Fig. 6 which also had to be dismantled for transport. These small tables are similar in construction and format to that shown in Fig. 7. The top of these small tables is supported by three panels, the front and the two sides of the table,

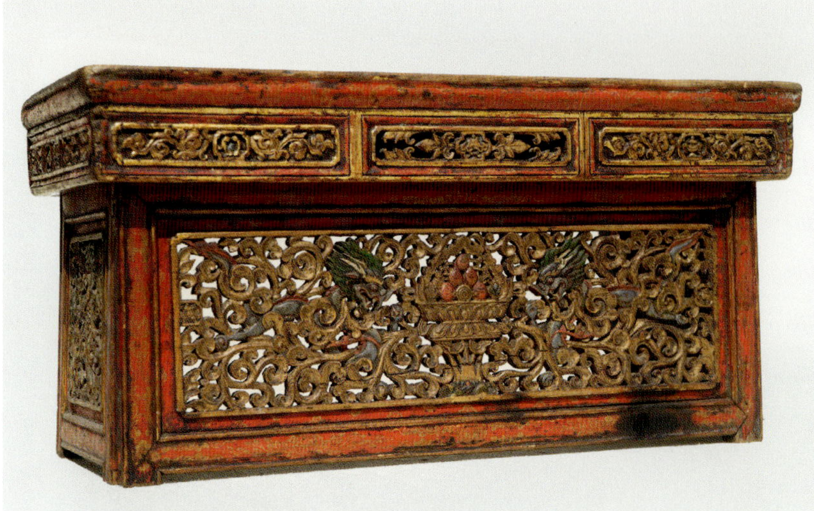

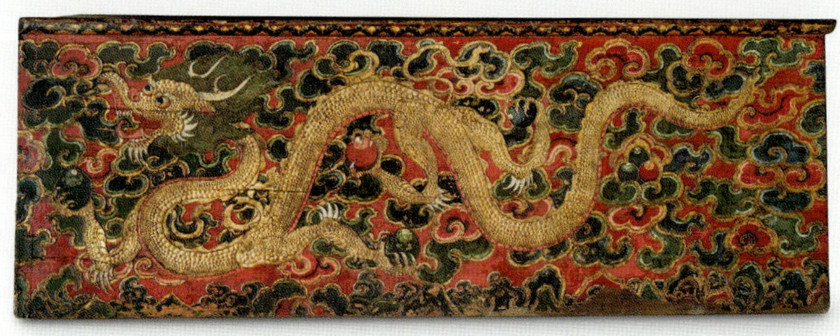

Fig. 7: Folding table (Tib. *lteb lchog*), wood, front and side panels carved in openwork and painted. Central Tibet, 17th c., 57×29×28 cm, H2N collection

Fig. 8: Long table for offerings and butter lamps (Tib. *khri lchog*), wood, painted with a golden dragon holding jewels surrounded by clouds. Central Tibet, 16th c., 136.5×35.5×48 cm, H2N collection

which could be folded up in the frame beneath the tabletop. The frame provides good protection to the often beautifully worked front side (Fig. 7) and the similarly designed side panels during transport on pack animals.

The motifs in the decoration of this table – snow lions on the sides and flaming jewels between dragons facing each other on the front – are often also seen on Tibetan chests. A particularity of this and some other finely decorated tables is the openwork carving, which adds special character to the golden scrollwork.

A further type of Tibetan table is a long, narrow table (Tib. *khri lchog*), usually rather low, on which religious offerings and butter lamps were placed. As is the case for the folding tables, the front panel of these tables extends to the floor providing an ideal surface for rich decoration in relief carving or painting (Fig. 8). Many offering tables date from the 16th to 18th centuries. Later, primarily small cabinets were made for this purpose.

CHESTS

Chests (Tib. *sgam*) are by far the most common type of early (prior to the 19th century) Tibetan furniture. They are represented in the Buddeberg collection by four significant examples. Chests no. 1 (Fig. 9) and no. 2 (Fig. 10) are typical of most Tibetan chests: a rectangular box with a lid. It consists of a top panel and borders on all four sides, which fit closely over the top of the chest. The decoration on the front border of the lid continues down the side and bottom of the chest front, providing a frame for the decoration in the field. On chest no. 1 this decoration is a pattern of interlocking *swastikas*, on chest no. 2 an irregular order of the Seven Auspicious Symbols of the *Chakravartin* (Sanskrit; Tib. *'khor los sgyur ba'i rgyal po*), which promise good fortune. The centre of the front of the chest is occupied by a dragon in a lobed medallion.

The dragon on chest no. 1 is shown in three-quarter view with its long, wide-open mouth. The head of the dragon with its long snout, curved horns and wild mane has more similarity with the representations of dragons on embroideries from the early Ming Dynasty (1368–1644), so around 1400 (Hong Kong Museum of Art [ed.] 1995: 201), than with textiles from the Wanli period (1573–1619) (ibid.: 203). This allows chest no. 1 to be dated to the 16th (15th?) century. The medallion with the dragon stands out from a latticework of interlocking circles and squares, which together with tendrils in the corners complete the field. This pattern of vertical, horizontal and diagonal lines connecting large circles is well known from textiles of the Ming Dynasty. Over two or three centuries it was adapted in different variations which were popular in Tibet as painted patterns on furniture as well as on woven cloth (see chest Fig. 12). In Tibetan it was called *kati rimo* (brocade pattern).

Chest no. 2 (Fig. 10) has a central medallion with a dragon as well. It is holding a bowl containing the "Wheel of the Law". This dragon is also an early representation in three-quarter view with a long snout, but could be somewhat younger than the dragon on chest no. 1 (Fig. 9). On chest no. 2, circles with the Chinese character *Shou*, symbol for the Chinese god of long life, *Shoulao*, surround the dragon medallion. These are accompanied by loosely placed auspicious symbols and flattering silk ribbons. Part of the decoration is in flat bas-relief, modelled in a gesso of glue and gypsum (Tib. *kyung bur*) before the paint is applied. The chests are constructed of thin, wooden panels, joined together with glue, without the use of nails. A typical feature is the reinforcement of the edges by regularly spaced

Fig. 9: Large chest ("chest no. 1") (Tib. *sgam*), wood with iron fittings, front side painted with a lobed dragon medallion in the centre of a *kati rimo* design. Central Tibet, 16th (15th?) c., 44.5×82×30 cm

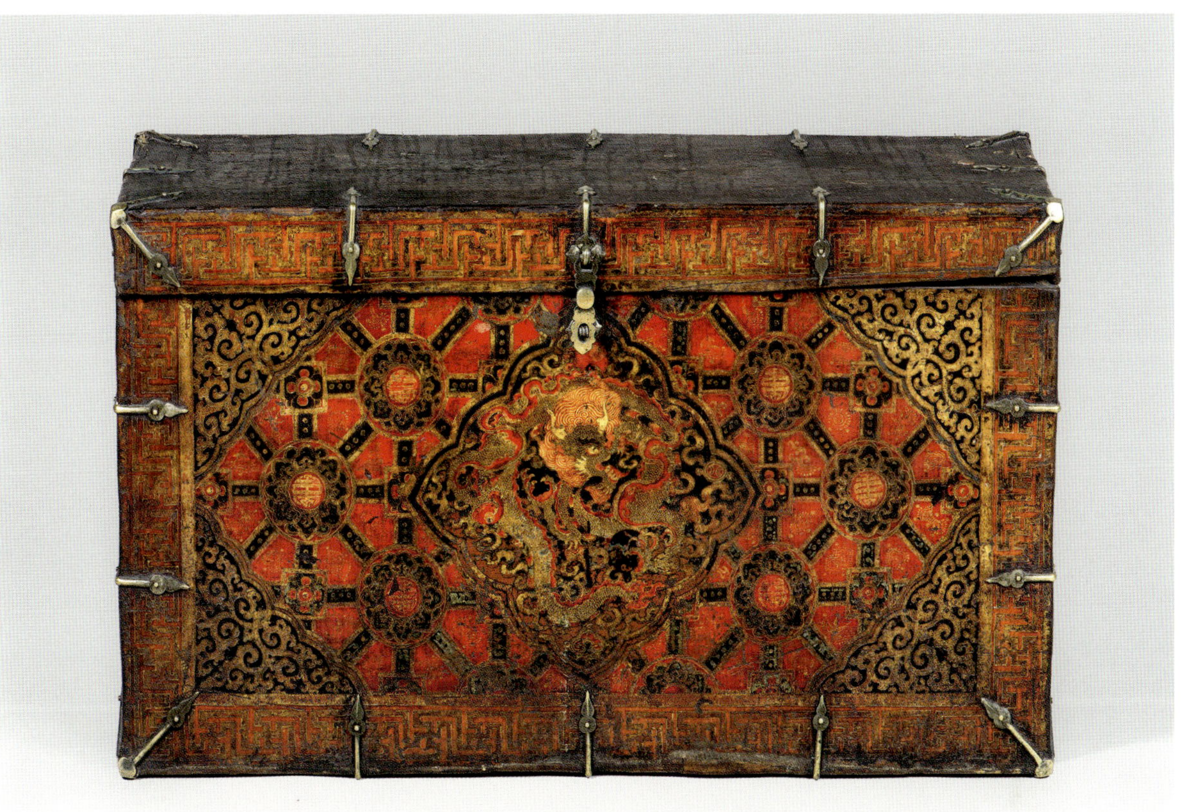

Fig. 10: Large Chest ("chest no. 2") (Tib. *sgam*), wood with iron fittings, front side painted with a dragon in a large lobed medallion, surrounded by *Shou* and other auspicious symbols. Central Tibet, 17th c., 56×91×38 cm

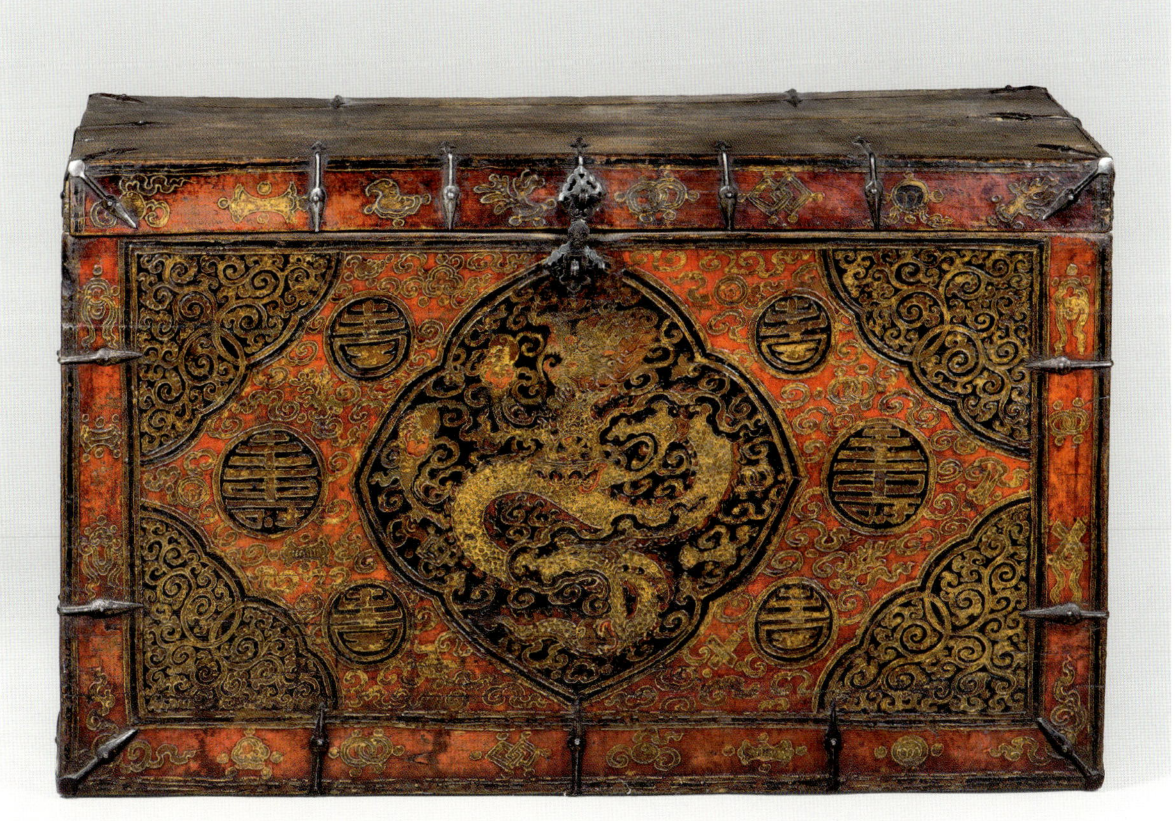

Detail of Fig. 5

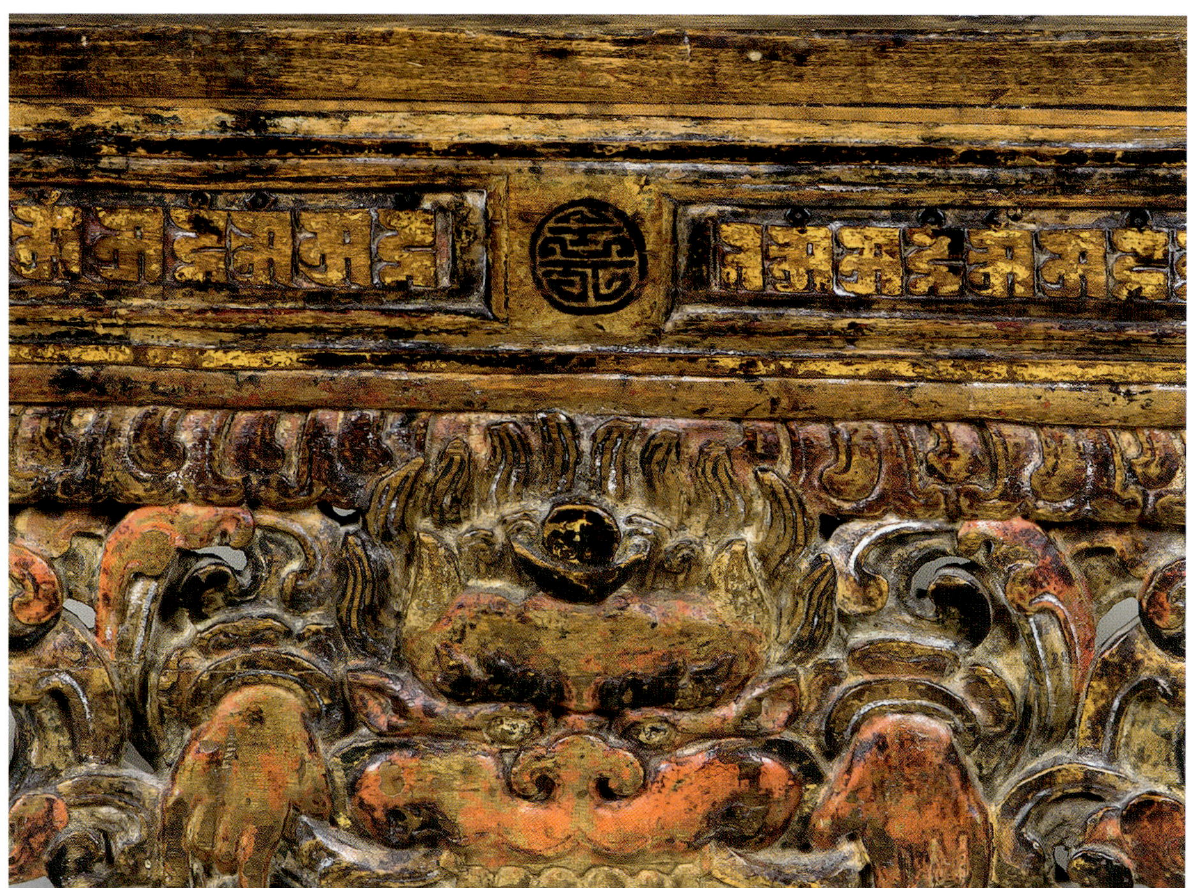

Detail of Fig. 9

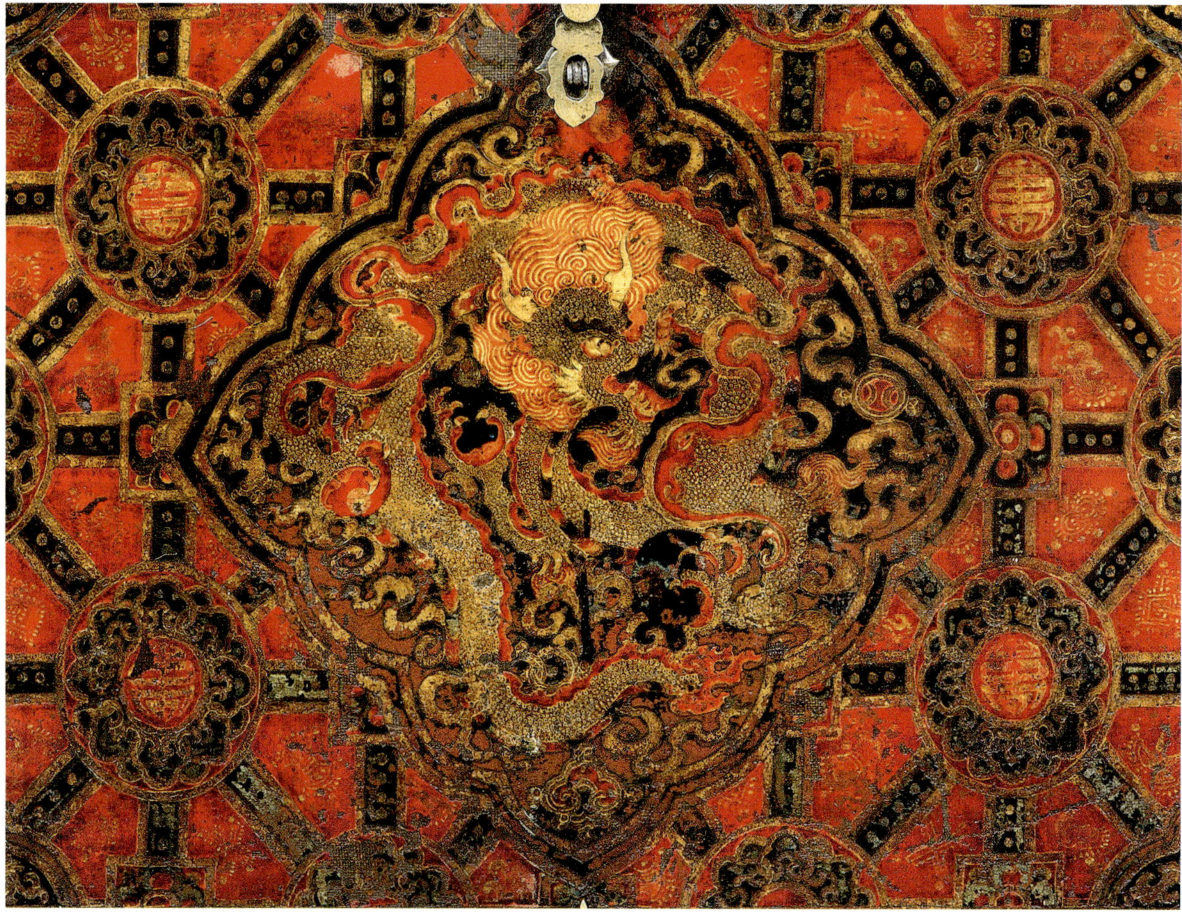

Detail of Fig. 12

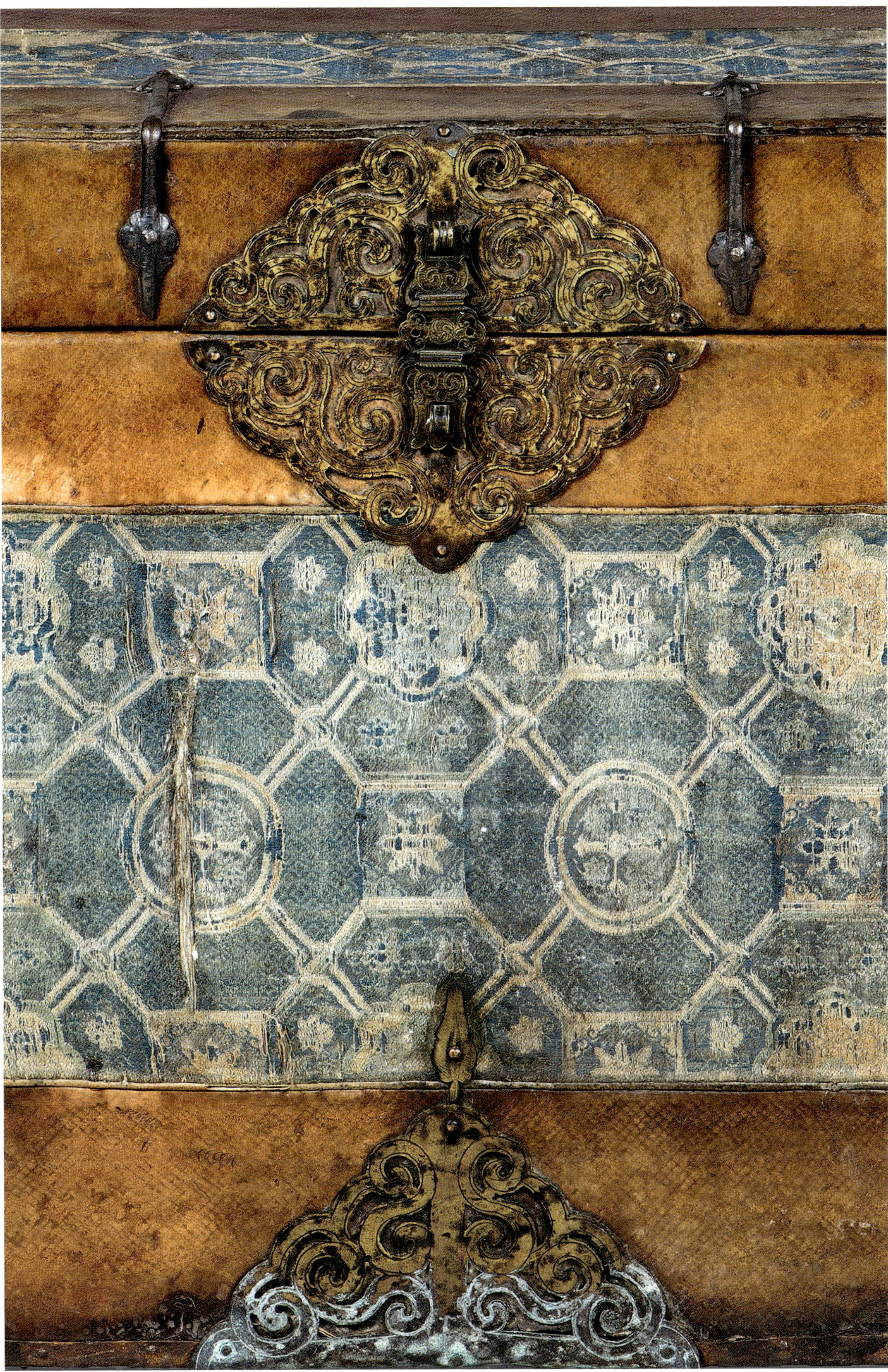

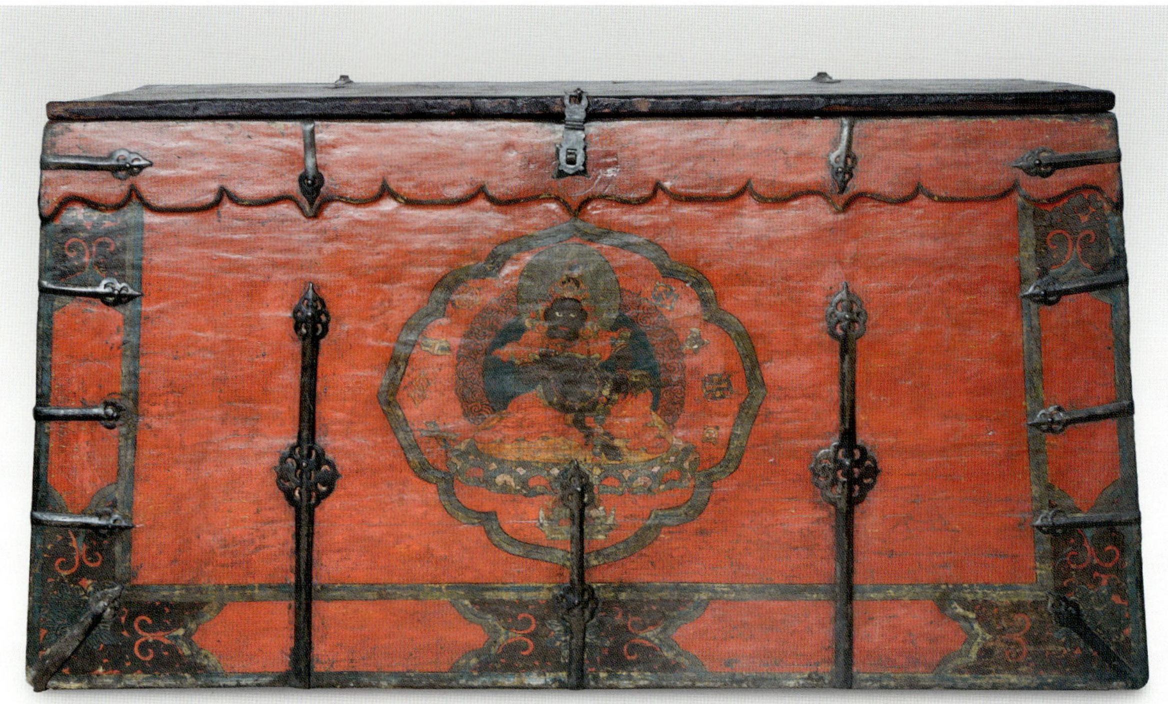

Fig. 11: Large chest with sloping sides (Tib. *rten sgam*), wood with long iron fittings, front side painted in red with Jambala, the god of wealth, in a medallion. South Tibet, Lhoka, 15th c., 104×36×59 cm, H2N collection

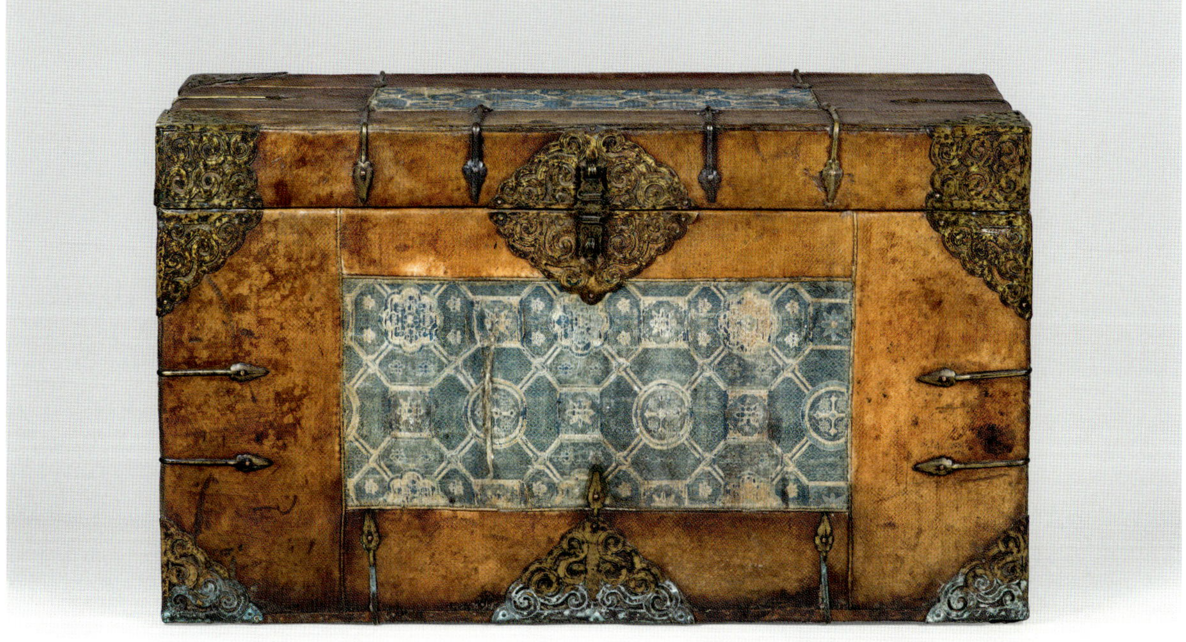

Fig. 12: Small chest ("chest no. 3") (Tib. *sgam chung*), wood clad with leather, a Ming brocade in *kati rimo* design is inserted in the centre of the front side and the lid, large openwork brass fittings at the edges and around the lock. Central Tibet, 17th c., 52×91×38 cm

angular metal fittings with arrowhead-like ends, usually of hand-wrought iron.

While most Tibetan chests have this characteristic box-lid, there are some chests with just a flat lid that rests on the edges of the sides of the chest or is recessed within (Fig. 11). It is assumed that this represents an older form (Corona & Hulse Corona 2004: 31). These other chests stand out by a number of special features from the main type of Tibetan chests. They are usually made of thicker panels, which suggest that they originated in an area where wood was readily available, probably Lhoka. Their painted decorations are not only different from the main type but also different from each other. Some are adorned with a large medallion depicting Jambala, the god of wealth, on the front (Fig. 11). Those chests which additionally have a freely drawn painting of figures on the front side are more

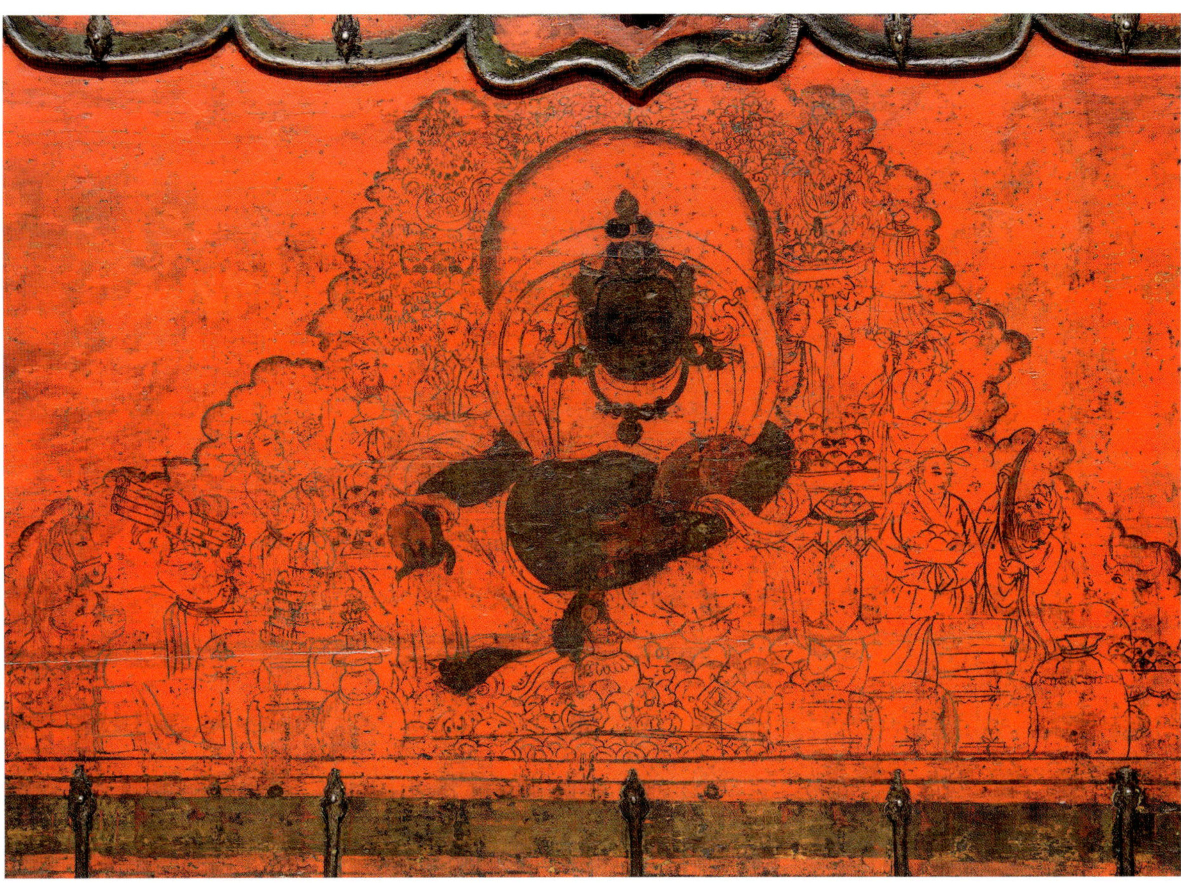

Fig. 13: Large chest (Tib. *sgam*), wood, on the front side Jambala, the god of wealth, surrounded by men and pack animals bringing treasures. Central Tibet, 15th c., 114×55×71 cm, H2N collection

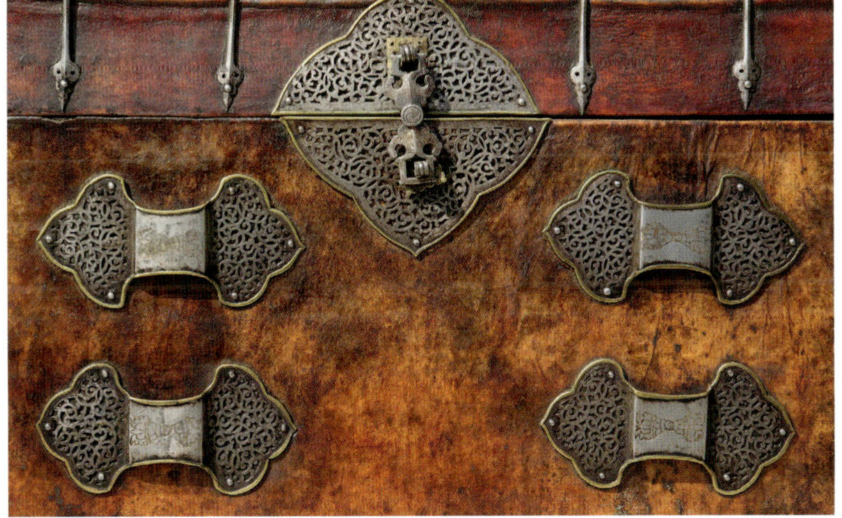

Fig. 14: Chest for transport on pack animals (Tib. *sgam chung*), wood clad with leather, iron fittings mounted in brass. Central Tibet, 18th/19th c., 63×39.5×24 cm, H2N collection

seldom (Fig. 13). Chests can differ in other respects, showing a great richness in variety. Some are trapezoidal (Fig. 11), smaller at the top, and the angular iron fittings can extend to add decoration.

Chest no. 3 (Fig. 12) in the Buddeberg collection is an example of the type of chest that was made for several centuries in this size and form for transport on pack animals: wooden chests covered in leather. To add to the beauty of this piece, a Ming period brocade is inlaid on the lid and in the front. The corners are reinforced with brass parts showing an openwork design to protect the chest during transport. Other chests of this type have metal fittings on the front through which leather straps can be inserted to buckle the chest on the pack animal (Fig. 14). These iron fittings were produced in a complex, openwork pattern and are mounted in a brass border. They are the only decoration on this chest and demonstrate Tibetan craftsmen's great ironworking skill. Although these leather-covered transport chests are always very similar in form and dimensions, they show great variations in the outer appearance. On an unusual very early example (Fig. 15) the edges are broadly covered with green-dyed shark skin instead of leather. The central surfaces of the lid, front and side panels are decorated with gold foil on a red lacquer background. The front shows a pair of phoenixes, the symbol for the Chinese empress. Leaves and tendrils in a style typical for the Yuan Dynasty (1280–1367) surround the phoenixes.

Medium-sized and smaller chests were also made entirely of leather (Tib. *sgo sgam*). Due to the large herds of yak, sheep and goats, leather is a readily available material in Tibet. It can easily be worked. Tibetan leather chests come in different forms and various types of construction. The lids of leather chests always have sides that cover the top

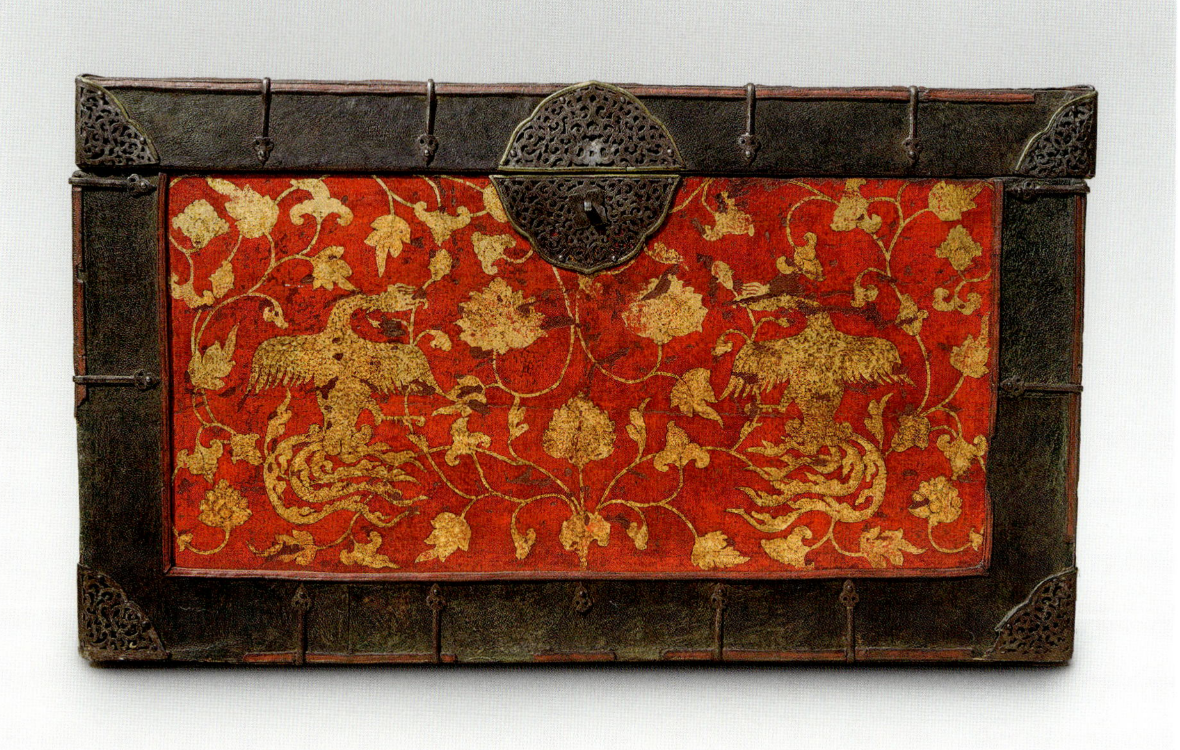

Fig. 15: Chest for transport on pack animals (Tib. *sgam chung*), wood, broad edges coated with shark skin, iron fittings, lid, front and sides with gold-leaf decorations on red lacquer. Central Tibet, 14th/15th c., 74.5×34.5×42.5 cm, H2N collection

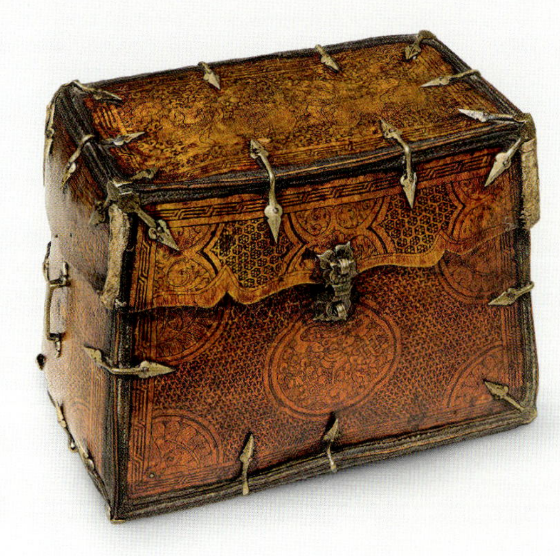

Fig. 16: Small leather chest with brass mountings (Tib. *ko sgam*), lid, front and sides decorated with painting on gold foil, the Eight Auspicious Symbols (Sanskrit *Aṣṭamaṅgala*, Tib. *bkra shis rtags brgyad*) in the central medallion on the front side. Central Tibet, 16th/17th c., 28×17×21 cm, H2N collection

edges of the chest itself. They are often trapezoidal, as shown in Fig. 16. The sides are individual pieces of leather sewn together with triple seams at the edges. As is the case for wooden chests, the edges and corners are strengthened and protected by metal straps with the typical arrowhead ends, here in brass. The chest is richly painted. The principle decoration is a pair of snow lions on the lid and a medallion showing the Eight Auspicious Symbols (Tib. *bkra shis rtags brgyad*) on the front. The meander-like borders and the two filler motifs on the front (rosettes in hexagons and a net of interlocking Y-figures) are identical with those on a lacquered and gilded tubular leather container (Anninos 2000: 110), so it can be assumed that they were made in the same period (15th century), if not in the same workshop. The chest was decorated by covering it entirely with gold foil, on which the snow lions, the Eight Auspicious Symbols and other details were drawn in fine black and brown lines. Cutting out part of the gold foil created the less refined geometric patterns.

Chest no. 4 (Fig. 17) is unique in several ways. In contrast to most other Tibetan chests, it can be geographically identified; it comes from Kham in eastern Tibet, a once well-forested region. This explains the use of solid planks in its construction, which obviates the need for iron fittings. This impressive piece of furniture was created in East Tibet at a time when in Central Tibet high quality chests had ceased to be produced. The tiger is the emblematic animal of the Khampa people. The tiger skin painted on a red background appears to be protecting the chest, and so it was intended. Not all monasteries could afford a real stuffed tiger to protect the temple, such as the one hanging in Khorchag (Fig. 18), but the painted skin on the chest served the same purpose.

Fig. 17: Small chest ("chest no. 4") (Tib. *sgam chung*), wood, with a front-facing painted tiger skin hanging over the lid and front. Kham, East Tibet, 19th c., 50×71×37 cm

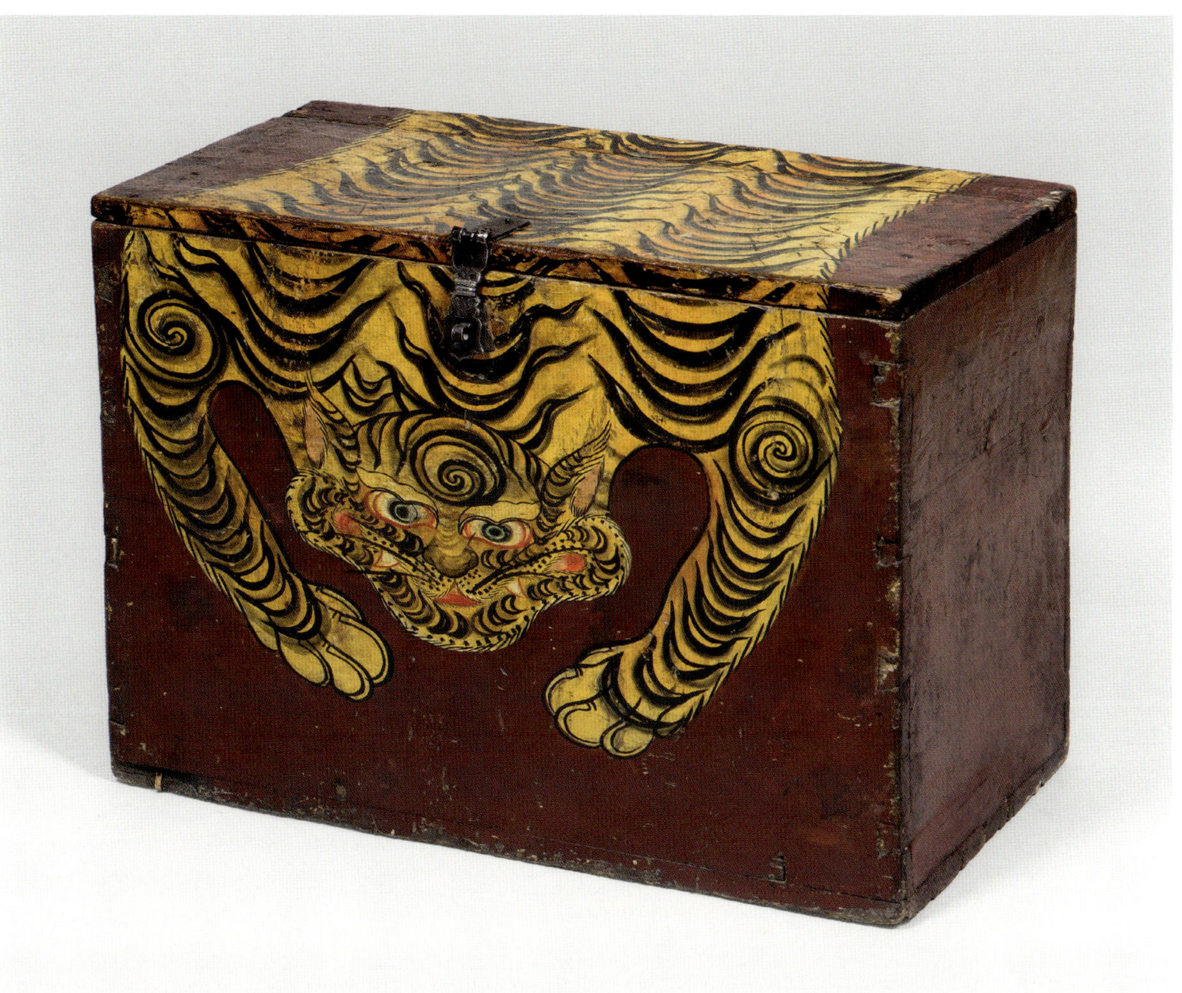

Fig. 18: Stuffed tiger and snow leopard with ceremonial scarves (Tib. *kha btags*). Khorchag monastery (Tib. *'khor chags dgon pa*). Purang District, Southwest Tibet, 1994

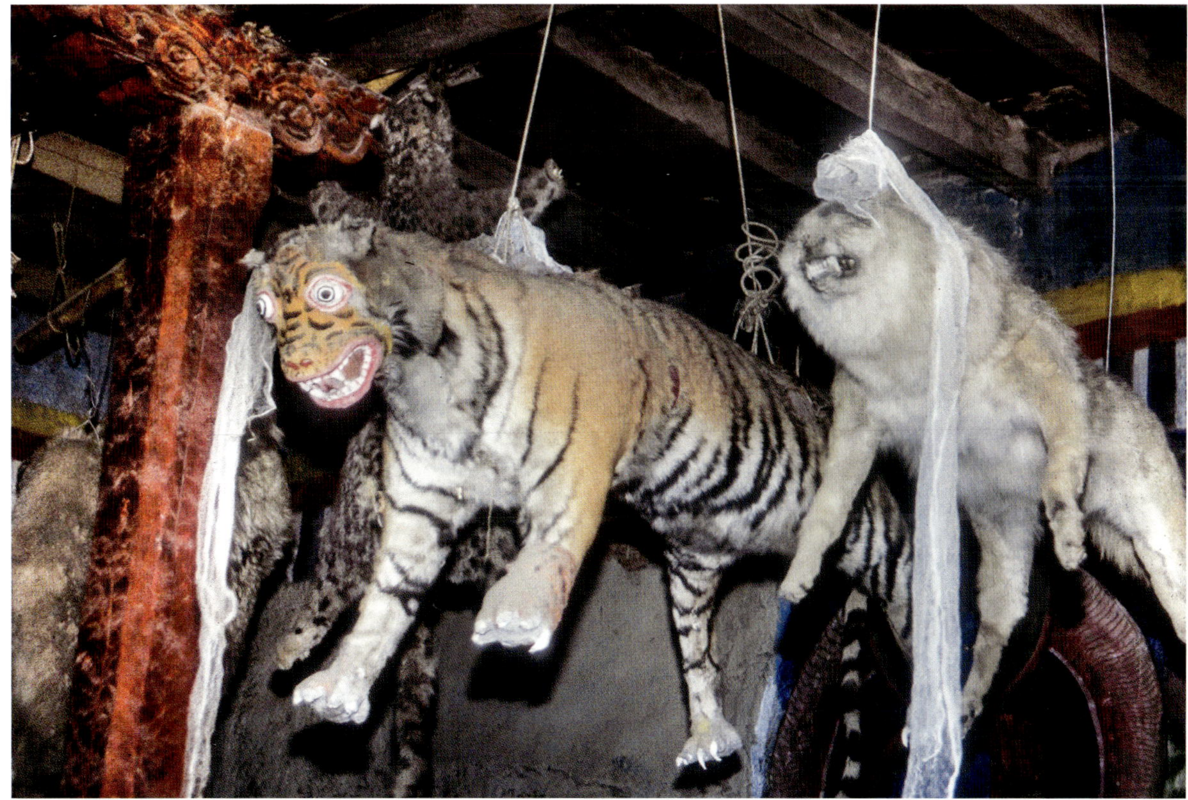

Fig. 19: Large *torma* (Tib. *gtor ma*). Ramoche monastery, Lhasa, Central Tibet, 2006

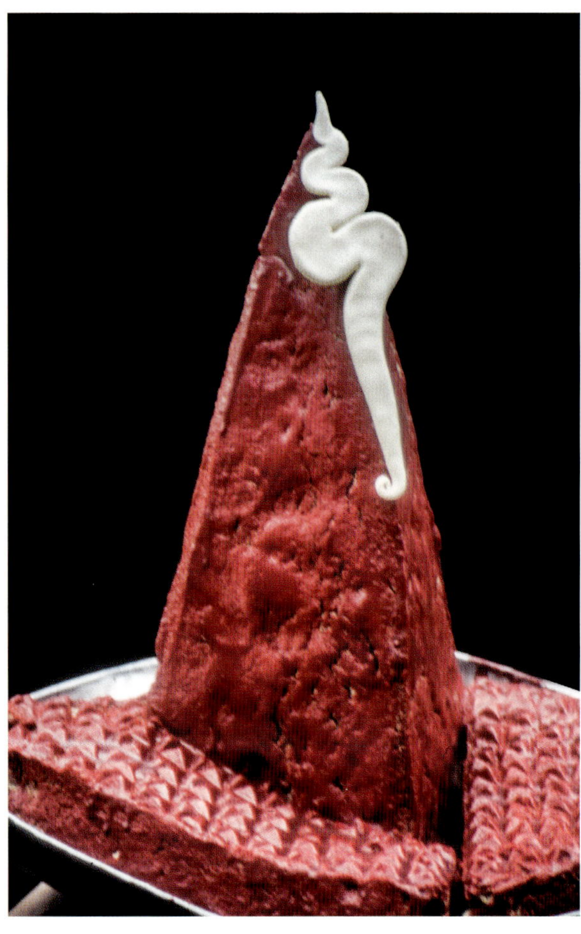

Fig. 20: Small cabinet for the storage of torma (Tib. *gtor sgam*), wood, on the front animals painted in gold leaf. Central Tibet, 16th/17th c., 36×30.5×33 cm, H2N collection

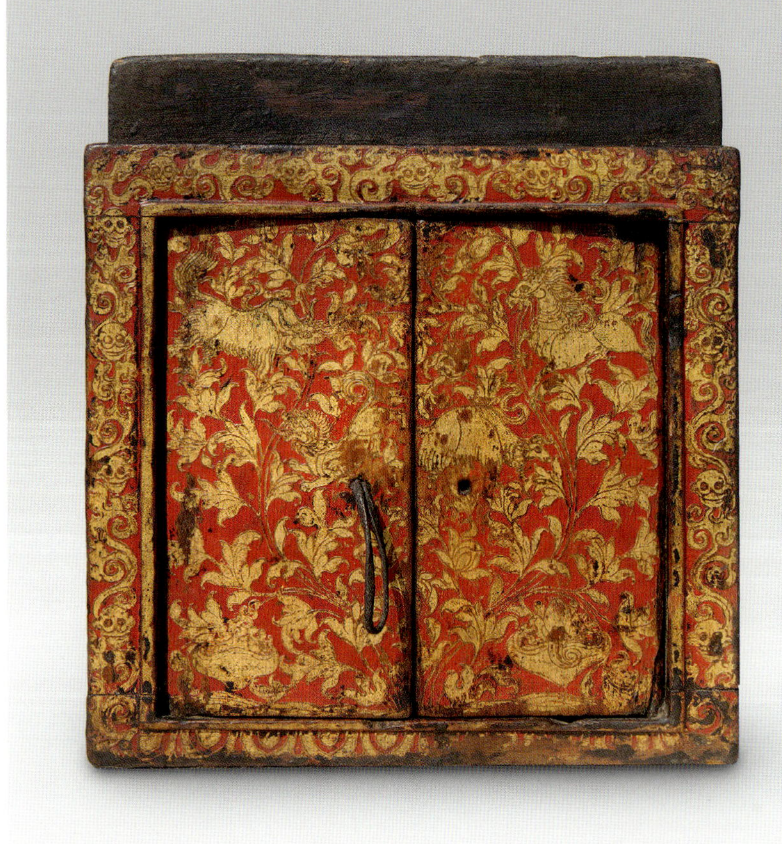

CABINETS

Chests normally have a lid on top, convenient for storing objects and materials that can easily be lowered into them. Many things, however, are better kept in a piece of furniture that is accessible from the front, cabinets and cupboards of varying sizes. In Tibetan temples, *torma* are a primary example, offering cakes formed from dough of roasted barley flour and butter. They are offered to deities to solicit their benevolence. *Torma* are only prepared once a year, but are used daily in religious ceremonies (Fig. 19 shows a freshly made *torma* in Ramoche monastery in Lhasa). They are kept in a *torgam*, a low, small cabinet with two doors, to protect them from mice and dust. Small *torgam*, such as the one in Fig. 20, may well be the oldest form of Tibetan cabinets. The decoration of this *torgam*, with skulls painted on the frame, suggests that it once was in a *Gonkhang*, a temple for guardian deities. On the doors in gold foil on a red background are animals: yak, horse, he-goat and mastiff. These animals are connected to Mahakala (Tib. *mgon po nag po chen po*), one of the most important *Dharmapala*, protectors of the Buddhist doctrine. Between the golden foliage at the bottom of the doors one can recognise two skull bowls. The left one is filled with blood, the right one with the "wrathful offering of the five senses" (which can be better recognised on the *torgam* in Fig. 21 and will therefore be described there).

Among the five cabinets in the Buddeberg collection two are *torgam* (Figs. 21 and 22). The upper halves of the doors of the *torgam* in Fig. 21 show the faces of the *Dharmapala* Mahakala, to whom the previously described *torgam* was also dedicated. Mahakala is represented as a wrathful deity with wide-open eyes, gaping mouth and flaming eyebrows, a third eye and a crown of five skulls. Recognised as one of the most powerful deities, Mahakala is often invoked. This *torgam* would have been used to keep the *torma* that were offered to him daily. The lower parts of the doors show two representations of the *torma* used in the Mahakala cult. On the left door, in a white skull cup resting on a tripod of three skulls, the wrathful offering of the five senses is shown. The five organs of sense are represented: two eyes for sight, two ears for hearing, a nose for smell, three tongues for taste, and a heart in the form of a lotus bud for touch. The skull cup on the right door holds a flaming, triangular *torma*. The side panels of this *torgam* are decorated with fruit and vases filled with flowers and a branch of red coral.

The small cabinet of Fig. 22 was probably also used as a *torgam*, although its painting does not suggest this at first

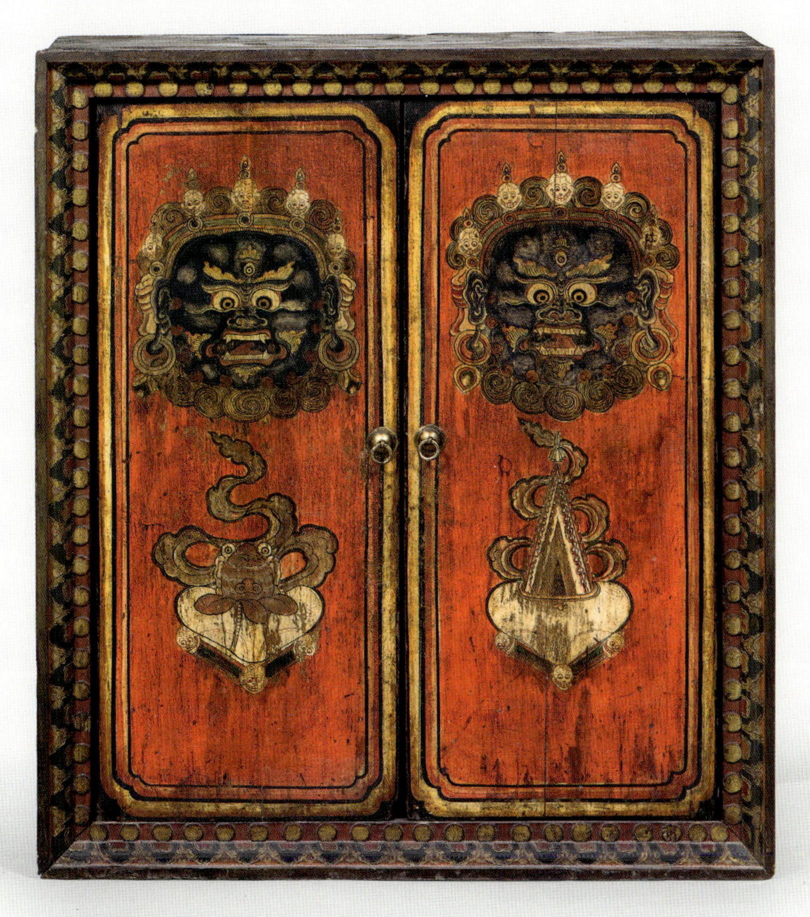

Fig. 21: Small cabinet for the storage of *torma* (Tib. *gtor sgam*), wood, on the doors faces of the *Dharmapala* Mahakala and skull cups filled with the "Five Senses" and a flaming *torma*. Central Tibet, 18th /19th c., 102×90×37 cm

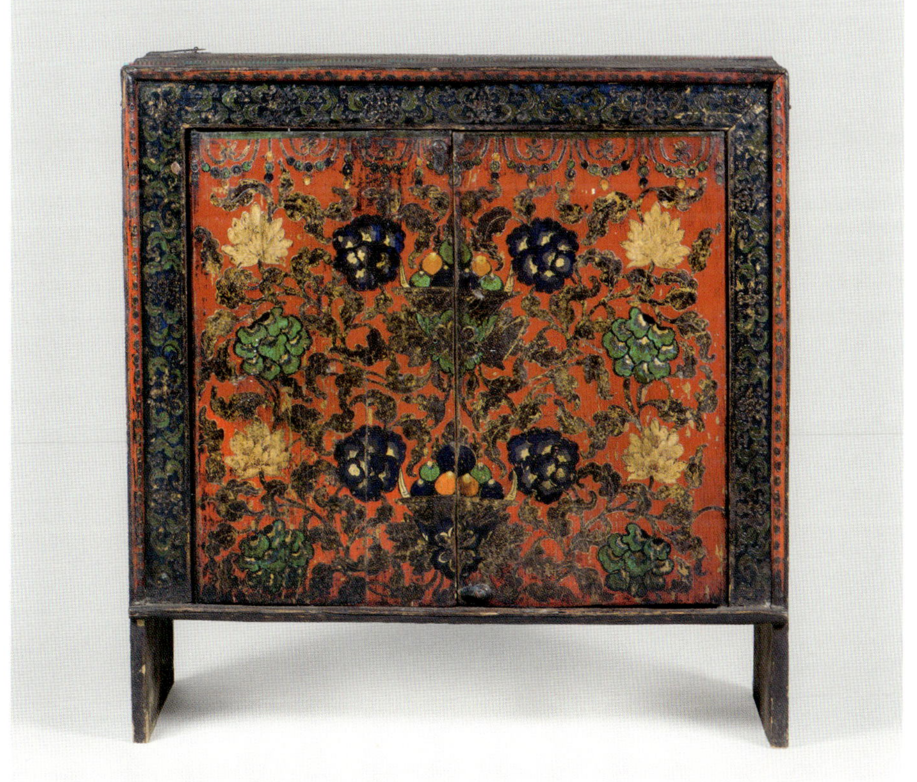

Fig. 22: Small cabinet for the storage of *torma* (Tib. *gtor sgam*), wood, the doors painted with foliage and flowers. Central Tibet, 18th/19th c., 81.5×82×31.5 cm

Fig. 23: Lectern (Tib. *dpe sgam*), wood, painted with scrolls of leaves and the Chinese auspicious character Double *Xi* (for double fortune). Central Tibet, 18th/19th c., 89.5×87.5×30.5 cm

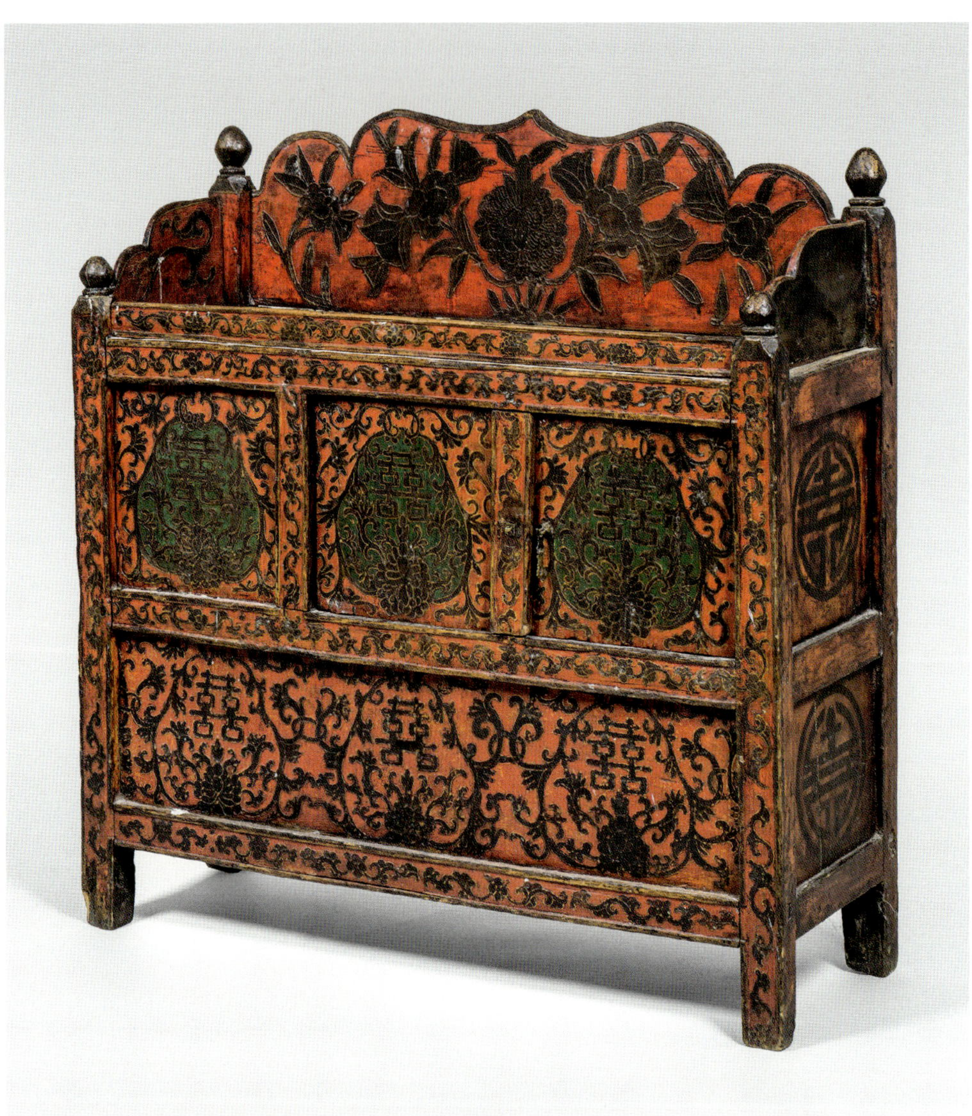

Fig. 24: Pair of cabinets with winged doors (Tib. *chod sgam*), wood, doors decorated in gold foil with identical representations of dragons in three-quarter view on each panel. Central Tibet, 18th c., each cabinet 77×34.5×84.5 cm, H2N collection

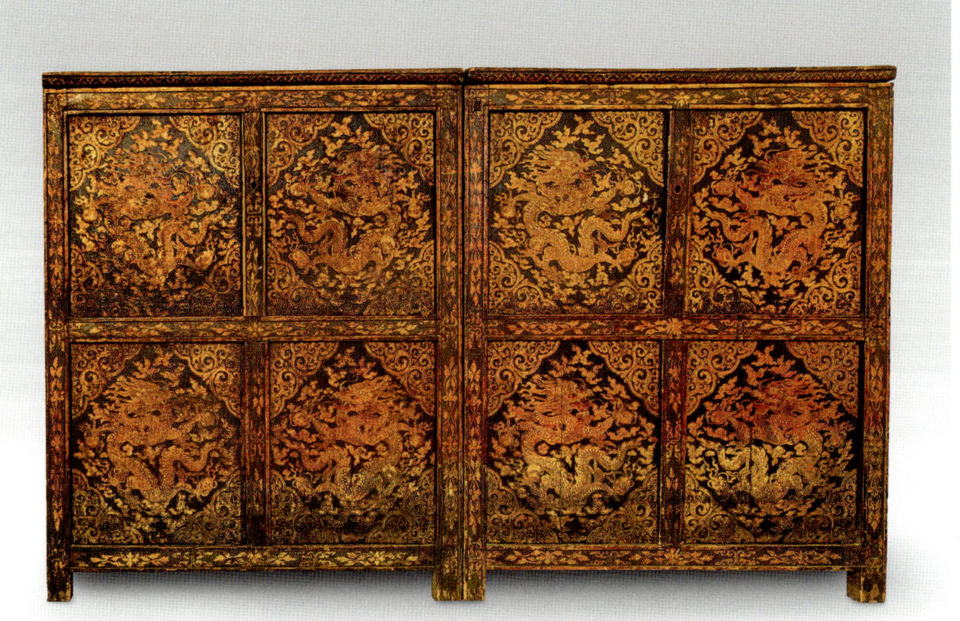

Fig. 25: Cabinet (Tib. *sgam*), wood, on the front fine painting of the four mythical animals of the "Four Dignities": tiger, dragon, *Garuda* and snow lion in medallions. Central Tibet, 18th/19th c., 88×95×53 cm

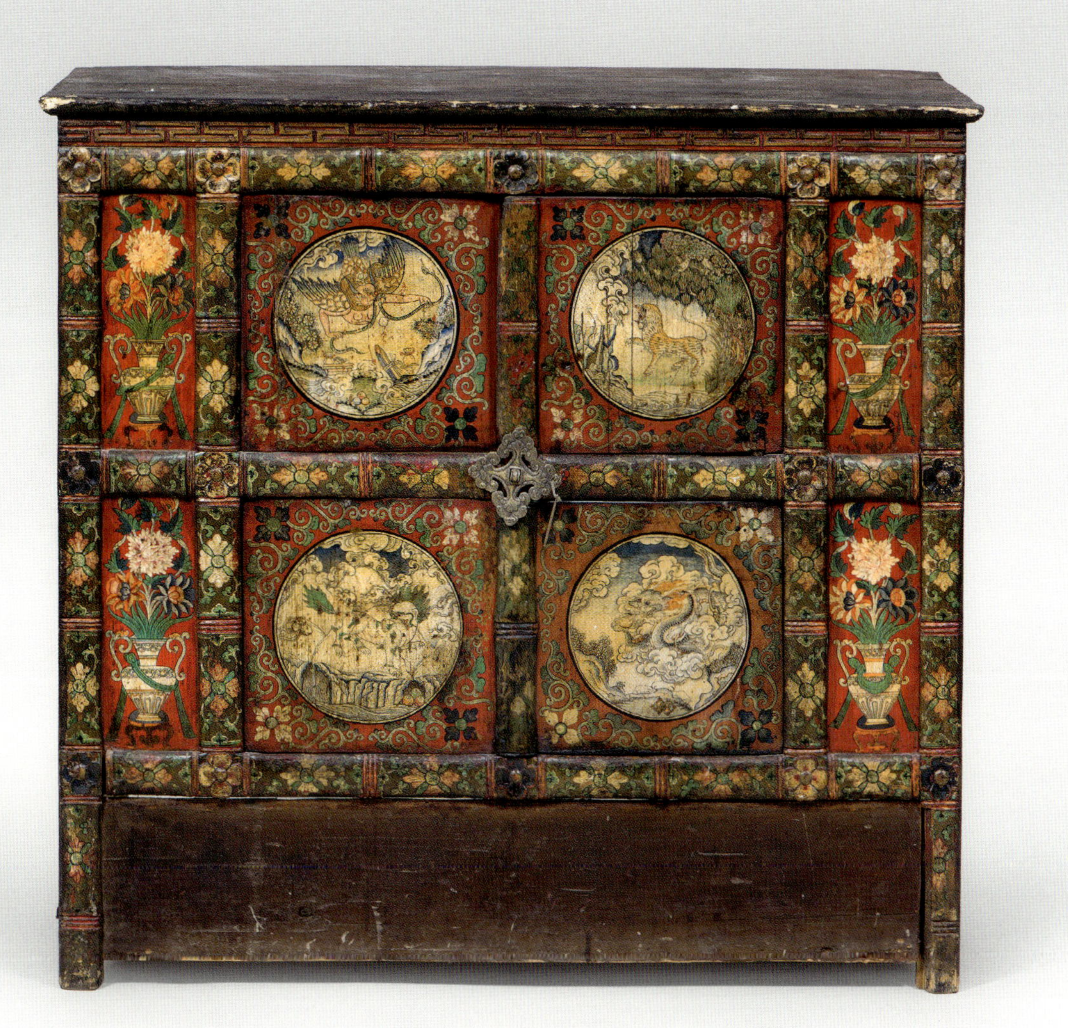

Detail of Fig. 25

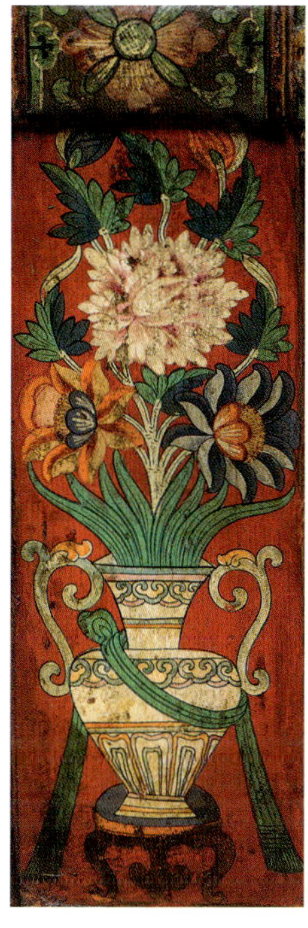

glance. The front is decorated with dense foliage and blue, green and white flowers, four of each. Their form suggests peonies or chrysanthemums, both particularly favoured in Chinese art. In the middle, two more flowers bear two skull cups, one above the other, which are filled with the Seven Jewels, flanked by elephant tusks. On *thangkas*, such piles of jewels are often shown placed before deities as a sign of devotion. Thus the jewels in the cups on this cabinet indicate devotion to the deity whose *torma* were stored in it. Elephant tusks often flank or frame the Seven Jewels and other piles of jewels, reinforcing their function as offerings. Chains of pearls and jewels adorn the top of the doorframe. They appear in similar form as the upper border of murals in many Tibetan temples. This also underlines the ritual function of this cabinet.

Notched panels forming the back and sidewalls of the structure of the upper part of the cabinet are a significant feature of another cabinet (Fig. 23). Such pieces of furniture are called *pegam*, derived from the Tibetan word for book, *dpe cha*, and for chest, *sgam*, as they were originally designed for use as a lectern. Important elements of their construction are the four corner posts, which on the present and most other examples are crowned with lotus buds. The black decoration stands out on a red background, whereby it is possible that the black design was originally covered with gold foil, lost due to aging of the glue (Corona & Hulse Corona 2004: 40). The front of the *pegam* is decorated with complex foliage, which encloses six identical stylised Chinese characters, that for Double *Xi* which represents double fortune: material and spiritual fortune, on earth and in heaven. The squares and horizontal lines represent the earth, the vertical lines the heavens. Large images of *Shou*, the Chinese symbol for the god of long life, are painted on the side panels. This *pegam* was meant to give its user double fortune and a long life.

Fig. 26a and 26b:
Large altar cabinet (Tib. *chod sgam*), solid wood, richly painted, in the upper part behind the doors three niches for bronze statues of seated deities. Kham, East Tibet, 19th/20th c., 171×131.5×48 cm

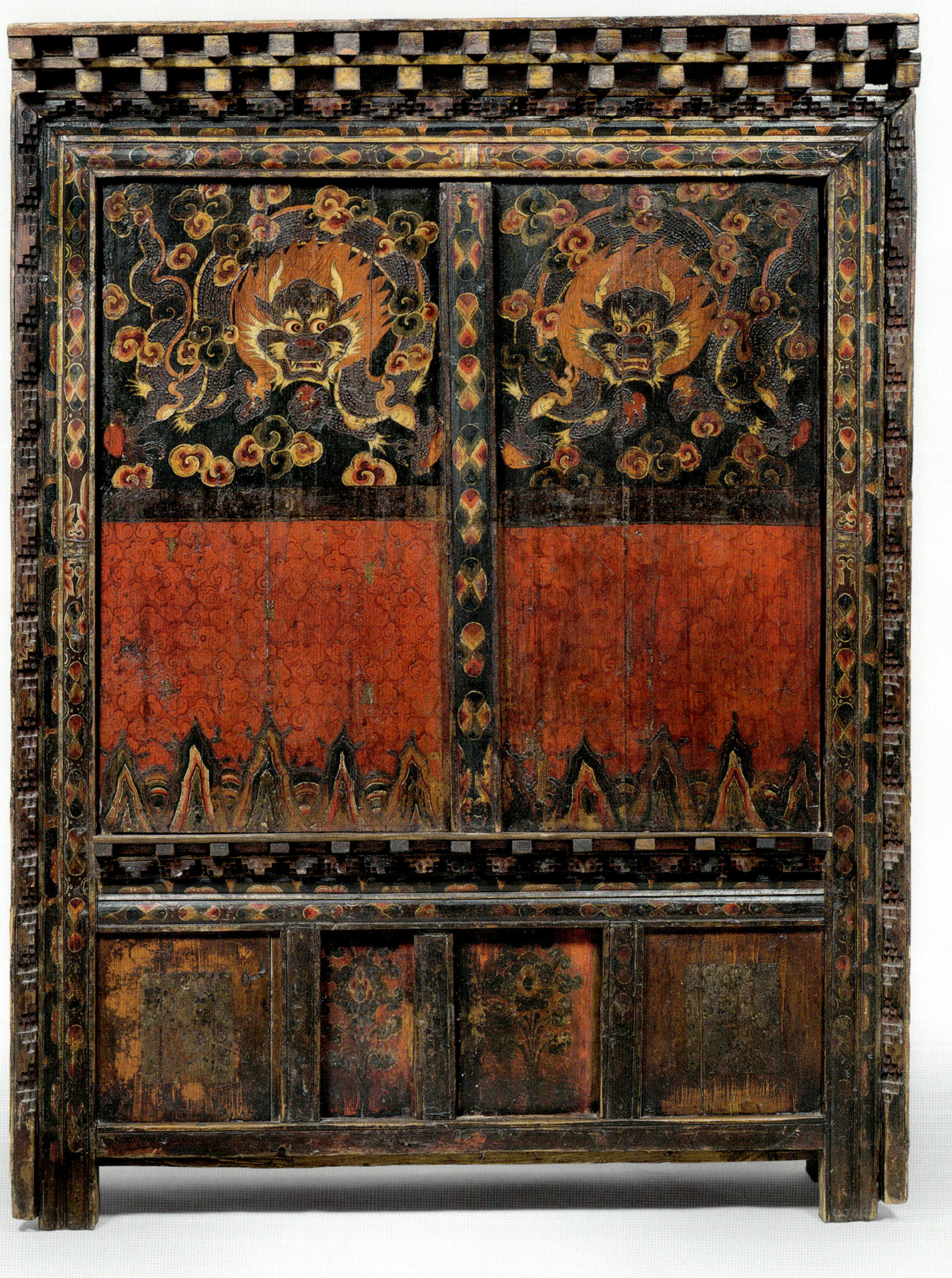

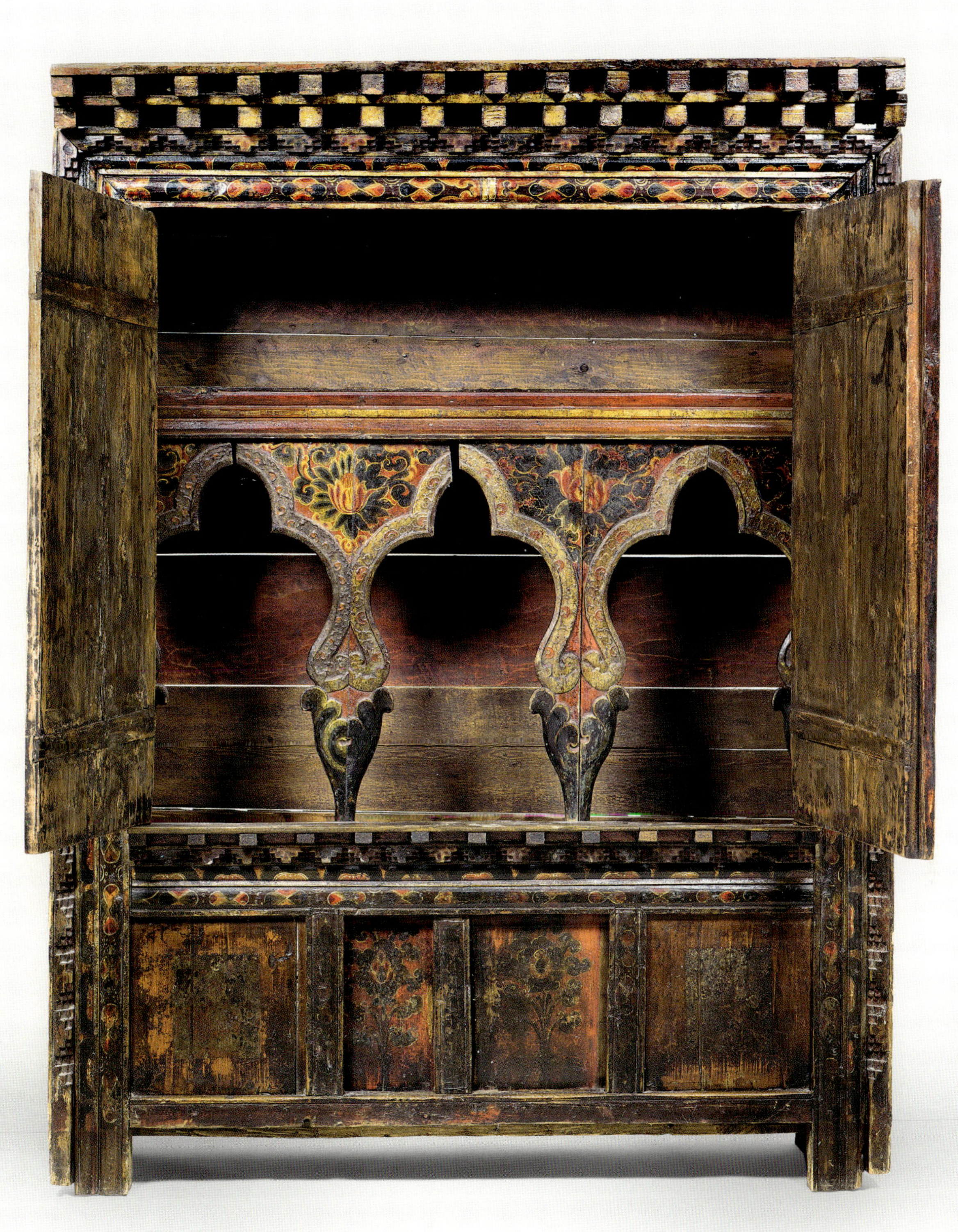

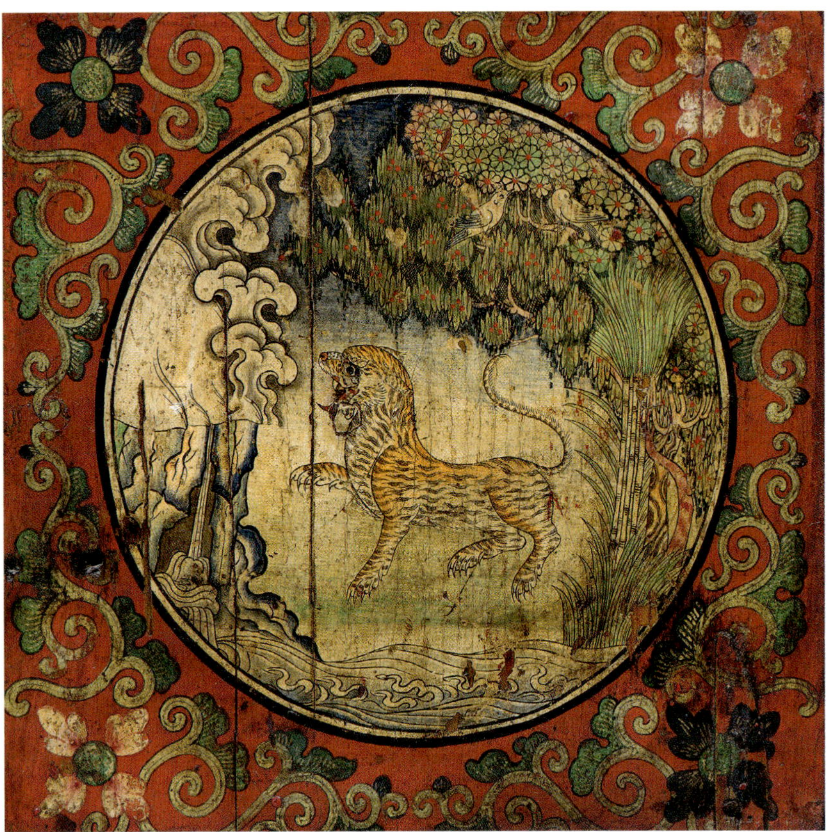

Detail of Fig. 25

After the zenith of Tibetan chests in the 18th century, their function as storage furniture for both religious and worldly goods was taken over by cabinets. *Torgam* and *pegam*, well represented in the Buddeberg collection are a rare minority among Tibetan cabinets. The great majority of Tibetan cabinets as they were produced from the end of the 17th century on are similar to the pair in Fig. 24. They consist of a frame construction of two rows, one above the other, of two panels, seldom three, all the same size. Typically, as in the illustration, they were often made in pairs, the doors hinged to open in opposite directions to be opened from the middle. The decoration was often gold foil on a red background, or, as in this example, on a dark blue background. The dragon in three-quarter view is surrounded by small clouds as it was similarly represented on imperial robes. The corners of the panels show a composition of foliage, similar to that common on the front side of chests. This continuation of traditional decoration was broken in the 19th and 20th centuries, when cabinets were produced in greater numbers.

The restrained design gives way to a multi-coloured painting, sometimes even with figural representations. However, they are seldom so finely painted as the medallions on the doors of the small cabinet in Fig. 25. In the centre of the painting are the four mythical animals: tiger, dragon, the mythical bird Garuda and the snow lion. As a group they represent the "Four Dignities", the qualities and attitudes that a *Bodhisattva* aims to attain on the way to enlightenment: confidence, mild fortitude, fearlessness, and a clear awareness or wisdom. In these medallions, the four animals are shown in a landscape of water, clouds, mountains and trees. On the four smaller panels on the front of the cabinet are Vases of Immortality filled with peonies, a symbol for eternal life. They have two handles, typical for their depiction on Tibetan furniture.

The altar cabinet (Fig. 26) in the Buddeberg collection is remarkable in several respects: its size, massive construction with architectural elements, and its division into an upper and lower part with the respective doors. The two large upper doors open to reveal an altar with three niches. Altar cabinets of this type come from Kham in eastern Tibet (Corona & Hulse Corona 2004: 56). Because of the abundance of wood in this province, cabinetmakers could use the material more liberally than in Central Tibet. One can see from the uneven surface on the insides of the doors that the boards were not sawn but hewn with an axe or chisel. The individual parts of the cabinet are joined by tongue-and-groove, without the use of nails. The top beam is carved with a double row of square blocks, an architectural element reminiscent of the ends of roof beams of Tibetan temples. Below this is a carved three-dimensional pattern of stepped cubes, the *chotseg* (Tib. *chos brtsegs*), a pattern often found around temple doors. It continues down the side posts of the altar cabinet. Within this carved frame is an inner frame painted with figures that recall the form of an hourglass. The painting on the upper half of the doors shows a face-on view of a dragon's head. The surrounding clouds recall their appearance on imperial robes of the late Qing Dynasty (1644–1911), equally the range of mountains at the base of the doors. When opened, the doors give view to the altar, which was designed to contain three seated deities, as one can recognise from the forms of the mandorlas surrounding the niches.

STAND FOR AN ALTAR FIGURE

Wooden stands for altar figures are a rare type of Tibetan furniture. The example in the Buddeberg collection (Fig. 27) captivates with the two snow lions on the front, whose raised front paws appear to support atlas-like the missing statue. In accordance with tradition, they are painted white with green accents in their flowing manes. A finely drawn

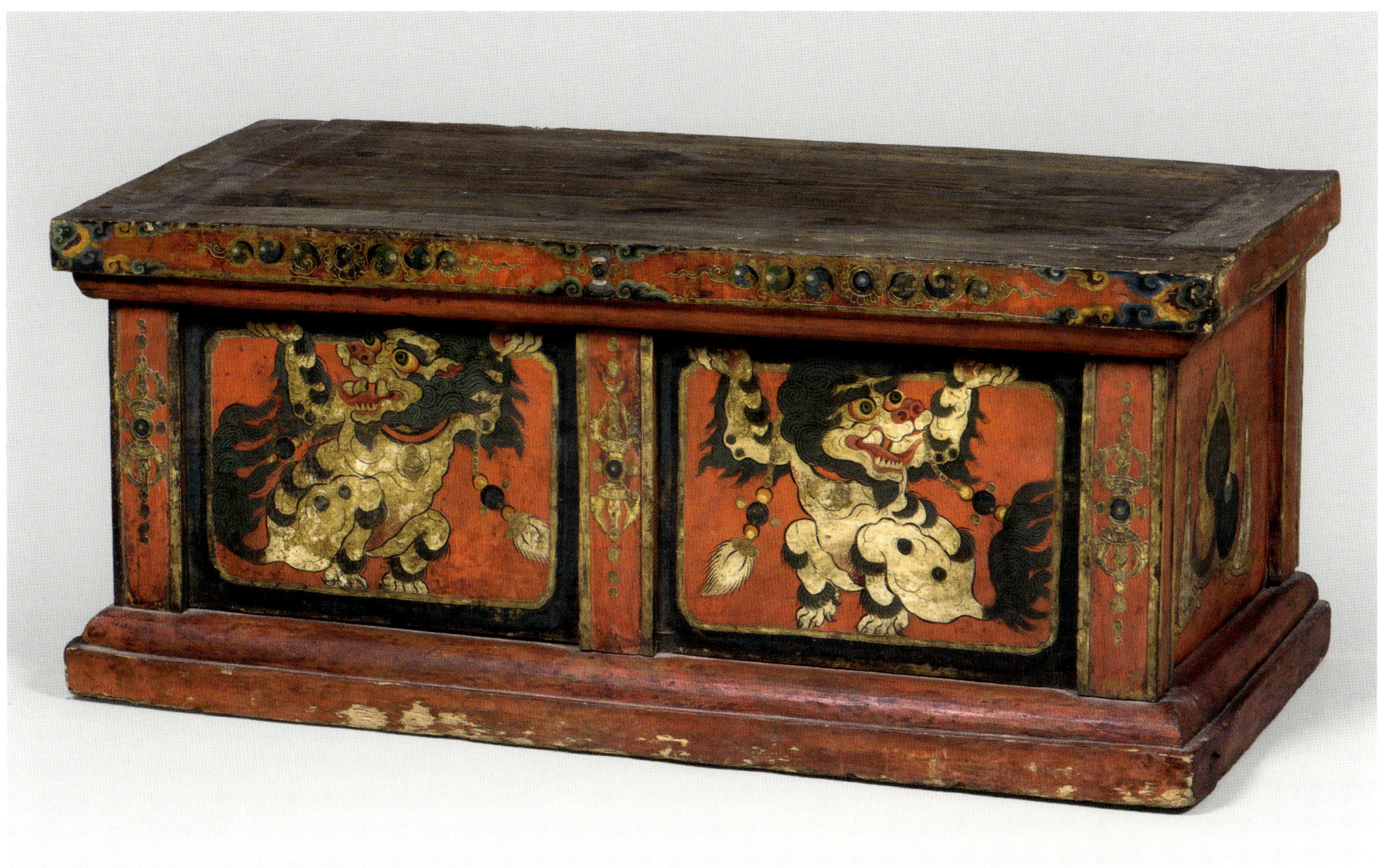

Fig. 27: Stand for an altar statue, wood, painted with two snow lions sitting opposite each other carrying the weight of the statue atlas-like. Central Tibet, 14th–16th c., 41.5×100×48 cm

vajra (thunderbolt, Tib. *rdo rje*) is shown on each of the posts that frame the panels with the snow lions.

Pairs of lions on stands for statues have a long tradition that goes back to earlier Indian examples. They first appear in India around the beginning of the first millennium in the Kushan Dynasty (1st century BC–2nd century AD), both in Gandhara and Mathura, continuing in the Gupta Dynasty (ca. 320–550 AD), then enjoying their heyday in the era of the eastern India Pala Dynasty (ca. 750–1161 AD) in the 10th to 12th centuries. From there, also via Nepal and Kashmir, the two lions on the bases for statues found their way into Tibetan art, particularly on bronzes and murals. While most of these Tibetan representations of the lions follow the Indian style, those on the base in the Buddeberg collection in Fig. 27 are stylistically Chinese.

It is astounding that Tibetan furniture is aligned in its decoration almost exclusively to Chinese templates, whereas sculpture and painting in Central Tibet are influenced by the styles of the Pala Dynasty and Nepal, thus following the Indian style canon. One can only speculate about this strict stylistic dichotomy. It dates back at least to the beginning of the 14th century, when there were two very different styles of painting in Central Tibet, as can be recognised in the murals in Shalu monastery. Although these significant works were financed primarily by the Yuan emperor, most sections were executed in a style influenced by Pala and Nepal art, while – in contrast – a few walls are in the very clearly different Chinese style. There must have been at that time a conscious decision to follow completely the tradition of Indian and Nepalese art for religious painted and sculpted works. Just as clearly, the decoration of furniture continued to be based on Chinese models, over time following the changes in their style and form as in China, though often with a significant time delay. This can be particularly well observed in the representation of dragons.

Detail of Fig. 26

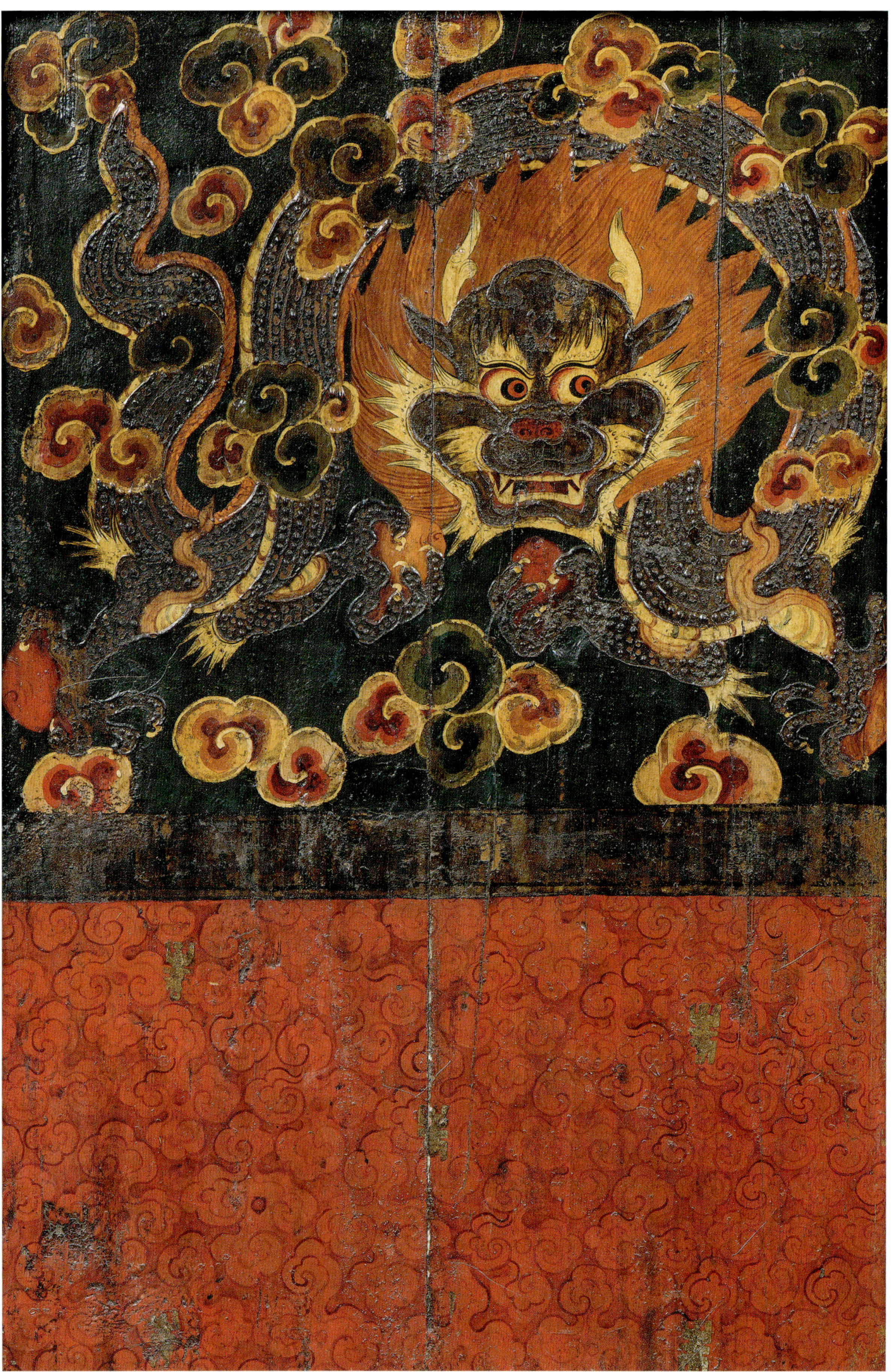

GLOSSARY

Aṣṭamaṅgala
Eight Auspicious Symbols, Tib. *bkra shis rtags brgyad*, conch shell, parasol, wheel, endless knot, pair of fish, vase, lotus, banner.

Bodhisattva
Sanskrit; Tib. *byang chub sems dpa'*, a highly compassionate being on the way to buddhahood that acts for the welfare of all other living beings.

Chakravartin
Sanskrit; Tib. *'khor los sgyur ba'i rgyal po*, literally: "the one who turns the wheel", an ideal monarch.

chotseg
Tib. *chos brtsegs*, literally "the stacking of religious law", a triangular pattern of tiny cubes cut in relief.

Dharmapala
Sanskrit; Tib. *chos skyong*, protector of the teachings of Buddha.

Four Dignities
They represent sacred qualities and attitudes that a *Bodhisattva* develops on the path to enlightenment; symbolised by the four animals: tiger for confidence, snow lion for gentle power, Garuda for fearlessness and the dragon for clear awareness.

gesso
Tib. *kyung bur*, a mixture of gypsum and chalk used as a primer on canvas or wood.

Gonkhang
Tib. *mgon khang*, temple for guardian deities.

kati rimo
Tib. *kha ti ri mo*, brocade pattern.

Kham
Tib. *khams*, region in East Tibet, today the eastern part of the Tibet Autonomous Region, the western part of Sichuan Province, the northernmost part of Yunnan Province and the southernmost part of Qinghai Province.

khorlam
Tib. *khor lam*, pilgrim's corridor around or inside a temple.

kīrtimukha
Sanskrit, literally "face of victory", mythological guardian creature with a lion's face originating from the Skanda Purana.

khyisu
Tib. *khyi su*, dog-legged, cabriole legs.

Lantsa
Sanskrit; ornamental script for religious Sanskrit texts which have been translated into Tibetan.

Lhoka
Tib. *lho kha sa khul*, Prefecture in the south of Tibet.

Makara
Sanskrit; Tib. *chu srin ma ka ra*, mythological creature made up of elephant, crocodile, snake and dragon.

Mandorla
A body halo around a deity in sculpture or painting.

mantra
A repeated prayer.

pegam
Tib. *dpe sgam*, stand or lectern to hold a book.

Serkhang
Tib. *gser khang*, one of the main temple halls.

torgam
Tib. *gtor sgam*, small chest or box for the storage of *torma*.

torma
Tib. *gtor ma*, offering cake made of butter and *tsampa*.

tsampa
Tib. *tsam pa*, roasted barley flour.

vajra
Sanskrit; Tib. *rdo rje* ritual object, thunderbolt.

Vase of immortality
The vase filled with ambrosia is one of the Eight Auspicious Symbols.

zipak
Tib. *zigs pa*, mythological animal with a pig's snout, personifying the guardian function for devotees.

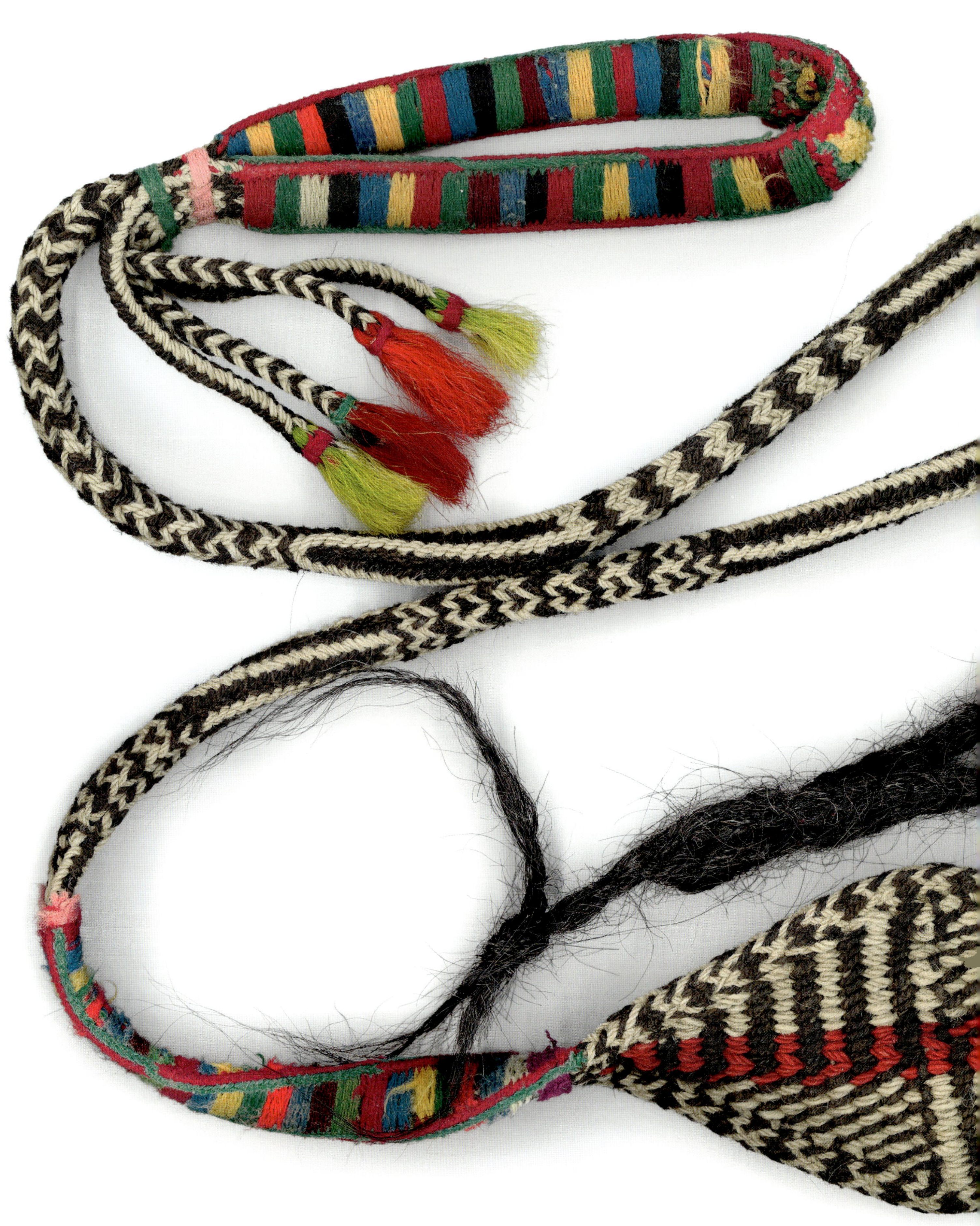

APPENDICES

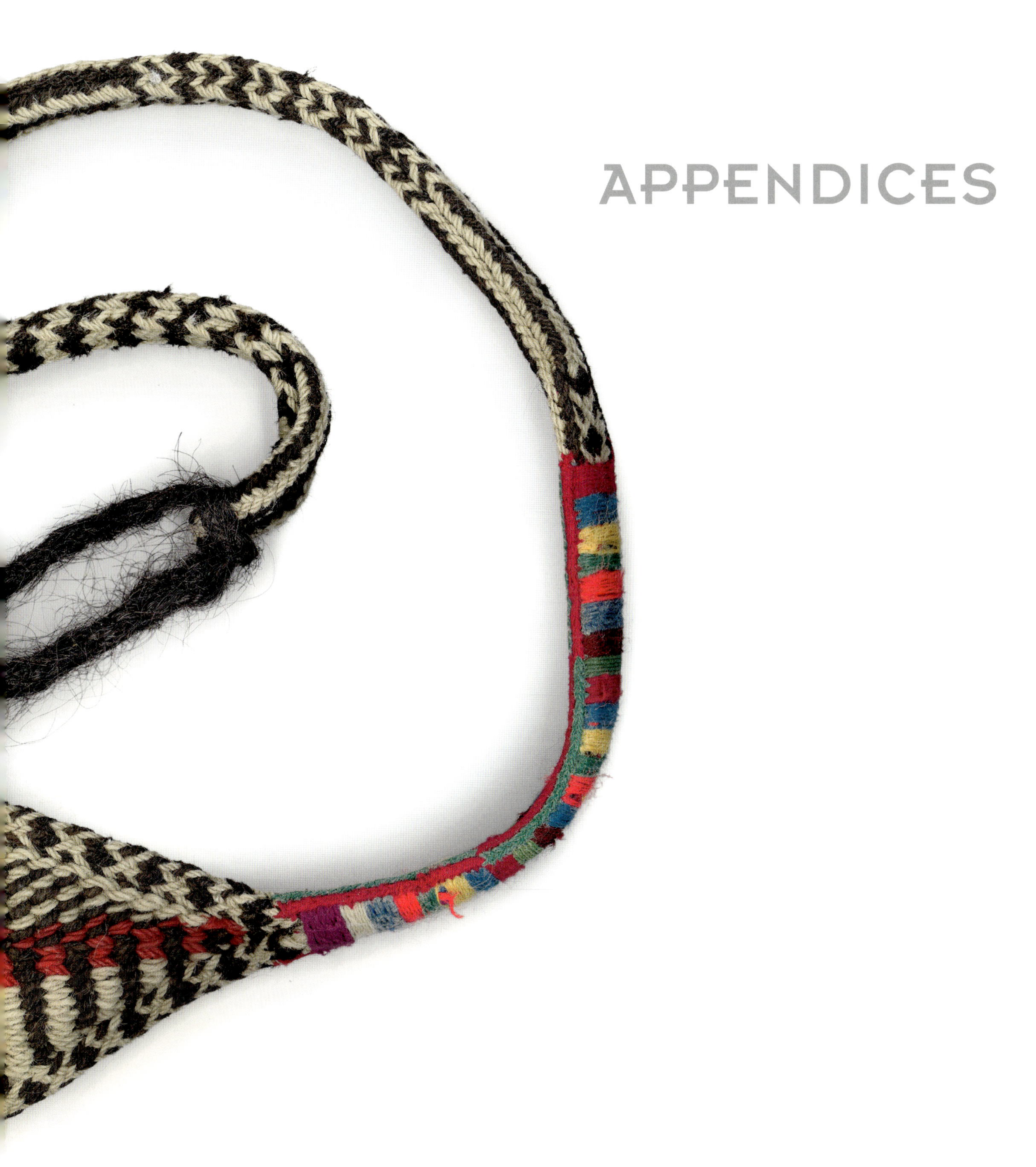

Elena Tsareva

CATALOGUE OF TIBETAN RUGS

Preceding double page: herders' slingshot; cf. Fig. 30 in the contribution by Kalantari

It was my pleasure to be able to research and document this extensive collection of Tibetan pile weavings, which are still so little known in Europe and America, also little known to myself, before I inspected and discovered their unique features, studying them both in Starnberg and St. Petersburg between March 2014 and April 2016.

The collection consists of 197 items, of which more than a dozen are from China and Khotan. Detailed analyses of 120 items are given here of which six are from China and one from Khotan, included for the purpose of comparison. The other 77 items were not researched in detail due to their similarity to more exemplary pile weavings of the same type. This explains the gaps in the otherwise consecutive numbers of the catalogue items discussed.

The extensive details for each item result from this intense learning experience, evident in the long descriptions in the article, which explains the unusual, unique peculiarities found in Tibetan pile weavings. As mentioned there, some still defy explanation, with question marks in the details for a few items. Some items I inspected before I understood enough about the Tibetan techniques to describe them properly.

It is my hope that my analyses will help others to solve these questions and further the appreciation and understanding of Tibetan pile weavings.

The dimension of the items in the catalogue are first that of the warp (excluding possible fringes), then that of the weft. For those with a textile border, the dimensions are those of the visible area of the rug's surface.

C9: *Masho* over-saddle rug

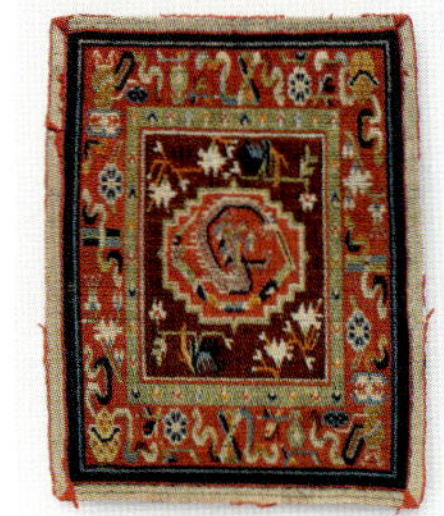

72×55 cm. Tibet. Second half 19th century. PATTERN: stepped central rosette, with curled dragon. Main border with Buddhist symbols; inner row of buds. WARP: cotton; Z?S. Deeply depressed. Density: 90 warps/dm. WEFT: wool; Z1; off light rose and light grey mix, of different thickness. Two parallel shoots in a unit. Density: 18 units/dm. PILE: wool; Z3 (light rose; plied together rose [Z2] and purple [Z1]); Z2S (ivory); otherwise Z2. Height: 3 mm (sky); 4.5 mm (dark blue); 5 mm (lemon-yellow, purple-red); otherwise 4 mm. BASIC LOOPS: asym. open left, long leg; loops on 1 warp; regular sym. and asym. open left. SINGLES: as, with bottom packing loop; otherwise sym., with similar loop. PAIRED: left side: asym.; right side: asym. long leg, with packing bottom loop. LONG ROW: left end: sym., otherwise sym. with packing bottom loop; right end: asym. long leg, with packing bottom loop; in between: basic asym. long leg. CURVED LINES: sym., with open loop on one warp; otherwise small asym. OTHER IRREGULARITIES: eccentric weave; offset effect; also packing combined with sharing. LOOPING DENSITY: 47–48 (horiz.) × 19–21 = 912–1,008 basic loops/sq dm (approx.). COLOURS (10): purple-red, light rose, orange, lemon-yellow, grass-green (with yellow fibres), dark blue; sky, ivory, light rose plied together with red-purple. FINISH: all edges are covered with cherry-colour twill, heavily damaged. ADDITIONAL INFORMATION: makes a set with C10 *makden* under-saddle rug. A masterpiece.

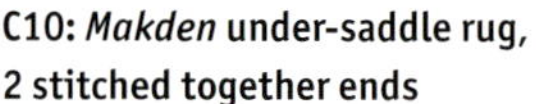

C10: *Makden* under-saddle rug, 2 stitched together ends

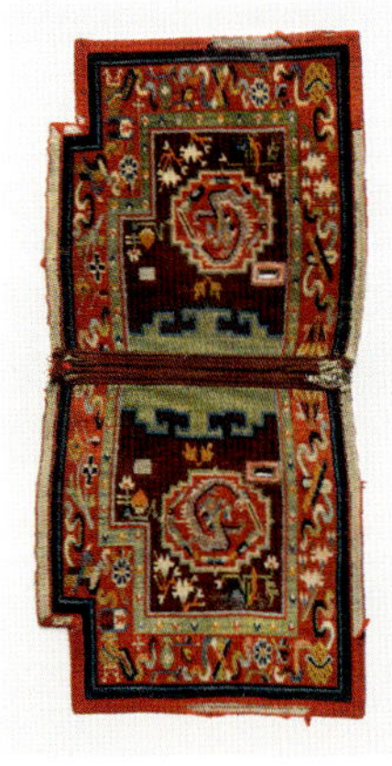

125×59 cm. Tibet. Second half 19th – early 20th century. PATTERN: stepped central rosette, with curled dragon; Buddhist symbols' border. WARP: cotton; Z?S. Deeply depressed. Density: 92–96 warps/dm. WEFT: wool; ivory; Z1; two parallel shoots in a unit. Density: 24 units/dm. PILE: wool; Z3 (green, sky, ivory); otherwise Z2. Height: 4–6 mm. BASIC LOOPS: asym. long leg; open and closed loops; regular asym. and sym. SINGLES: regular as, with bottom loop; otherwise regular sym. PAIRED: left side: regular asym. open left; right side: asym. long leg, with packing bottom loop. LONG ROWS: left end: asym. long leg, with packing bottom loop; right end: sym.; in between: basic asym. long leg. OTHER IRREGULARITIES: eccentric weave (in dragon figures); offset effect; carving effect; also packing combined with sharing. LOOPING DENSITY: 46–48 (horiz.) × 24 = 1,104–1,152 basic loops/

sq dm (approx.). COLOURS (11): dark claret, bright-red, purple/rose, dark rose (faded), orange, olive-yellow, grass-green (with yellow fibres), dark blue, sky, off light sky, ivory. FINISH: all edges are trimmed with cherry-colour twill. ADDITIONAL INFORMATION: makes set with C9 *masho* over-saddle rug. Carving effect caused by different pile wear. Heavily damaged trimming. A masterpiece.

C11: *Makden* under-saddle rug in the shape of a butterfly for a high-ranking lama, 2 stitched together ends

Ca. 122×75 cm. Tibet. Late 19th – early 20th century (?). PATTERN: image of a bat, blossoming branches, mountain, still water images, on light blue background. WARP: cotton; white; Z?S; fine. Depressed. Density: 86 warps/dm. WEFT: wool; ivory; Z1. Two parallel shoots in a unit. Density: 26 units/dm. PILE: wool; Z3 (rose, golden-yellow, orange-red); Z2, Z4 (dark sky); otherwise Z2. BASIC LOOPS: asym. long leg; open loops; regular sym. SINGLES: sym., with packing bottom loop. PAIRED: left side: asym. open left; right side: asym. long leg, with packing bottom loop. LONG ROWS: left end: sym., diagonal; right end: asym. long leg, with packing bottom loop; in between: basic asym. long leg. OTHER IRREGULARITIES: offset effect and proper offset; also packing combined with sharing. LOOPING DENSITY: 43×26 = 1,118 loops/ sq dm. COLOURS (11): carmine, pink-red, very light pink, rose, orange-red, golden-yellow, olive-yellow mix, dark sky, very light grey-sky, olive, ivory (all pink-rose shades faded). FINISH: the back is covered with lining. ADDITIONAL INFORMATION: exclusively beautiful pattern in spite of the running red shades. Monastic work.

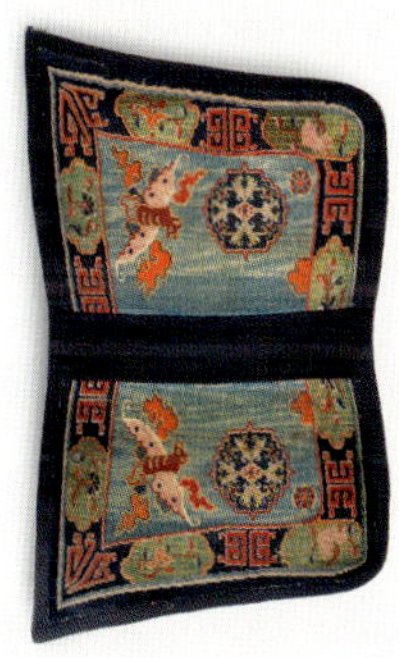

C12: *Makden* under-saddle rug in the shape of a butterfly, 2 stitched together ends

Ca. 117×66 cm. Tibet. Late 19th – early 20th century (?). PATTERN: bat and stepped rosette, with cross-shaped figure, on sky background; border with floral cartouches and stylised hieroglyphs. WARP: cotton; ivory; Z?S; fine. Depressed. Density: 92 warps/dm. WEFT: wool, Z2 and Z3; rose, rose and brown, light olive-brown. Two parallel shoots in a unit. Density: 26 units/dm. PILE: wool; Z3 (rose, bright red); otherwise Z2. Height: 1 mm (ivory); 3 mm (claret, bright red, grass-green, dark blue, dark green); 4 mm (orange, very light turquoise-sky); otherwise 2 mm. BASIC LOOPS: asym. long leg; open loops; regular sym. SINGLES: asym., with packing bottom loop; otherwise sym., of large size, with similar loop. PAIRED: right side: asym. long leg, with packing bottom loop; left: sym., otherwise asym., both diagonal. LONG ROWS: right end: asym. long leg, with packing bottom loop, continues to the left end; otherwise left end: pack of two diagonal sym.; in between: basic asym. long leg. OTHER IRREGULARITIES: offset effect; packs of two diagonal sym. angled on different directions by an asym. long leg in between; also packing combined with sharing. LOOPING DENSITY: 46 (horiz.) ×26 = 1,196 basic loops/sq dm (approx.). COLOURS (13): claret, bright red, rose, light rose, orange, yellow, grass-green, mix of grass-green and yellow, dark green, dark blue (motley), sky, off light turquoise-sky, ivory. Alternating rows of loops of close shades: green-yellow and yellow; sky and off light turquoise-sky, etc. FINISH: missing. ADDITIONAL INFORMATION: masterly methods of colouring of motifs.

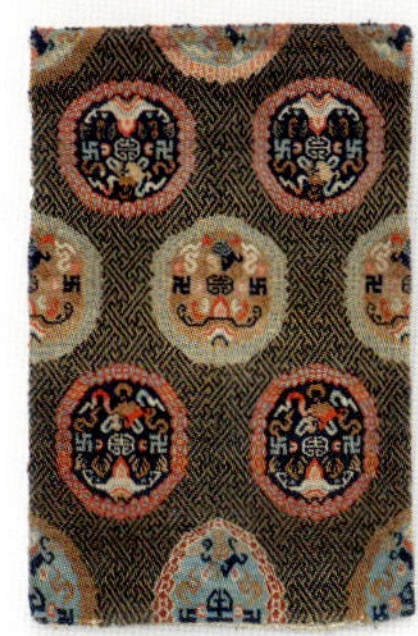

C13: *Khagangma* sitting or *masho* over-saddle rug for a high-ranking lama

86×56 cm. Tibet. 19th century. PATTERN: 5 complete, ½ and ¼ medallions on continuous diagonal *swastika* field pattern. WARP: cotton; ivory; Z?S. Depressed. Density: 76–80 warps/dm. WEFT: wool; ivory; Z1; of excellent quality. Two parallel shoots in a unit. Density: 30 units/dm. PILE: wool; Z3 (dark rose, light rose, ivory); otherwise Z2. Height: 3.5 mm (black-blue-green, light beige); 4 mm (bright red, very light rose, dark blue, ivory); otherwise 3 mm. BASIC LOOPS: asym. long leg; open loops; regular asym. and sym. SINGLES: asym., with packing bottom loop. PAIRED: left side: sym.; right side: asym. long leg, with packing bottom loop. LONG ROWS: left end: sym., otherwise asym., with bottom loop; right end: asym. long leg, with packing bottom loop; in between: basic asym. long leg. CURVED LINES: turning points: large-size diagonal sym. with bottom loop; below and above: diagonal tiny asym. with bottom loops. Other variants' probability. OTHER IRREGULARITIES: offset by means of loops on 3 and on 1 warp; all-over offset effect; also packing combined with sharing. LOOPING DENSITY: 38–40 (horiz.) ×30 = 1,140–1,200 basic loops/ sq dm (approx.). COLOURS (14): claret, bright red, dark rose (faded bright red), light rose (faded), off light rose, black-blue-green, dark blue, sky, light sky, off light sky, light chestnut, olive-brown, light beige (faded from camel-hair brown), ivory. FINISH: sides: missing; upper end: 1 cm plain weave, cut; bottom end: 1.5 cm plain weave and warp return loops. ADDITIONAL INFORMATION: restored right side bottom corner. A real work of art.

C14: Temple sitting rug, fragment

198×69 cm. China. Late 19th – early 20th century. WARP: cotton; ivory; Z?S. Depressed. WEFT: cotton; ivory; Z2S; fine. PILE: wool; Z2 (dark sky); Z2S (sky, dark blue); otherwise Z3. Height: 10 mm. KNOT: asym. open left; some loops on 3 warps. COLOURS (7): light cherry (faded), orange-pink, olive-green, sky, dark sky, dark blue, ivory. FINISH: edges are trimmed with crimson corduroy; back is lined with cotton twill, of light shade. ADDITIONAL INFORMATION: lined and framed, thus impossible to identify knot density. Most probably made for Tibet.

C15: *Khaden* sitting and sleeping rug, or wall hanging

164×86–88 cm. Tibet. 19th century. PATTERN: 3 medallions, with lion, tiger and *Garuda* winged creature; dragons in main border. WARP: cotton; Z?S. Depressed. Density: 76 warps/dm. WEFT: two parallel shoots in a unit. Density: 22 units/dm. PILE: wool; Z2 (cherry-red, light grey); Z2S (terracotta, off light rose, dark blue); otherwise Z3. Height: 3 mm, except for light grey, 2 mm. BASIC LOOPS: asym. long leg; open loops; regular sym. and asym. SINGLES: sym., with packing loop. PAIRED: left

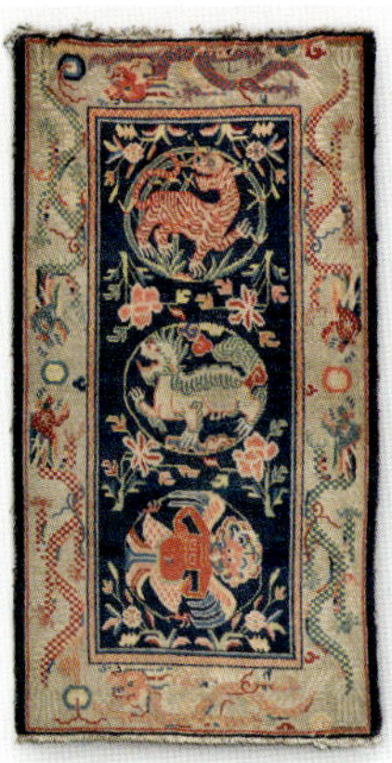

side: sym.; right side: asym. long leg, with packing bottom loop. LONG ROWS: left end: sym.; right end: asym. long leg, with packing bottom loop; in between: asym. long leg. CURVED LINES: by loops inserted over the wefts; increase of the edge loops' depression; offset. OTHER IRREGULARITIES: offsetting by missed warp and sharing; packing combined with sharing. LOOPING DENSITY: 38 (horiz.) ×22 = 836 knots/sq dm (approx.). COLOURS (15): cherry-red, pink-rose (faded bright red), off light rose, light grass-green, sky, dark blue, mid-blue, light grey; ivory; cherry-red plied together with rose, light green plied together with yellow and pink-rose, light green plied together with pink-rose, sky plied together with yellow, mid-blue plied together with rose, sky plied together with rose. FINISH: sides: regular weft return over side warp. ADDITIONAL INFORMATION: a rare masterpiece of design, weaving and art of making pile yarns of nuanced shades.

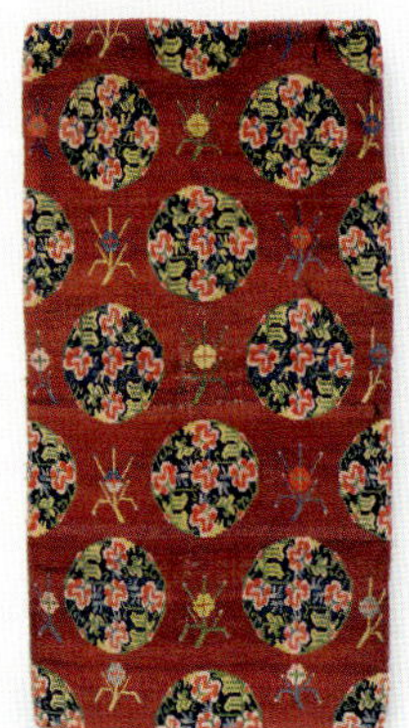

C16: *Khaden* sitting and sleeping rug for a high-ranking lama

149×79 cm. Tibet. 19th century (?). PATTERN: 8 complete floral rosettes, with ½ and ¼, on cherry background. WARP: wool; ivory; Z2S. Deeply depressed. Density: 70 warps/ dm. WEFT: wool; ivory; Z1; two parallel shoots in a unit. Density: 22 units/dm. PILE: wool; Z2. Height: 3 mm (cherry, orange-red, yellow, light sky, ivory); 4 mm (bright red, sky); otherwise 6 mm. BASIC LOOPS: asym. long leg; open loops on 1 warp; regular sym. SINGLES: sym., with packing bottom loop. PAIRED: left side: sym.; right side: asym. long leg, with packing bottom loop. LONG ROWS: left end: sym., deeply depressed; right end: asym. long leg, with packing bottom loop; in between: asym. long leg. CURVED LINES: additional left- and right-side packing loops; over weft loops; large size very deeply depressed sym. loops. OTHER IRREGULARITIES: all-over offset effect; also packing combined with sharing. LOOPING DENSITY: 35 (horiz.) ×22 = 770 basic loops/ sq dm (approx.). COLOURS (13): cherry, rose, light rose (faded), bright red, bright orange-red, yellow, soft yellow-green, cold green, very light turquoise (wool of different quality), sky, light sky, dark blue, ivory. FINISH: sides: regular return over two additional warps; ends: covered with trimming. ADDITIONAL INFORMATION: most probably made for Chinese market. The back is lined with white cotton panel.

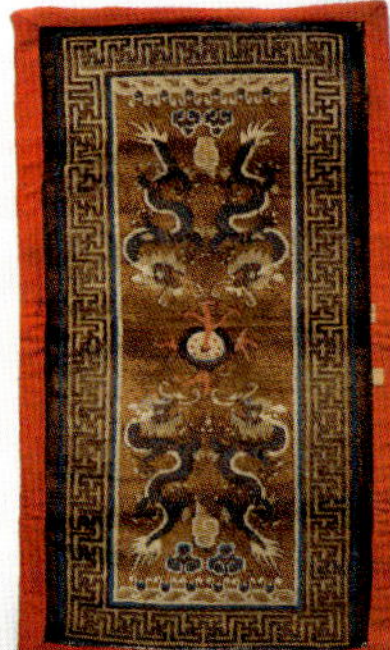

C17: Main carpet

145×74 cm. China. Late 19th century. PATTERN: 2 pairs of dragons; *swastika* meander border. WARP and WEFT: cotton. PILE: wool; pile of different height because of the wear. KNOTS: regular asym. open left. FINISH: lined and trimmed by red cloth. ADDITIONAL INFORMATION: included for comparison.

C18: *Masho* over-saddle rug for a high-ranking lama

75×59 cm. Tibet. 19th century. PATTERN: dragon, phoenix and lotuses. WARP: wool; ivory; Z2S; fine. Depressed. Density: 76 warps/dm. WEFT: wool; ivory; Z2S; strong ply. Two parallel shoots in a unit. Density: 28 units/dm. PILE: wool; Z2S (yellow, dark blue; bordeaux-red mix); Z3S (bright red, orange-grey mix); Z3 (rose, ivory, orange plied with yellow, grey, etc.); otherwise Z2. Height: 3–3.5 mm (olive); 4 mm (yellow); 5 mm (bordeaux-red, orange, cold green, dark blue); 7 mm (bright red); otherwise 6 mm. BASIC LOOPS: asym. long leg, open left; open loops; regular sym. and asym. SINGLES: asym. long leg, with packing bottom loop. PAIRED: left side: regular asym., mostly very small in size; right side: asym. long leg, with packing bottom loop. LONG ROWS: left end: sym., often nearly vertical; right end: asym. long leg, with packing bottom loop; in between: asym. long leg. CURVED LINES: diagonal sym. loops pushed by the neighbouring asym. long leg. OTHER IRREGULARITIES: packing combined with sharing. LOOPING DENSITY: 38 (horiz.) ×28 = 1.064 basic loops/sq dm (approx.). COLOURS (14–15): bordeaux-red (faded ends), bright red, pink (faded), rose, orange, orange-yellow-grey mix, gold-yellow (faded ends), cold green, dark blue, light off-sky, off sky-grey, olive, ivory; orange plied together with yellow. FINISH: sides: regular weft return over two additional warps; ends: covered by trimming. ADDITIONAL INFORMATION: other mixed colours variants probable. All-over trimming with dark blue cotton twill. Different pile wear produces carving effect. Masterful and elegant monastic work.

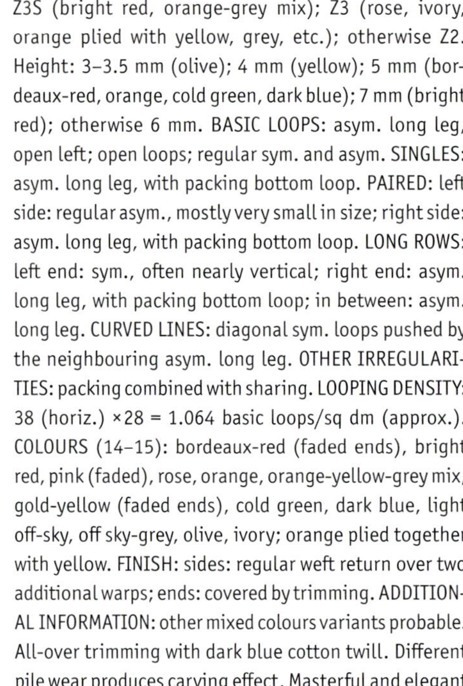

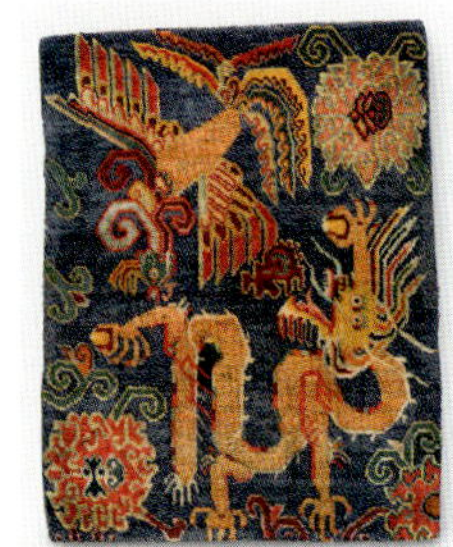

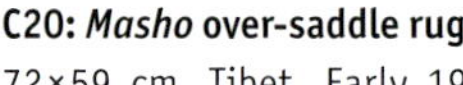

C20: *Masho* over-saddle rug

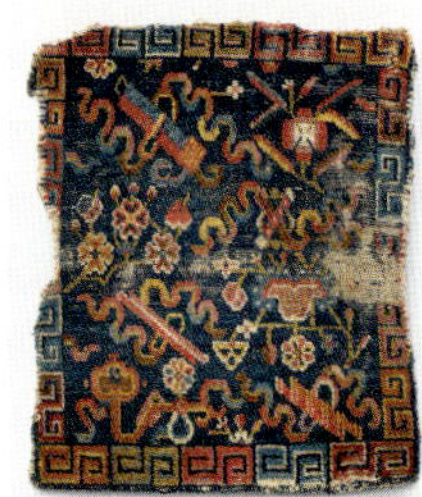

72×59 cm. Tibet. Early 19th century (?). PATTERN: Buddhist and floral motifs, on dark blue background; continuous thunder-line border. WARP: wool; ivory; Z2S; very fine and beautiful. Density: 76 warps/dm. WEFT: wool; ivory and shades of brown; Z2S. Three parallel shoots in a unit. Density: 23 units/dm. PILE: wool; Z2 (orange, dark cold green, light off-sky, mid-blue, dark blue; mustard); otherwise Z3. Height: 1 mm (light pink; worn); 2 mm (pink, light off-sky, dark cold green); 3 mm (claret, orange-red, gold-yellow, light olive, mid-blue); 4 mm (orange, dark blue, mustard, ivory); 5 mm (soft brown). BASIC LOOPS: asym. long leg; open loops; regular sym. SINGLES: asym., with bottom packing loop. PAIRED: left side: sym.; right side: asym. long leg, with packing bottom loop. LONG ROWS: left end: sym.; right end: asym. long leg, with packing bottom loop; in between: asym. long leg. CURVED LINES: very small single loops on deeply depressed pairs of warps and diagonal loops. OTHER IRREGULARITIES: offset, by sharing; also packing combined with sharing. LOOPING DENSITY: 38 (horiz.) ×23 = 874 basic loops/sq dm (approx.). COLOURS (14): claret, pink, light pink, orange-red, orange (changed to rust tint), gold-yellow, dark cold green, dark blue, mid-blue, light off-sky, light olive, mustard, soft brown, ivory. FINISH: sides and top end: missing; bottom: warp return loops. ADDITIONAL INFORMATION: bought at a bazaar, was used by a woman-seller as a sitting rug. Relates to dragon and floral types. Excellent monastic work.

C21: *Khaden* sitting and sleeping rug

149×82 cm. Tibet. Early 20th century. PATTERN: blue-and-ivory checkerbord, in red frame. WARP: wool; ivory and ivory plied together with brown; Z2S; fine. Depressed. Density: 60 warps/dm. WEFT: wool; ivory, with

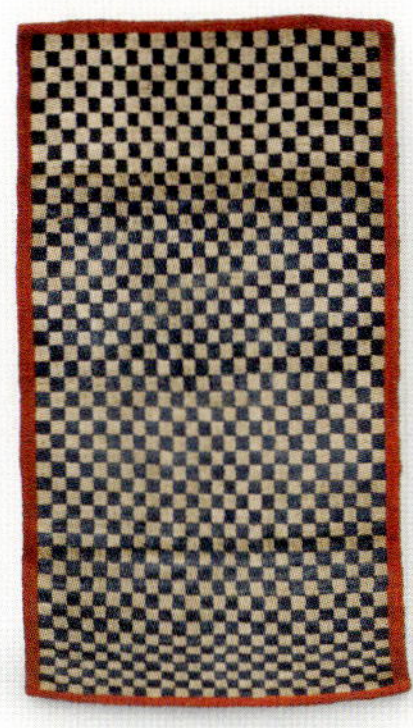

adding of coloured fibres; Z2S. One shoot in a unit. Density: 19 units/dm. PILE: yak hair and sheep wool; Z2S (yak hair, brown-black), loose spin and ply; Z3S (wool, ivory and red), very loose spin and ply (made without spindle). Height: 7 mm (ivory); 8 mm (red). BASIC LOOPS: asym. long leg; open; regular asym. and sym. LONG ROWS: left end: deeply depressed asym. long leg, packed from the top with a small sym.; right end: asym. long leg, with packing bottom loop; in between: asym. long leg open left. IRREGULARITIES: packing combined with sharing. LOOPING DENSITY: 30 (horiz.) × 19 = 577 basic loops/sq dm (approx.). COLOURS (3): red, ivory, brown-black (yak hair). FINISH: sides: regular weft return over side warp; ends: 2.5 cm plain weave folded over to the back and sewn down. ADDITIONAL INFORMATION: red dyestuff runs. Rural work. In wefts the weaver added red, brown, green fibres, probably whichever yarns were available.

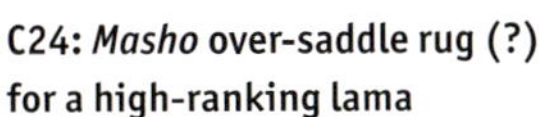

C24: *Masho* over-saddle rug (?) for a high-ranking lama

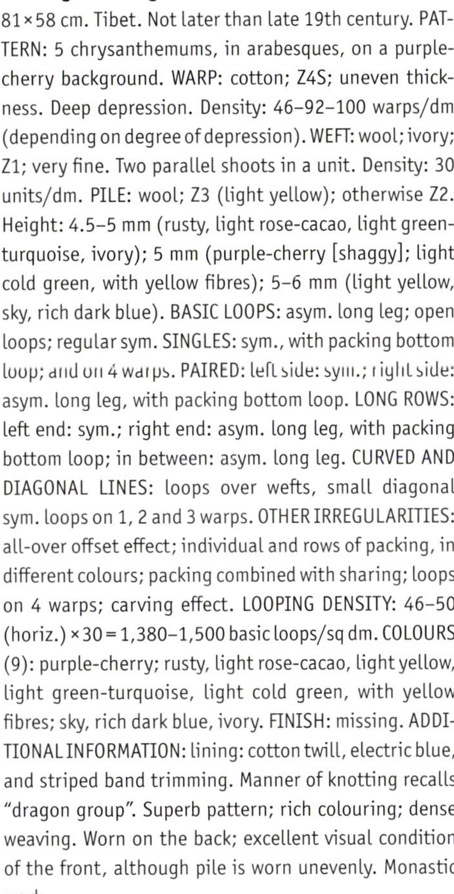

81 × 58 cm. Tibet. Not later than late 19th century. PATTERN: 5 chrysanthemums, in arabesques, on a purple-cherry background. WARP: cotton; Z4S; uneven thickness. Deep depression. Density: 46–92–100 warps/dm (depending on degree of depression). WEFT: wool; ivory; Z1; very fine. Two parallel shoots in a unit. Density: 30 units/dm. PILE: wool; Z3 (light yellow); otherwise Z2. Height: 4.5–5 mm (rusty, light rose-cacao, light green-turquoise, ivory); 5 mm (purple-cherry [shaggy]; light cold green, with yellow fibres); 5–6 mm (light yellow, sky, rich dark blue). BASIC LOOPS: asym. long leg; open loops; regular sym. SINGLES: sym., with packing bottom loop; and on 4 warps. PAIRED: left side: sym.; right side: asym. long leg, with packing bottom loop. LONG ROWS: left end: sym.; right end: asym. long leg, with packing bottom loop; in between: asym. long leg. CURVED AND DIAGONAL LINES: loops over wefts, small diagonal sym. loops on 1, 2 and 3 warps. OTHER IRREGULARITIES: all-over offset effect; individual and rows of packing, in different colours; packing combined with sharing; loops on 4 warps; carving effect. LOOPING DENSITY: 46–50 (horiz.) × 30 = 1,380–1,500 basic loops/sq dm. COLOURS (9): purple-cherry; rusty, light rose-cacao, light yellow, light green-turquoise, light cold green, with yellow fibres; sky, rich dark blue, ivory. FINISH: missing. ADDITIONAL INFORMATION: lining: cotton twill, electric blue, and striped band trimming. Manner of knotting recalls "dragon group". Superb pattern; rich colouring; dense weaving. Worn on the back; excellent visual condition of the front, although pile is worn unevenly. Monastic work.

C26: *Khaden* sitting and sleeping rug

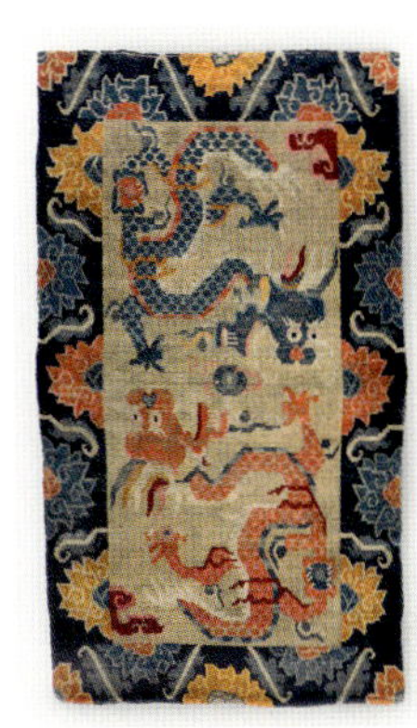

156 × 90 cm. Tibet. Late 19th – early 20th century. PATTERN: 2 dragons on light grey-beige background; halves of chrysanthemum and serrated leaves' framing. WARP: cotton; Z?S. Depressed. Density: 76 warps/dm. WEFT: wool; Z1; light mix and brown. Two parallel shoots in a unit. Density: 18 units/dm. PILE: wool; Z1 (very light rose); Z3 (pink, light yellow, ivory); otherwise Z2. Height: 2 mm (ivory); 3 mm (pink, very light rose, sky, beige); 4 mm (light yellow, very light sky, dark sky, dark blue); otherwise 5 mm. BASIC LOOPS: asym. long leg; open loops; regular asym. and sym. SINGLES: asym. long leg, with packing bottom loop. PAIRED: left side: regular asym.; right side: asym. long leg, with packing bottom loop. LONG ROWS: left end: regular asym., otherwise sym.; right end: asym. long leg, with packing bottom loop; in between: asym. long leg. CURVED LINES: sym. over wefts; diagonal loops, offset by sharing and loops on 1 warp. OTHER IRREGULARITIES: offset effect, packing; also packing combined with sharing. LOOPING DENSITY: 38 (horiz.) × 18 = 684 basic loops/sq dm. COLOURS (12): claret, pink, very light rose; orange-red (faded red), orange, gold-yellow, light yellow, dark blue; dark sky (shaggy), sky, light grey-beige, ivory; orange-red plied together with yellow. Alternating rows of close in colours shades. FINISH: sides: plain weft return; top end: covered with a band of thick woollen twill; bottom end: 1.5 cm of tabby, folded over to the back and sewn down. ADDITIONAL INFORMATION: worn pile. Some restoration of one of the corners. Monastic work.

C27: *Khagangma* sitting rug

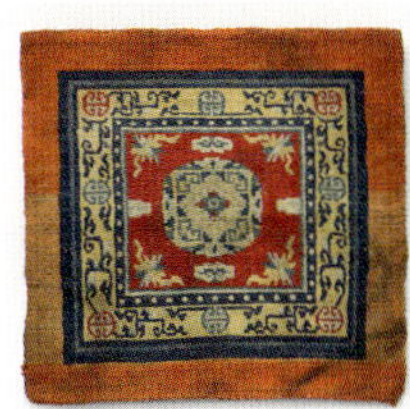

79 × 84 cm. Tibet. 19th century. PATTERN: central medallion, on red background; floral border; inner row of "pearls". WARP: wool; light rust and ivory; Z2S; silky. Density: 58 warps/dm. WEFT: wool; chocolate-brown; Z3; soft, shaggy, thick. Two parallel shoots in a unit. Density: 20 units/dm. PILE: wool; Z2. Height: 5 mm (yellow); 6 mm (sky, light sky, ivory); 7 mm (dark blue, cherry); 8–9 mm (rust, rust mixed with camel). BASIC LOOPS: asym. long leg; open loops; regular sym. and asym. open left. IRREGULARITIES: packing combined with sharing. LOOPING DENSITY: 29 (horiz.) × 20 = 580 basic loops/sq dm. COLOURS (8): cherry, rust (slightly running, abrash), rust, mixed with camel (abrash), yellow (thick), sky, light sky (shaggy), dark blue (shaggy), ivory (grey shade or just very dirty). FINISH: sides: plain weft return over 3 additional warps. Upper end 2.7 cm and bottom 1.7 cm folded over to the back and sewn down. ADDITIONAL INFORMATION: Trimming band in piled technique. Rural work.

C29: *Khaden* sitting and sleeping rug

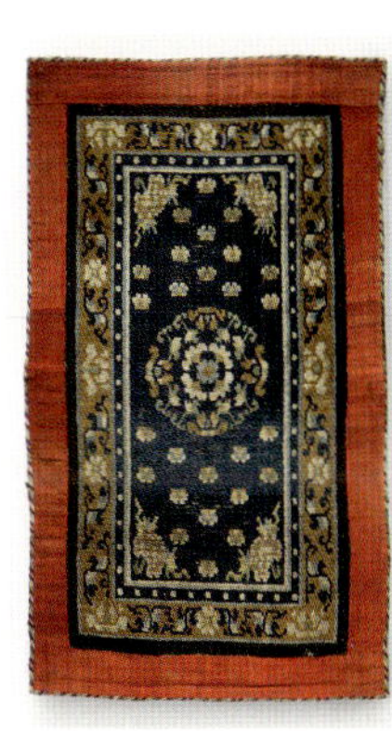

117 × 64 cm. Tibet. Late 19th – early 20th century. PATTERN: central floral rosette and rows of "buds", on dark blue background; floral border. WARP: wool; ivory; Z2S. Density: approx. 50 warps/dm. WEFT: wool; ivory and mix; Z1. Two parallel shoots in a unit. Density: 20 units/dm. PILE: wool; Z2 (light apricot, light yellow-green, light sky, black-brown); otherwise Z3. Height: 4 mm (yellow, ivory); 4–5 mm (light sky); otherwise 5 mm. BASIC LOOPS: asym. long leg; open loops; regular sym. SINGLES: sym., with packing bottom loop. PAIRED: left side: sym.; right side: asym. long leg, with packing bottom loop. LONG ROWS: left end: sym.; right end: asym. long leg, with packing bottom loop; in between: asym. long leg. CURVED LINES: long leg ends can run under a number of neighbouring loops of different colours. IRREGULARITIES: packing combined with sharing. LOOPING DENSITY: 25 (horiz.) × 20 = 500 basic loops/sq dm. COLOURS (10): rust, light apricot, yellow, light

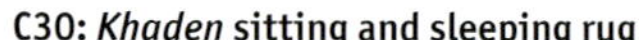

yellow-green, light sky, dark green, brown-red, brown, black-brown, ivory. FINISH: lining and trimming with red twill and diagonal ikat stripes' textiles. ADDITIONAL INFORMATION: wool of sky colour is poorly dyed: motley, actually sky-ivory. Rural work.

C30: *Khaden* sitting and sleeping rug

149×84 cm. Tibet. Late 19th century. PATTERN: 8 complete and ½ garland rosettes, on chestnut background; T-border. WARP: wool; ivory; Z2S; soft, loose spin and ply. Depressed. Density: 60–64 warps/dm. WEFT: wool; grey mix; Z1. Two parallel shoots in a unit. Density: 20 units/ dm. PILE: wool; thick yarns; Z2 (dark rose, also Z4; dark sky-blue; ivory, also Z3); otherwise Z3 (chestnut, also Z4). Height: 5 mm (ivory, also 6–7 mm); 6 mm (chestnut, cold dark green, dark blue; dark rose, also 7 mm); otherwise 7 mm. BASIC LOOPS: asym. long leg; open loops, on 1 warp; sym. loops on 1 warp; regular asym.; regular sym. SINGLES: (identified variant): closed loops, on 1 warp. LONG ROWS: right end: asym. long leg, with packing bottom loop; left end: sym. or asym.; in between: asym. long leg. OTHER IRREGULARITIES: numerous loops with horizontally arranged ends; packing loops combined with sharing. LOOPING DENSITY: 30–32 (horiz.) × 20 = 600–640 basic loops/sq dm. COLOURS (8): carmine, chestnut, dark rose; yellow, with green fibres; cold dark green; dark sky-blue; dark blue (abrash); ivory. FINISH: sides: regular return over two additional side warps; ends: missing. ADDITIONAL INFORMATION: Monastic work.

C31: Carpet

154×85 cm. Khotan (?) or China. 19th century. PATTERN: Large central rosette and floral motives, on dark blue background; diagonal *swastika* border. WARP: cotton; Z?S2. Light depression. Density: 64 warps/dm. WEFT: cotton; Z2. Two regular shoots in a unit. Density: 34 units/dm. PILE: wool; Z2S; Z3S (ivory); Z2S, Z4S (dark rose); excellent quality. Height: 3 mm (light pink, dark rose); 5 mm (ivory); 6 mm (dark blue); otherwise 4 mm. KNOT: asym. open left. KNOTTING DENSITY: 32 (horiz.) × 34 = 1,088 knots/sq dm. IRREGULARITIES: light reps effect; also packing combined with sharing. COLOURS (9): dark rose (slightly faded ends), light pink, light turquoise-blue, sky-blue, dark blue, mid-blue, ivory; plied together sky-blue and ivory, plied together light sky and ivory. FINISH: no finish visible because of the lining. ADDI-TIONAL INFORMATION: beautiful wool and colours. All-over trimming with cotton textile, of Tibetan work.

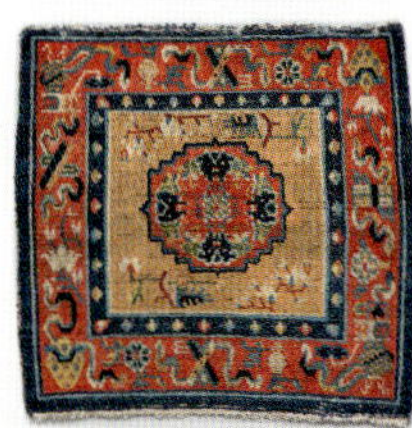

C32: *Khagangma* sitting rug or cushion cover

65×66 cm. Tibet. Late 19th century. PATTERN: stepped central rosette; Buddhist symbols in border. WARP: cotton; Z?S. Density: 78–79 warps/dm. WEFT: wool; Z1; ivory, light rose, chocolate-brown; very thick. One, mostly two parallel shoots in a unit. Density: 22 units/ dm. PILE: wool; Z2S (plied together claret and red); Z3 (light turquoise-green, sky); otherwise Z2. Height: 4 mm (lemon-yellow, cold green, ivory); otherwise 3 mm. BASIC LOOPS: asym. long leg; open loops; regular sym. SINGLES: regular sym. and sym. with packing bottom loop. PAIRED: left side: closed loop; right side: sym.; otherwise: left side: sym.; right side: asym. long leg with packing bottom loop. LONG ROWS: left end: sym., with packing bottom loop and packing right-side loop end; right end: asym. long leg, with packing bottom loop; in between: asym. long leg. CURVED AND DIAGONAL LINES: sharing, loops over wefts, loops of very large size. OTHER IRREGULARITIES: rows of packing; eccentric weave (paired and triple, central rosette); offset (by sharing); offset effect; also packing combined with sharing. LOOPING DENSITY: 36–38 (horiz.) × 22 = 792–836 basic loops/sq dm. COLOURS (14): deep orange-red, pink, light rose, orange-red, lemon-yellow, cold green, light turquoise-green (faded light green), dark blue, sky, claret plied together with red, pink plied together with ivory, beige (faded orange), very light camel, ivory. FINISH: sides: plain weft return over one additional warp; top: cut; bottom: 1 cm tabby, warp return loops. ADDITIONAL INFORMATION: exclusive masterpiece of weaving; possible other tricks of looping and colour shades. Image demonstrates all mentioned peculiarities of the described *khagangma's* structure. Monastic work.

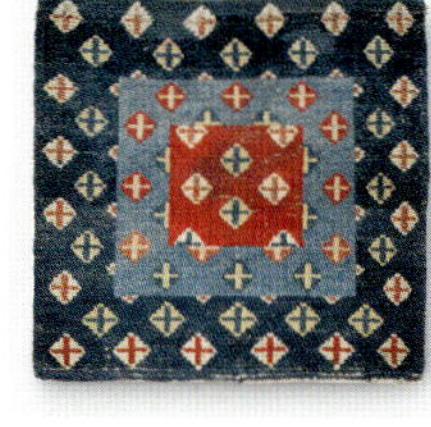

C33: *Khagangma* sitting rug for a high-ranking lama

62×65 cm. Tibet. 19th century. PATTERN: straight crosses, in ivory diamonds; on red (central square), sky-blue and dark blue background. WARP: wool, ivory, Z2S; cotton, Z2S. Light depression. Density: 60 warps/dm. WEFT: wool; ivory; Z1. Two parallel shoots in a unit. Density: 18 units/ dm. PILE: wool; Z2S; thick, loose spin and ply. Height: 5 mm (approx.), all over worn out, centre in particular. BASIC LOOPS: asym. long leg; open loops; regular asym. and sym. SINGLES: asym. long leg, with packing bottom loop. PAIRED: right side: asym. long leg, with packing bottom loop; left side: sym. LONG ROWS: left end: sym.; right end: asym. long leg, with packing bottom loop; in between: asym. long leg. OTHER IRREGULARITIES: packing; also packing combined with sharing. LOOPING DENSITY: 30 (horiz.) × 18 = 540 basic loops/sq dm. COLOURS (8): scarlet-red, pink (faded), yellow (faded), sky-blue (abrash, faded), dark green-blue, dark blue (abrash), silver-ivory, red plied with orange. FINISH: sides: plain weft return; top end: 2 cm tabby, folded over to the back and sewn down; bottom end: 1 cm tabby, 2.5 cm warp return loops. ADDITIONAL INFORMATION: some restoration of the ends. Original lining missing. Pair to C126.

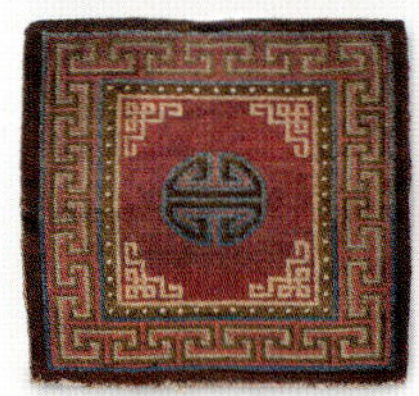

C34a and C34b: Pair of *khagangma* sitting rugs

69×77 cm (C34a), 70×77 cm (C34b). Tibet. Middle of the 19th century or earlier. PATTERN: central hieroglyph-shaped rosette (imitation of *Shou* character [?]), on cherry background; imitation of T-border; inner pearl border. WARP: wool; light mix; Z2S. Depressed. Density: 48 warps/dm. WEFT: wool; mix; Z1. Two parallel shoots in a unit. Density: 14 units/dm. PILE: wool, yak down; Z2 (light cherry, olive-green, with yellow fibres; ivory); Z3 (sky-blue, chocolate-brown); Z4 (light rose, light cherry). Height: 6 mm (olive-green, with yellow fibres; chocolate-brown, ivory); otherwise 7 mm. BASIC LOOPS: asym. long leg; open loops, on 1 warp; regular sym., often with very deep inclination (diagonal). SINGLES: asym.

long leg, with packing bottom loop. PAIRED: right side: asym. long leg, with packing bottom loop; left side: sym. LONG ROWS: left end: sym.; right end: asym. long leg, with packing bottom loop; in between: asym. long leg. DIAGONAL LINES: by very deep (nearly vertical) inclination of edged sym. loops. OTHER IRREGULARITIES: packing; sharing combined with packing. LOOPING DENSITY: 24 (horiz.) × 14 = 336 basic loops/sq dm. COLOURS (6): light cherry, light rose (faded ends); olive-green, with yellow fibres; sky-blue, chocolate-brown, ivory. FINISH: missing. ADDITIONAL INFORMATION: some knots are very large knots (approx. 2/cm); very irregular weave; all dye stuffs are poorly absorbed by the fibres.

C35: Wangden *Drumze khagangma* sitting rug

98 × 99 cm. Tibet. 19th century or earlier. PATTERN: ca. 5 × 5 cm, checkerboard, with central dots, on orange-red background. WARP: wool; ivory and brown mix, with yak or horse hair; Z2S. Density: 44 warps/dm. WEFT: wool; ivory mainly; Z1, of different thickness (spun without spindle). Two parallel shoots in a unit. Density: 8 units/dm. PILE: wool, Z2S. Height: 11 mm (off-blue); 12 mm (red, off-green). BASIC LOOPS: single-level warp-faced back structure; basic element: asym. long leg, on 2 active warps, sometimes with one warp in between; long ends of the long leg loops go under and over several neighbouring warps to the left; otherwise: closed loops. LONG ROWS: left end: asym.; right end: asym. long leg, with packing bottom loop on 2 warps; in between: asym. long leg. IRREGULARITIES: packing combined with sharing. LOOPING DENSITY: 22 (horiz.) × 8 = 176 basic loops/sq dm. COLOURS (3): orange-red; off-green, partly faded to yellow; off-blue. FINISH: sides: three rows of 8 cm long fringe (see also C148); top end: warp ends carefully plaited into a braid; bottom end: 2 cm tabby (2 units), with warp return loops. ADDITIONAL INFORMATION: archaic type.

C36: Horse blanket for a high-ranking lama

105 × 120–157 cm. Tibet. Not later than early 20th century. PATTERN: two phoenixes and chrysanthemums, on burgundy background; top band with floral meander. WARP: cotton; Z?S. Depressed. Density: 56–62 (in curves) warps/dm. WEFT: wool; off light grey mix; Z1. Two parallel shoots in a unit. Density: 19–21 units/dm. PILE: wool; Z3 (bright red); otherwise Z2. Height: 2 mm (light orange, very light orange); 3 mm (grass-green, light sky); 3–4 mm (dark cherry, sky); 4 mm (bright red, orange, yellow, rose-ivory); 4–5 mm (burgundy); 5 mm (light rose); 5–6 mm (pink-red, dark blue). BASIC LOOPS: asym. open left long leg loops; open loops on 1 warp; regular asym. and sym. loops. SINGLES: sym. and asym., both with packing bottom loop. PAIRED: left side: sym.; right side: asym. long leg and packing bottom loop; LONG ROWS: left end: sym.; right end: asym. long leg with packing bottom loop; in between: asym. long leg. CURVED LINES AND DIAGONAL LINES: "dancing warps" by method of inserting and dropping of additional warps; change of angle of depression; sym. loops over wefts; offset by use of sym. loops on 3 warps, with packing bottom loop; change of depression; bottom end in all-over offset; general offset effect. OTHER IRREGULARITIES: packing; sharing combined with packing; offset effect. LOOPING DENSITY: 47–48 (horiz.) × 19–21 = 912–1,008 basic loops/sq dm. COLOURS (15): dark cherry; burgundy (shaggy), bright red, pink-red, light rose (faded); orange; very light orange (faded ends), yellow; grass-green, with yellow fibres; sky; light sky, dark blue; light rose, plied together with ivory; green plied together with yellow. FINISH: perimeter in frame with a cotton twill band, of blue colour. ADDITIONAL INFORMATION: belongs to the "dancing warps" group (see also C89). Superb monastic work.

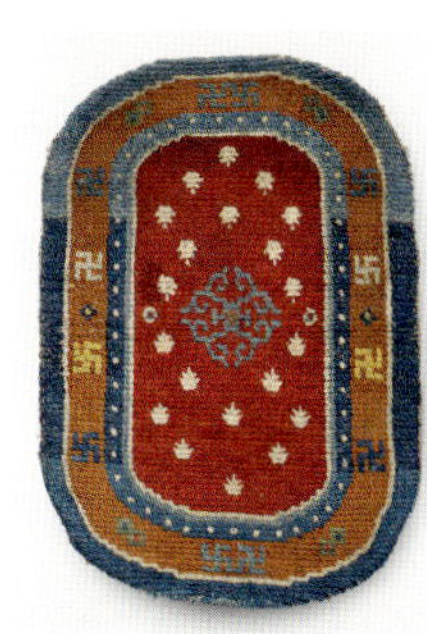

C37: *Masho* over-saddle rug, oval form

78 × 55.5 cm. Tibet. Second half 19th century (?). PATTERN: central medallion, with doubled *vajras* and "palms", on red background; *swastika* and pearl borders. WARP: wool; ivory; Z2S. Deeply depressed. Density: 50 warps/dm. WEFT: wool; Z1; ivory and chocolate-brown, also orange and grey. Two parallel shoots in a unit. Density: 14 units/dm. PILE: wool; silver-grey; Z2, Z4, of excellent quality. Height: 5 mm. BASIC LOOPS: asym. long leg; open loops; regular sym. LONG ROWS: left end: sym.; right end: asym. long leg, with packing bottom loop; in between: asym. long leg. IRREGULARITIES: packing; sharing combined with packing. LOOPING DENSITY: 25 (horiz.) × 14 = 350 basic loops/sq dm. COLOURS (9): cherry-red, chestnut, pink-red, yellow; cold green, plied together with yellow, off light blue, blue (abrash), dark blue (abrash), silver-grey. FINISH: sides: plain weft return over 3 additional warps; ends: tabby, folded over to the back and sewn down. ADDITIONAL INFORMATION: rural work.

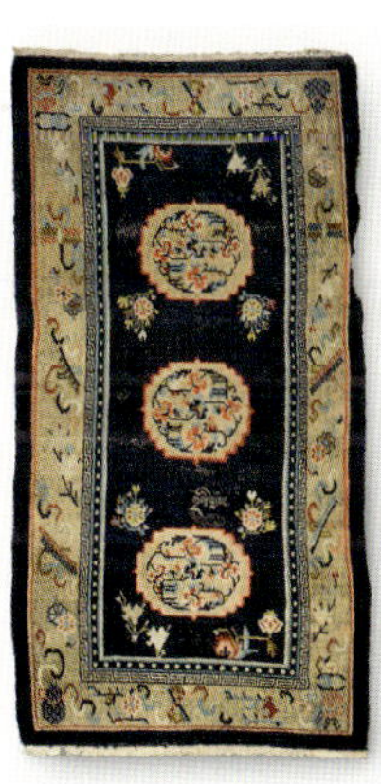

C38: *Khaden* sitting and sleeping rug

160 × 85 cm. Tibet. 1900s. PATTERN: 3 floral medallions and an inscription, on dark blue background; main border with Buddhist symbols; inner pearl border. WARP: cotton; ivory; Z?S. Density: 76 warps/dm. WEFT: wool; ivory-brown mix; Z1; loose, of different thickness (spun without spindle [?]). Two parallel shoots in a unit. Density: 24 units/dm. PILE: wool; excellent quality; traces of loose ply; Z1 (yellow, sky); Z1–Z2 (rose-pink); Z2–Z3 (sky); Z2S (light beige); Z3 (ivory); otherwise Z2. Height: 3 mm (light beige); 4 mm (carmine-red, yellow, dark blue, 2 shades); 6 mm (ivory); otherwise 5–5.5 mm. BASIC LOOPS: asym. long leg; open loops; closed loops, on 1 warp; regular asym.; regular sym. SINGLES: regular asym., otherwise closed loop, on 1 warp. LONG ROWS: left end: sym. or closed loop, on 1 warp; right end: asym. long leg, with packing bottom loop; in between: asym. with packing bottom loops. CURVED LINES: open loops, depressed, Z1. OTHER IRREGULARITIES: packing; sharing combined with packing. LOOPING DENSITY: 38 (horiz.) × 24 = 912 basic loops/sq dm. COLOURS (12): carmine-red; light chestnut, rose-pink (faded ends), rose, yellow; grass-green, sky, very light sky-grey, dark blue, 2 shades; light beige, ivory. FINISH: sides: plain return over 3 additional warps; top end: missing; bottom end: 1.5 cm tabby, warp return loops. ADDITIONAL INFORMATION: structure may be more complicated.

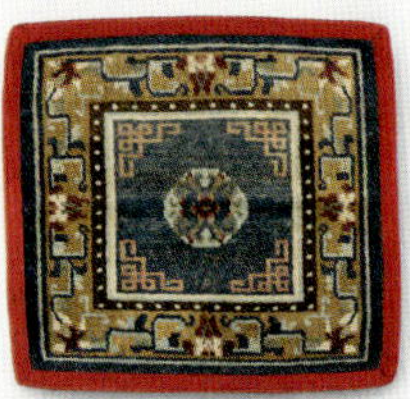

C39: *Khagangma* sitting rug
67.5×72.5 cm. Tibet. 19th century. PATTERN: floral medallion, on blue background; floral meander geometric style border; inner pearl border. WARP: hemp (?), wool; variants of ivory and off-grey mix; Z2S; shaggy. Density: 48 warps/dm. WEFT: hemp (?), wool; variants of ivory and off-grey mix; Z2S; two parallel shoots in a unit. Density: 16 units/dm. PILE: wool, yak hair; Z3. Height: 3 mm (off-sky, ivory); 3–4 mm (dark brown); 5 mm (claret); 5–6 mm (dark blue); otherwise 4 mm. BASIC LOOPS: asym. long leg; open loops; regular asym.; regular sym. LONG ROWS: left end: sym., with packed loop; right end: open loop otherwise plain asym. long leg; in between: asym. long leg. FINE VERTICAL LINES: right side: closed or open loop; left side: asym., made of Z3S2 yarns. DIAGONAL AND FINE VERTICAL LINES: left side: made of Z3S2 yarns regular asym.; right side: closed and open loops. OTHER IRREGULARITIES: packing; sharing combined with packing. LOOPING DENSITY: 24 (horiz.) ×16 = 384 basic loops/sq dm. COLOURS (11): claret; dark rose, 2 shades; off olive-green, off-green, off-sky; off-blue, dark blue, khaki, dark-brown, ivory. FINISH: lining and trimming. ADDITIONAL INFORMATION: beautiful soft colour scale.

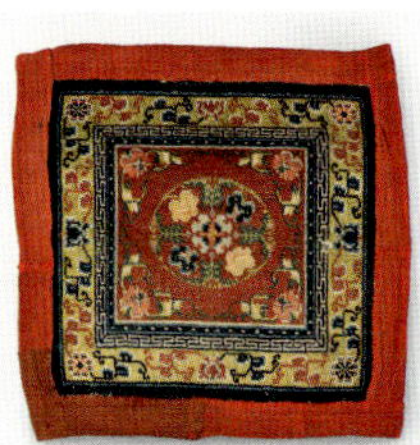

C40: *Khagangma* sitting rug
64×66 cm. Tibet. Second half 19th or early 20th century. PATTERN: central floral rosette, on cherry-red background; floral meander border; inner pearl border. WARP: wool, light grey mix; Z2S; fine. Depressed. Density: 68 warps/ dm. WEFT: wool; ivory; Z2S; loose spin and ply. Two parallel shoots in a unit. Density: 14 units/dm. PILE: wool; Z3. Height: 2 mm (orange-red, very light off grey-sky, ivory); 2–3 mm (cherry-red, light rose, cold green); 2–4 (violet); 3 mm (dark rose, light olive-green, dark sky, dark blue); 3.5 mm (yellow). BASIC LOOPS: asym. long leg; open loops; regular asym. and sym. SINGLES: sym., small and large. PAIRED: left side: sym.; right side: asym. long leg, with packing bottom loop. LONG ROWS: left end: sym.; right end: asym. long leg, with packing bottom loop; in between: asym. long leg. CURVED AND DIAGONAL LINES: sym., with packing bottom loop; also aggravation of depression. OTHER IRREGULARITIES: packing; sharing combined with packing. LOOPING DENSITY: 34 (horiz.) ×14 = 476 basic loops/sq dm. COLOURS (12): cherry-red; dark rose, light rose; orange-red, yellow; light olive-green, cold green, dark blue, dark sky, off grey-sky, ivory. FINISH: sides: plain weft return over 1 additional warp; back and ends are lined and trimmed: sides: wide handmade red woollen twill, colourated in running red dyestuff; back: machine-made dark blue cotton twill. ADDITIONAL INFORMATION: real work of art.

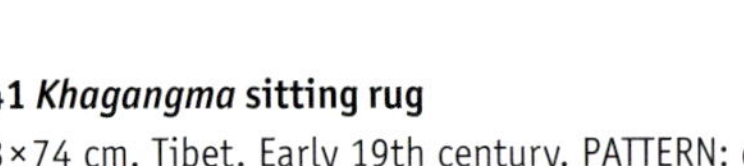

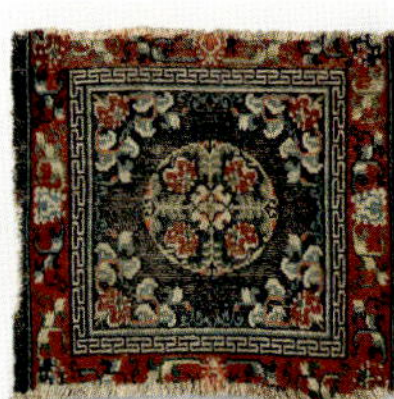

C41 *Khagangma* sitting rug
63×74 cm. Tibet. Early 19th century. PATTERN: central floral rosette, on off-blue background; flower with 2 branches border, on cherry background; inner T-border. WARP: wool; ivory; Z2S; very strong, rather thick. Alternating from very deep to small depression. Density: 66 warps/dm. WEFT: cotton; ivory; Z6S. Two parallel shoots in a unit. Density: 20 units/dm. PILE: wool; Z2, Z4 (mostly); very fine elementary threads. Height: medium short; 2–4 mm. BASIC LOOPS: asym. long leg; open loops; closed loops, on 1 warp; regular asym. and sym. SINGLES: sym. and sym. with packing bottom loop. PAIRED: left end: sym., with long leg from the right side; right end: asym. long leg, with packing bottom loop. LONG ROWS: left end: sym.; right end: asym. long leg, with packing bottom loop; in between: asym. long leg. CURVED AND DIAGONAL LINES: regular sym., with open loop; change of depression; offset by missed warps. OTHER IRREGULARITIES: packing; sharing combined with packing; sym. cross-loops (?). LOOPING DENSITY: 33 (horiz.) ×20 = 660 basic loops/sq dm. COLOURS (13): deep carmine, carmine, deep cherry, orange-red, yellow, dark grass-green, blue-green, dark blue, sky, off light sky, off-olive, ivory; plied together sky and off light sky. FINISH: missing. ADDITIONAL INFORMATION: heavily worn, splendid pattern and colours. Monastic work.

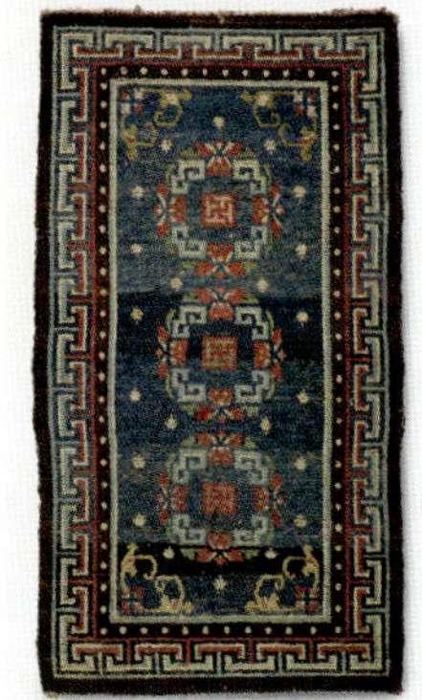

C46: *Khaden* sitting and sleeping rug
131×71 cm. Tibet. Mid-19th century (?). PATTERN: 3 geometric-style rosettes, with *swastikas*, on off-blue background; main T-border; inner pearl border. WARP: wool; Z2S; ivory/brown and brown. Density: 56 warps/ dm. WEFT: wool; Z1; mix of shades of brown and ivory; also orange. Two parallel shoots in a unit. Density: 20 (?) units/dm. PILE: wool, yak hair; Z3 (ivory); otherwise Z2. Height: 4 mm (cherry-red, old rose, green-yellow); 4–5 (ivory); otherwise 5 mm. BASIC LOOPS: asym. long leg; open loops; regular sym. SINGLES: asym. with packing bottom loop; otherwise sym., with packing bottom loop. PAIRED: left side: sym.; right side: asym. long leg, with packing bottom loop. LONG ROWS: left end: sym., with bottom loop; right end: asym. long leg, with packing bottom loop; in between: asym. long leg. CURVED AND DIAGONAL LINES: regular sym., with packing loop either on the right or on the left-side warp, depending on the pattern. OTHER IRREGULARITIES: packing; sharing combined with packing; offset effect. LOOPING DENSITY: 28 (horiz.) ×20 (?) = 480 (?) basic loops/sq dm. COLOURS (9): cherry-red, old rose, yellow, dark blue/ mid-blue/grey-sky (central field, abrash), off light sky (motley), dark olive, chocolate-brown, dark brown/ black-brown (yak hair, shaggy; abrash), ivory. FINISH: sides: plain weft return; top: 1 cm tabby, cut, later folded over to the back and sewn down; bottom: 1 cm tabby, warp return loops. ADDITIONAL INFORMATION: good balance of pattern. Rural work.

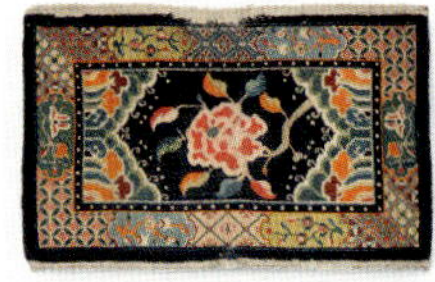

C48: *Masho* over-saddle rug
54×91 cm (woven horizontally). Tibet. 1st quarter 20th century. PATTERN: rose and "sea waves and clouds", on a black-blue background; 6 "blossoming branches" cartouches and complex lattice main border motifs; inner pearl border. WARP: cotton; Z?S. Deeply depressed. Density: 104 warps/dm. WEFT: wool, ivory and light mix; Z1; loose. Two parallel shoots in a unit. Density: 29–30 units/ dm. PILE: wool; Z3 (red); otherwise Z2. Height: 2 mm (red, brown-red; dark green, 2 shades; blue, black); otherwise 2 mm. BASIC LOOPS: asym. long leg; open loops; regular sym. SINGLES, INCLUDING FINE DIAGONAL LINES: regular sym., with packing bottom loop. PAIRED:

left side: regular sym.; right side: asym. long leg, with packing bottom loop. LONG ROWS: left end: large sym.; right end: asym. long leg, with packing bottom loop; in between: asym. long leg. CURVED LINES: offset by sharing; diagonal loops; terminal loops with packing loops on either left or right warp, depending on curve direction. Other variants possible. OTHER IRREGULARITIES: offset effect. LOOPING DENSITY: 52 (horiz.) ×29–30 = 1,508–1,560 basic loops/sq dm. COLOURS (13+): red, brown-red, rose, orange, lemon-yellow, 2 shades of dark green (one faded to green-blue), light olive-green; blue, sky, light sky (motley), ivory, black. Numerous "intermediate" shades in mixture of fibres of colours of close tints. FINISH: sides: plain return over 4 additional warps; top: 2 cm tabby, tiny loops; bottom: 1.5 cm tabby, warp return loops. ADDITIONAL INFORMATION: masterful work, with perfectly arranged pattern. Design similar to C127. Damaged in the centre. Lattice motifs are typical for Chinese silks.

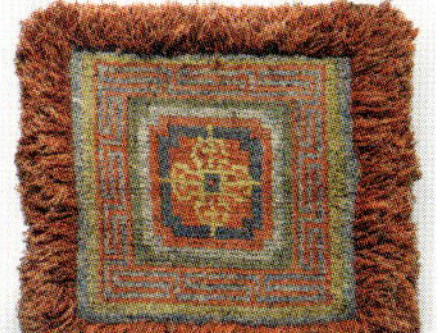

C49: Wangden *Drumze khagangma* sitting rug, with fringe

72×76 cm. Tibet. Late 19th – early 20th century. PATTERN: double *vajras* in central square; key-meander main border; plain lines of different colours narrow frames. WARP: wool, dark brown, some light mix; mid-type and overcoat yak hair; Z2S2. Density: 56 warps/dm. WEFT: wool, ivory and brown; Z1, of different thickness (spun without spindle). Two parallel shoots in a unit. Density: 8.5 units/dm. PILE: wool; Z2S; Z2S2, dyed unevenly. Height: 10 mm in the centre; 20 mm at the sides and ends. BASIC LOOPS: single-level (back warp face) type. Basic units: asym. long leg, with long ends pack under 2, 4 and 6 neighbouring warps to the left, some overrunning the belonging unit; open and closed loops; regular asym. and sym. SINGLES: regular sym., with bottom packing loop on 1 warp. PAIRED: left side: regular asym.; right side: asym. long leg. LONG ROWS: left end: regular asym.; right end: asym. long leg; in between: regular sym., otherwise asym. long leg. FINE LINES: made by pairs of asym. long leg. CURVED LINES: regular asym. and packing with different in colour long legs of neighbouring loops. OTHER IRREGULARITIES: numerous unsystematic irregularities, most probably formed asym. in result of weavers' mistakes; packing; sharing combined with packing. LOOPING DENSITY: 23 (horiz.) ×8.5 = 195.5 basic loops/sq dm. COLOURS (7): red; yellow; off olive-green; light green (faded, close to yellow); off dark blue, off light blue, blue. FINISH: sides: plain weft return; top: warp ends are plaited into a braid, at the corner tied together to make a huge loop; bottom: edge warps are wrapped round to make a 2.5 cm trimming. Seven rows of red-colour pile make an all-over the perimeter fringe, approx. 6 cm long. ADDITIONAL INFORMATION: soft colour scale, with dominating red shades; cold colour scale yarns have motley shades. Nomadic type weave, but of perfect monastic execution.

C53: Main carpet, quarter (?) of the bottom part

177×133 cm. China. Early 19th century. PATTERN: 2 imperial dragons; borders: waves and rainbow motifs. WARP: cotton; Z?S. Density: 49–50 warps/dm. WEFT: cotton; Z?S. Two regular shoots. Density: 26 units/dm. PILE: wool and hair; different quality and different height; in general hard; Z3 (grass-green, light green); otherwise Z2. Height: 2–3 mm (light green); 3 mm (brown-black); 3–4 mm (grass-green); 4 mm (rust-red); 4–5 mm (off grey-blue), 5 mm (dark rose-brown, mid-blue, camel-beige); 5–6 mm (terracotta-red, ivory); 6 mm (light pink, rose-cacao); 6–7 mm (light camel-brown). KNOT: regular asym. open left, depressed. KNOT Density: 24 (horiz.) ×26 = 642 knots/sq dm. COLOURS (14): terracotta-red, dark rose-brown, light pink, rose-cacao, rust-red, grass-green, light green, off grey-blue, mid-blue, camel-beige, light camel-brown, brown-black, ivory. FINISH: right side: side warps wrapped round by wefts; left side and top: cut; bottom: 2 cm tabby, 7 cm warp return loops. ADDITIONAL INFORMATION: typical for Chinese carpets manner of "drawing" small details, for example eyes. Heavily worn on the front and the back.

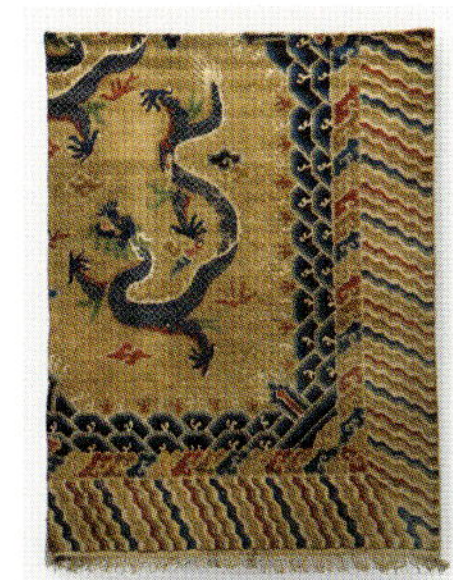

C55: *Khaden* sitting and sleeping rug

130×73 cm. Tibet. Middle of the 19th century. PATTERN: 3 close to square geometric in style medallions and "palms", on blue background; T-border, variant; narrow key-border. WARP: wool, Z2S; ivory and ivory mixed with brown. Density: 58 warps/dm. WEFT: wool; light mix; Z1. Two parallel shoots in a unit. Density: 20 units/dm. PILE: wool; Z3 (ivory); otherwise Z2. Height: 2 mm (orange, worn in the middle); 3–5 mm (off cherry-red); 4 mm (light yellow-green, ivory); 5–6 mm (red); otherwise 5 mm. BASIC LOOPS: asym. long leg; open loops, on 1 warp; regular sym. and asym. SINGLES: sym., with packing bottom loop. PAIRED: left: sym.; right: asym. long leg, with packing bottom loop. LONG ROWS: left end: sym., of large size; right end: asym. long leg, with packing bottom loop; in between: asym. long leg. CURVED LINES: regular asym., otherwise sym., with packing bottom loop; depending on place in structure loops can look upwards. OTHER IRREGULARITIES: offset effect. LOOPING DENSITY: 29 (horiz.) ×20 = 580 basic loops/sq dm. COLOURS (9): off cherry-red, red, orange, light yellow-green, light sky, blue, dark dark brown, ivory, brown plied with black. FINISH: sides: plain return over 3 additional warps; top: cut, wrapped round (late); bottom: 1 cm tabby, warp return loops. ADDITIONAL INFORMATION: good colours and dyestuffs. Worn in the centre. Rural work; comparable to C46, m.b. also to C29.

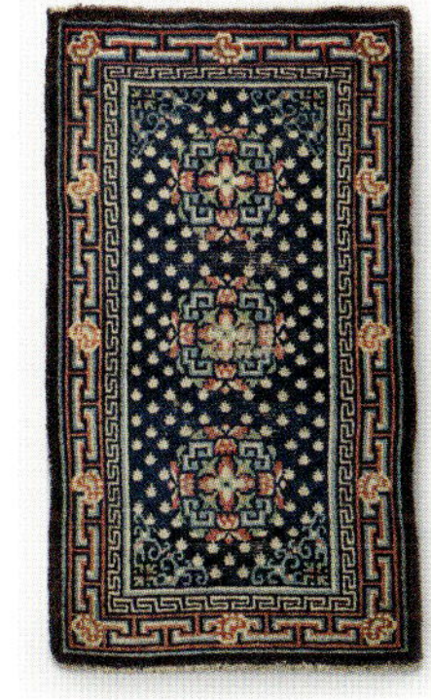

C56: *Khaden* sitting and sleeping rug

154×87–90 cm. Tibet. First quarter 20th century. PATTERN: 2 dragons, on beige background; non-separated border, with half-chrysanthemums and serrated leaves. WARP: cotton; Z?S. Depressed. Density: 84 warps/dm. WEFT: wool; ivory; Z1. Two parallel shoots in a unit. Density: 22 units/dm. PILE: wool; Z3 (off light turquoise); otherwise Z2. Height: 3 mm (dark sky, beige); 4–5 mm; (orange-red); 5 mm (orange); otherwise 4 mm. BASIC LOOPS: asym. long leg; open loops; regular sym. and asym. SINGLES: asym., with packing bottom loop. PAIRED: left: sym.; right: asym. long leg, with packing bottom loop; LONG ROWS: left end: sym.; right end: asym. long leg, with packing bottom loop; in between: asym. long leg. OTHER IRREGULARITIES: offset, by shar-

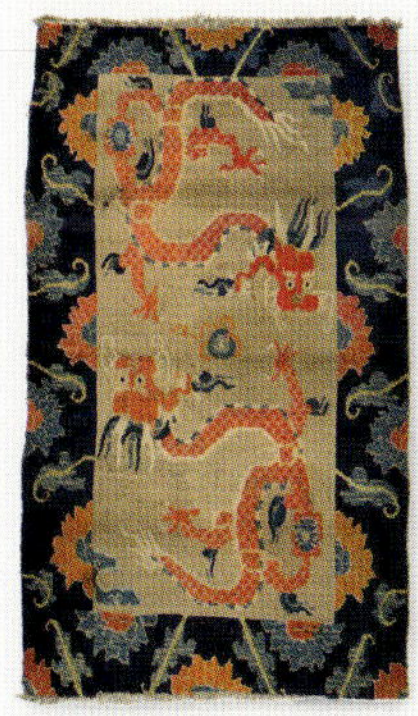

ing. LOOPING DENSITY: 42 (horiz.) ×22 = 924 basic loops/sq dm. COLOURS (13): bright red, very light rose, pink, very light pink-beige, orange-red, orange, lemon-yellow, off light turquoise, dark blue, dark sky, off light sky, beige, ivory. FINISH: sides: plain return over 3 additional warps; ends: cut. ADDITIONAL INFORMATION: worn on the back. Commercial product.

C57: *Masho* over-saddle rug

71×57 cm. Tibet. 19th century. PATTERN: central medallion with lion-dog image and corner peony (?) blossoms, on deep sky-blue background; border with images of dragons and phoenixes. WARP: wool; ivory; Z(?)S; fine. Depressed. Density: 56 warps/dm. WEFT: wool; light mix; Z1. Two parallel shoots in a unit. Density: 20 units/dm. PILE: wool; Z3 (ivory); otherwise Z2. Height: 2 mm (orange, worn in the middle); 3–5 mm (off cherry-red); 4 mm (light yellow-green, ivory); 5–6 mm (red); otherwise 5 mm. BASIC LOOPS: asym. long leg; sym. open loops; regular asym. SINGLES: asym. long leg, with packing bottom loop. LONG ROWS: left end: asym. loop, otherwise regular asym., of very small size and with strong depression; right end: asym. long leg, with packing bottom loop; in between: asym. long leg. DIAGONAL AND CURVED LINES: regular asym., with packing bottom loop; depressed paired loops; other variants. OTHER IRREGULARITIES: offset and offset effect. LOOPING DENSITY: 28 (horiz.) ×20 = 560 basic loops/sq dm. COLOURS (13): crimson, off cherry-red, bright red, orange-rose, orange, light grass-green, dark blue, deep sky, dark brown, ivory, red plied with brown, green plied with ivory, brown plied with black (can be more). FINISH: back is lined with ivory felt and lined with blue cotton textile; edges are trimmed with wide band of red-colour woollen cloth. ADDITIONAL INFORMATION: not possible to identify all structural elements because of lining and trimming. Charming piece, with masterly designed pattern and elaborated colouring, including usage of red-and-ivory yarns for representing dragon scales. Professional commercial work, probably for Chinese market.

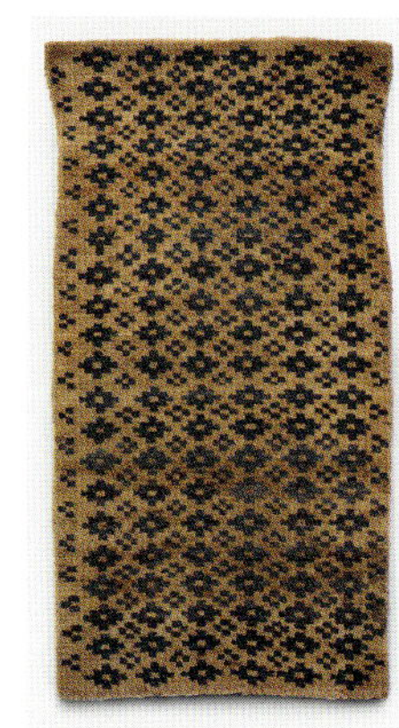

C58: *Khagangma* sitting rug for high-ranking lama, large fragment

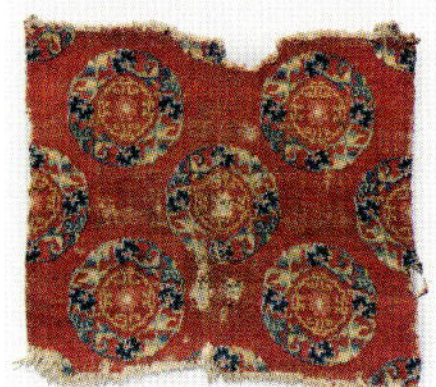

70×80 cm. Tibet. Not later than early 19th century. PATTERN: 5 garland rosettes, with halves and quarters, on cherry-red background. WARP: wool; ivory; Z2S; fine. Depressed. Density: 80 warps/dm. WEFT: wool; ivory; Z2S; fine. One shoot in a unit. Density: 24 units/dm. PILE: wool; Z3S (rich cherry-red); Z3 (old rose; rust, faded to olive-brown; sky); otherwise Z2S. Height: 2 mm (light turquoise, sky); 2.5 mm (light turquoise-green, with yellow fibres); 2–3 mm (ivory); 2–4 mm (rich cherry-red), 3 mm (rust, faded to olive-brown, mid-blue); 3–4 mm (camel-yellow); 4 mm (old rose); 4–5 mm (dark blue). BASIC LOOPS: asym. long leg; open sym. loops; regular sym. SINGLES: sym., diagonal, with packing bottom loop. LONG ROWS: left end: sym., deeply slanted; right end: asym. long leg, with packing bottom loop; in between: asym. long leg. DIAGONAL AND CURVED LINES: specifically arranged packing loops of diagonal sym.; single loops. OTHER IRREGULARITIES: packing; sharing combined with packing. LOOPING DENSITY: 36 (horiz.) ×24 = 864 basic loops/sq dm. COLOURS (11): rich cherry-red, old rose, camel-yellow; light turquoise-green, with yellow fibres; light turquoise, sky, mid-blue, dark blue; rust-brown, faded to olive-brown; ivory (shaggy). FINISH: sides: plain weft return over 3 additional warps. Ends: missing, except for a tiny bit of plain weave (2 cm). ADDITIONAL INFORMATION: losses of sides and ends; strong general wear. Excellent in quality weave, elegant colouring, refined pattern balance – the best of the type in the collection, a model example of early monastic work.

C59: *Khaden* sitting and sleeping rug for a high-ranking lama

149×76 cm. Tibet. Ca. 1900. PATTERN: alternating rows of small stepped diamonds and straight crosses, on ivory background. WARP: cotton; Z3S; white. Depressed. Density: 56 warps/dm. WEFT: wool; ivory and brown; Z1. Two parallel shoots in a unit. Density: 24 units/dm. PILE: wool; Z3 (dark blue); Z5 (faded rust). Height: long pile. BASIC LOOPS: regular asym. open left (dominate); asym. long leg; sym. loops; regular sym. IRREGULARITIES: packing; sharing combined with packing. LOOPING DENSITY: 28 (horiz.) ×18 = 504 basic loops/sq dm. COLOURS (2): dark blue, ivory (faded light rust-brown). FINISH: sides: plain weft return over 2 additional warps. Top end: tabby, with sumakh-type finish; bottom end: similar finish, warp return loops. ADDITIONAL INFORMATION: rural work.

C60: *Sabden* main carpet, large fragment (missing left border)

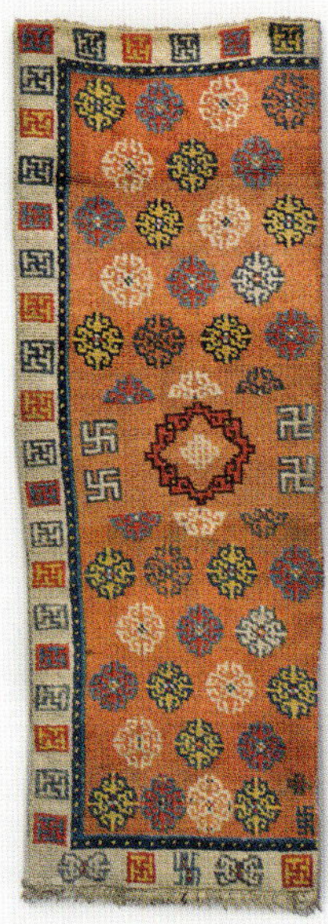

192×72 cm. Tibet. Second half 19th century. Pattern: central geometric diamond-shaped medallion, otherwise 4 *swastikas* and rows of small rosettes; on rust background; main border with *swastikas*, on ivory background; inner pearl border. WARP: wool; ivory; Z2S; two side warps: plied together ivory and brown yarns; thick. Density: 52 warps/dm. WEFT: wool; ivory and light mix; Z1; thick. Two parallel shoots in a unit. Density: 16 units/dm. PILE: wool; thick; Z2 (dark blue); Z4 (off-pink); otherwise Z3. Height: 4 mm (off-pink, dark brown); 4–5 mm (dark blue); 5 mm (off-sky); otherwise 4 mm. BASIC LOOPS: asym. long leg; loops on 1 warp; regular sym. SINGLES: asym., with bottom packing loop. PAIRED: left side: sym., of large size; right side: asym. long leg, with packing bottom loop. LONG ROW: left end: asym. long leg, with packing bottom loop; right end: sym., of large side; in between: basic asym. long leg. IRREGULARITIES: packing combined with sharing. LOOPING DENSITY: 26 (horiz.) ×16 = 416 basic loops/sq dm. COLOURS (10): carmine, off-pink, orange-red, rust, yellow, dark blue, off-blue, off-sky, off grey-sky, dark brown, ivory. FINISH: sides: regular weft return over 2 additional warps; bottom end: 1 cm tabby, loose ends; top end: cut. ADDITIONAL INFORMATION: missing left side border. Low looping density correlated with thickness of yarns. Good professional rural (nomadic ?) work; most probably made to order. Rust-colour background yarns can imitate camel hair.

C61: *Tsuktruk khaden* sitting and sleeping rug for a high-ranking lama, 5 stitched together panels

156×75.5 cm, panels: 14.5 cm, 16.5 cm, 15.5 cm, 15 cm, 15 cm. Tibet. 19th century (?). PATTERN: all-over deep crimson colour. WARP: wool; ivory; Z2S; fine. Density: 62–72 warps/dm. WEFT: wool; ivory and brown; Z1, Z2; thick. One (several 2) shoot in a unit. Density: 40 units/dm. PILE: wool; Z2S. Height: 10 mm. BASIC LOOPS: sym. loops, on 1 warp, with one warp in between. IRREGULARITIES: all-over offset. LOOPING DENSITY: 35 (horiz.) ×40 = 1,400 basic loops/sq dm. COLOURS (1): deep crimson-red. FINISH: sides: plain weft return. Ends: missing. ADDITIONAL INFORMATION: wide cotton band stitched along the back sides and ends. Perfect, archaic in style weave, comparable with archaeological findings of the Central Asian Early Iron period.

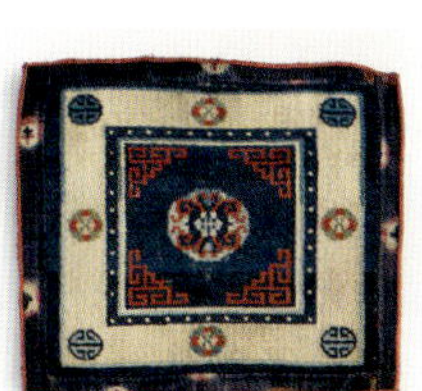

C63: *Khagangma* sitting rug

56×66 cm. Tibet. Second half 19th century (?). PATTERN: small central medallion, on dark blue background; wide ivory-colour border, with 4 imitations of *Shou* hieroglyphs and 4 4-petal rosettes; narrow pearl border. WARP: wool; ivory; Z2S. Density: 54 warps/dm. WEFT: wool; ivory; Z2S. Two parallel shoots in a unit. Density: 17 units/dm. PILE: wool; Z2, Z3; a few Z6. Height: 4 mm (rose, sky); otherwise 5–6 mm. BASIC LOOPS: asym. long leg; open loops; regular asym. and sym. SINGLES: sym., with packing bottom loop. PAIRED: left side: sym.; right side: asym. long leg, with packing bottom loop. LONG ROWS: left end: sym.; right end: asym. long leg, with packing bottom loop; in between: asym. long leg. IRREGULARITIES: packing; sharing combined with packing; loops over wefts. LOOPING DENSITY: 27 (horiz.) ×17 = 459 basic loops/sq dm. COLOURS (7): cherry, rose, cold green/olive-green (abrash); dark blue (abrash), sky, light sky, ivory (faded light rust-brown). FINISH: all edges trimmed with reserve-technique textile band and red tape. ADDITIONAL INFORMATION: regular weave; well-composed pattern. Monastic work in rural tradition (?).

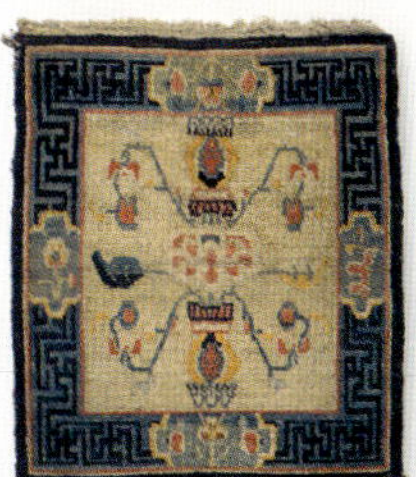

C64: *Masho* over-saddle rug

67×58 cm. Tibet. Not later than early 20th century. PATTERN: vase, with flowers, on light camel-yellow background; *swastika* meander border, with 4 floral cartouches. WARP: wool; ivory; Z2S. Density: 92 warps/dm. WEFT: wool; light mix; Z1. Two parallel shoots in a unit. Density: 21 units/dm. PILE: wool; Z2. Height: 3 mm (olive-green); 5 mm (off-yellow); 6 mm (light camel-yellow); otherwise 4 mm. BASIC LOOPS: asym. long leg; open loops, on 1 warp; regular sym. and asym. SINGLES: regular asym. PAIRED: left side: sym.; right side: asym. long leg, with packing bottom loop. LONG ROWS: left end: sym.; right end: asym. long leg, with packing bottom loop; in between: asym. long leg. IRREGULARITIES: packing; sharing combined with packing; offset effect. LOOPING DENSITY: 46 (horiz.) ×21 = 966 basic loops/sq dm. COLOURS (12): claret, red, rose, off light rose, orange, off light yellow, light camel-yellow, olive-green, light turquoise, off light turquoise, dark sky, dark blue. FINISH: sides: plain return over 1 additional warp; top: 1 cm, cut; bottom: missing. ADDITIONAL INFORMATION: monastic work, probably for Chinese market. Comparable in composition and function to C48, C89, C91, and C101.

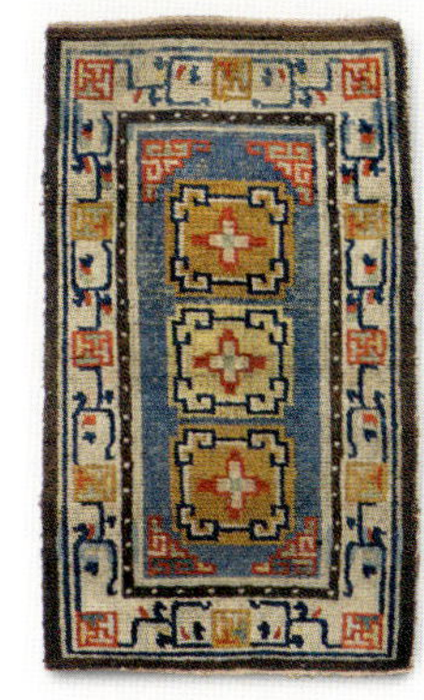

C65: *Khaden* sitting and sleeping rug

110×66 cm. Tibet. Second half 19th century. PATTERN: 3 rectangular-shaped medallions, with central cross, on sky background; *swastika* and floral meander main border, inner pearl border. WARP: wool; Z2S; ivory. Density: 58 warps/dm. WEFT: wool; ivory and light grey mix; Z1. Two parallel shoots in a unit. Density: 17 units/dm. PILE: wool; Z2. Height: 5 mm (mustard); 7 mm (dark blue, light turquoise); otherwise 6 mm. BASIC LOOPS: asym. long leg; open loops, on 1 warp; regular sym. and asym. PAIRED: left side: asym.; right side: asym. long leg, with packing bottom loop. LONG ROWS: left end: sym., of very large size; right end: asym. long leg, with packing bottom loop; in between: long leg asym. open left. IRREGULARITIES: packing; sharing combined with packing. LOOPING DENSITY: 29 (horiz.) ×17 = 493 basic loops/sq dm. Loose structure. COLOURS (12): cherry-red, off light rose (faded), yellow, green/turquoise-yellow, dark blue-green, off light turquoise, dark blue, sky (motley), mustard, off light grey, brown-black, ivory. FINISH: sides: plain weft return over 2 additional warps; bottom: 1 cm tabby, warp return loops; top: 1 cm tabby on the front, 1 cm turned over to the back, sewn down. ADDITIONAL INFORMATION: rural work; poor design and simple weave. Comparable in style and composition to C46, C55, C155, and C157.

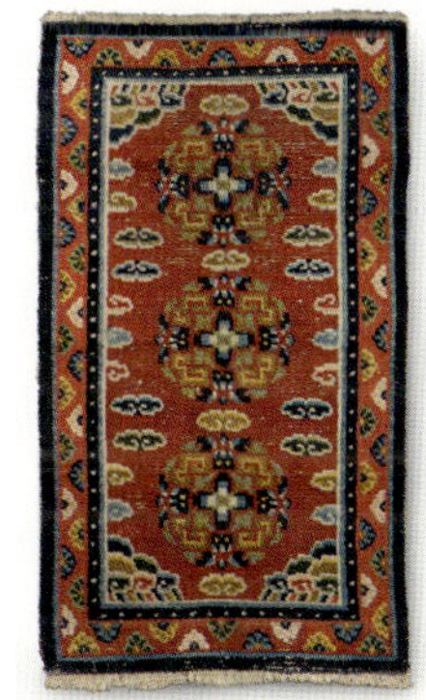

C66: *Khaden* sitting and sleeping rug

129×72 cm. Tibet, under Khotan influence. Early 20th century. PATTERN: 3 large medallions and cloud motifs, on cherry-red background; half-lotus border, inner pearl border. WARP: wool; ivory; Z2S; ruined. Depressed. Density: 56 warps/dm. WEFT: wool; light mix; Z2S; loose, thick. Two parallel shoots in a unit. Density: 28 units/dm. PILE: wool; Z2, Z3. Height: 5 mm (sky); 7 mm (cherry-red, olive-green, light green-olive); 9 mm (ivory); otherwise 6 mm. BASIC LOOPS: asym. long leg; open loops, on 1 and on 2 warps; regular sym. LONG ROWS: left end: sym.; right end: asym. long leg, with packing bottom loop; in between: asym. long leg. IRREGULARITIES: packing; sharing combined with packing. LOOPING DENSITY: 28 (horiz.) ×28 = 784 basic loops/sq dm. COLOURS (9): cherry-red, light pink, yellow, dark blue, sky, olive-green, light green-olive, khaki, ivory. FINISH: sides: plain return over 2 additional warps; bottom end: 1.5 cm tabby, warp return loops; top: 2 cm tabby, cut.

C67: *Khagangma* sitting rug

67×72 cm. Tibet. Mid-19th century. PATTERN: large central rosette, on dark blue background; wide T-border and inner pearl border. WARP: wool; light mix; Z2S; fine. Depressed. Density: 48 warps/dm. WEFT: wool; ivory; Z1. Two parallel shoots in a unit. Density: 17 units/dm. PILE: wool; Z3 (yellow, light sky, sky); Z2, Z2S (very light rose); otherwise Z2. Height: 3 mm (yellow); 3–5 mm (off light rose); 5 mm (light sky, sky, mid-dark blue, ivory); 7 mm (light turquoise); otherwise 6 mm. BASIC LOOPS:

asym. long leg; open loops; on 1, otherwise on 2 warp; regular sym. and asym. SINGLES: sym., with packing bottom loop. PAIRED: left side: asym; right side: asym. long leg, with packing bottom loop. LONG ROWS: left end: sym., otherwise asym.; right end: asym. long leg, with packing bottom loop; in between: asym. long leg. CURVED LINES: additional loops on wefts, with loop ends pulled upwards; change of angle and direction of depression. OTHER IRREGULARITIES: packing; sharing combined with packing; offset effect. LOOPING DENSITY: 24 (horiz.) × 17 = 408 basic loops/sq dm. COLOURS (11): carmine, light rose, off light rose, yellow, light turquoise, light sky, sky (motley), mid-blue (shaggy), dark blue, dark brown (motley), ivory. FINISH: sides: plain weft return over 3 additional warps; ends: cut. ADDITIONAL INFORMATION: reasonably worn front and shaggy back. Excellent colour balance and pattern, although simple. Comparable in structure to C55.

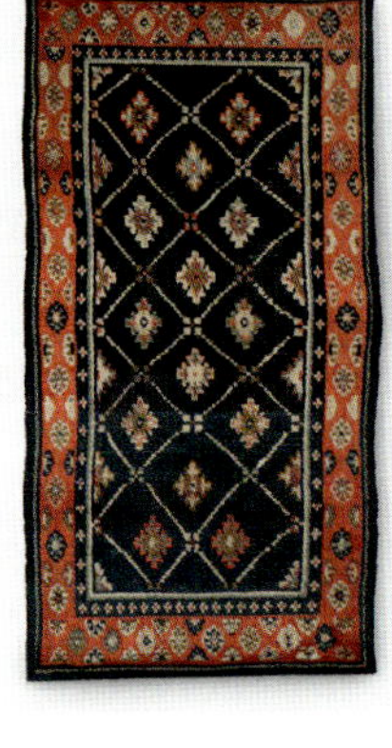

C68: *Khaden* rug for a high-ranking person
149×80 cm. Tibet. Last third 19th century. PATTERN: large floral rosettes, 5 complete, ½ along the edges and ¼ in the corners, on dark blue background. WARP: cotton; ivory; Z2S. Density: 72 warps/dm. WEFT: wool; ivory mix; Z2. Two parallel shoots in a unit. Density: 26 units/dm. PILE: wool; mainly Z2. Height: 3 mm (salmon); 5 mm (yellow); 6 mm (cherry-red, grass-green, dark blue); otherwise 4 mm. BASIC LOOPS: all-over asym. open left, with long leg and packing bottom loop, on 1 warp; otherwise without loops (description is probably incomplete). IRREGULARITIES: sharing combined with packing. LOOPING DENSITY: 29 (horiz.) × 26 = 754 basic loops/sq dm. COLOURS (9): cherry-red, light pink-rose, salmon, yellow, grass-green (with yellow shade), dark blue, dark sky, light sky (abrash), ivory. FINISH: sides: plain weft return over 3 additional warps; ends: covered by trimming. ADDITIONAL INFORMATION: excellent wool. Professional commercial product.

C69: *Khaden* sitting and sleeping rug
152×80 cm. Tibet. Last third 19th century (?). PATTERN: diagonal lattice with cross-shaped figures, on blue background; border: multi-petal rosettes, on bright red background. WARP: cotton; white; Z2S; fine. Density: 64 warps/dm. WEFT: wool; brown mix; Z1. Two parallel shoots in a unit. Density: 15 units/dm. PILE: wool; Z3. Height: 6 mm (bright red); otherwise 7 mm. BASIC LOOPS: asym. open left, with long leg; open and closed loops, on 1 warp; regular sym. and asym. SINGLES: asym. open left. LONG ROWS: left end: regular asym.; right end: asym. long leg, with packing bottom loop; in between: asym. long leg. IRREGULARITIES: packing; sharing combined with packing; rows of sharing knots. Sym. knots across 1 and 2 wefts. LOOPING DENSITY: 29 (horiz.) × 20 = 580 basic loops/sq dm. COLOURS (7): bright red, rose, dark blue, off-turquoise, chestnut, faded violet, ivory. FINISH: sides: plain weft return over side warps; ends: 1 cm of plain weave, cut. ADDITIONAL INFORMATION: worn. Made for sale. Impressive pattern, although alien to Tibet.

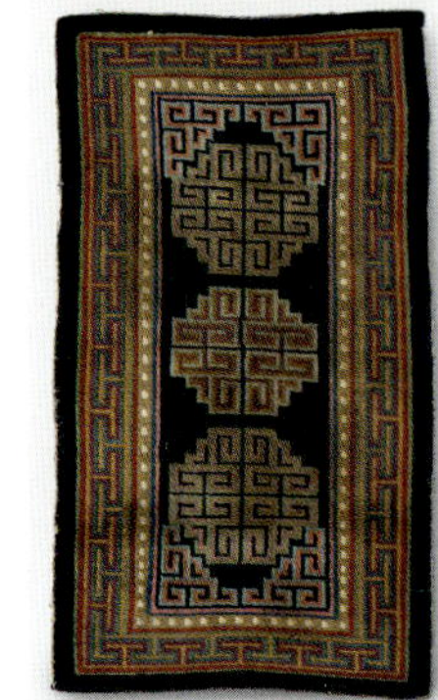

C71: *Khaden* sitting and sleeping rug
147×81 cm. Tibet. 1st half 20th century. PATTERN: three large geometric rosettes, on black-blue background; main T-border; inner pearl border. WARP: wool; ivory; Z2S; fine. Very deep depression. Density: 44 warps/dm. WEFT: wool; light mix; Z1. Two parallel shoots in a unit. Density: 14 units/dm. PILE: wool; Z3. Height: 3–4 mm. BASIC LOOPS: asym. open left, with long leg; open and closed loops, on 1 warp; regular sym. LONG ROWS: left end: sym., nearly vertical; right end: asym. long leg, with packing bottom loop; in between: asym. long leg. IRREGULARITIES: packing; sharing combined with packing. LOOPING DENSITY: 22 (horiz.) × 14 = 308 basic loops/sq dm. COLOURS (14): crimson, cherry-red, dark rose (faded bordeaux), green, green-blue, turquoise, blue, violet-blue, blue, black-blue, red-brown olive, khaki, ivory. FINISH: sides: plain weft return over 2 additional side warps (hemp [?]); ends: missing. ADDITIONAL INFORMATION: unusual for Tibet pattern, with imitation of Chinese recurring-line rosettes.

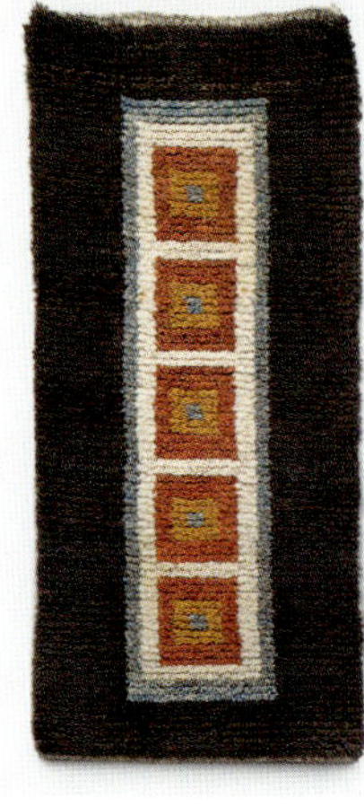

C72: *Khaden drumze* temple sitting rug for a lama
164×74 cm. Tibet. Late 20th century. PATTERN: row of 5 squares, with yellow centre; wide black-brown framing. WARP: wool, ivory and hair, grey-brown; mostly mixed, sometimes plied together; Z2S. Density: 45 warps/dm. WEFT: wool, ivory and light mix; Z1; very thick, spun without spindle. Two shoots in a unit. Density: 7 units/dm. PILE: wool, yak hair; Z2S2 (grey, ivory); otherwise Z2S; loose. Height: 20 mm. BASIC LOOPS, AND GENERAL STRUCTURE: warp-faced back technique, single-level (on 3 warps, otherwise on 1). Basic loops: asym. long leg; open loops, on 2 warps; regular asym. and sym. LONG ROWS: left end: sym.; right end: asym. long leg, with packing bottom loop; in between: asym. long leg. IRREGULARITIES: packing; sharing combined with packing. Accidental asym. loops with very long leg over 5–7 warps. LOOPING DENSITY: 15 (horiz.) × 7 = 105 basic loops/sq dm. COLOURS (6): orange, yellow, off-sky, also off-sky mixed with grey, black-brown (yak hair), ivory. FINISH: sides: plain weft return; bottom end: warp ends plaited into a fine braid; top end: warp ends are plaited into a broad band. ADDITIONAL INFORMATION: classic shape for monastic use. Very soft and shaggy black-brown yak-hair yarns. Off-sky is motley. Ends finish similar to C77. Monastic work.

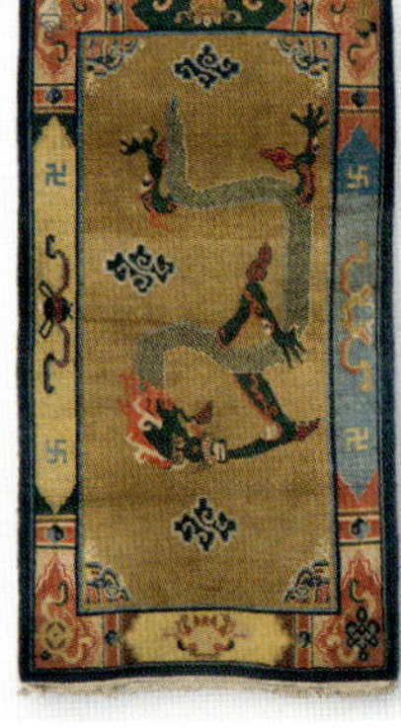

C73: *Sabden* main carpet
160×87 cm. Tibet. Not later than early 20th century. PATTERN: green dragon, on cacao-beige background; border: 4 cartouches, with Buddhist symbols. WARP: cotton; ivory; Z?S. WEFT: wool; ivory and light pink; Z2S. Two parallel shoots in a unit. PILE: wool; Z3 (warm shades); otherwise Z2. Height: 4 mm (cherry-red, bright red, off light rose, dark cold green, off light turquoise-sky, ivory); 4–5 mm (light pink, yellow, cacao); otherwise 5 mm and 5–6 mm. BASIC LOOPS: asym. long leg; open loops, on 1 warp; regular sym. and on 3 warps. LONG ROWS: left end: variants of sym., and sym. with bottom loop; right end: asym. long leg, with packing bottom loop; in between: long leg asym. open left. CURVING AND FINE LINES: vertical rows of loops on 1 warp,

additional single-level and sym. loops (dragon's eye). OTHER IRREGULARITIES: offset (with additional loops); packing, also in different colours (ivory and sky); sharing; sharing combined with packing. COLOURS (12): off-purple, cherry-red, bright red, light pink, off light pink, yellow, dark cold green (abrash, shaggy), sky, off light turquoise-sky, dark blue, cacao-beige, ivory. FINISH: sides: plain weft return over 1 additional warp; bottom end: 1 cm warp return loops; top end: 1.5 cm tabby, cut. ADDITIONAL INFORMATION: excellent professional work. Impression of carving caused by different wear of pile yarns. Light shades: 2nd and 3rd use of dye baths. Copy of a Chinese carpet; many common for Chinese and Tibetan weaving manner's tricks. Most probably made for Chinese market.

C75: Pillow front panel (?)

37×64 cm. Tibet. Early 20th century. PATTERN: blossoming branch and two birds, on light rust background. WARP: wool; ivory; Z2S; fine. Density: 68 warps/dm. WEFT: wool; ivory; Z3. One shoot in a unit. Density: 35 units/dm (?). PILE: wool; Z3 (pink, gold-yellow); otherwise Z2. Height: 5–6 mm. BASIC LOOPS: asym. long leg; open loops, on 1 warp; regular asym. and sym., some on 3 warps. SINGLES: sym., with packing bottom loop. PAIRED: left side: asym.; right side: asym. long leg, with packing bottom loop. LONG ROWS: left end: asym.; right end: asym. long leg, with packing bottom loop; in between: asym. long leg. IRREGULARITIES: packing; sharing combined with packing; offset (by side loop on 1 warp). LOOPING DENSITY: 34 (horiz.) ×35 = 1,190 basic loops/sq dm. COLOURS (8): bright red, pink, light rust, gold-yellow, dark green, dark blue, off light sky, olive-brown. FINISH: sides: plain weft return over 1 additional warp; ends: folded over to the back and sewn down. ADDITIONAL INFORMATION: Chinese-style pattern.

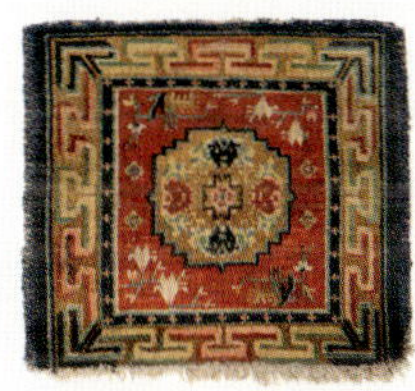

C76: *Khagangma* sitting rug

70×78 cm. Tibet. Third quarter 19th century (?). PATTERN: stepped medallion, on carmine background; main T-border; inner stripe: row of tiny straight crosses. WARP: cotton; ivory; Z?S. Depressed. Density: 68 warps/dm. WEFT: wool; brown mix; Z1. Three parallel shoots in a unit. Density: 16 units/dm. PILE: wool; Z3 (pink, yellow, sky/ivory); otherwise Z2. Height: 4 mm (carmine, light yellow, yellow, yellow-green); 7 mm (black); 10 mm (dark blue at the edges of the rug); otherwise 5 mm. BASIC LOOPS: asym. long leg; open loops; regular sym. SINGLES: asym. with packing bottom loop. PAIRED: left side: sym.; right side: asym. long leg, with packing bottom loop. LONG ROWS: left end: sym.; right end: asym. long leg, with packing bottom loop; in between: asym. long leg. CURVED LINES: combination of loops and diagonal sym. OTHER IRREGULARITIES: packing; sharing combined with packing; numerous loops. LOOPING DENSITY: 34 (horiz.) ×16 = 544 basic loops/sq dm. COLOURS (11): carmine, pink (faded tips), yellow, light yellow, yellow-green, green, dark blue (motley), brown, black, ivory, sky plied together with ivory (motley). FINISH: sides: plain weft return; ends: missing. ADDITIONAL INFORMATION: strong wear, losses and spots suggest long active usage. Monastic work (?).

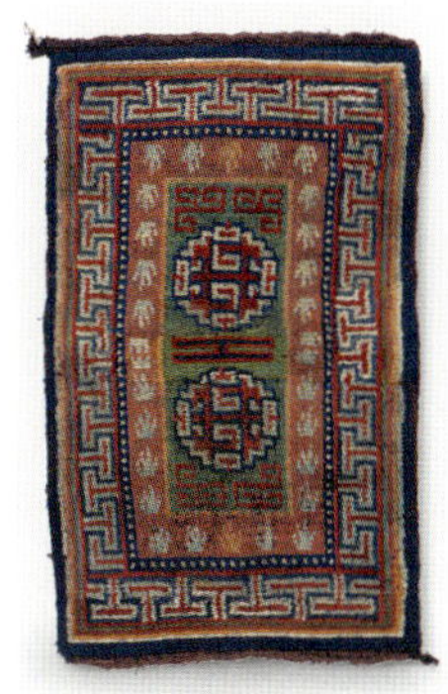

C77: Wangden *Drumze masho* over-saddle rug

101×67 cm. Tibet. Not earlier than late 19th century. PATTERN: 2 stepped rosettes, on green background; T-border; inner: "palms" and pearl border. WARP: yak hair (?); dark brown; Z2S; fine. Density: 123–124 warps/dm. WEFT: yak under hair (?); brown; Z4; soft, loose ply. 2 parallel shoots in a unit. Density: 14 units/dm. PILE: wool; Z1 (ivory/light sky mix); Z2 (cold motley green); otherwise Z3. Height: worn, 5 mm all over. BASIC LOOPS: warp-faced back, single-level looping; basic loops: asym. long leg, long end under 2 warps; open and closed sym. loops on 2 warps; regular sym. SINGLES: asym. long leg, on 2 upper shed warps, with packing bottom loop. LONG ROWS: right end: asym. long leg, with packing bottom loop; left end: sym. loops, otherwise closed loop; in between: asym. long leg. IRREGULARITIES: packing; sharing combined with packing; unusually long legs (comparable to C72). LOOPING DENSITY: 31/32 (horiz.) ×14 = 434/448 basic loops/sq dm. COLOURS (7): dark cherry-red, orange, cold green (motley), dark blue; mid-blue, ivory; plied together ivory and dark blue; plied together ivory and shades of off light sky; mix of ivory and light sky fibres. FINISH: sides: plain weft return. Ends: warp ends plaited into a flat braid. ADDITIONAL INFORMATION: artistically close to C71, although different in structure, more complicated in design and earlier in age. Commercial rural work (?).

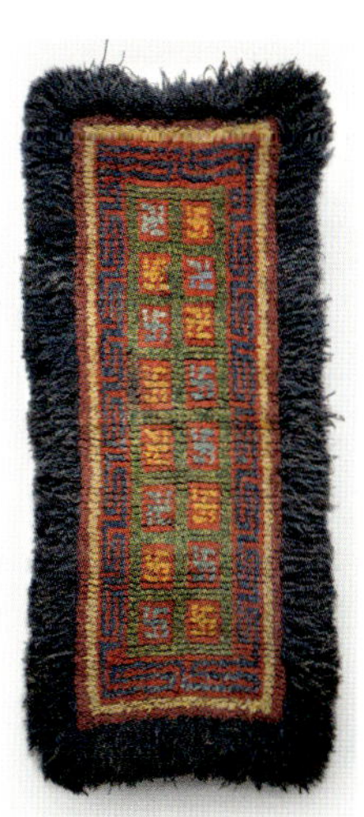

C78: Wangden *Drumze* temple sitting rug (?)

169×60 cm. Tibet. Late 19th century (?). PATTERN: 2×8 square rosettes, with *swastika* image, on grass-green background; inner key-border. WARP: wool; ivory, and mix of ivory and brown yak or horse hair; Z2S. Density: 60–68 warps/dm. WEFT: 1) wool, ivory; camel hair, rust-brown; Z2S; loose spin and ply; 2) yak under hair, black-brown, plied together with wool, grey mix; Z2S; very soft; 3) yak hair, black-brown, plied together with wool, dark brown, soft; Z2S; all over loose (can be other variants). Yarns spun by hand, without spindle. 2 parallel shoots in a unit. Density: 6 units/dm. PILE: wool; Z3x2 (orange-red); Z4x2 (ivory/white); otherwise Z2S2. Height: 20 mm (orange-red, light sky, ivory/whight); 25 mm (yellow); 30 mm (lemon-yellow, green-yellow, mid-blue); 35 mm (light violet-red); 45 mm (bright red); fringe: 120–130 mm (dark blue). BASIC LOOPS: single-level (warp-faced back) weave. Basic units: asym. open left, on 2 upper shed warps, with long leg; open sym. loops, on 1 and 2 warps; regular sym. LONG ROWS: right end: asym. long leg, with packing bottom loop; left end: closed loop; in between: sym. long leg. OTHER IRREGULARITIES: packing; sharing combined with packing. LOOPING DENSITY: 23 (horiz.) ×6 = 138 basic loops/sq dm. COLOURS (9): dark cherry, bright red, orange-red, yellow, lemon-yellow, green-blue, mid-blue, light sky, ivory/white. FINISH: sides: plain weft return over 2 additional warps; bottom end: 2.5 cm tabby, warp return loops. Fringe: 9 rows of dark blue loops at the sides and 5 at the ends (yarns from even to motley). ADDITIONAL INFORMATION: sides trimmed with a tape. All threads, except yellow, orange-red and violet-red, are poorly dyed and regularly contain fibres of different colours. Nonetheless, it represents the developed tradition (compare to C72, C77, C148); monastic work.

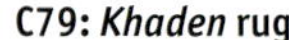

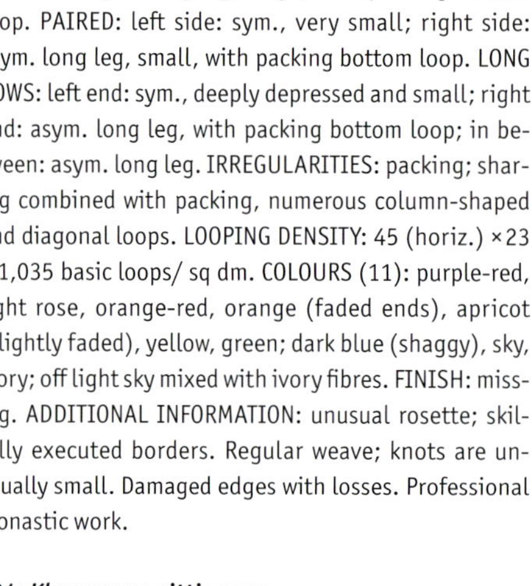

C79: *Khaden* rug

121×71 cm. Tibet. 3rd quarter 19th century (?). PATTERN: stepped central rosette, quarters in the corners and "palms", on dark blue background; pearl border. WARP: wool; dark brown; Z2S; poor quality. Depressed. Density: 48 warps/dm. WEFT: wool; ivory; Z1. Two parallel shoots in a unit. Density: 18 units/dm. PILE: wool; Z2S; faintly plied. Height: 7 mm. BASIC LOOPS: asym. long leg; open sym. loops, on 2 warps; regular sym. and asym. (?). SINGLES: regular sym., with bottom packing loop. PAIRED: left: regular asym.; right: asym. long leg. IRREGULARITIES: packing; sharing combined with packing; numerous diagonal and very large loops. LOOPING DENSITY: 24 (horiz.) ×18 = 422 basic loops/sq dm. COLOURS (9): cherry-red, fuchsin (faded), cold green, motley cold green, dark blue; sky, dark purple-brown, ivory; purple plied together with sky. FINISH: sides: plain weft return over 3 additional warps; bottom end: warp return loops; top end: missing. ADDITIONAL INFORMATION: some details of weaving are also typical for Chinese manner of looping. All-over "palms" speak for a special function. Fuchsin dye suggests a late 1860s dating.

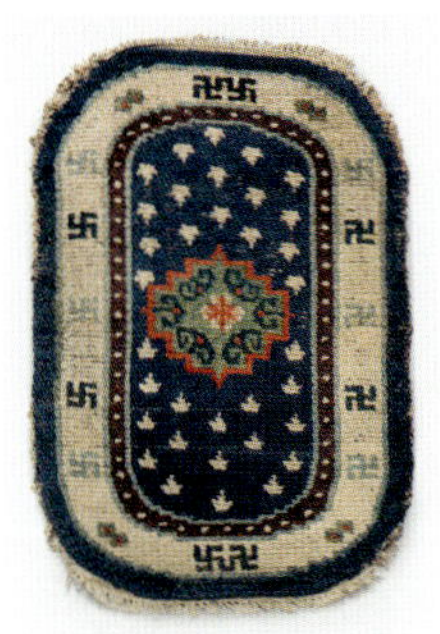

C82: *Masho* over-saddle rug, oval

80×56 cm. Tibet. Mid-19th century or earlier. PATTERN: stepped central rosette and "palms", on dark blue background; ivory-ground main border, with spare *swastikas*; inner pearl border, on purple-brown ground. WARP: wool; ivory; Z2S. Deeply depressed. Density: 47–48 warps/dm. WEFT: 1) wool, probably yak hair; black-brown; Z1; very loose; 2) wool; ivory; Z2. Two parallel shoots in a unit. Density: 15 units/dm. PILE: wool; Z3, Z4; loose ply. Height: 5–6 mm. BASIC LOOPS: asym. long leg; open and closed loops, on 1 warp; regular asym. and sym. PAIRED: left side: sym.; right side: asym. long leg, with packing bottom open loop. LONG ROWS: left end: sym., otherwise asym., deeply depressed, with bottom loops on 1 and on 2 warps; right end: asym. long leg, with packing bottom open loop; in between: asym. long leg. IRREGULARITIES: packing; sharing combined with packing; numerous short rows of sym. loops. LOOPING DENSITY: 23–34 (horiz.) ×15 = 345–360 basic loops/sq dm. COLOURS (9): scarlet-red, orange-pink, salmon, off grass-green, dark blue, sky, off-blue, purple-brown, ivory. FINISH: sides: plain weft return. ADDITIONAL INFORMATION: restoration of edges. Traces of running red-colour trimming. Rural work.

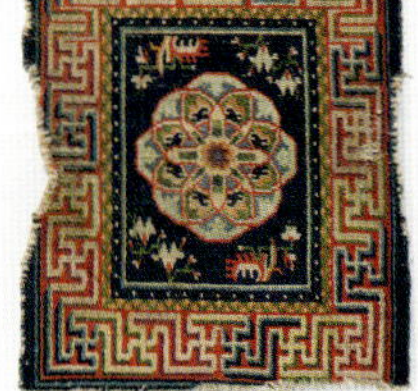

C83: *Masho* over-saddle or sitting rug

63×56 cm. Tibet. Not later than ca. 1900. PATTERN: large lobed rosette and 4 flowers, on blue ground; *swastika* meander main border; inner pearl border. WARP: cotton; white; Z3S; fine. Depressed. Density: 90 warps/dm. WEFT: wool; ivory; Z1; loose. Two parallel shoots in a unit. Density: 23 units/dm. PILE: wool; Z2. Height: 2 mm (apricot, dark green, off light sky mix with ivory); otherwise 3 mm. BASIC LOOPS: asym. long leg; closed and open loops on 1 warp; regular asym. and sym. loops. SINGLES: asym. long leg, large, with packing bottom loop. PAIRED: left side: sym., very small; right side: asym. long leg, small, with packing bottom loop. LONG ROWS: left end: sym., deeply depressed and small; right end: asym. long leg, with packing bottom loop; in between: asym. long leg. IRREGULARITIES: packing; sharing combined with packing, numerous column-shaped and diagonal loops. LOOPING DENSITY: 45 (horiz.) ×23 = 1,035 basic loops/ sq dm. COLOURS (11): purple-red, light rose, orange-red, orange (faded ends), apricot (slightly faded), yellow, green; dark blue (shaggy), sky, ivory; off light sky mixed with ivory fibres. FINISH: missing. ADDITIONAL INFORMATION: unusual rosette; skilfully executed borders. Regular weave; knots are unusually small. Damaged edges with losses. Professional monastic work.

C84: *Khagangma* sitting rug

61×68 cm. Tibet. Late 19th century. PATTERN: oval medallion, with corner blossoms, on off light grey ground; main T-border; inner pearl border. WARP: wool; ivory; S2Z. Depressed. Density: 60 warps/dm. WEFT: wool; ivory; S2Z; fine. Two parallel shoots in a unit. Density: 18 units/dm. PILE: wool; Z3, Z3S (off light camel-grey). Height: 2.5–5 mm (off light camel-grey); 3–4 mm (orange-red, mid-blue); 4–5 mm (dark blue); otherwise 3 mm. BASIC LOOPS: asym. long leg; open loops; regular sym. SINGLE: sym., otherwise sym. with bottom open loop on 1 warp. PAIRED: left side: sym.; right side: asym. long leg, with packing bottom loop: LONG ROWS: left end: sym.; right end: asym. long leg, with packing bottom loop; in between: asym. long leg. CURVED LINES: diagonal sym. (left side) and sym. with packing bottom loop (right side). IRREGULARITIES: packing; sharing combined with packing. LOOPING DENSITY: 28 (horiz.) ×18 = 504 basic loops/sq dm. COLOURS (9): carmine-red, dark rose, orange-red, yellow, turquoise-green (abrash, mixed with yellow), dark blue, mid-blue, off light camel-grey, ivory. FINISH: sides: complicated weft return over 3 additional warps; bottom end: 1 cm tabby, folded over to the back and sewn down; top end: missing. ADDITIONAL INFORMATION: good colours; professional work; uneven wear of pile, off-grey background in particular.

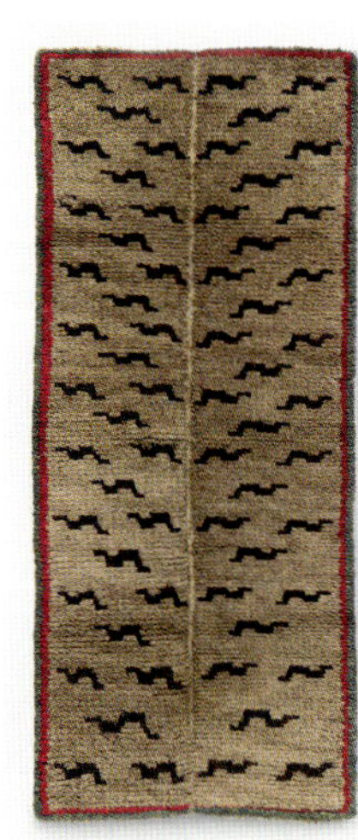

C85: *Tsuktruk khaden* sitting and sleeping rug for a lama (?), 2 stitched together panels

141×61.5 cm; panels: 31 cm and 30.5 cm. Tibet. 20th century. PATTERN: tiger skin motif, blue on ivory ground; narrow red-line framing. WARP: cotton; ivory; Z2S; fine. Density: 42 warps/dm. WEFT: wool; ivory, grey (little); Z2S; thick, loose spin and ply. Density: 6–7 shoots in a unit. PILE: wool; Z3; Z2S2 (carmine, very loose spin and ply); otherwise Z2 (?). Height: 8–10 mm, 9–17 mm (uneven shaving). BASIC LOOPS: single-level sym. open loops, on 1 warp, with one warp in between. LOOPING DENSITY: 21 (horiz.) ×12.5 = 262.5 basic loops/sq dm. COLOURS (4): crimson, cacao (faded to ivory), turquoise, dark blue-green. FINISH: sides: plain weft return; ends: cut. ADDITIONAL INFORMATION: archaic weave; traditional shape and sacred pattern.

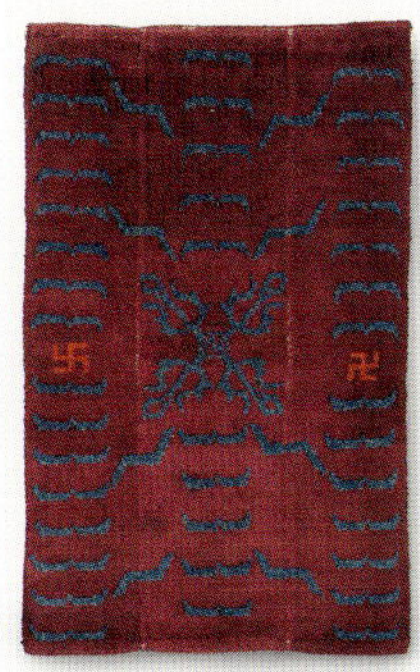

C86: ***Tsuktruk* sitting and sleeping rug for a lama, 3 stitched together panels**
88×54.5 cm; panels: 16.5 cm, 20.5 cm, 17.5 cm. Tibet. Late 20th century. PATTERN: 1 images of double *vajra* motif, on dark claret ground with "tiger-skin" motifs. WARP: wool; ivory; S10; fine. Density: 61 warps/dm. WEFT: yak under hair (?); dark brown; Z1; loose and thick. Two parallel shoots in a unit. Density: 32 units/ dm. PILE: wool; Z6 (dark claret); otherwise Z3. Height: 4 mm. BASIC LOOPS: single-level weave; basic element: sym. Open loops on 1 warp, with 1 warp in between. IRREGULARITIES: all-over offset. LOOPING DENSITY: 30 (horiz.) ×32 = 960 basic loops/sq dm. COLOURS (3): dark claret, red, blue. FINISH: sides: plain weft return over 1 additional warp; bottom end: 1.4 cm tabby, folded over to the back and sewn down; top end: 2 cm tabby and 1 cm looped end folded over to the back and sewn down. ADDITIONAL INFORMATION: archaic in shape and weave. Probably made to order. Comparable to C85.

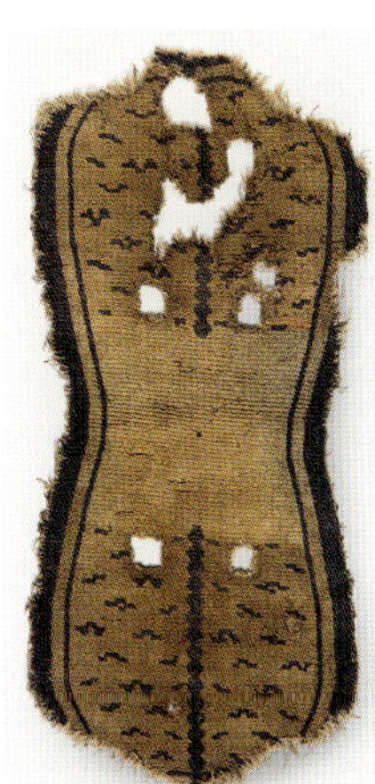

C87: ***Makden* under-saddle rug, oval**
122×58 cm. Tibet. 3rd quarter 19th century (?). PATTERN: "tiger skin", in navy-blue colour, on light camel-hair colour ground. WARP: wool; ivory; Z2S; tight twist, thick. Density: 54 warps/dm. Dropped warps' trick. WEFT: 1) wool; ivory; Z1; 2) hemp (?); brown-grey; Z2S. From one to four parallel shoots in a unit. Density: 14 units/ dm. PILE: wool, Z2S, Z3S–Z5S; very loose. Height: 5 mm. BASIC LOOPS: asym. long leg; open loops; regular asym. and sym. PAIRED: left side: asym. and sym.; right side: asym. long leg with packing bottom loop. LONG ROWS: left end: asym.; right end: asym. long leg, with packing bottom loop; in between: asym. long leg. DIAGONAL LINES: specific closed diagonal loops, on 2 warps; across the weft loops; diagonal loops; open loops in different to basic loop colour; offset effect by long-leg ends. OTHER IRREGULARITIES: dropped warp trick (sides), packing; sharing combined with packing; offsetting. LOOPING DENSITY: 27 (horiz.) ×14 = 378 basic loops/sq dm. COLOURS (2): light camel-hair colour (faded red, fuchsin [?]), navy-blue. FINISH: sides: complicated unusual type, with interwoven and floating side wefts, hemp in particular; ends: missing. ADDITIONAL INFORMATION: rarely identified shape and pattern. Archaic structural details. Navy-blue pile threads dyed after plying of yarns, thus motley. Heavily damaged by intensive wear, with losses; square holes for saddle belts.

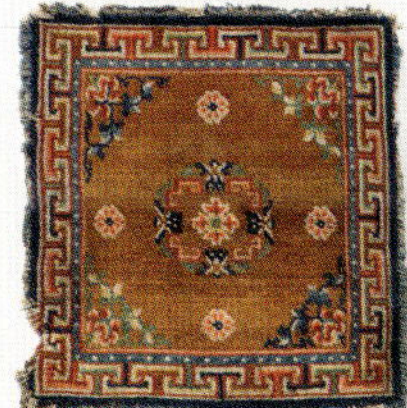

C88: ***Khagangma* sitting rug**
82×77 cm. Tibet. 19th century. PATTERN: small central rosette, four 8-petal rosettes, corner blossoming branches on rust-brown ground; T-border; inner pearl border. WARP: wool; ivory/grey/brown mix; Z2S. Density: 60 warps/dm. WEFT: wool; ivory/grey/brown mix; Z3. One shoot in a unit. Density: 20 units/dm. PILE: wool; Z2 (light purple, rose, orange-red, sky, dark blue); otherwise Z3; excellent quality. Height: 4–5 mm (ivory); 5 mm (cherry); 5–6 mm (rose, dark blue); 6–7 mm (yellow); 7 mm (orange-red, sky, rust-brown); 7–8 mm (light purple, turquoise-green). BASIC LOOPS: asym. open left, with long leg; open loops, on 1 warp; regular sym. SINGLES: asym. long leg, with packing bottom loop. PAIRED: left side: sym.; right side: asym. long leg, with packing bottom loop. LONG ROWS: left end: sym.; right end: asym. long leg, with packing bottom loop; in between: asym. long leg. IRREGULARITIES: packing; sharing combined with packing. Numerous sym. loops over wefts, in curved lines in particular. LOOPING DENSITY: 30 (horiz.) ×20 = 600 basic loops/sq dm. COLOURS (10): light purple, cherry, rose, orange-red, yellow, turquoise-green (with yellow fibres), dark blue, sky, rust-brown, ivory. FINISH: sides: 1.5 cm tabby; bottom: 3 cm tabby, warp return makes loops; top: remains of tabby, folded over to the back and sewn down. Remains of made by asym. loops sky-colour fringe, in asym. loops, all over the perimeter. ADDITIONAL INFORMATION: motley colours. Worn, with losses of edges; uneven pile wear.

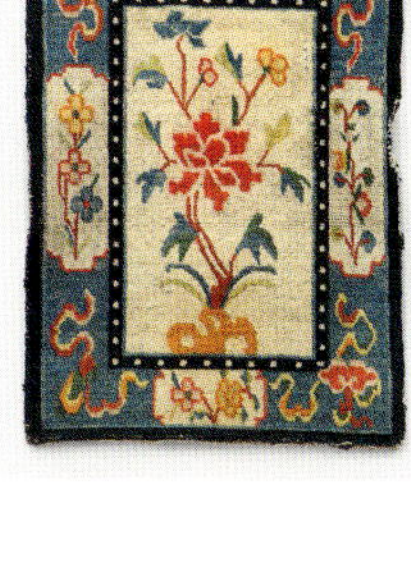

C89: ***Masho* over-saddle rug**
80×58 cm. Tibet. Late 19th (?) century. PATTERN: blossoming flower, on ivory background; main border: 4 flower cartouches and Buddhist symbols; inner pearl border. WARP: wool; ivory and ivory plied together with off-blue; Z2S; very fine. Depressed. Density: 74 warps/ dm. WEFT: wool; ivory and off-blue mix; Z4. Two parallel shoots in a unit. Density: 22 units/dm. PILE: wool; Z2; good quality. Height: 3 mm (light sky); 4 mm (bright red, yellow, light turquoise, sky); 6 mm (dark blue); otherwise 5 mm. BASIC LOOPS: asym. long leg; open loops; regular sym. and asym. SINGLES: asym.; with packing bottom loop. PAIRED: left side: asym. right side: sym., with packing bottom loop. LONG ROWS: left end: sym., of small size, and packing bottom loop; right end: asym. long leg, with packing bottom loop; in between: asym. long leg. CURVED LINES: "dancing warps" by method of inserting and dropping of additional warps; change of angle of depression. OTHER IRREGULARITIES: additional warps; offset, packing; regular sharing; sharing combined with packing; offset effect. LOOPING DENSITY: 37 (horiz.) ×22 = 814 basic loops/sq dm. COLOURS (11): bright red (shaggy), rose (faded ends), yellow, orange, green, light turquoise, light olive-green, dark blue, sky (motley), light sky, ivory. FINISH: sides: missing; bottom: 1 cm tabby, warp return loops. ADDITIONAL INFORMATION: very complicated, beautiful and highly professional weave, comparable to C36, C73, etc. The pattern probably represents an early canon in the "blossoming branch on ivory ground" group (see C91). Worn, particularly on the back; damaged edges, the sides especially.

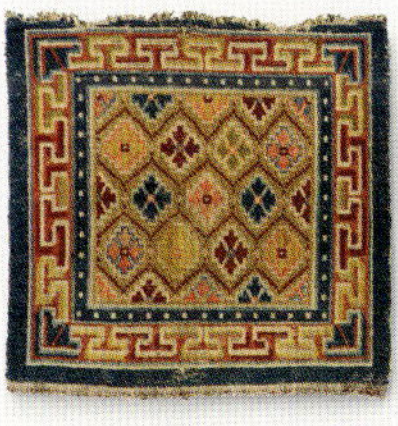

C90: ***Khagangma* sitting rug**
76×82 cm. Tibet. 20th century. PATTERN: hexagonal lattice, with four cross-arranged arrow-shaped figures. T-border; inner pearl border. WARP: wool; ivory; Z2S. Density: 58 warps/dm. WEFT: wool; some ivory, otherwise grey and dark brown; Z1. Two parallel shoots in a unit. Density: 18 units/dm. PILE: wool; Z3. Height: 2.5 mm (off-sky); 2–3 mm (gold yellow); 3 mm (pink, beige); otherwise 4 mm. BASIC LOOPS: asym. long leg; open loops; regular asym. and sym. IRREGULARITIES: diagonal loops, combined with loops. LOOPING DENSITY: 29 (horiz.) ×18 = 522 basic loops/sq dm. COLOURS (8): dark claret, cherry-red, pink (runs), gold-yellow, dark

blue, off-sky, beige, ivory. FINISH: sides: plain return over 2 additional warps; bottom: 1.5 cm tabby, warp return loops; top end: missing. ADDITIONAL INFORMATION: comparatively simple weave and pattern. Professional work, commercial product.

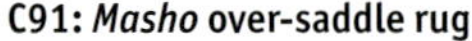

C91: *Masho* over-saddle rug

70×55 cm. Tibet. Early 20th century. PATTERN: 4 blossoming branches, on light yellow ground; main border: four flower cartouches on *swastika* meander. WARP: cotton; ivory; Z?S. Density: 42 warps/dm. WEFT: wool; ivory, also dark brown; Z1. Two parallel shoots in a unit. Density: 28 units/dm. PILE: wool; Z2; otherwise Z4 (red-rose) and Z2S (plied together sky and ivory). Height: 3 mm (pink, claret, off-sky); 2–4 mm (light yellow); 3–5 mm (off cherry-red); 4 mm (yellow, orange, olive-green); otherwise 5 mm. BASIC LOOPS: asym. long leg; open loops; regular sym. and asym. SINGLE: asym. long leg, with sym. packing bottom loop. PAIRED: left side: sym.; right side: asym. long leg, with packing bottom loop. LONG ROWS: left end: sym., of large size mainly; right end: asym. long leg, with packing bottom loop; in between: long leg asym. open left. IRREGULARITIES: packing; regular sharing and combined with packing; all-over offset. LOOPING DENSITY: 21 (horiz.) ×28 = 588 basic loops/sq dm. COLOURS (15): claret, bright red (runs), rose (faded red), off light pink (faded), orange-yellow (faded orange, runs), yellow, light yellow, dark olive-green, olive-green, off light turquoise (faded to grey), dark blue, mid-blue (faded to green-grey), brown, ivory, plied together sky and ivory. FINISH: sides: plain weft return; ends: cut. ADDITIONAL INFORMATION: early aniline period: late 19th or early 20th century. Typical for "flowers on ivory ground" group complicated weave (compare to C64, C89; also "rose, waves and mountains" type [C48, C101]).

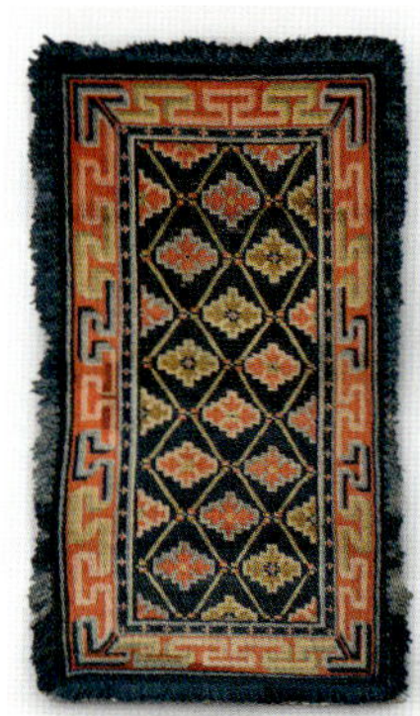

C92: *Khaden* sitting and sleeping rug

131×71 cm. Tibet. 1st half 20th century. PATTERN: diamond lattice with stepped diamonds, on dark blue background; T-border; inner pearl border. WARP: cotton; white; Z2S. Density: 68 warps/dm. WEFT: wool; light mix; Z1. Two parallel shoots in a unit. Density: 20 units/dm. PILE: wool; Z3. Height: 2 mm (ivory); otherwise 5–6 mm. BASIC LOOPS: asym. long leg; open loops; regular sym. and asym. PAIRED: left side: asym.; right side: asym. long leg, with packing bottom loop. LONG ROWS: left end: sym.; right end: asym. long leg, with packing bottom loop; in between: asym. long leg. IRREGULARITIES: packing; sharing combined with packing. LOOPING DENSITY: 34 (horiz.) ×20 = 680 basic loops/sq dm. COLOURS (9): bright red, pink, yellow, grass-green mixed with yellow, sky, off dark blue, light chestnut, sky mixed with ivory, ivory. FINISH: sides: specific edging in shape of alternating 2–3 short rows of packing loops and 3 units of wefts, with plain weft return; bottom end: 1 cm tabby, cut; top end: 2 cm tabby, folded over to the back and sewn down. All-over dark blue fringe, sym., 3–4 cm long. ADDITIONAL INFORMATION: professional work, commercial product.

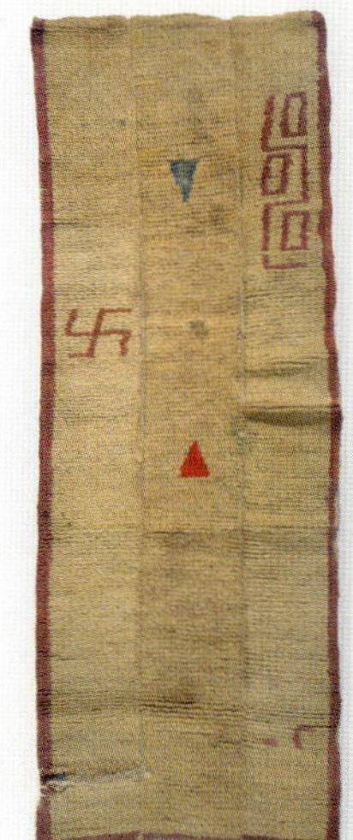

C93: *Tsuktruk khaden* sitting and sleeping rug of 3 panels

200×71.5 cm; panels: 24 cm, 23.5 cm, 24 cm. Tibet. 1st half 20th century. PATTERN: red-colour *swastika*, zigzag, with 3 ovals, and blue-colour triangle, on ivory ground; broad red line along the sides. WARP: wool; ivory Z2; fine. Density: 50 warps/dm. WEFT: wool; ivory; Z2S; loose spin and ply, fine. 14–15 shoots in a unit. Density: 13–14 units/dm. PILE: wool; Z3; of different quality. Height: 5 mm (in the middle); otherwise 10 mm. LOOPING: open sym. loops on 1 warp, with one warp in between. LOOPING DENSITY: 25 (horiz.) ×15 = 375 basic loops/sq dm. COLOURS (4): bright red, dark rose-red, off-yellow, dark sky (runs). FINISH: sides: plain return over 3 additional warps; top: cut, wrapped round (late); bottom: 1 cm tabby, warp return loops. ADDITIONAL INFORMATION: rural work. Large yellow-colour stains.

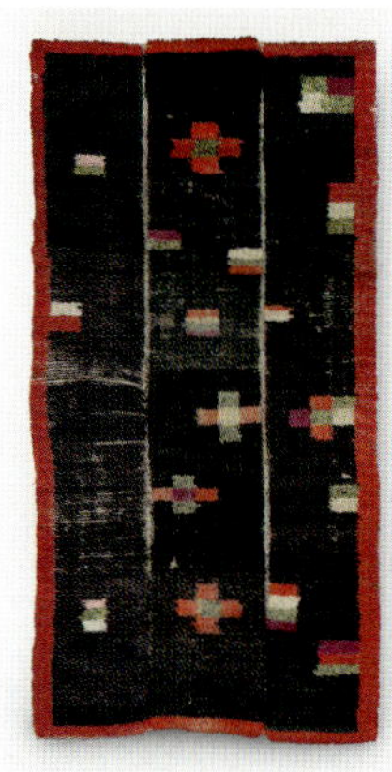

C95: *Tsuktruk khaden* sitting and sleeping rug of 3 panels

144×73 cm; panels: 25 cm, 24.5 cm, 23.5 cm. Tibet. 20th century. PATTERN: large crosses and 3-colour rectangles. WARP: wool, originally ivory; S1. Density: 24 warps/dm. WEFT: wool; originally ivory; Z1. 4 regular shoots in a unit. Density: 20 units/dm. PILE: wool; Z1 (brown-black); otherwise Z2. Height: 9 mm (black-brown); 10 mm (off-red); 10–11 mm (off grass-green); 12 mm (ivory), 15 mm (bright red); otherwise 11 mm. LOOPING: open sym. single-level loops, on 2 active warps, with 1 warp in between. LOOPING DENSITY: 8 (horiz.) ×20 = 160 basic loops/sq dm. COLOURS (8): bright red (runs), off-red (faded), crimson (runs), pink (faded), lemon-yellow (faded), off grass-green (faded), brown-black, ivory. FINISH: sides: plain weft return over 2 additional warps; bottom and top ends: 1 cm tabby, folded over to the back and sewn down. ADDITIONAL INFORMATION: rural work; running red and crimson dye.

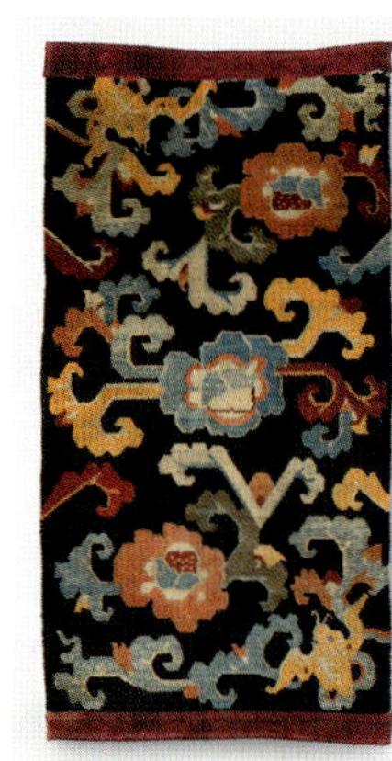

C96: *Khaden* sitting and sleeping rug for a high-ranking lama

154×85 cm. Tibet. Early 20th century (?). PATTERN: large-scale floral motifs, on black background. WARP: cotton; ivory; Z?S. Density: 30 warps/dm. WEFT: wool; light grey mix, pinkish; Z2S; very loose. Two shoots in a unit. Density: 20 units/dm. PILE: wool; Z2 (dark claret, yellow); otherwise Z3. Height: 5 mm (claret); 6 mm (off light rose, off sky); 7 mm (bright red, off faded pink, black); otherwise 8 mm. BASIC LOOPS: asym. long leg; open and closed loops; regular sym. and asym. SINGLES: asym. long leg, with packing bottom loop; otherwise: regular asym., with closed bottom loop. PAIRED: left side: sym.; right side: asym. long leg, with packing bottom loop. LONG ROWS: left end: sym.; right end: asym. long leg, with packing bottom loop; in between: asym. long leg. CURVED LINES: made by asym. singles, with closed bottom loop. OTHER IRREGULARITIES: packing; sharing combined with packing. Loops can be closed in case used with single asym. LOOPING DENSITY: 15 (horiz.) ×20 = 300 basic loops/sq dm. COLOURS (9): dark claret, bright red (faded ends), pink (totally faded), off light rose (faded to ivory, shaggy), orange, yellow, dark green (faded to green-grey), off-sky, black. FINISH: sides:

plain weft return over 2 additional warps; ends: trimmed with a band of crimson corduroy. ADDITIONAL INFORMATION: bold, impressive pattern of unusual character. No pile of ivory colour. Professional monastic (?) work. Most probably made to order.

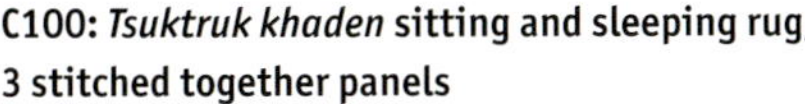

C100: *Tsuktruk khaden* sitting and sleeping rug, 3 stitched together panels

179×74 cm. Tibet. Late 19th – early 20th century. PATTERN: ivory and blue checkerboard central field; red and blue lines' framing. WARP: goat or yak under hair and hair (?); light brown and grey mix; Z2S; loose ply; rather fine. Density: 50 warps/dm. WEFT: light brown and grey mix; Z2S; week ply, but not loose. Two regular shoots in a unit (one is "hidden"). Density: 10 units/dm. PILE: wool; Z3 and Z6; loose, no ply. Height: 18 mm (red); otherwise 10–11 mm. LOOPING: single-level; open sym. loop on 1 warp, with one warp in between. LOOPING DENSITY: 30 (horiz.) × 10 = 300 basic loops/sq dm. COLOURS (3): pink-red (faded), blue (faded to grey), off violet-blue; other colours, i.e. mixture of rose, turquoise, and light blue, are totally faded out to ivory. FINISH: sides: plain weft return; ends: folded over to the back and sewn down. ADDITIONAL INFORMATION: the texture is very elastic, as if knitted. Rural work.

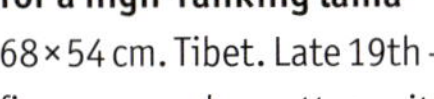

C101: *Masho* over-saddle rug

76×58 cm. Tibet. Not later than early 20th century. PATTERN: central rose, on dark blue ground, with mountains, sea and cloud motifs in the corners; main border: 4 floral cartouches, octagonal compartment, with diamonds' motifs and diagonal lattice with 4-petal motifs; inner: T-border. WARP: cotton; ivory; Z2S; fine. Deep depression. Density: 96 warps/dm. WEFT: wool; brown and ivory; Z1. Two parallel shoots in a unit. Density: 26 units/dm. PILE: wool; Z3 (pink); otherwise Z2. Height: 2 mm (beige); 5 mm (pink, mid-blue); otherwise 4 mm. BASIC LOOPS: asym. long leg; open loops; regular sym. and asym. SINGLES: regular asym., with packing bottom loop. PAIRED: left side: sym.; right side: asym. long leg, with packing bottom loop; otherwise both sym. LONG ROWS: left end: sym., often of large size;right end: asym. long leg, with packing bottom loop; in between: asym. long leg. CURVED AND DIAGONAL LINES: change of depression; loops over wefts; diagonal loops; offset by sharing. OTHER IRREGULARITIES: packing; sharing combined with packing. LOOPING DENSITY: 50 (horiz.) × 26 = 1,300 basic loops/sq dm. COLOURS (15+): dark claret, pink (faded ends), light rose, orange-rose, orange-red, gold-yellow, green, off-green (faded), sky, light sky, dark blue, mid-blue, light lilac (faded), beige, ivory, mix of orange-rose and claret. FINISH: all edges missing. ADDITIONAL INFORMATION: a masterpiece: elegant pattern, deep clean colours; excellent weave. Running red spots at the sides: traces of removed trimming. Compare pattern and structure to C48.

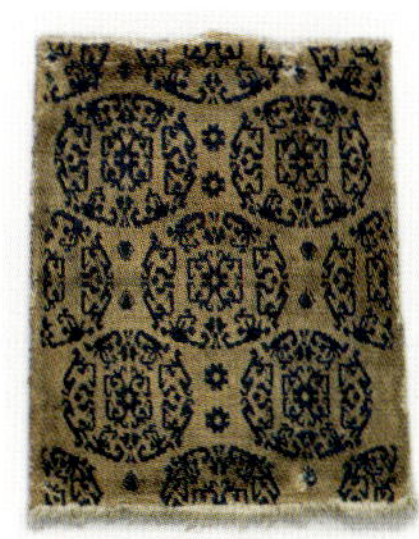

C102: *Khagangma* sitting rug for a high-ranking lama

68×54 cm. Tibet. Late 19th – early 20th century. PATTERN: five openwork rosettes, with halves and quarters. WARP: cotton; white; Z1; and wool; ivory; Z2; plied together 3S; very loose ply. Deep depression. Density: 84 warps/dm. WEFT: wool; ivory; Z2; fine; and cotton; white; Z1; thick. Three parallel shoots in a unit; otherwise yak hair (?); purple-brown, Z1; one shoot in a unit. Other variants. Density: 24 units/dm. PILE: wool; Z2; Z3. Height: 4 mm. IDENTIFIED BASIC LOOPS: asym. open left long leg, with packed bottom open loop. LOOPING DENSITY: 42 (horiz.) × 24 = 1,008 basic loops/sq dm. COLOURS: seen: black-blue and either totally faded or chemically washed out to camel-hair colour light rose, dark green, black-brown and other unrecognised pigments. FINISH: sides: plain weft return; bottom end: missing; top end: 1.5 cm tabby, folded over to the back and sewn down. ADDITIONAL INFORMATION: from the condition of the colouring, belongs to the early aniline period, for Tibet that was most probably early 20th century. The size suggests use as *masho* over-saddle rug, although it does not have typical for *masho* symmetrical damages at the sides. Central "rosette" is clumsy, other patterns have regular shapes.

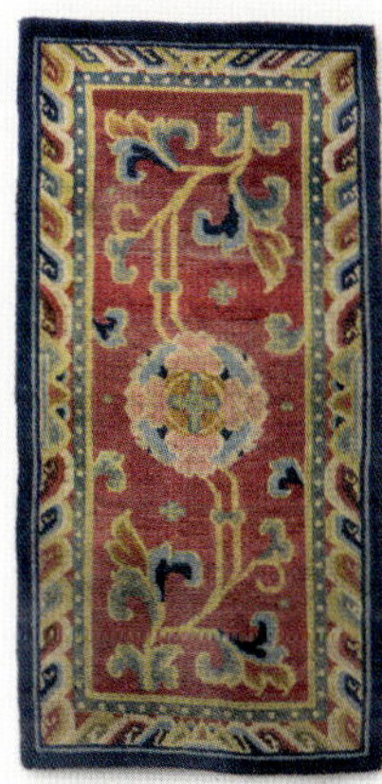

C103: *Khaden* sitting and sleeping rug (?)

156×78 cm. Tibet. 20th century. PATTERN: central rosette, with two branches, on red ground; sea waves and mountains' border, inner pearl border. WARP: wool; light mix and several dark brown; Z2S. Depressed. Density: 56 warps/dm. WEFT: wool; light grey mix; Z1. Two parallel shoots in a unit. Density: 15–16 units/dm. PILE: wool; Z2 (carmine, dark yellow, dark blue); otherwise Z3. Height: 3 mm (carmine, grass-green, ivory); 3–4 mm (yellow); 4 mm (sky, light olive, off green-sky); 6 mm (dark yellow); otherwise 5 mm. BASIC LOOPS: asym. long leg; open loops; regular sym. and asym. PAIRED: left side; sym.; right side: asym. long leg, with packing bottom loop. CURVED LINES: loops over wefts; change of depression; sharing, offset. LONG ROWS: left end: sym., often of large size; right end: asym. long leg, with packing bottom loop; in between: asym. long leg. OTHER IRREGULARITIES: packing; regular sharing and sharing combined with packing; offset. LOOPING DENSITY: 28 (horiz.) × 26 = 728 basic loops/sq dm. COLOURS (16): dark red-purple, 2 shades of carmine (Z2, Z3), 2 shades of light rose, yellow, dark yellow, grass-green fibres mixed with yellow (motley), off green-sky, off light turquoise, sky, dark blue, light olive (faded), beige, ivory, red purple plied together with rose. FINISH: plain weft return over 3 aditional warps; bottom end: 1.5 cm of tabby, warps return to make loops/frings; top end: 1.5 cm tabby, cut. ADDITIONAL INFORMATION: excellent shiny wool; superb pattern and colouring; well-designed, gracious pattern, although unusual (?) for Tibet, with Chinese "accents". Similar to other perfectly made items structure corresponds to pattern peculiarities.

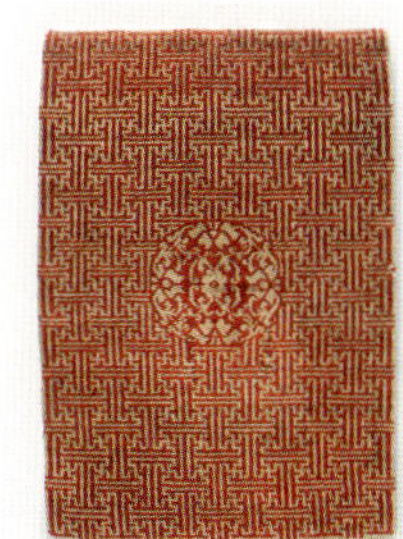

C108: *Khagangma* sitting rug for a high-ranking lama

82×58 cm. Tibet. 19th century. PATTERN: elegant claret openwork floral rosette on an all-over straight *swastika* lattice, off-rose ground. WARP: wool; ivory; Z2S; fine. Density: 78 warps/dm. WEFT: wool; ivory; Z1. Two parallel shoots in a unit. Density: 24 units/dm. PILE: wool; Z2 (claret); Z4 (off light pink); slightly shaggy. Height: 4 mm (off light pink); 5 mm (claret). BASIC LOOPS: asym.

long leg; open loops; regular sym. and asym. SINGLE LOOP: asym. long leg. PAIRED: left side: sym.; right side: asym. long leg, with packing bottom loop. LONG ROWS: left end: sym. or rather asym.; right end: asym. long leg, with packing bottom loop; in between: asym. long leg. CURVED AND DIAGONAL LINES: offset, in central medallion in particular; sym. loops over wefts; small asym. on the over-the-wefts' warps; loops with ends pointed against general pile direction. OTHER IRREGULARITIES: packing; sharing; sharing combined with packing. LOOPING DENSITY: 39 (horiz.) × 24 = 936 basic loops/sq dm. COLOURS (2): claret, off light rose. FINISH: plain weft return over 2 aditional warps; bottom end: 1 cm tabby, warps return makes fringe loops; top end: 1 cm tabby, cut. Both ends folded over to the back and sewn down. ADDITIONAL INFORMATION: professional manufacture. Another masterpiece, with simple and gracious design and weave: an example of minimalism in Tibetan carpet weaving tradition. Slightly shaggy surface speaks for a long and intensive usage.

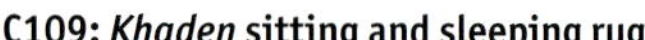

C109: *Khaden* sitting and sleeping rug

148 × 85 cm. Tibet. 1st quarter 20th century. PATTERN: diagonal lattice with cross-shaped motifs, on ivory ground. WARP: wool; ivory; Z2S. Density: 60 warps/dm. WEFT: wool; ivory; Z3. One shoot in a unit. Density: 14 units/dm. PILE: wool; Z2 (dark claret, orange, olive-green); otherwise Z3. Height: 5 mm (carmine, pink); 6 mm (dark rose, golden-yellow); 7 mm (orange, off sky-blue); 8 mm (dark green, light beige); 9 mm (dark claret). BASIC LOOPS: asym. long leg; open loops, on 1 warp; regular sym. SINGLES: asym. open left, with long leg. PAIRED: left side: sym.; right side: asym. long leg, with packing bottom loop. LONG ROWS: left end: sym.; right end: asym. long leg, with packing bottom loop; in between: asym. long leg. IRREGULARITIES: packing; sharing; sharing combined with packing. LOOPING DENSITY: 30 (horiz.) × 14 = 420 basic loops/sq dm. COLOURS (11): dark claret, carmine (faded), pink, dark rose, gold-yellow, orange, two shades of dark green (alternate), off sky-blue, light beige, ivory. FINISH: plain weft return; bottom end: 2 cm tabby, warps return make fringe loops; top end: missing. ADDITIONAL INFORMATION: model of simply woven rug, if we can speak about simplicity in terms of Tibetan carpet weaving. Probably made to order for a high-ranking lama.

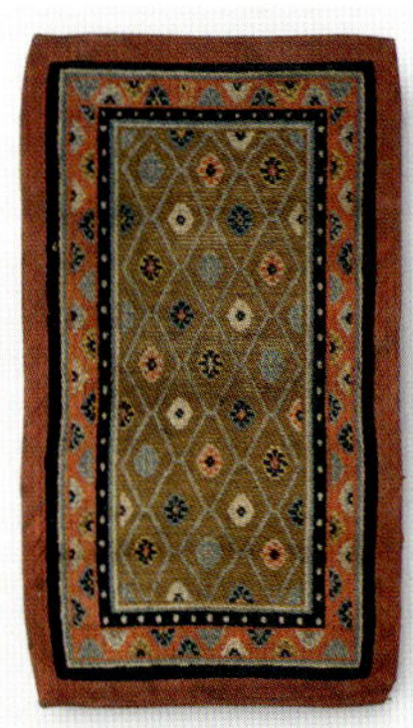

C110: *Khaden* sitting and sleeping rug

135 × 73 cm. Tibet. 20th century. PATTERN: diagonal lattice, with small rosettes, on mustard ground; broad border, with half-rosettes; inner pearl border. WARP: wool; ivory; Z2S; fine. Depression. Density: 48 warps/dm. WEFT: wool; light mix; Z1. Two parallel shoots in a unit. Density: 14 units/dm. PILE: wool; Z3 (off-sky, ivory); otherwise Z2. Height: 5 mm (off light sky); 6 mm (off sky, mustard); 7–8 mm (off light rose); 8 mm (ivory); otherwise 7 mm. BASIC LOOPS: asym. long leg; open loops; regular sym. and asym. SINGLES: asym. long leg, with sym. packing bottom loop, on 2 warps; also sometimes with asym. packing closed loop, on 1 warp, above leg's end. PAIRED: left side: small asym., sometimes with open bottom packing loop; right side: asym. long leg, with packing bottom loop. LONG ROWS: left end: sym., otherwise asym., with bottom packing loop; right end: asym. long leg, with packing bottom loop; in between: long leg asym. open left. IRREGULARITIES: packing; sharing; sharing combined with packing. LOOPING DENSITY: 24 (horiz.) × 14 = 336 basic loops/sq dm. COLOURS (9): light crimson, off light rose, orange-red, yellow, dark blue (1st bath), off-sky (2nd bath), off light sky (3rd bath), mustard, ivory. FINISH: plain weft return; ends: covered with red twill trimming; lined with ivory twill back. ADDITIONAL INFORMATION: simple rural work, most probably for commerce. Seen only on the back are tiny red loops which can be marks separating each period of work. Worn, especially in the centre.

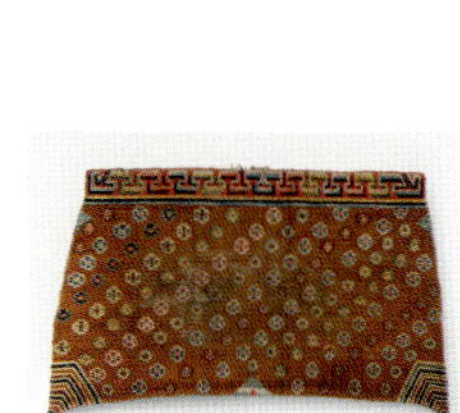

C111: Horse blanket

92 × 140/163 cm. Tibet. Ca. 1900. PATTERN: diagonal rows of small 8-petal rosettes, on rust background; "rainbow" in bottom corners and concentric triangle in between; T-motif along the upper end. WARP: cotton; ivory; Z2S. Density: 64 warps/dm. WEFT: wool; light brown mix; Z1. Two parallel shoots in a unit. Density: 20 units/dm. PILE: wool; Z3 (yellow); Z2S (rust, loose); Z3S (light rose, loose); otherwise Z2. Height: 7 mm (ivory, sky); 6 mm (off sky, mustard); 7–8 mm (off light rose); 8 mm (ivory); 9 mm (light rose, yellow); 8–10 mm (black); 9–10 mm (yellow-green); otherwise 8 mm. BASIC LOOPS: asym. long leg; open loops, on 2 warps; regular sym. SINGLE: asym. long leg, with bottom packing loop. PAIRED: left side sym.; right side: asym. long leg, with packing bottom loop. LONG ROWS: left end: sym.; right end: asym. long leg, with packing bottom loop; in between: asym. long leg. DIAGONAL LINES: offset by sharing. OTHER IRREGULARITIES: packing; sharing, sharing combined with packing. LOOPING DENSITY: 32 (horiz.) × 20 = 640 basic loops/sq dm. COLOURS (10): bright red, light rose, red-chestnut, rust, yellow, yellow-green, cold green, sky, black, ivory. FINISH: plain weft return; ends: covered with twill trimming. ADDITIONAL INFORMATION: professional regular weave; simple structure and pattern. Worn in the middle.

C113: *Khaden* sitting and sleeping rug for a high-ranking lama

163 × 83 cm. Tibet. 19th century (?). PATTERN: 8 complicated oval medallions, also ½ and ¼ along the side and in the corners, on diagonal *swastika* lattice background. WARP: cotton; ivory; Z?S. Density: 62 warps/dm. WEFT: 1) wool; ivory, also ivory mixed with brown and other shades; Z1, Z3; thick; 2) cotton; Z1; thick. Two parallel shoots in a unit. Density: 25 units/dm. PILE: wool; Z3 (purple-red, mustard); otherwise Z2. Height: 7 mm (bright red, mustard, black-green); 6–7 mm (purple-red); otherwise 6 mm. BASIC LOOPS: asym. long leg; open loops; regular sym. SINGLE: very large angled sym., with bottom packing loop; otherwise regular sym. PAIRED: left side: sym.; right side: asym. long leg, with bottom packing loop. LONG ROWS: left end: sym.; right end: asym. long leg, with packing bottom loop; in between: asym. long leg. DIAGONAL LINES: by offset. IRREGULARITIES: all-over offset; regular sharing and sharing combined with packing. LOOPING DENSITY: 32

(horiz.) ×25 = 800 basic loops/sq dm. COLOURS (10): purple-red, bright red, rose (faded ends), sky, very light sky, mustard, black-green, ivory. FINISH: weft return over 4 additional warps; bottom end: remains of loops; upper end: missing. ADDITIONAL INFORMATION: professional weave, although mistakes in pattern. Some shaggy pile yarns. Numerous variants of colour and pile material quality in wefts.

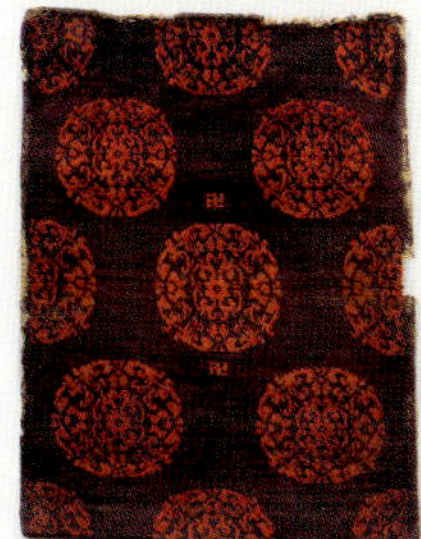

C114: *Masho* over-saddle rug for a high-ranking lama

82×60 cm. Tibet. 19th century. PATTERN: five large purple-red medallions, also ½ along the sides and ¼ in corners; on purple-blue ground. 2 tiny *swastikas*. WARP: cotton; ivory; Z4S. Density: 74 warps/dm. WEFT: ivory; wool or camel hair; Z3. One shoots in a unit. Density: 28 units/dm. PILE: wool; Z2S. Height: 2.5–3 mm (red is slightly longer). BASIC LOOPS: asym. long leg; open loops; individual. DIAGONAL LINES: diagonal loops on 1 warp. LOOPING DENSITY: 37 (horiz.) ×28 = 1,036 basic loops/sq dm. COLOURS (2): purple-red, purple-blue. FINISH: weft return over 4 additional warps; bottom end: 1.5 cm tabby, 1.3 cm long warp return loops; top end: 1 cm tabby, folded over to the back and sewn down. ADDITIONAL INFORMATION: refined piece; pattern and structural indices comparable to C108 (earlier).

C115: Long sitting rug for monastery services, fragment

165×77 cm. Tibet. Early 20th century (?). PATTERN: row of squares, with central stepped medallion in each; *swastika* main border. WARP: wool; ivory; Z3S; thick; 3 side warps: brown mélange; Z2S; finer and of different quality than ivory. Deep depression. Density: 48–50 warps/dm. WEFT: wool; ivory; Z2S. Two parallel shoots in a unit; because of deep depression we see only waving shoots. Density: 14 units/dm. PILE: wool; Z4. Height: 7 mm the longest. BASIC LOOPS: asym. long leg; open loops; regular sym. IRREGULARITIES: all pile elements are very large. LOOPING DENSITY: 24–25 (horiz.) ×14 = 336–350 basic loops/sq dm. COLOURS (10): cherry-red, pink-red (motley), rose (faded pink-orange), orange, yellow, dark grass-green, green-blue, dark blue, sky (motley), ivory. FINISH: sides: complicated weft return over three additional warps; ends: missing. ADDITIONAL INFORMATION excellent wool. All colours but blue scale and ivory are running. Monastic work (?). No proper structural description, as this was the first item I checked before I understood the details of the Tibetan manner of weaving.

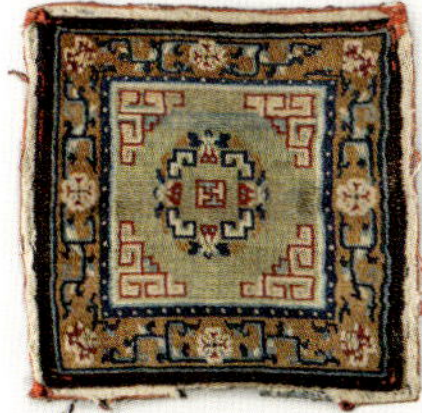

C116: *Khagangma* sitting rug

76×78 cm. Tibet. 19th century. PATTERN: delicate rosette, with central *swastika*, on light olive ground; wavy branches and rosettes border; inner pearl border. WARP: wool; ivory; Z2S. Density: 60 warps/dm. WEFT: wool; ivory; Z2S; thick and loose, excellent quality. Two parallel shoots in a unit. Density: 18 units/dm. PILE: wool; Z3 (sky, beige); otherwise Z2. Height: 5 mm (claret, dark brown); 6 mm (off light rose, light olive-green); 7 mm (ivory); otherwise 4 mm. BASIC LOOPS: asym. open left, with long leg (short end often goes practically parallel to wefts); open loops; regular sym. SINGLE: asym. long leg, with bottom packing loop. PAIRED: left side: sym.; right side: asym. long leg, with bottom loop. LONG ROWS: left end: large sym.; right end: asym. long leg, with packing bottom loop, often very large; in between: asym. long leg. DIAGONAL LINES: additional inserted parallel to wefts' thread, Z3 (length of loop basis); loops over wefts, also with upward looking ends. OTHER IRREGULARITIES: offset, in borders in particularly; regular sharing and sharing combined with packing, inserted between a loop and the main lower weft additional bits of wefts (for curving reasons); other specific tricks. LOOPING DENSITY: 32 (horiz.) ×25 = 800 basic loops/sq dm. COLOURS (8): claret, off light rose, sky (motley), dark blue, light olive-green, beige, dark brown, ivory (superb quality of wool). FINISH: all edges are covered by felt and cotton tabby lining. ADDITIONAL INFORMATION: heavily worn pile, particularly in the centre. Exclusive methods of making diagonal lines. Domestic weave.

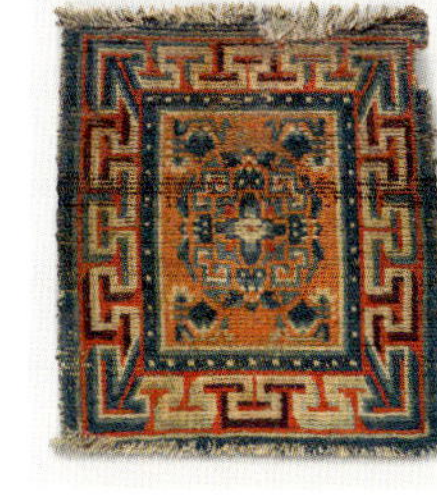

C117: *Khagangma* sitting rug

56×51 cm. Tibet. 19th century (?). PATTERN: large central rosette and corners branches, on rust-orange background; T-border; inner pearl border. WARP: cotton; ivory; Z4S. Depressed. Density: 71 warps/dm. WEFT: wool, ivory; yak hair (?), brown-black; mixture of fibres of different colours; Z1 (?); loose, very thick. Shooting: 1) two parallel shoots in a unit; 2) brown-black, with one shoot in a unit. Density: 17 units/dm. PILE: wool; Z3S. Height: worn. BASIC LOOPS: asym. long leg; open loops; regular sym. LONG ROWS: left end: sym.; right end: asym. long leg, with packing bottom loop; in between: long leg asym. open left. IDENTIFIED IRREGULARITIES: sharing, combined with packing; unusual set of wefts. LOOPING DENSITY: 35.5 (horiz.) ×17 = 603.5 basic loops/sq dm. COLOURS (11): purple-red, bright red, rose, salmon, rust-orange, light yellow, light turquoise, dark blue, dark sky, light grey-blue, ivory. FINISH: regular return; ends: missing. ADDITIONAL INFORMATION: heavily worn, losses of pile and edges, ends in particular. Professional work: masterful regular weave; excellent execution of pattern, beautiful colours.

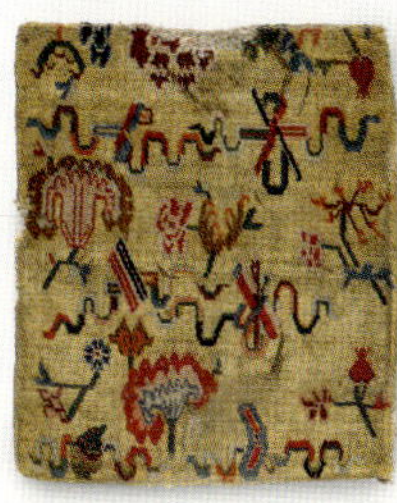

C118: *Masho* over-saddle rug for a high-ranking lama

68×58 cm. Tibet. Early 20th century. PATTERN: Buddhist symbols, on light gold-yellow ground. WARP: cotton; ivory; Z?S. Density: 100 warps/dm. WEFT: wool; ivory; Z1; thick. Two parallel shoots in a unit. Density: 50 units/dm. PILE: wool; Z2S (gold-yellow, dark cold green); otherwise Z2 and Z4. Height: 1 mm (chocolate-brown); 2 mm (deep cherry-purple, rose, light grey-sky); 3 mm (crimson, orange-red, dark cold green, off mid-blue); 4 mm (olive-grey); 5 mm (gold-yellow, dark blue). BASIC LOOPS: asym. long leg; open loops; regular sym. SINGLE: sym., regularly diagonal. PAIRED: left side: sym.; right side: asym. long leg, with bottom loop. LONG ROWS: left end: large sym.; right end: asym. long leg, with packing bottom loop; in between: asym. long leg. DIAGONAL LINES: loops over wefts; diagonal, in singles and initial in a row sym. loops' in particular. OTHER IRREGULARITIES: all-over offset, by different tricks; sharing; regular packing and combined with sharing. COLOURS (12): deep cherry-purple, crimson (runs), rose, orange-red, gold-yellow, dark cold green, light green-sky, dark blue, off mid-blue, olive-grey, chocolate-brown, ivory. FINISH: sides: regular weft return over 7 additional warps; bottom end: 1.5 cm tabby, warps make fringe loops; upper end: cut and sewn down. ADDITIONAL INFORMATION: heavily worn pile; felt patch. Exclusive pattern and colouring. Professional weave, with rare and individual tricks.

C119: Sculptured horse crupper rug

49×52 cm. Tibet. 19th century. PATTERN: large round rosette in upper part, two lotuses below; mountain peaks, sea sprays' motif at the bottom and the sides. WARP: wool; ivory and light mix (different quality and thickness; ivory is finer); Z2S; fine. Depressed. Density: 60 warps/dm. WEFT: wool; light mix; Z2S. Two parallel shoots in a unit. Density: 19 units/dm. PILE: wool and camel hair (?); Z2 (soft brown), Z2, Z4 (claret); Z3 (pink, light yellow, olive-brown, ivory), Z3, Z6 (off-sky); otherwise Z4 (other variants possible). Height: 3 mm (light grey, ivory); 3–4 mm (deep blue, olive-brown); 4–5 (claret, off light sky); 6 mm (dark rose); otherwise 4 mm. BASIC LOOPS: asym. long leg; open loops; regular sym. and asym. SINGLE: asym.; also asym. with packing bottom loop; otherwise, seldom sym. LONG ROWS: left end: sym.; right end: asym. long leg, with packing bottom loop; in between: long leg asym. open left. DIAGONAL AND CURVED LINES: usage of thick, Z4 and Z6 loops to angle the neighbouring fine elements (in this case rose colour); sharing of loops of different colours; change of angle of depression; additional loops. OTHER IRREGULARITIES: sharing, packing; areas with all-over offset, by sharing (in rosette in particular); carving effect. LOOPING DENSITY: 30 (horiz.) ×19 = 570 basic loops/sq dm. COLOURS (16): sheep wool: dark claret, dark rose, rose, off light rose, light yellow, light emerald-green, sky-green, turquoise, off light turquoise, deep blue, sky; camel down: soft brown, olive-brown, 2 shades of light grey, ivory. FINISH: all edges and folded over to the back and sewn down (late finish [?]). ADDITIONAL INFORMATION: excellent wool; heavily worn pile. Exclusive pattern and colouring.

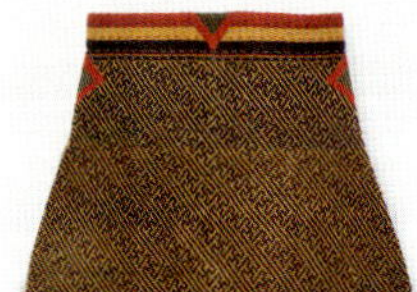

C120: Horse blanket

102×95/141 cm. Tibet. 19th or early 20th century. PATTERN: diaper motif, of linked *swastikas*. Black, yellow and red bands along the upper end. Single triangles at both sides and upper end band. WARP: wool or camel hair; dark ivory; Z2S. Density: 64 warps/dm. WEFT: identical to warps: wool or camel hair, dark ivory (continuation of warps, which are released thanks to the trapping sides' narrowing); Z2S. Density: 22 units/dm (for details see "additional information" below). PILE: wool; Z3 (bright red); otherwise Z2. Height: 5 mm (bright red, dark green); otherwise 6 mm. BASIC LOOPS: asym. long leg; open loops; regular sym. SINGLE: sym., with packing bottom loop. PAIRED: (very few) left side: sym.; right side: asym. long leg. LONG ROWS: left end: sym.; right end: asym. long leg, with packing bottom loop; in between: asym. long leg. DIAGONAL LINES: loops over wefts; diagonal looping; mainly by all over offset, determined by the applied manner of using released warps as wefts (see "additional information"). OTHER IRREGULARITIES: number of warps reduces by one after each 3–4 rows of loops to produce a one-warp offset; sharing, packing, sharing combined with packing. LOOPING DENSITY: 32 (horiz.) × 22 = 704 basic loops/sq dm. COLOURS (4): bright red, dark gold-yellow (shaggy), dark green, black (shaggy). FINISH: sides: weft return; in diagonal parts loose warps enter the shed and work as wefts; bottom end: 1.5 cm tabby, warps make fringe loops; upper end: 1.5 cm tabby, cut. ADDITIONAL INFORMATION: number of warps reduces by one, thus knots get one-warp offset.

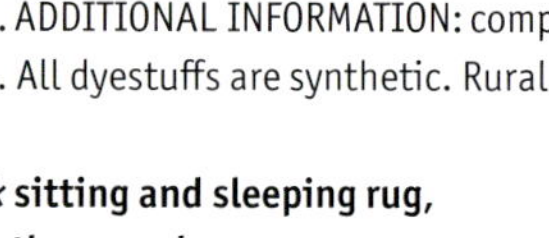

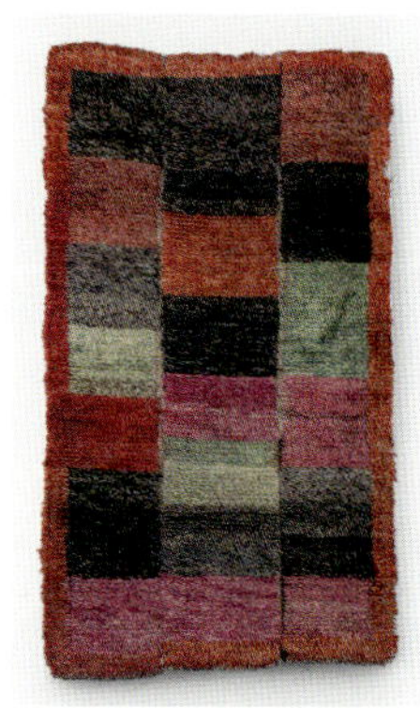

C121: *Tsuktruk*, 3 stitched together panels

136×77 cm; panels: 26 cm, 26 cm, 25 cm. Tibet. 20th century. PATTERN: 3 rows of large squares, of different colours; off-red framing. WARP: wool (?); ivory; S1; very fine and elastic. WEFT: wool; ivory and dark brown; Z1; loose; 4–6 shoots in a unit. PILE: wool; Z3. Height: ca. 20 mm. LOOPING: single-level open sym. loops, on 1 warp, with one warp in between. COLOURS (8): crimson, claret, red, off-red, green, off-blue, grey, ivory. FINISH: sides: plain weft return; ends: folded over to the back and sewn down. ADDITIONAL INFORMATION: comparable to C79 and C95. All dyestuffs are synthetic. Rural work.

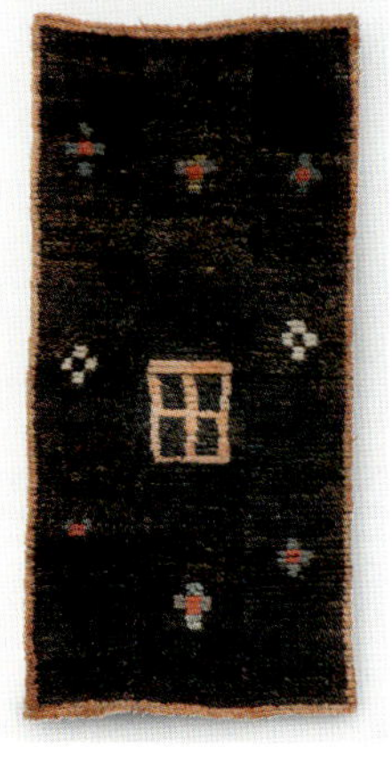

C122: *Tsuktruk* sitting and sleeping rug, 3 stitched together panels

139×63 cm; panels: 21 cm, 21 cm, 21 cm. Tibet. Early 20th century (?). PATTERN: 4-checks square in the middle, spare crosses, on black-blue ground; motley orange-red frame. WARP: wool (?); ivory; S2; very fine and strong. Density: 56 warps/dm. WEFT: wool (?); ivory; S2; fine and strong. Density: 17 units/dm: 9–12 shoots in left-side panel unit; 7–10 in central; 16–18 in right-side panel. PILE: wool; Z2, Z3 (orange), Z4, also without spin (grass-green, ivory/sky). Height: 10 mm (orange, grass-green, green, lilac); 15 mm (bright red, orange, electric blue). LOOPING: single-level sym. open loops; variants: 1) on 2 and 3 warps, with no gaps in between; 2) on 1 and 2 warps, with 1 warp in between; 3) on 1 warp, with 1 warp in between. COLOURS (9): bright red, orange, grass-green, green, electric blue, black-blue (runs), grey, ivory/sky, ivory. FINISH: sides: plain weft return; bottom end: 2 cm tabby; top end: 1 cm tabby; folded over to the back and sewn down. ADDITIONAL INFORMATION: comparable to C79, C95, C121 in particular, although it appears to be much earlier. Rural work.

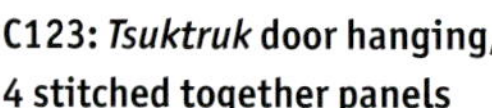

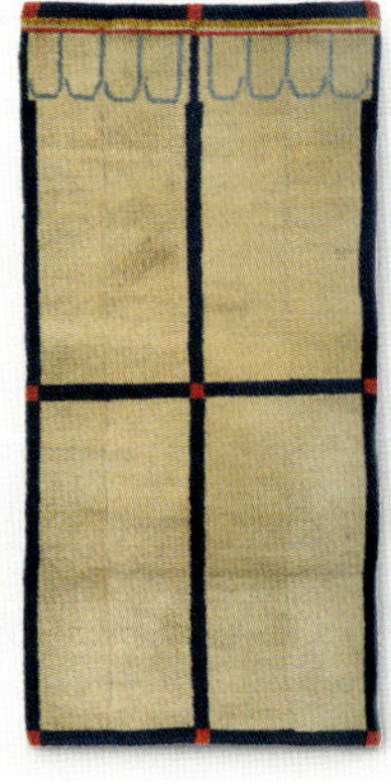

C123: *Tsuktruk* door hanging, 4 stitched together panels

155×75 cm; panels: 19 cm, 18.5 cm, 18.5 cm, 19 cm. Tibet. 20th century. PATTERN: straight dark blue cross on ivory ground; lambrequin pattern along the top end. WARP: wool; ivory; S1; very fine. Density: 56 warps/dm. WEFT: cotton and wool (?); white; flat unspun strands, excellent quality. 1 shoot in a unit. Density: 4–6 units/dm. PILE: wool; Z3. Height: 5 mm (ivory in the centre), 7 mm (dark blue in the centre); 9 mm (ivory at the sides); 10 mm (crimson-red, gold-yellow, sky-blue); 11 mm (dark blue at the sides). LOOPING: single-level open loop on 1 warp, with 1 warp in between; all-over offset. LOOPING DENSITY: 28×4–6 = 112–168 knots/dm. COLOURS (5): crimson-red, gold-yellow, sky-blue, dark blue, ivory. FINISH: sides: plain weft return; ends: folded over to the back and sewn down. ADDITIONAL INFORMATION: regular professional weave; rare type, should be a door hanging for a yurt or for a stationary house.

C125: *Khagangma* sitting rug

72×70 cm. Tibet. 19th century. PATTERN: central rosette and four creatures, on claret background; border with Buddhist symbols; narrow: key-motif; inner pearl border. WARP: cotton; white; Z2S. Depressed. Density: 40 warps/ dm. WEFT: wool; 1) rose, Z1; 2) brown mixed with ivory, Z2S. Two parallel shoots in a unit. Density: 26 units/dm. PILE: wool; Z3 (rose, mustard, ivory); otherwise Z2. Height: 6 mm (pink, turquoise-green); 6–7 mm (mustard); otherwise 7 mm. BASIC LOOPS: asym. long leg; open and closed loops, on 1 warp; regular sym. SINGLE: closed loops on one warp. PAIRED: left side: large sym.; right side: asym. long leg, with packing bottom loop. LONG ROWS: left end: large sym.; right end: asym. long leg, with packing bottom loop; in between: asym. long leg. CURVED LINES: pushing loops; sym. loops over wefts; change of depression. OTHER IRREGULARITIES: packing; sharing, also sharing combined with packing; offsetting; small regular asym.; short lines of eccentric weave. LOOPING DENSITY: 20 (horiz.) ×26 = 520 basic loops/sq dm. COLOURS (9): claret, pink (faded bright red), rose (faded ends), camel (faded yellow), turquoise-green (faded green, shaggy), dark blue, sky, mustard, ivory. FINISH: regular weft return over 1 additional warp; ends: cut. ADDITIONAL INFORMATION: practically unused, although missing a large part of the left-side border; some home-made restoration. Excellent professional weave; elegant well-balanced pattern and colouring.

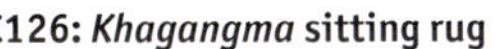

C126: *Khagangma* sitting rug

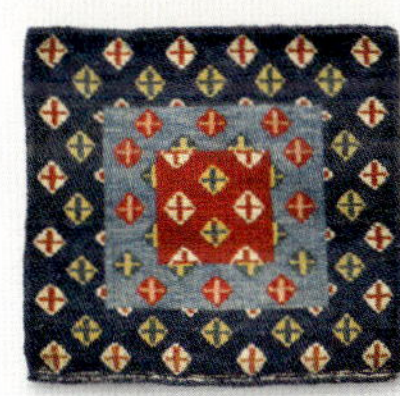

61×64 cm. Tibet. 19th century. PATTERN: concentric squares of dark blue, off grey-sky and central scarlet-red colour, with regular rows of diagonal diamonds with small straight crosses and half-crosses inside. WARP: wool; ivory; Z2S; fine, excellent quality. Depressed. Density: 60 warps/dm. WEFT: wool; ivory; Z1. Two parallel shoots in a unit. Density: 18 units/dm. PILE: wool; Z2S; also Z4 (scarlet-red, ivory); some with loose ply. BASIC LOOPS: asym. long leg; open loops; regular asym. and sym. SINGLES: asym. long leg, with packing bottom loop. PAIRED: left side: sym.; right side: asym. long leg, with packing bottom loop. LONG ROWS: left end: sym.; right end: asym. long leg, with packing bottom loop; in between: asym. long leg, some with additional bottom loop. IRREGULARITIES: sharing combined with packing. LOOPING DENSITY: 30 (horiz.) × 18 = 540 basic loops/sq dm. COLOURS (7): scarlet-red, pink (faded), yellow (faded), dark green-blue (abrash), dark blue (abrash), light grey-sky (abrash, faded), silver-ivory. FINISH: sides: plain weft return; bottom end: 1.2 cm tabby; top end: 1.5 cm tabby, folded over to the back and sewn down. ADDITIONAL INFORMATION: original lining missing. Restoration of ends: 1.5 cm of the top and 1 cm of the bottom, on Z2S warps. A masterpiece: excellent regular weave and archaic pattern. Pair to C33.

C127: *Masho* over-saddle rug for a high-ranking lama

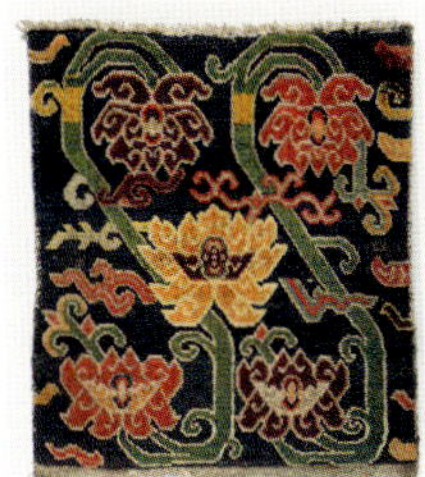

64×57 cm. Tibet. 19th century. PATTERN: 5 lotuses on curving stems, on off dark blue background. WARP: cotton; ivory; Z?S. Deeply depressed. Density: 68 warps/dm. WEFT: wool; ivory and variants of mix; Z1. Two parallel shoots in a unit. Density: 27 units/dm. PILE: wool, camel hair (?); Z2, Z4 (some single loops). Height: 3 mm (dark blue); 5 mm (light rose); 6 mm (orange); 6 mm (deep purple, light camel hair-grey); otherwise 4 mm. BASIC LOOPS: asym. long leg; open loops; regular asym. and sym. SINGLES: asym. long leg, with packing bottom loop. PAIRED: left side: sym.; right side: asym. long leg, with packing bottom loop. LONG ROWS: left end: sym.; right end: asym. long leg, with packing bottom loop; in between: asym. long leg. CURVED LINES: change of depression; sym. over weft loops; very large diagonal sym. OTHER IRREGULARITIES: sharing, and sharing combined with packing; large sym. single-level knots on 1 front warp (unseen from the back); LOOPING DENSITY: 34 (horiz.) × 27 = 918 basic loops/sq dm. COLOURS (10): deep purple, red-rose (shaggy), light rose, orange, yellow, yellow-green (motley), turquoise, dark blue (abrash); light camel hair-grey (camel hair), ivory. FINISH: sides: missing; bottom end: warp return loops; top end: cut. ADDITIONAL INFORMATION: another example of individualistic monastic (?) work. Home-made dyeing (motley shades and abrash of cold colour scale). Strong wear on the front and some on the back, which was protected by lining, now missing.

C129: *Khaden* sitting and sleeping rug

130×66 cm. Tibet. Mid-19th century. PATTERN: 2 stepped medallions, "palms" and *swastikas*, on mid-blue ground; T-border; inner pearl border. WARP: wool; light mix; Z2S. Density: 56 warps/dm. WEFT: wool; rust and light grey mix; Z2S. Two parallel shoots in a unit. Density: 16 units/dm. PILE: wool, yak hair; Z2, Z4 (light yellow); Z2 (mid-blue); Z2S (black-blue, black-brown); Z3S (dark orange-red, light sky); Z4S (ivory). Height: 3 mm (dark blue); 5 mm (light rose), 6 mm (orange); 6 mm (deep purple, light camel-grey); otherwise 4 mm. BASIC LOOPS: asym. long leg; open loops, on 1 and 2 warps; regular asym. and sym. SINGLES: regular asym. or asym. with packing bottom loop on 2 warps. PAIRED: left side: large asym. loop; right side: asym. long leg, with packing bottom loop. LONG ROWS: right end: asym. long leg, with packing bottom loop; left end: asym.; in between: asym. long leg, mainly with bottom loops. IRREGULARITIES: sharing combined with packing, all large knots and loops are angled because of their size; also regular asym. are pushed from below by loops on 1 warp and look asym. if shared, although they are not. LOOPING DENSITY: 28 (horiz.) × 16 = 448 basic loops/sq dm. COLOURS (8): dark orange-red, light orange-red, light yellow, mid-blue (motley), black-blue, black-brown (yak, ruined), ivory, plied together sky and mid-blue. FINISH: sides: regular weft return over 2 additional warps; bottom end: 1.5 cm tabby, warp return loops; top end: cut. ADDITIONAL INFORMATION: belongs to the large loop cluster. Numerous individual tricks, including inserted loops on 1 and 2 warps, etc., there are so many that it is impossible to describe them all. Pile is too short for loops of the size, thus many long legs "jump out" from the texture, in left border in particular. In spite of all that the rug looks very attractive and definitely belongs to a classic artistic type of *khadens*, with "central medallion and palms" pattern.

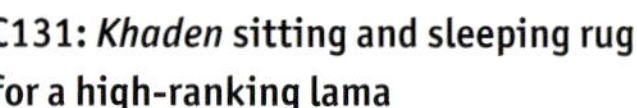

C131: *Khaden* sitting and sleeping rug for a high-ranking lama

160×86 cm. Tibet. Ca. 1900. PATTERN: dragons, phoenixes and large lotus, on black-blue ground. WARP: cotton; white; Z?S. Depressed. WEFT: wool; ivory; Z1. Two parallel shoots in a unit. PILE: wool; Z3 (ivory); otherwise Z2. Height: 4 mm (green-blue); 5 mm (off green-turquoise, sky, black-blue); 5–6 mm (dark cold green); otherwise 6 mm. BASIC LOOPS: asym. long leg; open and closed loops, on 1 warp; regular sym. and asym. LONG ROWS: left end: large sym. or asym.; right end: asym. long leg, with packing bottom loop; in between: asym. long leg. CURVED LINES: loops over wefts; loops on one warp, sharing, change of depression, eccentric weave, etc. OTHER IRREGULARITIES: packing; sharing combined with packing; offsetting. COLOURS (12): dark terracotta (shaggy), bright red (runs), light rose, light beige-rose, yellow, off green-turquoise (with yellow fibres), dark cold green, green dark blue (shaggy, looks blue from the front and green from the back), sky, light sky, black-blue (very shaggy), ivory. FINISH: regular weft return; bottom end: 2 cm of tabby, warp return makes loops; top end: 1.5 cm tabby, folded over to the back and sewn down. ADDITIONAL INFORMATION: structural description is not complete. Excellent professional weave and pattern, monastic work.

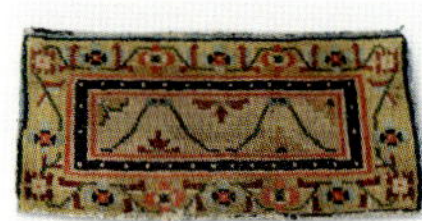

C135: Cushion cover (?)

24×53–57 cm. Tibet. Early 20th century. PATTERN: detail of diagonal lattice composition, with halves of cross-shaped motifs, on off-yellow ground; border: floral meander. WARP: cotton; white; Z?S. Depressed. Density: 74 warps/dm. WEFT: wool; ivory and light mix; Z1; very thick. Two parallel shoots in a unit. Density: 24 units/dm. PILE: wool; Z4 (mustard); otherwise Z3. BASIC LOOPS: asym. long leg; open and closed loops, on 1 warp; regular sym. LONG ROWS: left end: sym.; right end: asym. long leg, with packing bottom loop; in between: asym. long leg. IRREGULARITIES: packing; sharing combined with packing; offsetting; loops over wefts. LOOPING DENSITY: 37 (horiz.) × 24 = 888 knots/sq dm. COLOURS (11): claret, orange-red, light rose, off light rose, light apricot, yellow, dull green, off light sky, dark blue, light mustard, ivory. FINISH: missing. ADDITIONAL INFORMATION: All loops are extremely tiny while yarns are shaggy, thus it is impossible to identify all details of structure. All colours faded except for claret, orange-red, dull green and dark blue. Rural work (?).

C137: *Khaden* sitting and sleeping rug for a high-ranking lama (?)

170×93 cm. Tibet. 2nd quarter 19th century. PATTERN: 3 peonies and waving sea, on dark blue ground. WARP: cotton; white; Z?S. Depressed. Density: 82 warps/dm. WEFT: wool; light mix; Z1. Two parallel shoots in a unit. Density: 22 units/dm. PILE: wool; Z3 (light rose); otherwise Z2. Height: 4 mm (light rose, yellow, light grey-turquoise, dark blue, dark-cacao); 6 mm (mid-blue, ivory); 5–6 mm (sky); otherwise 5 mm. BASIC LOOPS: asym. long leg; open and closed loops, on 1 warp; regular sym.; asym. on 1 warp. PAIRED: left side: regular asym.; right side: small-size asym. long leg, with packing bottom loop: LONG ROWS: left end: large sym. or asym.; right end: asym. long leg, with packing bottom loop; in between: asym. long leg. CURVED LINES: loops over wefts; loops on one warp, change of depression and size of loops. OTHER IRREGULARITIES: packing; sharing combined with packing. LOOPING DENSITY: 41 × 22 = 902 basic loops/sq dm. COLOURS (16): dark pink, light rose (faded), off light rose, orange (shaggy), yellow (faded), light turquoise-green, turquoise, light sky, sky, off light grey-sky, mid-blue, dark blue, dark cacao (faded), light grey (faded fuchsin), ivory, sky (Z1) plied together with pink (Z1). FINISH: all edges are trimmed with lining. ADDITIONAL INFORMATION: Blue-green scale can contain additional shades. Fuchsin dye points to 1860s. No running dye-stuffs: the impression arises because of very light, nearly colourless shades of sky and rose. Excellent weave. Rare pattern.

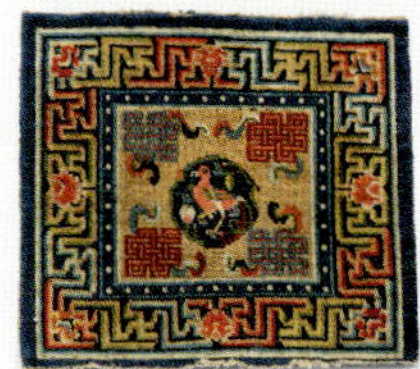

C141: *Khagangma* sitting rug

63×73 cm. Tibet. Late 19th – early 20th century. PATTERN: small round central medallion, with bird image; endless knots (*gerehs*) in corners, on camel-hair colour ground; *swastika* meander and small roses' main border; inner pearl border. WARP: cotton; ivory; Z?S. Density: 72 warps/dm. WEFT: wool; ivory; Z1 and mix, plied; shaggy. Two parallel shoots in a unit. Density: 23 units/ dm. PILE: wool; Z2. Height: 3 mm (off light turquoise, dark blue); 3–5 mm (orange-red); 5 mm (claret); otherwise 4 mm. BASIC LOOPS: asym. long leg; open loops; regular sym.; asym. on 1 warp. SINGLES: asym. long leg loop, with packing bottom loop. PAIRED: left side: sym.; right side: asym. long leg, with packing bottom loop. LONG ROWS: left end: large sym.; right end: asym. long leg, with packing bottom loop; in between: asym. long leg. CURVED LINES: asym. loops over wefts. OTHER IRREGULARITIES: packing; sharing combined with packing. LOOPING DENSITY: 36 × 23 = 828 basic loops/sq dm. COLOURS (10): claret, rose, orange-red, yellow, light olive-green, off light turquoise, dark blue, sky, camel hair, ivory. FINISH: sides: regular weft return over side warps; trimmed with ivory woollen textile; ends: cut. ADDITIONAL INFORMATION: absolutely charming pattern, regular professional weave. Worn out from the front, although with no losses, due to proper balance of pile height and looping density. The back was covered by lining, thus is in good condition, although there are some bottom end losses.

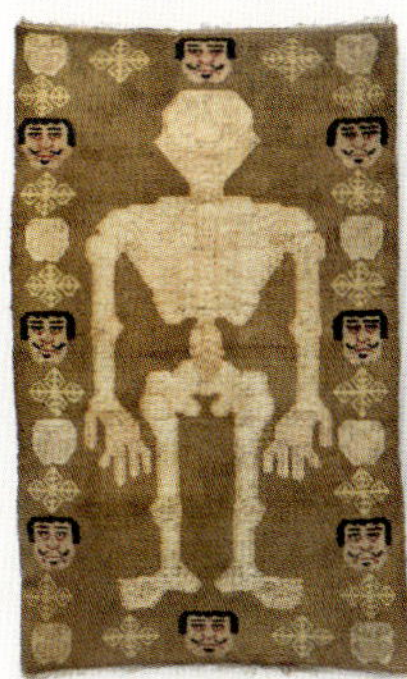

C142: *Khaden* sleeping and sitting rug (?)

126×77 cm. Central Asia (?). Early 20th century. PATTERN: Tantric subject: central skeleton image; masks, mans' heads and doubled *vajras* along the edges. WARP: cotton; Z?S. Density: 56 warps/dm. WEFT: cotton; Z2, Z3. Two parallel shoots in a unit. Density: 25 units/dm. PILE: pashmina (?); Z3 (yellow); otherwise Z4. Height: 4 mm. BASIC KNOT: asym. open left. IRREGULARITIES: offset (mainly in depictions of palms, knees and feet). KNOT DENSITY: 28×23 = 672 knots/sq dm. COLOURS (7): carmine, pink, 2 shades of rose (one totally faded), off rose, light yellow (faded), ivory. FINISH: sides: regular weft return; bottom end: missing; top end: 5 cm tabby. ADDITIONAL INFORMATION: bottom part heavily worn; upper part totally matted (camel-hair undercoat or pashmina [?]).

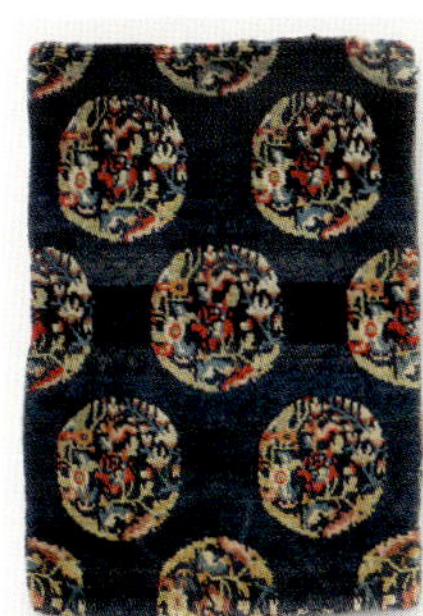

C143: *Masho* over-saddle rug for a high-ranking lama

82×55 cm. Tibet. 19th century (?). PATTERN: 5 floral rosettes, with ½ and ¼, on dark blue ground. WARP: wool; Z2S; fine. Density: ca. 90 warps/dm. WEFT: wool; light mix; Z1. Two parallel shoots in a unit. Density: 24 units/dm. PILE: wool; Z3 (ivory); otherwise Z2. Height: 6 mm (orange); 6–7 mm (olive-green, dark blue); 7 mm (rose, brownish-red, ivory); 7–8 mm (sky); 8 mm (bright red, yellow). BASIC LOOPS: asym. long leg; open loops; regular sym. and asym. SINGLES: sym. PAIRED: left regular asym.; right: asym. long leg, with packing bottom loop. LONG ROWS: left end: sym.; right end: asym. long leg, with packing bottom loop; in between: asym. long leg. CURVED LINES: loops' ends point upwards; all over packing loops and loops over wefts; additional loops at the beginning and at the end of lines of colour units. OTHER IRREGULARITIES: packing; sharing combined with packing. KNOT Density: 36×23 = 828 knots/sq dm. COLOURS (9): bright red, brownish-red, rose, orange, yellow, olive-green, sky, dark blue, ivory. FINISH: sides: regular weft return; trimmed with ivory wool; ends: cut. ADDITIONAL INFORMATION: excellent weave, individual tricks for making curving lines. Difference in colouring of the crossover central band suggests its heavy damage and reweaving. This cannot be stated for sure because from the back the rug is completely closed by lining. The latter also hampered the proper study of density and other structural parameters. Blue scale is slightly motley.

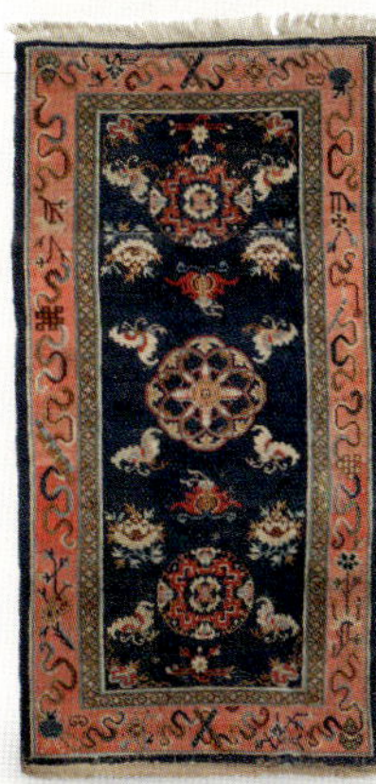

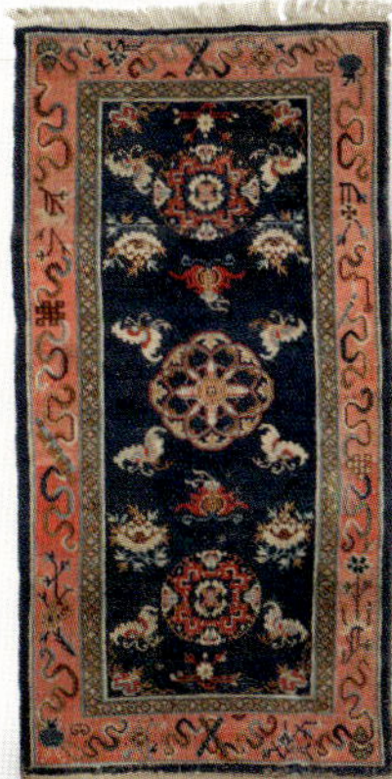

C145: *Khaden* sitting and sleeping rug

165×80 cm. Tibet. Late 19th century. PATTERN: 3 round medallions and pairs of butterflies, on dark blue ground; main border: Buddhist symbols, on rose ground; inner: offset rows of small crosses. WARP: wool; ivory; Z2S; fine, excellent quality. Depression. Density: 76 warps/dm. WEFT: wool; light mix and brown; Z1; fine. Two parallel shoots in a unit. PILE: wool; Z3 (rose, sky); otherwise Z2; also Z4 and Z6 to make extra large loops. Height: 3 mm (dark red-purple, yellow, ivory); otherwise 2 mm. BASIC LOOPS: asym. long leg; open loops; regular sym. SINGLES: sym., large, with packing bottom loop. PAIRED: left side: regular sym.; right side: asym. long leg, with packing bottom loop. LONG ROWS: left end: sym.; right end: asym. long leg, with packing bottom loop; in between: asym. long leg. CURVED LINES: asym. loops over wefts, otherwise large angled Z4 and Z6 sym. loops; also change of depression. OTHER IRREGULARITIES: packing; sharing combined with packing; offset by missed warps trick and loops on 1 warp. COLOURS (11): dark red-purple, bright red, rose (motley), off light rose, yellow, dark olive-green (worn), dark blue, sky, rust, camel-brown, ivory. FINISH: sides: regular weft return over 2 additional warps; bottom end: 3 cm tabby, warp return loops; top end: remake. ADDITIONAL INFORMATION: excellent individual professional work. Rare pattern.

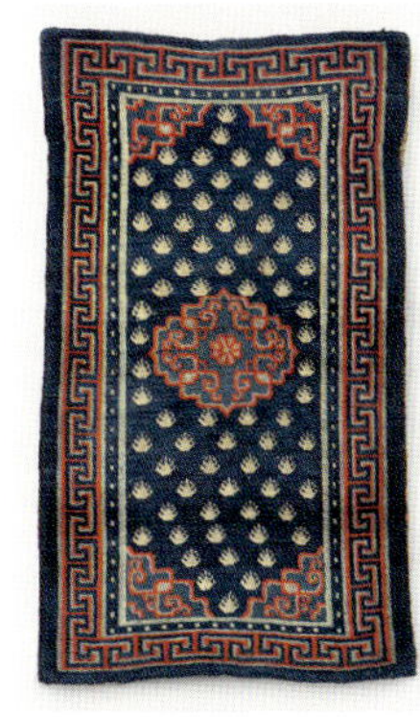

C146: *Khaden* sitting and sleeping rug

121×69 cm. Khotan (?). 20th century. PATTERN: large stepped medallion and imitation of "palms" (7-fingers), on off-blue ground; main T-border; inner pearl border. WARP: wool; ivory; Z3S. Depressed. Density: 54 ends/cm. WEFT: wool; ivory; Z2, S1 (added). Density: 22 shoots/dm. PILE: wool and camel hair (?); Z4. Height: 6 mm. BASIC KNOTS: regular asym. open left knots; loops on 1 warp. LOOPING DENSITY: 27×22 = 594 knots/dm. COLOURS (6): orange-red, rose, off light turquoise, mid-blue, off-grey, ivory (camel hair [?]). FINISH: original finish missing. ADDITIONAL INFORMATION: numerous repairs, sides and corners restored. Manner of weaving, colour scale and type of rosette speak for non-Tibetan manner of carpet weaving.

C147: Sculptured horse crupper rug

43×60 cm. Tibet. 20th century. PATTERN: chrysanthemum and two branches, with endless knot in each. WARP: wool; ivory; Z2S; very fine. Deeply depressed. Density: 80 warps/dm. WEFT: wool; ivory; S1, S2Z. Two parallel shoots in a unit. Density: 40 units/dm. PILE: wool; Z3 (ivory); otherwise Z2. Height: 4–5 (light pink); 5 mm (carmine, rust-yellow, olive-green, sky); 6 mm (purple); otherwise 4 mm. BASIC LOOPS: asym. long leg; open loops; regular sym. and asym. SINGLE: regular asym. with a packing bottom loop. PAIRED: left side: sym.; right side: asym. long leg, with bottom packing loop. LONG ROWS: left end: sym.; right end: asym. long leg, with packing bottom loop; in between: asym. long leg. IRREGULARITIES: sharing, packing; offset effect, by sharing. CURVED LINES: by virtue of high density and deep depression. LOOPING DENSITY: 40 (horiz.) ×40 = 1,600 basic loops/sq dm. COLOURS (12): purple, carmine, pink, light pink (faded ends), rust-yellow, orange, olive-green, grass-green, sky, dark blue, light lilac, ivory. FINISH: back and edges are covered with cotton lining. ADDITIONAL INFORMATION: lining (cotton), together with very high looping, prevents exact identification of weaving peculiarities. Complicated form; unusual pattern.

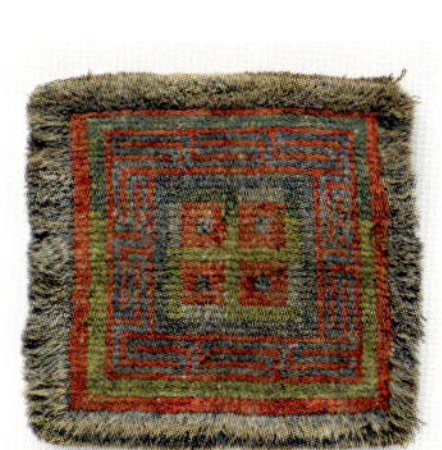

C148: Wangden *Drumze khagangma* sitting rug

71×76 cm. Tibet. 19th century. PATTERN: 4 central squares; kind of key-border and green and red lines' outer framing. WARP: wool; brown, mixed with yak or horse hair; Z2S. Density: 56 warps/dm. WEFT: wool; 1) ivory and dark brown, Z1; 2) ivory and rust plied together; Z2S; loose and thick; spun without a spindle. Two parallel shoots in a unit. Density: 6 units/dm. PILE: wool; Z2S2. Height: 20–45 mm; fringe: 50–60 mm. BASIC LOOPS: single-level weave (warp-faced back); asym. long leg, on 2 and 4 active warps, with, otherwise without one warp in between; open sym. loops, on 1 and on 2 active warps; regular sym. on 2 active warps. SINGLES: regular sym., on 3 active (upper row) warps. PAIRED: regular sym., on 2 active warps. TRIPLE: variants, for example: asym. long leg on 4 active warps, with bottom packing loop on 2 warps. LONG ROWS: left end: asym. long leg, otherwise sym., on 2 active warps; right end: asym. long leg, with packing bottom loop, with and without warp in between, loop can be on 1, otherwise on 2 active warps; in between: asym. open left, long leg. IRREGULARITIES: packing; sharing combined with packing; unusual change of gaps between the loops and in number of active warps in loops. LOOPING DENSITY: 23 (horiz.) × 6 = 138 basic loops/sq dm. COLOURS (4): orange-red (motley), off green-blue/green-yellow (mixture of different shades), off-blue (motley, abrash), off-grey. FINISH: sides: plain weft return over 2 additional warps; bottom end: warp ends plaited into a braid, at the corner terminate with a rope. All-over fringe: 6–5 cm long, of motley off-blue yarns. ADDITIONAL INFORMATION: stable developed tradition, with special individual devices (compare to C72, C77 and C78 in particular). All yarns are home-dyed and regularly contain fibres of different colours. Strong dense weave prevented the loss of pile loops. Excellent design and splendid colour scale, in spite of (or probably thanks to) motley and abrash shades. Monastic work.

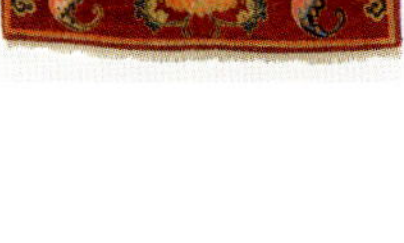

C153: *Khagangma* sitting rug (?) for a high-ranking lama

52 × 93 cm. Tibet. Not later than early 20th century. PATTERN: three bats and blossoming lotus, with branches, on deep cherry ground; narrow orange-red framing. WARP: cotton; white; Z?S. Density: 94 warps/dm. WEFT: wool; light rose; Z1. Two parallel shoots in a unit. Density: 36 units/dm. PILE: wool; Z3 (orange, camel); otherwise Z2; excellent quality. Height: 2 mm (deep cherry); 4 mm (dark green, dark sky, camel); 6 mm (light rose, light sky); otherwise 5 mm. BASIC LOOPS: asym. long leg; open loops; regular sym. and asym. SINGLES: sym., with packing bottom loop. PAIRED: left side: regular asym.; right side: asym. long leg, with packing bottom loop. LONG ROWS: left end: asym., otherwise sym.; right end: asym. long leg, with packing bottom loop; in between: asym. long leg. CURVED LINES: asym. loops over wefts; eccentric weave (additional short row of loops); diagonal sym.; offset; other tricks' probability. OTHER IRREGULARITIES: packing; sharing combined with packing. LOOPING DENSITY: 47 × 36 = 1,692 basic loops/sq dm. COLOURS (13): deep cherry, pink (faded), light rose, orange-red (faded ends), orange, dark green, light sky, dark sky, dark blue, camel, brown, ivory, off light pink plied together with sky (Z2). FINISH: sides: complicated weft return over 3 additional warps; bottom end: 1.5 cm tabby, warp return loops; top end: cut. ADDITIONAL INFORMATION: real masterpiece: superb pattern, fantastic weaving structure, excellent pile wool; brilliant colours speak for professional monastic work. High density for 5–6 mm long pile; difference in pile wear produces impression of carving. Cherry runs a little bit at the bottom, most probably as a result of over-dyeing and wrong drying after washing.

C154: *Khaden* sitting and sleeping rug for a high-ranking lama

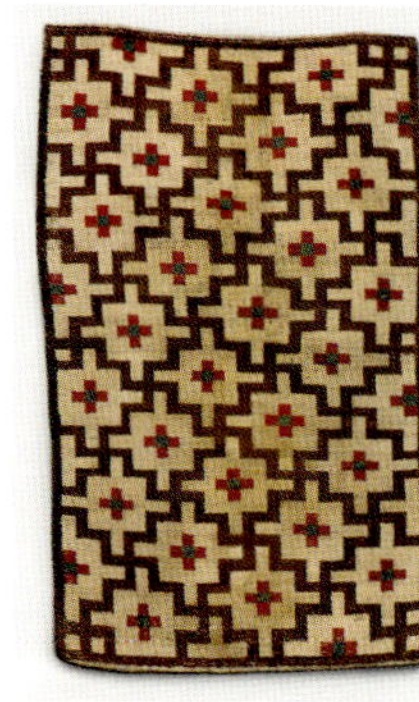

140 × 87 cm. Tibet. Mid-19th century (?). PATTERN: *swastika* lattice, with straight crosses, on ivory ground. WARP: cotton; ivory; Z2S. Deep depression. Density: 58 warps/dm. WEFT: wool; ivory; Z1. Two parallel shoots in a unit. Density: 17 units/dm. PILE: wool; yak hair; Z2S; excellent quality. Height: 2.5 mm (bright red, grass-green); 5 mm (chocolate-brown); otherwise 3.5 mm. BASIC LOOPS: asym. long leg; open loops; regular sym. and asym. LONG ROWS: left end: asym., otherwise sym.; right end: asym. long leg, with packing bottom loop; in between: asym. long leg. IRREGULARITIES: packing; sharing combined with packing; diagonal loops by change of warp depression. LOOPING DENSITY: 29 × 17 = 493 basic loops/sq dm. COLOURS (6): claret, bright red (corroded), grass-green, dark green (corroded), chocolate-brown (yak hair), ivory. FINISH: sides: regular weft return over 2 additional warps; ends: 2 cm tabby, folded over to the back and sewn down. ADDITIONAL INFORMATION: highly professional work. Rather worn, repaired upper end centre. Masterpiece of design minimalism, with dramatic, psychologically strong pattern.

C155: *Khaden* sitting and sleeping rug

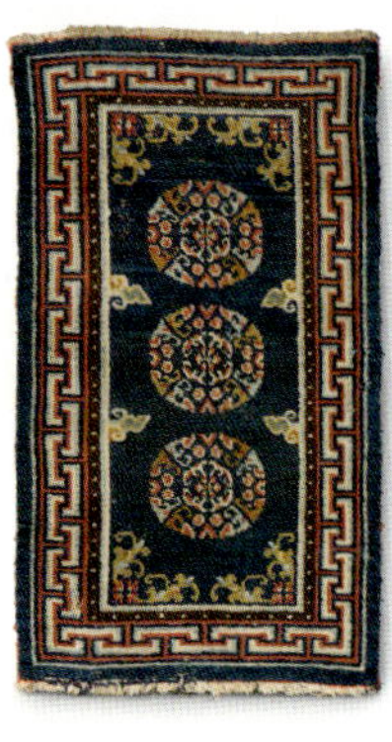

129 × 72 cm. Tibet. 19th century. PATTERN: three medallions and corner floral motifs, on blue ground, main T-border; inner pearl border. WARP: wool; ivory and light mix; Z2S; pretty loose. Density: 52 warps/dm. WEFT: wool; ivory and light mix; Z1; loose. Two parallel shoots in a unit. Density: 16 units/dm. PILE: wool; yak undercoat; Z3. Height: 2 mm (ivory); 3 mm (rust); 4 mm (rose); 4.5 mm (red, dark blue). BASIC LOOPS: asym. long leg; open and closed loops, on 1 warp; regular asym.; and sym., usually large. SINGLES: sym., otherwise asym., with packing bottom loop. PAIRED: left side: regular asym.; right side: asym. long leg, with packing bottom loop. LONG ROWS: right end: asym. long leg, with packing bottom loop; left end: asym., otherwise sym.; in between: asym. long leg. CURVED LINES: numerous additional open and closed loops, diagonal loops of large size; sym. with open loop on 2 warps. OTHER IRREGULARITIES: packing; sharing combined with packing. LOOPING DENSITY: 26 × 16 = 416 basic loops/sq dm. COLOURS (14): cherry-red, rose, light rose, yellow, olive-green, off light sky, light sky, sky, dark blue, rust, light chestnut, chocolate-brown (yak), ivory. FINISH: sides: regular weft return over 2 additional ivory-and-brown warps; bottom end: 2 shoots of weft, warp return makes 1 cm long loops; top end: missing. ADDITIONAL INFORMATION: professional rural work; classical pattern. Pile wear in the centre. Red spots at the end: traces of running red-colour lining.

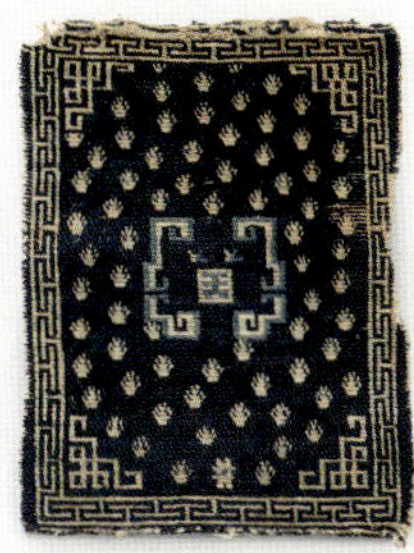

C157: *Khagangma* sitting rug

70×54 cm. Tibet. 20th century. PATTERN: strange square-shaped central figure and imitations of "palms", on dark blue ground; T-border. WARP: wool; ivory; Z2S; fine. Density: 82 warps/dm. WEFT: wool; ivory; Z1; loose and thick. Two parallel shoots in a unit. Density: 18 units/dm. PILE: wool; Z3. Height: 5.5 mm. BASIC LOOPS: asym. long leg; open loops; regular asym. SINGLES: regular asym., with packing bottom loop. LONG ROWS; left end: asym.; right end: asym. long leg, with packing bottom loopin between: asym. long leg. IRREGULARITIES: packing; sharing combined with packing. LOOPING DENSITY: 41×18 = 738 basic loops/sq dm. COLOURS (4): off light grey-sky, sky, dark blue, ivory. FINISH: missing. ADDITIONAL INFORMATION: heavily worn centre, top end and losses of right side texture. Numerous mistakes in pattern, including the central figure, wrongly shaped palm motif and T-border. Was most probably made from memory by a beginner-weaver, asym. also confirmed by regular, simple, "domestic" in character structure. Upper ⅓ part was woven in a different texture and shade of dark blue yarns. One crimson dot in central figure.

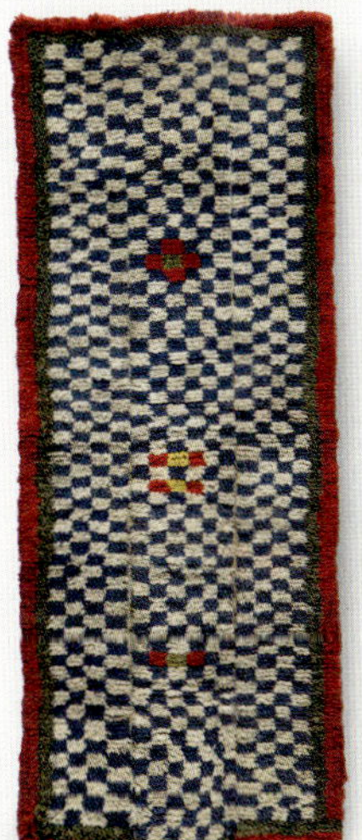

C158: *Tsuktruk khaden*, 3 panels

182×70 cm; panels: 22.3 cm, 23 cm, 23 cm. Tibet. 20th century. PATTERN: blue-and-ivory checkerboard; central red crosses and red framing. WARP: wool; ivory; S1. Density: 48 warps/dm. WEFT: wool; ivory and red; Z1; fine; 16–20 shoots in a unit. Density: 11 units/dm. PILE: wool; Z2S (yellow, blue); otherwise Z3S. Height: 16 mm (green); 20 mm (blue); otherwise 21–22 mm. LOOPING: sym. single-level open loop, on 2 active warps, with 2 warps in between. Density: 24×11 = 264 knots/dm. COLOURS (5): carmine-red, yellow, green (with yellow fibres), blue, ivory. FINISH: sides: plain weft return over 2 additional warps; ends: 1.5 cm tabby, folded over to the back and sewn down. ADDITIONAL INFORMATION: very simple, most probably rural work. Central square borders are marked with additional red wefts.

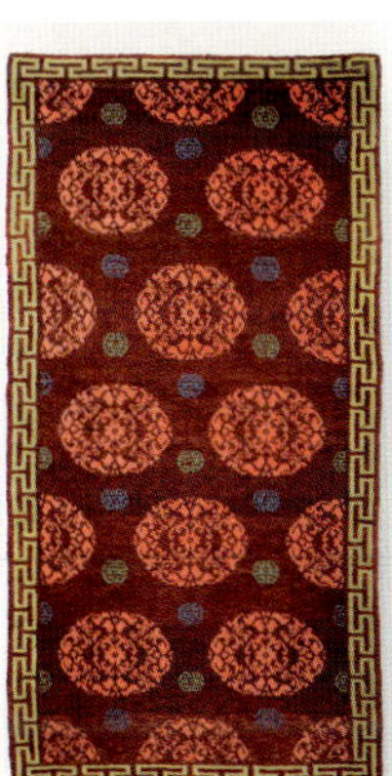

C159: *Khaden* sitting and sleeping rug

168×85 cm. Tibet. Late 20th century. PATTERN: 8 floral rosettes, with ½ along the side and ¼ in the corners; intermediate *Shou* hieroglyphs, on cherry ground; unframed T-border. WARP: cotton; ivory; Z?S. Density: 76–80 warps/dm. WEFT: wool; ivory; Z1; loose. Two parallel shoots in a unit. Density: 25 units/dm. PILE: wool; Z2. Height: 8 mm. BASIC LOOPS: asym. long leg; open loops; regular sym. SINGLES: sym., with packing bottom loop. PAIRED: left side: sym.; right side: asym. long leg, with packing bottom loop. LONG ROWS: left end: sym.; right end: asym. long leg, with packing bottom loop; in between: asym. long leg. IRREGULARITIES: packing; sharing combined with packing. LOOPING DENSITY: 38–40×25 = 950–1,000 basic loops/sq dm. COLOURS (5): claret, pink, yellow, green, blue. FINISH: edges are covered by trimming. ADDITIONAL INFORMATION: regular, definitely commercial weave. Synthetic dyestuffs, most probably vat-dyeing.

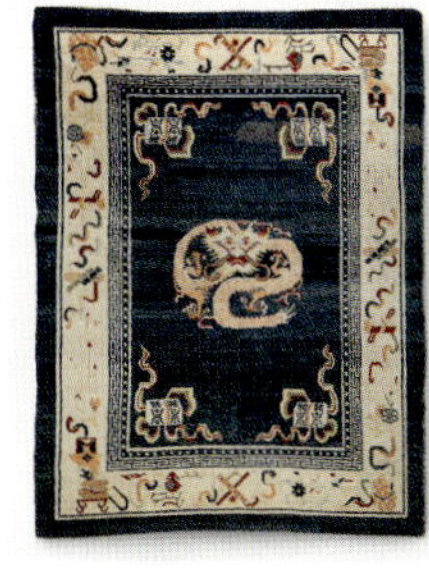

C160: *Sabden* main carpet

242×180 cm. Tibet. Ca. 1900. PATTERN: dragon, on blue background; main border with Buddhist symbols; inner: T- and pearl borders. WARP: cotton; ivory; Z?S. Density: 60 warps/dm. WEFT: cotton; ivory; Z1; irregular in a number of shoots. Density: 14 units/dm. PILE: wool; Z1; also Z2–Z3 in large knots. Height: 8–9 mm. BASIC LOOPS: asym. long leg; open loops; regular asym. and sym. SINGLES: sym., of large size. PAIRED: left side: sym.; right side: asym. long leg, with packing bottom loop. LONG ROWS: left end: sym., otherwise asym., with upward-pointing ends; right end: asym. long leg, with packing bottom loop; in between: asym. long leg. CURVED LINES: large-size sym.; asym. loops, with upward-pointing ends. OTHER IRREGULARITIES: packing; sharing combined with packing; LOOPING DENSITY: 30×14 = 420 basic loops/sq dm. COLOURS (11): dark carmine, rose, light rose, light yellow, off light yellow, off grey-green, light sky, off light sky, dark blue (motley, abrash), ivory. FINISH: sides: plain weft return over 3 additional warps; ends: tabby, folded over to the back and sewn down. ADDITIONAL INFORMATION: copy of classic 19th century Chinese carpet. Commercial product. Chemically washed.

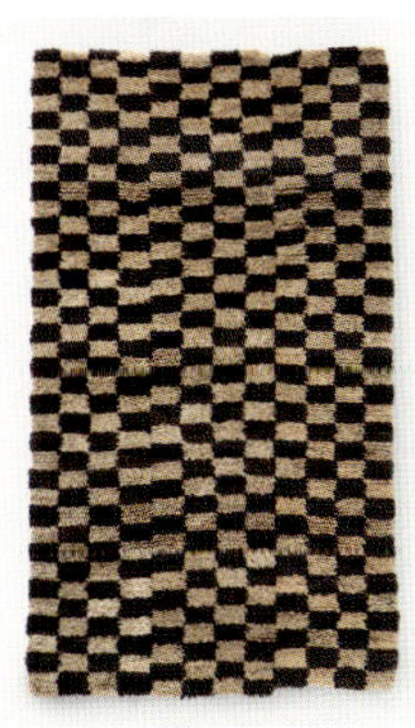

C163: *Tsuktruk khaden* sitting and sleeping rug for a high-ranking lama, of 3 panels

139×80 cm; panels: 26.5 cm, 27 cm, 26.5 cm. Tibet. 20th (?) century. PATTERN: light off-brown and black coloured checkerboard. WARP: wool; ivory; S2Z; strong spin and loose ply, high quality. Density: 41 end/dm. WEFT: wool; ivory; Z1; fine; 14–10–9 (according to panels) shoots in a unit. Density: 17–24 units/dm. PILE: wool, Z3; yak hair, Z2; some S-ply of both. Height: 12–15 mm long. LOOPING: sym. single-level open loops on 1 warp, with 1 warp in between. IRREGULARITIES: offset; all over strong reps effect. DENSITY: 21×14–15 = 294–315 loops/dm. COLOURS (2): off light rose (faded), black (yak hair). FINISH: sides: plain weft return over 2 additional warps; ends: 2 cm tabby, with reps effect, folded over to the back and sewn down. ADDITIONAL INFORMATION: excellent wool, with a lot of lanoline. Archaic pattern and weave.

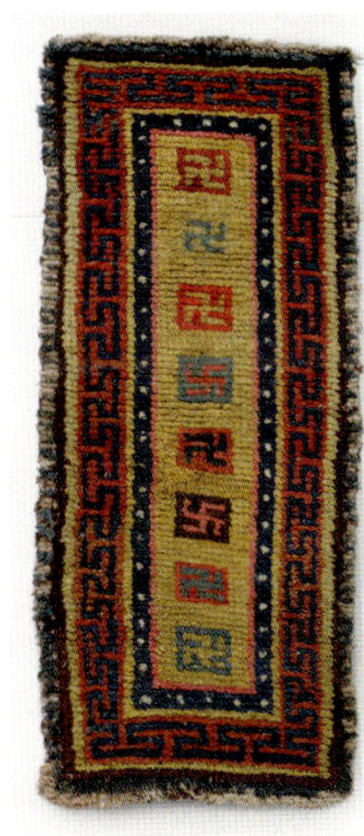

C164: Wangden *Drumze khaden* sitting and sleeping rug

147×62 cm. Tibet. 19th century. PATTERN: 8 squares with "sun" and "moon" *swastikas*, on yellow ground; main T-border; inner pearl border; 5 framing lines; unusual details. WARP: wool; ivory; yak hair, brown-black; ivory and black plied together; Z2S. Density: 63 warps/dm. WEFT: wool; ivory; yak hair, brown-black; ivory and black mix; Z1. 2–3 yarns in a shoot; 2 shoots in a unit. Density: 4 units/dm. PILE: wool; Z3, Z3S; loose spin and ply. Height: 11–12 mm. Side and ends' edge rows of dark blue pile is much longer. BASIC LOOPS: single-level weave (warp-faced back) on 2 active warps, otherwise on 1; with 1 warp in between, otherwise without; asym. long left, with long leg; open sym. loops, on 1, otherwise on 2 active warps; regular sym. loops on 2 active warps. SINGLES: regular sym., on 2 active warps. PAIRED: regular sym., on 2 active warps. LONG ROWS: right end: asym.

long leg, with packing bottom loop; left end: sym., with tiny bottom packing loop on 1 warp; in between: asym. long leg (the description is not complete because of numerous difficulties in identification of variants). IRREGULARITIES: packing; sharing combined with packing; numerous very large left-side sym. loops; accidental asym. loops with very long legs, which float under a short row of different in colour left-side loops. LOOPING DENSITY: 32×4 = 128 basic loops/dm. COLOURS (10): claret-red, pink-red, pink, olive-yellow, sky, mid-blue, lemon-yellow, dark blue, purple-brown, ivory (cold scale shades are motley). FINISH: sides: plain pair of wefts' return over side warps; ends: warps' ends plaited into a braid. ADDITIONAL INFORMATION: individual unique structure, comparable to C72. Excellent colours and design.

C165: *Khagangma* sitting rug

63×68 cm. Tibet. Early (?) 19th century. PATTERN: central field with curved dragon rosette, very wide main border with Buddhist symbols, two inner borders, a pearl border, and one with short, diagonal bands. WARP: wool; ivory; Z2S; tight spin and ply. Density: 32 warps/dm. WEFT: wool; ivory/brown mix; Z1. Two parallel shoots in a unit. Density: 24 units/dm. PILE: wool; Z2 (dark blue, light brown); otherwise Z3. Height: 2 mm (off-turquoise), 3 mm (ivory); 4 mm (cherry-red, green); otherwise 5 mm. BASIC LOOPS: asym. long leg; open loops; regular sym. LONG ROWS: left end: sym.; right end: asym. long leg, with packing bottom loop; in between: asym. long leg. IRREGULARITIES: packing; sharing combined with packing. LOOPING DENSITY: 16×14 = 224 basic loops/sq dm. COLOURS (7): cherry-red, light rose, green, off light turquoise (abrash), off dark blue (abrash, shabby), light brown, ivory. FINISH: sides: plain weft return over 2 additional warps; bottom end: 1.5 cm tabby, warp return loops; top end: 1.5 cm tabby, folded over to the back and sewn down. ADDITIONAL INFORMATION: supposedly one of the earliest items in the collection. Pattern suggests Central Asian nomadic influence.

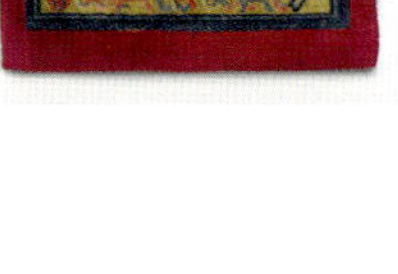

C166: *Masho* over-saddle rug or *khagangma* sitting rug

64×55 cm. Tibet. 19th century. PATTERN: central field with curved dragon rosette; very wide main border, with Buddhist symbols; inner: row of short diagonal bands and a pearl border. WARP AND WEFT: impossible to identify because of extremely dense weave and padding. PILE: wool; Z3 (light sky); otherwise Z2. Pile height: 5 mm (dark blue); 6 mm (dark blue/sky); otherwise 4 mm. BASIC LOOPS: asym. long leg; open loops; regular asym. and sym. Dense weave. SINGLES: asym. with bottom loop, otherwise sym., with bottom loop. PAIRED: left: sym.; right: asym. long leg with a packing bottom loop. LONG ROWS: left end: sym.; right end: asym. long leg, with packing bottom loop; in between: asym. long leg. IRREGULARITIES: packing; sharing combined with packing; eccentric weave; all-over sharing in dragon motif. COLOURS (14): terracotta, bright red, orange-red, light pink, off-pink, orange-rose, old rose (faded orange-red), yellow, sky, light sky, dark blue (shabby), off light grey, dark blue plied together with sky, ivory. FINISH: back and edges are covered with felt padding and black cotton lining. ADDITIONAL INFORMATION: monastic work; one of the most artistically elaborate items in the collection; impossible to identify exact colour scale because of the unwashed condition.

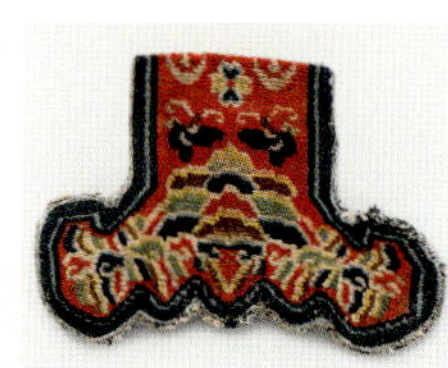

C167: Horse crupper ornament

36×53 cm. Central Tibet. 1920s or earlier. PATTERN: flower, 2 butterflies, mountain and scrolls, on red ground. WARP: wool; ivory and ivory plied with brown (coloured by running red of the pile); Z2S; very fine. Density: 58 warps/dm. WEFT: wool; ivory; Z2S (also coloured by running red). Two parallel shoots in a unit. Density: 21 units/dm. PILE: wool; Z3 (bright red, yellow); otherwise Z2. Height: 3–4 mm (light rose, green); 5 mm (ivory); otherwise 4 mm. BASIC LOOPS: asym. long leg; open loops; regular asym. and large-size sym. loops. LONG ROWS: left end: asym. long leg, with packing bottom loop, otherwise large-size sym.; right end: asym. long leg, with packing bottom loop; in between: asym. long leg. IRREGULARITIES: sharing, packing; numerous additional open and closed loops. LOOPING DENSITY: 29 (horiz.) ×21 = 609 basic loops/sq dm. COLOURS (8): bright red (runs), light rose, yellow, green, sky, black-blue, brown, ivory. FINISH: all edges covered with cotton trimming. ADDITIONAL INFORMATION: heavily worn pile. Warps used by the weaver are too fine to identify loop structure.

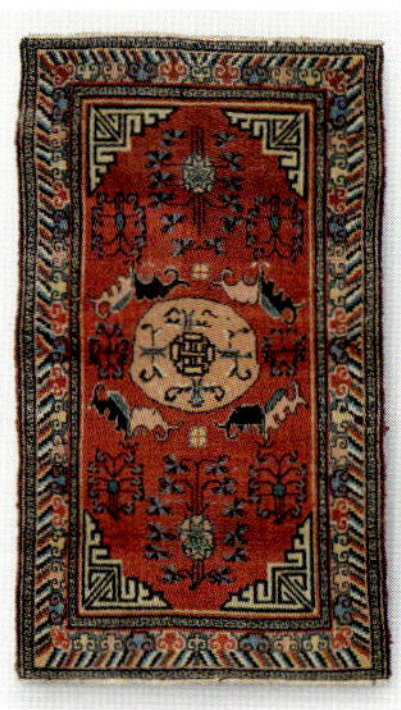

C168: *Sabden* floor carpet

138×81 cm. China (?). Late 19th century. PATTERN: central rosette and floral motifs, on cherry-red background; main border with sea spray motif; T-border guard stripes. WARP: cotton; white; Z?S. Overdepressed. Density: 70 warps/dm. WEFT: cotton; white; Z?S. Two shoots in a unit. Density: 38 units/dm. PILE: wool; Z2S. Height: 3 mm. Knot: asym. open left. Density: 35 (horiz.) ×38 = 1,330 basic loops/sq dm. COLOURS (8): cherry-red, yellow, lemon-yellow, cold green, sky, dark blue, cacao, ivory. FINISH: original finish missing.

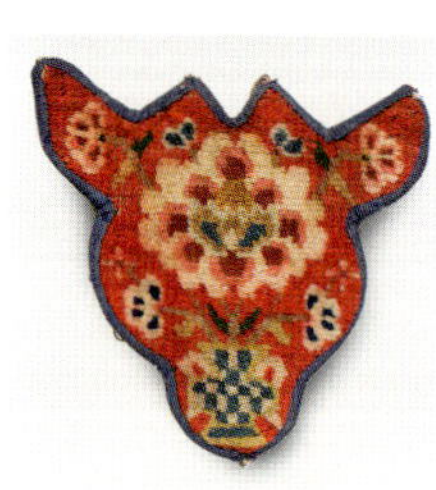

C176: *Takyab* horse, mule or donkey forehead cover

25.5×25 cm. Tibet. 19th century. PATTERN: peony in vase, on red ground. WARP: cotton; ivory; Z?S. Depression. Density: 100 warps/dm. WEFT: wool; ivory; Z1. Two parallel shoots in a unit. Density: 45 units/dm. PILE: wool; Z2. Height: 3 mm (pink, yellow plied together with claret); 5 mm (yellow, sky-blue); 6 mm (black-blue); otherwise 4 mm. BASIC LOOPS: asym. long leg; open loops; regular sym. and asym. open left. SINGLE: asym. with a packing bottom loop. PAIRED: left side: asym.; right side: asym. with a packing bottom loop. LONG ROWS: left end: regular sym.; right end: asym. long leg, with packing bottom loop; in between: asym. long leg. IRREGULARITIES: sharing, packing. LOOPING DENSITY: 50 (horiz.) ×45 = 2,250 basic loops/sq dm. COLOURS (12): claret, bright red (runs), rose-red, off light pink, yellow, dark emerald-green, off dark green, dark sky, black-blue, light camel, ivory, yellow plied together with claret. FINISH: all edges and trimmed with cotton textile. ADDITIONAL INFORMATION: shaggy pile; some wear. Masterpiece of design.

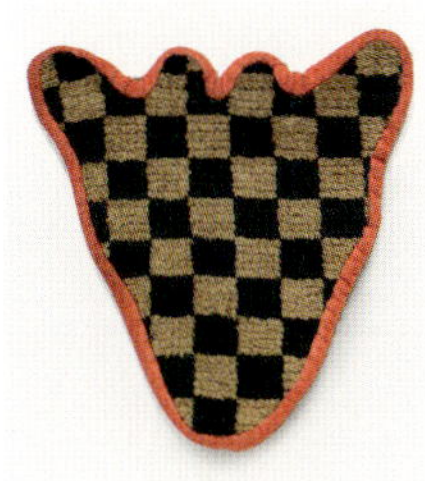

C177: *Takyab* horse, mule or donkey forehead cover, remake

23×21 cm. Tibet. Woven part: early 20th century. PATTERN: light camel-hair colour and black-blue checkerboard. WARP: wool (?); ivory; Z2S. Density: 70 warps/dm. WEFT: wool; light mix; Z1. Two parallel shoots in a unit. Density: 26 units/dm. PILE: wool; Z2. Height: 5 mm. BASIC LOOPS: asym. long leg; open loops; regular sym. and asym. open left. LONG ROWS: left end: sym.; right end: asym. long leg, with packing bottom loop; in between: asym. open left long leg. IRREGULARITIES: sharing, packing; offsetting. LOOPING DENSITY: 35 (horiz.) ×26 = 910 basic loops/sq dm. COLOURS (2): camel-hair colour, black-blue. FINISH: the back and edges are covered with pink cotton lining and trimming. ADDITIONAL INFORMATION: home-made rather clumsy re-use of a fragment from an apparently early 20th century rug.

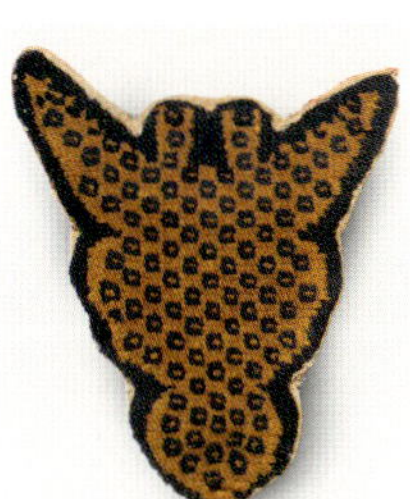

C184: *Takyab* horse, mule or donkey forehead cover

25×22 cm. Tibet. 19th century. PATTERN: imitation of leopard pelt. WARP: wool; ivory and grey mix; Z2S. Deeply depressed. Density: 100 warps/dm. WEFT: light mix; Z1. Two parallel shoots in a unit. Density: 28 units/dm. PILE: wool; Z1(?); thick. Height: 5 mm. BASIC LOOPS: asym. long leg; open loops; regular sym. and asym. open left. LONG ROWS: left end: sym.; right end: asym. long leg, with packing bottom loop; in between: long leg asym. open left. IRREGULARITIES: sharing, packing; offsetting; some tricks are not identified because of the lining. APPROX. DENSITY OF LOOPING: 50 (horiz.) ×28 = 1,400 basic loops/sq dm. COLOURS (2): camel-yellow, dark blue. FINISH: the back is covered with a fragment of old decorated cotton lining, and trimmed with striped cotton twill; stitching is made by silk threads. Three stitched to the edges' leather tassels. ADDITIONAL INFORMATION: many indices are unrecognised because of a high looping density and lining. Masterpiece of weaving and design, the best and probably the earliest of the type.

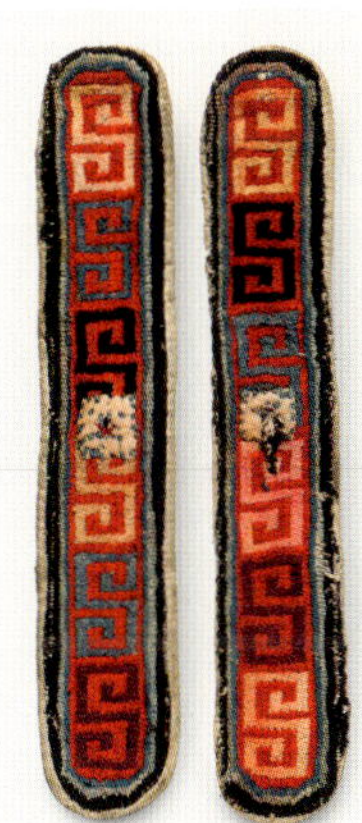

C190: A pair of horse equipment belts

60.5×9.5 cm and 60.5×10 cm. Tibet. 20th century. PATTERN: row of S-motifs. WARP: wool; ivory; Z2S. Density: 30 warps/dm. WEFT: wool; ivory; Z1. Two parallel shoots in a unit. Density: 20 units/dm. PILE: wool; loose; Z2S (brown-black); Z3 (bright red, rose); otherwise Z2. Height: 4 mm (off light blue); 5 mm (yellow, ivory); 5–6 mm (sky); otherwise 6 mm. BASIC LOOPS: basic: asym. long leg; open loops; regular sym. and asym. LOOPING DENSITY: 15 (horiz.) ×20 = 300 basic loops/sq dm. COLOURS (9): dark claret, bright red (runs), pink, yellow, sky, off light blue, dark blue, black-brown, ivory. FINISH: the back and edges are covered with cotton lining and trimmed. ADDITIONAL INFORMATION: patches in the centre of each. Rare items.

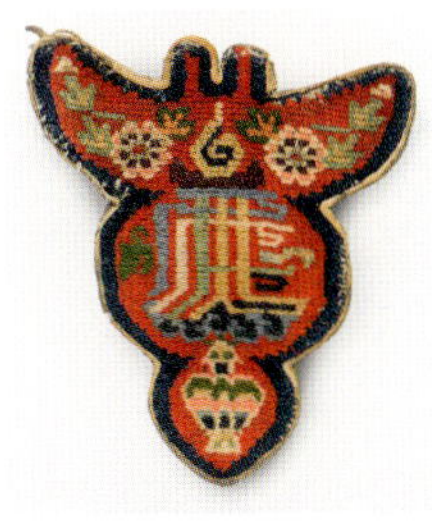

C193: *Takyab* horse, mule or donkey forehead cover

29.5×26 cm. Tibet. Late 19th – early 20th century. PATTERN: large central hieroglyph, multipetal small rosettes, a "pearl". WARP: wool; ivory; Z2S. Density: 80 warps/dm. WEFT: wool; ivory; Z1. Two parallel shoots in a unit. Density: 30 units/dm. PILE: wool; Z3; of unrecognised shade; otherwise Z2. Height: 3 mm (purple, bright red); 4 mm (orange, ivory); 4–5 mm (off sky); otherwise 5 mm. BASIC LOOPS: asym. long leg; open loops; regular sym. PAIRED: left side: sym.; right side: asym. long leg, with packing bottom loop. LONG ROWS: left end: sym.; right end: asym. long leg, with packing bottom loop; in between: long leg asym. open left. IRREGULARITIES: sharing, packing; loops over wefts. LOOPING DENSITY: 50 (horiz.) ×28 = 1,400 basic loops/sq dm. COLOURS (14): cherry-red, claret, bright red, light rose, orange-rose (faded), yellow, dark emerald-green (with yellow fibres), off light turquoise (with yellow fibres), sky, dark blue, purple-blue, light camel hair, light olive-grey, ivory. FINISH: back side and edges covered with woollen cloth lining and leather strip trimming. Cotton rope and two leather tassels stitched to the upper edge. ADDITIONAL INFORMATION: strong wear of upper part makes sculptured effect. A masterpiece.

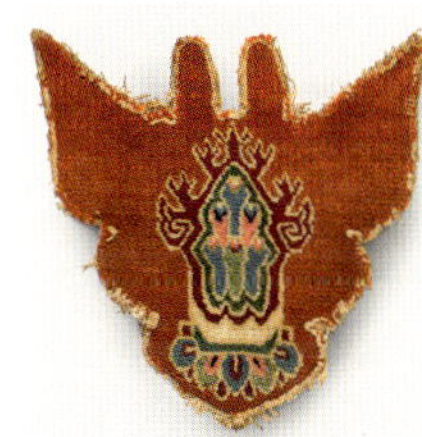

C195: *Takyab* horse, mule or donkey forehead cover

29×28 cm. Tibet. 20th century. PATTERN: complex vertical figure, of mythological character, on rust ground. WARP: cotton; white; Z?S. Density: 120 warps/dm. WEFT: cotton; white; Z1. Two parallel shoots in a unit. Density: 32 units/dm. PILE: wool; Z3 (yellow), Z2, Z4 (rust); otherwise Z2. Height: 4 mm (purple, pink, light yellow), otherwise 5 mm. BASIC LOOPS: asym. long leg; open loops; regular sym. SINGLE: sym., with packing bottom loop. PAIRED: left side: sym., small; right side: asym. long leg, with packing bottom loop. LONG ROWS: left end: sym.; right end: asym. long leg, with packing bottom loop; in between: asym long leg. open left. IRREGULARITIES: sharing, short rows of packing; loops over wefts. LOOPING DENSITY: 60 (horiz.) ×32 = 1,920 basic loops/sq dm. COLOURS (9): purple, pink (faded ends), rust, light yellow, grass-green, dark green, sky, dark blue, ivory. FINISH: all edges are covered with a band stitched over the end rows of loops. ADDITIONAL INFORMATION: unusual motif can be a variant of Goddess of Animals' image. Professional work, probably made to order.

Britta Schwenck

TEXTILE-TECHNICAL ANALYSIS OF NINE[1] TIBETAN TEXTILES[2]

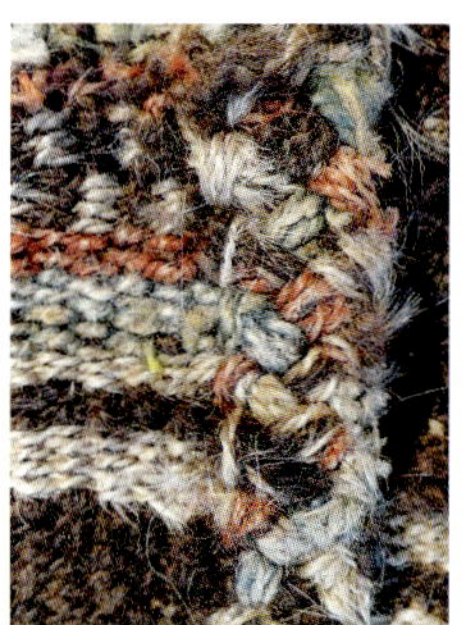

T11 (Fig. 23): Striped, heavy all-purpose blanket
Animal hair (yak, goat?). 145×143 cm. WEAVE: plain weave. PATTERN: coloured warp stripes. COMMENT: six panels sewn together, end finishing at one side. WARP: animal hair (yak, goat?), plied S-spun 2 Z-spun yarns (hereafter abbreviated: "plied S2Z"), 3–4 warps/cm, white, red, blue, green, brown. WEFT: animal hair (yak, goat?), plied S2Z, alternating in stripes of undyed white and brown. SEWING THREAD: animal hair (yak?), plied S2Z, dark brown. SEAMS: selvedges sewn together with overcast stitching. END FINISHING: Warp ends braided parallel to the weft (see Seiler-Baldinger 1991: 134), still existent on one side, frayed (?) on the other.

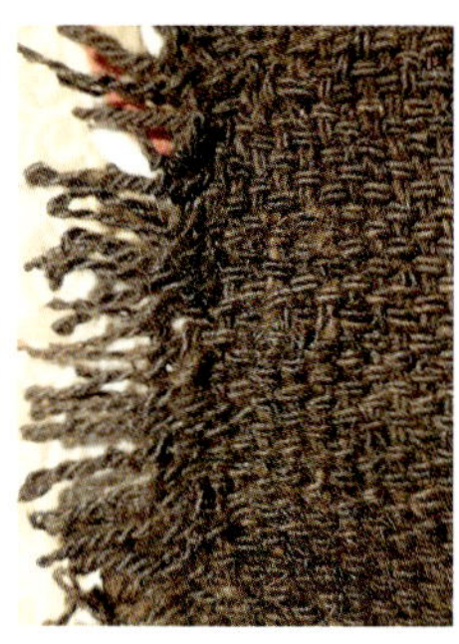

T13 (w/o Fig.): Fragment of tent fabric
Animal hair (yak?). 52×23/33 cm. WEAVE: plain (Panama 2/2). COMMENT: top edge hemmed, under edge with fringes. WARP: yak hair (?), tightly spun Z, 10 warps/cm, undyed dark brown. WEFT: yak hair (?), tightly spun plied S2Z, 6 wefts/cm, undyed dark brown. SEWING THREAD: animal hair (yak?), plied S2Z, thick undyed black. SEAMS: on one side with overcast stitching. END FINISHING: fringe of 4 or 2 pairs of warps twisted together.

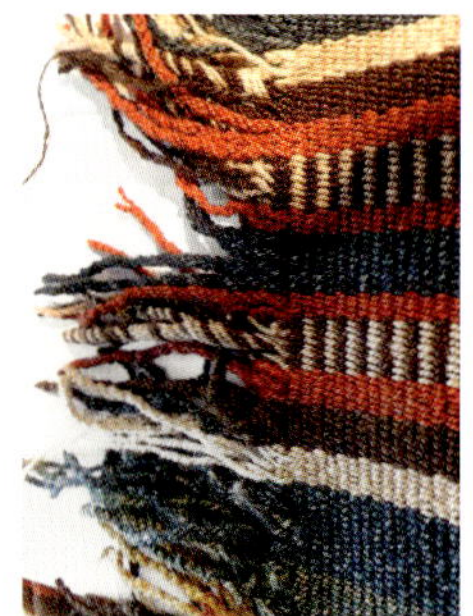

T31 (Fig. 24): Striped all-purpose blanket
Wool (sheep). 132×142 cm. WEAVE: plain weave. PATTERN: coloured warp stripes. COMMENT: six panels sewn together, one edge hemmed, the other fringed. WARP: wool (?), tightly spun plied S2Z, 12–14 warps/cm, white, yellow, red, green, brown. WEFT: wool (?), plied S2Z, 5 wefts/cm; light blue. SEWING THREAD 1: wool (?), plied S2Z, dark brown. SEWING THREAD 2: wool (?), plied S2Z, white. SEAMS: selvedges sewn together with overcast stitching (sewing thread 1). One warp end is hemmed with running stitches, using tripled thread (sewing thread 2). END FINISHING: Fringes of 4 or 8 warps twisted together in Z-twist.

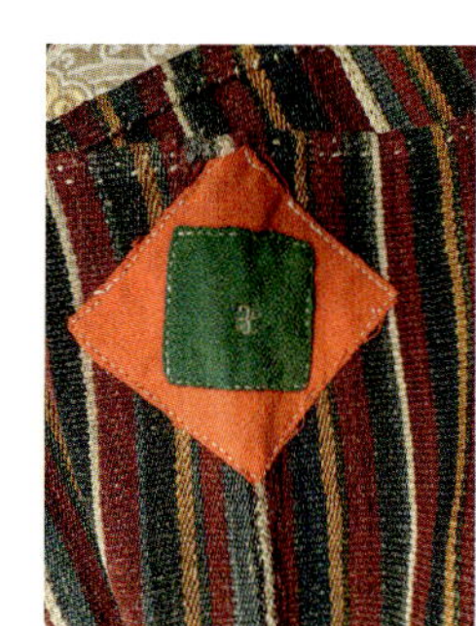

T41 (Fig. 25): Striped all-purpose blanket
Wool (sheep?). 167×178 cm. WEAVE: plain weave. PATTERN: coloured warp stripes and small embroidery in red thread; textile appliqué on one of the selvedges. COMMENT: eight panels sewn together and hemmed at both ends. WARP: wool (?), plied S2Z, 12–20 warps/cm, white, yellow, red, light blue, dark blue, green. WEFT: wool (?), plied S2Z, 5 wefts/cm, brown. SEWING THREAD 1: wool (?), plied S2Z, white. SEWING THREAD 2: cotton (?), plied S2Z, white. SEWING THREAD 3: cotton (?), plied S4Z, red. SEAMS: the 8 panels are sewn together at their selvedges (sewing thread 1). Seam with overcast stitching (sewing thread 1), crêpe fabric appliquéd with running stitch (?). In addition, small embroidery in red (sewing thread 3).

Appliqué
FABRIC 1: crêpe, plain weave. WARP (?) wool, S-twist, tightly spun (overspun), 20 warps/cm, red. WARP (?): wool, S-twist, tightly spun (overspun), 14 wefts/cm, red. FABRIC 2: crêpe, plain weave. WARP (?): wool, S-twist, tightly spun (overspun), 20 warps/cm, green. WEFT (?): wool, S-twist, tightly spun (overspun), 18 wefts/cm, green.

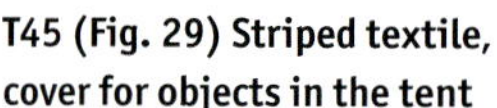

T45 (Fig. 29) Striped textile, cover for objects in the tent
Animal hair (yak, goat, sheep?). 75×204 cm. WEAVE: plain with supplementary wefts. PATTERN: coloured stripes with a central ornamental stripe. COMMENT: seven panels sewn together, one edge hemmed, the other fringed. WARP: animal hair or wool (?), plied S2Z, 16 warps/cm, white, yellow, rose, red, blue, green, brown. WEFT: animal hair (yak?), plied S2Z, 4 wefts/cm, brown. SUPPLEMENTARY WEFT: animal hair (?), tightly plied S2Z, white, red, blue. SEWING THREAD: wool (?), plied S2Z, brown. SEAMS: panels sewn together at the selvedges with overcast stitching. Seams also with overcast stitching. END FINISHING: the fringes on the lower edge have been added. Z2S, twisted together. Light brown fringes in S2Z, each with 2 plied warps.

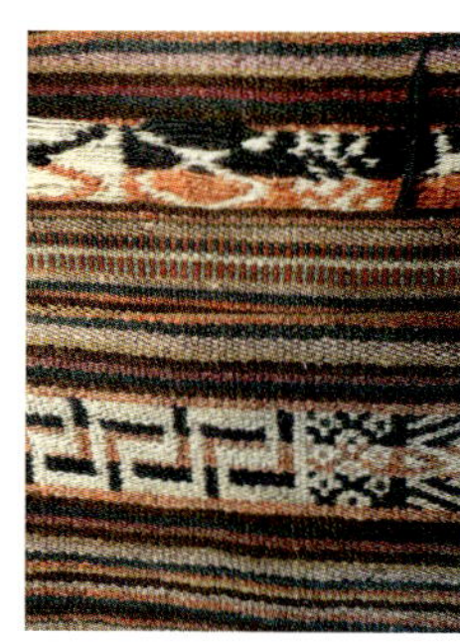

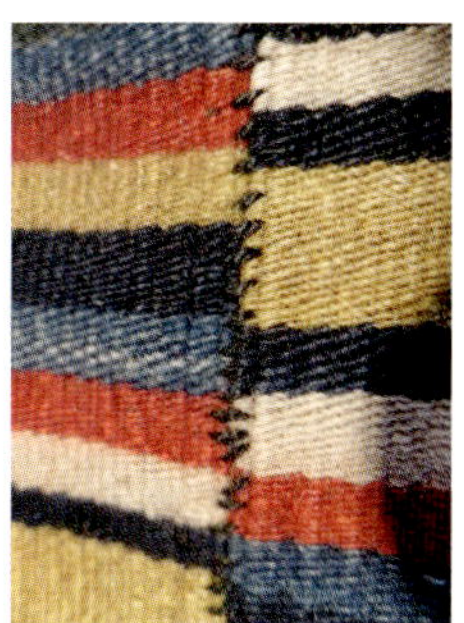

T51 (Fig. 20): Striped textile, apron or hip cloth
Wool (sheep). 84×85 cm. WEAVE: S-twill 2/2. PATTERN: coloured weft stripes. COMMENT: four narrow panels sewn together; upper and lower edges hemmed. WARP: wool (?), tightly plied S2Z, 12 warps/cm, undyed brown. WEFT: wool (?), lightly spun Z, 32–34 wefts/cm, white, yellow, red, green, light and dark blue. SEWING THREAD: wool (?), plied S2Z, black (probably undyed). SEAMS: the 4 panels are sewn together at their selvedges with overcast stitching. The ends are hemmed with running stitches using doubled thread.

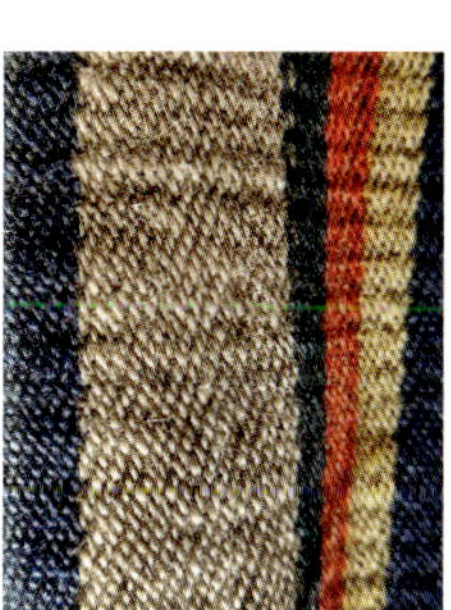

T52 (Fig. 17): Striped textile, apron
Wool (sheep). 62×68 cm. WEAVE: S-twill 2/2. PATTERN: coloured weft stripes. COMMENT: three narrow panels sewn together, upper and lower edges hemmed. WARP 1: wool (?), plied S2Z, 12 warps/cm, undyed dark brown. WARP 2: wool (?), S2Z, 10 warps/cm, natural colours, undyed. WEFT: wool (?), Z-spun, 26–30 wefts/cm, white, yellow, red, dark blue, green (yarn-dyed). SEWING THREAD: wool (?), S2Z, black. SEAMS: the 3 panels are sewn together at the selvedges with overcast stitching. Double thread was used for the hemming.

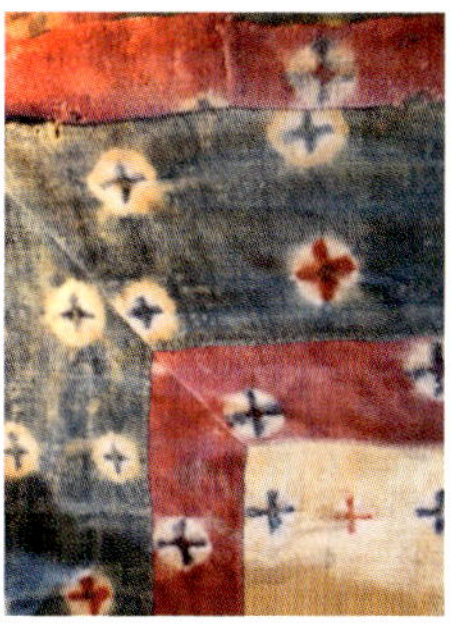

T71 (Fig. 11): Cover for a long cushion in *nambu* textile
Wool (sheep?). 232×86 cm. WEAVE: S-twill 2/2. PATTERN: plangi (tie-dye) technique (?). COMMENT: different coloured strips cut to size and sewn together. Originally, the textile had a nap, now worn away and only evident in a few places, for example along the seams on the reverse. WARP: wool (?), tightly S-spun, 12 warps/cm, white, yellow, red, green (garment-dyed). WEFT: wool (?), Z-spun, 8–10 wefts/cm in the same colours. SEWING THREAD: wool (?), plied S2Z, undyed brown. SEAMS: the pieces are sewn together with running stitches, along some cut edges with overcast stitching.

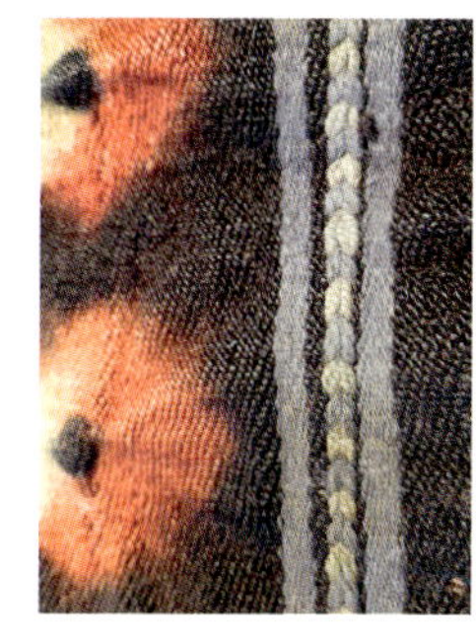

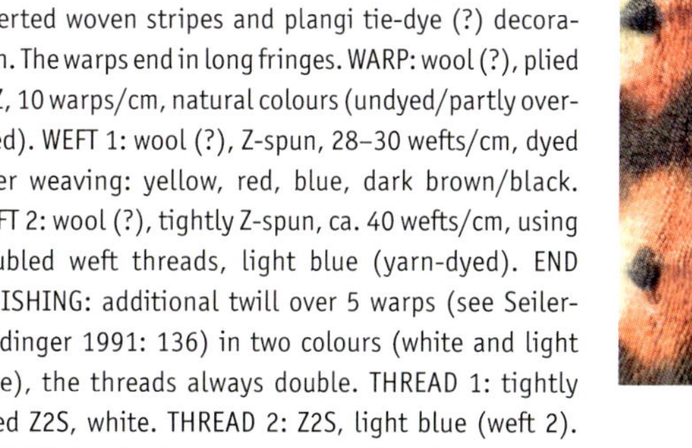

T91 (Fig. 21): Long sash
Wool (sheep). 320×16 cm. WEAVE: S-twill 2/2. PATTERN: inserted woven stripes and plangi tie-dye (?) decoration. The warps end in long fringes. WARP: wool (?), plied S2Z, 10 warps/cm, natural colours (undyed/partly overdyed). WEFT 1: wool (?), Z-spun, 28–30 wefts/cm, dyed after weaving: yellow, red, blue, dark brown/black. WEFT 2: wool (?), tightly Z-spun, ca. 40 wefts/cm, using doubled weft threads, light blue (yarn-dyed). END FINISHING: additional twill over 5 warps (see Seiler-Baldinger 1991: 136) in two colours (white and light blue), the threads always double. THREAD 1: tightly plied Z2S, white. THREAD 2: Z2S, light blue (weft 2). FRINGES: in sets, three pairs of warp threads in S-twists (of 2 threads each in Z-twist), knotted together at their ends, long fringes with blended colours (garment-dyed).

NOTES

1 Eight of the nine textiles analysed here are described and illustrated in the contribution by Christiane Kalantari. The number of the illustration – "Fig." – is given with each analysis.

2 The types of fibres were identified solely from optic and tactile impression and are, therefore, uncertain. This is indicated by the question marks.

LIST OF REFERENCES

Ahmed, Monisha 2002:
Living Fabric. Weaving among the Nomads of Ladakh Himalaya. Bangkok.

[Aisin Gioro Pu Yi] 1983:
From Emperor to Citizen. The Autobiography of Aisin-Gioro Pu Yi. Peking (2nd edition; First edition: 1964).

Anninos, Tony 1997:
Painted Tibetan Furniture. In: *Arts of Asia* 27, 1: 47–65.

Anninos, Tony 2000:
Tibetan Leather Boxes. In: *Arts of Asia* 30, 1: 101–117.

Anonymous 1987:
Der tiefgründige Weg des Phowa. Meditationsanweisung der Karma-Kagyu Linie. Vienna.

Anonymous n.d.:
Chinese Nichols Rugs. In: Internet Antique Gazette. Reference Information on Antiques & Fine Art Topics. http://www.internetantiquegazette.com/oriental_carpets_rugs/1373_chinese_nichols_rugs/ (last accessed 11 May 2016).

Appel, Michaela 2008:
Friedl Martin. In: Jean-Loup Rousselot (ed.): *450 Jahre Völkerkunde in München, 850 Jahre München*. Munich 2008: 27.

Appel, Michaela & Bernd During & Thomas Huck (eds.) 2014:
"... ein Land voller Rätsel und Geheimnisse". Briefe aus Ladakh von Amalie und Sebastian Schmitt 1907–1913. Munich.

Appel, Michaela & Christine Stelzig (eds.) 2012:
Netzwerk Exotik. 150 Jahre Völkerkundemuseum München. Munich.

Asian Art Museum of San Francisco (ed.) 1992:
Beauty, Wealth and Power. Jewels and Ornaments of Asia. San Francisco.

Bartholomew, Terese Tse 2006:
Hidden Meanings in Chinese Art. San Francisco.

Beer, Robert 2003:
The Handbook of Tibetan Buddhist Symbols. Chicago, London.

Beger, Bruno 1998:
Mit der deutschen Tibetexpedition Ernst Schäfer 1938/39 nach Lhasa. Wiesbaden.

Bellezza, John Vincent 2000:
Images of Lost Civilization. The Ancient Rock Art of Upper Tibet. http://www.asianart.com/articles/rockart/ (last accessed 15 September 2016).

Bellezza, John Vincent 2013:
Death and Beyond in Ancient Tibet: Archaic Concepts and Practices in a Thousand-Year-Old Illuminated Funerary Manuscript and Old Tibetan Funerary Documents of Gathang Bumpa and Dunhuang. Vienna.

Bidder, Hans 1979:
Carpets from Eastern Turkestan Known as Khotan, Samarkand and Kansu Carpets. Accokeek (Maryland), Tübingen (2nd edition, reprint of the 1964 London edition).

Brauen, Martin 1980:
Feste in Ladakh. Graz.

Brauen, Martin 1982:
Volksglauben. In: Claudius C. Müller & Walter Raunig (eds.): *Der Weg zum Dach der Welt*. Innsbruck, Frankfurt/M. 1982: 244–274.

Brescius, Moritz von & Friederike Kaiser & Stephanie Kleidt (eds.) 2015:
Über den Himalaya. Die Expedition der Brüder Schlagintweit nach Indien und Zentralasien 1854 bis 1858. Cologne, Weimar, Vienna.

Buckley, Chris 2011:
Living Hands. Tibetan Arts and Artisans. Hong Kong.

Buckley, Chris 2014:
Local Colour. In: *HALI* 179 (Spring 2014): 60–69.

Bunker, Emma C. 2001:
The Cemetery at Shanpula, Xinjiang. Simple Burials, Complex Textiles. In: Dominik Keller & Regula Schorta (eds.): Fabulous Creatures from the Desert Sands. Central Asian Woolen Textiles from the Second Century BC to the Second Century AD. (*Riggisberger Berichte*, 10) Riggisberg 2001: 15–45.

Bunn, Stephanie 2010:
Nomadic Felts. (*Artistic Traditions in World Cultures*) London.

Casey, Jane 2008:
Seats of Power: Tantric Carpets and Textiles from the Himalayas. In: Anna Maria Rossi & Fabio Rossi Ltd. (eds.): *Tantric Carpets from the Himalayas*. London: 7–12.

Chodrak, Trinley & Kesang Tashi 2000:
Of Wool and Loom. The Tradition of Tibetan Rugs. Bangkok.

Clarke, John 1997:
Tibet. Caught in Time. Reading.

Clarke, John 2006:
A History of Ironworking in Tibet. Centers of Production, Styles, and Techniques. In: Donald J. LaRocca (ed.): *Warriors of the Himalaya. Rediscovering the Arms and Armor of Tibet*. New York 2006: 21–33.

Coad, Sam (ed.) 2014:
Wangden / Style. An Exhibition of Early Tibetan Wangden Rugs. Bristol.

Cole, Thomas J. 1990a:
A Tribal Tradition. In: *HALI* 12 (No. 1, Issue 49, February 1990): 16–29.

Cole, Thomas J. 1990b:
A Commentary on Tibetan Carpets. In: *Arts of Asia* 20, 3: 166–173.

Cole, Thomas 2003:
In the Plateau Style. In: *HALI* 131 (November/December 2003): 78–81.

Cole, Thomas 2004:
Dream Weavers: Textile Art from the Tibetan Plateau. Singapore.

Cole, Thomas 2011:
Patterns of Life. The Art of Tibetan Carpets. New York.

Corona, Luca & Camilla Hulse Corona 2004:
Tibetan Furniture: Construction, Form and Function.
In: David Kamansky (ed.): *Wooden Wonders. Tibetan Furniture in Secular and Religious Life*. Pasadena, Chicago 2004: 23–60.

Dagyab Rinpoche, Loden Sherap 1992:
Buddhistische Glückssymbole im tibetischen Kulturraum.
Eine Untersuchung der neun bekanntesten Symbolgruppen.
(*Diederichs Gelbe Reihe, 93: Tibet*) Munich.

Dalai Lama Tenzin Gyatso & Jeffrey Hopkins 2002:
Kālachakra Tantra. Der Einweihungsritus. Der Ritualtext von Kädrup Geleg Pälsangpo mit detaillierten Erläuterungen. Berlin.

Darchen, Karma Trinley 2012:
Secrets of Tibetan Weaving. The Greensmith Collection. Chiang Mai.

Das, Sarat Chandra 1902:
Journey to Lhasa and Central Tibet. London.

De Jong, Koos 2013:
Dragon & Horse. Saddle Rugs and Other Horse Tack from China and Beyond. Amsterdam, Hong Kong.

Denwood, Philip 1974:
The Tibetan Carpet. Warminster.

Desrosiers, Sophie 1982:
Beschreibung einer tibetischen Schleuder.
In: Claudius C. Müller & Walter Raunig (eds.):
Der Weg zum Dach der Welt. Innsbruck, Frankfurt/M. 1982: 177.

Eco, Umberto 1972:
Einführung in die Semiotik. Munich.

Eiland, Murray L. 1979:
Chinese and Exotic Rugs. Boston.

Eiland, Murray L. & Murray Eiland 1998:
Oriental Rugs. A Complete Guide. London.

Eliade, Mircea 1987:
The Sacred and the Profane. The Nature of Religion. New York.

Emery, Irene 1980:
The Primary Structures of Fabrics. An Illustrated Classification.
Washington, D.C.

Engelhardt, Isrun 2003:
The Ernst-Schäfer-Tibet-Expedition 1938–1939. New Light on the Political History of Tibet in the First Half of the 20th Century.
In: Alex McKay (ed.): *Tibet and Her Neighbours. A History*.
London 2003: 187–195.

Engelhardt, Isrun (ed.) 2007:
Tibet in 1938-1939. Photographs from the Ernst Schäfer Expedition to Tibet. Chicago.

Everding, Karl-Heinz 1993:
Tibet: Lamaistische Klosterkultur, nomadische Lebensformen und bäuerlicher Alltag auf dem "Dach der Welt".
(*DuMont Kunstreiseführer*) Cologne.

Flood, Finbarr Barry 2009:
Objects of Translation: Material Culture and Medieval "Hindu-Muslim" Encounter. Princeton.

Ford, Jim 1987:
Der Tibeter-Teppich seit 1959. In: Hans Hongsermaier (ed.):
Tibeter-Teppiche. Innsbruck 1987: 80–112.

Ford, Jim & Barbara Ford 1989:
Der Stellenwert der Sammlung in der Teppichkunst. In:
Mimi Lipton (ed.): *Tigerteppiche aus Tibet*. Stuttgart 1989: 151–184.

Francke, Hermann 1898:
Ein Besuch im buddhistischen Kloster Hemis (Ladāk). In: *Globus. Illustrierte Zeitschrift für Länder- und Völkerkunde* 73, 1898: 1–8.

Francke, Hermann 1921:
Durch Zentralasien in die indische Gefangenschaft. Herrnhut.

Goepper, Roger & Jaroslav Poncar 1996:
Alchi. Ladakh's Hidden Buddhist Sanctuary. The Sumtsek. London.

Goldstein, Melvyn C. & Cynthia M. Beall 1990:
Nomads of Western Tibet. The Survival of a Way of Life.
Berkeley, Los Angeles.

Gonick, Gloria 2015:
Early Carpets and Tapestries on the Eastern Silk Road.
Woodbridge (Suffolk).

Grönbold, Günter 1991:
Tibetische Buchdeckel. (*Bayerische Staatsbibliothek. Ausstellungskataloge*, 54) Munich.

Gropp, Gerd 1989:
A. H. Francke und die Kalmücken. In: Walther Heissig & Claudius C. Müller (eds.): *Die Mongolen*. Volume 2.
Innsbruck, Frankfurt/M. 1989: 106–108.

Gyalpo, Tsering et al. 2012:
Khorchag. (*Studies and Materials on Historical Western Tibet*, volume 1)
Lhasa.

Hackmack, Adolf 1924:
Chinese Carpets and Rugs. Tientsin.

Harris, Tina 2013:
Geographical Diversions: Tibetan Trade, Global Transactions.
(*Geographies of Justice and Social Transformation*, 18)
Athens (Georgia), London.

Heissig, Walther & Claudius C. Müller (eds.) 1989:
Die Mongolen, volumes 1 & 2. Munich.

Heller, Amy 2009:
Hidden Treasures of the Himalayas. Tibetan Manuscripts, Paintings and Sculptures of Dolpo. Chicago.

Hirsch, Udo 1991:
The Fabric of Deities & Kings. In: *HALI* 13
(No. 4, Issue 58, August 1991): 104–111.

Hoffman, Michael E. & Lobsang P. Lhalungpa 1983:
Tibet. The Sacred Realm. Photographs 1880–1950. New York.

Holzammer, Markus 2003:
Der Apotheker Joseph Schedel: Tagebücher aus Japan (1886–1899) und China (1909–1921). (*Beiträge zur Wirtschafts- und Sozialgeschichte BWSG*, 97) Stuttgart.

Hong Kong Museum of Art (ed.) 1995:
Heaven's Embroidered Cloths. One Thousand Years of Chinese Textiles. Hong Kong.

Houston, Mary G. 1920:
Ancient Egyptian, Mesopotamian and Persian Costume and Decoration. London.

Hubel, Reinhard G. 1965:
Ullstein Teppichbuch. Eine Teppichkunde für Käufer und Sammler. Berlin, Frankfurt, Vienna.

Hummel, Siegbert 1949:
Elemente der Tibetischen Kunst. (*Forschungen zur Völkerdynamik Zentral- und Ostasiens*, issue 3) Leipzig.

Hummel, Siegbert 1956/57:
Schleuder und Tierbalgboot in Tibet. In: *Bulletin der Schweizerischen Gesellschaft für Anthropologie und Ethnologie* 33: 42–48.

Hummel, Siegbert 1993:
Mythologisches aus Eurasien im Ge-sar-Heldenepos der Tibeter. Ulm.

Jettmar, Karl & Volker Thewalt 1985:
Zwischen Gandhāra und den Seidenstraßen: Felsbilder am Karakorum Highway. Entdeckungen deutsch-pakistanischer Expeditionen 1979–1984. Mainz/Rhein.

Jones, Schuyler 1996:
Tibetan Nomads. Environment, Pastoral Economy, and Material Culture. (*The Carlsberg Foundation's Nomad Research Project*) London.

Kalantari, see also: Papa-Kalantari

Kalantari, Christiane & Tsering Gyalpo 2011:
On Ornament, Textiles and Baldachins Depicted on the Ceilings of Buddhist Cave Temples in Khartse Valley, Western Tibet. Form, Function and Meaning. Kunstgeschichte-ejournal.net.: http://www.kunstgeschichte-ejournal.net/306/1/Kalantari_und_Gyalpo_102.pdf (last accessed 15 June 2016).

Kamansky, David (ed.) 2004:
Wooden Wonders. Tibetan Furniture in Secular and Religious Life. Pasadena, Chicago.

Kater, Michael H. 2006:
Das "Ahnenerbe" der SS, 1935–1945. Ein Beitrag zur Kulturpolitik des Dritten Reiches. (*Studien zur Zeitgeschichte,* volume 6) Munich (4th edition).

Kick, Wilhelm 1982:
Alexander von Humboldt und die Brüder Schlagintweit. In: Claudius C. Müller & Walter Raunig (eds.): *Der Weg zum Dach der Welt.* Innsbruck, Frankfurt/M. 1982: 75–77.

Kleidt, Stephanie 2015:
Lust und Last. Die Sammlungen der Gebrüder Schlagintweit. In: Moritz von Brescius & Friederike Kaiser & Stephanie Kleidt (eds.): *Über den Himalaya. Die Expedition der Brüder Schlagintweit nach Indien und Zentralasien 1854 bis 1858.* Cologne, Weimar, Vienna 2015: 113–137.

Klimburg-Salter, Deborah 1982:
The Silk Route and the Diamond Path. Esoteric Buddhist Art on the Trans-Himalayan Trade Routes. Los Angeles.

Köpke, Wulf & Bernd Schmelz (eds.) 2005:
Die Welt des tibetischen Buddhismus. (*Mitteilungen aus dem Museum für Völkerkunde Hamburg*, new series, volume 36) Hamburg.

Körner, Hans 1982:
Die Brüder Schlagintweit – Hermann, Adolph, Robert und Emil – Familie, Forschungsreise in Indien und Hochasien, Werke, Sammlungen und Nachlaß, Bibliographie. In: Claudius C. Müller & Walter Raunig (eds.): *Der Weg zum Dach der Welt.* Innsbruck, Frankfurt/M. 1982: 62–75.

Krotkov, Jasmine 1991:
Tibetan Rug Design in History. In: *Oriental Rug Review* 11/2: 6–10.

Kuløy, Hallvard Kåre 1996:
Tibetan Rugs. Bangkok (6th edition).

Landon, Perceval 1905:
Lhasa. An Account of the Country and People of Central Tibet and of the Progress of the Mission sent there by the English Government in the year 1903–4. Volume 1. London.

Lange, Diana 2012:
"Local Handicraft Made by Tibetan Village Artisans". Globale Einflüsse und ihre Folgen für das lokale Handwerk in Zentraltibet. In: *Zentralasiatische Studien* 41: 89–106.

LaRocca, Donald J. 2006:
Warriors of the Himalaya. Rediscovering the Arms and Armor of Tibet. New York.

Leeper, Arthur Alden 1984:
Origins of the Tibetan Pile Rug Tradition: Archaeological Evidence. In: Diana K. Myers (ed.): *Temple, Household, Horseback: Rugs of the Tibetan Plateau.* Washington, D.C. 1984: 21–25.

Lindgren, Uta 1982:
Die naturwissenschaftlichen Forschungen der Brüder Schlagintweit in Hochasien. In: Claudius C. Müller & Walter Raunig (eds.): *Der Weg zum Dach der Welt.* Innsbruck, Frankfurt/M. 1982: 98–104.

Lipton, Mimi (ed.) 1989:
Tigerteppiche aus Tibet. Stuttgart.

Lorentz, Hans Achim 1972:
A View of Chinese Rugs from the Seventeenth to the Twentieth Century. London, Boston.

Lorentz, Hans Achim 1975:
Chinesische Teppiche 17.–20. Jahrhundert. Geschichte, Ästhetik, Symbolik. Munich.

Lu, Hongqi 2003:
Antique Carpets of China. Beijing.

Mauch, Peter 1987:
Die alten tibetischen Teppiche. In: Hans Hongsermeier (ed.): *Tibeter-Teppiche.* Innsbruck 1987: 13–79.

Mergenthaler, Markus 2010: Der Traum vom Himalaja ... in München. In: Claudius Müller & Markus Mergenthaler (eds.): *Tibet. Religion Kunst Mythos.* Dettelbach 2010: 183–192.

Meyer, Fernand 1987:
Trésors du Tibet. Paris.

Mierau, Peter 2006:
Nationalsozialistische Expeditionspolitik. Deutsche Asien-Expeditionen 1933–1945. (*Münchner Beiträge zur Geschichtswissenschaft*, volume 1) Munich.

Miller, Daniel 2009:
An Early Origin for Tibetan Carpets. In: Daniel Miller (ed.): *Auspicious Carpets. Tibetan Rugs and Textiles.* San Francisco 2009: 75–78.

Morris, Charles W. 1981:
Symbolik und Realität. Frankfurt/M.

Müller, Claudius C. & Walter Raunig (eds.) 1982:
Der Weg zum Dach der Welt. Innsbruck, Frankfurt/M.

Myers, Diana K. 1984:
Temple, Household, Horseback: Rugs of the Tibetan Plateau. Washington, D.C.

Nawang, Tsering Shakspo 2008:
The Culture of Ladakh through Song and Dance. Leh.

Page, John & Serina Page 1990:
The Woven Mystery. Old Tibetan Rugs. London.

Pallis, Marco 2004:
Peaks and Lamas. A Classic Book on Mountaineering, Buddhism and Tibet. Washington, D.C.

Papa-Kalantari, see also: Kalantari

Papa-Kalantari, Christiane A. 2000:
Die Deckenmalereien des gSum-brtsegs in Alchi (Ladakh). Studie zu den Textildarstellungen eines frühen buddhistischen Tempels aus dem westtibetischen Kulturkreis. Vienna.

Papa-Kalantari, Christiane A. 2002:
The Ceiling Paintings of the Alchi gsum brtsegs: Problems of Style
In: Eva Allinger & Deborah E. Klimburg-Salter (eds.):
Buddhist Art and Tibetan Patronage. Ninth to Fourteenth Centuries. (*Proceedings of the 9th Seminar of the International Association for Tibetan Studies, 2000*) Leiden 2002: 85–113.

Pearce, Chris (ed.) 1992:
Woven Jewels, Tibetan Rugs from Southern California Collections. Pasadena (California).

Piaget, Jean 1973: *Der Strukturalismus*. Olten.

Piccus, Robert P. 2011:
Sacred & Secular. The Piccus Collection of Tibetan Rugs. Chicago.

Pinner, Lesley 1983:
Die Struktur einiger chinesischer Teppiche und die Verwendung von "Einschieb-" und kettenteilenden Knoten. In: *HALI* 5 (No. 3): 272–275.

Polter, Stefan B. 1982:
Nadelschau in Hochasien: Englische Magnetforschung und die Brüder Schlagintweit. In: Claudius C. Müller & Walter Raunig (eds.): *Der Weg zum Dach der Welt*. Innsbruck, Frankfurt/M. 1982: 78–98.

Reynolds, Valrae 1999:
From the Sacred Realm. Treasures of Tibetan Art from the Newark Museum. Munich, London, New York.

Rhodes, Nicholas & Deki Rhodes 2006:
A Man of the Frontier. S.W. Laden La (1876-1936). His Life and Times in Darjeeling and Tibet. Kolkata.

Richtsfeld, Bruno J. 2010/11 (ed.):
August Hermann Franckes (1870–1930) Bearbeitung der Serindien- und Ladakh-Sammlung Francke/Körber im Völkerkundemuseum München aus dem Jahre 1928. Die Serindien-Sammlung des Staatlichen Museums für Völkerkunde München I.
In: *Münchner Beiträge zur Völkerkunde* 14, 2010/2011: 65–128.

Ronge, Veronika 1978a:
Das tibetische Handwerkertum vor 1959. (*Beiträge zur Südasienforschung, Südasien-Institut, Universität Heidelberg*, volume 43) Wiesbaden.

Ronge, Veronika 1978b:
Tibetische Brettchenweberei. In: *Zentralasiatische Studien* 12: 237–251.

Ronge, Veronika 2005: Zeugnisse der Vielfalt:
Kleidung in Tibet. In: Wulf Köpke & Bernd Schmelz (eds.): Die Welt des tibetischen Buddhismus. (*Mitteilungen aus dem Museum für Völkerkunde Hamburg*, new series, volume 36) Hamburg 2005: 525–547.

Rossi, Anna Maria & Fabio Rossi Ltd. (eds.) 2008:
Tantric Carpets from the Himalayas. London.

Sabahi, Taher 2001: *Teunis Wollesen Collection. Teppiche vom Dach der Welt*. Turin.

Schäfer, Ernst 1943:
Geheimnis Tibet. Erster Bericht der Deutschen Tibet-Expedition Ernst Schäfer. Munich.

Schäfer, Ernst 1949:
Fest der weißen Schleier. Eine Forscherfahrt durch Tibet nach Lhasa, der heiligen Stadt des Gottkönigtums. Braunschweig.

Schäfer, Ernst 1950:
Über den Himalaja ins Land der Götter. Auf Forscherfahrt von Indien nach Tibet. Hamburg, Berlin.

Schlagintweit, Stefan 1982:
Die Brüder Schlagintweit. Ein Abriß ihres Lebens.
In: Claudius C. Müller & Walter Raunig (eds.):
Der Weg zum Dach der Welt. Innsbruck, Frankfurt/M. 1982: 11–13.

Schlim, Jean Louis 2001:
König Ludwig II. von Bayern. Traum und Technik. Munich.

Seeberger, Max 1982:
Die wissenschaftlichen Instrumente der Brüder Schlagintweit auf ihren Forschungsreisen in Hochasien.
In: Claudius C. Müller & Walter Raunig (eds.): *Der Weg zum Dach der Welt.* Innsbruck, Frankfurt/M. 1982: 104–111.

Seiler-Baldinger, Annemarie 1991:
Systematik der textilen Techniken. (*Basler Beiträge zur Ethnologie*, volume 32) Basel (new, completely revised and enlarged edition).

Singer, Jane Casey 1996:
Gold Jewelry from Tibet and Nepal. London.

Skorupski, Tadeusz 1983:
Tibetan Amulets. (*White Orchid Books*) Bangkok.

Smejkal, Alex 1990:
Kult und Alltag in Tibet. Die tibetischen Sammlungen in der Völkerkunde-Abteilung des Niedersächsischen Landesmuseums Hannover. Hanover.

Snellgrove, L. David & Tadeusz Skorupski 1977:
The Cultural Heritage of Ladakh. Warminster (2 volumes).

Spuhler, Friedrich 1987:
Die Orientteppiche im Museum für Islamische Kunst Berlin. (*Veröffentlichungen des Museums für Islamische Kunst*, volume 1) Munich.

Spuhler, Friedrich 2007:
On the Long Journey from East to West. Dragons from Tibet. In: Annette Hagedorn & Avinoa Shalem (eds.): *Facts and Artefacts. Art in the Islamic World: Festschrift for Jens Kroeger on his 65th Birthday.* Leiden 2007: 251–262.

Staudigel, Otfried 2008:
Gewebte Bilder, Enträtselte Motive. Doppelseitige Brettchengewebe aus Birma, Tibet und Tunesien - Woven Images Unravelled Motifs. Double-Faced Tablet-Woven Bands from Burma, Tibet and Tunisia. Norderstedt.

Stein, Rolf Alfred 1972:
Tibetan Civilization. Stanford (California).

Tanavoli, Parviz 1998:
Horse & Camel Trappings from Tribal Iran. Teheran.

Taring, Rintschen Dölma 1992:
Ich bin eine Tochter Tibets. Lebenszeugnisse aus einer versunkenen Welt. Berne, Munich, Vienna (2nd edition).

Tsareva, Elena 1984:
Salor Carpets. In: *HALI* 6 (No. 2): 126–135.

Tsareva, Elena 2005:
Some Notes on the Structure of Classical Chinese Carpets. In: Hans König & Rupert Waterhouse (eds.): *Glanz der Himmelssöhne. Kaiserliche Teppiche aus China. 1400-1750.* Cologne, London 2005: 187–208.

Tsareva, Elena 2008:
K voprosu o datirovanii rannih turkmenskih kovrov (salory, saryki, naselenie Srednei Amudaryi). In: *Trudy Margianskoi arkeologicheskoi ekspeditsii.* [On the Issue of Dating of Early Turkmen Carpets (Salor, Saryks, Populations of the Middle Amu Darya) In: *Transactions of the Margiana archaeological expedition*]. T. 2. Moscow 2008: 234–244.

Tsareva, Elena 2011:
Turkmen Carpets. Masterpieces of Steppe Art, from 16th to 19th Centuries. The Hoffmeister Collection. Stuttgart.

Tsareva, Elena 2015:
Istoriya formirovaniya I rasprostraneniya vorsovyh tehnik (evraziiskaya traditsiya) [History of Origin and Spread of Piled Techniques (Eurasian Tradition)]. In: *Radlovskii sbornik* 2015: 67–81.

Tsareva, Elena 2016:
Turkmen Carpets. The Neville Kingston Collection. Stuttgart.

Tucci, Giuseppe 1935:
On some Bronze Objects Discovered in Western Tibet. In: *Artibus Asiae* 5, 2/4: 105–116.

Tucci, Giuseppe 1941:
Indo-Tibetica IV. Gyantse ed i suoi monasteri. Parte I. Descrizione generale dei tempi. (*Reale Accademia d'Italia. Studi e documenti*, 1) Rom.

Tucci, Giuseppe 1973:
Transhimalaya. Delhi, Bombay, London.

Utzinger, Rudolf 1923:
Masken. (*Orbis Pictus/Weltkunst-Bücherei*, volume 13) Berlin.

Van Grevenbroek, Bob & Charles Gay 2009:
A Primer on Old Tibetan Carpets. In: Daniel Miller (ed.): *Auspicious Carpets, Tibetan Rugs and Textiles.* San Francisco 2009: 133–146.

Walravens, Hartmut 2008:
Josef Schedel (1856–1943). Ein deutscher Apotheker in Ostasien. Nebst den Briefen von Justizrat Hans Rudelsberger und Professor Lucian Scherman. (*Neuerwerbungen der Ostasien-Abteilung*, special issue 17) Berlin.

Watt, James C. Y. 1998:
Textiles of the Mongol Period in China. In: *Orientations* 29, 3: 72–83.

Watt, James C. Y. & Anne Wardwell 1997:
When Silk was Gold. Central Asian and Chinese Textiles. New York.

Weigelt, Uta 2003:
Lucian Scherman (1864–1946) und das Münchner Museum für Völkerkunde. (*Münchner Beiträge zur Völkerkunde*, supplementary issue 2, 2003) Munich.

Weihreter, Hans 1988:
Schmuck aus dem Himalaja. Graz.

Weihreter, Hans 2001:
Westhimalaya. Am Rand der bewohnbaren Erde. Graz.

Weihreter, Hans 2002:
Thog-lcags. Geheimnisvolle Amulette Tibets. Augsburg.

Weihreter, Hans 2010:
Ladakh. Vergessene Feste. Botschaften im Fels. Graz.

Wild, Thomas 1998:
Seltene Teppiche aus Tibet – Wangden Drumtze. In: *Pazyryk. Das Jahrbuch der Pazyryk Gesellschaft*, volume 1. Munich 1998: 151–155.

Wild, Thomas 2009:
Yarlung Drumze. In: *HALI* 161 (Autumn 2009): 66–69.

Wild, Thomas 2014a:
Preface. In: Sam Coad (ed.): *Wangden / Style. An Exhibition of Early Tibetan Wangden Rugs.* Bristol 2014: 7–8.

Wild, Thomas 2014b:
Tibet's Tradition in Indigo. In: *HALI* 181 (Autumn 2014): 64–73.

Williams, Charles Alfred Speed 1941:
Chinese Symbolism and Art Motifs. A Comprehensive Handbook on Symbolism in Chinese Art through the Ages. Shanghai.

Worcester, Ted 2009:
Auspicious Carpets: A Tibetan View of Aesthetics. In: Daniel Miller (ed.): *Auspicious Carpets. Tibetan Rugs and Textiles.* Manila 2009: 15–36.

Zhang He 2010:
Figurative and Inscribed Carpets from Shanpula, Khotan: Unexpected Representations of the Hindu God Krishna. A Preliminary Study. In: *Journal of Inner Asian Art and Archaeology* 5: 59–93.

Zhang, Tracy Ying 2009:
Carpet Worlds: The Cultural Representation and Production of Tibetan Carpets. Burnaby.

Sitting rug (*khagangma*) with tiger design. 19th century, 56×62.5 cm. Karl Steiner collection no. 19, MFK inv. no. 2015-80-7

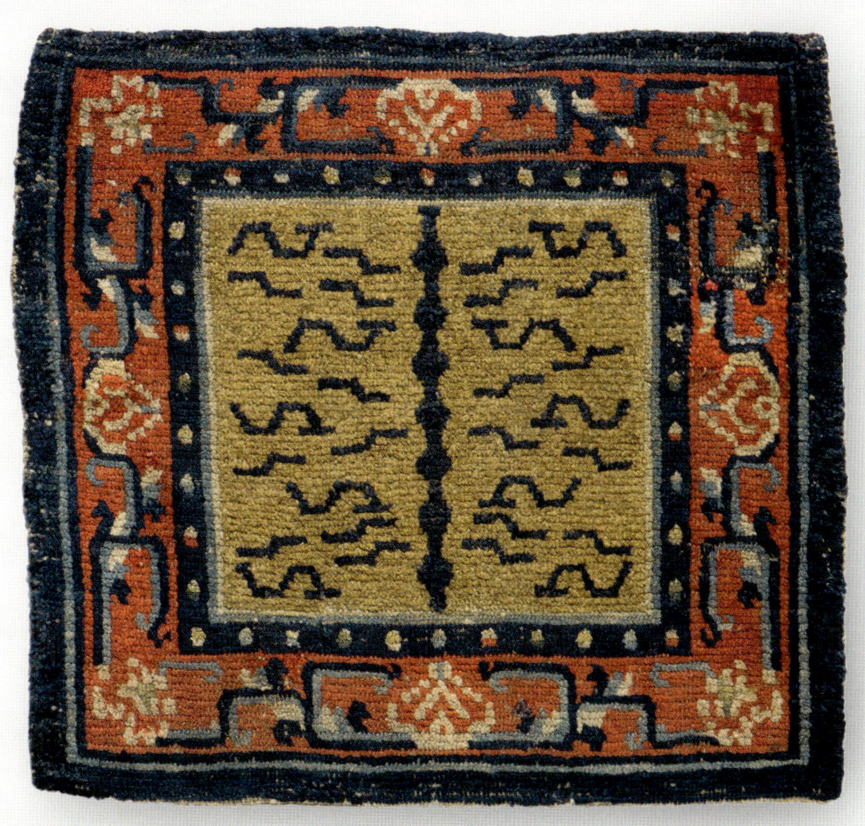

Sitting rug (*khagangma*). Ca. 1900, 71.5×78 cm. Karl Steiner collection no. 20, MFK inv. no. 2015-80-8

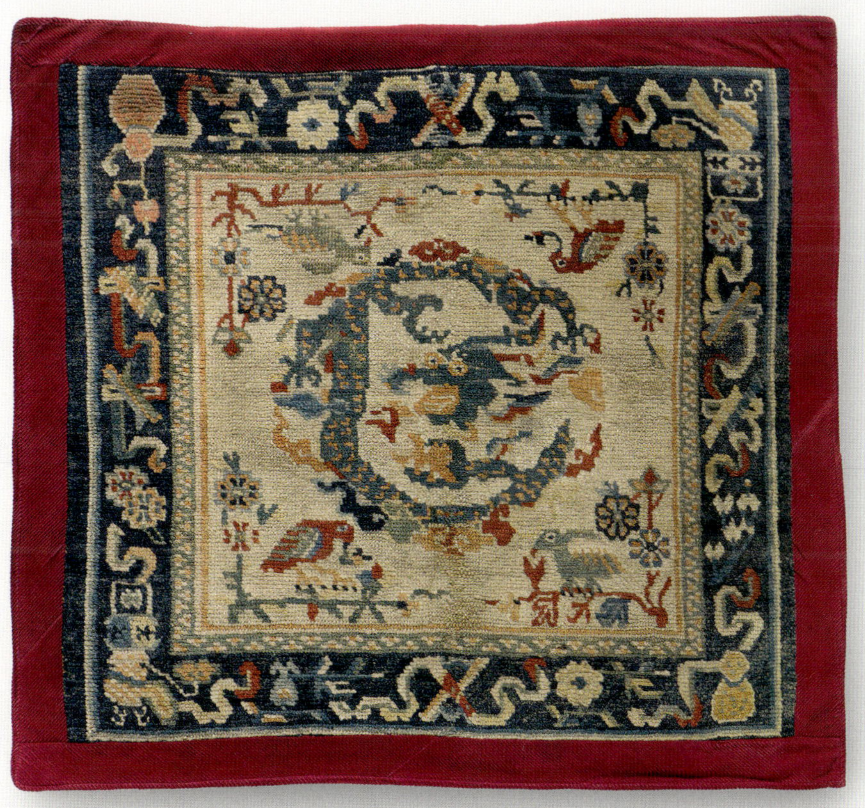

IMAGES AND CONCORDANCES[1]

PHOTOGRAPHS

© M. Buddeberg
6, 21, 23, 27, 30 top, 33, 34, 36, 37, 38, 40, 41, 42, 44, 45, 46, 49, 51–57, 89, 92 (Figs. 42, 43), 94, 149, 160 (Fig. 12), 161 (Fig. 16), 169–171, 194 (Figs. 2, 3), 196 (Figs. 4, 5), 201 (Fig. 13), 220

© S.Ch. Das
133 (Fig. 7)

© M. Franke, Museum Fünf Kontinente
Front cover, 2 (Frontispiece), 8, 10, 12, 13, 15, 17, 18 (photograph by E. Krause), 19 (photograph by E. Krause), 22, 25 (*C15*), 29 (*C117*), 35 (*T10*), 59, 60 (*C166*), 63, 64, 66 top and bottom left, 68, 70 (Fig. 10), 71 (Fig. 12), 73 (Fig. 14; *C141*), 75, 76 (Fig. 20), 77 (Fig. 22), 78 (Fig. 25), 79 (Fig. 27), 82–85, 88, 90, 91, 92 (Fig. 44), 93 (Fig. 46), 95 (Fig. 49), 96–99, 101 (Fig. 58), 102 (Fig. 60), 103, 105–109, 112, 113, 117–119, 120 (*C50**), 121–123, 125–127, 128 (*C77*), 131 (*C35*), 132 (Fig. 5; *C49*), 134 (*C77*), 136 (*C67*), 137 (*C155*), 139 (*C58*), 141 (*C137*), 142 (*C137*), 143 (*C131*), 144 (*C131*), 145 (*C24*), 146 (*C24*), 148 (*C20*), 150 (Fig. 2a: *C9*; Fig. 2b: *C10*), 151 (Fig. 3a: *C139**; Fig. 3b: *C140**), 152 (*C20*), 153 (*C82*), 154 (*C37*), 155 (*C83*), 156 (*C136**), 157 (*C11*), 158 (*K. Steiner no. 4; MFK inv. no. 2015-80-2*), 159 (*C36*), 161 (Fig. 13: *C105**; Fig. 14: *C147*; Fig. 15: *C167*), 162 (Fig. 17: *C170**; Fig. 18: *C171**; Fig. 19: *C176*; Fig. 20: *C177*; Fig. 21: *C178**; Fig. 22: *C181**), 163 (Fig. 23: *C183**; Fig. 24: *C184*; Fig. 25: *C185**; Fig. 26: *C195*; Fig. 27: *K. Steiner no. 45, MFK inv. no. 2015-80-20*; Fig. 28: *K. Steiner no. 48, MFK inv. no. 2015-80-22*), 164 (*C171**), 165 (*C185**), 166 (*C191**), 167 (*C192**), 168 (*C94*), 172 (*C61*), 173 (*C93*), 174 (*C94*), 175 (*C122*), 176 (*C123*), 177 (*C72**), 178 (*C49*), 180 (*C18*), 182 (*C18*), 183 (*C6**), 184 (*C73, MFK inv. no. 2015-31-8*), 185 (*C6**), 186 (*Bhutan 38*), 187 (Fig. 5: *Bhutan 32*; Fig. 6: *C120*), 188 (Fig. 7: *C193*; Fig. 8: *C49*), 189 (*K. Steiner no. 31, MFK inv. no. 2015-80-17*), 190 (*C19, MFK inv. no. 2015-31-23*), 192 (*T45*), 200 (*T71*), 204 (*T52*), 205 (*T62*), 206 (*T62*), 207 (*T78*), 208 (*T78*), 209 (Fig. 20: *T51*), 210 (Fig. 22: *T96*; Fig. 23: *T11*), 211 (*T31*), 212, 213 (*T41*), 214 (*T95*), 215 (Fig. 27: *T101*; Fig. 28: *T21*), 216, 217, 218 (*T45*), 219 (*T113*), 226/227 (*J45*), 228 (*K41*), 229 (*M161*), 231 (*K1*), 232 (Fig. 3: *K3*; Fig. 4: *K2*; Fig. 5: *K5*; Fig. 6: *K7*), 233, 234 (Fig. 7: *K6*; Fig. 8: *K4*; Fig. 9: *K43*; Fig. 10: *K28*; Fig. 11: *K12*), 235 (Figs. 12a, b: *K14*; Fig. 13: *K10*, Figs. 14a, b: *K9*), 236 (*K11*), 237 (Figs. 15a, b: *K13*; Fig. 16a, b: *K16*; Figs. 17a, b: *K22*; Figs. 18a, b: *K24*; Figs. 19a, b: *K73*; Figs. 21a, b: *K17, K18*; Fig. 22: *K76*), 238, 239, 240 (Figs. 23a, b: *K20, K21*; Fig. 24: *K19*), 241 (Figs. 25a, b: *K34a, b*; Fig. 26: *K15*; Fig. 27: *K41*; Fig. 28: *K42*; Fig. 29: *K23*; Figs. 30a, b: *K8a, b*), 242 (Fig. 31: *K50*; Figs. 32a, b: *K29a, b*; Fig. 33: *K30*), 243 (Fig. 34: *K31*; Fig. 35: *K37*; Figs. 36a, b: *K39*), 244, 245, 246 (Fig. 37: *K33*; Fig. 38: *K32*), 247 (Fig. 39: *K47*; Fig. 40: *K48*; Fig. 41: *K45*; Fig. 42: *K74*; Fig. 43: *K38*; Figs. 44/1–3: *K25*), 248, 249, 250 (Figs. 45/1–2: *K36*; Fig. 47: *K70*; Fig. 48: *K71*), 251 (Figs. 46a–d: *K60, K61, K64, K65*; Fig. 49: *K72*; Fig. 50: *M141*; Fig. 51: *M151*), 252 (*J43*), 257 (Fig. 7: *J3*; Fig. 8: *J8*; Fig. 9: *J7*; Fig. 10: *J4*), 258, 259, 260 (Fig. 11: *J5*; Fig. 12: J43; Fig. 13: J44; Fig. 14: J45), 261 (Fig. 15: J46; Fig. 16: J47), 262, 263, 264 (*J48*), 265 (Fig. 18: *J49*; Fig. 19: *J50*; Fig. 20: *J51*), 266 (Fig. 21: *J52*; Fig. 22: *J53*; Fig. 23: *J54*); 267 (Fig. 24: *J55*; Fig. 25: *J56*), 268, 269, 270 (Fig. 26: *J57*; Fig. 27: *J58*; Fig. 28: *J59*), 271 (Fig. 29: *J24*; Fig. 30: *J17*; Fig. 31: *J23*), 272, 273, 276, 278/279 (*F6*), 280, 283 (Fig. 5: *F3*), 285 (Fig. 9: *F1*; Fig. 10: *F2*), 288 (Fig. 12: *F4*), 291 (Fig. 17: *F5*), 293 (Fig. 21: *F9*; Fig. 22: *F7*), 294 (Fig. 23: *F8*), 295 (Fig. 25: *F10*), 296 (Fig. 26a: *F11*), 297 (Fig. 26b: *F11*), 298 (Fig. 26: *F10*), 299 (Fig. 27: *F6*), 300 (*F11*), 302/303 (*T113*), 304–331, 339, Back cover (*C57*)

© E. Geer
147

© H. Harrer
138

© A. Heller
193: Repro from Heller 2009: 107, Fig. 76

© Ch. Kalantari
197, 198 (Figs. 7, 8), 199 (Figs. 9, 10), 201 (Fig. 12), 202 (Figs. 14, 15), 203

© Karma Trinley Darchen
170

© H. F. Neumann
282, 283 (Fig. 6), 284 (Figs. 7 and 8), 288 (Fig. 11), 289, 290, 291 (Fig. 18), 292, 294 (Fig. 24)

© rangeland.herders.html
89 (Fig. 39)

© Reproline Genceller
30/31 (Fig. 6: *T59a*), 63 (Figs. 2 and 3, drawings by Denwood 1974, figs. 46 and 53), 191 (*Silk 11*), 222 (Fig. 32: *Band 1*; Fig. 33: *Band 14*), 223 (Figs. 34a, b: *Bands 17a, b*; Fig. 35: *Band 18*), 224 (*Band 20*)

© B. Schwenck
332, 333

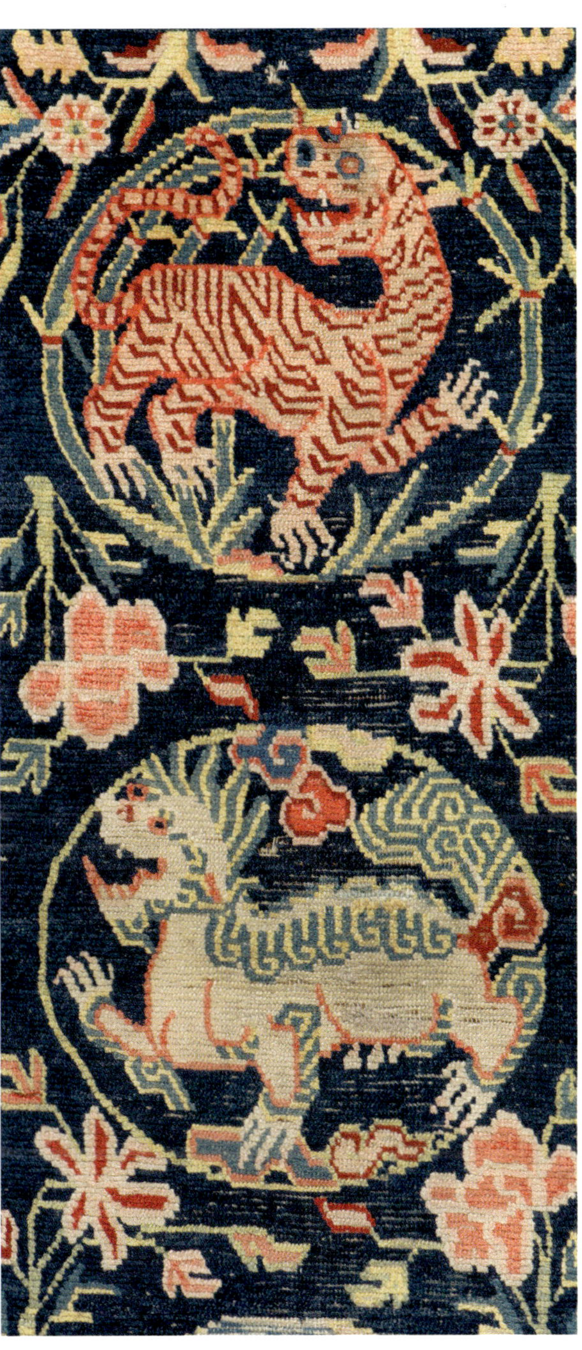

Detail of Fig. 2 in the contribution by Michael Buddeberg. Rare rug from the Wollesen collection with two of the symbolic animals of the "Four Dignities"

© S. Shapiro (MAE RAS)
100 (Fig. 56a)

© H. Staunton
(Archive no.: PRM 1999.23.1.33.2, Copyright: Pitt Rivers Museum, University of Oxford) 140

© E. Tsareva
66 (Fig. 6 right), 73 (Figs. 15c, d; 16a–c), 74 (Figs. 17b, c), 76 (Figs. 21a–c), 77 (Figs. 23b–d), 78 (Figs. 24a, b), 79 (Figs. 26a, b; 28b–d), 80 (Figs. 29a, b), 86 (Figs. 34a, b; 35b, c), 87 (Figs. 36a, b; 37b, c), 93 (Figs. 45a, b), 95 (Figs. 50a–c), 100 (Figs. 56b, c), 101 (Fig. 57 b), 102 (Figs. 59a–c), 104 (Fig. 62d), 110, 111 (Figs. 71b, c), 114 (Figs. 74a–c; 75c)

© N. Tsareva
101 (Fig. 57c)

© H. Weihreter
253, 254, 255, 256, 274, 275

© L. Weir
133 (Fig. 6)

© Th. Wild
130 (Fig. 1 right; Fig. 2), 132 (Fig. 4)

© Zhang He
130 (Fig. 1 left)

DRAWINGS

© E. Tsareva: Drawings, N. Tsvetkova: Computer graphics
69, 70 (Figs. 9a–c), 71 (Figs. 11a, b; 13a, c), 73 (Figs. 15a, b), 74 (Fig. 17a), 77 (Fig. 23a), 79 (Fig. 28a), 81, 86 (Fig. 35a), 87 (Fig. 37a), 104 (Figs. 62a–c), 111 (Fig. 71a), 114 (Figs. 75a, b)

NOTE

1 Collection numbers (C numbers) with a * are knotted items which were not examined by Elena Tsareva. Therefore their technical data are not included in the catalogue.

IMPRINT

This publication accompanies the exhibition
From the Land of the Snow Lion
Tibetan Treasures from the 15th to 20th Centuries:
The Justyna and Michael Buddeberg Collection
Museum Fünf Kontinente, Munich
9 December 2016 to 18 June 2017

Museum Fünf Kontinente
Bavarian State Museums
Maximilianstraße 42 · 80538 Munich
T +49 (0)89 210 136 100 · F +49 (0)89 210 136 247
www.museum-fuenf-kontinente.de

Director
Christine Kron

Curator
Bruno J. Richtsfeld

Exhibition Design
DIE WERFT, Munich
Matthias Nolz, Christian Raißle, Swen Sieber

Marketing, Press, and Social Media
Dorothee Schäfer, Robert Fin Steinle, Ricarda Berendson

Artistic and Cultural Promotion
Cornelia Hübler

Illustrations
Front cover and frontispiece:
Pair of snow lions, repoussé work,
gilded copper, partially coloured.
Central Tibet, 18th century,
25.5×26 and 25.5×23 cm

Back cover:
Tibetan saddle rug.
19th century, 71×57 cm

Edited by
Michael Buddeberg and Bruno J. Richtsfeld
for the Museum Fünf Kontinente, Munich

Editorial Team
Michael Buddeberg, Starnberg
Bruno J. Richtsfeld, Munich
Uta Weigelt, Singapore
Lawrence E. Fogelberg, Bad Homburg v.d.H.
Markus Voigt, Ramsgate (GB)

Copyediting
German/English: Ulrich Berkmann, Mainz
English: Paul Harris, Cologne

Translation of the Contributions
English-German: Ute Weber, Heidelberg
German-English: Sabine Lang, Christiansholm
Paul Harris, Cologne
Lawrence E. Fogelberg, Bad Homburg v.d.H.

Project Management Hirmer Verlag
Jürgen Kleidt, Munich

Photography of the Buddeberg collection
Marianne Franke, Museum Fünf Kontinente

Reproductions
REPROLINE GENCELLER, Munich
Tuncay Genceller, Anke von der Hagen

Cover Design and Book Layout
Ines von Ketelhodt, k und m design, Flörsheim am Main

Type and Paper
Officina Sans (Book/Bold), Insignia LT Std (Roman)
Gardamatt Art 150 g/m2

Publisher
Hirmer Verlag GmbH
Nymphenburger Straße 8, 80636 Munich, www.hirmerverlag.de

Printing and Binding
Printer Trento S.r.L., Trento

Printed in Italy

Bibliographical information of the German National Library
The German National Library records this publication in the German National Bibliography; detailed bibliographical data is available on the Internet at http://dnb.de

German edition: ISBN 978-3-7774-2624-2
English edition: ISBN 978-3-7774-2626-6

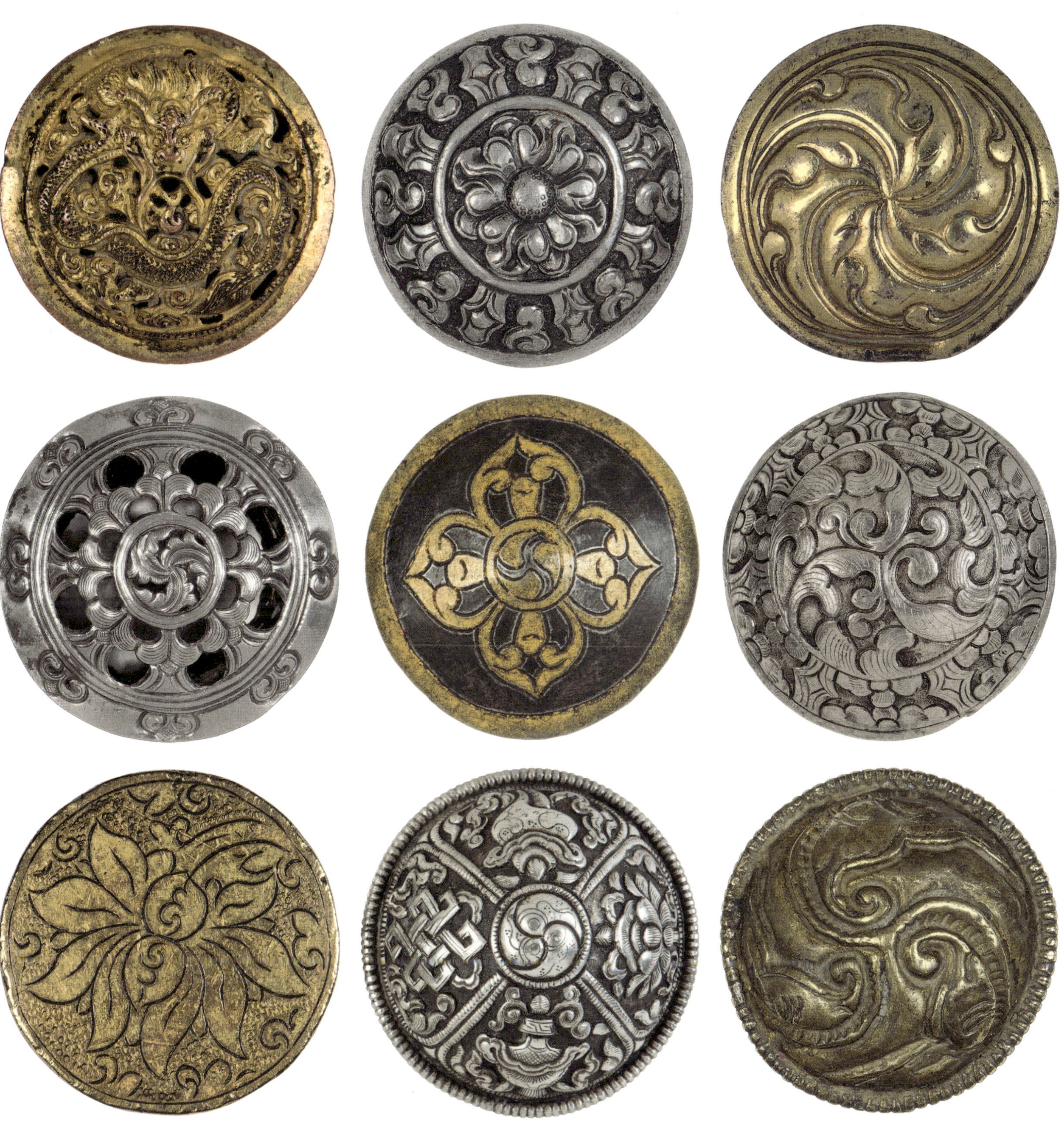

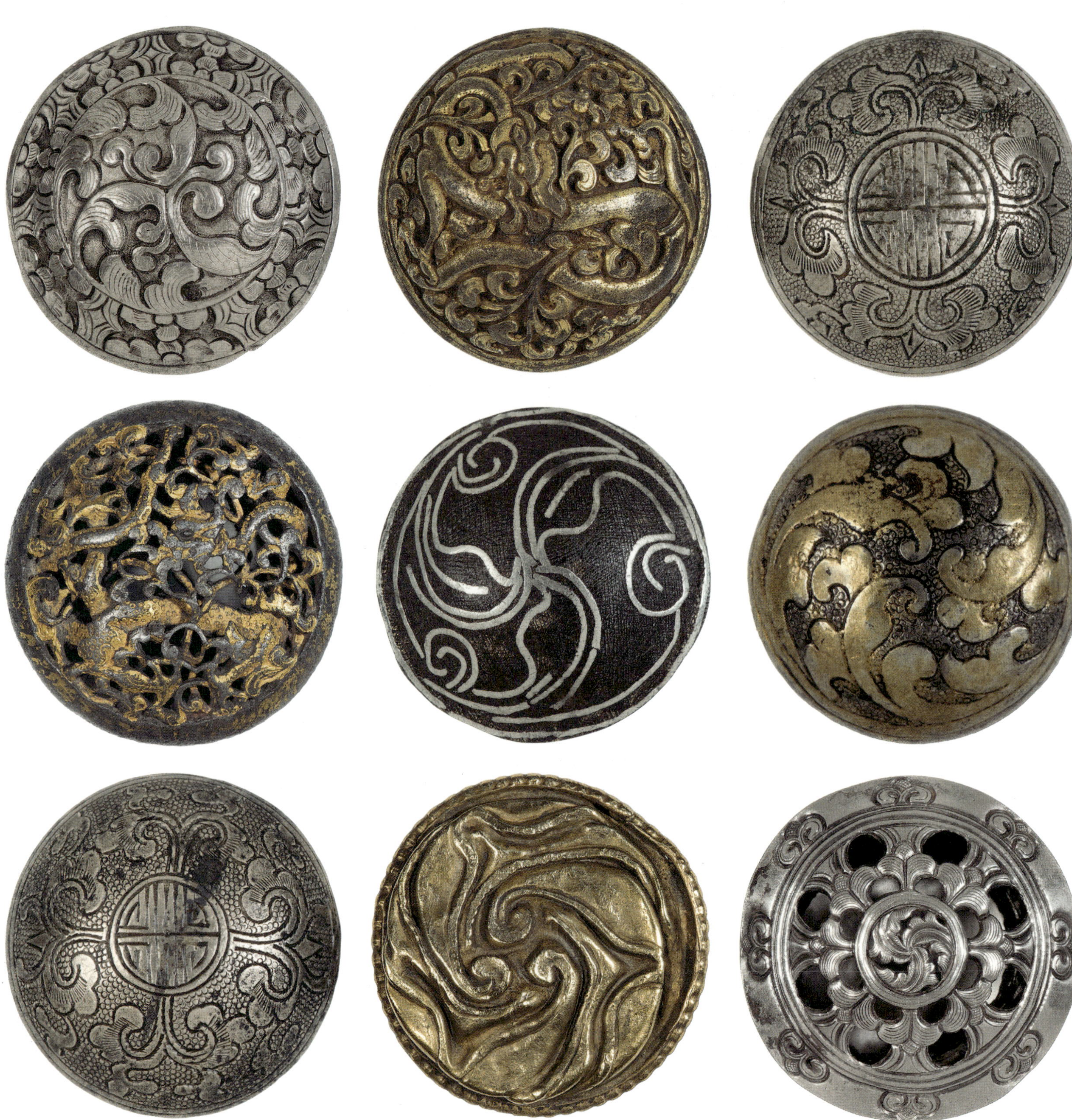